MW00711330

A

DICTIONARY

IN

HINDEE AND ENGLISH:

COMPILED FROM

APPROVED AUTHORITIES.

BY

J. T. THOMPSON,

DELHI.

CALCUTTA :

PRINTED FOR THE COMPILER, AT THE BAPTIST MISSION PRESS:

AND SOLD BY

MESSRS. THACKER AND CO., ST. ANDREW'S LIBRARY ; MESSRS. OSTELL AND LEPAGE, BRITISH
LIBRARY ; AND P. S. D'ROZARIO AND CO., TANK SQUARE, CALCUTTA.

MDCCCXLVI.

This scarce antiquarian book is included in our special *Legacy Reprint Series*. In the interest of creating a more extensive selection of rare historical book reprints, we have chosen to reproduce this title even though it may possibly have occasional imperfections such as missing and blurred pages, missing text, poor pictures, markings, dark backgrounds and other reproduction issues beyond our control. Because this work is culturally important, we have made it available as a part of our commitment to protecting, preserving and promoting the world's literature. Thank you for your understanding.

PREFACE.

So far back as the year 1785, Proposals had been set forth in England, by Capt. William Kirkpatrick, of the Hon. Company's Military Service, and Persian Secretary to the Commander-in-Chief in India, to publish a Hindee Vocabulary, of which the materials were all ready, but a delay in preparing the Naguree types, prevented its publication at the time when a Vocabulary of Persian, Arabic, and English, by that eminent Linguist, was offered to the public, in the course of the same year. Since that period, however, the proposed work appears never to have been published, either in England, where the Proposals had been issued, or in India, where numerous other works, to aid the Oriental student, have successively appeared in print. A Hindee Dictionary, therefore, remained a Desideratum still, as the other works adverted to, only afford assistance to the Oriental Student, in the Arabic, Persian, Oordoo, Sunskrit, Bengalee, and Marhatta languages respectively, and not in Hindee ; with the exception of a slender Glossary affixed to an edition of the Prem Sagur. To enable the student, then, to acquire this language, spoken by the generality of Hindoos, and over a vast extent of country, he was left, for a series of years, with the above scanty exception, to Oordoo Dictionaries, embodying a necessarily limited portion of Hindee vocables, and to the Selections from Hindee works, prepared for the use of the junior branches of the Military Service, by the Hindee Professor of the College of Fort William. The portion of Hindee words found in Oordoo Dictionaries, could alone have been directly useful to the student in his researches into the language, as the English meanings were all provided therein. But the vocables in the Selections, though numerous, and embracing six Hindee works, yet possessed not the facility of acquisition, which the former collection afforded, from not one of the selected works being accompanied by a Glossary, or even a free translation. So that, when the student has, with creditable labour, read through 268 quarto pages of Hindee composition, selected from native authors, he has only, unless he possess some other mode of acquiring the meaning of the words, had the benefit of so many natives speaking in his hearing, or making him repeat their language without any explanatory medium. The disadvantages of such a plan of instruction, are, however, sufficiently counterbalanced by the labours of the Professor of Hindee, in his edition of the Prem Sagur, above adverted to, to which is affixed a Vocabulary of the principal terms occurring in that work. This vocabulary, though a very limited one, is justly appreciated by every student of Hindee ; and not a few of those who have had the privilege of consulting it, have wished to see, based on it, a larger work of the kind, aiding not only in the perusal and due understanding of the Prem Sagur, but of such other Hindee works

also, which are studied in order to pass an examination, or with a view to a more extensive acquaintance with the language.

A few years after the publication of Capt. Price's Vocabulary of the principal terms
occurring in the Prem Sagur, just alluded to, the Rev. M. T. Adam of Benares,
published his most acceptable Vocabulary of the Hindee language, containing upwards
of 20,000 words ; but with the meanings in Hindee, instead of English. This was certainly a great benefit conferred on the students of Hindee, both native and European ;
yet it must be allowed, that the meanings not having been given in English, is a considerable drawback on the advantages which the European student may hope to derive
from consulting the work.

Seventeen years have now elapsed since the publication of the last mentioned Hindee
Vocabulary, and no attempt, it would appear, has been made to offer to the students of
Hindee, and the Patrons of Hindee literature, a work formed on the plan of Adam's
Hindee Vocabulary, but with the significations in English. A work of the kind has
often been mentioned as desirable, and the Compiler of the following sheets, in common with others, has frequently felt the want of such a publication, or a Hindee and
English Dictionary on an enlarged scale ; and he moreover ventured to solicit two eminent Oriental scholars, of considerable attainments, the one in Sunskrit, and the other
in Hindee, to undertake such a work, for the benefit of European Students of Hindee
in general, and of the junior branches of the Military Service in particular ; but he regrets to say, his application was not successful ; the Sunskrit scholar not deeming the
language sufficiently defined, and the Hindee scholar possessing no leisure from professional duties. The Compiler indeed possessed the nucleus of such a work, commenced
some thirty years ago, but on his becoming acquainted with the above eminent scholars, he for a time forbore to resume his contemplated work ; however, on being disappointed in his application to them, of whom one has quitted India, and the other,
will not, it is likely, stay long in it, the Compiler once more proposed the subject to a
third gentleman, who was likely, with benefit to Indian Literature, to have undertaken
the work : but he too has left India.

In the meantime, a communication was made to the Compiler on the part of a gentleman who is a great proficient in Hindee, and a liberal patron of useful undertakings ; requesting he would undertake a work based on Price's and Adam's Vocabularies, and amplified by all the additional terms to be found in the works of Wilson,
Hunter and Shakespear, and in the Hindee portion of the Compiler's own Oordoo and
English Dictionary. After due consideration, the compiler entered on the preparation
of the work required, and availing himself of the materials in his possession, prosecuted, and through the help of a gracious Providence, finished the Compilation now offered to the reading portion of the Community in general, and to Students of Hindee, and
the Patrons of its Literature in particular ; and which, as it is the largest collection of
Hindee words yet published, with the meanings in English, he has thought proper to
designate, *A Hindee and English Dictionary.* The collection consists of about 30,000

words, which, with their significations, have been derived from, or collated with the best authorities.

There is no department of study, the compiler conceives, which the present work will not be found to be helpful in advancing; and terms are to be met with in it, both simple and abstract. The Hindee, as generally spoken, does certainly not offer the requisite terms; but Hindee works do, and the parent language of nearly Twenty cognate languages, does possess the required facility of expression. It will surely, therefore, not be considered a fault in the present compilation, that it embraces, and even abounds with terms purely Sunskrit; since in our ordinary conversation with natives, we never hesitate to make use of words, both of Sunskrit, Persian, and Arabic origin; and such derivations must necessarily serve to enrich the language, whether spoken or written. Besides, have Colleges and other Seminaries of learning in India, all the standard works they require, to advance the studies of their students and pupils? and as it must be confessed they have not, it may be further asked, Whence are the technical and abstract terms required for Hindee composition or translation, to be obtained? Not surely from the Oordoo, to any considerable extent, as admissions from it, would be thought to mar the purity of the language. Nor yet from the spoken Hindee of the generality of Hindoos, who it is known mainly use the language, as its colloquial standard can hardly be said to be yet fixed. But to the Parent Sunskrit we may very properly look for such terms, suited as it is for composition in every department of science, and affording, as it does, the greatest facilities for the readiest expression of ideas. This leaning towards, and dependance on the Sunskrit, are the more justifiable, as such peculiarity is not claimed for the Hindee alone; for about Twenty other languages possess it, and languages too, which are spoken within or on the borders of the British territories, such as the Bengalee, the Assam, the Ooriya, Nepalese, Mugudh, Bhugelkhund, Marhatta, Bundelkhund, Cashmere, Punjabee, Sindh, Bilochee, Kutch, Goojratee, Kunkun, Bikanere, Oodypore, Marwar, and Bruj languages; all of which may be said, to abound more or less with Sunskrit terms. Dr. Carey indeed thought, that there were scarcely any words to be found in the languages of the north, which were not of Sunskrit origin: and what that eminent scholar and late distinguished Professor of Sunskrit, Bengalee, and Marhatta, in the College of Fort William, asserted of the Bengalee language, is equally applicable to the Hindee, that it is almost entirely derived from the Sunskrit: that considerably more than three-fourths of the words are pure Sunskrit; and that those composing the greatest part of the remainder are so little corrupted, that their origin may be traced without difficulty. It was also Dr. Carey's opinion, that "most of the above cognate languages, are copious, and were they duly cultivated, would be found capable of being employed in every kind of composition with advantage. Most of the elegancies of style, and delicate shades of meaning, may in their present state, be expressed by them with great facility; and should literature become an object of more general pursuit in India, and the colloquial languages be more employed in different species of style and composition, the capacities

also, which are studied in order to pass an examination, or with a view to a more extensive acquaintance with the language.

A few years after the publication of Capt. Price's Vocabulary of the principal terms
occurring in the Prem Sagur, just alluded to, the Rev. M. T. Adam of Benares,
published his most acceptable Vocabulary of the Hindee language, containing upwards
of 20,000 words ; but with the meanings in Hindee, instead of English. This was certainly a great benefit conferred on the students of Hindee, both native and European ;
yet it must be allowed, that the meanings not having been given in English, is a considerable drawback on the advantages which the European student may hope to derive
from consulting the work.

Seventeen years have now elapsed since the publication of the last mentioned Hindee
Vocabulary, and no attempt, it would appear, has been made to offer to the students of
Hindee, and the Patrons of Hindee literature, a work formed on the plan of Adam's
Hindee Vocabulary, but with the significations in English. A work of the kind has
often been mentioned as desirable, and the Compiler of the following sheets, in common with others, has frequently felt the want of such a publication, or a Hindee and
English Dictionary on an enlarged scale ; and he moreover ventured to solicit two eminent Oriental scholars, of considerable attainments, the one in Sunskrit, and the other
in Hindee, to undertake such a work, for the benefit of European Students of Hindee
in general, and of the junior branches of the Military Service in particular ; but he regrets to say, his application was not successful ; the Sunskrit scholar not deeming the
language sufficiently defined, and the Hindee scholar possessing no leisure from professional duties. The Compiler indeed possessed the nucleus of such a work, commenced
some thirty years ago, but on his becoming acquainted with the above eminent scholars, he for a time forbore to resume his contemplated work ; however, on being disappointed in his application to them, of whom one has quitted India, and the other,
will not, it is likely, stay long in it, the Compiler once more proposed the subject to a
third gentleman, who was likely, with benefit to Indian Literature, to have undertaken
the work : but he too has left India.

In the meantime, a communication was made to the Compiler on the part of a gentleman who is a great proficient in Hindee, and a liberal patron of useful undertakings ; requesting he would undertake a work based on Price's and Adam's Vocabularies, and amplified by all the additional terms to be found in the works of Wilson,
Hunter and Shakespear, and in the Hindee portion of the Compiler's own Oordoo and
English Dictionary. After due consideration, the compiler entered on the preparation
of the work required, and availing himself of the materials in his possession, prosecuted, and through the help of a gracious Providence, finished the Compilation now offered to the reading portion of the Community in general, and to Students of Hindee, and
the Patrons of its Literature in particular ; and which, as it is the largest collection of
Hindee words yet published, with the meanings in English, he has thought proper to
designate, *A Hindee and English Dictionary.* The collection consists of about 30,000

words, which, with their significations, have been derived from, or collated with the best authorities.

There is no department of study, the compiler conceives, which the present work will not be found to be helpful in advancing; and terms are to be met with in it, both simple and abstract. The Hindee, as generally spoken, does certainly not offer the requisite terms; but Hindee works do, and the parent language of nearly Twenty cognate languages, does possess the required facility of expression. It will surely, therefore, not be considered a fault in the present compilation, that it embraces, and even abounds with terms purely Sunskrit; since in our ordinary conversation with natives, we never hesitate to make use of words, both of Sunskrit, Persian, and Arabic origin; and such derivations must necessarily serve to enrich the language, whether spoken or written. Besides, have Colleges and other Seminaries of learning in India, all the standard works they require, to advance the studies of their students and pupils? and as it must be confessed they have not, it may be further asked, Whence are the technical and abstract terms required for Hindee composition or translation, to be obtained? Not surely from the Oordoo, to any considerable extent, as admissions from it, would be thought to mar the purity of the language. Nor yet from the spoken Hindee of the generality of Hindoos, who it is known mainly use the language, as its colloquial standard can hardly be said to be yet fixed. But to the Parent Sunskrit we may very properly look for such terms, suited as it is for composition in every department of science, and affording, as it does, the greatest facilities for the readiest expression of ideas. This leaning towards, and dependance on the Sunskrit, are the more justifiable, as such peculiarity is not claimed for the Hindee alone; for about Twenty other languages possess it, and languages too, which are spoken within or on the borders of the British territories, such as the Bengalee, the Assam, the Ooriya, Nepalese, Mugudh, Bhugelkhund, Marhatta, Bundelkhund, Cashmere, Punjabee, Sindh, Bilochee, Kutch, Goojratee, Kunkun, Bikanere, Oodypore, Marwar, and Bruj languages; all of which may be said, to abound more or less with Sunskrit terms. Dr. Carey indeed thought, that there were scarcely any words to be found in the languages of the north, which were not of Sunskrit origin: and what that eminent scholar and late distinguished Professor of Sunskrit, Bengalee, and Marhatta, in the College of Fort William, asserted of the Bengalee language, is equally applicable to the Hindee, that it is almost entirely derived from the Sunskrit: that considerably more than three-fourths of the words are pure Sunskrit; and that those composing the greatest part of the remainder are so little corrupted, that their origin may be traced without difficulty. It was also Dr. Carey's opinion, that "most of the above cognate languages, are copious, and were they duly cultivated, would be found capable of being employed in every kind of composition with advantage. Most of the elegancies of style, and delicate shades of meaning, may in their present state, be expressed by them with great facility; and should literature become an object of more general pursuit in India, and the colloquial languages be more employed in different species of style and composition, the capacities

also, which are studied in order to pass an examination, or with a view to a more extensive acquaintance with the language.

A few years after the publication of Capt. Price's Vocabulary of the principal terms
occurring in the Prem Sagur, just alluded to, the Rev. M. T. Adam of Benares,
published his most acceptable Vocabulary of the Hindee language, containing upwards
of 20,000 words ; but with the meanings in Hindee, instead of English. This was certainly a great benefit conferred on the students of Hindee, both native and European ;
yet it must be allowed, that the meanings not having been given in English, is a considerable drawback on the advantages which the European student may hope to derive
from consulting the work.

Seventeen years have now elapsed since the publication of the last mentioned Hindee
Vocabulary, and no attempt, it would appear, has been made to offer to the students of
Hindee, and the Patrons of Hindee literature, a work formed on the plan of Adam's
Hindee Vocabulary, but with the significations in English. A work of the kind has
often been mentioned as desirable, and the Compiler of the following sheets, in common with others, has frequently felt the want of such a publication, or a Hindee and
English Dictionary on an enlarged scale ; and he moreover ventured to solicit two eminent Oriental scholars, of considerable attainments, the one in Sunskrit, and the other
in Hindee, to undertake such a work, for the benefit of European Students of Hindee
in general, and of the junior branches of the Military Service in particular ; but he regrets to say, his application was not successful ; the Sunskrit scholar not deeming the
language sufficiently defined, and the Hindee scholar possessing no leisure from professional duties. The Compiler indeed possessed the nucleus of such a work, commenced
some thirty years ago, but on his becoming acquainted with the above eminent scholars, he for a time forbore to resume his contemplated work ; however, on being disappointed in his application to them, of whom one has quitted India, and the other,
will not, it is likely, stay long in it, the Compiler once more proposed the subject to a
third gentleman, who was likely, with benefit to Indian Literature, to have undertaken
the work : but he too has left India.

In the meantime, a communication was made to the Compiler on the part of a gentleman who is a great proficient in Hindee, and a liberal patron of useful undertakings ; requesting he would undertake a work based on Price's and Adam's Vocabularies, and amplified by all the additional terms to be found in the works of Wilson,
Hunter and Shakespear, and in the Hindee portion of the Compiler's own Oordoo and
English Dictionary. After due consideration, the compiler entered on the preparation
of the work required, and availing himself of the materials in his possession, prosecuted, and through the help of a gracious Providence, finished the Compilation now offered to the reading portion of the Community in general, and to Students of Hindee, and
the Patrons of its Literature in particular ; and which, as it is the largest collection of
Hindee words yet published, with the meanings in English, he has thought proper to
designate, *A Hindee and English Dictionary.* The collection consists of about 30,000

words, which, with their significations, have been derived from, or collated with the best authorities.

There is no department of study, the compiler conceives, which the present work will not be found to be helpful in advancing; and terms are to be met with in it, both simple and abstract. The Hindee, as generally spoken, does certainly not offer the requisite terms; but Hindee works do, and the parent language of nearly Twenty cognate languages, does possess the required facility of expression. It will surely, therefore, not be considered a fault in the present compilation, that it embraces, and even abounds with terms purely Sunskrit; since in our ordinary conversation with natives, we never hesitate to make use of words, both of Sunskrit, Persian, and Arabic origin; and such derivations must necessarily serve to enrich the language, whether spoken or written. Besides, have Colleges and other Seminaries of learning in India, all the standard works they require, to advance the studies of their students and pupils? and as it must be confessed they have not, it may be further asked, Whence are the technical and abstract terms required for Hindee composition or translation, to be obtained? Not surely from the Oordoo, to any considerable extent, as admissions from it, would be thought to mar the purity of the language. Nor yet from the spoken Hindee of the generality of Hindoos, who it is known mainly use the language, as its colloquial standard can hardly be said to be yet fixed. But to the Parent Sunskrit we may very properly look for such terms, suited as it is for composition in every department of science, and affording, as it does, the greatest facilities for the readiest expression of ideas. This leaning towards, and dependance on the Sunskrit, are the more justifiable, as such peculiarity is not claimed for the Hindee alone; for about Twenty other languages possess it, and languages too, which are spoken within or on the borders of the British territories, such as the Bengalee, the Assam, the Ooriya, Nepalese, Mugudh, Bhugelkhund, Marhatta, Bundelkhund, Cashmere, Punjabee, Sindh, Bilochee, Kutch, Goojratee, Kunkun, Bikanere, Oodypore, Marwar, and Bruj languages; all of which may be said, to abound more or less with Sunskrit terms. Dr. Carey indeed thought, that there were scarcely any words to be found in the languages of the north, which were not of Sunskrit origin: and what that eminent scholar and late distinguished Professor of Sunskrit, Bengalee, and Marhatta, in the College of Fort William, asserted of the Bengalee language, is equally applicable to the Hindee, that it is almost entirely derived from the Sunskrit: that considerably more than three-fourths of the words are pure Sunskrit; and that those composing the greatest part of the remainder are so little corrupted, that their origin may be traced without difficulty. It was also Dr. Carey's opinion, that "most of the above cognate languages, are copious, and were they duly cultivated, would be found capable of being employed in every kind of composition with advantage. Most of the elegancies of style, and delicate shades of meaning, may in their present state, be expressed by them with great facility; and should literature become an object of more general pursuit in India, and the colloquial languages be more employed in different species of style and composition, the capacities

also, which are studied in order to pass an examination, or with a view to a more extensive acquaintance with the language.

A few years after the publication of Capt. Price's Vocabulary of the principal terms occurring in the Prem Sagur, just alluded to, the Rev. M. T. Adam of Benares, published his most acceptable Vocabulary of the Hindee language, containing upwards of 20,000 words ; but with the meanings in Hindee, instead of English. This was certainly a great benefit conferred on the students of Hindee, both native and European ; yet it must be allowed, that the meanings not having been given in English, is a considerable drawback on the advantages which the European student may hope to derive from consulting the work.

Seventeen years have now elapsed since the publication of the last mentioned Hindee Vocabulary, and no attempt, it would appear, has been made to offer to the students of Hindee, and the Patrons of Hindee literature, a work formed on the plan of Adam's Hindee Vocabulary, but with the significations in English. A work of the kind has often been mentioned as desirable, and the Compiler of the following sheets, in common with others, has frequently felt the want of such a publication, or a Hindee and English Dictionary on an enlarged scale ; and he moreover ventured to solicit two eminent Oriental scholars, of considerable attainments, the one in Sunskrit, and the other in Hindee, to undertake such a work, for the benefit of European Students of Hindee in general, and of the junior branches of the Military Service in particular ; but he regrets to say, his application was not successful ; the Sunskrit scholar not deeming the language sufficiently defined, and the Hindee scholar possessing no leisure from professional duties. The Compiler indeed possessed the nucleus of such a work, commenced some thirty years ago, but on his becoming acquainted with the above eminent scholars, he for a time forbore to resume his contemplated work ; however, on being disappointed in his application to them, of whom one has quitted India, and the other, will not, it is likely, stay long in it, the Compiler once more proposed the subject to a third gentleman, who was likely, with benefit to Indian Literature, to have undertaken the work : but he too has left India.

In the meantime, a communication was made to the Compiler on the part of a gentleman who is a great proficient in Hindee, and a liberal patron of useful undertakings ; requesting he would undertake a work based on Price's and Adam's Vocabularies, and amplified by all the additional terms to be found in the works of Wilson, Hunter and Shakespear, and in the Hindee portion of the Compiler's own Oordoo and English Dictionary. After due consideration, the compiler entered on the preparation of the work required, and availing himself of the materials in his possession, prosecuted, and through the help of a gracious Providence, finished the Compilation now offered to the reading portion of the Community in general, and to Students of Hindee, and the Patrons of its Literature in particular ; and which, as it is the largest collection of Hindee words yet published, with the meanings in English, he has thought proper to designate, *A Hindee and English Dictionary*. The collection consists of about 30,000

words, which, with their significations, have been derived from, or collated with the best authorities.

There is no department of study, the compiler conceives, which the present work will not be found to be helpful in advancing; and terms are to be met with in it, both simple and abstract. The Hindee, as generally spoken, does certainly not offer the requisite terms; but Hindee works do, and the parent language of nearly Twenty cognate languages, does possess the required facility of expression. It will surely, therefore, not be considered a fault in the present compilation, that it embraces, and even abounds with terms purely Sunskrit; since in our ordinary conversation with natives, we never hesitate to make use of words, both of Sunskrit, Persian, and Arabic origin; and such derivations must necessarily serve to enrich the language, whether spoken or written. Besides, have Colleges and other Seminaries of learning in India, all the standard works they require, to advance the studies of their students and pupils? and as it must be confessed they have not, it may be further asked, Whence are the technical and abstract terms required for Hindee composition or translation, to be obtained? Not surely from the Oordoo, to any considerable extent, as admissions from it, would be thought to mar the purity of the language. Nor yet from the spoken Hindee of the generality of Hindoos, who it is known mainly use the language, as its colloquial standard can hardly be said to be yet fixed. But to the Parent Sunskrit we may very properly look for such terms, suited as it is for composition in every department of science, and affording, as it does, the greatest facilities for the readiest expression of ideas. This leaning towards, and dependance on the Sunskrit, are the more justifiable, as such peculiarity is not claimed for the Hindee alone; for about Twenty other languages possess it, and languages too, which are spoken within or on the borders of the British territories, such as the Bengalee, the Assam, the Ooriya, Nepalese, Mugudh, Bhugelkhund, Marhatta, Bundelkhund, Cashmere, Punjabee, Sindh, Bilochee, Kutch, Goojratee, Kunkun, Bikanere, Oodypore, Marwar, and Bruj languages; all of which may be said, to abound more or less with Sunskrit terms. Dr. Carey indeed thought, that there were scarcely any words to be found in the languages of the north, which were not of Sunskrit origin: and what that eminent scholar and late distinguished Professor of Sunskrit, Bengalee, and Marhatta, in the College of Fort William, asserted of the Bengalee language, is equally applicable to the Hindee, that it is almost entirely derived from the Sunskrit: that considerably more than three-fourths of the words are pure Sunskrit; and that those composing the greatest part of the remainder are so little corrupted, that their origin may be traced without difficulty. It was also Dr. Carey's opinion, that "most of the above cognate languages, are copious, and were they duly cultivated, would be found capable of being employed in every kind of composition with advantage. Most of the elegancies of style, and delicate shades of meaning, may in their present state, be expressed by them with great facility; and should literature become an object of more general pursuit in India, and the colloquial languages be more employed in different species of style and composition, the capacities

of these languages would be developed, and the languages themselves carried to a degree of refinement, of which we have now but a faint idea."

If then, as Dr. Carey states, the greater part of the words in the above languages be derived from the Sunskrit, the Hindee, as being one of them, would certainly be enriched, and its capacities improved by drawing from that original source. The compiler therefore hopes that he will be pardoned for having added to his compilation so largely from the parent language, terms, familiar, it may be, only to the learned part of the population, but hardly in use among the other classes of natives. But who is there, that does not desire to speak, and write, and discourse, in a style above that of rustics or unlettered men, if he wishes to express himself with accuracy, aptitude, and an elegance that should charm, or command admiration? since the model of the dialect, observes Dr. Carey, which is spoken by ploughmen, menial servants, or labouring mechanics, is not that, on which the learned in any country form their language. Let then the European scholar not hesitate, in his conversation and composition, to adopt a style that shall shew his attainments to be on a par with those of the learned men of the country, at the same time that his judicious selection of universally-understood terms, shall render his communication level with the capacities of all classes of people.

In the work now offered to the Public, the Compiler has endeavoured to give the commonest words in use in Hindee, selected from various publications, or known to be in general use; but fearing he may have overlooked some of the easiest terms, he begs the indulgent consideration of such as may be disposed to censure him for his seeming neglect, which, however, he assures them, was not intentional. While on the other hand, the Compiler takes this opportunity of stating, that certain terms, not at all calculated to promote the study of any science, and admitted into their works, without a due degree of discrimination, by others in the same field of labour, though never to be met with in the usual English Dictionaries, have by him been studiously omitted.

Having now noticed what appears to be an early attempt, if it be not indeed the earliest, to publish a Hindee Dictionary; and shown what helps have since been provided to promote the study of Hindee, directly and indirectly; together with the want that still exists for such a work: it only remains for the compiler to acknowledge with deep gratitude to his Maker, that his life has been mercifully spared, and his health continued, to enable him to finish *THE HINDEE AND ENGLISH DICTIONARY*, which he has now much pleasure in offering to a Liberal Public; from whom, for a period of Fourteen years, he has experienced the most unexampled support in his Oordoo publications: and the compiler therefore trusts, that should the present work be found likely to be useful to the Student, or of assistance in composition or translation, the wonted Patronage of that Public will not be withheld, but kindly extended to it.

J. T. THOMPSON.

Delhi, the 6th Oct. 1846.

THE DEVU-NAGUREE ALPHABET.

Vowels.

अ आ इ ई उ ऊ ऋ ॡ ऌ ए ऐ ओ औ अं अः

Consonants.

क	च	ट	त	प	य	श
ख	छ	ठ	थ	फ	र	ष
ग	ज	ड	द	ब	ल	स
घ	झ	ढ	ध	भ	व	ह
ङ	ञ	ण	न	म	—	क्ष

The Symbols of the Vowels.

ा ि ी ु ू ृ ॄ ॢ ॣ े ै ो ौ ं ः

Numerical Figures.

१ २ ३ ४ ५ ६ ७ ८ ९ १० २० १००

Final Vowels with a Consonant.

क	का	कि	की	कु	कू	कृ	कॄ	के	कै	को	कौ	कं	कः
ख	खा	खि	खी	खु	खू	खृ	खॄ	खे	खै	खो	खौ	खं	खः
ग	गा	गि	गी	गु	गू	गृ	गॄ	गे	गै	गो	गौ	गं	गः
घ	घा	घि	घी	घु	घू	घृ	घॄ	घे	घै	घो	घौ	घं	घः
च	चा	चि	ची	चु	चू	चृ	चॄ	चे	चै	चो	चौ	चं	चः
छ	छा	छि	छी	छु	छू	छृ	छॄ	छे	छै	छो	छौ	छं	छः
ज	जा	जि	जी	जु	जू	जृ	जॄ	जे	जै	जो	जौ	जं	जः
झ	झा	झि	झी	झु	झू	झृ	झॄ	झे	झै	झो	झौ	झं	झः
ट	टा	टि	टी	टु	टू	टृ	टॄ	टे	टै	टो	टौ	टं	टः
ठ	ठा	ठि	ठी	ठु	ठू	ठृ	ठॄ	ठे	ठै	ठो	ठौ	ठं	ठः
ड	डा	डि	डी	डु	डू	डृ	डॄ	डे	डै	डो	डौ	डं	डः
ढ	ढा	ढि	ढी	ढु	ढू	ढृ	ढॄ	ढे	ढै	ढो	ढौ	ढं	ढः
ण	णा	णि	णी	णु	णू	णृ	णॄ	णे	णै	णो	णौ	णं	णः
त	ता	ति	ती	तु	तू	तृ	तॄ	ते	तै	तो	तौ	तं	तः
थ	था	थि	थी	थु	थू	थृ	थॄ	थे	थै	थो	थौ	थं	थः
द	दा	दि	दी	दु	दू	दृ	दॄ	दे	दै	दो	दौ	दं	दः

ध	धा	धिं	धी	धु	धू	धृ	धॄ	धे	धै	धो	धौ	धं	धः
न	ना	नि	नी	नु	नू	नृ	नॄ	ने	नै	नो	नौ	नं	नः
प	पा	पि	पी	पु	पू	पृ	पॄ	पे	पै	पो	पौ	पं	पः
फ	फा	फि	फी	फु	फू	फृ	फॄ	फे	फै	फो	फौ	फं	फः
ब	बा	बि	बी	बु	बू	बृ	बॄ	बे	बै	बो	बौ	बं	बः
भ	भा	भि	भी	भु	भू	भृ	भॄ	भे	भै	भो	भौ	भं	भः
म	मा	मि	मी	मु	मू	मृ	मॄ	मे	मै	मो	मौ	मं	मः
य	या	यि	यी	यु	यू	यृ	यॄ	ये	यै	यो	यौ	यं	यः
र	रा	रि	री	रु	रू	रृ	रॄ	रे	रै	रो	रौ	रं	रः
ल	ला	लि	ली	लु	लू	लृ	लॄ	ले	लै	लो	लौ	लं	लः
व	वा	वि	वी	वु	वू	वृ	वॄ	वे	वै	वो	वौ	वं	वः
श	शा	शि	शी	शु	शू	शृ	शॄ	शे	शै	शो	शौ	शं	शः
ष	षा	षि	षी	षु	षू	षृ	षॄ	षे	षै	षो	षौ	षं	षः
स	सा	सि	सी	सु	सू	सृ	सॄ	से	सै	सो	सौ	सं	सः
ह	हा	हि	ही	हु	हू	हृ	हॄ	हे	है	हो	हौ	हं	हः
ळ	ळा	ळि	ळी	ळु	ळू	ळृ	ळॄ	ळे	ळै	ळो	ळौ	ळं	ळः

COMPOUND CONSONANTS.

Double Letters.

[illegible] [illegible] [illegible] [illegible] [illegible] ।
[illegible] [illegible] [illegible] [illegible] [illegible] ।
[illegible] [illegible] [illegible] [illegible] [illegible] ।
[illegible] [illegible] [illegible] [illegible] [illegible] ।
[illegible] [illegible] [illegible] [illegible] [illegible] ।
[illegible] [illegible] [illegible] [illegible]
[illegible] [illegible] [illegible] [illegible] ॥
[illegible] [illegible] [illegible] [illegible] ।
[illegible] [illegible] [illegible] [illegible] ।
[illegible] [illegible] [illegible] [illegible] [illegible] ।
[illegible] [illegible] [illegible] [illegible] [illegible] ।
[illegible] [illegible] [illegible] [illegible] [illegible] ।
[illegible] [illegible]
[illegible] [illegible] [illegible] [illegible] ॥
[illegible] [illegible] [illegible] [illegible] ।
[illegible] [illegible] ।
[illegible] [illegible] ।
[illegible] [illegible] [illegible] [illegible] [illegible] ।
[illegible] [illegible] [illegible] [illegible] ।
[illegible]
[illegible] [illegible] [illegible] [illegible] ॥
[illegible] [illegible] ।

[illegible] [illegible] ।
[illegible] [illegible] ।
[illegible] [illegible] [illegible] [illegible] [illegible] ।
[illegible] [illegible] [illegible] ॥
[illegible] [illegible] [illegible] [illegible] ।
[illegible] [illegible] [illegible] ।
[illegible] [illegible] [illegible] ।
[illegible] [illegible] [illegible] [illegible] [illegible] ।
[illegible] [illegible] [illegible] [illegible] [illegible] ।
[illegible] [illegible] [illegible]
[illegible] [illegible] [illegible] [illegible] ॥
[illegible] [illegible] [illegible] [illegible] ।
[illegible] [illegible] [illegible] ।
[illegible] [illegible] [illegible] ।
[illegible] [illegible] ।
[illegible] [illegible]
[illegible] [illegible] [illegible] [illegible] ॥
[illegible] [illegible] [illegible] [illegible] [illegible] ।
[illegible] [illegible] [illegible] [illegible] [illegible] ।
[illegible] [illegible] [illegible] [illegible] [illegible] ।
[illegible] [illegible] [illegible] [illegible] [illegible] ।
[illegible] [illegible] [illegible] [illegible] [illegible] ।

[illegible] [illegible] [illegible] [illegible]
[illegible] [illegible] [illegible] [illegible] ॥

[illegible] [illegible] [illegible] [illegible] [illegible] ।
[illegible] [illegible] [illegible] [illegible] [illegible] ।
[illegible] [illegible] [illegible] [illegible] [illegible] ।
[illegible] [illegible] [illegible] [illegible] [illegible] ।
[illegible] [illegible] [illegible] [illegible] [illegible] ।
[illegible] [illegible] [illegible] [illegible]
[illegible] [illegible] [illegible] [illegible] ॥

[illegible] [illegible] [illegible] [illegible] ।
[illegible] [illegible] [illegible] [illegible] ।
[illegible] [illegible] [illegible] [illegible] [illegible] ।
[illegible] [illegible] [illegible] [illegible] [illegible] ।
[illegible] [illegible] [illegible] [illegible] [illegible] ।
[illegible] [illegible] [illegible] [illegible] ।
[illegible] [illegible] [illegible] [illegible] [illegible] ।
[illegible] [illegible] [illegible] [illegible] [illegible] ।
[illegible] [illegible] [illegible] [illegible] [illegible] ।
[illegible] [illegible] [illegible] [illegible] [illegible]
[illegible] [illegible] [illegible] [illegible] ॥

A
DICTIONARY,
HINDEE AND ENGLISH.

अ

अ uh, The first letter of the Nagree alphabet, and inherent short vowel; an inseparable particle signifying negation or privation, as अचल; as a negative prefix to words beginning with a vowel. अ is changed to अन्, as अ and अंत, form अनंत; an interjection of pity.

अऋणी ú-rin-ee, *adj.* Free from debt, or obligation.

अंक unk, *s. m.* A mark or spot, a cypher, a numerical figure, number, letter of the alphabet, mark on cloth to shew the price; the flank or part above the hip; embrace.

अंकक únk-uk, *s. m.* An accountant, an arithmetician.

अंकरी únk-ree, *s. f.* The barb of an arrow, a hook, tenter, catch; a circle.

अंकना únk-na, *v. a.* To mark, page a book, distinguish a thing by some mark. *v. n.* To be valued, prized, examined, approved of.

अंकवार unk-wár, *s. f.* An embrace, the bosom. *Unk-war bhurna, v. a.* To embrace.

अंकुस únk-us, ⎫ *s. m.* The iron hook with

अंकुस únk-oos, ⎬ which elephants are guided or driven, a goad. *Unkoos marna*, To reduce to submission, to reduce to obedience.

अंकाना unk-ána, *v. a.* To cause to value, prize, examine (*as cloth*), to approve of. [ment.

अंकाव unk-áo, *s. m.* Valuation, appraise-

अंकित únk-it, *adj.* Marked, spotted, stained, paged.

अंकुर ún-koor, ⎫

अंकुरा un-kóora, ⎬ *s. m.* A sprout or shoot.

अंकुसी ún-koosee, *s. f.* A hook, a tenter.

अंकी únk-ree, *s. f.* A kind of vetch (*Vicia sativa*); wet grain; a young sprout.

अंखरी únkh-ree, *s. f.* An eye or glance of the eye.

अंखाना unkh-ána, *v. n.* To be angry or displeased, to be peevish or fretful.

अंखियां unkh-iyán, *s. f. pl.* The eyes.

अंगरखा ung-ur-khá, *s. m.* A coat, gown, jacket, doublet.

अंगीकार ung-ee-kár, *s. m.* An agreement, a promise, acquiescence. *Ungeekar kurna, v. a.* To accept, receive, agree to.

अंगीकृत ung-ee-krít, *adj.* Agreed, promised, acceded to.

अंगीठी ung-ée-thee, *s. f.* A chafingdish, brasier.

अंगुरी úngoo-ree, *s. f.* A finger, a finger's breadth.

अंगूठा ungóotha, *s. m.* The thumb. *Ungootha dikhana*, An attitude adopted by women in blandishment as a token of prohibition; to brave, defy.

अंगूठी un-góo-thee, *s. f.* A ring worn on the finger.

अंगोछा un-góchha, *s. m.* A cloth which Hindoos fasten round the waist when bathing, and afterwards wipe themselves with; a towel, a handkerchief.

अंत unt, *s. m.* End, completion; perdition, destruction; mind, heart; a boundary, limit; intelligence, news, account of. *adj.* Final, ultimate. *adv.* After all, at last; in, within; elsewhere, somewhere else.

अंतर úntur, *adv.* Within, between, amongst; without, except. *s. m.* Interval, intermediate space, intermission; period, term, difference; opportune time; midst, the midst; the heart, the supreme soul. *adj.* Other, similar.

अंतरगति úntur-gúti, *s. f.* The emotions of the heart, inward sensations.

अंतरजामी úntur-jamee, *adj.* Pervading the inward parts, acquainted with the heart (*an epithet of the Deity*).

B

अंतर्ध्यान unturdhyán, *adj.* Out of sight, vanished, disappeared, concealed. *s. m.* Disappearance. *Unturdhyan hona, v. n.* To vanish, disappear, be concealed.

अंतर्पट unturpút, *s. m.* A curtain, a skreen.

अंतरिया unturíya, *s. m.* Intermittent, an intermitting fever.

अंतरीछ untureéksh, *s. m.* The sky or atmosphere. *adv.* In the air, out of sight.

अंधा úndha, *adj.* Blind, dark. *Undha dhoond,* Blind, blindly. *Undha dhoond rona,* To weep excessively. *Undha dhoond lootana,* To squander, spend extravagantly.

अंधाकूवा úndha-kóoa, ⎫ *s. m.* A well filled
अंधाकूप úndha-kóop, ⎭ up with rubbish, a dry well, a well overgrown with bushes or weeds, one, of which the mouth is hidden.

अंधेर undhér, *s. m.* Darkness, misfortune. calamity, injustice, violence, tumult, tyranny, oppression, outrage. *Undher kurna, v. a.* To act unjustly, tyrannize, oppress.   [ness.

अंधेरा undhéra, *adj.* Dark. *s. m.* Dark-
अंधेरी undhéree, *adj. f.* Dark. *Undheree rat,* A dark night. *Undheree kothree, s. f.* A dark room ; the belly, the womb.

अंब umb, *s. m.* A mangoe, a mangoe tree.

अंबर úmbur, *s. m.* The sky or atmosphere ; clothes, apparel.

अंबारी umbáree, *s. f.* A canopy, a litter used on an elephant or camel.   [goe.

अंबिया úmbiya, *s. f.* A small unripe mau-

अंस uns, *s. m.* Part, division, portion, share ; right, possession ; essence ; a degree of a circle, of latitude or longitude, &c. (*in arithmetic*) a fraction ; the numerator of a fraction.

अंसिक únsik, *s. m.* A partner, a proprietor.

अंसी únsee, *adj.* A partner, sharer, coheir.

अकत uóot, *s. m.* One who has no offspring, (*met.*) An unmarried man ; a stupid person, blockhead, dunce.

अकर úkur, *s. f.* Crookedness ; strut, airs. *Ukurbaz,* An affected person, a fop, a swaggerer. *Ukurbazee, s. f.* Swaggering, strutting, airs.

अकड़ना úkurna, *v. n.* To writhe, ache, be cramped, become stiff or rigid, to stiffen ; to strut affectedly, to give one's self airs.

अकड़बाई ukurbáee, *s. f.* The cramp.

अकरा úkra, *part. pass.* Stiff, affected.

अकड़ैत ukryt, *adj.* An affected person, a swaggerer, a fop.

अकंटक ukúntuk, *adj.* Free from thorns, literally or metaphorically.

अकथ ukúth, *adj.* Not to be told or related, beyond description, unspeakable, unutterable ; unfit to be spoken, obscene.

अकंपित ukúmpit, *adj.* Firm, unshaken.

अकरा úkra, *adj.* Dear, costly. *s. f.* A kind of vetch.

अकर्कश ukúrkkus, *adj.* Soft, not hard.

अकरनी ukúrnee, *adj.* Inconsistent, indecent, unsuitable, not to be done.

अकर्म úkurm, *s. m.* Bad action, sin, vice, wickedness.

अकर्मक ukúrmuk, *adj.* Intransitive (*a verb*).

अकर्मण्य ukurmunyúh, *adj.* Useless, unprofitable, good for nothing.   [out work.

अकर्मा úkurma, *adj.* Idle, unoccupied, with-

अकर्मी úkurmee, *adj.* Wretch, sinner.

अकल्पित úkulpit, *adj.* Not artificial, not made.

अकल्यान úkulyan, *adj.* Ominous, portentous, of bad omen, unlucky, inauspicious.

अकस्मात् ukusmát, *adv.* Immediately, accidentally, without a cause, unexpectedly, suddenly, instantly, presently, unawares, abruptly.

अकाज ukáj, *s. m.* Hurt, injury, loss, detriment, prejudice ; uselessness.

अकाजी ukajée, *adj.* Useless (*animal, thing, or person*) ; a retarder.

अकाम úkam,   ⎫ *adj.* Unprofitable, fruit-
अकारथ ukáruth, ⎭ less, yielding no return, vain.

अकारन úkarun, *s. m.* Absence or non-existence of a cause. *adv.* Causelessly.

अकाल ukál, *s. m.* Unseasonableness, famine, scarcity, extremity, pinch. *adj.* Unseasonable, premature, untimely. *Ukal-phúl, s. m.* A fruit produced out of season.

अकिंचन úkinchun, *adj.* Poor, wretched miserable, destitute, needy, indigent.

अकीर्ति úkeertti, *s. f.* Infamy, disgrace.

अकुलाना ukoolána, *v. n.* To be agitated, distracted, confused, confounded, out of order ; to tire, weary ; to be astonished.

अकुलीन ukooléena, *adj.* Not noble, plebeian, low, mean, ignoble, of mean extraction, of low origin or race.

अकुलीनी ukooléenee, *adj. f.* Not of good family, ignoble, base (*woman*).

अकुशल úkooshul, *adj.* Unlucky, inauspicious.

अकोर ukór, *s. f.* A bribe.

अकोरी ukóree, *adj.* One who receives a bribe.

अकोल ukól, *s. m.* A plant, the oil of which is used in enchantments (*Alangium hexapetalum*).

अकंद úkwund, *s. m.* Swallow-wort.

अकृत्रिम úkritrim, *adj.* Inartificial, not made.

अक्रूर **úkroor**, *adj.* Not cruel, mild, humane, gentle.

अखूर **ukhúr**, *adj.* Undisciplined (*soldier*), barbarous.

अखण्ड **ukhúnd**, *adj.* Unbroken, whole, entire, all.

अखण्डित **ukhúndit**, *adj.* Unbroken; continuous; unrefuted.

अखूत **ukhút**, *s. m.* Fried grain, whole grain used in religious ceremonies.

अखय **úkhuy**, *adj.* Everlasting, not liable to decay, durable, permanent. *Ukhuy bur*, Name of a tree; an undecayable tree.

अखरोट **ukhrót**, *s. m.* A walnut; the fruit of the Aleurites triloba, also, is so called.

अखल **ukhúl**, *adj.* All, the whole, every, entire.

अखाड़ा **ukhára**, *s. m.* A palæstra or place for wrestling, a scene, any place of assembly, a court or circus. [entire.

अखिल **ukhíl**, *adj.* All, the whole, every,

अख्यात **ukhyát**, *adj.* Unknown, obscure, not famous.

अगड़बगड़ **úgur-búgur**, *s. m.* Trifling employment or talk, trifles, trash, trumpery. *adj.* Promiscuous, composed of odds and ends.

अगणित **úgunit**, *adj.* Innumerable, not counted, not reckoned.

अगति **ugúti**, *adj.* Without character, dishonoured, disgraced; one whose funeral ceremonies have not been performed. *s. f.* Disgrace, distress, inconvenience; damnation, condemnation.

अगम **úgum**, ⎫ *adj.* Impassable, inac-
अगम्य **ugúmyuh**, ⎭ cessible, impervious, deep, unfathomable, unfordable, bottomless; unaccomplishable, incomprehensible; difficult of acquirement, unattainable.

अगर **úgur**, *s. m.* Wood of aloes.

अगरवाला **ugurwála**, *s. m.* A race of merchants of the *Vys* tribe from *Ugroha*, west of Delhi.

अगरी **ugurée**, *adj.* Of the colour of *Ugur*, i. e. wood of aloes.

अगला **úgla**, *adj.* Prior, preceding, first, foremost, former, chief, principal; ancestor; ancient; other, next.

अगवा **úgwa**, *adj.* Foremost. *s. m.* A guide, a forerunner, harbinger; one who adjusts a marriage.

अगवाई **ugwaée**, *s. f.* Guidance.

अगवाड़ा **ugwára**, *s. m.* The front, the forepart; the space in the front of a house.

अगवानी **ugwánee**, *s. m.* A guide, harbinger.

अगवाही **ugwáhee**, *s. f.* Conflagration.

B 2

अगस्ति **ugústi**, *s. m.* A sage celebrated in Hindoo mythology: he is represented of short stature, and to have been born in a water jar: he is famed for having swallowed the ocean when it had given him offence: at his command also the *Vindhya* range of mountains prostrated itself, and so remains.

अगहन **úghun**, *s. m.* The eighth Hindoo month (*during which the sun is in Scorpio, and the moon is full near Orion's head*); Nov.-Dec.

अगाऊ **ugaóo**, *adv.* Before, in front. *Ugaoo jana*, *v. n.* To advance, to meet a person.

अगाड़ी **ugáree**, *adv.* Before, in front, forward, further on, onward. *s. f.* The ropes with which a horse's forefeet are tied; the front, forepart. *Ugáree pichháree lugána*, To confine (*especially a horse*). *Ugáree marna*, *v. a.* To attack in front, to defeat a hostile army in a pitched battle.

अगाध **ugádh**, *adj.* Unfathomable, very deep, bottomless.

अगाधता **ugadhtá**, *s. f.* Depth.

अगासी **ugásee**, *s. m.* A turband; a terrace in front of an upper room.

अगिन **úgin**, *s. m.* A bird, a sort of lark.

अगिनबाव **uginbáo**, *s. m.* The farcy in horses, an eruptive disease in men.

अगिया **úgiya**, *s. m.* A bird (*Alauda aggiya*).

अगुआ **úgooa**, *s. m.* A guide, a harbinger.

अगुण **úgoon**, *adj.* Unskilful, without merit, ineffectual, void of good qualities, bad. *s. m.* A defect, a fault.

अगुप्त **úgoopt**, *adj.* Unhidden, unconcealed.

अगुरु **úgooroo**, *s. m.* A fragrant wood, aloe wood, or agallochum (*Aquillaria agallocha*); another tree which produces Bdellium (*Amyris agullocha*); the Sisoo tree (*Dalbergia Sisoo*). *adj.* Light, not heavy.

अगूढ़ **úgoorh**, *adj.* Easy, manifest, evident. *Ugoorh bhao*, *adj.* Open, honest, candid.

अगोचर **úgochur**, *adj.* Unperceived, imperceptible, invisible, covert, unseen, unwitnessed. *s. m.* The invisible, Supreme.

अगोड़ी **ugóree**, *adv.* In advance, beforehand.

अगोरना **ugórna**, *v. a.* To watch.

अगोरिया **ugóriya**, *s. m.* A watchman.

अगोलना **ugólna**, *v. a.* To watch.

अगौनी **ugóunee**, *s. f.* The going or sending forward, to meet and receive a visitant with honor. *Ugounee kurna*, *v. a.* To advance and meet the bridegroom, to go to meet a visitant on the road.

अग्नि **úgni**, *s. m.* Fire; the god of fire and the regent of the south-east quarter; one of the *poorans*; the fire of the stomach, the digestive faculty, appetite.

अग्निक úgnik, *s. m.* An insect of a scarlet colour, the lady-bird.

अग्निगर्भ ugni-gúrbh, *s. m.* The sun-stone or a fabulous gem, supposed to contain and impart solar heat.

अग्निपरीचा úgni-puréeksha, *s. f.* The fiery ordeal, by a heated iron or boiling oil, or passing through fire.

अग्निप्रस्तर úgni-prústur, *s. m.* Fire-stone, flint, or any stone producing fire.

अग्निबाण ugni-bán, *s. m.* Arrow of fire, a rocket.

अग्निमणि úgni-múni, *s. m.* The sun-stone.

अग्निसंस्कार úgni-sunskár, *s. m.* Funeral ceremonies, as burning a dead body, or any ceremony performed with consecrated fire.

अग्र ugr, *s. m.* The forepart of a thing. *adj.* Prior, first.

अग्रगामी ugr-gámee, *adj.* Preceding, going before. *s. m.* Forerunner.

अग्रग्रास ugr-grás, *s. m.* The first morsel.

अग्रसर ugr-súr, *s. m.* A guide, *adj.* Preceding, going before, a leader.

अग्रसोच ugr-sóch, *s. m.* Foresight, providence, precaution.

अग्रसोची ugr-sóchee, *adj.* Provident, endued with foresight.

अग्रास ugrás, ⎱ *s. m.* Victuals offered
अग्रासन ugrásun, ⎰ in oblations, sacrifices, &c. to the gods.

अघ ugh, *s. m.* Sin, guilt, wickedness.

अघनाशक ugh-náshuk, *adj.* Purifying, freeing from sin.

अघमय ugh-múy, *adj.* Sinful.

अघाई ugháee, *s. f.* Satiety, surfeiting.

अघाना ughána, *v. a.* To surfeit, satiate. *v. n.* To surfeit, to be satiated. *adj.* Satiated, rich, affluent.

अघोर ughór, *s. m.* A name of *Siv. adj.* Formidable, terrible.

अघोरपंथ ughór-punth, *s. m.* A particular religious order among Hindoos.

अघोरपंथी ughór-púnthee, ⎱ *adj. (used sub-*
अघोरी ughóree, ⎰ *stantively)* An order of religious mendicants professing the *ughorpunth* : they eat every thing, however filthy, even human carcases ; hence, a gross or filthy feeder.

अङ unk, *s. m.* Mark, spot, figure, number, letter of the alphabet ; flank or part above the hip ; the body ; embrace ; mark on cloth to shew the price.

अङ्कुक únkuk, *s. m.* An accountant, arithmetician.

अङ्कना unkna, *v. n.* To be valued, prized, examined, approved of.

अङ्करी unkree, *s. f.* A kind of vetch (*Vicia sativa*) ; wet grain ; a young sprout.

अङ्कविद्या unk-vídya, *s. f.* Arithmetic.

अङ्कसी unksee, *s. f.* A hook, a tenter.

अङ्काना unkána, *v. a.* To cause to value, to examine (*as cloth*), to approve of.

अङ्काव unkáo, *s. m.* Valuation.

अङ्कित unkit, *adj.* Marked, paged, examined, valued.

अङ्कूर unkoor, ⎱ *s. m.* A plantlet, a seed-
अङ्कूरा unkóora, ⎰ bud, a shoot or sprout, a germ.

अङ्कूश unkoosh, ⎱ *s. m.* The iron hook with
अङ्कूस unkoos, ⎰ which elephants are guided or driven.

अङ्कूर unkór, *s. m.* A sprout, a germin.

अङ्ग ung, *s. m.* A limb or member, the body.

अङ्गाई ungráee, *s. f.* Stretching the limbs, a yawning.

अङ्गाना ungrána, *v. n.* To yawn, stretch the limbs, oscitate.

अङ्गना ungna, ⎱ *s. m.* A yard, area,
अङ्गनाई ungnáee, ⎰ court, inclosed space adjoining to a house.

अङ्गरखा ungurkha, *s. m.* A coat, a doublet.

अङ्गराई ungráee, *s. f.* Stretching of the limbs, a yawning.

अङ्गली únglee, *s. f.* A finger. *Pyr kee únglee,* A toe. *Kúlum kee únglee,* Fore-finger. *Beech kee únglee,* Middle finger. *Kun únglee,* Little finger. *Unglee ka nok,* Tip of the finger.

अङ्गा unga, *s. f.* A maid whose business it is to hold, watch, and amuse a child ; a kind of nurse. *s. m.* A coat.

अङ्गारा ungára, *s. m.* A firebrand, embers, sparks remaining in ashes. *Ungáron pur lotna,* To be agitated or tormented (*particularly from jealousy*).

अङ्गारि ungári, *s. f.* A small portable fire-pan.

अङ्गिया úngiya, *s. f. m.* Bodice, stays.

अङ्गी ungée, *adj.* Corporeal, bodily.

अङ्गीकार ungeekár, *s. m.* An agreement, a promise, avowal, conceding to, acceptance of a proposal. *Ungeekár kúrna, v. a.* To accept, receive, agree to.

अङ्गूल úngool, *s. m.* The thumb, a finger.

अङ्गूली úngoolee, ⎱ *s. f.* A finger, a finger's
अङ्गूरी úngooree, ⎰ breadth.

अङ्गूष्ठ úngooshth, *s. m.* The thumb.

अङ्गूठा ungóotha, *s. m.* The thumb. *Un-*

giotha dikhána, An attitude adopted by women, in blandishment, as a token of prohibition ; to brave, defy.

अंगूठी ungóothee, *s. f.* A ring worn on the finger.

अंगेट ungét, }
अंगोट ungót, } *s. f.* Appearance, person.

अंगेठी ungéthee, *s. f.* A chafing-dish.

अंगोछा ungóchha, *s. m.* A cloth which Hindoos fasten round the waist when bathing, and afterwards wipe themselves with ; a towel, a hand-kerchief.

अंगोरा ungóra, *s. m.* A midge, a gnat.

अचंचल úchunchul, *adj.* Fixed, unmoved, firm, inactive.

अचंड úchund, *adj.* Gentle, not passionate.

अचंभा uchúmbha, *s. m.* Wonder, a wonderful thing, astonishment ; cause of astonishment.

अचकरी úchkuree, *s. f.* Lasciviousness, wantonness, wickedness.

अचक्षु úchukshoo, *adj.* Blind. *s. f.* Spectacles.

अचतानापचताना uchtána-puchtána, *v. n.* To repent, lament some neglect, grieve, be sorry.

अचतूर úchutoor, *adj.* Stupid, inactive.

अचपल úchpul, *f.* } *adj.* Restless, incon-
अचपला úchpula, *m.* } stant, playful,
अचपली úchpulee, *f.* } wanton ; brisk.

अचपलाहट uchpuláhut, } *s. f.* Restless-
अचपली úchpulee, } ness, inconstancy, wantonness ; playfulness, vivacity.

अचर úchur, *adj.* Immovable ; inanimate.

अचरच úchruch, } *s. m.* Wonder, admira-
अचरज úchruj, } tion, astonishment.
adj. Astonishing.

अचल úchul, *adj.* Immovable, fixed, incapable of motion. *s. m.* A mountain, an aged person. *Neel uchul,* The blue mountain near Bala-sore.

अचला úchula, *s. f.* The earth.

अचानक uchánuk, } *adv.* Suddenly,
अचानचक uchánchuk, } unawares, unexpectedly.

अचाना uchána, *v. a.* To wash or rinse the mouth after eating ; to drink.

अचार uchár, *s. m.* Conduct, common practice, usage, a rule of conduct.

अचार्य ucháruj, *s. m.* A spiritual guide or teacher, a learned *pundit.*

अचिक्कन úchikkun, *adj.* Rough, unpolish-ed.

अचिंत úchint, *adj.* Thoughtless.

अचिंता úchinta, *s. f.* Disregard, absence of thought or consideration.

अचीता úcheeta, *adj.* Unwished for ; not painted (*paper, &c.*)

अचूक úchook, *adj.* Unerring, sure ; (*hence*) a good marksman.

अचेत úchet, *adj.* Out of mind or senses, senseless, thoughtless, stupid. *Uchet hona, v. n.* To be insensible, to be thoughtless.

अचैन úchyn, *adj.* Uneasy, uncomfortable.

अच्युत úchyoot, *adj.* Fixed, permanent, imperishable, eternal. *s. m.* A name of *Vishnoo* or God.

अच्छुत úchchhut, *adj.* Infallible, indelible. *s. m. pres. part.* Remaining, existing, continuing ; whole grain, whole rice used in religious ceremonies, fried grain. *Uchchhut tiluk, s. f.* The ceremony of putting a few grains of rice on the forehead of an image when addressed, or of a *brahmun* when invited to an entertainment.

अच्छयवृक्ष úchchhy-bríchh, *s. m.* An unde-cayable tree.

अक्षर úchchhur, } *s. m.* A letter of the al-
अक्षर ukshur, } phabet.

अक्षरी úchchhuree, *adj.* Scientific, letter-ed, writing an elegant hand.

अच्छा úchchha, *adj.* Good, excellent, pleasant, righteous, healthy, well, sound ; lucky. *Uchchha hona, v. n.* To recover. *Uchchha kurna, v. a.* To cure, recover. *Uchchha lugna, v. n.* To become, beseem, be pleasing, be agreeable.

अच्छोदन uchchhódun, *s. m.* The chase, hunting.

अक्षौहिणी uchchhóuhinee, *s. f.* A complete army consisting of 109,350 foot, 65,610 horse, 21,870 chariots, and 21,870 elephants.

अच्छुय úchhuy, *adj.* Imperishable.

अच्छरौटी uchhróutee, *s. f.* Orthography ; a mode of playing on a stringed instrument so as to express the words of a song.

अच्छवानी uchhwánee, *s. f.* Caudle.

अछूता uchhóota, *adj.* Intangible (*victuals dressed for religious persons, &c.*), inviolable.

अज uj, *adv.* To-day, now. *s. m.* A he-goat.

अजगर újgur, *s. m.* A large serpent, the Boa constrictor.

अजगत újgoot, *adj.* Wonderful, astonishing

अजनम újunm, *adj.* Unborn and unbegotten.

अजमूद ujmóod, } *s. m.* Parsley (*Apium*
अजमोदा ujmóda, } *involucratum*), com-
mon carraway (*Carum Carui*), a kind of lovage (*Ligusticum Ajowan*).

अजय újy, *adj.* Not victorious, unsuccess-ful, subdued. *s. m.* Defeat.

अजर újur, *adj.* Free from decay, ever young, not subject to decrepitude, or the infirmi-ties of age, undecayable, imperishing.

अजवायन ujwáyun, *s. f.* The seed of a plant of the dill kind (*Ligusticum Ajowan*).

अजम अयम } újush, *adj.* Infamous.

अजहु újhoo, } *adv.* To-day also, even
अजहूं újhoon, } now, just now, yet, immediately.

अजा úja, *s. f.* A she-goat, illusion, the unreality of the universe.

अजार ujár, *s. m.* Canvas (*cloth made of hemp*).

अजात uját, *adj.* Expelled from his caste (*a man*).

अजाती ujátee, *s. m.* A man who has lost his caste.

अजान uján, *adj.* Ignorant, simple, innocent, indifferent, careless.

अजानी ujánee, *s. f.* Ignorance, simplicity.

अजित újit, *adj.* Unconquered; unexcelled, unsurpassed.

अजिन újin, *s. m.* A hide, used as a seat, bed, &c. by the religious student; generally the hide of an antelope.

अजिर ujír, *s. m.* An area, court, yard.

अजी ujée, An interjection to call or bespeak attention: in Bengal, it is used to an inferior, or in cases of great intimacy only; but in the western provinces, it is often addressed to a superior as a term of respect.

अजीत ujéet, *adj.* Invincible, unsubdued, impregnable.

अजीतवर्ण ujéet-burn, *s. m.* Leprosy (*of a bad kind*).

अजीर्ण ujéern, *s. m.* Indigestion; surfeit, flatulence. *adj.* Undecayed, unimpaired.

अजीव ujéev, *adj.* Lifeless, dead.

अजुक्त ujóokt, } *adj.* Unfit. *s. f.* Vio
अजुगत ujóogut, } lence, oppression, compulsion.

अजूठा ujóotha, *adj.* Untouched, untasted (*victuals*).

अजों újon, *adv.* Hitherto, to this day.

अजोड़ ujór, *adj.* Without joining; peerless, scarce.

अजोत ujót, *adj.* Without splendour, dull.

अझोल ujhól, *adj.* Of steady pace (*an elephant*).

अज्ञु úgyu, *adj.* Idiot, stupid, ignorant.

अज्ञा úgya, *s. f.* Command, order, permission.

अज्ञाकारी úgya-káree, *adj.* Acting according to orders, obedient.

अज्ञात ugyát, *adj.* Ignorant, simple, innocent; unknown.

अज्ञान ugyán, *adj.* Ignorant, witless, unknowing, a simpleton, stupid, unwise. *s. m.* Ignorance.

अज्ञानता ugyánta, *s. f.* Ignorance, stupidity, simplicity.

अज्ञानपन ugyanpún, *s. m.* Ignorance, foolishness, stupidity, simplicity.

अज्ञानी ugyánee, *adj.* Ignorant, unwise.

अंचल únchul, } *s. m.* The end or border
आंचल ánchul, } of a cloth, veil, shawl, &c.; the breast (*of a woman or lactescent animal*).

अंचला únchla, *s. m.* The end or border of a cloth, veil, shawl, &c.; a sheet used among *Jógees*.

अंजन únjun, *s. m.* A collyrium or application to the eye-lashes to darken and improve them, a universal article of the eastern toilet; particular applications, as lamp black, antimony, and another kind called *rusanjun*.

अंजनसार unjunsár, *s. m.* Collyrium.

अंजनहारी unjunháree, *s. f.* A stye or stithe on the eyelids.

अंजना únjna, *v. n.* To have the eyes tinged with *únjun*.

अंजना únjuna, *s. f.* The mother of *Hunoomán*; a lizard.

अंजनिका únjunika, *s. f.* A kind of newt or lizard.

अंजनी únjunee, *s. f.* A woman, perfumed with sandal, &c.; a medicinal plant used as a sedative and laxative.

अंजुला únjula, } *s. m.* The cavity formed
अंजुलि únjuli, } by putting the hands together and holding the palms as if to receive water; a measure, as much as can be held in both hands so disposed.

अटक útuk, *s. f.* Prevention, stop, obstruction, bar, obstacle; name of a river, the Atock.

अटकना útukna, *v. n.* To be stopped, to be prevented, to adhere, cease, rest, stick, stop.

अटकल útkul, *s. f.* Guess, conjecture, judgment, opinion, quantity, size. *Utkulbáz, adj.* Adroit at guessing; an appraiser. *Utkulna, v. a.* To guess, conjecture, judge, estimate, think. *Utkul-púchchoo, s. m.* One who guesses at a venture, or without grounds on which to judge. *adv.* At random.

अटकलना útkulna, *v. a.* To guess, to conjecture, to judge, to think.

अटका útka, *s. m.* The pot in which victuals are dressed for the public at the door of the temple at *Jugunnath*, *part. past.* Aground, stopped, hindered.

अटकाना utkána, *v. a.* To stop, to hinder, to prevent, restrain, detain, coerce.

चटकाव **utkáo**, *s. m.* Stop, prevention, hinderance, restraint, detention.

चटखेल **utkhél**, *adj.* Wanton.

चटखेली **utkhélee**, *s. f.* Wantonness, an affected (*also a graceful*) pace or mode of walking.

चटट **útut**, *adj.* Coarse, strong (*cloth*).

चटम **útun**, *s. m.* A balcony, an upper room.

चटना **útna**, *v. n.* To be contained; to be filled; to wander, perambulate, walk about. *Kooa ut gya*, The well is filled up.

चटनी **útnee**, *s. f.* The notched extremity or horn of a bow.

चटपटी **útputee**, } *adj.* Inconsider-
चटपटांगी **utputángee**, } ate, irregular, unstudied, thoughtless. *Utputee bat, s. f.* Confused or inconsistent speech, prevarication.

चटम **útum**, *s. m.* A heap.

चटल **útul**, *adj.* Immovable, permanent, fixed, of determined resolution, incontrovertible, unchangeable, irrevocable, irrefragable. *Utultá, s. f.* Incontrovertibility, immovableness.

चटवटखटवाट **utwát-khutwát**, *s. f.* The state of a person who in great affliction, remains bed-rid. *Utwánee Khutwánee lena*, To be confined to bed in great trouble or affliction.

चटवि **útvi**, *s. f.* Forest, grove, wilderness.

चटा **úta**, *s. f.* An upper room or story, a balcony.

चटारी **utáree**, *s. f.* A thatched upper room.

चटाल **utál**, *s. f.* A stack, rick (*of grass, corn, &c.*), a heap of baggage, &c.

चटाला **utála**, *s. m.* A heap; furniture.

चटूट **utóot**, *adj.* Not liable to be broken; inexhaustible.

चटेक **uték**, *adj.* Without support.

चटेर **utér**, *s. f.* Name of a town.

चटेरन **utérun**, *s. m.* A skein or bundle of thread, a reel; the lounge (*in the manage*).

चटेरना **utérna**, *v. a.* To make up thread into skeins, to reel; to lounge a horse.

चटोक **utók**, *adj.* Unquestioned, uninterrupted, unrestrained, without hinderance.

चटोल **utól**, *adj.* Unpolished (*stones or jewels; and hence, of persons*), rude, unmannerly.

चट्टाल **uttál**, *s. m.* An upper room or pavilion.

चट्टालिका **uttálika**, *s. f.* A thatched upper room.

चट्टी **úttee**, *s. f.* A hank or bundle of thread; a cant word for a turban.

चठखेली **uthkhélee**, *s. f.* Playfulness, wantonness.

चठतालीस **uthtálees**, *adj.* Forty-eight.

चठतीस **uthtées**, *adj.* Thirty-eight.

चठल **úthul**, *s. m.* Bathing of the bride and bridegroom together, the third day after marriage.

चठवाटीचठवाटी **uthwátee-khutwátee**, *s. f.* The state of being confined to bed through sickness, &c.

चठवारा **uthwára**, *s. m.* The eighth day after any other; a week.

चठसठ **úthsuth**, *adj.* Sixty-eight.

चठहत्तर **uthhúttur**, *adj.* Seventy-eight.

चठारेस **utháees**, *adj.* Twenty-eight.

चठानवे **uthánweh**, *adj.* Ninety-eight.

चठारह **utháruh**, *adj.* Eighteen. *Utháruhbhar*, Various, of different kinds.

चठावन **utháwun**, *adj.* Fifty-eight.

चठासी **uthásee**, *adj.* Eighty-eight.

चठेल **úthel**, *adj.* Not capable of being pushed out of its place, unanswerable, irrefragable.

चर **ur**, *s. f.* Contention, contrariety, obstinacy.

चढ़ंग **úrung**, *s. f.* A manufacturing town.

चढ़ंगा **urúnga**, *s. m.* A mode of wrestling with the feet; an obstacle.

चढ़तला **úrtula**, *s. m.* Defence, protection.

चढ़ना **úrna**, *v. n.* To stop, hesitate. *Ur kurna*, To stop, be obstinate (*as a horse*).

चढ़ंगा **urbúnga**, *adj.* Crooked, uneven.

चढ़ढ़ंग **urburúng**, *s. m.* Foolish actions.

चढ़ढ़ंगी **urburúngee**, *adj.* Inconsiderate.

चढ़ढ़ **úrbur**, *s. m.* Words without meaning. *adj.* Uneven, rugged. *Urbur bukna, v. a.* To speak inconsiderately or without meaning, to rave, talk absurdly, babble.

चढ़बन्द **úrbund**, *s. m.* A cloth worn by Hindoos, passing from the waist between the thighs and fastening behind.

चढ़यल **úryul**, *adj.* Obstinate, perverse, mulish.

चढ़हट **úrhut**, *s. f.* Agency, commission, sale by commission.

चढ़ारा **urára**, *s. m.* High steep banks of a river or tank.

चढ़ाना **urána**, *v. a.* To make to stop; to fasten one thing to another. *s. m.* Name of a tune.

चढ़ानी **uranee**, *s. f.* A large fan or parasol.

चढ़ूआ **uróoa**, *adj.* Obstinate, perverse, mulish, restiff.

चढ़ूसा **uróosa**, *s. m.* A medicinal plant (*Justicia adhenatoda and ganderussa*).

चढ़ेआना **úrey ána**, *v. n.* To protect, to become a protection.

অরৈৰ urynch, *s. f.* Enmity.

অডোল udól, *adj.* Not capable of being shaken or moved; immovable, fixed, unshaken.

অরোপরোস úros-purós, *s. m.* Neighbourhood.

অরঢাই urháee, *adj.* Two and a half; or when used with a noun of number, twice and a half the aggregate number. *s. f.* A full gallop.

অনি úni, *s. m.* The edge or point of a sharp weapon.

অনিমন únimun, } *s. m.* A superhuman
অনিমা únima, } faculty; the subtle and invisible state assumable by austere devotion and the performance of magical rites, or as possessed by a deity.

অনী únee, *s. f.* The point or edge of any sharp instrument, (*as, of an arrow, spear, &c.*)

অনু únoo, *s. m.* An atom. *adj.* Atomic, small, minute.

অন্তনা úntna, *v. n.* To be contained, to be tightened, to be filled up, (*a well, tank, &c.*)

অন্তৱানা untwána, *v. a.* To make contain, to cram into.

অন্তা únta, *s. m.* A ball, a marble. *Unta ghur, s. m.* A billiard-room.

অন্তাকোরী únta-kóree, *s. f.* A cord with which cattle are tied neck and heels.

অন্তাচিত úntachít, *adj.* Unlucky.

অন্থলুনা unthlúna, *v. a.* To twist, writhe. *v. n.* To swagger, strut, give one's self airs, walk affectedly.

অন্দ und, *s. m.* Palma christi (*Ricinus vulgaris*); an egg.

অন্দ und, } *s. m.* A testicle, or the scro-
আন্র anr, } tum; semen genitale.

অন্দকোষ undkósh, *s. m.* The scrotum, the testicles; rupture, hernia.

অন্দুজ undúj, *adj.* Oviparous, as, a serpent, a fish, a bird, a lizard.

অন্দা únda, *s. m.* An egg. *Unda dena,* To lay an egg.

অন্দেল undél, *adj.* Oviparous; with egg (*a bird*).

অতথা útutha, *adj.* Powerless, without authority.

অতন útun, *s. prop.* Kamdeo, the god of love among the Hindoos.

অতর্পিত úturpit, *adj.* Unsatisfied.

অতল útul, *s. m.* A particular hell, or division of the infernal regions; the portion immediately below the earth.

অতলস্পর্শ útul-spúrsh, *adj.* Very deep, bottomless.

অতসী útsee, *s. f.* Flax (*Linum usitatissimum*).

অতা úta, *s. m.* Father.

অতাঈ utáee, *s. m. f.* One who sings and dances gratis.

অতি úti, *prep.* Over, beyond (*in point of time, place or degree*), gone by, passed over, exceeding, surpassing, very, over, much, very much, &c.; it implies general excess or pre-eminence. *adv.* Exceedingly.

অতিকা útika, *adv.* Much, excessively.

অতিকাল utikál, *s. m.* Delay.

অতিগন্দ utigúnd, *s. m.* The sixth of the twenty-seven astrological *yogs* or periods.

অতিগতি utigúti, *adv.* Very much, very great.

অতিগন্ধ utigúndh, *s. m.* A fragrant grass, lemon-grass (*Andropogon schœnanthus*).

অতিগর্ব্বিত útigúrbbit, *adj.* Arrogant, proud.

অতিগুপ্ত utigóopt, *adj.* Very secret, closely hidden or concealed.

অতিচার utichár, *s. m.* The passage of a planet from one zodiacal sign to another, in a shorter than common period.

অতিজাগর utijágur, *adj.* Very wakeful, restless. *s. m.* The black curlew.

অতিজীর্ণ utijéern, *adj.* Very old.

অতিতীক্ষ্ণ uti-téekshn, *adj.* Very pungent, sharp, hot, or acrid.

অতিথি útithi, *s. m.* A guest, pilgrim, stranger, person entitled to the rights of hospitality. *Utithi kriya, s. f.* Hospitality, considered as a religious duty. *Utithi-seva, s. f.* Service of a guest, hospitality.

অতিদান útidan, *s. m.* Munificence.

অতিদাহ útidah, *s. m.* Great heat; violent inflammation.

অতিদুর্গত úti-dóorgut, *s. f.* Great difficulty or distress.

অতিদুষ্কর úti-dóoshkur, *adj.* Very arduous, very difficult.

অতিদূর útidóor, *s. m.* A great distance, afar off.

অতিদোষ útidósh, *s. m.* A great fault.

অতিপরাক্রম úti-purákrum, *s. m.* Great power.

অতিপাতক úti-pátuk, *s. m.* A heinous sin.

অতিপাতকী úti-pátukee, *adj.* A great sinner, flagrantly criminal.

অতিপান utipán, *s. m.* Excessive drinking, inebriety.

অতিবক্তা uti-búkta, *adj.* A great talker, a babbler.

चतिवल útibul, *adj.* Strong, powerful.

चतिबार útibar, *adv.* Frequently.

चतिबेल utibél, *adv.* or *adj.* Much, excessive, unlimited, frequently.

चतिभार utibhár, *s. m.* A great or excessive burden.

चतियोग्य utijógyuh, *adj.* Very worthy.

चतिरिक्त útirikt, *adj.* Excessive, exceeding.

चतिरोग útirog, *s. m.* Consumption (*Phthisis pulmonalis*).

चतिवक्ता úti-vukta, *adj.* A great talker, a babbler.

चतिविकट úti-vikut, *s. m.* A fierce elephant. *adj.* Very fierce, very formidable; hard, difficult.

चतिविष útivish, *adj.* Antidote, exceeding or subduing poison.

चतिविषा úti-visha, *s. f.* A tree used in medicine, the bark is also used in dyeing: it is of three kinds, white, red and black (*Atis* or *Betula*.)

चतिशुक्त útishukt, *adj.* Very powerful.

चतिशक्ति úti-shukti, *s. f.* Great power.

चतिशक्तिता úti-shuktitá, *s. f.* Heroic valour, prowess.

चतिशय útishuy, *adj.* Much, excessive.

चतिशीत útisheet, *adj.* Excessively cold.

चतिसंचय útisúnchuy, *s. m.* A hoard, a great accumulation.

चतिसार utisár, *s. m.* Diarrhœa or dysentery. *Utisárkee, adj.* Dysenteric. *Utisáree, adj.* Afflicted with dysentery; cathartic.

चतिहास útihas, *s. m.* A horse-laugh, violent laughter.

चतीत uteet, *s. m.* A wanderer, pilgrim, a mendicant among Hindoos. *adj.* Past, elapsed.

चतीतकाल uteet-kál, *s. m.* (*In gram.*) The preterite tense.

चतीस utées, *s. m.* A medicinal root.

चतीसार uteesár, *s. m.* Dysentery.

चतीक्ष्ण úteekshn, *adj.* Blunt, not sharp, dull, obtuse. *Uteekshntá, s. f.* Bluntness.

चतुल útool, } *adj.* Not weighed, incapa-
चतोल útol, } ble of being weighed; unequalled, unparalleled.

चतृप्त útript, *adj.* Unsatisfied, restless.

चतृप्ति útripti, *s. f.* Insatiableness, voraciousness.

चतेज úteja, *adj.* Dark, dim, dull. *s. m.* Insignificance, feebleness, imbecility.

चत्युन्त útyunt, *adj.* or *adv.* Much, very much, excessive, great.

चत्युल्प útyulp, *adj.* Very small, very little.

चत्याचार útyachar, *s. m.* Deviation from prescribed observances, contemning religious and moral laws.

चत्याचारी útyacharee, *adj.* Transgressing.

चत्यावश्यक utyávushyuk, *adj.* Indispensably necessary, very requisite, of great importance.

चत्र utr, *adv.* In this place, here, herein.

चथु úthu, *conj.* (*inceptive or premising particle used to introduce a remark, question, affirmation, &c.*) Thus, so, then, hence, further, now, moreover, henceforth.

चथुक úthuk, *adj.* Unwearied, untired, insensible of fatigue.

चथर्वन uthúrvun, *s. m.* The fourth Ved.

चथुल úthul, *adj.* Unsteady, unstable, wavering.

चथ्वा úthwa, *conj.* Or.

चथा útha, *adj.* Deep, unfordable, unfathomable, out of man's depth.

चथाईन uthácen, *s. f.* A place where people meet for counsel, or to converse and amuse themselves.

चथाह utháh, *adj.* Bottomless, very deep, unfathomable.

चथित uthít, } *adj.* Unstable, unsteady,
चस्थित ústhit, } wavering.

चद ud, *adj.* Half. *Ud-pukka,* Half-ripe.

चदकचा údukcha, *s. m.* A cloth for carrying things in, a covering.

चदखिला údkhila, *adj. m.* Half-blown (*a flower, &c.*).

चदखोला udkhóla, *adj. m.* Half-open.

चदगड़ा údgurha, *adj. m.* Half-driven (*as a stake*).

चदुंड údund, *adj.* Unpunished. *s. m.* Impunity.

चदत्त údutt, *adj.* Not given.

चदत्ता údutta, *adj. f.* Not given in marriage (*a female*).

चदभव údbhou, *s. m.* Act of being born or of springing up (*as plants from seed*), birth, production.

चदमूवा údmooa, } *adj. m.* Half-dead.
चदमरा údmura, }

चदुया úduya, *adj.* Unfeeling, unmerciful, destitute of pity.

चदर्श údursh, } *adj.* Unseen, unforeseen.
चदृष्ट údrisht, } *s. m.* Casual and unforeseen danger, fortune, luck.

चदर्शन údurshun, *s. m.* Disappearance. *adj.* Invisible.

c

बदूरसा údursa, *s. m.* A kind of very fine muslin ; a kind of sweetmeat.

बदलबदल údul-búdul, } *s. m.* Exchange,
बदलाबदला údla-búdla, } alteration.

बदलाबदला करना údla-búdla kúrna, *v. a. m.* To exchange, swop or barter ; confuse, displace.

बदली बदली करनी údlee búdlee kúrnee, *v. a. f.* To exchange, swop or barter ; confuse, displace.

बदवान udwán, } *s. f.* Braces for tight-
बदवायन udwáyun, } ening the tape of a bedstead.

बदहन údhun, *s. m.* Water set to boil for dressing victuals.

बदाता údata, } *adj.* Illiberal, avaricious,
बदानी údanee, } stingy.

बदिति úditi, *s. f.* The proper name of the mother of the gods.

बदिति नन्दन úditi-núndun, *s. m.* A deity.

बदिन údin, *s. m.* An unlucky day.

बदिष्ट údisht, *s. m.* Misfortune, fate.

बदृश्यु údrishyu, *adj.* Invisible, unseen.

बदृष्ट údrisht, *adj.* Unseen, unforeseen.

बदी úddhee, *s. f.* Half a dumree (*a small coin*), half a piece of cloth.

बदोत údot, } *adj.* Without splendour.
बद्योत údyot, }

बदौरी udóuree, *s. f.* A kind of food eaten by Hindoos.

बद्भुत údbhoot, *adj.* Surprising, wonderful, admirable. *s. m.* Surprise, astonishment.

बद्रुक údruk, *s. f.* Ginger, in an undried state (*Amomum zinziber*).

बद्रुकी údrukee, *s. f.* A kind of sweetmeat.

बद्रोह údroh, *s. m.* Mildness, moderation, the absence of tyranny and oppression.

बद्रोही údrohee, *adj.* Innocuous, mild.

बद्वन्द údwund, *adj.* Quiet, tranquil, free from strife.

बद्वायन udwáyun, *s. f.* Braces for tightening the tape of a bedstead.

बद्वितीय údwiteeyu, } *adj.* Peerless, match-
बद्वित údwyt, } less, unequalled ; only, sole, without a second.

बद्वेष udwesh, *adj.* Harmless, not malicious.

बद्वेषी údweshee, *adj.* Harmless, inoffensive.

बध údhuh, *prep.* Down, downwards, below (*in place, rank or degree*) ; the reverse of उत oot.

बध udh, (*in comp.*) Half.

बधंग udhúng, *s. m.* Palsy affecting one side or half the body, hemiplegia.

बधंगी udhúngee, *adj.* Affected with hemiplegia, palsied ; paralytic.

बधकुचरा udh-kúchra, *adj. m.* Half-dressed victuals.

बधकच्चा udh-kúchcha, *adj. m.* Half-ripe.

बधकपाली udh-kupálee, *s. f.* A pain affecting half the head ; a nut of areca shaped like a hemisphere (*so named, probably, from two kernels being contained in one shell : and to such a nut the virtue is ascribed of curing the disease of the same name*).

बधकर údh-kur, *s. m.* Half the tax or duty of any kind (*the other half being remitted*).

बधकूहा udh-kúha, *adj. m.* Half-spoken, half-uttered

बधन údhun, } *adj.* Poor, destitute, in-
बधनी údhunee, } digent.

बधपक्का udh-púkka, *adj.* Half-ripe.

बधपुत údbput, *s. m.* A prince, a commander, a master.

बधबुना udh-búna, *adj. m.* Half-made, half-prepared.

बधबुर údhbur, *adv.* Half-way, in the middle.

बधबीच údhbeech, *adv.* In the middle.

बधम údhum, *adj.* Inferior, low, mean, vile, despicable, wretched, contemptible.

बधमूआ údh-mooa, } *adj.* Half-dead.
बधमरा údh-mura, }

बधर údhur, *adj.* Low, inferior, below ; low, vile. *s. m.* The lip, the lower lip ; pudendum muliebre.

बधर údhur, *s. m.* Empty space, the space between heaven and earth. *adj.* Suspended, separate, at a distance. *adv.* In the middle.

बधरसा údhursa, *s. m.* A half piece of cloth ; a sort of cloth.

बधरामृत údhur-ámrit, *s. m.* The moisture, honey or nectar of the lips.

बधर्म údhurm, *s. m.* Injustice, irreligion, unrighteousness, impiety, immorality, sin, crime. *adj.* Unjust, impious.

बधर्मचारी údhurm-cháree, *adj.* Unrighteous, wicked.

बधर्मता udhurmtá, *s. f.* Unrighteousness.

बधर्मपना údhurm-púna, *s. m.* Injustice, crime.

बधर्मिष्ठ údhurmishth, *adj.* Very wicked.

बधर्मी údhurmee, *adj.* Unjust, wicked, unrighteous, sinful, criminal, immoral, impious.

चचचच **údhwun**, *adj.* Half of any thing.

चचचाच **udhwár**, *s. f.* A half (*generally applied to pieces of cloth*).

चचान **udhán**, *s. m.* Oils, unguents.

चचार **údhar**, } *s. m.* Food, aliment, vic-
चाचार **ádhar**, } tuals, nourishment, support.

चचासिच **údharmik**, *adj.* Unjust, unrighteods, wicked.

चचाचीची **údha-séesee**, *s. f.* Pain affecting the half of the head, hemicrania.

चचि **údhi**, *prep.* Over, above, upon; it implies superiority (*in place, quality, or quantity*), and is the reverse of चचू *up*.

चचिच **údhik**, *adj.* Exceeding, excessive, greater, moreover, more than, most, additional, extra, augmented.

चचिकता **udhiktá**, *s. f.* Excess, addition.

चचिकाई **udhikáee**, *s. f.* Increase, augmentation, abundance, excess; oppression.

चचिकाना **udhikána**, *v. a.* To augment, increase.

चचिकार **udhikár**, *s. m.* A kingdom, a government, an estate; the bearing of royal insignia, dominion, possession, authority, rule, title, a right, a privilege, an inheritance.

चचिकारी **udhikáree**, *adj.* Possessing a right, title, or privilege. *s. m.* A proprietor, a master, an owner, one invested with power and authority, a ruler, a director.

चचिकत **ádhikrit**, *s. m.* A superintendant in general; an inspector of receipts and disbursements, an auditor of public accompts.

चचिप **údhip**, } *s. m.* An owner, a lord,
चचिपति **údhiput**, } or master; a king.

चचिमांच **udhi-máns**, *s. m.* Fleshy excrescences on the eye, cancer of the eye.

चचिमाच **udhimás**, *s. m.* An intercalary month, formed of the aggregate days, omitted in reckoning the lunar year.

चचियाना **udhiyána**, *v. a.* To halve, to divide.

चचिराज **udhiráj**, *s. m.* A great or supreme king, superior prince, a sovereign, an emperor.

चचिराज्युच **udhirájyuh**, *s. m.* Empire, supreme sway.

चचीन **udhéen**, } *adj.* Obedient, submis-
चचीन **adhéen**, } sive, humble, docile, subject to the control of another, subservient; dependant.

चचीनता **udheentá**, *s. f.* Submission, obedience, obsequiousness, servility, humility, servitude, subjection, dependance, slavery.

चचीनी **udhéenee**, *s. f.* Submission, humbleness, obsequiousness; petition.

चचीर **udhér**, *adj.* Confused, perplexed; unsteady (*lit. or met.*); impatient, hasty, precipitate, irresolute.

चचीरज **údheeruj**, *s. m.* Confusedness, perplexity, unsteadiness. *adj.* Perplexed, confused, unsteady, impatient.

चचीरजा **udhéerja**, } *adj.* Confused, per-
चचीरजी **udhéerjee**, } plexed.

चचीरता **udheertá**, *s. f.* Haste, precipitation, irresolution, fickleness, unsteadiness, want of firmness; confusion, perplexity, impatience.

चचीचर **udhéeshwur**, *s. m.* An emperor, a king paramount over all the neighbouring princes.

चचूरा **udhóora**, *adj.* Half-ready, half-dressed; immature (*a fœtus*); unfinished. *Udhoora jána, v. n.* To miscarry (*a female*).

चचीर **udhér**, *adj.* Middle-aged, just past the prime of life (*applied most frequently to women*).

चचेचा **udhéla**, *s. m.* Half a pice or *pysa* (*a small coin*).

चचेची **udhélee**, *s. f.* Half a rupee.

चचेयं **údhyrj**, *adj.* Unsteady, feeble, irresolute.

चचेयां **udhyrjá**, *s. m.* Instability, want of firmness.

चचीतर **udhótur**, *s. f.* A fine kind of cloth.

चचीमुच **udhómookh**, *adj.* With the head downwards (*as the Hindoos practise in the tupusya*), looking downwards, drooping the head (*from grief or shame*); headlong; inverted, turned upside down.

चचीरी **udhóuree**, *s. f.* Half a hide (*of a thick strong kind*).

चचून **údhyun**, *s. m.* Study, reading, especially of the sacred books; one of the six duties of a brahmun.

चचूक्ष **udhyúksh**, *s. m.* A master, a lord, a chief, a governor, a superintendant.

चचाान **udhyána**, *v. a.* To halve, to divide.

चचापुक **udhyápuk**, *s. m.* A teacher, one who instructs in the sacred books.

चचापन **udhyápun**, *s. m.* Instructing, teaching the sacred books.

चचाायु **udhyáyu**, *s. m.* A section, or division of a book; a chapter, or lecture of the Veds; a chapter, a lesson.

चन **un**, A prefix of negation, privation or diminution, used properly before words beginning with a vowel only, चच being adopted before consonants: in Hindee, however, चन frequently occurs with consonants; so, चनचन **únunt**, चनदेचा **úndekha**.

चनचाना **unkhána**, *v. n.* To be angry, or displeased, to be peevish, or fretful.

बनमड़ úngurh, *m. f.* ⎫ *adj.* Unwrought
बनमड़ा úngurha, *m.* ⎬ unformed; un
बनमड़ी úngurhee, *f.* ⎭ educated; unlicked, unpolished, unfinished, unset (*as a ring or
jewel*). *Ungurhee bat*, Inconsistent or ill-arranged
speech.

बनगिनत úngunit, ⎫ *adj.* Uncounted, in
बनगिनत ungínut, ⎬ numerable, num
बनगिनती úngintee, ⎭ berless, countless.

बनगिना úngina, *adj.* Uncounted, numberless. *Ungina muheena*, The eighth month of a
woman's pregnancy.

बनघ únugh, *adj.* Sinless, innocent.

बनचाहत únchahut, *adj.* Not desired.

बनचित únchit, *adj.* Unawares, suddenly,
unexpectedly.

बनछीला únchheela, *adj.* Unpared (*as
fruit, &c.*), unlicked, rude, awkward, boorish.

बनजमा únjuna, *adj.* Unborn.

बनजल únjul, *s. m.* Victuals and food.

बनजला únjula, *adj.* Unburnt.

बनजस únjus, *s. m.* Infamy.

बनजान unján, *adj.* Unwitting, unintentional, not knowing, ignorant. *s. m.* A stranger.

बनजाना unjána, *adj.* Unknown, ignorant.

बनजाने unjáneh, *adv.* Ignorantly, not
knowing, unwittingly.

बनजामा unjáma, *adj.* Barren (*land*) in
which nothing will grow.

बनदेखा úndekha, *adj.* Unseen, invisible.

बनधीन únudheen, *adj.* Independant.

बनधोया úndhoya, *adj.* Unwashed; unclean

बनन्त únunt, *adj.* Boundless, illimitable;
endless, eternal; infinite, innumerable. *s. m.* A
name of the serpent said to support the earth; a
name of *Vishnoo*; name of several plants; a cord
with fourteen knots, which the Hindoos tie on
their arm on the 14th day of *Bhadon sookl-puksh*,
which is sacred to *Vishnoo*, and called *Ununt-
choudus.*

बनन्तता ununttá, *s. f.* Eternity.

बनन्तराशि únunt-ráshi, *s. f.* (*In arithmetic*) Infinite quantity.

बनन्तरूप ununt-róop, *adj.* Multiform.

बनन्तवात ununt-vát, *s. m.* Rigidity or paralysis of the muscles of the face and neck.

बनन्त्य únuntyuh, *adj.* Unbounded, infinite, eternal. *s. m.* Immortality; eternity; infinity.

बनपढ़ा únpurha, *adj.* Illiterate, uninformed.

बनपत्य únputyuh, *adj.* Childless, having
no progeny.

बनपुराध únupuradh, *s. m.* Innocence.
adj. Innocent, sinless.

बनपुराधी únupuradhee, *adj.* Innocent,
sinless.

बनपेख únupekh, *adj.* Disregarding, unheeding.

बनपेखा únupeksha, *s. f.* Carelessness, indifference, disregard.

बनबनाव únbunao, *s. m.* Discord, dissension, misunderstanding.

बनबियाहा únbiyaha, *adj.* Unmarried.

बनबेधा únbedha, *adj.* Unbored, unperforated.

बनबोल únbol, *adj.* Silent, speechless,
mute.

बनभिलाष únubhilash, *s. m.* Indifference,
absence of desire.

बनभिलाषी únubhilashee, *adj.* Indifferent.

बनमना únmuna, *m.* ⎫ *adj.* Thoughtful,
बनमनी únmunee, *f.* ⎬ agitated, regretting, out of humour, sad, troubled in mind, dissatisfied, displeased, vexed, sickly.

बनजुष únjush, *s. m.* Infamy.

बनरस únrus, *s. m.* Want of flavour or
enjoyment; disgust, nauseousness, coolness or
misunderstanding between friends.

बनरीत únreet, *s. f.* Unmannerliness, ill-
behaviour.

बनर्थ únurth, *adj.* Unmeaning, fruitless,
abortive; absurd, improper, nonsensical.

बनल únul, *s. f.* Fire; a plant (*Plumbago
zeylanica and rosea*).

बनवट únwut, *s. m.* A ring furnished with
little balls and worn on the great toe.

बनवधान únuvudhan, *adj.* Careless, inattentive. *s. m.* Inadvertence, inattention, carelessness.

बनवधानता únuvudhantá, *s. f.* Inadvertence, inattention.

बनवसर únuvusur, *adj.* Occupied, busy,
having no leisure; unseasonable, inopportune.
s. m. Want of leisure or opportunity; unseasonableness, inopportuneness.

बनवस्था únuvustha, *adj.* Unstable, unsteady; incontinent. *s. f.* Instability, absence of
fixed state or condition; uncertainty, doubt; incontinence, dissoluteness.

बनसमझा únsumjha, *adj.* Not understood,
not knowing.

बनसिख únsikh, *adj.* Unlearned.

बनसुना únsoona, *adj.* Unheard, not
noticed, disregarded. *Unsoonee kurna*, v. n. To
pretend not to hear (*what is spoken*); to disregard.

अनहंकार únhunkar, *s. m.* Absence of pride, humility.

अनहंकारी únhunkaree, *adj.* Humble, not proud.

अनहित únhit, *adj.* Without affection, an enemy. *s. m.* Enmity, disaffection.

अनाकार únakar, *adj.* Shapeless, without form.

अनाक्रान्ता únakranta, *s. f.* A sort of prickly nightshade (*Solanum jacquini*).

अनगम्यह únagumyuh, *adj.* Unapproachable; inaccessible; unobtainable.

अनाचार únachar, *s. m.* Improper conduct, irreligion, neglect of moral or religious observance. *adj.* Immoral, ill-behaved, indecent.

अनाचारी únacharee, *adj.* Immoral, indecorous, indecent.

अनाज unáj, *s. m.* Grain.

अनाड़ी unáree, *adj.* Unskilful, clumsy, artless, awkward, inexpert. *s. m. f.* A novice, bungler, simpleton.

अनातुर únatoor, *adj.* Well, vigorous, free from sickness or pain.

अनाथ únath, *adj.* Husbandless, without a protector, lord or master, without chief or sovereign; helpless.

अनादर únadur, *s. m.* Disrespect; affront.

अनादि únadi, *adj.* Without beginning, eternal as it respects beginning, unborn, uncreate.

अनादित्व unadi-twúh, *s. m.* Eternity.

अनायास únay-as, *s. m.* Ease, facility. *adj.* Easy.

अनार्पन unarpún, *s. m.* Silliness, clumsiness, inexpertness, ignorance, awkwardness.

अनाश्यह únashyuh, *adj.* Indestructible.

अनाहार únahar, *s. m.* Abstinence, starvation.

अनाहारी únaharee, *adj.* Fasting.

अनिच्छा únichchha, *s. f.* Indifference, absence of wish or desire.

अनित्यह únityuh, *adj.* Not for ever; frail, perishable, transient, not everlasting, transitory, temporary, fugitive.

अनित्यता unityutá, *s. f.* Transient or limited existence.

अनिद्र únidr, *adj.* Awake, sleepless.

अनिन्दित únindit, *adj.* Unreproachable.

अनिपुण únipoon, *adj.* Unskilled, not conversant.

अनिरुद्ध únirooddh, *adj.* Unobstructed, unrestrained.

अनिर्णय únirnuy, *s. m.* Uncertainty.

अनिर्मल únirmul, *adj.* Dirty, foul.

अनिर्वचनीय únirvuchuneéyuh, } *adj.* Not
अनिर्वाच्य unirvachyuh, } fit to be spoken; indescribable, indefinable.

अनिल únil, *s. m.* Air or wind, considered also as a deity.

अनिवारित únivarit, *adj.* Unchecked, unimpeded, unopposed, unforbidden.

अनिषिद्ध únishiddh, *adj.* Unprohibited, unforbidden.

अनिष्ट únisht, *adj.* Undesired, ominous, evil, bad, unlucky.

अनिष्ठा únishtha, *s. m.* Unsteadfastness, unsteadiness.

अनी únee, *s. f.* The point or edge of any sharp instrument (*as, of an arrow, spear, &c.*).

अनीकिनी uneékinee, *s. f.* An army, a host, forces; a certain force, 1-10th of an *Ukshóuhinee*, consisting of 2187 elephants, and as many cars, 6561 horse, and 10,935 foot.

अनीति uneéti, *s. f.* Injustice, immorality, impropriety, rudeness, unmannerliness, impolicy, ill-conduct.

अनु únoo, *prep.* After (*in time, place, rank and degree*), according to, in imitation to; it is the reverse of अभि úbhi.

अनुकम्पा únoo-kúmpa, *s. f.* Tenderness, compassion, pity.

अनुकूल únookool, *adj.* Co-inciding, friendly to, assisting, acting in concert with, favourable or conformable to.

अनुकूलता únoo-kóolta, *s. f.* A co-incidence, a being in concert, a concert, concord, good will, consent.

अनुक्त únookt, *adj.* Not spoken, not told, not mentioned. *s. m.* A trope.

अनुक्रम únookrum, *s. m.* Order, method, a succession, a series.

अनुखल únookhal, *s. m.* A creek.

अनुग únoog, *adj.* Following, succeeding. *s. m. f.* A follower, a servant, a dependant.

अनुगत únoogut, *adj.* Gone after, dependant on, attached to.

अनुगामी únoo-gámee, *adj.* Following, consequent upon, devoted to, imitating. *s. m.* A companion, a follower; one who goes behind or after.

अनुग्रह únoogruh, *s. m.* Favour, grace, kindness, indulgence; conferring benefits, promoting good, and preventing ill.

अनुचर únoochur, *s. m.* A companion, a follower, a servant, an attendant.

अनुचरी únoo-chúree, *s. f.* A female companion.

अनुचित únoochit, *adj.* Unfit, improper, unbecoming.

बनुज únooj, *adj.* Younger, junior. *s. m.* A younger brother.

बनुझ्रा únoogya, *s. f.* An order, command, injunction.

बनुताप unootáp, *s. m.* Repentance, regret, remorse.

बनुतापी unootápee, *adj.* Penitent, regretting.

बनुतारा únoo-tára, *s. m.* A satellite.

बनुत्तर únoottur, *adj.* Unable to answer, silent, without reply. [daily.

बनुदिन únoodin, *adj.* and *adv.* Every day,

बनुनासिक únoo-násik, *adj.* Nasal, uttered through the nose.

बनुपल únoopul, *s. m.* A second (*of time*).

बनुपस्थित únoopusthit, *adj.* Not ready, not present.

बनुपान unoopán, *s. m.* A fluid vehicle (*in medicine*); or that which is swallowed after the medicine.

बनुबन्धी únoo-búndhee, *adj.* Connected with, attached.

बनुभव únoobhuvuh, ⎱ *s. m.* Apprehension,
— únoobhou, ⎰ the exercise of the understanding independent of memory; comprehension, guess, inference, perception, supposition, hypothesis, experience; result, consequence.

बनुभूत unoobhóot, *adj.* Experienced, felt, guessed, perceived, indicated.

बनुमति únoo-múti, *s. f.* An order, a command, permission, advice.

बनुमरण únoo-múrun, *s. m.* A widow's burning on a separate pile from her deceased husband.

बनुमान únooman, *s. m.* Inference, guess, hypothesis, logical conclusion.

बनुराग únoorag, *s. m.* Affection, love, passion, attachment. [with.

बनुरागना unoorágna, *v. n.* To be in love

बनुरागी únoo-rágee, *part. act.* Making friendship, loving, caressing. *adj.* Impassioned, in love.

बनुराधा únoo-rádha, *s. f.* The 17th Nukshutruh or lunar mansion, designated by a row of oblations (*stars in Libra*).

बनुरूप unooróop, *adj.* Like, resembling, corresponding with. *s. m.* Conformity.

बनुरोध unooródh, *s. m.* The accomplishing of a desired object for another person, obligingness, service.

बनुसन्धान únoo-sundhán, *s. m.* Inquiry, investigation, searching.

बनुसरना unoo-súrna, *v. n.* To follow, to be consequent upon, to follow a person, to follow upon some previous circumstance.

बनुसार unoosár, *adj.* Following, answering to, according with. *s. m.* Conformity to usage, &c.

बनुसारी únoo-sarée, *adj.* Following; according with or to.

बनुस्वार únooswar, *s. m.* In grammar the nasal character or bindee °.

बनूठा unóotha, *adj.* Rare, wonderful, uncommon (*generally applied to things or animals*).

बनूप unóop, *adj.* Incomparable, best.

बनऋणी únrinee, *adj.* Unindebted, free from debt.

बनेक unék, *adj.* Many, much, abundant.

बनेककाल unek-kál, *adv.* A long time.

बनेकरूप unek-róop, *adj.* Multiform; of various kinds or sorts; fickle, of variable mind.

बनेकविध unek-vídh, *adj.* Various, of many kinds, in different ways.

बनेकाकार unek-akár, *adj.* Multiform.

बनोखा unókha, *adj.* Rare, uncommon, wonderful (*generally applied to man*).

बनोना únona, *adj.* Saltless.

बन्तःकरण úntuh-kurun, *s. m.* The understanding, the heart, the will, the conscience, the soul.

बन्तःपाती úntuh-pátee, *adj.* Included.

बन्तःपुर untuh-póor, *s. m.* The queen's apartments, the inner or female apartments.

बन्तःशरीर untuh-shuréer, *s. m.* The internal and spiritual part of man, the conscience, the soul.

बन्त unt, *s. m.* End, completion; death; a boundary, a limit; perdition, destruction; mind, heart. *adv.* After all, at last; in, within, elsewhere, somewhere else. [of.

बन्त unt, *s. m.* Intelligence, news, account

बन्तकाल untkál, *s. m.* Dying moment, hour of death. [cast.

बन्तुज úntuj, *s. m.* A shoodr or man of low

बन्त्री úntree, ⎱ *s. f.* Entrails, intestines,
बत्री úntree, ⎰ bowels, gut.

बन्तर úntur, *adv.* Within, between, amongst; without, except. *s. m.* Interval, intermediate space; period, term; difference; hole or rent; midst, the midst; the heart, the supreme soul. *adj.* Other, similar.

बन्तर्गति úntur-gáti, *s. f.* The emotions of the heart, inward sensations. *adj.* Forgotten.

बन्तरंग unturúng, *s. m.* A relative, a near friend.

बन्तर्जात untur-jat, *adj.* Inborn, inbred, innate.

बन्तर्दुष्ट untur-dóosht, *adj.* Internally bad, wicked, vile.

अंतरपट unturpút, *s. m.* A curtain, a skreen.

अंतरवेद unturbéd, *n. prop.* Name of the country between the *Gunga* and *Jumna rivers,* called in Persian Dooabuh, the Doab.

अंतरा úntura, *adj.* In the middle, among; near at hand; without, except. *s. m.* A verse, any verse of a song excepting the first.

अंतरातप úntura-túp, *s. f.* A tertian ague.

अंतरापत्यः úntur-apútyuh, *adj. f.* Pregnant.

अंतराल unturál, *s. m.* Included space.

अंतरिया únturiya, *s. f.* A tertian ague.

अंतरित únturit, *adj.* Inward, internal.

अंतरिक्ष unturíksh, *s. m.* The sky or atmosphere.

अंतरी úntree, *s. f.* Entrails, intestines, bowels, gut. *Untriyan julna,* To be very hungry. *Untriyan kool-hoowullah purhna,* To be very hungry: (*lit. The belly repeating, There is but one God*). *Untree ka bul khólna,* To eat a bellyful after starving. *Untriyen men ag lugna,* To be very hungry.

अंतरीप unturéep, *s. m.* A promontory, a headland, a cape, as, *Koomaree-untureep,* Cape Comorin.

अंतरीक्ष untureéksh, *s. m.* The sky or atmosphere. *adv.* In the air, out of sight.

अंतरजामी úntur-jámee, *adj.* Pervading the inward parts, acquainted with the heart (*an epithet of the Deity*).

अंतरद्वार untur-dwár, *s. m.* A private door within a house.

अंतरध्यान úntur-dhiyán, *s. m.* A disappearing, a vanishing away; profound inward meditation. *adj.* Out of sight, vanished, disappeared, concealed.

अंतरपट unturpút, *s. m.* A curtain, a skreen.

अंतरभाव untur-bháo, *s. m.* Internal or inherent nature or disposition.

अंतरभूत untur-bhóot, *adj.* or *adv.* In the midst.

अंतरमनस úntur-múnus, *adj.* Sad, perplexed.

अंतरजामी úntur-jámee, *adj.* Pervading the inward parts, heart-searching or pervading, acquainted with the heart (*an epithet of the Deity*).

अंतरवत्नी úntur-vútnee, *s. f.* A pregnant woman.

अंतरवेदी úntur-védee, *s. f.* The name of a country, the Doab, or country between the Gunga and Jumna rivers.

अंतिम úntim, *adj.* Final, ultimate.

अंत्यज untyúj, *s. m.* A shoodr or man of the fourth tribe.

अंत्यजन्म úntyu-júnma, *s. m.* A man of the shoodr or fourth tribe.

अंत्यजन्मनी úntyu-júnumnee, *s. f.* A woman of the shoodr or fourth tribe.

अंत्यवर्ण úntyuvúrn, *s. m. f.* A man or woman of the shoodr or fourth tribe.

अंत्र untr, *s. f.* The entrails, the bowels, the viscera.

अंध undh, *s. m.* Darkness. *adj.* Blind.

अंधकार undhkár, *s. m.* Darkness.

अंधकूप úndh-koop, *s. m.* A blind well, one of which the mouth is hidden or overgrown by weeds.

अंधतमस undh-túmus, *s. m.* Great darkness.

अंधता undh-tá, *s. f.* Blindness.

अंधला índhla, } *adj.* Blind, dark, dim.
अंधा úndha, } *Undhlapán, s. m.* Blindness, intellectual blindness, acting as if one were blind.

अंधियारा undhiyára, *adj.* Dark.

अंधेर undhér, *s. m.* Misfortune, calamity, injustice, violence, tumult, outrage, tyranny, oppression; darkness. *Undher kurna, v. a.* To act unjustly, to tyrannize, to oppress.

अंधेरा undhéra, *adj.* Dark, blind. *s. m.* Darkness.

अंधेरी undhéree, *adj. f.* Dark. *s. f.* Darkness.

अंधेरी कोठरी undhéree-kóthree, *s. f.* A dark room; the belly, womb.

अंन unn, *s. m.* Food, victuals, grain, boiled rice; corn. *Unn-data, s. m.* A benefactor.

अंनकूट unn-kóot, *s. m.* A festival celebrated by Hindoos, on the day following the *dewálee,* by offering a large quantity of meats to their gods.

अंनजल únnjul, } *s. m.* Victuals and
अंनपानी únn-pánee, } drink; support, maintenance, subsistence.

अंनपूर्णा unnpóorna, *s. m.* Satiety of food. *n. prop.* The name of a goddess, the Ceres of the Hindoos.

अंनप्राशन unn-práshun, *s. m.* The ceremony of giving a child *kheer* or milk and rice for the first time when six months old.

अंनरस unn-rús, *s. m.* Chyle.

अंनहीन unnhéen, *adj.* Destitute of food, needy.

अंना únna, *s. m.* The husband of a nurse.

अंनी únnee, *s. f.* A nurse or female attendant on a child.

अंमेल únmel, } *adj.* Discordant, heteroge-
अंमिल únmil, } neous.

अन्मोल únmol, *adj.* Invaluable, beyond price.

अन्य únyuh, *adj.* Another, other, different.

अन्यजन्म únyujúnum, *s. m.* Another birth, regeneration.

अन्यत्र unyútr, *adv.* Elsewhere, in another place.

अन्यथा únyutha, *adv.* Otherwise, in a different manner, inaccurately, untruly. *adj.* Contrary.

अन्यमनस् únyumúnus, *adj.* Fickle, versatile, absent.

अन्याय únyayuh, *s. m.* Injustice, outrage, impropriety.

अन्यायी únyayee, *adj.* Unjust, oppressive, lawless.

अन्यान्य unyónyuh, *adj.* Reciprocal, mutual.

अन्वय únvuy, *s. m.* Race, lineage; interpretation, making out the natural order or connexion of poetical style.

अन्वित únvit, *adj.* Connected with, joined, possessed of, fraught with, inherent in.

अन्वेषण unvéshun, *s. m.* Inquiry, search, research.

अन्वेषी unvéshee, *adj.* Searching, inquisitive.

अन्ह्वाना unhwána, *v. a.* To wash, bathe, cause to bathe.

अन्हान unhán, *s. m.* Bathing.

अन्हाना unhána, *v. n.* To bathe, to wash.

अन्होनहार únhonhar, *adj.* Hopeless, unpromising; improbable.

अन्होना únhona, *adj.* Impossible.

अप úpuh, *prep.* Under, below (*denoting inferiority, secrecy, disappearance, slyness, &c.*); ill amiss, bad; the reverse of अधि *udhi.*

अपंथ úpunth, *s. m.* A wrong or bad road, a devious track; heresy.

अपंथी úpunthee, *adj.* One who has lost his way; devious; heretical.

अपंपा úpumpa, *s. m.* One's self (*used in the accusative case only*), as, *Upumpa buchána,* To guard or protect one's self.

अपक úpuk, *adj.* Unripe.

अपकर्म úpkurm, *s. m.* A mean or unworthy action, wickedness.

अपकलंक upkulunk, *s. m.* An indelible disgrace.

अपकार úpkar, *s. m.* A hindrance, a detriment, an injury.

अपकृष्ट úpkrisht, *adj.* Bad, inferior, deteriorated.

अपक्व úpukk, *adj.* Raw, unripe, imperfect, immature.

अपक्वता upukktá, *s. f.* Immaturity.

अपचय úpchuy, *s. m.* Loss, detriment, waste.

अपजस úpjus, *s. m.* Infamy, ignominy, dishonour.

अपजसी úpjusee, *adj.* Infamous, unfortunate.

अपटक úputuk, *adj.* One whose hands and feet are become useless, paralytic.

अपटु úputoo, *adj.* Unskilled, awkward, incapable, uncouth; ineloquent.

अपति úputi, *s. f.* Discredit, disgrace.

अपतिया úputiya, ⎱ *adj.* Faithless, trea-
अपतियारा úputiyara, ⎰ cherous.

अपतिव्रता uputi-vrúta, *adj. s. f.* Unchaste (*a woman*); a courtezan.

अपत्य úputyuh, *s. m.* Offspring, male or female.

अपथ úputh, *s. m.* The want of a road; a bad road.

अपथ्य upúthyuh, *adj.* Indigestible, unwholesome.

अपना úpna, *m.* ⎱ *pron. poss.* Of or belong-
अपनी úpnee, *f.* ⎰ ing to self, own. *Upnee gdona,* To sing one's own praises, to egotize.

अपनाना upnána, *v. a.* To make a thing one's own, to convert or appropriate to one's own use.

अपनायत upnáyut, *s. f.* Family, relations, kindred, kin.

अपबुष्य úpubushyu, ⎱ *adj.* Absolute, inde-
अपबुस úpubus, ⎰ pendent.

अपबाद upubád, *s. m.* Complaint, accusation, censure.

अपबित्र úpubitr, *adj.* Unclean, defiled, impure.

अपभाषा úpubhasha, *s. f.* Low, vulgar or obscene language.

अपभ्रंश upubhrúnsh, ⎱ *s. m.* Common or
अपभंश upubhúnsh, ⎰ vulgar talk, a vulgar term, ungrammatical language.

अपमान upumán, *s. m.* Disgrace, dishonour, affront, disrespect, contempt.

अपमानित upumánit, *adj.* Disrespected, disgraced.

अपमानी upumánee, *adj.* Disgraced, abased, dishonourable, disreputable.

अपमान्य upumányuh, *adj.* Disreputable, dishonourable.

अपमृत्यू úpumrityoo, *s. f.* An inauspicious death, an untimely death, sudden death, dying of some casualty, not of sickness or decay.

अपयश úpjush, *s. m.* Infamy, ignominy, disgrace, dishonour.

अपजशी upjúshee, *adj.* Infamous, unfortunate.

अपर úpur, *adj.* Another, other.

अपरंपार upurumpár, *adj.* Boundless, infinite.

अपराजय upurájuy, *s. m.* Not a defeat; victory, invincibleness.

अपराजित úpurajit, *adj.* Unconquered, invincible, unerring, not vanquished, not defeated.

अपराजिता upurajíta, *s. f.* A twining shrub (*Clitoria ternatea*); also a name applied to several plants.

अपराध upurádh, *s. m.* Offence, crime, fault, transgression, guilt, sin.

अपराधी upurádhee, *s. m.* A criminal, sinner, offender, transgressor, one culpable.

अपराह्न upuráhun, *s. m.* Afternoon, the last watch of the day.

अपरिपाटी upuripátee, *s. f.* Deviation from established custom.

अपरिमित úpurimit, *adj.* Not measured; immoderate, unlimited.

अपरीक्षा úpureeksha, *s. f.* Want of trial or proof; an improper or insufficient trial of any thing.

अपर्श úpurs, *s. m.* The state of a hindoo after bathing, previous to worship or to eating, during which it is unlawful for him to touch any one; leprosy.

अपलक्षण úpulukshun, *s. m.* A bad omen, bad sign.

अपलक्षण upulúkshuna, *adj. m.* Of a bad sign or suspicious appearance, unlucky, ominous.

अपलज्ज upulújj, } *adj.* Impudent, im-
अपलज्जी upulujjee, } modest, shameless.

अपलज्जा upulújja, *s. f.* Impudence, shamelessness.

अपवर्ग upuvúrg, *s. m.* Liberation, deliverance, emancipation, final beatitude, the deliverance of the soul from the body and exemption from further transmigration.

अपवाद upuvád, *s. m.* Complaint, reproach, accusation, censure, blame.

अपवादी upuvádee, *m.* } *s.* A complainer,
अपवादित upuvadín, *f.* } an accuser.

अपवित्र úpuvitr, *adj.* Unclean, defiled, impure, profane.

अपवित्रता upuvitrtá, *s. f.* Uncleanness, filth, impurity.

अपशकुन upshúkoon, *s. m.* A portent, a bad omen, any unlucky or inauspicious object.

अपशब्द úpushubd, *s. m.* A disagreeable sound, wind broken backwards, ungrammatical language.

अपष्ट úpusht, *adj.* Hidden, secret; inevident, unintelligible, not clear.

अपसरा úpsura, *s. f.* A female dancer or courtezan in *Swurg*, the hindoo paradise.

अपसव्य upusúvyuh, *s. m.* Right (*not left*), the right side of the body. *adj.* Opposite, contrary.

अपस्मार upusmár, *s. m.* The epilepsy, falling sickness.

अपहरण upuhúrun, *s. m.* A plundering, a purloining.

अपहर्ता upuhúrtta, *s. m.* A robber, a plunderer, a thief.

अपह्नव upúhnuv, *s. m.* Denial, concealment.

अपक्ष úpuksh, *adj.* Without wings, without assistance or protection.

अपाक úpak, *adj.* Unripe, immature, raw. *s. m.* Immaturity; indigestion.

अपांग upáng, *s. m.* The outer corner of the eye; a sectarial mark or circlet on the forehead. *adj.* Maimed, crippled.

अपांगदर्शन upáng-dúrshun, *s. m.* A side glance, a leer, a wink.

अपात्र upatr, *adj.* Incapable, unfit, unworthy. *s. m.* An inferior or worthless person.

अपादान upadán, *s. m.* The taking from a thing; (*in gram.*) the ablative case.

अपान upán, *s. m.* The anus; wind broken backwards.

अपाप úpap, *adj.* Sinless, innocent, pure.

अपार upár, *adj.* Boundless, unbounded, interminable, excessive, impassable.

अपावन úpawun, *adj.* Defiling, polluting, impure.

अपाश्रय úpashruy, *adj.* Helpless, destitute.

अपाहुज upáhuj, *adj.* Lazy, cripple; a person who never visits any one.

अपीड úpeer, *adj.* Without pain.

अपीन upéen, *adj.* Light, lean.

अपीनस upéenus, *s. m.* Dryness of the nose, want of the pituitary secretion and loss of smell, cold.

अपेय úpeeyuh, *adj.* Unfit to be drunk, forbidden (*liquor*).

अपुच्छ úpoochchh, *adj.* Tailless.

अपुच्छा úpoochchha, *s. f.* A tree (*Dalbergia Sisu*).

अपुण्य úpoonyuh, *s. m.* Uncharitableness. *adj.* Wicked, bad.

अपुत्र úpootr, *adj.* Without offspring. *s. m.* A disreputable son.

अपुरुष úpooroosh, *adj.* Impotent, effeminate, unmanly.

चपूष्ट **úpoosht**, *adj.* Lean.

चपुष्पित **úpooshpit**, *adj.* Without flowers (*a tree or plant*), not bearing flowers, not in flower.

चपूजक **úpoojuk**, *adj.* Ungodly, irreligious, irreverent.

चपूज्य **úpoojyuh**, *adj.* That which is not worshipped, or is not a proper object of worship.

चपूत **úpoot**, *adj.* Childless; undutiful (*child*).

चपूर्ण **úpoorn**, *adj.* Not full, incomplete. *s. m.* A fraction.

चपूर्णकाल **upoorn-kál**, *adj.* Premature.

चपूर्णता **upoorn-tá**, *s. f.* Incompleteness.

चपूर्व **úpoorv**, *adj.* Unprecedented, unparalleled, eminent, excellent, uncommon, unheard of, new, admirable, remarkable, wonderful, extraordinary.

चपेचक **upékshuk**, *s. m.* An expectant. *adj.* Expecting, waiting for.

चपेचा **upéksha**, *s. f.* Expectation, hope.

चपेचित **upekshít**, *adj.* Expected, waited for, wished, hoped.

चपेची **upekshée**, *adj.* Expecting, hoping, an expectant; looking to.

चपेख **upékh**, *adj.* Invisible, unseen.

चपेय **upéyuh**, *adj.* Unfit to be drunk, forbidden (*liquor*).

चपौरुष **úpourush**, *adj.* Impotent, effeminate, unmanly.

चप्रकट **úprukut**, *adj.* Unmanifested, unapparent.

चप्रकाश **úprukash**, *adj.* Secret, private, hidden, not public or displayed, not manifest or evident.

चप्रचण्ड **úpruchund**, *adj.* Not violent, not strong or forcible, without dignity.

चप्रताप **úprutap**, *s. m.* Want of dignity or acuteness, of power or fortune; dulness, want of brilliancy.

चप्रतापी **úprutapee**, *adj.* Blunt, powerless, unfortunate.

चप्रतिष्ठा **úprutishtha**, *s. f.* Want of respectability.

चप्रतीत **úpruteet**, *adj.* Without credit.

चप्रतीती **úpruteetee**, *s. f.* Want of confidence or of credit, mistrust.

चप्रत्यच **úprutyuksh**, *adj.* Imperceptible, invisible, not evident, secret, absent, not present.

चप्रत्यय **úprutuy**, *s. m.* Doubt, distrust, disbelief, incredulity, mistrust, unbelief.

चप्रत्ययी **úprutuyée**, *adj.* Doubtful, mistrusting, sceptical.

चप्रथा **úprutha**, *s. f.* Deviation from custom, secrecy.

चप्रधान **úprudhan**, *adj.* Subordinate, secondary, mean, powerless.

चप्रभा **úprubha**, *s. f.* Want of splendour; darkness, dulness.

चप्रमाण **úpruman**, *adj.* Without proof, untrue, of doubtful authority.

चप्रवीण **úpruveen**, *adj.* Unskilful.

चप्रसन्न **úprusunn**, *adj.* Ungracious, unfavourable, displeased, dissatisfied, averse, unpropitious.

चप्रसाद **úprusad**, *s. m.* Disfavour, disapprobation.

चप्रसादी **úprusadee**, *adj.* That which is not presented to the deity.

चप्रसिद्ध **úprusiddh**, *adj.* Not famous, not well known; uncelebrated.

चप्राचीन **úpracheen**, *adj.* Modern, recent.

चप्राप्त **úprapt**, *adj.* Unobtained.

चप्राप्ति **úprapti**, *s. f.* Non-attainment, non-acquisition.

चप्रामाणिक **úpramanik**, *adj.* Unauthentic, unauthoritative.

चप्रमाण **úpramanyuh**, *s. m.* Absence or insufficiency of proof or authority.

चप्रिय **úpriyuh**, *adj.* Unamiable, not beloved, disagreeable, unkind, unfriendly.

चप्रीति **úpreeti**, *s. f.* Indifference, want of love, dislike, aversion, disgust, enmity, hatred, unfriendliness.

चप्रेम **úprem**, *s. m.* Want of love, aversion, hatred, enmity, dislike.

चफरारैं **uphráee**, *s. f.* Gluttony, a surfeit.

चफराना **uphrána**, *v. a.* To feed a person so that his belly swells; (*met.*) to give a person (*money, &c.*) to the utmost extent of his desire.

चफूर्णा **uphúrna**, *v. n.* To swell out (*the belly*), to gormandize, to eat to satiety; to become very rich.

चफल **úphul**, *adj.* Fruitless, barren, unfruitful; vain, unproductive, unprofitable.

चफलता **uphultá**, *s. f.* Barrenness, unprofitableness.

चफलित **úphulit**, *adj.* Not in fruit (*a fruit tree*).

चफीम **uphéem**, } *s. f.* Opium.
चाफू **áphoo**, }

चफेदा **uphéuda**, *adj.* Self-conceited, obstinate.

चफेन **úphen**, *adj.* Without foam.

चब **ub**, *adv.* Now, presently, just now.

चबका **úbka**, *adj. m.* } Of the present time,
चबकी **úbkee**, *adj. f.* } now.

चबकें **úbkeh**, *adv.* Now.

षबकेषी **ubkéshee,** *adj.* Without fruit, barren (*a tree*).

षबच **úbuch,** *adj.* That which has not escaped.

षबतरैं **ubtúeen,** *adv.* Till now.

षबतक **ubtúk,**
षबतलक **ubtúluk,** } *adv.* Till now, hitherto, yet, as yet, still.
षबतोरी **ub-tóree,**

षबतब **úbtub,** *adv.* Presently. *Ubtub hona,* To be at the point of death.

षबतें **ubtén,** *adv.* From this time, henceforth.

षबधा **ubdhá,** *s. f.* The segment of the base of a triangle.

षबधूत **ubdhóot,** *m.*
षबधूतनी **ubdhóotnee,** *f.* } *s.* One devoted to God but not attending on ceremonies; a kind of hindoo devotee who worships *Siv.*

षबधुय **úbudhyuh,** *adj.* Not deserving death, not be slain; sacred, inviolable.

षबनी **úbnee,** *s. f.* The earth, the world.

षबरक **úbruk,** *s. m.* Talc, mica.

षबल **úbul,** *adj.* Weak, feeble, infirm.

षबला **úbula,** *adj. f.* Weak, powerless. *s. f.* A woman.

षबलाई **ubláee,** *f.*
षबलापा **ubulápa,** *m.* } Weakness.

षबली **úbulee,** *adj.* Weak. *s. f.* A row, range, continuous line.

षबलोकन **ubulókun,** *s. m.* Sight, seeing.

षबष **úbush,** *adj.* Powerless, without choice.   [naked.

षबसन **úbusun,** *adj.* Without clothes,

षबसेडूर **úbseh-dóor,** (*An expression of those, who after reciting past misfortune, pray to be preserved from a return of it,*) Far be it from us!

षबाक **ubák,** *adj.* Speechless, silent, dumb.

षबिक्त **úbikt,** *adj.* Hidden, unintelligible; any invisible principle.

षबिक्त षबित **úbikt-gúnit,** *s. f.* Arithmetic of unknown quantities, algebra.

षबिचल **úbichul,** *adj.* Motionless, immovable, unmoved, unshaken, resolute, firm.

षबिचार **úbichar,** *s. m.* Want of consideration; injustice.

षबिचारी **ubicháree,** *m.*
षबिचारिनी **ubi-charínee,** *f.* } *adj.* Destitute of consideration or reflection; unjust (*woman or man*).

षबिद्या **úbidya,** *s. f.* Ignorance.

षबिनय **úbinuy,** *s. m.* Pertness, wantonness, want of submission.

षबिनाश **úbinash,** *s. m.* Exemption from loss, safety.

षबिनाशी **ubináshee,** *adj.* Safe, entire, free from loss; everlasting, eternal, undecayable, imperishable.

षबिनीत **ubinéet,** *adj.* Wanton, pert, petulant.

षबिन्दु **úbindoo,** *adj.* Without dot or nasal character.

षबिबेक **úbibek,** *s. m.* Want of discrimination, indiscretion.

षबिबेकता **ubibektá,** *s. f.* Indiscreetness, indiscretion.

षबिबेकी **úbibekee,** *adj.* Indiscreet, inconsiderate, void of discretion.

षबिरोध **úbirodh,** *s. m.* Without contention; tranquillity, quietness.

षबिरोधी **úbirodhee,** *m.*
षबिरोधिनी **úbirodhinee,** *f.* } *adj.* Quiet, tranquil.

षबिलम्ब **úbilumb,** *s. m.* Quickness, diligence.

षबिश्वास **úbishwas,** *s. m.* Want of confidence, distrust, incredulity.

षबिश्वासी **úbishwasee,** *m.*
षबिश्वासिन् **úbishwasin.** *f.*
षबिश्वासिनी **úbishwasinee,** *f.* } *adj.* Without confidence, distrustful.   [ferent.

षबिषन **úbisun,** *adj.* Without desire, indif-

षबी **ubée,** *adv.* Now, exactly now.

षबुद्धि **úbooddhi,** *s. f.* Ignorance. *adj.* Ignorant, stupid.

षबुद्धिमान् **úbooddhi-mán,** *adj.* Unwise, ignorant, foolish.

षबुध **úboodh,**
षबूझ **úboojh,** } *adj.* Stupid, foolish, ignorant, void of understanding.

षबे **ubéh,** *interj.* (*used by way of contempt*) Holla! you fellow! you rascal! sirrah.

षबेर **ubér,** *s. f.* Delay, lateness.

षबोध **úbodh,** *s. m.* Ignorance, stupidity. *adj.* Ignorant, stupid; puzzled, perplexed.

षबोधगम्य **úbodh-gúmyuh,** *adj.* Incomprehensible.   [ble.

षबोधनीय **úbodh-néeyuh,** *adj.* Unintelligi-

षबोल **úbol,** *adj.* Silent.

षब्ज **ubj,** *s. m.* The nymphæa or lotus; the moon; a conch; a tree (*Eugenia acutangula*); the physician of the gods; a large number, million of millions.

षब्धि **úbdhi,** *s. m.* The ocean.

षब्धिकफ **ubdhi-kúph,** *s. m.* Cuttle-fish bone.

षब्धयग्नि **ubdh-yúgni,** *s. m.* Submarine fire.

षभक्त **úbhukt,** *s. f.* Want of desire or faith, disregard, indifference, not believing, not attached to.

अभक्ति úbhukti, *s. f.* Incredulity, unbelief, want of devotion to.

अभक्तिमान् úbhukti-mán, *adj.* Unbelieving, undevoted to.

अभय úbhuy, *adj.* Fearless, undaunted. *s. m.* The root of a fragrant grass (*Andropogon muricatum*).

अभयदान úbhuy-dán, ⎱ *s. m.* Assurance of
अभयवाक् úbhuy-vák, ⎰ safety or protection, encouragement.

अभया úbhuyá, *s. f.* Yellow myrobalan (*Terminalia citrina*).

अभरण ubhúrun, *s. m.* Jewels, ornaments, decoration.

अभरम úbhurum, *adj.* Without credit or respect or character, disgraced, dishonoured. *Ubhurum kurna, v. a.* To disgrace.

अभाग úbhag, *s. m.* Misfortune, adversity.

अभागा úbhaga, *m.* ⎫
अभागिनी úbhaginee, *f.* ⎬ *adj.* Unfortu-nate, destitute,
अभागी úbhagee, *f.* ⎭ wretched, forlorn.

अभाग्य úbhagyuh, *s. m.* Misfortune. *adj.* Unfortunate, wretched.

अभार úbhar, *adj.* Light (*not heavy*).

अभाव úbhao, *s. m.* Non-existence, non-entity, a deficiency; annihilation, death.

अभि úbhi, *prep.* Before (*in time and place*), against, with respect to; (*it is the reverse of* अनु *ánoo*.)

अभिचार ubhichár, *s. m.* An incantation to destroy.

अभिजित úbhijit, *s. m.* A division of time, the eighth *moohoortt* or hour; the 21st constellation or lunar asterism.

अभिधान ubhidhán, *s. m.* A name, an appellation; a vocabulary, a dictionary.

अभिनव ubhinóu, *adj.* Recent, new.

अभिन्न úbhinn, *adj.* Undivided. *s. m.* An integer, a whole number.

अभिप्राय ubhipráyuh, *s. m.* Meaning, intention, design, wish, purpose, desire, scope, sentiment, opinion, sense; the main purport of a book.

अभिवाद ubhibád, *s. m.* Obeisance, a bow or prostration to a person addressed by name; also, an opprobrious or unfriendly speech.

अभिभूत ubhibhóot, *adj.* Subdued, defeated, humbled, overcome.

अभिमत úbhimut, *adj.* Approved, chosen; wished, desired; agreed, accepted; assented to.

अभिमतता ubhimuttá, *s. f.* Desire, love; agreeableness, desirableness.

अभिमान ubhimán, *s. m.* Pride, haughtiness, self-conceit, arrogance.

अभिमानता ubhimantá, *s. f.* Pride, arrogance.

अभिमानी ubhimánee, ⎱ *adj.* Proud, haugh-
अभिमान्य ubhimányuh, ⎰ ty, arrogant.

अभिमुख ubhimóokh, *adj.* Present, facing, in front of, approaching. *adv.* Towards; in front or presence of.

अभिमुखता ubhimookhtá, *s. f.* Presence, proximity.

अभिलाष ubhilásh, *m.* ⎱ *s.* Wish, desire,
अभिलाषा ubhilásha, *f.* ⎰ inclination.

अभिलाषी ubhilashée, *adj.* Wishing, desiring.

अभिवाद ubhivád, *s. m.* Opprobrious or unfriendly speech.

अभिवादन ubhivádun, *s. m.* Obeisance, a bow or prostration to a person addressed by name.

अभिषिक्त ubhishíkt, *adj.* Anointed to office, installed, imbued with, inaugurated, enthroned.

अभिषेक ubhishék, *s. m.* Bathing, sprinkling; the word is often used for initiation, royal unction, &c., sprinkling with the water of the Ganges, or water in which various articles have been immersed, being an essential part of the rites; also, for a religious ceremony, including the presentation of a variety of articles, fruits, gems, &c., along with water or fluid substances, for the bathing of the idol to which worship is offered.

अभिसारिका ubhi-sárika, *adj. f.* A woman who makes or keeps an assignation, a lewd woman.

अभिसारिणी ubhisarinée, *f.* ⎱ *adj.* Going to
अभिसारी ubhisáree, *m.* ⎰ an appointment or assignation.

अभी ubhée, *adv.* Just now, exactly now, immediately, instantly, presently, already.

अभीत úbheet, *adj.* Fearless, undaunted.

अभीति ubheetí, *s. f.* Fearlessness.

अभीप्सित ubhéespit, ⎱ *adj.* Beloved, desir-
अभीष्ट ubhéesht, ⎰ ed, wished for.

अभूं úbhoon, *adv.* Hitherto, yet.

अभूत úbhoot, *adj.* Non-existent, not existing, not past.

अभेद ubhéd, ⎱ *adj.* Alike, indiscriminate,
अभेव ubhéo, ⎰ indivisible, inseparable, impenetrable; known, public. *s. m.* A similarity; identity, absence of difference or distinction.

अभोजी úbhojee, *adj.* Fasting.

अभोज्य ubhójyuh, *adj.* Unfit to be eaten, not eatable.

अभ्यागत ubhiyágut, *s. m.* A guest, a visitor. *adj.* Arrived.

अभ्यास ubhiyás, *s. m.* Study, practice, exercise, the frequent repetition of a thing in order to fix it on the mind.

षभ्यासी ubhiyásee, *adj.* Studious, practising, exercising, repeating.

षभ ubhr, *s. m.* The sky or atmosphere, a cloud, talc.

षभक úbhruk, *s. m.* The mineral substance called talc.

षमकाधमका úmka-dhúmka, } *s. m.* Trifles,
षमाधमका úmka-dhúmka, } trifling; a person of little estimation.

षमङ्गल úmungul, *s. m.* A disaster, a calamity, an evil omen, inauspiciousness, ill luck. *adj* Inauspicious, unlucky, evil.

षमचूर umchóor, *s. m.* Parings of the mango dried in the sun.

षमनुष्यह úmunooshyuh, *adj.* Unmanly.

षमनुष्टा umunooshtá, *s. f.* Unmanliness.

षमनोनीत úmunoneet, *adj.* Disapproved; reprobate.

षमनोयोग úmunojog, *s. m.* Inattention.

षमनोयोगी umunojógee, *adj.* Inattentive.

षमनोहर úmunohur, *adj.* Disagreeable, displeasing, unattractive.

षमता úmumta, *s. f.* Disinterestedness, indifference, stoicism.

षमर úmur, *adj.* Immortal, exempt from death, long-lived, everlasting; the Deity; the name of a Sunskrit lexicographer.

षमर्ता umurtá, *s. f.* Immortality.

षमरपद umur-púd, *s. m.* The state of an immortal, immortality.

षमरलोक umur-lók, *s. m.* Heaven, the region of immortality.

षमरा úmra, *s. m.* The hog-plum (*Spondias magnifera*).

षमराई umráee, *s. f.* A garden of mangoe trees.

षमरावती úmur-áwutee, *s. f.* The capital or celestial city of *Indr.*

षमरूत umróot, *s. f.* A guava (*Psydium pyriferum*).

षमर्याद úmurjad, } *s. f.* Disrespect, in
षमर्यादा úmurjada, } dignity, dishonour alight, affront.

षमल úmul, *s. m.* Intoxication. *adj.* Pure, clean, bright.

षमलतास umultás, *s. m.* Cassia fistula.

षमलपत्ती úmul-púttee, *s. f.* A kind of stitching.

षमलिन úmulin, *adj.* Clean, pure.

षमात्युह umátyuh, *s. m.* A minister, counsellor, a senator, a statesman, an adviser.

षमाना umána, *v. n.* To be contained, to go into.

षमानी úmanee, *adj.* Incredulous, inattentive; without pride, humble, modest.

षमान्युह úmanyuh, } *adj.* Incredi-
षमाननीय umanunéeyuh, } ble.

षमावट umáwut, *s. m.* The inspissated juice of the mangoe.

षमावस umáwus, } *s. f.* The conjunc-
षमावस्या umawúshyuh, } tion of the sun and moon, the change of the moon or day of new moon.

षमिट úmit, *adj.* Indelible, not defaced.

षमित úmit, *adj.* Unmeasured.

षमी úmee, *s. f.* The water of life, nectar.

षमुक úmook, *adj.* Such a one, a certain person.

षमुख्यह úmookhyuh, *adj.* Inferior, ordinary.

षमूर्त úmoortt, *adj.* Formless, shapeless, unembodied.   [origin.

षमूल úmool, *adj.* Destitute of a root or

षमृत úmrit, *s. m.* The food of the gods, ambrosia, nectar; immortality, any thing sweet, water, wine, a guava; final emancipation.

षमृत्ता umrittá, *s. f.* Immortality.

षमृती úmritee, *adj.* Nectarious. *s. f.* A kind of cloth.

षमेध्यह umédhyuh, *s. m.* Fæces, excrement.

षमोघ umógh, *adj.* Productive, fruitful; infallible, effectual.

षमोल umól, *adj.* Invaluable.

षम्ब umb, *s. m.* A mangoe, a mangoe tree.

षम्बुत úmbut, *adj.* Sour.

षम्बुताना umbutána, *v. n.* To grow sour, to be acidulated.

षम्बर úmbur, *s. m.* The sky or atmosphere; clothes, apparel; a perfume (*Ambergris*).

षम्बराई úmbur-áee, *s. f.* A mangoe orchard or grove.

षम्बा úmba, *s. f.* Mother.

षम्बारी umbáree, *s. f.* A canopy, a litter used on an elephant or camel.

षम्बिका úmbika, *s. f.* A name of *Bhuwánee*, wife of *Siv.*   [goe.

षम्बिया úmbiya, *s. f.* A small unripe mangoe.

षम्बू úmboo, *s. m.* Water.

षम्बूज úmbooj, } *s. m.* The lotus (*Nym-*
षम्भोज umbhój, } *phæa nelumbo*).

षम्बोल umból, *adj.* Silent, speechless.

षम्मा úmma, *s. f.* Mother.

षम्रा úmra, *s. m.* The hog-plum (*Spondias magnifera*).

षम्रूत umróot, *s. m.* A guava (*Psydium pyriferum*).

चम uml, *adj.* Acid, sour. *s. m.* Sourness, acidity.

चमता umltá, *s. f.* Sourness, acidity.

चमान úmlan, *s. m.* Globe amaranth (*Gomphrena globosa*). *adj.* Clean, clear.

चयतन újutun, *adj.* Without endeavour, easy, without pains.

चयथार्थ újutharth, *adj.* Improper; unrighteous, not true.

चयन úyun, *s. m.* A road, a path; the half year, i. e. the sun's course north or south of the equator.

चयश újush, *s. m.* Dishonour, infamy.

चयाना uyána, *adj.* Ignorant, unknowing, witless, simple.

चयुक्त újookt, *adj.* Unfit, incompatible. *s. m.* Violence, oppression, compulsion.

चयूत újoot *adj.* Ten thousand.

चयोग्युह újógyuh, *adj.* Unfit, incompatible, incompetent, unable, unsuitable.

चयोग्यता ujogyutá, *s. f.* Unfitness, unsuitableness, incongruity, impropriety.

चयोध्या ujódhiya, *adj.* Not to be warred against. *s. f.* The capital of Ram, the modern Oude.   [casia.

चरई úruee, *s. f.* The root of Arum colo-

चरकट úrkut, *s. f.* Vigilance, activity, cleverness, ingenuity.   [Arcot.

चरकाट urkát, *s. m.* A city in the *Dúkkhin*,

चरकाटी urkátee, *s. m.* A pilot. *adj.* Belonging to *Urkát*, or *Arcot. Urkátee roopyya*, An Arcot rupee.

चरक्षित úrukshit, *adj.* Unprotected, undefended.

चरगुजा úrguja, *s. m.* A perfume of a yellowish colour and compounded of several scented ingredients.

चरगुजी urgújee, *adj.* Dyed with *úrguja*, (*as garments, &c.*)

चरगा úrga, *adj.* Separate, apart, distinct.

चरगाई urgáee, *s. f.* Being silent.

चरगाना urgána, *v. a.* To separate, put on one side. *v. n.* To be separated, set apart.

चरघ urúgh, } *s. m.* An oblation of eight
चर्घ urgh,   } ingredients offered to a god or a brahman.

चरझना úrujhna, *v. n.* To be ravelled or intangled, involved (*as thread or the hair, or, met. the heart*); to be bound (*as in fetters, &c.*); to quarrel without cause or unreasonably.

चरणा úrna, *s. m.* (*or úrna-bhynsa*), A wild buffalo; cow dung found dried in the forest, (*used as fuel by the native apothecaries in the preparation of medicines.*)

चरणी úrnee, *s. f.* A female wild buffalo.

चरण्ड úrund, *s. m.* The tree from which castor-oil is made (*Ricinus vulgaris or Palma Christi*).

चरण्डी úrundee, *s. f.* The fruit of the Palma Christi.

चरण्युह urunyúh, *s. m.* A forest, a wilderness.

चरना úrna, *v. n.* To stop, hesitate.

चरपना urupna, *v. n.* To present an offering.

चरबराना urburána, *v. n.* To hurry, be confused, confounded, perplexed, agitated, embarrassed.

चरविन्द úrwind, *s. m.* The lotus (*Namphæa nelumbo*).

चरवी úrwee, *s. f.* A species of Arum, the root of which is used for food (*Arum colocasia*); called also, *ghóyan, ghóoyan,* and in Bengal, *kuchchoo.*

चरस úrus, *adj.* Without juice, sapless, insipid, tasteless; dull, flat (*as a composition*).

चरसुत्ता ursútta, *s. m.* Guess, conjecture, valuation, appraisement; a mediator, a broker.

चरसेलेनैना urséeleh-nyna, *adj.* Having weak eyes, with eyes as if just awake.

चरहट úrhut, *s. m.* An engine for raising water.

चरहर úrhur, *s. f.* A kind of pulse (*Cytisus cajan*).

चराजक úrajuk, *adj.* Destitute of a king (*a country*).

चराधना urádhna, *v. n.* To worship, adore.

चरारा urára, *s. m.* Marks of nails left after scratching.

चरि úri, *s. m.* An enemy.

चरिष्ट úrisht, *s. m.* Garlick, the neemb tree (*Melia azad-dirachta*), a crow, good fortune, happiness, misfortune, sign or symptom of death.

चरी úree, *f. interj.* (*used in calling to or addressing, commonly in a disrespectful way*), Ho! O! hear, you!

चरीति úreeti, *s. f.* Unpoliteness, incivility, bad manners.

चरु úroo, *conj.* And.

चरूई úrooee, *s. f.* Sickness of stomach arising from pregnancy.

चरूचि úroochi, *s. f.* Sickness at stomach, nausea; aversion, dislike; want of appetite, disrelish, disgust.

चरून úroon, *s. m.* The sun; the dawn; the colour of the dawn, dark red.

चरूनाई uroonáee, *s. f.* The dawn; the colour of the dawn, dark red.

चरूनोदय úroon-óduy, *s. m.* The first appearance of the dawn, break of day.

उरसोपल uroon-ópul, *s. m.* A ruby.

उरस úroos, *s. m.* A medicinal plant or tree, (*Justicia adhatoda and gandarussa*).

उरे úreh, *m. interj. (used in calling to or addressing, commonly in a disrespectful way),* Holla ho ! O ! hear you !

उरेब uréb, *s. m.* Guilt.

उरोग uróg, *adj.* Free from disease, healthy, well. *s. m.* Health.

उरोगी urógee, *adj.* Well, in health.

उर्क urk, *s. m.* The sun ; a plant (*Calatropis gigantea*), swallow-wort (*Asclepias gigantea*).

उर्कदिन urk-din, *s. m.* A solar day.

उर्कमण्डल urk-múndul, *s. m.* The disc of the sun.

उर्कवर्ष urk-vúrsh, *s. m.* A solar year.

उर्कांश urk-áns, *s. m.* A digit or twelfth of the sun's disc.

उर्काश्मन urk-áshmun, *s. m.* A crystal lens ; a ruby.

उर्कोपल urk-ópul, *s. m.* The sun-stone ; a ruby ; a crystal lens.

उर्गजा úrguja, *s. m.* A perfume of a yellowish colour and compounded of several scented ingredients.

उर्गजी úrgujee, *adj.* Dyed with *úrguja* (*as garments, &c.*).

उर्गुनी úrgunee, *s. m.* A rope stretched, or a wooden rod or bamboo placed horizontally for drying clothes on or for similar purposes.

उर्घ urgh, *s. m.* Mode of worship; an oblation of eight ingredients to a god or a *brahmun*; act of pouring out water in honour of a deity (*the sun, moon, &c.*) while performing worship ; price, value.

उर्घा úrgha, *s. m.* A vessel shaped like a boat, used by the Hindoos for performing libation in their worship of idols.

उर्चुक úrchuk, *adj.* Worshipping, a worshipper, an adorer.

उर्चुना úrchuna, *v. a.* To worship, honour, treat with ceremony. *s. f.* Worship, the homage paid to deities and to superiors.

उर्चा úrcha, *s. f.* Worship, adoration ; an image.

उर्चि úrchi, *s. m.* Flame ; light, splendour, radiance.

उर्चित úrchit, *adj.* Worshipped, reverenced, respected, saluted.

उर्जुन úrjun, *s. m.* Act of acquiring ; gain, acquisition.

उर्जुना úrjuna, *v. a.* To gain, acquire.

उर्जून úrjoon, *s. m.* A celebrated hero, the third son of *Pandoo*; a tree (*Terminalia alata glabra*).

उर्णुव úrnuv, *s. m.* The ocean.

उर्तुला úrtula, *s. m.* A patron, a protector.

उर्थ urth, *s. m.* Intention, purpose, object, design, motive ; sake, cause; meaning, signification, acceptation ; property, wealth, goods, riches substance ; request, begging. *Tupusyárth,* For devotion's sake, for devotional purposes.

उर्थशास्त्र urth-shástr, *s. m.* The science which teaches how to obtain things, as friends, money, or any other object.

उर्थसिद्धि urth-síddhi, *s. f.* Success.

उर्थात urthát, *adv.* That is to say, viz.

उर्थान्तर urth-ántur, *s. m.* Another meaning.

उर्थी úrthee, *adj.* Supplicating, craving, desirous, the having an object to accomplish ; self-interested, designing. *s. m.* A petitioner. *s. f.* A bier.

उर्थीय urthéeya, *s. m.* A follower, a client, a protegee, a person recommended.

उर्दावा urdáwa, *s. m.* Coarsely-ground meal.

उर्दास urdás, *s. f.* Representation, offering to a deity.

उर्द्ध urddh, *adj.* Half.

उर्द्धचन्द्र urddh-chúndr, A crescent, a half-moon, a semicircle.

उर्द्धभाग urddh-bhág, *s. m.* A half.

उर्द्धरात्र urddh-rátr, *s. f.* Midnight.

उर्द्धाङ्ग urddháng, *s. m.* Half the body ; palsy affecting one side or the upper or lower part of the body, hemiplegia.

उर्द्धाङ्गी urddhángee, *adj.* One afflicted with the hemiplegia. *s. f.* A wife.

उर्पुन úrpun, *s. m.* The making an offering ; delivering, entrusting ; an offering. *Urpun kúrna, v. a.* To present an offering, deliver, entrust.

उर्पना úrpna, *v. a.* To present an offering.

उर्ब urb, *adj.* One hundred millions. *Urb khurb,* Innumerable.

उर्बाक urbák, *adj.* Low, inferior, vile. *adv.* Former, prior in time.

उर्बूद úrbood, *adj.* One hundred millions.

उर्भुक úrbhuk, *s. m.* A child, a pupil.

उर्राटा urráta, *s. m.* A long and prolonged sound (*as from the discharge of artillery or the fall of a building*).

उर्राना urrána, *v. n.* To produce a continued sound (*as a mill: the word being an imitation of the sound*).

उर्षपर्ष úrshpursh, *s. m.* Partial bathing (*throwing a very little water on the head with one's hand instead of bathing*), sprinkling or aspersion ; act of touching.

ঊর্হন্ত úrhunt, *s. m.* A *soogút* or follower of the doctrines of *Bouddh.*

উলংকার ulunkár, *s. m.* Ornament (*of dress*), trinket, jewel ; rhetorick.

উলংকৃত ulunkrít, *adj.* Adorned, ornamented, embellished.

উলংগ úlung, *adj.* Naked. *s. f.* Side, way, corner, entrenchments. *Is ulung,* On this side.

উলুক úluk, *s. f.* A ringlet, curl or lock of hair.

উলুকনন্দা úluk-núnda, *s. f.* A stream that runs from the Himaluy mountains, and falls into the Ganges near Sreenugur.

উলুকাবলি úluk-avuli, *s. f.* A row of side curls. [omen.

উলুক্ষুন úlukshun, *s. m.* A bad sign or ill

উলুক্ষুনী úlukshunee, *adj.* Unfortunate, ill-fated.

উলুখ úlukh, } *adj.* Invisible, unseen ; a
উলুক্ষ úluksh, } form of salutation among a class of mendicants.

উলুগ úlug, } *adj.* Separate, apart, dis-
উল্গা úlga, } tinct, loose, aloof, aside. asunder ; unconfined. *Ulug ulug, adv.* Separately.

উলুগথুলুগ úlug-thúlug, *adv.* Apart.

উলুগনী úlgunee, *s. f.* A line for hanging clothes on.

উল্গা úlga, *adj.* Separate, apart, distinct, free, loose, unconfined. *s. m.* A sandal.

উলুগাই ulgáee, *s. f.* Separation.

উলুগানা ulgána, *v. a.* To separate, disjoin, put on one side.

উলুংকার uluṇkár, *s. m.* Ornament (*of dress*), trinket, jewel ; rhetorick.

উলুংকৃত ulunkrít, *adj.* Adorned, ornamented, embellished.

উলুঙ úlung, *adj.* Naked. *s. f.* Side, way, corner, entrenchments. *Is ulung,* This side.

উলুরবুলুর úlur-búlur, *s. f.* Trifling talk or employment.

উলুতনী últunee, *s. f.* The rope round the neck of an elephant in which the driver puts his feet as in stirrups.

উলুতা últa, } *s. m.* Cotton strongly im-
আলতা álta, } pregnated with the dye of lac ready to be used for dyeing, &c. (*principally used by the Hindoo women for staining their feet red*).

উলবেলপুনা ulbél-púna, *s. m.* Foppishness, spruceness, airs and blandishments.

উলবেলা ulbéla, *adj.* Artless, simple, innocent. *s. m.* A fop, a beau.

উলুম úlum, *adj.* Enough, abundance ; able, adequate or equal to.

ঊলুস úlus, *s. m.* Laziness, sloth, idleness, drowsiness, inactivity. *adj.* Lazy, idle, indolent.

উলসানা ulsána, *v. n.* To doze, be drowsy ; to slacken.

উলসী úlsee, *s. f.* Linseed (*Linum usitatissimum*).

উলাপ uláp, *s. m.* Discourse, conversation. *s. f.* Prelude to singing.

উলাপনা ulápna, *v. n.* To tune the voice, to run over th edifferent notes previous to singing, to catch the proper key, to sing, to tune.

উলাব uláv, *s. m.* A bonfire.

উলি úli, *s. m.* A large black bee, a scorpion, an Indian cuckoo (*Cuculus indicus*), a crow, spirituous liquor.

উলী ulée, *s. m.* A large black bee, fabled to be enamoured of the lotus. *s. f.* A female friend.

উলীক uléek, *s. m.* Falsehood, untruth, any thing displeasing or disagreeable. *adj.* False, unpleasing.

উল্যাবুল্যা ulyya-bulyya, *s. f.* Sacrifice, victim ; lighted wisps with which the hindoos divert themselves at the season of the *dewálee.*

উলোকন úlokun, *s. m.* Disappearance, invisibility.

উলোনা úlona, } *adj.* Not salt, fresh, salt-
উলোনা úlona, } less, insipid.

উলোপ ulóp, *adj.* Concealed, defaced, retired, run out, destroyed ; apparent.

উলোপনা ulópna, *v. a.* To conceal, hide one's self, lie hid.

উলোল ulól, *s. f.* Gambol (*generally applied to a horse*). *adj.* Steady.

উলোলকুলোল ulólkulól, *s. f.* Gambols, playsomeness, wantonness.

উলৌকিক úloukik, *adj.* Unpopular, not current, supernatural.

উল্প ulp, *adj.* Little, small, few, short.

উল্পতা ulp-tá, *s. f.* Smallness, minuteness ; inferiority, insignificance.

উল্পপ্রভাও úlp-prubháo, *adj.* Insignificant, of little weight or consequence.

উল্পপ্রমাণ úlp-prumán, *adj.* Of little authority.

উল্পপ্রমাণুক úlp-prumánuk, *adj.* Credulous, resting on little evidence ; of little weight or authority.

উল্পবল úlp-bul, *adj.* Feeble, of little strength.

উল্পবুদ্ধি úlp-bóoddhi, *adj.* Ignorant, silly, unwise.

উল্পমাত্র ulp-mátr, *s. m.* A little, a little only ; a short time, a few moments.

উল্পশক্তি ulp-shúkti, *adj.* Weak, feeble.

अल्पायु ulp-áyoo, *adj.* Short-lived ; young, of few years.

अल्पाहार ulp-áhar, *adj.* Moderate, abstemious. *s. m.* Moderation, abstinence.

अल्पाहारी ulp-aharée, *adj.* Moderate, abstemious.

अल्लाना ullána, *v. n.* To bawl, scream, squeak.

अल्हड़ ulhúr, *adj.* Young, untaught (*animal*), unskilful.

अल्हाना ulhána, *v. n.* To rejoice, to be cheerful.

अल्हैया ulhyya, *s. f.* Name of a *raginee* or musical mode.

अवंतिका uvúntika, *s. f.* Name of a city, the modern *Oujein*.

अव úvub, *prep.* From, down from, off, away : it is the reverse of उ and is sometimes used to denote deprivation, disgrace, disjunction, &c.

अवकाश uvukásh, *s. m.* Leisure, opportunity ; interval, space.

अवकेशी uvukéshee, *adj.* Barren.

अवगत uvugút, *adj.* Known, understood.

अवगति uvugúti, *s. f.* Knowledge in general.

अवगाह uvugáh, } *s. m.* Bathing, ablu

अवगाहन uvugáhun, } tion.

अवगीत uvugéet, *adj.* Detested, reproached, wicked, vile. *s. m.* Reproach, blame.

अवगुन úvugoon, } *s. m.* Defect, blemish,

ओगुन óugoon, } vice.

अवज्ञा uvúgya, *s. f.* Contempt, despite, disregard, disrespect.

अवतरना uvutúrna, *v. a.* To descend, especially as an incarnation of the Deity.

अवतार uvutár, *s. m.* Birth, descent, incarnation, especially of a deity from heaven ; the appearance of any deity upon earth, but more particularly the mythological incarnations of *Vishnoo* in ten principal forms, viz. *Mútsya*, a fish; *Kuchchúp*, a tortoise ; *Vuráh*, a boar ; *Nrisingh*, a man-lion ; *Vámun*, a dwarf; *Pursoorám* ; *Ram* ; *Krishn* ; *Boodh* ; and *Kúlkee*; a pious or distinguished person, in the language of respect or flattery, is also called an *Uvutár*, a descent or incarnation of the deity ; a *teerth* or sacred place ; translation, translating ; crossing.

अवदीच uvudéech, *s. m.* A tribe of *Goojratee* brahmuns.

अवध úvudh, *s. f.* Agreement, promise, engagement ; the province of *Ujoddhya* or *Oude*.

अवधान uvudhán, *adj.* Cautious, attentive. *s. m.* Caution, attention.

अवधि úvudhi, *s. m.* Limit. *adv.* As far as, as long as.

अवधि úvudhi, *s. m.* The ocean.

अवध्य úvadhyuh, *adj.* Not fit to be slaughtered.

अवम uvúm, *adj.* Low, vile, inferior.

अवयव uvuyúv, *s. m.* A limb, a member.

अवरोध uvuródh, *s. m.* The seraglio of a palace, the queen's apartment, a place, a covering ; hindrance, obstruction.

अवलम्ब uvulúmb, *s. m.* Asylum, protection. *adj.* Depending, hanging down.

अवलम्बित úvu-lúmbit, *adj.* Quick, expeditious ; alighting, descending ; protected, cherished.

अवलोकन úvu-lókun, *s. m.* View, sight, the looking at any object, the surveying of any object.

अवलोकना úvu-lókna, *v. a.* To see.

अवलोकित úvu-lókit, *s. m.* A *Jyn* saint. *adj.* Seen.

अवश úvush, *adj.* Subject to another ; helpless.

अवशिष्ट uvushísht, *adj.* Left, remaining.

अवशेष uvushésh, *s. m.* A residue, a remnant, a surplus.

अवश्युह uvúshyuh, *adv.* Certainly, necessarily, positively, actually, really.

अवश्युक uvushyúk, *adj.* Necessary, inevitable, indispensable.

अवश्युकता uvushyuktá, *s. f.* Necessity, obligation ; certainty.

अवसर úvusur, } *s. m.* Occasion, time, op-

ओसर óusur, } portunity, leisure, a moment.

अवसान uvusán, *s. m.* Conclusion, termination, cessation ; death, boundary, limit.

अवस्तुता uvustootá, *s. f.* Insubstantiality, unreality.

अवस्था úvustha, *s. f.* State, condition, any particular state varying with the progress of time, as youth, age, &c.

अवाई uváee, *s. f.* Approach, advance ; a saddle-cloth adorned with fringes, &c.

अवाच्युह uváchyuh, *adj.* Dumb, speechless.

अवार uvár, *s. f.* Delay ; injustice, tyranny.

अविचल úvichul, *adj.* Motionless, unmoved, unshaken, resolute, firm.

अविचार úvichar, *s. m.* Want of judgment or discrimination, want of consideration, injustice.

अविचारित uvichárit, *adj.* Ill judged or investigated, unconsidered.

अविचारी uvicháree, *m.* } *adj.* Desti-

अविचारिणी uvichárinee, *f.* } tute of consideration or reflection ; unjust (*woman or man*).

अविद्या úvidya, *s. f.* Ignorance.

अविनय úviny, *s. m.* Pertness, wantonness, want of submission.

অবিনাশ úvinash, *s. m.* Exemption from loss, safety.

অবিনাশী úvinashee, *adj.* Safe, entire, free from loss, everlasting, eternal.

অবিনীত uvinéet, *adj.* Misbehaving, acting ill or improperly.

অবিনীতা uvinéeta, *s. f.* An unchaste or disloyal woman.

অবিন্দু úvindoo, *adj.* Without point or dot.

অবিরোধ úvirodh, *s. m.* Without contention, tranquillity, quietness.

অবিরোধিনী úvirodhinee, *f.*⎫ *adj.* Quiet,
অবিরোধী úvirodhee, *m.* ⎭ tranquil.

অবিলম্ব úvilumb, *s. m.* Quickness, diligence.

অবিবাদী úvivadee, *adj.* Not disputatious.

অবিবেক úvivek, *s. m.* Want of discrimination or judgment, indiscretion.

অবিবেকতা úvivekta, *s. f.* Indiscreetness, indiscretion, inconsiderateness, imprudence, want of judgment.

অবিবেকী úvivekee, *adj.* Indiscreet, inconsiderate, void of discretion, undiscriminating.

অবিশেষ úvishesh, *s. m.* A want of distinction. *adj.* Indiscriminate.

অবিশ্বাস úvishwas, *s. m.* Want of confidence, distrust, incredulity, unbelief, suspicion, mistrust.

অবিশ্বাসী úvishwasee, *m.* ⎫ *adj.* Without confi-
অবিশ্বাসিন্ úvishwasin, *f.* ⎬ dence, dis-
অবিশ্বাসিনী úvishwasinee, *f.* ⎭ trustful, unbelieving, mistrustful.

অবিষ úvish, *adj.* Anti-venemous, antidote, not poisonous.

অবের uvér, *s. f.* Delay, lateness.

অব্যক্ত úvyukt, *s. m.* The Supreme Being, or Universal Spirit; the soul; nature, temperament. *adj.* Indistinct, unapparent, invisible, imperceptible.

অব্যয় uvyúy, *s. m.* An indeclinable word, a particle; a name of *Vishnoo*. *adj.* Economical, parsimonious.

অব্যবস্থা úvyuvustha, *adj.* Irregular, without rule.

অব্যবস্থিত úvyuvusthit, *adj.* Not regulated, undisciplined, not put in order.

অব্যবহিত úvyuvuhit, *adj.* Not interposed, joined, united.

অব্যাকুল úvyakool, *adj.* Calm, firm, composed.

অব্যাপ্তি úvyapti, *s. f.* The not diffusing itself. *adj.* Not pervading.

অশুকুন úshukoon, *s. m.* A bad omen, a portent.

অশুকুনী úshukoonee, *adj.* Portentous, ill-omened.

অশক্ত úshukt, *adj.* Unable, incompetent, powerless.

অশক্তি úshukti, *s. f.* Inability, incapability, weakness, impotence.

অশক্য úshukyuh, *adj.* Impossible, impracticable. [portent.

অশগুন úshugoon, *s. m.* A bad omen, a

অশগুনী úshugoonee, *adj.* Portentous, ill-omened.

অশঙ্ক úshunk, *adj.* Fearless, undaunted; secure, certain.

অশন úshun, *s. m.* Eating, food; also the *Sun* tree on which the *tusur* silk-worm feeds (*Terminalia alata tomentosa*).

অশরণ úshurun, *adj.* Without shelter, helpless.

অশরীরী úshureeree, *adj.* Incorporeal.

অশান্ত úshant, *adj.* Restless, anxious, unresigned.

অশান্তি úshanti, *s. f.* Anxiety, restlessness.

অশাবন্ত ushawúnt, *adj.* Fearful, unquiet, pitiful.

অশাবরী ushawúree, *s. f.* A *raginee* or musical mode; a kind of pigeon, a sort of cotton cloth.

অশাস্ত্র úshastr, *adj.* Unlawful, illegal, irregular, inconsistent.

অশাস্ত্রীয় úshastreeyuh, *adj.* Contrary to law, inconsistent with the rules of science.

অশিক্ষিত úshikshit, *adj.* Untaught, ignorant.

অশিষ্ট úshisht, *adj.* Unpolite, undisciplined, unpolished, ungoverned, neglected, under the dominion of evil habits arising from a neglected education, rude, barbarous, savage, profligate.

অশুগুন úshoogoon, *s. m.* A bad omen, a portent.

অশুচি úshoochi, *adj.* Impure, foul, unclean (*ceremonially*). *s. f.* Impurity.

অশুদ্ধ úshooddh, *adj.* Incorrect, impure, inaccurate, mistaken. *Ushooddhya, adj.* One who speaks or reads wrong.

অশুদ্ধতা úshooddhta, *s. f.* Inaccuracy, uncleanness, impurity.

অশুভ úshoobh, *adj.* Unfavourable, inauspicious, unbecoming, unpropitious, bad, evil. *s. m.* Misfortune, calamity, inauspiciousness, unhappiness, distress.

অশেষ úshesh, *adj.* Boundless, endless, infinite, entire, all.

অশোক úshok, *adj.* At ease, unmolested. *s. m.* Ease, tranquillity; cheerfulness, a plant (*Jonesia asoca*).

वशोच úshoch, *s. m.* Content, tranquillity, the absence of care.

वशोभा úshobha, *s. f.* Ugliness, want of elegance. *adj.* Shapeless, ill-made, ugly.

वशोच úshouch, *s. m.* Impurity; mourning.

वश्नान ushnán, *s. m.* Bathing.

वश्मरी úshmree, *s. f.* The stone or gravel (*the disease*); strangury.

वश्र úshr, *s. m.* A tear.

वश्रद्धा úshruddha, *s. f.* Aversion, disgust, loathing, contempt; distrust, disbelief.

वश्लेखा ushlékha, *s. f.* The ninth *nukshutr* or lunar mansion containing 5 stars.

वश्लोक ushlók, *s. m.* Verse, distich.

वश्व úshwuh, *s. m.* A horse.

वश्वगन्धा úshwuh-gúndha, *s. f.* A plant (*Physalis flexuosa*).

वश्वत्थ úshwutth, *s. m.* The holy fig-tree (*Ficus religiosa*).

वश्वपति úshwupúti, *s. m.* Lord or master of horse, a person of rank attended by horsemen, a horseman.

वश्वमेध úshwumedh, *s. m.* The actual or emblematic sacrifice of a horse: this sacrifice is one of the highest order, and when performed a hundred times entitles the sacrificer to the dominion of *swurg* or paradise: it appears to have been originally typical; the horse and other animals being simply bound during the performance of certain ceremonies: the actual sacrifice is an introduction of a later period.

वश्वयूज ushwuyóoj, *s. f.* The first lunar mansion.

वश्ववार ushwuvár, *s. m.* A horseman.

वश्वशाला úshwushála, *s. f.* A stable.

वश्वारूढ ushv-aróorh, *adj.* Mounted on a horse. *s. m.* A horseman.

वश्विनी úshwinee, *s. f.* The first of the 24 constellations in the moon's path; hence, considered its mansions: it consists of 3 stars in the head of Aries, and is so named from *Ushwuh*, a horse, because represented by a symbol of a horse's head.

वषाढ ushárh, *s. m.* The hindoo third solar month (*June-July, during which the sun is in Gemini, and the full moon is near Usharha* वषाढा *more properly called Poorv-asharha* पूर्वाषाढा *or Oottus-asharha* उतराषाढा *a constellation in Sagittarius*).

वषाढी ushárhee, *s. f.* Day of the full moon in *Usharh*.

वष usht, *adj.* Eight.

वष्टधातू úsht-dhatoo, *s. m.* The eight metals, reckoned as follows by the hindoos, viz., gold, silver, copper, brass, tin, bell-metal, lead and iron.

वष्टधातवी usht-dhátee, *s. f.* A mixed metal of iron and others, a compound of eight metals.

वष्टप्रहर úsht-prúhur, *adj.* Incessant, unremitting, the whole day and night.

वष्टम úshtum, *a.* The eighth.

वष्टमंगल úsht-múngul, *s. m.* A horse with a white face, tail, breast and hoofs; a collection of eight lucky things to be assembled on certain occasions, as at a coronation, &c., as a lion, bull, an elephant, a water jar, a fan, a flag, a trumpet, and a lamp; or a *brahmun*, a cow, fire, gold, ghee, the sun, water, and a king.

वष्टमी úshtumee, *s. f.* The eighth day of the moon.

वष्टसिद्धि úsht-síddhi, *s. m.* The eight *siddhis*, a superior order of beings; a personification of the powers and laws of nature; when they are subjected to the will by holiness and austerities, whatever the fancy desires, may, it is said, be obtained; universal sovereignty may be acquired, and implicit obedience to any command enforced; the magnitude, weight, or levity of the body may be rendered invisible, and transported in an instant to any part of the universe.

वष्टांग ushtáng, *s. m.* Eight parts of man, viz., the hands, feet, thighs, breast, eyes, head, words and mind.

वष्टांगप्रणाम ushtáng-prunám, *s. m.* Prostration in salutation or adoration, so as to touch the ground with the eight principal parts of man, viz., the hands, feet, thigh, breast, eyes, head, words and mind.

वष्टादश ushtadúsh, *adj.* Eighteen.

वसंख्य úsunkhyuh, *adj.* Countless, innumerable.

वसंगत úsungut, *adj.* Improper, absurd, bad.

वसंयोग úsunjog, *s. m.* Want of opportunity.

वसंशय úsunshuy, *adj.* Undoubted.

वसकुत úskut, *s. f.* Drowsiness, slothfulness.

वसकुती úskutee, *adj.* Drowsy, lazy.

वसगन्ध úsgundh, *s. m.* A plant used medicinally (*Physalis flexuosa*).

वसुज्जुन úsujjun, *adj.* Unfit, untrue, improper, not good or fit, not respectable or of good family.

वसत úsut, *adj.* Unholy, ungodly, nonexistent, untrue, false.

वसती úsutee, *adj.* Disloyal or unchaste (*a wife*).

वसत्य úsutyuh, *adj.* Untrue, false. *s. m.* Untruth.

वसती úsutyee, *adj.* Liar, untrue.

वसन úsun, *s. m.* A tree (*Terminalia alata tomentosa*).

ख‌स‌न‌ख **úsuntoosht**, *adj.* Discontented, dissatisfied, displeased.

ख‌स‌न‌ख **úsuntokh**, ⎫ *s. m.* Discontent, displeasure.
ख‌स‌न‌ख **úsuntosh**, ⎭ pleasure.

ख‌स‌न‌ख **úsunman**, *s. m.* Disrespect.

ख‌स‌भ‌ख **úsubhyuh**, *adj.* Rude, unfit for society, unpolite.

ख‌स‌म‌ख‌ख **úsmunjus**, *s. m.* Doubt, suspense, uncertainty ; unconformity, disparity, difference.

ख‌स‌म‌ख **úsumuy**, *adv.* Out of season, premature. *s. m.* A time of misfortune, an improper time, a time of distress.

ख‌स‌म‌ख **úsumurth**, *adj.* Powerless, feeble, weak ; unable, incompetent.

ख‌स‌म‌ख **úsuman**, *adj.* Different ; unlike ; unequal.

ख‌स‌म‌ख **úsumapt**, *adj.* Unfinished, incomplete.

ख‌स‌म‌ख‌ि **úsumapti**, *s. f.* Incompleteness.

ख‌स‌म‌ख **úsumpoprn**, *adj.* Incomplete, not entire. [united.

ख‌स‌म‌ख **úsumbuddh**, *adj.* Not joined or

ख‌स‌म‌ख **úsumbhuv**, *adj.* Uncommon, inconsistent, incompatible, improbable, unlikely, unreasonable.

ख‌स‌म‌ख **úsummut**, *adj.* Dissentient, differing from ; averse, contrary.

ख‌स‌म‌ख‌ि **úsummuti**, *s. f.* Dissent, difference of opinion ; dislike, aversion.

ख‌स‌म‌ख **úsumman**, *s. m.* Disrespect, disgrace.

ख‌स‌र‌ख **úsurun**, *adj.* Unprotected, helpless.

ख‌स‌ह‌ख **úsuhújj**, *adj.* Intolerable, insufferable.

ख‌स‌ह‌ख **úsuhun**, *adj.* Impatient, not bearing with, unable to endure.

ख‌स‌ह‌न‌ख **úsuhunéeyuh**, *adj.* Unbearable, insufferable.

ख‌स‌ह‌ख‌ख **úsuhujyuh**, *adj.* Intolerable, unbearable.

ख‌सा‌ख‌ख **úsakshat**, *adv.* Not in the presence of, in the absence of.

ख‌सा‌ख‌ी **úsakshee**, *s. m.* False testimony, without evidence.

ख‌सा‌ख‌ख **úsakshyuh**, *s. m.* A want of testimony. *adj.* Without credit or reputation.

ख‌सा‌ख **úsakh**, *adj.* Without credit or reputation.

ख‌सा‌ख‌ी **úsakhee**, *s. m.* False testimony, without evidence.

ख‌सा‌ख **úsath**, *adj.* Addicted to bad company.

ख‌सा‌ख‌ी **úsathee**, *adj.* Upstart, stranger, unknown person.

ख‌स‌ध **úsaddh**, *adj.* Without desire or energy ; lazy.

ख‌स‌ध **úsadh**. *adj.* Evil-minded ; without desire or energy ; lazy.

ख‌स‌ध‌ू **úsadhoo**, *adj.* Unrighteous, bad, immoral, wicked.

ख‌सा‌ध‌ु‌ता **úsadhootá**, *s. f.* Wickedness.

ख‌सा‌ध‌्‌य **úsadhyuh**, *adj.* Unable, weak, incapable ; impossible, incurable.

ख‌स‌म‌र्‌थ **úsamurth**, *adj.* Powerless, weak.

ख‌सा‌र **úsar**, *adj.* Sapless, pithless ; vain, unprofitable ; hollow (*like a reed*) ; foolish, weak of understanding.

ख‌सा‌व‌धा‌न **úsavdhan**, *adj.* Careless, inadvertent.

ख‌सा‌व‌न्‌त **úsavunt**, *adj.* Fearful, unquiet, pitiful.

ख‌सा‌व‌र‌ी **úsawúree**, *s. f.* A musical mode ; a kind of pigeon ; a sort of cotton cloth.

ख‌सि **úsi**, *s. m.* A sword, a scimitar.

ख‌सि‌द्‌ध **úsiddh**, *adj.* Not effected ; invalid, false ; unripe ; imperfect, incomplete ; unaccomplished.

ख‌सी‌ं‌चा **úseencha**, *adj.* Not watered, not irrigated (*a field, &c.*).

ख‌सी‌मा **úseema**, *adj.* Unbounded, unlimited.

ख‌सी‌स **úsees**, *s. m.* Blessing, benediction, return of compliment from a hindoo superior (*a brahmun*).

ख‌सी‌र्‌बा‌द **useerbád**, *s. m.* A benediction, blessing ; salutation.

ख‌सू **úsoo**, *s. m.* Life, breath ; the five vital breaths or airs of the body ; reflection, thought, or the heart as the seat of it ; affection.

ख‌सू‌ख **úsookh**, *s. m.* Sorrow, uneasiness, restlessness, affliction, pain.

ख‌सू‌ख‌ी **úsookhee**, *adj.* Uneasy, unhappy, sorrowful, restless, afflicted.

ख‌सू‌ग‌न **úsoogun**, *s. m.* Bad omen, a portent.

ख‌सू‌द्‌ध **úsooddh**, *adj.* Incorrect, impure, inaccurate ; mistaken.

ख‌सू‌र **úsoor**, *s. m.* A demon. (*The Usoors are considered demons of the first order, and in constant hostility with the gods*).

ख‌सू‌झ **úsoojh**, *adj.* Invisible, incorporeal.

ख‌सू‌या **usóoya**, *s. f.* Detraction, malice, slander.

ख‌से‌व‌न **usevun**, *s. m.* Disobedience, inattention. *Useva, s. f.* Disobedience.

ख‌सों **úson**, *adv.* This year.

ख‌सो‌क **úsok**, *s. m.* Ease, tranquillity, cheerfulness ; a shrub (*Jonesia asoca*).

ख‌सो‌ग **úsog**, *s. m.* Ease, tranquillity ; a tree (*Uvaria longifolia*).

उसोगी **úsogee**, *adj.* At ease, unmolested.

उसोच **úsoch**, *adj.* Not contrivable, impossible to be effected by reflection or study, not to be regretted.

उसोची **úsochee**, *adj.* Careless, indifferent, unconcerned.

उसोज **usój**, *s. m.* The sixth solar month.

उसोभा **úsobha**, *adj.* Shapeless, ill-made, ugly.

उस्त **ust**, *s. m.* Setting of the sun. *Ust hóna*, To set (*the sun*).

उस्तब्यस्त **ustubyúst**, *adj.* Dispersed, scattered, confused, agitated, perplexed, helter skelter, in confusion.

उस्ताचल **ustáchul**, *n. prop.* A mountain in the west, behind which the sun is supposed to set.

उस्तुत **ústoot**, *s. f.* Praise, eulogy, glorification, an anthem, a hymn.

उस्त्र **ustr**, *s. m.* A missile weapon, a weapon in general.

उस्त्रविद्या **ustr-vídya**, *s. f.* The military science.

उस्त्रवेद **ustr-véd**, *s. m.* The science of arms and war. [less.

उस्त्रहीन **ustr-héen**, *adj.* Unarmed, defence-

उस्थुल **ústhul**, } *s. m.* Place, site, soil,
स्थुल **sthul**, } dry or firm ground ; place or stand of a hindoo mendicant.

उस्थान **usthán**, *s. m.* Place, abode, residence.

उस्थावर **usthávur**, *adj.* Moveable, moving, not fixed.

उस्थि **ústhi**, *s. m.* A bone.

उस्थिपञ्जर **ústhi-púnjur**, *s. m.* A skeleton.

उस्थिभङ्ग **usthi-bhúng**, *s. m.* A fracture ; a plant of supposed efficacy in fractures (*Cissus quadrangularis*).

उस्थिभेद **usthi-bhéd**, *s. m.* Fracturing, breaking or wounding a bone.

उस्थिर **ústhir**, *adj.* Restless, unsteady ; unstable, uncertain.

उस्थिरता **ústhirta**, *s. f.* Unsteadiness, instability, fickleness, mutability.

उस्थिवत **usthivút**, *adj.* Bony, osseous.

उस्थिशोष **usthi-shókh**, *s. m.* Dryness and decay of the bones.

उस्थिसन्धि **usthi-súndhi**, *s. f.* Uniting of a broken bone.

उस्थ्यर्ज **ústhyrj**, *s. m.* Instability, unsteadiness.

उस्नेह **usneh**, *adj.* Harsh, unkind. *s. m.* Unkindness, want of affection.

उस्पर्शनीय **úspursh-néeyuh**, *adj.* Impure, not to be touched.

उस्पर्शी **úspursee**. *adj.* Intangible.

उस्पष्ट **úspusht**, *adj.* Indistinct.

उस्पृश्यूह **úsprish-yúh**, *adj.* Not to be touched.

उस्मरुन **usmurun**, *s. m.* Forgetfulness, forgetting.

उस्मृति **úsmriti**, *s. f.* Want of memory, forgetfulness.

उसर **usr**, *s. m.* A corner ; hair ; blood ; a tear.

उसरि **úsri**, *s. f.* Ten millions.

उस्सी **ússee**, *adj.* Eighty.

उहुम **úhum**, *pron.* I.

उहुन **úhun**, *adv.* Do not, not, no, nay.

उहुंकार **uhunkár**, *s. m.* Pride, egotism, arrogance, haughtiness, conceit.

उहुंकारी **uhunkáree**, } *adj.* Haughty, arro-
उहुंकृत **uhunkrít**, } gant, proud, self-important.

उबुंमति **úbum-múti**, *s. f.* Spiritual ignorance ; conceit ; self-love.

उह्रुह **úhruh**, *s. m.* A reservoir for collecting rain-water to water the fields ; fuel made of cow-dung. [ful.

उहुर्षित **úhurshit**, *adj.* Unhappy, sorrow-

उहुल्युह **uhúlyuh**, *n. prop.* Wife of *Gotum* and daughter of *Brumha* ; one of the *oopsurus*.

उहन **úhan**, *interj.* Do not, no, nay.

उहाहाबा **úha-hába**, *interj.* Expressive of surprise, pain, pleasure, &c., ah ! aha !

उहुर्निशि **úhur-níshi**, *adv.* Day and night.

उहार **uhár**, *s. m.* Starch, glue, paste ; aliment, food, victuals.

उहार्ना **uhárna**, *v. a.* To paste, to starch.

उहिंसुक **úhinsuk**, *adj.* Uninjurious, harmless, inoffensive, innocuous.

उहिंसा **úhinsa**, *s. f.* Harmlessness, doing injury to nothing.

उहि **úhi**, *s. m.* A serpent.

उहित **úhit**, *s. m.* Enmity, want of affection. *adj.* Hostile, inimical ; hurtful, prejudicial.

उहितकारी **úhit-káree**, *adj.* Adverse, inimical, acting unkindly. [inimical.

उहितमना **úhit-múna**, *adj.* Hating, adverse,

उहिफेन **uhi-phén**, *s. m.* The saliva or venom of a snake.

उहीर **uhéer**, *s. m.* A cowherd, a cast or tribe whose business it is to attend on cows.

उहीरनी **uhéernee**, } *s. f.* A female of the
उहीरी **uhéeree**, } *uheer* tribe, a cowherdess.

उहेह **úheh**, } *interj.* O ! sign of the voca-
उहो **úho**, } tive.

बरेतुक úhetook, *adj.* Causeless, ground-less. [ing.

बरेर uhér, *s. f.* Prey, game, chase, hunt-

बरेरिया uhériya,) *s. m.* A sportsman, a
बरेरी uhéree,) hunter.

बरेर uhéroo, *s. f.* A plant (*Asparagus racemosus*).

बरो úho, *interj.* O! holla! wonderful!

बरोराच uhorátr, *adv.* Day and night.

बक्ष uksh, *s. m.* A die, cubic or oblong, for playing with, the spots on dice.

बक्षत úkshut, *adj.* Infallible, indelible. *s. m. pres. part.* Remaining, existing, continuing; whole grain, whole grains of rice used in religious ceremonies, fried grain.

बक्षततिलक úkshut-tiluk, *s. f.* The cere-mony of putting a few grains of rice on the forehead of an idol when addressed, or of a *brahmun* when invited to an entertainment.

बक्षभाग uksh-bhág, *s. m.* A degree of lati-tude.

बक्षय úkshuy, *adj.* Imperishable, unde-cayable, durable, permanent.

बक्षयता ukshuy-tá, *s. f.* Durability, im-perishableness.

बक्षयबृक्ष úkshuy-bríksh, *s. m.* An unde-cayable tree.

बक्षयलोक ukshuy-lók, *s. m.* Heaven, the imperishable world or region.

बक्षर úkshur, *s. m.* A letter of the al-phabet.

बक्षरी úkshuree, *adv.* Scientific, lettered, writing an elegant hand.

बक्षांश ukshánsh, *s. m.* A degree of lati-tude or longititude.

बक्षि úkshi, *s. m.* An eye.

बक्षितारा úkshi-tára, *s. f.* The pupil of the eye.

बोहिणि ukshóuhinee, *s. f.* A complete army consisting of 109,350 foot, 65,610 horse, 21,870 chariots, and 21,870 elephants.

च्या

बा A, The second vowel in the Nagree alphabet, nearly corresponding to *a* in *all*. A particle of reminiscence, Ah! Oh! a particle of com-passion, Ah! Alas!

बाबभाव áobháo, *s. m.* A welcome.

बाः ah, *interj.* Aye aye! oh aye!

बांक ank, *s. m.* A numerical figure, a num-ber; a mark, a spot, a letter of the alphabet; the flank or part above the hip; the body; embrace; mark on cloth to shew its price.

बांकना ánkna, *v. a.* To mark a thing, to page a book, to write down numbers; to value, appraise, examine, approve of.

बांकरी ánkree, *s. f.* A tendril, cirrhus.

बांकरी ánkree, *s. f.* The barb of an arrow; a hook, a tenter; a circle.

बांकुस ánkoos, *s. m.* The hook or iron with which elephants are driven, a goad.

बांकुस मारना ánkoos márna, *v. a.* To re-duce to submission, to bring to obedience.

बांख ankh, *s. f.* The eye.

बांख बंजनी ankh-únjunee, *s. f.* A stye on the eye-lids.

बांख बानी ankh ánee, *v. n.* To have an inflammation in the eyes, to be blear-eyed.

बांख किसीको देखनी ankh kísee kee dékhnee, To receive education in any one's company.

बांख किसीसे रोषन करना ankh kísee seh róshun kúrna, To meet (*visit*) a friend or person of rank.

बांख खुटकनी ankh khútuknee, *v. n.* To have pain in the eyes.

बांख घूरकना ankh ghoorúkna, *v. n.* To look on with anger.

बांख चूरना ankh chúrna, *v. n.* To have eyes marked by debauch.

बांख चुरानी ankh churánee, *v. a.* To be angry, to be intoxicated.

बांख चमकानी ankh chumkánee, *v. a.* To make the eyes dance, to roll one's eyes in anger or as a blandishment.

बांख चीर चीर देखना ankh cheer-cheer)
dékhna,)
बांख चीरके देखना ankh chéerkeh dékhna,) *v. n.* To look with great attention and deep medi-tation, or with anger.

बांख चुरानी ankh chooránee, *v. a.* (*To steal eyes*). Not to attend to, to avert the eyes through shame, to avoid the sight of any one.

बांख छिपानी ankh chhipánee, *v. a.* (*To hide one's eyes*). To be ashamed of an improper act.

बांख झपकना ankh jhúpukna, *v. n.* (*To move the eye-lids quickly*). To fear.

बांख ठंडी करनी ankh thúndee kúrnee, *v. a.* To have consolation by meeting friends, to be glad.

बांख डबडबानी ankh dubdubánee, *v. n.* The eyes to fill with tears.

बांख दाबनी ankh dábnee, *v. a.* (*To shut one's eyes*). To forbid by signs.

बांख दिखानी ankh dikhánee,) *v. a.* (*To*
बांख दिखलानी ankh dikhlánee,) *shew* one's eyes). To frighten, to deter, to browbeat.

बांख देखके कुछ करना ankh dékhkeh koochh kúrna, To do any thing after consulting the incli-nation of another.

आंख नह रूखनी aṅkh nuh rúkhnee, To have no hope or expectation; to be mentally blind.

आंख पथरानी aṅkh puthránee, v. n. To become dim (the eyes) from long expectation.

आंख पसारना aṅkh pusárna, v. a. To open one's eyes, to stare, to be wise and prudent, to discriminate, to discern, to be judicious.

आंख फड़कनी aṅkh phúruknee, v. n. To feel a pulsation in the eye. (Considered, if in the right eye of a man, or the left of a woman, as an omen of some desirable event, whilst the contrary affection is regarded unlucky.)

आंख फूटनी aṅkh phóotnee, v. n. To be blind.

आंख फूटी पीड़ गई aṅkh phóotee peer gyee, The eye is lost and the pain is gone. (Spoken of a contention which has ceased, from the object of it being lost to both parties.)

आंख फेरनी aṅkh phérnee, v. a. To shew aversion after friendship.

आंख फेर लेना aṅkh pher léna, v. a. To turn away the eyes (as, from grief, displeasure, &c.).

आंख फोड़नी aṅkh phórnee, v. a. To make blind; to expect or watch in vain.

आंख फोड़ा aṅkh-phóra, s. m. A midge that flies into the eyes at night.

आंख बंद कर लेनी aṅkh bund kur lénee, v. a. To turn from another, to treat one with neglect; to die.

आंख बचाना aṅkh buchána, v. a. To steal away privately and unseen.

आंख बदलना aṅkh búdulna, v. a. To withdraw one's favour or affection from any one.

आंख बराबर न कर सकना aṅkh burábur nuh kur súkna, v. n. (Not to be able to look steadfastly in another's face.) To be ashamed.

आंख भरके देखना aṅkh bhúrkeh dékhna, v. a. To look till one's curiosity is fully satisfied.

आंख भरलाना aṅkh bhur-lána, v. n. To have eyes full of tears, to be ready to cry.

आंख मारनी aṅkh márnee, v. a. To wink. to stop any one by a sign, to make amorous signs with the eyes.

आंख मिंच जाना aṅkh mínch jána, v. n. To die, to perish.

आंख मिचौवल aṅkh-michóuwul, m. } s.
आंख मिचौली aṅkh-michóulee, f. } Blind-man's buff. [steadfastly.

आंख मिलनी aṅkh mílnee, v. n. To look

आंख मिलानी aṅkh milánee, v. a. To contract friendship.

आंख मूंद के एक चीज का इख्तियार करना aṅkh moond keh ek cheez ka ikhtiyár kúrna, v. a. To choose or accept precipitately or inconsiderately.

आंख मूंदौरा aṅkh moondóura s. m. Blind-man's buff.

आंख रखनी aṅkh rúkhnee, v. a. To love, to entertain friendship; to have hopes; to discern.

आंख लगानी aṅkh lugánee, v. a. To contract friendship or affection for any one, to fall in love.

आंख लड़नी aṅkh lúrnee, To meet with one's lover unexpectedly.

आंख लड़ानी aṅkh lúranee, v. a. To wink as a hint, to communicate a secret by signs.

आंख सूर्ख करनी aṅkh soorkh kúrnee, v. a. To be angry.

आंख सेंकनी aṅkh sénknee, To contemplate the beauty of any one.

आंख से गिरना aṅkh-seh girna, v. n. To become contemptible.

आंख से देखके कुछ करना aṅkh-seh dékhkeh koochh kúrna, To do any thing knowingly and with reflection.

आंखें देखना áṅkhen dékhna, v. a. To study one's temper or inclination; to behave respectfully towards another.

आंखें नीली पीली करना áṅkhen néelee péelee kúrna, v. a. To change the colour of the face from excess of anger.

आंखों का गुलाबी करना áṅkhon ka goolábee kúrna, Is applied to a look of intoxication or wantonness.

आंखों पर बैठना áṅkhon pur bythna, v. n. To be beloved, to sit or cause to sit in a very elevated place, to become dignified.

आंखों में आना áṅkhon men ána, v. n. To intoxicate (especially applied to wine).

आंखों में खाक डालना áṅkhon men khak dálna, v. a. To commend or puff wares of an inferior quality; to pilfer or snatch away any thing quickly and privately.

आंखों में खुड़कना áṅkhon men khóorukna, v. n. To be seen with envy and dislike.

आंखों में घुर करना áṅkhon men ghur kúrna, v. a. To be beloved or esteemed; to persist in one's erroneous opinions.

आंखों में चर्बी छाना áṅkhon men chúrbee chhána, v. n. To be wilfully blind, to pretend from pride not to know one's old acquaintance.

आंखों में फिरना áṅkhon men phírna, v. n. To be always present in one's eyes, to be ever in one's mind.

आंखों में रात काटना áṅkhon men rat kátna, v. a.
आंखों में रात ले जाना áṅkhon men rat le jána, v. n. }
To pass the night awake.

आंग ang, s. m. The body; a limb or member.

आंगन **ángun,** } *s. m.* A yard, area, court,
आंगना **ángna,** } inclosed space adjoining to a house.

आंच **anch,** *s. f.* Heat, flame of a fire (*not of a candle*), blaze, glare.

आंचर **ánchur,** *s. m.* The end or border of a cloth, veil, shawl, &c.

आंचल **ánchul,** *s. m.* The end or border of a cloth, veil, shawl, &c.; the breast (*of a woman or lactescent animal*).

आंजन **ánjun,** *s. m.* A collyrium or application to the eye-lashes to darken and improve them, antimony.

आंजना **ánjna,** *v. a.* To tinge the eyes with *anjun.*

आंसू **ánjhoo,** *s. m.* A tear.

आंट **ant,** *s. f.* A knot; envy.

आंटना **ántna,** *v. a.* To fill (*a well, tank, &c.*) *v. n.* To come or go into, to reach.

आंटसांट **ant-sant,** *s. f.* Partnership; intrigue.

आंटी **ántee,** *s. f.* A handful, a skein of thread, a bundle of grass, &c., a wisp, a small fagot.

आंठी **ánthee,** *s. f.* Stone of fruit; coagulation.

आंड **and,** } *s. f.* A testicle.
आंड़ **anr,** }

आंडू **ándoo,** *adj.* Having large testicles. *Ándoo-byl, s. m.* A bull.

आंत **ant,** *s. f.* Entrails, gut, intestine, tripe. *Ant áona, v. n.* To be afflicted with the coming down of the rectum. *Ant girna, v. n.* To void white glutinous stools.

आंधी **ándhee,** *s. f.* Storm, tempest, gale. *Andhee hóna, v. n.* To engage keenly in a bad action.

आन **an,** *adj.* Other, different. *s. f.* Order, command.

आंव **anv,** *s. m.* The glutinous whitish matter or mucus voided by those afflicted with a tenesmus; affection of the bowels. *Anv bythna,* To be afflicted with a tenesmus, or to be in the act of discharging the *anv.*

आंवलनाल **ánwul-nal,** *s. f.* The navel-string, &c. of an infant.

आंवला **ánvla,** *s. m.* A kind of myrobalans (*Phyllanthus emblica*).

आंस **ans,** *s. f.* The fibrous part of any thing.

आंसू **ánsoo,** *s. m.* A tear.

आक **ak,** *s. m.* Curled-flowered gigantic swallow-wort (*Asclepias gigantea*); a sprout of sugar-cane.

आकम्पन **ákumpun,** *v. m.* Shaking, trembling.

आकम्पित **akúmpit,** *adj.* Shaken, trembling.

आकर **ákur,** *s. f.* Mine, quarry, spring, source; multitude; the den of a lion or tiger.

आकर्ष **akúrsh,** *s. m.* Attraction, fascination; magnetic attraction; a magnet, a loadstone; spasm.

आकर्षक **akúrshuk,** *s. m.* A loadstone, a magnet, any thing which draws or attracts. *adj.* Attractive.

आकर्षण **akúrshun,** *s. m.* Attraction, drawing, attracting. [tive.

आकर्षिक **akurshík,** *adj.* Magnetic, attrac-

आकर्षित **akúrshit,** *adj.* Attracted, drawn.

आकर्षी **akurshée,** *adj.* Attractive.

आकल **ákla,** *adj. m.* Fleet, swift; peevish.

आकली **áklee,** *s. f.* Motion, agitation (*especially of a carriage*).

आकांक्षा **akánksha,** *s. f.* Wish, desire, expectation; purpose, intention.

आकांक्षित **akánkshit,** *adj.* Desirous; desired, wished, expected.

आकांक्षी **akánkshee,** *adj.* Desirous, full of hope, waiting, expecting, wishing; asking, inquiring, expectant.

आकार **akár,** *s. m.* Form, appearance, aspect, shape, statue, likeness; hint, sign, token; the letter आ, also the symbol of the vowel which represents the letter आ when joined to a consonant.

आकाल **akál,** *s. m.* Scarcity, famine.

आकाश **akásh,** *s. m.* The fifth element, æther, the sky, atmosphere, the heavens, the firmament, space; the subtle and etherial fluid, supposed to fill and pervade the universe, and to be the peculiar vehicle of life and sound.

आकाशदीया **akásh-déeya,** *s. m.* A lamp which the hindoos hang aloft on a bamboo in the month of *Kartik,* an elevated lantern, a beacon.

आकाशनीम **akásh-neem,** *s. m.* A plant growing on the *neem* trees (*a kind of Epidendron.*)

आकाशपुवन **akásh-púwun,** *s. m.* } A plant
आकाशबेल **akásh-bél,** *s. f.* } growing on other trees, air-plant or dodder (*Cuscuta reflexa*).

आकाशबृत्ति **akásh-brítti,** *s. f.* Subsistence not derived from any certain funds, or depending on any particular person; casual subsistence; living from hand to mouth.

आकाशबृत्ती **akásh-brittee,** *adj.* (used substantively), One whose subsistence is fortuitous.

आकाशमण्डल **akásh-múndul,** *s. m.* The atmosphere, the celestial sphere.

आकाशवाणी **ukásh-vánee,** *s. f.* A voice from heaven; revelation, an oracle.

आकाशी **akáshee,** *adj.* Aerial, airy, unsubstantial, celestial; atmospherical.

आकाशीवर्ण akáshee-búrn, *adj.* Cerulean, azure.

आकिंचन akínchun, *s. m.* Poverty.

आकूल ákool, *adj.* Confounded, perplexed; agitated, confused, troubled, distressed.

आकूलता akóolta, *s. f.* Agitation, distress.

आकूलित akóolit, *adj.* Agitated, disturbed, distracted.

आकृति ákriti, *s. f.* Shape, form, figure, likeness, an image; the body; species.

आकृष्ट akrísht, *adj.* Attracted, drawn.

आक्रम ákrum, *s. m.* Ascending, superiority, surpassing, surmounting; invasion, a seizing.

आखुत ákhut, *s. m.* Whole or unbroken rice used in oblations.

आखा ákha, *s. m.* A riddle, a sieve; a bag filled with grain (*two such bags being carried by a bullock or camel*).

आखूपाषान ákhoo-pashán, *s. m.* A kind of mineral, a loadstone.

आखेट akhét, *s. m.* The chase, hunting; a pursuing; terror, fright.

आखेटिक akhétik, *s. m.* A hound.

आखोट akhot, *s. m.* The walnut tree.

आख्या ákhya, *s. f.* A name, appellation, term.

आख्यात akhyát, *adj.* Said, spoken; denominated, named.

आग ag, *s. f.* Fire.

आग उठाना ag oothána, *v. a.* To raise disturbance, enrage, provoke.

आग करना ag kúrna, *v. a.* To make any thing exceedingly warm; to excite envy or anger.

आगत águt, *a.* Come, arrived.

आग देना ag déna, *v. a.* To burn a hindoo corpse.

आग पुरना ag purna, *v. n.* To be enraged; as, *méres báton-seh óospur ag púrtee hy,* he is enraged at my words.

आग बरना ag burna, *v. n.* To be enraged, to be very angry.

आग बरसना ag búrusna, *v. n.* To rain fire (*applied to the extreme heat of the sun, or to a hot fire of cannon or musketry in battle*).

आग बुझाना ag boojhána, *v. a.* To extinguish fire; to appease a tumult, to pacify a quarrel, to still resentment.

आग भकना ag bhúkna, ⎤ *v. a.* To speak
आग फाँकना ag phánkna, ⎦ idle words, to boast.

आगम águm, *s. m.* Futurity; a shastru containing spells and incantations; a shastru or work on sacred science.

आगम ज्ञानी águm-jánee, ⎤ *s. m.* Knowing
आगम ज्ञानी águm-gyánee, ⎦ the future; a prognosticator, diviner, foreteller.

आगमन águmun, *s. m.* Coming, arriving, arrival.

आगमना agmuná, *s. m.* The advanced guard. *adj.* Adventurous, venturesome, forward, early (*as fruit*).

आगम बक्ता águm-búkta, *s. m.* A foreteller, a predictor; *Siv.* one who tells the doctrines of *águm.*

आगम बांधना águm-bándhna, *v. a.* To determine the future, to foretell.

आगम विद्या águm-bídiya, *s. f.* The art or science of foretelling or divining.

आगमें किसीकी अछना ag-men kísee-kee ⎤ júlna,
आगमें किसीकी छोटना ag-men kísee-kee ⎬ lótna,
आगमें घिरकी अछना ag-men ghyr-kee ⎦ júlna,
v. n. To bring reproach, to accuse, to suffer for another.

आगमें पानी डाछना ag-men pánee dálna, *v. a.* To extinguish fire; to appease a tumult, to pacify a quarrel, to still resentment.

आगमें छोटना ag-men lótna, *v. n.* To be afflicted with grief or melancholy.

आग लगना ag lúgna, *v. n.* To be set on fire, to be enraged, to be very hungry.

आग लुगाके पानी ले दोरना ag lugákeh pánee leh dóurna, To pretend to appease a quarrel which one has purposely excited, to play tricks, to deceive.

आग लगाना ag lugána, *v. a.* To set on fire, to inflame; to enrage, to cause disturbance.

आग लगेपर बिल्लीका मूत ढूंढना या मांगना ag lúgeh-pur billee-ka moot dhóondhna ya mángna, To put off, to delay or excuse one's self on vain pretences.

आगलान्त agulánt, *adv.* Up to the neck.

आग लेनेको आना ag léneko ána, To come to get fire (*is spoken of a friend who goes to visit another and leaves him quickly*).

आगवा ágwa, *s. m.* A pommel.

आग सुलगाना ag soolgána, *v. a.* To inflame; to excite sedition, to foment a quarrel clandestinely.

आग होना ag hóna, *v. n.* To be enraged.

आगा ága, *s. m.* The front, the forepart; the space in front of a house, the forepart of a turband.

आगाध agádh, *adj.* Very deep.

आगा पीछा करना ága péechha kúrna, *v. n.* To hesitate, waver, boggle, demur, stand shill-I-shall-I.

F

आगामी **agámee**, *adj.* Coming, about to come; future.

आगार **agár**, *s. m.* A house, a dwelling.

आगू **ágoo**, *adj.* Forward. *adv.* Before, heretofore.

आगे **ágeh**, *adv.* Before, in front, fore, beyond, more, ago, already, formerly, forwards, farther, onwards; henceforward, along; then, hence, rather, sooner.

आगे आना **ágeh-ána**, *v. n.* To come forward, advance; to return, revert.

आगे धरलेना **ágeh dhur-léna**, To get before, outstrip, surpass, pass (*as a horse in a race*).

आगे लाना **ágeh lána**, *v. n.* To advance (*actively*), to bring forward.

आग्रह **agrúh**, *s. m.* Favour, patronage; seizing, taking; surpassing, surmounting; power, ability.

आग्रहायण **agruháyun**, *s. m.* A month so called, the first of the hindoo year according to some systems, (*November-December*).

आग्रहायणी **agruháyunee**, *s. f.* The name of a constellation consisting of 3 stars, 1 of which is Orionis, figured by an antelope's head, hence also मृगशिरस् **mrígshiras**; the day of full moon in the month Agruháyun.

आघार **aghár**, *s. m.* Ghee or clarified butter.

आङ्ग **ang**, *s. m.* A soft delicate form, or body.

आचमन **áchmun**, *s. m.* Rincing the mouth, sipping water before religious ceremonies, meals &c., from the palm of the hand, and spitting it out again.

आचरण **áchurun**, *s. m.* Manner of life, conduct, behaviour, custom, practice, institute, religious observance, usage.

आचार **achár**, *s. m.* An established rule of conduct, an ordinance, institute, a precept; custom, practice, usage, a religious observance; pickles. *Achar vurjjit, adj.* Irregular, out of rule; out of cast.

आचारी **acháree**, *adj.* Practising (*what is good*), strict in the observance of religious ceremonies.

आचार्यः **acháryuh**, *s. m.* A spiritual guide or teacher; he who invests the student with the sacrificial thread, and instructs him in the *Veds*, the law of sacrifice, and religious mysteries; a name of *Drona* the teacher of the *Pandoos.*

आचार्या **achárya**, *s. f.* A spiritual preceptress.

आचार्यानी **acharyánee**, *s. f.* The wife of an *Acháryuh* or holy teacher.

आच्छादन **achchhádun**, *s. m.* Cloth, clothes; a covering, a sheath, mantle, cloak, &c.

आच्छे **áchhen**, *adj. plur.* Good, excellent.

आज **aj**, *adv.* To-day. Aj-kul, Now-a-days, to-day or to-morrow, of late, in a few days. Aj-kul kúrna, or Aj-kul butána, To procrastinate. Aj-keh din, To-day. Aj-kee rat, To-night. Aj-keh roz, To-day.

आजा **ája**, *s. m.* A paternal grand-father.

आजाना **ajána**, *v. n.* To come suddenly, befall, happen; to come.

आजीव **ajéev**, *s. m.* Livelihood, profession, subsistence.

आजीविका **ajéevika**, *s. f.* Means of supporting life, livelihood, subsistence, profession.

आज्ञा **ágya**, *s. f.* Command, order, permission, an injunction, a precept.

आज्ञाकार **agyakár**, } *adj.* Acting according to order, obedient, ministrant, obsequious.
आज्ञाकारी **agyakáree**, }

आज्ञापत्र **agya-pútr**, *s. m.* An edict, a written order.

आज्ञाभङ्ग **agya-bhúng**, *s. m.* Disobedience, insubordination.

आञ्जनेय **anjunéyuh**, *s. m.* A name of the monkey Hunoomán.

आञ्जिनेय **anjinéyuh**, *s. m.* An insect, a kind of newt.

आटरूष **átroos**, *s. m.* A tree (*Justicia adhenatoda, &c.*).

आटा **áta**, *s. m.* Flour, meal, farina.

आटि **áti**, *s. m.* The *Sarali*, a bird so called (*Turdus ginginianus*).

आठ **ath**, *adj.* Eight. *Ath ath ánsoo róna,* To shed floods of tears, to weep exceedingly. *Ath púhur,* All the twenty-four hours; constantly, day and night. *Ath khúmba,* A canopy supported by eight posts.

आठवाँ **athwán**, *adj.* Eighth.

आड़ **ar**, *s. f.* A screen, shelter, concealment, protection; an horizontal line drawn across the forehead; prevention, stop, hinderance.

आड़ना **árna**, *v. a.* To prop, shelter, protect, defend, stop.

आडम्बर **adúmbur**, *s. m.* Charge sounded by musical instruments; commencement; pride, arrogance; anger, passion; happiness, pleasure.

आड़वाड़ **arwár**, *s. f.* A stop. *adj.* Stopping.

आड़ा **ára**, *adj.* Oblique, crooked, across, athwart, cross, transverse.

आड़ि **ári**, *s. f.* A bird, the *Sarali* (*Turdus ginginianus*).

आड़ी **áree**, *s. f.* A tone or tune in music. *part.* A protector, defender, supporter.

आड़ू **ároo**, *s. m.* A peach.

আৰ্‌ আৰ্জা áreh-ána, *v. n.* To protect, become a protection.

আৰ্ arh, *s. f.* A kind of fish.

আৰ্‌হত arhut, *s. f.* Agency ; commission, brokerage, sale by commission.

আৰ্হ্য árhyuh, *adj.* Wealthy, rich, opulent.

আণি áni, *s. m. f.* The edge of a sword. the pin of the axle of a cart ; a limit, a boundary.

আতঙ্গ atung, *s. m.* Fear, apprehension ; disease, sickness ; affliction, pain ; parade, ostentation, show, pomp.

আত at, *s. m.* Custard apple (*Annona squamosa or reticulata*).

আততায়িন attáyin, *s. m. f.* ⎫ A felon, a
আততায়ী attáyee, *s. m.* ⎭ thief, a murderer, incendiary.

আতপ átup, *s. m.* Sun-beams, sunshine.

আতা áta, *s. m.* A custard apple.

আতিথেয় atithéyuh, ⎫ *adj.* Proper for a
আতিথ্য atíthyuh, ⎭ guest ; hospitable, attentive to a guest.

আতী পাতী átee-pátee, *s. f.* The name of a game.

আতুর átoor, *adj.* Diseased, distressed, anxious, distracted, agitated, restless, afflicted.

আতু átoo, *s. f.* A female teacher or governess.

আত্ম atm, *s. m.* Soul, self. *Atm-páluk,* Selfish. *Atm-ghat,* Self-murder. *Atm-námee,* Self-evident.

আত্মগুপ্তা atm-góopta, *s. f.* A plant, Cowach (*Carpopogon pruriens*).

আত্মঘাত atm-ghát, *s. m.* Self-murder, suicide.

আত্মঘাতক atm-ghátuk, *s. m.* One who commits suicide.

আত্মঘাতী atm-ghátee, *adj.* Committing suicide ; a suicide.

আত্মজ atmúj, *adj.* Springing from one's self. *s. m.* A son.

আত্মজা atmúja, *s. f.* A daughter.

আত্মজ্ঞান atmgyán, *s. m.* The knowledge of spirit, self-knowledge.

আত্মনামী atm-námee, *adj.* Self-evident.

আত্মপালক atm-páluk, *adj.* Selfish.

আত্মবুদ্ধি atm-bóoddhi, *s. f.* Self-knowledge.

আত্মবোধ atm-bódh, *s. m.* Spiritual instruction.

আত্মবিদ্যা atm-vídya, *s. f.* Spiritual knowledge.

আত্মশক্তি atm-shúkti, *s. f.* Inherent or own power.

আত্মশ্লাঘা atm-shlágha, *s. f.* Self-applause, vanity, self-flattery, egotism, boasting.

আত্মসংযম atm-súnjum, *s. m.* Self-restraint, stoicism.

আত্মসন্দেহ atm-sundéh, *s. m.* Internal doubt.

আত্মহত্যা atm-hútya, *s. f.* Suicide, self-destruction.

আত্মহিত atm-hít, *adj.* Beneficial to one's self.

আত্মা átma, *s. m.* The soul, the body, the self, the mind, the understanding.

আত্মিক átmik, *adj.* Relating to mind, to one's self.

আত্মীয় atméeyuh, *adj.* Cognate, related to, of kin ; belonging to one's self, related to one's self, own.

আথর্ব্বণ athúrvvun, *s. m.* A *brahmun* versed in the *Uthúrvun Ved* ; a collection of prayers, &c., delivered by Uthúrvun a sage.

আদন্ত ad-unt, *adj.* From the first till the last, from the beginning to the end. *s. m.* The beginning and the end.

আদর ádur, *s. m.* Respect, reverence, act of treating with attention and deference, politeness.

আদরমান adurmán, *s. m.* Respect and honour.

আদর্শ ádursh, *s. m.* A mirror ; a commentary, original manuscript from which a copy is taken ; a specimen, a sign.

আদা áda, *s. m.* Ginger in the undried state.

আদান adán, *s. m.* Taking, receipt, acceptance.

আদানপ্রদান adán-prudán, *s. m.* Giving and taking.

আদি ádi, *adj.* First, prior ; pre-eminent. *adj.* (in comp.) Other, &c.

আদিক ádik, *adj.* Relating to the beginning ; and the rest, etcetera.

আদিকারণ ádi-kárun, *s. m.* A primary cause.

আদিত ádit, *adv.* From the beginning ; etcetera, and the like.

আদিত্য ádityuh, *s. m.* A deity in general ; a deity of a particular class ; the *ádityus* are 12 in number, and are forms of *Sóoryuh* or the sun, and appear to represent him as distinct in each month of the year ; the sun.

আদিত্যবার adityuwár, *s. m.* Sunday.

আদিত aditwuh, *s. m.* Priority, precedence.

আদিপুরষ ádi-póoroosh, *s. m.* One of the names of *Vishnu*.

2 F

आदेश ádesh, *s. m.* An order, a command, a salutation of *Jogees*; in grammar, a substitute.

आदौ adóu, *adv.* In the beginning.

आद्युह ádyuh, *adj.* First, initial.

आद्यन्त adyúnt, *s. m.* First and last, beginning and end. *adj.* From the first till the last, from the beginning to the end.

आद्रा ádra, *s. f.* The sixth lunar mansion (*probably Orionis*); the beginning of the rainy season.

आधा ádha, *adj.* Half. In comp. it becomes adh, udh, or ud; as udh-móoa, or ud-mooa, Half-dead.

आधान adhán, *s. m.* Conception, pregnancy; a ceremony performed previous to conception as conducive to it; a pledge, a deposit; a surety.

आधानिक adhánik, *s. m.* A ceremony performed after cohabitation to procure or favour conception.

आधार adhár, *s. m.* A patron, supporter, one on whom dependance is placed for assistance; food, aliment, victuals, nourishment; comprehension, location; a dike, a canal; a basin round the foot of a tree.

आधारी adháree, (*in comp.*) An eater; as, *Doodh-adháree*, One who lives on milk.

आधार्मिक ádharmmik, *adj.* Unjust, unrighteous.

आधासीसी ádha-séesee, *s. f.* A pain affecting the half of the head, Hemicrania.

आधि ádhi, *s. m.* Mental agony, anxiety; expectation, calamity; a pledge, a pawn; location, fixing, scite, &c., engagement.

आधिक्या adhíkyuh, *s. m.* Excess, an overplus, abundance.

आधिपत्य ádhi-pútyuh, *s. m.* Sovereignty, government; lordship.

आधीन adhéen, *adj.* Submissive, obedient, dependant, humble, docile.

आधीनता adhéenta, ⎫ *s. f.* Submission,
आधीनताई adheentáee, ⎭ obedience, obsequiousness, servility, humility.

आधुनिक ádhoonik, *adj.* Recent, modern, belonging to the present time.

आधुनिकता ádhoonikta, *s. f.* Recentness, the being modern, novelty.

आध्यापक adhyápuk, *s. m.* A teacher, a scriptural preceptor.

आन an, *s. f.* Order, command; bashfulness, modesty, shame; an oath; a graceful attitude; affectation, pride. *adj.* Other, different.

आनंद ánund, *s. m.* Pleasure, delight, felicity, happiness, joy, ease; God, Supreme Spirit. *Anund-kúnd*, Root (*or source*) of happiness.

आनक ánuk, *s. m.* A large military drum beaten at one end; a small drum or tabor; a kettle drum.

आनन ánun, *s. m.* Mouth, face, visage. *s. f.* Order.

आनन्द ánund, *s. m.* ⎫ Pleasure, delight,
आनन्दता anundtá, *s. f.* ⎭ felicity, happiness, joy, ease. *Anund-kúnd*, Root (*or source*) of happiness.

आनन्दमय anund-múy, *adj.* Blissful, made up, consisting of, happiness. *s. m.* The Supreme Spirit.

आनन्दित anúndit, ⎫ *adj.* Joyful, happy,
आनन्दी anúndee, ⎭ glad, rejoiced, delighted.

आना ána, *v. n.* To come, to be. *An-púrna*, To happen. *s. m.* The sixteenth part of a rupee.

आनाकानी anakánee, *s. f.* Turning a deaf ear, overlooking, winking at, purposely neglecting.

आनुकूल्य anookóolyuh, *s. m.* Help, assistance, patronage.

आनुपूर्व्य anoopóorv, *s. f.* Order, method, a rank, a row.

आनुमानिक anoománik, *adj.* Capable of being inferred, probable, specious.

आन्तरीक्ष antureéksh, *adj.* Heavenly, celestial, produced in the sky. *s. m.* The firmament.

आन्त्रिक antrík, *adj.* Visceral, relating to the bowels.

आन्दु ándoo, *s. m.* The chain or rope with which the feet of elephants are tied up.

आन्ना ánna, *v. a.* To bring.

आप ap, *pron.* Self, selves, yourselves, you Sir (*used instead of the personal pronoun of the second person by an inferior when addressing his superior.*) *Ap-swárthee, adj.* Selfish, seeking the interest of self.

आप ap, *s. m.* Water.

आपआप ap-ap, *s. m.* Selfishness, egotism.

आपकाज ap-káj, ⎫ *adj.* Attending to
आपकाजी ap-kájee, ⎭ (*one's*) own business, engaged in (*one's*) own affairs.

आपत áput, ⎫ *s. f.* Misfortune, calamity,
आपत्ति apútti, ⎭ adversity, an evil.

आपत्काल aput-kál, *s. m.* Season of distress.

आपद ápud, ⎫ *s. f.* Misfortune, calamity,
आपदा ápuda, ⎭ an accident, danger, adversity, an evil.

आपद्ग्रस्त apud-grúst, *adj.* Unfortunate, unhappy, in misfortune.

आपन ápun, *pron.* Self.

आपनिक apuník, *s. m.* An emerald.

আবদ **apúnn**, *adj.* Unfortunate, afflicted; gained, obtained, acquired; a refuge, one who comes for shelter or protection.

আবরূপ **áproop**, *s. m.* and *adj.* Self, self-formed, the Deity.

আপস **ápus**, *pron. recip.* Themselves, one another; hence, *s. f.* Kindred, brotherhood, fellowship. *Apus men rúhna,* is applied to signify adultery, &c. (*in the dialect of women*).

আপা **ápa**, *s. f.* An elder sister. *pron.* Self.

আপী **apée**, *s. f.* The twentieth lunar mansion.

আপ্ত **apt**, *adj.* Trusted, confidential; gained, obtained; true. [degree.

আপ্তা **aptá**, *s. m.* Quotient; equation of a

আপ্লব **aplúv**, ⎫ *s. m.* Bathing.
আপ্লাব **apláv**, ⎭

আপকূট **apkóot**, *s. m.* An initiated householder. *adj.* Bathed.

আফূ **áphoo**, *s. f.* Opium.

আবাধা **abádha**, *s. f.* Segment of the base of a triangle.

আবরণ **ábhurun**, *s. m.* Ornament, decoration, as jewels, &c.

আভা **ábha**, *s. f.* Beauty; splendour; light.

আভাষ **ábhash**, ⎫ *s. m.* A preface, a preamble, an introduction.
আভাস **ábhas**, ⎭

আভিমুখ **ábhi-mookh**, *s. m.* Presence, being in front of or face to face.

আভীর **abhéer**, *s. m.* A cow-keeper, sprung from a brahmun and female of the medical tribe or the *Umbusth.*

আভূষণ **abhóoshun**, *s. m.* Jewels, ornaments.

আম **am**, *adj.* Raw, undressed, unripe. *s. m.* Provisions, victuals (*undressed*); the mango tree or fruit; sickness, disease.

আময় **ámuy**, *s. m.* Sickness, disease.

আমর্ষ **ámursh**, *s. m.* Wrath or rage, anger; envy, impatience of another's success.

আমলা **ámla**, *s. m.* Emblic myrobalan (*Phyllanthus emblica*).

আমবাত **amvát**, *s. m.* Constipation or torpor of the bowels, with flatulence and intumescence, the wind being supposed to be chiefly affected.

আমশূল **am-shóol**, *s. m.* The cholic, pain arising from indigestion.

আমাতিসার **áma-tisár**, *s. m.* Dysentery.

আমান্ন **ámánn**, *s. m.* Raw rice or grain; provisions (*undressed*).

আমিষ **ámish**, *s. m.* Flesh; enjoyment; an object of enjoyment, a pleasing or beautiful object, &c.

আমোদ **amód**, *s. m.* Fragrance, odour, a diffusive perfume; pleasure.

আম্নসাম্ন **ámna-sámna**, *s. m.* Confronting.

আম্নেসাম্নে **ámneh-sámneh**, *adv.* Opposite, face to face, over against.

আম্বর **ámbur**, *s. f.* Amber.

আম্বাত **ambát**, *s. m.* A swelling which comes without pain, and goes off as easily without medicine; a windy tumour.

আম্র **amr**, *s. m.* The mango-tree (*Mangifera Indica*).

আম্লিকা **ámlika**, *s. f.* The tamarind tree.

আয়ুহ **áyuh**, *s. m.* Receipt, gain, profit.

আয়ত **áyut**, *adj.* Long, wide. *s. m.* Sunbeam, sunshine.

আয়ত্ত **áyutt**, *adj.* Docile, tractable, dependant.

আয়ত্ততা **ayutt-tá**, *s. f.* Docility, tractableness, humility.

আয়ুসু **ayúsoo**, *s. m.* Order, command.

আয়া **áya**, *s. f.* An ayah or female attendant on children.

আয়াস **ayás**, *s. m.* Fatigue, weariness.

আয়ু **áyoo**, ⎫
আয়ুর্দা **áyoorda**, ⎬ *s. f.* Age, duration of life.
আয়ুর্বল **áyoorbul**, ⎪
আয়ুস **ayós**, ⎭

আয়োধ **ayódh**, *s. m.* A weapon in general.

আর **ar**, *s. f.* A goad.

আরম্ভ **árumbh**, *s. m.* A beginning, a commencement; an introduction, a prologue.

আর্চা **árcha**, *s. f.* Worship, an image.

আরুজ **áruj**, *adj.* Respectable, venerable.

আরুত **árut**, *adj.* Distressed, grieved, afflicted.

আর্তা **árta**, *s. m.* A ceremony attending marriage. When the bridegroom first comes to the house of the bride, he is received by her relations, who present to him, and more particularly round his head, a platter painted and divided into several compartments, in the middle of which is a lamp made of flour, filled with *ghee*, and having several wicks lighted.

আর্তি **árti**, *s. f.* Pain, distress, affliction.

আর্তী **ártee**, *s. f.* A ceremony performed in adoration of the gods by moving circularly, round the head of the idol, a platter containing a burning lamp with several wicks.

আরনা **árna**, *v. n.* To stop.

আরম্ভ **árumbh**, *s. m.* A beginning, a commencement; an introduction, a prologue.

আরস **árus**, *s. m.* Idleness, laziness, inactivity.

आरसी árusee, *adj.* Idle, lazy, indolent, inactive.

आरसी ársee, *s. f.* A mirror (*particularly a mirror on the thumb used by hindoo females*).

आरस्य árusyub, *s. m.* Insipidity, want of flavour or spirit.

आरा ára, *s. m.* A saw ; a shoemaker's knife or awl ; the name of a district, *Arrah* in *Shahabad.*

आराति aráti, *s. m.* An enemy.

आराधन arádhun, *s. m.* Accomplishment, gratifying ; worship, devotion, supplication.

आराधना arádhna, *v. a.* To worship, adore, practise devotion, serve, to accomplish. *s. f.* Service, worship, adoration.

आराम arám, *s. m.* A pleasure garden, a grove.

आरी áree, *s. f.* A small saw, a hand saw, an awl.

आरीया áreeya, *s. m.* A plant of the gourd kind.

आरूक árook, *s. m.* A drug brought from the hills, of cooling properties.

आरूंधना aróondhna, *v. a.* To strangle. *Kunth-aróodhun,* Strangulation.

आरूढ aróorh, *adj.* Mounted on a horse or any thing else, ascended, risen. *Megh-aróorh,* Seated on a cloud.

आरोग्य árogyub, *s. m.* Health. *adj.* Healthy.

आरोप aróp, *s. m.* A transmutation, a change.

आरोपन arópun, *s. m.* Planting.

आरोपित arópit, *adj.* Deposited, intrusted ; transformed, changed into, feigned.

आरोहन aróhun, *s. m.* Rising, ascending ; the rising or growing of new shoots ; a ladder, a staircase.

आर्त artt, *adj.* Pained, afflicted ; disturbed, confounded.

आर्द्र ardr, *adj.* Wet, moist, damp.

आर्द्रक árdruk, *s. m.* Ginger, in the undried state.

आर्द्रा árdra, *s. f.* The 6th lunar mansion.

आर्बुद árbul, *s. f.* Age, duration of life.

आर्य áryuh, *adj.* Of a good family, respectable, venerable.

आर्सी ársee, *s. f.* A mirror (*particularly a mirror on the thumb used by hindoo females*).

आल al, *s. f.* The name of a tree, from the root of which a red colour is extracted for staining leather, dying silk, &c. (*Morinda citrifolia*). *s. m.* Yellow orpiment.

आलंबन alúmbun, *s. m.* Dependance ; a support, a protector.

आलय áluy, *s. m.* A house.

आलवाल alwál, *s. m.* A basin for water round the root of a tree.

आलस álus, *s. m.* Idleness, slothfulness, laziness. *adj.* Idle, slothful, lazy.

आलसी álusee, *adj.* Idle, slothful, lazy.

आलस्य alúsyub, *s. m.* Idleness, slothfulness, laziness. *adj.* Idle, slothful, apathetic.

आलस्यी álusyee, *adj.* Drowsy, slothful.

आला ála, *s. m.* A small recess in a pillar or wall for holding a lamp, &c. *adj.* Wet ; runing (*as a sore*).

आलान alán, *s. m.* The post to which an elephant is tied, or the rope that ties him.

आलाप aláp, *s. f.* Prelude to singing. *s. m.* Speaking to, addressing, conversation ; enumeration of the questions in an arithmetical or algebraic sum.

आलापचारी alapcháree, *s. f.* The act of tuning the voice previous to singing.

आलापना alápna, *v. a.* To tune the voice, to run over the different notes previous to singing, to catch the proper key, to sing, to tune.

आलि áli, ⎱ *s. f.* A woman's female
आली álee, ⎰ friend, a damsel.

आलिंगन alíngun, *s. m.* Embracing, the clasping any one in the arms, an embrace.

आलिंगी alíngee, *adj.* Embracing.

आली álee, *s. f.* A woman's female friend, a damsel. *s. m.* A scorpion.

आलीरंग álee-rúng, *s. m.* A colour extracted from the al tree (*Morinda citrifolia*).

आलू áloo, ⎱ *s. m.* An esculent root (*Arum*
आलू áloo, ⎰ *campanulatum*), a potatoe. *Rut-áloo,* A yam ; *Shukurkúnd,* A sweet potatoe.

आलेप alép, *s. m.* Liniment.

आलोक alók, *s. m.* Sight, seeing, looking ; light ; flattery, complimentary language, panegyric.

आलोकन alókun, *s. m.* Sight, seeing, looking.

आल्हा álha, *s. prop.* Name of a *hindoo* soldier and poet, from whom a species of poetry takes its name.

आवक áwuk, *s. m.* Insurance.

आवती áwutee, *s. f.* Approach, advance ; the coming of an army, the approach of friend ; the season in which merchandize is expected.

आवन áwun, *s. m.* Coming, approach. *Awun awun,* Tidings of approach.

आवनेहार aonehár, *adj.* That which is to come, he that shall come.

आवरून awurún, *s. m.* A shield ; a covering.

आवर्दा áwurda, *s. f.* The allotted period of any one's life, a life time, an age.

আৱনী áwunon, *v. n.* To come.

আৱভক্তি áobhukti, ⎫ *s. f.* A civil recep-
আৱভগত áobhugut, ⎬ tion or salutation,
আৱভগতি áobhuguti ⎭ welcome, courte-
ousness.

আৱলি áwuli, *s. f.* A row, a range, a continuous line ; a series, a dynasty, a lineage.

আৱশ্যক awushyúk, *adj.* Necessary, indispensable, expedient. *s. m.* Necessity, expediency.

আৱশ্যকতা awúshyukta, *s. f.* Necessity,
indispensableness, inevitability.

আৱা áwa, *s. m.* A potter's-kiln.

আৱাৈ awáee, *s. f.* Report, mention.

আৱাগমন áwa-gúmun, ⎫ *s. m.* Transmi-
আৱাগৱন áwa-gúwun, ⎬ gration, coming
and going.

আৱাজাৈ áwa-jáee, *s. f.* Coming and going, intercourse, dancing after.

আৱাতী awátee, *s. f.* Approach, advance ;
the coming of an army ; the approach of a friend ;
the season in which merchandize is expected.

আৱাস awás, *s. m.* A house.

আৱাহন awáhun, *s. m.* Calling, summons.

আবিৰ্ভাৱ ávirbhao, *s. m.* An unfolding, a
developing, a manifesting, manifestation, presence,
becoming visible.

আবিৰ্ভূত avirbhóot, *adj.* Unfolded, developed, manifested, appeared.

আবিষ্ট avisht, *adj.* Possessed (*by a demon,
&c.*) ; possessed, engrossed (*by any sentiment or
feeling*).

আৱৃত avrít, *adj.* Enclosed, surrounded (*by
a ditch, wall, &c.*)

আৱৃত্তি avrítti, *s. f.* Order, method ; a re-
pitition of the same thing, a revolution.

আশুক্ত áshukt, *adj.* Fond, attached, enamoured, addicted, devoted to, strongly inclined
to ; able, powerful.

আশুক্তি áshukti, *s. f.* Attachment, fondness ; power, ability, might.

আশুন্কা áshunka, *s. f.* Fear, apprehension,
awe, terror, danger, peril ; doubt, uncertainty.

আশুন áshun, *s. m.* A tree (*Terminalia
alata tomentosa*), on which the tusur silk-worm
feeds.

আশুয় áshuy, *s. m.* Meaning, intention,
aim, scope, an object of desire.

আশা ásha, *s. f.* Hope, desire ; dependance, reliance, trust.

আশাঢ় ashárh, *s. m.* A hindoo month
containing part of June and July, and commencing
when the sun enters Gemini ; the name of the
20th and 21st mansions in the *hindoo* Zodiac.

আশাপ্রাপ্ত asha-prápt, *adj.* Successful, possessing the object hoped for.

আশাবন্ধ asha-búndh, *s. m.* Confidence,
trust, expectation.

আশাভঙ্গ asha-bhúng, *s. m.* Disappointment.

আশাৱন্ত ashawúnt, *adj.* Expectant, dependant ; hoping, having hope.

আশাহীন asha-héen, *adj.* Desponding,
despairing.

আশিস áshis, *s. f.* Blessing, benediction,
bestowing or wishing a blessing upon others.

আশীৰ্বচন asheer-vúchun, *s. m.* A blessing, a benediction.

আশীৰ্বাদ asheerbad, *s. m.* ⎫ Benediction,
আশীস ashées, *s. f.* ⎬ blessing,
return of a compliment from a brahmun.

আশ্চৰ্য áshchurj, *s. m.* Surprise, astonishment, amazement. *adj.* Astonishing, wonderful.

আশ্চৰ্যতা ashchurjyutá, *s. m.* Wonderful-
ness ; wonder, astonishment.

আশ্রম áshrum, *s. m.* Abode, residence ; a
religious order, of which there are four kinds referable to the different periods of life ; as 1st, That of
the *bruhmucharee* or student ; 2d, That of the *gri-
hust* or householder ; 3d, That of the *vunuprusth*
or anchorite ; and 4th, That of the *bhikshook* or
beggar ; a college, a school ; a hermitage, the
abode of retired devotees or sages.

আশ্রুয় áshruy, ⎫ *s. m.* Cheating, fraud, cir-
আশ্রা áshra, ⎬ cumvention ; proximity,
vicinity ; a retreat, an abode, an asylum ; a house ;
a means of defence, having recourse to protection
or sanctuary ; trust, reliance, hope ; a patron, a
protector.

আশ্রিত áshrit, *adj.* One who relies on another ; a refugee, a protegee ; a dependant.

আশ্রীত ashryt, *adj.* Hopeful, trusting, confident.

আশ্বাস ashwás, *s. m.* Completion, cessation, comfort.

আশ্বিন áshwin, *s. m.* The 6th hindoo
month (*September-October*), commencing when
the sun enters Virgo, and in which the moon is
full near the stars in the head of Aries.

আষাঢ় ashárh, *s. m.* The hindoo 3d solar
month (*June-July, during which the sun is in
Gemini, and the full moon is near asharha, more
commonly called poorvusharha or otturasharha
constellations in Sagittarius*).

আস as, *s. f.* Hope, dependance, reliance,
trust.

আসকত áskut, *s. f.* Laziness, tardiness.
Askutána, v. n. To be lazy. *Askutee, adj.* Lazy,
remiss.

আসকতানা askutána, *v. n.* To be lazy.

আষকতী áskutee, *adj.* Lazy, remiss.

আষক্ত ásukt, *adj.* Diligent, zealously active ; fond, enamoured, addicted, devoted to ; intent or attached strongly to ; trusting to, confiding in ; eternal.

আষক্তি ásukti, *s. f.* Attachment to one object or pursuit, diligence, application.

আষন ásun, *s. m.* A tree on which the *tusur* silk-worm feeds (*Terminalia aluta tomentosa*) ; a stool, a seat, a small carpet on which the hindoos sit at their worship ; a carpet to sit on ; stay, abiding, posture, attitude, sitting (*especially the attitudes adopted by jogees in their devotional exercises, of which they reckon eighty-four*) ; the inside or upper part of the thigh ; the withers of an elephant, the part where the driver sits. *Asun túleh ána*, To come under subjection. *Asun jórna*, To sit on the hams. *Asun dólna*, Spoken of a holy man, who perceiving by supernatural intelligence that some one in distress has called on him, interposes in his behalf. *Asun seh asun jórna*, To sit close in contact with another person. *Asun lugána*, To sit obstinately in a given posture till one's request be obtained. *Asun márna*, To sit (*particularly in an attitude practised by jogees or devotees*), to retain one's seat firmly on horseback.

আষনী ásunee, *s. f.* A small carpet, &c., on which hindoos sit and perform poojas.

আষপাষ aspás, *s. m.* Vicinity, circumference. *adv.* Around, about, on all sides.

আষমন্তাত asumuntát, *adv.* All around, on every side ; wholly, altogether.

আষুয় ásuy, *s. m.* Meaning, intention, aim, scope, an object of desire ; an asylum, abode or retreat.

আষব ásuv, *s. m.* Rum, spirit distilled from sugar or molasses.

আষা ása, *s. f.* Hope, dependance, reliance, trust.

আষাবন্ত asa-wúnt, *adj.* Expectant, dependant.

আষাবরী asáwuree, *s. f.* A musical mode or *raginee* ; a kind of pigeon ; a sort of cotton cloth.

আষিষ ásik, *s. m.* Benediction, blessing ; instruction.

আষিষবাদ asirbád, } *s. m.* Benediction,
আষীবাদ aséerbad, } blessing.

আষিন ásin, *s. m.* The 6th *hindoo* month in which the moon is full near the stars in the head of Aries (*September-October*).

আষীন aséen, *adj.* Sitting, seated.

আষীস asées, *s. f.* Blessing, benediction ; return of compliment from a *hindoo* superior (*a brahmun*).

আষুর ásoor, *s. m.* An *Usoor* or demon ; a form of marriage, in which the bridegroom gives to the bride, her father and paternal kinsmen, as much as he can afford.

আষুরী ásooree, *s. f.* Of or belonging to the *Usoors*, devilish, demoniacal ; a division of medicine, surgery, curing by cutting with instruments, applying the actual cautery, &c. *Asooree maya, s. f.* Deception of demons.

আষ্কত áskut, *s. f.* Laziness, tardiness. *Askutána, v. n.* To be lazy. *Askutee, adj.* Lazy, remiss.

আষ্কতী áskutee, *adj.* Lazy, remiss.

আষ্তিক ástik, *s. m.* A believer, pious, faithful.

আষ্থা ástha, *s. f.* Prop, stay, place or means of abiding ; effort, pains, care.

আষ্পদ áspud, *s. m.* A place, a situation ; dignity, rank.

আষ্রম ásrum, *s. m.* Abode, residence ; a religious order (*of which there are four kinds referable to the different periods of life ; as 1st, That of the bruhmucharee or student ; 2d, That of the grihusth or householder ; 3d, That of the vanuprusth or anchorite ; and 4th, That of the bhikshook or beggar*).

আষ্রা ásra, *s. m.* Means of defence or protection, trust, reliance, hope, defence, asylum, retreat, refuge, shelter, abode, house.

আষ্রিত asrít, *adj.* One who relies on another, a refugee, a protegee.

আষ্রীত asryt, *adj.* Hopeful, trusting, confident.

আস্বাদ aswád, *s. m.* Savour, relish.

আস্বাস aswás, *s. m.* Completion, cessation, comfort.

আহ ah ! An interjection, aha ! ah !

আহুত áhut, *s. f.* Sound, noise.

আহুরজাহুর áhur-jáhur, *s. f.* Coming and going.

আহলা áhla, *s. m.* Inundation, flood, overflow.

আহা áha, *interj.* Ah ! aha ! alas ! Oh !

আহার ahár, *s. m.* Food.

আহি áhi, Is.

আহুত áhoot, } *s. m.* Offering oblations
আহুতি áhooti, } with fire to the deities, a burnt-offering.

আহ্নিক áhnik, *s. m.* The constant or daily ceremonies of religion ; constant occupation, daily work. *adj.* Daily, diurnal.

আহ্নিকী áhnikee, *adj.* Of or belonging to a day.

আহ্লা áhla, *s. m.* Inundation, deluge, flood, overflow.

आह्लाद ahlád, *s. m.* Joy, gladness, delight, mirth, exultation, festivity.

आह्लादित ahládit, *adj.* Joyful, glad, delighted, pleased, merry, elated in mind, rejoiced.

आह्वान ahbán, *s. m.* A call, invitation, summons.

आक्षेप akshép, *s. m.* Reproof, reproach, an irony, a sarcasm; abuse, reviling, censure, blame.

———————

इ

इ i, the third vowel of the Nagree alphabet, corresponding to *I* short, and pronounced like that letter in *tin, hill,* &c. When compounded with a preceding consonant, its symbolical mark is ि, and it is placed on the left-hand of the letter, though sounded after it.

इंदूआ índooa, *s. m.* A round fold or roll used in carrying a burthen on the head.

इंदूई índooee, *s. f.* A round ornament for the top of the head.

इंदारा índára, *s. m.* A large well of masonry.

इंदूर índoor, *s. m.* A rat, mouse.

इंद्र índr, *s. m.* The regent of the visible heavens and of the inferior divinities; the Indian Jove.

इंद्राणी indránee, *s. f.* The wife of Indruh; a medicine or plant (*Vitex negundo*).

इंद्रायुन indráyun, *s. f.* Colocynth, wild gourd (*Cucumis colocynthis, a fruit of beautiful appearance but bitter taste*); hence, a beautiful but worthless person is called *Indrayun ka phul,* The fruit of indrayun.

इंद्रासन indrásun, *s. m.* The seat or throne of Indruh.

इंद्री índree, *s. f.* An organ of sense, the organs of action and perception (*the hindoos reckoning those of action to be the hand, the foot, the voice, the organ of generation, and the organ of excretion; and those of perception to be the mind, the eye, the ear, the nose, the tongue, and the skin*); the privities. *Indree joolláb,* A diuretick medicine

इंधन índhun, *s. m.* Fuel; wood, grass, &c., used for the purpose.

इक ik, *adj.* One. *Iksár, adj.* Alike, similar.

इकचित्त ik-chítt, *adj.* Of one mind.

इकछुत राज íkchhut-ráj, *s. m.* Universal dominion. *Ikchhut-raj kurna, v. a.* To hold universal dominion.

इकटक íktuk, *s. m.* A fixed looking at any thing without closing the eyes.

G

इकुट्ठ ikúttha, *m.*
इकठा íktha, *m.*
इकुट्ठी ikútthee, *f.* } *adj.* Collected together, in one place.
इकठी íkthee, *f.*

इकठोरा ikthóura, *m.* } *adj.* Collected together, in one place.
इकठोरी ikthóuree, *f.*

इकला íkla, *adj. m.* Alone, only.

इकलाई ikláee, *s. f.* Singleness, loneliness.

इकलौता iklóuta, *adj.* Only, single, alone.

इकसार iksár, *adj.* Alike, similar.

इक्का íkka, *adj.* Single, incomparable, unique, superexcellent. *s. m.* An earring of a single pearl; an ornament worn on the wrist, often hollow, containing perfume; a champion who serves alone, without being attached to any corps; a single-horse gig or buggy or native carriage, commonly used at Patna.

इंगित íngit, *s. m.* Hint, sign, gesture; going, motion; inquiry, research.

इच्छुक ichchhúk, *adj.* Wishing, desirous.

इच्छन íchchhun, *s. m.* An; seeing, sight.

इच्छा íchchha, *s. f.* Wish, desire. *Ichchha-bhójun,* Desirable food, or food agreeable and abundant, to the utmost desire.

इच्छूक ichchhóok, *adj.* Wishing, desirous.

इठलाना ithlána, *v. a.* To walk affectedly or coquettishly, to express tenderness or kindness by gesture.

इत it, *adv.* Here, hither.

इतना ítna, *adj. m.* As much as this, thus much, so much, so many. *Itneh-men,* In the mean time, mean-while, mean-time.

इतर ítur, *adj.* Affected, giving one's self airs, playful, wanton, coquetish; other, different; low, vile. *Itur lók, adj.* The low people, people of low caste; other people.

इतराना itrána, *v. a.* To give one's self airs, to act with affectation, to act in an unnatural or unusual manner.

इतराया itráya, *m.* } *adj.* Affected, playful,
इतराई itráee, *f.* } wanton.

इतवार itwár, *s. m.* Sunday.

इति íti, *adj. m.* This much, so much. *conj.* A word usually written at the end of a book, letter, &c., signifying that it is finished; conclusion, enough (*finis*).

इतिहास itihás, *s. m.* History, traditional accounts of former events, heroic history, story, fable.

इतेक iték, *adj.* So much, thus much.

इतौ itóu, *adj.* This much, so much.

इत्यादि ityádi, *conj.* Et cetera, and so forth.

ए, ईंधुर, *adv.* Here, hither, on this side. *Idhur oodhur*, About, around, up and down, here and there.

ए॰द्वारा indára, *s. m.* A large well of masonry.

ए॰दुरेखा índoo-rékha, *s. f.* A digit of the moon.

ए॰द्र indr, *s. m.* The regent of the visible heavens and of the inferior divinities.

ए॰दुरजाल indurjál, *s. m.* Deception, cheating, juggling; trick or stratagem in war.

ए॰द्रजाली indr-jálee, *adj.* A juggler, a conjurer; deceptive, unreal.

ए॰दुरजौं indurjóu, *s. m.* A medicinal seed (*Sparrow's tongue, Nerium antidysentericum*).

ए॰द्रनील indr-néel, *s. m.* A sapphire.

ए॰द्रनीलक indr-néeluk, *s. m.* An emerald.

ए॰दुरप्रस्थ indurprústh, *s. m.* A name of the ancient city of Delhi.

ए॰द्रप्रोहिता indr-próhita, *s. f.* The asterism Pooshya.

ए॰दुरबुधू índurbúdhoo, *s. f.* An insect (*a species of acarus of a scarlet colour and like velvet*) the wife of Indruh.

ए॰दुरजौं indurjóu, *s. m.* A medicinal seed (*Sparrow's tongue, Nerium antidysentericum*).

ए॰द्राणी indránee, *s. f.* The wife of Indruh; a medicine or plant (*Vitex negundo*).

ए॰द्रायुन indráyun, *s. f.* Colocynth, wild gourd (*Cucumis colocynthis*), the fruit of the Coloquintida plant (*a fruit of beautiful appearance but bitter taste, hence, a beautiful but worthless person is called Indrayun ka phul, The fruit of indrayun*)

ए॰द्रासुन indrásun, *s. m.* The seat or throne of Indruh.

ए॰द्रियुह índriyuh, ⎱ *s. f.* An organ of sense,
ए॰द्री índree, ⎰ the organs of action and perception (*the hindoos reckoning those of action to be the hand, the foot, the voice, the organ of generation, and the organ of excretion; and those of perception to be the mind, the eye, the ear, the nose, the tongue, and the skin*); the privities.

ए॰द्रियग्यान índriyu-gyán, *s. m.* The faculty of perception, sense, consciousness.

ए॰धन índhun, *s. m.* Fuel; wood, grass, &c., used for the purpose.

ए॰ब ib, *adv.* Thus, as, in like manner.

ए॰भ ibh, *s. m.* An elephant.

ए॰भपालुक ibh-páluk, *s. m.* The driver or keeper of an elephant.

ए॰मरती ímrutee, *adj.* Nectarious. *s. f.* A kind of sweetmeat; a small vessel for drinking out of; a kind of cloth.

ए॰मली ímli, ⎱ *s. f.* Tamarind tree and its
ए॰मली ímlee, ⎰ fruit.

ए॰लायुचा iláyucha, *s. m.* A kind of silk cloth.

ए॰लायुची iláyuchee, ⎱ *s. f.* Large carda-
ए॰लाची ilánchee, ⎰ mums.

ए॰लीश iléesh, *s. m.* A fish, the Hilsa or Sable (*Clupea alosa*).

ए॰ल्ला ílla, *s. m.* A wart.

ए॰ष्ट isht, *part.* Desired, wished, approved; worshipped, adored, reverenced, respected; cherished, beloved. *s. m.* A god, a deity, an object, a beloved person, any thing wished for.

ए॰ष्टतुम isht-túm, *adj.* Beloved, best beloved, dearest, most desired.

ए॰ष्टतर isht-túr, *adj.* Dearer, more dear, more desired.

ए॰ष्टता isht-tá, *s. f.* Desirableness, reverence, respect.

ए॰स्तुम्भ ístumbh, ⎱ *s. m.* The trunk of a tree,
स्तुम्भ stumbh, ⎰ a column, pile, post, pillar.

ए॰स्त्री ístree, *s. f.* A woman; a wife. *s. m.* A smoothing iron. *Istree kúrna, v. a.* To iron or smooth with an iron.

ए॰स्थिर ísthir, ⎱ *adj.* Settled, steady, firm,
स्थिर sthir, ⎰ fixed.

ए॰स्थिरता isthirtá, ⎱ *s. f.* Rest, tranquillity,
स्थिरता sthírta, ⎰ steadiness.

ए॰स्पृहा íspriha, *s. f.* Inclination, desire, wish.

ए॰ह ih, *pron.* This. *Ih-lok, s. m.* The present world. *Ihi,* This very. *Ihi-thán,* Here, in this very place.

ए॰हकाल ih-kál, *s. m.* This life.

ए॰हलोक ih-lók, *s. m.* This life, this world.

ए॰क्षू íkshoo, *s. f.* Sugar-cane.

ए॰क्षूकांड ikshoo-kánd, *s. m.* A species of sugar-cane (*Saccharum munja*).

ए॰क्षूमती íkshoo-mútee, *s. f.* The name of a river in Bengal, the Issamutty.

ए॰क्षूमेही íkshoo-mehée, *adj.* Diabetic.

ए॰क्षूरस ikshoo-rús, *s. m.* The juice of the sugar-cane.

ए॰क्षूसार ikshoo-sár, *s. m.* Molasses, raw or unrefined sugar.

_____

ई

ई ee, The fourth vowel of the Nagree alphabet, pronounced like *ee* in *feel, keel*, &c. and when compounded with a consonant it is expressed by the symbol ी.

एंट eent, *s. f.* A brick.

एंटगारी eent-gáree, *s. f.* Brick-work.

एंटाया eentáya, *s. m.* A kind of dove.

एंधूआ eendhooa, *s. m.* A roll or round fold on which a burthen is carried on the head.

एंदूर eendoor, *s. m.* A rat, a mouse.

एंधन eendhun, *s. m.* Fuel; wood, grass, &c., used for the purpose.

एख eekh, *s. f.* Sugar-cane.

एठ eeth, *part.* Desired, wished, approved; worshipped, adored, reverenced, respected; cherished, beloved. *s. m.* A god, a deity, an object, a beloved person, any thing wished for.

एतुर eetur, *part. act.* Acting affectedly.

एदृश eedrísh, *adv.* Thus, such, resembling this.

एधुर eedhur, *adv.* Here, hither.

एंदूर eendoor, *s. m.* A rat, a mouse.

एर्ष eersha, *s. f.* Envy, spite.

एर्षालू eershaloo, *adj.* Envious.

एअ eeah, *s. m.* Lord, a name of *Siv*; also of the same as regent of the north-east quarter; a ruler, a master.

एश eesha, *s. f.* The shaft of a plough.

एशान eeshán, *s. m.* A name of *Siv*; light, splendour. *Eeshan-kon, s. m.* North-east.

एशिता eeshita, *s. f.* ⎫ Superiority, su-
एशित्वूं eeshitwúh, *s. m.* ⎭ premacy, one of the eight attributes of divinity.

एश्वर eeshwur, *s. m.* Ruler, master, lord; the Supreme Ruler of the universe, God, the supreme; a name of *Siv*, of *Kamdev*, of *Doorga*, of *Lukshmee*, of *Suruswutee*, or of any other of the *Suktees* or female energies of the deities.

एश्वरता eeshwurtá, *s. f.* Godhead, divinity.

एश्वरभाव eeshwur-bháo, *s. m.* The divine nature.

एश्वराधीन eeshwur-adheen, *adj.* Subject to or dependent on God.

एश्वराधीनता eeshwur-adheentá, *s. f.* Dependance upon or subjection to God.

एश्वराराधन eeshwur-arádhna, *s. f.* Worship of God.

एषत् eeshut, *adv.* A little, somewhat.

एस ees, *s. m.* Lord, a name of *Siv*, also of the same as regent of the north-east quarter; a ruler, a master.

एहां eehan, *adv.* Hither.

एहा eeha, *s. f.* Wish, desire; effort, exertion.

एक्षुन eekshun, *s. m.* Sight, seeing; the eye.

ऊ

ऊ oo, The fifth vowel of the *Nagree* alphabet, corresponding to *oo* in good. When it follows a consonant in the same syllable, it is placed under the letter, and is expressed by its symbol, as उ *interj.* Oh! denoting pain.

ऊंगुल óongul, *s. m.* ⎫ A finger; a finger's
ऊंगली óonglee, *s. f.* ⎭ breadth.

ऊंचनीच oonch-neech, *adj.* Ups and downs of life, vicissitude, high and low, particulars.

ऊंचाई ooncháee, *s. f.* ⎫
ऊंचाऊ ooncháoo, *s. m.* ⎬ Height, eleva-
ऊंचास oonchás, *s. f.* ⎪ tion.
ऊंचाहट ooncháhut, *s. f.*⎭

ऊंचाना oonchána, *v. a.* To raise, to take up.

ऊंडेलना oondélna, *v. a.* To pour.

ऊकुटना óokutna, ⎫ *v. a.* To dig up slowly
ऊकताना ooktána, ⎭ any thing buried in the ground, to extract a secret gradually and artfully, to pump.

ऊकरू óokroo, *s. m.* The posture of sitting on the hams with the soles of the feet on the ground.

ऊकत óokut, ⎫ *s. f.* Speech, voice, lan-
ऊक्ति óokti, ⎭ guage; contrivances, invention. *Ookut bunána, v. a.* To make up a story, to invent, to contrive. *Ookut lena, v. a.* To discover, to find out.

ऊकताना ooktána, *v. n.* To fret, to be melancholy or dejected; to be out of humour with, to be tired of, to tire.

ऊकतारू ooktároo, *part.* Instigator, promoter.

ऊकतारना ooktárna, *v. a.* To promote, to forward.

ऊकुलना óokulna, *v. n.* To boil.

ऊकूसना ookúsna, *v. n.* To be excited, to be moved, to try to move.

ऊकसाना ooksána, *v. a.* To excite, to move.

ऊकालना ookálna, *v. a.* To boil water.

ऊकेलना ookélna, *v. a.* To turn up.

ऊकत óokt, *adj.* Spoken.

ऊक्ति óokti, *s. f.* Speech, voice, language; contrivances, invention.

ऊखुटना óokhutna, *v. n.* To trip.

ऊखुरना óokhurna, *v. n.* To be rooted up, plucked up or raised up, to slip out (as a bone, &c.). *Ookhurna pookhurna,* To be plucked or rooted up.

ऊखराना ookhrána, ⎫ *v. a.* To root up,
ऊखारना ookhárna, ⎭ break or pluck up, eradicate, extirpate; dislocate.

উখলী óokhlee, *s. f.* A wooden mortar.

উখাড় ookhár, *s. f.* Rooting up, extirpation.

উখাড় পুখাড় ookhál-pookhál, *s. m.* Cholera morbus.

উখেড়্বানা ookherwána, *v. a.* To cause to pluck up.

উগত óogut, *part.* Growing, springing up; production.

উগনা óogna, *v. n.* To grow, to be produced, to spring (as plants), to rise (as the moon). *Oogtehee jul-jana,* To be withered immediately on springing up (is applied to a hope or expectation which is blasted in the bud).

উগল্না oogúlna, *v. a.* To spit out, to vomit; (met.) to refund property surreptitiously obtained.

উগানা oogána, *v. a.* To cause to grow, &c.

উগাল oogál, *s. m.* That which is spit out after chewing any thing (especially betel leaf.) *Ap ka oogal mera oodhar,* Your worship's leavings are my nourishment; i. e. You, sir, are my support and benefactor. *Oogaldan, s. m.* A spitting-pot.

উগাহনা oogáhna, *v. a.* To gather, collect, accumulate.

উগাহী oogáhee, *s. f.* Usury; the trade of lending money on interest of one-fourth part, the payment of which is received by instalments.

উগ্র óogr, *s. m.* Wrath, anger.

উগ্রা óogra, *adj.* Angry, cruel, wrathful.

উঘুরনা óoghurna, *v. n.* To be uncovered, discovered, opened, pulled off.

উঘারনা ooghárna, *v. a.* To uncover, discover, unveil, open, pull off, unclose, bare.

উঘারু ooghároo, *s. m.* One who uncovers or unveils.

উচকনা oochúkna, *v. n.* To rise, to be raised or lifted; to leap, bound, spring up.

উচকানা oochkána, *v. a.* To lift or raise up.

উচক্কা oochúkka, *s. m.* A thief, a pickpocket.

উচক্কী oochúkkee, *s. f.* A female thief or pick-pocket.

উচটনা óochutna, *v. n.* To separate; to be separated (as plaster from a wall); to slip, slide, rebound (as a sword striking a hard body obliquely); to be broken or interrupted (sleep).

উচরঙ oochrúng, *s. m.* A moth.

উচরনা oochúrna, *v. n.* To speak, pronounce, utter.

উচুলনা oochúlna, *v. n.* To separate, to be separated.

উচলানা oochlána, *v. a.* To order a person to separate (one thing from another).

উচাটনা oochátna, *v. a.* To divide, separate. *Oochat hóna,* To be tired, to be disgusted.

উচানা oochána, *v. a.* To lift up a burden.

উচারনা oochárna, *v. a.* To pronounce, to speak out, to utter.

উচিত óochit, *adj.* Proper, becoming, fit, suitable, convenient.

উচেলনা oochélna, *v. a.* To separate one thing from another.

উচ oochch, *adj.* High, tall, lofty.

উচতা oochchutá, *s. f.* Height.

উচচুরনা oochchúrna, *v. n.* To separate (as the skin from the flesh, &c.); to be uttered, spoken or pronounced. *v. a.* To speak, utter, tell.

উচচাটন ooch-chátun, *s. m.* } The act of
উচাটী oochátee, *s. f.* } vexing, or rendering sorrowful, vexation.

উচচান ooch-chán, *s. f.* Height.

উচচার ooch-chár, *s. m.* } Pronunciation,
উচচারন ooch-chárun, } utterance, articulation, expression, enunciation.

উচচারনা ooch-chárna, *v. a.* To pronounce, speak out, utter, articulate, express.

উচচারিত oochcharít, *adj.* Pronounced, uttered, articulated.

উচছাহ ooch-chháh, *s. m.* Joy, gladness.

উচছীন ooch-chhín, *adj.* Ruined, laid waste, destroyed.

উচছীষ্ট ooch-chhísht, *s. m.* Food left or rejected, crumbs, fragments, leavings, orts.

উচছ্বাস oochchh-wás, *s. m.* Breath, breathing; hope, expectation; division of a book.

উচছুরনা oochchhúrna, } *v. n.* To leap or
উচছুলনা oochchhúlna, } bound, to spring or sprout up (as water in a fountain), to spring or fly up.

উচছলানা oochchh-lána, *v. a.* To order another to throw up any thing.

উচছালনা oochchhálna, *v. a.* To throw up, to toss up a thing (as a ball, &c.) and catch it in the hand.

উজুদ oojúd, *adj.* Inconsiderate, rash, ignorant, clownish.

উজুরনা oojúrna, *v. n.* To become desolate.

উজুরবানা oojurwána, *v. a.* To lay waste by the hands of a third person.

উজরাপুজরা óojra-póojra, *part.* In ruins, desolate.

উজুলনা oojúlna, *v. n.* To become clean, to shine, to be bright.

উজলা óojla, *adj.* Clear, shining, luminous, bright, splendid.

উজলানা oojlána, *v. a.* To cause to cleanse, to brighten.

उजवाना oojwána, *v. a.* To cause a person to pour from one vessel to another.

उजागर oojágur, *s. m.* Splendor, brightness. *adj.* Famous, celebrated; light, bright, splendid.

उजार oojár, *adj.* Desert, desolate, ruined, ruinous, demolished, deserted, abandoned.

उजारना oojárna, *v. a.* To lay waste, desolate, demolish, injure, expose to loss.

उजान ooján, *s. m.* The direction or part of a river which is opposite to the course of the stream, up the stream.

उजालना oojálna, *v. a.* To cleanse, polish (*metals or jewels*).

उजाला oojála, *s. m.* Splendor, brightness, light. *adj.* Clear, shining, luminous, bright.

उजाली oojálee, *s. f.* Splendor, glare. *adj.* Bright, clear, light.

उज्जल óojjul, ⎫ *adj.* Clean, bright, lumi-
उज्जवल óojjwul, ⎭ nous, splendid, clear, pure, shining; blown, expanded.

उज्जवलता oojjwultá, *s. f.* Splendour, radiance.

उज्जलित óojjulit, *adj.* Pure, clean, clear.

उज्जैन oojjyn, *s. m.* The city of *Oojein*, formerly the capital of *Vikrumadítyuh*: it is one of the seven sacred cities of the hindoos, and the first meridian of their geographers.

उझुकना oojhúkna, *v. a.* To peep, to spy.

उझुर oojhúr, ⎫ *adj.* Ignorant, illiterate,
उज्झुर oojjhúr, ⎭ clownish.

उझुलना oojhúlna, *v. n.* To flow or be poured from one vessel into another. *v. a.* To throw or pour quickly from one vessel into another.

उझालना oojhálna, *v. a.* To pour from one vessel into another.

उटुक्करलिस ootúkkur-lys, *adj.* Precipitate, rash, acting without consideration.

उटुंगन ootúngun, *s. f.* A river near Gwalior; a plant.

उठुंगन oothúngun, *s. m.* A prop or support.

उठना óothna, *v. n.* To rise up, be raised, to spring; to be abolished.

उठबैठ ooth-byth, *s. f.* Restlessness; a kind of exercise.

उठवाना ooth-wána, *v. a.* To cause to lift or raise up, or remove, &c.

उठवैया ooth-wyya, *s. m.* One who rises.

उठाईगीरा oothácee-géera, *s. m.* A pilferer, a purloiner, a petty thief.

उठान oothán, *s. f.* Act of appearing. *s. m.* An area or court; rising, ascension, appearing.

उठाना oothána, *v. a.* To lift, take or raise up, elevate, hoist, take or bear away, produce, invent, cause, gain, get, enjoy, abolish, excite, rouse, support, bear, carry, remove, receive, suffer, exhibit, contract debts or purchase on credit, expend.

उठाबैठी óotha-bythee, *s. f.* Act of frequently rising up and sitting down; inconstancy.

उडुगन óorgun, *s. plur.* The stars, the starry firmament.

उडचलना oor-chúlna, *v. n.* To walk with a stately or affected gait.

उडुन óorun, *adj.* Flying.

उडना óorna, *v. n.* To fly.

उडनागन oor-nágun, *s. f.* A flying serpent.

उडुप óorup, *s. m.* A raft, a float.

उडुस óorus, *s. m.* A bug.

उडाऊ ooráoo, *s. m.* A spendthrift, an extravagant person, prodigal.

उडाक oorák, *adj.* Capable of flying, fledged.

उडान oorán, *s. f.* Act of flying.

उडाना oorána, *v. a.* To cause to fly; to squander or spend extravagantly, dissipate, blow up or away, disperse, filch; to entice. *Oorana poorana,* To squander.

उडूप oodóop, *s. m,* A raft, a float.

उडहुंगन oorhúngun, *s. m.* Any thing placed under a vessel to prevent its oversetting; a prop, a support.

उडहुक करना oorhúk kúrna, *v. n.* To seek or cry for an absent person (*applied to a child only*).

उडहुकना oorhúkna, *v. n.* To overset.

उडहुकपर oorhúk-pur, *adj.* A broach, a tilt.

उडहुना óorhna, *v. a.* To put on clothes.

उडहाना oorhána, *v. a.* To cause to clothe.

उडहैया oorhyya, *part.* A wearer or putter on of a dress.

उडहौना oorhóuna, *s. m.* Clothing.

उंडेलना oondélna, *v. a.* To pour.

उत oot, *adv.* There, thither.

उतकल óotkul, *n. prop.* The province of Orissa.

उतना óotna, *adj. m.* As much as that, so much, so many.

उतरन óotrun, *s. f.* A fragment, any thing taken off from the body; cast off clothes. *Rin seh óotrun hóna,* To be freed from debt.

उतरना ootúrna, *v. n.* To descend, alight, halt, bait, disembark, land, dismount, subside, decrease, pass over, cross, go off, fall off, decay, fade, flag, be freed from debt, become insipid, flatten, fall in value or in dignity.

উতরওয়ানা ooturwána, *v. a.* To cause to descend or alight.

উতরানা ootrána, *v. a.* To take down or pull down (*by the hands of a third person, as, to do it one's self, is ootarna*); to boil over.

উতলা óotla, *adj.* Shallow.

উতান ootán, } *adj.* Supine, lying on the
উত্তান oottán, } back; shallow.

উতার ootár, *s. m.* Descent, declination. *Ootar dena,* To bring down; (*met.*) to disgrace, to dishonour.

উতারন ootárun, *s. f.* A fragment.

উতারনা ootárna, *v. a.* To cause to alight or descend, to bring down; to degrade; to cause to pass over, to convey over; to take off, to tear off, strip off, to cut off, or break off (*a portion of any thing*); to unload, disembark, dismount, discharge; to make a return or recompense. *Ootareh hooeh,* Engaged with a desperate resolution in any enterprise: (*metaphor taken from cavalry, who dismount to fight on foot with a determination to conquer or die*).

উতারা ootára, *s. m.* A descent; crossing or passing (*over a river, &c.*); an answer; cast off clothes; disgrace, degradation; ransom; self-devotion.

উতাবল ootáwul, *s. f.* Quickness, speed, despatch.

উতাবলা ootáola, *adj. m.* Swift, quick, speedy, precipitate, rash.

উতাবলী ootáolee, *adj. f.* Swift, quick, speedy. *s. f.* Haste, speed, rashness, impatience.

উতীর্ন ootéerun, *adj.* Worn, cast off (*clothes, jewels, &c.*).

উত্কন্ঠা ootkántha, *s. f.* Regretting, missing any thing.

উত্কৃষ্টভূম óotkrisht-bhoom, *s. m.* A good soil.

উত্তপ্ত oottúpt, *adj.* Anxious, excited.

উত্তম óottum, *adj.* Excellent, best, principal, first, chief.

উত্তমপুরুষ óottum-póoroosh, *s. m.* An excellent man.

উত্তর óottur, *s. m.* An answer, the north. *adj.* Posterior, latter, behind, northern, superior, high. *Ootturardh,* The latter half.

উত্তরফল্গুনী óottur-phúlgoonee, *s. f.* The twelfth lunar mansion containing two stars, figured by a bed.

উত্তরভাদ্রপদ óottur-bhádrpud, *s. m.* The 27th lunar mansion, figured by a conch, and comprehending two stars of which one is Andromeda.

উত্তরা óottura, *adj.* Northern, northerly. *s. f.* North wind, boreas.

উত্তরাধিকার óottur-adhikár, *s. m.* An inheritance.

উত্তরাধিকারী óottur-adhikáree, *s. f.* An heir, a successor.

উত্তরায়ন óotturáyun, *s. m.* The half of the year during which the sun is to the north of the equator, the summer solstice.

উত্তরার্ধ óotturárdh, *adj.* The last half.

উত্তরাষাঢ়া oottur-ashárha, *s. f.* The 21st lunar mansion, figured by an elephant's tooth, or a bed, and containing two stars, one of which is in Sagittarius.

উত্তরাহ oottur-áha, *adj.* Of or belonging to the north, northern.

উত্তরোত্তর óottur-óttur, *adv.* More and more, further and further.

উত্তীর্ন ootéern, *adj.* Arrived, got over a difficulty, delivered, rescued.

উত্তুঙ্গ óottoong, *adj.* High, lofty, tall.

উত্তু óottoo, *s. m.* Plaits of cloth. *Márkur oottoo bunáya bookeh-tueen,* He beat him to a mummy (*lit. till his body became marked like the plaits in cloth*). *Oottoo kurna, v. a.* To plait. *Oottoo-gur,* A plaiter.

উত্থান ootthán, *s. m.* Effort, rising up, manly exertion, battle, joy. *Ootthan ekadushee,* or *devuthán,* The eleventh of the *shookl-puksh* of *Kartik,* when *Vishnoo* is said to awake from sleep: (*during the four months that he is supposed to sleep it is unlawful to marry*).

উত্থাপন ootthápun, *s. m.* The act of raising a thing up, in arithmetic the producing of the answer or result.

উত্পত্তি ootpútt, } *s. f.* Birth, origin, crea-
উত্পত্তি ootpútti, } tion, production.

উত্পন্ন ootpúnn, *adj.* Born, produced; gained; occurred. *s. m.* Proceeds, profit, produce.

উত্পল ootpúl, *s. m.* A blue lotus (*Nymphea cerulea*); a plant (a *Costus*).

উত্পাটন ootpátun, *s. m.* The rooting up of a thing, eradication.

উত্পাত ootpát, *s. m.* A portent, a phenomenon; violence, injustice, injury.

উত্পাদন ootpádun, *s. m.* The producing or creating of a thing.

উত্প্রেক্ষা ootpréksha, *s. f.* Indifference, carelessness; comparison; illustration (*in poetry or rhetoric*).

উত্সর্গ ootsúrg, *s. m.* Abandoning, quitting, resigning, retiring from; giving, donation; any precept or rule.

উত্সব óotsuv, *s. m.* A festival, a jubilee, public rejoicing; impatience; wrath.

উত্সাহ ootsáh, *s. m.* Effort, perseverance, energy, fortitude; happiness, joy.

उताहोस ootaáhee, *adj.* Active, persevering.

उथलना oothúlna, *v. n.* To overturn, to overset.

ऊथलपूथल óothul-póothul, *adj.* Topsy turvy, higgledy piggledy. *s. f.* Confusion, interchange.

ऊथला óothla, *adj.* Shallow.

उथलाना oothlána, *v. a.* To cause to turn over or overset.

उदक óoduk, *s. m.* Water.

उदधि oodúdhi, *s. m.* The ocean.

उदय óoduy, *s. m.* The eastern mountain, behind which the sun is supposed to rise ; rising, ascending ; light, splendour ; prosperity, good fortune. *Ooduy hona, v. n.* To rise (*as the sun, &c.*)

उदयास्त ooduyást, *s. m.* From sun-rise to sun-set ; from *ooduyachul*, where the sun is supposed to rise, to *ustachul*, where it is supposed to set.

उदयी ooduyée, *adj.* Prosperous, flourishing.

उदर óodur, *s. m.* The belly.

उदरपिशाच oodur-pishách, *adj.* A glutton, voracious, one who devours every thing, flesh, fish, &c., one who is a devil for his belly.

उदरामय óodur-ámuy, *s. m.* Diarrhea, dysentery.

उदरावेष्ट oodur-avésht, *s. m.* The tape worm.

उदरिनी óodur-ínee, *s. f.* A pregnant woman.

उदरिन oodurín, ⎫
उदरी ooduree, ⎬ *adj.* Fat, corpulent.

उदरिल ooduríl, *adj.* Fat, corpulent.

उदरी óoduree, *s. f.* Enlargement of the abdomen from dropsy or flatulency. *adj.* Abdominal.

उदात्त oodátt, *s. m.* The acute accent, a high or sharp tone ; gift, donation ; a musical instrument, a large drum.

उदात्ता oodátta, *adj.* Liberal, giving, a donor, great, illustrious ; dear, beloved.

उदान oodán, *s. m.* One of the five vital airs, that which rises up the throat and passes into the head.

उदार oodár, *adj.* Generous, liberal, munificent ; great ; unperplexed ; gentle.

उदारता oodárta, *s. f.* Generosity, liberality, munificent.

उदास oodás, *s. m.* Unsettledness, retiredness. *adj.* Unsettled, retired, lonely, forlorn, dejected, sorrowful, sad ; apathetic.

उदासी oodásee, *s. f.* Solitude, loneliness, sadness, dejection. *adj.* Unsettled, solitary, lonely, retired, dejected.

उदासीन oodaséen, *s. m.* A class of mendicants of the Punjab, an hermit or anchorite, a cynic, a misanthrope, a stoic.

उदाहत oodáhut, *s. f.* Brownness.

उदाहरण oodá-hurun, *s. m.* An example or illustration, a simile, a comparison, an opposite argument, one of the five modes of logical reasoning.

उदित óodit, *adj.* Risen (*as the sun*) ; distinguished, conspicuous (*as valour, &c.*).

उदुम्बर oodóombur, *s. m.* The glomerous fig tree (*Ficus glomerata*) ; a sect of brahmuns.

उदूखल oodóokhul, *s. m.* A gum resin, Bdellium.

उद्गत óodgut, *adj.* Vomited, cast up.

उद्गार oodgár, *s. m.* Vomiting ; sound.

उद्घाटन ood-ghátun, *s. m.* The rope and bucket of a well, a leathern bucket used for drawing water ; an instrument or means of opening a key, &c.

उद्घाटित ood-ghátit, *adj.* Done with effort, exerted ; opened.

उद्दिम óoddim, *s. m.* Strenuous and continued efforts, exertion, endeavour, labour ; calling, employment, trade.

उद्दीपन ood-déepun, *adj.* Exciting, inflaming as passion ; blazing, glowing of a luminous body.

उद्दीप्त ooddéept, *adj.* Illuminated.

उद्देश ooddésh, *s. m.* A scope, a vestige, a trace.

उद्धुक ooddhúk, *s. m.* Asthma, act of gasping or panting, plethora in the vessels of the head, head-ache, indigestion.

उद्धत ood-dhút, *adj.* Rude, arrogant, ill-behaved. *s. m.* A king's wrestler.

उद्धार ood-dhár, *s. m.* Debt (*especially not bearing interest*), deduction, discharge, deliverance, salvation, raising up from any place or state.

उद्धारना ood-dhárna, *v. a.* To liberate, discharge.

उद्भव oodbhúvuh, *s. m.* Birth, production.

उद्यत oodyút, *s. m.* A section, a chapter, the division of a book. *adj.* Raised, held up ; active, persevering, labouring diligently and incessantly.

उद्यम oodyúm, *s. m.* Strenuous and continued effort, exertion, perseverance, endeavor, labour ; calling, employment, trade.

उद्यान oodyán, *s. m.* A royal garden ; purpose, motive.

उद्योग oodyóg, *s. m.* Exertion, perseverance, strenuous and continued endeavour.

उद्योगी oodyógee, *adj.* Active, laborious, persevering, one who makes effort.

उद्योत oodyót, *s. m.* Light, lustre.

उद्र oodr, *s. m.* An offer.

उद्विग्न oodvígn, *adj.* Perplexed, dejected, anxious, troubled, filled with thought.

उद्वेग oodvég, *s. m.* Regret, agitation, consternation, fear; perplexity, dejection, anxiety, uneasiness, exertion, care; the fruit of the Areca catechu, betel-nut.

उद्वेगी oodvégee, *adj.* Perplexed, anxious, perturbed, agitated.

उद्वोध oodvódh, *s. m.* Recollection, the recognizing of a thing.

उधर óodhur, } *adv.* There, thither, on
उधर óodhur, }   that side, on the other side. *Oodhur seh,* From that or the other side.

उधरा óodhra, *adj. m.* Opened, undone, unrolled (*as the seam in a garment, or thread which was rolled up in a clue*).

उधार oodhár, } *s. m.* Debt (*especially not
उद्धार ooddhár, }   bearing interest*), deduction, discharge, deliverance, salvation, raising up from any place or state.

उधारना oodhárna, *v. a.* To liberate, to discharge.

उधेड़ oodhér, *s. m.* Unravelling, unwearing. *Oodher-boon,* Perplexity.

उधेड़ना oodhérna, }
उधेड़नौं oodhérnoun, } *v. a.* To undo, to unravel, unfold.
उधरना oodhérna, }

उन oon, *pron. plur.* Those, them.

उनचास oonchás, *adj.* Forty-nine.

उनतालीस oontálees, *adj.* Thirty-nine.

उनतीस oontées, *adj.* Twenty-nine.

उनसठ óonsuth, *adj.* Fifty-nine.

उनासी oonásee, *adj.* Seventy-nine.

उनीस oonées, *adj.* Nineteen.

उन्नत oonnút, *adj.* High, tall.

उन्नति óonnuti, *s. f.* Increase, advancement, prosperity; rising, ascending.

उन्मत्त óonmutt, } *adj.* Insane, frantic, mad;
उन्मद óonmud, }   drunk, intoxicated, lustful, furious, extravagant.

उन्मत्तता oonmutt-tá, *s. f.* Insanity, intoxication.

उन्माद oonmád, *s. m.* Madness, extravagance.

उन्मादा oonmáda, *adj.* Mad, insane, extravagant.

उन्मान oonmán, *s. m.* A measure of size or quantity.

उन्मुख óonmookh, *adj.* Looking upwards.

उन्मेष oonmésh, *s. m.* Winking, twinkling of the eye-lids.

उनहार oonhár, *s. f.* Manner, appearance. *adj.* Like, resembling.

उप oop, A preposition which usually conveys the idea of vicinity or resemblance in an inferior degree.

उपकरण oopkúrun, *s. m.* The insignia of royalty; implements, materials, means; helping, assisting.

उपकार oop-kár, *s. m.* Favour, protection, help, assistance, benefit, kindness.

उपकारक oopkáruk, *adj.* A friend, a protector, one who befriends.

उपकारी oopkáree, *adj.* Assisting, helping, beneficent, a benefactor; subsidiary, subservient.

उपक्रम óopkrum, *s. m.* Deliberate commencement or undertaking; a beginning in general; a stratagem.

उपगत óopgut, *adj.* Promised, agreed.

उपगम oopgúm, *s. m.* Agreement, promise; approach, approximation.

उपगृह óopgruh, *s. m.* A prisoner, a man or animal in confinement; favour, encouragement; assistance.

उपपुंग oopúng, *s. m.* A kind of musical instrument.

उपचार oopchár, *s. m.* Service; physicking, the practice of medicine; practice, profession usage; a present, a bribe.

उपज oopúj, *s. f.* Any thing spoken or sung extempore, the burthen of a song, the chorus, variations in music.

उपजतन oopjútun, *s. m.* Preparation, exertion.

उपजना oopújna, *v. n.* To spring up, grow, be produced, shoot forth.

उपजाऊ oopjáoo, *adj.* Fertile.

उपजाना oopjána, *v. a.* To create, produce, make grow, cultivate.

उपजित óopjit, *adj.* Produced, propagated.

उपजीवन oopjéevun, *s. m.* Subsistence, means of living.

उपजीविका oop-jéevika, *s. f.* Livelihood, means of support, subsistence.

उपजीवी oopjeevée, *adj.* Dependant, living by or on.

उपटन óoptun, } *s. m.* A composition of
उपटना óoptuna, } perfumes, flour, &c. used to rub the body with.

उपठना óoputhna, *v. n.* To be tired or to be sick of a business.

उपुड़ना oopúrna, *v. n.* To be rooted out, to be pulled out, to be skinned; to be imprinted with the mark of any thing.

उपताप ooptáp, *s. m.* Disease; haste, hurry; heat, pain, misfortune.

उपदंश oopdúnsh, *s. m.* A relish or something to promote drinking; the venereal disease.

उपदा óopda, *s. f.* A present, an offering to a king or great man, &c.; a bribe.

उपदेश oopdésh, *s. m.* Advice, counsel, exhortation, admonition, information, instruction.

उपदेशक oopdéshuk,) *s. m. f.* An adviser,
उपदेशी oopdéshee,) instructor, admonisher, a guide, specially a spiritual guide.

उपदेशिन् oopdéshin, *adj.* Advising, an adviser.

उपद्रव oopúdro, *s. m.* A portent, any natural phenomenon so considered; violence, injury, injustice, tyranny, excess, insult.

उपधातु óopdhatoo, *s. m.* An inferior mineral, a semimetal, of which, seven are specified, viz. pyrites, sulphate of copper, talc, antimony, red orpiment, yellow orpiment, and calx of brass; secondary secretion, as the milk, menses, adeps, sweat, teeth, hair, and lymph.

उपनय oopnúy,) *s. m.* The initiation
उपनयन oopnúyun,) of the three first classes; investiture with a peculiar thread or cord worn over the left shoulder, and under the right; the cord of the *Brahmun* is of cotton, *moonj* or *koosa* grass; of the *Kshutree*, of *sun* or flax; and of the *Vys*, of wool: the youths are invested, respectively, from 8 to 16, from 11 to 22, and from 12 to 24 years of age.

उपनिषद् óopnishud, *s. f.* A portion of the religious writings of the *hindoos*: the theological part, and the *Vedant* or argumentative part of the *Veds*, either detached from, or comprised in the principal work.

उपनेत्र óopnétruh, *s. m.* Spectacles, glasses for the eye.

उपपति óop-púti, *s. m.* A paramour, a gallant.

उपपातक óop-pátuk, *s. m.* A heinous crime, as killing a cow, selling a daughter, atheism, &c.

उपमा óopma,) *s. f.* A resemblance,
उपमान oopmán,) comparison, simile, that thing to which another is likened.

उपमिति óopmíti, *s. f.* Resemblance, comparison, a likeness, a picture, image, &c.

उपयुक्त oopuyóokt, *adj.* Fit, proper, right, becoming, worthy, qualified; adapted to, suitable, appropriate.

उपर óopur, *prep.* Above, on, over.

उपरना oopúrna, *s. m.* A scarf.

उपरला óopurla, *adj.* Superficial, the outside of a garment (*opposed to the lining*).

उपरवाईतरवाई oopurwáee-turwáee, *s. f.* Surfeit, mort de chien, cholera morbus.

उपरस óoprus, *s. m.* A secondary mineral, as red chalk, bitumen, &c.; a subordinate flavour.

उपरान्त oopránt, *adv.* After, afterwards.

उपराला ooprála, *s. m.* Aid, assistance. *Ooprála kurna, v. a.* To take one's part, protect, stickle for.

उपरि óopuri, *adv.* Above, up.

उपरोध oopuródh, *s. m.* Partiality, protection, support, defence, favour, kindness.

उपरोंछा oopróuncha, *s. m.* A towel or cloth for wiping the body. *adj.* Superficial.

उपर्ना oopúrna, *s. m.* A scarf, a covering (*sheet*).

उपर्ला oopúrla, *adj.* Superficial; the outside of a garment (*opposed to the lining*).

उपरवाईतरवाई oopurwáee-turwáee, *s. f.* Surfeit, mort de chien, cholera morbus.

उपल óopul, *s. m.* A rock or stone, a precious stone or jewel.

उपलक्षण óoplukshun, *s. m.* A synecdoche of a part for a whole, or of a quality for that in which it resides.

उपला óopla, *s. m.* Cakes of dried cowdung.

उपलिप्त ooplípt, *adj.* Smeared, plastered.

उपली óoplee, *s. f.* Cakes of dried cowdung of a small size.

उपलेप ooplép, *s. m.* Plastering, smearing, anointing.

उपलेपन ooplépun, *s. m.* Smearing, plastering with cowdung, &c.

उपवन óopvun, *s. m.* A garden, a grove, an artificially planted wood.

उपवर्णन óopvurnun, *s. m.* Minute description.

उपवास oopvás, *s. m.* A fast, fasting.

उपवासी oopvásee, *adj.* Fasting, one who observes a fast.

उपविद्या óopvidya, *s. f.* Profane science, inferior sort of knowledge.

उपविष óopvish, *s. m.* Factitious poison; a narcotic, any deleterious drug, as opium, Datura, &c.

उपवीत oopvéet, *s. m.* The thread or cord worn by the three first classes of *hindoos* over the left shoulder and under the right.

उपवेद oopvéd, *s. m.* A division of *hindoo* science deduced immediately from the *Veds*: four works are included under this denomination, and severally entitled, *Ayoosh, Gundhurvuh, Dhunoosh,* and *Sthaputyuh;* the first, it is said, was delivered to mankind by *Bruhma, Indruh, Dhunwunturi,* and five other deities, and comprises the theory of disorders and medicines, with the practical methods of curing diseases; the second, or music, was invented and explained by *Bhurut;* the third, *oopuved* was composed by *Vishwamitruh* on the fabrication and use of arms and implements handled in war by the tribe of *Kshuttrees*; and *Vish-wukurma* is said to have revealed the fourth in various treatises on sixty-four mechanical arts, for the improvement of such as exercise them.

उपशम oopushúm, *s. m.* Tranquillity, calmness, patience.

उपशांत oopshánt, *adj.* Calm, tranquil; appeased, pacified.

उपशांति oopshánti, *s. f.* Tranquillity, calm; appeasing, allaying.

उपशांती oopshántee, *adj.* Tranquil, calm, appeased.

उपशास्त्र óopshashtruh, *s. m.* Sciences connected with, or derived from the *shastruh.*

उपस oopús, *s. f.* Stink, staleness, putrefaction, rottenness.

उपसना oopúsna, *v. n.* To become musty, to rot.

उपसर्ग oopsúrg, *s. m.* A portent, a natural phenomenon supposed to announce future evil; a disease, possession by an evil spirit; a particle prefixed to roots, &c., a preposition.

उपस्त्री óopstree, *s. f.* A concubine.

उपस्थ oopústh, *s. m.* The male or female organs of generation.

उपस्थित óopusthit, *adj.* Present, ready; approached, approximate.

उपहास oopuhás, *s. m.* Derision, scorn, laughter, fun, sport, ridicule, laughing at any one.

उपाख्यान oopákhyan, *s. m.* A tale, a story, a narration.

उपांग oopáng, *s. m.* The sectarial mark made with Sandal, &c. on the forehead.

उपार्णा oopárna, *v. a.* To root up, extirpate, eradicate.

उपादान oopadán, *s. m.* Abstraction, restraining the organs of sense and perception; cause, motive; immediate or proximate cause.

उपाध oopádh, *s. f.* Violence, injury, injustice, tyranny.

उपाधि oopádhi, *s. m.* Virtuous reflection; a discriminative or distinguishing property; deception, disguise; a title, a discriminative appellation, a nick name.

उपाधी oopádhee, *adj.* Violent, unjust.

उपाध्याय oopádhyayuh, *s. m.* A spiritual preceptor.

उपाध्याया oopadhyáya, *s. f.* A female preceptor.

उपाध्यायी oopadhyáyee, } *s. f.* The wife of
उपाध्यानी oopadhyánee, } a teacher.

उपाना oopána, *v. a.* To create, produce, earn, get; to adopt as an expedient or remedy, to contrive, to prepare.

उपाय oopáeh, *s. m.* A means, expedient, plan, way, contrivance, scheme, preparation, redress, remedy.

उपायी oopáyee, *adj.* Resorting to expedients, contriving, remedying; contriver; expert in the use of means.

उपार्जन oopárjun, *s. m.* Earning, acquiring property.

उपार्जित oopárjit, *adj.* Acquired, gained, earned.

उपालंभ oopalúmbh, *s. m.* Abuse, reviling; deferring, delaying.

उपाव oopáo, *s. m.* Remedy, redress.

उपास oopás, *s. m.* A fast, fasting.

उपासक oopásuk, *s. m.* A worshipper; a servant.

उपासना oopásna, *s. f.* Worship, adoration, service, attendance on a superior, sedulity, supplication, prayer, intercession. *v. a.* To reverence, to worship.

उपासा oopása, *adj.* Hungry, one who fasts.

उपासी oopásee, *adj.* Serving, worshipping.

उपास्य oopásyuh, *adj.* Worthy of being worshipped, deserving of service, of honour, &c.

उपेक्षा oopékshya, *s. f.* Trick, deceit, one of the minor expedients in war; abandoning, abandonment.

उफन्ना oophúnna, *v. n.* To boil over.

उबुकना oobúkna, *v. n.* To vomit.

उबकाई oobkáee, *s. f.* Act of vomiting.

उबकाना oobkána, *v. a.* To vomit.

उबटन óobtun, *s. m.* A paste for scouring the skin previous to bathing.

उबटना óobutna, *v. a.* To rub on the body a detergent application called *oobtun.*

उबुलना óobulna, *v. n.* To boil.

उबलाना ooblána, *v. a.* To cause to boil (*by the hands of another*); to boil any thing with such violence that it is spilled.

उबुसना oobúsna, *v. n.* To rot, to putrefy.

उबसाना oobsána, *v. a.* To cause to rot.

उबाकना oobákna, *v. a.* To vomit.

उबाना oobána, *v. a.* To sow, to plant.

उबारना oobárna, *v. a.* To set at liberty, liberate, release.   [boil.

उबालना oobálna, *v. n.* To boil, to make

उभक óobhuk, *s. m.* A bear.

उभय óobhuy, *pron.* Both.

उभुरना óobhurna, *v. n.* To swell, to rise up, to overflow, to unlade (*a cart or boat*).

उभरा óobhra, *part.* Unladen (*as a cart or boat*). *Oobhra kurna, v. a.* To unlade (*a cart or boat*).

উভরাবা **oobhrána**, *v. a.* To fill a vessel till it run over.

উভারনা **oobhárna**, *v. a.* To take away, to steal.

উভানা **oobhána**, *v. a.* To alarm, to disturb.

উভার **oobhár**, *s. m.* Swelling, plumpness, tumefaction, prominence.

উভারনা **oobhárna**, *v. a.* To plump up, to raise up, to excite, to persuade.

উমং **óomung**, *s. f.* Excessive joy, transport, exultation, ambition.

উমংনা **óomungna**, *v. n.* To advance with joy.

উমংগী **óomungee**, *adj.* Aspiring, ambitious.

উমুন্দা **oomúndna**, *v. n.* To overflow, to fall (*as tears*), to swell, to increase or be poured out (*as a river, clouds, an army, the heart, &c.*).

উর **oor**, *s. m.* The bosom, the breast. *Oor lena*, *v. a.* To embrace, to caress, to fondle.

উরগ **óorug**, *s. m.* A snake.

উরগস্থান **oorug-sthán**, *s. m.* The infernal regions below the earth.

উরতু **óortoo**, *s. m.* Crimpling, plaits (*as of clothes*).

উরতুগর **oortoo-gúr**, *s. m.* A crimpler or plaiter of clothes.

উরলা **óorla**, *adj.* Hithermost, of this side.

উরিহনা **ooríhna**, *s. m.* Reproach, reproof.

উরু **óoroo**, *s. f.* The upper part of the thigh. *adj.* Large, great, ample.

উরেব **ooréb**, *s. f.* Complication, deception.

উর্দ **oord**, উর্দ্ধ **oordh**, } *s. f.* A kind of vetch (*Dolichos pilosus*).

উর্দাবেগনী **óorda-bégnee**, *s. f.* A female armed attendant in the *hurum*.

উর্দ্র **oordr**, *s. m.* An otter.

উর্দ্ধং **oordhúng**, *s. m.* A disease occasioned by the mounting of wind upwards.

উর্বসী **óorbusee**, *s. f.* The name of a courtezan, or female dancer in the heaven of *Indruh*; an ornament worn on the breast.

উর্বরা **óorwura**, *s. f.* Fertile soil, yielding every kind of crop; land in general.

উলং **oolúng**, *adj.* Naked.

উলুচনা **oolúchna**, *v. a.* To throw out the water from any thing, to drain.

উলঝুন **óoljhun**, *s. f.* Involution, entanglement, complication.

উলুঝনা **oolújhna**, *v. n.* To be entangled, to ravel, to be involved (*in difficulties*). *v. a.* To quarrel, to debate.

উলুঝপুলুঝ আনা **óolujh-póolujh jána**, *v. n.* To be entangled, to ravel, &c.

উলঝানা **ooljhána**, *v. a.* To entangle, to ravel or entwist (*as thread*), to involve, busy or engage (*in difficulties, business, &c.*), to embroil.

উলঝাও **ooljháo**, *s. m.* Entanglement, perplexity, intricacy, complication, involution.

উলঝেরা **ooljhéra**, *s. m.* Entanglement.

উলটকুঁবল **óolut-kúnwul**, *s. m.* Name of a flower.

উলটনা **óolutna**, *v. a.* To pervert, subvert, thwart, reverse, overturn, reply. *v. n.* To be reversed, turned over or turned back, to return.

উলটপুলট **óolut-póolut**, *adj.* Higgledy piggledy, topsy turvy. *s. f.* Confusion, interchange.

উলটা **óolta**, *part.* or *adj.* Reversed, turned back. *s. m.* Reverse, opposite, contrary, reverted, turned back; pease pudding, a kind of pudding made of the meal of any pulse.

উলটানা **ooltána**, *v. a.* To overturn, turn over, overset, upset, pervert, thwart, reverse, invert, return.

উলটানা পুলটানা **ooltána-pooltána**, *v. a.* To reverse, modify; to interchange.

উলটা পুলটা **óolta-póolta**, *adj.* Topsy turvy, higgledy piggledy.

উলুথনা **oolúthna**, *v. n.* To undulate, to be agitated (*as the ocean by storms*).

উলথা **óoltha**, *s. m.* Translation (*of a writing*).

উলুরনা **oolúrna**, *v. n.* To lie down, to rest.

উলুলনা **oolúlna**, *v. n.* To be overset, to be laid on one side.

উলুহনা **oolúhna**, *s. m.* A complaint, an accusation. *v. n.* To grow, to vegetate. *Ooluhna dena*, *v. a.* To reproach, complain (*to*), accuse.

উলারনা **oolárna**, *v. a.* To cause to sleep.

উলালনা **oolálna**, *v. n.* To overset, to lay over to one side.

উলাহনা **oolàhna**, *s. m.* Reproach, complaint.

উলেচনা **ooléechna**, *v. a.* To throw up water, to bale.

উলু **óoloo**, উলবা **óolwa**, } *s. f.* A kind of grass (*Saccharum cylindricum.*)

উলূক **oolóok**, *s. m.* An owl.

উলূখল **oolóokhul**, *s. m.* Bdellium, a gummy substance; a wooden mortar used for cleansing rice.

উলেন্দনা **ooléndna**, *v. a.* To pour water.

উল্কা **óolka**, *s. f.* A firebrand; fire falling from heaven, a meteor, &c.; flame; fire.

উল্মূক **óolmook**, *s. m.* A firebrand, wood burning or burnt to charcoal.

উল্লংঘন **oollúnghun**, *s. m.* The transgressing of a rule or custom; transgression.

ऊलू óolloo, *s. m.* An owl; (*met.*) a stupid fellow, a blockhead, a fool.

ऊलूपन oolloopún, *s. m.* Stupidity, foolishness.

ऊशीर ooshéer, *s. f.* The root of a fragrant grass (*Andropogon muricatum*).

ऊषण ooshúnna, *v. n.* To boil.

ऊष óosha, ⎱ *s. m.* Early morning,
ऊषाकाल óosha-kal, ⎰ dawn, day-break.

ऊष्ट्र óoshtruh, *s. m.* A camel.

ऊष्ण ooshn, *adj.* Hot, warm; pungent, acrid. *s. m.* Heat, warmth.

ऊष्णता ooshn-tá, *s. f.* Heat, warmth.

ऊष्णीष ooshnéesh, *s. m.* A turban, a diadem.

ऊष्मता óoshmta, *s. f.* Heat, warmth.

ऊष्मा óoshma, *s. f.* Wrath; warmth.

ऊस्त óosta, *s. m.* A barber.

ऊस्न óosna, *part.* Boiled. *Oosnana, v. a.* To cause to boil.

ऊसन्न oosúnna, *v. n.* To boil.

ऊसरना oosúrna, *v. n.* To retreat, shrink from, recede.

ऊसल पूसल जाना óosul-púsul jána, *v. n.* To be agitated, to be tossed, to get into confusion.

ऊसाना oosána, *v. a.* To winnow.

ऊसान्ना oosánna, *v. a.* To boil.

ऊसारना oosárna, *v. a.* To remove, to put out of place.

ऊसारा oosára, *s. m.* A porch, portico, peristyle, vestibule.

ऊसास oosás, *s. m.* Breath, breathing, respiration.

ऊसासना oosásna, *v. n.* To breathe.

ऊसिजना oosíjna, *v. n.* To boil.

ऊसीजना ooséejna, ⎱ *v. a.* To boil.
ऊसीझना ooséejhna, ⎰

ऊसीर ooséer, *s. f.* A fragrant root of grass used in making tatties (*Andropogon muricatum*).

ऊसीसा ooséesa, *s. m.* A pillow, cushion, head of a bed or resting place.

ऊसेवना oosévna, *v. a.* To throw out the water from boiled rice.

ऊसकाना ooskána, *v. a.* To light a fire or candle; to excite, to instigate.

ऊहूरना oohúrna, *v. a.* To subside (*a swelling or inundation*).

ऊ

ऊ oo, The sixth vowel of the *Naguree* alphabet: it has the sound of *oo* in food.

ऊः ooh, An interjection used to express sudden pain or distress, Oh!

ऊंघ oongh, *s. f.* Nodding, sleepiness.

ऊंघना óonghna, *v. n.* To nod from sleepiness, to doze, to slumber, to droop.

ऊंघाई oongháee, ⎱ *s. f.* Drowsiness, nodding, doze, sleepiness,
ऊंघास oonghás, ⎰ drooping.

ऊंचा óoncha, *adj.* High, tall, above, steep, loud. *Ooncha bol bolna,* To speak with pride. *Ooncha soonna,* To be hard of hearing. *Oonchakanee, s. f.* Deafness. *Ooncheh bol ka moonh neecha,* The proud ones are degraded.

ऊंचाई ooncháee, ⎱ *s. f.* Height, elevation,
ऊंचान oonchán, ⎰ steepness, eminence, tallness.

ऊंट oont, *s. m.* A camel.

ऊंटकटारा oont-kutára, *s. m.* Name of a thistle of which camels are fond (*Eschinops echinatus*).

ऊंटनी óontnee, *s. f.* A female camel.

ऊंहीं óonheen, *adv.* Exactly in that manner, so.

ऊई óoee, *interj.* Oh!

ऊक ook, *s. f.* Error, slip.

ऊकना óokna, *v. n.* To vomit.

ऊख ookh, *s. f.* A sugar-cane (*Saccharum officinarum*).

ऊखारी ookháree, *s. f.* A sugar-cane field.

ऊटपटंग oot-putúng, *s. m.* Absurdity, nonsense, what is without meaning or foundation. *adj.* Poor, helpless, destitute, in disorder.

ऊटपटंगी oot-putúngee, *adj.* One who speaks inconsiderately or without preparation.

ऊन oon, *s. f.* Wool.

ऊनी oonée, *adj.* Woollen.

ऊत oot, *s. m.* One who dies without leaving issue, an unmarried man; a stupid person, blockhead, dunce.

ऊद ood, ⎱ *s. m.* An otter.
ऊदबिलाव ood-biláo, ⎰

ऊदा óoda, *s. m.* Brown. *adj.* Of a brown colour.

ऊदाई oodáee, ⎱ *s. f.* Brownness.
ऊदाहट oodáhat, ⎰

ऊधम óodhum, *s. m.* Noise, impudence, rebellion, disturbance.

ऊधमी óodhumee, *adj.* Making noise, impudent, rebellious.

ऊधर óodhur, ⎱ *adv.* There, thither, on
ऊधर óodhur, ⎰ that side, on the other side.

ऊन oon, *s. f.* Wool. *adj.* Less, defective, minus.

ऊनी óonee, *adj.* Woollen.

ऊपर óopur, *adv.* Above, up, up, upon, upwards, over, outside, past. *s. m.* Top, outside, exterior. *Oopur seh*, From above, over, as, *Toofan oopur seh chula gya*, The storm passed over.

ऊपरी óopuree, *adj.* Foreign.

ऊभ oobh, *s. m.* Oppressive heat, langnor occasioned by heat.

ऊभना óobhna, *v. n.* To be agitated or oppressed with heat; to be angry or dissatisfied.

ऊबट óobut, *adj.* Impassable, steep; inaccessible.

ऊर्द्ध oorddh, *adj.* High, on high, above. *Oorddh-bahoo, adj.* With arms aloft or raised up (*a posture of Jogees*). *Oorddh-poond, s. m.* A peculiar line, delineated on the forehead by the worshippers of *Vishnoo. Oorddh-sans, s. m.* Deep inspiration, gasp.

ऊर्द्धरेता oorddh-réta, *s. m.* An order of religious mendicants, the *sunyasee*, the *Rishi*; one who lives in perpetual chastity.

ऊर्द्धसांस oorddh-sans, *s. m.* Deep inspiration, gasp.

ऊलू óoloo, ऊलूआ óolooa, } *s. f.* A kind of grass (*Saccharum cylindricum*).

ऊषण óoshun, *s. m.* Black pepper.

ऊषर óoshur, *adj.* Barren (*land*), a spot with saline soil.

ऊह ooh, *s. m.* Reasoning.

———

ऋ

ऋ ri, The seventh vowel of the *Naguree* alphabet: it has the sound of *ri* in rich, and its symbolical character is ृ, which is thus combined ऋ र.

ऋग्वेद ríg-ved, *s. m.* The first of the four *Veds.*

ऋचा rích-a, *s. f.* A sentence or *muntruh* of the *Rig-ved*; a magical invocation, a mystical prayer of the *veds.*

ऋजु ríj-oo, *adj.* Straight; straight metaphorically, as in morals.

ऋण rin, *s. m.* Debt; (*in Algebra*), negative quantity, minus.

ऋणग्रस्त rin-grúst, *adj.* Indebted, involved in debt.

ऋणमार rin-már, *s. m.* One who does not pay his debts.

ऋणमुक्ति rin-móokti, *s. f.* Discharge of a debt.

ऋणमोक्ष rin-móksh, *s. m.* Paying a debt.

ऋणशोधन rin-shódhun, *s. m.* Payment or discharge of a debt.

ऋणिया ríniya, *s. m. f.* A debtor.

———

ऋणी rín-ee, *adj. m.* Indebted. *s. m.* A debtor.

ऋतु rít-oo, *s. f.* Season, weather: the *hindoos* divide the year into six seasons, each consisting of two months, viz. *vusunt, greeshm, vursha, surud, him,* and *shishir*; the menstrual evacuation.

ऋतुप्राप्त rít-oo-prápt, *adj.* Fruitful, fertile, &c., productive in due season.

ऋतुमती rít-oo-mútee, *s. f.* A woman during menstruation.

ऋतुस्नान rítoo-snán, *s. m.* Bathing after menstruation.

ऋद्ध riddh, *adj.* Prosperous, thriving, rising, &c.

ऋद्धि ríd-dhee, *s. f.* A medicinal plant; wealth, possession, property; increase, prosperity; a name of the goddess *Parvutee.*

ऋन rin, *s. m.* Debt.

ऋनी rín-ee, *s. m.* A debtor.

ऋषि ríshi, *s. m.* A *ved*, or sacred composition; a sanctified personage so called; a sage or saint: there are several orders of these *rishis*, as the *Muhurshi, Devurshi, Rajurshi,* &c. the uncompounded name is especially applied to seven ancient sages, beginning with *Vushishth*, who hold in mythology an exalted and mysterious rank, and who form in astronomy the asterism of the Greater Bear; the *Rishi* of a *muntruh* or mystic prayer in the *Veds*, is the sage by whom it is supposed to have been remembered or recited.

ऋषी rísh-ee, *s. f.* The wife of a *Rishi.*

ऋषीश rish-éesh, *s. m.* Chief of the *Rishis.*

ऋक्ष riksh, *s. m.* A bear; a star, a constellation.

———

ॠ

ॠ ree, The eighth vowel in the *Naguree* alphabet: it has the sound of *ree* in reed, and when combined its symbol is ॄ thus placed beneath the letter ॠ.

ॠ ree, *s. f.* The mother of the gods; also of the demons; a name of *Siv*; an *Usoor* or demon.

———

ऌ

ऌ lri, or li, The ninth vowel of the *Naguree* alphabet, having the power of *lri*, but more usually considered to be expressed by *li* in Lily.

———

ॡ

ॡ lree, or lee, The tenth vowel in the *Naguree* alphabet: it has the sound of *lee* in leek.

ए

ए e, or eh, The eleventh vowel in the *Naguree* alphabet, corresponding very nearly to *e* in esquire, hempen : its symbol is placed above the letter it may be combined with, as ते.

ए eh, *interj*. O! a respectful particle of address.

एक ek, *adj*. One. *Eka-ekee*, All at once. *Ek-ad*, Some few. *Ek-bargee*, All at once. *Ek-dust*, All together, entire. *Ek-san*, *adj*. Alike, similar. *Ek-seh din nuh ruhneh*, Is used to denote a change of condition, most commonly from good to evil, but sometimes the reverse. *Ek kee dus soonanee*, To reply ten (*words*) for one : (*spoken of a person who replies with many words, especially in giving abuse*). *Ek-lukht*, Altogether, entirely. *Ek-nuh-ek*, One or other.

एकक ék-uk, *adj*. Alone, solitary.

एककाल ek-kál, *s. m*. One or the same time.

एककालीन ek-kaléen, *adj*. Coeval, belonging to the same period, simultaneous, contemporary.

एकगुरु ek-góoroo, *s. m*. A spiritual brother, pupil of the same preceptor.

एकग्रामीण ek-graméen, *adj*. Of the same town or village.

एकचित्त ék-chitt, *adj*. Thinking of one thing only, intent upon, absorbed in ; of one mind, agreeing, concurring.

एकटक éktuk, *s. m*. A fixed look, stare.

एकठा ekúttha, ⎫ *adj*. Together, collected.
एकठा ekthá ⎭ *Ektha*, or *Ekuttha kúrna*, To gather, to collect.

एकतराज्वर ekutúra-jwur, *s. m*. A tertian ague.

एकता ékta, *s. f*. Unity, oneness ; union ; equality.

एकतान ektán, *adj*. Closely attentive, having the mind fixed on one only object. *s. m*. Musical unison.

एकताल ektál, *s. m*. Harmony, unison, the accurate adjustment of song, dance and instrumental music.

एकतीर्थिं ek-téerthin, *s. m*. A spiritual brother, an associate in religious offices or objects.

एकत्र ekútr, *adv*. In one place, collectedly, together.

एकदा ekdá, *adv*. Once, at once, at the same time.

एकदुःखसुख ék-dookh-sookh, *adj*. Sympathizing, having the same joys and sorrows.

एकदृश ek-drísh, *adj*. One-eyed, single-eyed.

एकपक्ष ekpúksh, *adj*. An associate, a firm ally or partizan.

एकपत्नी ek-pútnee, *s. f*. A faithful wife, one devoted to her husband.

एकभुक्त ek-bhúkt, *adj*. Worshipping one Deity.

एकभुक्ति ek-bhúkti, *adj*. Of one faith ; believing in one Deity.

एकराशि ek-ráshi, *s. f*. A heap, a crowd.

एकरूप ekróop, *adj*. Like, similar, same, resembling.

एकुल ékul, *adj*. Alone, solitary.

एकलौता ek-lóuta, *adj*. Only-begotten (*son*).

एकवर्ण ek-vúrn, *adj*. Of one caste or tribe ; of one colour. *s. m*. One unknown quantity (*in algebra*).

एकवर्णी ek-vúrnee, *s. f*. Beating time, marking musical measure by clapping the hands, or the instrument which does so, a castanet.

एकशरण ek-shúrun, *s. m*. One only hope and refuge, especially applied to a Deity.

एकशरीर ek-shuréer, *adj*. Of one body or blood.

एकसा éksa, ⎫ *adj*. Alike, similar, resembling, of the same quality.
एकसार eksár, ⎭

एकाई ekáee, *s. f*. Unanimity.

एकाएकी eknékee, *adv*. All at once, suddenly.

एकांत ekánt, *adj*. Aside, apart, alone.

एकाकार ekakár, *adj*. Alike, uniform, of the same form.

एकाकी ekákee, *adj*. Solitary, alone.

एकाग्रह ekágruh, *adj*. Intent, closely attentive, fixed on one object ; undisturbed, unperplexed.

एकाग्रता ek-agrutá, *s. f*. Close and undisturbed attention.

एकादशी eká-dúsee, *s. f*. The eleventh day of the lunar fortnight.

एकाधिपति ek-ádhi-púti, *s. m*. A sovereign, a monarch.

एकांत ekánt, *adj*. Aside, apart, alone ; solitary, uninhabited, lonely, retired.

एकाक्ष ekáksh, *s. m*. A crow. *adj*. One-eyed.

एकैक ekyk, *adj*. Singly, one by one.

एर er, *s. f*. Striking with the heel, spurring. *Er marna*, To spur.

एरगुज ergúj, *s. m*. A medicinal plant, used for the cure of ring-worms.

एड़ी éree, *s. f*. The heel. *Eree dekho*, Look at your heel (*look at home*): a phrase used to obviate the effect of an evil eye.

एतद्र्थ **étudurth**, *adv.* Therefore, for this reason.

एतना **étna**, *adj. m.* As much as this, so much.

एतवार **etwár**, *s. m.* Sunday.

एता **éta**, *adj. m.* So much, thus much.

एताओता **etáota**, *adv.* On this account, for this reason.

एतावन्मात्र **etáwun-mátr**, *adj.* Thus much, only this.

एमन **ém-un**, *s. m.* A musical mode.

एरन्द **ér-und**, *s. m.* The castor oil plant (*Palma Christi* or *Ricinus communis*).

एराफेर **er-a-phér**, *s. m.* } Exchange, in-
एराफेरी **er-a-phéree**, *s. f.* } terchange; barter; dancing attendance.

एरी **ér-ee**, *interj.* O! a vocative particle for females.

एलवा **élwa**, *s. m.* Aloes (*Aloe perfoliata*).

एला **él-a**, *s. f.* Small cardamums, the seed of the *Electeria Cardamomum*, or *Alpinia Cardamomum.*

एव **ev**, *adv.* As, like.

एवम **évum**, *adv.* So, like, thus; and.

ऐ

ऐ **uy**, The twelfth vowel of the *Naguree* alphabet: it has the sound of y in *Jypoor*, and its symbol in combinations is thus placed over the letter `ै`.

ऐंच **uynch**, } *s. m.* Reserve, drawing.
ईंच **eench**, }

ऐंचना **uynchna**, } *v. a.* To draw, attract,
ईंचना **éenchna**, } pull.

ऐंटा **uynta**, *s. m.* A snail.

ऐंठ **uynth**, *s. f.* A coil, twist, convolution, twistening, tightening; strut.

ऐंठना **uynthna**, *v. a.* To tighten. *v. n.* To writhe, cramp, twist; to strut, stalk, walk affectedly.

ऐंडना **uyndna**, *v. n.* To strut, to stalk.

ऐकाधिपत्य **uyk-ádhi-pútyuh**, *s. m.* Sole monarch.

ऐकाहिक **uykáhik**, *adj.* Quotidian.

ऐक्य **uykyuh**, *s. m.* Oneness, unity, equailty; an aggregate, a total.

ऐगून **úygoon**, *s. m.* Unskilfulness, stupidity.

ऐन्द्रजालिक **úyndur-jálik**, *adj.* Belonging to legerdemain, magical; deceptive, illusory. *s. m.* A juggler.

ऐरावती **úyravutee**, *s. f.* The *Ravee* river in the *Punjab*.

ऐश्वर्य्य **uyshwúryuh**, *s. m.* Grandeur, glory, pomp, wealth, greatness, majesty, state; superhuman power, the divine faculties of omnipresence, omnipotence, invisibility, &c.; supremacy, dominion, sway, power, might.

ऐसा **úysa**, *adj.* Such, like this, so, resembling, like (*particularly when joined to other words as, murd-uysa, Like a man*). *Uysa tysa, or Uysa wysa,* So so, indifferent, indifferently.

ऐसे **úyseh**, } *adv.* Thus.
ऐसें **úysen**, }

ऐसों **úyson**, *adv.* This year.

ऐहिक **úyhik**, *adj.* Pertaining to the present state; worldly, local, of this world, of this place.

ओ

ओ **o**, The thirteenth vowel in the *Naguree* alphabet, it has the sound of o in go, and its symbol `ो` when combined is made thus को.

ओ **o**, The vocative interjection O! an interjection of calling, ho, hola; of reminiscence, ho, ah; of compassion, ah, oh. *conj.* And.

ओं **ong**, *conj.* The mystical monosyllable *Om.*

ओंठ **onth**, *s. m.* The lip.

ओंदा **ónda**, *adj.* Deep.

ओंध **ondh**, *s. m.* The cord with which rafters of frames for thatching on are pulled into their places and fastened till the roof is finished.

ओंधा **óndha**, *adj.* Upside down, overturned.

ओक **ok**, *s. m.* A house, a dwelling; an asylum, a place of refuge; sickness at the stomach, inclination to vomit; a draught of water from the hollow of the hand.

ओकना **ókna**, *v. n.* To vomit.

ओखली **ókhlee**, *s. f.* A wooden mortar.

ओघ **ogh**, *s. m.* Multitude, aggregate (*in general*), a collection.

ओछा **óchha**, *adj.* Light, of little consequence, absurd, trifling, fickle, fruitless, silly, capricious. *Ochha hona*, To want.

ओंकार **ónkar**, *s. m.* The mysterious name of the Deity.

ओजस् **ójus**, *s. m.* Light, splendour; manifestation, appearance; strength; vitality, vital warmth and action as appearing especially in the foetus.

ओझ **ojh**, *s. m.* Entrails, stomach, guts.

ओझड **ójhur**, *s. f.* A thrust, a push.

ओझल **ójhul,** *s. f.* Privacy, retirement. *adj.* Private, hid. *Ojhul kurna,* To conceal, screen, &c. *Ojhul hona,* To be concealed, &c.

ओझा **ójha,** *s. m.* A wizard, sorcerer, magician.

ओट **ot,** *s. f.* Protection, shade, shelter, screen, covering, concealment, partition. *Ot kurna,* To conceal, skreen, &c. *Ot hona,* To be concealed, &c.

ओटना **ótna,** *v. a.* To defend, skreen, shelter; to thrumb, separate the seed from cotton; to catch (*a ball &c.*).

ओठा **óta,** *s. m.* A partition wall or skreen.

ओठ **oth,** *s. m.* The lip.

ओढ़न **órun,** *s. m.* A shield, a target.

ओरा **óra,** *s. m.* A basket, a pannier.

ओढ़ना **órhna,** *v. a.* To put on (*dress*). *s. m.* A sheet, cloak, or mantle.

ओढ़नी **órhnee,** *s. m.* A smaller sheet, a veil or woman's mantle.

ओंधा **ónda,** *adj.* Deep.

ओत **ot,** *s. f.* Overplus, surplus; abatement, convalescence.

ओता **óta,** *adj.* So much, so many.

ओदन **ódun,** *s. m.* Boiled rice.

ओदनी **ódunee,** *s. f.* A plant (*Sida cordifolia, &c.*).

ओदा **óda,** *adj.* Wet, moist, damp.

ओधे **ódheh,** *adj.* Possessing a right or title to. *s. m.* A proprietor, one invested with power and authority.

ओप **om,** *s. f.* Beauty, lustre, elegance, brilliancy, brightness, polish.

ओपची **ópchee,** *s. m.* A man armed with weapons or clothed in mail. *Opchee khánuh, s. m.* A guard-house or post of armed men

ओम् **om,** *adv.* The mystic name of the Deity prefacing all the prayers and most of the writings of the *hindoos*; a name of *Vishnoo,* of *Shiv,* and of *Bruhm,* it therefore implies the *Indian triad,* and expresses *the three in one.*

ओर **or,** *s. f.* Origin; boundary, limit; way, side (*ward*). *Oos or,* That way, on that side, thitherward. *Or nibahna,* To be constant to, protect (*for ever*).

ओरमा **órma,** *s. m.* A particular kind of sewing, stitching together two breadths.

ओरी **óree,** *adj.* Partial; sidesman, protector, patron. *s. f.* The eaves of a house.

ओल **ol,** *s. m.* A vegetable, the root of which is eaten (*Arum campanulatum*); a hostage.

ओलती **óltee,** *s. f.* The eaves of a roof.

ओला **óla,** *s. m.* Hail; a kind of sweetmeat. *Ola ho-jana,* To become cold. *Jon sir moondaya ton oleh pureh,* I had no sooner shaved my

head than a shower of hail came on: (*spoken of one who has just engaged in an enterprize which turns out unfortunate*).

ओष **osh,** *s. f.* Dew. *Os pur-jánee,* To fall in value, to be deprived of importance, splendour, &c., to become less in demand than formerly.

ओषधि **óshudhi,** } *s. f.* An annual plant
ओषधी **óshudhee,** } or deciduous herb; one that dies after becoming ripe; an ingredient of a medicine.

ओष्ठ **oshth,** *s. m.* The lip, especially the upper.

ओष्ठरोग **óshth-róg,** *s. m.* Any morbid affection of the lips.

ओष्ठी **óshthee,** *s. f.* A creeper, bearing a red flower, to which the lip is commonly compared (*Bryonia grandis* or *Momordica monodelpha, &c.*).

ओस **os,** *s. f.* Dew. *Os pur-janee,* To fall in value, to be deprived of importance, splendour, &c., to become less in demand than formerly.

ओसबर्ग **os-búrg,** *s. m.* Name of a medicine.

ओसर **ósur,** *s. f.* A heifer.

ओसरा **ósra,** *s. m.* Turn, vicissitude. *Osra-osree,* By turns, alternately.

ओसीसा **oséesa,** *s. m.* The head of a bed or resting-place; a pillow, a cushion.

ओहो ** óho,** *interj.* Heigh! ho!

औ

औ **ou,** The fourteenth vowel of the *Naguree* alphabet, having the sound of *ou* in our; its symbol is ौ and it is combined thus औा.

औ **ou,** *conj.* And, also.

औंगी **óungee,** *s. f.* Silence, dumbness.

औंडा **óunda,** *adj.* Deep.

औंधना **óundhna,** *v. n.* To lower (*as the sky*).

औंधा **óundha,** *adj.* Upside down, overturned. *Oundha-bukht, s. m.* Misfortune, adverse fortune. *Oundhee peshanee, adj.* Short-sighted; unfortunate.

औंधाना **oundhána,** *v. a.* To turn upside down, to reverse, to overturn, to spill.

औंला **óunla,** *s. m.* A fruit, a kind of Myrobalans (*Phyllanthus emblica*).

औंलासार **óunla-sár,** *s. m.* A sort of brimstone.

औगाह **ougáh,** *adj.* Deep.

औगी **óugee,** *s. f.* A whip like a waggoner's, about seven cubits long, used in training horses; an ornamental edging of superior country shoes (*peculiar to Delhi*).

ऊगुण óugoon, *s. m.* Defect, blemish, vice.

ऊगुणी óugoonee, *adj.* Without virtue or science, ignorant.

ऊघट óughut, *adj.* Inaccessible, steep; unfrequented.

ऊचक óuchuk, ⎤ *adv.* Suddenly, unawares,
ऊचट óuchut, ⎦ unexpectedly.

ऊछ ouchh, *s. m.* A root from which an orange colour is extracted (*Morinda citrifolia*).

ऊझुर óujhur, *s. f.* A thrust, a push.

ऊटन óutun, *verbal noun.* Boiling, evaporation by boiling. *s. m.* A knife used for cutting tobacco.

ऊटना óutna, *v. a.* To boil (*as milk*), to evaporate over a fire. *v. n.* To consume with rage or vexation.

ऊतरना outúrna, *v. n.* To descend (*as in incarnation of the Deity, &c.*) on earth.

ऊतार outár, ⎤ *s. m.* Birth, descent, in-
अवतार uvutár, ⎦ carnation, especially of a deity from heaven; the appearance of any deity upon earth, but more particularly the mythological incarnations of *Vishnoo* in ten principal forms which are well known, viz. *Mutsya*, a fish; *Kuchhhup*, a tortoise; *Vurah*, a boar; *Nrisingh*, a man-lion; *Vamun*, a dwarf; *Pursooram*; *Ram*; *Krishn*; *Boodh*; and *Kulkee*; a pious or distinguished person, in the language of respect or flattery, is also called an *Uvutar*, a descent or incarnation of the deity; a *teerth* or sacred place; translation, translating; crossing.

ऊतसूकयुह outsóokyuh, *s. m.* Anxiety, perturbation, regret.

ऊदात oudát, *adj.* White (*the colour*).

ऊदान oudán, *s. m.* Gratis, what is given over and above or without purchase.

ऊदार्युह oudáryuh, *s. m.* Munificence, liberality.

ऊदास्युह oudásyuh, *s. m.* Solitude, loneliness.

ऊनेंपौनें óuneh-póuneh, *adv.* More or less.

ऊबट óubut, ⎤ *adj.* Impassable, steep,
ऊबहट oubhút, ⎦ inaccessible, devious.

ऊर our, *conj.* And, also. *adj.* More, other. *Ourek*, Another, separate, distinct, else. *Our-nuheen-to*, And if not then and otherwise. *Ourhee*, Quite different, extraordinary.

ऊरस óurus, *adj.* A legitimate child, *i. e.* by a wife of the same tribe.

ऊर्द्देहिक ourddh-déhik, *adj.* Obsequies of a deceased person; whatever is given or performed in remembrance of a wealthy person deceased.

ऊरुवानल óuruv-ánul, *s. m.* Submarine fire.

ऊषुध óushudh, *s. f.* A medicament, a drug, any herb, mineral, &c. used in medicine.

ऊषधि óushudhi, *s. m.* A deciduous plant, an annual production, as grass, &c.

ऊषधीय óushudh-éeyuh, *adj.* Medicinal.

ऊसन óusna, *v. n.* To become musty, to rot, to putrify.

ऊसर óusur, *s. m.* Occasion, time, opportunity, leisure.

ऊसान ousán, *s. m.* Sensation, sense; courage; presence of mind.

ऊसूच óusooch, *adj.* Without consideration, heedless.

ऊसर ousér, *s. m.* Anxiety, solicitude.

क

क kub, The first consonant of the *Nagree* alphabet, and having the sound of *K*, as in *Kirk*.

कंकन kúnkun, *s. m.* A bracelet or ornament of the wrist.

कंकर kúnkur, *s. m.* A nodule of limestone, limestone, stone, gravel.

कंकरा kúnkura, *s. m.* A stone ball with which boys play, a marble, pebble.

कंकरी kúnkuree, *s. f.* A small round stone or pebble.

कंकालिन kunkálin, *s. f.* A kind of witch, hag or sorceress.

कंकेला kunkréla, *adj.* Gravelly.

कंकरोल kunkról, *s. m.* A kind of gourd (*Momordica mixta*).

कंखजुरा kunkhujóora, *s. m.* A centipede (*Scolopendra*)

कंखी kúnkhee, *s. f.* A side glance, a squint, a sly look. *Kunkhiya*, *s. f.* A side glance, ogle. *Kunkhiya dekhna*, To ogle, leer.

कंगन kúngun, *s. m.* An ornament worn on the wrists by *hindoo* women, bracelet.

कंगना kúngna, *s. m.* A thread tied round a bridegroom's wrist.

कंगनी kúngnee, *s. f.* A cornice; a small grain, millet (*Panicum Italicum*).

कंगरोड़ kungrór, *s. m.* The ridge of the back, the spine; name of a bird (*water-fowl*).

कंगुलता kúngulta, *s. f.* Penury, poverty.

कंगाल kungál, *adj.* Poor, friendless, miserly. *Kungal-banka*, Poor and proud. *Kungaltur*, Vain-glorious. *Kungulta*, *s. f.* Penury, poverty.

कंचन kúnchun, *s. m.* Gold; a caste of people whose females are dancers. *Kunchun-ban*, A real *Kunchun* or one by birth. *Kunchun-khuchit*, *adj.* Inlaid with gold.

कंचनी kúnchunee, *s. f.* A female *kunchun*, a dancing girl, a strumpet, courtezan.

कंच kúnchoo, ⎱ *s. f.* A bodice or
कंचुकी kúnchookee, ⎰ jacket.

कंज kunj, *s. m.* A lotus.

कंजर kúnjur, *s. m.* A caste of people generally employed in selling ropes, &c. They also catch and eat snakes.

कंजा kunja, *adj.* Blue-eyed.

कंजिया kúnjiya, *s. f.* A small stythe or sty.

कंजूस kunjóos, *s. m.* A miser, a niggard.

कंजूसी kunjóosee, *s. f.* Stinginess, meanness, penuriousness, niggardliness.

कंटक kúntuk, *s. m.* A thorn ; a bad man ; a mean enemy.

कंटकारी kuntkáree, *s. f.* A sort of prickly nightshade (*Solanum jacquini*).

कंटर kúntur, *adj.* Miserly.

कंटिया kúntiya, *s. f.* A fishing-hook ; a vessel for keeping oil.

कंठ kunth, *s. m.* Windpipe, or the lump on the windpipe, the throat, the larynx, Adam's apple ; the bosom ; voice. *adj.* By-heart, committed to memory. *Kunth-aroondhun,* Strangulation. *Kunth phootna, v. n.* To be broken, the voice (*of a boy, becoming hoarse as he approaches to puberty*). *Kunth-mala, s. f.* A kind of necklace of gold and jewels ; the bronchocele or goitre ; scrofula. *Kunth kurna,* To get by heart.

कंठला kúnthla, *s. m.* A necklace composed of pieces of gold, silver, &c., put on children to avert evil.

कंठा kúntha, *s. m.* A necklace or rosary of large beads made of silver, crystal, or the earth of *kurbula.*

कंठाग्रह kunthágruh, *adj.* By rote, by memory.

कंठाभरण kunth-ábhurun, *s. m. pl.* The ornaments of the neck.

कंठी kúnthee, *s. f.* A short necklace.

कंड्राना kundrána, *v. n.* To bristle ; to dislike or abhor.

कंड्री kúndree, *s. m.* Name of a vegetable, a kind of mustard.

कंडा kúnda, *s. m.* Dry cow-dung picked up in the fields, &c., used for fuel ; a reed ; a bush.

कंडारी kundáree, *s. m.* A helmsman, a steersman.

कंडाल kundál, *s. m.* A kind of hautboy.

कंडी kúndee, *s. f.* Scraps of dried cow-dung.

कंडेरा kundéra, *s. m.* A cleaner of cotton.

कंत kunt, *s. m.* A husband, a sweetheart.

कंथा kunthá, *s. m.* An apparatus.

कंद kund, *s. m.* A bulbous or tuberous root ; one of an esculent sort (*Arum companulatum*) ; garlic ; an affection of the feminine organ.

कंदुर kúndur, *s. m. f.* ⎱ An artificial or na
कंदरा kúndra, *s. f.* ⎰ tural cavern, a chasm in a mountain.

कंदुल kúndul, *s. m.* A gum (*Sagapenum*).

कंदला kúndla, *s. m.* A precipice ; a cave ; a kind of silver thread.

कंदसार kundsár, *s. m.* A stag, buck, deer.

कंदा kúnda, ⎱ *s. m.* A squill (*Erythroni*
कंद्रा kúndra, ⎰ *um Indicum*).

कंदा करना kúnda kúrna, *v. a.* To engrave (*as seals, &c.*). *Kundakar, s. m.* An engraver.

कंदासा kundása, *s. m.* A priapus, obelisk, the ling or lingum.

कंध kundh, ⎱ *s. m.* The shoulder. *Koon*
कंधः kóonduh, ⎰ *duh jharna,* To prepare to fly (*a bird*).

कंधा kúndha, *s. m.* The shoulder. *Kundha dena,* To carry a dead body.

कंधियाना kundhiyána, *v. a.* To shoulder, to place on the shoulder.

कंधेली kundhélee, *s. f.* A kind of pannel or pack-saddle.

कंवल kúnwul, *s. m.* The lotus (*Nymphæa nelumbo*). *Kunwulbad,* The jaundice. *Kunwul nyn, adj.* Having eyes like the flower of the lotus. *Kunwulduh, s. m.* Very deep water abounding with lotuses.

कंस kuns, *s. m.* A proper name ; the uncle and enemy of *Krishn,* by whom he was slain ; as the foe of the deity, he is considered an *Usoor* or demon.

ककड़ी kúkree, *s. f.* A kind of cucumber (*Cucumis utilissimus*).

ककना kúkna, *s. m.* ⎱ A ring worn on the
ककनी kuknee, *s. f.* ⎰ wrist, a bracelet.

ककरोंदा kukrónda, *s. m.* A fruit (*Celsia*).

ककहरा kukúbra, *s. m.* The alphabet.

कका kúk-a, *s. m.* A paternal uncle.

ककोरना kukórna, *v. a.* T scrape (*the earth as fowls do*), to hollow, to excavate.

ककरी kúkhree, *s. f.* The armpit ; soreness of the armpit.

ककोरी kukhóuree, *s. f.* A painful suppurating tumour in the armpit.

कगर kúgur, *s. m.* Edge, corner, border ; architrave.

ककुन kúnkun, *s. m.* A bracelet or ornament of the wrist.

ककुर kúnkur, *s. m.* A nodule of limestone.

ककुरा kún-kur-a, *s. m.* A stone ball with which boys play, a marble.

ककुरी kún-kur-ee, *s. f.* A small round stone or pebble.

कंगन **kún-gun**, *s. m.* An ornament worn on the wrists by *hindoo* women.

कंगना **kúng-na**, *s. m.* A thread tied round a bridegroom's wrist.

कंगनी **kúng-nee**, *s. f.* A cornice; a small grain (*Panicum Italicum*).

कंगरोर **kung-rór**, *s. m.* The ridge of the back, the spine; name of a bird (*water-fowl*).

कंगुलता **kún-gul-ta**, *s. f.* Penury, poverty.

कंगाल **kun-gál**, *adj.* Poor, friendless, miserly. *Kungal-banka*, Poor and proud. *Kungal-tar*, Vain-glorious.

कंगालिन **kun-gál-in**, *s. f.* A kind of witch, hag or sorceress.

कंगूरी **kungóoree**, *s. f.* The lobe of the ear.

कंघा **kúng-ha**, *s. m.* } A comb. *Kunghee*
कंघी **kúng-hee**, *s. f.* } *sunwárna*, To adjust the hair which has been disordered in sleep. *Kunghee kurna*, To comb (*the hair*).

कच **kuch**, *s. m.* Rawness; simplicity; hair.

कचक **kúch-uk**, *s. f.* Pain (*of a wound*), limp. *Kuchukna*, *v. n.* To strain, sprain, twist; to limp; to pain.

कचकच **kúch-kuch**, *s. m.* Debate, altercation. *Kuchkuchahut*, *s. f.* The act of debating, &c.

कचकचाना **kuch-kuch-ána**, *v. n.* To swarm, to be very abundant, to be gritty.

कचकना **kuch-úk-na**, *v. n.* To strain, sprain, twist; to pain.

कचकरा **kúch-kur-a**, *s. m.* Tortoise-shell.

कचकाना **kuch-ká-na**, *v. a.* To strain, sprain, twist.

कचकेला **kuch-kél-a**, *s. m.* A kind of plantain which is eaten boiled or cooked as a vegetable.

कचरा **kúchra**, *s. m.* An unripe melon of a very diminutive kind.

कचनार **kuch-nár**, *s. f.* A tree, the flowers of which are a delicate vegetable (*Bauhinia variegata*).

कचपुच **kuch-puch**, *s. f.* Crowd. *adj.* Close, thick, stuffed together.

कचपचिया **kuch-púchiya**, *s. m.* The pleiades.

कचपन **kuch-pún**, *s. m.* Rawness, simplicity.

कचबच **kuch-búch**, *s. m. pl.* Infants, brats, children; family.

कचमच **kuch-múch**, *s. f.* Unintelligible or incorrect language, babble, nonsense.

कचरा **kúch-ra**, *s. m.* The raw *khurbooza* or melon; clay.

कचरी **kúch-ree**, *s. m.* A fruit (*Cucumis Madraspatensis*).

कचला **kúch-la**, *s. m.* Clay.

कचलोन **kuch-lón**, *s. m.* A kind of salt said to promote digestion.

कचलोहिया **kuch-lóhiya**, *s. f.* Untempered steel.

कचलोहू **kuch-lóhoo**, *s. m.* Bloody ichor discharged with purulent matter.

कचहरी **kuch-úh-ree**, *s. f.* A hall or court of justice, townhall, court, office.

कचाई **kuch-áee**, *s. f.* Rawness; indigestion, surfeit.

कचालू **kuch-á-loo**, *s. m.* An esculent root (*Arum colocasia*).

कचिया **kúch-i-ya**, *s. m.* A reaping hook or sickle.

कचियाना **kuch-i-yá-na**, *v. n.* To be frightened, to draw back, to shrink.

कचियाहट **kuch-i-yá-hut**, *s. f.* Abhorrence.

कचूआर **kuch-oo-ár**, *s. m.* Bauhinia variegata.

कचूमर **kuch-óo-mur**, *s. m.* A kind of pickle. *Kuchoomur kur dalna*, To cut to pieces.

कचूर **kuch-óor**, *s. m.* A plant or drug (*Circuma reclinata or zerumbet*).

कचेरा **kuch-ér-a**, *s. m.* The name of a tribe.

कचौरी **kuch-óu-ree**, *s. f.* A kind of pastry made of wheaten flour and pulse.

कच्चा **kúch-cha**, *adj.* Unripe, crude, immature; raw, built of unbaked earth; silly; inexperienced; false.

कच्चू **kúch-choo**, *s. m.* A plant (*Arum colocasia*).

कच्छप **kuch-chhúp**, *s. m.* A tortoise, a turtle.

कच्छी **kúch-chhee**, *s. m.* A horse (*with a hollow back*) from the province of *Kuchchh* on the banks of the *Sind*.

कछ **kuchh**, *s. m.* A tortoise, turtle; privities.

कछना **kúchh-na**, *s. m.* A kind of breeches which cover very little of the thigh. *v. n.* To be washed.

कछनी **kúchh-nee**, *s. f.* A smaller kind of breeches.

कछलंपट **kuchh-lúm-put**, *adj.* Incontinent, lewd, dissolute, libertine, lecher.

कछवाहा **kuchh-wá-ha**, *s. m.* A tribe of *Rajpoots* claiming descent from *Koos*, the son of *Ram Chundur*. The *Rajas* of *Jynugur* are of this family.

कछारना **kuch-hár-na**, *v. a.* To wash, to rinse.

कछू **kúchh-oo**, *neut. pron.* (*in Bruj*) Any, some, something, little, whatever.

कछूआ **kuchhóo-a**, *s. m.* A tortoise, a turtle. *Kuchhooa-dabur, adj.* Uneven-bottomed (a river), deep and shallow alternately.

कछोटी **kuch-hóu-tee**, *s. f.* A cloth worn between the legs to conceal the privities.

कजरा **kúj-ra**, *s. m.* Lamp-black, used for painting the eyes.

कजरारा **kuj-rá-ra**, *adj.* Black (*eyes*) without painting.

कजलौटी **kuj-lóu-tee**, *s. f.* A pot for keeping *kujjul;* an iron instrument like snuffers, used to receive smoke, prepare and keep lamp-black.

कजाचित **kuj-á-chit**, *adv.* Perhaps, should.

कज्जल **kúj-jul**, *s. m.* Lamp-black, soot, collyrium prepared from soot.

कंचन **kún-chun**, *s. m.* Gold; a caste of people whose females are dancers. *Kunchun-ban,* A real *Kunchun,* or one by birth. *Kunchun-khuchit, adj.* Inlaid with gold.

कंचनी **kún-chun-ee**, *s. f.* A female *Kunchun,* a dancing girl, a strumpet.

कंचु **kún-choo**, *s. f.* A bodice or jacket.

कंज **kunj**, *s. m.* A lotus.

कंजर **kún-jur**, *s. m.* A caste of people generally employed in selling ropes, &c. They also catch and eat snakes.

कंजा **kún·ja**, *adj.* Blue-eyed.

कंजिया **kún-ji-ya**, *s. f.* A small stythe or stye.

कंजूस **kun-jóos**, *s. m.* A miser, a niggard. *Kunjoosee, s. f.* Stinginess, meanness, penuriousness.

कट **kut**, *s. m.* Black colour to mark chintz with. *s. f.* The reins, the loins, the waist. *Kut-kehree, adj.* Having a waist elegant as the lion's (*epithet of a woman*).

कटक **kút-uk**, *s. m.* An army.

कटकना **kút-kun-a**, *s. m.* A picture or model (*or wood*); plan, scheme, sketch, regulation. *adj.* Shrewd, cunning.

कटकरंज **kut-kur-únj**, } *s. f.* The febri-
कटकलेजी **kut·kul-éj-ee**, } fuge nut (*Guilandina Bonducella:* or *Cesalpinia bonducella*).

कटखना **kut-khún-a**, *adj.* Inclined to bite.

कटखाना **kut-khá-na**, *v. a.* To bite.

कटघरा **kut-ghúr-a**, *s. m.* A wooden cage; a railing, a palisade.

कटना **kút-na**, *v. n.* To be cut; to be clipped or cut off; to be spent or passed (*time, life, &c.*); to be abashed, to be interrupted; to die of wounds.

कटनास **kutnás**, *s. m.* A bird (*Coracias*).

कटनी **kút-nee**, *s. f.* The season for cutting grain, harvest.

कटफल **kút-phul**, *s. m.* A small tree found in the north-west of *Hindoostan,* the bark and seeds of which are used in medicine, and as aromatics: the fruit also is eaten: the common name is *Kayuphul.*

कटबंधन **kut-bún-dhun**, *s. m.* A clog or ring of wood with which the feet of elephants are fastened.

कटर **kút-ur**, *adj.* Cruel, relentless. *subs.* Caitiff.

कटरना **kút-ruh-na**, *v. n.* To be cut, to be cut off, intercepted, divided, separated, or stopt up (*as, a road by being infested with thieves, &c.*).

कटरा **kút ra**, *s. m.* A market, suburbs, the market town belonging to a fort.

कटवाना **kut-wá-na**, *v. a.* To cause to cut, to cause to be bitten.

कटहर **kut-húr**, *s. m.* A wooden cage in which wild beasts are kept.

कटहरा **kut-úh-ra**, *s. m.* A wooden cage; a railing, a palisade.

कटहल **kut-húl**, *s. m.* A fruit and tree, the jack and fruit (*Artocarpus integrifolia*).

कटहा **kutuhá**, *adj.* Inclined to bite, snapping, snappish.

कटा **kút-a**, *s. f.* Killing, slaughter. *Kuta kurna,* To slaughter, murder.

कटाना **kut-ána**, *v. a.* To cause to cut or bite.

कटार **kut-ár**, *s. m.* A dagger; a polecat.

कटारा **kut-á-ra**, *s. m.* A medicinal plant (*Globe thistle; Echinops echinatus*).

कटारिया **kut-á-ri-ya**, *s. m.* A kind of silk cloth with stripes in the form of daggers.

कटारी **kut-á-ree**, *s. f.* A dagger.

कटाल **kut-ál**, *s. m.* Flood, spring tide (*Bengalee*).

कटाव **kut-áo**, *s. m.* A kind of flowering on clothes. *adj.* Cutting.

कटासा **kut-á-sa**, *adj.* Inclined to bite.

कटाह **kut-áh**, *s. m.* A shallow boiler for oil or butter, &c.

कटाक्ष **kut-áksh**, *s. m.* A leer, a glance or side look, ogling.

कटि **kút-i**, } *s. f.* The hip, the buttocks,
कटी **kút-ee**, } the reins, the loins, the waist. *Kut-kehree, adj.* Having a waist elegant as the lion's (*epithet of a woman*).

कटित **kút-it**, *s. m.* Vent, sale.

कटिया **kutiya**, *s. f.* A fishing hook.

कटीला **kut-ée-la**, *adj.* Thorny; name of a plant; active, brave (*a soldier*).

कटु **kút-oo**, *s. m.* Pungency, or a pungent taste; a flower (*Michelia Champaca*). *adj.* Pungent; fierce, impetuous, hot.

कटुता **kutoo-tá**, *s. f.* Pungency, sharpness; testiness, irritability.

कड़ूबी kut-óo-see, *s. f.* Smut, obscenity.

कड़ेब kutéo, *s. f.* Bad habit.

कड़ोरा kut-ó-ra, *s. m.* A brass bowl, a cup, goblet, &c. of metal, a shallow cup.

कड़ोरी kut-ó-ree, *s. f.* A small bowl or cup of metal.

कड़ोल kut-ól, *s. m.* A man of an inferior and degraded tribe, a *Chundal*; a plant (*perhaps Cowitch, Dolichos pruriens*).

कड़र kut-túr, *adj.* Inclined or addicted to bite (*a horse*).

कट्टा kút-ta, *adj.* Robust, able-bodied, athletic, strong. *s. m.* A large louse.

कट्था kut-thá, *s. m.* A land measure (*the twentieth part of a beegha*); a corn measure containing five *seers*.

कठंदर kut-hún-dur, *s. m.* The wind dropsy, tympany.

कठ kuth, *s. m.* Contraction of *Kath*.

कठगुलाब kuth-goláb, *s. m.* A kind of rose (*Rosa chinensis*).

कठघरा kuth-ghúra, *s. m.* A wooden cage; a railing, a palisade.

कठफोड़ा kuth-phóra, *s. m.* A wood-pecker (*Picus*).

कठबंदन kuth-bún-dun, *s. m.* A wooden ring with which the feet of elephants are fastened.

कठबिरकी kuth-bir-óo-kee, *s. f.* A toad.

कठबेला kuth-bél-a, *s. m.* A flower (*Jasminum multiflorum*).

कठमस्ता kuth-mús-ta, *adj.* Very stout and lusty.

कठहर kut-húr, *adj.* Hard.

कठरा kúth-ra, ⎱ *s. m.* A tub, tray, plate,
कठड़ा kúth-ra, ⎰ platter, trough, young male buffalo.

कठरी kúth-ree, *s. f.* A small tub, trough.

कठला kúth-la, *s. m.* A wooden ornament or charm hung on the neck of a child.

कठहंसी kuth-húnsee, *s. f.* Affected or forced smiles (*with internal displeasure*).

कठिंजर kút-hín-jur, *s. m.* A plant worshipped by the *hindoos*, commonly called *Toolsee* (*Ocymum sanctum, or sacred basil*).

कठिन kút-hin, *adj.* Difficult, obscure; painful, troublesome, acute, hard, solid; unkind, severe.

कठिनता kut-hintá, *s. f.* Firmness, hardness; severity; difficulty, obscurity.

कठिनहृदय kúthin-hríduy, ⎱ *adj.*
कठिनान्तःकरण kúthin-ántuh-kúrun ⎰ Hardhearted, harsh, cruel, severe, unkind.

कठिनी kút-hin-ee, *s. f.* Chalk (*for writing with*).

कठिया kút-hi-ya, *s. m.* A trencher, a platter; a snare, trap, trepan.

कठिल kut-híll, *s. m.* (*Momordica Charantia*).

कठोर kut-hór, ⎱ *adj.* Hard, solid; severe,
कठोल kut-hól, ⎰ relentless, cruel, callous.

कठोरता kut-hór-ta, *s. f.* Hardness, firmness; relentlessness, cruelty, severity, rigor.

कठौती kut-hóu-tee, *s. f.* A tub, plate, trencher, platter.

कड़ kur, *s. f.* The seed of safflower (*Carthamus tinctorius*).

कड़क kúr-uk, *s. f.* A crash, a crack; thunder; agility.

कड़कड़ा kúr-kur-a, *adj.* Hard, stiff, strong.

कड़कड़ाना kur-kur-á-na, *v. n.* To give such a sound as oil or butter when boiling.

कड़कना kúr-uk-na, *v. n.* To crack, crackle; to thunder.

कड़का kúr-ka, ⎱ *s. m.* Pœan, song of
कड़को kúr-ka, ⎰ triumph.

कड़खा kur-khá, *s. m.* Commemoration, mention; encouraging soldiers in time of battle by pointing out the good effects of steadiness and valour, extolling the actions of former heroes, &c.; war-song to encourage combatants.

कड़खैत kur-khyt, *s. m.* A kind of bar, and officer in Indian armies whose business it is to encourage the soldiers by the exhortations called *Kurkha*.

कड़ना kúr-na, *v. a.* To perforate.

कड़रून kur-ur-bóon, *s. m.* Name of a plant.

कड़वा kúr-wa, *adj.* Bitter, acrid; strong, virulent; hard-hearted; brave. *Kurwa kurna*, To give or expend unwillingly. *Kurwa hona*, To be enraged. *Kurweh kuseleh din*, Hard and cruel times.

कड़वातेल kúrwa-tel, *s. m.* Mustard oil, bitter-oil.

कड़वाहट kur-wá-hut, *s. f.* Bitterness.

कड़वी kúr-wee, *s. f.* Stubble of a sort of grain.

कड़ही kur-hée, *s. f.* A dish consisting of the meal of pulse (*Chuna or Cicer arietinum*) dressed with sour milk.

कड़ा kúr-a, *adj.* Hard, stiff; harsh, obdurate. *s. m.* A ring worn on the wrists, ankles, &c., a ringlet, bracelet, the handle of a door, or any thing in form of a ring. *adj.* Arch, sly, knowing, penetrating, sharp, harsh, cruel.

कड़ाकड़ kur-a-kúr, *s. m.* Successive crashes.

कड़ाका kur-á-ka, *s. m.* The crash made by breaking any thing; a rigid fast (*in which nothing of food or drink has entered the mouth*).

कटारा kur-á-ra, *s. m.* The perpendicular bank of a river, &c., side, brink, bank.

कटाह kur-áh, *s. m.* A shallow iron boiler (*in which sugar, &c., is boiled*), caldron.

कटाही kur-á-hee, *s. f.* A frying pan.

कटी kúr-ee, *s. f.* A rafter, a beam ; a ring used to manacle or to fetter with.

कटोड़ kur-ór, } *adj.* Ten millions. *Kuror-*
कटोर kur-ór, } *putee,* Possessor of a crore of rupees. *Kuror-khookh, s. m.* A liar.

कटबना kúrb-na, *v. n.* To be extracted, drawn, pulled out ; to escape, rise, slip, issue, spring ; to be delineated, drawn or painted (*as a picture*).

कटी kúr-hee, *s. f.* A dish consisting of the meal of pulse (*Chuna or Cicer ariatinum*) dressed with sour milk.

कटूआ kur-hóoa, *s. m.* A loan, a debt ; a premium on a loan ; a deduction from the sum lent.

कन kun, *s. m.* Grain, coin, a grain, a minute particle, an eye of corn, a spark or facet of any gem.

कनकि kún-ki, *s. f.* Ground rice, or the scraps that fly off in pounding rice to separate it from the husk.

कनरस kúu-rus, *s. m.* Taking a pleasure in hearing (*music, &c.*). *Kunrusiya, s. m.* A lover of music, an amateur.

कनिका kún-i-ka, *s. f.* Fine sand (*particularly grittiness or sand in bread*), an atom ; a small particle, a grain, a kind of rice.

कनेर kunér, *s. m.* A tree (*Cascaria ovata*).

कनटक kún-tuk, *s. m.* A thorn ; a bad man ; a mean enemy.

कनटकारी kunt-ká-ree, *s. f.* A sort of prickly night-shade (*Solanum jacquini*).

कनटकी kúntukee, *adj.* Thorny, prickly ; vexatious, annoying.

कनटार kun-tár, *adj.* Prickly, thorny.

कनटिया kún-ti-ya, *s. f.* A fishing-hook ; a vessel for keeping oil.

कनठ kunth, *s. m.* Windpipe, or the lump on the windpipe, the throat, the larynx, Adam's apple ; the bosom ; voice. *adj.* By heart, committed to memory. *Kunth-aroondhun,* Strangulation. *Kunth-phootna, v. n.* To be broken, the voice (*of a boy, becoming hoarse as he approaches to puberty*). *Kunth-mala, s. f.* A kind of necklace of gold and jewels ; the bronchocela, or goitre ; scrofula. *Kunth kurna,* To get by heart.

कनठभूषा kunth-bhóosha, *s. f.* A collar or short neck-lace.

कनठमनि kunth-mún-i, *s. m.* A jewel worn on the throat.

कनठल kúnth-la, *s. m.* A necklace composed of pieces of gold, silver, &c., put on children to avert evil.

कनठहस्थ kunt-hústh, *adj.* By heart.

कनठा kúnt-ha, *s. m.* A necklace or rosary of large beads made of silver, crystal, or the earth of *Kurbulla.*

कनठाग्रह kunt-hágruh, *adj.* By rote, by memory.

कनठाभरन kunt-há-bhur-un, *s. m. pl.* The ornaments of the neck.

कनठी kúnt-hee, *s. f.* A short necklace.

कत kut, *ind.* Where ? whither ? why ? how ?

कतनई kut-núee, *s. f.* Spinning.

कतना kút-na, *v. n.* To be spun.

कतरन kútrun, *s. f.* } Parings, clippings.
कतरा kútra, *s. m.* }

कतरना kút-ur-na, *v. a.* To clip, to cut (*as with scissors*), to cut out, to pare.

कतरनी kút-ur-nee, *s. f.* Scissors.

कतरबेोंत kut-ur-béont, *s. m.* Cutting out ; (*met.*) meditation, consultation, anxiety.

कतरा kutra, *s. m.* Parings, clippings.

कतराई kut-rá-ee, *s. f.* Price paid for cutting out (*clothes, &c.*). *adj.* Sideways.

कतराना kut-rá-ua, *v. a.* To cause to clip, to cut out ; to leave the high road, stealing away by by-paths, to go round about, to shrink, to slink away (*from*), to edge or go sideways. *Kutrakur chulna,* To desert one's companion, to cut the society of any one.

कताई kut-á-ee, *s. f.* Spinning, the price paid for spinning. *Kutaee kurna,* To spin.

कताना kut-á-na, *v. a.* To get spun, to cause to spin.

कतारा kut-á-ra, *s. m.* A kind of sugarcane.

कतीरा kut-ée-ra, *s. m.* A gum resembling tragacanth obtained from the *Sterculia urens.*

कतल kut-túl, *s. f.* A lump of stone, brick or earth.

कतान kut-tán, *s. m.* A knife, a dagger. (*Bengalee*).

कतथक kut-thúk, *s. m.* A story-teller ; a kind of singer.

कथ kuth, *s. m.* The astringent vegetable extract which the natives eat with betel-leaf; it is the produce of a species of mimosa (*Chadira*) catechu, terra japonica.

कथक kut-húk, *s. m.* A narrator, a relator, one who recites a story, or who publicly reads and expounds the *Poorans.*

कथन kut-hún, *s. m.* Saying, narrating, relating.

कथन kúth-na, *v. a.* To tell, to say, to relate.

कथा kut-há, *s. f.* A story, tale, fable, relation, narrative.

कथिक kút-hik, *s. m.* A story teller by profession, a narrator, or relator.

कथित kút-hit, *adj.* Spoken, said, told, related.

कथोपकथन kuth-óp-kut-hun, *s. m.* Conversation, free intercourse; a dialogue, a conference; narration.

कद kud, *adv.* When?

कदन kúd-un, *s. m.* A killer, a destroyer; killing, destroying.

कदम kúd-um, कदम्ब kúd-umb, } *s. m.* A tree (*Nauclea orientalis*).

कदम्बपुष्पी kúdumb-póoshpee, *s. f.* A plant the flowers of which resemble those of the *Kudumb*, commonly called *Moondeerse*.

कदर kúd-ur, *s. m.* A white sort of Mimosa.

कदर्युह kud-úr-yuh, *adj.* Avaricious, miserly.

कदल kúd-ul, *s. m. f.* कदलक kúd-luk, *s. m.* कदली kúd-lee, *s. f.* } The plantain or banana tree (*Musa sapientum*).

कदा kúd-a, *adv.* When? at what time?

कदाकर kúd-akar, *adj.* Ill-formed, ugly.

कदाचार kúd-a-char, *adj.* Wicked, profligate, abandoned, following evil practices.

कदाचित kud-á-chit, कदापि kud-á-pi, } *adv.* Sometimes, at some time or other; should, perhaps.

कदीमा kud-ée-ma, *s. m.* An iron crow; a Pumpkin (*Cucurbita pepo*).

कदी kúd-hee, कदु kúd-hoo, } *adj.* Ever, some time or other.

कन kun, *s. m.* Appreciating, valuing (*a field*); a weevil; grain, corn; a grain, a minute particle. *Kun kurna*, To value. *Kun-koot, s. f.* Appraisement of a crop on the field, valuation.

कनक kún-uk, *s. m.* Gold; the plant *Dhutoora* or thorn apple (*Datura metel*).

कनकटा kun-kút-a, *adj.* Ear-cropt, earless.

कनकटी kun-kút-ee, *s. f.* A disorder in the ears.

कनखजूरा kun-khuj-óo-ra, *s. m.* A centipede (*Scolopendra*).

कनरी kún-ree, *s. f.* A musical mode or *raginee*.

कनपटी kun-pút-ee, *s. f.* The temple (*the upper part of the side of the face*).

कनफटा kun-phút-a, *s. m.* A *jogee* or *hindoo* mendicant with slit ears.

कनरस kunrus, *s. m.* Taking a pleasure in hearing (*music, &c.*).

कनरसिया kunrúsiya, *s. m.* A lover of music, an amateur.

कनवाई kun-wá-ee, *s. f.* Boring the ears.

कनशुलाई kun-shul-áee, *s. f.* A kind of *Scolopendra* or *Julus* which is said to get into the brain through the ears, and by its bite to occasion excessive pain and even death.

कनहूर kun-húr, *s. m.* A rudder.

कनहूरा kun-húr-a, *s. m.* Attention, listening.

कनहुरीला kunhuréela, *s. m.* A steersman.

कनहा kun-há, *s. m.* An officer employed by government to value the crops on the field.

कनहाई kunháee, *s. f.* Valuation of crops of grain. *n. prop. m.* The name of *Krishn*.

कनाकुचू kun-a-kúch-oo, *s. m.* The name of a vegetable, a species of Arum.

कनागत kun-á-gut, *s. f.* A *shraddh* or religious ceremony performed daily by *hindoos*, during the dark half of the month *Asin*, in honor of deceased ancestors, or *pitri* : hence that fortnight is called *Kun-a*.

कनिक kún-ik, *s. m.* Wheaten flour.

कनियाना kun-i-yá-na, *v. a.* To go to one side, to avoid one, to dodge, to shun.

कनियाहट kun-i-yá-hut, *s. f.* Shyness.

कनिष्ठ kún-ishth, *adj.* Small, little. *s. m.* A younger brother.

कनिष्ठा kun-ísh-tha, *s. f.* The little finger.

कनिहा kun-i-há, *adj.* Revengeful.

कनीरा kun-ée-ra, *s. m.* A caste of people, generally arrow-makers.

कने kún-eh, *prep.* Near, to, with, &c.

कनेटी kun-ét-ee, *s. f.* Pulling the ears.

कनेर kun-ér, कनेल kun-él, } *s. f.* A flower (*Nerium odorum*, single).

कनैया kun-úy-ya, *s. m.* The ceremony of boring the ears.

कनोजिया kun-óu-ji-ya, *adj.* Inhabitant of Canouge.

कनौठा kun óut-ha, *s. m.* Any situation in an apartment close to an angle of the wall.

कनौंड kun-óund, *s. m.* Diffidence, bashfulness.

कनौंडा kun-óun-da, *adj.* Diffident, bashful, favoured; standing in awe of, or afraid to meet another.

कनौरा kun-óu-ra, *adj.* Standing in awe of another. *Kunoura kurna*, To gain ascendency over another, or make him stand in awe.

कन्त kunt, *s. m.* A husband, sweetheart.

कन्ठ kúnt-ha, *s. m.* An apparatus or band round the neck of a *jogee* to carry things on.

कन्द kund, *s. m.* A bulbous or tuberous root; one of an esculent sort (*Arum companulatum*); garlic; an affection of the feminine organ.

कन्दल kún-dul, *s. m.* A gum (*Sagapenum*).

कन्दला kúnd-la, *s. m.* A precipice; a cave; a kind of silver thread.

कन्दसार kund-sár, *s. m.* A stag, buck, deer.

कन्द्रा kúnd-ra, } *s. m.* A squill (*Erythroni-*
कुन्द kún-da, } *um Indicum.*

कन्ध kundh, } *s. m.* The shoulder. *Koon-*
कून्दा kóonda, } *da jharna,* To prepare
कन्धा kúnd-ha, } to fly (*a bird*).

कन्धियाना kund-hi-yá-na, *v. a.* To shoulder, to place on the shoulder.

कन्धेली kund-hél-ee, *s. f.* A kind of pannel or pack-saddle.

कन्ना kún-na, *s. m.* The notches on the two sides of the upper leather of a shoe; the part of a paper kite to which the string is tied.

कन्नादार kun-na-dár, *s. m.* A kind of shoe or slipper.

कन्नी kún-nee, *s. f.* A spark of a diamond or other gem; bran. *Kunnee katna,* To undermine a person, or effect his ruin by clandestine means.

कन्यका kún-yu-ka, *s. f.* A girl, a maiden; the Socotrine aloe (*Aloe perfoliata*).

कन्या kún-ya, *s. f.* A little girl, a girl nine years old; a daughter; a virgin; the sign Virgo. *Kun-ya-dan,* Dowry, virgin-giving, giving a girl in marriage.

कन्हरेला kunh-réc-la, *s. m.* A steersman.

कन्हाई kun-há-ee, *s. f.* Valuation of crops of grain.

कन्हैया kun-hy-ya, *n. prop.* A name of *Krishn.*

कपकपी kup-kúp-ee, *s. f.* Shivering, trembling, quaking, perturbation.

कपट kúp-ut, *s. m.* Fraud, deceit, cheating, circumvention, trick, spite, rancour, adulteration, subterfuge. *adj.* Designing, insincere.

कपटता kuput-tá, *s. f.* Deceitfulness.

कपटलेख kuput-lékh, *s. m.* A forged document.

कपटवेष kuput-vésh, *s. m.* Disguise.

कपटवेषी kúput-veshée, *adj.* Disguised, in masquerade. *s. m.* A hypocrite.

कपटी kúp-ut-ee, *adj.* Insincere, fraudulent, dishonest, a rogue, a cheat, false, deceitful, hypocritical; adulterated.

कपड़ kúp-ur, *s. m.* Cloth. *Kupurchhan kurna,* To strain. *Kupurchhun, adj.* Impalpable

(*powder*); deep (*consultation*); thoroughly sifted (*intelligence, &c.*).

कपड़कोठा kúpur-kótha, *s. m.* A tent.

कपड़ा kúp-ra, *s. m.* Cloth; clothes, dress, habit. *Kupra puhunna,* To put on clothes. *Kupron seh hona,* To have the menses.

कपड़े kúpreh, *s. m. pl.* Dress, apparel. *Kupreh rungna,* To become a mendicant. *Kupreh ko jhol dena,* To give an alarm. *Kupreh-wupreh,* Clothes.

कपना kúp-na, *v. n.* To shiver, tremble, quake, quiver. *adj.* Trembling.

कपरकूट kup-ur-kóot, *adj.* Pounded up with rags (*clay for making crucibles, &c.*).

कपरधूल kup-ur-dhóol, *s. m.* A kind of gauze.

कपाट kup-át, *s. m.* A door, a shutter, the leaf or pannel of a door.

कपार kup-ár, *s. m.* The skull, the cranium; fate, destiny.

कपारी kup-á-ree, *adj.* Shrewd, sly. *s. m.* A caste in Bengal who sells greens, &c.; a title of *Shiv,* who carries a skull in his hand and a chain of skulls round his neck; a cavesson. *Urdh-kuparee,* Pain of half the head, hemicrania; an areca nut having two kernels, or rather one of those kernels which are convex on one side and flat on the other, where it was in contact with its fellow. (*These nuts, from the doctrine of signatures, are said to be a remedy for the Hemicrania*).

कपाल kup-ál, *s. m.* The head, forehead; the skull, the cranium; fate, destiny. *Kupal phootna,* To be unfortunate. *Kupal khoolna,* To have a favourable turn of fortune.

कपाली kup-á-lee, *s. m.* A title of *Shiv.* *Kupalee-usun,* An attitude of mendicants in worship, standing on their heads. *Kupalee-kriya,* A ceremony among *hindoos*; when a dead body is burning and nearly reduced to ashes, the nearest relation breaks the skull with the stroke of a bamboo and pours melted *ghee* into the cavity; hence, *Kupal kriya kurna,* To think intensely, to beat or cudgel one's brains.

कपास kup-ás, *s. f.* Cotton (*undressed*); the cotton plant (*Gossypium herbaceum*).

कपि kúp-i, *s. m.* An ape or monkey.

कपित्थ kup-ítth, *s. m.* The elephant or wood apple (*Feronia Elephantium,* or *Cratæva Valanga*).

कपिला kúp-i-la, *s. f.* A brown-coloured cow.

कपूत kup-óot, } *s. m.* A bad or degene-
कपूत्र kup-óotr, } rate son.

कपूती kup-óo-tee, *s. f.* Degeneracy.

कपूर kup-óor, *s. m.* Camphor; also, name of a flower.

कपूर कचरी kup-oor-kúch-ree, *s. f.* A sort of medicine.

कपूरी kup-óo-ree, *s. f.* A kind of betel-leaf.

कपोत kup-ót, *s. m.* A pigeon or dove, especially the spotted-necked pigeon.

कपोल kup-ól, *s. m.* The cheek. *Kupol-gendoos*, A small pillow of a circular shape to rest the cheek upon.

कफ kuph, *s. m.* Phlegm, one of the three humors of the body; watery froth or foam in general.

कफनाशन kuph-náshun, *adj.* Antiphlegmatic.

कफी kuphée, *adj.* Phlegmatic.

कब kub, *adv.* When. *Kubtuk, adv.* Till when. *Kubkub, adv.* When? *Kubka,* or *Kubkeh,* or *Kubkee,* Since when? Of what time? *Kublo,* Till when? How long?

कबड्डी kub-úd-dee, *s. f.* A game among boys, who divide themselves into two parties; one of which takes its station on one side of a line or ridge, called *pala*, made on the ground, and the other on the other. One boy, shouting *kubbuddee kubuddee,* passes this line and endeavours to touch one of those on the opposite side; if he is able to do this, and to return to his own party, the boy that was so touched is supposed to be slain, that is, retires from the game; but if the boy who made the assault be seized and unable to return, he dies, or retires in the same manner. The assault is thus made from the two sides alternately, and that party is victorious of which some remain after all their opponents are slain. [Prison bars?]

कबन्ध kub-úndh, *s. m.* A headless trunk, especially retaining the powers of action.

कबरा kúb-ra, *adj.* Grey, dirty white, variegated.

कबार kub-ár, *s. m.* A door.

कवि kúb-i, *s. m.* A poet.

कवित kúb-it, *s. m.* A sort of verse used by the *hindoos,* poetry.

कविता kúb-it-a, *s. f.* Poetry, a poem.

कवीश्वर kub-ée-shwur, *s. m.* An eminent poet, a prince of poets.

कभी kúb-hee, } *adv.* Ever, some time or
कभू kúb-hoo, } other. *Kubhee kubhee,* Sometimes, now and then, at times. *Kubhee keh,* Of sometime, sometime ago. *Kubhee nuh kubhee,* Sometime or other.

कमठ kúm-uth, *s. m.* A tortoise, a turtle.

कमठा kúm-tha, *s. m.* A bow (*made of bamboo*).

कमरा kúm-rha, *s. m.* A gourd (*Cucurbita pepo*).

कमण्डल kum-ún-dul, *s. m.* An earthen or wooden water-pot used by the ascetic and religious student.

कमन kúm-un, *adj.* Libidinous, desirous; beautiful, desirable.

कमनीय kum-un-éeyuh, *adj.* Pleasing, beautiful, desirable.

कमरख kúm-rukh, *s. m.* A fruit (*Averrhoa carimbola*).

कमल kúm-ul, *s. m.* The lotus (*Nelumbium speciosum* or *Nymphæa nelumbo*).

कमलबाइ kum-ul-báeh, *s. m.* A disorder, the jaundice.

कमला kúm-ul-a, *s. m.* The caterpillar or larva of a brown moth, covered with fine bristles, which, on handling it, adhere to the skin and excite itching: it is destructive to trees; the palmer-worm. *s. f.* A name of the goddess *Lukshmee*; an excellent woman.

कमलिनी kum-lín-ee, *s. f.* A number of lotus flowers, or a place abounding with them.

कमली kúm-lee, *s. f.* A small blanket.

कमवाना kum-wá-na, *v. a.* To cause to work, to earn, to use (*as razors, &c.*).

कमाई kum-á-ee, *s. f.* Earning, gain; work, performance.

कमाऊ kum-á-oo, *adj.* Laborious, one who earns (*a livelihood*).

कमाना kum-á-na, *v. a.* To earn; to work, to perform; to perpetrate, to commit (*crime*), to do (*good*); to clean (*leather or a privy*); to lessen, to abate.

कमासूत kumásoot, *s. m.* A journeyman, a servant, a workman, earner.

कमीला kum-ée-la, *s. m.* A plant or drug.

कमेरा kum-ér-a, *s. m.* A workman, journeyman, an assistant.

कमोद kum-ód, *s. m.* A dyeing drug, being the dust from the outside of the capsules of *Rottlera tinctoria*; said to be, also, a purgative medicine and aphrodisiac.

कमोदिनी kum-ó-din-ee, *s. f.* A sort of water-lily, described as expanding its petals during the night, and closing them in the day time (*Menyanthes Indica,* or *Cristata*).

कमोरी kum-ó-ree, *s. f.* A small earthen vessel.

कम्प kump, *s. m.* Shivering, tremour, trembling, quaking, perturbation, shaking.

कम्पन kumpún, *s. m.* Trembling, quivering.

कम्पना kúmp-na, *v. n.* To tremble.

कम्पमान kumpmán, *adj.* Trembling.

कम्पाना kum-pá-na, *v. a.* To cause to tremble, to shake, to agitate.

कम्पाथ kum-pá-ha, ⎫ adj. Tremulous, fear-
कम्पित kúm-pit, ⎭ ful, shaking, trembling.

कम्बल kúm-bul, ⎫ s. m. A blanket.
कम्मल kúm-mul, ⎭ s. m. A blanket.

कम्बोज kum-boj, s. m. A country in the north of India, Camboj or Cambay.

कर kur, s. m. The hand. s. m. f. Tribute, duty, custom, fee, tax, toll, impost, royal revenue.

करकच kúr-kuch, s. m. A kind of salt, sea salt made by evaporation.

करकनाथ kur-uk-náth, s. f. A species of fowl whose bones even are black.

करकरा kur-kúr-a, s. m. Bad coin; a bird (Numidian crane).

करकराहट kur-kur-á-hut, s. f. Cracking, crackling noise.

करकस kúr-kus, adj. Piercing, harsh; obdurate, violent, sharp, contumelious.

करकसा kúr-kus-a, s. f. A termagant, scold.

करकाना kur-ká-na, v. a. To strain, sprain, break.

करगदा kur-gúd-a, s. m. A string worn round the waist.

करगहन kur-gúh-un, s. m. Protection.

करंज kur-únj, s. m. A plant (Galedupa arborea).

करन kúr-un, s. m. Cause, instrument; making, acting, doing; to make, to do; the ear, the helm of a boat.

करन kúr-un, s. m. An astrological division of time, of which there are eleven, 7 moveable and 4 fixed, and 2 are equal to a lunar day.

करनी kúr-nee, s. f. Action, business; a trowel; (in arithmetic), a surd or irrational quantity.

करतब kúr-tub, s. m. Action, business, deed; skill, art.

करतल kúr-tul, s. m. The palm of the hand.

करताल kur-tál, s. m. ⎫ A musical in-
करतालो kur-tá-lee, s. f. ⎭ strument, a kind of small cymbal; the word may also imply beating time with the hands.

करती kúr-tee, s. f. The skin of a calf stuffed and placed near the mother to make her give milk.

करतूत kur-tóot, s. f. Action, business.

करदा kúr-da, s. m. Exchange, balance made to make up a deficiency in coin, or the difference between the price of new things and old given in exchange.

करदिखलाना kur-dikh-lána, v. a. To realize.

करधुमरी kur-dhúm-ree, s. f. A girdle, zone, cordon.

करन kúr-un, s. m. Lace cut into small pieces and put on a cap.

करनफूल kur-un-phóol, s. m. A kind of ear-ring.

करनहार kurunhár, s. m. Doer, maker.

करना kúr-na, v. a. To do, make, form, perform, execute, effect, act, administer, avail, set, thrust, use, cone. s. m. A kind of citron (Citrus medicus); making, doing, &c.

करनेवाला kurneywála, s. m. Maker, doer.

करबो kúr-bee, s. f. The stalk of joar or bajra (Holcus sorgum and spicatus).

करम kúr-um, ⎫ s. m. Business, act, ac-
कर्म kurm, ⎭ tion; fortune, fate, destiny, office; accus. case; hindoo worship, devotion; name of a bird. Kurumbhog, s. m. Fulfilling of destiny.

करमचारी kur-um-chá-ree, s. m. An inferior officer to collect the revenue from a certain division of a village, the village accountant.

करमेवा kurméywa, s. m. A kind of vegetable.

करलगूआ kur-lúg-oo-a, adj. Uxorious.

करलाना kur-lá-na, v. a. To effect, to settle. r. n. To shriek.

करवट kur-wút, s. f. Sideways, sleeping on the side, turning from side to side. Kurwut lena, To turn (in bed). Kurwut kurna, To turn over.

करवाना kur-wá-na, v. a. To cause to make or do.

करवाल kur-wál, ⎫ s. m. A rudder, a
करवारा kur-wá-ra, ⎭ paddle.

करवीर kur-wéer, s. m. A fragrant plant or flower (Oleander or Nerium odorum).

करशोथ kur-shóth, s. m. Œdematous swelling of the hands.

करसी kúr-see, s. f. Small lumps of cowdung dried for fuel.

करहा kur-há, s. f. The loins.

करांत kur-ánt, s. m. A saw.

करांती kur-án-tee, s. m. A sawyer.

करा kúr-a, adj. Hard, adulterated, false or bad (as coin).

कराकूल kur-a-kóol, s. m. A bird, a kind of heron or curlew.

कराना kur-á-na, v. a. To cause to be done or made, to actuate, to effect.

करायल kur-á-yul, s. m. Rosin, resin.

करारा kur-a-rá, adj. Hard, stiff.

कराल kur-ál, s. m. Rosin, pitch. adj. Great, large; high, lofty; formidable, terrible.

करांहना kur-áh-na, *v. n.* To sigh and utter ah! from pain, to groan, to moan.

कराही kur-á-hee, *s. f.* A flat vessel of iron, brass, or earth, in which food is boiled or fried. *Kurahee chatna,* To lick the pots (*from indigence or extreme avarice*); hence, applied as a reproach to a bridegroom if it rain on his wedding procession. *Kurahee lena,* A species of ordeal, in which oil is made boiling hot in the vessel above described, a small piece of gold, as a ring, is put in it, and the suspected person is to take it out. If he do this without injury to his hand, he is pronounced innocent.

करिल kúr-il, *s. m.* A sprout, a shoot.

करीर kur-éer, *s. m.* The shoot of a bamboo; a thorny plant growing in deserts and fed upon by camels (*Capparis aphylla*).

करील kur-éel, *s. m.* A plant (*Capparis spinosa*).

करुना kúr-oo-na, *s. f.* Tenderness, pity, compassion, mercy. *Kuroona-nidhan,* Abode of tenderness and mercy (*an epithet of the Deity*).

करुणात्मक kúroon-átmuk, *adj.* Compassionate, tender.

करुणामय kúroon-ámuy, *adj.* Gentle, compassionate.

करूआ kur-óo-a, *s. m.* An earthen pipkin, a pot with a spout. *Kurooa-chouth,* A *hindoo* holy-day celebrated in the month *Kartik.*

करेकर kur-ekúr, *adj.* Abreast.

करेरा kur-éra, *adj.* Hard, stiff, vehement.

करेला kur-éla, *s. m.* A vegetable of a bitter taste (*Momordica charantia*).

करैत kur-uyt, *s. m.* A snake (*of a very venemous kind*).

करोड़ kur-ór, ⎫ *adj.* Ten millions. *Kuror-*
करोर kur-ór, ⎭ *putee,* Possessor of a *crore* of rupees. *Kuror-khookh, s. m.* A liar.

करोरा kur-ó-ra, *s. m.* A tax-gatherer, an inspector, an overseer.

करोत kur-ót, *s. m.* A saw.

करोनी kur-ó-nee, *s. f.* Milk that sticks to the bottom of the pot after boiling.

करौंदा kur-óun-da, *s. m.* A fruit, the corinda (*Carissa carandus*).

कर्क kurk, *s. m.* A crab; the sign Cancer.

कर्कट kur-kút, *s. m.* A crab; a sign of the zodiac, *Cancer*; a kind of bird, the Numidian crane.

कर्कश kur-kúsh, *adj.* Violent; hard; intangible; cruel; unfeeling, unmerciful; harsh, unkind; miserly.

कर्का kur-ká, ⎫ *s. m.* Pæan, song of
कर्का kur-ká, ⎭ triumph.

कर्केतर kurk-étur, *s. m.* A kind of gem or precious stone.

कर्चूर kur-chóor, *s. m.* A plant (*Curcuma reclinata*).

कर्चूरक kur-chóo-ruk, *s. m.* Zedoary (*Curcuma zerumbet*).

कर्छनी kur-chhún-ee, *s. f.* An iron skimmer.

कर्छा kur-chhá, *s. m.* A large spoon, a ladle.

कर्छाल kur-chhál, *s. f.* A bound, spring, jump.

कर्छी kur-chhée, *s. f.* A spoon; a skein (*a ringlet*).

कर्छूल kur-chhóol, *s. f.* An iron spoon; a sword made of soft iron.

कर्रा kúr-ra, *adj.* Stiff, hard; harsh, obdurate.

कर्ण kurn, *s. m.* The ear; the helm of a boat, &c. *Kurn-phool, s. m.* A kind of ear-ring.

कर्णकीटी kurn-kéetee, ⎫ *s. f.* An insect
कर्णजलूका kurn-julóoka, ⎭ or worm with many feet, and of a reddish colour (*Julus cornifer*); a small centipede.

कर्णगूथ kurn-góoth, *s. m.* The wax of the ear.

कर्णदर्पण kurn-dúrpun, *s. m.* An ear-ring, an ornament of the ear.

कर्णधार kurn-dhár, *s. m.* A supercargo, pilot or helmsman.

कर्णपाक kurn-pák, *s. m.* Inflammation of the outer ear.

कर्णपाली kurn-pálee, *s. f.* An ornament of the ear, a garland or string of jewels pendent from it.

कर्णपूर kurn-póor, *s. m.* The capital of *Raja Kurn,* the ancient name of *Bhaugulpore.*

कर्णप्रतिनाह kurn-prutináh, *s. m.* A disease of the ear, suppression of the excretion or wax, which is supposed to have dissolved and to pass by the nose and mouth.

कर्णफल kurn-phúl, *s. m.* A sort of fish (*Ophiocephalus kurrawey*).

कर्णफूल kurn-phóol, *s. m.* A kind of ear-ring.

कर्णमद्गूर kurn-múdgoor, *s. m.* A sort of sheat-fish (*Silurus unitus*).

कर्णमल kurn-múl, *s. m.* The excretion or wax of the ear.

कर्णमुकूट kurn-mookóot, *s. m.* An ornament of the ear; an ear-ring.

कर्णमूल kurn-móol, *s. m.* A parotis, or swelling near the ear.

कर्णलतिका kurn-lutiká, *s. f.* The lobe of the ear.

कर्णवेधन kurn-véd-hun, *s. m.* Perforating the ears.

कर्णवेधनी kurn-ved-hun-ée, *s. f.* An instrument for perforating the ear.

कर्णशूल kurn-shóol, *s. m.* Ear-ache.

कर्णसाव kurn-sráv, *s. m.* Discharge of ichorous matter from the ear.

कर्णाट kur-nát, *s. m.* A country, the modern *Carnatic*; the name however was anciently applied to the central districts of the peninsula, including *Mysore*.

कर्णाटी kur-na-tée, *s. f.* One of the *raginees*, or female personifications of the musical modes.

कर्णालङ्कार kurn-alunkár, *s. m.* An earring, or ornament of the ear.

कर्णिनी kurninée, *s. f.* A disease of the uterus, prolapsus or polypus uteri.

कर्णी kúr-nee, *s. f.* Action, business; a trowel.

कर्णी kúrnee, *s. m.* The name of a mountain, one of the seven principal ranges of the mountains, dividing the universe.

कर्तरी kúrt-tur-ee, *s. f.* A pair of scissors, or shears.

कर्तव्य kurt-túv-yuh, *adj.* Proper to be done, what ought to be done, necessary, incumbent, practicable, proper, fit.

कर्तव्यता kurt-túv-yuta, *s. f.* Practicability, propriety, fitness, necessity, obligation.

कर्ता kúrt-ta, *s. m.* Maker, Creator (*the Divine Being*), author, doer, agent; nominative (*in gram.*); a proprietor, master; a husband.

कर्तार kurt-tár, *s. m.* The Creator, maker; an author, doer.

कर्तृ kúr-tri, *adj.* An agent, a doer, a maker.

कर्तृत्व kur-trít-wuh, *s. m.* Agency, management, rule, government.

कर्द kurd, कर्दम kur-dúm, } *s. m.* Mud, mire, clay.

कर्दन kurdún, *s. m.* Grumbling of the bowels, *borborygmi*.

कर्धनी kúr-dhun-ee, *s. f.* A waist-band, girdle, zone, cordon.

कर्पास kur-pás, *s. m.* Cotton.

कर्पासी kur-pás-ee, *s. f.* The cotton tree.

कर्पूर kur-póor, *s. m.* Camphor.

कर्पूरक kur-póo-ruk, कर्पूरक kur-bóo-ruk, } *s. m.* Zedoary (*Curcuma zerumbet*).

कर्पूरतैल kurpóor-tyl, *s. m.* Camphor liniment.

कर्पूरमणि kurpóor-múni, *s. m.* A white mineral used medicinally.

कर्बुदार kurboo-dár, *s. m.* Mountain ebony; blue barleria.

कर्बुरा kúrboora, *s. f.* Trumpet flower (*Bignonia suaveolens*); a sort of Basil (*Ocymum gratissimum*).

कर्म kurmm, करम kúr-um, } *s. m.* Action, act, office, fortune, fate, destiny; accusative case; hindoo worship, devotion; name of a bird. *Kurm-bhog, s. m.* Fulfilling of destiny.

कर्मकाण्ड kurm-kánd, *s. m.* The body of religious ceremonies, commanded in the hindoo laws, or established by custom.

कर्मकार kurm-kár, *adj.* A worker. *s. m.* A blacksmith.

कर्मकारक kurm-ká-ruk, *s. m.* One who does any work; accusative case.

कर्मच्युत kurm-chyóot, *adj.* Dismissed from office.

कर्मदुष्ट kurm-dóosht, *adj.* Immoral, disreputable.

कर्मभोग kurm-bhóg, *s. m.* Fulfilling of destiny; the suffering of the consequences of actions, whether good or bad.

कर्मयोग kurm-yóog, *s. m.* The fourth and present age of the world, the iron age.

कर्मविपाक kurm-vip-ák, *s. m.* The consequences of actions.

कर्मशील kurm-shéel, *adj.* Assiduous, laborious; one who perseveres in his duties without looking forward to their reward.

कर्मशुद्ध kurm-shóoddh, *s. m.* Approved occupation.

कर्मशूर kurm-shóor, *adj.* Assiduous, laborious.

कर्मसिद्धि kurm-síddhi, *s. f.* Success, accomplishment.

कर्माधर्मी kúrma-dhúrmee, *adj.* Devout, virtuous; fortunate, accidental.

कर्मिष्ठ kurm-íshth, *adj.* Active, assiduous, diligent.

कर्मी kúr-mee, *adj.* Relating to any work, doing works, fortunate.

कर्मेन्द्रिय kurm-éndri-yuh, *s. m.* An organ of action: five are reckoned, the hand, the foot, the larynx, or organ of the voice, the organ of generation and that of feculent excretion.

करा kurrá, *adj.* Hard, adulterated, false or bad (*as coin*).

करना kur-rá-na, *v. n.* To be hard or stiff.

कर्षक kúr-shuk, *adj.* A cultivator of the soil, one who lives by tillage.

कर्षण kúr-shun, *s. m.* Ploughing, cultivating the ground; drawing or attracting.

कर्षफल kursh-phúl, *s. m.* Beleric myrobalan (*Terminalia belerica*).

कर्षिणी kúr-shin-ee, *s. f.* A medicinal sort of moon plant; the bit of a bridle.

कल kul, *s. m.* To-morrow, yesterday; the fourth period of the *hindoos*. *s. f.* Ease, tranquillity, peace, relief, quiet, rest; a trap, a machine, a lock. *Kul kee bat,* News of yesterday, something that happened very lately. *Kul-mukul, s. f.* Uneasiness, disquiet, trouble. *Kul ka admee,* An automaton, a puppet; (*met.*) a very weak person. *Kul ka ghora,* A very well trained and obedient horse.

कलकल kúl-kul, *s. m.* Wrangling; a confused noise, the murmuring or buz of a crowd.

कलकी kúl-kee, *s. m.* The tenth *hindoo* incarnation, yet to happen. The deity is expected to assume the appearance of a *brahmun*, who is to be born in the town of *Sumbhul,* and in the family of *Vishnoo Surma*; he will ride on horseback and put to death all the wicked.

कलगा kúl-ga, *s. m.* A flower, the cockscomb (*Amaranthus*), prince's feather.

कलंक kúl-unk, *s. m.* A spot or mark, abuse, calumny, accusation, reflection, aspersion, suspicion, scandal, obloquy, defamation, blemish, brand, stigma.

कलंकित kul-unkít, *adj.* Calumniated, defamed.

कलंकिनी kul-ún-kin-ee, *f.*
कलंकी kul-ún-kee, *m.* } *adj.* Stained, blemished, charged with any thing disgraceful; liable to reproach; disgraced, reviled.

कलजुहवा kul-júh-wan, *adj.* Dark-complexioned, sallow.

कलजिभा kul-jíb-ha, *adj.* Malignant, ill-omened, whose curses prevail.

कलुंज kul-únj, *adj.* An animal struck with a poisoned weapon.

कलत्र kul-útr, *s. f.* A wife.

कलप kúl-up, *s. m.* Die for the hair; starch.

कलपना kúl-up-na, *v. n.* To be grieved, to grieve.

कलपाना kul-pá-na, *v. a.* To grieve, to distress.

कलम kúl-um, *s. m.* A pen, a reed for writing with.

कलमकल kul-mukúl, *s. f.* Distraction, trouble.

कलमलाना kul-mul-á-na, *v. n.* To fidget, to writhe, to flutter.

कलमी kúl-mee, *s. f.* Convolvulus repens, used as an esculent vegetable.

कलवल kúl-wul, *s. f.* Misfortune, calamity.

कलवार kul-wár, *s. m.* A distiller, a vender of spirituous liquors.

कलुष kúl-ush, *s. m.* A dome, cupola, spire, or the ornament on the top of a dome, a pinnacle; a water-pot. *Kulus sthapun kurna, v. a.* To make an offering of a jar of water to any deity: five twigs of the following trees deemed sacred being previously placed in it, viz. the *Ushwutth* (*Ficus Religiosa*), *Vut* (*Ficus Indica*), *Oodoombur* (*Ficus Glomerata*), *Shumee* (*Mimosa Albida*), and *Amra* (*Hog-plum*) or mango.

कलुश kúl-sha, *s. m.* A pinnacle.

कलशिरा kul-shír-a, *adj.* Block-headed. *s. m.* Man.

कलसी kúl-see, *s. f.* A water-pot, a little spire on the top of a dome or pinnacle.

कलह kúl-uh, *s. m.* Quarrel, strife, contention.

कलहकार kúluh-kár, *s. m.* Quarrelsome, turbulent.

कलहकारिणी kúluh-kárinee, *s. f.* A quarrelsome woman.

कलहकारी kúluh-káree, *adj.* Quarrelsome, factious, turbulent.

कलहारा kuluhára, *adj.* Quarrelsome, contentious.

कलही kúl-uh-ee, *s. f.* A scold, a termagant, a vixen.

कला kúl-a, *s. f.* The sixteenth part of the moon's diameter, a digit of the moon; a division of time, about eight seconds, the sixtieth part of a degree; part, portion; art, trick. *Kula-basee, s. f.* Turning over head and heels, tumbling, juggling. *Kula nuh budna,* To disobey, decline, not to succeed. *Kula nuh lugna,* Not to have an advantage, not to avail.

कलाई kul-á-ee, *s. f.* Wrist; a kind of pulse; leguminous seeds in general.

कलाना kul-á-na, *v. a.* To parch grain.

कलाप kul-áp, *s. m.* Assemblage, multitude; a grammar of the *Sunskrit* language.

कलाबत्तून kúl-a-buttóon, *s. m.* Gold thread, a silver thread.

कलार kul-ár, *s. m.* A distiller, a seller of spirituous liquors, a tavern-keeper, an innkeeper.

कलारिन kul-ár-in, *s. f.* Female of *Kular.*

कलावन्त kul-a-wúnt, *s. m.* A kind of singer or musician.

कलाहक kul-á-huk, *s. m.* A musical instrument.

कलि kúli, *s. m.* The fourth age of the world, according to the *hindoos,* the iron age or that of vice: the commencement of the *Kuli-yoog* or age is placed about 3101 years anterior to the Christian era, the number of its years are 432,000, at the expiration of which the world is to be destroyed.

कलि kúl-i, }
कली kúl-ee, } *s. f.* A bud, an unblown flower blossom ; quicklime ; the fourth age of the world.

कलिक kúlik, *s. m.* A curlew.

कलिंग kúl-ing, *s. m.* The febrifuge nut plant (*Cæsalpinia* or *Guilandina Bonducella*) ; the name of a country : the name *Kuling* is applied in the *Poorans* to several places, but it especially signifies a district on the Coromandel coast, extending from below *Cuttack* to the vicinity of *Madras.*

कलिंगा kúl-in-ga, *s. f.* A plant, commonly called *Teoree*, the bark of which is used as a purgative.

कलियाना kul-iyá-na, *v. n.* To blossom, to bloom, to bud.

कलियूग kúli-yóog, *s. m.* The fourth or present age of the world, which Mr. Bently supposes to have commenced 3102 years before the Christian era.

कली kúl-ee, *s. f.* A bud, an unblown flower blossom ; quicklime ; the *Kuli-yoog* or 4th age of the *hindoos.*

कलीसा kuléesa, *s. m.* A christian church, a congregation of believers.

कलूटा kul-óo-ta, *adj.* Black (*complexioned*).

कलेऊ kul-éoo, *s. m.* Cold meat, stale victuals, a luncheon, a breakfast.

कलेजा kul-éj-a, *s. m.* The liver ; (*met.*) courage, spirit, magnanimity, heart. *Kuleja oolut-na,* To be fatigued with excessive vomiting. *Kuleja phutna,* To be disturbed with grief or jealousy. *Kuleja thunda kurna,* To obtain one's wish, to get ease. *Kuleja julna kisee ka,* To suffer sorrow, to mourn. *Kuleja kampna,* To be afraid, to suffer cold. *Kuleja pur samp phirna,* To suffer jealousy or envy. *Kuleja seh luga rukhna,* To caress, embrace, love exceedingly. *Kulejeh men dal rukhna,* To love or esteem exceedingly.

कलेवर kul-éwur, *s. m.* The body.

कलेवा kul-é-wa, *s. m.* Cold meat, stale victuals, a luncheon, a breakfast.

कलेस kul-és, *s. m.* Sickness, pain, trouble, distress, vexation, affliction, torment, quarrel, contention.

कलोर kul-ór, *s. m.* A heifer.

कलोल kul-ól, *s. f.* Wantonness, friskiness, play, sport, frolic, gambol.

कलोंजी kul-óun-jee, *s. f.* A small, blackish, triangular, pyramidical shaped seed of a very pungent smell used medicinally (*Nigella Indica*)

कल्क kulk, *s. m.* Sediment, the deposit of oil, ghee, &c., dirt, filth ; ordure, fæces ; sin, fraud ; the *Beleric myrobalan* ; the wax of the ear. *adj.* Sinful, wicked.

कल्प kulp, *s. m.* A *shastr* or sacred work, one of the six *Vedangs,* and comprehending the description of religious rites ; a day and night of *Bruhma,* a period of 4,320,000,000 of solar sydereal years or years of mortals, measuring the duration of the world, and as many, the interval of its annihilation ; a destruction of the world ; a sacred precept, practice prescribed by the *Veds* for effecting certain consequences ; optionality, alternative, doubt ; resolve, purpose, any act of determination ; propriety, fitness.

कल्पतरु kulp-túroo, }
कल्पवृक्ष kulp-bríksh, } *s. m.* One of the fabulous trees of *Indru's* heaven ; a tree which yields whatever may be desired.

कल्पक्षय kulp-kshúy, *s. m.* The destruction of all things, the end of the world.

कल्पना kúlpun-a, *s. m.* A scheme, a contrivance, a plan, a forgery, an imitation.

कल्पांत kulp-ánt, *s. m.* The destruction of the world, the end of the *Kulp,* or four ages of its existence.

कल्पित kúl-pit, *adj.* Made, arranged, artificially produced or constructed.

कल्युह kúlyuh, *s. m.* The dawn or break of day. *adv.* Yesterday, to-morrow. *adj.* Healthy, recovered from sickness ; deaf and dumb.

कल्याण kul-yán, *s. m.* Welfare, happiness, prosperity, good fortune ; name of a musical mode sung at night ; a leguminous shrub (*Glycine debilis*). *adj.* Happy, well, right, prosperous, lucky.

कल्याणवचन kulyán-vúchun, *s. m.* Good wishes.

कल्याणी kulyan-ée, *adj.* Happy, lucky, prosperous ; auspicious, propitious.

कल्लर kúl-lur, *adj.* Barren, sterile (*land*) ; salt (*as food*).

कल्लाना kul-lá-na, *v. n.* To burn, to be inflamed (*as the skin by rubbing pepper, &c. on it*).

कल्लापूरवर kúlla-púrwur, *s. m.* A kind of sweetmeat.

कल्लोल kullól, *s. m.* Joy, happiness, pleasure.

कल्ह kulh, *s. m.* Yesterday, to-morrow.

कवच kúwuch, *s. m.* Armour, mail ; a drum used in battle, or kettle drum ; a tree (*Hibiscus populneoides*) ; an amulet, a writing carried about the person as a charm.

कवचपत्र kúwuch-pútr, *s. m.* A tree, commonly called *Bhojputr :* pieces of the bark of this tree inscribed with mystical verses serve as amulets, &c.

कवयी kúwuyee, *s. f.* A kind of flat fish, remarkable for going by land from one spot to another (*Coius coboius*).

कवꕠ kúwul, ⎱ *s. m.* A mouthful ; a kind
कवꕠ kúwuk, ⎰ of fish ; an astringent
wash for cleaning the mouth, a gargle.

कवि kúvi, *s. m.* A poet.

कविता kúvit-a, ⎱ *s. f.* Poetry, a poem.
कविताई kuvit-áee, ⎰

कꗪꕡ kush-ér-oo, *s. m.* A kind of grass
(*Scirpus kysoor*); a root (*Cyperus tuberosus*) ;
one of the nine divisions of *Jumboo dweep*.

कꗪमोर kush-méer, *s. m.* The name of a
country, *Cashmeer*.

कꗪयꕠ kúsh-yup, *s. m.* The name of a *mooni* or deified sage, the son of *Murichi* and father
of the immortals, gods and devils ; a kind of deer.

कꗪ kush, *s. m.* The touchstone ; assay ;
the decoction of a colouring substance.

कꗪꕠꕠ kushún, *s. m.* Touch or test of gold
by the touchstone.

कꗪायꕠꕠ kusháyuh, *s. m.* Astringency.

कꗪावꕠ kush-á-wut, *s. f.* An astringent.

कꗪोटी kush-óu-tee, *s. f.* A touchstone.

कꗪꕠ kusht, *s. m.* Want, penury, affliction,
pain, distress, hardship, vehemence, violence,
acuteness (*of pain*), agony, difficulty ; bodily pain
or uneasiness.

कꗪꕠꕠ kusht-kúr, *adj.* Giving pain or
trouble.

कꗪꕠ kushtí, *s. f.* Test, trial ; pain, trouble.

कꗪꕠ kush-tée, *adj.* Suffering a painful and
tedious labour (*a woman*) ; afflicted, suffering, in
want.

कꕠ kus, *s. m.* Strength, power ; assay, a
touchstone ; the decoction of a colouring substance.

कꕠꕠ kús-uk, *s. f.* Pain, stitch, affliction.

कꕠꕠꕠ kús-uk-na, *v. n.* To suffer pain, to
be painful.

कꕠकꕠꕠ kus-kús-a, *adj.* Gritty, sandy (*as
bread*).

कꕠꕠꕠ kús-koot, *s. m.* Bell-metal.

कꕠꕠ kús-un, *s. m.* Rack, torment, torture.

कꕠꕠ kús-na, *v. a.* To tighten, tie, brace ;
to assay, try, prove, examine ; to fry in melted
butter. *s. m.* A bundle, wallet.

कꕠमꕠꕠꕠ kus-mus-ána, *v. n.* To move, to
shake.

कꕠꕠꕠ kus-wá-na, *v. a.* To cause to
tighten, tie, bind, &c.

कꕠꕠ kús-a, *adj.* Tight, tense, strait.

कꕠꕠ kus-á-ee, *s. m.* A butcher. *adj.*
Cruel, hard-hearted.

कꕠꕠꕠ kus-á-na, *v. a.* To cause to try, to
prove or assay ; to cause to tighten. *v. n.* To be
spoiled (*curds, &c.*) by standing in a metal vessel.

कꕠꕠया kus-á-ya, *adj.* Ready, tied up.

कꕠꕠꕠ kus-ár, *s. m.* A sweetmeat.

कꕠꕠꕠ kus-áo, *s. m.* Astringency.

कꕠꕠवꕠ kusawút, ⎱ *s. f.* An astringent.
कꕠꕠꕠꕠ kusahút, ⎰

कꕠꕠꕠ kus-ee-lá. *adj.* Strong, vigorous.

कꕠꕠꕠ kus-ées, *s. m.* Martial vitriol (*Sulphas ferri*).

कꕠꕠꕠꕠꕠ kús-eh-kus-áeh, *part.* Tied up,
prepared, ready.

कꕠꕠꕠ kus-ér-a, *s. m.* A brazier or pewterer.

कꕠꕠꕠ kus-ér-oo, *s. m.* A root (*Cyperus tuberosus*).

कꕠꕠꕠ kus-él-a, *adj.* Astringent.

कꕠꕠꕠꕠ kus-óun-dee, *s. f.* A kind of pickle ;
a plant (*Cassia sophera*).

कꕠꕠꕠ kus-óu-tee, *s. f.* A touchstone.

कꕠꕠꕠ kus-tóo-ra, *s. f.* An oyster.

कꕠꕠꕠ kus-tóo-ree, *s. f.* Musk, the animal
perfume so called, as brought from *Cashmeer*, *Nepal*, and western *Assam*, and *Bootan*, the latter is
said to be the best.

कꕠꕠ kúh-na, *v. a.* To tell, say, recount,
relate, bid, order, call, affirm, assert, aver, avow,
declare, acquaint, advise, speak. *s. m.* Saying, advice, order. *Kuh dena*, To tell, bid, order, &c.

कꕠꕠावꕠ kuh-ná-wut, *s. f.* A proverb, saying, an adage ; style.

कꕠꕠꕠ kuhúr-na, *v. n.* To groan.

कꕠꕠꕠꕠ kuh-rá-na, *v. n.* To groan (*as a
sick person*).

कꕠꕠꕠꕠ kuh-lá-na, *v. a.* To cause to say,
to call, to be called ; to parch. *v. n.* To wither ; to
become weak, to be lazy.

कꕠꕠꕠ ꕠꕠꕠ kuh-la-bhéj-na, *v. a.* To send
a message, to send and tell, to inform.

कꕠꕠꕠ kuh-wá-na, *v. a.* To cause to
speak.

कꕠꕠ kuhán, *adv.* Where? *Kuhan-tuk*,
How far? how long? to what degree? *Kuhan seh*,
Whence? *Kuhan ka kuhan*, To what degree! extremely, immensely.

कꕠꕠ kúha, *s. m.* Order, leave, saying,
word, call, confession, affirmation, advice. *pron.*
What? which? how? why?

कꕠꕠकꕠꕠ kuha-kuhée, *s. f.* Altercation,
expostulation.

कꕠꕠꕠ kuhána, *v. a.* To cause to speak, to
cause to tell, to be called.

कꕠꕠꕠ kuhánee, *s. f.* A tale, story, fable.

कꕠꕠꕠ kuhár, *s. m.* A palkee-bearer.

कꕠꕠꕠꕠ kuháwut, *s. f.* A proverb, saying,
an adage.

कषासूतन kuha-sóonee, *s. f.* Conversation, discussion, altercation.

कषीं kuhéen, *adv.* Somewhere, any where, wherever. *Kuheen nuh kuheen,* Somewhere or other.

कषी kuhée, *s. f.* A foraging party.

कषूं kuhóon, *adv.* Somewhere, anywhere.

कष kuksh, *s. m.* The arm-pit, the side or flank.

कषा kukshá, *s. f.* The end of the lower garment, which after the cloth is carried round the body is brought up behind and tucked into the waistband; a woman's girdle or zone.

का ka, *pron.* Whom? what? which? *postpos.* Of, belonging to. [stone.

कांकर kán-kur, *s. m.* A nodule of lime-

कंख kankh, *s. f.* The armpit.

कांखना kánkhna, *v. n.* To grunt.

कांखा kánkha, *s. m.* Straining (*when at stool, &c.*)

कांगन kán-gun, } *s. m.* A plant or its
कांगनी káng-nee, } seed (*Panicum italicum*).

कांगरी káng-ree, *s. f.* A chafing-dish.

कंच kanch, *s. m.* Glass; a disorder in which the *intestinum rectum* is prolapsed; a prolapsus ani. *Kanch nikulna, Ani procidentia.*

कांचा kancha, *adj.* Raw.

कांछा kánchha, *s. f.* Wish, desire, inclination.

कांजी kán-jee, *s. f.* A kind of pickle or vinegar made by steeping rice in water and letting the liquor ferment, which is kept for use sometimes twenty years.

कांटा kán-ta, *s. m.* A thorn, spine; a fork; small (*goldsmith's or apothecary's*) scales; a spur; a type; the tongue of a balance; fishing-hook; a fish-bone. *Kanta sa nikul jana,* To be freed from distress or injury. *Kanton pur ghuseetna,* (*lit. to drag upon thorns*), To extol or exalt one above his merits; (*used by a person who from humility disclaims the praises bestowed on him.*) *Kanteh boneh,* (*lit. to plant thorns*), To prepare distress or misfortune for one's self.

कांठ kán-tha, *adj.* Near, proximate.

कांड kand, *s. m.* A section, part, division; sport, exhibition.

कांडना kánr-na, *v. a.* To tread, to trample.

कांडली kánd-lee, *s. f.* Purslain (*Portulaca*).

कांडी kán-dee, *s. f.* A rafter; a sentence of the *Vedas.*

कांदा kán-da, *s. m.* An onion.

कांडू kán-doo, *s. m.* A sugar-boiler; a tribe whose business it is to fry corn, prepare sweetmeats, &c.

कांदो kán-do, *s. m.* Mud, slime.

कांधना kándh na, *v. a.* To assist, to protect.

कांधा kán-dha, *s. m.* The shoulder. *Kandha hilana,* To shrug up the shoulders. *Kandha dena,* To assist; to carry away the dead.

कांपना kámp-na, *v. n.* To shiver, tremble, quake, shake.

कांस kans, *s. f.* A species of grass (*Saccharun spontaneum*).

कांसा kán-sa, } *s. m.* Bell-metal, white
कांस्य káns-yuh, } copper or brass, queen's-metal, any amalgam of zinc and copper.

कांस्यकार kansyukár, *s. m.* A brazier, a pewterer, a worker in white or bell-metal.

कांसमील kansyunéel, *s. m.* Blue vitriol considered as a collyrium.

कांक्षा kánk-sha, *s. f.* Wish, desire, inclination.

काई káee, *s. f.* The green scum on the surface of stagnant pools, or the green mould that sticks to walls and pavements, scum, fur, paste.

कायफल káe-phul, *s. m.* A medicine, an aromatic bark (*Fragaria vesca*).

काक kak, *s. m.* A crow. *Kakpuksh, s. m.* Tresses.

काकरा kák-rá, *s. m.* A kind of leather.

काकरा शिंगी kákra-síngee, *s. f.* A medicine.

काकुन kakún, *s. m.* A leprosy with black and red spots, considered incurable.

काकपीलु kak-péeloo, *s. m.* A kind of ebony.

काकवन्ध्या kak-búndhya, *s. f.* A woman that bears only one child.

काकमद्गु kak-múdgoo, *s. m.* A water-hen, a gallinule.

काकमर्द kak-múrd, *s. m.* The colocynth or bitter apple.

काका ká-ka, *s. m.* A paternal uncle.

काकी ká-kee, *s. f.* Aunt.

काकूंजकी ka-kóonj-kee, *s. f.* Ranunculus.

काकोल kakól, *s. m.* A poisonous substance of a black colour, possibly the berry of the Cocculus Indicus; a division of the infernal regions or hell.

काकोली kakólee, *s. f.* A vegetable substance used in medicine, described as sweet and cooling, allaying fever, removing phlegm, &c., it is said to be a root brought from *Nepal* or *Morung.*

काख kakh, *s. f.* The armpit.

काख चखाई kakh-ulaee, *s. f.* A painful suppurating tumour in the armpit.

काग kag, *s. m.* A crow; a raven.

कच kach, *s. m.* Glass; alkaline ashes, any salt of potash or soda in a glassy or crystalline state; crystal, quartz or glass; a disease of the eyes.

कचमनि kach-múni, *s. m.* Crystal, quartz.

कचमल kach múl, *s. m.* Black salt or soda.

कचलवन kach-lúvun, *s. m.* Black salt, a medicinal salt, prepared by calcining fossil salt and the fruit of the emblic myrobalan together: it consists chiefly of muriate of soda, with a small quantity of iron, lime and sulphur, and is a tonic aperient.

कचा ká-cha, *adj.* Unripe, raw, simple, unknowing.

कछ kachh, *s. m.* A cloth worn round the hips passing between the legs and tucked in behind; the upper part of the thigh.

कछन káchhun, *s. f.* A female gardener.

कछना káchh-na, *v. a.* To bind on or tie up the *Kachh* or upper part of the thigh; to skin, to gather.

कछनी káchh-nee, *s. f.* A cloth worn over the *Kachh*, or upper part of the thigh.

कछी kách-hee, *s. m.* A gardener who cultivates and sells pot-herbs.

कज kaj, *s. m.* Business, occupation, a work, an action, affair.

काजल kájul, *s. m.* Lampblack (*with which the eyelids are painted*). *Kajul kee kothree*, A place from going into which, on an affair, the being engaged in which, brings disgrace or suspicion on one's character.

काजी ká-jee, *adj.* Busy, employed.

काजे ká-jeh, *prep.* By reason of, for the sake of.

कांचन kán-chun, *s. m.* Gold. *adj.* Golden, of gold.

कांचनमय kánchun-muy, *adj.* Golden.

कट kat, *s. f.* A cut, incision, execution; scum; virulence. *Kat kurna, v. a.* To wound, to cut. *Kat khana,* To bite.

कटकूट kat-kóot, *s. f.* Clippings, chips, scraps. *Katkoot kurna,* To clip, cut out; to deduct.

काटना kát-na, *v. a.* To cut, clip; to bite, corrode, erode; to reap; to saw; to stop, stay; to waste, spend, pass away (*time*), to pass (*a road*); to interrupt, intercept; to shame, make ashamed. *Kat dalna,* To cut off, amputate.

काटो katóo, *s. m.* Cutter. *adj.* Corrosive.

काठ kath, *s. m.* Wood, timber, stock, block, a pair of stocks; a scabbard. *Kath-pootles, s. f.* A puppet, a toy. *Kat chubana,* To fare hardly. *Kath ka oolloo, s. m.* A sad blockhead. *adj.* Impenetrable, blockhead. *Kath kee bhumbo, s. f.* A sad blockhead (*woman*). *Kath keera,* A bug.

L

Kath men paon dena, To be imprisoned, to be in the stocks. *Kath menduk,* A toad. *Kath hona,* To pine away; to be petrified with astonishment. *Kath kubar,* Wooden articles.

काठरा káth-ra, *s. m.* A wooden pot.

काठिन्य kat-hín-yuh, *s. f.* Difficulty; hardness; cruelty.

काठी kát-hee, *s. f.* Body; scabbard; shape; wood, timber; appearance, person; a saddle.

कारा ká-ra, *s. m.* A young buffalo.

कढ karh, *s. m.* Membrum virile.

कढना kárh-na, *v. a.* To draw forth (*as a sword*), to draw, draw off, skin, take out, extricate; to draw lines or figures, work flowers on cloth, draw figures in needle-work, to draw, paint, delineate.

कढा kár-ha, *s. m.* A decoction.

काना ká-na, *adj.* Blind of one eye, one-eyed. (*Fruits, nuts, &c.*) whose kernel is rotten, or which has no kernel; foolish, stupid. *Kunabatee kurna,* To talk or whisper in the ear; to consult, advise. *Kana-phooses, s. f.* Whispering. *Kana-teeree, s. f.* The name of a grass. *Kanakanee kurna,* To whisper. *Kanes-kouree,* A cowrie with a hole in it.

कानी ká-nee, *adj. f.* A woman blind of one eye.

कांड kand, *s. m.* A chapter, a section, part, division; sport, exhibition.

कातना kát-na, *v. a.* To spin.

कातर ká-tur, *adj.* Distressed, agitated with distress, confused, perplexed, disordered; timid, timorous, gentle. *s. m.* A large kind of fish (*Cyprinus catla*).

कातरता katurtá, *s. f.* Timidity, agitation.

कातिक ká-tik, *s. m.* The second or seventh *hindoo* month (*October-November*) when the moon is full near *Krittika* or the Pleiades.

कादर ká-dur, *adj.* Timid, timorous, confused, distressed.

कादराए kaduráee, ⎫ *s. f.* Timidity, timorousness.
कादरी ká-dur-ee, ⎭

कादा kada, ⎫ *s. m.* Slime, mud, mire.
कादो ká-dou, ⎭

कान kan, *s. m.* The ear. *adj.* Blind of one eye. *Kan metna,* To pull the ears, chastise. *Kan bhurna,* To excite dissention by tale-bearing. *Kan pur joon nu-chulna,* To be very negligent or careless. *Kan pur rukhna,* To remember; to abstain. *Kan pur hath dhurna,* To refuse, deny. *Kan pukurna,* To confess inferiority. *Kan phootna, v. n.* To be deaf. *Kan phorna,* To make a noise. *Kan phoonkun,* To tell tales, to excite quarrels; to tutor. *Kan jhookana,* To desire to hear. *Kan dhurna,* To hear, listen, attend, be attentive. *Kan dubakur chuleh jana*, To run away. *Kan dubana*, To turn back the ears, as a horse does when preparing to bite. *Kan deh soonna*, To hear attentively. *Kun dena*, To hear, to be attentive. *Kan sulaee*, *s. f.* Name of an insect. *Kan ka purda*, The tympanum. *Kan katna*, To get the better of, surpass, overcome, outwit. *Kan khureh kona*, To be alarmed. *Kan khol dena*, (*lit.*) To open one's ears ; to inform ; to make acquainted with, warn, caution. *Kun lugna*, To get into one's confidence. *Kan mulna*, To admonish, punish, chastise. *Kun-myl*, *s. m.* Ear-wax. *Kan-myl-wala*, A person whose employment it is to pick or clean the ears. *Kan men oonglee deh ruhna*, To stop one's ears, to turn a deaf ear to what is said. *Kan men bat marna*, To pretend not to hear. *Kan men purna*, To be heard (*a speech*). *Kan men tel dalna*, (*lit.* to pour oil in the ear,) To pretend not to hear. *Kan men tel dalkur so ruhna*, To be inattentive or negligent. *Kan men kuhna*, To whisper, to tell. *Kan nuh hilana*, To be silent. *Kanoukan kuhna*, To whisper. *Kan hilana*, To acquiesce in. *Kan honeh*, To understand, comprehend, be warned or take example.

कान kan, *s. f.* Modesty, shame, respect. *s. m.* A husband. *Kan kurna*, To be ashamed. *Kan chhorna*, To be impudent. *Kan nuh kurna*, To treat with disrespect.

कानन ká-nun, *s. m.* A forest, desert, wood.

कानफल kán-phul, *s. m.* A fruit.

कानी ká-nee, *s. f.* Resentment, spite.

कान्त kant, *s. m.* Husband. *adj.* Pleasing, agreeable, beautiful.

कान्ता kán-ta, *s. f.* Wife, beloved ; beauty, splendor ; light, a lovely or desirable woman.

कान्ति kánti, *s. f.* Splendour, lustre.

कान्यकुब kanyu-kóobj, *s. m.* A country, the modern *Kunouj*.

कान्ह kanh, *s. m.* A husband ; one of the names of *Krishn*.

कान्हड़ा kánh-ra, *s. m.* A musical mode ; a kind of nightingale.

कापुरुष ká-poo-róosh, *adj.* A contemptible man.

काफल ká-phul, *s. m.* A bitter seed.

काविष ká-bish, *s. f.* An earth with which earthen ware is varnished.

काबेरी ka-bér-ee, *n. prop.* Name of a river, the *Carery*.

काम kam, *s. m.* Desire, wish, inclination ; the god of love, Cupid ; business, action, act, deed, affair, matter, work, use, occupation, employment ; packet, mail, post-bag. *Kam ana*, To come into use, be of use, avail, stand in stead, to be wanted ; to be smitten, to be slain in the field. *Kam tumam kurna*, To accomplish, to finish ; to kill, to make away with. *Kam tumam hona*, To

be finished, killed, or made away with. *Kam chulana*, To carry on business. *Kam rukhna*, To make use of. *Kamkaj*, Business, occupation. *Kamkajee*, *adj.* Laborious, active, alert. *Kamkel*, *s. f.* Amorous dalliance, coition. *Kam men lana*, To employ, to use. *Kam nikalna*, To carry into effect, to accomplish one's desire.

कामकेलि kam-kéli, *s. f.* Amorous dalliance, coition.

कामदेव kam-déo, *n. prop.* Cupid, the son of *Vishnoo*, and *Rookminee*, and husband of *Ruti* (*Venus*).

कामधेनु kam-dhén-oo, *n. prop.* A cow belonging to *Indr*, said to grant every thing requested of her ; a cow that gives much milk.

कामना kám-na, *s. f.* Desire, wish, inclination.

कामयित्री kamyitrí, *adj.* Libidinous, lustful, desirous.

कामराज kam-ráj, *s. m.* Sonchus.

कामरी kám-ree, *s. f.* A blanket.

कामरूप kam-róop, *s. m.* A district lying east of Bengal, formerly independent, now part of Assam. *adj.* Pleasing, beautiful ; taking any or every shape at will.

कामरूपिन् kam-róop-in, *adj.* Pleasing, beautiful.

कामरूपी kam-róop-ee, *adj.* Pleasing, beautiful ; a native of *Camroop*.

कामला kamulá, *s. f.* A complaint, jaundice, excessive secretion or obstruction of bile.

कामातुर kam-á-toor, } *adj.* Distracted or
कामार्त kamárt, } agitated with love or lust, lascivious, libidinous, lustful.

कामान्ध kam-ándh, *adj.* Blind by lust, lustful.

कामारि kamári, *s. m.* A mineral substance used in medicine, a sort of pyrites.

कामार्थी kam-ár-thee, *s. m.* A person who carries baskets filled with Ganges water.

कामिन् ká-min, *s. m.* An amorous man, an uxorious husband ; the ruddy goose, a pigeon, a sparrow ; a boy dressed in female attire who dances in the season of the *holes*.

कामिनी ká-min-ee, *s. f.* A loving or affectionate woman. *adj.* Libidinous, cupidinous.

कामी ká-mee, *adj.* Libidinous, lustful, impassioned, fond, wanton ; cupidinous ; loving ; busy. *s. f.* A lump of gold.

कामुक ká-mook, *adj.* Cupidinous, desirous, lustful, libidinous.

कामुकी ká-moo-kee, *s. f.* A woman libidinous or lustful.

कामोदक ka-mó-duk, *s. m.* Oblation of water to deceased friends, &c., exclusive of those for whom it is directed by law.

कामोदा ka-mó-da, *s. f.* A *raginee*, one of the female personifications of the musical modes, sung in the night.

काम्पना kamp-ná, *v. n.* To shiver, tremble, quake, shake.

काम्बोज kam-bój, *s. m.* A horse of the breed of *Camboge. n. prop.* A country in the north of India, *Camboge, Cambay,* or *Khumbach.*

काम्य kám-yuh, *adj.* Agreeable, desirable, amiable.

काम्यकर्म kám-yuh-kurm, *s. m.* A supererogatory work performed at pleasure or through the desire of some advantage.

काम्यदान kám-yuh-dan, *s. m.* An acceptable or desirable gift.

कायुः kayuh, *s. m.* } The body, appearance,
काया kaya, *s. f.* } person.

कायक ká-yuk, *adj.* Bodily, personal.

कायफल káe-phul, *s. m.* A medicine, an aromatic bark (*Fragaria vesca*).

कायर ká-yur, *adj.* Cowardly, timid, timorous.

कायस्थ ká-yusth, *s. m.* The Supreme Being; a cast or tribe, the *Cayeth* or writer caste, proceeding from a *Kshuttree* father, and *Soodr* mother.

काया ká-ya, *s. f.* The body, appearance, person.

कारक ká-ruk, *adj.* An agent, acting, doing. *s. m.* Action, especially in grammar; case (*in gram.*)

कारज ká-ruj, *s. m.* Business, an action, affair, work, profession, &c.

कारण ká-run, *s. m.* Cause, motive, principle; account, reason, occasion, action, agency; an instrument or means.

कारा ká-ra, *s. m.* A black snake. *adj.* Black.

कारागार ka-ra-gár, *s. m.* A gaol, a place of confinement. [doer.

कारी ká-ree, (*in comp.*) Making, maker,

कारू ká-roo, } *adj.* An artist, an
कारूकर ka-roo-kúr, } artificer, an agent, a maker, a doer.

कारूनिक ká-roo-nik, *adj.* Compassionate, tender, kind.

कार्त्तवीर्य kárttuh-béeryuh, *s. m.* A king, also called *Urjoon*, a celebrated hero, distinct from the *Pandoo* prince; one of the *Jyn Chukruvurtees* or emperors of the world.

कार्तिक kárt-tik, *s. m.* The eighth month (*October—November*) when the moon is full near the Pleiades.

कार्तिकोत्सव kart-tik-ót-suv, *s. m.* The day of full moon in the month *Cartik*, a festival.

L 2

कार्पण्य kar-pún-yuh, *s. m.* Poverty, indigence.

कार्पास kar-pás, *s. f.* The cotton plant (*Gossypeum*); cotton cloth, &c.

कार्पासी kar-pá-see, *adj.* Made of cotton, cottony, &c.

कार्मिक kárm-mik, *adj.* Worked, embroidered, intermixed with coloured thread (*cloth, &c.*)

कार्मुक kárm-mook, *s. m.* A bow.

कार्य kár-yuh, } *s. m.* Cause, origin; mo-
—— karj, } tive, object; affair, business, an action, a work, profession, &c.

कार्यचिन्ता karj-chínta, *s. f.* Prudence, caution, consideration.

कार्यसिद्धि karj-síddhi, *s. f.* Accomplishment, success, fulfilment of any object or purpose.

कार्षक kár-shuk, *s. m.* A husbandman.

कार्षापण kár-sha-pun, *s. m.* A weight or measure of silver, equal to 16 *puns* of *cowries*; a weight of copper, equal to 80 *Ruttees*; a weight of shells equal to the same number of *cowries*; a husbandman.

कार्षिक kár-shik, *s. m.* A weight; a husbandman.

काल kal, *s. m.* Time; a name of *Yumuh* or *Jum*, the supposed regent of the dead; death; season, age; dearth, famine; angel of death; calamity; (*met.*) a snake; (*in Bruj*) To-morrow. *Kal-bitana*, or —*katna*, or —*gunwana*, To waste one's time, to spend time. *Kal-bus hona*, To be in the hands of death, to be seized by fate. *Kal-purna*, The coming or happening of a famine.

कालक ká-luk, *s. f.* Blackness; one of the expressions of quantity (*corresponding to our a, b, x, y, &c.*) in *Beej gunit*, or Algebra; freckle, mark, stain, spot.

कालकील kal-kéel, *s. m.* A confused or mingled sound, a tumult.

कालकूट kal-kóot, *s. m.* A kind of poison, destroying even the regent of death; the poison of a snake.

कालुख kalukh, *s. m.* Freckle, mark, stain, spot.

कालगन्ध kal-gúndh, *s. m.* A kind of Cobra de capella.

कालचक्र kal-chúkr, *s. m.* A cycle, a given revolution of time; a period.

कालञ्जर ka-lún-jur, *s. m.* A name of *Shiv*; a rock in *Bundelkhund*, the modern *Callinjer*; the adjacent country; an assembly of religious mendicants; *Callinjer* is one of the places at which such assemblies meet, being enumerated in the *Veds* amongst the *Tupusya-sthans*, or spots adapted to practices of austere devotion.

कालधर्म kál-dhurm, *s. m.* Death, dying.

कालनिर्य्यास kal-nir-yás *s. m.* A fragrant and resinous substance, Bdellium.

कालप्रभात kal-prub-hát, *s. m.* The sultry season, autumn, the two months following the rainy season.

कालमा kál-ma, *s. m.* Suspicion, calumny.

कालमेषिका kal-mésh-ik-a, *s. f.* Bengal madder; black Teoree.

कालमेषी kal-mésh-ee, *s. f.* A plant (Serratula or Conyza anthelmintica); Bengal madder (Rubia Manjeeth).

कालराति kal-rá-tri, *s. m.* A particular night, one of which occurs on the 7th day of the 7th month of every 77th year: after such a period of life, a man is considered exempt from attention to the usual ordinances.

काललुवण kal-lúv-un, *s. m.* A factitious and purgative salt.

कालसर्प kal-súrp, *s. m.* The black and most deadly variety of the cobra (Coluber naga).

कालसार kal-sár, *s. m.* The black antelope.

कालसूत्र kal-sóotr, *s. m.* One of the twenty-one hells.

कालक्षेप kal-kshép, *s. m.* The passing or spending of time; the enduring of suffering.

काला ká-la, *adj.* Black, dark. *s. m.* A snake; time; a name of Krishn. Kala-dana, A purgative seed (Convolvulus nil?) Kala-jeera, s. m. Seeds of the Nigella indica. Kala-moonh kurna, To break off all connexion with another; to disgrace; to copulate; to expel. Kala-numuk, s. m. A kind of rock salt impregnated with sulphur and bitumen, which leaves a hepatic flavour in the mouth (it is much used medicinally). Kaleh-burun, Of the colour of a snake. Kaleh kos, A great distance. Kaleh-bal, s. m. The lower part of the belly, the pubes.

कालागुरु kála-góoroo, *s. m.* A black kind of Aloe wood or Agallochum.

कालाञ्जनी kal-án-jun-ee, *s. m.* A small shrub used as a purgative.

कालान्तर kalántur, *s. m.* Interval, intermediate time; process of time.

कालापत्ती kála-púttee, *s. f.* The act of calking a ship or boat. Kala-puttee kurna, To calk (a ship, &c.)

कालापन kalapún, *s. m.* Blackness.

कालिंदी kál-in-dee, *s. f.* A name of the river Jumna.

कालिक kál-ik, *s. m.* The curlew; blackness, a black colour; a fault or flaw in gold, &c.; a line of hair extending to the navel; ink or blacking, soot; a small bird, commonly called Syam.

कालिदास káli-dás, *n. prop.* A celebrated poet, author of Sucoontula, the Rughoo Vuns, the Nuloduy, and other poems: he was one of the nine poets or gems of Vikrumadityuh's court, and is supposed to have flourished in the century preceding the Christian era; the name is however applied to more persons than one, and seems in some measure to have been used as an honourable title: the works attributed to this author are amongst the most elegant compositions in the Sanskrit language.

कालिन्दी kál-in-dee, *s. f.* The river Jumna.

कालिया ká-li-ya, *s. m.* A serpent said to have been vanquished by Krishn. *adj.* Black (complexion).

काली ká-lee, *adj. f.* Black. *s. f.* The Hecate of the hindoos, and wife of Shiv, to whom human sacrifices are offered; the Nile; ink. *s. m.* A fabulous serpent with a hundred and ten hoods said to have been vanquished by Krishn. Kalee-mirch, s. f. Black pepper. Kalee-boon, s. m. Name of a plant. Kalee toolsee, s. f. Basil (Ocymum basilicum). Kalee-duh, Name of a whirlpool in the river Jumna, where the serpent Kalee is said to have lived. Kalee-mittee, s. f. Black lead.

कालीन kaléen, *adj.* Timely, seasonable, relating to time.

कालीहुर ka-lee-húr, *s. m.* A buck, deer.

कालेश्वर kal-ésh-wur, *s. m.* A drug.

काल्पनिक kálp-nik, *adj.* Feigned, forged, contrived, factitious. *s. m.* A hypocrite.

काल्पनिकता kálp-nik-ta, *s. f.* Hypocrisy.

कावर ká-wur, *s. f.* The baskets in which the hindoos carry about the Ganges water.

कावादेना káwa-déna, *v. a.* To ring or lounge (a horse, &c.); to trick, to sham.

काव्य kávyuh, *s. m.* A poem, a poetical composition.

काव्यचोर kávyuh-chóur, *s. m.* A plagiarist.

काश kash, *s. f.* Cough, catarrh; a species of grass (Saccharum spontaneum). Kashwas, s. m. Asthma.

काशी ká shee, *s. f.* A celebrated city and place of pilgrimage, the modern Benares.

काष्ठ kashth, *s. m.* Wood.

काष्ठक kásh-thuk, *s. m.* Aloe wood or Agallochum.

काष्ठकीट kasht-kéet, *s. m.* A small insect or worm found in decayed wood.

काष्ठकूट kasht-kóot, *s. m.* The wood-pecker.

काष्ठी kashthée, *adj.* Of wood, wooden.

कास kas, *s. m.* Cough, catarrh. *s. f.* A species of reed or long grass of which rope is made (Saccharum spontaneum). Kas-swas, Asthma.

कासघ्न kas-úghn, *adj.* Removing or alleviating cough, pectoral.

कासघ्नी kas-ughnée, *s. f.* A sort of prickly nightshade (Solanum jacquini).

कासनाशिनी **kas-násh-in-ee**, *s. f.* A thorny plant, used as a remedy for the cough.

कासबी **kás-bee**, *s. m.* A weaver.

कासमर्द **kas-múrd**, *s. m.* A plant (*Cassia* or *Senna esculenta*).

कासालू **kas-á-loo**, *s. m.* An esculent root, a sort of yam.

कासीस **ka-sées**, *s. m.* Green vitriol, green sulphate of iron.

कास्त **kast**, *s. m.* Name of a plant (*Chara*).

काहन **ká-hun**, *s. m.* An aggregate number consisting of sixteen *puns*, or 1280 *cowries*.

काहलु **káh-lu**, *adj.* Mischievous.

काहलापूष्प **kah-la-póoshp**, *s. m.* Thorn-apple (*Datura metel*).

काहू **ká-hoo**, (*in Bruj*) *pron. adj.* Some, any, any one, any thing.

काहे **ká-heh**, *pron.* Why? wherefore? for what?

कि **ki**, *conj.* That, or.

किकि **kiki**, *s. m.* The blue jay.

किकियाना **kikiyána**, *v. n.* To shriek, to scream.

किंकुर **kín-kur**, *s. m.* A slave, a servant.

किंकिनी **kínk-in-ee**, *s. f.* A girdle of bells or tinkling ornaments worn by women.

किंग्री **kín-gree**, *s. f.* A sort of fiddle.

किचकिचाना **kich-kich-ána**, *v. n.* To grind (*or gnash*) the teeth.

किचराना **kich-rá-na**, *v. n.* To have a gummy running at the eyes, to be blear-eyed.

किचपिच **kich-pích**, *s. f.* Mud, mire, &c.

किचरपिचर होना **kích-ur-píchur hóna**, To be very wet.

किचरा **kích-ra**, *s. m.* The gummy substance that oozes out of the eyes.

किंचली **kínch-lee**, *s. f.* The slough (*of a snake, &c.*)

किंचित **kín-chit**, *adj.* A little, a part. *adv.* Something, somewhat.

कित्त **kitt**, *s. m.* A kind of sour dish; excrement, excretion, dirt.

किर **kir**, *s. m.* A worm. *Kir-khaya, adj.* Worm-eaten; marked with small-pox, pitted, spotted.

किरकिराना **kir-kir-ána**, *v. n.* To gnash the teeth with rage.

किरहा **kir-há**, *adj.* Worm-eaten; weevil-eaten.

कित **kit**, *adv.* Where? whither? *adj.* How many? how much?

कितेँ **kit-éen**, *postpos.* To, up to, for.

कितना **kít-na**, *m.* ⎫
कितनी **kít-nee**, *f.* ⎬ *adj.* How much? how
किता **kít-ta**, *m.* ⎭ many?

किदारबसंत **kidár-búsunt**, *s. m.* A musical mode.

किदारा **kid-á-ra**, *s. m.* A musical mode sung in the midnight of summer.

किधर **kíd-hur**, *adv.* Where? whither?

किन **kin**, *pron. interrog. pl.* Who? which?

किनवैया **kín-wyya**, *s. m.* A purchaser.

किनारी **kin-á-ree**, *s. f.* (*Gold or silver*) Lace; edge, border.

किंतू **kín-too**, *conj.* But.

किंतुघ्न **kintóoghn**, *s. m.* One of the eleven periods called *Kuruns*.

किंनर **kín-nur**, *s. m.* A kind of singer or chorister at the court of the gods; a demigod attached to the service of *Koover*, the god of riches.

किम **kim**, *relat. pron.* What? who? which? how?

किंपूरुष **kím-póoroosh**, *s. m.* A division of the universe, one of the nine *khunds* or portions into which the world is divided, and described as the country between the *Himachul* and *Himakoot* mountains; a despicable or low man.

कियारी **ki-yá-ree**, *s. f.* A bed (*of a garden*); a frame.

किरकिटी **kír-kit-ee**, *s. f.* A mote, or particle of dust fallen into the eye.

किरकिरा **kír-kir-a**, *adj.* Gritty, sandy.

किरकिराना **kir-kir-ána**, *v. n.* To be gritty, to grate.

किरतिया **kír-ti-ya**, *s. m.* A dancer, or singing boy.

किरन **kír-un**, *s. f.* A ray of light, a sun or moon beam.

किरनमय **kirún-muy**, *adj.* Radiant, bright, refulgent.

किरवान **kir-wán**, *s. f.* A sword.

किरात **kir-át**, *s. m.* A savage, a tribe of mountaineers who live by the chase, the *Kirhadæ* of Arrian.

किराना **kir-á-na**, *s. m.* Grocery. *v. a.* To adjust; to sift, separate by turning round in a winnowing fan (*differing from phutukna*).

किराव **kir-áo**, *s. m.* A small pea (*Pisum arvense*).

किरिया **kír-i-ya**, *s. f.* An oath.

किरीट **kir-éet**, *s. m.* A crest, a diadem.

किरौ **kir-óu**, *s. m.* A hollow tooth; endive. *adj.* Broken, rugged, tattered.

किर्च **kirch**, *s. f.* A splinter; a sword (*especially, a straight one to thrust with*).

किर्मी kírm-mee, *s. f.* The *Pulas* tree.

किल kil, *adv.* Certainly, indeed, verily; probably, possibly.

किलक kíl-uk, *s. f.* Splendour, lustre (*of a gem*).

किलकिंचित kil-kín-chit, *s. m.* Wanton or amorous pastime, or gestures.

किलकिलकांटा kilkil-kánta, *s. m.* A game among boys; one boy, having drawn several lines upon a stone, hides it, and the others, repeating the word *kilkil-kanta*, run about searching for it; whoever finds the stone, has a right to strike the boy who hid it, three times with his fingers on the back of the hand.

किलकिला kíl-kil-a, *s. m.* Peevishness, fretfulness, anger. *s. f.* Sound expressing joy, or the expression of pleasure by any sound or cry.

किलकिलाना kil-kil-ána, *v. n.* To be fretful, to snap, to snarl, to be peevish, to squable.

किलनी kíl-nee, *s. f.* A tick (*insect that infests dogs, &c.*), a doglouse.

कलाना kil-á-na, *v. a.* To winnon; to strike with the fist.

किलकारी kilkáree, *s. f.* The chattering (*of a monkey*), snarling; sound expressing joy. *Kilkaree marna, v. n.* To express pleasure by any sound or cry, to shout.

किली kíl-lee, *s. f.* A key, bolt.

किवांच kiv-ánch, *s. m.* A plant, cowitch (*Dolichos pruriens*).

किशोर kish-ór, *s. m.* A youth, a son, a lad, one from his birth to the end of his fifteenth year; a minor in law, becoming after his fifteenth year subject to suits at law.

किशोरा kish-ó-ra, *adj.* Young, infantine.

किश्त kisht, *s. f.* Check (*at chess*).

किस kis, *pron. interrog.* Whom? which? what? *Kisturuh*, In what manner? how? *Kiskudr*, How much? *Kis-kis*, Which? (*used interrogatively, and expressive of much, many, various*). *Kis-liyeh*, Why? wherefore.

किसनई kis-núee, *s. f.* Husbandry, agriculture.

किसान kis-án, *s. m.* A husbandman, ploughman, peasant, farmer.

किसारी kis-á-ree, *s. f.* A kind of pulse (*Lathyrus sativus*).

किसे kís-eh, *pron. inter. sing.* To whom? to what? to which?

की kee, *postpos.* (*fem. of ka*) Of, belonging to.

कीकर kee-kur, *s. m.* The Acacia tree.

कीच keech, } *s. f.* Dirt, mud, slime,
कीचड़ kée-chur, } mire.

कीट keet, *s. m.* An insect, a worm, a reptile; the dregs of oil in a lamp, or that collected in a *hookka* snake.

कीड़ा keer-há, } *adj.* Wormy, worm-eaten.
कीरहा keer-há, } en.

कीड़ा kée-ra, *s. m.* A worm, an insect, a maggot, a reptile, a snake, a leech.

कीधर kee-dhúr, *adv.* Whither, &c.

कीना kée-na, *3rd pers. sing. mas. perf. tense* (*of kurna, to do*), Done, made.

कीन्ना kéen-na, *v. a.* To purchase, to buy. *Keenwyya, adj.* A purchaser.

कीप keep, *s. f.* A funnel.

कीया kée-ya, *part. past*, or, *s. m.* Done, made; deed, doings.

कीर keer, } *s. m.* A parrot; parroquet.
कीरक kee-ruk, } quet.

कीरत kée-rut, } *s. f.* Praise, fame, renown.
कीर्ति keert-ti, } *Kee-rut-wan, adj.* Renowned.

कीरहा keeruhá, *adj.* Wormy.

कीरित kée-rit, *s. f.* Virtue.

कीर्तन kéert-tun, *s. m.* Speech, words; shouting for joy, singing aloud, singing in concert; celebrating, praising.

कीर्तना kéert-tuna, *s. f.* Fame, glory.

कीर्ती kéert-tí, *s. f.* Fame, renown, glory.

कीर्तिमान keertti-mán, *adj.* Praised, famous, celebrated.

कील keel, *s. f.* A small nail, peg, tack, stake, pin, bolt, wedge; the core of a boil. *Keelkanta*, Tools, apparatus, accoutrements.

कीलना kéel-na, *v. a.* To charm a snake so as to prevent his biting.

कीला kée-la, *s. f.* A small nail, tack, peg.

कु koo, A particle of depreciation prefixed to nouns, and implying, sin, guilt; reproach, contempt; diminution, littleness.

कुंगरा koong-ra, *adj.* Able-bodied, robust, athletic, stout. *Koongraee, s. f.* Strength, stoutness.

कुंचकी kóonch-kee, *s. f.* A bodice.

कुंज koonj, *s. m.* An arbour.

कुंजर kóon-jur, *s. m.* An elephant.

कुंजरा kóonj-ra, *s. m.* A caste whose business it is to sell vegetables. *Koonjrun, s. f.* Female of *Koonjra*.

कुंजल kóon-jul, *s. m.* An elephant, a large elephant.

कुंजी kóon-jee, *s. f.* A key.

कुंड koond, *s. m.* An abyss, a pool, spring; a pit for sacrifice; a hole in the ground for receiving and preserving consecrated fire; a well, a basin of water, especially consecrated to some holy purpose or person.

कुंडल kóon-dul, *s. m.* A large ring worn in the ears; a circle; a halo round the sun or moon. *Koondul marna*, To coil, to form a coil.

कुंडलिया koon-dúl-iya, *s. m.* A species of *Hindee* stanza, which invariably ends with the word with which it began: it is hence compared to a circle or the coil of a snake, the opposite ends of which unite.

कुंडली kóond-lee, *s. m.* A coil, ring, curl, hoop; a snake. *Koondlee bunāna*, To curl.

कुंडी kóon-dee, *s. f.* A chain or iron catch to fasten a door.

कुंद koond, *s. m.* A flower (*Jasminum grandiflorum*).

कुंदन kóon-dun, *s. m.* Pure gold.

कुंदनकूट koon-dun-kóot, *s. m.* A medicine (*Olibanum*).

कुंदरा kóond-ra, *s. m.* A stack, a rick.

कुंदला kóond-la,} *s. m.* A kind of tent.
कुंदला kóond-la,}

कुंदी kóon-dee, *s. f.* The act of calendering (*cloth*). *Koondee kurna*, To calender (*cloth*), to beat, to cudgel. *Koondeegur*, *s. m.* A calenderer.

कुंबा kóom-ba, *s. m.* Tribe, cast, family, brotherhood.

कुंभ koombh, *s. m.* A water-pot; the sign Aquarius. *Koombh ka mela*, The twelfth year fair of *Hurdwar*, a celebrated *Hindoo* pilgrimage. *Koombhnee*, The sixth-year fair.

कुंवर kóon-wur,} *s. m.* An unmarried
कुंवारा koon-wá-ra,} boy, a son, a child; the son of a Raja, a prince, heir-apparent.

कुंवारी koon-wá-ree, *s. f.* A maiden, a virgin, a princess, a daughter, a young lady fit for marriage.

कुकर्म koo-kúrm, *s. m.* Wickedness, sin, depravity, villainy.

कुकर्मकारी kóokurm-karée, *adj.* Wicked, depraved.

कुकर्मा koo-kurmá, *adj.* Wicked, bad.

कुकर्मी koo-kúr-mee, *adj.* Wicked, vicious.

कुकरोंदा kook-rón-da, *s. m.* A plant (*Celsia*).

कुकुर koo-koor, *s. m.* A dog; a *Kshuttree*.

कुकुरमूता kóokoor-móota, *s. m.* A mushroom, a toadstool.

कुकूनुक kookóo-nuk, *s. m.* Weakness of the eyes in infants.

कुक्कुट kóokkoot, *s. m.* A gallinaceous fowl, a cock, a wild cock (*Phasianus Gallus*).

कुक्कुटव्रत kook-koot-vrút, *s. m.* A religious observance, (*worship of Shiv*) held by women on the seventh of the light fortnight of *Bhadon*, especially for the sake of obtaining offspring.

कुक्कुटी kóok-koo-tee, *s. f.* A hen.

कुक्कुर kóok-koor, *s. m.* A dog.

कुक्कुरी kóok-koo-ree, *s. f.* A bitch.

कुक्रिया kóo-kri-ya, *s. f.* A crime, a sin, a wicked action.

कुक्षि kóok-shi, *s. m.* The belly, the cavity of the abdomen.

कुख्याति koo-khyáti, *s. f.* Evil report, infamy.

कुंकुम kóom-kóom, *s. m.* Saffron (*Crocus sativus*).

कुंकुमा kóom kóom-a, *s. m.* A vessel in which the *goolal* or red mixture is contained with which they play at the *holee*.

कुच kooch, *s. m. f.* A breast, a pap, the bosom.

कुचंदन koo-chún-dun, *s. m.* Red sanders (*Pterocarpus santulinus*); sappan or log wood.

कुचर koo-chúr, *adj.* Censorious, detracting.

कुचलना kóo-chul-na, *v. a.* To bruise, to crush. *Koochul-dalna*, *v. a.* To bruise, &c.; to overlay.

कुचला kóoch-la, *s. m.* A vomic nut (*Strychnos nux vomica*).

कुचली kóoch-lee, *s. f.* The canine teeth.

कुचाग्रह kooch-ágruh, *s. m.* A nipple.

कुचाल koo-chál, *s. f.* Misbehaviour, misconduct. *Koo-chales*, *adj.* Of bad conduct or behaviour, ill-behaved. [ear.

कुचिया kóoch-i-ya, *s. m.* The lobe of the

कुचेला koochéyla, *adj.* Ill-clothed, dressed in dirty or tattered garments.

कुछ koochh, *neut. pron.* Any, anything, aught, some, something, somewhat, a little, whatever. *Koochh our gana*, To give a false explanation, to tell a different story. *Koochh-ek*, Some little, some few. *Koochh toom neh puru paya*, Have you found a treasure? (*an expression addressed to one who seems inordinately pleased without apparent cause.*) *Koochh toom neh khwab dekha*, What! have you dreamt this, or seen a vision? (*an expression used to a person who relates improbabilities: or to depict the astonishment of the speaker at any unexpected act of another*). *Koochh seh kooch hona*, To be entirely changed. *Kooch nuh kooch*, Some at least, something or other. *Koochh nuheen*, Nothing. *Koochh ho*, Whatever may happen, come what may.

कुज kooj, *s. m.* The planet Mars; Tuesday.

कुंजजीवन kóoj-lee-bun, *s. m.* A forest frequented by elephants.

कुजाति koo-já-ti, *adj.* Base, of mean extraction or bad cast ; one who has lost his cast, an outcast.

कुंज koonj, *s. m.* A place overgrown with creeping plants, a bower, an arbour.

कुंजर koon-júr, *s. m.* An elephant.

कुंजी kóon-jee, *s. f.* A key.

कुट koot, *s. m.* A medicine (*Costus arabicus*).

कुटकी kóot-kee, *s. f.* A medicine ; a gnat ; estrangement from or desertion of friends.

कुटकुट kóot-koot, *s. m.* Nibbling, itching, scratching.

कुटज koo-túj, *s. m.* A medicinal plant (*Echites antidysenterica*) ; the seeds are used as a vermifuge.

कुटना kóot-na, *s. m.* A pimp.

कुटनाई koot-ná-ee, *s. f.* The wages of a pimp.

कुटनाना koot-ná-na, *v. a.* To entice, seduce, inveigle, wheedle, coax.

कुटनापा koot-ná-pa, *s. m.* Pimping.

कुटनी kóot-nee, *s. f.* A bawd, a procuress.

कुटनुट koo-tún-nut, *s. m.* A plant (*Bignonia indica*).

कुटाया koo-tá-ya, *s. m.* Solanum jacquini.

कुटार koo-tár, *s. m.* An impatient little horse.

कुटिर kóo-tir, *s. m.* A cottage, a hut.

कुटिल kóo-til, *adj.* Crooked, bent ; perverse, untoward, cruel ; dishonest, fraudulent.

कुटिलता kootiltá, *s. f.* Crookedness ; guile, dishonesty.

कुटी kóo-tee, *s. f.* A cottage, a hut.

कुटीर koo-téer, *s. m.* A small house, a hut, a hovel.

कुटुम kóo-toom, ⎱ *s. m.* Kin, family,
कुटुम्ब kóo-toomb, ⎰ tribe, cast, relative, a kinsman, a connexion ; offspring, progeny, race.

कुटुम्बिन koo-toom-bín, ⎫ *s. m.* A house-
कुटुमी kóo-too-mee, ⎬ holder, a pater-
कुटुम्बी kóo-toom-bee, ⎭ familias.

कुटुम्बिनी koo-toom-bín-ee, *s. f.* The wife of a householder and mother of a family, a matron.

कुटेव koo-téo, *s. f.* A bad habit.

कुहनी kóott-nee, *s. f.* A bawd, a procuress.

कुटार koot-tár, *s. m.* Copulation.

कुठर koot-húr, *s. m.* The post round which the string of the churning stick winds.

कुठाकू koot-há-koo, *s. m.* A bird, the wood-pecker.

कुठार koot-hár, *s. m.* An axe.

कुठारी koot-há-ree, *s. f.* An axe ; an earthen vase prepared for melting gold, silver, &c., a crucible.

कुरुकना koo-rúk-na, ⎱ *v. n.* To cluck,
कुरकुराना koor-koo-rá-na, ⎰ to cackle (*a laying hen*) ; to speak angrily, murmur, grumble.

कुरमा kóorma, *s. m.* Tribe, cast, family, race.

कुरुक kóo-rook, *adj.* A clucking (*hen*). *s. f.* Clucking (*of a hen*).

कुदंग koo-dhúng, *adj.* Unmannerly, illbred, rude. *Koodhungee, s. f.* Unmannerliness, rudeness.

कुरहन koor-hún, *s. f.* Grief, sorrow, lamentation.

कुरहना kóorh-na, *v. n.* To grieve, mourn, lament, pine, repine, vex, be afflicted, be angry or disgusted.

कुदंब koo-dhúb, *adj.* Ill-shaped, ill-mannered, ugly, rude.

कुरहाना koor-há-na, *v. a.* To vex, afflict, grieve, trouble, anger, disgust, displease.

कुनब kóon-ba, *s. m.* Tribe, cast, family, brotherhood.

कुंहित kóont-hit, *adj.* Ashamed.

कुंद koond, *s. m.* An abyss, pool, spring ; a pit for sacrifice ; a hole in the ground for receiving and preserving consecrated fire ; a well, a basin of water, especially consecrated to some holy purpose or person.

कुंदल kóon-dul, *s. m.* A large ring worn in the ears ; a circle ; a halo round the sun or moon.

कुंदलिया koon-dul-íya, *s. m.* A species of *Hindee* stanza, which invariably ends with the word with which it began ; it is hence compared to a circle or the coil of a snake, the opposite ends of which unite.

कुंदली kóond-lee, *s. f.* A coil, ring, curl, a snake. *Koondlee bunana*, To curl.

कुंदी kóon-dee, *s. f.* A chain or iron catch to fasten a door.

कुतप koo-túp, ⎱ *s. m.* The eighth hour
कुतुप koo-tóop, ⎰ or portion of the day ; about noon.

कुतरन kóot-run, *s. m.* That which is gnawed or bitten off with the teeth.

कुतरना koo-túr-na, *v. a.* To cut with the teeth.

कुतर kóot-roo, *s. m.* A puppy ; a cutter.

कुतिया kóo-ti-ya, *s. f.* A bitch.

कुतूनुक kootóonuk, *s. m.* Weakness of the eyes in infants.

कुतूहल koo-tóo-hul, *s. m.* Eagerness, desire ; show, exhibition, sport, pleasure, diversion.

pastime, festivity; a spectacle. *Kootoohulee, adj.* Sportive, fond of sport or festivity.

कुत्ता kóot-ta, *s. m.* A dog.

कुत्रापि koo-trá-pi, *adv.* Wherever, any where, somewhere,

कुत्सा kóot-sa, *s. f.* Reproach, contempt, censure, calumny.

कुत्सित kóot-sit, *adj.* Low, vile, contemptible; contemned, reviled.

कुद्कना koo-dúk-na, } *v. n.* To leap, bound,
कुद्राना kood-rá-na, } jump, frisk, caper, skip.

कुद्वाना kood-wá-na, *v. a.* To cause to dandle.

कुदाना koodána, *v. a.* To dandle; to cause to leap; (*met.*) to provoke.

कुदाया koodáya, *s. m.* A kind of dove.

कुदार koo-dár, *s. m.* A pick-axe.

कुदाल koo-dál, *s. m.* A hoe or kind of spade, a pick-axe or mattock.

कुदाली koo-dá-lee, *s. f.* A small mattock, a spade, hoe, dibble.

कुदृष्टि kóo-drishti, *s. f.* Weak sight, evil eye.

कुदृल kood-dúl, *s. m.* Mountain ebony.

कुद्दाल kood-dal, *s. m.* Mountain ebony (*Bauhinia variegata*); a kind of spade or hoe.

कुनख koo-núkh, *s. m.* A disease of the nails.

कुनखी koo-nukhée, *adj.* Having bad or diseased nails.

कुनबा kóon-ba, *s. m.* Tribe, cast, family, brotherhood.

कुनीति koo-néeti, *s. f.* Bad behaviour, ill-manners; impolicy, misgovernment.

कुनतुल koon-tul, *s. m.* Hair.

कुन्द koond, *s. m.* A kind of Jasmin (*Jasminum grandiflorum*).

कुन्दन kóon-dun, *s. m.* Pure gold.

कुन्दरकुट koon-dur-kóot, *s. m.* A medicine.

कुन्दरा kóond-ra, *s. m.* A stack, a rick.

कुन्दला kóond-la, *s. m.* A kind of tent.

कुन्दी kóon-dee, *s. f.* The act of calendering (*cloth*). *Koondee kurna*, To calender (*cloth*); to beat, to cudgel. *Koondeegur, s. m.* A calenderer.

कुन्दूरू kóondooroo, *s. f.* The resin of the *Boswelia thurifera*, gum Olibanum, or frankincense.

कुपथ koo-púth, *s. m.* Deviation, aberration, immorality, profligacy, a bad road; heterodox doctrine, heresy.

कुपथगामी kóoputh-gámee, *adj.* Wicked, going in a bad or wrong road.

कुपरामर्ष koo-pur-á-mursh, *s. m.* Bad advice.

कुपात्र koo-pátr, *adj.* Unworthy, unfit.

कुपित kóo-pit, *adj.* Incensed, angry, offended.

कुपुत्र koo-póotr, *s. m.* A disobedient or wicked son.

कुपुरुष koo-póoroosh, *s. m.* A low or vile man; a poltroon.

कुपूत koo-póot, *s. m.* A bad or degenerate son.

कुप्पा kóop-pa, *s. m.* A large leathern vessel for holding oil, ghee, &c. *Kooppa loorhna*, The decease of a king, &c. *Kooppa hona*, To become very fat.

कुप्पी kóop-pee, *s. f.* A small leathern vessel for holding oil, ghee, &c.; a vial, a skin, a leathern bottle.

कुब koob, *s. m.* A hump.

कुबजा kóob-ja, }
कुबरा kóob-ra, } *adj.* Hump-backed, crooked.
कुबज koobj, }
कुबर्बा kóorbba, }

कुबुर koobúr, *s. m.* A hump.

कुबेर koo-bér, *s. m.* The Indian Plutus, the god of wealth.

कुर्ब्बा kóorb-ba, *adj.* Hump-backed.

कुभार्जा koo-bhár ja, *s. f.* A bad wife.

कुभाव koo-bháo, *s. m.* Ill-temper, bad disposition, ill-treatment.

कुमकुम kóom-koom, *s. m.* Saffron.

कुमत koomút, } *s. f.* Foolishness, stupidity, indiscretion.
कुमति koo-mut-i, } *adj.* Stupid, foolish; wicked, vicious, injudicious.

कुमद kóo-mud, } *s. m.* A white esculent lotus, that expands its petals during the night, and closes them in the day-time (*Nymphæa esculenta*).
कुमूद kóo-mood, }

कुमन्त्रना koo-mún-trun-a, *s. m.* Bad counsel, ill advice, intrigue.

कुमाच koo-mách, *s. m.* A kind of unleavened bread. *Koomuch-sa moonh*, A broad face.

कुमार koo-már, *s. m.* A boy; the son of a raja, a prince.

कुमारिका koo-má-ri-ka, } *s. f.* A maiden,
कुमारी koo-má-ree, } a virgin, a princess, a daughter, a young lady fit for marriage.

कुमार्ग koo-márg, *s. m.* A bad road; a bad course.

कुमूद kóo-mood, *s. m.* A white esculent lotus that expands its petals during the night, and closes them in the day-time (*Nymphæa esculenta*).

M

कुमुदिनी koo-moo-dín-ee, *s. f.* A place abounding in lotuses, &c.

कुमेद्य koo-méd-ya, } *s. m.* A small
कुमेंध्य koo-méndh-ya, } elephant.

कुमेरु kooméroo, *s. m.* The southern hemisphere or pole.

कुम्भ koombh, *s. m.* A water-pot; the sign Aquarius. *Koombh ka mela*, The twelfth-year fair of *Hurdwar*, a celebrated *Hindoo* pilgrimage. *Koombhnee*, The sixth-year fair.

कुम्भकार koombh-kár, *s. m.* A potter.

कुम्भकामला koombh-kámla, *s. f.* A bilious affection, a sort of jaundice.

कुम्भला kóombh-la, *s. f.* A plant, the flowers of which are compared to those of the *Nauclea cadamba*.

कुम्भिका koombhi-ká, *s. f.* A disease of the eyes, hordeolum or stye.

कुम्भीपाक koom-bhee-pák, *s. m.* A hell in which the wicked are supposed to be baked like a potter's vessels.

कुम्भीर koom-bhéer, *s. m.* The crocodile of the Ganges, the long-nosed alligator.

कुम्हलाना koomh-lá-na, } *v. n.* To wither,
कुमलाना koom-lá-na, } fade, blast, droop, be blighted, dry up.

कुम्हार koom-hár, *s. m.* A potter.

कुम्हारनी koomhárnee, *s. f.* A potter's wife or a female potter.

कुम्हारी koom-há-ree, *s. f.* An animal resembling a wasp, which builds its house of clay.

कुम्हीर koomhéer, *s. m.* An alligator, a crocodile.

कुरकुरी kóor-koo-ree, *s. f.* Belly-fretting.

कुरंग koo-rúng, *s. m.* A deer.

कुरंड koo-rúud, *s. m.* Corundum stone (*Adamantinus corundum*).

कुर्थी kóor-thee, *s. f.* A kind of vetch (*Dolichos biflorus*).

कुरूस koorús, *s. m.* Bad taste, badness of juice or flavour. *adj.* Bad in taste or flavour.

कुरसत koorsut, *s. m.* A kind of coarse sugar.

कुरीति koo-réeti, *s. f.* Misconduct, bad manners.

कुरु kóo-roo, *n. prop.* An ancient sovereign of *Delhi* and the country around. *Koorookshetr*, n. prop. The country near *Delhi* where the great battle was fought between the *Kouruv*, and the *Pandur*. *Koroo-bunsee*, *adj.* Of the race of *Kooroo*.

कुरु kóoroo, *s. m. Kooroo* or *Oottur Kooroo*, the most northerly of the four *Muha Dweeps*, or principal divisions of the known world; by other systems it is considered as one of the nine divisions or *Vurshus* of the same: in both cases, however it is the country beyond the northernmost range of mountains, extending to the frozen ocean.

कुरूल kóo-rool, *s. m.* A curl or lock of hair, especially on the forehead.

कुरूवक koo-roo-vúk, *s. m.* The crimson amaranth; a purple species of Barleria; also a yellow kind.

कुरुविन्द kooroo-vínd, }
कुरुविल kooroo-víll, } *s. m.* A ruby.
कुरुविल्व kooroo-vílv, }

कुरूप koo-róop, *adj.* Deformed, ugly. *s. m.* Ugliness.

कुरूपता kooroop-tá, *s. f.* Ugliness.

कुरूपी koo-roopée, *adj.* Ugly, ill-made, frightful, deformed.

कुरेलना koo-rél-na, *v. a.* To poke.

कूर्कूट kóor-koot, *s. f.* Sweepings, rubbish.

कूर्कूरी koorkoorée, *s. f.* Belly-fretting.

कूर्छाल koor-chhál, *s. f.* A bound, spring, jump.

कूर्म koorm, *s. m.* A tortoise, a turtle; the second *Hindoo* mythological incarnation.

कूर्मी koor-mée, *s. m.* A tribe of husbandmen.

कूर्याल koor-yál, *s. f.* The state of a bird sitting at ease and in security, trimming its wings with its beak; (hence) ease, security, hope, confidence of success. *Kooryal men ghoolela lugna*, To be disappointed or fall into misfortune in the moment of security, or when sure of success.

कूरी kóor-ree, *s. f.* Gristle, cartilage.

कूर्सुत kóor-sut, *s. m.* A kind of coarse sugar.

कुल kool, *s. m.* Family, pedigree, race, tribe or caste, relations, household.

कुलकुला kóol-koo-la, *s. m.* Gargling.

कुलकुली kóol-koo-lee, *s. f.* The itch.

कुलुच्छन koo-lúch-chhun, *s. m.* Misconduct, bad temper; ugliness.

कुलुच्छना koo-lúch-chhun-a, *adj.* Of bad signs or features, ugly, ill-tempered, ill-omened.

कुलचा kóol-cha, *s. m.* Capital, principal, stock in trade.

कुलुंज koo-lúnj, *adj.* Cutting behind in walking (a horse).

कुलुंजन koo-lún-jun, *s. m.* A plant (*Alpinia galanga* or *Galanga major*); a seed (*Nigella sativa*).

कुलटा kóol-ta, *s. f.* An unchaste woman, one by whom the family honour is injured, a prostitute.

कुलटी kóol-tee, *s. f.* Red arsenic.

कुलतारण kool-tá-run, *s. m.* A youth who is a credit to his family, the saviour of his family.

कुलुत्था kool-út-tha, *s. f.* A blue stone used in medicine, and applied as a collyrium to the eyes, also as an astringent to sores.

कुलथी kóol-thee, *s. f.* A kind of vetch (*Dolichos biflorus*).

कुलदेवी kool-dév-ee, *s. f.* The goddess of a family, any female deity worshipped in particular by a family through successive generations.

कुलद्रोही kool-dró-hee, *s. m.* One who brings disgrace or reproach on his family.

कुलधर्म kool-dhúrm, *s. m.* Practice or observance peculiar to a tribe or cast, peculiar duty of cast or race.

कुलनाश kool-násh, *s. m.* A reprobate, an out-cast. [a family.

कुलपति kool-pút-i, *s. m.* Head or chief of

कुलपालक kool-pál-uk, *adj.* Nourishing or providing for a family.

कुलपालि kool-pá-li, *s. f.* A chaste woman.

कुलपूज्य kool-póoj-yuh, *s. m.* The object of worship or of reverence of a family; a family priest.

कुलवधू kool-búd-hoo, *s. f.* A virtuous woman of a noble family.

कुलबुला kóol-boo-la, *adj.* Vermicular.

कुलबुलाना kool-boo-lá-na, *v. a.* To itch; to fidget; to writhe (*as a worm or snake*); to grumble or rumble (*the bowels*).

कुलबुलाहट kool-boo-lá-hut, *s. f.* Vermicular motion.

कुलबोर kool-bór, *adj.* One who disgraces his family.

कुलबोरना kool-bór-na, *v. a.* To disgrace one's family.

कुलमा koolma, *s. m.* A sausage.

कुलवन्त kool-wúnt, } *adj.* Of a good or no-
कुलवान kool-wán, } ble family, of noble descent.

कुलवन्ती kool-wún-tee, *adj. f.* Chaste, of pure or noble descent; a gentlewoman.

कुलवान kool-wán, *adj.* Well-born, of good or noble family, of noble descent.

कुलहुर kóol-hur, *s. m.* A kind of firework.

कुलहुरा kóol-hur-a, *s. m.* A cup larger than *koolhiya*, an earthen vessel to drink out of.

कुलक्षण koo-lúk-shun, *s. m.* Misconduct, bad temper, ugliness.

कुलक्षणा koo-lúk-shun-a, *adj.* Of bad signs or features, ugly, ill-tempered, ill-omened.

कुलांच koo-lánch, *s. f.* A bound, spring, leap, jump, bounce. *Koolanch marna*, To bound or skip.

कुलाचार kool-a-chár, *s. m.* Practice or observance peculiar to a tribe or cast, peculiar duty of cast or race.

कुलाल koo-lál, *s. m.* A potter.

कुलाहुल koo-lá-hul, *s. m.* A loud and confused sound, a great and indistinct noise, tumult, uproar.

कुलहिया kóol-hi-ya, *s. f.* A cup, a small round vessel. *Koolhiya men goor phorna* (*lit. to break a lump of coarse sugur in a small cup*), To endeavour to do with few hands a work which requires many. *Koolhiya lugana*, Cupping.

कुलीजन koo-lée-jun, *s. m.* A drug (*the root of Piper betel*).

कुलीन koo-léen, *adj.* Noble, of respectable descent, well-born, of a good family, genteel.

कुलीनता koo-léen-ta, } *s. f.* Nobility, re-
कुलीनाई koo-leen-áee, } spectability of descent, gentility.

कुलीना koo-lée-na, *s. m.* A kind of pickle.

कुल्ला kóol-la, *s. m.* } Gargling or rinsing
कुल्ली kóol-lee, *s. f.* } the mouth, washing the mouth.

कुल्हाड़ी kool-há-ree, *s. f.* An axe, a hatchet.

कुवच koo-vúch, *adj.* Abusive, censorious, detracting.

कुवेर koo-vér, *s. m.* The Indian Plutus, the god of wealth.

कुश kóoshu, *s. m.* A species of grass used in many solemn and religious observances, hence called sacrificial grass (*Poa cynosuroides*), the sacred grass of the *Hindoos*.

कुशल kóoshul, *s. m.* } Welfare,
कुशलक्षेम koo-shul-kshém, *s. f.* } happiness, well-being, health, prosperity, safety.

कुशलता kooshultá, *s. f.* Well-being, health, happiness, welfare.

कुशल kóo-shul-a, *adj.* Happy, well, right.

कुशली kooshulée, *adj.* Auspicious, favourable; happy, prosperous.

कुशासन koosh-á-sun, *s. m.* A seat or mat made of the *Kooshu* grass.

कुशील koo-shéel, *adj.* Ill-behaved, rude, wicked; evil-disposed, ill-tempered.

कुशीलता koosheeltá, *s. f.* Misbehaviour, misconduct; bad disposition, ill temper.

कुष्ठ koosht, *s. m.* Leprosy, of which eighteen varieties are enumerated, seven great or severe, and eleven of minor importance.

कुष्ठ kooshth, *s. m.* A plant (*Costus speciosus*).

कुष्ठनाशन kooshth-ná-shun, *s. m.* White mustard; a sort of yam.

कुष्ठनाशिनी kooshth-ná-shin-ee, *s. f.* A plant (*Psoralia corylifolia*).

कुशी **kóosh-thee**, *adj.* Leprous ; a leper.

कुष्मांड **kooshmánd**, *s. m.* A pumpkin gourd ; a drug ; a religious ceremony, a certain rite performed as a penance or expiation.

कुसंग **koo-súng**, *s. m.* Bad company.

कुसरात **koos-rát**, *s. f.* Health, happiness, welfare.

कूसल **kóosul**, *adv.* Well, happy.

कुसीद **koo-séed**, *s. m.* Usury, the profession of usury ; any loan or thing lent to be repaid with interest.

कुसीदा **koo-sée-da**, *adj.* A money-lender.

कुसीदिक **koo-sée-dik**, *adj.* One who follows the profession of usury.

कुसुम **kóo-soom**, *s. m.* A flower with which clothes are dyed red, bastard saffron, safflower (*Carthamus tinctorius*) ; the menstrual discharge ; ophthalmia, disease of the eyes.

कुसुमांजन **koo-soom-án-jun**, *s. m.* The calx of brass used as a collyrium.

कुसुम्भ **kóo-soombh**, *s. m.* Safflower (*Carthamus tinctorius*).

कुसुम्भा **kóo-soom-bha**, *s. m.* The die of safflower ; (*met.*) an infusion of *bhung* (*Cannabis sativa*) used for intoxication.

कुसुम्भी **kóo-soom-bhee**, *adj.* Cloths dyed with safflower.

कुस्वप्न **koo-swúpn**, *s. m.* A bad dream, night-mare.

कुहनी **kóoh-nee**, *s. f.* The elbow.

कुहरा **kóoh-ra**, *s. m.* Fog, mist.

कुहराम **kooh-rám**, *s. m.* Lamentation, weeping.

कुहासा **koo-há-sa**, *s. m.* A fog, a mist.

कुही **kóo-hee**, *s. f.* A species of hawk.

कुहूक **kóo-hook**, *s. f.* The notes of the *kokila* or *koyel*.

कुहूकना **kóo-hook-na**, *v. n.* To sound (*as koyels do*).

कूआं **kóo-an**, *s. m.* A well.

कूंच **koonch**, *s. m.* The little red and black seed which goldsmiths use for weights (*Abrus precatorius*).

कूंची **koon-chée**, *s. f.* A brush.

कूंज **koonj**, *s. m.* The name of a bird, perhaps the crane.

कूंत **koont**, *s. m.* Conjecture, guess.

कूआ **kóo-a**, *s. m.* A well ; angle or corner (*of the eye*) ; slice, division (*of the jack fruit*) ; Cocoon (*of the silk worm*).

कूआर **kooár**, *s. m.* The sixth *Hindoo* month (*Sept.-Oct.*)

कूआरपना **kooar-púna**, *s. m.* The state of a bachelor or virgin, celibacy.

कूआरा **koo-á-ra**, *s. m.* An unmarried person, a bachelor.

कूआरी **koo-á-ree**, *s. f.* A maid, a virgin.

कूक **kook**, *s. f.* Sobbing, crying. *Kook marna*, To cry, to sob.

कूकना **kóok-na**, *v. n.* To sob, cry, scream ; to vociferate or call (*as the kokil*). *v. a.* To wind up (*a watch, clock, &c.*)

कूकर **kóo-kur**, *s. m.* A dog.

कूकरचाल **kookur-chál**, *s. f.* A trot.

कूकरमूता **kookur-móota**, *s. m.* A mushroom (*growing on wood*), a toadstool.

कूकरी **kóok-ree**, *s. f.* A bundle of thread ; maize, Indian corn (*Zea mais*) ; the gripes.

कूकू **kóo-koo**, *s. m.* Cooing ; a dove ; an omelet.

कूचिका **kóochika**, *s. f.* A small brush or hair pencil.

कूचिया **kóo-chi-ya**, *s. f.* A small tamarind ; part of the ear, the lobe.

कूच्छा **kóo-chha**, *s. m.* A tuft, cluster.

कूट **koot**, *s. m.* Paper used to make pasteboard. *s. f.* Mimickry ; illusion ; fraud, deceit, trick ; falsehood.

कूटता **kóot-ta**, *s. f.* Falsehood, fraud.

कूटना **kóot-na**, *v. a.* To pound, beat, bray, macerate ; to cudgel.

कूटार्थभाषिता **koot-árth-bháshita**, *s. f.* A tale, a story, a fiction.

कूरा **kóo-ra**, *s. m.* Sweepings, dirt, rubbish.

कूर्ब **koorb**, *adj.* Foolish, stupid, simpleton.

कूंडा **kóon-da**, *s. m.* A vessel (*earthen*) for kneading bread in, a platter. *Koonda karhna*, To prosper.

कूंडी **kóon-dee**, *s. f.* A vessel (*of stone*) in which snuff, *bhung*, &c. are ground.

कूत **koot**, *s. m.* Survey, a task, guess, appraisement ; estimate ; the base of a right angled triangle.

कूतुक **kóo-tuk**, *s. m.* One of the rules in arithmetic or algebra.

कूतना **kóot-na**, *v. a.* To value, to appraise.

कूद **kood**, *s. f.* A spring, jump, leap, bound.

कूदना **kóod-na**, *v. n.* To leap, bound, jump, (*met.*) rejoice ; to boast. *Koodna-phandna*, To jump about, to leap, (*about, as for joy.*)

कूनाई **koo-náee**, *s. f.* A scrap.

कूंडला **koondla**, *s. m.* A kind of tent.

कूप **koop**, *s. m.* A well ; a hole, a hollow.

कूपी **koo-pée**, *s. f.* A small well.

कूपेरा **kóo-py-ra**, *adj.* Unlucky.

कूबर **kóo-bur**, *s. m.* A hump.

कूमांष **koo-mánchh**, *s. m.* A kind of bread.

कृषहदेनी kóom-hul-dénee, *v. n.* To break into a house by penetrating through the wall.

कूर koor, *adj.* Cruel, savage, pitiless ; violator.

कूरनी kóornee, *s. f.* A scoop.

कूर्म kóorm, *s. m.* A tortoise, a turtle ; the second *Hindoo* mythological incarnation.

कूल kool, *s. m.* A bank, a shore ; a heap, a mound ; a pond or pool.

कूला kóo-la, *s. m.* The hip.

कूली kóo-lee, *s. m* A labourer, porter, carrier, a cooley.

कूवरा kóovra, *s. m.* A hump-backed man.

कूहरा kóoh-ra, *s. m.* } Fog, mist.
कूहा kóo-ha, *s. f.* }

कृत krit, *adj.* Done, made, performed ; fit, proper. *s. f.* Fruit, consequence ; the first of the four ages of the world, the golden age or *Sut joog. adv.* Completely finished.

कृतघ्नी krit-úgh-nee, *adj.* Ungrateful, not acknowledging former good offices, neglectful of favours, an ingrate.

कृतघ्नता krit-ughn-táee, *s. f.* Ingratitude.

कृतग्य krit-úg-yuh, *adj.* Grateful, remembering former aid or favors.

कृतग्यता krit-úg-yut-a, *s. f.* Gratitude.

कृतयुग krít-yoog, *s. m.* The first of the four ages of the world, the *Sut-yoog.*

कृतार्थ krit-árth, *adj.* The granting of supplication, the fulfilment of a request, successful, having obtained one's purpose or accomplished one's design.

कृतार्थता kritárth-ta, *s. f.* Success, accomplishment of an object.

कृत्तिका krít-ti-ka, *s. f.* The third of the lunar mansions, or constellations in the moon's path, consisting of six stars ; and corresponding to the pleiades.

कृत्रिम krít-rim, *adj.* Made, factitious, artificial, the reverse of what is naturally or spontaneously produced.

कृत्रिमपुत्र krit-rim-póotr, *s. m.* An adopted son ; one of the twelve kinds recognized in law.

कृत्रिममित्र krit-rim-mítr, *s. m.* An acquired friend, one on whom benefits have been conferred or from whom they have been received.

कृदन्त krid-unt, *s. m.* Derivative from a verb ; name of a treatise on syntax.

कृपण kríp-un, *adj.* Miserly, avaricious.

कृपणता kríp-un-ta, *s. f.* Stinginess.

कृपा kríp-a, *s. f.* Tenderness, compassion, favor, kindness, pity, mercy, affection, bounty.

कृपाण krip-án, *s. m.* A sword, a scimitar or sacrificial knife.

कृपानिधान krip-a-nidhán, *s. m.* The abode of mercy, the mansion of kindness.

कृपालु krip-á-loo, *adj.* Compassionate, tender, merciful, liberal, kind, benevolent, obliging, propitious.

कृपामय kripa-múy, *adj.* Compassionate.

कृपासिंधु kripa-sindhóo, *s. m.* Ocean of grace, mercy or kindness.

कृपाहीन kripa-héen, *adj.* Unfeeling, unkind, hard-hearted.

कृमि krím-i, *s. m.* A worm, an insect in general ; lac, the red dye, which is in fact an insect.

कृमिघ्न krim-íghn, *adj.* Vermifuge, anthelmintic. *s. m.* A shrub used in medicine, as an anthelmintic, commonly called *Birung* (*Erycibe paniculata*).

कृमिज krím-ij, *s. m.* Agallochum.

कृमिजा krím-ij-a, *s. f.* Lac, a red dye so called.

कृमिदन्तक krími-dúntuk, *s. m.* Tooth-ache with decay of the teeth.

कृमिल krím-il, *adj.* Having worms, wormy.

कृमिला krím-il-a, *s. f.* A fruitful woman, one bearing many children.

कृमिहर krimi-húr, *adj.* Anthelmintic, vermifuge.

कृमी krímee, *adj.* Affected with worms.

कृश krish, *adj.* Small, thin, little, minute ; spare, emaciated.

कृशता krísh-ut-a, *s. f.* Smallness, slenderness, spareness, leanness, thinness, emaciatedness.

कृशांगी krish-án-gee, *s. f.* A woman with a slender shape.

कृषक krish-úk, *s. m.* A husbandman, a peasant.

कृषाण krish-án, *s. m.* A husbandman, ploughman, peasant, farmer.

कृषि kríshi, *s. f.* Husbandry, agriculture ; ploughing, cultivating the soil, &c.

कृष्ण krishn, *adj.* Black, dark blue. *n. prop.* One of the *Hindoo* mythological incarnations : he is distinct from the ten *Uvutars* or incarnations, being identified with the deity.

कृष्णचरण krishn-chúr-un, *s. m.* A plant (*Poinciana pulcherrima*).

कृष्णजटा krishn-jút-a, *s. f.* The Indian spikenard.

कृष्णजीरक krishn-jée-ruk, *s. m. Culonji*, a plant having a small black seed which is used for medical and culinary purposes (*Nigella Indica*).

कृष्णता krishn-tá, *s. f.* Blackness.

कृष्णतामर krishn-támr, *s. m.* A kind of Sandal wood, of a dusky copper hue.

कृष्णपक्ष krishn-puksh, *s. m.* The dark half of a month, the fifteen days during which the moon is in the wane.

कृष्णफल krishn-phul, *s. m.* A fruit, the *Corinda.*

कृष्णलवण krishn-lúvun, *s. m.* A factitious salt, either that prepared by evaporation from saline soil, or the medicinal kind, a muriate of soda.

कृष्णलोह krishn-lóh, *s. m.* The loadstone.

कृष्णसार krishn-shár, ⎫ *s.m.* The black
कृष्णसारंग krishn-shár-ung, ⎭ antelope.

कृष्णानदी krishna-núd-ee, *s. f.* A river, possibly the river *Kistna* in the Decan.

कृष्णावास krishn-a-vás, *s. m.* The holy fig-tree (*Ficus religiosa*).

कृष्णाश्रित krishn-á-shrit, *adj.* Devoted to or the votary of *Krishn.*

कृशता krís-ut-a, *s. f.* Slenderness, spareness, leanness.

के keh, *postpos.* Of *Ooskeh pas*, near him.

केओरा keo-rá, *s. m.* A flower (*Pandanus odoratissimus*).

केंचुआ kenchwa, *s. m.* An earthworm.

केकड़ा kék-ra, *s. m.* A crab.

केकर kék-ur, *adj.* Squint-eyed.

केका kék-a, *s. f.* The cry of a peacock.

केकी kék-ee, *s. m.* A peacock.

केचूक kéch-ook, *s. m.* An esculent root (*Arum colocasia*).

केरा kér-a, *s. m.* A sapling.

केतकी két-kee, *s. f.* A flower (*Pandanus odoratissimus*).

केता két-a, *pron.* How much? how many?

केतिक két-ik, *adj.* Some, a few, a little.

केतु két-oo, *s. m.* The dragon's tail or descending node; in astronomy the ninth of the planets; in mythology, a demon; a comet, a falling-star, &c.

केतुतारा kétoo-tára, *s. f.* A comet.

केतुमाल ket-oo-mál, *s. m.* One of the nine great divisions of the known world, the western portion or *Vursh* of *Jumboo Dweep.*

केतुरत्न ketoo-rútn, *s. m.* Lapis lazuli.

केदार ked-ár, *s. m.* A field; a mountain; the modern *Kedar*, part of the *Himalaya* mountains.

केंदु kén-doo, *s. m.* A sort of ebony (*Diospyros tomentosa*).

केंदुक kén-dook, *s. m.* A sort of ebony, that yields a species of tar (*Diospyros glutinosa*).

केंद्र kendr, *s. m.* The poles; the centre of a circle.

केयूर keyóor, *s. m.* A bracelet worn on the upper arm.

केल kel, *s. f.* Amorous dalliance, coition.

केलन kél-un, *s. f.* A daughter-in-law.

केला kéla, *s. m.* A plantain (*tree or fruit*), banana.

केलि kél-i, ⎫ *s. f.* Play, sport, pastime,
केली kél-ee, ⎭ amusement, amorous dalliance, coition.

केवरा kév-ra, *s. m.* A flower (*Pandanus odoratissimus*).

केवर्त्त kev-urtt, ⎫ *s. m.* A fisherman.
केवट kév-ut, ⎭

केवल kév-ul, *adj.* One, alone, only, solely, completely, peculiarly; all, entire, whole. *s. m.* A species of knowledge, probably that of the unity of God. *adv.* Completely, peculiarly, only, solely.

केवांच kev-ánch, *s. f.* Cowitch (*Dolichos pruriens*).

केवार kev-ár, *s. m.* The shutter or fold of a door, a door.

केवली kév-lee, *s. f.* Horoscope, nativity.

केश kesh, *s. m.* The hair of the head, a cock's comb.

केशर késh-ur, *s. m.* A plant, called also *Nagesur* (*Mesua ferrea*); a shrub used in dying (*Rottleria tinctoria*).

केशरिन् késh-ur-in, ⎫ *s. m.* A lion.
केशरी késh-ur-ee, ⎭

केशवेश kesh-vésh, *s. m.* A tress or fillet of hair.

केशाकेशी késh-a-késh-ee, *conj.* Pulling the hair mutually, hair to hair.

केशी keshée, *s. f.* A lock of hair on the crown of the head.

केसर kés-ur, *s. m.* Saffron (*Crocus sativus*).

केसरिया kes-ur-íya, *adj.* Yellow or saffron-coloured.

केहरी keh-ree, *s. m.* A lion.

कै ky, *pron.* How many? *adj.* Several. *conj.* Or, either. *Ky-ek*, or *Ky-oo-ek*, Some few.

कैंचली kynch-lee, *s. f.* The slough or skin of a snake.

कैराटक ky-rá-tuk, *s. m.* A species of poison, one of the fixed kinds.

कैत kyt, *s. m.* A tree (*Feronia elephantum*).

कैथा ky-thá, *s. m.* An intoxicating drink made from the fruit of the *Kyt.*

कैथी kyt-hée, *s. f.* The *Kytkee-Naguree* characters used chiefly by *Kayusths* about *Patna* and the adjacent country.

कैन kyn, *s. f.* A bamboo twig.

कैरी kyree, *s. f.* A small unripe mango. *Kyree-ankh, s. f.* A wall-eye, an eye the pupil of which is grey

कैल kyl, *s. f.* A sprout, a shoot.

कैलास ky-lás, *s. m.* The mountain *Kylas*, the fabulous residence of *Koover*, and favourite haunt of *Shiv*; it is placed by the *Hindoos* amongst the *Himalaya* mountains, and the name is given to one of the loftiest peaks lying on the north of the *Manus* lake.   [terman.

कैवर्त ky-vúrtt, *s. m.* A fisherman, a waterman

कैवल्य ky-vályuh, *s. m.* Eternal emancipation, future happiness.

कैसा ky-sa,⎫ *pron.* How? in what man-
कैसे ky-seh,⎬ ner? what sort of? What
कैसो ky-so,⎭ like? *Kysahee,* Howsoever.

को ko, *pron.* Who? which? what? *postpos.* To, for.

कोई kó-ee, *s. f.* The water-lily (*Nymphæa lotus*); the pulp of the jack fruit (*Artocarpus integrifolia*).

कोई kó-ee,⎫ *pron.* Any, any one. any
कोऊ kó-oo,⎬ body, some one. *a.* Some
body. *Koee-sa,* certain, somebody, something. *Koee nuh koee,* Somebody or other, some or other. *Koee nukeen,* Nobody, none. *Koee dum men,* Soon, shortly, immediately.

कोएरी koerée, *s. m.* A planter, a husbandman, a gardener, a *Hindoo* cast whose profession is husbandry.

कोएला koéla, *s. m.* Charcoal.

कोंचना kónch-na, *v. a.* To prick, pierce, stab, gore.

कोंडा kónd-ha, *s. m.* A gourd, a sweet pumpkin (*Cucurbita pepo*).

कोंपल kón-pul, *s. f.* A young shoot, a bud, an unblown flower.

कोक kok, *s. m.* The ruddy goose (*Anas caserca*).

कोका kó-ka, *s. m.* A foster-brother, nurse's child; a small nail, a tack; a kind of lotus.

कोकिनी kó-kin-ee, *adj.* Short.

कोकिल kó-kil,⎫ *s. m.* The black or Indian
कोईल kó-eel,⎬ cuckoo (*Cuculus*): the *kokil* makes a prominent figure in *Hindoo* poetry, and is supposed by his musical cry to inspire pleasing and tender emotions.

कोकिलबयनी kókil-bynee, *adj.* Speaking like a *kokil*, eloquent as the *kokil*.

कोख kokh,⎫ *s. f.* The womb, the abdo-
कोखा ko-khá,⎬ men, hypochondrium.

कोखबंद kokh-búnd, *adj.* Barren.

कोंकुन kón-kun, *s. m.* The name of a country, *Konkan,* in the peninsula.

कोजागर ko-já-gur, *s. m.* The day of full-moon in the month *Aswin* (*Sept.-Oct.*): who is awake? the call of *Lukhmee,* who descending on this night promised wealth to all that were awake, hence the night is spent in festivity and games of chance in honor of the goddess.

कोट kot, *s. m.* A fort, redoubt, stronghold, castle.

कोटर kó-tur, *s. m.* A kind of greens; holes made by birds in trees.

कोटि kóti, *adj.* A crore or ten millions.

कोट्ट kott, *s. m.* A fort, a castle, a stronghold.

कोठ koth, *s. m.* A species of leprosy with large round spots; ring-worm, impetigo.

कोठरी kóth-ree, *s. f.* A room, chamber, apartment, closet.

कोठा kót-ha, *s. m.* A house built of burnt-bricks or stone; a story, a floor.

कोठी kót-hee, *s. f.* A small (*brick*) house, a warehouse, a granary, dwelling, mansion, barrack, chamber, bank, chest, bin, storehouse, factory; a banking-house; the chamber of a gun, the inside or shaft of a well; the womb; the ferrule or mounting at the end of a scabbard. *Kotheewal,* A wholesale merchant, a warehouse-keeper.

कोठौर kothóur, *adv.* Out of place.

कोर kor, *s. m.* The leprosy.

कोरना kór-na, *v. a.* To dig out, to scoop, bore, hollow, excavate.

कोरबाला kor-bá-la, *s. m.* The name of a bird, of a snake, and of a flower.

कोरा kó-ra, *s. m.* A whip, a lash. *Kora kurna,* To whip; to reduce to obedience; to put a horse to his speed by whipping. *Kora marna,* To lash.

कोरी koree, *s. f.* A score, twenty.

कोरह korh, *s. m.* The leprosy. *Korh-men khaj nikulna,* In leprosy to catch the itch: (*met.*) to have one misfortune added to another.

कोरहना kórh na, *v. a.* To vex, to afflict, to grieve.

कोरही kór-hee, *adj.* A leper

कोन kon, *s. m.* A corner, an angle. *Konuhdar, adj.* Cornered, angled.

कोना kó-na, *s. m.* Corner, side. *Kona-koothra, s. m.* A corner of a room, house, &c., hole and corner, every corner.

कोनि kó ni, *adj.* Having a crooked arm.

कोतल kotul, *s. m.* A led-horse. *Kotulkush, s. m.* A surcingle, particularly for fastening body-clothes.

कोतमीर kotméer, *s. f.* A kind of greens, coriander.

कोथ koth, *s. m.* Inflammation and ulceration of the angles of the eye-lids ; gangrene.

कोदो kodo,　 कोद्रव kodrúv, } *s. m* A small grain (*Paspalum frumentaceum*).

कोना kóna, *s. m.* A corner, an angle, a side. *Konadar, adj,* Cornered, angular.

कोन्त kont, *s. f.* A spear.

कोप kop, *s. m.* Wrath, rage, passion, anger.

कोपज्वलित kop-jwúlit, *adj.* Enraged, inflamed with wrath. 　[with anger.

कोपदीप्त kop-déept, *adj.* Incensed, inflamed

कोपन kopún, *adj.* Passionate, wrathful.

कोपना kópna, *v. n.* To be angry, to be wrathful, to rage. *s. f.* A passionate woman.

कोपवान kopwán, *adj.* Passionate, angry.

कोपवेग kop-vég, *s. m.* Violence, impetuosity of passion.

कोपाकुल kopa-kóol, *adj.* Furious, enraged.

कोपान्वित kopan-wít, *adj.* Passionate, angry, rageful, wrathful.

कोपिनी kopínee, *f.* } *adj.* Angry, passionate, wrathful.
कोपी kopée, *m.* }

कोपीन kopéen, *s. f.* A cloth worn (*round the waist*) between the legs.

कोबी kobée, *s. f.* A cabbage.

कोमल kómul, *adj.* Soft, bland, tender, mild, placid.

कोमलता komultá, *s. f.* Softness, placidity, tenderness, mildness, agreeableness.

कोमलताई komul-tá-ee, *s f.* Softness.

कोयन kó-yun, *s. m.* A corner, an angle.

कोयल kó-yul, *s. f.* A bird (*Cuculus*) ; a flower (*Clitoria ternatea*).

कोयला kó-yul-a, *s. m.* Charcoal.

कोर kor, *s. f.* Edge, border, margin, side, point. *s. m.* A crore or ten millions.

कोरक kó ruk, *s. m.* A bud, an unblown flower.

कोरा kó-ra, *adj.* New, unused, unhandled, unbleached, fresh (*applied chiefly to earthen vessels, cloth, or paper*). *Koreh ruhna,* To be disappointed.

कोरंगी ko-rún-gee, *s. f.* Small cardamums.

कोरी kó-ree, *s. f.* A virgin.

कोरो kóro, *s. m.* A rafter.

कोल kol, *s. m.* A creek, a bay ; any long narrow passage, a lane ; embracing, an embrace ; a tribe of mountaineers, the *Coles ;* a country, *Calinga,* the modern sea coast from *Cuttack* to *Madras.*

कोला kolá, *s. m.* A jackal.

कोलाहल ko-lá-hul, *s. m.* Uproar, clutter, tumult, mirth, a confused or mingled sound, a noise made by many, or a great an indistinct noise.

कोलिया kó-li-ya, *s. m.* A lane.

कोलियाना ko-li-yá-na, *v. a.* To embrace, to take in the lap.

कोली kó-lee, *s. m.* A weaver.

कोलू kó-loo, *s. m.* An oilman, a cast whose business it is to sell oil.

कोलेह kó-leh, *adv.* Lap, bosom, embrace.

कोल्हू kúl-hoo, *s. m.* An oilman's press. *Kolhoo-men purwa dena,* To macerate (*any thing*) in a press, &c.

कोविदार ko-vi-dár, *s. m.* A species of Ebony (*Bauhinia variegata*).

कोश kosh, *s. m.* A measure of about two miles ; a piece added to the end of a sleeve, a cuff.

कोशना kósh-na, *v. a.* To curse.

कोशल kó-shul, *s. m. f.* A name of the city of *Ujodhya* (*Oude*) or neighbouring district.

कोष kosh, *s. m.* A sheathe, a scabbard ; a judicial trial by oath or ordeal, attesting a deity and touching or drinking water three times in which some idol has been washed ; a testicle or the scrotum ; a nutmeg ; a dictionary or vocabulary.

कोषला kó-shul-a, *s. f.* The country south of *Ujodhya* (*Oude*) or *Ujodhya* itself.

कोषवृद्धि kósh-bríddhi, *s. f.* Swelled testicle, enlargement of the scrotum, from Hernia humoralis, or hydrocele, &c.

कोष्ठ koshth, *s. m.* A granary, a place in which grain is kept ; an apartment ; any viscus, as the heart, lungs, stomach, bowels, &c.

कोष्ठाग्नि koshth-ágni, *s. m.* The digestive faculty, the gastric juice.

कोसना kós-na, *v. a.* To curse.

कोसली kóslee, *s. m.* New leaves just sprouting.

कोसा kósa, *s. m.* Curse, malediction.

कोहनी kóh-nee, *s. f.* The elbow.

कोहर kó-hur, *s. m.* Fog, mist ; name of a fruit.

कोही kó-hee, *s. f.* A species of hawk (*Falco cristatellus*).

कौ kou, *postpos.* Of, belonging to.

कौं koun, *postpos.* Denoting the objective case, To, for.

कौंध koundh, *s. f.* Splendour, brightness, flash (*as of lightning*).

कोंधना koundh-na, *v. n.* To lighten, to flash.

कोंधा kound-ha, *s. m.* Lightning.

कोंला koun-la, *s. m.* A kind of orange.

कोरा kou-ra, *s. m.* A shell of a large kind.

कोरियाला kou-ri-yá-la, *s. m.* A kind of snake; a wealthy person.

कोड़ी kóu-ree, *s. f.* A small shell used as coin (Cypraea monita); money, fare, hire; a gland; the point of the sternum, or ensiform cartilage. *Kouree-book, adj.* Venal. *Phootee kouree, or Kanee kouree,* A bit of money of the lowest value, (*fig.*) a farthing.

कोतुक kóu-took, *s. m.* Joy, pleasure, happiness; sport, pastime, diversion, play, trick, show, a scene or spectacle.

कोतुकी kóu-took-ee, *s. m.* A tumbler, a dancer, one who contributes to divert by exhibitions, &c. *adj.* Sportive, of pastime or diversion.

कोन koun, *pron.* Who? which? what? *Kounsa,* Which? what? what sort of?

कोपीन kou-péen, *s. m.* A privy part, a small piece of cloth worn over the privities.

कोमार kou-már, *s. m.* Youth, childhood. *Koumaree, adj.* Maiden, virgin.

कोमुद kóu-mood, *s. m.* The month *Kartik* (October-November).

कोमुदी kóu-moo-dee, *s. f.* Moonlight.

कोर kour, *s. m.* A mouthful.

कोरपंडु kour-pún-doo, *s. m.* The *Kouruvus,* and the *Panduvus,* the patronymics of two families descended from *Kooroo* by their respective fathers *Dhritarashtruh* and *Pandoo.*

कोरव kóu-ruv, *s. m.* A descendant of *Kooroo.*

कोल koul, *adj.* Of a good family, well-born. *s. m.* A mouthful.

कोलुव koulúv, *s. m.* One of the astrological periods called *Kuruns.*

कोला kóu-la, *s. m.* Corner, side (*of a room,* &c.); embrace, bosom, armful; a kind of orange.

कोलिक koulík, *adj.* Ancestral.

कोलिया kóu-li-ya, *s. f.* A small mouthful.

कोलियाना kou-li-yá-na, *v. a.* To take in the arms, or the lap, to embrace.

कोली kóu-lee, *s. f.* Embrace, grasp of the arms.

कोवा kóu-va, *s. m.* A crow.

कावोंठी kóu-va-thén-thee, *s. f.* A flower (Clitoria ternatea).

कोश koush, *s. m. Canyakoobj* or *Canouje,* the ancient city, so called.

कोशुल kóu-shul, *s. m.* Happiness, welfare, &c.

कोशुली kóu-shul-ee, *s. f.* Greeting, salutation, friendly inquiry; a respectful present.

कोशुल्युह kou-shúl-yuh, *s. m.* Good fortune, well-being, &c.

कोशिकी kóu-shik-ee, *s. f.* Name of a river.

कोशेयुह kou-shéyuh, } *adj.* Silken, of silk.
कोशेय kou-shéyuh, }

कोसोंभ kóu-soombh, *adj.* Dyed with safflower.

कोस्तोभ kóu-stoobh, *s. m.* The jewel of *Krishn* suspended on his breast.

क्या kyá, *pron.* What? how? why? whether, or.

क्यारी kyá-ree, *s. f.* A bed (*of a garden*); a frame.

क्यों kyón, *adv.* Why? wherefore? how? well? what? then, because.

क्योंकर kyón-kur, *adv.* Why? how?

क्योंकि kyón-ki, *adv.* Because that.

क्रंदन krún-dun, *s. m.* Weeping, lamenting.

क्रम krum, *s. m.* Order, method; uninterrupted progress.

क्रमि krúm-i, *s. m.* An insect, a worm.

क्रय kruy, *s. m.* Buying, purchase.

क्रयविक्रय kruy-bík-ruy, *s. m.* Trade, traffic, buying and selling.

क्रांति krán-ti, *s. f.* Ascending, surmounting either in a literal or figurative sense; the sun's course on the globe, the ecliptic; declination of a planet; splendour, lustre.

क्रांतिमंडल kránti-múndul, *s. m.* The ecliptic.

क्रिमी krím-ee, *s. m.* A worm, an insect; lac, which is the accumulation of an insect.

क्रिया krí-ya, *s. f.* Deed, an act, action; a religious act; obsequies; a verb; an oath. *Kriya-kurm, s. m.* The performance of obsequies.

क्रियेंद्रिय kriyén-driyuh, *s. m.* An organ of action, as the hand, foot, voice, organ of generation and that of excretion.

क्रीड़ा krée-ra, *s. f.* Sport, play, pastime, pleasure, amusement, game.

क्रीड़ारतन kréera-rutn, *s. m.* Copulation.

क्रीड़ावत kreera-vút, *adj.* Sporting, sportive.

क्रीत kreet, *adj.* Bought, purchased.

क्रीतक krée-tuk, *s. m.* A son bought from his natural parents, and adopted as male issue.

क्रीता krée-ta, *s. m.* A son, one of the twelve kinds acknowledged by the ancient *Hindoo* law; he who is purchased from his natural parents.

क्रीमिज krím-ij, *s. m.* The *Ugooroo* or aloe wood.

क्रूद्ध krooddh, *adj.* Angry, wrathful.

क्रूध kroodh, *s. f.* Anger, passion.

क्रूर kroor, *adj.* Cruel, pitiless, hard-hearted, harsh, savage ; formidable, terrible.

क्रूरकर्मा kroor-kúrma, *adj.* Fierce, cruel, unrelenting.

क्रूरकोष्ठ kroor-kóshth, *s. m.* Torpid or costive bowels unaffected by strong purgatives.

क्रूरता kroor-tá, *s. f.* Cruelty, fierceness.

क्रूरदृश kroor-drísh, *adj.* Mischievous, villanous ; evil-eyed.

क्रोध krodh, *s. m.* Anger, wrath, passion, rage.

क्रोधन kró-dhun,
क्रोधिन kró-dhin, } *adj.* Passionate, angry, wrathful, choleric.
क्रोधी kró-dhee,

क्रोधना krodhuná, *s. f.* A passionate woman, a vixen.

क्रोधमय krodh-múy, *adj.* Angry, passionate.

क्रोधवर्जित krodh-vúrjit, *adj.* Free from wrath, mild, calm. [lent.

क्रोधवस krodh-vús, *adj.* Passionate, vio-
क्रोधी krodhée, *adj.* Angry, passionate.

क्रोश krosh, *s. m.* A measure of distance, a league, a *Cos* containing 4,000 cubits ; some make the *Cos* 8,000 cubits.

क्रौञ्च krounch, *s. m.* One of the *Dweeps*, or principal divisions of the world.

क्लान्त klant, *adj.* Wearied ; depressed in spirits or exhausted.

क्लान्तमन klant-múna, *adj.* Low-spirited, languid, melancholy.

क्लान्ति klánti, *s. f.* Fatigue, weariness.

क्लिश्मित klísh-it, } *adj.* Distrest, afflicted,
क्लिष्ट klisht,   } wearied.

क्लीव kleev, *s. m.* The neuter gender ; an eunuch. *adj.* Weak, impotent ; idle, slothful.

क्लेद kled, *s. m.* Wetness, dampness, moisture.

क्लेश klesh, *s. m.* Pain, affliction or distress ; pain from disease, anguish ; worldly occupation, care, trouble.

क्लेशित kleshít, *adj.* Pained, distressed, afflicted.

क्लैव्य klyv, *s. m.* Absence of virility, impotence ; the neuter gender ; unmanliness, cowardice, &c.

ख

ख khuh, The second consonant of the *Naguree* alphabet : it is a guttural and has the sound of the English kh.

ख khuh, *s. m.* Heaven ; sky or æther ; vacuity.

खंकली khúnk-lee, *s. f.* A plant (*Polypody*), a kind of moss.

खंखर khun-khúr, *adj.* Dry and crackling.

खंखारना khun-khár-na, *v. a.* To hem, hawk, expectorate.

खंगर khún-gur, *s. m.* Semi-vitrified bricks.

खंगाल डालना khungál dálna, *v. a.* To murder privately.

खंगालना khun-gál-na, *v. a.* To wash, rinse.

खंगैल khún-gyl, *adj.* Tusked.

खंजन khún-jun, *s. m.* A small bird, a wagtail.

खंजरी khúnj-ree, *s. f.* A small tambourin, a timbrel.

खंड khund, *s. m.* Side, quarter, division of the earth, region, division of a house, apartment ; part, piece, fragment, portion ; a chapter, section ; sugar (*coarse*) ; the songs of *Pudmawut*.

खंडन khún-dun, *s. m.* The act of reducing any thing to pieces, the rescinding of an order, the refuting of an argument, the removing of any calamity, the thwarting of any scheme ; breaking, dividing.

खंडन करना khúndun kúrna, *v. a.* To cut up, to quarter, to cut to pieces; to divide ; to refute.

खंडना khúnd-na, *v. a.* To refute.

खंडर khún-dur, *s. m.* A ruinous and broken-down building, ruins of a town or house, &c.

खंडरीच khund-réech, *s. m.* A small bird, a wagtail.

खंडला khúnd-la, *s. m.* A flake, a slice (*especially of fish*), a division or piece (*of land*).

खंडित करना khúndit kúrna, *v. a.* To refute, in'errupt, prevent.

खंडिता khún-dit-a, *s. f.* A woman, who, provoked at the infidelities of her husband or lover, is rather abusive, speaks her mind freely, but is supposed to retain no malice in her breast.

खंध khundh, *s. m.* District, province, division, section.

खंधोर khun-dhór, *adj.* Turbid.

खंती khún-tee, *s. f.* A paddle for digging the ground, a dibble.

खंदाना khun-dá-na, *s. m.* A pit from which earth has been dug out to make bricks or pottery ; a notch in a log of wood.

खंभ khumbh, *s. m.* A pillar, a post. *Khum thokna, v. a.* To strike the hands against the arms preparatory to wrestling, &c., to challenge (*as wrestlers do*).

खोखोरना khukhórna, *v. a.* To scoop, scrape.

खुग khug, *s. m.* A bird ; air, wind. *Khug-ra, s. m.* The adjutant bird.

खगोल khugól, *s. m.* The vault or circle of the heavens, the planisphere ; the same represented artificially, the armillary sphere.

खगोलविद्या khúgol-vídya, *s. f.* Astronomy.

खचना khúch-na, *v. n.* To be set (*as a jewel*).

खचर khúch-ur, *s. m.* A cloud.

खचा khúch-a, } *adj.* Set (*as a jewel*),
खचित khúch-it, } set with jewels, inlaid.

खजूर khuj-óor, *s. m.* A date, or date tree (*Phenix dactylifera*) ; wild date (*Elate sylvestris or Phenix sylvestris*) ; a kind of sweetmeat. *Khuj-oor-chhuree*, A kind of silk cloth stained with waving marks like the traces of the old leaves on the trunk of the date tree.

खजूरा khujóora, *s. m.* The ridge of a thatched roof.

खजूरिया khujóoriya, *s. m.* A date.

खंज khunj, *adj.* Lame, crippled, limping.

खंजन khún-jun, *s. m.* A small bird, the wagtail (*Motacilla alba*).

खंजरी khúnj-ur-ee, *s. m.* A small tambourin, a timbrel.

खंजरीट khunj-réet, *s. m.* A wagtail.

खंजा khún-ja, *s. f.* A species of metre, a stanza of two lines, one of 32, the other of 30 feet.

खट khut, *adj.* Six. *Khut-rus*, Six tastes. *Khut-shastr*, The six philosophical sciences of the Hindoos (*called otherwise Khut-durshun*), viz. *Niyayu*, Logic, taught by *Gotum* ; *Vysheshik*, taught by *Kunad* : it agrees with *Niyayu* in some points and differs in others ; *Mimansa*, taught by *Jymuni* : it consists of rules for the construction and right interpretation of the *Veds* ; *Vedant*, taught by *Vyasdev* : the science of theology ; *Sankhyu*, taught by *Kupil* : the followers of this sect disbelieve in a Creator, saying that the universe is from all eternity ; *Patun-jul*, introduced by *Shesunag* : it agrees in every point with *Sankhyu*, excepting that it makes God to be the Creator.

खट khut, *s. f.* A bedstead.

खटकना khút-uk-na, *v. n.* To wrangle, to offend, to wrankle, to pierce (*as a thorn*) ; to doubt, to be apprehensive. *s. m.* Doubt, hesitation, disgust.

खटका khút-ka, } *s. m.* Apprehension, sus-
खटक khút-uk, } picion, doubt, suspense, abodement ; sound of footsteps.

खटकाना khutkána, *s. m.* Rapping, thumping, rattling (*of a door, &c.*)

खटखटाना khut-khut-ána, *v. a.* To knock, tap, pat, rap.

खटगीर khut-géer, *s. m.* A bug.

खटछप्पर khut-chhúppur, *s. m.* A bedstead with curtains.

खटना khút-na, *v. n.* To last.

खटपट khút-put, *s. f.* Wrangling, contention, quarrel ; clashing of weapons.

खटमल khút-mul, *s. m.* A bug.

खटमीठा khut-méet-ha, *s. m.* A mixed taste of sour and sweet ; agreeable.

खटराग khut-rág, *s. m.* Wrangling ; singing discordantly.

खटरिया khút-ri-ya, *s. m.* An insect.

खटवा khút-wa, *s. f.* A bedstead.

खटवारा khutwára, *s. m.* A dunghill.

खटाई khut-á-ee, *s. f.* Acidity, sourness ; an acid.

खटाका khut-á-ka, *s. m.* A crash.

खटापटी khut-a-pút-ee, *s. f.* Wrangling.

खटाल khut-ál, *s. m.* Spring-tide.

खटाव khut-áo, *s. m.* A pin with which a boat is fastened.

खटास khut-ás, *s. m.* A polecat.

खटिया khút-i-ya, *s. f.* A bedstead, a bier. *Khooda kureh ooskee khutiya nikleh*, God grant his bier may be carried out, or he may die (*a common form of cursing*).

खटीक khut-éek, *s. m.* A hunter, one who lives by killing and selling game.

खटोला khut-ó-la, *s. m.* A small bedstead.

खट्टा khút-ta, *adj.* Acid, sour. *Khutta-sag, s. m.* The herb sorrel. *Khutta-sa, adj.* Sourish, acetous, acescent.

खट्टास khuttás, *s. m.* The civet or zibet cat (*Viverra zibetha*), a polecat.

खट्टिक khút-tik, *s. m.* A hunter, one who lives by killing and selling game.

खट्टू khút-too, *s. m.* A labourer.

खट्टा khút-wa, *s. f.* A bedstead.

खरूंख khurúnkh, *adj.* Dry, dried up.

खरुक khúr-uk, *s. f.* A cow-house or cowshed ; an imitative sound. *Khuruk jana*, To take warning, to be apprized. [clang

खरुकना khúr-uk-na, *v. n.* To rustle, rattle,

खरका khúr-ka, *s. m.* Doubt, apprehension ; a toothpick.

खरखराना khur-khur-ána, *v. n.* To creak, clatter, rattle, jar ; to grind the teeth ; to snore.

खरखराहट khur-khur-áhut, *s. f.* Creaking, clatter, rattling, jarring (*as a door*), snoring.

खरुग khúr-ug, *s. m.* A sword or scimitar.

खरबुड़ाहट khurburáhut, } *s. f.* Hurry,
खरबुड़ी khúr-bur-ee, } bustle, commotion, tumult, uproar ; noise of horse's feet in galloping ; griping on going to stool.

खुरमंडल khúr-mun-dul, *s. f.* Wrangling.

खुरसान khur-sán, *s. m.* A whetstone, a grindstone.

खुरा khúr-a, *adj.* Erect, upright, standing up, standing, steep, high, aground, ready, ripe, perpendicular. *Khura kurna*, To raise, station, place, stay or stop, stick up, place erect, procure a fictitious person for some purpose. *Khura hona*, To stand up, be erect, rise, stand. *Khura ruhna*, *v. n.* To stand, stay, remain standing.

खुराऊं khur-á-oon, *s. m.* Pattens (*wooden*). *Khuraoondar*, A kind of shoes fastened to pattens.

खुरिया khúr-i-ya, *s. f.* Chalk.

खुरिल khúr-il, *s. f.* A mortar.

खुरी khúr-ee, } *s. f.* Chalk.
खुरीमिट्टी khúr-ee-míttee, } *Kut-khuree*, *s. f.* A species of steatites with which children learn to write, and which is used in giving a polish to stucco.

खुरुआ khúr-oo-a, *s. m.* An ornament worn on the wrist, a bracelet.

खुरेखुरे khúr-eh-khúr-eh, *adv.* Soon, immediately, instantly, presently, quickly.

खुर्ग khurg, *s. m. f.* A sword.

खुरह khurh, *s. f.* Straw.

खुन्द khund, *s. m.* Side, quarter, region, division of a house, apartment; part, piece, fragment, portion; a chapter, section; sugar (*coarse*); the songs of *Pudmawut*; a flaw in a jewel.

खुन्दन khún-dun, *s. m.* Breaking, dividing, cutting, reducing to pieces, rescinding an order, refuting an argument, removing of any calamity, thwarting of any scheme.

खुन्दन करना khúndun kúrna, *v. a.* To cut up, to quarter, to cut to pieces, to divide; to refute.

खुन्दना khúnd-na, *v. a.* To refute.

खुन्दित khund-ít, *adj.* Cut, torn, broken in pieces; destroyed; refuted, controverted; scattered, dispersed.

खुन्दित करना khúndit kúrna, *v. a.* To refute, prevent, interrupt.

खुन्दिता khún-dit-a, *s. f.* A woman, who, provoked at the infidelities of her husband or lover, is rather abusive, speaks her mind freely, but is supposed to retain no malice in her breast.

खुतरानी khut-rá-nee, *s. f.* The female of *Khutree*.

खुतवारा khut-wá-ra, *s. m.* A dunghill.

खुत्ता khútta, *s. m.* A grain-pit, a cavity in which grain is kept.

खुत्री khút-ree, *s. m.* One of the four *Hindoo* casts, a man of the military tribe. *Khutranee*, *s. f.* The female of *Khutree*.

खुदबुदाना khud-bud-ána, *v. n.* To simmer, to make a boiling noise.

खुदिर khúd-ir, *s. m.* A tree, the resin of which is used in medicine, *Kuttha* or catechu (*Mimosa catechu*).

खुदिरोपम khud-ir-ópum, *s. m.* The *Babool* (*Acacia Arabica*).

खुदी khúd-ee, *s. f.* A grass that grows in ponds.

खुदेर khud-er, *s. f.* Pursuit.

खुदेरना khud-ér-na, *v. a.* To pursue, to hunt.

खुन khun, *s. m.* A division of a house, a story (*of a building*), a flight of rooms; a mine; a certain day of the fortnight, as the full, change, &c., of the moon.

खुनुकना khún-uk-na, *v. n.* To jingle, to ring.

खुनदाना khun-dá-na, *s. m.* A pit from which earth has been dug to make bricks or pottery; a notch in a log of wood.

खुप्ता khúp-ta, *s. m.* A broken tile; a slice of mango.

खुपुत khúp-ut, *adj.* Expended. *s. f.* Vent, sale.

खुप्ती kúp-tee, *s. f.* Vent, sale, expense; request; a lunatic.

खुपना khúp-na, *v. n.* To be dried up or absorbed; to sell, go off, be expended or made away with; to remain, join, mix with, enter, penetrate. *s. m.* A company (*of travellers, &c.*)

खुपरा khúp-ra, *s. m.* A tile; an arrow with a broad point.

खुपरी khúp-ree, *s. f.* A small tile; the skull.

खुपरैल khup-ryl, *s. f.* A tiled house, tiling, building of tiles.

खुपाच khup-ách, *s. f.* A piece torn off from a bamboo, a splinter; a very lean person.

खुपाना khup-á-na, *v. a.* To dry up, destroy, make away with, despatch, ravage.

खुपूर khúp-oor, *s. m.* The betel tree (*Areca faufel*, or catechu).

खुपुर khúp-pur, *s. m.* The skull, the cranium; a chafing dish; an earthen cup used by *jogees*; the vessel in which the blood of a victim is offered.

खुबसा khúb-sa, *s. m.* Slime.

खुब्बा khúb-ba, *adj.* Left-handed.

खुम khum, *s. m.* A pillar, a post. *Khum thonkna*, *v. a.* To strike the hands against the arms preparatory to wrestling, &c.; to challenge (as wrestlers do).

खुमुस khumus, *adj.* Sultry.

खुमसाई khumsáee, *s. f.* Sultriness.

खुमाच khumách, *s. f.* A musical mode.

खमीछुन khúm-ee-lun, *s. m.* Lassitude, weariness, sleepiness.

खम्बा khúmba, } *s. m.* A pillar, a post.
खम्भ khumbh, }

खर khur, *s. f.* Grass, straw. *s. m.* An ass.

खरंक khúr-unk, *adj.* Dry, dried up.

खरंजा khúr-un-ja, *s. m.* Pavement, causey.

खरक khúr-uk, *s. f.* A cow-house, or cow-shed.

खरकाना khur-ká-na, *v. a.* To thump, to shake; to frighten away, to put to flight; to sell.

खरखरा khur-khúr-a, *s. m.* A currycomb.

खरखरिया khur-khúr-iya, *s. f.* A chair, a litter.

खरछरा khur-chhúr-a, *adj.* Rough.

खरपा khúr-pa, *s. m.* A sandal; the seam of a garment which extends from the arm-pit down the side.

खरबर khúr-bur, *s. f.* Noise of horse's feet in galloping; tumult, uproar.

खरउल khúr-ul, *s. m.* A stone for grinding medicine on, a mortar.

खरभ khurb, *s. f.* Straw.

खरहरा khur-húr-a, *s. m.* A currycomb.

खरहा khurhá, *s. m.* A hare, a rabbit.

खरहारना khur-hár-na, *v. a.* To sweep.

खरही khúr-hee, *s. f.* A stack, a rick; a kind of grass.

खरा khúr-a, *adj.* Pure, prime, best sort, genuine, honest, candid, sincere, strict.

खराई khur-á-ee, *s. f.* Purity, excellence, probity, rectitude, trustiness, honesty, candour.

खराका khur-á-ka, *s. m.* A crashing noise.

खरहुंड khur-a-húnd, *s. f.* The stalk of burnt grass.

खरी khúr-ee, *s. f.* Oil-cake; chalk.

खरोंट khur-ónt, *s. f.* A scratch with the nail.

खरोंटना khur-ónt-na, *v. a.* To scratch.

खरोचना khur-óch-na, } *v. a.* To scrape, to
खरोतना khur-ót-na, } scratch.

खर्ज khurj, *s. f.* The bass (*in music*).

खर्जूर khúrj-joor, *s. m.* The date tree and its fruit.

खर्जूररस khurjjoor-rús, *s. m.* The juice or extract of the wild date, *Taree*, used to leaven bread, and as an intoxicating liquor, when in a state of spontaneous fermentation.

खर्रा khúr-ra, *s. m.* The rough draught of a letter or any writing; an iron instrument to rub horses with, a currycomb; an ulcer with hardness of the skin on the back of the foot.

खर्राटा khur-rá-ta, *s. m.* Snoring. *Khurra-ta marna,* To snore.

खर्ब khurbb, *s. m.* A large number, ten million millions, a billion. *adj.* A dwarf, short, low, of little size or stature.

खल khul, *s. m.* A worthless person, a malicious person; sediment, deposit of oil, &c., an oil-cake; a pit. *adj.* Low, vile, base; mischievous; bad, wicked.

खलुंगा khul-ún-ga, *s. m.* A park.

खलखलाना khul-khul-ána, *v. n.* To rumble, to grumble (*the bowels*).

खलड़ा khúl-ra, *s. m.* Skin, hide.

खलड़ी khúl-ree, *s. m.* Skin, hide, membrane; the prepuce, foreskin.

खलता khúl-ta, *s. f.* Worthlessness, wickedness, villainy; filthiness.

खलबल khúl-bul, *s. f.* Hurry, bustle, agitation, commotion, alarm, tumult, hurlyburly.

खलबलाना khul-bul-ána, *v. n.* To boil, bubble; to be agitated or tossed up and down.

खलारी khul-ár-ee, *s. f.* The place in which salt is boiled (*in Bengal*).

खलार khul-ár, *s. f.* A hollow, bottom.

खलि khúli, *s. m.* Sediment of oil or oil-cake.

खलियान khul-i-yán, *s. m.* A granary.

खलियाना khul-i-yá-na, *v. a.* To skin, to flay.

खलिश khúlish, } *s. m.* A kind of fish
खलेश khulésh, } (*Trichopodus colisa*).

खलिहान khuli-hán, *s. m.* A threshing-floor.

खली khúl-ee, } *s. f.* The dregs of mus-
खली khúl-lee, } tard-seed, &c., after the oil is pressed out, oil-cakes.

खलेल khul-él, *s. m.* Scented oil; a hole made by children for playing at trap-ball or marbles.

खलोक्ति khul-ókti, *s. f.* Abuse, low or wicked language.

खल्ल khull, *s. m.* A mill, a stone or vessel for grinding drugs, &c.

खल्ला khúl-la, *s. m.* A shoe.

खल्लिट khúllit, *adj.* Bald, morbidly troubled with falling of the hair.

खवा khúv-a, *s. m.* The shoulder.

खशरीर khu-shuréer, *s. m.* A celestial or immortal body.

खसकंत khus-kúnt, *s. f.* Separation, running away.

खसकाना khuskána, *v. a.* To remove, shove out of the way, to slide away, draw back.

खसखस khús-khus, *s. f.* The poppy-head;

the scented roots of a species of grass (*Andropogon muricata*) used for door-screens in the hot weather, which being sprinkled with water, serve to cool the rooms.

खसखस रस khuskhus-rús, *s. m.* Poppy-juice, opium.

खसखसा khús-khus-a, *s. m.* Grinding the teeth.

खसखसाना khus-khus-ána, *v. n.* To grind the teeth.

खसरा khús-ra, *s. m.* A day-book, field-book, waste-book, rough drawings, draught (*of an account*); a scab; a kind of eruptive disease.

खसाना khus-á-na, *v. n.* To ruin, fall in, sink; to open, loosen.

खसोटना khus-ót-na, *v. a.* To pull, pluck, pull the hair, scratch, tear.

खस्फटिक khuh-sphútik, *s. m.* Crystal, the sun gem; the moon gem.

खंग khang, *s. m.* A tusk.

खंच khanch, *s. m.* Slime, mud.

खांचा khán-cha, *s. m.* A tray, a basket, a pannier; a cage, a hen-coop.

खंड khand, *s. m.* Sugar (*coarse*).

खांडना khánd-na, *v. a.* To excavate, to pound.

खांडा khán-da, *s. m.* A straight double-edged sword, cutlass, cleaver (*butcher's*); a flake or slice (*of fish*). *Khandeh keh dhar-pur chulna*, To arbitrate, to decide.

खांसना kháns-na, *v. n.* To cough.

खांसी khán-see, *s. f.* A cough.

खाई kháee, *s. f.* A ditch, a moat, a trench.

खाऊ kháoo, *s. m.* A glutton.

खाग khag, *s. m.* The horn of a rhinoceros.

खाज khaj, *s. f.* The itch.

खाजा khá-ja, *s. m.* A sweetmeat like pie-crust.

खाट khat, *s. f.* A bedstead; a bier, a cot or bedstead on which dead bodies are conveyed to the pile.

खात khat, *s. f.* Manure. *s. m.* A pit, a subterraneous granary.

खाता khá-ta, *s. m.* The act of eating; daily account, waste-book. *Khata-baree, s. f.* A storehouse.

खाती khá-tee, *s. f.* A cast generally employed as cart-wrights. *s. m.* A carpenter.

खाद khad, *s. f.* Dung, manure.

खाद्य khád-yuh, *adj.* Edible, fit to be eaten. *s. m.* Food, victuals.

खान khan, *s. f.* A mine; (*met.*) a nest, a heap, abundance, receptacle.

खानखूर khankhúr, *s. m.* A pit, a shaft (*of a mine*); any thing very dry.

खाना khána, *v. a.* To eat; to embezzle; (*met.*) to get, suffer, take, receive, hold, contain. *s. m.* Food, dinner, eating. *Kha jana*, To eat up, devour. *Khana peena*, Meat and drink, food, board, fare.

खानि kháni, *s. f.* A mine; (*met.*) a nest, a heap, abundance, receptacle.

खानहारा khanhára, *s. m.* Eater, devourer.

खाबड़ khabur, *adj.* Uneven.

खार khar, *s. m.* Alkali, potash.

खारा khá-ra, *adj.* Salt, brackish. *s. m.* A net (*in which straw is tied*).

खारी kharee, *adj.* Salt, brackish.

खारूआ khá-roo-a, *s. m.* A coarse kind of red cloth of cotton.

खाल khal, *s. f.* Skin, hide; bellows; a rivulet, river, canal, creek, inlet. *Khal khynchna*, To take the skin off, to flay.

खाओ khao, *s. f.* Manure.

खिंचना khínch-na, *v. n.* To be drawn, pulled or tightened, to be drawn or delineated (*a picture, &c.*); to be borne or suffered. *Khinchana, v. a.* To cause to draw or endure.

खिंचावट khincháwut, *s. f.* Drawing, tightening.

खिंदना khindna, *v. n.* To be scattered.

खिंदाना khin-dá-na, *v. a.* To scatter.

खिंदरी khínd-ree, *s. f.* A pallet, a beggar's bedding.

खिचड़ी khích-ree, *s. f.* A dish made of pulse and rice boiled together, the flower of the ber tree (*Zizyphus jujuba*); earnest to dancing women when they are engaged for an entertainment; a mixed heap of gold and silver coin; a barbarous mixture of two languages, a langua franca or jargon.

खिचना khích-na, *v. n.* To be pulled, to be drawn, to be extracted, to be endured, to stretch.

खिचवाना khichwáua, *v. a.* To cause to draw, pull, extract, stretch.

खिचा khích-a, *part. past,* or *adj.* Tense, tight; fine, slender.

खिचाव khich-áo, *s. m.* Drag, pull, draught; tenseness, tightness.

खिजलाना khij-lá-na, *v. a.* To vex, tease, irritate, trouble, disturb, molest. *v. n.* To get angry.

खिजाना khij-á-na, *v. a.* To vex, tease, irritate, trouble, disturb, molest.

खिझ khijh, *s. f.* Fretfulness, vexation, teasing.

खिझलाना khijh-lá-na, ⎫ *v. n.* To be angry,
खिझना khíjh-na, ⎰ to fret, to be vexed.

खिझाना khij-há-na, *v. n.* To fret, to be vexed.

खिड़की khir-kee, *s. f.* A window, casement, gate, back-door, wicket, sallyport, shutter.

खिन्न khinn, *adj.* Distress, suffering pain or uneasiness; wearied, exhausted.

खिरकिन khír-kin, *s. f.* A window.

खिरन khír-un, *s. f.* A black ring painted on a tambourin.

खिरनी khír-nee, *s. f.* A tree and its fruit (*Mimusops kauki*).

खिरसा khír-sa, *s. m.* A dish made with biestings, or the milk of a cow just calved.

खिलखिलाना khil-khil-ána, *v. n.* To laugh heartily, to giggle, titter.

खिलजाना khil-jána, *v. n.* To blossom, bloom; to laugh, to be delighted.

खिलना khíl-na, *v. n.* To blow (*as a flower*), to flower; to be delighted, to laugh.

खिलवाड़ khil-wár, *adj.* Humorous, playful, funny, pleasant, entertaining.

खिलादेदार khiláee-dáee, *s. f.* A dry nurse. *Khilaee-pilaee*, Charge of maintenance.

खिलाऊ khiláoo, *s. m.* Given to eat, feeder. *adj.* Causing to bloom.

खिलाड़ khil-ár, खिलाड़ी khil-ár-ee, } *adj.* Playsome.

खिलाना khil-ána, *v. a.* To cause or give to eat, to feed; to cause to take (*an oath, &c.*); to cause to suffer (*as, mar khilana,* To cause to be beaten); to cause to play, to allow to play, to amuse, play with, dandle; make to blossom (*a flower*).

खिलार khil-ár, *adj.* Playsome.

खिलौड़ khil-óur, *adj.* Playful, addicted to gaming.

खिलौना khil-óu-na, *s. f.* A plaything, a toy, a bawble, gewgaw.

खिल्ली khíl-lee, *s. f.* Joke, jest, humour. *Khillee-baz, adj.* Humorous, playsome, funny. *Khillee-bazee, s. f.* Humour, fun, play, jocularity.

खिल्लू khíl-loo, *adj.* Humorous, playsome, funny.

खिस khis, *s. f.* Grinning, shewing the teeth, a tooth.

खिसकना khís-uk-na, *v. n.* To stir, slip, slip away, to sheer off. *Khisuk jana, v. n.* To slip away, steal away, slide.

खिसकाना khis-ká-na, *v. a.* To remove, shove out of the way, slide away, draw back.

खिसना khís-na, *v. n.* To fall, to sink (*as a terrace*); to drop off; to become old, decline in years.

खिसुलना khís-ul-na, *v. n.* To slip. *adj.* Slippery.

खिसलुहा khis-luhá, *adj.* Slippery.

खिसलाव khis-láo, *s. m.* Slipperiness, slipping.

खिसलाहट khis-lá-hut, *s. f.* Slipperiness.

खिसाना khis-á-na, खिसाय रहना khisáeh rúhna, } *v. n.* To flinch, draw back, to be abashed.

खिसियाना khis-iyá-na, *v. n.* To grin. *adj.* Fretful, peevish, bashful, abashed.

खिसियाहट khis-iyá-hut, *s. f.* Vexation, fretfulness.

खीच kheech, *s. m.* Reluctance, repugnance.

खीज kheej, *s. f.* Anger, vexation.

खीजना khéej-na, *v. n.* To be angry, to be vexed.

खीर kheer, *s. f.* Rice-milk.

खीरा khée-ra, *s. m.* A cucumber (*Cucumis utillissimas*).

खीरी khée-ree, *s. f.* An udder.

खील kheel, *s. f.* Parched grain inflated or puffed out by heat so as to appear like froth.

खीली khée-lee, *s. f.* Betel-leaf made up with the different ingredients.

खीस khees, *s. f.* Loss; a grin; shrug; biestings.

खीसना khées-na, खीस निकालना khées nikálna, } *v. n.* To grin.

खीसा khée-sa, *s. m.* A rubber (*used in baths*); a pocket.

खीह kheeh, *s. f.* An alkaline earth, fossil alkali.

खोंदला khóond-la, *s. m.* A hollow of a tree.

खोंदुलना khoon-dúl-na, *v. a.* To trample, tread, beat or work with the feet.

खूंस khoons, *s. m.* Animosity, spite, rancour.

खूंसाना khoon-sá-na, *v. n.* To be angry.

खूख khookh, *adj.* Poor.

खुजलाना khooj-lá-na, *v. n.* To itch, scratch, tickle.

खुजलाहट khooj-lá-hut, *s. f.* Itching, scratching, titillation.

खुजली khóoj-lee, *s. f.* The itch.

खुजाना khoo-já-na, *v. a.* To scratch, to rub gently with the nails.

खुझराहा khoojh-rá-ha, *adj.* Stingy.

खुटकना khoo-túk-na, *v. a.* To nibble; to doubt.

खुटका khóot-ka, *s. m.* Apprehension, suspicion, doubt, suspense; sound of footsteps.

खुटाई khoo-tá-ee, *s. f.* Perfidy.

खुटी khóot-tee, *s. f.* A treasure, hoard; a gnat.

खुहरा khóor-la, *adj.* Rough. *s. m.* A henhouse.

खपहला khóond-la, *s. m.* A hollow of a tree.

खूंटी khóot-tee, *s. f.* A purse.

खुदना khoodna, *v. n.* To be dug, to be engraved.

खुदवाना khood-wá-na, } *v. a.* To cause to
खुदाना khoo-dá-na, } delve, dig, engrave, carve.

खुदे khóod-deh, *s. f.* The spaces in a necessary between the little brick partitions; the space from which a tooth has fallen out or been extracted.

खुधा khóod-ha, *s. f.* Hunger.

खुधार्थ khood-hárth, *adj.* Distressed with hunger, hungry.

खुनसाना khoon-sá-na, *v. n.* To be angry.

खुनसी khóon-see, *adj.* Angry.

खुबना khóob-na, *v. a.* To affect, penetrate, stick into; to adorn.

खुर khoor, *s. m.* } A (*cloven*) hoof, a
खुरी khóo-ree, *s. f.* } horse's hoof.

खुरचन khóor-chun, *s. f.* Pot-scrapings.

खुरचना khóo-ruch-na, *v. a.* To scrape.

खुरचनी khóo-ruch-nee, *s. f.* A scraper, a scoop or shovel.

खुरुंद khóo-rund, *s. m.* A scab.

खुरपा khóor-pa, *s. m.* An instrument for scraping grass for horses; the knee-pan, patella.

खुरपी khóor-pee, *s. f.* A scraper, a weeding knife, the tool with which grass is scraped up for horses; a shovel for cleaning out a bird-cage.

खुरमा khóor-ma, *s. m.* A kind of sweetmeat.

खुरांट khoo-ránt, *adj.* Very old.

खुरिया khoo-rí-ya, *s. m.* The knee-pan; an instrument like a cup formed of a cocoanut shell or other material, with which clothes are marked with stripes.

खुरी khóoree, *s. f.* A (*cloven*) hoof.

खुरेरना khoo-rér-na, *v. a.* To run after, to persecute, to catch, to enclose.

खुरखुरा khóor-khoo-ra, *adj.* Rough.

खुल खेलना khool-khélna, *v. a.* To indulge openly in vices which were formerly practised in secret.

खुलजाना khool-jána, *v. n.* To be opened.

खुलना khóol-na, *v. n.* To be opened, revealed, expanded, untied or unfolded, disclosed or uncovered, let loose or be loose, laid aside (*restraint*), dispersed (*clouds*), clear up (*the sky*), be broken (*meditation, &c.*)

खुलवाना khoolwána, *v. a.* To cause to open.

खुलाना khoolána, *v. a.* To open or cause to open.

खुलेबंदों khóoleh-bundon, *adv.* Freely, unceremoniously, openly.

खुसरफुसर khóosur-phoosur, *s. m.* Whispering.

खूंच khoonch, *s. f.* The tendo Achillis, hamstring. *Khoonch marna,* To hamstring.

खूंट khoont, *s. m.* A corner, an angle; ear-wax; station, portion.

खूंटला khóont-la, *s. m.* A drug.

खूंटा khóon-ta, *s. m.* A wooden stake.

खूंदना khóond-na, *v. a.* To dig up (*as the earth with the feet*).

खूखी khóo-khee, *s. f.* A little girl.

खूजिया khóo-ji-ya, *adj.* A searcher, inquirer, investigator, inquisitive.

खूझा khóoj-ha, *s. m.* Sediment, dregs, mouldiness of vinegar, &c.

खूटना khóot-na, *v. a.* To pluck, to pick the leaves, &c. of vegetables.

खूठी khóot-hee, } *s. f.* A scab.
खूथी khóot-hee, }

खूड khoor, *s. m.* A furrow.

खूद khood, *s. f.* Refuse.

खूद्र khoodr, *adj.* Small, mean.

खूद्राना khood-rá-na, *v. n.* To trot.

खूमना khóom-na, *v. n.* To wax old.

खेकसा khék-sa, *s. m.* A mark, a sign.

खेचर khéch-ur, *s. m.* A *Vidyadhur*, or kind of demigod.

खेटक khét-uk, *s. m.* Spoil, chase, hunting. *s. f.* A weapon, the club of *Bulram*.

खेटकी khét-uk-ee, *s. m.* A sportsman, a hunter.

खेरा khér-a, *s. f.* A village.

खेरी khér-ee, *s. f.* A kind of iron or steel, a sort of steel made in India.

खेत khet, *s. m.* A field, a field of battle, ground; a holy place. *Khet-chhorna, v. a.* To flee from the field of battle. *Khet rukna,* To remain on the field (*of battle*), to be killed.

खेती khét-ee, *s. f.* Husbandry; crop. *adj.* Arable.

खेतीबाड़ी khétee-báree, *s. f.* Husbandry, agriculture.

खेतीहुर khetee-húr, *s. m.* A peasant, a husbandman.

खेद khed, *s. m.* Sorrow, grief, affliction, distress; pain.

खेदना khéd-na, *v. a.* To run after, to persecute, to pursue.

खेदा khéd-a, *s. m.* The trap or enclosure in which elephants are caught.

खेदित khéd-it, *adj.* Sorrowful, repentant ; afflicted, distressed, pained.

खेप khep, *s. f.* A trip, voyage ; a piece of base metal inserted in coin, or cracked coin ; a term in algebra ; something added to a sum ; an apartment. *Khep kurna,* To sustain a loss.

खेपना khép-na, *v. a.* To pass the time.

खेपा khép-a, *adj.* An idiot, a madman, a fool.

खेपिया khép-i-ya, *s. m.* A voyager.

खेमकुशल khem-kóoshul, *s. f.* Health.

खेरी khér-ee, *s. f.* After-birth. *Kherhee, s. f.* Membranes in which the fœtus is enveloped, secundines, placenta.

खेल khel, *s. m.* Play, game, sport, fun, pastime.

खेलखिलाड़ी khel-khil-áree, *adj. f.* Playsome, wanton ; an unchaste (*woman*), an adulteress, strumpet.

खेलना khél-na, *v. a.* To play, to sport. *Khelut (Bruj) part. pres.* Playing, play.

खेवुक khéwuk, } *s. m.* A waterman, a row-
खेवुट khéwut, } er, a boatman.

खेवना khéo-na, *v. a.* To row, punt, paddle ; suffer, endure (*pain, calamity, &c.*)

खेवा khéwa, *s. m.* Fare, ferry-money, price of passage in a boat, passage-money ; crossing over a river.

खेश khesh, *s. m.* A kind of cloth, diaper, damask ; a sheet or wrapper of such cloth.

खेसरा khés-ra, *s. m.* A kind of cloth.

खैंच khynch, *s. f.* Pulling, drawing ; scarcity.

खैंचना khynch-na, *v. a.* To pull, draw, tighten ; delineate, paint.

खैंचाखैंची khyncha-khynchee, *s. f.* Pulling and hawling.

खयाल khy-ál, (*Bruj*) *s. m.* Play, sport, fun, pastime.

खैर khyr, *s. m.* A tree (*Mimosa catechu*).

खैरा khy-ra, *adj.* Brown. *s. m.* A sprat (*or fish very like one*) ; a tree (*Mimosa catechu*).

खैला khy-la, *s. m.* A young bullock, a steer.

खोआ khó-a, *s. m.* Plaster ; coarse brick-dust ; milk, inspissated by boiling.

खोआना khoána, *v. a.* To cause to lose or part with.

खोई khó-ee, *s. f.* The dry part of sugar-cane after expressing the juice ; clothes folded up and put on the head as a defence against rain.

खोंखना khónkh-na, *v. n.* To cough.

o

खोंखी khón-khee, *s. f.* A cough.

खोंच khonch, *s. f.* A cut or rent in cloth, &c.

खोंचना khónch-na, *v. a.* To thrust, to stuff.

खोंचा khónch-a, *s. m.* A thrust, stuffing.

खोंचाखांची khóncha-khánchee, *s. f.* Thrusting ; mutual wrangling or quarrelling.

खोंची khón-chee, *s. f.* Any thing stuffed into another, as grass into thatch ; trifling purchases ; part of grain which is to be parched taken as payment for parching it ; something paid by those who draw water at a well to the *bihishtee* who attends there with his bucket, for the use of it.

खोंटा khón-ta, *adj.* Deficient, adulterated, bad (*as coin*), false, deceitful. *s. m.* A tent-pin, a pin, a peg, nail ; protection. *Khonteh ke bul koodna,* To become insolent relying on protection ; (*the idea seems to be taken from a person's teasing an animal, which, being fastened by a rope is unable to get at him : so that the khonta is only indirectly a protection by restraining the adversary.*)

खोंदकल khónd-kul, *s. m.* A hollow.

खोंदला khónd-la, *adj.* Toothless, hollow.

खोंता khón-ta, } *s. m.* A bird's nest.
खोंधा khón-dha, }

खोंपा khón-pa, *s. m.* The hair of the head braided or tied up on the top of the head.

खोंसना khóns-na, *v. a.* To stuff, thrust in, cram.

खोखला khókh-la, *adj.* Hollow, excavated (*as a tooth or a tree, &c.*)

खोखा khó-kha, *s. m.* A boy ; a bill of exchange of which the amount has been paid remaining in the hand of him who has paid it by way of voucher.

खोज khoj, *s. m.* Search, inquiry, quest ; trace, mark.

खोजखाज khoj-kháj, *s. f.* Vexation ; inquiry.

खोजना khój-na, *v. a.* To search for, to inquire after, to seek, explore.

खो जाना kho-jána, *v. n.* To be lost.

खोजिया khojíya, *adj.* A searcher, inquirer, investigator, inquisitive.

खोट khot, *s. f.* A blunder, vice, blemish, defect, fault.

खोटा khó ta, *adj.* Perfidious, counterfeit, false, faulty, defective.

खोटाई kho-tá-ee, *s. f.* Perfidy ; vice, blemish, falseness, faultiness, defectiveness.

खोद khod, *s. m.* A push, thrust, pass.

खोदना khód-na, *v. a.* To dig, to delve, to hollow ; to search for.

खोदनी khód-nee, *s. f.* Searching ; a spade.

खोदर khó-dur, *s. m.* A certain pace (*of a horse*).

खोदरा khód-ra, *adj.* Pock-marked.

खोदबेवाद khod-bewád, *s. m.* Search, inquiry.

खोना khó-na, *v. a.* To lose, part with, to get rid of, to waste, to squander. *s. m.* Losing ; a leaf which contains a parcel of betel or flowers, &c.

खोप khop, *s. f.* A cave, a corner ; a rent, a fissure.

खोपरा khóp-ra, *s. m.* A cocoanut, rather the kernel of a cocoanut, kernel.

खोपरी khóp-ree, *s. f.* The skull, a shell, pate. *Khopree kha-jana, v. a.* To spend or lavish another's property.

खोपा khó-pa, *s. m.* The hair of the head braided or tied up on the top of the head.

खोबार khobár, *s. m.* A hogsty.

खोया khó-ya, *s. m.* Refuse.

खोर khor, *s. f.* An alley ; a covering ; the rage or curse of a god.

खोरी khó-ree, *s. f.* An alley.

खोल khol, *s. m.* A case, sheath, hollow (*as of a tree, &c.*), a cavity.

खोलरा khól-ra, *s. m.* A hollow (*as of a tree, &c.*)

खोलना khól-na, *v. a.* To open, to loose, to shine, to expand, untie, unravel, set sail or unmoor (*a ship, &c.*)

खोलबंदी khol-bún-dee, *s. f.* The changing or removing of a horse's shoes.

खोसना khós-na, *v. a.* To take or snatch away ; to pull out hairs.

खोसा khó-sa, *adj.* Having little or no beard (*a man*). *s. m.* Rind, peel, skin, shell.

खोह khoh, *s. m.* A cavern, an abyss, a pit.

खौर khour, *s. f.* The marks which *Hindoos* make on their foreheads with Sandal-wood, saffron, &c.

खौरा khóu-ra, *s. m.* The rot (*among sheep*), the falling off of the hairs.

खौलना khóul-na, *v. n.* To boil, to be agitated by heat.

ख्यात khyát, *adj.* Famous, celebrated, notorious.

ख्याति khyáti, *s. f.* Fame, celebrity, notoriety.

ख्यात्यापन्न khyat-ya-púnn, *adj.* Famous.

ख्याल khyál, *s. m.* Play, sport, fun, pastime.

ख्रीस्त khreest, *n. prop.* The Lord Jesus Christ, the Saviour of the world.

खिस्तियान khris-ti-yán, *s. m.* A christian, a follower of the Lord Jesus Christ.

ग

ग guh, The third consonant of the *Naguree* alphabet, answering to G, in *Good*.

गं gung, (*used in compos.*) A river, a stream. *Do-gung*, In two streams (*a river*).

गंगा gún-ga, *s. f.* The river Ganges.

गंगाजमनी gúnga-júmnee, *s. f.* A kind of ear-ring.

गंज gunj, *s. m.* A scaldhead (*Tinea capitis*).

गंजा gún-ja, *adj.* Scaldheaded, bald.

गंजिया gun-jí-ya, *s. f.* A wallet, a bag (*in which grass-cutters keep their sickle, &c.*)

गंझैल gun-jhyl, *adj.* Addicted to the use of *ganjha.*

गंठजोरा gunth-jóra, *s. m.* Knot-joining. *Gunth-jora bandhna, v. a.* To tie together the skirts of the mantles of the bride and bridegroom ; a ceremony attending marriage performed by the *Poorohit* or officiating priest.

गंठकटा gunth-kúta, *s. m.* A cut-purse.

गंडा gún-da, *s. m.* A ring, a circle ; a kind of horse-collar, a knotted string tied round the neck of a child, &c., as a charm ; the number four.

गंडासा gun-dá-sa, *s. m.* A sort of axe, a pole-axe.

गंडी gún-dee, *s. f.* A circle, particularly that which *Ramchundruh* is said to have drawn round *Seeta*, to protect her from *Rawun.*

गंडेरी gun-dér-ee, *s. f.* A segment, cut, or portion of sugar-cane.

गंद gund, *s. f.* Stink, filth, ordure, smell.

गंदक gunduk, *s. f.* Brimstone. *Gunduk ka utr,* Sulphuric Acid.

गंदना gúnd-na, *s. f.* A leak (*Allium porrum*).

गंदा gún-da, *adj.* Stinking, filthy, foul, nasty ; odious.

गंध gundh, *s. f.* Perfume, odour, scent.

गंधक gún-dhuk, *s. f.* Brimstone.

गंधराज gundh-ráj, *s. m.* Gardenia florida.

गंधर्व gun-dhúrv, *s. m.* A celestial musician, a class of demi-gods. *Gundhurv-byah, s. m.* A kind of marriage. *Gundhurv-geet, s. m.* A kind of song or singing.

गंधार gundhár, *s. m.* A musical mode.

गंधी gún-dhee, *s. m.* A person who sells rose-water, essences and utr, a perfumer ; a green bug.

गंधीला gun-dhée-la, *adj.* Stinking.

संभीर gum-bhér, *adj.* Deep; serious, thoughtful, sedate, grave.

संबाव gun-wá-oo, *adj.* Squanderer.

संबाबा gun-wá-na, *v. a.* To lose, throw away, get rid of, discharge, spend in vain, waste, squander, pass, trifle.

संबार gun-wár, *s. m.* A countryman, villager; clown, boor, churl, rustic, peasant.

संबी gunwee, *adj.* Relating to a village or the country, rustic.

गबन gúg-un, *s. m.* Sky, firmament, atmosphere, heaven.

गबनधूल gugun-dhóol, *s. f.* Dust of the *Ketkee* flower (*Pandanus odoratissimus*).

गबनभेर gugun-bher, *s. m.* A pelican (*Pelecanus onocrotalus*).

गबरी gúg-ree, *s. f.* A water-pot.

गंगा gungá, *s. f.* The river Ganges.

गंगाजमनी gúnga-júmnee, *s. f.* A kind of ear-ring.

गंगाजल gunga-júl, *s. m.* The water of the Ganges.

गंगातीर gunga-téer, *s. m.* The bank of the Ganges.

गंगाद्वार gunga-dwár, *s. m.* The place where the Ganges enters the plains, *Huridwar.*

गंगापार gunga-pár, *s. m.* The (*further*) bank of the Ganges.

गंगापुत्र gunga-póotr, *s. m.* A man of a mixed and low caste, employed to remove dead bodies; a brahmun who conducts the ceremonies of pilgrimage at some places on the Ganges, especially at *Benares.*

गंगाजात्रा gunga-játra, *s. f.* Pilgrimage to the Ganges; carrying a sick person to the river side to die there.

गंगाक्षेत्र gunga-kshétr, *s. m.* The river Ganges, and two cos on either of its banks.

गच guch, *s. m.* Mortar, plaster, cement, old mortar knocked off walls, &c.; the floor.

गचगीना guch-géena, *adj.* Short and fat (person).

गचपच gúchpuch, *adj.* Crowded, stuffed together, close, thick.

गज guj, *s. m.* An elephant; a measure of length, the *Gus*, a yard, a measure of two cubits.

गजगमनी guj-gúmunee, } *adj. f.* Walking
गजगौनी guj-góunee, } (*stately*) like an elephant: an epithet made use of to express a graceful gait in a female.

गजगाह guj-gáh, *s. m.* A string composed of several tassels, made of the hair of a species of ox, and suspended as an ornament from an elephant's neck, or is fastened to a horse's ears, extending on both sides to the saddle.

गजदंत guj-dúnt, *s. m.* A name of *Gunesh*; ivory, the elephant's tooth.

गजनाल guj-nál, *s. m.* A large gun or cannon.

गजनी gúj-nee, *s. f.* Bole, earth.

गजपति guj-pút-i, *s. m.* The master or rider of an elephant, the title of a *rajah.*

गजपाटल guj-pá-tul, *s. m.* Lampblack (*with which the eye-lids are painted*).

गजपाल guj-pál, *s. m.* An elephant driver or keeper.

गजमोती guj-mó-tee, *s. m.* A large pearl: it is a popular idea of the *Hindoos* that the finest pearls are to be found in the heads of elephants.

गजर gúj-ur, *s. m.* The chimes rung at the expiration of a watch or *puhur* of the day or night; but sometimes restricted to those at the close of the fourth; the word *puhur* being more commonly used for the middle chimes.

गजरभत guj-ur-bhútt, *s. m.* A dish of boiled carrots.

गजरा gúj-ra, *s. m.* The leaf of the carrot; a kind of jewel, an ornament for the wrist, a bracelet; the waving lines on *mushroo* (a kind of silk cloth).

गजराज guj-ráj, *s. m.* A large elephant.

गजराहार gujra-hár, *s. m.* A wreath or necklace of flowers; a gold ornament of the same form.

गजा gúj-a, *s. m.* Part of a cart; a kind of sweetmeat.

गजाना guj-á-na, *v. n.* To work, to ferment.

गझा gujhá, *s. m.* Winning.

गझिन gujhín, *adj.* Thick (*a forest, &c.*)

गंज gunj, *s. m.* A scaldhead (*Tinea capitis*).

गंज gunj, *s. m.* A mine, a jewel-mine; a treasury, a jewel room, the place where plate, &c. is preserved; a mart, a place where grain, &c. is stored for sale.

गंजा gún-ja, *adj.* Scaldheaded, bald.

गंजिया gun-jí-ya, *s. f.* A wallet, a bag (*in which grass-cutters keep their sickle, &c.*)

गटरमूल gut-ur-múl, *s. m.* A nick-name for a monkey.

गटपट gút-put, *adv.* Higgledy-piggledy.

गट्टा gút-ta, *s. m.* The part of the pipe which fixes into the top of the metal part of a *hookka*; the ankle.

गट्ठा gút-tha, *s. m.* A bundle, package, pack; root of onion, turmerick, &c., a clove of garlic.

गठकटा gúth-kuta, *s. m.* A cut-purse.

गठकटी guth-kút-ee, *s. f.* The practice of a cut-purse.

गठना gúth-na, *v. n.* To be joined or arranged together; to be tied or knotted together; to unite, connect; collude.

गठबंधन guth-bún-dhun, ⎱ *s. m.* Binding
गठजोरा guth-jó-ra, ⎰ or joining in a knot; tying the knot, a *Hindoo* ceremony attending marriage, at which the bride and bridegroom's clothes are fastened together, and a procession takes place to a river or piece of water.

गठर gut-húr, *s. m.* A large bundle, a bale, a pack.

गठरी gúth-ree, *s. f.* A bundle, parcel, packet; total, amount; crew, pack, junto. *Guthree bandhna, v. a.* To pack up, bundle, gather (*money, &c.*) *Guthree kurna, v. a.* To add (*figures*).

गठवाना guth-wá-na, *v. a.* To cause to join or to adhere.

गठाना gut-há-na, *v. a.* To attach, connect, join, tie.

गठाव gut-háo, *s. m.* Connexion, joining together. *Guthao-ganthna, v. a.* To contrive well.

गठिया gút-hi-ya, *s. f.* A bump; pains in the joints; a back, sack; bundle, package.

गठियाबाव guthiya-báo, *s. f.* Rheumatism.

गठी gút-hee, ⎱ *s. f.* A ball, pack; a
गठिया gút-i-ya, ⎰ small bundle.

गठीला gut-hée-la, *adj.* Knotty; robust.

गठूवा gut-hóo-a, *s. m.* Knots in cloth.

गरंथ gur-únth, *s. m.* A game, tipcat; a mode of incantation performed for the destruction of any person (*marun*), to secure his affection (*mohun*), to subject him to obedience (*bus kurun*), to imprison him or deprive him of the power of action or speech (*stumbhun*), to drive him away (*oochchatun*), or to call him (*akurshun*). Certain words are pronounced over an effigy of the person or his name in writing, which is afterwards buried.

गरक gúr uk, *s. m.* A kind of fish (*a sort of gilt-head*).

गरगराना gur-gur-ána, *v. n.* To gurgle; thunder; roll; roar (*as a tiger*), to rumble.

गरगूदर gur-góo-dur, *s. m.* Any old tattered clothes, rags and tatters.

गरन gúr-un, *s. f.* A swamp, morass.

गरना gúr-na, *v. n.* To penetrate, enter, be driven into the earth (*as a stake, &c.*), be fixed, to fix, lie, sink, be buried.

गरबर gúr-bur, *adv.* Higgledy-piggledy.

गरबरा gúr-bur-a, *s. m.* Bustle, confusion; motion of the bowels, borborygmi.

गरबराहट gur-bur-áhut, *s. f.* Confusion, fright, alarm, bustle.

गररिया gur-úr-iya, *s. m.* A shepherd or goatherd.

गरुलवण gur-lúv-un, *s. m.* Rock or fossile salt, especially that found in the district of *Sambhur* in the province of *Ajmere*.

गरवा gúrwa, *s. m.* A kind of water-pot; a flower-pot carried about by musicians and dancing women at the feast of *busunt punchumee*, as an offering to people of rank, from whom they receive presents in return.

गरवाना gur-wá-na, *v. a.* To cause to be buried or driven into the earth.

गरहा gúr-ha, *s. m.* A cavity, a hole, a pit, an abyss.

गराना guróna, *v. a.* To cause to penetrate, &c.

गरियार gur-i-yár, *adj.* Stout-hearted, stiff-necked, stubborn, obstinate.

गरियारी gur-i-yáree, *s. f.* Obstinacy, stubbornness.

गरूवा gúr-oo-wa, *s. m.* A kind of water-pot; a flower-pot carried about by musicians and dancing women at the feast of *busunt punchumee*, as an offering to people of rank, from whom they receive presents in return.

गरेरिया gur-ér-iya, *s. m.* A shepherd or goatherd.

गरोना gur-ó-na, *v. a.* To pierce, perforate, bore, stick into.

गड्डी gúd-dee, *s. f.* A bundle of paper containing ten quires.

गढ़ gurh, *s. m.* A fort, a castle.

गढ़त gur-hút, *s. f.* Form, make, fashion.

गढ़ना gúrh-na, *v. a.* To malleate, form by hammering; to make, form, shape, fashion. *v. n.* To be driven down (*as a stake*), to be buried, sunk, &c. to be made, formed or fashioned.

गढ़वार gurh-wár, *adj.* Coarse, thick.

गढ़ा gúr-ha, *s. m.* A cavity, a hole, a pit, an abyss.

गढ़ाई gur-há-ee, *s. f.* The price of making jewellery.

गढ़ाना gurhána, *v. a.* To cause to form by hammering, to cause to make.

गढ़िया gúr-hi-ya, *s. f.* A pike, a javelin, spear.

गढ़ी gúr-hee, *s. f.* A small fort, a castle.

गढ़ेला gur-hél-a, *s. m.* A cavity, a hole, a pit, an abyss.

गढ़या gur-hy-ya, *s. f.* A small tank or pond. *s. m.* A barrier.

गण gun, *s. m.* A flock, multitude, troop, tribe, class, &c.; a body of troops equal to 29 chariots, 81 horse, and 135 foot; troops of inferior deities considered as *Shiv's* attendants, and under the especial superintendence of *Gunes*.

गणक gún-uk, *s. m.* An arithmetician, astrologer, a calculator of nativities.

गणकी gún-uk-ee, *s. f.* The wife of an astrologer.

गणता gun-tá, *s. f.* Arithmetic.

गणद्रव्यह gún-druv-yuh, *s. m.* Public property, common stock.

गणना gún-na, *v. a.* To count, to reckon up by number, to calculate.

गणनीय gun-un-éeyuh, *adj.* Numerable, to be counted or reckoned.

गणिका gún-ik-a, *s. f.* A courtezan, a harlot.

गणित gún-it, *adj.* Numbered, counted, reckoned, calculated. *s. m.* Computation, arithmetic, numeration. *Gun-it-kar, s. m.* An astrologer, an arithmetician.

गणेश gun-ésh, *s. m.* A name of *Shiv; Gunes* the son of *Shiv* and *Parvutee:* he is the god of wisdom, and remover of obstacles, whence in the commencement of all undertakings, the opening of all compositions, &c.; he receives the reverential homage of the *Hindoos:* he is represented as a short fat man with the head of an elephant, and the present appellation with other similar compounds alludes to his office as chief of the various classes of subordinate gods, who are regarded as *Shiv's* attendants.

गण्ड gund, *s. m.* A cheek, the whole side of the face including the temple; a boil, a phlegmonoid pimple; a mark, a spot; a rhinoceros.

गण्डक gún-duk, *s. m.* A rhinoceros.

गण्डकी gún-duk-ee, *s. f.* A river in the north of India, the *Gunduk.*

गण्डमाला gund-má-la, *s. f.* Inflammation of the glands of the neck, &c.

गण्डा gún-da, *s. m.* A ring, a circle; a knotted string tied round the neck of a child, &c. as a charm; the number four (*as, a gunda of cowries or four cowries*).

गण्डासा gun-dá-sa, *s. m.* An axe, a pole-axe.

गण्डि gún-di, *s. m.* Goitre or Bronchocele.

गण्डी gún-dee, *s. f.* A circle, particularly that which *Ramchundur* is said to have drawn round *Seeta* to protect her from *Rawun.*

गण्डेरी gun-dér-ee, *s. f.* A segment cut or portion of sugar-cane.

गण्य gún-yuh, *adj.* That which may be numbered.

गत gútuh, *adj.* Gone; obtained, gained.

गत gut, } *s. f.* Going, moving, motion,
गति gút-i, } procedure, march, pace, gait; state, condition, course of events, fate, fortune; funeral rites, salvation; custom, habit, usage, way. *Gut kurna, v. a.* To perform funeral rites.

गते gút-eh, *adv.* Softly, gently, slowly.

गदका gud-ká, *s. m.* A foil for fencing with; a mace, a club.

गद्गद gúd-gud, *adj.* Rejoicing, joyful.

गद्गदा gúd-gud-a, *s. m.* A grain (*Guilandina Bonducella*).

गदबूदा gud-búd-a, *adj.* Corpulent, fat.

गद्दला gúd-la, *adj.* Turbid, muddy, dull, dirty.

गद्दलाई gud-lá-ee, *s. f.* Muddiness, dulness.

गद्दहा gud-há, *s. m.* An ass.

गदा gúd-a, *s. f.* A club, a mace.

गदाधर gud-a-dhúr, *s. m.* A name of *Vishnoo* or *Krishn*, the mace-bearer.

गदेल gud-él, *s. m.* A child.

गदेला gud-él-a, *s. m.* A thick bedding.

गद्दुद gúd-gud, *adj.* Rejoicing, joyful.

गदर gúd-dur, } *adj.* Half-ripe (*fruit*).
गदरा gúd-ra, }

गदी gúd-dee, *s. f.* A cushion, pad, pack-saddle, bedding or any thing stuffed; a seat; a sovereign's throne.

गद्य gúdyuh, *s. m.* Prose.

गधा gúd-ha, *s. m.* An ass.

गधापूरना gúdha-póorna, *s. m.* Boerhavia diffusa.

गन gun, *s. m.* A troop, tribe, flock, class, multitude; *Shiv's* attendants.

गनना gún-na, *s. m.* Sugar-cane (*Saccharum officinarum*). *v. a.* To count, reckon, calculate, number, compute.

गन्दना gúnd-na, *s. m.* A leek (*Allium porrum*).

गन्ध gundh, *s. f.* Perfume, odour, scent, smell, fragrance.

गन्धक gún-dhuk, *s. f.* Brimstone.

गन्धकाष्ठ gundh-káshth, *s. m.* A fragrant wood, as sandal, aloe wood, &c.

गन्धमादन gundh-má-dun, *s. m.* The name of a particular mountain; sulphur.

गन्धरस gundh-rus, *s. m.* Myrrh.

गन्धराज gundh-ráj, *s. m.* Gardenia florida; sandal; any sweet smelling flower.

गन्धर्व gun-dhúrvv, *s. m.* A celestial musician; a class of demigods supposed to inhabit *Indru's* heaven, and form the orchestra at all the banquets of the principal deities; the soul after death, and previous to its being born again according to the notion of the *Hindoos;* a kind of deer.

गन्धवह gúndh-wuh, *s. m.* The wind. *adj.* Smelling, fragrant.

गन्धसार gundh-sár, *s. m.* Sandal.

गन्धार gun-dhár, *s. m.* A musical mode.

गप gup, *s. f.* Prattle, tattle, talk, chat, tattling. *Gup marna, v. a.* To prattle, tattle.

गुपकना gupúkna, *v. a.* To swallow, to gulp.

गुपशुप gúp-shup, *s. f.* Prattle, tattling, tattle.

गुप्पी gúp-pee, *adj.* A tattler, an idly talker.

गुबरू gubróo, *s. m.* A clown, young man, stripling, lad, an uninformed youth; a bridegroom.

गुबहस्ति gub-hús-ti, *s. f.* A ray of light, a sun or moon beam.

गभीर gub-héer, *adj.* Deep, profound, sagacious; thick, impervious (*as a forest*); serious, thoughtful, sedate, grave.

गुमक gúm-uk, *s. f.* Sound of the kettle-drum, violent shake or clash in music.

गुमकीला gum-kée-la, *adj.* Spicy, fragrant, odoriferous.

गुमत gúmut, *s. m.* A road.

गुमन gúm-un, *s. m.* Going, the act of going.

गुमनागुमन gumun-águm-un, *s. m.* Coming and going, access and egress, intercourse.

गुमाना gumána, *v. a.* To pass (*time*).

गुमिन gúm-in, *s. m.* A passenger.

गंभीर gum-bhéer, *adj.* Deep (*as water, but applied metaphorically to sound, intellect, &c. as in English*); serious, thoughtful, sedate, grave.

गभीरता gum-bhéer-ta, *s. f.* Depth (*of water*); depth of thought, profoundness; depth of sound.

गम्य gum-yuh, *adj.* Attainable, accessible.

गम्यता gumyutá, *s. f.* Accessibility; perceptibility.

गया gúy-a, *s. f.* A city in the province of *Behar,* a celebrated place of pilgrimage: it is said to have been rendered holy by the benediction of *Vishnoo,* who granted its sanctity to the prayers of its dying chief killed by the deity; a cow. *past part.* Gone, went.

गयाली guy-á-lee, *s. m.* A class of *Guya brahmuns,* who officiate in certain religious ceremonies, performed by pilgrims at that place.

गर gur, *s. m.* Sickness, disease; poison, an antidote.

गरगया gur-gúy-a, *s. f.* A sparrow.

गरगराना gur-gur-ána, *v. n.* To gurgle; to thunder; roll; roar (*as a tiger*); to rumble.

गुरुजना gúr-uj-na, *v. n.* To thunder, to roar, to bellow.

गरबता gurubtá, *s. f.* Pride; a proud woman.

गरभ gurúbh, *s. m.* The fœtus or embryo.

गुर्रा gúr-ra, *adj.* Bayish (*colour in a horse or pigeon*).

गरल gúr-ul, *s. m.* The venom of a snake, or venom in general.

गरली gur-lée, *adj.* Venemous, poisonous.

गुर्व gúr-wa, *adj.* Heavy; important; respectable; demure.

गुर्वापन gur-wa-pún, *s. m.* Respectability.

गुरा gúr-a, *s. m.* The throat, neck.

गरारा gur-á-ra, *s. m.* A sack (*for holding the walls of a tent, &c.*)

गुरारी gur-á-ree, *s. f.* An instrument for twisting thread or string.

गुरानवन guránwun, *s. m.* A tether.

गरिमा gúr-im-a, *s. f.* Importance, self-importance, vanity of mind, a boast.

गुरी gúr-ee, *s. f.* The kernel of a cocoanut.

गुरुर gúr-roor, *s. m.* In *Hindoo* mythology the regent of birds; a large vulture; a large kind of heron (*Ardea argala*), a gigantic crane or adjutant bird.

गर्ग gurg, *s. m.* One of the ten principal *Moonis* or saints.

गुर्गुज gúr-guj, *s. m.* A scaffold; a tower, a bastion, a cavalier.

गुर्गुरी gúr-gur-ee, *s. f.* A water-vessel, a guglet.

गर्ज gurj, *s. m.* The roaring of elephants; the rumbling of clouds, thunder; bellowing, roaring, roar.

गर्जन gúr-jun, *s. m.* Sound, noise; passion, wrath; the rumbling of clouds, &c.; thundering, thunder, bellowing, roaring.

गर्जी gúr-ji, *s. m.* The muttering of clouds, or distant thunder.

गर्त gurtt, *s. m.* A hole in general.

गर्दभ gurd-dúbh, *s. m.* The white lotus; an ass.

गर्दभी gurd-dúbh-ee, *s. f.* An insect, a kind of beetle springing from cow-dung.

गर्व gurb, *s. m.* Vanity, pride.

गर्बता gúrb-ta, *s. f.* Pride; a proud woman.

गर्ववंती gurbwúntee, *s. f.* A proud woman.

गर्भ gúrbh, *s. m.* A fœtus or embryo; pregnancy; the belly; the inside, the middle; the bed of the Ganges when the river is fullest, that is, on the 14th day of the dark half of the month *Bhadr,* or in the height of the rains: as high as the river flows at this period, so far extends the *Gurbh,* after which the *Teer* or proper bank begins, and extends for 150 cubits, this space is holy ground.

गर्भदा gurbh-dá, *s. f.* A shrub so called.

गर्भदास gurbh-dás, *s. m.* Son of a slave-girl.

गर्भपातक gurbh-pá-tuk, *s. m.* A red kind of *Morunga* supposed to produce abortion.

गर्भरूप gurbh-róop, *adj. m.* } A child, an
गर्भरूपी gurbh-róop-ee, *f.* } infant.

गर्भवती gurbh-vút-ee, s. f. A pregnant female.

गर्भश्राव gurbh-shráv, s. m. Abortion, miscarriage.

गर्भाधान gurbh-a-dhán, s. m. A ceremony performed prior to conception (being supposed conducive to future impregnation).

गर्भिनी gur-bhín-ee, s. f. A pregnant woman.

गर्री gúr-ree, s. f. An instrument for twisting thread or string.

गर्व gurvv, s. m. Pride, arrogance.

गर्ववर gurv-vúr, adj. Proud, haughty, arrogant.

गर्वित gurv-vít, adj. Proud, haughty; conceited.

गर्हन gur-hún, s. m. Censuring, censure, blame, reproach.

गर्हा gur-há, s. f. Abuse, censure, reproach.

गर्ह्य gúrh-yuh, adj. Low, vile, contemptible.

गल gul, s. m. The neck, throat. Gul bukiyan dalna, v. n. To throw one's arms around another's neck. Gul dena, v. a. To throttle, to choke; to execute by hanging.

गलका gúl-ka, s. f. A boil.

गलगंड gul-gund, s. m. Inflammation, enlargement of the glands of the neck.

गलगल gúl-gul, s. m. A citron; name of a bird; mixture of lime and linseed oil forming a kind of mortar impenetrable to water.

गलजंद्रा gul-júnd-ra, s. m. A handkerchief used as a sling for the arm.

गलंदा gul-ún-da, adj. Stentorophonic, or loudly sounding.

गलतनी gúl-tun-ee, s. f. Part of the headstall of a bridle.

गलना gúl-na, v. n. To melt, dissolve, waste, be dissolved, be wasted away.

गलनी gúl-nee, s. f. Wasting, consumption.

गलंदा gul-ún-da, adj. Abusive, foul-mouthed.

गलफटाकी gul-phut-ákee, s. f. Scolding; bragging, boasting. Gulphutakee kurna, v. a. To scold; to lie; to brag.

गलफरा gúl-phur-a, s. m. The jaws; the angle of the mouth.

गलफूट gul-phóot, s. f. Vaunt, vaunting.

गलफूला gul-phóo-la, adj. Chubby.

गलबही gul-búhee, s. f. Throwing the arms on the neck.

गलबाह gul-váh, s. f. An embrace, throwing the arms on the neck.

गलहूर gul-húr, s. m. The Goitre.

गलहार gul-hár, adj. Soluble, corruptible.

गलही gul-hée, s. f. The forecastle (of a boat, &c.); a prow.

गलहेंदा gulhénda, adj. Abusive.

गलह्या gul-hy-ya, s. m. Forecastle-man, boatswain.

गुला gúl-a, s. m. The throat, neck, gullet; voice. adj. Rotten, melted, wasted. Gula oothana (lit. to lift up the throat), To apply acrid substances, such as pepper, &c., to the uvula of a child, when it becomes hoarse, or loses its voice from the relaxation of that part. Gula-bundhana, To ensnare one's self, especially in the bonds of love. Gula-bythna or -purna, To be hoarse. Gula-phansna, To hang, to choke. Gula-dubana, To strangle. Gula dena, To waste. Gula-katna, To cut the throat. Gula-ghontna, To throttle, choke, strangle, hold by the throat. Guleh-purna, To seek the friendship of one who is averse from it. Guleh-puree-bujas sidh, We should make a virtue of necessity. Guleh ka har hona, To seek and persist in a quarrel or dispute, tease, plague, to importune; to seek with ardour the friendship or affection of any one; to persecute with kindness or attention. Guleh lugna, To embrace. Guleh mundhna, To importune.

गलाना gul-á-na, v. a. To melt, dissolve; to soften; to waste away, squander. Gulanehwala, s. m. A menstruum, a solvent.

गलार gul-ár, s. m. The name of a bird.

गलाव gul-áo, s. m. Solution, fusion. Gulaoo, adj. Soluble, septical, weakening, melter, dissolver.

गलावट gul-á-wut, s. f. Solution, dissolving.

गलित gúl-it, adj. Fallen, dropped.

गलियाना gul-i-yána, v. a. To abuse; to cram (a horse, &c.), to force food or medicine down the throat.

गलियारा gul-i-yára, s. m. A street or lane.

गली gúl-ee, s. f. A lane. Gulee buh gulee, From street to street. Gulee-koocha, s. m. A narrow lane.

गलेगंड gul-eh-gúnd, s. m. A kind of bird (the Adjutant or Ardea Argalla).

गलाला gul-lá-la, s. m. Gargarism.

गवन gúwun, s. m. Going, moving.

गवाख guwákh, s. f. The light that is admitted by a window, a skylight.

गवाना guwána, v. a. To cause to sing.

गवाक्ष guwáksh, s. f. A skylight, a hole to admit light, a lattice, window, an air-hole, a loop hole, a round window, a bull's eye, &c.

गवेरक guvérook, s. m. Red chalk.

गवेया guwy-ya, s. m. A singer.

गब्य gúvyuh, *adj.* Of or belonging to a cow.

गस्तान gustán, *adj. f.* A foolish dissolute woman.

गस्तांगर gustangúr, *adj. m.* A clown, ignorant, foolish.

गह guh, *s. f.* A handle.

गहक gúhuk, *s. f.* The emotion of intoxication.

गहकना gúhuk-na, *v. n.* To be agitated by intoxication.

गहकी gúh-kee, *s. f.* Purchase. *s. m. f.* A purchaser.

गहगहाना guh-guh-ána, *v. n.* To quiver, shake or undulate.

गहुन gúhun, *s. m.* An eclipse; thicket, wood, forest.

गहना gúh-na, *s. m.* Jewels, ornaments; a pledge, a pawn. *v. n.* To lay hold of, handle, seize, catch, take; to blush.

गहनी gúh-nee, *s. f.* Oakum; act of calking. *adj.* Pledged. *Guhnee-dhurna, v. a.* To pawn, to pledge.

गहरा gúh-ra, *adj.* Deep. *Guhra rung,* Deep colour.

गहवा gúh-wa, *s. m.* Pincers, forceps.

गहवारा guhwára, *s. m.* A swing, a cradle.

गांगन gán-gun, *s. m.* The name of a disorder.

गांजना gánj-na, *v. a.* To store, hoard; to stir, agitate; to churn.

गांजर gán-jur, *s. f.* A kind of grass or verdure.

गांजा gán-ja,   ⎱ *s. m.* The hemp plant
गांझा gán-jha, ⎰ (*Cannabis sativa*). The fructification when nearly ripe, is bruised and smoked for intoxication: the leaves dried are ground in water and drank for the same purpose: in this state it is called *bhung* and *subzee.*

गांठ ganth, *s. m.* A knot; joint, articulation; a bundle. *Ganth purna,* is applied to the fixing of enmity towards any one in the breast. *Gunth-dar, adj.* Knotted. *Ganth ka poora, adj.* Rich, wealthy. *Ganth ka khona,* To act to one's own prejudice. *Ganth kholna,* The untying of a knot; prodigality, expense; to open the purse; removal of prejudice.

गांठउखड़ना ganth-ookhúrna, *s. m.* A dislocation.

गांठगठीला ganth-guthéela, *adj.* Knotty (*as a stick*), compact (*as a man*).

गांठना gánth-na, *v. a.* To tie, knot, join, make adhere, stick, cobble, put together; to reduce to obedience or subjection; to attach.

गांड gand, *s. f.* The anus, privities. *Gand ghulut, adj.* Dead, stupid.

गांडर gán-dur, *s. f.* A kind of grass of which *khus khus* is the root (*Andropogon muricatum*).

गांडा gán-da, *s. m.* Sugar-cane.

गांडीव gan-déev, *s. m.* The bow of *Urjoon;* any bow.

गांडू gán-doo, *s. m.* A catamite, a sodomite (*Cinædus*).

गांथना gánth-na, *v. a.* To lay bricks in mortar, to string, to put or tie in order on a string, &c.

गांव gáon, *s. m.* A village.

गांवना gáno-na, *v. a.* To sing.

गांसना gáns-na, *v. a.* To pierce, transfix, spit (*as a fowl, &c.*)

गांसी gán-see, *s. f.* The iron point of an arrow.

गाए gáeh, *s. f.* A cow.

गागर gá-gur,   ⎱ *s. f.* A water-vessel, a
गागरी gag-rée, ⎰ guglet.

गाछ gachh, *s. m.* A tree.

गाछमिर्च gachh-mírch, *s. f.* Cayenne pepper (*Capsicum annuum*).

गाज gaj, *s. f.* Scum, froth; a thunderbolt. *Gaj-mara, adj.* Thunder-struck; afflicted, unfortunate.

गाजन gajun, *s. m.* Sounding, roaring.

गाजना gáj-na, *v. n.* To sound, to thunder; to roar as a lion or other wild beast; to be pleased, happy, cheerful, delighted.

गाजर gá-jur, *s. f.* A carrot (*Daucus carota*).

गाजाबाजा gája-bája, *s. m.* The sound or clangour of various musical instruments.

गाड़थोप gar-thóp, *s. f.* Burying, burial.

गाड़ना gár-na, *v. a.* To bury, set, drive down, fix, sink.

गाड़र gá-dur, *s. f.* A sheep.

गाड़रू gád-roo, *s. m.* A charm or *muntur* against venom or the bite of a snake.

गाड़ा gá-ra, *s. m.* A ditch, pit, cavern, an ambuscade; a cart, a carriage. *Gareh bythna,* To be concealed, to lie in ambush.

गाड़ी gá-ree, *s. f.* A cart, car, coach, carriage.

गाड़ीवान garee-wán, *s. m.* A carter, a coachman, a carman.

गाढ़ garh, *s. f.* A difficulty.

गाढ़ा gár-ha, *adj.* Thick, close, dense; sly, shrewd, knowing, wise; strong (*as tea*).

गांड gand, *s. f.* The anus, privities. *Gand-ghulut, adj.* Dead, stupid.

गांडर gán-dur, *s. f.* A grass of which *khus khus* is the root (*Andropogon muricatum*).

गांडा gán-da, *s. m.* Sugar-cane.

गांडीव gan-déev, *s. m.* The bow of *Urjoon*; any bow.

गात gat, *s. f.* The body; apparel.

गाता gá-ta, *s. m.* Paste-board.

गाती gá-tee, *s. f.* A plaid.

गातू gá-too, *s. m.* A celestial chorister.

गात्र gá-trub, *s. m.* The body; a limb, a member.

गायक gá-thuk, *s. m.* A musician, a singer; a chaunter of the *Poorans* or sacred poems.

गाथा gá-tha, *s. f.* A verse, a stanza; metre, rhythm; a song, a chaunt, or verse to be chaunted or sung.

गाद gad, *s. f.* Sediment.

गादना gád-na, *v. a.* To ram down.

गादर gá-dur, *adj.* Half-ripe (*grain*). *s. m.* A heap, stack, rick.

गादी gá-dee, *s. f.* A cushion, pad, pack-saddle, a thin mattress, bedding or any thing stuffed; a seat; a sovereign's throne.

गान gan, *s. m.* A song, singing.

गान्धर्व gan-dhúrbb, *s. m.* A heavenly chorister; a song, singing; a form of marriage, that which requires only mutual and amorous agreement.

गाना gá-na, *v. a.* To sing.

गान्धार gan-dhár, *s. m.* One of the seven primary notes of music; a country, *Candahar*, between the north of India and Persia.

गान्धारी gan-dhá-ree, *s. f.* One of the tutelary female deities of the *Jyns*.

गान्धिक gán-dhik, *s. m.* A vender of perfumes, a perfumer; a kind of worm having a strong fetid smell.

गाब gab, *s. m.* A tree, the fruit of which contains a glutinous astringent juice, with which the bottoms of boats are smeared, and in which nets are soaked (*Diospyros glutinosa, Embryopteris glutinifera*).

गाभ gabh, *s. m.* Pregnancy.

गाभना gábh-na, *v. a.* To snub.

गाभा gá-bha, *s. m.* A new leaf springing from the centre of a plantain tree.

गाभिन gá-bhin, *adj.* Pregnant (*an animal, as cow, buffalo, &c.*)

गाम gam, *s. m.* A village.

गामिनी gám-in-ee, *adj. f.* Going, moving.

गामूक gá-mook, *adj.* Going, locomotive.

गम्भीर्युह gam-bhéer-yuh, *s. m.* Depth (*of water, sound, &c.*)

गाय gáeh, *s. f.* A cow. *Gowmans*, Beef.

गायक gá-yuk, *s. m.* A singer. *adj.* Singing.

P

गायत्रिन् ga-yuh-trín, *s. m.* A tree that yields the resin formerly called Terra Japonica (*Mimosa catechu*).

गायत्री gá-yuh-tree, *s. f.* A measure of verse in the *Veds*, a stanza of 24 syllables, or 4 lines of 6 syllables each; a sacred verse from the *Veds* to be recited only mentally; this is usually personified and considered as a goddess, the metaphorical mother of the three first classes, in their capacity of twice-born; investiture with the sacred and distinguishing string, &c., being regarded as a new birth: there is but one *Gayutree* of the *Veds*, but according to the system of the *Tantrikus*, a number of mystical verses are called *Gayutrees*, each deity has one in particular, &c., The repetition of the *Gayutree* is considered necessary to salvation.

गायन gá-yun, *s. m.* A singer. *adj.* Singing, a singer.

गार gar, *s. f.* Abuse.

गारना gár-na, *v. a.* To strain; to squeeze; to milk.

गारा gá-ra, *s. m.* Mud (*kneaded or*) prepared for making pottery, prepared clay; a musical mode.

गारी gá-ree, *s. f.* Abuse.

गाल gal, *s. m.* A cheek; a sort of tobacco.

गाला gá-la, *s. m.* A pod of cotton; a ball of carded cotton.

गालि gá-li, *s. m.* A curse, execration, or imprecation.

गाली gá-lee, *s. f.* Abuse. *Galee-gulouj, s. f.* Reciprocal abuse. *Galiyan,* Indecent songs (*sung*) at marriages. *Galee denee,* To abuse, revile, call names, scold.

गावघू gáo-ghupoo, *adj.* Deceitful, alluring.

गावदी gáo-dee, *adj.* A simpleton, blockhead.

गावघी gáwa-ghee, *s. m.* Cow's clarified butter.

गाह gah, *s. m.* An alligator, a shark.

गाहक gá-huk, *s. m.* A chapman, purchaser, taker or seizer.

गाहना gáh-na, *v. a.* To calk, thrash, tread; to inquire, search, seek. *Gahi-gahi, adv.* With much inquiry, research. *plu. per. par.* Having inquired or sought repeatedly.

गाही gá-hee, *s. f.* Five (*an aggregate made up of five parts*).

गिंजाई gin-jáee, *s. f.* Name of an insect.

गिचपिचिया gich-pích-iya, *s. m.* The Pleiades.

गिटकारी git-ká-ree, *s. f.* A particular vocal sound in singing; quavering? shake?

गिटकौरी git-kóu-ree, *s. f.* A pebble.

गिड़गिड़ाना gir-gir-ána, v. a. To beseech, implore earnestly and humbly.

गिनती gín-tee, s. f. Number, reckoning, account; muster.

गिनना gín-na, v. a. To count, reckon, number.

गिनवाना gin-wána, v. a. To cause to count.

गिद्ध giddh, s. m. A vulture.

गिंगजाई gin-jáee, s. f. Name of an insect.

गिनती gín-tee, s. f. Number, reckoning, account; muster.

गिन्ना gín-na, v. a. To count, reckon, number.

गिरगिट gír-git, s. m. A lizard; a chameleon.

गिरथापन gír-tha-pun, s. m. Economy.

गिरना gír-na, v. n. To fall, to drop, to sink, to tumble down. *Girteh-purteh, adv.* With difficulty, with much ado.

गिर पड़ना gír-pur-na, v. n. To fall.

गिरहस्त gir-húst, adj. A householder, a peasant, a husbandman.

गिरहस्ताश्रम gírhust-ásrum, s. m. The state or abode of a *Girhust* or householder.

गिरहस्ती gir-hús-tee, s. f. Husbandry, housewifery, household.

गिराना gir-á-na, v. a. To cause to fall, to fell, to overturn, or overthrow, to abase, to cast, throw or break down; to spill, to drop, to shed; to strike. *Gira dena,* To throw, beat, cast or break down.

गिरि gír-i, s. m. A mountain, a hill. *adj.* Venerable, respectable, worshipful.

गिरिजा gír-ij-a, s. f. A name of the goddess *Parvutee,* as daughter of the personified *Himaluy* mountain.

गिरिर gír-ir, s. m. A hyena.

गिरिवर gír-i-wur, s. m. A mountain, a hill.

गिरिसार gir-i-sár, s. m. The *Muluya* mountains, situated in the south of India.

गिलट gil-ut, s. m. A protuberance, hard swelling, gland, knot, tumour, scirrhus.

गिलटी gíl-tee, s. f. A gland.

गिलहरी gil-úh-ree, s. f. A squirrel.

गिलियर gíl-i-yur, adj. Lazy.

गिलौंदा gil-óun-da, s. m. The flower of the *Muhooa (Bassia latifolia)* after it has fallen off.

गिलौ gilóu, s. m. *Minispermum glabrum.*

गिलौरी gil-óu-ree, s. f. Betel-leaf prepared and folded up.

गिल्ली gíll-lee, s. f. A span (*measure of circumference, i. e. the circle formed by joining the ends of the thumb and forefinger*); an ear of Indian corn (*Zea mays*) from which the seeds have

been taken out; the short stick in the game of tip-cat, which is struck by the longer one called *dunda. Gillee or Goollee-dunda khelna,* To play at tip-cat.

गींज geenj, s. f. A dish generally used in *Moohurrum.*

गींजना géenj-na, v. a. To crumple.

गीटम gée-tum, s. m. A coarse kind of carpet not coloured.

गीत geet, s. m. A song, singing. *Geet gana,* To sing.

गीता gée-ta, s. f. A name often applied to books as the *Bhagwut Geeta,* which is often called *Geeta* only.

गीदड़ gée-dur, s. m. A jackal (*Canis aureus*).

गीदड़भबकी géedur-bhúb-kee, s. f. Bullying, bluster, bravado.

गील geel, } s. f. A road.
ग्यल gyl, }

गीला gée-la, adj. Moist, damp, wet. *s. m.* A wild creeper (*Mimosa scandens*).

गुंगना góon-goo-na, adj. Milk-warm, tepid; snuffling, snuffler.

गुंगनाना goon-goo-ná-na, v. n. To be milk-warm; to snuffle, sing slowly or with a low voice.

गुंगनापन goon-goonapún, s. m. Tepidity.

गूंज goonj, s. f. Echo, buzzing, resounding, hollow sound.

गूंज goonj, s. m. The seed of *Abrus precatorius,* or the shrub itself. *Goonj-har, s. m.* A necklace composed of the *Goonja* seed.

गुंजरना goon-júr-na, v. n. To roar, to growl.

गुंजान goon-ján, adj. Thick, close.

गुंजानी goon-já-nee, s. f. Thickness, closeness.

गूंझा góon-jha, adj. Grave.

गुंथवाना goonthwána, v. a. To cause to string, &c.

गुंदेला goon-dél-a, adj. Producing gum (*a tree*).

गूंधना góondh-na, v. n. To be kneaded, plaited, &c.

गूंधावट goondh-áwut, s. f. Plaiting, braiding.

गूगल góog-gool, s. m. Name of a tree or gum (*Amyris agallocha*); Bdellium.

गुच्छा góoch-chha, s. m. A bunch, a cluster (*of fruit*), ear of corn.

गुच्छेदार gooch-chheh-dár, s. f. A kind of turband.

गुजरात gooj-rát, n. prop. A district of India, *Guzerat.*

गुजिया góo-ji-ya, s. f. An ear-ring; a kind of sweetmeat.

गूझन góo-jhun, *adv.* Thickly, closely.

गूंज goonj. } *s. m.* The seed of *Abrus*
गूंजा góon-ja, } *precatorius*, or the shrub itself. *Goonj-har, s. m.* A necklace composed of the *Goonja* seed.

गूंजत goonjút, *adj.* Buzzing, humming, making a low murmuring sound.

गूंजान goon-ján, *adj.* Thick, close.

गूंजानी goon-já-nee, *s. f.* Thickness, closeness.

गूटकना góo-tuk-na, *v. n.* To coo as a dove; to swallow.

गूटका góot-ka, *s. m.* A ball prepared by devotees, by putting which in their mouths they are supposed to become invisible; a sweetmeat swallowed as a bolus without chewing; a small book worn as an amulet.

गूटिका góo-ti-ka, *s. f.* A pill, a bolus, any small globe or ball.

गूठला góoth-la, *adj.* Being set on edge (*the teeth*).

गूठली góoth-lee, *s. f.* A kernel, stone (*of fruit*), seed.

गूर goor, *s. m.* Molasses, treacle, raw sugar. *Goorumba*, Mangoes boiled with meal and sugar, resembling mangoe-fool.

गूरगूराना goor-goo-rána, *v. n.* To rumble (*the bowels*).

गूरगूरी góor-goo-ree, *s. f.* A small *hookka*, a kind of pipe for smoking.

गूरूच goo-rúch, *s. m.* A medicine (*Menispermum glabrum*).

गूरपूस्प goor-póosp, } *s. m.* A kind of *Bas-*
गूरफूल goor-phóol, } *sia* (*B. latifolia*) bearing flowers which are sweet, and from which a spirituous liquor is distilled; the nuts afford an oil used instead of butter.

गूराना goo-rá-na, *v. a.* To dig; to cause to dig.

गूरिया goo-ri-ya, *s. m.* A seller of *Goor*, *s. f.* A doll.

गूडी góod-dee, *s. f.* A child's kite; a pinion.

गूरहुल góor-hul, *s. m. Hibiscus syriacus.*

गून goon, *s. m.* A quality, an attribute or property in general (*but especially of excellence, &c.*); skill, understanding, cleverness, virtue, mode, method, manner, merit; a string, rope, small track-rope, a property of humanity, of which three are particularized, viz. the *Sutwuh, Rujuh,* and *Tumuh,* or principles of truth or existence, passion, or foulness, and darkness or ignorance; a favour, a kindness. *Goon-kurna*, To benefit. *Goon-ka pulta dena*, To repay a benefit. *Goon-chhandna*, To pass over a person's good qualities. *Goon-gahuk, adj.* Purchasing skill or merit, patro-

nising learning. *s. m.* A discerner of merit, a patron of learning. *Goon manna*, To acknowledge a favour. *Goon-nidhan*, Abode of skill or merit; skilful.

गूनखान goon-khán, (*lit. mine of merit*) *adj.* Very worthy, skilful or learned.

गूनगान goon-gán, *s. m.* Panegyric, praise.

गूनगान करना goon-gán kúrna, *v. a.* To sing, celebrate, prattle, (*or crow*) as infants.

गूनता góon-ta, *s. f.* Excellence; multiplication.

गूनभ्रंश goon-bhrúnsh, *s. m.* The loss of all good qualities.

गूनमूय goon-múy, *adj.* Possessed of merit.

गूनवंत goon-wúnt, } *adj.* Possessing attri-
गूनवान goon-wán, } butes but especially those of excellence; possessed of talent or virtue; virtuous, skilful, accomplished.

गूनसागर goon-ságur, *adj.* Endowed with all good qualities, an ocean of virtue or excellence.

गूनस्तूति goon-stóoti, *s. f.* Panegyric, encomium.

गूनहीन goon-héen, *adj.* Void of merit.

गूना góo-na, *s. m.* (*in comp.*) Fold, turn, time; as *Sou-goona*, A hundred-fold.

गूनिन góo-nin, } *adj.* Endowed with
गूनियन góo-ni-yun, } good qualities; skilful.

गूनी góo-nee, *adj.* Skilful, virtuous, dexterous, possessed of any quality or art; a snake-catcher, one who charms snakes, a sorcerer, conjurer.

गूनेश्वर goon-ésh-wur, *s. m.* The name of a mountain, according to some, *Chitrkote* or *Comptah* in *Bundelcund*.

गूथना góoth-na, *v. n.* To be plaited, to be threaded, to be strung.

गूथवां góoth-wan, *adj.* Plaited or strung together.

गूद good, *s. m.* } The anus.
गूदा góo-da, *s. f.* }

गूदकीलक good-kée-luk, } *s. m.* Piles.
गूदांकूर good-án-koor, }

गूदगूदा góod-goo-da, *adj.* Soft, plump.

गूदगूदाई good-goo-dáee, } *s. f.* Titil-
गूदगूदाहट good-goo-dá-hut, } lation.
गूदगूदी góod-goo-dee, }

गूदगूदाना good-goo-dána, *v. a.* To tickle, to titillate.

गूदग्रह good-grúh, *s. m.* Constipation, flatulence, &c.

मुद्क्रिया goo-dúr-í-ya, *adj.* Clothed in patched garments or rags; a tatterdemalion; one who lets quilts for hire. *Goodriya-peer, s. m.* A tree near a town or village on which people tie up rags in the manner of votive tablets, which they believe to be efficacious for the accomplishment of their wishes.

गद्दी gŏod-ree, *s. f.* A pallet, a beggar's bedding, quilts, &c.; a daily market.

गुदा gŏo-da, *s. f.* The anus.

गुदा gŏod-da, *s. m.* A baby, doll; a wind-gall; a bough, a branch.

गरी gŏod-dee, *s. f.* Nape of the neck.

गुन goon, *s. m.* A quality, an attribute or property in general (*but especially of excellence, &c.*); skill, cleverness, virtue, mode, method, manner, merit; a small track-rope; a property of humanity of which three are particularized, viz. the *Sutwuh, Rujuh,* and *Tumuh,* or principles of truth or existence; passion or foulness, and darkness or ignorance; a favour, or kindness. *Goon kurna,* To benefit. *Goon ka pulta dena,* To repay a benefit. *Goon chhandna,* To pass over a person's good qualities. *Goon-gahuk, adj.* Purchasing skill or merit, patronizing learning. *s. m.* A discerner of merit, a patron of learning. *Goon-manna,* To acknowledge a favour.

गुनगुना gŏon-goo-na, *adj.* Milk-warm; snuffling.

गुनगुनाना goon-goo-ná-na, *v. n.* To be milk-warm; to snuffle, sing slowly or with a low voice.

गुनवंत goon-wúnt, गुनवान् goo-wán, *adj.* Possessing attributes but especially those of excellence; possessed of talent or virtue; virtuous, skilful, accomplished.

गुनी gŏo-nee, *adj.* Skilful, virtuous, dexterous, possessed of any quality or art; a snake-catcher, one who charms snakes, a sorcerer.

गुप्त goopt, *adj.* Preserved, protected; hidden, concealed; invisible, withdrawn from sight. *s. m.* An appellation forming especially the second member of the name of a *Vysyuh* or man of the third class. *adv.* Privately, secretly.

गुप्तमति gŏopt-gut-i, *s. m.* A spy or secret emissary.

गुप्ति gŏop-ti, *s. f.* Concealing, concealment; preserving, protecting.

गुप्ती gŏop-tee, *s. f.* A hidden sword.

गुफा gŏo-pha, *s. f.* A cave.

गुबरौता goob-róu-ta, *s. m.* A beetle found in dunghills or old cowdung (*Scarabeus* or *Stercorarius? copris*).

गुभाना goo-bhá-na, गुभोना goo-bhó-na, *v. a.* To thrust, stick into.

गुभीला goo-bhée-la, *s. m.* Hard lumps in the intestines produced by costiveness, scybala.

गुमटा goomta, *s. m.* A swelling or tumour from a blow.

गुमडी gŏom-tee, *s. f.* गुमट gŏom-mut, *s. m.* } A tower, a bastion.

गुमरा gŏom-ra, गुमड़ा gŏom-ra, } *s. m.* A protuberance, a bump, a swelling.

गुमरी gŏom-ree, *s. f.* Vertigo.

गुमसा gŏom-sa, *adj.* Musty.

गुरजना goo-rúj-na, *v. n.* To snarl.

गुराई goo-rá-ee, *s. f.* Fairness, whiteness, yellowness, pale redness.

गुरिया goo-ri-ya, *s. f.* A bead (*of a rosary, &c.*)

गुरु gŏo-roo, *s. m.* A spiritual parent or director from whom the youth receives the initiatory *muntr* or prayer, and who conducts the ceremonies necessary at various seasons of infancy and youth, up to the period of investiture with the characteristic thread or string; this person may be the natural parent or the religious preceptor; a religious teacher, one who explains the law and religion to his pupil, instructs him in the *Shastrus,* &c.; a father, or any venerable male relation; a spiritual guide, preceptor, tutor, pastor, teacher; the planet Jupiter. *adj.* Heavy, weighty; important; honourable, respectable; great, eminent; difficult, arduous; best, excellent. *Gooroo-mookh hona,* To receive from a *Gooroo* the initiatory *muntr* or mystical prayer peculiar to the deity adopted for worship in particular, who is thence termed the *Isht-dev,* or chosen god; to become a scholar. *Gooroo-luksh, s. m.* Knowledge which can be acquired from a living instructor only.

गुरुकार्य goo-roo-káryuh, *s. m.* A serious or momentous affair; the business or office of a spiritual teacher.

गुरुजन goo-roo-jún, *s. m.* An elder, a venerable person.

गुरुतर gŏo-roo-tur, *adj.* More important, highly honourable, weighty.

गुरुदेवत goo-róo-dy-wút, *s. m.* The eighth lunar constellation.

गुरुपाक goo-roo-pák, *adj.* Difficult of digestion.

गुरुरत्न gooroo-rútn, *s. m.* A topaz.

गुरुवाइन gooroo-wáin, *s. f.* The wife of a spiritual teacher.

गुरुवार goo-roo-wár, *s. m.* Thursday.

गुर्ग gŏor-ga, *s. m.* A servant boy, brat; vagabond.

गुर्गाबी goor-gá-bee, *s. f.* A kind of shoe or slipper.

गुर्गुरी gŏor-goo-ree, *s. f.* Ague, the cold fit of a fever, a quotidian fever.

गुर्च goorch, *s. f.* A creeping plant (*Menispermum glabrum*).

गुर्जर gŏorj-jur, *s. m.* A district in the south-west, Guserat. *m. pl.* The people of *Guserat.*

गूझेरी góorj-jur-ee, *s. f.* One of the *Raginees* or female personifications of music.

गूरी góor-ree, *s. f.* Parched barley.

गूर्विनी góorv-vi-nee, ⎫ *s. f.* A pregnant
गूर्वी góorv-vee, ⎭ woman.

गूलगूला gool-goo-la, *s. m.* Sweet cakes fried in butter, or wheat flower, sugar and *duhee*, with anise and cardamom seeds made into dumplings and fried in ghee. *adj.* Soft.

गूलगूलाना gool-goo-lá-na, *v. a.* To soften, to mollify.

गूलगूलाहट gool-goo-lá-hut, *s. f.* Softness.

गूलगूथना gool-góoth-na, *adj.* Plump, handsome, chubby.

गूलचूला gool-chúl-a, *s. m.* A musketeer, a shooter of ball; a gunner.

गूलझूरी gool-jhúr-ee, *s. f.* Conglomeration, knot. *Gooljhuree dil-kee, s. f.* Grief, displeasure, mental uneasiness.

गूलहूती gool-hút-tee, *s. f.* Rice-gruel, or rice and water boiled together and seasoned with salt.

गूलाई goo-lá-ee, *s. f.* Roundness, rotundity.

गूलाबजामन gooláb-jámun, *s. f.* The rose-apple (*Eugenia jambos*).

गूलाल goo-lál, *s. m.* A farinaceous powder dyed red, which the *Hindoos* throw on each other during the indecent festivities and drunken frolics of the *holee*. *Goolal-chushm, adj.* Red-eyed. *Goolal-baree, s. f.* A royal pavilion or tent. *Goolalee, adj.* Of the colour of the *goolal* or stained with it.

गूली góo-lee, *s. f.* A pill, a bolus, any small globular substance; a disease.

गूलूगा goo-lóo-ga, *s. m.* A monkey's pouch.

गूलेल goo-lél, ⎫ *s. f.* A pellet-bow.
गूलेल goo-lyl, ⎭

गूल्फ goolph, *s. m.* The ankle.

गूल्म goolm, *s. m.* The division of an army, a body of troops consisting of 9 platoons, or 9 elephants, 9 chariots, 27 horse, and 45 foot; the spleen; a disease, according to some, a chronic enlargement of the spleen, but it appears to be an induration of the mesenteric glands so as to be perceived externally.

गूल्ला góol-la, *s. m.* A pellet shot from a pellet-bow.

गूल्ली góol-lee, *s. f.* A kind of pigeon. *s. f.* A whetstone, a polishing stone.

गूवाक goo-wák, *s. m.* The betel-nut tree (*Areca faufel* or *catechu*).

गूवैया goo-wy-ya, (*gossip*) *s. f.* A woman's female friend. *adj.* Eloquent, conversible.

गूश्त goosht, *s. m.* Cabal.

गूह gooh, *s. f.* Human excrement. *Gohee, adj.* Defiled with excrement.

गूहत góo-hut, *part.* Covered, concealed; plaiting the hair.

गूहना góoh-noun, *v. a.* To thread, to string; to plaid, to braid.

गूहराना gooh-rá-na, *v. n.* To bawl, to call out. *v. a.* To assist.

गूहांजनी gooh-án-jun-ee, *s. f.* A sty (*in the eye*).

गूहा góo-ha, *s. f.* A cave, a cavern.

गूहाई goo-há-ee, *s. f.* Meconium (*of infants*).

गूहार goo-hár, *s. f.* An assistant, aid; bawling; tumult, alarm.

गूह्य góohyuh, *adj.* Concealable, requiring concealment. *s. f.* The anus, the parts of the body which decency requires to be concealed.

गूह्यक góoh-yuk, *s. m.* A kind of demigod attendant upon *Koover*, the god of riches, and guardian of his treasures.

गू goo, *s. f.* Human excrement.

गूंगा góon-ga, *adj.* Dumb.

गूंगाई goon-gá-ee, *s. f.* Dumbness.

गूंज goonj, *s. f.* Echo, buzzing, resounding, hollow sound, roar.

गूंजना góonj-na, *v. n.* To resound, hum, buzz, growl, roar.

गूंझा góon-jha, *s. m.* A sort of sweetmeat.

गूंरा goonra, *s. m.* A beam (*of a ship*); the cross timbers (*of a boat*).

गूंथना góonth-na, *v. a.* To thread, string, plait; to stitch; to spit or put on a spit. *Goonthwana, v. a.* To cause to string, plait; stitch; put on a spit.

गूंद goond, *s. f.* Gum.

गूंदना góond-na, *v. a.* To knead; to plait, braid, plat, weave.

गूंदनी góond-nee, *s. f.* A tree yielding a sort of gummy fruit.

गूंदला góond-la, *adj.* Round, circular. *s. m.* A ring, a circle.

गूंधन góon-dhun, *s. m.* Dough; plaiting, braid.

गूंधना góondh-na, *v. a.* To knead (*flour, &c.*); to plait, braid, plat, weave.

गूआ góo-a, *s. f.* Betel-nut.

गूइयां gooiyán, *s. m.* A partner (*at any game*).

गूगूल góo-gul, *s. m.* A tree or gum (*Amyris agallocha*); Bdellium.

गूगली góog-lee, *s. f.* A cockle-shell.

गूजर góo-jur, *s. m.* A cast of *Rajpoots* originally from *Goojrat*.

गूजरी góoj-ree, *s. f.* The female of *Goojur ;* an ornament worn on the wrists and feet; an earthen image representing a milk-maid ; a musical mode.

गूजी goojée, *s. f.* A stick, a club.

गुढिया gooríya, *s. m.* A doll.

गूढ़ goorh, *adj.* Abstruse, difficult, obscure, abstracted ; secret, mysterious, enigmatical ; hidden, concealed.

गूढ़ता góorh-ta, *s. f.* Abstruseness, secrecy, concealedness.

गूढ़पात goorh-pát, *s. m.* A snake.

गूढ़पुरुष goorh-póo-roosh, *s. m.* A spy, a secret emissary, a disguised agent, a scout.

गूढ़बक्ता goorh-búkta, *s. m.* A pedagogue, a pedant.

गूढ़मार्ग goorh-márg, *s. m.* A subterraneous passage, a defile, a bye-road, or secret way.

गूढ़ार्थ goorh-árth, *adj.* Of obscure or hidden meaning.

गूथ gooth, *s. m.* A round ball of cotton.

गूथना góoth-na, *v. a.* To plait, braid, thread, string ; to stitch ; to spit or put on a spit.

गूदड़ góo-dur, *s. m.* A quilt ; a bundle of old clothes ; any old tattered cloths ; a kind of silk stuff. *Goodur-khyl, adj. (applied only to females)* Foolish, unmannerly, rude. *Goodur seena,* To stitch together. *Goodur ka lal,* or *Goodur men gundoura nikulna,* Good proceeding from evil.

गूदड़ी góod-ree, *s. f.* A quilt (*especially a mendicant's*) ; a bundle.

गूदर góo-dur, *adj.* Fat, plump.

गूदा góo-da, *s. m.* Brain, marrow, kernel, pith, crumb.

गूदिया goo-dí-ya, *adj.* Desirous, wishing.

गूधना góodh-na, *v. a.* To knead (*flour, &c.*)

गूमरा goomra, *s. m.* A bump, a swelling.

गूलर goolur, *s. f.* A wild fig (*Ficus guleria*).

गूह gooh, *s. f.* Human excrement.

गूहरिया goo-húr-i-ya, *s. m.* A dunghill, a place where excrement is thrown.

गूही góo-hee, *adj.* Defiled with excrement.

गृञ्जन grín-jun, *s. m.* Poisoned flesh, the meat of an animal destroyed by poison ; garlic.

गृध्र gridhr, *s. m.* A vulture.

गृध्रा grídh-ra, *adj.* Desirous, greedy, covetous.

गृध्रू grídh-roo, *adj.* Covetous, cupidinous, greedy.

गृध्रूता grídh-roo-ta, *s. f.* Covetousness, greediness, extreme and illiberal desire.

गृह grih, *s. m.* A house, dwelling, mansion, habitation in general ; a wife.

गृहकपोतक grih-kup-ó-tuk, *s. m.* A pigeon, a tame or domestic pigeon.

गृहतटी grih-tút-ee, *s. f.* A terrace in front of a house, a threshold.

गृहनाशन grih-ná-shun, *s. m.* A pigeon.

गृहपति grih-pút-i, *s. m.* A householder ; a householder of particular merit, giving alms and performing all the prescribed ceremonies, &c. ; virtue, especially of a householder, as hospitality, &c.

गृहभूमि grih-bhóo-mi, *s. f.* The scite of a habitation.

गृहवाटिका grih-vá-tik-a, *s. f.* A garden or grove near a house.

गृहस्थ grí-husth, *s. m.* A householder, a man of the second class, or he who after having finished his studies and been invested with the sacred thread, performs the duties of the master of a house, and father of a family ; a peasant, a husbandman.

गृहस्थाश्रम gríhusth-áshrum, *s. m.* The profession or condition of a house-holder or married man.

गृहस्थी gri-húst-hee, *s. f.* Husbandry, house-keeping, housewifery, household ; the duties of a householder.

गृहिणी grí-hin-ee, *s. f.* A wife.

गृहीत gri-héet, *adj.* Taken, attached, seized, caught.

गृह्य gríh-yuh, *adj.* A partisan, of or belonging to a side or party ; to be taken or seized ; domestic, of or belonging to a house ; a book containing directions for religious rites.

गेंठ genth, *s. f.* Name of a fish.

गेंदुक gén-duk, *s. m.* Marigold.

गेंडा gén-da, *s. m.* A rhinoceros.

गेंदू gén-doo, *s. m.* A ball for playing with.

गेंद gend, *s. m.* An elephant. *s. f.* A ball for playing with. *Gend-tures, s. f.* Playing at ball.

गेंदा géu-da, *s. m.* Marigold ; a ball.

गेंदी gén-dee, *s. f.* A ball (*to play with*).

गेगटा gég-ta, *s. m.* A crab.

गेगली gég-lee, *s. f.* A trollop.

गेरी gér-ee, *s. f.* Name of a game, knocking a stick over a line by throwing another stick at it.

गेदरा géd-ra, *adj.* Simple, ignorant, silly.

गेदा géd-a, *s. m.* A young unfledged bird ; (*met.*) an infant.

गेपा gép-a, *s. m.* A nipple.

गेबर géb-ur, *s. m.* Name of a bird.

गेरू gér-oo, *s. m.* A kind of red earth or ochre.

गेरूवा gér-oo-a, *adj.* Covered with or coloured like *geroo.*

गेरूई gér-oo-ee, *adj.* Of the colour of *geroo.* *s. f.* The smut, mildew.

गेल्ा gél-a, *adj.* Simple.

गेश्न geshn, } *s. m.* A professional singer, an actor, a mimic;
गेश्नू gésh-noo, } a chaunter of the *Sam Ved.*

गेब geb, *s. m.* A house, a dwelling.

गेहूं géhoon, *s. m.* Wheat.

गेहूंआं géhoo-an, *s. m.* The colour of wheat; a sort of grass. *adj.* Of the colour of wheat, swarthy.

गैंत gynt, } *s. f.* A pickaxe.
गैंती gyn-tee, }

गैंडा gyn-da, *s. m.* A rhinoceros.

गैना gy-na, *s. m.* A bush; a small bullock.

गैनी gy-nee, *s. f.* A small car or carriage drawn by the bullocks called *gyna.*

गैया gy-ya, *s. f.* A cow.

गैरा gy-ra, *s. m.* A sheaf (*of corn*).

गैरिक gy-rik, *s. m.* Red earth or ochre.

गैल gyl, *s. f.* A road.

गैहरी gyh-rée, *s. f.* Demurrage.

गो go, *s. f.* A cow.

गोंठ gonth, *s. m.* A kind of wide stitch or sewing.

गोंठा gón-tha, *s. m.* Dried cow-dung.

गोंडली gónd-lee, *s. f.* Name of a tree.

गोंद gond, *s. f.* Gum. *Gond-danee, s. f.* A vessel in which gum is kept to seal letters with. *Gond-kush,* An instrument for spreading gum with (*in sealing letters*).

गोंदनी gónd-nee, *s. f.* A reed of the leaves of which coarse mats are made (*Typha*).

गोंदा gón-da, *s. m.* A thin dough or pap made of flour of *Cicer arietinum* for feeding birds.

गोंदी gón-dee, *s. f.* Name of a tree (*Cordia*).

गोकर्ण go-kúrn, *s. m.* A span; a kind of deer (*the neel gow?*); a mule.

गोकुल gó-kool, *s. m.* A herd of kine, a multitude of cattle; a cow-house or station.

गोखरू gókh-roo, *s. m.* A plant (*Ruellia longifolia, and in Bengal, Tribulus lanuginosus*); an ornament (*bells tied round the ankles*); a joint. *Bura gokhroo, Pedalium murex.*

गोचना góch-na, *v. a.* To catch, seize.

गोचर gó-chur, *s. m.* Perception, information. *adj.* Known, perceived.

गोचरी gó-chur-ee, *adj.* Visible, seen, perceived.

गोजर gó-jur, *s. m.* A centipede (*Scolopendra*).

गोजागरिक go-já-gur-ik, *adj.* Happy, fortunate, auspicious.

गोट got, *s. f.* A counter, piece or man at back gammon, chess, &c.; the hem of a garment.

गोटा gó-ta, *s. m.* (*Gold or silver*) Lace or edging (*rather narrow*).

गोटी gó-tee, *s. f.* The small-pox, a pock.

गोर gor, *s. m.* The leg, foot.

गोरना gór-na, *v. a.* To dig, to scrape.

गोरी gó-ree, *s. f.* Taking away. *Goree kurna,* To take away, steal, walk off with.

गोन gon, *s. f.* A sack, bag (*of coarse cloth*), the sacks fastened on the sides of a beast of burthen to carry grain in.

गोत got, *s. m.* Parentage, lineage, pedigree, stock of a family.

गोतम go-tum, *n. prop. Boodha;* also the author of the *Nyayuk* philosophy, or logic, and his doctrines corresponded with those of Aristotle.

गोती gó-tee, *adj.* One of the same stock or family, a relative.

गोत्र gotr, *s. m.* Family, race, lineage, kin; a genus, a class or species.

गोत्रज go-trúj, *s. m.* A relation; in law the term is nearly equivalent to the *gentile* of Roman law, and is applied to kindred of the same general family who are connected by offerings of food and water, and stands opposed to the *Bundhoo* or cognate kin, who do not partake in the offerings to the common ancestors.

गोद god, } *s. f.* The lap, bosom, embrace; the elephantiasis.
गोदी gó-dee, } *God lena,* To adopt (*a child*). *God pusarna,* To ask, beg.

गोदना god-na, *v. a.* To prick, puncture, dot, mark with dots (*the skin*). *s. m.* Marks of tattooing.

गोदंत go-dúnt, *s. m.* Yellow orpiment; a cow's tooth; a fossil substance of a white colour, apparently an earthy salt.

गोदावरी go-dá-wur-ee, *s. f.* The name of a river in the peninsula, the *Godaveri.*

गोदोहनी go-dóh-nee, *s. f.* A milk-pail.

गोधरा gódh-ra, *s. m.* A bough, a branch.

गोधा gó-dha, *s. f.* A leathern fence worn by archers on the left arm to prevent its being injured by the bow-string.

गोधम gó-dhoom, } *s. m.* Wheat.
गोधूम go-dhóom, }

गोधूली go-dhóo-lee, *s. f.* } Evening, twilight.
गोधूरा go-dhóu-ra, *s. m.* }

गोधेनु go-dhén-oo, *s. f.* A milch-cow.

गोनस go-nus, *s. m.* A large kind of snake, considered to be the same with the Boa or Bor.

गोप gop, *s. m.* A herdsman, a cowherd, a milkman. *s. f.* A gold-necklace.

गोपन go-pún, *s. m.* Concealment. *Gopun kurna,* To conceal, to hide.

गोपनीय go-pun-éeyuh, *adj.* Fit to be concealed.

गोपरस gop-rús, *s. m.* Gum myrrh.

गोपाल go-pál, } *s. m.* A cowherd, a
गोपालक go-pá-luk, } cow-keeper or protector; a king, a sovereign.

गोपी gó-pee, *s. f.* The female of *Gop (a cowherd)*; a female cowherd.

गोपीचन्दन gópee-chúndun, *s. m.* A species of white clay.

गोपग्वाल gop-gwál, *s. m.* A cowherd.

गोफन go-phún, } *s. f.* A sling(*for throw-*
गोफिया gó-phi-ya, } *ing with*).

गोबर gó-bur, *s. m.* Cow-dung. *Gobur khana,* To do penance (*by eating cow-dung*).

गोबरगनेश go-bur-gun-ésh, *adj.* Fat.

गोबरी gó-bur-ee, *s. f.* Plaster made of cow-dung.

गोबरोंडा gob-rón-da, *s. m.* A beetle found in cow-dung (*Scarabeus*).

गोभी gó-bhee, *s. f.* A term in card-playing; name of a medicinal herb (*Hieracium*). *Soofyd gobhee, Cacalia sonchifolia.*

गोमय go-múy, *s. m.* Cow-dung.

गोमुख gó-mookh, *s. m.* A hole in a wall made by thieves, &c.; a breach.

गोमुखी gó-moo-khee, *s. f.* A cloth-bag containing a rosary, the hand being thrust in, counts the beads; the chasm in the *Himaluy* mountains through which the Ganges flows, erroneously conceived by the *Hindoos* to be of the shape of a cow's mouth.

गोमूत्र go-móotr, *s. m.* Cow's urine.

गोमेदक go-méd-uk, *s. m.* A gem of a yellowish or tawny colour (*a topaz*), a precious stone brought from the *Himaluy* and *Indus*, described as of four sorts, white, pale yellow, red, and dark blue, perhaps varieties of agate.

गोमेदसन्निभ gómed-súnnibh, *s. m.* Chalcedony or opal.

गोमेध go-médh, *s. m.* The offering or sacrifice of a cow.

गोरस go-rús, *s. m.* Milk, butter-milk, curdled or coagulated milk.

गोरसहा go-rus-há, *adj.* (*a child*) Reared with the milk of cattle. *s. m.* A sodomite.

गोरसी go-rús-ee, *s. f.* A vessel for holding milk, &c., a milk-pail.

गोरा gó-ra, *adj.* Fair (*complexioned*).

गोरू gó-roo, *s. m.* An ox, a cow. *Gorooa-dhookan, s. m.* Twilight (*the time of bringing home the cows*). *Gorooaree bera, s. f.* Evening.

गोरूत gó-root, *s. m.* A measure of distance equal to two *cros* or *cos*.

गोरोचना go-róch-na, *s. f.* A bright yellow pigment prepared from the urine of a cow or vomited in the shape of scibulæ by the animal; it is employed in painting and dyeing and is of especial virtue in marking the foreheads of the *Hindoos* with the *Tiluc* or sacred mark; it is also used in medicine as a sedative, tonic, and anthelmintic remedy, &c.

गोल gol, *s. m.* A circle, a ball, any thing round or globular; a water-jar. *adj.* Round. *Gol-phul, s. m.* The testicle. *Golgol, adj.* Round. *Golsa, adj.* Roundish.

गोलक gó-luk, *s. m.* } A widow's illegiti-
गोलिका gó-lik-a, *s. f.* } mate son or daughter.

गोलमिर्च gol-mirch, *s. f.* Black-pepper (*Piper-nigrum*).

गोला gó-la, *s. f.* A globe, a sphere, a *mundul*; a large water-jar. *s. m.* A granary; a cannon-ball; a ball; a large beam of wood; a kind of pigeon; the kernel of a cocoanut.

गोलाई golá-ee, *s. f.* Roundness.

गोलाकार golakár, *adj.* Round, globular.

गोलादुंडा go-la-dún-da, *s. m.* Name of a game, tip-cat.

गोलाध्याय goladhyáyuh, *s. m.* The division of mathematical science which treats of the spheres, spherics.

गोलार go-lar, *s. m.* Roundness.

गोलारा go-lá-ra, *adj.* Round.

गोली gó-lee, *s. f.* A bullet, a ball, a globule; a pill; a jar. *Golee marna,* To shoot a ball at.

गोलोक gó-lok, *s. m.* The heaven of *Vishnoo.*

गोवना gó-wun-a, *v. a.* To conceal, hide.

गोवर्द्धन go-wurd-dhún, *s. m.* A celebrated hill in *Vindravun*, or the country about *Muthoora*, it is said to have been upheld by *Krishn* upon one finger to shelter the cowherds from a storm excited by *Indr*, as a test of the divinity of the former.

गोशाल go-shál, *adj.* A cow-house.

गोष्ट gosht, *s. f.* Plot, cabal, conspiracy.

गोष्ठ goshth, *s. m.* A cowpen, a fold for cattle, a station of cowherds.

गोष्ठी gósht-hee, *s. f.* An assembly, a meeting; conversation, discourse; family connexions, but especially the dependant or junior branches.

गोष्पद gósh-pud, *s. m.* A measure, as much as a cow's footstep will hold; the mark or impression of cow's foot; a cow's foot or hoof.

गोसव gó-suv, *s. m.* The sacrifice of a cow, one of the grand sacrifices of the *Hindoos* in former times, and not permitted in the present age or *Kulijoog.*

गोसांई go-sáeen, *s. m.* The deity; a saint, a holy person; the descendants of the disciples of *Chytunyuh of Nuddea.*

गोसंया go-syn-ya, *s. m.* The deity.

गोस्तन gó-stun, *s. m.* A cluster of blossoms, a nosegay.

गोस्तनी go-stún-ee, *s. f.* A grape.

गोस्थान gó-sthan, *s. m.* A cowpen, a station for cattle.

गोवना gówuna, *v. a.* To hide, conceal.

गोह goh, *s. m.* A lizard, a guana; a gangetic alligator.

गोहत्या go-hútya, *s. f.* Killing a cow.

गोहरा góhur-a, *s. m.* Cakes of dried cow-dung; an ally, succourer, an assistant.

गोहरी gó-hur-ee, *s. f.* Demurrage.

गोहार go-hár, *s. m.* Tumult, uproar.

गोहूं gó-hoon, *s. m.* Wheat.

गोहुअन gó-hoo-un, गोहुना gó-hoo-na, } *s. m.* A species of snake, the Boa.

गोक्षुर gók-shoor, *s. m.* A plant (*Ruellia longifolia,* and *Tribulus languinosus*).

गो gou, *s. m. f.* A cow, one of the cow species. *Gou-dan, s. m.* Gift of a cow.

गों goun, *s. f.* Opportunity, advantage. *Goun-geer,* Controller, uncontrolled, ruler, invested with authority, self-interested. *Goun-ghat, s. f.* Power, opportunity.

गोख goukh, *s. m.* A portico.

गोछुई gou-chhúee, *s. f.* A sprout.

गोछी gouchhee, *s. f.* A hole or pit.

गोड़ gour, *s. m.* The district of *Gour,* the central part of Bengal; the ruins of its capital called by the same name are still extensive. *m. pl.* The inhabitants of *Gour* (*brahmuns*).

गोड़ा góu-ra, *s. m.* A cast of *Hindoos* in *Oorissa,* who are generally *palkee* carriers and bearers; a musical mode.

गोड़िया góu-ri-ya, *s. m.* Inhabitant of *Gour;* hence the followers of *Chytunyuh of Nuddea* are so called: this philosopher flourished in the year 1407 of *Salivahun,* about A. D. 1350.

गोड़ी góu-ree, *s. f.* Rum or spirit distilled from *Goor* or molasses; a musical mode.

गोदान góu-dan, *s. m.* Gift of a cow.

गोना góu-na, *s. m.* Bringing home a wife. *Gounhar, s. m.* The company who attend the bride when bringing home.

गोर gour, *adj.* Fair-complexioned.

गोरव gou-rúv, *s. m.* Reputation, respectability, venerableness, consequence or weight.

गोरवित góu-ruv-it, *adj.* Venerable, respectable.

गोरा góura, *s. m.* A cock-sparrow.

गोरिया góu-ri-ya, *s. f.* A sparrow.

गोरी góu-ree, *s. f.* A musical mode.

गोशाला gou-shá-la, *s. m.* A cow-house.

गोष gouh, *s. f.* Perseverance.

गोहुर्ह gou-húr-ha, *s. m.* An ally, succourer, an assistant.

ग्यारह gyáruh, *adj.* Eleven. *Gyruhwan, adj.* Eleventh.

ग्रथित grúth-it, *adj.* Strung, tied together, or in order.

ग्रन्थ grunth, *s. m.* A book or composition in prose or verse, a code, the book of the *Sikh* religion composed by the *gooroo Nanuk Shah.*

ग्रन्थकार grunth-kár, *s. m.* An author, bookmaker, writer, compiler.

ग्रन्थि grúnth-i, *s. m.* The joint or knot of a reed or cane, &c., and figuratively of the body; a tie, the knot of a cord, &c.

ग्रस्त grust, *adj.* Inaccurately pronounced, slurred, uttered with the omission of a letter or syllable.

ग्रह gruh, *s. m.* A house, a dwelling; a plant. *Gruh-sthapun,* Invoking the presence of the nine planets.

ग्रहण grúhun, *s. m.* Taking, seizure, receiving, acceptance; assent, agreement; an eclipse.

ग्रहणी grúhun-ee, *s. f.* Diarrhœa, dysentery.

ग्रहपीड़ा gruh-péera, *s. f.* The influence of an unpropitious planet.

ग्रहपूजा gruh-póoja, *s. f.* Worship of the sun and the other planets.

ग्रहराज gruh-ráj, *s. m.* The sun; the moon; the planet Jupiter.

ग्रहाधार gruha-dhár, *s. m.* The constellation *Dhroov* or the polar star, from its remaining fixed amidst the planetary movements.

ग्रहाधीन gruha-dhéen, *adj.* Subject to planetary influence.

ग्रहामय gruhamúy, *s. m.* Epilepsy, convulsions, demoniacal possession which the complaint is supposed to be.

ग्रहीता gruhée-ta, *adj.* Taking, disposed to take.

ग्राम gram, *s. m.* A village, a hamlet, an inhabited place in the midst of fields and meadow land, where men of the servile class mostly reside, and where agriculture thrives; a scale in music, an octave.

ग्रामणी grám-un-ee, *s. m.* A barber. *s. f.* A whore, a harlot; a female peasant or villager.

ग्रामयाजक gram-yájuk, *s. m.* The village priest, one who conducts the ceremonies for any or all classes, and is consequently considered as a degraded *brahmun*; it also applies to the attendant of an idol.

ग्रामवासी gram-vásee, *s. m.* A villager.

ग्रामिक gramík, *adj.* Village, rude, rustic.

ग्रामीण gra-méen, *adj.* A villager, a rustic, village; vulgar, rude.

ग्राम्य grám-yuh, *s. m.* Rustic or homely speech; the *Prakrit*, and the other dialects of India except the *Sunskrit.* *adj.* Rustic (*in discourse*); village-born, produced in or relating to a village.

ग्राम्यधर्म्म gram-yuh-dhúrmm, *s. m.* Copulation.

ग्राम्याश्व gram-yáswuh, *s. m.* An ass (*lit. village horse*).

ग्रास gras, *s. m.* A mouthful or a quantity equivalent to a mouthful, a lump of rice, &c., of the size of a peacock's egg.

ग्रह grah, *s. m.* Taking, either by seizure or acceptance; a shark; according to some the gangetic alligator, according to others, the water elephant (*the hippopotamus ?*).

ग्राहक grá-huk, *s. m.* One who takes or seizes, one who accepts.

ग्राह्य gráh-yuh, *adj.* Worthy of acceptance, fit to be received.

ग्रीवा grée-va, *s. f.* The neck; the back part of the neck, the nape, the tendon of the *Trapezium* muscle.

ग्रीष्म greeshm, *s. m.* The hot season comprehending two months, about June, July; heat, warmth. *adj.* Hot, warm.

ग्रेह greh, *s. m.* A dwelling, a house.

ग्रैव gryv, *s. m.* A necklace, a close necklace or collar.

ग्रैष्म gryshm, *adj.* Belonging or relating to the hot season.

ग्रैष्मी grysh-mee, *s. f.* Double jasmin.

ग्लान glan, *adj.* Wearied, languid, feeble, exhausted by fatigue, disease, &c.

ग्लानि glá-ni, *s. f.* Languor, lassitude, fatigue of body or depression of mind.

ग्वाल gwal, ग्वाला gwá-la, } *s. m.* A cowherd.

ग्वालिन gwá-lin, *s. f.* The female of *Gwal*, wife of a cowherd.

ग्वेंड gwynd, *adv.* Near.

ग्वेंडा gwyn-da, *s. m.* Suburb, vicinage. *Gwendeh, adv.* Near.

घ

घ ghuh, The fourth consonant of the *Naguree* alphabet, being the aspirate of the preceding letter, and corresponding with *gh.*

घंघोरना ghun-ghór-na, घंघोलना ghun-ghól-na, } *v. a.* To rinse; to mix any liquid by stirring it about.

घंच ghunch, *s. m.* The neck.

घंटा ghún-ta, *s. m.* A bell, a clock, an hour.

घंटाली ghun-tá-lee, *s. f.* A small bell.

घघरा ghúgh-ra, *s. m.* घघरी ghúgh-ree, *s. f.* } A petticoat.

घुचाघुच ghuch-a-ghúch, *adj.* Thick.

घट ghut, *s. m.* A water-pot; the body. *s. f.* Mind, heart, thought, soul.

घटक ghút-uk, *s. m.* A mediator, go-between, an ambassador, attorney, messenger; an agent who ascertains or invents genealogies and negociates matrimonial alliances.

घटती ghút-tee, *s. f.* Diminution, decrease; alleviation, abatement, decline.

घटदासी ghut-dásee, *s. f.* A bawd or procuress.

घटन ghútun, *s. m.* Occurring.

घटना ghút-na, *v. n.* To abate, decrease, lessen, decline, waste, dwindle, to be depressed.

घटनीय ghut-née-yuh, *adj.* Liable to abatement, or decrease, or diminution.

घटंत ghut-únt, *s. f.* Decrease.

घटवार ghut-wár, घटवाल ghut-wál, } *s. m.* A wharfinger.

घटहा ghut-há, *s. m.* An offender, transgressor.

घटा ghút-a, *s. f.* Cloudiness, gathering of the clouds, clouds; crowds.

घटातोप ghut-a-tóp, *s. m.* A covering for a *palkee*, a carriage, or any article of furniture.

घटाना ghut-á-na, *v. a.* To decrease, lessen, abate, diminish, allay, reduce.

घटाव ghut-áo, *s. m.* Deficiency, reduction, abbreviation, falling (*as of a river or of the price of any thing*), depreciation.

घटावना ghut-áo-na, *v. a.* To reduce, to cause to subside or fall.

घटिका ghút-i-ka, *s. f.* The ancle; a *moohoort* or 30th part of a day and night; a *dund* or period of 24 minutes.

घटिया ghút-i-ya, *adj.* Low-priced.

घटी ghút-ee, *s. f.* The *Ghuree*, or Indian clock, a plate of iron or mixed metal on which the hours are struck; diminution, abatement, decrease; alleviation.

घट्ट ghutt, *s. m.* A *ghat*, a quay or landing place, steps on the side of a river, &c., leading to the water's edge.

घट्टा ghút-ta, *s. m.* Corn of the foot.

घट्टी ghút-tee, *s. f.* A small or inferior landing place, private stairs, &c.

घुरघुराना ghur-ghur-ána, *v. n.* To thunder.

घुरना ghúr-na, *v. a.* To make, form, forge, work (metals).

घड़ा ghúr-a, *s. m.* A water-pot, an earthen pot, a pitcher, jar.

घड़िया ghúr-i-ya, *s. f.* A crucible; a honey-comb; the womb.

घड़ियाल ghur-i-yál, *s. m.* A crocodile; a plate of brass for beating time.

घड़ियाली ghur-i-yálee, *s. m.* The person who attends the *ghuriyal* and strikes the hours.

घड़ी ghuree, *s. f.* Fold, plait.

घड़ी ghúr-ee, *s. f.* An hour or the space of 24 minutes; an instrument for measuring time, a clock, watch, &c. *Ghuree men tola ghuree men masha*, Expresses a person of a changeable disposition.

घड़ोंचा ghur-ón-cha, *s. m.* } A stand for
घड़ोंची ghur-ón-chee, *s. f.* } water-pots, &c.

घड़ोला ghur-ó-la, *s. m.* A pot, a pitcher.

घंटा ghún-ta, *s. m.* A bell, also a plate of iron or mixed metal struck as a bell; a clock, an hour.

घंटाली ghun-tá-lee, *s. f.* A small bell.

घंटाशब्द ghun-ta-shúbd, *s. m.* Bell-metal.

घंटिका ghún-ti-ka, *s. f.* The uvula or soft palate.

घंटू ghún-too, *s. m.* A string of bells, tied on an elephant's chest, &c., by way of ornament.

घतिया ghutiya, *s. m.* A murderer.

घन ghun, *adj.* Material, solid; gross; compact; hard, firm; impenetrable; very, much. *s. m.* A number, an assemblage or quantity; (*in arithmetic*) the cube of a number; (*in geometry*) a solid.

घन ghun, *s. m.* Gathering of the clouds, clouds; an anvil, a sledge-hammer.

घनगरज ghun-gúr-uj, *s. m.* Thunder, any loud noise. *adj.* Loud-sounding.

घनघन ghún-ghun, *s. f.* An imitative sound.

घनघनाना ghun-ghun-ána, *v. n.* To jingle, ring, tinkle, to sound like a wheel in revolution.

घनघेरा ghun-ghér-a, *s. m.* A petticoat.

घनघोर ghun-ghór, *s. m.* Cloudiness, gathering of the clouds. *adj.* Cloudy, overcast; loud-sounding.

घनज्वाला ghun-jwá-la, *s. f.* Lightning, a flash of lightning.

घनतनवरन ghun-tun-vúr-un, *adj.* Whose body is of the colour of the clouds, an epithet of *Krishn*.

घनता ghun-tá, *s. f.* Firmness, compactness; thickness, solidity.

घनफल ghun-phúl, *s. m.* The contents of a solid (*in geometry*).

घनमूल ghun-móol, *s. m.* Cube root (*in arithmetic.*)

घनश्याम ghun-shyám, *adj.* Black as a cloud, &c. *s. m.* Black clouds.

घनसार ghun-sár, *s. m.* Camphor; mercury, or some peculiar form of it.

घना ghún-a, *adj.* Thick, close, confused, numerous, much, many.

घनेरा ghun-ér-a, *adj.* Much, many.

घनेस ghun-és, *s. m.* A bird (*Buceros malabaricus*).

घपची ghúp-chee, *s. f.* The grasp of the two arms.

घबराना ghub-rá-na, *v. n.* To be confused, confounded, perplexed, agitated, embarrassed, &c.

घबराहट ghub-rá-hut, *s. f.* Confusion, perplexity, agitation, perturbation, alarm, consternation.

घमंड ghúm-und, *s. m.* Pride, haughtiness, arrogance, conceit.

घमंडी ghum-ún-dee, *adj.* Proud, haughty, arrogant.

घमरौल ghum-róul, *s. f.* Crowd, confusion in a general engagement.

घमस ghúm-us, *s. f.* Heat, closeness.

घमसान ghum-sán, } *s. m.* Battle, en-
घमासान ghum-a-sán, } gagement.

घमाघम ghum-a-ghúm, *adj.* Thick, crowded. [the sun.

घमाना ghum-á-na, *v. n.* To sun, to bask in

घमूई ghum-óo-ee, *s. f.* Name of a plant.

घमोरी ghum-ó-ree, *s. f.* The prickly-heat.

घर ghur, *s. m.* House, dwelling, home, apartment, drawer, compartment, groove. *Ghur kurna*, To fix, settle, establish a family. *Ghur khokur tumasha dekhna*, To ruin one's self and spend the time in idle pleasures. *Ghur ghalna*, To ruin. *Ghur chulana*, To provide for one's household expenses. *Ghur doobona*, To ruin one's self and family. *Ghur doobna*, To be ruined. *Ghur dwaree, s. f.* A kind of tax, poll-tax, hearth-money. *Ghur-buhghur, adj.* To or in every house, from house to house. *Ghurbus-a, adj.* At home; indolent, inactive. *Ghur byth-jana*, To be ruined. *Ghur hona*, Expresses affection and unanimity between husband and wife.

घुरऊ ghur-úóo, *adj.* Domestic, household.

घुरत gbúr-ut, *s. f.* Make, form.

घुरनई ghur-núee, *s. f.* A raft made with pots, a float (*of pots*).

घुरना ghúr-na, *v. a.* To make, form, malleate, forge, work (*metals*).

घुरनी ghúr-nee, *s. f.* A wife.

घुरबराव ghur-bur-áo, *s. m.* Household furniture, &c.

घुरबार ghúr-bar, *s. m.* Family, household goods. *Ghurbar busana,* To consummate a marriage. *Ghurbar hona,* To undergo the consummation of a marriage.

घुरबारी ghúr-bá-ree, *s. f.* Housewifery, domestic concerns.

घुरर ghúr-ra, *s. m.* A rattling noise in the throat which dying people are afflicted with, pain, agony, pang.

घुरराटा ghur-rá-ta, *s. m.* Snoring.

घुरवाला ghur-wá-la, *s. m.* A housekeeper, master of a house.

घुरवाली ghur-wá-lee, *s. f.* Mistress of a house; house-keeping.

घुराना ghur-á-na, *s. m.* Family, household.

घुरामी ghur-á-mee, *s. m.* A thatcher.

घुरी ghúr-ee, *s. f.* An hour, or the space of 24 minutes; a fold, a plait. *adj.* Folded (*as clothes*).

घुरेला ghur-él·a, *adj.* Domestic, tame.

घुरऊआ ghur-óo-a, *s. m.* A small house which children make to play in.
घुरौंदा ghur-óun-da,

घुरघंट ghúr-ghut, *s. m.* A kind of fish (*Silurus*).

घुरघुर ghúr-ghur, *s. m.* The name of a river, the *Gogra* or *Ghogra*; the sound of gurgling, rumbling, &c.

घुर्म ghurm, *s. m.* Heat; the hot season; sun-shine; sweat, perspiration.

घुरशुन ghúr-shun, *s. m.* Grinding, pounding.

घुरशुनी ghúr-shun-ee, *s. f.* Turmeric.

घुलऊआ ghul-óo-a, *s. m.* A small quantity given above the quantity purchased, to boot.

घुसुन ghús-un, *s. f.* The act of rubbing.

घुसना ghusná, *v. n.* To be rubbed, to be
घिसना ghisná, abraded, to be worn, to fret, wear. *v. a.* To rub, rub off, whet; to beat. *adj.* Apt to be worn by rubbing.

घुसिटना ghús-it-na, *v. n.* To be dragged, to be trailed, to trail.

घुसियारा ghus-iyára, *s. m.* A grass-cutter.

घुसियारिन ghus-iyár-in, *s. f.* The wife of a grass-cutter.

घुसीटना ghus-éet-na, *v. a.* To drag, pull, trail.

घुसीला ghus-ée-la, *adj.* Grassy.

घुहुर ghúhur, *s. f.* Thunder. *Ghuhurna,* *v. n.* To thunder.

घुहराना ghuh-rána, *v. n.* To thunder; (*met.*) To roar, to bawl.

घुस्मुर ghús-mur, *adj.* Gluttonous, voracious.

घुस्रा ghús-ra, *adj.* Mischievous, hurtful.

घाइल ghá-il, *adj.* Wounded.

घाई gháee, *s. f.* Cudgelling; stratagem, fraud, a decoy; number five (*in reckoning*); the interval between the fingers or toes, the junction of the fingers, the space at the root where the fingers separate; the angle formed by a branch with the trunk of a tree, or space at the root of the branch; a cut or stroke with the broad sword or cudgel (*of which there are twelve cuts*).

घाईन gha-éen, *s. f.* (*One*) time, turn.

घाऊघुप gháoo-ghup, *adj.* Living from hand to mouth, improvident, spendthrift.

घांटी ghán-tee, *s. f.* Adam's apple, the larynx; wind-pipe.

घागस ghá-gus, *s. m.* A large kind of fowl.

घाघ ghagh, *adj.* Old, aged, experienced; sly, wily, shrewd.

घाघरा ghágh-ra, *s. m.* A petticoat; name of a river, *Gogra* or *Ghogra;* a plant (*Xanthium indicum*).

घाट ghat, *s. f.* A landing-place; a quay, wharf, ferry, ford, pass, bathing-place on a river side. *Ghat-mar,* *s. m.* A smuggler. *Ghat marna,* *v. a.* To smuggle.

घाट ghat, *s. m.* Mode, manner, shape; offence; want, abatement, reduction; deficiency, loss, detriment. *adj.* Abated, less.

घाटा ghá-ta, *s. m.* Acclivity, ascent; deficiency, abatement, reduction.

घाटिया ghá-ti-ya, *s. m.* A *brahmun* who sits at a *ghat* of the *Ganges, Jumna,* &c., to keep the clothes of the bathers.

घाटी ghá-tee, *s. f.* A strait, a pass (*in a mountain,* &c.), a ravine.

घात ghat, *s. f.* Aim, design, snare, ambuscade, ambush, opportunity; killing, slaughter; a bruise, a blow; product (*of a sum in multiplication*). *Ghat kurna,* To waylay, lie in ambush, kill. *Ghat takna,* To watch an opportunity.

घातक ghá-tuk, *s. m.* A murderer, maimer, an enemy.

घातन ghá-tun, *s. m.* Killing, slaughter; a murderer.

घाता ghá-ta, *s. m.* Name of a plaything.

घाती ghátee, *adj.* Murderous, felonious.

घातुक ghá-took, *adj.* Mischievous, injurious, murderous, cruel, savage, violent, ferocious.

घन ghan, *s. f.* As much as is thrown in at one time into a mill or mortar, &c.

घानी ghá-nee, *s. f.* An oil-mill (*or oil-press*); a sugar-mill.

घाबरा gháb-ra, *adj.* Confused, confounded.

घाम gham, *s. f.* Sunbeams, sunshine; heat (*of the sun*).

घामड़ gha-múr, *adj.* Simple, artless; a clown, a blockhead.

घायल ghá-yul, *adj.* Wounded.

घल ghal, *s. f.* Mischief.

घालुक ghá-luk, *s. m.* A destroyer, desolator, one who ruins.

घालना ghál-na, *v. a.* To desolate, ruin; to thrust in, to throw.

घालमेल ghálmel, *adj.* Jumbled.

घाव ghao, *s. m.* A wound, a sore. *Ghao ka nishan, s. m.* A scar.

घावघूप ghaoghúp, *adj.* Living from hand to mouth, improvident, spendthrift.

घास ghas, *s. f.* Meadow or pasture, grass, straw, hay, fodder. *Ghas-pat, s. f.* Sweepings.

घिंघाना ghin-ghá-na, *v. n.* To be hoarse.

घिघियाना ghighiyána, *v. a.* To falter, be unable to speak (*from fear, joy, &c.*), appear very humble, coax, wheedle, fawn, beseech, implore. *Ghighee bundh jana, v. n.* To falter, be unable to speak (*from shame or fear, &c.*)

घिचपिच ghich-pich, *adj.* Thick, confused, muddy. *Ghich-pich bukna, or bolna,* To speak thick.

घिन ghin, *s. f.* Disgust, shame, bashfulness. *Ghin dena,* To reproach, abash. *Ghin khana,* To be disgusted, to have the stomach turned.

घिनघिना ghín-ghin-a, *adj.* Disgusting.

घिनाना ghin-ána, *v. n.* To be disgusted. *adj.* Disgusting.

घिनियाना ghiniyána, *v. n.* To be disgusted.

घिनौना ghin-óu-na, *adj.* Disgusting, abominable, nauseous, fulsome.

घिया ghi-ya, *s. m.* Name of a vegetable, a pompion (*Cucurbita lagenaria*). *Ghiya toruee, s. f.* A vegetable (*Luffa pentandra*).

घिरना ghír-na, *v. n.* To be surrounded, enclosed, to be collected around; to gather (*as the clouds*).

घिरनी ghír-nee, *s. f.* A pulley; an instrument for twisting ropes; a kind of pigeon, the tumbler. *Ghirnee khana,* To go round.

घिरांद ghir-ánd, *s. f.* Stink (*particularly of urine*).

घिराना ghir-ána, *v. a.* To cause to surround or enclose.

घिसना ghís-na, *v. n.* To be rubbed, to be abraded. *v. a.* To rub; to beat. *adj.* Apt to be worn by rubbing.

घिसनी ghís-nee, *adv.* By rubbing; as *Ghisnee chulna,* To move along, rubbing on the ground, as a child on his buttocks before he is able to walk.

घिसाना ghis-ána, *v. a.* To cause to rub, abrade, wear.

घिसाव ghis-áo, *s. m.* } Attrition, rubbing, friction, abrasion.
घिसावट ghis-áwut, *s. f.* }

घिसियाना ghis-iyána, *v. a.* To trail, to drag.

घी ghee, *s. m.* Butter clarified by boiling and straining.

घीकवार gheek-wár, *s. m.* A medicinal plant (*Aloe perfoliata*).

घीला ghée-la, *s. m.* The name of a very large wild creeper.

घुंगौना ghoon-góu-na, *s. m.* A toy, a child's rattle.

घुंघची ghóongh-chee, *s. f.* A small red and black seed (*Abrus precatorius*).

घुंघरू ghóongh-roo, *s. m.* A small bell; an ornament worn round the ankles, with bells fastened to it.

घुंडी ghóon-dee, *s. f.* A button.

घुंसी ghóon-see, *adj.* Malicious; a receiver of bribes.

घुटना ghóot-na, *s. m.* The knee. *Ghootnon chulna,* To crawl about on the knees (*as a child*).

घुटना ghóot-na, *v. n.* To be rubbed, to be suffocated.

घुटाई ghoo-tá-ee, *s. f.* Perfidy.

घुटाना ghoo-tá-na, *v. a.* To shave clean, to polish.

घुर ghoor, *s. m.* A horse. *Ghoor-churha,* A horseman, trooper, one on horseback. *Ghoor-churhee, s. f.* A female on horseback; riding. *Ghoor-dour, s. m.* A race course, horse-race. *Ghoor-buhul, s. f.* A four-wheeled carriage for riding in drawn by horses, a chariot. *Ghoor-moonha, adj.* Horse-faced. *Ghoor-sal, s. m.* A stable.

घुरुकना ghoo-rúk-na, *v. a.* To brow-beat, to reprimand, to frown at.

घूरकी ghóor-kee, *s. f.* Rebuff, brow-beating, rebuke, frowning at.

घुरचुरहा ghoor-chúrha, *s. m.* A horseman.

घुरचुरही ghoor-chúrhee, *s. f.* A female on horseback; riding.

घुरदौड़ ghoor-dóur, *s. m.* A race-course.

घुरबघल ghoor-búhul, *s. f.* A two-wheeled carriage for riding in drawn by horses.

घुरमुंहा ghoor-móonha, *adj.* Horse-faced.

घुरसना ghoorúsna, *v. a.* To curl.

घुरसाल ghoor-sál, *s. m.* A stable.

घुन ghoon, *s. m.* Name of an insect found in timber (*destructive to wood, meal, grain, and flour*), a weevil; rancour.

घूना ghóo-na, *adj.* Destroyed by the *ghoon*, weevil-eaten.

घूना ghóo-na,
घूना ghóo-na, } *adj.* Secret, cautious, designing, malicious, spiteful, revengeful, bearing malice, rancorous.

घूंदी ghóon-dee, *s. f.* A button.

घुन ghoon, *s. m.* An insect found in timber (*destructive to wood, meal, and flour*), a weevil; rancour.

घुनगौना ghoon-gouna, *s. m.* A plaything.

घूना ghóo-na, *adj.* Destroyed by the *ghoon*, weevil-eaten.

घूनिया ghóo-ni-ya, *adj.* Designing, malicious, spiteful, revengeful, bearing malice, rancorous.

घप ghoop, *adj.* Dark.

घुमघूमा ghoom-ghóo-ma, *s. m.* Revolution, going round; subterfuge, evasion, prevarication; doubt, suspense, hesitation. *Ghoom-ghoo-ma-na, v. a.* To revolve; to prevaricate.

घुमंड ghoo-múnd, *s. f.* Gathering of the clouds.

घूमरा ghóom-ra, *s. m.* Name of a plant (*Phlomis*); name of an insect.

घूमरी ghóom-ree, *s. f.* The vertigo, swimming of the head, giddiness.

घुमाना ghoo-má-na, *v. a.* To turn round, whirl, cause to turn, wheel, roll, brandish, circulate, encircle; to beguile, delude. *Ghoomana phirana,* To prevaricate.

घुरकना ghoo-rúk-na, *v. a.* To brow-beat, reprimand, frown at, chide.

घुरकी ghóor-kee, *s. f.* Rebuff, brow-beating, rebuke, frowning at.

घुरघूरा ghóor-ghoo-ra, *s. m.* The mole-cricket (*Gryllus Gryllotalpa*); a phagedenick ulcer or herpes exedens (*so named from digging in the flesh, as the mole-cricket does in earth or sand*).

घूरनस ghóor-nus, *s. m.* Tendo Achilles.

घुरनाना ghoor-ná-na, *v. n.* To snore.

घूरनी ghóor-nee, *s. f.* A vertigo, swimming in the head, rolling.

घुलना ghóol-na, *v. n.* To melt, dissolve, be dissolved; to be mellowed, to rot (*as fruit*); to become lean, to waste.

घुलमिल ghóol-mil, *part.* Dissolved, mixed, melted (*in kindness*).

घूलवा ghóolwa, *s. m.* To boot.

घुलवाना ghool-wá-na, *v. a.* To cause to mix with a liquid, to cause to dissolve.

घुलाऊ ghooláoo, *adj.* Melting.

घुलाना ghoo-lá-na, *v. a.* To melt, to dissolve.

घुलावट ghoo-lá-wut, *s. f.* Melting, dissolving. [ton.

घूवा ghóo-wa, *s. m.* A coarse kind of cot-

घस ghoos, *s. m.* Penetrating.

घसना ghóos-na, *v. n.* To be thrust in, to enter, penetrate; interfere, meddle.

घुसपैठ ghoos-pyth, *s. f.* Access.

घुसाना ghoo-sá-na, *v. a.* To thrust in, stuff in, cram, penetrate, force in, cause to penetrate or enter.

घुसिरना ghoosírna, *v. n.* To be thrust or stuffed in.

घुसेरना ghoo-sér-na, *v. a.* To thrust, stuff, cram, force or run in, pierce, insinuate, foist.

घूंगनी ghóong-nee, *s. f.* A sort of stir-about, or grain of any kind (*pulse or wheat, &c.*) boiled whole with sugar.

घूंगर ghóon-gur, *s. m.* A curl. *Ghoongur-waleh,* Curled hair.

घूंगी ghóon-gee, *s. f.* Cloths folded and put on the head as a defence against the rain; a cockle or snail, a small *ghonga*.

घूंघची ghóongh-chee, *s. f.* A small red and black seed (*Arbus precatorius*).

घूंघट ghóon-ghut, *s. f.* A veil; concealing the face with a veil, &c. *Ghoonghut karhna,* To draw a veil over the face. *Ghoonghut kurna, v. a* To veil; to draw back his neck (*a horse*). *Ghoon-ghut khana, v. a.* To be broken or defeated (*an army*).

घूंघर ghóon-ghur, *s. m.* A curl.

घूंघरू ghóongh-roo, *s. m.* A small bell; an ornament worn round the ankles, with bells fastened to it.

घूंट ghoont, *s. m.* A gulp, draught, pull.

घूंटना ghóont-na, *v. a.* To gulp, drink, swallow.

घूंटी ghóon-tee, *s. f.* A medicine consisting of aloes, spices and borax, given to new-born infants to clear out the meconium.

घूस ghoons, *s. m.* A bandicote rat.

घूंसा ghóon-sa, *s. m.* A blow of the fist, &c.

घूघू ghóo-ghoo, *s. m.* The ring-necked dove; an owl.

घूघबा ghóo-ghoo-a, *s. m.* An owl; a blockhead.

घूट ghoot, *s. m.* A gulp, draught.

घूटना ghóot-na, *v. a.* To gulp, drink, guzzle.

घूटी ghóo-tee, *s. f.* A medicine given to new-born infants ; the ankle-joint.

घून ghoon, *s. m.* Rancour, malice, spite.

घूना ghóo-na, *adj.* Designing, malicious, spiteful, revengeful, rancorous ; secret, cautious.

घूम ghoom, *adv.* Back, round about.

घूमघूमाला ghoom-ghoo-mála, *adj.* Loose (*as a robe*), full.

घूमघूमेला ghoom-ghoo-mél-a, *adj.* Revolving, circling round.

घूमना ghóomna, *v. n.* To go round, revolve, turn, roll, wheel, whirl. *sub.* Whirling, turning, &c. *Sir ghoomna,* To be giddy or dizzy, to swim (*the head*).

घूर ghoor, *s. m.* Staring ; a dunghill.

घूरची ghóor-chee, *s. f.* A twist in thread, entanglement.

घूरना ghóor-na, *v. a.* To stare at, to stare, to fix the eyes on ; to look at angrily.

घूरा ghóo-ra, *s. m.* Sweepings ; a dunghill.

घूरिया ghóo-ri-ya, *s. m.* A dunghill.

घूस ghoos, *s. m.* A bandicote rat (*Mus malabaricus : Mus giganteus*) ; a bribe.

घूसत ghóo-sut, *s. m.* A young owl.

घूसमघूसा ghóosum-ghóosa, *s. m.* Thumping and pulling, boxing, fisticuffs.

घूसा ghóo-sa, *s. m.* A thump, a blow of the fist, buffet ; a bandicote rat.

घेंटा ghén-ta, *s. m.* ⎫
घेंटी ghén-tee, *s. f.* ⎬ A pig.

घेगा ghég-a, ⎫ *s. m.* The bronchocele,
घेगहा gheg-há ⎭ goitre, or Derbyshire neck.

घेतला ghét-la, *s. m.* A kind of shoe.

घेपना ghép-na, *v. a.* To mix, mingle, unite into a paste (*as flour and water*).

घेर gher, *adj.* Round, surrounding, enclosing ; loose (*as a robe*) ; full ; winding, meandering. *s. m.* Circuit, circumference. *Gherghar kurna,* To surround, stop or hinder. *Gherdar, adj.* Full, loose (*a robe*), circular, extensive.

घेर gher, *s. m.* Calumny, reproach, complaint.

घेरना ghér-na, *v. a.* To surround, compass, encircle, invest, beset, blockade. *Gherna gharna,* To surround, &c.

घेरनी ghér-nee, *s. f.* A handle for turning a spinning-wheel, a winch.

घेरा ghér-a, *adj.* Round, surrounded. *s. m.* A circle, a circumference ; a siege, blockade, a fence ; vertigo. *Ghera dalna,* To surround, lay a siege, besiege. *Ghereh meu purna,* To be surrounded.

घेवर ghé-wur, *s. f.* A kind of sweetmeat.

घृणा ghrín-a, *s. f.* Reproach, blame, censure, &c. ; compassion, tenderness, pity ; abhorrence, disgust ; shame, bashfulness.

घृत ghrit, *s. m. Ghee,* clarified butter, or butter which has been boiled gently and allowed to cool : it is then used for culinary and religious purposes, and is highly esteemed by the *Hindoos.*

घृतकुमारी ghrit-koo-má-ree, *s. f.* The aloe (*Aloe perfoliata*).

घोंगा ghón-ga, *s. m.* A cockle ; or cockle-shell, a snail (*Cochlea helix*).

घोंट ghónt, *s. f.* A draught (*drink*).

घोंटना ghónt-na, *v. a.* To polish by rubbing ; (*met.*) to investigate ; to strangle. *s. m.* A stone, &c. with which any thing is polished ; the knee.

घोंसला ghóns-la, *s. m.* A (*bird's*) nest.

घोखना ghókh-na, *v. a.* To repeat, to iterate, to speak aloud.

घोघी ghóg-hee, *s. f.* A pocket, pouch, wallet ; a turtle dove.

घोट ghot, *s. f.* Polish.

घोटक ghó-tuk, *s. m.* A horse.

घोटना ghót-na, *v. a.* To polish ; calender ; to plod ; to shave.

घोटनी ghót-nee, *s. f.* A rubber.

घोटा ghó-ta, *s. m.* A wooden rubber.

घोटू ghotóo, *adj.* Polished, smooth (*words*).

घोड़ा ghó-ra, *s. m.* A horse. *Ghoreh ko surput phenkna,* To force a horse to his utmost speed ; the cock (*of a gun*). *Ghora churhana,* To cock a gun.

घोपा ghó-pa, *s. m.* A cloth with a part folded like a sugar-loaf to cover the head and worn over the body in cold or wet weather.

घोयां ghó-yan, *s. f.* An esculent root (*Arum colocasia*).

घोर ghor, *s. m.* Horror, horribleness ; trepidation ; dread, awe, the sound of a drum. *Ghor ghoontna,* To be inwardly displeased, to conceal one's dislike or indignation. *adj.* Frightful, horrible, terrific, awful ; deep (*colour of a horse, or sleep*). *Ghor nidra,* Deep sleep.

घोरदर्शन ghór-dur-shun, *adj.* Terrific, of horrid or frightful appearance.

घोररूप ghor-róop, *adj.* Frightful, hideous. *s. m.* A hideous appearance.

घोररूपी ghor-roopée, *adj.* Frightful, horrible, hideous.

घोराकृति ghor-ákrití, *adj.* Frightful, hideous, of horrible aspect or form.

घोल ghol, *s. m.* Buttermilk.

घोलघुमाव ghol-ghoo-máo, *s. m.* Evasion, subterfuge.

घोलना ghól-na, *v. a.* To mix with a liquid, to dissolve.

घोलमेल ghol-mél, *s. m.* Mixture, mixing.

घोला ghó-la, *s. m.* An intoxicating potion made of *bhung* or opium ; a solution ; name of a fish. *Gholeh men dalna*, To involve in difficulty.

घोष ghosh, *s. m.* A station of herdsmen ; a cast of milk-men ; a cowherd.

घोषना ghósh-na, ⎱ *s. f.* Speaking aloud,
घोखना ghókh-na, ⎰ making a great noise ; crying, proclaiming.

घोसी ghó-see, *s. m.* A *Moosulman* cowherd or milk-man.

घौर ghour, *s. f.* A bunch (*of plantains*).

घौड ghoud, ⎱ *s. f.* A bunch or cluster of
घौर ghour, ⎰ grapes, dates or plantains.

घ्रान ghran, *s. m.* The nose ; smell, smell-ing. *adj.* Smelling.

घ्रानतपन ghran-túr-pun, *s. m.* Fragrance, odour, a fragrance, a perfume.

घ्रानेंद्रिय ghran-én-driyuh, *s. f.* The nose, the sense of smelling.

घ्रात ghrat, *adj.* Smelled.

च

च chub, The twentieth letter of the al-phabet, and first of the second or palatial class of consonants, having the sound of *Ch* in *Church.*

चंगबाव chung-báo, *s. m.* Name of a disorder.

चंगर chún-gur, *s. m.* Tray, trough.

चंगा chún-ga, *adj.* Healthy, cured, sound. *Chunga bunana*, To correct, punish, put to right, chastise. *Bhula-chunga, adj.* In health and vigour ; perfect, good.

चंगूर chun-góor, *adj.* Excellent.

चंगेर chun-gér, *s. f.* A flower-pot, a tray.

चंगेरा chun-gér-a, *s. m.* A large basket, a trough or tray.

चंगेरी chun-gér-ee, *s. f.* A small basket.

चंचनाना chun-chun-ána, *v. n.* To throb or shoot (*as a boil, &c.*) ; to make the noise butter does in a frying pan.

चंचल chún-chul, *adj.* Trembling, tremul-ous ; restless, wanton, playful, fickle ; perishable, transitory.

चंचलता chún-chul-ta, *s. f.* Perishableness ; restlessness, unsteadiness, wantonness.

चंचलपुना chunchulpúna, *s. m.* Playfulness, wantonness.

चंचलाई chun-chul-áee, *s. f.* Restlessness, playfulness ; perishableness.

चंचलाना chun-chul-ána, *v. n.* To be play-ful, wanton, unsteady, or restless.

चंचलाहट chun-chul-áhut, *s. f.* Restless-ness, unsteadiness, wantonness, fickleness.

चंठ chunt, *s. m.* A miser.

चंडाल chun-dál, *s. m.* An inferior cast of *Hindoos* ; (*met.*) a miser, a merciless wretch, an outcast.

चंडोल chun-dól, *s. m.* The rear-guard ; a sort of sedan ; the name of a bird ; a plaything consisting of four little earthen pots joined together.

चंद chund, *s. m.* The moon. *Chund-mookh, s. m.* Face bright or beautiful as the moon. *Chund-mookhee,* or *Chund-budunee, adj.* Having a face splendid as the moon.

चंदन chún-dun, *s. m.* Sandal-wood or tree, sanders (*Sirium myrtifolium* or *Santalum album*).

चंदला chúnd-la, *adj.* Bald. *s. m.* Baldness.

चंदवा chúnd-wa, *s. m.* A small canopy, an awning.

चंदा chún-da, *s. m.* An assessment, contri-bution, subscription ; the moon.

चंदिया chún-di-ya, *s. f.* The crown of the head.

चंदेल chun-déel, ⎱ *s. m.* A tribe of *Raj-*
चंदेला chun-dél-a, ⎰ *poots* who claim de-scent from the moon.

चंदेहा chun-dée-ha, *adj.* Silvery, white.

चंदेरी chun-dér-ee, ⎱ *s. f.* Name of a place.
चंदेल chun-dél, ⎰

चंदेली chun-dél-ee, *s. f.* Cambrick (*made at Chundel*).

चंद्र chundr, *s. m.* The moon, considered as a planet or a deity. *Chundr-mookhee, adj.* Having a countenance beautiful as the moon.

चंद्रुक chun-drúk, *s. m.* The eye in a pea-cock's tail ; a finger nail.

चंद्रकला chundr-kúl-a, *s. f.* A digit or one-sixteenth part of the moon's orb or diameter.

चंद्रगुप्त chundr-goopt, *s. m.* The reputed Registrar of Jum's court.

चंद्रबंसी chundr-bún-see, *s. m.* Descendant of the moon ; the name of a tribe of *Khuttrees,* who claim descent from the moon.

चंद्रभागा chundr-bhá-ga, *s. f.* The name of a river, the *Chinab,* one of the five streams of the *Punjab. Chundrbhag,* is the name of a mountain, part of the *Himaley* range, where the river is said to have its source.

चंद्रमा chundr-ma, *s. m.* The moon.

चंद्ररेणु chundr-rén-oo, *s. m.* A plagiarist, a poetical thief.

चंद्रलेखा chundr-lék-ha, *s. f.* A plant (*Serratula anthelmintica*) ; a digit of the moon.

चंद्रवल्लरी chundr-vúllur-ee, *s. f.* A kind of Asclepias (*A. acida*) ; rue.

चंद्रबाला chundr-vála, *s. f.* Large cardamoms.

चंद्रसंभव chundr-sum-bhúvuh, *s. f.* Small cardamoms.

चंद्रहार chundr-hár, *s. m.* An ornament of dress, a sort of necklace composed of circular pieces of gold, silver, &c.

चंद्र chundra, *adj.* Bald ; wise, intelligent.

चंद्रातप chundr-á-tup, *s. m.* Moonlight.

चंद्राना chundrána, *v. n.* To be withered or dried up (*a tree*), to cease to grow.

चंद्रिका chúnd-rik-a, *s. f.* Moonlight ; the moon-beams ; a small fish (*Zeus oblongus*); large cardamoms.

चंद्रिल chún-dril, *s. m.* A potherb (*Chenopodium album*).

चंद्रोदय chundr-ó-duy, *s. m.* An awning, a cloth or sheet spread over the large open courts of *Hindoo* houses, &c. upon festival occasions ; moon-rise ; a kind of collyrium.

चंपक chúm-puk,) *s. m.* A tree bearing a
चंपा chúm-pa,) yellow fragrant flower (*Michelia champaca*).

चंवर chún-wur, *s. m.* An instrument made of peacock's feathers, &c. waved over the head of a sovereign, used to whisk off flies, &c., and also made of the tail of the Bos grunniens, a species of ox.

चक chuk, *s. m.* Landed property, landed estate, a farm. *Chuk-bundee, s. f.* Defining or marking the boundaries of an estate.

चक chuk, *s. m.* A shepherd, or goatherd.

चकई chuk-úee, *s. f.* A toy, a whirligig ; a duck, the female of *chukwa*.

चकचका chuk-chúk-a, *adj.* Shining, resplendent.

चकचकी chuk-chúk-ee, *s. f.* A kind of dagger worn on the waist. *adj. f.* Resplendent.

चकछंदी chuk-chhóon-dee, *s. f.* A musk-rat (*Sorex cærulescens : Sorex cæruleus*).

चकता chúk-ta, *s. m.* A scraping of the skin, a scrape, a scar ; a slice, &c. *Chukta dena,* or —*lena,* To scar.

चकताना chuktána, *v. a.* To sod, to turf.

चकती chúk-tee, *s. f.* The hide of a rhinoceros (*of which shields are made*) ; a patch of leather, a slice, a patch ; the round of a cheese, a round plate of metal, &c., a litter, an epistle. *adj.* Compressed, flattened.

चकनाचूर chuk-na-chóor, *s. m.* Scraps, small pieces, atoms, filings. *Chukna-choor hona,*

To be dashed to pieces, to shatter. *Chukna-choor kurna,* To shatter, shiver, break to pieces.

चकमा chúk-ma, *s. m.* A boot, a stocking.

चकरबा chuk-úr-ba, *s. m.* Revelry. *Chukurba muchana, v. a.* To revel, to riot.

चकरा chúk-ra, *s. m.* A kind of dish made of pulse.

चकरानी chuk-rá-nee, *s. f.* Woman servant.

चकला chúk-la, *s. m.* A brothel ; a kind of cloth made of silk and cotton ; a division of a country containing several *purgunahs. adj.* Wide, broad ; round. *Chuklehdar, s. m.* The governor of a province or country. *Chuklehdaree, s. f.* The government of a province or country ; a round plate on which bread is rolled.

चकलाई chuk-láee, *s. f.* Breadth.

चकलाना chuk-lá-na, *v. a.* To extend in breadth, to widen.

चकवा chúkwa, *s. m.* The ruddy goose (*Anas casarca*) ; a whirlpool.

चकवी chúk-wee, *s. f.* The female of the water-fowl *chukwa.*

चकसूनी chuk-sóo-nee, *s. f.* A kind of grass.

चकाचाक chuk-a-chák, *s. f.* The sound of the repeated strokes of a sword, dagger, or mace.

चकचौंध chuk-a-chóundh, *s. f.* The state of being dazzled, radiance.

चकावर chuk-á-wur, *s. m.* A disease in horses.

चकावी chuk-á-wee, *s. f.* A ringworm.

चकित chúk-it, *adj.* Timid, fearful ; astonished.

चकेठा chuk-ét-ha, *adj.* With large eyes.

चकोत्रा chuk-ó-tra, *s. m.* A fruit of the lime kind, a citron, pompelmoose, shaddock (*Citrus decumanus*).

चकोर chuk-ór, *s. m.* The *Bartavelle* or Greek partridge (*Tetrao rufus: Perdix rufa*), fabulously said to subsist upon the moon-beams, and to eat fire at the full moon.

चकौंदा chuk-óun-da,) *s. m.* A species of
चकौंड chuk-óunr,) Cassia (*Cassia obtusifolia*), esteemed a remedy for ringworms.

चकस chuk-kús, *s. m.* A perch for birds (*particularly falcons*), a roost.

चक्का chúk-ka, *s. m.* Coagulated milk ; a carriage wheel, a circle. *adj.* Round ; thick (*as duhee, &c.*)

चक्कन chuk-kán, *adj.* Thick (*bhung, &c.*), blot, blotted, smeared.

चक्की chúk-kee, *s. f.* A millstone, a mill, grinder ; kneepan ; a thunderbolt.

चकु chúk-koo, *s. m.* A clasp-knife, a pen-knife.

चक्र chukr,
चकुर chúk-kur, } *s. m.* A whirlwind or whirlpool ; a circular missile weapon used principally by the *Sikhs,* a sharp discus or iron ring which they throw with great dexterity : (*it was with this instrument called Soodursun-chukr, that Narayan is said to have cut off the head of the Usoor Rahoo, when, after churning the ocean, the Soors or gods, and Usoors or demons fought for the umrit or nectar*) ; a circular course, the lounge (*in menage*) ; (*met.*) a misfortune, scrape, perplexity ; a side or quarter, as *Chuhoon chukkur men,* On the four sides, on all sides. *Chukr-dharee,* A peacock ; *Vishnoo. Chukr marna,* To wheel round, to whirl round. *Ghoreh ko chukkur dena,* To lounge a horse.

चक्रवत् chukr-vút, *adv.* In rotation, going round or revolving like a wheel.

चक्रवर्ती chukr-vúrttee, *s. m.* An emperor, a sovereign of the world, a universal monarch, the ruler of a *chukr* or country described as extending from sea to sea ; twelve princes beginning with *Bhurut* are especially considered as *Chukr-vurttees* ; a title of *brahmuns* in Bengal.

चक्रवाक chukr-vák, *s. m.* A bird, the ruddy goose (*Anas casarca*).

चक्रवान chukr-ván, *adj.* Circular, being in a ring or circle.

चक्राकार chukr-akár, *adj.* Circular.

चकित chúk-rit, *adj.* Astonished ; timid, fearful.

चकी chúk-ree, *s. f.* A round plate on which bread is rolled ; an assembly of singers.

चकेला chukréla, *adj.* Round, circular.

चख chukh, *s. m.* The eye.

चखना chúkh-na, *v. a.* To relish, taste.

चाचखी chukh-a-chúkh-ee, *s. f.* Discord.

चखाना chukh-á-na, *v. a.* To cause to taste.

चगुलना chug-úl-na, *v. a.* To eat without appetite.

चगेर chuger, *s. f.* A flower-pot.

चुगबाब chung-báo, *s. m.* Name of a disorder.

चुनगर chún-gur, *s. m.* Tray, trough.

चुनगा chún-ga, *adj.* Healthy, cured, sound. *Chunga bunana,* To correct, punish, put to right, chastise. *Bhula-chunga, adj.* In health and vigour ; perfect, good.

चुनगूर chun-góor, *adj.* Excellent.

चुनगेर chun-gér, *s. f.* A flower-pot, a tray.

चुनगेरा chun-gér-a, *s. m.* A large basket ; a trough, or tray.

चुनगेरी chun-gér-ee, *s. f.* A small basket.

चुचुर chúch-ur, *adj.* (*Land*) that has been cultivated or ploughed one year.

चुचरा chúch-ra, *s. m.* Name of a tree.

चुचुहिया chuchuhíya, *s. m.* A whistler.

चुचा chúch-a, *s. m.* Paternal uncle, father's brother.

चुची chúch-ee, *s. f.* Father's brother's wife, aunt.

चुचीर chuchéer, *s. m.* A line, stripe, score.

चुचेरा chuch-ér-a, *adj.* Descended from or related through a paternal uncle, as *Chucherabhaee, s. m.* A cousin, son of paternal uncle. *Chucheree buhin, s. f.* Daughter of paternal uncle, a female cousin.

चुचोरना chuch-ór-na, *v. a.* To suck (*a dry substance from which nothing can be obtained*).

चुचुल chúch-chul, *s. m.* Large breasts.

चुची chúch-chee, *s. f.* Father's brother's wife, aunt.

चुनचुनाना chun-chun-ána, *v. n.* To throb or shoot (*as a boil, &c.*) ; to make the noise butter does in a frying-pan.

चुनचुनाहट chun-chun-áhut, *s. f.* A throb, throbbing, a shooting pain.

चुनचुल chún-chul, *adj.* Trembling, shaking, moving, unsteady ; fickle, inconsiderate, inconstant, (*unsteady metaphorically*) ; playful, restless, wanton, perishable. *s. m.* A lecher, a libertine.

चुनचुलता chun-chul-tá, *s. f.* Restlessness ; perishableness ; fickleness, inconstancy, unsteadiness.

चुनचुलहृदय chúnchul-hríduy, *adj.* Capricious, fickle, false-hearted.

चुनचुला chún-chul-a, *s. f.* Lightning.

चुनचुलाई chun-chul-áee, *s. f.* Restlessness, playfulness.

चुनचुलाना chun-chul-ána, *v. n.* To be playful, wanton or restless.

चुनचुलाहट chun-chul-áhut, *s. f.* Restlessness, unsteadiness, wantonness.

चुचु chún-choo, *s. f.* A beak.

चुट chut, *adv.* Quickly, instantly. *s. f.* An excoriation, a sore, scab, cancer ; the noise of breaking up, snap. *Chut bhusum,* Eating up the whole, licking the platter clean. *Chut deh tootna,* To snap short, to break. *Chut kurna,* To eat, dissipate, make waste. *Chut hona, v. n.* To be dissipated or consumed.

चुटक chút-uk, *s. m.* A sparrow. *s. f.* A hen-sparrow ; a crash, a crack, a smack ; intelligence, gaudiness ; glitter, splendour, prime of life. *adj.* Intelligent, quick. *Chutuk seh, adv.* Deceiving. *Chutuk seh jana,* To pay with the fore topsail. *Chutukwaee, s. f.* Quickness.

चटकना chút-ók-na, *v. n.* To crackle (*as charcoal or wood on the fire*); to crack; to split.

चटकना chut-kún-a, *s. m.* A slap, box, blow, cuff.

चटका chút-ka, *s. m.* Scarcity. *Chutka lugana,* To thirst, to wish.

चटकाना chut-ká-na, *v. a.* To crack (*as a whip*); to snap the fingers (*in rejoicing*); to split; to fire off a musket; to irritate.

चटकारना chut-kár-na, *v. a.* To urge cattle by the clacking noise made by drawing the tongue from the palate.

चटकीला chut-kée-la, *adj.* Splendid, glittering, gaudy.

चटखना chut-úkh-na, *v. n.* To crackle (*as charcoal or wood on the fire*); to crack; to split.

चटकीरा chut-jée-ra, *s. m.* Name of a tree.

चटना chút-na, *adj. m.* Voracious (*man*).

चटनी chút-nee, *s. f.* A kind of acid sauce (*or marmalade*). *adj. f.* Voracious (*woman*).

चटपट chút-put, *adv.* Hastily, in a hurry, instantly.

चटपटा chút-put-a, *adj.* Active, hasty; stout; meat dressed with little sauce or gravy.

चटपटाना chut-put-ána, *v. n.* To be agitated, to flutter, palpitate, wince.

चटपटाहट chut-put-áhut, *s. f.* Agitation, flurry, flutter, palpitation.

चटपटिया chut-put-íya, *adj.* Active, quick, alert; hot (*with spices*).

चटपटी chut-pút-ee, *s. f.* Haste, hurry, quickness, agility.

चटवाना chut-wá-na, *v. a.* To make lick or lap up.

चटसाल chut-shál, ⎫ *s. f.* A school, an
चटसारी chut-sháree, ⎭ academy.

चटाई chut-áee, *s. f.* A mat. *Chutaee bichhana, v. a.* To mat, to spread a mat.

चटाक chut-ák, *s. f.* A crash, an explosion. *adj.* Intelligent.

चटाका chut-áka, *s. m.* A crash, an explosion, a smack (*or kiss*).

चटाचट chut-a-chút, *s. m.* Reiterated sound.

चटाखा chut-á-kha, *s. m.* A crash, an explosion, a smack (*or kiss*).

चटान chut-án, *s. f.* Rocky ground, block of stone, rock.

चटाना chut-ána, *v. a.* To make lick or lap up.

चटिया chút-iya, *s. m.* A pupil, a scholar.

चटूआ chut-óo-a, *s. m.* A kind of plaything; a sort of hawk.

चटोखा chut-ó-kha, *s. m.* A kind of dove.

चटोरा chút-ó-ra, *s. m.* An epicure, a glutton.

चट्टा chút-ta, *s. m.* A school-boy.

चट्टाबट्टा chútta-bútta, *s. m.* A plaything, a kind of rattle or clapper given to children.

चट्टी chúttee, *s. f.* Scarcity, want.

चट्ठा chut-thá, *s. m.* A bonne-bouche, dainties.

चड़ chur, *s. m.* Sound made by breaking a branch.

चड़चड़ chúr-chur, *s. m.* An imitative sound.

चड़चड़ाना chur-chur-ána, *v. n.* To crack, creak.

चड़पड़ाना chur-pur-ána, *v. n.* To smart, to palpitate, flutter, throb.

चड़बड़ बोलना churbur bólna, ⎫ *v. a.* To
चड़बड़ करना churbur kúrna, ⎭ chatter, prattle.

चड़बड़िया chur-bur-íya, *s. m.* A prattler, chatterer, an idle talker.

चड़र chúr-ur, *s. m.* An imitative sound.

चड्डा chuddha, *s. m.* The groin; a bubo.

चढ़के chúrh-keh, *adv.* Avowedly, designedly, excellently. *Churhta hona, v. n.* To excel.

चढ़ती chúrh-tee, *s. f.* Advantage, gain, rise.

चढ़ना chúrh-na, *v. n.* To ascend, mount, advance, attack, embark, board, rise, climb, soar, spread, swell, ride; to be strung (*a bow*); to be braced (*a drum*); to be offered up (*an oblation or sacrifice*). *Churhna ooturna, v. n.* To hire and dismiss; congressus.

चढ़न्दार chur-hun-dár, *s. m.* A passenger, supercargo.

चढ़बन्ना chúrh-bún-na, *v. a.* To find an opportunity.

चढ़वाँ churh-wán, *adj.* Rising up (*a shoe over the heel of the wearer*).

चढ़वाना churh-wá-na, *v. a.* To cause others to raise or to make ascend or to pull on, &c.

चढ़वैया churh-wy-ya, *s. m.* One who ascends, mounts, &c., a rider, mounter, climber.

चढ़ाई chur-háee, *s. f.* Ascent, acclivity, embarkation, attack, assault, irruption, rank, dignity; price paid for ascending, riding, embarking, &c.

चढ़ाना chur-há-na, *v. a.* To make ascend, embark, &c., to offer up oblations or sacrifice; to string (*a bow*); to brace (*a drum*); to raise, lift, take up, advance, apply, put, spread, bend, dye (*with colour*), pull, draw on, cock, fix (*a bayonet*), run.

चढ़ाव chur-háo, *s. m.* Ascent, rise, acclivity, attack, access, fit rank, dignity, flood-tide.

चूड़ी chúr-hee,   चूड़नी chúrh-nee,   } s. f. Preparation for battle.

चूड़ैत chur-hyt,   चूड़ैता chur-hyta,   } s. m. A trooper who does not ride his own horse, a rider.

चूड़ौवा chur-hóu-wa, s. m. A shoe rising up over the heel of the wearer.

चूनक chún-uk,   चूना chún-a,   } s. m. A kind of pulse, chick-pea (*Cicer arietinum*), vetches.

चूण chund, adj. Fierce, violent, passionate ; hot, warm ; pungent, acrid.

चूणता chund-tá, s. f. Warmth, pungency.

चूण्डवत् chund-wút, adj. Passionate, violent, warm.

चूण्डा chún-da,   चूण्डी chún-dee,   } s. f. A name of the goddess *Doorga*, applied especially to her fabulous incarnation for the purpose of destroying *Muhes Usoor*; this exploit forms the subject of a section of the *Markundeyuh Pooran*, and is particularly celebrated in Bengal at the *Doorga Pooja*, or festival held in honour of the goddess towards the close of the year (*October-November*) ; a passionate woman, a mischievous or furious woman.

चण्डावल chundáwul, s. m. The rear-guard.

चण्डाल chun-dál, s. m. An outcast, the generic name for a man of the lowest of the mixed tribes, born from a *Soodr* father and *Brahmunee* mother ; (*met.*) a miser, a merciless wretch.

चण्डालिन chun-dá-lin, s f. The female of *Chundal*.

चण्डिका chún-dik-a, s. f. The goddess *Doorga*.

चण्डीकूसुम chúndee-kóosoom, s. m. Red Oleander.

चण्डोल chun-dól, s. m. The rear-guard ; a sort of sedan ; the name of a bird ; a plaything consisting of four little earthen pots joined together.

चतर chút-ra,   चतुरा chút-oo-ra,   } adj. Wise, intelligent, cunning, clever.

चतरी chút-ree, s. f. A canopy, veil, a parasol ; a tent, a pavilion.

चतुर chút-oor, adj. Cunning, dexterous, ingenious, clever, sly, shrewd, wise, knowing, intelligent, expert, adroit, sagacious ; four.

चतुरता chút-oor-ta, s. f. Cunning, cleverness, slyness, wisdom, knowledge.

चतुरस्र chut-oor-úsr, adj. Four-cornered, quadrangular.

चतुरा chút-oo-ra, adj. Wise, intelligent, cunning, clever, expert.

चतुराई chut-oo-ráee, s. f. Cunning, cleverness, slyness, wisdom, knowledge, expertness.

चतुर्थ chút-oorth, adj. Fourth.

चतुर्दशी chut-oor-dúsh-ee, adj. The 14th day of the moon's age.

चतुर्भुज chut-oor-bhóoj, adj. Having four hands, an epithet of *Vishnoo*.

चतुर्भुजी chut-oor-bhóo-jee, adj. f. Having four hands, an epithet of *Devee*.

चतुर्मुख chut-oor-móokh, s. m. The deity *Bruhm*.

चतुर्योग chut-oor-yóog, s. m. The aggregate of the four *Yoogs* or ages of the *Hindoos*.

चतुर्वर्ग chut-oor-vúrg,   चतुर्भद्र chut-oor-bhúdr,   } s. m. The aggregate of four objects of human wishes, viz. virtue, love, wealth, and final beatitude.

चतुष्पथ chút-oosh-puth, s. m. A place where four roads meet.

चतुष्पद chut-oosh-púd,   चतुष्पदी chut-oosh-púd-ee, s. f.   } Verse, the metre of stanzas, especially consisting of four *puds* or lines.

चतुष्पदा chut-oosh-púd-a, s. m. An animal with four legs, a quadruped.

चम chun, s. m. A kind of sugar-cane.

चनक chún-uk, s. f. The bursting of the husk of a seed by exposure to the sun.

चनकना chún-uk-na, v. n. To burst and fall out (*as a seed from the husk*).

चना chún-a, s. m. A kind of pulse, chick-pea (*Cicer arietinum*), vetches.

चनेठ chun-éth, s. f. Spices given to cattle, drugs for oxen.

चन्द chund, s. m. The moon. *Chund-mookh, s. m.* A bright face or beautiful as the moon. *Chund-mookhee, or Chund-budunee, adj.* Having a face splendid as the moon.

चन्दन chún-dun, s. m. Sandal wood or tree (*Sirium myrtifolium*).

चन्दला chúnd-la, adj. Bald. s. m. Baldness.

चन्दवा chúnd-wa, s. m. A small canopy, an awning.

चन्दा chún-da, s. m. Assessment, contribution, subscription.

चन्दिया chún-di-ya, s. f. The crown of the head.

चन्देल chun-déel,   चन्देला chun-dél-a,   } s. m. A tribe of *Rajpoots* who claim descent from the moon.

चन्देहा chun-dée-ha, adj. Silvery, white.

चन्देरी chun-dér-ee,   चन्देल chun-dél,   } s. f. Name of a place.

चन्देली chun-dél-ee, s. f. Cambrick (*made at Chundel*).

चन्द्र chundr, *s. m.* The moon.

चन्द्रकला chundr-kúl-a, *s. f.* A digit, or one-sixteenth part of the moon's orb or diameter.

चन्द्रकान्त chundr-kánt, *s. m.* A fabulous gem, supposed to be formed of the congelation of the rays of the moon : a kind of crystal may perhaps be meant.

चन्द्रगुप्त chundr-góopt, *s. m.* The Registrar of *Yum's* court.

चन्द्रगोल chundr-gól, *s. m.* The orb or sphere of the moon.

चन्द्रग्रहण chundr-grúhun, *s. m.* Eclipse of the moon.

चन्द्रभागा chundr-bhá-ga, *s. f.* The name of a river, the *Chinab* one of the five streams of the *Punjab. Chundr-bhag,* The name of a mountain, part of the *Himaluy* range, where the river is said to have its source.

चन्द्रमणि chundr-mún-i, *s. m.* The moon-gem.

चन्द्रमण्डल chundr-múndul, *s. m.* The orb or disc of the moon, the lunar sphere.

चन्द्रमा chundr-má, *s. m.* The moon.

चन्द्ररेखा chundr-rékha, *s. f.* A digit of the moon.

चन्द्ररेणु chundr-rén-oo, *s. m.* A plagiarist, a poetical thief.

चन्द्रलेखा chundr-lék-ha, *s. f.* A plant (*Serratula anthelmintica*); a digit of the moon.

चन्द्रवंशी chundr-vúnsh-ee, *s. m.* A descendant of the moon; the name of a tribe of *Khuttrees* who claim descent from the moon.

चन्द्रवल्लरी chundr-vúllur-ee, *s. f.* A kind of Asclepias (*A. acida*).

चन्द्रवाला chundr-wála, *s. f.* Large cardamoms.

चन्द्रिका chún-drik-a, *s. f.* Moonlight; a small fish (*Zeus oblongus*).

चन्द्रोदय chundr-ó-duy, *s. m.* An awning, a cloth or sheet spread over the large open courts of *Hindoo* houses, &c., upon festival occasions; moon-rise; a kind of collyrium.

चन्द्रोपल chundr-ópul, *s. m.* Moon-gem.

चन्सूर chunsóor, *s. m.* Cress, cresses (*Lepidium sativum*).

चपकन chúp-kun, *s. f.* A kind of vest, a sort of coat. *Chupkundar, s. m.* A vest like a *chupkun.*

चपकना chúp-uk-na, *v. n.* To collapse.

चपका chúp-ka, *s. m.* Caprimulgus.

चपकाना chup-ká-na, *v. n.* To make adhere, to stick on; to compress; to threaten.

चपटना chup-út-na, *v. n.* To be flattened.

चपटा chúp-ta, *adj.* Flattened, compressed, shallow.

चपटाना chup-tá-na, *v. a.* To flatten.

चपटिही chup-tí-hee, *s. f.* Name of an insect.

चपुरचपुर chúp-ur-chúp-ur, *s. m.* An imitative sound of the noise of the mouth in eating.

चपुरना, chúp-ur-na, *v. n.* To flee, run away; to desist, deny.

चपरा chúp-ra, *s. m.* A kind of lac; clear land.

चपराऊ chup-rá-oo, *adj.* Brazen-faced. *s. m.* Slippers.

चपराना chup-rá-na, *v. a.* To falsify, to brazen.

चपरी chúp-ree, *s. f.* Cakes of cow-dung.

चपना chúp-na, *v. n.* To be abashed, to be bashful in company, to blush, submit, stoop; to be crushed or squeezed.

चपनी chúp-nee, *s. f.* A lid, a cover, top (*small*), the knee-pan. *Chupnee-bhur panee-men doob murna (lit. to drown one's self in a saucer-full of water),* To be greatly abashed. *Chupnee chatnee, (lit. to lick the pot-lid),* To be contented with little.

चपरास chup-rás, *s. f.* A buckle, breast-plate, clasp, badge.

चपरासी chup-rá-see, *s. m.* A messenger or other servant wearing a *chupras.*

चपुल chúp-ul, *adj.* Trembling, tremulous, shaking; wavering, unsteady; swift, expeditious; wanton, restless, volatile. *adv.* Swiftly.

चपुलता chup-ul-tá, *s. f.* Fickleness, inconstancy.

चपला chúp-ul-a, *s. f.* The goddess *Lukshmee* or fortune; lightning; a whore.

चपलात्मक chúpul-átmuk, *adj.* Of a fickle or inconstant nature.

चपाती chup-á-tee, *s. f.* A thin cake of unleavened bread.

चपाना chup-á-na, *v. a.* To abash; to place one thing on another, to pile.

चपेट chup-ét, *s. m.* The palm of the hand with the fingers extended. *s. f.* A slap, a blow; a sudden misfortune, risk.

चपेट chupet, *s. m.* A slap, a blow; a bastard. *adj.* Illegitimate.

चपोटी chup-ó-tee, *s. f.* An old worn-out turband.

चपन chúp-pun, *s. m.* A lid or cover of a pot (*large*).

चपल chúp-pul, *s. f.* A slipper.

चपा chúp-pa, *s. m.* A handbreadth.

चपी chúp-pee, *s. f.* Kneading the limbs.

चपू chúp-poo, *s. m.* An oar, a paddle. *Chuppoo marna, v. a.* To row.

चुपाड़ chup-hál, *s. f.* A place surrounded with marshes and mire.

चबनीरुड़ी chúbnee-húddee, *s. f.* Cartilage, gristle.

चबलाना chub-lá-na, *v. a.* To chew slowly.

चबवाना chub-wá-na, *v. a.* To cause to chew, &c.

चबाइ chub-áee, *s. f.* Mastication.

चबाना chub-á-na, *v. a.* To chew, gnaw, champ, masticate, bite (*the lip*). *Chuba chuba kur bat kurnee,* To speak with study or preparation; also, without reserve or haughtily or scornfully.

चबौला chub-áo-la, *adj.* Childish, boyish.

चबूतरा chub-óo-tra, *s. m.* A terrace or mound to sit and converse on; a custom-house; a police-office.

चबेना chub-én-a, *s. m.* } Parched grain to
चबेनी chub-én-ee, *s. f.* } exercise the teeth with when more substantial food is not at hand.

चभक chub-húk, *s. f.* Sting.

चमक chúm-uk, *s. f.* Glitter, splendour, flash, glare, gleam. *Chumuk-tumuk, s. f.* Splendour, refulgence, glitter.

चमकता chúm-uk-ta, *adj.* Bright, glittering.

चमकना chúm-uk-na, *v. n.* To glitter, shine, flash, glare, startle; to prosper; to be angry.

चमकाना chum-ká-na, *v. a.* To cause to glitter; to provoke, to make to start, to startle; to wave, brandish, flourish, brighten, burnish; to display.

चमकाव chum-káo, *s. m.* } Glitter,
चमकाहट chum-ká-hut, *s. f.* } splendour, much light, brilliancy, flourish, brightness.

चमगादड़ chum-gá-dur, *s. m.* }
चमगीदड़ chum-gée-dur, *s. m.* } A bat.
चमगुदड़ी chum-góod-ree, *s. f.* }

चमचुरुख chum-chúr-ukh, *adj.* Lean, meagre. *s. m.* A bat.

चमचमाना chum-chum-ána, *v. n.* To tingle; to sleep; to sparkle, shine, glitter.

चमचमाहट chum-chum-áhut, *s. f.* Brightness.

चमड़ा chúm-ra, *s. m.* Leather, a hide, a skin, the skin. *Chumra oodherna,* or, —*chhoorana,* or, —*nikulna,* To flay, to skin.

चमत्कार chum-ut-kár, *s. f.* A sort of grass; haste. *s. m.* Amazement; splendour; astonishment, surprise.

चमत्कारी chum-ut-káree, *adj.* Astonishing, sagacious, acute, unusual, surprising.

चमुत्कृत chumut-krít, *adj.* Surprised, astonished.

चमर chúm-ur, *s. m.* A fly-flapper, made of the Tibet cow's tail or *Soora-gao,* the Yak or Bos grunniens.

चमरख chúm-rukh, *s. f.* The apparatus of a spinning wheel; (*met.*) a lean woman.

चमरचमछी chúm-ur-búglee, *s. f.* A bittern.

चमरी chúm-ree, *s. f.* The Yak or Bos grunniens, of whose tail-hairs the *choures* is most usually made.

चमस chúm-us, *s. m.* A vessel used at sacrifices for drinking the juice of the acid asclepias, a kind of ladle or spoon; a plant commonly called *Khetpupra* (*Mollugo pentaphylla*).

चमाई chum-áee, *adj.* Copper-coloured.

चमाऊ chum-áoo, *s. f.* Slippers or shoes fixed to pattens.

चमार chum-ár, *s. m.* A worker in leather, a shoe-maker, cobbler, a tanner, a currier.

चमारी chum-á-ree, *s. f.* Female of *Chumar.*

चमू chúm-oo, *s. f.* An army; a squadron, a division of an army.

चमूकन chumóokun, *s. m.* A tick or louse infesting cattle.

चमेटा chum-ét-a, *s. m.* Box, thump, blow.

चमोटा chum-ó-ta, *s. m.* }
चमोटी chum-ó-tee, *s. f.* } A razor-strop.

चम्प chump, *s. m.* Mountain ebony (*Bauhinia variegata*).

चम्पक chúm-puk, } *s. m.* A tree bearing a
चम्पा chúm-pa, } yellow fragrant flower (*Michelia champaca*); a division of the jack fruit.

चम्पकबरनी chúm-puk-búrnee, *adj.* Of the colour of the *chumpa* flower, *i. e.* gold-coloured.

चम्पत होना chum-put hóna, *v. n.* To vanish, disappear, scamper off, run away.

चम्पा chúm-pa, *s. m.* A tree bearing a yellow fragrant flower (*Michelia champaca*). *Chumpaee, adj.* Of the colour of *chumpa.*

चम्पाकली chumpa-kúl-ee, *s. f.* A necklace, each piece of which resembles the unblown flowers of the *chumpa.*

चम्पाकेला chumpa-kél-a, *s. m.* A small kind of plantain.

चम्पावती chumpa-wút-ee, *s. f.* The district of *Chumpa* or *Bhagulpore* (*abounding in ebony trees*).

चम्पी chúm-pee, *adj.* Orange-coloured.

चम्पू chúm-poo, *s. f.* A work in which the same subject is continued through alternations in the composition of prose and verse.

चम्बुल chúm-bul, *s. f.* Name of a river in *Bundelkhund*.

चम्बा chúm-ba, *s. m.* A tribe of beggars who cut or scarify their skin.

चम्बू chúm-boo, *s. m.* A narrow-necked vessel for holding water.

चमेली chum-bél-ee, *s. f.* A flower (*Jasminum grandiflorum*).

चम्मुल chúm-mul, *s. m.*
चमला chum-la, *s. m.* } A beggar's cup.
चमली chúm-lee, *s. f.*

चय chy, *s. m.* An assemblage, a multitude; a heap, a collection; a mound of earth, raised to form the foundation of a building; a rampart or mound of earth, raised from the ditch of a fort.

चर chur, *s. m.* A ford, shoal, island; sound made by tearing cloth, &c.; a wagtail; forage, pasture; food. *adj.* Removeable, moveable, locomotive, moving, going; animate.

चरक chúr-uk, *s. m.* The author of a treatise on medicine, applied also to the work; leprosy.

चरकटा chur-kút-a, *s. m.* The person who cuts forage for cattle, elephant-keeper's underling.

चरका chúr-ka, *adj.* White-spotted (*as from leprosy*). *s. m.* A small wound, scratch.

चरकी chúr-kee, *s. m.* A leper.

चरखा chúr-kha, *s. m.* A spinning-wheel, a reel.

चरखी chúr-khee, *s. f.* A small spinning-wheel, a pully; the instrument with which the seed is separated from the cotton.

चरचना chúr-uch-na, *v. a.* To perfume the person of any one by plastering sandal-wood, &c. all over him, to apply (*perfumes to the body*).

चरचर chúr-chur, *s. m.* Prating, chattering; an imitative sound.

चरचुरा chúr-chura, *adj.* Talkative, chattering.

चरचराना chur-chur-ána, *v. n.* To crackle (*as wood in the fire*), to sputter, to chew with a cracking noise, to chide, scold, fret.

चरचेला chur-chél-a, *s. m.* A chatterer, a prater.

चरचूं chur-chóon, *s. m.* An imitative sound (*as of a carriage, wheel, &c.*); idle prattle.

चरचैत chur-chyt, *s. m.* A reasoner, a mentioner.

चरट chúr-ut, *s. m.* A wagtail.

चरन chúr-un, *s. m.* The foot; the feet of a verse; shoes, feeding, grazing.

चरनपतन chúrun-pútun, *s. m.* Prostration, falling at the feet.

चरनपतित chúrun-pútit, *adj.* Prostrate, fallen at the feet.

चरनसेवा chúrun-séva, *s. f.* Service, devotion.

चरनाभरन chúrun-ábhurun, *s. m.* An ornament on the feet.

चरनामृत chur-un-ámrit, } *s. m.* Ambrosia
चरनोदक churun-óduk, } of the feet (*implied in the expression*), the water with which an idol or a *Brahmun's* feet have been washed. *Churunamrit lena, v. a.* To wash the feet of a guest and sip the water.

चरती chúr-tee, *s. m.* One who does not fast.

चरन chúr-un, *s. m.* A foot; the feet of a verse; shoes.

चरना chúr-na, *v. n.* To graze, to feed. *s. m.* Half trowsers. *Churna churhana, v. a.* To put on half trowsers.

चरनामृत chur-un-ámrit, } *s. m.* Ambrosia
चरनोदक chur-un-óduk, } of the feet (*implied in the expression*), the water with which an idol or a *Brahmun's* feet have been washed. *Churunamrit lena, v. a.* To wash the feet of a guest and sip the water.

चरपरा chur-pur-a, *adj.* Acrid, hot (*as pepper*); smart (*in conversation*).

चरपराना chur-pur-ána, *v. n.* To smart.

चरपराहट chur-pur-áhut, *s. f.* Smarting, pungency.

चरपरिया chur-púr-iya, *adj.* Active, ingenious.

चरफर chúr-phur, *s. m.* Activity, cleverness, quickness.

चरफरा chúr-phur-a, *adj.* Active, clever, quick.

चरबुराएगी churburá-egee, *s. f.* Dexterity, expertness, activity.

चरबाना chur-bá-na, *v. a.* To brace a drum.

चरम chúr-um, *adj.* Last, ultimate, final; west, western.

चरमक्षाभृत chúrum-kshmá-bhrit, } *s. m.*
चरमाचल churum-áchul, } The western mountain behind which the sun is supposed to set.

चरवाई chur-wáee, *s. f.* Price paid for pasturage.

चरवाहा chur-wá-ha, *s. m.* A grazier, shepherd, feeder.

चरस chúr-us, *s. m.* The exudation of the flowers of hemp collected with the dew and prepared for use as an intoxicating drug; a leathern bucket, an urn.

चरसा chúr-sa, *s. m.* A hide, a skin.

चराई chur-áee, *s. f.* The price paid for pasturage; grazing, feeding, pasturage.

चराक chur-ák, *s. m.* An animal that grazes.

चराचर chur-a-chúr, *adj.* Moveable, locomotive; shaking, trembling, unsteady; sky, atmosphere; heaven.

चरान chur-án, *s. m.* Lea fallow, a meadow, a salt-marsh or meadow by the sea-shore.

चराना chur-ána, *v. a.* To graze, pasture, feed.

चराव chur-áo, *s. m.* Pasture-land.

चरित chúr-it, *s. m.* Fixed institute, proper or peculiar observance.

चरित्र chúr-itr, *s. m.* Instituted or peculiar observance or conduct; story, adventures, nature, temper, behaviour, disposition, motion, action, conduct, procedure, manner, carriage, quality, humour, use, custom; talent; history.

चरी chúr-ee, *s. f.* Unripe corn cut for the food of cattle. *adj.* Moveable, locomotive; trembling, shaking, unsteady.

चरूआ chúr-oo-a, *s. m.* A large pot.

चर्चक chúrch-uk, *s. m.* An arguer.

चर्चना chúrch-na, *v. a.* To consider, reflect, apprehend, conceive.

चर्चर chúr-chur, *s. m.* Prating, chattering; an imitative sound.

चर्चराना chur-chur-ána, *v. n.* To crackle (*as wood in the fire*), to sputter, to chew with a cracking noise, to chide.

चर्चा chúr-cha, *s. m. f.* Talking over past events, mention, mentioning, recapitulating former occurrences; inquiry, investigation; argument, report, discourse, discussion, consideration, careful perusal, prevalence, engagedness, attention to business; adoration; perfuming by smearing the whole body with sandal-wood, &c.

चर्चेला chur-chél-a, *s. m.* A chatterer, a prater. [tioner.

चर्चत chur-chyt, *s. m.* A reasoner, a men-

चर्म churm, *s. m.* Leather, a skin, a hide; a shield.

चर्मकार churm-kár, *s. m.* A shoe-maker, a currier or worker in leather.

चर्मचटका churm-chút-ka, } *s. f.* A bat.
चर्मचटी churm-chút-ee, }

चर्मनवती churm-un-vút-ee, } *s. f.* A river
चर्मवती churm-vút-ee, } that runs across *Bundelkhund* into the Ganges, the modern *Chumbul.*

चर्मतरंग churm-turúng, *s. m.* A wrinkle, a fold of skin.

चर्मन chúrm-un, *s. m.* Skin, hide, bark, &c.; a shield; a student's hide, usually that of an antelope.

चर्ममय churm-múy, } *adj.* Leather, made
चर्मी churmée, } of leather.

चर्मार churm-ár, *s. m.* A worker in leather.

चर्या chur-yá, *s. f.* Perseverance in religious austerities; due and regular observance of all rites or customs.

चर्रा churra, *s. m.* Thunder.

चर्राना churrána, *v. n.* To burst; to ache, to smart.

चर्व्वन chúrv-vun, *s. m.* Chewing, masticating.

चर्स churs, *s. m.* The exudation of the flowers of hemp collected with the dew and prepared for use as an intoxicating drug; a leathern bucket, or an urn.

चल chul, *s. f.* Going, dispersion; variation, departure from truth, failure in the performance of a promise or accomplishment of a prediction. *Chul dena, v. a.* To march (*as an army*); to beguile.

चलचलाव chul-chul-áo, *s. m.* Preparation for journey or departure.

चलचित्त chul-chítt, *adj.* Fickle, inconstant. *s. m.* Fickleness, mutability.

चलचित्तता chul-chitt-tá, *s. f.* Fickleness, unsteadiness, inconstancy.

चलत chúl-ut, *adj.* Current; saleable, vendible.

चलता chúl-ta, *s. m.* A tree producing an acid fruit (*Dillenia indica*). *part. act.* Going. *Chultee cheez, s. f.* Saleable goods, passable coin, &c.

चलदल chúl-dul, *s. m.* The holy fig tree.

चलन chúl-un, *s. m.* Habit, custom, process, course, fashion, conduct, behaviour; ceremony; currency. *adj.* Current. *Chulun chulna, v. n.* To behave.

चलनता chul-ún-ta, *adj.* Saleable, vendible.

चलना chúl-na, *v. n.* To move, go, proceed, walk, go off, pass (*as coin*), be discharged (*a gun, &c.*), to blow, flow, drive; behave; sail; work, answer, succeed, avail, last, serve, stand. *Chul-nikulna,* To turn out vicious, to exceed bounds. *Chuleh chulna,* To go along. *Chula jana,* To go along, be off, depart.

चलनी chúl-nee, *s. f.* A sieve. *adj.* Current, usual, fashionable.

चलफेर chul-phér, *s. m.* Motion.

चलबिचल chul-bi-chúl, *s. m.* Error, mistake.

चलबिधरा chul-bídh-ra, *adj.* Restive.

चलबिधराहट chul-bidh-ráhut, *s. f.* Restiveness.

चुलवा chúl-wa, *s. f.* A kind of fish (*Clupea cultrata*).

चुलाऊ chul-áoo, *adj.* Going; frail, inconstant, fickle; on the point of death.

चुलाचुल chul-a-chúl, } *s. f.* The bustle
चुलाचुली chul-a-chúl-ee, } of setting out on a journey, &c. setting about any thing. *adj.* Tremulous, unsteady; moveable and stationary.

चुलान chul-án, *s. f.* Clearance; remittance.

चुलाना chul-ána, *v. a.* To impel, set a going, make to go or pass, to drive; actuate, direct; to fire a musket or cannon, shoot at, do, hasten, forward, send, accustom, act, advance, utter, throw, thrust, use, walk.

चुलाव chul-áo, *s. m.* Habit, custom.

चुलावा chul-áwa, *s. m.* Movement, motion, going, custom.

चुलित chúl-it, *adj.* Current, usual; shaking, trembling; gone, departed.

चुलित्र chul-ítr, *s. m.* Nature, temper, behaviour, disposition, motion, action, conduct, procedure, manner, carriage, quality, humour, use, custom; talent; history.

चुलित्री chul-ít-ree, *adj.* Gay, sportive, changeable, inconstant, affected.

चुलू chúl-oo, *s. m.* A handful of water, water taken up in the hollowed palm of the hand for rinsing the mouth.

चुलूक chúl-ook, *s. m.* The hand hollowed as for holding a little water, &c.; a small pot, a gallipot, &c.; a handful of water.

चुलेन्द्रिय chuléndriyuh, *adj.* Sensitive, sensual, not having subdued senses or passions.

चुलो chúl-o, *interj.* Away! begone!

चुलौना chul-óu-na, *s. m.* A small stick with which the spinning-wheel is turned.

चुवाई chuwáee, *s. m.* Reporter, backbiter.

चुवाला chuwála, *s. m.* A chair, a sedan.

चुवाव chuwáo, *s. m.* A report, slander.

चुवि chúv-i, *s. f.* The pepper plant which yields long pepper.

चुविकी chúv-ik-ee, } (*Piper chavya*).
चुव chúv-yuh, }

चुषुक chúsh-uk, *s. m.* A vessel for drinking spirits with, a wine glass, &c.; any drinking vessel; spirituous liquor.

चुषुति chúsh-uti, *s. m.* Decay, infirmity.

चुषुक chús-uk, *s. f.* Pain, aching, throbbing pain, a stitch (*sharp lancinating pain*).

चुषुकना chús-uk-na, *v. n.* To throb, to ache.

चुष्का chús-ka, *s. m.* Love, ardent desire, a relish, habit, custom.

चुसना chús-na, *v. n.* To burst or split (*as tight cloth*).

चुसी chús-see, *s. f.* A species of itch peculiar to the palms of the hand and soles of the feet, said to be occasioned by insects.

चुहुकना chuhúk-na, *v. n.* To whistle (*as birds*).

चुहका chúh-ka, *s. m.* A kind of firework; the smarting of a wound, &c., by the application of a medicine. *Chuhka lugana*, To burn the skin slightly by fomenting.

चुहकार chuh-kár, *s. f.* Singing or chirping of birds.

चुहकारना chuh-kár-na, *v. n.* To sing or chirp (*birds*).

चुहकैट chuh-kyt, *adj.* Brawny, stout.

चुहचुहा chuh-chuhá, *adj.* Deeply-coloured.

चुहचुहाहट chuh-chuhá-hut, *s. f.* The singing or chirping of birds.

चुहचुहाना chuh-chuhána, *v. n.* To sing or chirp as birds.

चुहचुहिया chuh-chúhiya, *s. m.* A whistler.

चुहुलना chuhúl-na, *v. n.* To be fatigued, to be tired.

चुहुलपुहुल chúhul-púhul, *s. f.* Jollity, merriment, cheer, mirth.

चुहला chúh-la, } *s. m.* Dirt, mud, slime,
चिहला chíhla, } ooze, mire; a splinter of wood. *Chihla nikulna*, To fatigue, to be tired. *Chihla kurna*, To split to pieces.

चुहिये chúhiyeh, *adv.* Becoming; necessary, expedient.

चुही chuhée, *s. f.* Warbling.

चुहूँ chúhoon, *adj.* Four. *Chuhoon-or*, *adv.* On all sides.

चुहूँचुक chuhoon-chúk, } *adj.* Circumja-
चुहूँदिश chuhoon-dísh, } cent, all around.

चुक्षु chuk-shóo, *s. m.* The eye. *Chukshoo-rog*, *s. m.* Ophthalmia.

चाईन cháeen, *s. m.* A low class of *Hindoos*; the seed of tamarind.

चाईन cháeen, }
चाईनजूईन cháeen-jóoeen, } *s. f.* Scaldhead.

चांगला chang-la, *s. m.* A colour in horses.

चाँटना chánt-na, *v. a.* To press, to squeeze.

चांड chand, }
चांड chanr, } *s. f.* A prop.

चांद chand, *s. m.* The moon; the crown of the head; a white spot in the forehead of cattle, and many other things which are moon-like; an ornament; a month (*lunar*); a target (*to shoot at*). *Chand chhipana*, To change as the moon. *Chand-rat*, End of the month. *Chand-tara*, A robe made

8

of flowering muslin, &c. *Chand marna*, To fire at a mark. *Chand neh khet keeya*, The moon has risen.

चांदना chánd-na, *s. m.* Light. *Chandna-pukh*, *s. m.* The light fortnight of the moon.

चांदनी chánd-nee, *s. f.* The moon-beams, moonlight; name of a flower; a white cloth spread over a carpet; any thing white and shining. *Chandnee-chouk*, *s. m.* A wide and public street or market. *Chandnee-rat*, *s. f.* A moonlight night. *Chandnee ka mara jana*, *v. n.* To be affected with a disease supposed to proceed from a stroke of the moon (*a horse*).

चांदा chán-da, *s. m.* A subscription to raise a certain sum, an assessment, quota, share.

चांदी chán-dee, *s. f.* Silver (*pure*), plate; the crown of the head.

चांप champ, *s. f.* The lock of a gun; the stocks, the rack. *Champ churhana*, To cock a gun; to punish or torment by squeezing the ear with the lock of a gun.

चांपना chámp-na, *v. a.* To join; to stuff, cram, thrust in, press.

चांवल chán-wul, *s. m.* Rice.

चा cha, *s. f.* Tea. *Chadan*, *s. m.* Teapot.

चाए chae, *s. m.* Eagerness, pleasure, taste.

चाक chak, *s. m.* A potter's wheel; rings of earth forming a well; a mill-stone, mill.

चाकी chá-kee, *s. f.* A mill-stone, a mill; grinder.

चाखना chákh-na, *v. a.* To taste, relish, enjoy.

चांगला cháng-la, *s. m.* A colour in horses.

चाचर chá-chur, *s. m.* The pole round which they play at the festival of the *holee*; a fair or assemblage of people collected after the *holee*.

चाचा chá-cha, *s. m.* Paternal uncle, father's brother.

चाची chá-chee, *s. f.* Father's sister, or father's brother's wife, aunt.

चांचुल्य chan-chúl-yuh, *s. m.* Unsteadiness.

चाट chat, *s. f.* Longing, wish, itch, relish, taste; habit, custom; a delicacy, a bonne bouchee. *Chat lena*, To lick up.

चाटना chát-na, *v. a.* To lick, to lap.

चाटी chát-ee, *s. f.* A churn.

चार char, *s. f.* Turf; a hurt, a wound, a knock; a lever.

चांडाल chandál, *s. m.* An impure or degraded tribe, a *Pariah*, an outcaste.

चांडाली chandalée, *s. f.* A woman of the same tribe.

चातक chá-tuk, *s. m.* A bird, a kind of cuckoo (*Cuculus melano-leucus*).

चातुर chá-tur, *s. m.* A large net, a seine.

चातुर cha-tóor, *adj.* Clever, able, ingenious, shrewd, wise, knowing, cunning, sly; four.

चातुरी cha-tóo-ree, *s. f.* Dexterity, ability, cleverness.

चातुर्य cha-tóor-yuh, *s. m.* Cunning, shrewdness, slyness.

चातुर्वर्ण्यं chátoor-vúrnyuh, *s. m.* The aggregate of the four original casts, the *Brahmun*, *Khuttree*, *Vysyuh*, and *Soodr*.

चातुर्वेद chátoor-vyd-yuh, *s. m.* A priest, &c. versed in the four *Veds*.

चालाल chat-wál, *s. m.* A hollow made in the ground to receive a burnt-offering; any hole in the ground.

चांद्र chandr, *s. m.* The moon-gem; a month, a lunar month; the light fortnight, or half month during which the moon is on the increase. *adj.* Lunar.

चांद्रभागा chandr-bhága, *s. f.* A river in the *Punjab*, the *Chinab*.

चांद्रमस chandr-mús, *s. m.* The constellation *Mirgsira*; stars in Orion.

चांद्रायण chandr-áyun, *s. m.* A religious or expiatory observance, regulated by the moon's age; diminishing the daily consumption of food every day, by one mouthful, for the dark half of the month, and increasing it in like manner during the light half.

चाप chap, *s. m.* A bow.

चापपुट chap-pút, *s. m.* A tree (*Buchanania latifolia*).

चापल chá-pul, *s. m.* Unsteadiness (*literally or metaphorically*).

चाफंद cha-phúnd, *s. m.* A kind of fishing-net.

चाबना cháb-na, *v. a.* To chew, masticate, gnaw. *Chab chab baten kurnee*, To mince one's words, to speak little or haughtily.

चाबी chá-bee, *s. f.* A key.

चाभटपार्ना chábhut-párna, *v. a.* To craunch, to crush.

चाम cham, *s. m.* Hide, skin, leather. *Cham keh dam chulaneh*, *v. a.* To stretch to the utmost a temporary authority.

चामर chá-mur, *s. m.* The tail of the Bos grunniens, used to whisk off flies, &c.

चामरपूष्प chamur-póoshp, *s. m.* The betel-nut tree (*Areca faufel* or *catechu*).

चामीकर cha-mee-kúr, *s. m.* Gold.

चाय chá-yuh, *s. m.* Eagerness, pleasure, taste.

चार char, *adj.* Four. *Char-oongul*, *s. m.* A palm (*four inches*). *Char-oonglee*, *s. f.* Hand's-breadth. *Char-beesee*, *s. f.* Four-score. *Char-took*, *adj.* Broken (*into four pieces*).

চারগুণা char-góona, *adj.* Four-fold.

চারণ chá-run, *s. m.* A dancer or mimick, a kind of bard, reciter or panegyrist.

চারপথ char-púth, *s. m.* A meeting of two roads.

চারবাক char-vák, *s. m.* The head of a tribe of Atheists.

চারা chá-ra, *s. m.* Forage, fodder, food for cattle, bait for fish ; a young plant. *Chara dalna*, To bait.

চারু chá-roo *adj.* Beautiful, pleasing, agreeable, elegant.

চার্ব্বাক charv-vák, *s. m.* A sophist, a philosopher ; one acquainted with the doctrines of the schools, a sceptic in many matters of *Hindoo* faith, and considered by the orthodox as an atheist or materialist.

চার্ব্বী chárv-vee, *s. f.* A beautiful woman, a beauty ; understanding, intellect ; moonlight ; light, splendor.

চাল chal, *s. m.* The thatch or roof of a house. *s. f.* A colour in horses, roan ; gait, motion, movement, pace, procedure, habit, custom, practice, method, way. *Chal pukurna*, To prevail. *Chal chulna*, To behave. *Chal dhal, s. f.* Gait, motion, procedure, manners, behaviour, breeding, politeness. *Chal milna*, To smell a rat.

চালক chá-luk, *adj.* Laxative.

চালন chá-lun, *s. m.* A sieve, a strainer.

চালনা chál-na, *v. a.* To sift. *v. n.* To be mischievous. *Chalunhar*, A sifter.

চালনী chál-nee, *s. f.* A sieve, a strainer.

চালু chá-luh, *s. f.* A fish, a sort of sprat (*Clupea cultrata*).

চালা chá-la, *s. m.* Motion, departure ; (*met.*) a lucky moment.

চালী chá-lee, *adj.* Roguish, wicked, mischievous.

চালীস cha-lées, *adj.* Forty.

চালীসবাঁ cha-lées-van, *adj.* Fortieth ; (*hence*) the fortieth day after child-birth, death of a relation, &c.

চালীসা cha-lée-sa, *s. m.* A dimness of sight which is supposed to come on at forty years of age, and often to be removed on approaching the forty-eighth or fiftieth year ; the fortieth year of any era, or of the century.

চালীসী cha-lée-see, *s. f.* Quarantine kept after the death of a relation, child-birth, &c.

চাব cháo, *s. m.* Eagerness, pleasure, taste, desire ; a measure equal to four fingers ; a kind of bamboo. *Chao-chochla*, or *Chao-choz*, Fondness, endearment, fondling and toying.

চাবরী cháo-ree, *s. f.* Name of a bazar in *Delhi*.

চাবল chá-wul, *s. m.* Rice (*cleared of the husk and not dressed*).

চাস chas, *s. f.* Ploughing. *Chas kurna*, and *Chasna*, To plough.

চাসা chá-sa, *s. m.* A ploughman, a husbandman.

চাহ chah, *s. f.* Desire, wish, love, liking, affection, choice, want, appetite. *Chah-chit*, or *Chah-o-choz*, Love, affection, dalliance.

চাহুক chá-huk, *adj.* Affectionate.

চাহত chá-hut, *s. f.* Desire, will, wishing, volition, love, liking.

চাহনা cháh-na, *v. a.* To love, like, desire, wish for, will, want, demand, choose, need, require, pray, approve, ask for, crave, attempt, try, to see, look to, look for.

চাহা chá-ha, *s. m.* Love, affection, will.

চাহাচুহী cháha-chúhee, *s. f.* The love of one's country.

চাহিয়ে cháhiyeh, *adv.* Necessary, becoming, requisite.

চাহীতা cha-hée-ta, *adj.* Agreeable, desirable, beloved. *s.* A sweetheart, one beloved, a darling.

চাহীতী cha-hée-tee, *s. f.* A mistress, a sweetheart.

চাহো chá-ho, *imper.* Choose, either, or.

চিক chik, *s. f.* A pain in the loins ; a skreen made of split bamboos.

চিকটা chík-ta, *s. m.* A kind of *tussur* cloth.

চিকঠা chik-thá, *adj.* Filthy, greasy. *s. m.* An oil merchant.

চিকনা chík-na, *s. m.* Oil. *adj.* Clean, polished, smooth ; beautiful (*person*) ; greasy, oily, fat (*as meat*), glossy, sleek, slippery ; incontinent, lewd, wanton. *Chikna basun*, or, *—ghura bunna*, To be incontinent, incorrigible, deaf to admonition. *Chikna chanda, adj.* Beautiful. *Chiknee joroo, s. f.* A slippery wife. *Chiknee sooparee, s. f.* A kind of betel-nut prepared by boiling. *Chiknee soorut, adj.* Prosperous, affluent, flourishing. *Chiknee mittee, s. f.* Clay.

চিকনাই chik-náee, *s. f.* Fat of meat ; wantonness ; gloss, smoothness, polish.

চিকনানা chik-ná-na, *v. a.* To clean, polish, smooth, lubricate, sleek.

চিকনাহট chik-ná-hut, *s. f.* Cleanness, glossiness, sleekness, smoothness, polish ; greasiness ; beauty.

চিকনিয়া chík-ni-ya, *s. m.* Beau, spark.

চিকলনা chik-úl-na, *v. a.* To masticate, to chew (*slowly*).

চিকারনা chik-ár-na, *v. n.* To squeak.

चिकारा chik-á·ra, *s. m.* A kind of antelope found on the banks of the *Jumna*; a kind of fiddle.

चिकारी chik-áree, *s. f.* An insect like a musquito; smut (*obscenity*).

चिकित्सुक chík-it-suk, *s. m.* A physician, a practiser in medicine.

चिकित्सा chík-it-sa, *s. f.* The practice of medicine, healing, curing, administering or applying remedies, attendance of a physician on a patient.

चिकिन chík-in, *adj.* Flat-nosed.

चिकिल chík-il, *s. m.* Mud, mire.

चिकुर chik-óor, *s. m.* Hair; a lock of hair.

चिकुरा chik-óo-ra, *adj.* Rashly criminal, inconsiderately guilty, punishing or injuring others without consideration.

चिकोरना chik-ór-na, *v. a.* To peck.

चिकोरा chik-ó-ra, *adj.* Restless, inconstant.

चिक्क chikk, *s. m.* A musk rat.

चिककुट chík-kut, *adj.* Filthy, covered with grease and dirt.

चिककुन chik-kún, *adj.* Bland, soft, mild, unctuous, emollient.

चिककुनी chik-kunée, *s. f.* The betel-nut.

चिककुन chík-kun, *adj.* Clean; polished; beautiful (*person*); greasy, oily; incontinent, lewd, wanton.

चिककुस chík-kus, *s. m.* Barley meal.

चिकका chík-ka, *s. f.* A mouse.

चिककिन chik-kín-a, *adj.* Bland, unctuous, emollient.

चिककी chík-kee, *s. f.* A rotten betel-nut. *adj.* Flat-nosed.

चिकहुरुन chik-hóorun, *s. m.* Weed.

चिकहुरना chik-hóorna, *v. a.* To weed.

चिकहुरी chik-hóoree, *s. f.* A squirrel.

चिनगुट chin-gút, *s. m.* ⎫
चिंगरा chíng-ra, *s. m.* ⎬ A shrimp, or prawn.
चिंगरी chíng-ree, *s. f.* ⎭

चिंगनी chíng-nee, *s. f.* ⎫ A chicken.
चिंगा chín-ga, *s. m.* ⎭

चिंगी chín-gee, *s. f.* A spark of (*fire*); a wicked dwarf. *Chingee jhurnee*, or, —*chhootna*, or, —*nikulna*, To sparkle.

चिंगहार ching-hár, ⎫ *s. m.* Scream,
चिंगहारा ching-há-ra, ⎬ screech, clamour. *Chingharen marna*, To scream. *Chingharna*, *v. n.* To scream, to screech (*applied properly to the elephant*).

चिचरी chích-ree, *s. f.* A tick or louse (*of dogs and sheep*).

चिचरी चेंचना chichrhée khynchna, *v. a.* To scrawl, to score.

चिचिंदा chich-ín-da, *s. m.* A vegetable (*Beta vulgaris*).

चिचियाना chichi-yána, *v. n.* To squeak, shriek, bleat.

चिट chit, *s. f.* Rag, scrap. *Chit ookhur-na*, *v. n.* To splinter or have small pieces knocked off furniture.

चिटका chít-ka, *s. m.* A kind of grass or grain; mucus, slime.

चिटकारा chit-ká-ra, *s. m.* A speck, a scar; a clack with the tongue occasioned by an acrid taste. *Chitkara lugana*, To brand.

चिटकी chít-kee, *s. f.* Sunshine.

चिटटा chít-ta, *adj.* White, fair. *s. m.* A silver coin. *Chitta ookharna*, *v. a.* To splinter or knock small peices off furniture.

चिटटी chít-tee, *s. f.* The hen of the little birds called *Amaduvades* (*Fringilla amandava*).

चिटठा chit-thá, *s. m.* A memorandum of money paid, or the pay of servants of the state.

चिटठी chit-thée, *s. f.* A note, a letter, a billet. *Tulub chitthee*, *s. f.* A summons. *Chitthee-patee*, or, *Chitthee puttur*, *s. f.* Epistolary correspondence.

चिड chir, *s. f.* Vexation, irritation; aversion, antipathy. *Chir nikalna*, To banter.

चिड़चिड़ा chir-chír-a, *s. m.* A plant (*Achyranthes aspera*). *adj.* Cross, peevish, crabbed, fretful.

चिड़चिड़ाहट chir-chir-áhut, *s. f.* Peevishness, fretfulness.

चिड़ना chír-na, *v. n.* To be vexed, to vex, to be irritated, to fret, to be provoked.

चिड़पिड़ा chír-pir-a, *adj.* Fiery, hot (*as pepper*), acrid.

चिड़पिड़ाहट chir-pir-áhut, *s. f.* Acrimony.

चिड़ा chír-a, *s. m.* A sparrow. *Chiree*, *s. f.* A hen-sparrow.

चिड़ाना chir-ána, *v. a.* To vex, irritate, mock, provoke, offend, gibe, jeer.

चिड़िया chír-iya, *s. f.* A bird; a hen-sparrow (*a generic term*), a sparrow; a kind of sewing. *Chiriyah-khanuh*, *s. m.* An aviary.

चिड़ीमार chir-ee-már, *s. m.* A bird-catcher, a fowler.

चिड़ chirh, *s. f.* Abhorrence, abomination, dislike, vexation, provocation.

चिंता chín-ta, *s. f.* Thought, consideration, reflection, anxiety.

चिंतित chín-tit, *adj.* Thoughtful, reflective, anxious.

चित chit, *s. f.* Intellect, understanding, mind, life, soul, heart, memory; look, glance, sense. *Chit-chash*, Pleasing to the mind, satisfactory, what the heart desires. *Chit-chor*, Heart-stealer, heart-stealing, or heart-alluring. *Chit dena*, To pay attention. *Chit kurna*, To make up one's mind. *Chit lugun*, *adj.* Amusing, pleasant. *Chit lana*, *v. n.* To be attentive, attached, apply to.

चित chit, *adj.* Supine, lying flat on the back. *Chit kurna*, To throw (*one's adversary*) on his back (*a term in wrestling*), to discomfit, overcome in battle.

चितकबरा chit-kúb-ra, ⎫ *adj.* Piebald,
चितला chitla, ⎭ speckled, spotted.

चितना chít-na, *v. n.* To look, see, behold, appear; to be painted.

चितरना chitúrna, *v. a.* To paint.

चितरा chít-ra, *s. f.* Name of the fourteenth mansion of the moon (*Spica Virginis*).

चितला chít-la, *adj.* Piebald, speckled, spotted.

चितवन chít-wun, *s. f.* A sight, a look, a glance.

चितहट chit-hút, *s. f.* Reluctance, repugnance.

चिता chít-a, ⎫ *s. f.* A funeral pile.
चिताखा chit-ákha, ⎭

चितांग chit-áng, *adj.* Supine (*applied to animated beings*).

चिताचूरुक chit-a-chóoruk, *s. m.* A mark where a funeral pile has been, a mausoleum, a monument.

चिताना chit-ána, ⎫ *v. a.* To caution,
चिताओना chit-áo-na, ⎭ warn, apprize, inform, advise, suggest, remind, intimate, alarm.

चिताओनी chit-áo-nee, *s. f.* A token; admonition, warning.

चितेरा chit-ér-a, *s. m.* A person who paints flowers, &c. on wood, a painter.

चितौना chit-óu-na, *v. a.* To see, to look at, to behold.

चितकार chitkár, *s. m.* A cry, a scream.

चित्त chitt, *s. m.* The mind or faculty of reasoning, the heart considered as the seat of intellect.

चित्तप्रसन्नता chitt-prusúnn-ta, *s. f.* Happiness, gaity, joy. [able.

चित्तवान chittwán, *adj.* Kind-hearted, amiable.

चित्तविभ्रम chitt-vibhrúm, *s. m.* Madness, derangement.

चित्ता chítta, *s. m.* A medicinal plant (*Plumbago zeylanica*); application of a blister. *adj.* White.

चित्ताभोग chitta-bhóg, *s. m.* Consciousness of pleasure or pain, the attention of the mind to its own sensations.

चित्ती chíttee, *s. f.* A scar, spot, freckle, &c.; a kind of serpent; a *cowree* worn smooth by rubbing. *Chitteedar*, *adj.* Speckled. *Chittee lana*, To scar.

चित्य chít-yuh, *s. m.* A monument, or any mark of the scite of a funeral pile.

चित्या chit-yáh, *s. f.* A funeral pile.

चित्र chitr, *v. a.* A picture, painting, delineation, writing, &c. a circular ornament, a sectarial mark on the forehead.

चित्रकार chitr-kár, *s. m.* A portrait-painter, a painter.

चित्रकारी chitr-káree, *s. f.* Portrait-painting, painting.

चित्रकूट chitr-kóot, *s. m.* A mountain in *Bundelkhund*, the modern *Compteh*, and first habitation of *Ram* in his exile.

चित्रगर chitr-gúr, *s. m.* A portrait-painter, a painter.

चित्रगुप्त chitr-góopt, *s. m.* A name of *Yum*; *Yum's* registrar, said to record the vices and virtues of mankind, the recording angel or infernal registrar. [Myna.

चित्रनेत्र chitr-nétra, *s. f.* A small bird, the

चित्रपदा chitr-púd-a, *s. f.* A creeper (*Cissus pedata*) a kind of metre.

चित्रपर्णिका chitr-púrnik-a, ⎫ *s. f.* A plant
चित्रपर्णी chitr-púrnee, ⎭ (*Hemionites cordifolia*) Bengal madder (*Rubia manjeth*).

चित्रपादा chitr-páda, *s. f.* The *Myna*, a small bird so called.

चित्रविचित्र chitr-bichítr, ⎫ *adj.* Of various
चित्रविचित्र chitr-vichítr, ⎭ colours, variegated.

चित्रभोजन chitr-bhó-jun, *s. m.* Change of diet, eating of unusual food.

चित्रल chitrúl, *s. m.* Variegated or spotted (*the colour*).

चित्रशाला chitr-shála, *s. f.* A gallery of pictures, a picture-room.

चित्रा chítra, *s. f.* Name of the fourteenth mansion of the moon (*Spica Virginis*). *adj.* Variegated, spotted, speckled.

चित्रांग chitr-áng, *s. m.* A kind of snake; a plant (*Plumbago zeylanica*); yellow orpiment; vermilion.

चित्रिणी chitrín-ee, *s. f.* The second (*Hindoo*) division of women.

चिथरा chíth-ra, *s. m.* A rag, tatter.

चिथड़िया chit-hur-íya, *adj.* Tattered, ragged, clothed in rags.

चिथाड़ना chit-hár-na, *v. a.* To tear to pieces; to fill a paper with writing or scribbling; to abuse, revile, treat with indignity.

चिनग chín-ug, *s. f. Ardor urinæ.*

चिनगना chín-ug-na, *v. n.* To throb, to shoot (*as a boil, &c.* to cry, to screech.

चिनगारी chin-gá-ree, *s. f* A spark (*of fire*).

चिनगी chín-gee, *s. f.* A spark (*of fire*); a wicked dwarf. *Chingee jhurnee, or, —chhootna, or, —nikulna,* To sparkle.

चिनचिनाना chin-chin-ána, *v. n.* To scream, squeak, squall.

चिनन chín-tun, *s. m.* Study.

चिनना chín-tun-a, *v. a.* To study, to think.

चिना chín-ta, *s. f.* Reflection, consideration, recollection, care, doubt, danger, risk, anxiety, thought, peril.

चिनाकुल chinta-kóol, *adj.* Disturbed in thought or distracted by any idea.

चिनाना chin-tá-na, *v. a.* To cause to study.

चिनापर chinta-púr, *adj.* Thoughtful, anxious.

चिनामनि chinta-múni, *s. m.* A fabulous gem, supposed to yield its possessor whatever may be required.

चिनावत् chinta-vút, *adj.* Thinking, thoughtful.

चिनावेश्मन् chinta-véshmun, *s. m.* Council-house or room.

चिनित chín-tit, *adj.* Thoughtful, anxious, reflective.

चिनिया chín-ti-ya, *s. f.* Reflection, consideration, thinking.

चिन्न chinn, *s. m.* A kind of grain (*Panicum miliaceum*).

चिन्ह chinh, *s. m.* A scar, mark, spot, stain, sign, symbol, token by which any thing is known, feature, signature. *Chinh churhana,* To stigmatize.

चिन्हार chin-hár, *s. m.*   ⎰ An acquaint-
चिन्हारी chin-há-ree, *s. f.* ⎱ ance.

चिपकना chíp-uk-na, *v. n.* To stick, adhere, collapse; to spread or sink (*as ink on damp paper*); to be compressed. *Chipuk jana,* To fall in love at first sight.

चिपचिपा chíp-chip-a, *adj.* Clammy, viscid, glutinous, adhesive.

चिपचिपाना chip-chip-ána, ⎱ *v. n.* To ad-
चिपटना chíp-ut-na,   ⎰ here, to cohere, to stick.

चिपचिपाहट chip-chip-áhut, *s. f.* Viscosity, glutinousness, tenacity, stickiness.

चिपटा chíp-ta, *adj.* Clammy, viscous, glutinous.

चिपटाना chip-tá-na, *v. a.* To sod, turf, to apply patches, stick.

चिपराहा chip-rá-ha, *adj.* Bleared (*as the eyes*).

चिपरी chíp-ree, *s. f.* Small cakes of dried cow-dung.

चिपना chipna, *v. n.* To be concealed.

चिपरा chíp-ra, *s. m.* Gum (*of the eyes*).

चिप्पक chip-púk, *adj.* Shallow. *s. f.* Name of a bird.

चिप्पख chip-púkh, *s. m.* A sparrow-hawk.

चिप्पी chíp-pee, *s. f.* A patch on paper.

चिबावला chibáo-la, *adj.* Childish, boyish.

चिबिल chíb-il,   ⎱ *adj.* Unpolite, childish,
चिबिल्ला chib-ílla, ⎰ boyish. *Chibillapun, s. m.* Boyishness, childishness.

चिबुक chíb-ook, *s. f.* The chin.

चिमचिमा chím-chim-a, *s. m.* Oil become viscous by age.

चिमटना chim-út-na,   ⎱ *v. n.* To adhere, to
चिमड़ना chim-úr-na, ⎰ stick. *Chimut ruhna, v. n.* To cleave to.

चिमटा chím-ta, *s. m.* Tongs, forceps.

चिमटाना chim-tá-na, *v. n.* To adhere, to cling to.

चिमटी काटना chímtee kátna, *v. a.* To pinch.

चिमठा chim-thá, *adj.* Elastic, tough.

चिमड़ा chimrá, *adj.* Tough, ductile, flexible, hardy.

चिमड़ाई chim-ráee, *s. f.* Power, vigour, flexibility, ductility.

चिमड़ाना chim-rá-na, *v. n.* To toughen, grow tough.

चिमड़ाहट chim-rá-hut, *s. f.* Toughness, flexibility.

चिमड़ी chim-rée, *adj.* Infrangible (*a quill for instance*), hard.

चिमसा chím-sa, *adj.* Glutinous (*as oil by long keeping*).

चिमि chími, *s. m.* A parrot; a plant, from the fibres of which coarse cloth and rope are made.

चिर chir, *adj.* Long (*time*).

चिरंजी chir-ún-jee, *adj.* Long-lived.

चिरकना chir-úk-na, *v. a.* To have a scanty stool.

चिरकारी chir-káree, *adj.* Dilatory, tedious, slow.

चिरकाल chir-kál, *s. m.* A long period. *adv.* Always, eternally. *Chirkal seh, adv.* Long ago.

चिरकुट chir-kóot, *s. m.* A bit, a piece, a rag.

चिरकुढिया chir-koo-tíya, *adj. s. m.* A tatterdemalion, ragged.

चिरक्रिया chír-kriya, *adj.* Dilatory, tedious, slow.

चिरचिरा chír-chir-a, *s. m.* A medicinal plant (*Achyranthes aspera*) ; a child.

चिरचिराना chir-chir-ána, *v. n.* To crackle (*as wood in the fire*), to sputter, to chew with a cracking noise, to chide.

चिरचिराहट chir-chir-áhut, *s. f.* Peevishness, fretfulness.

चिरजीवना chir-jéev-na, *v. n.* To be long-lived.

चिरजीवी chir-jéev-ee, *adj.* Long-lived.

चिरजीविन chírun-jéevin, *s. m.* A crow; *Vishnoo. adj.* Long-lived.

चिरुंटी chir-ún-tee, *s. f.* A woman married or single, who continues to reside after maturity in her father's house; a young woman.

चिरतिक्त chír-tikt, *s. m.* A kind of Gentian (*Gentiana Cherayta*).

चिरतन chir-útn,
चिरंतन chir-ún-tun, } *adj.* Old, ancient, antiquated, long lasting.

चिरना chír-na, *v. n.* To be torn or split, to split.

चिरवाना chir-wá-na, *v. a.* To cause to tear or to be torn.

चिरस्थायी chir-sthayée, *adj.* Long enduring, lasting or remaining for a long time.

चिरांद chir-ánd, *s. f.* The smell of burning leather, hair, &c.

चिराना chir-ána, *v. a.* To cause to tear or be torn, cause to split.

चिरायु chiráyoo, *adj.* Long-lived. *s. m.* A Deity, a Divinity.

चिरिंटी chir-ín-tee, *s. f.* A woman staying in her father's house.

चिरोंजी chir-ón-jee, *s. f.* Nut of the *Chironjia sapida*, and the tree.

चिरौरी chir-óu-ree, *s. f.* Beseeching, begging, requesting.

चिल्क chíl-uk, *s. f.* Refulgence, glitter.

चिल्कना chíl-uk-na, *v. n.* To glitter, to shine.

चिलचिलाना chil-chil-ána, *v. n.* To shriek, scream, screech.

चिलराह chil-rá-ha, *adj.* Lousy.

चिलम chíl-um, *s. m.* The part of a *hookka* which contains the tobacco and fire.

चिलमची chíl-um-chee, *s. f.* A wash-hand bason of metal with a cover to it ; part of a *hookka* fixed under the *chilum.*

चिलवन chil-wún, *s. f.* A skreen for keeping out the glare, a venetian-blind, a lattice.

चिलवान chil-wán, *s. m.* A shutter.

चिलूहला chilúhla, *adj.* Splashy, muddy, slimy.

चिलहोरना chil-hór-na, *v. a.* To peck.

चिलिक chíl-ik, *s. f.* Twitch, stitch.

चिल्ल chill, *s. m.* The Bengal kite (*Falco cheela*).

चिल्लर chillúr, *s. f.* A louse. *Chillur marna, v. a.* To louse.

चिल्ला chílla, *s. m.* A bowstring; gold threads put in the borders of a turband. *Chilla khynchna, v. a.* To bend a bow ; to prepare for battle. *Chilla churhana, v. a.* To bend a bow.

चिल्लाना chil-lá-na, *v. n.* To scream, shriek, roar, bawl, bellow, cry out, exclaim.

चिल्लाहट chil-lá-hut, *s. f.* Cry, out-cry, scream.

चिल्ली chíl-lee, *s. f.* A kind of dish made of eggs ; a blockhead, one who plays mischievous pranks.

चिल्हवांस chilh-wáns, *s. m.* The flesh of a kite (*the eating of which is said to produce madness*) ; screaming like a kite.

चिहाना chihána, *v. a.* To embellish, decorate.

चिहिकना chihíkna, *s. m.* Warbling of the nightingale, &c. ; the sound of fireworks.

चिन्ह chinh, *s. m.* A mark of any kind, a spot, stain, sign, symbol, &c. ; a banner, a standard ; a symptom.

चींटी chéen-tee, *s. f.* Small ant.

चींथना chéenth-na, *v. n.* To be bruised by being trod upon.

चींऊटा cheeóon-ta, *s. m.* Large black ant.

चींऊटी cheeóon-tee, *s. f.* The diminutive of *cheeoonta.*

चींऊरा cheeóo-ra, *s. m.* Rice parched and eaten raw.

चीक cheek,
चीकड़ chee-kúr, } *s. f.* Mud, slime.

चीकट chée-kut, *s. f.* A mixture of oil and dust. *adj.* Greasy or dusty (*as cloth*).

चीख cheekh, *s. f.* A scream, screech, shriek. *Cheekh marna,* To scream, screech, shriek, cry.

चीखना chéekh-na, *v. n.* To roar, scream. *v. a.* To taste.

चीखूर chee-khóor, *s. m.* A squirrel.

चीठी chee-thée, *s. f.* A note, letter, billet.

चीतुर cheetúr, *s. m.* Hips, buttocks. *Cheetur tekna,* To get rest, to sit down.

चीतना chéet-na, *v. a.* To wish, think or imagine ; to draw, to paint.

चीतल chée-tul, *s. m.* A certain animal of the forest (*perhaps a leopard or panther, or some other spotted animal).* adj. Spotted, variegated, speckled (*colour*).

चीता chée-ta, *s. m.* Painting; thought, wish; understanding, wisdom; leopard or panther (*Felis jubata*; *Hunting leopard*); a medicinal plant (*Plumbago zeylanica*).

चीथना chéeth-na, *v. a.* To rend, to tear.

चीन cheen, *s. m.* A sort of grass (*Panicum miliaceum*); a country, China; a sort of cloth.

चीनकपूर cheen-kupóor, *s. m.* Camphor.

चीनपिष्ट cheen-píshth, *s. m.* Minium or red-lead (*brought in cakes or lumps from the hills on the north-west of Bengal, and between it and China*).

चीनी chée-nee, *s. f.* Sugar (*coarse, being perhaps so named from Cheen, China, whence it might have been first brought to India; as sugar-candy is called Misree, apparently from Misr, Egypt*). adj. Belonging to, or produced in China, Chinese.

चीन्ह cheenh, *s. m.* A mark, a token by which any thing is known.

चीन्हना chéenh-na, *v. a.* To know, to recognize.

चीन्हा chéen-ha, *s. m.* An acquaintance.

चीपड़ chée-pur, *s. f.* Rheum of the eyes.

चीर cheer, *s. m.* Rent, slit, strip; attire; tearing, rending, splitting, slitting. *s. f.* Cloth; a sort of covering or dress for women, clothes, attire; the Pine tree (*Pinus longifolia*). *Cheer nikulna,* To break through troops.

चीरना chéer-na, *v. a.* To rend, tear, split, slit, rip, cleave, saw, harrow.

चीरा chée-ra, *s. m.* Incision, cut, wound, slit; virginity; a turband. *Cheera ootarna, v. a.* To deflower. *Cheera-bund,* A virgin.

चीरी chee-rée, *s. f.* The ends or hem of a garment.

चीरेता chee-ry-ta, *s. m.* The Gentian plant (*Gentiana Cherayta*).

चील cheel, *s. f.* A kite (*Falco cheela*). *Cheel jhuputta marna,* To snatch.

चीलर chée-lur, } *s. f.* A louse.
चीलहर cheel-húr, }

चीवर chée-vur, *s. m.* The tattered dress of a *Bouddh* mendicant, or of any mendicant.

चीवरिन chée-vur-in, *s. m.* A *Bouddh* or *Jyn* mendicant.

चुआन choo-án, *s. f.* A reservoir, a cistern. *Chooan-khaee, s. f.* A deep ditch with water springing at the bottom.

चूंगी chóon-gee, *s. f.* A tax gathered daily from grain merchants, being as much grain as a man can grasp in his hand.

चूंचूना chóon-choo-na, *s. m.* Ascarides.

चूंधला chóondh-la, *s. m.* Blinkard. *Choondh-lana, v. n.* To be purblind, to see dimly.

चूंधा chóon-dha, *adj.* Blinkard; bad (*as a hand-writing*).

चुकती chóok-tee, *s. f.* Settlement.

चुकना chóok-na, *v. n.* To be finished, to be completed, to be fixed; to be agreed upon, to be adjusted.

चुकाई choo-káee, *s. f.* A task, agreement, adjustment, decision. *Chookaee dena,* To escape one's notice, to give one the slip.

चुकाना choo-ká-na, *v. a.* To finish, complete, settle, adjust; to fix the price of.

चुकौता choo-kóu-ta, *s. m.* A task, agreement, adjustment, decision, settlement.

चुकड़ chook-kúr, *s. m.* A small tank or pit, a shallow hole with water in it.

चुकार chook-kár, *s. m.* The roaring of a lion.

चुकी chóok-kee, *s. f.* Deceit, fraud. *Chook-kee dena, v. a.* To deceive, to play tricks.

चुक्र chookr, *s. m.* Sorrel; sourness; acid seasoning.

चुक्रिका chóo-kri-ka, *s. f.* Wood sorrel (*Oxalis monodelpha*), according to other authorities (*Rumex vesicarius*).

चुगन chóo-gun, *s. f.* A plait or fold in a garment.

चुगना chóog-na, *v. n.* To peck, to pick up food with the beak, to pick up food, to feed. *Choog lena, v. a.* To select, choose, cull.

चुगाना choo-gá-na, *v. a.* To cause to peck or pick up food with the beak.

चुंगी chóon-gee, *s. f.* A tax gathered daily from grain merchants, being as much grain as a man can grasp in his hand.

चुचकारना chooch-kár-na, *v. n.* To fondle, to chirp to, to cheer by making the noise occasioned by drawing in the breath with lips protruded.

चुचकारी chooch-ká-ree, *s. f.* Blandishment.

चुचाना choo-chá-na, *v. n.* To drop, to be drenched with water, to be dripping wet with sweat, water, &c.   [bosom.

चुचि chóochi, *s. m.* The female breast or

चुचचूर chooch-chúr, *s. m.* Large breasts.

चुटकी chóot-kee, *s. f.* A pinch; snapping of the fingers; the hammer of a gun; a mode of printing cloth or *goolbudun*; an ornament worn on the toes. *Chootkee bhurna,* or, —*lena,* To nip, to pinch; to throw out provoking insinuations. *Chootkiyon men oorana,* To put one off with a joke.

चुटकुला choot-kóo-la, *s. m.* Pleasantry, facetiousness, wit, humor; conondrum. *Choot-koola-sa, adj.* Amusing.

चूट्ला chóot-la, *s. m.* A cue or lock of hair worn behind.

चूटाना choo-tá-na,
चूटालना choo-tál-na, } *v. a.* To wound.

चूटिया chóo-ti-ya, *s. m.* A spy to thieves, the head of a gang of thieves. *s. f.* A lock of hair left on the head when the rest is shaved.

चुटियाना choo-ti-yána, *v. a.* To wound.

चूटीला choo-tée-la, *adj.* Wounded, bruised, stricken.

चूर choor, *s. f.* An imitative sound.

चूरूआ chóo-roo-a, *s. m.* A dish prepared from parched rice.

चूरैल choo-ryl, *s. f.* The ghost of a woman who died while pregnant; a hag, a fury; a dirty woman, slut, slattern.

चूनचूना chóon-choon-a, *s. m.*
चूनचूनी chóon-choo-nee, *s. f.* } Ascarides.

चूनट chóo-nut, *s. f.* Plaiting (*cloths*), plaits.

चूनन chóo-nun, *s. m.* Rumple, crease.

चूनरी chóon-ree, *s. f.* A mode of dying cloths, in which they are tied in different places previous to dipping them in the dye, so as to prevent the parts tied from receiving the colour, also, cloths dyed in this manner.

चूनवाना choon-wá-na,
चूनाना choo-ná-na, } *v. a.* To cause to pick, choose, select, arrange, put in order, &c. *Choona lena, v. a.* To plait (*cloth*); to kill by building a person into a wall.

चूनावट choo-ná-wut, *s. f.* A plait, plaiting.

चूनौटा choo-nóu-ta, *s. m.* A box for holding the lime used to chew along with betel; the folding of the cloth called *saree*, worn by women.

चूनौटी choo-nóu-tee, *s. f.* A small box for holding the lime used to chew along with betel; a small spoon used to take out the lime; encouraging troops in the time of battle (*for which purpose there is an officer in Indian armies*); selecting from an army the fittest men for a desperate enterprize; a practice which formerly prevailed at *Benaras*, (*on the 11th of Jeth, shookl puksh, the inhabitants were wont to swim across the river, and forming themselves into two parties, to fight with swords, clubs, &c.*)

चूंदी chóon-dee, *s. f.* A procuress, a bawd.

चूंधला chóondh-la, *adj.* Blinkard.

चूंधलाना choondh-lá-na, *v. n.* To be purblind, to see dimly.

चूंधा chóon-dha, *adj.* Dim, purblind, dim-sighted.

चूनना chóon-na, *v. a.* To gather, pick, choose, select, cull; to pick up food (*as birds*); to place in order, arrange; to plait (*cloth*). *s. m.*

Ascarides. *Durwasa choonna,* To close a door with bricks. [rides.

चूनी chóon-nee, *s. f.* A small ruby; asca-

चूप choop, *adj.* Silent. *interj.* Silence! (*the word ruh being understood*). *s. f.* Silence, as *Choop lugnee*, or *Choopkee lugnee, v. n.* To be struck dumb.

चूपका chóop-ka, *adj.* Silent.

चूपकी chóop-kee, *s. f.* Silence.

चूपचाप choop-cháp,
चूपाचूप choop-a-chóop, } *adj.* Silent. *adv.* Furtively, by stealth, silently.

चूपचूपाना choop-choo-pána, *v. n.* To keep silence. *Choop-choopateh, adv.* Silently, secretly.

चूपूरना choo-púr-na, *v. a.* To varnish, cover, smooth, anoint; palliate, besmear.

चूपरा choopra, *adj.* Plausible though false.

चूपरी chóop-ree, *adj. f.* Oiled, greasy; smooth, plausible. *Choopree bat, s. f.* Flattery, soft words. *Choopree rotee, s. f.* Cakes rich with clarified butter.

चूपी chóop-pee, *s. f.* Silence.

चूभकी chóobh-kee, *s. f.* A plunge in water, dip.

चूभना chóobh-na, *v. n.* To be stuck or thrust into, to pierce, to be pricked, pierced, goaded, stabbed, to penetrate.

चूभाना choo-bhá-na, *v. a.* To stick into, thrust into, pierce, goad, stab, prick.

चूमा chóo-ma,
चूमा chóo-ma, } *s. m.* A kiss. *Chooma-chatee, s. f.* Dalliance.

चूमाना choo-má-na, *v. a.* To cause to kiss.

चूमकार choom-kár, *s. m.*
चूमकारी choom-ká-ree, *s. f.* } A sound with the lips by which dogs and horses are called.

चूमकारना choom-kár-na, *v. a.* To coax, speak kindly to, soothe (*by drawing in the breath with protruded lips*).

चूमबुक chóom-buk, *s. m.* A kisser, a lecher; a rogue, a cheat; the loadstone, a magnet; extract (*from a book &c.*); a general scholar, one who knows parts in a variety of books; the upper part or middle of a balance.

चूमबन chóom-bun, *s. m.* Kissing; a kiss.

चूममुक choom-muk, *s. m.* The load-stone.

चूरकी chóor-kee, *s. f.* Lock of hair.

चूरकूट chóor-koot, *s. m.* Powder.

चूरुगना choo-rúg-na, *v. n.* To chirp; to prate, to prattle.

चूरचूरा chóor-choo-ra, *adj.* Crisp, acrid.

चूरमूरा chóor-moo-ra, *s. m.* An imitative sound.

चूराना choo-rá-na, *v. a.* To steal, filch, rob.

चुरी chóo-ree, *s. f.* Bangles or rings made of glass, &c., and worn on the wrist ; a kind of bracelet ; a small well.

चुरगना chóo-roog-na, *v. n.* To gabble, to prattle.

चुर्त choort, *s. f.* Nap, drowsiness, nodding.

चुरी chóor-ree, *s. f.* Dregs.

चुल chool, *s. f.* Itching, scratching.

चुलचुल chóol-chool, *s. m.* Wantonness, inconstancy.

चुलचुलाना chool-choo-lána, *v. n.* To itch, to titillate.

चुलचुली chool-chóo-lee, *s. f.* Wantonness, inconstancy.

चुलबुला chóol-boo-la, *adj.* Restless, fidgetting ; airy, gay.

चुलबुलाना chool-boo-lána, *v. n.* To be restless, to be agog, to fidget, to be fidgetty.

चुलबुलापन chool-boo-lápun, *s. m.* Gaiety.

चुलबुलाहट chool-boo-láhut, *s. f.* Restlessness ; gaiety.

चुलबुलिया chool-boo-líya, *adj.* Restless, fidgetting ; airy, gay. [drip.

चुलाना choolána, *v. a.* To distil, cause to

चुलाव choo-láo, *s. m.* A kind of dish.

चुल chooll, *s. m.* A blear eye.

चुला chóol-la, *adj.* Blear-eyed.

चुली chóol-lee, *s. f.* A fire-place, a chimney.

चुलू chóol-loo, *s. m.* A handful, the palm of the hand contracted so as to hold water. *Chool-loo-bhur panee men doob murna* (*lit. to drown one's self in a handful of water*), To be greatly ashamed. *Choolloo choolloo sadhna*, To get a habit of drinking by gradual increase. *Choolloo men coolloo hona*, To be intoxicated with a mouthful.

चुलहाई chool-háee, *adj. f.* Lewd, libidinous (*woman*).

चुलहारा chool-hára, *adj. m.* Lascivious, lewd.

चुसकना choo-súk-na, *v. n.* To throb.

चुसकी chóos-kee, *s. f.* A mouthful of drink.

चुसकर choo-súk-kur, *s. m.* One in the habit of sucking (*met. a tippler*).

चुसनी chóos-nee, *s. f.* A child's coral.

चुसी chóos-see, *s. f.* The juice of fruits.

चुहचुह chóoh-choo-ha, *adj.* Deeply-coloured.

चुहचुहाना chooh-choo-hána, *v. n.* To glow as a colour, to die a deep colour, to blush (a flower).

चुहल chóo-hul, *s. f.* Mention ; cheer, jollity, mirth, merriment, festivity. *Choohul kurna*, To carol, to make merry.

चुहला chóoh-la, *s. m.* A large wooden peg, a tent-pin.

चुहली chóoh-lee, *adj.* Comic.

चुहिया choohiya, *s. m.* A little mouse.

चूंगी chóongee, *s. f.* Toll, tax, duty.

चूंचुहाट choon-chuhát, *s. f.* Singing of birds.

चूंची chóon-chee, *s. f.* Breast, bubby, dug, nipple.

चूंटा chóon-ta, *s. m.* A large ant.

चूंटी chóon-tee, *s. f.* A small ant.

चूंथना chóonth-na, *v. a.* To gather (a flower), to claw, pinch.

चूंधला chóondh-la, } *adj.* Dim, purblind,
चूंधा chóon-dha, } dim-sighted.

चूंमा chóon-ma, *part. pass.* Kissed.

चूआन choo-án, *s. f.* A reservoir, a cistern. *Chooan-khaee, s. f.* A deep ditch with water springing at the bottom.

चूक chook, *s. f.* An error, fault, inadvertency, blunder, mistake, failing, miss. *adj.* Sour, acid. *s. m.* A medicine made of boiled lemon juice and pomegranates.

चूकना chóok-na, *v. n.* To blunder, mistake, depart from, err, miss, fail, miscarry.

चूका chóo-ka, *s. m.* A kind of sorrel (*Rumex vesicarius*) ; a kind of earthen pot.

चूख chookh, *s. m.* A medicine, orris-root, orrice, or iris-root.

चूची chóo-chee, *s. f.* Breast, pap, nipple, teat, dug.

चूट choot, *s. m.* A crack, a noise.

चूर choor, *s. m.* A silver or gold ornament worn by *Hindoo* widows ; the ring fastened to elephants' teeth.

चूरा chóo-ra, *s. f.* A single lock of hair left on the crown of the head at the ceremony of tonsure ; a peacock's crest ; any crest, plume, diadem, &c. ; the head ; top, summit ; a kind of bracelet. *s. m.* The rings fastened to elephants' teeth ; a kind of food made of parched rice.

चूरामनि chóora-mún-i, *s. m.* A jewel worn in a crest, or a diadem ; the *Goonja* (*Abrus precatorius*).

चूराला choo-rála, *s. f.* A kind of grass (*Kyllinga monocephala*). *adj.* Crested, having a lock of hair on the crown of the head.

चूरावत choo-ra-wút, *adj.* Crested, having a lock of hair, &c. on the top of the head.

चूरी chóo-ree, *s. f.* Bangles or rings made of glass, &c. and worn on the wrist. *Chooreedar, Drawers, or sleeves, made too long, so as to be crumpled into plaits.

चून choon, *s. m.* Flour ; lime.

चूतड़ chóo-tur, *s. m.* The backside, bum, buttock, hip, rump. *Chootur bujana,* To be overjoyed. *Chootur sukorna,* To loiter, to hang back. *Chootur seh kan ganthna,* To speak equivocally, to use far-fetched expressions.

चून choon, *s. m.* Flour ; lime.

चूना chóo-na, *v. n.* To leak, drop, distil, to be filtered, to ooze, exude ; to drop from the tree when ripe (*fruit*). *s. m.* Lime. *Choona-pusnee, s. f.* A dancing girl. *Choona lugana,* To defame.

चूनी chóo-nee, *s. f.* Pulse split or ground very coarsely ; a spark or small ruby or other gem.

चूपड़ chóo-pur, *s. m.* Grease.

चूपड़ी chóop-ree, *adj. f.* Oiled, greasy, smooth, plausible. *Choopree bat, s. f.* Flattery, soft words. *Choopree rotee, s. f.* Cakes rich with clarified butter.

चूभ choobh, *s. m.* Prick, puncture.

चूमकपत्थर chóomuk-putthúr, *s. m.* A magnet.

चूमन chóomun, *s. m.* Kissing.

चूमना chóom-na, *v. a.* To kiss.

चूमा chóo-ma, *s. m.* A kiss. *Chooma-chatee, s. f.* Dalliance.

चूर choor, *s. m.* Powder, filings, atoms. *adj.* Bruised. *Choor-choor, adj.* Broken to atoms. *Choor ruhna,* To sot. *Choor kurna,* To break into small pieces, to shatter. *Choor hona,* To be broken into small pieces ; to be enamoured of, to be in love, to dote ; to be tired. *Nusheh men choor hona,* To be intoxicated.

चूरन chóo-run, *s. m.* A powder composed of medicines for promoting digestion.

चूरा chóo-ra, *s. m.* Filings ; saw-dust ; grain reduced to coarse particles to be chucked into the mouth.

चूरी chóo-ree, *s. f.* A bread rich with clarified butter ; a bracelet.

चूर्ण choorn, *s. m.* Powder, dust, any pulverulent or minute division of substance ; fossile alkali, efflorescent salt ; aromatic powder, pounded sandal, &c.

चूर्णकुन्तल choorn-kóon-tul, *s. m.* A lock of hair, a curl or curling hair.

चूर्णखण्ड choorn-khúnd, *s. m.* Pebble, gravel, hardened fragments of earth, or brick ; limestone nodule, commonly known in India by the name of *Kunkur.*

चूरना chóor-na, *v. a.* To reduce to very small pieces or to atoms.

चूरमा chóor-ma, *s. m.* A kind of sweetmeat made of sugar and crumbled bread.

चूल chool, *s. f.* A tenon, the part of a joiner's work which fits into another (*as a dovetail*);

a pivot upon which a door turns (*as on a hinge*); an axle-tree arm. *Choolen ookhurna,* or, —*dheelee hona,* To be tired, worn out with labour.

चूला chóo-la, *s. f.* A crest.

चूल्हा chóol-ha, *s. m.*
चूल्ही chóol-hee, *s. f.* } A fire-place.

चूव्ना chóov-na, *v. n.* To drop, to leak, to ooze, to exude.

चूस्ना chóos-na, *v. a.* To suck.

चूसनी chóos-nee, *s. f.* Child's coral, a sucking stick for children.

चूहड़ choo-húr, *s. m.* The act of hunting by deceiving game with a stalking horse.

चूहरा chóoh-ra, *s. m.* A *Hindoo* sweeper.

चूहरी chóoh-ree, *s. m.* The wife of a *Choohra,* a *Hindoo* sweeper-woman.

चूहना chóoh-na, *v. a.* To suck.

चूहा chóo-ha, *s. m.* A rat, a mouse. *Chooheh-dan, s. m.* A mouse-trap. *Chooheh-mar, s. m.* A sparrow-hawk, cormorant, a mouser.

चूही chóo-hee, *s. f.* A mouse.

चेंचपेंच chench-pench, *s. m.* Brats.

चेंची chén-chee, *s. f.* A needle-case.

चेंचेंकरना chen-chen-kúrna, *v. n.* To chatter, chirp, murmur, grumble, squeak.

चेंरा chén-ra, *adj.* Young, little.

चेंप chenp, *s. m.* The acrid resin of fruits and trees.

चेट chet, *s. m.* A servant, a slave.

चेटक chét-uk, *s. f.* A miracle ; a deception.

चेटी chét-ee, *s. f.* A female servant.

चेरा chér-a, *s. m.* A servant.

चेरी chér-ee, *s. f.* A female servant or slave.

चेत chet, *s. m.* Memory, remembrance, thought, perception, consciousness ; circumspection.

चेतन chét-un, *adj.* Alive, living, feeling. *s. m.* Reason, rationality, caution ; soul, self ; understanding, intelligence, wisdom, reflexion.

चेतना chét-na, *v. a.* To remember, think of, advise, reflect, be aware, perceive ; to recover the senses, to be roused. *s. f.* Action.

चेता chét-a, *s. m.* An admonisher.

चेना chén-a, *s. m.* Millet (*Panicum Italicum*).

चेपना chép-na, *v. a.* To stick together.

चेराई cher-áee, *s. f.* Slavery.

चेरायता cher-áyuta, *s. m.* The Gentian plant (*Gentiana Cherayta*).

चेरी chér-ee, *s. f.* A female servant, a slave-girl.

चेला chél-a, *s. m.* A slave brought up in the house ; a pupil, a disciple ; a servant.

चेली chél-ee, *s. f.* A slave girl, a female servant.

चेवली chéo-lee, *s. f.* Silk (*cloth*).

चेष्टा chésh-ta, *s. f.* Application, endeavour, effort, exertion, motion, exercise, search, appearance, bodily act or function.

चेंटा chynta, *s. m.* Black ant.

चेत chyt, *s. m.* The twelfth *Hindoo* month (*March-April*).

चैतन्य chy-tún-yuh, *s. m.* Soul, spirit, the Deity considered as the essence of all being ; reason, understanding, caution, perception, the possession of the proper use of the faculties ; an animal or sentient being. *adj.* In possession of the senses, awake, rational, sensitive, cautious, attentive, aware, perceiving.

चैत्र chytr, *s. m.* The twelfth *Hindoo* month (*March-April*).

चैन chyn, *s. m.* Ease, relief, repose, tranquillity ; denying a bet in gaming, imposture.

चैना chy-na, *s. m.* A kind of corn.

चैला chy-la, *s. m.* A billet of wood cut for burning, &c.

चोंकना chónk-na, *v. a.* To prick, pierce.

चोंगला chóng-la, *s. m.* A joint of bamboo used to send letters in.

चोंगा chón-ga, *s. m.* A funnel.

चोंच chonch, *s. f.* Beak, bill ; a point.

चोंचला chónch-la, *s. m.* Playfulness, blandishments, endearing arts and expressions, coquetry, toyishness.

चोंटला chónt-la, *s. m.* The ribbon with which hair is tied or braided at the end, the cue or lock of hair behind ; false hair mixed with the real.

चोंटी chón-tee, *s. f.* The hair braided behind (*tail*), braid, cue ; top, apex, summit, pinnacle ; an ornament worn on the head by women. *Chontee asman-pur ghisna,* To be very vain or aspiring. *Chontee-kut,* A slave. *Chontee kutwana,* To be a slave, to be obedient. *Chontee kissee-kee hath men ana,* To have a power over one, to subdue.

चोंडा chón-da, *s. m.* The head ; hair braided on the top of the head.

चोंथना chónth-na, *v. a.* To scratch, to claw.

चोंधलाना chondh-lá-na, *v. n.* To be purblind, to see dimly.

चोंधी chón-dhee, *s. f.* Dimness, dulness of sight.

चोंप chomp, } *s. f.* Wish, desire, fondness ; alacrity, avidity ;
चोंप choump, } a gold ornament worn on the front teeth.

चोआ chó-a, *s. m.* A perfume ; the pod or skin of any kind of pulse ; a wind-fall (*fruit*).

चोआर cho-ár, *s. m.* A mountain robber, a mountaineer and outlaw.

चोआन cho-án, *s. f.* Dropping, dripping.

चोआना cho-á-na, *v. a.* To cause to drip, to distil, drop, filter, draw off.

चोकुर chó-kur, *s. m.* Husk of wheat, bran.

चोख chokh, *adj.* Sharp, pungent, keen. *s. m.* A medicine, orris-root.

चोखा chó-kha, *adj.* Pure, unadulterated, genuine, neat, good, choice, fine, sharp, pungent, keen ; clever, dexterous ; pleasing, delightful, beautiful.

चोखाई cho-khá-ee, *s. f.* Purity, sharpness.

चोखी chó-khee, *adj. f.* Sharp (*tone in music*).

चोगा chó-ga, *s. m.* Food of birds brought up from the crop ; food of birds in general. *Choga budulna,* To bill, caress as doves by joining bills.

चोंगा chón-ga, *s. m.* A funnel.

चोचला chóch-la, *s. m.* Playfulness, blandishments, endearing arts and expressions, coquetry, toyishness.

चोज choj, *s. m.* Subtileness, beauty.

चोजी chó-jee, *adj.* Subtile.

चोट chot, *s. f.* A hurt, bruise, blow, damage ; fall ; spite ; effort, attempt, assiduity ; desire, wish, aim. *Chot-pur chot,* One misfortune follows another, misfortunes come not singly. *Chot-bandhna,* To defend ; to bind up the edge of a sword, &c. ; to restrain by magic. *Chot khana,* To be hurt, to receive a blow ; to suffer loss.

चोटा chó-ta, *s. m.* Discount or premium independent of interest ; treacle.

चोटियाना cho-ti-yána, *v. a.* To seize by the hair.

चोटी chó-tee, *s. f.* A lock of hair left on the top of the head, the plait or tie of hair behind, a cue ; top, summit, summit of a hill ; a petticoat. *Chotee ka hona,* To excel, to be pre-eminent or unrivalled.

चोट्टा chót-ta, *s. m.* A thief.

चोर chor, *s. m.* A bodice or jacket.

चोथ choth, *s. m.* Cow-dung.

चोंधला chóndh-la, *adj.* Blinkard.

चोंधलाना chondh-lána, *v. n.* To be purblind, to see dimly.

चोंधी chón-dhee, *s. f.* Dimness, dulness of sight.

चोप chop, *s. f.* Desire, wish, hope.

चोभा chobhá, *s. m.* A nail ; a kind of victuals given upon great occasion, marriages, &c. ; prey ; puncture.

चोया chó-ya, *s. m.* Husk of grain ; the scale of a fish ; a hole dug in the sandy bed of a river which has dried, in which water is found.

चोर chor, *s. m.* A thief, a robber. *Chor-baloo, s. f.* A quicksand. *Chor-chukar, s. m.* A thief. *Chor-khana, s. m.* By-room, concealed drawer. *Chor-durwaza, s. m.* Trap-door. *Chor-dhor, s. m.* Plaintiff and defendant ; all the parties of a lawsuit ; a thief and what he has stolen. *Chor-sumeen,* A quagmire, bog. *Chor-seerhee, s. f.* Back-stairs. *Chor-khirkee, s. f.* A back-door, a by-door. *Chor-gulee, s. f.* A by-road, back-lane. *Chor lugna, v. n.* To be injured, to be damaged. *Chor lugna shuma-ko,* To waste a candle by a thief being attached to it. *Chor-muhull, s. m.* The apartments of the concubines of great men. *Chor-mundoora, s. m.* A game played by children. *Chor-muheechnee, s. f.* Hide and seek.

चोरपूसपी chor-póospee, *s. f.* A kind of grass (*Andropogon aciculatum*).

चोराना cho-rá-na, *v. a.* To steal.

चोरी chó-ree, *s. f.* Theft, roguery, robbery, stealth. *Choree-choree, adv.* By stealth, clandestinely.

चोला chó-la, *s. m.* A bodice, a garment worn by a bride at her marriage, a waistcoat, the body of a gown, a jacket ; a small betel-basket ; a country, the modern *Tanjore,* the name is also supposed to apply to a part of *Beerbhoom* in Bengal.

चोली chó-lee, *s. f.* A bodice, a waistcoat, the body of a gown, a jacket ; a small betel-basket.

चोवा chó-wa, *s. m.* A perfume ; the pod or skin of any kind of pulse ; a wind-fall (*fruit*).

चोष्य chósh-yuh, *adj.* Any thing (*fruit especially*) capable of being sucked, as a mango, &c.

चोहुरनीचला chóhur-néechla, *s. m.* The lower jaw.

चोहला chóh-la, *s. m.* A large peg or pin.

चौ chou, *s. m.* A back-tooth ; ploughshare. *adj.* (in compos.) Four. *Chou-bughla, s. m.* A kind of jacket not open under the arms. *Chou-bundee, s. f.* Giving a horse new shoes ; the fastenings of baggage. *Chou-bheer, adv.* On all sides, all round. *Chou-paruh, adj.* Four-pieced. *Chou-pas, adv.* All round, around. *Chou-puhul, adj.* Four-sided. *Chou-tuh, adj.* Of four folds. *Chou-joogee, adj.* Of the four ages or great (*Hindoo*) periods of the world. *Chou-muhulla, adj.* Of four stories (*a house,* &c.) *Chou-mookhee, adj.* Four-faced, having four faces. *Chou-mekha,* Tying the elbows behind.

चौअन्नी chóu-unnee, *s. f.* A (*silver*) four-anna piece, a quarter rupee.

चौंक chounk *s. f.* The act of starting, start.

चौंकना chóunk-na, *v. n.* To start, boggle, start up from sleep. *Chounk oothna,* To start, to wince. *Chounk purna,* To bounce, start up.

चौंकेल choun-kél, *s. m.* An untamed animal, a boggler.

चौंगा choún-ga, *s. m.* Wheedling. *Chounga kurna,* To wheedle out of money.

चौंगी choún-gee, *s. f.* Wheedling. *Choungee-baz, s. m.* A wheedler. *Chounges-bazee, s. f.* Sharping, &c.

चौंडू choún-doo, *s. m.* A blockhead.

चौंतरा choún-tur-a, *s. m.* A terrace or mound to sit and converse on ; a custom-house ; a police-office.

चौंतीस choun-tées, *adj.* Thirty-four.

चौंधियाना choun-dhi-yána, *v. n.* To be confused, frightened out of one's senses, amazed, dazzled or astonished.

चौंरा choún-ra, *s. m.* An apartment under ground for grain.

चौंरी choún-ree, *s. f.* An instrument for driving away flies, a fly-flapper.

चौंसर choún-sur, *s. m.* A game ; a garland of flowers.

चौक chouk, *s. m.* A market ; a square of a city ; a court-yard ; a square place filled, at marriages and on other occasions of rejoicings, with sweetmeats, which after certain ceremonies are distributed. *Chouk-bhurna,* or *Chouk-poorna,* To fill a *Chouk* or square place with sweetmeats on some occasion of rejoicing. *Chouk-putta,* A seat on which the people sit and eat in the *chouka.*

चौकुर chou-kúr, *adj.* Good, well, fine, excellent.

चौकुरा choú-kura, *s. m.* A ring of two pearls worn in each ear.

चौकुरी choú-kur-ee, *s. f.* A bound, a spring, a bounce ; a ring of pearls worn in the ear by men. *Choukuree bhurna,* To leap, bound, bounce. *Choukuree bhoolna,* To forget one's bound, i. e. to be fascinated, to have one's senses benumbed. *Choukuree mar bythna,* To squat.

चौकुन्ना chou-kún-na, *adj.* Cautious, alert, circumspect, sly, on one's guard, wary.

चौकस choú-kus, *adj.* Cautious, watchful, accurate, diligent, active, clever, alert, circumspect, intelligent ; full weight.

चौकसाई chou-kus-áee, *s. f.* Attention, circumspection, watchfulness, alertness, caution.

चौकसी choú-kus-ee, *s. f.* Watching, diligence, attention ; four people employed together, or eating out of the same dish or plate.

चौका choú-ka, *s. m.* The space in which *Hindoos* cook or eat their victuals ; a square slate of marble, &c. ; a square space of ground ; the four front teeth ; the cube of a measure called *bans.*

चौकी chóu-kee, *s. f.* A frame to sit on, stool, bench, chair; guard or watch; watching; the post where a guard is stationed; an ornament worn on the breast. *Choukeedar, adj.* Keeping guard. *s. m.* A watchman. *Choukeedaree, s. f.* The business of a watchman; the pay or hire of a watchman. *Choukee marna,* To smuggle. *Choukee dena,* To watch, guard, mount guard.

चौकोना chou-kó-na, } *adj.* Four-cornered,
चौकोर chou-kór,   } square.

चौखट chóu-khut, *s. m. f.* Frame of a door; the upper and lower piece of the frame of a door.

चौखी chóu-khee, *adj. f.* Sharp (*tone in music*).

चौखूंटा chou-khóon-ta, *adj.* Square.

चौगरा chou-gúr-a, *s. m.* A rabbit, hare.

चौगुन chou-gá-nub, *adj.* Quadruple, four-fold.

चौगान chou-gán, *s. m.* A game resembling cricket (*or tennis*) but played on horse-back; the bat or club with which the game is played, a mall, a plain. *Chougan-gah,* A place for that game. *Chougan-basee, s. f.* Playing of the game of *chougan.*

चौगानी chou-gá-nee, *s. f.* A straight *hookka-*snake or tube for smoking through.

चौगुना chóu-goo-na, *adj.* Four-fold, quadruple.

चौघरा chóu-ghur-a, *s.* A small box of gold or silver with four partitions for holding perfumes.

चौर chour, *adj.* Spoiled, destroyed.

चौरचौपट chour-chóu-put, *adj.* Abandoned, vicious; damaged.

चौरा chóu-ra, *adj.* Wide, broad. *Chourachukla, adj.* Extensive, spacious.

चौराई chou-rá-ee, *s. f.* Breadth, extent, width, extension; boasting. *Chouraee marna,* or, —*kurna,* To boast, to give one's self airs.

चौरान chou-rán, *s. m. f.* Width, breadth.

चौराना chou-rá-na, *v. a.* To increase in breadth, expand, widen.

चौडोल chou-dól, *s. m.* A kind of sedan with two poles.

चौतरका chou-túr-ka, *s. m.* A mitre; a kind of tent.

चौतरा chou-túr-a, *s. m.* A terrace or mound to sit and converse on.

चौतारा chou-tá-ra, *s. m.* A four-stringed musical instrument.

चौताल chou-tál, *s. m.* A mode in music.

चौतीया chou-tee-ya, *s. f.* A quartan (*ague*).

चौथ chouth, *s. f.* The fourth lunar day; the fourth part; hence, tribute (*collected by the Mahrattas*).

चौथा chóu-tha, *adj.* Fourth. *Choutheh, adv.* In the fourth place, fourthly.

चौथाई chou-thá-ee, *s. f.* The fourth part, a quarter.

चौथिया chóu-thi-ya, *s. m.* One who receives the *chouth* (*a tribute*); a quartan ague.

चौथी chóu-thee, *s. f.* The fourth day; a ceremony performed on the fourth day after marriage.

चौदंत chou-dúnt, *adj.* Crossing their teeth in fight (*elephants*); sturdy, robust, stout.

चौदंती chou-dún-tee, *s. f.* Boldness.

चौदस chóu-dus, *s. f.* The fourteenth day of the lunar fortnight.

चौदह chóu-duh, *adj.* Fourteen. *Choudhwan, adj.* Fourteenth.

चौदानिया chou-dá-niya, *s. m.* } An orna-
चौदानी chou-dá-nee, *s. f.* } ment (*formed of four pearls*) worn in the ears.

चौधर chou-dhúr, *adj.* Robust, active, vigorous, corpulent.

चौधराई chou-dhur-áee, *s. f.* The business of a *Choudhuree* (*the headman of a trade*).

चौधरी chóu-dhur-ee, *s. m.* The headman of a trade. (*In Bengal, a title of landholders superior to Tuallookdar*).

चौपट chóu-put, *adj.* Ruined, destroyed, levelled, flat, plain. *Chouput kurna,* To level, destroy.

चौपड़ chóu-pur, *s. f.* The name of a game played with oblong dice; the cloth on which it is played.

चौपती chou-pút-tee, } *s. f.* A small tract,
चौपत्री chou-pút-ree, } an essay, a pamphlet, a pocket-book. [sedan.

चौपहला chou-púh-la, *s. m.* A kind of

चौपा chóupa, *adj.* Four-footed.

चौपाई chou-páee, *s. f.* A sort of metre or verse consisting of four feet (*pud*) or lines.

चौपार chou-pár, *s. m.* A kind of summer-house or pavilion (*generally built jointly by several people as a resting place common to them all*); a quadruped, an animal, a beast.

चौपाला chou-pá-la, *s. m.* A litter, a sedan.

चौपायुह chou-páyuh, *s. m.* An animal, a beast, a quadruped.

चौबर chou-búr, *adj.* Stout, robust, bold.

चौबार chou-bár, *s. m.* Summer-house, an assembly, court, town-hall.

चौबारा chou-bá-ra, *s. m.* A shed.

चौबीस chou-bées, *adj.* Twenty-four.

चौबे chóu-beh, *s. m.* A *Brahmun* acquainted with the four *Veds* (*now, however, the term is applied to the descendants of such though not learned*).

चौमासा chou-má-sa, *s. m.* The rainy season.

चौमुख chóu-mookh, *s. m.* A lamp-stand with partitions; a name of *Bruhma*.

चौमुखा chou-moo-kha, *adj.* Having four burners, &c. (*a lamp*). *s. m.* A lamp-stand with four partitions; a kind of *puta* or wooden scimitar for fencing with.

चौमुखी chóu-moo-khee, *s. f.* Name of a *Hindoo* goddess; the seed of a tree called *Roodraksh* (*Scævola lobelia*, or, *Elæocarpus ganitrus*).

चौरंग chou-rúng, *s. m.* A practice of the sword exercise; cutting the four legs of an animal off at one blow. *Chourung katna, v. a.* To cut off the four legs of an animal at one blow. *Chourung marna,* To lose the use of the limbs by illness.

चौरस chóu-rus, *adj.* Level, even.

चौरसाई chou-rus-áee, *s. f.* Equality of surface, evenness, levelness.

चौरसाना chou-rus-ána, *v. a.* To level.

चौरा chóu-ra, *s. m.* A terrace or mound to sit and converse on; the place where *Hindoo* women are burned (*more properly, where the living widow or sutee is immolated*).

चौरान्वे chou-rán-weh, *adj.* Ninety-four.

चौरासी chou-rá-see, *adj.* Eighty-four. *s. f.* Morris-bells worn on the ankles by dancing girls.

चौराहा chou-rá-ha, *s. m.* A cross road.

चौरी chóu-ree, *s. f.* A summer house.

चौलकर्म chóul-kurmm, *s. m.* The ceremony of tonsure, cutting off all the hair from the head of a child three years old except one lock on the crown.

चौलुरा chou-lúr-a, *s. m.* } A necklace of
चौलुरी chou-lúr-ee, *s. f.* } four strings.

चौलाई chou-láee, *s. f.* A kind of greens (*Amaranthus polygamus*).

चौवन chouwún, *adj.* Fifty-four.

चौवा chóu-wa, *s. m.* A quadruped (*particularly oxen*); a handbreadth.

चौवाई chou-wáee, *s. f.* A tempest, hurricane, commotion (*q. d. wind blowing from four quarters*).

चौस chous, *s. m.* Flour, powder.

चौसठ chóu-suth, *adj.* Sixty-four.

चौसर chóu-sur, *s. m.* The name of a game played with oblong dice, or what the game is played on.

चौहट्टा chou-hútta, *s. m.* A place where four streets meet.

चौहत्तर chou-húttur, *adj.* Seventy-four.

चौहान chou-hán, *s. m.* A cast of *Rajpoots.*

च्युत chyoot, *adj.* Fallen, dropped, oozed out; fallen from or off; deviated from, erred, strayed.

छ

छ chhub, The seventh consonant in the *Naguree* alphabet. Its sound is expressed by *chh. adj.* Six. *Chhuh-sat, s. m.* Trick, cheat, juggle.

छुई chhuee, *s. f.* Pulmonary consumption; a thatched roof on a boat; a stuffed pad to prevent bullocks being hurt when loaded. *adj.* Abolished.

छंकाना chhun-ká-na, *v. a.* To concentrate, to cause to strain.

छंकाहट chhun-ká-hut, *s. f.* Concentration, causing to strain.

छंछाना chhun-chhun-ána, *v. n.* To simmer; to sound; to smart, to pain.

छंटना chhúnt-na, *v. n.* To grow thin; to diminish; to be extracted or separated.

छंटवाना chhunt-wá-na, *v. n.* To cause to clean rice; to cause to select, prune, lop, clip.

छंटाई chhun-táee, *s. f.* Cleaning or separating (*grain, &c.*); the price paid for cleaning.

छंटाव chhun-táo, *s. m.* Detachment on forage; beating rice to clear it from the husk.

छंहाई chhun-háee, *s. f.* Shadiness.

छकरा chhúk-ra, *s. m.* A kind of carriage, a cart, car.

छकराना chhuk-rá-na, *v. a.* To slap, to cuff.

छकना chhúk-na, *v. n.* To be content, satiated, gratified; to be afflicted, harassed; astonished. *Chhuk jana,* To be satisfied or satiated.

छकाई chhuk-áee, *s. f.* Satiety.

छकाना chhuk-ána, *v. a.* To pamper, cloy, satiate; to chastise.

छककुर chhuk-kúr, *s. f.* A slap, blow, cuff.

छक्का chhúk-ka, *s. m.* The sixth (*at cards, &c.*); a cage with a net attached to it. *Chhukka punja kurna,* To deceive, play tricks.

छग chhug, *s. m.* A goat.

छगरी chhúg-ree, *s. f.* A she-goat of small breed.

छगली chhúg-lee, *s. f.* A she-goat; a kind of Convolvulus (*C. argenteus*), or more probably *C. pres-capræ*.

छगुनी chhúg-oo-nee, *s. f.* Child's coral.

छछूरी chhu-chhúree, *s. f.* The root of a certain tree (*of the phapond*).

छज chhuj, *adj.* Bushy.

छज्जा chhúj-ja, *s. m.* Gallery; the expanded branches of a tree.

छंछनाना chhun-chhun-ána, *v. n.* To simmer; to sound; to smart, to pain.

छटना chhút-na, *s. m.* A kind of sieve. *v. n.* To decay, to separate, to be pruned, to be picked out.

छटपटाना chhut-put-ána, *v. n.* To toss, tumble about, flounder.

छठवां chhútwan, *adj.* Sixth.

छठहा chhut-há, *adj.* Waspish, peevish.

छटांक chhut-ánk, *s. f.* The sixteenth part of a *ser*, two ounces.

छटा chhút-a, *s. f.* Splendour, brilliancy, lustre, refulgence, a glory; assemblage, number; a straight or continuous mark or line.

छटाभा chhut-ábha, *s. f.* Lightning.

छठ chhutth, } *s. f.* The sixth day of a lu-
छठ chhuth, } nar fortnight.

छठा chhutha, *adj.* Sixth.

छठी chhút-thee, } *adj. f.* Sixth. *s. f.* A
छठी chhút-hee, } religious ceremony performed on the sixth day after child-birth. *Chhuthee ka dood yad dilana,* To correct or chastise.

छड़ chhur, *s. f.* The pole of a spear; spikenard.

छड़ना chhúr-na, *v. a.* To beat rice, to separate the husk from it.

छड़ा chhúr-a, *s. m.* An ornament made of pearls worn in the ears. *adj.* Alone.

छड़ी chhúr-ee, *s. f.* A switch, cane, rod, wand; a procession of the followers of *Shah Mudar.*

छड़ीला chhur-ée-la, *s. f.* A kind of fragrant moss.

छन chhun, *s. m.* A moment or instant.

छनिक chhún-ik, *adj.* Perishable, temporary, momentary, inconstant, uncertain.

छंटना chhúnt-na, *v. n.* To grow thin; to diminish; to be extracted or separated.

छंटवाना chhunt-wána, *v. n.* To cause to clean rice, to cause to select, prune, lop, clip.

छंटाई chhun-táee, *s. f.* Cleaning or separating (*grain, &c.*); the price paid for cleaning.

छंटाव chhun-táo, *s. m.* Detachment on forage; beating rice to clear it from the husk.

छत chhut, *s. f.* A roof, a cloth stretched across the roof of a room, a platform. *Chhut busana,* or, —*patna,* or, —*lugana, v. a.* To ceil, to cover the inner roof of a building.

छतनार chhut-nár, *adj.* Bunchy, flat.

छतर chhut-túr, *s. m.* An umbrella.

छत्ता chhútta, *s. m.* A honeycomb.

छतीस chhut-tées, *adj.* Thirty-six.

छतीसी chhut-tée-see, *adj. f.* Prude, prudish.

छत्र chhutr, *s. m.* A parasol, an umbrella, the Indian *Chhuttah.*

छत्रधारी chhutr-dháree, } *s. m.* One enti-
छत्रपति chhutr-púti, } tled to carry an umbrella, *i. e.* a *raja,* prince, &c.; a house set apart for the charitable entertainment of strangers, guests, &c.

छत्रभंग chhutr-bhúng, *s. m.* Widowhood; subversion of dominion, loss of empire, deposition, &c.

छत्रा chhút-ra, *s. f.* A kind of fennel (*Anethum sowa*); a pungent seed, coriander; a mushroom; anise.

छत्रिनी chhút-rin-ee, *s. f.* A female of the *Chhuttree* cast. *adj.* Bearing a parasol or umbrella.

छत्री chhút-ree, *s. m.* The second of the four *Hindoo* casts. *s. f.* A tester or covering of a bed, a small umbrella; a frame made of bamboos for pigeons to settle upon.

छत्तर chhut-wúr, *s. m.* A house, a dwelling; a bower, an arbor.

छदाम chhud-ám, *s. m.* (*In money*) Six *dam,* or the fourth part of a pice (*pysa*).

छद्म chhudm, } *s. m.* Disguise, mas-
छद्मन् chhúdm-un, } querade; trick, deceit, fraud.

छद्मतापस chhudm-tápus, *s. m.* A religious hypocrite, a false brother.

छन chhun, *s. m.* A moment, an instant; a sound made by the falling of a drop of water upon a warm plate, a hissing noise.

छनकाना chhun-ká-na, *v. a.* To concentrate, to cause to strain.

छनकाहट chhun-ká-hut, *s. f.* Concentration, causing to strain.

छनछनाना chhun-chhun-ána, *v. n.* To simmer; to sound; chink; to smart, to pain.

छनवाना chhun-wána, *v. a.* To cause to sift or strain.

छनाक chhun-ák, *s. m.* The sound (*hissing*) of a drop of water falling on a hot plate, a hissing noise; the sound of the breaking of earthen ware.

छनिक chhún-ik, *adj.* Perishable, temporary, momentary, inconstant, uncertain.

छंद chhund, *s. m.* Poetical metre, it is also applicable particularly to the metre of the *Veds*; a measure (*in music*); meaning, intention, purport, opinion; wish, desire. *adj.* Solitary, secret, private.

छंदना chhúnd-na, *v. n.* To be tied.

छंदपातन chhund-pátun, *s. m.* A hypocrite, a pretended and false ascetic.

छंदबंद chhund-búnd, *s. m.* Trick, cheating, deceiving.

छंदी chhún-dee, *adj.* Deceitful.

छंदोग chhun-dóg, *s. m.* A reciter or chanter of the *Sam Ved.*

छन्न chhún-na, *v. n.* To be strained, to be percolated. *s. m.* A sieve, a cloth through which any thing is sifted.

छुप chhup, *s. m.* Squash. *Chhup-chhup*, The sound occasioned by water when struck with the hand.

छुपई chhup-úee, *s. m.* A kind of measure of *Hindee* verse.

छुपकाना chhup-ká-na, *v. a.* To dash or throw water.

छुपना chhúp-na, *v. n.* To be printed or stamped ; to be concealed, hidden, absent, to disappear, to lurk.

छुपरी chhúp-ree, *s. f.* Puddle.

छुपवाना chhupwána, *v. a.* To cause to print.

छुपाई chhup-áee, *s. f.* Edition, the price of printing, the act of printing.

छुपाका chhup-áka, *s. m.* The sound produced by striking water, squash.

छुपाना chhup-ána, *v. a.* To hide, conceal, secrete; to cause to print.

छुप chhúp-uy, *s. m.* A kind of measure of *Hindee* verse.

छुपपन chhup-pún, *adj.* Fifty-six.

छुपर chhúp-pur, *s. m.* A thatched roof.

छुपरखुट chhup-pur-khút, *s. m.* A bedstead with curtains.   [er.

छुपरबन्द chhup-pur-búnd, *s. m.* A thatch-

छुपरबन्दी chhup-pur-bún-dee, *s.f.* Thatching.

छुब chhub, *s. f.* Beauty, splendour, brilliancy ; shape, form figure. *Chhub-tukhtee, s. f.* Handsomeness. *Chhubi-chheen, adj.* Small in shape, deficient in splendour, small or slender.

छुबरा chhúb-ra, *s. m.* A sort of basket.

छुबीला chhub-ée-la, *adj.* Handsome, comely, graceful.

छुबीस chhub-bées, *adj.* Twenty-six.

छुमछुमाना chhum-chhum-ána, *v. n.* To shine, to glitter ; to sound.

छुमुंड chhum-únd, *s. m.* An orphan, a fatherless son.

छुमना chhúm-na, *v. a.* To pardon, forgive.

छुय chhuy. *s. f.* Mortality, frailty, destruction.

छुयरोग chhuy-róg, *s. m.* Consumption.

छुया chhúy-a, *s. m.* Victim, shade, shadow ; a boy.

छुयासठ chhyásuth, *adj.* Sixty-six.

छुर chhur, *s. f.* Spikenard; shaft, pole, pike, staff, flagstaff, flag.

छुरछोबी chhur-chhó-bee, *s. f.* Jakes, a necessary.

छुरिन्द chhur-ín-da, *adj.* Alone, single, free (*not burdened, as a traveller, not having a load*).

छुर्द chhurd, } *s. f.* Vomiting, sickness,
छूर्दि chhúrdi, } reaching.

छुर्दिकारिपू chhúrdi-ka-ríp-oo, *s. m.* Small cardamoms (*an anti-emetic*).

छुर्रा chhúr-ra, *s. m.* Small shot.

छुल chhul, *s. m.* Wickedness, fraud, circumvention, stratagem, trick, deception, knavery, artifice, evasion, excuse, subterfuge, pretence. *Chhul-bul, s. m.* Force and fraud, stratagem, artifice, trick.

छुलुक chhúl-uk, *s. f.* Running over, overflow.

छुलुकना chhúl-uk-na, *v. n.* To be spilt, to overflow, to spill.

छुलकाना chhul-ká-na, *v. a.* To spill.

छुलुंगना chhul-úng-na, *v. n.* To skip.

छुलछुलाना chhul-chhul-ána, *v. a.* To murmur.

छुलछुलाहट chhul-chhul-áhut, *s. f.* Murmur.

छुलछिद्र chhul-chhídr, *s. m.* Plot, stratagem.

छुलछिद्री chhul-chhíd-ree, *adj.* Deceitful, fraudulent.

छुलना chhúl-na, *v. a.* To deceive, cheat, evade, make excuses. *s. m.* Tricking, deceiving.

छुलनी chhúl-nee, *adj.* Battered. *s. f.* A sieve. *Chhulnee kurna, v. a.* To batter.

छुलांग chhul-áng, *s. f.* Skipping, jumping, a spring, skip, leap. *Chhulangen marna*, To spring, to jump.

छुलावा chhul-áwa, *s. m.* Ignis fatuus, will-o'-the-wisp.

छुलिया chhúl-i-ya, } *adj.* Deceitful, fraudu-
छुली chhúl-ee, } lent, artful, treacherous, false, perfidious, betrayer. *s. m.* A cheat, deceiver.

छुल्ला chhúl-la, *s. m.* A ring (*ornamental*). *Chhulledar, adj.* Annular.

छुल्ली chhúl-lee, *s. f.* Skin, bark, rind, &c.

छुवि chhúv-i, *s. f.* Beauty, splendour, brilliance ; light, lustre.

छुवैया chhuwy-ya, *s. m.* A thatcher.

छाईं chhá-een, *s. f.* Discolouration.

छाई chháee, *s. f.* Ashes.

छन chhan, *s. f.* Shade, shadow ; the reflection of any object in a mirror, &c. *Chhan-banh, s. f.* Auspices.

छांट chhant, *s. f.* Refuse ; parings, &c. ; selection, fashion of clothes. *Chhant kurna*, To vomit, to disgorge. *Chhant lena*, To select, choose. *Chhant-chhutao*, Retrenchment.

छाँटन chhán-tun, *s. f.* Cutting, slip, chip.

छाँटना chhánt-na, *v. a.* To vomit ; to separate the husk from grain by pounding it in a mortar ; to husk ; to pare, clip, prune, lop, crop, trim, dress, clean, select.

छाँदना chhánd-na, *v. a.* To emit ; to leave, let go, release, forsake, abandon, to loose ; to vomit.

छाँद chhand, *s. f.* A tether, trammel, net.

छाँदना chhánd-na, *v. a.* To tether, fasten, tie, bind.

छाँदा chhán-da, *s. m.* Share, part (*among fukeers*).

छाँव chháon, ⎱ *s. f.* Shade, shadow, the
छाँह chhanh, ⎰ reflection of any object in a mirror, &c. *Chkanh-banh, s. f.* Auspices.

छाँहारा chhan-hára, *adj.* Umbrageous.

छाक chhak, *s. m.* Luncheon, ready prepared food carried out by labourers and husbandmen when they proceed to their daily work.

छाकना chhák-na, *v. a.* To clear the water of a well, &c.

छाग chhag, *s. m.* A he-goat.

छागल chhá-gul, *s. m.* A he-goat. *s. f.* A leathern bottle with a spout to it, a goat-skin.

छागिका chhá-gi-ka, ⎱ *s. f.* A she-goat.
छागी chhá-gee, ⎰

छाछ chhachh, *s. f.* Buttermilk.

छाज chhaj, *s. m.* A kind of basket used in winnowing or clearing grain.

छाजना chháj-na, *v. a.* To thatch ; to befit, to become.

छार chhar, *s. f.* A bank of a river. *Chhar-chitthee, s. f.* A permit, a pass.

छारछुरेला chhar-chhur-él-a, *s. m.* A medicinal herb.

छात chhat, *s. f.* Roof. *adj.* Thin, feeble, emaciated.

छाता chhá-ta, *s. m.* A large umbrella.

छाती chhá-tee, *s. f.* An umbrella.

छाती chhá-tee, *s. f.* Breast, dug, bubby. *Chhatee-bhur,* Breast-high. *Chhatee bhur-ana,* To weep. *Chhatee bhur-jana,* To be chest-foundered. *Chhatee-pur putthur rukhna,* To have patience. *Chhatee-pur moong dulna (lit. to grind pulse on the breast),* To do any thing in the presence of another person by which he is vexed. *Chhatee phutnee,* To break the heart with grief or sorrow, to sympathize. *Chhatee peetna,* To regret, repent, lament. *Chhatee thokna,* To encourage ; to assure. *Chhatee thundee hona,* To be pleased or overjoyed. *Chhatee julna,* To have the heart-burn ; to lament. *Chhatee ka putthur,* Nuisance, pest. *Chhatee ka jum (lit. the destroyer of the heart),* Is applied to a person or thing the presence of which is

unpleasant, a pest, a nuisance. *Chhatee kholkur milna,* To meet frankly. *Chhatee gudranee,* The breast to swell (*in young women*). *Chhatee lugana,* To lament, to grieve. *Chhatee lugana, or, Chhatee-seh lugana,* To fondle. *Chhatee nikalkur chulna,* To stalk, to strut.

छात्र chhatr, *s. m.* A scholar, a pupil, a disciple, a tyro or novice.

छादन chhá-dun, *s. m.* Covering, a covering, a screen, &c.

छादान chha-dán, *s. m.* A water-bag.

छादित chhá-dit, *adj.* Covered, concealed.

छान chhan, *s. f.* A roof, a frame of bamboo for thatching.

छानबिनान chhan-bin-án, *s. m.* Investigation.

छानवे chhán-web, *adj.* Ninety-six.

छानस chhá-nus, *s. f.* Chaff.

छाना chhá-na, *v. a.* To thatch, shade, cover, roof, spread. *Chha-jana,* To spread, to lie, to overshadow. *Chha lena,* To cloud, overspread, darken, overcast.

छानना chhán-na, *v. a.* To strain, percolate, filter, sift ; to search, canvass, investigate. *Chhan lena,* To cull, to select. *Chhan marna,* To search, rummage, explore, canvass.

छाप chhap, *s. f.* Stamp, print, copy, impression ; a seal, seal-string.

छापना chháp-na, *v. a.* To print, to stamp.

छापा chhá-pa, *s. m.* Edition, impression, stamp, print, seal, &c. *Chhapeh-khanuh, s. m.* Printing-office. *Chhapeh-wala,* Printer.

छापा chhá-pa, *s. m.* Denominational marks representing a lotus, trident, &c. delineated on the body by the *Vyshnuvs* or worshippers of *Vishnoo*.

छापाविद्या chhápa-vídya, *s. f.* The art of printing.

छाया chhá-ya, *s. f.* Shade, shadow, reflected image ; darkness, obscurity. *s. m.* Apparition, spectre, shade ; (*met.*) somewhat resembling ; a mode in music.

छायातरु chháya-túr-oo, *s. m.* A large tree, one that gives shade or shelter.

छायानट chha-ya-nút, *s. m.* A musical mode.

छायापथ chha-ya-púth, *s. m.* Æther, the firmament. [parasol.

छायामित्र chha-ya-mítr, *s. m.* A *chhata* or

छार chhar, *s. f.* Ashes, dust ; a large clod of earth.

छारछुबेला chhar-chhub-éela, *s. m.* A kind of fragrant moss.

छारू chhá-roo, *s. m.* The thrush (*disease*), blister.

छाल chhal, *s. f.* Peel, skin, rind, bark. *Chhal ootarna,* To peel, to decorticate.

छाला chhá-la, *s. m.* A blister, pustule, pimple ; skin.

छालिया chhá-li-ya, *s. f.* A kind of betel-nut.

छावना chháo-na, *v. a.* To thatch, to shade, to cover, to roof, to spread. *Chha jana,* To spread, to lie. *Chha lena,* To cloud, overspread, darken.

छावनी chháo-nee, *s. f.* Cantonments, barracks or huts for soldiers; thatching, the act of thatching.

छिंकवाना chhink-wá-na, } *v. a.* To cause
छिंकाना chhin-ká-na, } to stop, to cause to seize, to cancel, to strike out.

छिकुनी chhík-oo-nee, *s. f.* Wand, stick.

छिक्कन chhikkún, *s. m.* Sneezing.

छिंगुली chhín-goo-lee, *s. f.* The little finger.

छिचड़ा chhích-ra, *s. m.* Sink, slough (*of a wound*), skin.

छिचड़ैल chhich-ryl, *adj.* Lean, skinny.

छिछड़ा chhíchh-ra, *s. m.* The prepuce.

छिछला chhíchh-la, *adj.* Shallow.

छिछलाई chhichh-láee, *s. f.* Shallowness.

छिछली chhíchh-lee, *s. f.* The play of ducks and drakes.

छिछोरा chhi-chhó-ra, *adj.* Trifling, puerile, airy.

छिटकना chhi-túk-na, *v. n.* To be scattered, dissipated, or dispersed, to spirt, to spread. *Chhitukna chandnee ka,* The diffusion of moonlight.

छिटकनी chhit-kun-ee, *s. f.* A bolt.

छिटकाना chhit-ká-na, *v. a.* To dissipate, disperse, squirt, scatter, strew, desert.

छिटकी chhít-kee, *s. f.* Small shot, speck. *Chhitkee dena,* To flicker, to spot, to mark with strokes or touches. *Chhitkee dalna,* To splash. *Chhitkee kurna,* or, —*lugana,* To spot, to speck, &c.

छिड़कना chhir-úk-na, *v. a.* To sprinkle. *Chhiruk-kur bechna,* To sprinkle water on stale or faded vegetables or fruits to make them appear fresh ; to puff off goods.

छिड़कवाना chhir-uk-wána, *v. a.* To cause another to sprinkle.

छिड़काना chhir-ká-na, *v. a.* To cause to sprinkle.

छिड़काव chhir-káo, *s. m.* Sprinkling, watering.

छिड़ना chhír-na, *v. n.* To be touched, excited, plagued on.

छिन chhin, *s. m.* A moment or instant. *Chhin-bhur men,* In a moment.

छिनविधंस chhin-bidhúns, *adj.* Fading, frail, passing away quickly.

छिनेक chhin-ék, *adv.* A little while.

छितनी chhít-nee, *s. f.* A basket (*without a cover, like a tray*).

छितरना chhit-úr-na, *v. n.* To be scattered ; to be spread about.

छितराना chhit-rá-na, *v. a.* To scatter, to strew ; to spread.

छितरी chhít-ree, *s. f.* A small basket without lid or handle.

छिती chhít-ee, *s. f.* The earth. *Chhitee-chhan,* Covering the earth, prostrate on the ground. *Chhitee-chhan, v. n.* To be dispersed or scattered.

छिदना chhíd-na, *v. n.* To be pierced or bored.

छिदाना chhid-ána, *v. a.* To cause to pierce, to perforate.

छिद्र chhidr, *s. m.* A hole, a vacuity, a perforation, &c.; fault, defect, flaw (*moral or physical*).

छिद्रित chhid-rít, *adj.* Perforated, pierced, having holes or openings.

छिन chhin, *s. m.* A moment or instant. *Chhin bhur men,* In a moment.

छिनकना chhin-úk-na, *v. a.* To winnow, to sift. *v. n.* To go away offended.

छिनकाना chhin-kána, *v. a.* To cause to stop, to cause to seize, to cancel, strike out.

छिनविधंस chhin-bidhúns, *adj.* Fading, frail, passing away quickly.

छिनुला chhín-ul-a, *s. m.* A fornicator.

छिनवाना chhin-wá-na, *v. a.* To cause to snatch.

छिनाना chhin-ána, *v. a.* To seize, snatch, pluck, &c.

छिनाल chhin-ál, *s. f.* A harlot, a prostitute. *Chhinal-pun,* or, *Chhinal-puna, s. m.* Whoredom, prostitution, harlotry.

छिनाला chhin-ála, *s. m.* Fornication. *Chhinala kurna,* To whore, commit adultery.

छिनाव chhin-áo, *s. m.* Seizure.

छिनेक chhin-ék, *adv.* A little while.

छिन्न chhinn, *adj.* Cut, divided.

छिन्नभिन्न chhinn-bhínn, *adj.* Cut up, destroyed, scattered.

छिन्नरूहा chhinn-róoha, *s. f.* A tree (*Menispermum glabrum*).

छिन्नवेशिका chhinn-véshik-a, *s. f.* A plant also called *Uknidhi* (*Cissampelos hexandra*).

छिन्नसंशय chhinn-súnshuy, *adj.* Confirmed, confident, free from doubt.

छिन्ना chhín-na, *s. f.* A whore, a harlot ; a tree (*Menispermum glabrum*).

छिपकली chhip-kúl-ee, } s. f. A lizard.
छिपकी chhíp-kee,

छिपका chhíp-ka, s. m. Sprinkling.

छिपना chhíp-na, ⌉ v. n. To be concealed,
छुपना chhúp-na, } hidden, absent, to
छूपना chhóop-na, ⌋ disappear, to lurk.
Chhip jana, To retire, withdraw.

छिपा chhíp-a, adj. Close, hidden, concealed. *Chhipa ruhna*, To abscond. *Chhipa-chhipee,
adv.* Underhand, secretly.

छिपाना chhip-ána, ⌉ v. a. To conceal,
छुपाना chhoop-ána, } hide, secrete.
छुपाना chhup-ána, ⌋

छिपाव chhip-áo, s. m. Secrecy, concealment.

छिमा chhím-a, s. f. Pardon, quarter, forgiveness, absolution. *Chhima-jog, adj.* Pardon-
able. *Chhima kurna, v. a.* To pardon, forgive,
excuse.

छियानब्बे chhiya-núvveh, adj. Ninety-six.

छियालीस chhiya-lées, adj. Forty-six.

छियासठ chhiyá-sut, adj. Sixty-six.

छियासी chhiyá-see, adj. Eighty-six.

छिलका chhíl-ka, s. m. Crust, husk, shell,
peel, scale, rind, bark, skin. *Chhilka ootarna*, To
blanch, peel, husk, decorticate.

छिलना chhíl-na, v. n. To be excoriated.

छिलवाना chhil-wána, v. a. To cause to skin
or excoriate, &c.

छिलौरी chhil-óu-ree, s. f. A whitlow, blister, felon.

छिललूर chhil-lúr, s. m. The husk of *chuna*.

छिहत्तर chhi-húttur, adj. Seventy-six.

छी chhee, interj. Tush! tut! fy! foh!

छींक chheenk, s. f. Sneezing, sneeze.
Chheenk lanewala, A sternutatory (*medicine*).

छींकना chhéenk-na, v. n. To sneeze.

छींका chhéenk-a, s. m. A network of strings
or cords to hang any thing on (*as a burthen at
either end of a yoke or pole, &c.*), the cords of a
buhungee.

छींचना chhéench-na, v. a. To throw out
water.

छींट chheent, s. f. Chintz.

छींटना chhéent-na, v. a. To sprinkle.

छींटा chhéen-ta, s. m. Shot, spot, splash.
Chheenta marna, To sprinkle, bedrop.

छींका chhée-ka, s. m. A sling for carrying
baskets, &c.

छीछरा chhéechh-ra, s. m. The skinny and
rejected part of meat, a piece of flesh.

छीजना chhéej-na, v. n. To decrease, to
pine away.

छीट chheet, s. f. Spot, splash, chintz.

छीटना chhéet-na, v. a. To scatter, to
sprinkle.

छीन chheen, adj. Wasted, emaciated, decayed; slight, slender, little.

छीतर chhée-tur, s. m. Brogue, shoe.

छीदा chhée-da, adj. Thin, not close (*said
of a person or animal whose legs are much separated*).

छीन chheen, adj. Wasted, decayed; slight,
slender, little.

छीनना chhéen-na, v. a. To snatch, pull,
tear, pluck, rob. *Chheena-chhanee kurna*, To
scramble. *Chheen lena*, To snatch up, acquire,
take possession of, seize, pluck, bereave, deprive.

छीप chheep, s. f. Discoloration or spot on
the skin; fishing-rod; the act of a buffalo's pushing with his horns.

छीपना chhéep-na, v. a. To print clothes;
to push with the horn as a buffalo; to draw up
the rod in fishing.

छीपी chhée-pee, s. m. A cloth-printer.

छीमी chhée-mee, s. f. A pod, legume, husk.

छीर chheer, s. m. Milk.

छीलन chhée-lun, s. f. Parings.

छीलना chhéel-na, v. a. To peel, skin, ex-
coriate, pare, bark (*a tree, &c.*), erase, scrape.
Chheelna-chhalna, or, *Chheel-chhal kurna, v. a.*
To pare, peel, &c. [ger.

छुंगलिया chhóong-liya, s. f. The little fin-

छुछकारना chhoochh-kárna, v. a. To drive
away contemptuously; to set on or encourage a
dog.

छुछली chhóochh-lee, s. f. The play of a
dog or cat with game, &c.

छुछवाना chhoochh-wána, v. a. To conjure,
to exorcise.

छुछुंदरी chhoo-chhóon-dur-ee, s. f. The
musk rat or shrew.

छुछुंदर chhoo-chhóon-dur, s. f. Mole,
musk rat (*Sorex cærulescens*); a squib. *Chhoo-
chhoondur chhorna*, To backbite, calumniate,
excite resentment.

छुट chhoot, adv. But, except, save; (*in
compos.*) little, small, as, *Chhoot-bhya, s. m.* Middling class of people. *Chhoot-puna, s. m.* Childhood.

छुटकरा chhóot-kur-a, s. m. Deliverance.

छुटका chhóot-ka, adj. Little, small, less,
younger, junior, least.

छुटकाना chhoot-kána, v. a. To release, set
at liberty.

छुटकारा chhoot-kára, s. m. Exemption,
liberty, liberation, disengagement, deliverance,
release, discharge.

छुटखेला chhoot-khél-a, *adj.* Dissolute.

छुटखेली chhoot-khél-ee, *s. f.* Dissoluteness.

छुटना chhóot-na, *v. n.* To be adrift, discharged, got rid of, to be let go or let off, to be left or abandoned, to slip (*from*), to escape, to be liberated, loose, dishevelled (*the hair*), to cease, to get loose, to leave, remain, slip away, to be dismissed.

छुटपन chhoot-pún, *s. m.* Infancy, childhood.

छुटान chhoo-tán, ⎫ *s. f.* Leisure, time.
छुटानी chhoo-tá-nee, ⎭

छुटापा chhoo-tá-pa, *s. m.* Littleness.

छुटी chhóot-tee, *s. f.* Leave, discharge, release, acquittal, time, leisure, cessation, disengagement, intermission, dismission, permission, freedom.

छुरवाना chhoor-wána, *v. a.* To cause to let go, to cause to set free.

छुराना chhoorána, *v. a.* To set free, to free, liberate, extricate, get rid of, discharge, remove, deliver, dismiss; separate, except.

छुरावा chhoo-rá-wa, *s. m.* Deliverance, setting free.

छुरौती chhoo-róu-tee, *s. f.* Ransom.

छुतूहरा chhoo-túh-ra, *adj.* Defiled by touching, foul, corrupt, polluted (*applied to vessels, dishes, &c.*)

छुद्र chhoodr, *adj.* Mean, low, little, trifling.

छुधा chhóo-dha, *s. f.* Hunger.

छुपना chhóop-na, *v. n.* To be concealed, hidden, to be absent, to disappear, to lurk.

छुपाना chhoo-pá-na, *v. a.* To conceal, to hide.

छुरा chhóo-ra, *s. m.* A large knife, an amputating knife; a razor. *Chhoora-chhooree, s. f.* Snick and snee, fighting with knives.

छुरी chhóo-ree, *s. f.* A knife, scalpel. *Chhooree-tuleh dum lena,* To be patient in difficulties. *Chhooree-kutaree, s. f.* Snick and snee, fighting with knives; quarrel.

छुलुकना chhoo-lúk-na, ⎫ *v. a.* To
छुलछुलाना chhool-chhool-ána, ⎭ make water slowly (*as mares, &c. in heat*).

छुलाना chhoo-lána, *v. a.* To cause to touch.

छुलोहला chhoo-lóoh-la, ⎫ *adj.* Puerile, finical, boyish.
छुलोहला chhoo-lóh-la, ⎭

छुवाव chhoo-wáo, *s. m.* Resemblance, likeness.

छुहाना chhoo-há-na, *v. a.* To whitewash.

छुहारा chhoo-hára, *s. m.* A date (*Phœnix dactylifera*).

छुहावट chhoo-há-wut, *s. f.* Touch.

छूलू chhóol-loo, *adj.* Boyish, silly.

छूआना chhoo-ána, *v. a.* To cause to touch, &c.

छूआनी chhoo-ánee, *s. f.* Caudle given to a lying-in woman.

छूई chhóo-ee, *s. f.* Chalk.

छूकी chhóo-kee, *s. f.* A gnat.

छूछला chhóochh-la, *adj.* Foolish, silly, empty.

छूछा chhóo-chha, *adj.* Empty, hollow. *s. m.* Conjuration.

छूछी chhóo-chhee, *adj.* Contemptible, despicable, mean. *s. f.* A pipe, a tube, canula.

छूट chhoot, *s. f.* Remission, leaving; striking off hand or playing loose in fencing; radiance or splendour of jewels, reflection of a mirror, &c.; giving money off hand or at will to jugglers, &c. at entertainments.

छूटना chhóot-na, *v. n.* To be adrift, to be discharged, to spout, to be got rid of, to escape, to be liberated, to be loose, to be dishevelled (*the hair*); to cease, get loose, leave, remain, slip away, to be dismissed, to be let go, to be abandoned, to be left.

छूत chhoot, *s. f.* Defilement, contamination, touch.

छूना chhóo-na, *v. a.* To touch, meddle with, feel.

छेंक chhenk, *s. f.* ⎫ Sequestration of
छेंकाव chhenkáo, *s. m.* ⎭ goods. *Chhenk lena,* To confiscate.

छेंकना chhénk-na, *v. a.* To detain, prevent, stop, retain, bar, restrain, arrest.

छेंकवैया chhenk-wy-ya, *s. m.* A confiscator.

छेंकाव chhen-káo, *s. m.* Sequestration of goods.

छेंचना chhénch-na, *v. a.* To mince, to hack, to pound.

छेक chhek, *adj.* Domesticated, tame (*as a bird or beast*).

छेकना chhék-na, *v. a.* To stop, detain, prevent, retain, bar, restrain.

छेकोक्ति chhek-ókti, *s. f.* Indirect speech, insinuation, double entendre, hint, &c.

छेर chher, *s. f.* The act of irritating, irritation, vexing, &c. *Chher-chhar,* or *Chher-khanee, s. f.* Stricture, animadversion; the act of vexing, provoking, exciting, &c.

छेरना chhér-na, *v. a.* To irritate, vex, excite, fret, trouble, disturb, molest, abuse, insult, aggress, touch, handle, stir up, interrupt; to play on a musical instrument.

छेरा chhér-a, *s. m.* Touch, provocation, excitement, &c.

छेत्र chhetr, *s. m.* A geometrical figure; field, land, plantation; a sacred or holy place (*as Kooroo-kshetr*).

छेतफल chhetr-phul, *s. m.* The measurement (*or superficial contents*) of a field, of a triangle or other geometrical figure.

छेद chhed, *s. m.* A hole, an orifice; the denominator of a fraction; the divisor.

छेदक chhéd-uk, *s. m.* That which penetrates, any thing to bore a hole with.

छेदन chhéd-un, *s. m.* A hole, an orifice.

छेदना chhéd-na, *v. a.* To pierce, bore, perforate, penetrate.

छेना chhén-a, *s. m.* Curd; a small kind of cymbal. [cer.

छेनी chhén-ee, *s. f.* A chisel, punch, piercer.

छेम chhem,
छेमकुशल chhem-kóoshul, } *s. f.* Welfare.

छेमुनकुरी chhemun-kúr-ee, *s. f.* A sort of kite (*Falco ponticerianus*).

छेमउंद chhém-und, *s. m.* A fatherless son.

छेरना chhér-na, *v. n.* To have a bad digestion.

छेरी chhér-ee, *s. f.* A goat.

छेलू chhél-oo, *s. m.* A medicinal plant (*Conyza anthelmintica*).

छेव chheo, *s. m.* A mark, a piece of wood cut off. *Chheo murna*, To line out, mark.

छेवना chhéo-na, *v. a.* To pierce or to bleed a *tar* tree, to extract *tares*; to mark.

छेवनी chhéo-nee, *s. f.* A chisel, punch, piercer.

छेवुर chhéwur, *s. m.* Cuticle, skin.

छेवा chhéwa, *s. m.* Spaces, comma, &c.

छैया chhy-ya, *s. m.* Victim; shade, shadow; a boy.

छैल chhyl,
छैला chhyla, } *s. m.* A fop, a beau.

छैलछिकनिया chhyl-chíkniya, *s. m.* A coxcomb, a fop.

छैलापन chhyla-pún, *s. m.* Spruceness.

छोआ chhó-a, *s. m.* Treacle.

छोंक chhonk, *s. f.* Seasoning, relish.

छोंकन chhónk-un, *s. m.* Spices with which food is seasoned.

छोंछलाकरना chhónchla-kúrna, *v. a.* To fondle.

छोंछी chhónch-hee, *s. f.* Bodkin, case for needles; a small cup for children.

छोकरा chhók-ra, *s. m.* A boy.

छोकरी chhók-ree, *s. f.* A girl.

छोछो chho-chho, *s. f.* A nurse; bosom. *Chhochho kurna*, To fondle.

छोटा chhó-ta, *adj.* Little, small, less, younger, junior, least, &c. *Chhota-bura, adj.* Varied, variegated, various, great and small, high and low.

छोटाई chho-táee, *s. f.* Smallness.

छोड़ना chhór-na, *v. a.* To let go, emit fire, emit, forgive, forsake, leave, quit, desert, except, free, loose, omit, pardon, release, shoot, fire (*a gun, &c.*), spare, abandon, abdicate, abstain, breathe, resign, discharge, lay aside.

छोड़ा chhó-ra,
छोड़ाव chho-ráo, } *s. m.* Release, omission, leaving, sparing, letting go.
छोड़ावा chho-rá-wa,

छोड़ावना chho-ráo-na, *v. a.* To set free, deliver, dismiss, separate, except.

छोड़ौती chho-róu-tee, *s. f.* Ransom.

छोत chhot, *s. f.* Impurity, defilement.

छोनी chhó-nee, *s. f.* The earth.

छोप chhop, *s. m.* A coat of paint, &c. *Chhop-chhap kurna*, To shuffle up; to plaster or repair a wall, &c.

छोपना chhóp-na, *v. a.* To fill up, shut; paint, dye.

छोर chhor, *s. m.* Border; edge; end; a tow-boat.

छोरुन chhorún, *s. m.* Abandoning, leaving.

छोरा chhó-ra, *s. m.* A boy. *Chhora-chhoree, s. m.* Boy and girl; children.

छोरी chhó-ree, *s. f.* A girl.

छोलना chhól-na, *v. a.* To peel, skin, excoriate, pare, erase, scrape. *Chholnee, s. f.* A scraper.

छोह chhoh, *s. m.* Affection; anger.

छोहरा chhóh-ra, *s. m.* A boy, a lad.

छोही chhó-hee, *adj.* Affectionate; angry.

छौंक chhounk, *s. f.* Seasoning, relish.

छौंकन chhóunk-un, *s. m.* Spices with which food is seasoned.

छौंकना chhóunk-na, *v. a.* To season.

छौकुन chhóu-kun, *s. m.* A scrambler.

छौकना chhóuk-na, *v. a.* To scramble.

छौना chhóu-na, *s. m.* Young of any animal.

छौनी chhóu-nee, *s. f.* Cantonments, barracks.

छौर chhour, *s. m.* The shaving of the head or beard.

छौलिया chhou-líya, *adj.* Gay, cheerful.

ज

ज juh, The third letter of the second class of consonants, corresponding to the letter *j* in jam.

जंतु jún-too, *s. m.* An animal, a sentient being, creature.

जंत्र juntr, *s. m.* An amulet ; a musical instrument ; an instrument, an engine.

जंद्रा jún-dra, *s. m.* A pitchfork.

जक juk, *s. m.* When treasure, &c., is buried, an animal (*sometimes a man*) is killed and buried with it as a guard : this animal is called *Juk*, and receives orders to allow no one else to take up the treasure, &c. ; (*met.*) a miser, called also, *Juk ka goomashta*, or agent.

जकरना júk-ur-na, *v. a.* To tighten, draw tight (*as a knot*), bind, fasten, tie, piuion.

जकरबंद juk-ur-búnd, *adj.* Tight.

जख jukh, *s. m.* A sort of demi-god or fairy, an attendant on *Koover*, the Indian Plutus.

जखनी júkh-nee, *s. f.* A female *Jukh* or a fairy.

जग jug, *s. m.* The world, the universe. *Jug-bundhoo, s. m.* Friend of the world. *Jug-jugut, s. m.* The universe ; a feast, entertainment, sacrifice or religious ceremony in which oblations are presented.

जगजगा júg-jug-a, *s. m.* Brass tinsel, thin plates of brass used in decoration.

जगजगाहट jug-jug-áhut, *s. f.* Splendour, much light, glitter.

जगत् júg-ut, *s. m.* The world, the universe ; a buttress.

जगत उजागर júgut-oojágur, *adj.* Enlightening the world.

जगतदुःखी jugut-dóo-khee, *s. m.* A tyrant.

जगतक्षय jugut-kshúy, *s. m.* The destruction of the world.

जगती júg-ut-ee, *s. f.* The earth ; people, mankind ; a sort of metre. *adj.* Moveable, locomotive, transitory.

जगतीतल jug-tée-tul, *s. m.* The world, the earth, sublunary things.

जगत्कर्ता jugut-kúrta, *s. m.* A name of *Bruhm*; the creator of the world.

जगत्प्राण jugut-prán, *s. m.* Air, wind.

जगदम्बा jugud-úmba, *s. f.* Mother of the world, an epithet of a *Hindoo* goddess.

जगदाधार jugud-ádhar, *s. m.* Air, wind ; a stay or supporter of the universe.

जगदीश jugud-éesh, *s. m.* An epithet of *Vishnoo* and of *Shiv* ; lord of the world or universe.

जगद्विनाश jugud-vinásh, *s. m.* The expiration of a *Kulp* or period of the world's existence.

जगना júg-na, *v. n.* To awake, to rouse, to be awake. *Jugta, adj.* Awake.

जगन्नाथ jugun-náth, *s. m.* A form of *Vishnoo* ; a peculiar and celebrated idol of this name is worshipped on the Coromandel coast in Orissa, and pilgrimages are made to the shrine of *Jugusnath*, from all parts of India.

जगमगा jug-múg-a, *adj.* Glittering, splendid.

जगमगाना jug-mug-ána, *v. n.* To glitter, to shine.

जगमगाहट jugmug-áhut, *s. f.* Glitter, splendour, glare, much light.

जगर júg-ur, *s. m.* Armour, mail.

जगह júg-uh, *s. f.* Place, station, quarter, room, vacancy, stead. *Juguh chhorna, v. a.* To leave a blank.

जगहर júg-hur, *s. m.* Wakefulness (*occasioned by apprehension or disease*) ; coughing at night, vigils, vespers.

जगज्योति jug-a-jyóti, *s. f.* Splendour, much light.

जगाना jug-ána, *v. a.* To awake, wake, rouse from sleep.

जगेश्वर jug-éshwur, } *s. m.* A name of
जगनेश्वर jugun-éshwur, } *Vishnoo* and *Shiv* ; God of the universe.

जगोपवीत jugo-pubéet, *s. m.* The sacrificial thread or cord, worn by the three first classes of *Hindoos* over the left shoulder and under the right.

जघन jug-hún, *s. m.* Mons veneris ; the hip and loins.

जघन्युह jug-húnyuh, *adj.* Last, hindmost ; low, vile, base.

जघन्य jug-húnya, *s. m.* A *Soodr* or man of the fourth tribe.

जंगम júng-um, *s. m.* A *Hindoo* mendicant who has matted hair and rings a bell. *adj.* Locomotive, moveable, removeable, in motion, mendicant, that which has motion as opposed to that which is stationary.

जंगल jún-gul, *adj.* Desert, solitary, waste, jungle, wild, &c. *s. m.* A forest, a wood. *Jungul phirna*, or, —*jana*, To ease one's self.

जंगला júng-la, *adj.* Wild. *s. m.* A musical mode ; woody country, forest.

जंगली júng-lee, *adj. f. m.* Wild, savage, barbarian, clown, boor. *Junglee piyas*, Squills (*Erythronium Indicum*). *Junglee billee, s. f.* A wild cat. *Junglee singhara, s. m.* Hermodactyl. *Junglee kouwa, s. m.* A raven.

जंघा júng-ha, *s. f.* The leg ; the thigh.

जचना júch-na, *v. n.* To be examined, tried, proved, assayed.

जचावट juch-áwut, *s. f.* Test, trial, examination, proof.

जजमान juj-mán, *s. m.* A customer, a person to whose custom *Brahmuns*, barbers, and some others, have a legal claim.

जजमानी juj-mánee, *s. f.* The stipend paid by a *jujman* ; wife of a *jujman*.

अज्ञाज jun-jál, *s. m.* Trouble, difficulty, plague, embarrassment, perplexity; a swivel, &c.

अज्ञाली jun-já-lee, *s. m.* Molester.

अट jut, ⎱ *s. f.* Matted hair, the hair
अटा jút-a, ⎰ matted as worn by the god *Shiv*, and by ascetics; the long hairs occasionally clotted together, and brought over the head so as to project like a horn from the forehead, at other times allowed to fall carelessly over the back and shoulders; the root of a tree, a fibrous root; spikenard.

अटना jút-na, *v. a.* To pilfer, steal, defraud, snatch or seize by force.

अटाजूत jut-a-jóot, *s. f.* The braided hair of *Shiv* rolled on his head.

अटाधारी jut-a-dháree, *adj.* Whose hair is matted. *s. f.* The cockscomb flower (*Celosia cristata*).

अटामांसी jut-a-mánsee, *s. f.* Indian spikenard (*Valeriana Jutamansi*).

अटायू jut-ayóo, *s. m.* A fabulous bird mentioned in the story of *Ram*, as the son of *Uroon*, killed by *Rawun*; Bdellium.

अटाल jut-ál, *adj.* Wearing clotted hair.

अटाला jut-ála, *s. f.* Spikenard.

अटि jút-i, *s. f.* Waved-leaf fig tree (*Ficus venosa*).

अटित jút-it, *adj.* Clotted, matted; set, studded (*with jewels, &c.*). *s. f.* Set work of jewels, &c.

अटिन jút-in, *s. m.* Waved-leaf fig tree.

अटिनी jút-in-ee, *adj.* Having clotted hair.

अटिल jút-il, *s. m.* A lion. *s. f.* Indian spikenard; long-pepper; orris-root. *adj.* Having clotted or entangled hair.

अटूल jút-ool, *s. m.* A freckle, a mark.

अटर jut-húr, *s. m.* The belly.

चटरमूद jut-hur-nóod, *s. m. Cassia fistula.*

अटरा jút-hur-a, *adj.* Hard, firm; bound, tied.

अटरानल jut-hur-ánul, *s. m.* The uneasy sensation arising from hunger.

अटराम jut-hur-ám, *s. m.* Dropsy, water in the abdomen.

अड jur, *s. f.* A root, origin, foundation, base, basis. *s. m.* An inanimate body, what is void of life, a blockhead, idiot, dolt. *Jur ka bhed*, Essence. *adj.* Cold, frigid, chilly, stupid, apathetic, idiotic.

अड्क्रिय jur-kríyuh, *adj.* Dilatory, working slowly.

अड्ता júr-ta, *s. f.* Coldness, chilliness; apathy, stupidity; immoveableness, stiffness, rigidity, torpor.

अड्न júr-un, *s. f.* The act of setting jewels.

अड्ना júr-na, *v. a.* To strike, shake off; to join, make adhere; to stud, bestud, set jewels, fix, enchace.

अड्पेड jur-pér, *s. f.* Root and branch. *Jurper-seh ookharna, v. a.* To extirpate.

अड्वट júr-wut, *s. f.* The trunk of a tree.

अड्वाना jur-wána, *v. a.* To cause to set with jewels.

अड्हून jur-hún, *s. m.* Rice cropped at the end of the rainy season.

अड्रा júr-a, *s. f.* Cowach. *s. m.* Cold, frost, winter; idiocity, fatuity, stupidity; dulness, apathy, sluggishness of mind or body.

अड्ाई jur-áee, *s. f.* Price of setting jewels; the act of setting jewels.

अड्ाऊ jur-áoo, *adj.* Set, studded with jewels.

अड्ाना jur-ána, *v. n.* To be cold. *v. a.* To cause to stud, to cause to set jewels.

अड्ाव jur-áo, *s. m.* ⎱ Setting of jewels.
अड्ावट jurá-wut, *s. f.* ⎰

अड्ावर jur-áwur, ⎱ *s. f.* Warm clothes,
अड्ावल jur-áwul, ⎰ winter-dress.

अड्ित júr-it, *part.* Set (*with jewel, &c.*), studded.

अड्िया júr-iya, *s. m.* A jeweller, one who sets jewels; a striker.

अड्ी júr-ee, *s. f.* The root of a medicinal herb.

अड्ीबूटी júr-ee-bóotee, *s. f.* Medicinal herbs, drugs, simples.

अड्ूल júr-ool, *s. m.* A freckle, a mark.

अत jut, *s. f.* Manner, fashion, kind.

अतन jút-un, *s. m.* Carefulness, remedy, care, effort, endeavour.

अतनी jút-un-ee, *adj.* Careful.

अताना jut-ána, *v. a.* To inform of, caution, warn, apprize, to remind, to declare, to admonish; to proclaim, make known.

अतारा jut-ára, *s. m.* Lineage, family, pedigree, genealogy, dynasty.

अति jút-i, *s. f.* A kind of musical rhythm (*generally sung at the holes*).

अती jút-ee, *adj.* Faithful to the marriage bed (*a man*), religious person, devotee, a particular order of devotees; a sage whose passions are completely under subjection.

अतू jút-oo, *s. m.* Lac, a red dye, or animal pigment analogous to cochineal.

अतूक jút-ook, *s. m.* Lac; asafœtida.

अतूका jút-oo-ka, *s. f.* A plant commonly called *chukwut*; a bat.

अतूपूबक jút-oo-póotruk, *s. m.* A man at chess or backgammon, &c.

जत्रु **jút-roo**, *s. m.* The collar bone, the clavicle.

जथा **jút-ha**, *s. m.* A company, band, gang, party, class. *Jutha bandhna*, To form a party.

जथा **jút-ha**, *adv.* As, so, like, in the manner of, according to, to the utmost of. *Jutha jog*, In a proper manner, suitably, properly.

जथार्थ **jut-hárth**, *adv.* In fact, exactly, truly.

जद **jud**, *adv.* As, while, whilst, when, as soon as, at the time when. *Jud-tuk*, or, —*tuluk*, or, —*lug*, *adv.* Till, until, yet, whilst, as long as, while. *Jud-nuh-tud*, *adv.* Constantly.

जद्बातद्बा **júdba-túdba**, *adv.* So so.

जदुबंशी **júdoo-búnshee**, *adv.* Of the race of *Judoo*.

जद्यपि **júd-yupi**, *adv.* Though, although.

जन **jun**, *s. m.* Man, individually or collectively, a man, mankind, a person, an individual. In comp. it has a plural sense; as *Stree-jun*, Women.

जनक **jún-uk**, *s. m.* A father, a progenitor; the name of a king, sovereign of *Mithila*, and father of *Seeta*.

जनकपुर **junuk-póor**, *s. m.* The metropolis of *Rajah Junuk*, in the district of *Tirhoot*.

जनंगम **junúng-um**, *s. m.* A *Chundal*, a man of a low or degraded tribe.

जनआनबर **jun-jáuwur**, *s. m.* Man and beast.

जनता **jún-ut-a**, *s. f.* Mankind, a number of men.

जनन **jún-un**, *s. m.* Birth, production; family, race, lineage.

जनना **jún-na**, *v. n.* To be born.

जननी **jún-un-ee**, *s. f.* A mother; tenderness, compassion. *adj.* A parent, a progenitor.

जनरव **jun-rúv**, *s. m.* Noise, clamour; the sound of human voices.

जनलोक **jún-lok**, *s. m.* One of the seven *Loks* or *Hindoo* divisions of the world; the division said to be inhabited by pious men after their decease; a superior sort of paradise.

जनवाद **jun-vád**, *s. m.* News, rumour, report.

जनवासा **jun-wás-a**, *s. m.* The place at the bride's house where the bridegroom and his train are received.

जनश्रुति **jun-shróo-ti**, *s. f.* News, tidings, intelligence.

जना **jún-a**, *s. m.* A person, individual. *part. pass.* Born; a son.

जनाई **jun-áee**, *s. f.* A midwife.

जनाजात **jun-a-ját**, *adv.* Man by man, one by one (*person*).

जनान्तिक **jun-án-tik**, *s. m.* Secret communication, whispering, speaking aside, &c.

जनाना **jun-ána**, *v. a.* To deliver, bring to bed; to inform, remind, tell, warn, point out, shew, seem. *s. m.* Midwifery.

जनाव **jun-áo**, *s. m.* A signal.

जनाश्रय **jun-áshruy**, *s. m.* A temporary hall.

जनिका **jún-ik-a**, *s. m.* Double entendre, an expression having more than one meaning.

जनित **jún-it**, *adj.* Produced.

जनिता **jún-it-a**, *s. m.* A father.

जनित्री **jún-it-ree**, *s. f.* A mother.

जनी **jún-ee**, *s. f.* A woman in general; a mother; the wife of a son or brother's son, &c.; birth, production; a maid-servant; daughter-in-law.

जनु **jún-oo**, *s. m.* Birth, engenderment.

जनुक **jún-ook**, *conj.* To wit, though, although.

जनेऊ **jun-éoo**, *s. m.* The brahminical thread; a flaw in a jewel.

जनेत **jun-ét**, *s. f.* The company and attendants at a marriage feast.

जनेवा **jun-éwa**, *s. f.* A kind of grass (*Doob: Agrostis linearis*).

जनो **jún-o**, *s. m.* The brahminical thread. *adv.* Like as, as.

जनोदाहरण **jun-odahúr-un**, *s. m.* Fame, glory.

जन्ता **jún-ta**, *s. m.* An instrument for drawing wire.

जन्ताना **jun-tána**, *v. a.* To squeeze, to press.

जन्तार **jun-tár**, *s. m.* An amulet.

जन्तु **jún-too**, *s. m.* An animal, a sentient being, a creature, any being endowed with animal life; it is more usually applied however to beings of the lowest organization.

जन्तुघ्न **junt-óoghn**, *s. m.* A plant and vermifuge.

जन्तुफल **juntoo-phúl**, *s. m.* Glomerous fig-tree (*Ficus glomerata*).

जन्तुला **júntoo-la**, *s. f.* A kind of grass (*Saccharum spontaneum*).

जन्त्र **juntr**, *s. m.* A machine in general, any instrument or apparatus, an engine; a musical instrument; an amulet; juggling; an observatory; a dial.

जन्त्रमन्त्र **júntr-muntr**, *s. m.* Juggling, conjuring, enchanting by figures and incantations.

जन्त्री **jún-tree**, *s. f.* An instrument for drawing wire; a conjurer, a juggler, a wizard.

जन्द्रा **jún-dra**, *s. m.* A pitchfork.

जन्ना **jún-na**, *v. n.* To produce young, to be delivered (*of child*), to be born.

अम्ब junm, *s. m.* Birth, production, life.

अम्बकील junm-keel, *s. m. Vishnoo*, the bolt or stay of life.

अम्बद jun-múd, *s. m.* A father.

अम्बदाता junm-dáta, *s. m.* Father; God (*as the giver of life or author of existence*).

अम्बदिन júnm-din, *s. m.* Birth-day.

अम्बम् jun-mún, *s. m.* Birth, production.

अम्बना júnm-na, *v. n.* To be born.

अम्बपबी junm-pút-ree, *s. f.* Horoscope, nativity. *Junm-putree kee bidh milna*, To meet one's fate.

अम्बभूमि junm-bhóomi, *s. f.* } Birth-place.
अम्बस्थान junm-sthán, *s. m.* }

अम्बरोगी junm-rógee, *adj.* Valetudinarian.

अम्बाना jun-mána, *v. a.* To beget; to make vegetate.

अम्बान्तर junm-ántur, *s. m.* Regeneration, another birth, another state of existence.

अम्बान्तरीय junm-ántur-éeyuh, *adj.* Acquired in a former birth.

अम्बान्ध junm-ándh, *adj.* Born blind.

अम्बिन júnm-in, *s. m.* An animal, an existent being.

अम्बजय jun-mejúy, *n. prop.* The son and successor of *Rajah Pureekshit*.

अम्बोत्सव junm-ótsuv, *s. m.* A festival commemorating the birth of *Krishn*.

अम्ब jún-yuh, *s. m.* A father; the friend, attendant, or companion of a bridegroom.

अम्बा jún-yah, *s. f.* The friend of a mother; the relation or companion of a bride, a bridesmaid, &c.

अम्बासा junwása, *s. m.* The place at the bride's house where the bridegroom and his train are received.

अम्बाई jun-háee, } *adv.* Man by man, every
अम्बार jun-hár, } one.

अप jup, *s. m.* Silent repetition of the names of a deity, silent meditation, muttering prayers, repeating inaudibly passages from the *Shasters*; adoration, charms, names of a deity, counting silently the beads of a rosary, &c.

अपत jup-út, *part.* Repeating prayers, worshipping.

अपतप jup-túp, *s. m.* Devotion, adoration.

अपना júp-na, } *v. a.* To count one's
अपनौ júp-noun, } beads, to repeat the name of God internally, to recite the bead-roll, to make mention, to repeat prayers inaudibly.

अपपरायण júp-pur-áyun, *s. m.* A sage, one devoted to religious meditation.

अपसाला jup-mála, *s. f.* A rosary.

अपा júp-a, *s. f.* The flower of the plant *hoor-hoor* (*Cleome viscosa*).

अपोतपी júp-ee-túp-ee, *s. m.* An adorer.

अब jub, *adv.* When, at the time when, as soon as. *Jub-tuk*, or, —*tuluk*, or, —*tores*, *adv.* Till when, whilst, as long as. *Jub-tub*, Now and then. *Jub-juh*, Whenever. *Jub-ka-tub*, *adv.* At the time when, at the proper moment. *Jub-kubhee*, or, *Jub-kubhoo*, Whenever. *Jubki*, *adv.* At the time when, when, since. *Jub-lug*, *adv.* Till when, whilst, as long as. *Jub-nuh-tub*, *adv.* Now and then, perpetually. *Jubhee*, *adv.* At the very time. *Jub seh*, Since.

अबडा júb-ra, *s. m.* The jaw, or the part of the face from the corners of the mouth to the jaws.

अबदना jub-úd-na, *v. n.* To be filled, to be folded.

अबदा jub-úd-da, *adj.* Rigid, stiff, awkward.

अबदिया jub-úd-diya, *adj.* Ill-shaped.

अभा jub-há, } *s. m.* The jaw.
अभडा jubh-ra, }

अम jum, *s. m.* Pluto, the supposed regent of worlds below, or judge of departed souls, death. *Jum-doot*, *s. m.* Messenger of death. *Jum-deeya*, *s. m.* A lamp or illumination sacred to Pluto, lighted on the 13th of *Kartik, Krishn-puksh*, i. e. Three days before the *dewalee*.

अमक júm-uk, *s. m.* Repeating of a word in different significations (*in rhetoric*); a twin, *s. f.* The state of succeeding or going on well.

अमकना júm-uk-na, *v. n.* To succeed, go on well, fit, to be assembled. *Dookan jumkee*, Buyers and sellers are collected in the shop. *Lurace jumkee*, The fight was joined. *Mujlis jumkee*, The assembly is full. *Mookudduma jumka*, The cause is begun to be debated.

अमकाना jum-kána, *v. a.* To adjust, go on well, settle, fix; to assemble, crowd together.

अमघट jum-ghút, *s. m.* Crowd, multitude.

अमजम jum-jum, *adv.* Always, constantly, perpetually.

अमदग्नी jumud-úgnee, *n. prop.* Name of *Pursooram's* father.

अमदूत jum-dóot, *s. m.* Messenger of death.

अमधर jum-dhúr, *s. m.* A dagger.

अमना júm-na, *v. n.* To germinate, grow; to be coagulated, congealed or frozen, to consolidate; to be collected, to clot; to adhere, stick, cohere, set; to pace in the manege.

अमराज jum-ráj, *n. prop.* The regent of death.

अमबाई jum-háee, *s. f.* Gaping, yawning. *Jumhaee lena*, To gape, to yawn.

जमहाना jum-hána, *v. n.* To gape, to yawn.

जमाई jum-áee, *s. m.* A son-in-law.

जमाना jum-ána, *v. a.* To collect ; sum up ; coagulate, freeze or make ice ; congeal, consolidate ; to pace in the manege.

जमालगोटा jum-al-góta, *s. m.* A purgative nut (*Jatropha curcas : Croton Tiglium*).

जमाव jum-áo, *s. m.* A crowd or multitude ; a collection, accumulation, accretion ; coagulation.

जमावट jum-áwut, *s. f.* Coagulation, agglutination, congelation, consolidation.

जमुना júm-oona, *n. prop. f.* The river *Jumna.*

जमोगना jum-óg-na, *v. a.* To ascertain.

जम्पती júm-put-ee, *s. m. dual,* Husband and wife.

जम्बाल jum-bál, *s. m.* An aquatic plant (*Vallisneria*).

जम्बाला jum-bála, *s. m.* A fragrant plant (*Pandanus odoratissimus*).

जम्बीर jum-béer, *s. m.* Common lime (*Citrus acida*) ; a plant called by some a sort of basil, with small leaves.

जम्बु júm-boo, *s. f.* A fruit tree, the rose apple (*Eugenia Jambu*).

जम्बुक júm-book, *s. m.* A jackal ; a low man ; the rose apple.

जम्बुद्वीप jumbóo-dweep, *s. m.* One of the *Pouranic* divisions of the earth, including the whole of *Hindoostan,* and said to be so named from the preceding plant abounding in it, and implying according to the *Poorans,* the central division of the world, or the known world ; according to the *Bouddhas,* it is confined to India.

जम्बूल jum-bóol, *s. m.* A fragrant plant (*Pandanus odoratissimus*) ; the rose apple.

जम्भीरी jum-bhéer-ee, *s. m.* The lime or citron, apparently of more than one species ; a plant, considered to be a kind of basil with small leaves.

जय juy, *s. m. f.* Triumph, promotion, advancement, preferment, conquest, victory, bravo ! huzza ! all hail ! *s. m.* A kind of *moong* or bean (*Phaseolus mungo*).

जयजयकार juy-juy-kár, *s. m.* Rejoicings triumph, exultation.

जयजयवन्ती juy-juy-wúntee, *s. f.* Name of a musical mode.

जयढक juy-dhúk, *s. m.* A kind of drum.

जयध्वनि juy-dhwúni, *s. m.* Shout of victory.

जयत juyt, *s. m.* A plant (*Æschynomene sesban*) ; name of a musical mode.

जयन्ती juy-úntee, *s. f.* A tree (*Æschynomene sesban*) ; a flag, a banner.

जयपत्र juy-pútr, *s. m.* Record of victory or triumph ; in law, the sealed and written award of the judge in favor of either party.

जयपाल juy-pál, *s. m.* A king, a sovereign ; (it is also the appellation of several celebrated *Hindoo princes*) ; a tree (*Croton Tiglium*).

जयमङ्गल juy-múngul, *s. m.* The royal elephant.

जयमान juy-mán,
जयवन्त juy-wúnt,
जयवान juy-wán,
जयिनी juyín-ee,
जयी júyee,
} *adj.* Victorious.

जयमाल juy-mál, *s. f.* Necklace or garland of victory.

जयशब्द juy-shúbd, *s. m.* A shout or song of victory, or the exclamation *Juy Juy.* [rious.

जय्या júy-ya, *adj.* Able to conquer, victo-

जर jur, *s. f.* A root. *s. m.* A fever.

जरठ júr-tha, *adj.* Hard, solid ; hard-hearted, cruel, harsh ; old, decayed, infirm. *s. m.* Decripitude.

जरन jur-ún, *s. m.* Cumin-seed ; a plant, yielding a pungent seed (*Nigella indica*) ; old age, becoming old and infirm.

जरत् júr-ut, *adj.* Old, ancient, advanced in years ; infirm, decayed.

जरती júr-ut-ee, *s. f.* An old woman.

जरन júr-un, *s. f.* Burning.

जरना júr-na, *v. n.* To burn.

जरा jur-a, *s. f.* Decripitude, the general relaxation and debility consequent upon old age, or old age itself ; a tree (*Mimusops kauki*) ; a female demon.

जरांश jur-ánsh, *s. m.* Paroxysm of a fever.

जरातूर jur-a-tóor, *adj.* Infirm, decrepid, debilitated, old.

जराना jur-ána, *v. a.* To burn, kindle, inflame, light, make jealous. [uterus.

जरायु jur-áyoo, *s. m.* The womb, the

जरायुज jur-áyooj, *adj.* Viviparous, born from the womb, as man and other animals.

जरासन्ध jur-a-súndh, *s. m.* A proper name, a celebrated king and warrior, sovereign of *Mugudh,* father-in-law to *Kuns,* and foe to *Krishn :* he is said to have been slain in single combat by *Bheem.*

जरासन्धजित् jur-a-sundh-jít, *s. m. Bheemsen,* the third of the *Pandoo* princes.

जरीब jur-éeb, *s. f.* A sort of wooden dart with an iron point. *Jureeb chulana,* To throw the *jureeb.*

जरूथ júr-ooth, *s. m.* Skinniness, flesh flaccid with old age.

जर्झर júrj-ur, *s. m. Indr's* banner or emblem; an aquatic plant (*Vallisneria*). *adj.* Old, infirm.

जर्झरीका jur-jur-éeka, *adj.* Rugged, perforated, full of holes; old, decayed.

जर्ण jurn, *adj.* Old, decayed.

जर्तिल jurt-tíl, *s. m.* Sesamum, growing wild.

जल jul, *s. m.* Water; frigidity (*moral, mental or physical*). *adj.* Cold, stupid, apathetic, idiotic.

जलकण्टक jul-kún-tuk, *s. m.* An aquatic plant (*Trapa bispinosa*); a crocodile.

जलकपि jul-kúp-i, *s. m.* The gangetic porpoise or water-ape.

जलकाक jul-kák, *s. m.* The diver or water-crow.

जलकाङ्क्ष jul-kánksh, *s. m.* An elephant.

जलकिराट jul-kir-át, *s. m.* A shark, or according to some, a large alligator (*who moves preeminently among the watery herds*).

जलकुक्कुड jul-kóo-kur, *s. m.* A water-hen, a diver.

जलकुक्कुटी júl-kóok-kootee, *s. f.* The black-headed gull.

जलकुन्तल jul-kóon-tul, *s. m.* An aquatic plant (*Vallisneria*).

जलकूपी jul-kóo-pee, *s. f.* A whirlpool; a pond, a pool; a spring, a well.

जलकूर्म jul-kóormm, *s. m.* The gangetic porpoise.

जलकेश jul-késh, *s. m.* An aquatic plant (*Vallisneria*).

जलक्रीडा jul-kréera, *s. f.* Sporting, or gamboling in the water, bathing for pleasure or amusement.

जलगुल्म jul-góolm, *s. m.* A whirlpool; a turtle, a tortoise; a piece of water, a lake.

जलचर jul-chúr, *adj.* Aquatic, moving or going in water (*an animal*).

जलज jul-új, *s. m.* A fish; a lotus; a shell.

जलजन्तु jul-júntoo, *s. m.* A fish, or any marine, aquatic, or amphibious animal.

जलजन्तुका jul-júntoo-ka, *s. f.* A leech.

जलजल्प jul-júl-a, *adj.* Indignant, outrageous. [nant.

जलजलाना jul-jul-ána, *v. n.* To be indig-

जलजलाहट jul-jul-áhut, *s. f.* Indignation, rage, passion, anger.

जलजा jul-já, *s. f.* A plant, said to be a sort of *Bassia* growing in or near water. *adj* Water-born, aquatic.

जलडिम्ब jul-dímb, *s. m.* A bivalve shell.

जलतरंग jul-tur-úng, *s. m.* The musical glasses, or harmonicon; playing on glasses or china bowls by rubbing the edges; a brass vessel in which water is put and the edges are beaten with two sticks.

जलतरंजी jul-tur-únjee, *s. f.* Name of a musical instrument.

जलतापिक jul-tápik, } *s. m.* The *Hilsa* or
जलताल jul-tál, } Sable fish (*Clupea alosa*).

जलथल jul-thúl, *s. m.* Ground half covered with water, marshy ground.

जलुद júl-ud, *s. m.* A cloud; a fragrant grass (*Cyperus rotundus*).

जलदाशुन jul-dáshun, *s. m.* The *Sal* tree (*Shorea robusta*).

जलधर jul-dhúr, *s. m.* A cloud; the ocean; a grass (*Cyperus rotundus*).

जलधारा jul-dhára, *s. f.* A steam or current of water.

जलुधि júl-udh-i, *s. m.* The ocean.

जलुन júl-un, *s. m.* Burning, heat, inflammation; passion, vexation.

जलनकूल jul-un-kóol, *s. m.* An otter.

जलना júl-na, *v. n.* To burn, to be burnt, to be kindled; (*met.*) To get into a passion, to be enraged, to rage. *Jul oothna,* To break out (*as fire*). *Jul pukna,* To be in a passion, to rage. *Jul boojhna,* To brand, to burn to ashes. *Juleh pur non lugana,* (*lit. to throw salt on a burn*), To triumph over insult.

जलनिधि jul-nídhi, *s. m.* The ocean.

जलनिर्गम jul-nírgum, *s. m.* A drain, a water-course, a pipe along a wall or building for carrying off water; a water-fall, the descent of a spring, &c.

जलनीम jul-néem, *s. m.* A drug (*Herpestes monniera*).

जलनीली jul-néelee, *s. f. Vallisneria.*

जलन्धर jul-un-dhúr, *s. m.* The dropsy.

जलपच्छी jul-púch-chhee, *s. f.* Water-fowl.

जलपति jul-pút-i, *s. m. Vuroon,* the mythological deity presiding over the watery element, the *Hindoo* Neptune.

जलपाई jul-páee, *s. f.* An olive; the *Eleocarpus serratus.*

जलपान jul-pán, *s. m.* Drinking (*of water*), eating, taking light food between meals, a luncheon.

जलपिप्पली jul-píppullee, *s. f.* An aquatic plant (*Commelina salicifolia, &c.*)

जलप्रष्ठजा jul-prishth-ja, *s. f.* An aquatic plant (*Pistia stratiotes*).

জলপ্রিয় jul-príyuh, *s. m.* The *chatuk* (*Cu-culus melanoleucos*) ; a fish.

জলবন্ধক jul-búndhuk, *s. m.* A dam, a dike, rocks or stones impeding a current.

জলবন্ধু jul-búndhoo, *s. m.* A fish.

জলবৃল jul-búl, *part.* Burnt up or con-sumed with fire.

জলবরী jul-búhee, *s. f.* Swimming, strik-ing with the arms and legs in water.

জলবুদ্বুদ jul-bóod-bood, *s. m.* A bubble of water.

জলব্রহ্মী jul-brúhmee, *s. f.* A kind of potherb (*Hilancha repens*).

জলভূ jul-bhóo. *s. m.* A cloud ; an aquatic plant (*Commelina salicifolia or bengalensis*).

জলময় jul-múy, *s. m.* A deluge, flood, inundation. [sect.

জলমষিকা jul-múkshika, *s. f.* A water in-

জলমানুষ jul-mánoos, *s. m.* A waterman, a mermaid.

জলমার্গ jul-márg, *s. m.* A drain or issue from a pond.

জলমার্জার jul-márjar, *s. m.* An otter.

জলমূর্তি jul-móortti, *s. m. Shiv*, of whom one form is water, implying his omnipresence.

জলযন্ত্র jul-yúntr, *s. m.* A water-work, a machine for raising water, &c., any contrivance connected with that element.

জলযন্ত্রগৃহ jul-yuntr-gríh, *s. m.* A house or fabric erected in the midst of water, or sub-terraneous apartments constructed in the bank of a river, for retiring to in the hot season ; a sum-mer-house, &c.

জলরঙ্ক jul-rúnk, *s. m.* A kind of crane, feeding on small fish chiefly, and therefore haunt-ing swamps, &c.

জলরঙ্কু jul-rúnkoo, *s. m.* A gallinule.

জলরঞ্জ jul-rúnj, *s. m.* The *Vuk*, a kind of crane.

জললতা jul-lút-a, *s. f.* A wave, a billow.

জলবানা jul-wána, *v. a.* To cause to burn.

জলবিরাল jul-vir-ál, *s. m.* An otter.

জলবিষুব jul-vísh-oov, *s. m.* The autumnal Equinox, the moment of the Sun's entering *Libra*, occurring near the close of the annual rains.

জলবৃশ্চিক jul-vrísh-chik, *s. m.* A prawn or shrimp (*water-scorpion*).

জলব্যূধ jul-vyúdh, *s. m.* A kind of fish, a sort of pike.

জলবৈয jul-wy-ya, *s. m.* A burner.

জলশয় jul-shúy, *s. m. Vishnoo*, who is supposed to sleep, borne by his serpent couch above the ocean, during the four months of the periodical rains in India.

জলশায়ী jul-sháee, *s. m. Vishnoo*, as sleep-ing on the waters.

জলসূচি jul-sóochi, *s. m.* A fish, a sort of pike (*Esox scolopax*) ; the gangetic porpoise ; an aquatic plant (*Trapa bispinosa*). *s. f.* A leech.

জলসূত jul-sóot, *s. f.* The guinea-worm (*Filaria medinensis*).

জলসেনী jul-sén-ee, *s. f.* Sleeping in water by way of mortification ; a fish.

জলহৃহ jul-húh, *s. m.* A small water (*or summer*) house.

জলহাস jul-hás, *s. m.* Cuttle fish bone, considered as the indurated foam of the sea.

জলা júl-a, *s. m.* A lake.

জলাকার jul-akár, *s. m.* Appearance or semblance of water. [cat.

জলাখু jul-ákhoo, *s. m.* An otter or water-

জলাঞ্চল jul-ánchul, *s. m.* A natural water-course or channel ; a plant (*Vallisneria*).

জলাধার jul-adhár, *s. m.* A pond, a lake, a reservoir, any piece of water.

জলানা jul-ána, *v. a.* To burn, kindle, in-flame, fire, light, make jealous.

জলাবুলা júl-a-búl-a, } *adj.* Fretful, pas-
জলাভুনা jul-a-bhóona, } sionate, hot-tempered ; scorched.

জলাময় jul-amúy, *adj.* Full of water, wet.

জলাম্বিকা jul-ám-bik-a, *s. f.* A well.

জলার্ণব jul-árnuv, *s. m.* The rainy season ; the sea of fresh water ; an inundation, a flood, a deluge.

জলার্দ্রা jul-árdra, *adj.* Wet, charged with aqueous moisture.

জলালুকা jul-álooka, } *s. f.* A leech.
জলালোকা jul-alóka, }

জলাবন jul-áwun, *s. f.* Firewood.

জলাশয় jul-áshuy, *s. m.* A pond, a tank, a lake, a reservoir, or any piece of water ; the ocean ; a fragrant grass (*Andropogon muricatum*). *adj.* Stupid, dull, cold, apathetic.

জলিকা júl-ik-a, } *s. f.* A leech.
জলুকা júl-ook-a, }

জলিয়া júl-iya, *s. m.* A fisherman.

জলেচ্ছ্যা jul-éch-chhya, *s. f.* A plant (*Heliotropium indicum*).

জলেন্ধন jul-éndhun, *s. m.* Submarine fire.

জলেবী jul-éb-ee, *s. f.* A kind of sweetmeat.

জলেশ্বর jul-ésh-wur, *s. m.* The mythologi-cal deity of water, *Vuroon* ; the ocean.

জলোকা jul-óka, *s. f.* A leech.

জলোচ্ছ্বাস jul-ochchh-wás, *s. m.* A drain or channel, made on purpose for carrying off an ex-cess of water, or such a channel made naturally by the overflow of a river, &c.

अज्ञोदर jul-ódur, *s. m.* Dropsy.

अज्ञोरगो jul-órgee,
अज्ञोकस jul-óukus, } *s. f.* A leech.
अज्ञोका jul-óuka,

अज्ञप julp, *s. m.* Dissention, wrangling; prate, babble.

अज्ञपाक julp-ák, *adj.* A chatterer, talking much and foolishly or improperly.

अव jou, *s. m.* Barley. *Jou jou hisab lena,* To take a strict account, the mark between the joints of the finger.

अवत्री juwútree, *s. f.* Mace.

अवन júv-un, *s. m.* A courser, a fleet horse; a country, Ionia or Greece; a Greek or Mahomedan.

अवा júwa, *s. m.* Mark in the joints of the fingers; a flower, the China rose (*Hibiscus rosa sinensis*); a clove of garlic, a kind of stitch in needle-work. *Juwedar,* Served in a particular manner.

अवाई juwáee, *s. m.* A son-in-law.

अवाखार juwakhár, *s. m.* Impure salt-petre.

अवांकुर juwánkoor, *s. m.* The young shoots of barley presented by *Brahmuns* to their disciples at the feast of *Nouratr.*

अवापुष्प juwapóosp, *s. m.* The China rose, the plant or its flower.

अवार juwár, *s. m.* The rise or flow of the tide.

अवारा juwára, *s. m.* Indian corn.

अवाला juwála, *s. m.* Grain mixed with barley as food for cattle.

अवाली juwálee, *s. f.* Mixed wheat.

अवासा juwása, *s. m.* A prickly bush of which *tattees* are made, and which is eaten by camels (*Hedysarum alhagi*).

अस jus, *s. m.* Name, character, celebrity, reputation, fame, renown, luck. *Jus-upjus, s. m.* Good and evil, or the favourable and unfavourable traits of one's character.

असपत jus-pút,
असपति jus-pút-i, } *adj.* Reputable, renowned.

असवन्त jus-wúnt,
असस्वी jus-swée,
असी jús-ee, } *adj.* Famous, illustrious, renowned, celebrated.

अस just,
अस्ता jústa, } *s. m.* Pewter.

अर्त júhan, *adv.* Where, in which place, which place. *Juhan tuhan,* Here and there, everywhere. *Juhan ka tuhan,* Everywhere, in the same place as before. *Juhan juhan, adv.* Wherever. *Juhan kuheen, adv.* Wherever. *Juhan-tuk, adv.* As far as. *Juhan-seh,* Whence, from which place. *Juhan-tuhan phirna,* To straggle, to wander.

अर्ती juhéen, *adv.* Wherever.

अहा júha, *s. f.* A plant, the flowers of which resemble those of the *kudumb.*

अहानक juhánuk, *s. m.* The period of the total destruction of the world.

अहु júh-noo, *s. m.* The name of a king or saint.

अहुतन्या júhnoo-túnya, *s. f.* The Ganges: the river in its course is said to have disturbed the devotions of the saint *Juhnoo,* upon which he drank up its waters; having released them at the intercession of the gods, he is thus considered the parent of the stream.

जा ja, *pron. sing.* Whom, what, which, any one.

जाई jáee, *adj. f.* Born. *s. f.* A daughter.

जाकर ján-kur, *s. m.* Money (*or other pledge*) left for a thing purchased, while it is carried away to be finally approved.

जांगर ján-gur, *s. m.* The thigh and leg.

जांघ jangh, *s. f.* The thigh.

जांघुल ján-ghul, *s. m.* A kind of heron (*Ardea indica*).

जांघिया ján-ghi-ya, *s. m.* A kind of breeches that do not cover the thigh.

जांच janch, *s. m.* Trial, examination, test, assay, proof.

जांचना jánch-na, *v. a.* To examine, enquire into, ascertain, try, prove, assay.

जांत jant, *s. f.* A wooden trough for raising water.

जांता ján-ta, *s. f.* A stone-mill for grinding corn, a handmill of two stones, one over the other; a pair of bellows.

जाकर já-kur, *s. m.* Money (*or other pledge*) left for a thing purchased, while it is carried away to be finally approved.

जाग jag, *s. m.* A religious sacrifice, vigils.

जागत já-gut, *s. f.* Watchfulness, waking.

जागतीज्योति jágtee-jyót, *adj.* Possessed of or exerting miraculous powers.

जागना jág-na, *v. n.* To awake, to be awake, to wake.

जागरन jág-run, *s. m.* Vigil, wakefulness, keeping watch, sitting up at night (*in a religious ceremony or prayers*), vespers.

जागर्ति ja-gúrt-ti, *s. f.* Waking, vigilance.

जागुह já-guh, *s. f.* Place.

जागा já-ga, *s. m.* A cast of *Hindoos.*

जागाबंदी jága-búndee, *s. f.* Drowsiness, sleepiness.

जागू ja-góo, *adj.* Wakeful, watchful.

जांगुल ján-gul, *s. m.* The francoline partridge.

आंगली jáng-lee, *adj.* Rural, picturesque, diversified with hill, vale, wood, and water (*country*); wild, *jungles*, barbarous, savage. *s. f.* Cowach (*Carpopogon pruriens*).

आंगूल ján-gool, *s. m.* Poison, venom.

आंगुलि ján-goo-li, } *s. m.* A snake-
आंगुलिक ján-goo-lik, } catcher, a dealer in antidotes, a snake doctor, one who pretends chiefly by charms to cure the bite of snakes or other venemous animals.

आंगुली ján-goo-lee, *s. f.* Knowledge of poisons, the possession of charms or drugs, and employment of them as antidotes; a potherb (*Luffa acutangula*).

आचक já-chuk, *s. m.* A suitor, a solicitor, a candidate, a beggar, a person who goes about singing for charity, a petitioner, one who asks or solicits.

आचना jách-na, *v. a.* To want, need, require, implore, solicit, ask, beg.

आजक ja-júk, *s. m.* A *Brahmun*, who presides at the performance of a religious ceremony, an officiating priest; a player on cymbals or on the tabour.

आजम já-jum, *s. f.* A cloth thrown over the carpet to sit on.

आठ jat, *s. m.* A tribe of *Rajpoots*.

आटलि ját-li, *s. m. f.* A plant (*Bignonia suave-olens*).

आठ jath, *s. m.* The axis of an oil or sugar mill which presses the grain or the canes; a post placed by *Hindoos* in the centre of a tank to mark its being dedicated.

आड़ jar, *s. m.* The gums (*of the teeth*).

आड़ा já-ra, *s. m.* Cold, coldness; the winter.

आड़ी já-ree, *s. f.* A row of teeth.

आड्य jádyuh, *s. m.* Coldness, apathy; folly, stupidity, dullness or coldness of intellect; coldness, frigidity.

आत jat, *adj.* Born, produced, engendered; a child, offspring. *s. m.* Kind, sort, class, species, cast, sect, tribe, race; birth, production.

आतक ja-túk, *s. m.* A mendicant; astrological calculation of a nativity.

आतकर्म jat-kúrm, *s. m.* A sacrificial ceremony directed to be performed at the birth of a child.

आतपांत jat-pánt, *s. f.* Pedigree.

आति já-ti, *s. f.* Kind, sort, species, class, tribe; birth, production; lineage, race, family.

आतिलखन játi-lúkshun, *s. m.* Specific or generic distinction or characteristic; mark of tribe or caste.

आतिस्वभाव játi-swubháo, *s. m.* Specific or generic character or nature.

आतिहीन jati-héen, *adj.* Outcaste, void of caste.

आती já-tee, *s. f.* Great-flowered jasmin (*Jasminum grandiflorum*); mace, nutmeg.

आतीपत्री játee-pútree, *s. f.* Mace.

आतीफल jatee-phúl, *s. m.* Nutmeg.

आतीरस jatee-rús, *s. m.* Gum myrrh.

आत्य játyuh, *adj.* Well-born, of good family.

आत्यन्ध jat-yúndh, *adj.* Born blind.

आत्रा já-tra, *s. f.* A moment (*generally implying a fortunate moment*); pilgrimage; departure, march, journey; procession, a festival.

आत्री já-tree, } *s. m.* A pilgrim.
आत्रू já-troo, }

आदव ja-dúv, *s. m.* The lineage of *Krishn*, one of that race.

आन jan, *s. m.* A conjurer, an astrologer. *part.* Knowing. *adj.* Wise, intelligent. *Janboojh-kur*, *adv.* Knowingly, wilfully, purposely.

आनत janút, *adj.* Knowing, understanding.

आनना ján-na, *v. a.* To know, to understand, to comprehend, to suppose, to trust.

आननौ jan-nóun, *v. a.* To know, understand, to comprehend, to suppose.

आनपछान jan-puh-chán, *s. m.* An acquaintance, an intimate friend.

आनबूझके jan-bóojh-keh, *adv.* Knowingly, wilfully, purposely.

आनहार jan-hár, *adj.* Going, passing away.

आना já-na, *v. n.* To go, be, pass, reach, continue. *Jata-ruhna*, To be lost, missing, to die, disappear, vanish, go away, pass away.

आनु já-noo, *s. m.* The knee.

आनुफलक jánoo-phúluk, *s. m.* The knee-pan or patella.

आनुसन्धि jánoo-súndhi, *s. f.* The knee joint.

आने अनजाने jáneh-unjáneh, *adv.* Wittingly or unwittingly.

आने देना jáneh-déna, *v. a.* To liberate, let go; to excuse, pass over (*as a fault*). *Janeh-do*, Never mind, let alone, don't.

आनो já-no, *v. n.* To go; understand, suppose; that is, videlicet, to wit.

आन्ना ján-na, *v. a.* To know, understand, comprehend, suppose, believe, deem, think, fancy, conceive, judge, account, esteem, to trust.

आप jap, *s. m.* Repeating inaudibly passages from the *shasters*, charms, names of a deity, silent meditation, muttering of prayers, counting silently one's beads.

जापक já-puk, } s. m. One who counts his
जापी já-pee, } beads, or recites passages of the *Veds*, prayers, &c., inaudibly.

जाब jab, s. m. Muzzle for large cattle; a net for fruit; a sort of grass.

जाबी já-bee, s. f. Muzzle for small cattle.

जाम jam, s. m. The rose-apple (*Eugenia jambos*, &c.); the eighth part of a day, watch of three hours.

जामन já-mun, s. f. A fruit and tree so called (*Calyptranthes caryophyllifolia; Eugenia Jambolana*). s. m. Sour milk used to coagulate fresh milk, runnet, coagulator.

जामनी jám-nee, adj. Grecian, Mahomedan, or their language.

जामाता ja-má-ta, s. m. Son-in-law, daughter's husband.

जामात्रि ja-má-tri, s. m. A daughter's husband, a son-in-law; a husband, a lord or master; the sun-flower (*Helianthus annuus*).

जामिनी já-min-ee, s. f. Night.

जामी já-mee, s. f. A virtuous and respectable woman; a sister.

जाम्बव jám-bub, s. m. The rose-apple, the fruit.

जाम्बुवत jam-bóo-wút, s. m. A fabulous bear, father-in-law to *Krishn*.

जायपुत्री jae-pútree, s. f. Mace.

जायफल jae-phúl, s. m. Nutmeg (*Myristica moschata*).

जाया já-ya, s. f. A wife, one wedded according to the perfect ritual. adj. m. Born. s. m. A son.

जायापती jáya-pút-ee, s. m. dual, Husband and wife.

जार jar, s. m. A paramour, a gallant; virulence.

जारज já-ruj, s. m. f. An adulterine, the child of a woman by her gallant.

जारन já-run, s. m. Firewood, fuel.

जारना jár-na, v. a. To light, kindle, burn, inflame.

जारनौं jar-nóun, v. a. To burn, kindle, inflame, light.

जारुल já-rul, s. m. A kind of wood (*Lagerstræmia flos reginæ*).

जारू ja-róo, part. Burning.

जाल jal, s. m. A net; a sash; a window, a lattice, an eyelet, or loophole; magick, conjuring, illusion, supernatural deception. *Jaldar, adj.* Reticulated. *Jal-lukree, s. f. Valerian.*

जालन्धर ja-lún-dhur, s. m. A country situated in the north-west of India, apparently part of *Lahore*, and perhaps the modern *Jullindhur*.

जालन्धर jal-ún-dhur-a, adj An inhabitant of *Jalundhur*.

जाला já-la, s. m. Cobweb, a pellia; a jar; a speck on the eye, a cataract.

जालिक já-lik, s. m. A spider; a fisherman; a hunter using nets.

जालिकी já-lik-ee, adj. A cheat, a rogue, a vagabond, a conjurer or juggler; one who employs nets, &c., for a livelihood.

जालिनी já-lin-ee, s. f. A painting room.

जालिया já-liya, s. m. A cheat, a rogue, a conjuror.

जाली já-lee, adj. Illusory, deceptive. s. f. Net-work; the integument in which a foetus is enveloped; a coil; a caul; a lattice, grate, trelliswork. *Jales purna*, Expresses the hardening of the stone of a mango.

जाल्म jalm, s. m. A low man, one of a degraded tribe or business. adj. Cruel, harsh, severe; inconsiderate, rash, acting without thinking.

जावक já-wuk, s. m. The red colour procured from the *lakh* insect.

जावत्री já-wut-ree, } s. f. Mace (*the spice
जाविची já-wít-ree, } so called*).

जावनीभाषा jáwunee-bhásha, s. f. The language of the Greeks or of the Mahomedans.

जावां já-wan, adj. Twins.

जासू ja-sóo, pron. From or of whom.

जाहि já-hi, pron. rel. sing. In the dative case, to whom, to whomsoever.

जाही já-hee, s. f. A flower (*Jasminum grandiflorum*); a fire-work resembling that flower.

जिगजिगिया jig-jíg-iya, adj. Fawning.

जिगजिगी jig-jíg-ee, s. f. An exclamation expressive of surprise and pleasure. *Jigjigee kurna, v. a.* To fawn.

जिगीषा jig-ée-sha, s. f. Emulation, wish to excel or overcome.

जिंघि jín-ghi, s. f. Bengal madder (*Rubia manjith*).

जिजिया jíj-iya, s. f. A sister, a dug, a breast.

जिग्यासा jigyása, s. f. Asking, inquiring.

जिठानी jithá-nee, s. f. Husband's elder brother's wife.

जित jit, adv. Where.

जितक्रोध jit-kródh, adj. Of subdued passion, not to be provoked or made angry.

जितना jít-na, m. } adj. How much, so
जितनी jít-nee, f. } much, as much as, as many. *Jitneh-men*, In as much (*time*) as.

जिता jít-a, } adj. As much as, as many
जितेक jit-ék, } as.

जिताता jit-átma, *adj.* Self-subdued, void of passion.

जिताना jit-ána, *v. a.* To cause to win or conquer.

जितेन्द्रिय jit-éndriyuh,
जितेन्द्री jit-éndree, } *s. m.* An ascetic, a sage, one who has completely subdued his passions.

जितेन्द्रियता jit-éndriyuta, *s. f.* Continence, subjugation of the senses or passions.

जितेन्द्रिय jit-éndriya, *adj.* Having subdued the senses.

जित्या jit-yá, *adj.* Conquerable, vincible.

जित्वरी jit-wúr-ee, *adj.* Victorious, triumphant. *s. f.* The city of *Benares.*

जिधर jídhur, *adv.* Where, wherever, whither, there. *Jidhur tidhur, adv.* Whither, here and there ; every where.

जिन jin, *pron. rel. inflec. pl.* Whom, what, which. A negative particle, No, not. A prohibitive particle, Don't. *s. m.* A *Jin,* the generic name of the personage peculiar to the *Jyn* sect, who is ranked by them as superior to the gods of the other sects ; a saint and teacher : twenty-four *Jins* are supposed to flourish in an *Uvusurpini,* or *Jyn* age, and their writers enumerate those of the ages past, present, and to come ; a *Buddh,* a generic term applied to the chief saints of the *Buddh* sect, in the same manner as to those of the *Jyns.*

जिभारा jib-hára, *adj.* Abusive, foul-tongued, talkative.

जिम jim, *conj.* Like, as, in such manner as.

जिमाना jim-ána, *v. a.* To feed, to entertain.

जियरा jíyura, *s. m.* Life, soul. *adj.* (*met.*) Beloved.

जियाना jiyána, *v. a.* To give life, to vivify, recover any thing almost dead ; to foster, to patronize ; to cause to live.

जियूड़ा jiyóora,
जिवड़ा jív-ra, } *s. m.* Life, soul, sweetheart, beloved ; annual wages to washermen and others.

जियौठ jiyóuth, *adj.* Brave, courageous.

जिलाना jil-ána, *v. a.* To give life to ; to vivify, animate, recover any thing almost dead ; to foster, patronize.

जिवाना jiwána, *v. a.* To feed, to entertain ; to give life, to vivify, recover any thing almost dead ; to cause to live ; to foster, to patronize.

जिस jis, *pron. rel. sing.* That, what, who, whom, which, any one. *Jis-tis,* Whomever, whatever, some or other. *Jis-jis,* Whichever, each of which. *Jis juguh, adv.* Where, wherever. *Jis dum, adv.* When, while, whilst. *Jis turuh, adv.* What fashion or manner, (in) what manner, according to, as. *Jis-turuf, adv.* Wherever. *Jis-*

kudr, adv. To what degree, as, as much as, whatever, whatsoever. *Jis-kisee-ka,* Of whomever, whosesoever. *Jis-kisee-ko,* To whomever.

जिहिं jihin, *infl. pron.* That, what, who, whom.

जिह्वा jiv-há, *s. f.* The tongue.

जिह्वामूल jiv-ha-múl, *s. m.* The fir of the tongue.

जिह्वास्वाद jiv-ha-swád, *s. m.* Licking, lapping.

जी jee, *s. m.* Life, soul, self, spirit, mind. *Jee oothana,* To withdraw one's friendship or desire. *Jee boora kurna,* To vomit, to have a nausea ; to be displeased. *Jee burhana,* To be moderately desirous. *Jee bikhurna, v. n.* To faint. *Jee bhurjana,* To be at ease and contented. *Jee ajana,* To have the mind suddenly fixed (*on any thing*). *Jee bhur-ana,* To be touched with compassion or seized with grief. *Jee buhlana,* To amuse one's self, to dissipate reflection. *Jee pana,* To understand one's temper ; to be highly pleased ; to escape from misfortune. *Jee panes kurna,* To harass, to tease, to plague, to perplex. *Jee-pur kisee-kah chulna,* To obey. *Jee-pur khelna,* To risk one's life, to run the hazard. *Jee puseejna,* or, —*pighulna,* or, —*pighul jana,* To be compassionate, to feel affection. *Jee pukra jana,* To be sorry. *Jee phut jana,* To be broken-hearted. *Jee phir jana,* To be contented ; to be satiated or disgusted. *Jee julana,* To befriend ; to plague, to perplex. *Jee julna,* To be vexed or troubled in mind. *Jee chahna,* To desire. *Jee chhipana,* or, —*choorana,* To do a work carelessly or lazily, to neglect. *Jee chulana,* To act bravely. *Jee chulna,* To desire. *Jee-dan,* Granting life, pardoning a capital crime, permission. *Jee-dan kurna,* To grant life, to pardon a capital crime. *Jee dhurukna,* To have a palpitation of the heart. *Jee doob jana,* To faint. *Jee rukhna,* To be easily pleased, to please. *Jee-seh ootur jana,* To sink in the opinion of another ; to be broken-hearted. *Jee-seh marna,* To kill. *Jee kurna,* or, —*hona,* To desire, to wish for. *Jee khol keh keochh kurna,* To do with pleasure or cheerfully. *Jee kee uman mangnee,* To preface a discourse with excuses. *Jee keh budul jee dena,* To take up the cause of another. *Jee ghut jana,* To detest. *Jee lugana,* To excite desire or love, to place or fix the mind. *Jee lugna,* To contract affection for any person or thing, to hanker after. *Jee lena,* To penetrate one's thoughts ; to excite one's desire ; to kill. *Jee marna,* To mortify one's desire, to displease. *Jee milana,* To contract friendship. *Jee-men ana,* To come into the mind, to occur to the recollection. *Jee-men jul jana,* To be tormented with envy or jealousy. *Jee-men jee ana,* To be comforted. *Jee-men ghur kurna,* To be pleasant, agreeable or acceptable. *Jee nikulna,* To die ; to desire or love excessively ; to fear exceedingly. *Jee harna,* To be discouraged, to be depressed from fear, to be spiritless. *Jee hut jana,* To detest.

Y

जी jee, *adv.* Yes. *s. m.* Sir, master, madam.

जीका jée-ka, *s. f.* Pension, livelihood.

जीगुराना jeen-goo-rána, *v. n.* To corrugate, to wrinkle.

जीत jeet, *s. f.* Winning, victory.

जीतना jéet-na, *v. a.* To win, conquer, overcome, beat.

जीतब jée-tub, *s. m.* Life, existence.

जीतवन्त jeet-wúnt, ⎫ *s. m.* A winner.
जीतबैया jeet-wyya, ⎭

जीता jée-ta, *adj.* Alive, living; over, more, above. *Jeetejee, adj.* Alive, living.

जीतिया jée-ti-ya, *s. f.* Name of a *Hindoo* fast observed by women, who have lost several children, to preserve the remainder.

जीतू jee-tóo, *s. m.* A winner.

जीधर jée-dhur, *adv.* Where, wherever, there.

जीन jeen, *s. m.* An old man.

जीना jée-na, *v. n.* To live. *s. m.* Living.

जीभ jeebh, *s. f.* The tongue. *Jeebh burhana,* To be loquacious and abusive; to pursue pleasures beyond one's reach. *Jeebh pukurna,* To silence; to interrupt one's discourse; to criticise minutely. *Jeebh jhookana,* To pretend to wealth falsely. *Jeebh chatna,* To long after or covet unattainable enjoyment. *Jeebh chulana,* To boast beyond one's ability. *Jeebh dab keh bat kuhna,* To speak with reserve. *Jeebh katna,* To forbid by signs; to grant the request of a petitioner; to be struck with terror or astonishment. *Jeebh nikalna,* To be extremely fatigued or thirsty.

जीभारा jee-bhá-ra, *adj.* Plain-spoken, loquacious.

जीभी jée-bhee, *s. f.* An instrument for cleaning the tongue; a bit of a bridle.

जीमना jéem-na, *v. a.* To eat.

जीमार jee-már, *adj.* Capital (*as a crime*); mortifying one's desires.

जीरक jée-ruk, *s. m.* Cumin-seed.

जीरन jée-run, *adj.* Old, decayed; digested.

जीरा jée-ra, *s. m.* Cumin-seed.

जीर्ण jeern, *s. m.* An old man. *adj.* Old, ancient; withered, decayed; digested.

जीर्णता jeern-tá, *s. f.* Old age; infirmity, decay.

जीर्णवस्त्र jeern-vústr, *s. m.* Old, worn, or tattered raiment.

जीर्णवृद्धक jeern-vrúdh-nuk, *s. m.* A fragrant grass (*Cyperus rotundus*).

जीर्णि jéer-ni, *s. f.* Old age, infirmity, decay; digestion.

जील jeel, *s. f.* A high note or tone in singing or music opposite to the bass, the treble.

जीव jeev, *s. m.* Animated being, animal; life, existence; the sentient soul, the emanation of the deity which, it is believed, is incorporated with the animal body, and gives it life, motion, and sensation, hence also called *Jeevatmun*; it is opposed to that abstract state of the soul *Purmatmun,* in which, by meditating upon its own divine nature and origin, the spirit is supposed to be set at liberty from human feelings and passions.

जीवू jéeoo, *s. m.* A sweetheart, a lover. *interj.* Bravo!

जीवक jée-vuk, *s. m.* A tree (*Pentaptera tomentosa*); a medicinal plant, considered as one of the eight principal drugs, classed together under the name *Ushtvurg*; an animal, any being endowed with life.

जीवगर jeev-gúr, ⎫ *adj.* Resolute, bold,
जीवट jee-wút, ⎭ brave, courageous.

जीवजीव jeev-jeev, *s. m.* A kind of bird, supposed to be a sort of pheasant.

जीवञ्जीव jeev-un-jéev, *s. m.* A kind of bird, supposed to be a pheasant; the *Chukor* or Greek partridge.

जीवरा jéev-ra, *s. m.* The soul, life; a sweetheart, beloved; annual wages to washermen and others.

जीवत jée-wut, *part.* Living, alive. *adj.* Victorious.

जीवतिया jéev-tiya, *s. f.* A *Hindoo* fast observed by women who have lost several children to preserve the remainder.

जीवतोका jee-wútto-ka, *s. f.* A woman whose children are living.

जीवत्पति jée-wut-pút-i, *s. f.* A wife whose husband is alive.

जीवधन jéev-dhun, *s. m.* Living property, live stock, wealth in flocks and herds.

जीवन jée-wun, *s. m.* Life, existence; livelihood, living, profession; water; a son.

जीवनी jée-wun-ee, *s. f.* Jasmin.

जीवनोपाय jéevun-opáyuh, *s. m.* Livelihood, means of subsistence.

जीवनौषध jeev-nóu-shudh, *s. m.* A drug to revive the dead.

जीवुत jée-wuut, *adj.* Alive, living, existent.

जीवन्तिक jee-wún-tik, *s. m.* A fowler, a birdcatcher.

जीवन्तिका jee-wún-tik-a, *s. f.* A parasite plant (*Epidendron tesseloides, and other species*); a plant (*Menispermum glabrum*).

जीवन्ती jee-wún-tee, *s. f.* A tree (*Celtis orientalis*); a plant (*Menispermum glabrum*);

the *Sun* or *Saun* tree (*Mimosa albida*); yellow myrobalan (*Terminalia chebula*).

जीवपुत्रक jeev-póotruk, *s. m.* A plant bearing seeds which are used in Rosaries.

जीवमन्दिर jeev-múndir, *s. m.* The body.

जीवमार jeev-már, *adj.* Capital (*as a crime*); mortifying (*one's desires*).

जीवसू jeev-sóo, *s. f.* The mother of living offspring.

जीवस्थान jeev-sthán, *s. m.* A joint, an articulation.

जीवातु jeev-átoo, *s. m.* A drug for re-animating the dead; life, existence.

जीवाधार jeev-adhár, *s. m.* The earth.

जीवात्मा jeev-átma, *s. m.* The vital principle, or spirit; that spiritual essence which renders bodies susceptible of motion or sensation.

जीवान्तक jeev-ántuk, *s. m.* A fowler, a bird-catcher.

जीविका jéevika, *s. f.* Livelihood, profession or occupation, by which a subsistence is obtained; pension.

जीवित jée-wit, *s. m.* Living, life, existence.

जीवितकाल jee-wit-kál, *s. m.* Period or duration of life, a life.   [tent.

जीविता jée-wit-a, *adj.* Living, alive, exis-

जीवितेश jee-wit-ésh, *s. m.* A name of *Yum*, regent of death; a lover, a husband; lord or master of existence; a drug to revive the dead.

जीवितेशा jee-wit-ésha, *adj.* Ruling life, master of being (*applicable to objects either of reverence or affection*).

जीवी jée-vee, *adj.* Alive, living, animate, a living being.

जीहारना jee-hárna, *v. n.* To be discouraged, to be depressed from fear, to be spiritless.

जुआरी joo-áree, *s. m.* A gambler.

जुंग joong, *s. f.* Emotion, impulse; a volume containing several books.

जुग joog, *s. m.* One of the four great *Hindoo* periods; a term used in the game of *chousur*; a pair. *Jooganoojoog*, Ages of ages, from age to age, for ages. *Joogjoog*, *adv.* Constantly, eternally. *Joog phorna*, or, —*phootna*, To cause a difference between friends, to fall out.

जुगत jóo-gut, *s. f.* Address, dexterity, contrivance, counsel, wit, a pun, art. *Joogut bolna*, To pun. *Joogut-baz*, Punster, quibbler. *Joogut-bazee*, *s. f.* A quibble, pun, witticism, economy.

जुगती jóo-gut-ee, *adj.* Artful, clever, cunning, economical, facetious, punning.

जुगनी jóog-nee, *s. f.* Fire-fly, glow-worm; an ornament worn round the neck.

जुगनू jóog-noo, *s. m.* The fire-fly (*Lampyris*); a jewel worn about the neck.

जुगल jóo-gul, } *adj.* Two, a pair, brace,
जुगम jóo-gum, } couple.

जुगाना joo-gá-na, *v. a.* To be careful of, to keep with care; to lend labour, *i. e.* To assist another in his work in expectation of similar assistance being returned hereafter.

जुगाल joo-gál, *adj.* Two.

जुगालना joo-gálna, *v. a.* To chew the cud.

जुगाली joo-gálee, *s. f.* The cud.

जुगुप्सन joo-góop-sun, *s. m.* } Censure,
जुगुप्सा joo-góop-sa, *s. f.* } abuse, reproach, reviling.

जुगुप्सित joo-góop-sit, *adj.* Censured, abused, reproached, reviled.

जुंग joong, *s. m. f.* A potherb (*Convolvulus argenteus*).

जुंगित jóong-it, *adj.* Outcast, deserted, injured, abandoned.

जुझ joojh, *s. m.* An engagement, a battle.

जुझाउ बाजना joo-jháoo bajna, *v. n.* To sound warlike instruments in battle.

जुटक jóo-tuk, *s. m. f.* The matted hair of *Shiv* or of ascetics; any knot or fillet of hair.

जुटना jóot-na, *v. n.* To close with, to engage in close fight, to unite, to close, to join (*as the edges of a wound*); to stay, wait.

जुटाना joo-tána, *v. a.* To conglutinate.

जुड़ना jóor-na, *v. a.* To be joined.

जुड़हा joor-há, *s. m.* Twins.

जुड़ाई joo-rá-ee, *s. f.* The price of joining, mending, &c.

जुड़ाना joo-rá-na, *v. a.* To cause to join, to cause to couple, to get mended; to tear the hair in token of grief and vexation.

जुड़हा joorhá, *s. m.* Twins.

जुत joot, (*in compos.*) With, connected with, united with, joined to, as, *Dhurmjoot*, *adj.* Virtuous.   [or yoke.

जुतवाना joot-wána, *v. a.* To cause to join.

जुताई joo-táee, *adj.* Arable. *s. f.* Tillage. *Jootana*, *v. n.* To be joined, to yoke; to be tilled.

जुतियाना joo-ti-yána, *v. a.* To beat with a slipper.

जुद्ध jooddh, *s. m.* Battle, war, fight.

जून joon, *s. m.* Time.

जोंहरी jóonh-ree, *s. f.* A kind of grain.

जुन्हाई joon-háee, *s. f.* The moonlight.

जुन्हार joon-hár, *s. m.* A kind of grain (*comprising many species, of which Indian corn is one*).

जुन्हैया joon-hy-ya, *s. f.* The moonlight.

जुवती jóo-but-ee, *s. f.* A young woman, a damsel.

जूबा jóo-ba, *adj.* Young.

जुरना jóor-na, *v. n.* To be procured or obtained, to come to hand, to be joined.

जुरनौ jóor-noun, *v. n.* To unite, to be joined.

जुरा देना joora-déna, *v. a.* To procure.

जुराना joo-rá-na, *v. n.* To be comforted or pacified. *v. a.* To procure.

जुरावन joo-rá-wun, *adj.* Procurable. *Joo-rao, s. m.* Procurement.

जूरुवा jóo-roo-wa, *s. f.* A wife.

जुल jool, *s. m.* Deceit, cheating, a trick. *Joolbaz, s. m.* A knave, a cheat.

जुवती jóo-wut-ee, *s. f.* A young woman, a damsel.

जुवराज joo-wuráj, *s. m.* A king's son, the heir-apparent, one appointed to the empire.

जुवा jóo-wa, *adj.* Young, juvenile. *s. m.* A yoke, a young man or one of the virile age, or from sixteen to seventy.

जुवार joo-wár, *s. m.* Large maize.

जुवारी joo-wá-ree, *s. m.* A gambler; a thread stretched over the bridge of a musical instrument beneath the cords, whereby the sound is said to improve.

जुषकुक joosh-kúk, *s. m.* The water of boiled pulse, pease soup, porridge, &c.

जुष joosht, *s. m.* The crumbs or remnants of a meal, or its leavings.

जुषता jóosh-ta, *adj.* Served, obliged, worshipped, gratified by service.

जुहार joo-hár, *s. f. Hindoo* salutation, obeisance.

जू joo, *adv.* Lord! master! sir!

जूआ joo-a, *s. m.* A yoke; a die, dice, a gaming, gambling. *Jooa khelna,* To gamble. *Jooah-khana,* A gambling-house.

जूआत joo-át, *s. m.* A yoke.

जूआरी joo-áree, *s. m.* A gambler; a thread stretched over the bridge of a musical instrument beneath the cords, whereby the sound is said to improve.

जूं joon, *s. f.* A louse. *Joon-moonha, adj.* Smooth-faced, hypocritical.

जूगत jóo-gut, *s. f.* Manner, mode; skill, cleverness; a pun, or double meaning. *Joogut-baz,* A punster, or rather one who is fond of uttering double meanings.

जूझना jóojh-na, *v. n.* To fight, to be killed in battle. *Joojh murna,* To die fighting.

जूट joot, *s. m.* The matted hair of *Shiv;* the clotted hair of an ascetic.

जूर joor, *adj.* Cold. *s. m.* Coldness, the cold.

जूरा jóo-ra, *s. m.* Cold; the hair done up in a knot behind, the hinder part of a turband.

जूरी jóo-ree, *s. f.* An ague.

जूतखोरा joot-khóra, *adj.* Beaten with slippers; infamous.

जूता jóo-ta, *s. m.* A shoe, slipper.

जूती jóo-tee, *s. f.* A shoe. *Jootee-khor, adj.* Beaten with slippers; mean, abject. *Jootee-pyzar, s. f.* Scuffle. *Jootee-karee, s. f.* Act of beating with slippers.

जूथ jooth, *s. m.* A band, a company, flock, herd.

जून joon, *s. m.* Time.

जूना jóo-na, *s. m.* A rope of grass; a ring of twisted grass laid under a round-bottomed jar to prevent it from oversetting.

जूवा jóo-wa, *s. m.* A yoke.

जूल jool, *s. m.* Guile.

जूष joosh,⎫ *s. m.* The water of boiled
जूस joos, ⎭ pulse, pease soup, porridge, broth, &c.

जूह jooh, *s. m.* A yoke.

जूहर jóo-hur, *s. m.* Pits filled with water at the bottom of mountains.

जूही jóo-hee, *s. f.* Jasmine (*Jasminum auriculatum*).

जृम्भ jrím-bha, *s. f.* Gaping, yawning.

जृम्भिनी jrím-bhin-ee, *s. f.* A kind of mimosa (*Mimosa octandra*).

जेह jeh, *pron.* Who, which, what.

जेट jet, *s. f.* A heap.

जेठ jeth, *s. m.* Husband's elder brother, name of the second *Hindoo* month (*May-June*). *adj.* Older, first-born.

जेठरा jéthra, *adj.* Elder, first-born; husband's elder brother.

जेठा jét-ha, *adj. m.* Elder, first-born; the first and strongest tint obtained from the *koosoom* flower (*Carthamus tinctorius*).

जेठानी jet-há-nee, *s. f.* The wife of a husband's elder brother.

जेठीमधु jéthee-múdhoo, *s. m.* Liquorice (*Glycirrhiza glabra*).

जेठौत jet-hóut, *s. m.* Husband's elder brother's son.

जेता jét-a, *adj.* As much as, so much. *Jeta-ki, adv.* Though, although.

जेतिक jét-ik, *adj.* As many, as much.

जेब jeb, *s. f.* A pocket. *Jeb-kutra, s. m.* A pickpocket.

जेय jéya, *adj.* Conquerable, fit or subject to be conquered.

जेर jer, *s. m.* The membrane in which the foetus is enveloped, the after-birth, secundines.

जेल jel, *s. m.* A string or line of captives chained together, a string of buckets passed over the Persian wheel.

जेवड़ा jéo-ra, *s. m.* A cord, a string.

जेवड़ो jéo-ree, *s. f.* A string, a cord, a worm.

जेवना jéo-na, *v. a.* To eat.

जेवनार jeo-nár, *s. f.* A treat, feast, entertainment, banquet.

जेवरी jév-ree, *s. f.* A cord, a string.

जेठ jesht, *adj.* Eldest, chief.

जेठ jeshth, *s. m.* Husband's elder brother, name of the second *Hindoo* month (*June-July*). *adj.* Older, first-born.

जेठा jesh-thá, *s. f.* One of the lunar mansions (*the eighteenth*).

जेहुर jéhur, *s. f.* A pile of pots filled with water and placed one over the other in order to be carried on the head; a ceremony preparative to marriage, in which pots filled with water are piled over one another, the whole is crowned with a bowl of *shurbut*, and the friends watch by it during the night.

जेहर jéhur, *s. f.* The name of a female ornament.

जे jy, *adj.* As much as.

जे jy, *s. m. f.* Triumph, promotion, advancement, preferment, conquest, victory, bravo! huzza! all hail! *Jyjykar, s. m.* Rejoicings, triumph, exultation. *Jyjykar kurna,* To huzza, shout. *Jymal, s. f.* Necklace or garland of victory.

जेजवंती jyjy-wúntee, *s. f.* A musical mode.

जेढक jy-dhúk, *s. m.* A kind of drum.

जेत jyt, *s. m.* A plant (*Æschynomene sesban*); a musical mode.

जेवरथ jytr-rúth, *s. m.* A hero, a victor, a conqueror.

जेता jytrá, *s. m.* A conqueror, a victor.

जेवी jytree, *adj.* Victorious, triumphant.

जेन jyn, *s. m.* A *Jyn,* a follower of the principles of a *Jin* or teacher of heterodox notions, the chief of which are, the supremacy of certain religious pontiffs over the gods of the *Hindoos,* a denial of the divine authority of the *Veds,* and a disregard of the distinction of castes.

जेपाल jypál, *s. m.* A plant (*Croton Tiglium*).

जेवर jybér, *adj.* As many times, as often as.

जेमान jymán, *adj.* Victorious.

जेमिनि jymíni, *s. m.* A celebrated saint and philosopher, founder of the *Oottur mimanss* school.

जेसा jysa, *adv. or adj.* In the manner which, what-like, as, such as, according as. *Jysa chahiyeh,* As may be desired, as it ought, sufficiently. *Jysa tysa,* As well as, so so. *Jysa ka tysa,* Precisely the same, unaltered. *Jysa ki,* As though, as if.

जेह्य jyhy, *v. fut.* Will go, will be.

जेह्यौ jyhóu, *2d pers. pl. fut. ten.* of To go.

जो jo, *pron. rel.* Who, what, which, that. *conj.* If, that, that which, because. *Jo jo,* Whoever, whatever. *Jo chees,* What thing, whatever. *Jo koochh,* Whatever. *Jo koee,* Whoever. *Joki,* Though, although, whichever.

जोआर jo-ár, *s. f.* A grain, Indian corn (*Sorghum vulgaris*). *s. m.* Flood-tide.

जोआर भाटा joar-bháta, *s. m.* The flood-tide, and ebb-tide.

जों jon, *adv.* As, when. *Jon-ton,* In some way. *Jonton-kurkeh, adv.* In any way, by some means, somehow or other, as it could be done. *Jon ka ton,* As originally, in the same way as it was, as it was, as in reality, unaltered.

जोंक junk, *s. f.* A leech. *Jonk lugana,* To apply leeches.

जोंकर jón-kur, *adv.* In any way.

जोंगुक jón-guk, *s. m.* Aloe wood or Agallochum.

जोंहीं jón-heen, *adv.* As soon as.

जोक jok, *s. f.* A leech.

जोख jokh, *s. f.* Weight.

जोखना jókh-na, *v. a.* To weigh.

जोखिम jó-khim, *s. f.* Risk, venture, peril, danger, achievement, enterprize. *Jokhim oothana,* To run the hazard, venture, risk.

जोखिमी jókhim-ee, *s. m.* A risker.

जोखों jókhon, *s. f.* Risk, venture.

जोग jog, *s. m.* Junction, fitting; a fortunate moment, opportunity, occasion; penance, devotion, intense meditation; certain divisions of a great circle, measured upon the Ecliptic. *adj.* Possible, capable, fit (in *compos.* it answers to, able, worthy, &c.)

जोगता jóg-ta, *s. f.* Suitableness, capability, ability, fitness.

जोगनी jóg-nee, *s. f.* A class of female deities supposed to be attendant on the goddess *Debee;* (in *astrology*) spirits governing periods of good and ill luck.

जोगमाया jog-máya, *s. f.* A person's assuming any number of forms of his own body at pleasure; a deceptive power which *Jogees* are supposed to possess.

जोगा jó-ga, *adj.* Opportune, fit, proper, able, capable, adequate, advisable, apposite, applicable.

जोगाभ्यास jogabhyás, *s. m.* The life and practice of a *Jogee.*

जोगिन jógin, *s. f.* Female of *Jogee.*

जोगिनी jó-gin-ee, *s. f.* A female fiend or spirit, supposed to be attendant on and created by *Doorga* ; (*in astrology*) spirits governing periods of good and ill luck.

जोगिया jógiya, *s. m.* A colour. *s. f.* A musical mode ; a kind of pigeon.

जोगी jógee, *s. m.* A *Hindoo* mendicant, a devotee ; a cast of *Hindoos* who are commonly weavers : they do not burn but bury their dead ; and the women are sometimes buried alive with their husband's corpse.

जोगेश jogésh, } *s. m.* A devotee,
जोगेश्वर jogésh-wur, } an adorer.

जोग्यु jógyuh, *adj.* Accomplished, fit, capable.

जोजन jójun, *s. m.* A measure of four *cos.*

जोट jot, *s. m.* A fellow, peer, one of a pair, a mate, a match. *adj.* Equal, even, not odd. *Jot bandhna,* To pair.

जोड़ jor, *s. m.* Junction, joint, joining, connexion, conjunction, a patch, a seam, society. *Jor dena,* To cast up, to add the sum. *Jortor, s. m.* Contrivance, arrangement, mechanism, joint, joining. *Jorjar, s. m.* Savings, collecting by small quantities, scraping together.

जोड़ती jór-tee, *s. f.* Calculation, reckoning.

जोड़न jórun, *s. m.* Solder ; runnet.

जोड़ना jórna, *v. a.* To join, mend, patch ; to add together ; to reckon, to cast or sum or add up ; to get or rather to save and scrape up a fortune, &c. ; to fabricate, cement, solder, unite, set (*a bone, &c.*), to tie, annex, affix, invent, contrive.

जोड़ा jó-ra, *s. m.* Joining, connexion, a pair, a couple ; a pair of shoes ; a suit (*of clothes*) ; alchymy.

जोड़ाई joráee, *s. f.* Joining.

जोड़ी jóree, *s. f.* A pair, a couple.

जोत jot, *s. f.* Cultivation, cultivated land, tillage.

जोत jot, } *s. f.* Brilliancy, lustre, light ;
जोति jóti, } the sunbeams ; the flame of a candle or lamp ; vision. *Jot-man, adj.* Luminous, bright. *Jotisuroop, adj.* Luminous, self-resplendent (*an epithet of God*).

जोतना jótna, *v. a.* To yoke, to plough, to till.

जोतार jotár, *s. m.* A ploughman, a husbandman.

जोतिष jótish, *s. m.* Astrology, astronomy.

जोतिषी jótishee, *s. m.* An astrologer, an astronomer.

जोती jótee, *s. f.* The string which suspends the scale of a balance.

जोधन jódhun, *s. m.* Fighting, battle.

जोधा jódha, *s. m.* A warrior, a combatant.

जोन jon, } *s. f.* Pudendum mulieris.
जोनि jóni, }

जोबन jóbun, *s. m.* Puberty, adolescence, prime, youth ; (*met.*) breast.

जोबनवती jóbun-wútee, *adj. f.* At the age of puberty, fit to be married, youthful.

जोय joe, } *s. f.* A wife.
जोरू jóroo, }

जोला jóla, *s. m.* Fraud, deceit. *Jola dena,* To deceive.

जोवत jówut, *part.* Sees, regards, observes.

जोवनो jóv-nou, *v. a.* To see, to look at, to regard.

जोशी jó-shee, *s. m.* An astrologer, an astronomer.

जोसी jósee, *s. m.* A tribe of *Hindoos.*

जोहना jóhna, *v. a.* To expect, to look out for.

जो jou, *conj.* If that. *adv.* When, what time. *Joulon,* As long as.

जौ jou, *s. m.* Barley ; the mark between the joints of the finger. *Jou jou hisab lena,* To take a strict account.

जौंकना jóunkna, *v. a.* To rail.

जौंरा भौंरा jóunra-bhóunra, *s. m.* A retired room, a vault.

जौंदरी jóund-ree, } *s. f.* A grain, *Joar*
जौंदी jóun-dee, } (*Holcus sorgum*).
जूमरी jóon-ree, }

जौतूक jou-tóok, *s. m.* Dower, nuptial present.

जौन joun, *pron.* Who, what, which.

जौनार jou-nár, *s. f.* A feast.

जौलग jóu-lug, *adv.* Until, as long as.

ग्यपित gyúpit, *adj.* Taught, expounded, made known.

ग्यप्ति gyúpti, *s. f.* Understanding, comprehension, the exercise of the intellectual faculty.

ग्यात gyát, *adj.* Known, comprehended, understood.

ग्यातसिद्धान्त gyát-siddhánt, *s. m.* A man completely versed in any science or *Shastr.*

ग्याता gyáta, *s. m.* One acquainted with any thing. *Gyatapooroos,* A learned man.

ग्यातान्वय gyatanwy, *s. m.* A name of *Vurddhuman,* the last *Jin* or *Jyn* pontiff.

ग्याति gyáti, *s. m.* A father ; a distant kinsman, one who does not participate in the oblations of food or water offered to deceased ancestors.

ज्ञात्रि gyátri, *adj.* Knowing, wise, intelligent.

ज्ञातेयुः gyatéyuh, *s. m.* Relationship, affinity.

ज्ञान gyán, *s. m.* Knowledge in general; understanding, intellect, intelligence; knowledge of a specific and religious kind, that which is derived from meditation, and the study of philosophy which teaches man the (*now fallen*) divine nature and origin of his immaterial part with the unreality of corporal enjoyments or worldly forms, and which, separating him during life from terrestrial objects, is supposed to secure him after death, a final emancipation from existence, and re-union with the universal spirit; or in other words, to exempt the soul from further transmigration. *Gyan dourana*, To meditate deeply.

ज्ञानदर्पणः gyan-dúrpun, *s. m.* One of the *Jyn* saints.

ज्ञानवान gyanwán, ⎱ *adj.* Wise, intelligent,
ज्ञानी gyánee, ⎰ knowing, judicious, a sage, one possessing religious wisdom.

ज्ञानिन gyanín, *s. m.* An astrologer, a fortune-teller, a man prescient of future events; a sage, one possessing religious wisdom or *gyan.*

ज्ञानिनी gyanín-ee, *adj.* Wise, intelligent.

ज्ञानेन्द्रिय gyanéndriyuh, *s. m.* An organ of perception or consciousness, the skin, tongue, eye, ear and intellect.

ज्ञापक gyápuk, *adj.* Making known, giving information, proclaiming. *s. m.* One who proclaims.

ज्ञापन gyápun, *s. m.* Making known, apprising, communicating, informing.

ज्ञापित gyápit, *adj.* Revealed, discovered, notified.

ज्या jyá, *s. f.* A mother; the earth; a bowstring.

ज्यानौं jyánoun, *v. a.* To cause to live, to give life to, to recover any one almost dead; to foster, to patronise.

ज्येष्ठ jyéshth, *adj.* Best, most excellent, pre-eminent; very old, oldest; elder, elder-born. *s. m.* The month *Jyeth* (*May-June*).

ज्येष्ठता jyeshth-tá, *s. f.* Seniority; superiority.

ज्येष्ठतात jyeshth-tát, *s. m.* A father's elder brother.

ज्येष्ठवर्ण jyeshth-vúrn, *s. m.* A *Brahmun*, as elder or best-born.

ज्येष्ठा jyeshthá, *s. f.* One of the asterisms considered as lunar mansions, the 18th comprising three stars, of which one is Scorpionis, figured by a ring or earring; the middle finger.

ज्यों jyon, *adv.* As, how much, the more so, when, as if. *Jyon ka tyon*, Precisely the same.

ज्योति jyóti, *s. f.* Light.

ज्योतिष jyótish, *s. m.* Astronomical and astrological science, astronomy, astrology.

ज्योतिषिक jyótishik, *s. m.* An astrologer.

ज्योतिषी jyótishee, *s. f.* A star, a planet, an asterism. *s. m.* An astrologer, or astronomer.

ज्योतिष्क jyotísk, *s. m.* A planetary or heavenly body; the generic term for the sun, the moon, a planet, an asterism, a star: the word in the *m. pl. Jyotishka*, implies all these five.

ज्योतिष्मान jyotishmán, *adj.* Luminous, splendid, resplendent, glorious.

ज्योतीरथ jyotéeruth, *s. m.* The pole-star.

ज्योत्स्ना jyótsna, *s. f.* Moonlight.

ज्योत्स्नाप्रिय jyótsna-príyuh, *s. m.* The *Chucor* or Greek partridge.

ज्योत्स्नावृक्ष jyotsna-vríksh, *s. m.* The tripod or tree of a lampstand, a candlestick.

ज्योत्स्नी jyótsnee, *s. f.* A moonlight night, or a night in which the moon is full.

ज्वर jwur, *s. m.* Fever, intermitting or continued.

ज्वरनाशक jwur-náshuk, *adj.* Anti-febrile, febrifuge.

ज्वराग्नि jwur-ágni, *s. m.* Feverish heat, or the hot paroxysm of fever.

ज्वरापहा jwur-ápuha, *s. f.* A plant (*Medicago esculenta*).

ज्वरी jwúree, *adj.* Febrile, feverish, affected with fever.

ज्वल jwul, *s. m.* Flame, blaze, light.

ज्वलका jwúlka, *s. f.* Flame.

ज्वलन jwúlun, *s. m. Ugni* or fire; burning, blazing.

ज्वलित jwúl-it, *adj.* Burnt; blazing, flaming.

ज्वार jwar, *s. f.* A grain, Indian corn, maize (*Holcus sorgum*).

ज्वाला jwá-la, *s. f.* Flame, blaze.

ज्वालाजिह्वा jwála-jivhá, *s. m. Ugni* or fire, whose tongue is flame.

ज्वालामुखी jwála-móokhee, *s. f.* A place where subterranean fires break forth, an object of veneration to the *Hindoos*; a volcano: a celebrated *Jwala-mookhee* or volcano exists near *Bulkh*, to which pilgrimages are made from *Hindoostan*, the soil abounding with hydrogenous gas which takes fire when coming in contact with the external air; otherwise, vents being made, a light is applied to the orifice and flame being kindled is fed by the stream of gas that escapes.

झ

झ jhuh, the ninth consonant of the *Nagaree* alphabet, the aspirate of the preceding letter, and corresponding in power to *jh*.

झं jhun, *s. m.* The sound of platters or of any vessels of metal striking against one another, clash of arms, as of swords, &c.

झंकार jhun-kár, *s. f.* Clinking, tinkling, ringing.

झंखना jhúnkh-na, ⎫ *v. n.* To be horror-
झंखनौं jhúnkhnoun, ⎭ struck, have the hair stand on end, to shudder, rave, chatter, lament.

झंखारा jhun-khára, *s. m.* An elk; a tree without leaves.

झंगा jhún-ga, *s. m.* An upper garment or vest, a coat, a gown.

झंझकार jhunjh-kár, *s. f.* Clinking, tinkling, ringing.

झंझट jhun-jhút, *s. m.* Wrangling, perplexity, encumbrance.

झंझटी jhún-jhut-ee, *adj.* Perplexing.

झंझना jhún-jhun-a, *adj.* Peevish, fretful.

झंझनाना jhun-jhun-ána, *v. n.* To tinkle, clink, tingle, ring, gingle, rattle.

झंझनाहट jhun-jhun-áhut, *s. f.* Peevishness; clinking, tinkling, ringing.

झंझरी jhúnjh-ree, *s. f.* A lattice.

झंडा jhún-da, *s. m.* A banner, a flag, an ensign, a streamer.

झंदूला jhun-dóo-la, *adj.* With thick handsome foliage (*a tree*), with a fine head of hair (*a child*).

झंवाना jhun-wána, *v. n.* To tan (*in the sun*). *v. a.* To wash the feet by rubbing *jhanwan*.

झक jhuk, *s. f.* Passion, emotion. *Jhuk marna*, To act fruitlessly or absurdly. *Jhukee, adj.* Passionate.

झकझोरी jhuk-jhóree, *s. f.* Scrambling and wrangling, snatching.

झकना jhúk-na, *v. n.* To rave, chatter, reflect, lament.

झकरी jhúk-ree, *s. f.* A milk-pail or vessel.

झकाझक jhuk-a-jhúk, *adj.* Shining, glittering with gold and silver, &c. brocade.

झकोर jhuk-ór, *s. m.* Loss, misfortune.

झकोरा jhuk-óra, *s. m.* Raining, a shower, a squall, a breeze, gust.

झकोरना jhuk-órna, *v. a.* To drive or beat as wind or rain in a squall, to shake.

झकोल jhuk-ól, *s. f.* The act of shaking in the water.

झकोलना jhuk-ólna, *v. a.* To shake.

झकझर jhuk-kár, *s. m.* A squall, a storm, a tempest.

झकी jhúk-kee, *s. m.* A chatterer, a prater, an useless talker.

झकना jhúkh-na, *v. n.* To chatter.

झगर jhug-úr, *s. m.* A kind of hawk.

झगरना jhug-úr-na, *v. n.* To wrangle, quarrel, dispute, cavil, contend, squabble.

झगरा jhúg-ra, *s. m.* Wrangling, quarrelling, contention, quarrel, squabble, strife. *Jhugra pukurna*, To engage in another's quarrel. *Jhugra rugra, s. m.* Squabbling and wrangling, brawl, squabble.

झगराना jhug-rána, *v. a.* To set a wrangling.

झगरालिन jhug-rálin, *f.* ⎫ *adj.* Quarrel-
झगरालू jhugráloo, *m.* ⎭ some, wrangling, disputatious, contentious; a brawler, an arguer.

झगा jhúg-a, *s. m.* An upper garment or vest, a coat, a gown. [shirt.

झगूला jhúg-oo-la, *s. m.* A child's frock or झुझर jhúj-jhur, *s. m.* A goglet.

झुझ jhujh, *s. m.* A long beard.

झुझकारना jhujh-kárna, *s. a.* To browbeat, to speak snappishly to.

झूझला jhújhla, *s. m.* A kind of sweetmeat.

झुझझुन jhun-jhun, *s. m.* An indistinct noise like the jangling of metal ornaments, a ringing, a rattling, &c.

झुझरी jhúnjh-ree, *s. f.* A lattice.

झुझझा jhunj-jhá, *s. f.* Wind, wind and rain, a hurricane, a gale; a sharp clanging sound, jangling; raining in large drops.

झुझानिल jhunj-jhánil, *s. m.* Wind with rain, a high wind in the rainy season, a typhoon or the sort of tempest frequent in the south-west monsoon.

झुझावात jhunj-jhawát, *s. m.* Wind with rain, a storm, a squall.

झट jhut, *adj.* Quick, instantly. *Jhut-seh*, or *Jhutput, adv.* Quickly, hastily.

झटक jhút-uk, *s. f.* Twitch, stitch, toss, throw, jerk, shake.

झटकना jhút-uk-na, *v. n.* To shake; to become lean. *v. a.* To touse, twitch, pull, jerk. *Jhutuk lena, v. a.* To snatch.

झटका jhút-ka, *part.* Slaughtered by cutting off the head (*in the Hindoo way*), broken asunder or torn by a sudden jerk, torn to pieces. *s. m.* A shake, a pull, a twitch.

झटकाना jhut-kána, *v. a.* To shake, to pull.

झटपट jhút-put, *adv.* Quickly, hastily.

झटास jhut-ás, *s. m.* Flap, clap, rain blown with a strong wind.

झुटि jhút-i, *s. m.* A small tree, a shrub, a bush.

झटिति jhút-it-í, *adv.* Quickly, speedily, instantly.

झुर jhur, *s. f.* Heavy rain; the heat from a fire. *s. m. f.* A kind of lock.

झुरकना jhúr-uk-na, } *v. a.* To browbeat,
झिरकना jhir-uk-na, } to speak snappishly to, to threaten, to jerk.

झुरकझुरकी jhúrka-jhurkee, *s. f.* Mutual wrangling.

झुरझुराना jhur-jhur-ána, *v. n.* To shake, to jerk.

झुरन jhúr-un, *s. f.* The act of falling off (*as of fruit from a tree*); snuff.

झुरना jhúr-na, *v. n.* To fall off (*as fruit, leaves, &c. from a tree*), emit, drop, fall, pour, shake, strain, to be sounded (*the noubut*), to be discharged (*a volley*).

झुरुप jhúr-up, *s. f.* Heat, fierceness (*as of pepper*), acrimony; sparring, contention.

झुरुपना jhúr-up-na, *v. n.* To spar, fight (*as cocks, &c.*), to contend.

झुरपाझुरपी jhúrpa-jhúrpee, *s. f.* Fighting (*particularly of birds*), sparring, contention.

झुरपाना jhur-pána, *v. a.* To fight (*cocks or other birds*), make to spar or contend.

झुरबरना jhur-búrna, *v. n.* To burn, to be all in flames.

झुरबेर jhur-bér, *s. m.* }
झुरबेरी jhur-béree, *s. f.* } A wild *ber* tree
झुरबेल jhur-bél, *s. f.* } (*Zizyphus jujuba*).

झुरवाना jhur-wána, *v. a.* To cause others to sweep.

झुराक jhur-ák, } *s. m.* Speed, haste,
झुराका jhur-áka, } hurry.

झुराखा jhur-ákha, *s. m.* A skylight.

झुराझुर jhur-a-jhúr, *adv.* Hastily, rapidly.

झुराना jhur-ána, *v. a.* To get swept; to cause to be exorcised.

झुरी jhúr-ee, *s. f.* Continued rain, showers, storm, wet weather; perquisites.

झुरोटा jhuróta, *s. m.* The end of the season (*of fruits, &c.*), going out of season.

झुनक jhún-uk, *s. f.* Ringing, tinkling, clinking, tingling.

झुनकना jhún-uk-na, *v. n.* To tinkle, clink, tingle, ring.

झुनडा jhún-da, *s. m.* A banner, a flag, an ensign, a streamer.

झुनडोला jhun-dóola, *adj.* With thick hand-

z

some foliage (*a tree*), with a fine head of hair (*a child*).

झुन jhun, *s. m.* The sound of platters or of any vessels of metal striking against one another, clash of arms (*as of swords, &c.*)

झुनक jhún-uk, *s. f.* Ringing, tinkling, clinking, tingling; clank, jingle.

झुनकना jhún-ukna, *v. n.* To tinkle, clink, tingle, ring, jingle.

झुनकार jhun-kár, *s. f.* Clinking, tinkling, ringing, clank, jingle, rattle.

झुनकारना jhun-kárna, *v. a.* To ring.

झुनवां jhún-wan, *s. m.* A kind of rice.

झुप jhup, *adj.* Quick. *adv.* Quickly. *Jhupseh, adv.* Quickly, in a trice. *Jhup khana, v. n.* To overset (*a paper kite in flying*).

झुपक jhúp-uk, *s. f.* Fanning, winking, &c.

झुपकना jhúp-uk-na, *v. a.* To fan, to move to and fro (*a fan*). *v. n.* To spring (*as a tiger*); to snatch; to wink.

झुपकाना jhup-kána, *v. n.* To wink, to twinkle.

झुपकी jhúp-kee, *s. f.* A snatch, a spring (*as of a tiger*), drowsiness, wink, twinkle.

झुपट jhúp-ut, *s. f.* A snatch, a spring (*as of a tiger*), rush, snap. *Jhuput lena,* To snatch, snap up.

झुपटना jhúp-ut-na, *v. n.* To snatch, to spring, to attack suddenly, to spring or pounce upon, to fly at, snap at.

झुपट्टा jhupútta, *s. m.* Assault, sudden attack; the spring of a tiger, a snatch. *Jhuputta marna,* To snatch.

झुपाझुपी jhup-a-jhúp-ee, *s. f.* Haste, hurry.

झुपाट jhup-át, *s. f.* Quickness.

झुपाना jhup-ána, *v. n.* To take a nap.

झुपास jhup-ás, *s. f.* A shower.

झुपासिया jhup-ásiya, *adj.* Deceitful, fraudulent.

झुबकाना jhub-kána, *v. a.* To astonish.

झुबिया jhúb-iya, *s. m.* An ornament.

झुबूषा jhúb-ooa, *adj.* Long-haired (*cattle or dogs*), shaggy; bent, curved, bending (*as the bough of a tree*).

झुब्बा jhúbba, *s. m.* A tassel.

झुब्बी jhúbbee, *s. f.* Trappings.

झुब्बूषा jhúbbooa, *adj.* Long-haired (*cattle or dogs*), shaggy; bent, curved, bending (*as the bough of a tree*).

झमक jhúm-uk, *s. f.* Glitter.

झमकडा jhúm-uk-ra, *s. m.* Splendour.

झमकना jhúm-uk-na, *v. n.* To glitter; to dance.

झमका jhúm-ka, *s. m.* Splendour, refulgence ; the clash or clatter of metallic substances.

झमकाना jhum-kána, *v. a.* To cause to glitter or dance.

झमकी jhúm-kee, *s. f.* Glance, glare, glitter.

झमझम jhúm-jhum, ⎫ *adv.* Heavily and
झमाझम jhum-ajhúm, ⎭ during the whole day (*raining*).

झमझमाना jhum-jhum-ána, *v. n.* To sparkle, shine, glitter.

झमरझमर jhúm-ur-jhúm-ur, *adv.* Drop by drop (*as small rain*).

झमाका jhum-áka, *s. m.* A heavy shower ; quickness, haste.

झमाझम jhum-ajhúm, *adv.* Heavily and during the whole day (*raining*).

झर jhur, *s. f.* Heavy rain ; the heat from a fire. *Jhur burna*, To burn, to be all in flames.

झरना jhúr-na, *s. m.* A skimmer ; a spring, a cascade. *v. n.* To spring, to flow ; to fall off (*as fruit, leaves, &c. from the tree*).

झरफना jhúr-uph-na, *v. n.* To spar, to fight (*as cocks, &c.*), to contend.

झरोखा jhur-ókha, *s. m.* A lattice, a window.

झरझर jhúr-jhur, *s. m.* A goglet.

झरना jhúr-na, *s. m.* A skimmer ; a spring, a cascade. *v. n.* To spring, to flow ; to fall off (*as fruit, leaves, &c. from the tree*).

झल jhul, *s. f.* Passion, anger, jealousy ; the heat from a fire.

झलक jhúl-uk, *s. f.* Brightness, glitter, glare, refulgence, reflection of light.

झलकना jhúl-uk-na, *v. n.* To shine, to glare.

झलका jhúl-ka, *s. m.* A blister.

झलकाना jhul-kána, *v. a.* To cause to shine, brighten, burnish.

झलकार jhulkár, *s. m.* Burning, brightness, splendour.

झलकी jhúl-kee, *s. f.* A glance.

झलझल jhúl-jhul, *s. m.* Glare, glitter.

झलझलाना jhuljhul-ána, *v. n.* To glitter, to glare ; to be in a passion ; to throb, ache, smart.

झलझलाहट jhuljhul-áhut, *s. f.* Glitter, glare, splendour ; smart.

झलना jhúl-na, *v. a.* To fan, to move to and fro (*as a fan*), to flap. *v. n.* To be soldered or repaired.

झलवाना jhul-wána, *v. a.* Causal of *Jhulna*.

झलहाया jhul-háya, *adj.* Suspicious ; jealous.

झलझल jhul-ajhúl, *adj.* Luminous, resplendent, embroidered. *s. f.* Splendour, glitter.

झलाना jhul-ána, *v. a.* To repair (*any thing of metal*), to solder.

झलाबोर jhul-abór, *adj.* Splendid, shining, covered with jewels and ornaments. *s. f.* Splendour.

झलार jhul-ár, *s. m.* A thicket, copse, underwood.

झाईं jháeen, *s. f.* Shadow ; a freckle or black mark on the face (*not a mole*).

झांक jhank, *s. f.* A peep. *s. m.* A herd of deer, a flock of birds, &c.

झांकना jhánk-na, *v. a.* To peep, to spy.

झांकड़ jhán-kur, *s. m.* Bushes, brambles, underwood.

झांकझोंकी jhánka-jhónkee, *s. f.* Peeping, bopeep.

झांक jhank, *s. m.* A kind of deer.

झांझ jhanjh, *s. f.* Cymbal ; anger, passion, pet, rage ; stillness, dreariness ; impatience (*in a horse expecting his corn*).

झांझट jhán-jhut, *s. f.* Wrangling, squabbling, quarrelling.

झांझा jhán-jha, *s. m.* The name of an insect, caterpillar, cabbage-worm.

झांझिया jhán-jhiya, *adj.* Passionate.

झांझी jhán-jhee, *s. f.* A kind of play. (*Children in the month of Asin go about at night, dancing, begging, and carrying on their heads earthen pots perforated on all sides, within which lamps are kept burning.*)

झांप jhamp, *s. m.* A matted shutter.

झांपना jhámp-na, *v. a.* To cover, to shut.

झांवरा jháonra, *adj.* Black.

झांवली jháon-lee, *s. f.* A wink, coquetry ; a hot wind. *Jhaonleebaz*, A coquette. *Jhaonlee lena*, To ogle.

झांवा jhánwa, *s. m.* Pumice stone, bricks burnt to cinder.

झांसना jháns-na, *v. a.* To debauch, to seduce, to wheedle, to coax ; to be inclined, to be agog, to be intent or set (*on*), to covet.

झांसू jhán-soo, *s. m.* A flatterer, wheedler, seducer.

झाऊ jháoo, *s. m.* A tree growing in marshy ground, whose tender branches are worked into baskets, and the dry wood is used as fuel (*Tamarix Indica*). [scum.

झाग jhag, *s. m.* Foam, froth (*of the ocean*),

झाझर jhájhur, *s. m.* Cymbals or bells for the ankles.

झाझा jhájha, *s. m.* An intoxicating mixture made with *bhung* or hemp.

झाट jhat, *s. m.* An arbour, a bower, a place overgrown with creepers ; a wood, a thicket.

झाटा jháta, *s. f.* Jasmin.

झाटीका jhatéeka, *s. f.* A plant (*Flacourtia cataphracta*).

झाड़ jhar, *s. m.* Bushes, brambles, bush, shrub, brake, underwood ; a kind of firework ; a lustre or chandelier ; a purge ; continued rain. *Jhar bandhna,* To rain without ceasing. *Jhar puhar,* Digression. *Jhar phoonk, s. f.* Juggling, conquering, hocus pocus (*particularly to cure the bite of a snake or a disease*). *Jhar jhutuk, s. f.* Sweeping. *Jhar jhunkhar, s. m.* Brambles, large dry bushes. *Jhar jhoor, s. f.* Sweepings ; perquisites ; thicket.

झाड़खंड jhar-khúnd, *adj.* Bushy. *s. m.* A forest, the forest of *Byjnath*.

झाड़न jhá-run, *s. f.* Sweepings ; a coarse cloth for wiping furniture, &c.

झाड़ना jhár-na, *v. a.* To sweep, brush, shift, clean, strain, knock off, dash, strike, flap, strike fire (*as with a flint*), to beat (*bushes, &c.*) *Jhar puchhor kur dekhna,* To try, to prove, to examine. *Jharna phoonkna,* To exorcise, to repeat spells or charms. *Jhar dalna,* To sweep out or away. *Jhar dena, v. a.* To brush, to clear away.

झाड़न्त jhar-únt, *adv.* Entirely.

झाड़ा jhára, *s. m.* A stool, a purge. *Jhara jhupteh jana,* To go to the necessary. *Jhara jhupta lena,* To search. *Jhara phirna,* or *Jhara jhutka phirna,* To walk among the bushes (*which means*) to go to the necessary. *Jhara dena,* To submit to search. *Dookan-jhara, s. m.* Sweepings of a (*druggist's*) shop, compound medicine.

झाड़ी jhá-ree, *s. f.* Forest, wood, underwood, brushwood, copse, bush, brake, shrub.

झाड़ू jhároo, *s. m. f.* A besom, broom, a comet. *Jharoo-kush,* or, *—burdar, s. m.* A sweeper ; the caste of *Hulalkhor*.

झापा jhápa, *s. m.* A narrow-mouthed basket.

झाबर jhá-bur, *s. f.* Marshy land, fen.

झाबा jhába, *s. m.* A leathern pot for measuring oil, ghee, &c.

झामक jhámuk, *s. m.* A burnt or vitrified brick.

झामर jhámur, *s. m.* A small whetstone, used chiefly by housewives for sharpening their spindles, needles, &c.

झामा jháma, *s. m.* Pumice stone, bricks burnt to cinder.

झारी jháree, *s. f.* A pitcher with a long neck and a spout to it, an ewer ; forest, wood, underwood, brush-wood.

झाल jhal, *s. m.* Sharpness, heat, fieriness (*as of pepper*), acrimony ; a large basket ; joining or soldering of metals.

झालना jhálna, *v. a.* To season (*pickles*) ; to polish, to clean (*plate*) ; to solder.

झालर jhá-lur, *s. f.* Fringe. *Jhalurdar, adj.* Fringed.

झालरा jhál-ra, *s. m.* A spring (*of water*).

झालरी jhálree, *s. f.* Cymbals.

झावू jháwoo, *s. m.* A tree (*Tamarix Indica*).

झिझक jhíjh-uk, *s. f.* A start.

झिझकना jhíjh-uk-na, } *v. n.* To start or
झुझकना jhújh-uk-na, } boggle, to feel the sensation of the limbs being asleep, or as if pins and needles were striking through them.

झिझकाना jhijh-kána, *v. n.* To start.

झिड़क jhír-uk, *s. f.* Threat, jerk.

झिड़कना jhír-ukna, } *v. a.* To browbeat,
झुड़कना jhúr-ukna, } speak snappishly to, scold, threaten, jerk.

झिड़काझिड़की jhirka-jhírkee, *s. f.* Mutual wrangling.

झिड़की jhírkee, } *s. f.* Rebuff, snappish-
झुड़की jhúrkee, } ness, frowning, jerk, repercussion.

झिड़झिड़ाना jhír-jhir-ána, *v. n.* To rage, rail, storm.

झिनहुड्ड jhín-hudda, *adj.* Raw-boned.

झिन्टी jhín-tee, *s. f.* A shrub (*Barleria cristata*).

झिनझिनी jhín-jhin-ee, *s. f.* The tinkling sensation felt when a limb is asleep.

झिरझिर jhír-jhir, *adj.* Running in a slender stream (*water, &c.*)

झिरझिरा jhír-jhir-a, *adj.* Very thin.

झिरझिराना jhir-jhir-ána, *v. n.* To trickle, to rill.

झिरी jhír-ee, *s. f.* A cricket.

झिलगा jhíl-ga, *s. m.* The netted bottom of a bed or couch when worn out and separated. *adj.* A couch or bed is said to be *jhilga,* when the bottom is worn out or broken.

झिलंगा jhil-únga, *s. m.* A kind of soldier.

झिलम jhíl-um, *s. f.* Armour, a coat of mail ; the visor of a helmet. *Jhilum ka top,* An iron helmet.

झिलमिल jhíl-mil, *s. m.* A kind of gauze ; a shutter, a venetian blind.

झिलमिला jhíl-mil-a, *adj.* Thin, sparkling.

झिलमिलाना jhíl-mil-ána, *v. n.* To undulate as the flame of a candle or as water, to twinkle, to scintillate.

झिल्ली jhíllee, *s. f.* A cricket ; a thin skin, a pellicle ; the membrane in which the fœtus is enveloped (*secundines*) ; the caul (*omentum*).

झीकना jhéekna,
झीखना jhéekhna,
झींकना jhéenkna,
} *v. n.* To grieve, lament, think of any thing with sorrow, recommend any thing seriously.

झींगट jhéengut, *s. m.* A steersman.

झींगा jhéen-ga, *s. f.* A shrimp, a prawn. *s. m. Cucumis acutangulus: Luffa acutangula.*

झींगुर jhéen-goor, *s. m.* A kind of insect, a cricket.

झीन jheen,
झीना jhéena,
} *adj.* Fine, subtile, thin.

झील jheel, *s. f.* A lake.

झीसी jhéesee, *s. m.* A shower.

झुकना jhóok-na, *v. n.* To nod, to bow, to stoop, to be bent, especially downwards (*as the bough of a tree*), to be tilted; to be angry, to be perplexed.

झुकाना jhoo-kána, *v. a.* To cause to stoop, to tilt, bend downwards; to bow, incline; to nod or make nod.

झुकाव jhoo-káo, *s. m.* The state of being bent downwards, stoop.

झुकावट jhoo-ká-wut, *s. f.* Stooping, nodding, bending downwards.

झुंझलाना jhoonjh-lána, *v. n.* To be peevish or fretful, to be petulant or irritable, to rage, to storm. *Jhoonjhlahut, s. f.* Peevishness, raging, storming.

झुठलाना jhoot-lána,
झूठलाना jhooth-lána,
} *v. a.* To belie, to falsify.

झुठालना jhoo-tálna,
झूठालना jhoo-thál-na,
} *v. a.* To prove to be false, to prove one in the wrong; to pollute victuals by touching them, &c. *Moonh jhootalna*, To eat something. *Moonha moonh jhootalna*, To give a man the lie to his face.

झूड़ jhoor, *s. m.* A bush, bramble.

झूंट jhoont, *s. m.* A shrub, a bush.

झूंड jhoond, *s. m.* A crowd, swarm, flock, troop; the buzzing noise of a crowd; a clump of trees. *Jhoond keh jhoond*, Crowds, &c., used intensively.

झूंडा jhóonda, *s. m.* A standard, a banner, a flag.

झूंडी jhóon-dee, *s. f.* A bush, a tuft of grass.

झूम jhoon, *s. f.* Slight resemblance.

झूनझूना jhóon-jhoon-a, *s. m.* A child's rattle.

झूनझूनी jhóon-jhoon-ee, *s. f.* Little bells worn on the feet.

झूमका jhóom-ka, *s. m.* The bell-shaped pendant of an ear-ring; the wain, *Ursa Major*; a bunch of flowers or fruit; name of a flower.

झूरना jhóor-na, *v. n.* To wither, to fade (*from grief*), to pine.

झूरमट jhóor-mut, *s. m.* A multitude, a crowd, assembly, ball; a battle, conflict; a shawl twisted round the head.

झुरियाना jhooriyána, *v. a.* To weed; to wipe, clean, and plaster a house, &c.

झूरी jhóo-ree, *s. f.* A wrinkle.

झुलकाना jhoolkána, *v. a.* To scorch, to singe (*as the small feathers of a plucked fowl*).

झूलना jhóolna, *v. n.* To swing, to dangle.

झुलस जाना jhóolus jána, *v. n.* To be scorched or singed.

झुलस देना jhóolus déna, *v. a.* To sear, to singe.

झुलुसना jhoolúsna, *v. n.* To be singed, scorched or seared.

झुलसाना jhoolsána, *v. a.* To cause to singe, to singe, sear, scorch.

झूलाना jhoolána, *v. a.* To swing, shove a swing in which others are, to rock (*a cradle*); to dangle, to hang; to make another (*as a dun*) dance after one.

झूला jhóolla, *s. m.* A shirt or vest that covers the body from the shoulder downwards.

झूंझ jhoonjh, *s. m.* A bird's nest.

झूंझुल jhóon-jhul, *s. f.* Petulance, peevishness, irritableness, rage.

झूंटर jhóon-tur,
झूंठर jhóon-thur,
} *s. f.* Ground that produces two crops yearly.

झूंठनझांठन jhóonthun-jhánthun, *s. f.* Leavings.

झूंडी jhóondee, *s. f.* A bush, a clump of grass.

झूट jhoot,
झूठ jhooth,
} *adj.* False. *s. m.* A lie, falsehood. *Jhooth mooth*, False, untrue. *adv.* Falsely. *Jhooth bolna*, To lie, to tell a lie, speaking falsehood.

झूटा jhóota,
झूठा jhóotha,
} *adj.* Liar, false; (*among Hindoos*) that which has touched food and is thereby defiled; offal, refuse, left (*food*). *s. m.* Leavings of food. *Jhoota jhata, s. m.* Offals, left food. *Jhootha chatna*, To eat leavings, to be very wretched. *Jhoothee nuh poochhna*, To refuse even common civility.

झूर jhoor, *s. m.* A bush, bramble.

झूना jhóona, *s. m.* A ripe cocoa-nut; a kind of muslin.

झूम jhoom, *s. m.* Abundance of foliage; waving, undulating. *Jhoom jhoom*, Gathering of the clouds.

झूमक jhóomuk, *s. f.* An assembly, a ball; (*met.*) a battle, an engagement.

झूमका jhóomka, *s. m.* The bell-shaped pendant of an ear-ring; the constellation of the bear.

झूमकी jhóomkee, *s. f.* A kind of ear-ring.

झूमझूम jhoom-jhoom, *s. m.* Gathering of the clouds.

झूमना jhóomna, *v. n.* To wave, move the head up and down, slumber, move loose, gather (*the clouds*).

झूरना jhóor-na, *v. a.* To pound, to grind; to shake fruit from the tree. *v. n.* To pine.

झूरा jhóora, *adj.* Withered.

झूल jhool, *s. f.* Body-clothes of cattle, housings, a bag, a wallet, a knapsack.

झूलना jhóolna, *v. n.* To swing (*for exercise*); to swing, dangle, hang, oscillate. *s. m.* A kind of poem.

झूला jhoola, *s. m.* A swing, the rope on which people swing.

झूसा jhóosa, *s. m.* Misling rain.

झूसी jhóosee, *s. f.* A town opposite *Allahubad.*

झोंक jhonk, *s. f.* A shove or push in swinging; the impulse of a squall or sudden blast of wind. *Jhonk dena,* To set fire to (*particularly straw, &c.*); to throw dust, &c.; to throw away (*the lives of men uselessly*). *Jhonk khana,* To roll.

झोंकना jhónkna, *v. a.* To cast, push, throw, toss; to cast fuel (*into an oven*).

झोंटा jhónta, *s. m.* ⎫ The hair of the back
झोंटी jhóntee, *s. f.* ⎬ part of the head; the motion of a swing. *Jhonta dena,* To shake one's head with violence.

झोंपड़ा jhómpra, *s. m.* ⎫ A cottage, a hut.
झोंपड़ी jhómpree, *s. f.* ⎭

झोंपा jhómpa, *s. m.* A bunch of fruit; a cloth with eyelets which covers the whole body; a spike.

झोंरा jhónra, *s. m.* A bunch, a cluster (*of fruit*).

झोक jhok, *s. f.* A jolt, a puff or gust.

झोका jhóka, *s. m.* A blow, a contact, collision, a gust, blast, breeze or current (*of wind*).

झोझ jhojh, *s. m.* A nest; the stomach; a pendulous belly.

झोझा jhójha, *s. m.* The stomach.

झोल jhol, *s. m.* Puckering or wrinkling (*as of ill made clothes*); a litter, brood, farrow, hatch, a birth.

झोला jhóla, *s. m.* A stroke of the sun; the palsy; a knapsack, a wallet.

झोली jhólee, *s. f.* A wallet.

झोंरा jhóunra, *adj.* Tawny.

झोंसा jhóunsa, *adj.* Greatly burnt or scorched.

झोर jhour, *s. f.* Squabbling; sounding all the strings of a musical instrument at once.

झोवा jhóu-wa, *s. m.* A tree (*Tamarix Indica*), whose branches when tender are made into baskets, and when dry are used as fuel: it grows in marshes; a basket without a cover.

———

ट

ट tuh, The eleventh consonant of the *Naguree* alphabet, and answers to the English *t* in tin.

टंकना túnk-na, *v. n.* To be stitched.

टंकार tunkár, *s. f.* The twang (*of a bowstring*).

टंकोरना tun-kór-na, *v. n.* To twang.

टंगना túng-na, *v. n.* To be hung, to be suspended.

टंगरी túng-ree, *s. f.* The leg.

टंच tunch, *adj.* Miserly; hard; untractable.

टंटा túnta, *s. m.* Wrangling, altercation, squabble, strife.

टक tuk, *s. f.* Temper, nature, disposition. *Tuk bandhna, v. a.* To stare, to gaze. *Tuk lugana, v. a.* To expect, to long for.

टकटकी túk-tuk-ee, *s. f.* Staring, fixed look, gaze. *Tuktukee bandhna,* To regard with a fixed look, to gaze.

टकना túk-na, *v. n.* To be stitched. *v. a.* To stare at, to aim, peep, see, spy, watch, view, behold, look, look for, attend.

टकराना tuk-rána, *v. a.* To knock together the heads of two people, to dash the head on something, to dash together, to butt. *v. n.* To grope in a dark place or passage.

टकसाल tuksál, *s. f.* A mint. *Tuksal ka khota, adj.* Spoilt in education. *Tuksal churhna, v. n.* To be educated. *Tuksal bahur, adj.* Uneducated, unpolished, rude, unclassical.

टकसालिया tuk-sáliya, ⎫ *s. m.* Officers of
टकसाली tuk-sálee, ⎭ the mint.

टका túk-a, *s. m.* Two pice of *Delhi*, nearly equal in value to a penny, English money, or about two-thirds of an anna.

टकाई tuk-áee, *s. f.* A tax, duty, collection, imposition; a cheap trull.

टकी túk-ee, *s. f.* Stare, fixed look; aim.

टकूवा túk-ooa, *s. m.* A spindle.

ਟਕੇਤ tuk-ét, ⎱ adj. Rich, possessed of rea-
ਟਕਤ tukyt, ⎰ dy money.

ਟਕੋਰ tuk-ór, s. f. The sound of a drum ;
a fillip, tap.

ਟਕੋਰਾ tuk-óra, s. m. A fillip, a tap ; a
very small unripe mango ; the sound of a drum.

ਟਕੋਰਨਾ tuk-órna, v. a. To foment.

ਟਕੋਨਾ tuk-óu-na, s. m. Two pice or two-
thirds of an anna of Delhi, nearly to a penny, English money.

ਟਕਦੇਸ਼ੀ tukk-déshee, s. m. A potherb
(Chenopodium album).

ਟਕਰ tukkúr, s. m. Shoving, pushing, push,
shouldering, knocking against, collision, striking a
blow, butt, butting, the knocking of head to head ;
equality. Tukkur khana, v. a. To stumble ; to be
dashed against any thing ; to meet with a loss or
misfortune. Tukkur puhar seh lenee, To enter the
lists against an antagonist of greatly superior force.
Tukkur marna, v. a. To knock against ; (met. from
the suppliant's striking their heads on the ground)
to pray ; to curse.

ਟਖਨਾ túkhna, s. m. The ankle joint.

ਟਗਰ túg-ur, s. m. Borax ; wanton play or
sport ; wandering of the mind, confusion, perplexity.

ਟਗੁਰਨਾ tug-úr-na, v. n. To roll.

ਟਗਰਾ túg-ra, adj. Squint-eyed.

ਟਗਰਾਨਾ tug-rána, ⎱ v. a. To roll.
ਟਘਰਾਨਾ tugh-rána, ⎰

ਟਗੁਰਨਾ tug-húr-na, v. n. ⎱ To roll.
ਟਘਰਾਨਾ tugh-rána, v. a. ⎰

ਟਗੁਹਲਨਾ tug-húlna, v. n. To roll ; to be
melted, to rarefy.

ਟਘਲਾਨਾ tugh-lána, v. a. To roll.

ਟਂਕ tunk, s. m. A kind of elephant or wood
apple ; Borax ; a spade or hoe ; a hatchet, or stone
cutter's chisel ; a sword, a scimitar, a sacrificial
hatchet or knife ; a weight equal to four mashas ;
a weight of silver put for a coin.

ਟਂਕਪਤਿ tunk-pút-i, s. m. The master of the
mint.

ਟਂਕਸ਼ਾਲਾ tunk-shála, s. f. A mint.

ਟਂਕਾ tun-ka, s. m. The jingle of plates,
dishes, &c.

ਟਂਕਾਨਕ tunk-ánuk, s. m. The mulberry
(Morus Indica).

ਟਂਕਾਰ tun-kár, s. m. Surprise, wonder ;
fame, notoriety ; the twang of a bow-string.

ਟਂਕੋਰਨਾ tun-kórna, v. n. To twang.

ਟਂਗ tung, s. m. The leg ; Borax.

ਟਂਗਜਾਨਾ tung-jána, ⎱ v. n. To be hung, to
ਟਂਗਨਾ túngna, ⎰ be suspended.

ਟਂਗਰੀ túng-ree, s. f. The leg.

ਟੁਂਗਿਨੀ túngin-ee, s. f. A plant (Cissampelos hexandra).

ਟਂਚ tunch, adj. Miserly ; hard, untractable.

ਟਟਕਾ tútka, adj. Fresh, new, recent.

ਟਟਰੀ tútree, s. f. The crown of the head ;
a fence, a hedge.

ਟਟਪੁਂਜਿਯਾ tut-póonjiya, adj. Bankrupt, or
reduced in circumstances (a merchant).

ਟਟਵਾਨੀ tutwánee, s. f. A pony mare.

ਟਟਿਯਾ tútiya, s. f. A skreen, a matted
shutter.

ਟਟਿਰੀ tutíree, ⎱ s. f. A bird, a sand-
ਟਟੀਹਰੀ tutéehree, ⎰ piper (Tringa goensis).

ਟਟੋਲਨਾ tu-tólna, v. a. To feel for, grope,
search for by feeling, touch, finger.

ਟਟੁਰ túttur, s. m. A matted shutter.

ਟਟੁਰੀ túttur-ee, s. f. A lie, a falsehood ; a
kettle-drum.

ਟਟਾ tútta, s. m. A skreen.

ਟਟੀ túttee, s. f. A skreen, a matted shutter ; a necessary office ; a frame for illumination.
Tuttee bundhna, v. n. To draw up men in a close
rank. Shikar kee tuttee kee ot bythna, To do
secretly ; to form an ambuscade.

ਟਟੂ túttoo, s. m. A pony.

ਟਟਿਯਾ tút-hiya, s. f. A flat dish used by
Hindoos.

ਟਂਟਾ túnta, s. m. Wrangling, altercation,
squabble, strife.

ਟਨ tun, s. m. Twang ; pride, conceit,
vanity. Tun tun, A sound.

ਟਨੁਕ tún-uk, s. f. A harsh sound.

ਟਨਕਾ túnka, s. m. The jingle (of plates,
dishes, &c.)

ਟਨਾ tún-a, s. m. Pudendum muliebre, clitoris.

ਟਨਾਨਾ tun-ána, v. a. To extend, to stretch.

ਟਪ tup, s. m. A spring, leap, bound, a
drop of rain or other liquid ; a sound.

ਟਪਕ túp-uk, s. f. Pain, throbbing ; sound
made by dropping. Tupuk nuwees, s. m. One who
reports erroneously what he pretends to have
overheard. Tupuk purna, To drip.

ਟਪਕਨਾ túp-uk-na, v. n. To drop when
ripe ; to drip, distil ; to throb, palpitate.

ਟਪਕਾ túp-ka, s. m. A drop of rain ; fruit
falling when ripe (particularly mangoes) ; a
windfal.

ਟਪਕਾਨਾ tup-kána, v. a. To cause to drip,
to distil.

टपकाव tup-káo, *s. m.* Distillation.

टपकी túp-kee, *s. f.* A small drop of rain; fruit falling when ripe (*particularly mangoes*); a windfall.

टपआना tup-jána, *v. n.* To jump over, to leap over.

टपना túp-na, *v. a.* To jump over. *Tup-a-toa, part.* Groping.

टप पड़ना tup púrna, *v. a.* To thrust one's self into other people's concerns, to intermeddle, to interfere.

टपाना tup-ána, *v. a.* To cause to jump over, to cause to leap; to make to bound.

टप्पा túppa, *s. m.* The post office; a mode in music; the bound of a ball, &c.; a sort of hook; a jump, a bound. *Tuppa khana, v. a.* To bound or ricochet (*a shot*). *Tuppa marna, v. a.* To sew or stitch with intervals; to read in a desultory manner.

टब्बर túbbur, *s. m.* Family.

टर tur, *adj.* Intoxicated; inattentive, regardless, like one intoxicated.

टरटर túrtur, *s. f.* Chattering.

टरटराना turturána, *v. a.* To chatter.

टरटरी túrturee, *s. f.* Chattering.

टरना túrna, } *v. n.* To give way, to shrink
टलना túlna, } from, flinch; to pass away, disappear, retire.

टर्रा túrra, *adj.* Wicked, vicious (*particularly a horse*); stout.

टर्राना turrána, *v. a.* To chatter.

टल आना tul jána, *v. n.* To get out of the way, to disappear, vanish, pass away.

टलना túlna, *v. n.* To give way, shrink from, flinch; to disappear, pass away, retire.

टलप túl-up, *s. f.* A piece, a fragment.

टलमलाना tulmul-ána, *v. n.* To totter; to tantalize.

टलाना tul-ána, *v. a.* To cause to disappear, to cause to give way.

टलूवा tul-óoa, *s. m.* A man who watches over a *tal* or stack of wood.

टलनवीसी túlleh-nuwéesee, *s. f.* Unprofitable employment, wasting of time.

टसक tús-uk, *s. f.* Shooting pain, stitch, throb.

टसकना túsuk-na, *v. n.* To move, to shake; to have pain, to decline in quality.

टसकाना tuskána, *v. a.* To move, to shake; to shoot with pain.

टसना túsna, *v. n.* To burst (*as tight cloth or a pillow stuffed too full*), to split, to crack.

टसवे tús-weh, *s. m.* Tears.

टहुक túhuk, *s. f.* Pain in the joints.

टहुकना túhuk-na, *v. n.* To pain.

टहटुहा tuhtuhá, *s. m.* Beauty, freshness or splendour, conspicuous at a distance.

टहना túhna, *s. m.* A branch or large bough of a tree.

टहनी túhnee, *s. f.* A branch.

टहुल túhul, } *s. f.* House-
टहुलटुकोर túhul-tukór, } wifery, housekeeping, duty, service, task, business, work, job, use, drudgery. *Tuhul tukor kurna, v. a.* To serve, to grudge. *Tuhul luganee, v. a.* To dance attendance.

टहुलना túhulna, *v. n.* To walk backwards and forwards, to take the air, to rove, to ramble.

टहुलनी túhulnee, *s. f.* A housewife.

टहलाना tuhlána, *v. a.* To lead about, to cause to walk backwards and forwards (*as a horse or child*); to make dance attendance.

टहुलूवा túh-looa, *s. m.* A manager of household concerns, a servant, a drudge.

टहुलूई tuh-loo-ée, *s. f.* A housewife.

टहों túhon, *s. m.* The voice of a new born child.

टहोका tuhóka, *s. m.* A blow.

टांक tank, *s. m.* A weight equal to four *mashas. s. f.* An iron pin; a stitch.

टांकना tánkna, *v. a.* To stitch, to cobble.

टांकर tánkur, *s. m.* A blackguard, a lecher, a libertine.

टांका tánka, *s. m.* A stitch; a tub made of stones; solder. *Tankeh lugana, v. a.* To stitch; to solder.

टांकी tánkee, *s. f.* A venereal chancre or shanker; a square piece cut out of a melon to examine its quality; a chisel. [to solder.

टांके लुगाना tánkeh lugána, *v. a.* To stitch;

टांग tang, *s. f.* The leg. *Tang oothana,* To copulate. *Tang dena,* To hang up, to hang; to be a catamite.

टांगन tán-gun, *s. m.* A kind of horse, a highland pony.

टांगना táng-na, *v. a.* To hang up, dangle, hang by a string, &c. (*not on a peg*).

टांगी tán-gee, *s. f.* A hatchet.

टांघन tán-ghun, } *s. m.* A kind of horse, a
टांगम tán-gun, } highland pony. *Tanghun-nooma, adj.* Like a *tanghun.*

टांच tanch, } *adj.* Perverse, audacious,
टांचड़ा tánchra, } troublesome.

टांट tant, *s. f.* The crown of the head.

टांठा tántha, *adj.* Powerful, strong, firm, solid.

 टंठाई tantháee, *s. f.* Solidity.

टंड tand, *s. f.* A stage, a raised seat, platform.

टांडा tánda, *s. m.* A venture (*of goods*); name of a place in *Oude*; the goods of a *Bunjara.*

टाट tat, *s. m.* Canvas, sackcloth. *Tatbaf, s. m.* A weaver of canvas. *Tatbafee, s. f.* Embroidery.

टाटक tátuk, *adj.* Fresh, new, recent; juggling.

टाटी tátee, *s. f.* A skreen, a matted shutter.

टारी táree, *s. f.* A small hatchet or axe.

टानना tánna, *v. a.* To stretch, to pull.

टाप tap, *s. f.* A stroke with the fore foot of a horse; the sound of horse's hoof in travelling; a frame made of bamboo for catching fish.

टापना tápna, *v. a.* To paw with the fore feet (*as a horse that is impatient*); to whore (*a low phrase*).

टापा tápa, *s. m.* A hen-coop. *Tapa-toee kurna,* To trifle; to grope, to rummage.

टापू tápoo, *s. m.* An island.

टाबर tábur, *s. f.* A small lake.

टारना tárna, *v. a.* To move out of the way.

टारी táree, *s. f.* Distance.

टाल tal, *verbal n. f.* Evasion, putting aside, putting off or out of the way, rejecting a request. *s. f.* A heap (*of grain,* &c.), a stack, a rick; baldness from age; a turn or trick in wrestling. *Tal kurna,* To put off; to heap. *Tal marna,* To heap; to turn the scale fraudulently in weighing.

टालटोल tal-tól, *s. m.* Evasion, prevarication, putting off, shuffling, chicane.

टालना tál-na, *v. a.* To evade, prevaricate, avoid, put off, postpone, defer; to drive out of the way, put or turn aside, ward off, fend, obviate, move, remove, prevent.

टालमटोल tal-mut-ól, *s. m.* Evasion, prevarication, putting off, shuffling, chicane, fraud, deceit.

टाला tála, *s. m.* Evasion; a rick, heap, stack. *Tala bala butana,* To put off.

टाली tálee, *s. f.* A sort of musical instrument.

टिकटिकी tíktik-ee, *s. f.* A lizard.

टिकठी tík-thee, *s. f.* A teapoy or stool.

टिकना tíkna, *v. n.* To stop, remain in any place, to be detained, to lodge, stay, tarry.

टिकली tíklee, *s. f.* A wafer, a small round cake; an ornament worn on the forehead.

टिकाऊ tikáoo, *adj.* Durable, lasting.

टिकाना tikána, *v. a.* To retain, fix in any place, stop, billet, lodge, station.

टिकाव tik-áo, *s. m.* Stability, permanance.

टिकिया tíkiya, *s. f.* A small cake of bread, a little cake of charcoal for the *hookka*, a wafer, a bolus.

टिकोर tik-or, *s. m.* A cataplasm, a poultice.

टिक्कूर tikkúr, *s. f.* A thick cake of bread.

टिक्की tíkkee, *s. f.* A small cake of bread. *Tikkee lugana, v. a.* To form a connexion, make interest, earn a scanty livelihood.

टिघुलना tig-húlna, *v. n.* To be melted, to rarefy.

टिटकारना titkárna, *v. a.* To urge an animal by *titkaree.*

टिटकारी titkáree, *s. f.* The noise made by drawing the tongue from the roof of the mouth, to make horses, &c. proceed.

टिटोहरा titéehra, *s. m.* } A sand piper
टिटोहरी titéehree, *s. f.* } (*Tringa goensis*).

टिट्टिभ títtibh, *s. m.* A bird (*Parra jacana* or *goensis*).

टिड्डा tídda, *s. m.* A grasshopper.

टिड्डी tíddee, *s. f.* A locust.

टिपका típka, *s. m.* A stain of any colour applied by the finger.

टिप्पन tippún, *s. f.* Annotation.

टिप्पनी tippunée, *s. f.* A gloss, a comment.

टिप्पस tippús, *s. f.* Pride, arrogance.

टिभाना tib-hána, *v. a.* To give a small daily allowance, such as merely to save one from starving. [ance.

टिभाव tibháo, *s. m.* A small daily allow-

टिमटिम tím-tim, *s. m.* A sound.

टिमटिमाना tim-tim-ána, *v. n.* To give a faint light.

टिलिया tíliya, *s. f.* A young hen.

टिलूआ til-óoa, *s. m.* A flatterer.

टिहरा tíhra, *s. f.* A small village.

टीट teent, *s. m.* The ripe fruit of *kureel*; a speck on the eye.

टीक teek, *s. f.* An ornament for the head and neck.

टीका téeka, *s. m.* A mark or marks made with coloured earths or unguents upon the forehead and between the eye-brows, either as an ornament or sectarial distinction; an ornament worn on the forehead; the nuptial gifts or engagement; inoculation. *s. f.* A commentary. *Teeka bhejna,* To send the nuptial gifts, which are presented by the relations of the bride to the bridegroom. *Teeka lena,* To accept the nuptial gifts.

टीकैत teekyt, *adj.* Invested with the *teeka* or badge of sovereignty.

टीटली téetlee, *s. f.* A sort of medicine.

टीरी téeree, *s. f.* A locust.

टीप teep, *s. f.* A note of hand, a check ; drawing a card ; raising the voice in singing ; the noting of any thing ; the act of pressing, compressing. *Teep lena, v. a.* To draw a card.

टीपटाप teep-táp, *s. f.* Ornament ; the act of pressing or compressing.

टीपना téepna, *v. a.* To press, to compress, to grope, feel, squeeze.

टीर teer, *s. f.* A transverse piece in cloths, or a breadth cut diagonally.

टील teel, *s. f.* A young hen ; a woman (*so named in contempt*).

टीला téela, *s. m.* A rising ground, a small hill, a mount, a ridge, a hillock.

टीस tees, *s. f.* A throb, throbbing, a shooting pain. *Tees marna,* To throb, shoot. *Teesna, v. n.* To palpitate, to throb.

टुंरिया tóoniya, *adj.* Tiny. *Tooniya tota,* A kind of parrot.

टुक took, *adj.* A little.

टुकड़ा tóok-ra, *s. m.* A piece, bit, portion, division, morsel. *Tookr-guda,* A beggar for a bit of bread.

टुकसा tóok-sa, *adj.* A little.

टुंग tóonga, *s. m.* Scut, a short tail.

टुंगार toongár, *s. f.* Pecking, nibbling of fruit, &c., more for amusement than from appetite.

टुच्चा tóoch-cha, *s. m.* A rake, a blackguard.

टुटुनाना toon-too-nána, *v. a.* To tune slowly.

टुंड toond, *s. m.* A hand or branch that has been cut off.

टुंडा tóon-da, *adj.* Handless, whose hands have been cut off, or one born without hands. *s. m.* The knob in the back part of a turband. *Toondehdar, s. m.* A turband which has a knob in the hinder part.

टुंडी tóondee, *s. f.* The navel. *adj. f.* Handless. *Toondiyan kusna,* or, —*churhana,* or, —*bandhna,* To tie the hands behind the back.

टुपाना too-pána, *v. a.* To have buried, to cause to cover.

टुभुक toobhúk, *s. f.* The sound of water dropping ; sound of guggling.

टुसकना too-súkna, *v. n.* To cry, to weep.

टुहुकना tóo-hook-na, *v. n.* To cry.

टूं toon, *s. m.* Ventris crepitus. *Toon kurna,* Crepitum ventris edere.

टुंगना tóongna, *v. a.* To peck, nibble, chew straws, &c., for amusement ; to pick ; to piddle.

टुंगाटांगी tóonga-tángee, *s. f.* Pecking and nibbling.

टुंडी tóon-dee, *s. f.* The navel ; a small branch or stump of a tree, broken at the end and leafless.

टूक took, } *s. m.* A piece, a little, a particle, an atom, a bit ; a single beat of a drum.
टूका tóoka, }

टूट toot, *s. f.* Fracture, breaking, break ; misunderstanding or coolness between friends, harm, loss, deficiency ; a passage omitted in the writing of a book, which is afterwards written in the margin. *Toot jana,* To be broken ; to become ill, to pine. *Toot purna,* To break in upon, to rush in, to be collected in crowds. *Toot ruhna,* To be distressed, to be weary, to be reduced to poverty, to pine away ; to be separated.

टूटना tóotna, *v. n.* To break, to be broken, to burst, fail, break forth or rush upon, to assault, to attack, to charge, to invade.

टूटा tóota, *part.* Broken, decayed. *s. m.* Loss, failure, deficiency. *Toota-phoota, adj.* Fragments, broken to pieces.

टूम toom, *s. m.* Trifles ; an ornament ; a frame for pigeons to perch on. *Toom tam, s. m.* A few trifles ; an ornament. *Toom dena,* To push gently.

टूसी tóosee, *s. f.* A bud.

टेंगरा téngra, *s. m.* }
टेंगरी téngree, *s. f.* } A fish (*Silurus*).

टेंगी téngee, *s. f.* Teasing.

टेंट tent, *s. m.* The ripe fruit of *kureel* ; a speck on the eye.

टेंटुर téntur, *s. m.* Name of a fruit.

टेंटा ténta, *s. m.* A large ripe fruit of *kureel* ; a fizgig ; speaking inconsiderately.

टेंटी téntee, *s. f.* Name of a fruit ; speaking inconsiderately.

टेंटुआ téntooa, *s. m.* The windpipe, the throat.

टेंटेन ténten, *s. m.* An imitative sound, an inarticulate sound.

टेक tek, *s. f.* A prop, a pillar, reliance ; a promise, a vow. *Tek ruhna,* To lean upon.

टेकन ték-un, *s. m.* A prop, support.

टेकना tékna, *v. a.* To support, to prop.

टेकर ték-ur, } *s. m.* Rising ground, a
टेकरा ték-ra, } height.

टेगरा tég-ra, *s. m.* Rising ground.

टेड़ा tér-a, *s. m.* The trunk of a tree ; an instrument for twisting coarse thread or twine.

टेढ़ा térha, *adj.* Crooked, bent, awry. *Terha kurna,* v. a. To bend, to crook, to distort. *Terha bera, adj.* Crooked.

टेढ़ाई terháee, *s. f.* Crookedness, obliquity.

टेढ़ी térhee, *s. f.* Pride, vanity, haughtiness; perverseness.

टेना téna, *s. m.* A cock of the breed of fowls called *tenee.*

टेनी tén-ee, *s. m.* A particular breed of fowls. *adj.* Tiny, small.

टेम tem, *s. f.* Snuff of a candle, the flame of a candle or lamp. *Temtam, s. m.* Dressing.

टेर ter, *s. f.* Tune; voice, call.

टेरना térna, *v. n.* To bawl, to roar to, to call loudly, to shout, to holla; to tune.

टेरा tér-a, *s. m.* A curtain. *adj.* Squint-eyed, cock-eyed.

टेलना télna, *v. a.* To remove.

टेलूआ tél-ooa, *s. m.* A beam.

टेव téo, *s. f.* Habit, custom.

टेवकी téokee, *s. f.* A prop, a pillar.

टेवना téona, *v. a.* To sharpen.

टेवा téwa, *s. m.* Calculation of nativity; habit, custom.

टेसू tésoo, *s. m.* The blossoms of the *Pulas* tree (*Butea frondosa*); a kind of play.

टेहरा téhra, *s. m.* A village.　　　[riage.

टेहला téhla, *s. m.* The customs of mar-

टोआ tóa, *s. f.* Act of feeling or groping.

टोआटोई toa-tóee, *s. f.* Searching, feeling for, feeling.

टोंटा tónta, *s. m.* A cracker, a serpent in fireworks; a joint of bamboo, &c.; a cartridge. *adj.* Handless.

टोंटी tóntee, *s. f.* A spout.

टोक tok, *s. f.* Hinderance, prevention; the influence of an evil eye.

टोकटाक tok-ták, *s. f.* Hinderance, prevention.

टोकना tókna, *v. a.* To interrogate, prevent, challenge, envy, accost; to look at with an evil eye.

टोकरा tókra, *s. m.* A large basket (*without a lid*).

टोकरी tókree, *s. f.* A small basket (*without a lid*).

टोकाटोकी tóka-tókee, *s. f.* Hinderance, prevention.

टोटका tótka, *s. m.* A charm, an amulet, a philter, a superstitious remedy.

टोटरू tótroo, *s. m.* A kind of turtle-dove.

टोटा tóta, *s. m.* Loss, deficiency, detriment; a cartridge; a candle's end.

टोड़ी tóree, *s. f.* The name of a musical mode or *raginee.*

टोनवा tónwa, *s. m.* A kind of hawk; enchantment.

टोनहा tonhá, *s. m.* A juggling man, a conjurer.

टोनहाई tonháee, *s. f.* A juggling woman, a female conjurer, a witch.

टोना tóna, *s. m.* Enchantment, fascination. *v. a.* To feel, grope, handle.

टोनाटानी tóna-tánee, *s. f.* ⎱ Hocus pocus, juggling.
टोनाटामन tona-támun, *s. m.* ⎰

टोप top, *s. m.* A hat, a cap, helmet, head, cover, thimble; bait; a stitch.

टोपा tópa, *s. m.* A helmet, cap, hat.

टोपी tópee, *s. f.* A hat. *Topeewala,* One who wears a hat, or an animal with a comb, crest, &c. It is used also to express the *Persian* or *Moghul* troops; but now more generally applies to every European (*from wearing a hat or cap*).

टोरा tóra, *s. m.* A ledge extending out from a wall, to keep off the weather, without pillars; eaves.

टोल tol, *s. m.* A company, a society; a hamlet. *Tol marna,* To dash one top against another while in motion.　　[town.

टोला tóla, *s. m.* A quarter or section of a

टोली tólee, *s. f.* A company, a society, a crowd.

टोनहा tounhá, *s. m.* A juggler, a conjurer.

ठ

ठ thuh, The aspirate of the preceding letter, corresponding to *th* in pent-house.

ठकठक thúk-thuk, *s. m. f.* Hard work, harassing labour, difficulties; a sound.

ठकठकाना thuk-thuk-ána, *v. a.* To tap, to rap, to pat.

ठकठकिया thuk-thúkiya, *s. m.* A stickler, a wrangler.

ठकठेला thuk-théla, *adj.* Stuffed together in a crowd, crowded.

ठकठोवा thuk-thóuwa, *s. f.* A small boat so called, a shallop, a skiff.

ठकुराई thuk-ooráee, *s. f.* Godship, divinity; chiefship, mastership.

ठकुरायन thuk-ooráyun, *s. f.* A female divinity or idol.

ठग thug, *s. m.* A robber, assassin, cutthroat; a cheat, impostor. *Thugbazee,* or, *Thugbidya, s. f.* Cunning, art, fraudulent dexterity. *Thug lana,* To rob, to cheat. *Thug lena,* To cheat.

ठगई thugúee, *s. f.* Robbery, theft, cheating.

ठगना thúgna, *v. a.* To cheat, to deceive.

ठगनी thúg-nee, *s. f.* A female robber or cheat.

ठगाई thug-áee, *s. f.* Robbery, theft, cheating.

ठगाना thugána, *v. n.* To be cheated.

ठगिन thúg-in, *s. f.* A female robber or cheat.

ठगिया thúg-iya, *s. m.* A cheater.

ठगौरी thug-óuree, *s. f.* Cheat, trick.

ठट thut, *s. m.* Bank, shore.

ठट्ठूर thutthúr, *s. m.* Frame made of bamboo for thatching, shell of a house.

ठट्ठा thutthá, *s. m.* Fun, sport, joking, jest ; name of a place. *Thuttha kurna,* To jest, joke, crack a joke, deride, ridicule. *Thutthehbaz,* A jester, a humorous person, a funny fellow, jocular, arch, waggish, comical, facetious. *Thutthehbazee, s. f.* Jesting, sporting, fun, jocularity. *Thuttha marna,* To jest, joke, deride, ridicule.

ठठ thuth, *s. m.* Throng, crowd.

ठठरा thúthra, *s. m.* A fence.

ठठरी thúthree, *s. f.* The frame of a matted skreen, the frame (*bamboo work*) of a thatched roof, shell of a house ; a bier ; a skeleton, a very thin person.

ठठकना thuthúkna, *v. n.* To stop, to stagnate, to stand amazed, to draw back in surprise, to shrink, to boggle.

ठठाना thuthána, *v. a.* To strike, beat ; beat one's own head, &c. (*in token of vexation*) ; harass one's self.

ठठेरा thuthéra, *s. m.* A brazier, a tinker. *Thuthereh thuthereh kee budluee,* A bargain between two people equally acute or knowing, diamond cut diamond.

ठठेरा thuthéra, *s. m.* The stalk of the *joar* (*Holcus sorgum*).

ठठेरी thuthéree, *s. f.* A female brazier or tinker.

ठठोर thuthór, ⎱ *adj.* Banterer, waggish,
ठठोल thuthól, ⎰ jocular, jocose, jester, wag.

ठठोली thuthólee, *s. f.* Fun, humour, sport, joking, jesting, jocularity, comicalness, derision.

ठड्डा thúdda, *s. m.* The beak of a paper kite.

ठंड thund, *s. f.* Coldness, cold, a cold.

ठंडक thún-duk, *s. f.* Coldness.

ठंडा thúnda, *adj.* Cold. *Kuleja thunda kurna,* To be pleased, to be happy (*by seeing a friend, son, &c.*) ; to have one's revenge gratified. *Thunda kurna, v. a.* To make cold, cool ; to ex-

tinguish ; to comfort, to assuage, to pacify, appease. *Thunda purna,* To abate (*anger, virility or wantonness*). *Thundu hona,* To become cold, to cool ; to be extinguished ; to be comforted or pacified ; to rest ; to lose virility.

ठंडाई thundáee, *s. f.* Refrigerant medicine ; the intoxicating drug made of *bhung.*

ठंडी thún-dee, *adj. f.* Cold. *Thundee sans bhurnee,* To sigh.

ठंढा thundhá, *adj.* Cold.

ठनकना thún-uk-na, *v. n.* To throb, to shoot (*as the pain of head-ache*) ; to jingle, tinkle, clink.

ठनठनाना thun-thun-ána, *v. n.* To jingle, to rattle.

ठनाक thun-ák, *s. m.* A jingle, tinkle, clink.

ठन्ना thúnna, *v. n.* To be fixed, to be ascertined.

ठपना thúp-na, *v. a.* To strike.

ठप्पा thúppa, *s. m.* An instrument for stamping leather with, a die, a stamp, a printing type ; printing.

ठरक thúruk, ⎱ *s. m.* Snore. *Thuruk par-*
ठरर thúr-ur, ⎰ *na, v. n.* To snore.

ठरा thúr-a, *s. f.* A kind of wine or spirituous liquor ; a kind of shoe worn by villagers.

ठरिया thúr-iya, *s. m.* A kind of earthen *hookka.*

ठर्रा thúrra, *s. f.* A kind of wine or spirituous liquor ; a kind of shoe worn by villagers.

ठस thus, An imitative sound, as of a musket ill charged or flashing in the pan.

ठसक thús-uk, *s. f.* State, dignity.

ठसकना thús-uk-na, *v. a.* To break a piece off of any vessel of earthen ware, by knocking two vessels together, without completely destroying it.

ठसनी thús-nee, *s. f.* A rammer.

ठसाठस thus-a-thús, *adj.* Filled, crowded.

ठस्सा thússa, *s. m.* A mould or form into which plates of metal, &c., are beat to take the form of pastes of ornaments, &c. ; pride, vanity.

ठहरना thuhúrna, *v. n.* To be stopped, to be fixed, to stop, stay, remain, abide, rest, stand, last, to be fixed on, concluded, settled, determined, proved.

ठहराना thuhrána, *v. a.* To fix, stop, determine, appropriate, settle, ascertain, appoint, fix on, demonstrate, prove, conclude or consider, ascribe.

ठहराव thuhráo, *s. m.* Settlement, fixture, permanence, appropriation, proof.

ठहाका thu-háka, *s. m.* A peal, a succession of loud sounds, an explosion. *Thuhakeh kee moolakat, s. f.* Meeting with great demonstrations of friendship.

ठाँ than, } *s. m. f.* Place, residence, a
ठाँव tháon, } situation.

ठाँसना tháns-na, *v. a.* To stuff, to cram.

ठा tha, *s. m.* A sound made by striking one
thing against another.

ठाकुर thá-koor, *s. m.* The divinity, an idol;
a lord, master, chief (*among Rajpoots*); a land-
holder; a barber.

ठाकुरद्वारा thákoor-dwára, *s. m.* An idol-
temple.

ठाट that, *s. m.* The frame of a roof for
thatching, on which the straw is laid; arrangement, adjustment.

ठाठ thath, *s. m.* State, dignity, equipage,
pomp; conveniency, plenty.

ठारा thára, *adj.* Erect.

ठारह tharh, *adj.* Steep.

ठारहना thárh-na, *v. n.* To be fixed, to
stand.

ठारहा tharhá, *adj. m.* } Erect, standing.
ठारही tharhée, *adj. f.* }

ठानठू than-thóo, *adj.* Worthy of belief,
trusty. *s. m.* The report of a musket.

ठान्ना thánna, *v. a.* To resolve or fix (*in the
mind*), to determine, be intent on, intend, set one's
heart on; to settle, perform.

ठार thar, *s. m.* Determination; snow,
frost.

ठाल thal, *s. m.* A branch.

ठाला thá-la, *s. m.* A branch. *adj.* Disengaged, at leisure, unemployed.

ठाली thá-lee, *s. f.* A branch.

ठासना thás-na, *v. a.* To stuff, cram, ram
down.

ठिकरा thík-ra, *s. m.* Fragment of an earthen vessel, a shard, potsherd; a vessel for carrying fire, such as mendicants use.

ठिकाना thik-ána, *s. m.* Residence, place,
station, site, abode, dwelling; boundary, limit,
fixing. *Thikana kurna, v. a.* To account for, to
search or trace an affair to its commencement.
Thikana dhoondhna, v. a. To seek a residence or
employment. *Thikaneh lugna, v. n.* To be killed, to
die, to be put an end to; to be terminated. *Thikaneh lugana, v. a.* To put to death, to kill, to waylay, to make away with, to despatch, assassinate;
to establish, settle, arrange, prove; find out one's
residence.

ठिङना thíng-na, *adj.* Short, dwarfish.

ठिङनाई thing-náee, *s. f.* Lowness (*of stature*).

ठिठक thithúk, *s. f.* The state of standing
amazed. *Thithuk juna*, or, — *ruhna. v. n.* To stop
short.

ठिठकना thithúkna, *v. n.* To stop, stagnate, stand amazed, draw back in surprise, shrink,
boggle.

ठिठुरना thithúrna, *v. n.* To be numbed or
benumbed, to be chill.

ठिठरा thíth-ra, *adj.* Numbed, numb, benumbed, torpid.

ठिठराहट thíth-ráhut, } *s. f.* Numbness,
ठिठुर thíth-oor, } numbedness,
chilliness, torpor, torpidness.

ठिठुरना thíth-oorna, *v. n.* To be numbed
or benumbed, to be chill. *Thithoorana, v. a.* To
chill, benumb, numb.

ठिठुरा thíth-oora, *adj.* Numbed, numb,
benumbed, torpid.

ठिनक thín-uk, *s. f.* Sob.

ठिनकना thín-uk-na, *v. n.* To sob.

ठिर thir, *s. f.* Frost; coldness.

ठिरना thír-na, *v. n.* To freeze, to be chilled.

ठिराना thir-ána, *v. a.* To cause to congeal.

ठिलिया thíl-iya, *s. f.* A water-pot.

ठीक theek, *adj.* Exact, even, accurate, complete, just, fit, meet, proper, reasonable, true, regular, right; (*met.*) parsimonious. *adv.* Exactly,
&c. *s. m.* Sum, addition. *Theek ana, v. n.* To fit,
correspond, suit, answer, apply. *Theek kurna, v. a.*
To put to rights, to correct, to adjust, to adapt,
fit; to beat. *Theek thak, adj.* Exact, fit, proper,
accurate. *adv.* Properly, fitly, accurately, ade-
quately. *Theek thak kurna, v. a.* To put to rights,
correct, adjust, fit.

ठीकमठीक theekum-théek, *adv.* Exactly,
truly, rightly.

ठीकमठीका theekum-théeka, *s. m.* Abuse.

ठीकरा théckra, *s. m.* A broken piece of
earthenware.

ठीकरी théek-ree, *s. f.* A broken piece of
earthenware, a potsherd; mons veneris. *Theekree
choonna, To be mad.*

ठीका théeka, *s. m.* Hire, fare, fixed price;
work done by contract, a task.

ठीप theep, *s. f.* A kind of lamp.

ठुकड़ा thóok-ra, *s. m.* A bit, a piece (*of
bread, &c.*)

ठुकराना thook-rána, *v. a.* To kick or strike
with the toes.

ठुड्डी thóod-dee, *s. f.* The chin; parched
grain. *Thooddee pukurna, To flatter, to curry
favour.*

ठुनकाना thoon-kána, *v. a.* To cause to
knock or hammer.

ठुनुक thóon-ook, *s. f.* Sob.

ठुनुकना thóon-ookna, *v. n.* To sob.

ठुमक thóom-uk, *s. f.* The act of waving or walking with a graceful easy air. *Thoomuk chal*, A dignified pace, stately gait, graceful carriage.

ठुमकना thóom-uk-na, *v. n.* To walk with grace and stateliness, to strut, to walk with dignity.

ठुमका thóom-ka, *adj.* Short, of low stature.

ठुमकी thóom-kee, *adj.* Lazy. *s. f.* The playing of a paper kite to keep it up when the wind is light.

ठुसकना thóo-suk-na, *v. a.* Peditum ciere, suppedere ; to weep but not aloud.

ठुसकी thóos-kee, *s. f.* Ventris crepitus surdus.

ठुसना thóos-na, *v. n.* To be stuffed, to be crammed.

ठुसाना thoo-sána, *v. a.* To cause to stuff.

ठूंटिया thoontiya, *s. m.* A eunuch.

ठूंठ thoonth, *s. m.* A stump, a branch of a tree (*broken off at the end and leafless*) ; an amputated hand.

ठूंठा thóon-tha, ठूंठिया thóon-thiya, } *adj.* Having the hand amputated ; having its branches lopped and leafless (*a tree*).

ठूंठी thóon-thee, *s. f.* Stubble.

ठेऊना théoo-na, *s. m.* The knee ; the pastern (*of a horse*).

ठेंगना théng-na, *adj.* Short, dwarfish.

ठेंगा théng-a, *s. m.* A stick, a small club ; a tool (*penis*).

ठेंगाबाजना thénga-bájua, *v. a.* To spoil.

ठेंठ thenth, *adj.* Pure, genuine ; contentious.

ठेंठी thén-thee, *s. f.* A cork, a plug ; a ball of ear-wax ; a *dhotee* or cloth reaching no further than the knee.

ठेक thek, *s. f.* A support, a prop ; a large sack filled with grain.

ठेका thék-a, *s. m.* A plug.

ठेकी thék-ee, *s. f.* Act of resting on the way (*a porter carrying a load*). *Thekee dena*, or, —*lugana*, To rest (*a porter carrying a load*).

ठेठ theth, *adj.* Pure, genuine ; contentious.

ठेपी thép-ee, *s. f.* A cork, a plug, a stopple. *Thepee moonh men dena*, To be silent.

ठेलुआ thélua, *v. a.* To shove, to push, to move forward by pushing. *s. m.* Acting the buffoon.

ठेला thél-a, *s. m.* A push, a shove. *Thela-thelee, s. f.* Shoving and shouldering.

ठेवना théona, *s. m.* The knee ; the pastern (*of a horse*).

ठेस thes, *s. m.* A knock, a blow, tripping against a stone, &c., a shove, a push, a thrust.

ठेसना thésna, *v. a.* To pierce ; to knock against ; to stuff, to cram, to ram in ; to eat ravenously.

ठेसरा thésra, *s. m.* Sneer, oblique reflection or innuendo.

ठोंकना thónk-na, *v. a.* To knock, to hammer ; to drive (*as a stake*) ; to thrust with the finger, to fillip, to drive, to beat, to tap, to thump. *Thonk dena*, To hammer or drive down, to knock. *Peeth thonkna*, To pat on the back.

ठोंग thong, *s. f.* The act of striking with a finger or beak, pecking.

ठोंगना thóng-na, ठोंगाना thon-gána, } *v. a.* To strike with the beak, to peck.

ठोंगा thón-ga, *s. m.* Striking with the beak.

ठोंठ thonth, *s. f.* Beak, bill (*of a bird*).

ठोकना thók-na, *v. a.* To beat, strike, drive (*as a stake*).

ठोकर thókur, *s. f.* Tripping or striking the foot against any thing, a beat of the foot, a kick, a stumble ; a stumbling-block.

ठोकर खाना thókur-khána, *v. a.* To trip, to stumble ; to meet with a loss or misfortune.

ठोकर लगना thókur lúgna, *v. n.* To strike against the foot (*a stumbling-block or obstacle*).

ठोकरा thókra, *s. m.* A fillip. *adj.* Hard (*as bad bread*).

ठोढ़ी thór-hee, *s. f.* The chin.

ठोर thor, *s. f.* Beak, bill.

ठोला thó-la, *s. m.* A cup for the food and drink of a bird in a cage ; the knuckles. *Thola marna, v. a.* To strike with the knuckles.

ठोस thos, *adj.* Solid, compact.

ठोसना thós-na, *v. a.* To stuff.

ठोसा thosa, *s. m.* The thumb presented in token of denial.

ठोसाई tho-sáee, *s. f.* Solidity.

ठौर thour, *s. f.* Place, room, residence. *adv.* Upon the spot. *Thour ruhna*, To be murdered, to be knocked down lifeless upon the spot.

———

ड

ड duh, The thirteenth consonant of the *Naguree* alphabet, or the third letter of the lingual or cerebral class of consonants. It is often confounded in pronunciation with a hard *r* or *l*, sounded as in the northumbrian bur. It has the sound of the English *d* in dun, and is pronounced by applying the tip of the tongue inverted to the palate.

डकराना duk-rána, *v. n.* To cry bitterly.

डुकार duk-ár, *s. f.* A belch, eructation, bellowing. *Dukarna, v. n.* To belch; to bellow, to low. *Dukar jana, or, — bythna, v. n.* To embezzle. *Dukar lena,* To belch.

डकैत dukyt, *s. m.* A robber, a pirate.

डकैती dukytee, *s. f.* Robbery, piracy.

डकौत duk-óut, } *s. m.* A caste of
डकौतिया duk-óu-tiya, } *Hindoos* descended from a *brahmun* on the father's and a *gwalin* on the mother's side. They subsist on alms on Saturday, and are skilled in astrology.

डग dug, *s. f.* A space, one step (*measure*).

डगडगाना dug-dug-ána, *v. n.* To shake; to burn brightly, to burn clear (*charcoal*). *Dugdugakur panee peena,* To drink greedily, or a large quantity at a draught.

डगमग dúg-mug, *adj.* Unsteady, tottering.

डगमगाना dug-mug-ána, *v. n.* To totter, stagger, shiver.

डगर dúg-ur, *s. f.* A road, a highway.

डगरना dúg-ur-na, *v. n.* To travel, to walk on the road, to roll.

डगराना dug-rána, *v. a.* To roll.

डग्गा dúg-ga, *s. m.* A lean, long-legged horse, a Rosinante, a garran.

डंक dunk, *s. m.* The sting of a reptile or wasp, &c., but particularly of a scorpion. *Dunk marna, v. a.* To sting.

डंका dún-ka, *s. m.* A double drum, a kettle-drum.

डंकिनी dún-kin-ee, *s. f.* A witch, a kind of female imp or evil being.

डंकियाना dun-ki-yána, *v. a.* To sting (*as a reptile*).

डंकीला dun-kée-la, *adj.* Armed with a sting, stinger.

डटना dút-na, *v. n.* To stop, to stand still.

डट्टा dútta, *s. m.* A plug, spigot, stopple, cork.

डंठा dút-ha, *s. m.* A stalk.

डढ़मूंडा durh-móonda, *adj.* Beard-shaven, beardless.

डढ़ियल durhi-yúl, *adj.* Having a long beard.

डंड dund, *s. m.* The arm above the elbow; a kind of exercise, placing the hands on the ground and then bending down so as almost to touch the earth with the breast.

डंडपेल dund-pél, *s. m.* One who exercises himself at the *dund.*

डंडवत dun-wút, *s. f.* *Hindoo* salutation, bow, obeisance, prostration.

डंडा dún-da, *s. m.* A staff, an ensign-staff; the beam of a pair of scales; a collector of market duties.

डंडिया dún-diya, *s. m.* A kind of garment for women; a collector of market duties.

डंडी dún-dee, *s. f.* The tube of the corolla of the *Nyctanthes arbortristis*, which is used for dying; a handle; the beam of a pair of scales. *s. m.* A mendicant who carries a staff in his hand. *Pug dundee, s. f.* A footpath, by-path, track.

डंडीर dun-déer, *s. f.* A line, stripe, score, lineament.

डंडौत dun-dóut, *s. f.* *Hindoo* salutation, bow, obeisance, prostration.

डुपटना dúp-ut-na, *v. n.* To call, bawl at, halloo, rebuke, gallop.

डुफ duph, *s. m.* A tambourin.

डुफारना duphár-na, *v. n.* To cry bitterly, to blubber, roar.

डुफाली duphá-lee, *s. m.* A kind of *Mahomedan* mendicant, who always plays upon a musical instrument called *duph*; a chatterer.

डुब dub, *s. m.* Strength, power, authority; a kind of pocket; the leather with which oil-pots are made. *Dubgur, s. m.* A currier.

डुबकना dúb-uk-na, *v. n.* To glitter.

डुबका dúb-ka, *s. m.* Fresh water drawn from a well. *adj.* Fat, corpulent.

डुबडुबाना dub-dub-ána, *v. a.* To fill with water or tears (*the eyes*). *Ankhen dub-dubana, or, Ansoo dubdubana,* To be on the point of shedding tears.

डुबरा dúb-ra, *s. m.* Marshy land, a puddle.

डुबराडुहरा dúbra-dúhra, *s. m.* A hole or pit of water, a puddle.

डुबरिया dúb-riya, *adj.* Left-handed.

डुबस dúb-us, *s. m.* Provisions, sea-stock, stores.

डुबोना dub-óna, *v. a.* To drown, immerse, flood; to ruin, &c.

डुब्बा dúbba, *s. m.* A leathern vessel for holding oil.

डुब्बू dúbboo, *s. m.* An iron spoon.

डमरू dúm-roo, *s. m.* A musical instrument, a sort of small drum shaped like an hour-glass, held in one hand, and beaten with the fingers.

ड्यन dyun, *s. m.* A car or litter carried on men's shoulders, a palankeen, a *dooly*; flying in the air, the flight of a bird.

डर dur, *s. m. f.* Fear, dread, awe.

डरना dúr-na, } *v. n.* To fear, be
डरुपना dúr-up-na, } frightened, dread.

डरुप dúr-úp, *adj.* Afraid.

डरपोकना dur-pók-na, *v. n.* A coward.

डरवैया dur-wy-ya, *adj.* Fearful; (*met.*) A coward.

डराऊ dur-áoo, *adj.* Terrible.

डराक dur-ák, *adj.* Fearful.

डराना dur-ána, } *v. a.* To frighten, scare,
डरावना dur-áona, } cause to fear, terrify, alarm, daunt, deter. *adj.* Frightful, terrible, terrifying.

डरालू duráloo, *adj.* Timid, fearing.

डलक dúl-uk, *s. m.* A sling, a basket, a *dalee,* carried on men's shoulders by means of a stick and ropes like the beam, and strings of a balance; presents of fruit, sweetmeats, &c., are usually sent in this manner. *s. f.* Glitter.

डलवा dúl-wa, *s. m.* A large basket (*without a lid*).

डलवाना dul-wána, *v. a.* To cause to throw down, or to throw, to occasion, &c.

डला dúl-a, *s. m.* A large lump, a clod; a large basket.

डलिया dúl-iya, *s. m.* A basket (*without a cover, like a tray*). [&c.]

डली dúl-ee, *s. f.* A lump (*of sugar, meat,*

डवा dúwa, *s. m.* A large wooden spoon.

डस dus, *s. m.* The string by which scales are suspended (*or held in the hand*); the threads of the warp at the end of a piece of cloth which are left unwoven; the end of a piece of cloth.

डसना dús-na, *v. a.* To bite or sting (*as a venemous animal*).

डसौना dus-óu-na, *s. m.* Bedding.

डहक dúhuk, *s. m.* A cavern, abyss, a pitfall.

डहकाना duh-kána, *v. a.* To deceive, disappoint, balk, tantalize; to spoil, throw away uselessly.

डहडहा duh-duhá, *adj.* Flourishing, blooming, green, fresh; pleasing.

डहडहाना duh-duhána, *v. a.* To flourish, to blossom.

डांक dank, *s. m.* Foil (*under precious stones*); the sting of a scorpion (*and sometimes of other animals*).

डांग dang, *s. f.* A stick, a club; the greatest height or summit of a mountain.

डांगर dán-gur, *adj.* Thin, lean. *s. m.* A lean beast, a starveling; the flowering stem of radishes or mustard; cattle.

डांटडपट dánt-duput, *s. f.* Gallop.

डांटना dánt-na, *v. a.* To snub, rebuke, threaten, menace.

डांठल dán-thul, *s. m.* Pedicle, petiole, footstalk.

डांठी dán-thee, *s. f.* A straw, stubble, pedicle, stalk.

डांड dand, *s. m.* Retaliation, punishment, penalty, fine, amercement, mulct, revenge, forfeit; an oar; the backbone; a stick; a line.

डांडना dánd-na, *v. a.* To retaliate, to take revenge, to fine, to punish.

डांड भरना dand-bhúrna, *v. a.* To pay a fine.

डांडलेना dand-léna, *v. a.* To take a fine, to fine, to amerce.

डांडा dán-da, *s. m.* Landmarks; road.

डांडामेंडा dánda-ménda, *s. m.* The frontier boundary between the lands of two proprietors.

डांडी dán-dee, *s. m.* A rower, a boatman.

डांवरू dáon-roo, *s. m.* A tiger's cub or whelp.

डांवाडोल danwadól, *adj.* Wandering without house or home, errant, ruined, lost, destitute. *Danwa dolee,* *s. f.* The wandering without house or home, destitute state.

डांस dans, *s. m.* The sting of a reptile; a large musquito, a gadfly.

डाक dak, *s. f.* A post (*for the conveyance of letters, also relay of horses or of palkee bearers*); a post-office; perpetual vomiting. *Duk lugnee,* To be seized with constant vomiting.

डाक dak, *s. m.* Husband of a *dakinee.*

डाकना dák-na, *v. a.* To vomit.

डाका dá-ka, *s. m.* An attack by robbers. *Daka purna,* or, — *dena,* or, — *dalna,* To rob.

डाकिन dá-kin, } *s. f.* A kind of female
डाकिनी dá-kin-ee, } imp or evil being; a witch, a termagant.

डाकिया dá-kiya, *s. m.* Robber; postman.

डाकी dá-kee, *adj.* Gluttonous.

डाकू dákoo, *s. m.* A robber, a pirate.

डाट dat, *s. f.* Threatening, snubbing, browbeating, checking.

डाटना dát-na, *v. a.* To snub, check, chide, threaten, to browbeat.

डाढ़ darh, *s. f.* A jaw-tooth or grinder.

डाढ़ी dár-hee, *s. f.* A beard.

डाब dab, *s. f.* A sacrificial grass (*Poa cynosuroides*). *s. m.* A sword-belt; an unripe cocoa-nut.

डाबक dá-buk, *s. m.* Fresh water drawn from a well.

डाबर dá-bur, *s. m.* A vessel for washing hands in; a round tank.

डाबरनैनी dábur-nynee, *adj.* Having large eyes (*epithet peculiar to women*).

डाभ dabh, *s. m.* A sacrificial grass (*Poa cynosuroides*). *s. m.* A forest.

डामर dám-ur, *s. m.* Resin, a torch.

डायन dá-yun, *s. f.* A witch.

डार dar, *s. f.* Branch, bough; line, row. *Dar kee dar,* Company, band.

डारना **dár-na**, *v. a.* To throw, fling, cast, drop, shed, pour, inject, lay, throw down, throw away.

डारिम **dár-im**, *s. m.* A pomegranate.

डाल **dal**, *s. f.* A branch, a bough. *Ek dal,* *adj.* Of one piece, without joining.

डालना **dál-na**, *v. a.* To throw down, to fling, cast, drop, shed, pour, inject, lay, put, push, set, shake, submit, throw, hurl, thrust, destroy, throw away; cause, occasion, produce, excite. *Dal dena, v. a.* To throw away, cast, cause, occasion, &c.

डाला **dála**, *s. m.* A litter, a large branch.

डालिम **dá-lim**, *s. m.* A pomegranate.

डाली **dálee**, *s. f.* A present of fruit, &c., a basket of fruit, &c.; a branch, a bough.

डाह **dah**, *s. f.* Malice, spite, envy, jealousy, burning.

डाहना **dáh-na**, *v. n.* To be malicious, to burn with spite; to be fused (*as metal*); to heat (*metal*).

डाहल **dá-hul**, *s. m.* The name of a country, also *Tripoora.* [ous.

डाही **dáhee**, *adj.* Malicious, spiteful, envi-

डाहुक **dá-hook**, *s. m.* A gallinule.

डिगना **díg-na**, *v. n.* To shake, vibrate, tremble, quaver, move; to shrink, to go back.

डिगर आना **digur jána**, *v. n.* To go away.

डिगाना **dig-ána**, *v. a.* To cause to shake or move.

डिगुर **dín-gur**, *s. m.* A fat man; a servant, a slave; a rogue, a cheat; a low or depraved man.

डिटना **dít-na**, } *v. a.* To see; to take
डिठना **díth-na**, } aim, to look at.

डिठियारा **dithiyára**, *adj.* Seeing, the opposite of blind.

डिन्दिम **dín-dim**, *s. m.* A musical instrument; a kind of small drum or tabour; a plant bearing a small fruit (*Carissa carandas*).

डिन्दिर **dín-dir**, *s. m.* Cuttle-fish bone considered to be the foam of the sea.

डिबरिया **díb-riya**, *adj.* Left-handed.

डिबिया **díb-iya**, *s. f.* A very small box.

डिब्बा **díbba**, *s. m.* A small box.

डिब्बी **díbbee**, *s. f.* A cartouch-box, a small box.

डिम **dim**, *s. m.* A dramatic entertainment, dramatic exhibition of battle or tumult.

डिम्ब **dimb**, *s. m.* An egg; a chrysalis; the bladder; the spleen; the uterus; any young animal.

डिम्बिका **dímbika**, *s. f.* A libidinous woman.

डिम्भ **dimbh**, *s. m.* Pride, vanity; any young animal; a fool, an idiot, a blockhead.

डिम्भ **dím-bha**, *s. f.* An infant.

डींग **deeng**, *s. m.* Pride, vaunting, boasting.

डींग मारना **deeng-márna**, *v. a.* To make boast (*of*), to boast.

डीठ **deeth**, *s. f.* Sight, look, glance, vision.

डीठबंद **deeth-búnd**, *adj.* Enchanting the sight, preventing one's seeing by conjuration, a juggler.

डीठबंदी **deeth-búndee**, *s. f.* Enchanting the sight, preventing by conjuration one's seeing.

डील **deel**, *s. m. f.* Stature; body, bulk, size.

डीह **deeh**, *s. m.* A haunt, place, dwelling, village.

डीहा **déeha**, *s. m.* A bank, a mound.

डुक **dook**, *s. m.* A blow with the fist.

डुकरिया **dook-ríya**, *adj. f.* Old (*woman*).

डुगडुगाना **doog-doog-ána**, *v. n.* To sound (*a kettle-drum*), to twinkle.

डुडु **dóon-doo**, } *s. m.* A kind of snake
डुडुभ **doon-dóobh**, } (*Amphisbæna*).

डुबकी **dóob-kee**, *s. f.* A dip, dive, plunge.

डुबवाना **doob-wána**, *v. a.* To cause to drown, &c.

डुबाना **doo-bána**, *v. a.* To cause to sink, to immerse, dip; to demolish, ruin, destroy.

डुबाव **doo-báo**, *adj.* Out of man's depth, deep (*enough to drown in*). *s. m.* Drowning.

डुबोना **doo-bó-na**, } *v. a.* To drown, im-
डुबोना **dub-óna**, } merse, flood; to ruin. *Dubo-dena, v. a.* To exhaust, to ruin, to demolish, to drown.

डुरियाना **doo-riyána**, *v. a.* To lead about (*as a horse*), to lead in hand.

डुलाना **doo-lána**, *v. a.* To move, shake, swing, agitate.

डुलि **dóoli**, *s. f.* A small turtle; a female turtle.

डुलिका **dóolika**, *s. f.* A small bird resembling a wagtail.

डूब **doob**, *s. m.* A dip, a dive, immersion.

डूबना **dóob-na**, *v. n.* To dive; to drown; to be immerged or deluged; to set, to sink; to be destroyed or ruined; to be absorbed (*in business, study, &c.*) *Dil doobna,* To faint.

डेग **deg**, *s. m.* Step, pace.

डेढ़ **derh**, *adj.* One and half. *Derh eent kee musjid joodee bunanee* (*lit. to build a separate mosque of a brick and a half*), To withdraw, through pride, from the society of others. *Derh pao,* Three eighths. *Derh pouwa,* A weight, three-eighths of a *ser. Derh bukayun miyan bagh men,* *lit.* The gentleman is in his garden consisting of a tree and a half, (*and the bukayun, Melia semper-*

virens, here mentioned, is a tree of no use or estimation) is applied to a person who assumes consequences without reason.

डेढ़गत **derh-gút,** *s. f.* A kind of dance.

डेना **dén-a,** *s. m.* A log tied to the neck of a vicious ox.

डेरा **dér-a,** *s. m.* A dwelling, a tent. *adj.* Squint-eyed.

डेल **del,** }
डेला **dél-a,** } *s. m.* A lump of earth.

डेवढ़ा **deórha,** *s. m.* Half as much again ; a mode of reckoning. [a half.

डेवढ़ाना **deorhána,** *v. a.* To take once and

डेवढ़ी **deórhee,** *s. f.* A threshold, a door, antichamber, porch.

डेवढ़ीदार **deorheedár,** *s. m.* A door-keeper.

डेहूर **déhoor,** *s. f.* A volley, several muskets discharged at once.

डेहूरी **déhooree,** *s. f.* A threshold, a door, antichamber, porch.

डैन **dyn,** *s. m.* Wings of birds.

डैना **dyna,** *s. m.* A branch, a bough.

डोई **dóee,** *s. f.* A wooden spoon, ladle.

डोंगर **dóng-ur,** *s. m.* A mountain.

डोंगा **dón-ga,** *s. m.* } A spoon ; a canoe ;
डोंगी **dón-gee,** *s. f.* } a trough.

डोंडी **dón-dee,** *s. f.* Proclamation by beat of drum.

डोंर **donr,** }
डोंरा **dónra,** } *s. f.* A species of snake.

डोक **dok,** *s. f.* Vomiting.

डोकना **dók-na,** *v. n.* To vomit.

डोकरा **dókra,** *adj. m.* Old (*man*).

डोकरी **dók-ree,** *adj. f.* Old (*woman*).

डोकी **dó-kee,** *part. act.* Vomiting.

डोब **dob,** *s. m.* A dip, a dive, a plunge, a dip (*in die or colouring*).

डोबदेना **dob-déna,** *v. a.* To dip in die or colouring.

डोबा **dó-ba,** *s. m.* A reservoir ; fainting.

डोम **dom,** } *s. m.* A low caste of *Hin-*
डोमरा **dómra,** } *doos* ; the name of a caste of Mahomedans, the males of which are musicians, and the females sing and dance in the company of females only.

डोमनपना **dómun-pún-a,** *s. m.* The art or practice of a male or female of the *dom* caste.

डोमनी **dóm-nee,** *s. f.* A female of the caste called *dom*.

डोर **dor,** *s. f.* String, cord, thread, rope. *s. m.* A fillet of thread or cord tied round the arm or wrist.

डोरक **dó-ruk,** *s. m.* A fillet of thread or cord tied round the arm or wrist ; it is also applied to the string tying a packet or parcel.

डोरा **dó-ra,** *s. m.* Thread, line, cord ; edge of a sword ; *Ankh ka dora*, A bloodshot eye, vessels distended with blood on the tunica conjunctiva of the eye (*from intoxication or other cause*). *Gurdun ka dora*, A graceful motion of the neck in dancing. *Doreh dalna, v. a.* To stitch a quilt ; to utter a long continued sound like the *Amaduvade* (*Fringilla amandava*).

डोरिया **dóriya,** *s. m.* Striped muslin ; a dog-keeper ; lace.

डोरी **dóree,** *s. f.* A string, cord, thread, rope.

डोल **dol,** *s. m.* A bucket for drawing water.

डोलची **dól-chee,** *s. f.* A small bucket for drawing water.

डोलडोल **doldol,** *s. m.* Roving, perambulating.

डोलना **dól-na,** *v. n.* To move, to shake or be shaken ; to roam, ramble, rove, wander ; to swing.

डोला **dó-la,** *s. m.* A kind of sedan ; a wife from an inferior family, married by a person of rank, who gives a present to her parents. She ranks below wives of equal family, but above concubines.

डोला **dó-la,** *s. m.* Manner ; coition.

डोलादेना **dóla-déna,** *v. a.* To give a daughter to a superior by way of tribute.

डोली **dó-lee,** *s. f.* A kind of sedan (*for women.*)

डौंजा **dóunja,** *s. m.* A scaffold.

डौंडी **dóun-dee,** *s. f.* Proclamation by beat of drum.

डौरही **dóurhee,** *s. f.* Threshold, door, antichamber. *adj. f.* Half as much again ; raised one half higher (*a tone in music*).

डौल **doul,** *s. m.* Manner, method, mode ; shape, fashion, form.

ढ

ढ **dhuh,** The fourteenth consonant in the *Naguree* alphabet, or the fourth of the third series, and aspirate of the preceding letter : it has the power of *dh* in Holy rood-house.

ढूंईदेना **dhúee-déna,** *v. a.* To force an invitation, by fixing one's self in a house till dinner comes on table.

ढंग **dhung,** *s. m.* Behaviour, manners, breeding, gracefulness, mode, method.

ढंढोरा **dhun-dhóra,** *s. m.* Publication or proclamation by beat of drum.

डंढोरिया dhun-dhóriya, *s. m.* A crier, a proclaimer by beat of drum.

डक dhuk, *s. m.* A weight.

डकना dhúk-na, *v. a.* To cover, to conceal. *s. m.* A lid, cover, potlid.

डकनी dhúk-nee, *s. f.* A lid, cover (*of a pot*).

डकार dhuk-ár, *s. f.* A belch, eructation, bellowing.

डकारलेना dhukár-léna, *v. n.* To belch.

डकेल dhuk-él, *s. m.* A shove, push, thrust.

डकेलदेना dhukél déna, *v. a.* To push, precipitate.

डकेलना dhuk-élna, *v. a.* To shove, push, justle.

डकेलू dhuk-éloo, *s. m.* A pusher.

डक्क dhukk, *s. m.* A city or district, *Dhacca* or *Dacca*; covering or disappearance.

डक्का dhúk-ka, *s. f.* A large or a double drum.

डंग dhung, *s. m.* Behaviour, manners, breeding, gracefulness, mode, method.

डठिया dhút-iya, } *s. f.* A cord used in-
डठी dhúttee, } stead of a bridle.

डठ्था dhut-thá, *s. m.* A plug, cork, bung.

डरकोंवा dhur-kóuwa, *s. m.* A raven.

डर्व dhúr-wa, *s. m.* The name of a bird, a kind of *myna*.

डंढोरा dhun-dhóra, *s. m.* Publication or proclamation by beat of drum.

डंढोरिया dhun-dhó-riya, *s. m.* A crier, a proclaimer by beat of drum.

डना dhuna, *v. n.* To be demolished, razed, destroyed.

डनेक dhun-ék, *s. m.* A bird with a very large bill (*Buceros*).

डपडपाना dhup-dhup-ána, *v. a.* To thump a drum (*as children do*).

डपना dhúp-na, *v. n.* To be covered, to be concealed or hidden. *s. m.* A cover, covering.

डब dhub, *s. m.* Shape, form; manners, breeding, behaviour, mode, method, manner, knack, knowledge, fashion, style, way, address, dexterity, art, position.

डबरा dhúb-ra, *adj.* Turbid.

डबेला dhub-éela, *adj.* Well-made, graceful.

डबूंवा dhub-óoa, *s. m.* A copper coin equal to a pice (*pysa*).

डमलाना dhum-lána, *v. n.* To roll.

डलुक dhúl-uk, *s. f.* Rolling, tilting.

डलुकना dhúl-uk-na, *v. n.* To roll, be spilt.

डलका dhúl-ka, *adj.* Blear-eyed; spilling.

डलकाना dhul-kána, *v. a.* To tilt, overturn, spill, pour, roll.

डलना dhúl-na, *v. n.* To be cast (*a metal*), to be poured out, to flow, spill; to roll; to incline, decline. *Din dhulna,* To decline the day (*towards evening*). *Dhultee phirtee chhaon* (*lit. rolling and turning shade*), is applied, to the changeable state of worldly concerns, (*met.*) to a person of a capricious or unsteady temper.

डलमुलाना dhul-mul-ána, *v. n.* To move from side to side, to totter.

डलाना dhul-ána, *v. a.* To cause to cast (*metal*), to cause to pour.

डलेत dhulyt, *s. m.* A person in the equipage of great men armed with sword and buckler; a constable, a targetier.

डवाना dhuwána, *v. a.* To cause to be knocked down, razed or demolished.

डहना dhúhna, *v. n.* To fall, to be demolished, to tumble down (*as a house, &c.*), to be razed, destroyed.

डहपूरना dhuh-púrna, *v. n.* To fall, to soss.

डाई dháee, *adj.* Two and a half.

डांकना dhánk-na, *v. a.* To cover, to shut.

डांग dhang, *s. f.* A precipice, cliff.

डांचा dhán-cha, *s. m.* A frame, a plan.

डांपना dhámp-na, *v. a.* To cover, conceal, hide.

डांसना dháns-na, *v. a.* To blame, to accuse.

डांस dhán-sa, *s. m.* Calumny, undeserved abuse, defamation.

डाक dhak, *s. m.* A tree (*Butea frondosa*).

डाका dhá-ka, *s. m.* A thick wood of *dhak* trees; a city or district, *Dhacca* or *Dacca*.

डाटा dhá-ta, *s. m.* A handkerchief tied over the turband and over the ears.

डाठी dha-thée, *s. f.* Rack, torment, torture; a noose or gin fastened on a horse's nose.

डारस dhá-rus, *s. f. m.* Firmness of mind, confidence, animation, encouragement, comfort.

डारस देना dharus déna, *v. a.* To animate.

डारस बंधाना dharus bundhána, *v. a.* To encourage, comfort, keep in spirits. [singer.

डारी dhá-ree, *s. m.* A kind of musician, a

डारहस dha-rhús, *s. m. f.* Firmness of mind, confidence, animation, encouragement, comfort.

डारहिन dha-rhín, *s. m.*] A kind of musi-
डारही dha-rhée, *s. f.* } cian, a singer.

डान dhan, *s. m.* Hedge, enclosure.

डाना dhá-na, *v. a.* To break, batter, knock down or raze (*a building, &c.*), to demolish.

डाबा dhá-ba, *s. m.* A net; the eaves of a house, extending three or four cubits beyond the wall, so that people may sit under them.

ढाल dhal, *s. m.* Declivity, slope. *s. f.* A shield, target, buckler.

ढालना dhál-na, *v. a.* To cast (*metal in fusion*); to pour out, tilt, spill; (*met.*) to do mischief, mar, spoil.

ढालवाँ dhal-wán, *adj.* Sloping, declivous; cast (*metal*).

ढाली dhá-lee, *s. m.* A warrior armed with a shield, a shield-bearer.

ढालू dhalóo, *adj.* Slant, sloping. *part. act.* Spoiling, doing mischief, casting, &c. *Dhaloo-bhar kurna,* To shift goods, &c., occasionally over shallows, &c.

ढाहा dhá-ha, *s. m.* The precipitous or high bank of a river.

ढिग dhig, *s. m. f.* Side; near, close to.

ढिठाई dhit-háee, *s. f.* Forwardness, assurance, impudence, audacity, audaciousness, boldness, presumption, presumptuousness, petulance, pertness.

ढिबका dhíb-ka, *s. m.* Protuberance.

ढिमढिमी dhím-dhim-ee, *s. f.* A kind of tambourin.

ढिल्लुर dhillúr, *adj.* Lazy.

ढीठ dheeth, } *adj.* Forward, impudent,
ढीठा dhee-thá, } familiar, bold, daring, presumptuous, confident. *pret. part. pass.* Seen.

ढीर्ह dheerh, *s. m.* Pregnancy; a large belly.

ढील dheel, *s. f.* Looseness, relaxedness, remissness, laziness, inattention, delay.

ढीला dhee-la, *adj.* Loose, not tight; remiss; lazy, inattentive, dilatory.

ढीलाई dhee-lá-ee, *s. f.* Looseness, remissness.

ढीहा dhee-ha, *s. m.* A rising ground.

ढूंढना dhóondh-na, *v. a.* To seek, to search for.

ढूंढनाढांढना dhóondhna-dhándhna, *v. a.* To search for, to seek.

ढूंढवाना dhoondhwána, *v. a.* To cause to seek.

ढूकना dhóok-na, *v. n.* To enter, penetrate; to take aim, look, have regard or inclination (*to*); to sympathize.

ढूकीलगाना dhóokkee-lugána, *v. a.* To take aim.

ढूलना dhóol-na, *v. n.* To be poured out, to be spilt, to roll.

ढुलवाना dhool-wána, } *v. a.* To cause to
ढुलाना dhoo-lána, } be carried; to spill (*water, &c.*)

ढूलाई dhoo-láee, *s. f.* Act of carrying; price paid for carrying, or for transporting.

ढूआ dhóoa, *s. m.* A bank, a mound, a clod of earth.

ढूंढधार dhoonr-dhánr, *s. m.* Search.

ढूंढ dhoondh, *s. m.* Search.

ढूंढन dhoon-dhún, *s. m.* Seeking, searching, investigating.

ढूंढना dhóondh-na, *v. a.* To seek, search for. *Dhoondhna-dhandhna,* To search for, seek.

ढूंढिया dhóon-dhiya, *s. m.* A mendicant of the sect of *Jyn.*

ढूकना dhóok-na, *v. n.* To shut, close; to steal on, draw nigh, approach; go into, enter.

ढूका dhóo-ka, *s. m.* Tapping or shoving, by way of calling the attention of one spoken to.

ढूका देना dhóoka déna, *v. a.* To peep, to tap.

ढूरवा dhóor-wa, *s. m.* A pea.

ढूली dhóo-lee, *s. f.* A bundle of one hundred betel-leaves. *s. m.* A drummer.

ढूसुर dhóo-sur, *s. m.* A caste of *Hindoos.*

ढेऊ dhéoo, *s. m.* A wave.

ढेंकली dhénk-lee, *s. f.* A mode of joining breadths of cloth or of cutting out cloth; a machine for drawing out water, being a lever supported on a long post, having a bucket suspended to one end, and a weight of earth or stone to the other.

ढेंका dhén-ka, *s. m.* A machine for pounding with.

ढेंरस dhén-rus, *s. m.* A kind of gourd.

ढेंरी dhén-ree, *s. f.* The capsule of the poppy (*or of the cotton tree*), a poppy-head; an ornament worn in the ear. [belly.

ढेंधा dhen-dhá, *s. m.* Pregnancy; a large

ढेर्ह dherh, *s. m.* Name of a tribe of workers in leather; a crow.

ढेरही dhér-hee, *s. f.* An ornament worn in the ear.

ढेर dher, *s. m.* A heap, accumulation. *adj.* Much, abundant, enough.

ढेरा dhér-a, *adj.* Squinting, squint-eyed.

ढेरी dhér-ee, *s. f.* A heap.

ढेला dhél-a, *s. m.* A clod of earth, a lump of clay, chalk, &c. *Dhela-chouth, s. f.* The fourth day of the bright part of the *Hindoo* month *Bhadon,* a festival on which the *Hindoos* pelt each other with stones, or throw them into each other's houses, and if abused, consider the abuse an honor.

ढेहा dhéha, *s. m.* A kind of *Hindoo* mendicant; a tribe of *Jats.*

ढैया dhy-ya, *s. m.* A measure of two and a half *ser.*

ढैयाटेकुर dhyya-tékur, *adj.* Desolated.

ढोआ dhó-a, *s. m.* Fruit and flowers presented by inferiors on festival days.

ढोंचा dhón-cha, *adj.* Four and a half.

ढोंड dhond, *s. f.* A capsule or seed-vessel (*especially of the poppy*).

ढोक dhok, *s. f.* Salutation.

ढोकना dhók-na, *v. a.* To drink, to tope.

ढोका dhó-ka, *s. m.* A piece of stone.

ढोटा dhó-ta, *s. m.* A child.

ढोना dhó-na, *v. a.* To carry, to bear.

ढोर dhor, *s. m.* Cattle.

ढोरा dhó-ra, *s. m.* The representation of a tomb carried about in the *Moohurrum*.

ढोरी dhó-ree, *s. f.* Eagerness, ardour.

ढोल dhol, *s. m.* A large drum.

ढोलक dhó-luk, } *s. f.* A small drum.
ढोलकी dhól-kee, }

ढोलकिया dho-luk-íya, *s. m.* A person that plays on the *dholuk*.

ढोलन dhó-lun, *s. m.* A friend, a sweetheart.

ढोलना dhól-na, *s. m.* A little amulet in the shape of a drum.

ढोला dhó-la, *n. prop.* Name of a famous lover in *Hindoostan. s. m.* A boy.

ढोलिया dhó-liya, *s. m.* A drummer.

ढोली dhó-lee, *s. f.* A bundle of one hundred betel-leaves. *s. m.* A drummer.

ढोंचा dhóun-cha, *adj.* Four and a half.

ण

ण nuh, The fifth letter of the third class of consonants in the *Nagures* alphabet, or the fifteenth consonant : it is scarcely ever used as an initial letter. It has the power of *n*, uttered with the point of the tongue pressed back on the palate.

त

त tuh, The first letter of the fourth or dental class of consonants, or the sixteenth consonant in the *Nagures* alphabet. It has the sound of *t* in most of the continental languages of Europe, or, as expressed in the provincial pronunciation of butter in Yorkshire.

तईं túee*n*, } *adv.* Till, up to, while, toward, near to, to, at (*or*
तक tuk, } *denoting after a genitive form, the objective case*).

तकतक tuk-tuk, *s. m.* The sound of feet.

तकना túk-na, *v. a.* To look at, to look, to observe, to aim at, to watch. *v. n.* To be looked at, to be stared at, to look.

तकला túk-la, *s. m.* A spindle.

तकली túk-lee, *s. f.* A weaver's reel.

तकवाही tuk-wá-hee, *s. f.* Watching, overseeing, superintending, looking sharp after (*as after a silversmith*).

तकान tuk-án, *s. m.* Motion, agitation, gesture.

तकाना tuk-ána, *v. a.* To aim.

तकीनी tuk-éenee, *s. f.* A small pillow.

तकूआ túk-ooa, *s. m.* A spindle.

तक्र tukr, *s. m.* Buttermilk, with a fourth part water.

तक्राट tukr-át, *s. m.* A churning stick.

तक्षक túk-shuk, *s. m.* One of the principal mythological *Nagus* or serpents of *patal*; a snake of a middle size and of a red colour.

तक्षनी túk-shun-ee, *s. f.* A carpenter's adze.

तक्षन tuk-shún, *s. m.* A carpenter.

तक्षशिला tuksh-shíl-a, *s. f.* The name of a city, the *Taxila* of *Ptolemy* in the *Punjab*.

तखरी túkh-ree, *s. f.* Scales.

तखान tukh-án, *s. m.* A carpenter.

तगना túg-na, *v. a.* To quilt, to stitch together.

तगर túg-ur, *s. m.* A tree (*Tabernæmontana coronaria*).

तगाई tug-áee, *s. f.* The price paid for quilting, &c.; the act of quilting.

तगाना tug-ána, *v. a.* To cause to be quilted, to get stitched together.

तग्गा túgga, *s. f.* A strand or thread of a twist.

तग्गी túggee, *s. f.* A strand or thread of a twist; a kind of fishing-line not used with a rod. *Ti-tuggee*, A thread of tree strands. *Chou-tuggee* One of four strands.

तङ्ग tún-ga, *s. m.* Two pice (*pysa*).

तचना túch-na, *v. n.* To be heated, to parch.

तचाना tuch-ána, *v. a.* To parch, to scorch.

तज tuj, *s. f.* The bay tree or its bark (*Laurus cassia*), woody cassia.

तजना túj-na, *v. a.* To abandon, desert, quit, leave.

तट tut, *s. m.* A field; a shore or bank.

तटस्थ tut-ústh, *s. m.* An indifferent person, one neither a friend nor a foe.

तर tur, *s. m.* Party, division, faction; an imitative sound.

तरुकना túr-uk-na, *v. n.* To be cracked, to be split, to burst, to crack.

तरका túr-ka, *s. m.* Dawn of day. *Turkeh, adv.* In the morning early, at dawn of day.

तरतराना tur-tur-ána, *v. n.* To trickle,

drop, patter, bluster, welter; to warp or crack with noise (*as a plank exposed to the sun*).

तकतकड़ाहट **tur-tur-áhut,** *s. f.* The act of dropping.

तकुप **tur-úp,** *s. f.* Haste, hurry, outrageousness, explosion, fury, leap, jump.

तकुपका **tur-púr-a,** *s. m.* The noise of falling water.

तकुपकी **tur-púr-ee,** *s. f.* Flutter, palpitation.

तकुपना **tur-úp-na,** ⎱ *v. n.* To flutter, palpitate, flounce, be
तकुफना **tur-úph-na,** ⎰ agitated, writhe, jump, spring, bound, wriggle, toss; to be very desirous about any thing.

तकुपाना **tur-pána,** *v. a.* To put in great agitation; to cause to flutter or stumble.

तकुपीला **tur-péela,** *adj.* Hasty, hurrying.

तकुफ **tur-úph,** *s. f.* Agitation, tossing about, palpitation.   [to palpitate.

तकुफकाना **tur-phur-ána,** *v. n.* To flutter,

तकुफकाहट **tur-phur-áhut,** *s. f.* Act of fluttering, palpitation.

तकुफना **tur-úph-na,** *v. n.* To flutter, to palpitate; to be very desirous about any thing, to be agitated, to writhe, jump, spring, bound, wriggle, toss.

तकुफाना **tur-phá-na,** *v. a.* To put in great agitation; to cause to flutter or stumble.

तक्रा **túr-a,** *s. m.* An island.

तक्राकरी **tur-ák-ree,** *s. f.* The beam of a balance.

तक्राका **tur-áka,** *adj.* Pretty, shewy, gaudy. *s. m.* The sound of striking.

तक्राग **tur-ág,** *s. m.* A pond, a pool, deep enough for the growth of the lotus and other aquatic flowers; a trap for catching deer.

तक्राड़ा **tur-ára,** *s. m.* Throwing water.

तक्राया **tur-áya,** *s. m.* Gaudiness in dress, wearing smart clothes. *Turayadar, s. m.* One who dresses well and is particular in having fine and well-made clothes.   [vanity.

तक्राबा **tur-áwa,** *s. m.* Show, ostentation,

तकुडल **tún-dool,** *s. m.* Rice (*cleaned from the husk*), any grain after threshing and winnowing; a vermifuge plant.

तकुडलु **tún-doo-loo,** *s. f.* A plant of which the seeds are used as a vermifuge.

तत् **tut,** *pron.* That.

ततरी **tútree,** *s. f.* A playful, wanton girl.

ततुहरा **tu-túh-ra,** *s. m.* A vessel for warming water, a kettle.

तताना **tut-ána,** *v. a.* To warm.

ततार **tutár,** *s. f.* Embrocation, pouring of water on a diseased part. *Tutarna, v. a.* To embrocate.

तत्काल **tútkál,** *adv.* At that time, then. *s. m.* Present, time being, or the time when an act occurs.

तत्कालऊधी **tutkal-údhee,** *s. m.* A man wise or intelligent for the time being, one having presence of mind, &c.

तत्क्षन **tut-kshún,** *s. m.* Time present, time being. *adv.* At that time, instantly, immediately.

तत्ता **tútta,** *adj.* Hot, fiery, passionate, furious, outrageous.

तत्पर **tutpúr,** *adj.* Diligent, attending to any thing closely and anxiously, engaged, attentive, addicted to, adept.

तत्र **tutr,** *adv.* There, therein.

तत्रभवत **tutr-bhúwut,** *adj.* Venerable, respectable, reverend.

तत्व **tútwuh,** *s. m.* An element, a principle, the essence; essential nature, the real nature of the human soul, considered in the *shasters*, as one and the same with the divine spirit animating the universe: the philosophical etymology of this word best explains its meaning, तद् that, *that divine being*, and त्व thou, that *very God* art *thou*; the Supreme Being or *Brumh*; truth, reality, the essential substance, opposed to what is illusory or fallacious; an element or elementary property differently enumerated in different systems, from the three which are the same with the three *goons*, to twenty-seven, which include the elements, organs, faculties, matter, spirit, life, and God; a first principle, an axiom; mind, intellect; slow time in music; a musical instrument.

तत्वज्ञान **tútwuh-gyán,** *s. m.* Knowledge of divine truth.

तथ **tuth,** *adj.* True, right.

तथा **tuthá,** *s. f.* Power, ability, might. *adv. or conj.* So, thus, ditto, and.

तथागुत **tutha-gút,** *s. m.* A *Jyn* or *Booddh.*

तथापि **tuthápi,** *adv.* Nevertheless, yet, even.

तथास्तु **tuthás-too,** *adv.* Be it so, yes.

तद् **tud,** *adv.* Then, at that time, afterwards, in that case, therefore, so soon. *Tud-untur, adv.* After that, after which. *Tud to, adv.* Then, in that case. *Tud 'bhee, adv.* Still, nevertheless, however, notwithstanding. *Tud seh, adv.* Thence, since that time. *Tud-hee, adv.* At that very time, in that case only.

तदा **túd-a,** *adv.* Then, at that time.

तदधन **tud-dhún,** *adj.* Miserly, niggardly.

तधी **tud-hée,** *adv.* At that very time.

तन **tun,** *s. m.* The body, person. *Tuni-tunha, adv.* Alone, solitary. *Tun-o-mun murna,* To restrain one's desires and be silent. *Tun-dih,* A person of application. *Tun-dihee, s. f.* Application, exertion, attention, diligence. *Tun-dooroost*, *adj.* Healthy, vigorous. *Tun-dooroostee*, *s. f.* Health, vigour. *Tun dena*, To pay attention. *Tun-purwur*, Careful of the body, over-attentive to the body. *Tun-purwuree*, *s. f.* Self-indulgence.

तनक **tún-uk**, *adj.* or *adv.* Slight, small, a little. *adv.* Slightly.

तनय **tún-uy**, *s. m.* A son; a male descendant.

तनया **tun-uyá**, *s. f.* A daughter.

तनिया **túniya**, *s. m.* A kind of covering for the waist.

तनी **tún-ee**, *s. f.* A string with which garments are tied; a daughter.

तनू **tún-oo**, *s. f.* The body.

तनुक **tún-ook**, *adj.* or *adv.* Slight, small, a little. *adv.* Slightly.

तनूरूप **tunoo-kóop**, *s. m.* A pore of the skin.

तनतनाना **tun-tun-úna**, *v. n.* To twang, to tingle.

तनतनाहट **tun-tun-áhut**, *s. f.* Sharp pricking pain from inflammation.

तन्ति **túnti**, *s. m.* A weaver.

तन्तु **túntoo**, *s. m.* A thread; offspring, race, descendants.

तन्तुकीट **tuntoo-kéet**, *s. m.* A silk-worm.

तन्त्र **tuntr**, *s. m.* One of the books held sacred by the *Hindoos*; a religious treatise teaching peculiar and mystical formula and rites for the worship of the deities, or the attainment of superhuman power; it is mostly in the form of a dialogue between *Shiv* and *Doorga*, who are the peculiar deities of the *Tantrikus*: there is a great number of these works, and their authority, in many parts of India, seems to have, in a great measure, superseded that of the *Veds*: according to one account, a *Tuntr* comprises five subjects, the creation and destruction of the world, the worship of the gods, the attainment of all objects, magical rites for the acquirement of six (*superhuman*) faculties, and four modes of union with spirit by meditation: a variety of subjects are, however, introduced into many of them; whilst some are limited to a single topic, as the mode of breathing in certain rites, the language of birds, beasts, &c.; a branch of the *Veds*, that which teaches *muntrus* or mystical and magical formulæ; demonstration, clear and right conclusion; raiment, vesture; a medicament, a drug; a principal medicament, or perhaps a charm, considered as producing medicinal effects; a charm, an enchantment.

तन्त्री **tún-tree**, *s. m.* A musician.

तन्द्रा **tún-dra**, *s. f.* Lassitude, exhaustion, weariness, syncope.

तन्द्रालु **tun-drá-loo**, *adj.* Slothful, sluggish, overcome with sleep or fatigue.

तन्द्री **tún-dree**, *s. f.* Sleepiness, drowsiness; lassitude, fainting, exhaustion.

तन्न **túnna**, *v. n.* To stretch, pull tight; to sit upright.

तन्नाना **tunnána**, *v. n.* To twang; to have a sharp pricking pain from inflammation.

तप **tup**, *s. m.* The hot season, summer; devout austerity, religious penance. *s. f.* Heat, warmth.

तपकना **tup-úk-na**, *v. n.* To throb, to palpitate. *Tupukna phoreh ka*, The throbbing of a phlegmon or boil, when coming to suppuration.

तपत **túp-ut**, *adj.* Hot, warm, fervent. *s. f.* Heat.

तपन **túp-un**, *s. m.* The sun; a division of hell, the hot season; mental distress, pining, grieving. *s. f.* Heat, glow, fervour, warmth, burning.

तपना **tupna**, *v. n.* To be glorified; to glow, be heated, frisk about.

तपनी **túp-un-ee**, *s. f.* The *Godaveree* river.

तपरी **túp-ree**, *s. f.* A mound, a small height, an acclivity.

तपस् **tup-ús**, *s. m.* Religious austerity, penance, mortification, the practice of mental or personal self-denial; a world, the region inhabited by saints or devotees after death; virtue, moral merit; duty, the special observance of certain things, thus the *Tupus* of a *Brahmun* is sacred learning; of a *Kshutree*, the protection of subjects; of a *Vys*, almsgiving to *Brahmuns*; of a *Soodr*, the service of the same sect; and of a *Rishi* or saint, feeding upon herbs and roots.

तपस्य **tup-úsyuh**, *s. m.* The month *Phalgoon* (February-March).

तपस्या **tup-ús-ya**, *s. f.* Devout austerity, religious penance, devotion.

तपस्विन **tup-uswín**, तपस्वी **tup-úswee**, *s. m.* An ascetic, a religious engaged in the practice of rigorous and devout penance.

तपस्वी **tup-ússee**, *s. m.* A devotee, a performer of austere devotion, an ascetic. *adj.* Devout, practising austere devotion. *Tupsee*, or *Tupussee-muchhlee*, *s. f.* The mango fish (*Polynemus paradisea*).

तपा **túp-a**, *s. m.* A worshipper, an ascetic, a devotee.

तपाना **tup-ána**, *v. a.* To pour out a libation; to heat, to warm, to cause to glow, to make another warm himself at the fire or in the sun.

तपास **tup-ás**, *s. f.* Sunshine, the sunbeams; toil, labour.

तपी **túp-ee**, *s. m.* A devotee, a worshipper.

तपोधन tup-ó-dhun, *s. m.* A devotee, an ascetic, one who performs religious penance.

तपोवट tup-ó-wut, *s. m.* A country, part of central India, or Holy land.

तप्त tupt, *adj.* Hot, warm, fervent, heated, inflamed, burnt with heat, pain or sorrow.

तप्तकृच्छ्र tupt-krich-chhrúh, *s. m.* A sort of penance, drinking hot water, milk, or *ghee*, for three days.

तप्पा túppa, *s. m.* Division, district, parish.

तब tub, *adv.* Then, at that time, so soon; afterwards. *Tub tuk*, Till then. *Tub-tores*, or, *Tub-tueen*, or, *Tub-lug*, *adv.* Till then, so long.

तबही tub-hée, *adv.* At that very time. *Tubhee-to*, Then indeed. *Tubhee-seh*, Thence, thenceforth.

तबे tub-úy, *adv.* Exactly then.

तमः túmub, *s. m.* Darkness, gloom; the quality of darkness, incident to humanity; illusion of mind, headstrong passion, anger; irascibility or promptitude to the vindictive passions.

तम tum, *s. m.* The third of the qualities incident to the state of humanity, the *Tumuh-goon*, or property of darkness, whence proceed folly, ignorance, mental blindness, worldly delusion, &c.; darkness, gloom; sorrow, grief.

तमक túm-uk, *s. f.* Vanity, arrogance, pride; growing red in the face.

तमकना túm-uk-na, *v. n.* To grow red (*in the face*); to be enraged without cause, or to break out into violence at a temperate and reasonable speech.

तमका túm-ka, *s. m.* A stroke of the sun.

तमत túm-ut, *adj.* Desirous, cupidinous, longing or hankering after.

तमतमाना tum-tum-ána, *v. n.* To grow red in the face; to glow, to sparkle, to twinkle, to flash.

तमतमाहट tum-tum-áhut, *s. f.* The state of growing red in the face, glow.

तमस túm-us, *s. m.* The third of the qualities incident to humanity, the *Tumuh-goon*, or property of darkness, whence proceed folly, ignorance, mental blindness, worldly delusion, &c.; darkness (*physical or moral*), gloom; sorrow, grief.

तमस्विनी tumuswín-ee, *s. f.* Night.

तमाल tum-ál, *s. m.* The sectarial mark made with *sandal*, &c., on the forehead; a tree bearing black blossoms (*Xanthocymus pictorius*).

तमालक tum-áluk, *s. m.* A kind of potherb (*Marsilea dentata*).

तमालिका tum-álika, *s. f.* A district in Bengal, the modern *Tumlook*.

तमाली tum-álee, *s. f.* A medicinal plant used as an emollient in affections of the mouth and fauces.

तमिस्रा tum-ísra, *s. f.* A dark night, or one during the wane of the moon. *s. m.* The dark half of the month, from the full to the change.

तमोगुण túmo-goon, *s. m.* The third of the qualities incident to the state of humanity, the property of darkness, whence proceed folly, ignorance, mental blindness, worldly delusion, &c.; darkness, gloom; sorrow, grief.

तमोघ्न tumóghn, *s. m.* The legislator of *Booddh*.

तमोलिप्ती tum-o-líptee, *s. f.* The district of *Tumlook* in Bengal.

तमोवृत tum-o-vrít, *adj.* Overcome with rage, fear, &c., or any of the effects of the property of darkness.

तम्बालू tum-bá-loo, *s. m.* A pot, pipkin.

तम्बिया túm-biya, *s. m.* A pot.

तम्बू túm-boo, *s. m.* A tent.

तम्बोल tum-ból, *s. m.* The betel leaf. *Tumbol ana*, To bleed from the bridle (*a horse's mouth*).

तम्बोलिन tum-bo-lín, *s. f.* A woman whose business it is to sell betel leaf; name of a tree.

तम्बोली tum-bó-lee, *s. m.* A caste whose business it is to sell betel leaf.

तर tur, *adv.* Under, beneath.

तरुच túr-uce, *s. f.* A star.

तरुक túr-uk, *s. f.* A beam, a rafter.

तरकारी tur-ká-ree, *s. f.* Esculent vegetables.

तरकुल túr-kool, *s. m.* The fruit of the *tar* tree (*Borassus flabelliformis*).

तरखा túr-kha, *adj.* Rapid (*a stream*).

तरंग tur-úng, *s. f.* A wave, an emotion; whim, conceit, fancy, caprice; becoming state and dignity.

तरंगिनी tur-un-gín-ee, *s. f.* A river.

तरंगी tur-ún-gee, *adj.* Braggart, fanciful, fantastical, whimsical.

तरछुट túr-chhut, *s. f.* Dregs, sediment, lees.

तरण túr-un, *s. m.* A raft, a float; *swurg* or paradise; crossing over, passing, going across; escaping, being saved; one who is saved or delivered.

तरणि túr-un-i, *s. m.* The sun; a ray of light; a float or raft.

तरणि túr-un-i, ⎫ *s. f.* A ship, vessel,
तरणी túr-un-ee, ⎭ boat; the succotrine aloe (*A. perfoliata*); a plant (*Hibiscus mutabilis*).

तरंड tur-únd, *s. m.* A raft or float, made of bamboos, &c. tied together, and sometimes floated upon jars or hollow gourds inverted; the float of a fishing line.

तरुखी tur-ún-dee, *adj.* A boat, a vessel.

तरतरा túr-tura, *s. m.* A kind of dish.

तरन túr-un, *s. m.* Passing over ; escaping, being saved ; one who is saved or delivered.

तरना túr-na, *v. n.* To cross over, to pass over, to be ferried ; to be saved.

तरन्त túr-unt, *s. m.* A fog ; a hard shower, a torrent of rain ; the ocean.

तरनी túr-un-tee, *s. f.* A boat.

तरपन túr-pun, *s. m.* A libation of water to the manes of deceased ancestors ; satisfaction, gratification.

तरफना túr-uph-na, *v. n.* To flutter, palpitate, flounce, be agitated, writhe, jump, spring, bound, wriggle, toss ; to be very desirous about any thing.

तरबूज tur-bóoj, *s. m.* A water-melon (*Cucurbita citrullus*).

तरल túr-ul, *adj.* Capricious, changeable, fickle, inconstant, ticklish, volatile, unsteady ; libidinous, lecherous, wanton.

तरला túr-la, *adj.* Lower, nethermost. *s. m.* A kind of bamboo ; bottom, depth, lower or under part.

तरव túr-uv, *s. m.* A tree.

तरवर túr-wur, *s. m.* Any large tree.

तरवरिया tur-wúr-iya, *s. m.* A sword ; a swordsman, a fencer.

तरवार tur-wár, *s. f.* A sword, a scimitar.

तरसना túr-us-na, *v. n.* To long, desire anxiously, be agog ; to pity.

तरा túr-a, *s. m.* The bottom of any thing.

तराइन tur-a-ín, *s. m.* Stars.

तराई tur-áee, *s. f.* A marsh, mead, meadow. *Turaee khewa, adj.* Living in, or near water (*water-fowl, water-spaniel, &c.*)

तराकड़ी turák-ree, *s. f.* The beam of a balance.

तरान tur-án, *s. m.* Revenue.

तराना tur-ána, *v. a.* To cause to pass over or swim ; to save.

तरी túr-ee, *s. f.* A boat.

तरू túr-oo, *s. m.* A tree.

तरूजीवन tur-oo-jéewun, *s. m.* The root of a tree.

तरून túr-oon, *s. m.* A kind of flower (*Achyranthes aspera ?*) ; a young man, one of the virile age. *adj.* Young, juvenile, adult ; new, fresh, novel.

तरूनाई tur-oon-áee, *s. f.* } Adolescence,
तरूनापन turoona-pún, *s. m.* } youth, puberty.

तरूनी túr-oo-nee, *s. f.* A young woman from 16 to 30 years of age, generally however one about the first age.

तरे túr-eh, *adv.* Under.

तरेरा tur-ér-a, *s. m.* The falling of water from a spout, or from any height.

तरेत tur-ét, *s. m.* A buoy.

तरेया tur-úy-ya, *s. f.* A star.

तर्क turk, *s. m.* Doubt, disputation, discussion, reasoning ; the science of reasoning, logic ; (*in logic*) a proposition.

तर्कविद्या turk-vídya, *s. f.* The science of reasoning or logic.

तर्कारी tur-káree, *s. f.* Esculent vegetables.

तर्कित túr-kit, *adj.* Doubtful, disputatious.

तर्किन turk-in, *s. m.* A logician, a disputant, a follower of the *Turk shastr.*

तर्किल túrk-il, *s. m.* Cassia tora.

तर्की túr-kee, *s. f.* A kind of ornament for the ears made of the leaves of the *tar* tree. *s. m.* A logician, a disputant, a follower of the *Turk shastr.*

तर्कू túrkoo, *s. f.* A spindle, an iron pin upon which the cotton is first drawn out ; it also serves as the distaff, the cotton being next transferred from it to the wheel.

तर्कुट túr-koot, *s. m.* Drawing out the cotton upon the distaff or upon the wheel.

तर्कुटी tur-kóo-tee, *s. f.* A spindle or a distaff.

तर्कुपिण्ड tur-koo-pínd, *s. m.* } A ball of
तर्कुपीठी tur-koo-péethee, *s. f.* } clay, &c. upon the lower end of the spindle to assist in giving it a rotatory motion.

तर्कुल túr-kool, *s. m.* The fruit of the *tar* tree (*Borassus flabelliformis*).

तर्कुलासुक tur-kool-ásuk, *s. m.* A concave shell or saucer in which the lower end of the spindle is placed and whirled round.

तर्कुशान turkoo-shán, *s. m.* A small whetstone for sharpening spindles, &c.

तर्खा túr-kha, *adj.* Rapid (*a stream*).

तर्जन túr-jun, *s. m.* Wrath, anger.

तर्जनी túr-jun-ee, *s. f.* The fore-finger.

तर्तराता tur-tur-áta, *adj.* Very greasy ; dripping with moisture.

तर्तराना turtur-ána, *v. n.* To bluster, to boast.

तर्तराहट turtur-áhut, *s. f.* Bluster, boast.

तर्पन túr-pun, *s. m.* Satisfaction, given or received ; either the act of pleasing or the state of being pleased ; satiety, fulness ; a religious rite, presenting water to the manes of the deceased.

तर्ब turb, *s. f.* A musical tone.

तरोना tur-rá-na, *v. n.* To grudge, grumble, murmur.

तुर्रारा turrára, *s. m.* Rapidity, flow. *Turrara bhurna*, To gallop.

तर्वरिया tur-wúr-iya, *s. m.* A sword; a swordsman, a fencer.

तर्वार tur-wár, *s. f.* A sword, a scimitar.

तर्ष tursh, *s. m.* Thirst; wish, desire.

तुर्षुन túr-shun, *s. m.* Thirst, thirsting; it is also used metaphorically.

तर्षित túrsh-it, *adj.* Thirsting, athirst, thirsty.

तर्स turs, *s. m.* Compassion, mercy. *Turs khana*, To compassionate, to pity.

तर्साना tur-sá-na, *v. a.* To cause to long, set agog, tantalize, tease, vex.

तर्सों túr-son, *adv.* The third day past or to come (*not including the present, i. e. two days intervening*).

तल tul, *s. m.* Depth, bottom, lowness, inferiority of position, the place under or underneath; the sole of the foot.

तलऊपर tul-óopur, *adj.* Upside down; confused.

तलक túl-uk, *adv.* Till.

तलछट túl-chhut, *s. f.* Dregs, refuse, scum, sediment, offals, leavings.

तलतलाना tultulána, *v. n.* To shake.

तलना túl-na, *v. a.* To fry.

तलपट túl-put, *adj.* Ruined, destroyed.

तलपना túl-up-na, } *v. n.* To flutter, to
तलफना túl-uph-na, } palpitate, be restless, be agitated, to flounce.

तलमलाना tul-mul-ána, *v. n.* To be tantalized; to grieve, to be agitated.

तलवरिया tul-wúr-iya, *s. f.* A scimitar. *s. m.* A swordsman, one armed with a scimitar, a sword-player, a fencer.

तलवार tul-wár, *s. f.* A sword, a scimitar.

तलवासना tul-wás-na, *v. a.* Spoken of the feet of an animal which are worn by treading on hard rocky ground.

तला túl-a, *s. f.* A leathern fence worn by archers on the left arm. *s. m.* The stand or support of any thing, that which is under or below it; the bottom of any thing; the sole of a shoe; protection.

तलातल túl-a-túl, *s. m.* One of the seven divisions of the infernal regions.

तलाव tul-áo, *s. m.* A pond, reservoir of water.

तलिहरू tul-ih-roo, *adj.* Inferior, next, below, one who acts at the command of another.

तली túl-ee, *s. f.* The bottom of any thing; the sole of a shoe; beneath; under; impalpable powder.

तलूआ túl-ooa, } *s. m.* The sole of the foot.
तलवा túl-wa, } *Tulooa chatna*, or, *Tulweh tuleh hath dhurna*, To flatter. *Tulweh suhlaneh*, (*lit. to stroke the soles of the feet*) Signifies excessive flattery, adulation. *Tuloon seh ag lugnee*, (*lit. burning in the soles of the feet*) Implies excessive anger.

तलेह túl-eh, *adv.* Below, down, beneath, under. *Tuleh-oopur, adj.* Upside down; confused. *Tuleh tuleh dekhna*, To see clandestinely. *Tuleh kee zumeen oopur honee*, Is used to express great disturbance and confusion.

तुलुय्या tul-úy-ya, *s. f.* A small pond.

तुलूह्य tul-úyha, *s. m.* A turtle dove.

तलिका túllika, *s. f.* A key.

तुवर्ग tuwúrg, *s. m.* The dental class of letters in the *Naguree* alphabet, beginning with त *tuh.*

तुशतरी túsh-tur-ee, *s. f.* A salver, a small plate, a saucer.

तुसर tús-ur, *s. m.* A shuttle; a kind of coarse silk the produce of a particular worm (*Bombyx paphia*), that feeds on the *asun* (*Terminalia alata tomentosa*), &c.

तुसला tús-la, *s. m.* A vessel used by *Hindoos* to dress their victuals in.

तुसकर tús-kur, *s. m.* A thief, a robber, a stealer; a kind of potherb (*Medicago esculenta*); a tree (*Vangueria spinosa*).

तुसकरता tuskur-tá, *s. f.* Thievishness, thieving.

तुसकरी túskur-ee, *s. f.* Theft; a passionate woman.

तुस्म tusm, *s. m.* A razor-strop.

तुस्सू tús-soo, *s. m.* An inch.

तुहुसनुहुस túhus-núhus, *adj.* Ruined, destroyed, dispersed.

तुहँ túhan, *adv.* Thither, there. *Tuhan tuhan*, In each place.

तुहाना tuhána, *v. a.* To fold, to ply, to wrap.

तुहीं tuhéen, *adv.* Thither, there, exactly there.

ता ta, *inflect. of the 3d pers. pron. sing.* Him, her, it, that.

तांगा tán-ga, *s. m.* A small two-wheeled car without covering, and on which one person only can sit. *Tanga-suwar*, One who rides on a *tanga*.

तांडव tán-duv, *s. m.* Dancing, especially with violent gesticulation, and particularly applied to the frantic dance of the god *Shiv* and his votaries.

तांत tant, *s. f.* A loom; cat-gut, sinew, the string of a musical instrument. *Tant bajee our rag boojha*, He understood from the first word *Tant bandhna*, To put to silence an idle talker.

तांता tán-ta, *s. m.* A string (*of camels, horses, &c.*), a drove ; a train, a series, a range, a row.

तांती tán-tee, *s. m.* A weaver.

तांबड़ा támb-ra, *s. m.* A copper colour (*in pigeons*) ; a false stone resembling a ruby.

तांबा tám-ba, *s. m.* Copper.

ताइत tá-it, *s. m.* An amulet or charm.

ताई tá-ee, *s. f.* An aunt, paternal uncle's wife, father's elder brother's wife ; an earthen frying pot.

ताऊ tá-oo, *s. m.* A paternal uncle, fa-
तानू tán-oo, } ther's elder brother.

ताक tak, *s. f.* Look, fixed regard, glance, peep ; aim, view, the act of aiming, pointing (*of a dog*). *Tak bandhna*, To covet, to point (*as a dog*). *Tak ruhna*, To aspire.

ताकना ták-na, *v. a.* To stare at, aim, peep, see, spy, watch, view, behold, look, look tor, attend.

ताकवाक ták-bak, *s. f.* Nick of time.

ताग tag, } *s. m.* Thread.
तागा tá-ga, }

तागतोड़ tag-tór, *s. m.* Lace.

तागना tág-na, *v. a.* To thread.

तागा tá-ga, *s. m.* Thread.

ताटंक tá-tunk, *s. m.* An ornament worn in the ear.

ताड़ tar, *s. m.* The palm tree (*Borassus flabelliformis*). *s. f.* Understanding. *Tarbaz, adj.* Intelligent, quick of apprehension. *Tarbazee, s. f.* Quickness of apprehension.

ताड़क tá-ruk, *s. m.* A reprover, punisher, chastiser.

ताड़ंक ta-rúnk, *s. m.* An ornament worn in the ear.

ताड़न ta-rún, } *s. m.* Beating, whipping,
ताड़ना tár-na, } punishment, admonition, reproof, penalty. *Tarna kurna*, To reprove, punish, chastise.

ताड़ना tár-na, *v. a.* To understand, conceive, comprehend, guess, apprehend.

ताड़नीय tar-néeyuh, *adj.* Reproveable, worthy of admonition, punishment, &c.

ताड़ी tá-ree, *s. f.* The juice of the palm tree (*toddy*) ; hilt of a dagger.

तांडव tán-duv, *s. m.* Dancing, especially with violent gesticulation, and particularly applied to the frantic dance of the god *Shiv* and his votaries.

तातः ta-túh, *adj.* Venerable, reverend, respectable.

तात tat, *s. m.* Father. *adj.* Hot, warm.

तातनी tat-née, *pron. inflect. f.* Of her, that or it.

तातनौ tat-nóu, *pron. inflect. m.* Of him, that or it.

तातूल ta-túl, *adj.* Hot, warm.

ताता ta-ta, *adj. m.* Hot, heating (*food*).

तातेह ta-téh, *pron. inflect.* From him, her, it, or that.

तात्कालिक tat-kálik, *adj.* Of that time or period.

तात्पर्य tat-púrj, *s. m.* Object, purpose, intent, design ; meaning, purport ; explanation ; the apprehension of an implied wish or thought ; need.

तद्‌आत्म्य tád-atm-yuh, *s. f.* Likeness, similarity.

तादृश्य tá-drish-yuh, *adj.* Such like, like him or it, &c.

तान tan, *s. f.* A tune, a tone, the key note in music ; stretching, tension, knitting (*eye-brows*).

तांडव tán-duv, *s. m.* Dancing with violent gesticulation.

तानतोड़ना tan-tórna, *v. a.* To crack a joke, to drop a word which shall excite quarrelling or induce conversation, to animadvert ; to strike up a tune.

ताना tá-na, *s. m.* The warp, the threads that are extended lengthwise upon a loom. *Tana bana kurna*, To fidget, to dance attendance. *Taneh tanna*, To wander here and there without profit.

ताना tá-na, *v. a.* To heat, prove, assay.

तानी tá-nee, *s. f.* The warp ; the price paid for weaving.

तांत्रिक tán-trik, *s. m.* A scholar, a man completely versed in any science ; a follower of the doctrine taught by the *Tuntrus*.

तानना tán-na, *v. a.* To extend, stretch, expand, pull, knit (*the eye-brows*). *Tumboo tanna*, To pitch tents.

ताप tap, *s. m.* Warmth, heat, burning (*moral or physical*) ; pain, sorrow, distress. *s. f.* Fever. *Tap-tillee, s. f.* An induration of the spleen, attended with, or preceded by fever ; splenitis, ague-cake.

तापक tá-puk, *s. m.* Fever, morbid heat. *adj.* Burning, inflaming, heating.

तापन tá-pun, *s. m.* The sun ; heating, inflaming.

तापना táp-na, *v. a.* To bask in the sun or before a fire, to warm one's self at (*or over*) a fire, to warm, to heat.

तापस tá-pus, *adj.* Performing penance. *s. m.* A practiser of devout austerities, a devotee, an ascetic.

तापित tapít, *adj.* Inflamed ; distressed, pained.

ताषी **tá-pee,** s. f. A name of the *Taptee* or *Surat* river; a name of the *Jumna* river. *adj.* Oppressed by heat, morbid, moral or physical; any thing heated or glowing.

ताप्य **tápyuh,** s. m. A mineral substance, sulphuret of iron, said to be procured from the *Tapee* river.

ताबड़तोड़ **tabur-tór,** *adv.* Successively, repeatedly. [copper.

तामचीनी **tam-chéenee,** s. f. Enamelled

तामड़ा **támra,** s. m. A gem of inferior value of a copper colour.

तामरस **tam-rús,** s. m. A lotus (*Nymphæa nelumbo*); copper; gold.

तामलकी **ta-múl-kee,** s. f. A plant (*Flacourtia cataphracta*).

तामलिप्त **tam-lípt,** s. f. A district in the south of Bengal, *Tumlook.*

तामस **tá-mus,** *adj.* Affected by or appertaining to the third quality, that of darkness or vice; partaking or influenced by the principle of inertness, ignorance or mental darkness, inert, stupid, ignorant. s. m. Darkness, illusion, irascibility; an incendiary, a malignant and mischievous man, a villain.

तामसी **tá-mus-ee,** *adj.* Dark, irascible, vindictive.

तामा **tá-ma,** } s. m. Copper.
ताम्बा **tám-ba,** }

तामेश्वर **tam-ésh-wur,** s. m. Calx or scoriæ of copper.

ताम्बूल **tam-bóol,** s. m. Betel-leaf, the areca nut.

ताम्बूलराग **tambool-rág,** s. m. A kind of pulse (*Ervum lens*).

ताम्बूलवल्ली **tambool-wúllee,** s. f. A small plant bearing a pungent leaf, with which the areca nut, a small quantity of caustic lime or chunam, and catechu, and occasionally cloves, cardamoms, &c., form the *Pan* or betel of the Asiatics (*Piper betel*).

ताम्बूली **tam-bóo-lee,** s. f. Betel (*Piper betel*) or its pungent leaf, which together with the areca nut is eaten very generally by the natives of the east. s. m. The *Pan* bearer of a prince or sovereign; a servant whose business it is to prepare and furnish the *Pan*.

ताम्ब्रा **tám-bra,** s. m. A copper colour (*in pigeons*); a false stone resembling a ruby.

ताम्र **tamr,** s. m. Copper; a kind of sandal wood represented as of a dark red colour and smelling like a lotus; a dark or coppery red.

ताम्रकर्णी **tamr-kúrnee,** s. f. A name of the female elephant of the west.

ताम्रकार **tamr-kár,** s. m. A brazier, a copper-smith.

ताम्रगर्भ **tamr-gúrbh,** s. m. Blue vitriol or sulphate of copper.

ताम्रपट्ट **tamr-pútt,** s. m. A copper plate, such as *Hindoo* grants of land, &c., are frequently inscribed on.

ताम्रपर्णी **tamr-púrnee,** s. f. A river in the peninsula and the district in its vicinity.

ताम्रपुष्प **tamr-póoshp,** s. m. A kind of ebony (*Bauhinia variegatu*); a plant (*Kempferia rotunda*).

ताम्रपुष्पा **tamr-póoshp-a,** s. f. Trumpet flower (*Bignonia suave-olens*).

ताम्रपुष्पी **tamr-póoshp-ee,** s. f. *Lythrum fruticosum.*

ताम्रफल **tamr-phúl,** s. m. *Alangium hexapetalum.*

ताम्रवर्णी **tamr-vúrnee,** s. f. The blossom of sesamum.

ताम्रवल्ली **tamr-wúllee,** s. f. Bengal madder (*Rubia manjith*).

ताम्रबीज **tamr-véej,** s. m. A kind of vetch.

ताम्रवृक्ष **tamr-vríksh,** s. m. A sort of sandal wood.

ताम्रसार **tamr-sár,** s. m. A red kind of sandal (*Pterospermum santolinum*).

ताम्राकू **tam-rákoo,** s. m. One of the eighteen divisions of the known continent.

तामिक **tám-rik,** s. m. A brazier, a copper-smith.

तामिका **tam-rík-a,** s. f. A copper vessel for marking time.

तामी **tám-ree,** s. f. A copper or metallic cup of prescribed capacity, and perforated by a small hole at the bottom, answering the purpose of an hour glass: it is put into a vessel of water, the water gradually filling it and the cup sinking marks the time that has elapsed.

तार **tar,** s. m. A high note or tone in music; a wire, a chord. [er.

तारक **tá-ruk,** *adj.* A protector, a preserv-

तारटूटना **tar-tóotna,** v. n. To be disjointed, to be separated.

तारण **tá-run,** s. m. A raft, a float; the act of freeing, salvation, deliverance; one that sets free or delivers.

तारणतारण **tárun-túrun,** s. m. f. The Saviour, and the person saved.

तारणा **tárna,** v. a. To free, rid, exempt from further transmigration, absolve from sin, save.

तारतम्य **tar-túm-yuh,** s. m. Distinction, discrimination.

तारतोड़ **tar-tór,** s. m. A kind of sewing or needle-work, open work, pulling out some threads, &c.

तारना **tár-na**, *v. a.* To free, to rid, to exempt from further transmigration, to absolve from sin, to save.

तारपतार **tar-put-ár**, *adj.* Dispersed, &c.

तार बांधना **tar bándhna**, *v. a.* To continue or repeat an action without interruption.

तारा **tára**, *s. m.* A star; the pupil of the eye. *Tareh ginna*, To count the stars, *i. e.* to get no sleep.

तारापथ **tara-púth**, *s. m.* The atmosphere, the firmament, heaven or sky.

तारामण्डल **tára-múndul**, *s. m.* The starry sphere.

तारिका **tá-rik-a**, *s. f.* The apple of the eye; a star.

तारिणी **tá-rin-ee**, *s. f.* A goddess peculiar to the *Jyns*; a name of *Doorga*; deliverer.

तारी **tá-ree**, *s. f.* The clapping of hands; a key; abstraction, absence of mind, absorption in thought or devotion.

ताऋ **ta-rúo**, *s. m.* The palate.

तार्किक **tark-ík**, *s. m.* A philosopher, a sophist, a follower of either of the six schools of *Hindoo* philosophy.

तार्किकः **tar-kik-úh**, *adj.* Relating or attached to the science of reasoning.

तार्ना **tár-na**, *v. a.* To free, to rid, to exempt from further transmigration, to absolve from sin, to save.

ताल **tal**, *s. m.* A pond; beating time in music, musical time or measure, chime; slapping or clapping the hands together or against the arms previous to fighting; a musical instrument of bell-metal or brass (*a sort of cymbal*) played with a stick; the palm tree (*Borassus flabelliformis*). *Tal dena*, To chime; to slap the hands on the arms before fighting. *Tal marna*, or, —*thokna*, To strike the hand against the arms preparatory to wrestling.

तालक **tá-luk**, *s. m.* A bolt, a latch, a kind of lock for fastening a door with.

तालपत्र **tal-pútr**, *s. m.* A hollow cylinder of gold with or without a ring attached to it, thrust through the lobe of the ear, and worn as an ornament.

तालपर्णी **tal-púrnee**, *s. f.* A sort of anise (*Anethum panmorium*).

तालपुष्पक **tal-póoshp-uk**, *s. m.* A medicinal application to the eyes.

तालमखाना **tal-muk-hána**, *s. m.* A medicinal herb (*Barleria longifolia*).

तालमूली **tal-móo-lee**, *s. f.* A plant (*Curculigo orchioides*).

तालवृन्त **tal-vrínt**, *s. m.* A fan.

ताला **tá-la**, *s. m.* A lock.

तालाख्य **tál-akhya**, *s. f.* A perfume.

ताली **tá-lee**, *s. f.* A sort of key or pin; clapping of the hands together; a species of the mountain palm (*Corypha taliera*); a plant (*Flacourtia cataphracta*). *Talee ek hath seh bujnee*, Is used to express an impossibility. *Talee bujana*, To clap the hands (*generally by way of censure and ridicule*); to hoot. *Talee marna*, To hoot.

तालू **tá-loo**, *s. m.* The palate, the ridge or slit in the root of the mouth; a disorder in horses, the lampreys.

ताव **tao**, *s. m.* A sheet of paper; proof, trial, essay; speed.

ताव **táo**, *s. m.* Heat; passion, rage; strength, power; splendour, dignity; twist, coil, contortion. *Tao dena*, To twist; to stroke the whiskers; to heat (*as iron*). *Tao pech khana*, To be heated; to be angry.

तावत **tá-wut**, *adv.* So much, so far, so many, unto, until, the correlative to यावत *yawut*.

तावना **táo-na**, *v. a.* To heat, to raise heat by blowing with bellows, to anneal; to prove, to assay; to twist.

ताश **tash**, *s. m.* Cloth of gold, brocade.

तास **tas**, *s. m.* The cards, a game at cards; brocade, cloth of gold.

तासू **tá-soo**, } *pron.* Of him, that or
तासुकौ **tasoo-kóu**, } it.

ताहि **tá-hi**, *pron.* To him, her, or it.

ताहिरी **tá-hir-ee**, *s. f.* A kind of dish, viz. rice boiled with *bur-ee*, which consists, of pulse (*Phaseolus radiatus*) ground in a wet state mixed with ginger, pepper, &c. and dried in small lumps.

तिकतिक **tik-tik**, *s. f.* A sound used in driving a cart.

तिकोनिया **tik-ó-niya**, *adj.* Triangular.

तिक्का **tíkka**, *s. m.* A small piece of flesh, a steak, a chop, a collop, a slice.

तिक्त **tikt**, *adj.* Bitter; fragrant. *s. m.* A bitter taste, bitterness; fragrance, perfume.

तिक्तक **tík-tuk**, *s. m.* A kind of gourd (*Trichosanthes diœca*); a sort of Gentian (*G. cherayta*).

तिक्तगन्धा **tikt-gún-dha**, *s. f.* A plant (*Lycopodium imbricatum*).

तिक्ततूम्बी **tikt-tóom-bee**, *s. f.* A bitter gourd.

तिक्तदुग्धा **tikt-dóog-dha**, *s. f.* A medicinal kind of moon-plant.

तिक्तपत्र **tikt-pútr**, *s. m.* A cucurbitaceous plant (*Momordica mixta*).

तिक्तपर्वन् **tikt-purwún**, *s. f.* A potherb (*Hilancha repens*); a plant (*Menispermum glabrum*).

तिक्तभद्रक **tikt-bhúd-ruk**, *s. m.* A kind of cucumber (*Trichosanthes diœca*).

तिक्तरोहिणिका **tikt-ro-hínika**, *s. f.* A medicinal plant.

तिक्तवल्ली tikt-wúllee, *s. f.* A plant (*Aletris hyacinthoides*).

तिक्तशाक tikt-shák, *s. m.* A plant (*Capparis trifoliata*).

तिक्तसार tikt-sár, *s. m.* A sort of Mimosa (*M. catechu*).

तिक्तिका tík-tik-a, *s. f.* A bitter gourd.

तिखरा करना tíkhra kurna, *v. a.* To trifallow, to plough three times.

तिखारना ti-khár-na, *v. a.* To confirm, to prove, to establish by argument; to inquire earnestly; to trifallow.

तिगुन tí-goon, *s. m.* A tone in music. *adj.* Threefold, triple.

तिगुना tí-goon-a, *adj.* Threefold.

तिग्म tigm, *s. m.* Heat, also the heat of spices, or pungency. *adj.* Hot, pungent, acrid; sharp (*as a weapon*).

तिच्चन tich-chún, *adj.* Sharp, virulent, bitter, severe.

तिजरी tíj-ree, } *s. f.* A tertian fever or
तिजारी tij-áree, } ague.

तिन्टी tín-tee, *s. f.* A plant, commonly called *Teoree.*

तित tit, *adv.* Thither, there.

तितना títna, } *adj.* So many, so much,
तितनी títnee, } *Titneh-men,* In so much (*time*).

तितरबितर títur-bítur, *adj.* Dispersed.

तितिक्षा titík-sha, *s. f.* Patience, resignation, sufferance, endurance.

तितिक्षित titíkshit, } *adj.* Patient, resign-
तितिक्षु titíkshoo, } ed.

तितिम्ब titímba, *s. m.* An obstacle, impediment, stratagem.

तितिल títil, *s. m.* One of the seven *Kuruns* or astronomical periods so called; a sort of sweetmeat made of sesamum, ground, and baked with sugar.

तितिर títtir, *s. m.* The Francoline partridge.

तितिरि títtiri, *s. m.* The Francoline partridge; the name of a *mooni*, and one of the early teachers of the *Tyttiri* or black *Yujoor Ved*; the *Yujoor Ved*, named after its teacher.

तिथ tith, } *s. f.* A lunar day, one thir-
तिथि títhi, } tieth of a whole lunation.

तिथिक्षय tithi-kshúy, *s. m.* Day of new moon.

तिदुरी ti-dur-ee, *adj.* Three-doored.

तिधुर tídhur, *adv.* There.

तिधारा tidhá-ra, *s. m.* A plant (*Euphorbia antiquorum*); the meeting of three streams.

तिन tin, *pron. pl. inflect.* Them, those. He, she, it, that. *Tinhen,* To them or those, &c.

तिनकना tín-uk-na, *v. n.* To flutter, palpitate, throb.

तिनका tín-ka, *s. m.* A straw, a bit of the stalk of grass. *Tinka danton men lena,* To make submission, confess inferiority, or ask for quarter. *Tinkeh choonna* (*lit. to pick straws*), To be intoxicated.

तिनतिरी tín-tir-ee, *s. m.* The tamarind tree.

तिन्नी tínnee, *s. f.* A kind of rice.

तिन्दु tín-doo, *s. m.* A species of ebony, from the fruit of which a kind of resin is obtained, that is used in India as pitch for caulking vessels, &c. (*Diospyros glutinosa*).

तिन्दुकी tín-doo-kee, *s. f.* The resinous fruit of a sort of ebony.

तिबारा tí-bára, *adj.* Thrice. *s. m.* A hall or room with three doors.

तिमि tími, *s. m.* A fabulous fish of an enormous size, said to be one hundred *Yojuns* long.

तिमिङ्गिल tim-ín-gil, *s. m.* A large fabulous fish.

तिमिङ्गिलगिल timingil-gíl, *s. m.* A fabulous fish larger than either of the preceding.

तिमित tímit, *adj.* Wet, moist, moistened, damp; steady, fixed, unmoved, unshaken.

तिमिर tímir, *s. m.* Darkness; gutta serena, total blindness from affection of the optic nerve.

तिमिष tím-ish, *s. m.* A kind of pumpkin gourd; a water melon.

तियुह tíyuh, *s. f.* A woman, a wife.

तिरकूटा tír-koo-ta, *s. m.* A mixture of dry ginger, long pepper, and black pepper.

तिरखा tír-kha, *s. f.* Thirst, desire.

तिरखूंटी tir-khóon-tee, *s. f.* A trivet.

तिरछा tír-chha, *adj.* Crooked, across, crosswise, bent, oblique, awry, askant; perverse; affected, foolish. *Tirchha dekhna,* To squint, to look askant. *Tirchha lugna, v. n.* To strike obliquely, to glance. *Tirchhee ankh kurna,* To look angrily, to cast unkind looks. *Tirchhee nuzur,* Leer, ogle, side glance, squint.

तिरछाना tir-chhá-na, *v. a.* To crook, to place in a transverse position, slant. *v. n.* To be perverse; to be affected.

तिरछियाना tir-chhi-yána, *v. n.* To edge, to go obliquely.

तिरतिराना tir-tir-ána, *v. n.* To trickle, to drop.

तिरना tír-na, *v. n.* To swim.

तिरपद tír-pud, *s. m.* A tripod.

तिरपन tír-pun, *adj.* Fifty-three.

तिरपोलिया tir-póu-liya, *s. m.* A building with three doors or arches.

तिरफुल tír-phul-a, *s. m.* A medicine composed of three myrobalans.

तिरबाचक tir-bá-chuk, *s. m.* An agreement confirmed three times.

तिरभंगा tir-bhún-ga, *adj.* Standing awry, or bending (*properly with legs, loins and neck bent*).

तिरभंगी tir-bhún-gee, *adj.* Having the position described under *tirbhunga*, an epithet of *Krishn. s. f.* A species of poetical measure.

तिरस tír-us, *adv.* Indirectly, underhandedly, secretly, covertly; crookedly, awry; a particle of abuse or depreciation.

तिरसठ tír-suth, *adj.* Sixty-three.

तिरसकार tir-us-kár, *s. m.* Disrespect, abuse, reproach.

तिरसकिया tir-us-kríya, *s. f.* Disrespect, contempt, reproach.

तिरसकृत tir-us-krít, *adj.* Reviled, abused, reproached, censured.

तिरा tír-a, (*contraction of Tera*), Thy, thine.

तिराना tir-ána, *v. a.* To cause to pass over or swim; to save.

तिरानवे tiránweh, *adj.* Ninety-three.

तिराव tir-áo, *s. m.* Swimming.

तिरास tir-ás, *s. f.* Thirst.

तिरास आना tiras-ána, ⎫ *v. n.* To be
तिरास लगना tiras-lúgna, ⎭ thirsty.

तिरासी tirásee, *adj.* Eighty-three.

तिरिया tír-iya, *s. f.* A woman, maid, female, wife.

तिरियाचरित्र tiriya-churítr, *s. m.* Female wiles.

तिरियाबेद tiriya-béd, *s. m.* The science of women, knowledge of women.

तिरियाराज tiriya-ráj, *s. m.* Amazon country, petticoat government.

तिरी tír-ee, *adj.* Three.

तिरीबिरी tíree-bíree, *adj.* Dispersed.

तिरेंद tir-énd, *s. m.* The float of a fishing line, a float or buoy.

तिरेंदा tirénda, *s. m.* A float.

तिरोहित tir-ó-hit, *adj.* Covered, concealed, hidden, removed or withdrawn from sight.

तिरौंदा tir-óunda, *s. m.* A buoy, beacon.

तिमिरा tír-mir-a, *s. m.* A spot of oil, &c. swimming on water; an ocular spectrum, or spark appearing before the eye from the internal state of that organ.

तिमिराना tir-mir-ána, *v. n.* To vibrate, dazzle, thrill, shake; to glisten as grease or oil swimming on water.

तिमिराहट tir-mir-áhut, *s. f.* Vibration.

तिमिरी tír-mir-ee, *s. f.* Vertigo, darkness (*Perhaps amaurosis or blindness from disease*).

तिरहूत tír-hoot, *s. f.* A district on the *Gunduk, Tirhoot.*

तिरहूतिया tirhóotiya, *adj.* Belonging to *Tirhoot*, produced in *Tirhoot*.

तिल til, *s. m.* A plant bearing an oily seed; the oil and seed being both much used in oriental cooking (*Sesamum orientale*): a mole or spot, compared to a seed of sesamum. *Tilon men tel nuheen kuhna,* (*lit. to say there is no oil in the seeds of sesamum, is*) To say snow is black, to deny the most evident truth.

तिलक tíl-uk, *s. m.* A mark or marks made with coloured earths or unguents upon the forehead, and between the eye-brows, either as an ornament or a sectarial distinction; a freckle, a mole, a natural mark on the person; a title, especially in composition, implying pre-eminence.

तिलका tíl-uk-a, *s. f.* A kind of necklace. *adj.* Spotted, freckled, a person having moles or spots; chief, principal.

तिलकूट til-kút, *s. m.* The farina of sesamum.

तिलकालक til-ká-luk, *s. m.* A mole or spot on the body; a man so marked.

तिलकूट til-kóot, *s. m.* A sweetmeat, composed of pounded sesamum and sugar.

तिलंगा til-ún-ga, *s. m.* An inhabitant of *Tylung*, in which the first soldiers were clothed and disciplined in the European manner; (*hence*) a soldier or rather sepoy.

तिलंगी til-ún-gee, *s. f.* A kind of (*child's*) kite.

तिलचट्टा til-chútta, *s. m.* A cock-roach (*Blatta*).

तिलचावली til-cháolee, *s. f.* Mixture composed of rice and sesamum seeds; a mixture of black and gray hairs in the head.

तिलचूरी til-chóoree, *s. f.* A kind of sweetmeat.

तिलुरा tí-lur-a, *s. m.* A necklace of three strings.

तिलतैल til-tyl, *s. m.* Sesamum oil.

तिलधेनु til-dhén-oo, *s. f.* Sesamum made up in the shape of a cow, for the purpose of being presented to *Brahmuns*.

तिलपर्णी til-púrnee, *s. f.* Red sanders (*Pterocarpus santolinus*).

तिलपिचट til-pích-chut, *s. m.* A sort of sweetmeat made chiefly of ground sesamum.

तिलपिंज til-pínj, ⎫ *s. m.* Barren sesamum,
तिलपेज til-péj, ⎭ bearing no blossom, or its seed yielding no oil.

तिलबर tíl-bur, *s. m.* A kind of bird.

तिलमय til-múy, *adj.* Made or composed of sesamum.

तिलमयूर til-muyóor, *s. m.* A kind of peafowl, marked with spots resembling the seed of the sesamum.

तिलशकरी til-shúk-ree, *s. f.* A kind of sweetmeat made of sesame and sugar.

तिलहा til-há, *adj.* Oily.

तिलाई til-áee, *s. f.* A small frying-pan.

तिलावड़ी til-áo-ree, *s. f.* A plain in the vicinity of *Sirhind*, abounding in robbers ; hence, it is applied to any situation of danger.

तिलूआ tíl-oo-a, *s. m.* A kind of sweetmeat (*eaten particularly by the Hindoos when the sun enters Capricorn*).

तिलोंहा til-ón-ha, *adj.* (*Spoken of a lamp*) Sloped so that the oil may reach the wick.

तिलोत्तमा til-óttum-a, *s. f.* One of the courtezans of *Swurg*, the paradise of the *Hindoos*.

तिलोदन til-óu-dun, *s. m.* A dish of milk, rice and sesamum.

तिल्ली tillee, *s. f.* The spleen or milt. *Tup-tillee, s. f.* Disorder of the spleen.

तिवारा tiwára, *s. m.* A hall or building with three doors.

तिवासी tiwásee, *adj.* Stale, three days old.

तिष tish, *s. f.* Thirst.

तिष्णा tísh-na, *s. f.* Thirst ; temptation.

तिष्यु tísh-yuh, *s. m.* The eighth *nukshutr* or lunar mansion, an asterism figured by an arrow, and containing three stars, of which one is *Cancri. adj.* Auspicious, fortunate, lucky.

तिष्या tísh-yah, ⎫ *s. f.* Emblic
तिष्युपुष्प tishyuh-póoshp, ⎭ myrobalan (*Phyllanthus emblica*), or auspicious flower.

तिस tis, *inflect. pron.* That, which, &c. *Tis-ooprant, adv.* Moreover. *Tis-pur,* or, *Tis-peh, adv.* Besides, over and above, moreover, yet, nevertheless, still, then, after that, thereon, whereat. *Tis-pur-bhee, adv.* Thereon, nevertheless, yet, still.

तिसरायत tis-rá-yut, *s. m.* A third person, an umpire.

तिसूत tisóot, *s. m.* Name of a medicine.

तिहत्तर tihúttur, *adj.* Seventy-three.

तिहरा tíhra, *adj.* Triple, three-fold.

तिहराना tihrána, *v. a.* To tertiate, to do the third time, to triple.

तिहरावट tihrá-wut, *s. f.* Triplication.

तिहरे tíh-reh, *pron.* Your, of you.

तिहाई tiháee, *s. f.* The third part ; the third part of a piece of cloth for making trousers.

तिहायत tiháyut, *s. m.* A third person ; a court of inquiry, three or four persons by whom any cause is arbitrated, an arbitrator.

तिहारी tiháree, *f.* ⎫
तिहारे tiháreh, *m.* ⎬ *pron.* Your, of you.
तिहारौ tihárou, *m.* ⎭

तिहिं tíhin, *pron. pl.* Those very, them, themselves.

तिहूं tíhoon, *adj.* Three.

तिक्षुन tíkshun, *adj.* Pungent, hot ; angry, passionate ; sharp, acute, penetrating, ardent, virulent, bitter, severe.

तीकुठ tée-kuth, *s. m.* Posteriors.

तीकूर tée-koor, *s. f.* A starchy substance obtained from the root of the *Curcuma angustifolia.*

तीक्षुन tée-kshun, *adj.* Hot, warm, pungent, ardent ; zealous, active, warm ; keen, intelligent ; angry, passionate ; sharp (*as a sword*), penetrating.

तीक्ष्णकंटक teekshn-kúntuk, *s. m.* Thorn apple (*Datura metel*).

तीक्ष्णकंद teekshn-kúnd, *s. m.* The onion.

तीक्ष्णकर्मं teekshn-kúrmmun, *adj.* Active, zealous.

तीक्ष्णगंध teekshn-gúndh, *s. m. Morunga Hyperanthera* ; the gum olibanum tree ; small cardamoms.

तीक्ष्णगंधा teekshn-gún-dha, *s. f.* Mustard seed ; orris root ; *Pandanus odoratissimus.*

तीक्ष्णतैल teekshn-tyl, *s. m.* Resin ; the milky juice of the *Euphorbia* ; spirituous or vinous liquor.

तीक्ष्णपत्र teekshn-pútr, ⎫
तीक्ष्णफल teekshn-phúl, ⎬ *s. m.* Coriander.

तीक्ष्णपुष्प teekshn-póoshp, *s. m.* Cloves.

तीक्ष्णरस teekshn-rús, *s. m.* Saltpetre.

तीक्ष्णशूक teekshn-shóok, *s. m.* Barley.

तीखा tée-kha, *adj.* Pungent, hot, warm ; angry, passionate ; sharp (*as a sword*), penetrating.

तीखी tée-khee, *adj. f.* Sharp (*tone in music*).

तीखूर tée-khoor, *s. f.* A starchy substance obtained from the root of the *Curcuma augustifolia.*

तीछन tée-chhun, *adj.* Ardent, sharp.

तीज teej, *s. f.* The third day of a lunar fortnight.

तीजा tée-ja, *s. m.* The third day after the death of a relation, on which oblations are offered (*used among Mahomedans*).

तीत téet, ⎫ *adj.* Bitter ; pungent, hot,
तीता téeta, ⎭ acrid.

तीतर tée-tur, *s. m.* A partridge (*Perdix*

Francolinus). Teetur keh moonh luchhmee (lit. good fortune proceeds from the mouth of the partridge, which is a small bird, of little estimation), A saying used when a person of mean understanding is chosen to decide in matters of which he is incompetent to judge.

तीतरी **téet-ree,** *s. f.* A butterfly; a sort of medicine.

तीता **téeta,** *adj.* Bitter; pungent, hot, acrid.

तीन **teen,** *adj.* Three.

तीनतेरह **teen-téruh,** *adj.* Dispersed, scattered, ruined.

तीनथान **teen-thán,** *s. m.* The private parts; penis (*only*).

तीय **téeyuh,** *s. f.* A woman or female in general.

तीयल **téeyul,** *s. f.* A suit (*of female's clothes*).

तीर **teer,** *s. m.* A shore, a bank; an arrow. *adv.* Near.

तीरथ **téeruth,** *s. m.* A holy spot visited by pilgrims, especially at sacred waters.

तीरभुक्ति **teer-bhóok-ti,** *s. m. Tirhoot,* a province in the east of central *Hindoostan,* lying on the north of *Behar:* being bounded on the west and east by the *Gundukee* and *Cousikee* rivers, on the south by the *Ganges,* and on the north by the skirts of the *Himaleh* mountains.

तीर्ण **teern,** *adj.* Crossed, passed over; spread, expanded.

तीर्णपदी **teern-púd-ee,** *s. f.* A plant (*Curculigo orchioides*).

तीर्थ **teerth,** *s. m.* Pilgrimage; a holy place, any place of pilgrimage as *Benares, Gya, Juggernauth,* &c. but especially particular spots along the course of sacred streams, as the *Ganges,* &c, and in the vicinity of some piece of water or sacred springs.

तीर्थराज **teerth-ráj,** *s. m.* The city of *Pryag* or *Allahabad.*

तीर्थराजी **teerth-rájee,** *s. f.* The city of *Benares,* the most eminent of the *Teerths* or places of pilgrimage.

तीली **tée-lee,** *s. f.* A bar (*as of a cage, &c.*); the calf of the leg.

तीवर **tée-wur,** *s. m.* A hunter, one who lives by killing and selling game; a fisherman, one who lives by fishing.

तीवरी **tée-wur-ee,** *s. f.* The wife of a hunter.

तीव्र **teevr,** *adv.* Much, excessively, endless. *adj.* Much, excessive, endless, unbounded, unlimited; pungent, hot, warm.

तीव्रवेदना **teevr-védna,** *s. f.* Agony, excessive pain, the pain of damnation.

तीव्रा **téev-ra,** *s. f.* A river in the east of Bengal.

तीस **tees,** *adj.* Thirty.

तीसरा **tées-ra,** *adj.* Third.

तीसरे **tées-reh,** *adv.* In the third place, thirdly.

तीसी **tée-see,** *s. f.* Flax (*Linum usitatissimum*).

तुंग **toong,** *adj.* High, tall.

तुक **took,** *s. f.* One line of a poem, a ryhme; a moment.

तुकला **tóok-la,** *s. m.* ⎫
तुकली **tóok-lee,** *s. f.* ⎬ A kind of paper kite.
तुकुल **tóok-kul,** *s. f.* ⎭

तुकाक्षीरी **took-ák-sheeree,** ⎫ *s. f.* The manna of bamboos.
तुगा **tóo-ga,** ⎬

तुंग **toong,** *adj.* High, tall, elevated, lofty. *s. m.* A tree (*Rottleria tinctoria*); top, vertex, altitude.

तुंगभद्र **toong-bhúdr,** *s. m.* A restive elephant, or one in rut. *s. f.* A river in the *Mysore* country, the *Toombhudr.*

तुंगी **tóongee,** *s. f.* A kind of basil (*Ocymum gratissimum*).

तुच्छ **toochchh,** *adj.* Void, empty; contemptible, despicable, worthless.

तुच्छद्रु **too-chchhúd-roo,** The castor oil tree, as having no sap.

तुड़वाना **toorwána,** ⎫ *v. a.* To cause to break.
तुड़ाना **too-rá-na,** ⎬

तुटी **too-túee,** *s. f.* A vessel with a spout.

तुतराना **toot-rána,** ⎫ *v. n.* To lisp, speak imperfectly as a child.
तुतलाना **toot-láua,** ⎬

तुत्थ **tootth,** *s. m.* A collyrium extracted from the *Amomum Zanthorhiza;* blue vitriol sulphate of copper, especially medicinally considered as an *unjun,* or application to the eyes.

तुत्थांजन **tootth-án-jun,** *s. m.* Blue vitriol, considered as a medicinal application to the eyes.

तुनकी **tóonkee,** *s. f.* A fine kind of bread or wafers thin as muslin.

तुनतुनाना **toon-too-nána,** *v. n.* To sound.

तुंद **toond,** *s. m.* The belly. *s. f.* The navel.

तुंदकूपी **toond-kóopee,** *s. f.* The navel.

तुंदपरिमार्ज **toond-purim-árj,** ⎫ *s. m.* A lazy man, a sloth, a sluggard, passing his whole time in stroking his sides.
तुंदपरिमृज **toond-purim-írj,** ⎬

तुंदिल **tóon-dil,** *adj.* Having a prominent or elevated navel.

तून toon, *s. m.* Toon, a tree of which the wood bears some resemblance to mahogany and is used for furniture, &c. (*Cedrela toona*). *adj.* Tormented, vexed, injured, cut, broken, cut down, &c.

तूनवाद toon-váyuh, *s. m.* A tailor.

तूपक tóo-puk, *s. f.* A musket.

तुम toom, *2d. pers. pron. pl.* You. *Toom ap*, You yourself. *Toom ko*, or, *Toomhon ko*, or, *Toomhen*, To you. *Toom tunou*, *pron. 2d. pers. mas. gen. pl.* Your, of you.

तुमाई too-máee, *s. f.* The price of carding.

तुमाना too-mána, *v. a.* To cause to be carded.

तुमुल tóo-mool, *s. m.* Mingled or tumultuous combat; uproar, clangour, tumult, tumultuous sound or noise; *Beleric myrobalan*.

तुम्बा tóom-ba, *s. m.* A hollowed gourd, the rind of a gourd in which beggars carry water, &c.

तुम्बिया tóom-biya, *s. m.* A pot.

तुम्बी tóom-bee, *s. f.* A long gourd (*Cucurbita lagenaria*); a small hollowed gourd, the rind of a gourd in which beggars carry water, &c.; a kind of pipe (*chiefly used by those who exhibit snakes*).

तुरई too-rúee, *s. f.* A kind of vegetable (*Cucumis acutangulus*).

तुरक tóo-ruk, *s. m.* A Turk; a soldier, a Mahomedan.

तुरग tóo-rug, *s. m.* A horse.

तुरगी tóo-rug-ee, *s. f.* A plant (*Physalis flexuosa*).

तुरगब्रह्मचर्यक tóorug-bruhm-chúryuk, *s. m.* Necessary celibacy, leading a life of continence in consequence merely of being without female society.

तुरगी tóo-rug-ee, *s. m.* A horseman, cavalier, &c. *adj.* Equestrian, riding, mounted, or carried on a horse.

तुरंग too-rúng, *s. m.* A horse.

तुरंगी too-rúng-ee, *s. f.* A plant (*Physalis flexuosa*).

तुरत too-rut, } *adv.* Quickly, instantly, directly.
तुरंत tóo-runt, }

तुरपन tóorpun, *s. f.* A kind of stitch.

तुरपना too-rúp-na, *v. a.* To sew (*in a particular manner*), to stitch.

तुरपाना toorpána, *v. a.* To stitch, darn, hem.

तुरमुती toormútee, *s. f.* A kind of hawk (*Falco fasciatus*, or *Falco dubius*).

तुरही túor-hee, } *s. f.* A trumpet, a clarion.
तुरी tóo-ree, }

तुरी tóo-ree, *s. f.* A brush, or a fibrous stick used by weavers to clean and separate the threads of the woof; a painter's brush or fibrous stick used for that purpose.

तुरीय too-rée-yuh, *s. m.* The divine Being, or universal Spirit.

तुरुष्क tóo-rooshk, *s. m.* Incense; a country, perhaps *Tooran* or *Toorkistan*, the original country of the Turks.

तुरुष्क too-róosh-ka, *s. m. pl.* The inhabitants of *Toorooshk*.

तुर्त toort, } *adv.* Instantly,
तुर्तफुर्त toort-phóort, } quickly, hastily,
तुर्ताव toortáo, } directly, presently, immediately. *Toortee phoortee*, *adv.* Hastily, quickly. [*pant.*]

तुर्तुरा tóortoora, *adj.* Nimble, active; flippant.

तुल tool, *adj.* Alike, like. *Tool bythna*, To be weighed against valuable things, which are to be given in alms; to sit straight and compact (*as in a boat which might be overset by sitting uneven or carelessly*). *Tool ruhna*, To stand front to front, ready for battle or opposed.

तुलतुलाना tool-too-lána, *v. n.* To become soft (*from moisture, as a mud wall in the rains, as a sore or boil when suppurating, or as fruit getting ripe*).

तुलना tóol-na, *v. n.* To be weighed or balanced; to be drawn up in array (*as one army against another*).

तुलसी tóol-see, *s. f.* A small shrub held in veneration by the *Hindoos*, Holy Basil (*Ocymum sanctum*): *Toolsee* is said to have been a nymph beloved by *Krishn*, and by him metamorphosed into this plant. *Toolsee ka heera*, Beads made of the wood of the *Toolsee* plant. *Toolsee duna*, A gold ornament. *Toolsee das*, *n. prop.* Name of a *Gosaeen*, and author of the *Toolseekrit-Ramayun*.

तुला tóo-la, *s. f.* Measure by weight; a measure or weight of gold and silver, 100 *pulus* or about 145 ounces troy; a balance, especially a fine balance, goldsmith's or assay scales; the sign *Libra* of the zodiac; the practice of being weighed against gold or any kind of valuable substance, which is afterwards given to priests.

तुलाकोटि tóola-koti, *s. f.* An ornament of the feet or toes; a hundred millions.

तुलाकोश toola-kósh, *s. m.* A sort of ordeal, in which the accused is tried by being weighed in a scale.

तुलाबीज toola-béej, *s. m.* The berry of the *Abrus precatorius*, from which the goldsmith's or jeweller's weight in India is taken; the berry weighs about $1\frac{7}{16}$ grain troy, the factitious weight about $2\frac{7}{8}$.

तुलावा tooláwa, *s. m.* Part of an Indian carriage, which rests on the axletree arm and supports the body of the carriage.

2 D

तुलिका tóolika, *s. f.* A small bird said to resemble the wagtail.

तुलिफुल्ला tóoli-phúl-a, *s. f.* The *Simul* or silk-cotton tree.

तुली tóo-lee, *s. f.* A steelyard ; a fibrous stick or brush used by weavers for cleansing the threads of the woof ; a painter's brush or fibrous stick used for that purpose.

तुल्य tóol-yuh, *adj.* Like, resembling, equal or analogous to.

तुल्यपान tool-yuh-pán, *s. m.* Drinking together.

तुवर toovur, *s. m.* A tribe of *Rajpoots.*

तुवरी tóo-wur-ee, *s. f.* A kind of lentil (*Cytisus cajan*).

तुष toosh, *s. m.* The husk or chaff of rice, &c. ; *Beleric myrobalan.*

तुषानल too-shá-nul, *s. m.* A conflagration of chaff, or of the husk of corn ; a capital punishment ; burning ; twisting dry straw, &c. around the limbs of a criminal, and setting it on fire.

तुषार too-shár, *s. m.* Frost ; cold ; thin rain, mist ; ice or snow.

तुषारा too-shára, *adj.* Cold, frigid, frosty.

तुषित tóo-shit, *s. m.* A kind of subordinate deity, one of a class of thirty-six.

तुष्ट toosht, *adj.* Pleased, satisfied, rejoiced, gratified.

तुष्टता tóosht-ta, *s. f.* Delight, satisfaction, gratification.

तुष्टि tóosh-ti, *s. f.* Pleasure, satisfaction, gratification, content.

तुस toos, *s. m.* The husk of corn or rice.

तुहिन tóo-hin, *s. m.* Frost, snow.

तू too, *pron.* 2d. *pers. sing.* Thou. *Too too,* Sound of calling a dog.

तूअर too-úr, *s. f.* A kind of pulse (*Cytisus cajan*).

तूं करना toon-tán kurna, *v. a.* To dispute, to wrangle, to abuse.

तूंबा tóom-ba, *s. m.* A hollowed gourd, the rind of a gourd in which beggars carry water, &c.

तूंबी tóom-bee, *s. f.* A small gourd ; the snout of a crocodile, alligator, &c. ; a kind of musical pipe (*chiefly used by those who exhibit snakes*).

तूकारना too-kárna, *v. a.* To thou.

तूण toon, *s. m.* A quiver ; a tree the wood of which bears some resemblance to mahogany, and is used for furniture, &c. (*Cedrela toona.*)

तूणीर too-néer, *s. m.* A quiver.

तूतई too-túee, *s. f.* A vessel with a spout.

तूतक tóo-tuk,

तूतिया tóo-tiya, } *s. m.* Blue vitriol, tutty.

तूतन tootún, *s. m.* Chips, clippings, filings, fragments.

तून toon, *s. m.* A quiver ; a tree the wood of which bears some resemblance to mahogany, and is used for furniture, &c. (*Cedrela toona*).

तूमना tóomna, *v. a.* To card or separate (*wool or cotton*) with the finger, preparatory to combing.

तूमरी tóom-ree, *s. f.* The snout of a crocodile, alligator, &c.

तूमिया tóo-miya, *s. m.* Thread made of carded cotton, in opposition to that made of what has been beat only.

तूना tóom-na, *v. a.* To card or separate (*wool or cotton*) with the finger, preparatory to combing.

तूर्ण toorn, *adv.* Quick, swift, quickly. *adj.* Quick, expeditious.

तूल tool, *s. m.* Resembling.

तूलनाली tool-nálee, *s. f.* A thick roll of cotton, from which it is drawn out in spinning.

तूली tóo-lee, *s. f.* A steelyard ; a weaver's fibrous stick or brush ; a pencil, a painter's brush, or a stick with a fibrous extremity, used as one ; a rod, &c., dipped into crucibles to try if their contents are in fusion.

तूवर tóo-wur, *s. m.* A tribe of *Rajpoots ;* a bull without horns though of an age to have them ; a beardless man ; a eunuch.

तूहिन tóo-hin, *s. m.* Snow, frost.

तूही tóo-hee, *pron.* Thou thyself.

तृण trin, *s. m.* Grass, any gramineous plant.

तृणजुम्भ trin-júmbh, *adj.* Graminivorous, one whose food is grass.

तृणजाति trin-játi, *s. m.* The vegetable kingdom.

तृणराज trin-ráj, *s. m.* A palmyra tree.

तृणवत् trin-wút, *adj.* Like grass, like a straw ; worthless, insignificant.

तृणूस trin-ús, *adj.* Grassy, made, &c. with grass.

तृणाग्नि trin-ágni, *s. m.* Conflagration of chaff ; burning a criminal wrapped up in straw.

तृतीय tri-téeyuh, *adj.* Third. *Triteeyuh prukriti, s. f.* A eunuch ; the neuter gender.

तृप्त tript, *adj.* Pleased, satisfied, contented.

तृप्तात्मा tript-átma, *adj.* Contented, satisfied, tranquil.

तृप्ति trípti, *s. f.* Pleasure, satisfaction, content.

तृफुल tri-phul-a, *s. f.* The three myrobalans.

तृमूर्त्ति tri-móortti, *s. f.* Trinity ; the three principal *Hindoo* gods.

तृषा tri-shá, *s. f.* Thirst, wish, desire; a plant (*Commelina salicifolia*).

तृषावन्त tri-sha-wúnt, *adj.* Thirsty.

तृषित trí-shit, *adj.* Thirsty, thirsting (*physically or metaphorically*).

तृष्णुज् trish-núj, *adj.* Thirsty (*physically or metaphorically*), desiring, longing for, cupidinous.

तृष्णा trísh-na, *s. f.* Thirst; ambition, desire, wish, avarice.

तृष्णाक्षय trish-nakshúy, *s. m.* Content, resignation, patience.

ते teh, *pron.* They, those. *postpos.* From, by, with, in, than.

तें ten, *prepos.* From, by, with, in.

तेंतालीस ten-tálees, *adj.* Forty-three.

तेंतीस ten-tées, *adj.* Thirty-three.

तेंडुआ tén-doo-a, *s. m.* A leopard (*Felis leopardus*).

तेंडू tén-doo, *s. m.* A fruit (*Diospyros ebenum* or *glutinosa*).

तेईस te-ées, *adj.* Twenty-three.

तेज tej, *s. m.* Ardour, splendour, glory, refulgence, strength, energy; fire; sharpness, pungency.

तेजनक tej-núk, *s. m.* A kind of reed (*Saccharum Sara*).

तेजनी téj-nee, *s. f.* A plant (*Aletris hyacinthoides*).

तेजपात tej-pát *s. m.* The leaf of the Laurus cassia, cassia.

तेजमान tej-mán, *adj.* Glorious, splendid, energetic.

तेजवती tej-wút-ee, *s. f.* An aromatic plant (*Pothos officinalis*).

तेजवन्त tej-wúnt, *adj.* Glorious, splendid, energetic.

तेजस téj-us, *s. m.* Splendour, light, lustre; dignity, consequence; strength, power; semen virile.

तेजस्कर tej-us-kúr, *adj.* Restorative, invigorating, provocative, tonic.

तेजस्वी tej-ús-wee, } *adj.* Glorious, luminous, brilliant, splendid, energetic; famous, celebrated.
तेजोमय tej-o-múy, }

तेजोमन्थ tej-o-múnth, *s. m.* A tree (*Premna spinosa*).

तेजोवती tej-o-wútee, *s. f.* A plant bearing a fruit resembling pepper.

तेता téta, *adv.* So much, thus much.

तेपची tép-chee, *s. f.* A kind of stitch.

तेमन tém-un, *s. m.* Wetting, moistening, moisture, wet, damp; a sauce or condiment.

तेमनी tém-un-ee, *s. f.* A chimney, a fireplace.

तेरा tér-a, *pron.* 2d *per. sing. gen. case,* Thy, thine.

तेरस tér-us, *s. f.* The thirteenth day of the lunar fortnight.

तेरह tér-uh, *adj.* Thirteen. *Teruhwan, adj.* Thirteenth.

तेरोस tér-oos, *s. m.* The third year past or to come, year before last, year after the next.

तेल tel, *s. m.* Oil. *Tel churhana, v. a.* To anoint the head, shoulders, hands, and feet of the bride and bridegroom with oil mixed with turmeric during the marriage ceremony.

तेलिन tél-in, *s. f.* Wife of an oilman.

तेलिया tél-iya, *s. m.* Name of a colour, dark bay. *Teliya soorung, adj.* Light bay coloured.

तेली tél-ee, *s. m.* A caste whose business is to sell oil, an oilman.

तेवन téwun, *s. m.* A garden, a pleasure garden or play-ground; play, sport, pastime.

तेवर téwur, *s. m.* Swimming or giddiness in the head.

तेवरस téo-rus, *s. m.* The third year past or to come, year before last, year after the next.

तेवराना teo-rá-ua, *v. n.* To have a swimming in the head, to be giddy, to be faint, to stagger, to fall down senseless from a blow.

तेवरी téo-ree, } *s. f.* A frown. *Teoree*
तेवरही téor-hee, } *churhana*, To frown.
तेवरी téo-ree, } *Teoree churhna*, A frown to come on.

तेवहार teo-hár, *s. m.* A holiday, a festival.

तेवों téon, *adv.* So, in like manner, as; at the same time, then.

तेवोंधा téon-dha, *adj.* Dim-sighted, purblind.

तेह teh, *s. m.* Anger, passion, vehemence.

तेहुर téhur, *s. m.* A female ornament worn round the ankles.

तेहा téha, *s. m.* Steadfastness, peremptoriness, perseverance, speaking with warmth, vehemence.

तेही téhee, *adv.* Exactly then.

ते ty, *adj.* So many. *Tyber,* So often.

तैं tyn, *pron.* Thou.

तैंतीस tyntées, *adj.* Thirty-three.

तैतिल ty-til, *s. m.* One of the astronomical periods called *Kurun*.

तैतिर tyt-tir, *s. m.* A flock of partridges, a Francoline partridge.

तैत्तिरीय tyt-tir-éeyuh, *adj.* Relating to the *Tittiri* portion of the *Veds,* as a student, a text, teacher, section of, &c.: the texts of this *Ved* being disgorged by *Yajnyuwulkyu* in a tangible form, and picked up by the rest of *Vysumpayunu's* disciples, who for the purpose assumed the shape of partridges.

तैत्तिरीयक **tyt-tir-eeyuk,** *s. m.* A follower of the *Tittiri* branch of the *Veds.*

तैरना **tyr-na,** *v. a.* To swim, to cross over.

तैल **tyl,** *s. m.* Oil, expressed oil, prepared from sesamum, mustard, &c.; storax, gum Benzoin, incense.

तैलकिट्ट **tyl-kítt,** *s. m.* The oil cake, a cake made of the oily seed, after expression.

तैलङ्ग **ty-lúng,** *s. m.* The part of the peninsula south of *Orissa,* the modern *Carnatic.*

तैलङ्गा **ty-lún-ga,** *s. m.* An inhabitant of the country called *Tylung,* or the *Carnatic ;* a sepoy or native foot soldier dressed in the European costume.

तैलचौरिका **tyl-chóurika,** *s. m.* A cockroach, or oil-stealer.

तैलमाली **tyl-má-lee,** *s. f.* A wick, the cotton of a lamp.

तैलस्फटिक **tyl-sphút-ik,** *s. m.* A sort of gem, (*Amber?*)

तैलिनी **ty-lin-ee,** *s. f.* The wick or cotton of a lamp.

तैलिशाला **tyli-sála,** *s. f.* An oil mill.

तैली **ty-lee,** *s. m.* An oilman, an oil grinder or preparer. *adj.* Relating or belonging to oil, oily, &c.

तैसा **tysa,** *adj.* Such. *adv.* So, in that manner, in like manner, at the same moment.

तो **to,** A conjunction introducing the answer to a conditional proposition ; Then, that ; as, *Jo too awega to pawega,* If thou wilt come, then shalt thou receive. An adverb denoting asseveration or emphasis ; as, *Myn to ata tha, pur oosneh aneh nuh deeya,* I was in fact coming, but he prevented me.

तों **ton,** *adv.* So, in that manner, then.

तोंद **tond,** *s. f.* A pot belly.

तोंदी **tón-dee,** *s. f.* The navel.

तोंदैल **ton-dyl,** } *adj.* Pot-bellied, gor-
तोंदैला **ton-dy-la,** } bellied, corpulent.

तोंहीं **ton-heen,** *adv.* Exactly then.

तोड़ **tor,** *s. m.* The breach made by a gun, &c.; the strength of a current ; whey. *Tor kurna,* To make a breach (*as a ball*). *Tor jor, s. m.* Cutting out (*as cloth by a tailor*); arranging a speech, &c. *Tor dalna,* To break and destroy, to pull down. *Tor tar, s.* Breaking and destroying ; plain speaking. *Tor dena,* To break, to spoil. *Tor phor, s.* Breaking, plain speaking. *Tor lena,* To gather, to pluck (*fruit*).

तोड़ **tor,** } *s. f.* A net work thrown over a
तोर **tor,** } woman's *palkee,* &c.

तोड़ता **tór-ta,** *s. m.* A dried pod of *toree,* kept for seed.

तोड़ना **tór-na,** *v. a.* To break, tear, rend, burst, split, demolish ; to change (*money*), to pluck or gather (*fruit, flowers,* &c.), to reduce (*in arithmetic*). *Dum torna,* To be at the point of death. *Rotee torna,* To eat the bread of idleness. *Torna jorna,* (*to break and join*), Expresses absolute power over any thing.

तोड़ुल **tó-rul,** *s. m.* A large thick ring worn on the wrist.

तोड़वाई **tor-wáee,** *s. f.* Price paid for breaking or changing coin.

तोड़वाना **tor-wána,** *v. a.* To cause to be broken, or to be changed (*coin*).

तोड़ा **tó-ra,** *s. m.* Scarcity, want ; a purse, a bag containing one thousand rupees ; the match of a gun ; a bank, an island, a bar ; a ploughshare ; a piece of rope ; an ornament like a chain. *Torehdar,* A matchlock.

तोड़ाना **to-rá-na,** *v. a.* To cause to be broken or changed (*as money*).

तोड़ी **tó-ree,** *s. f.* Mustard seed. *adv.* Till, up to.

तोतना **tót-na,** *v. a.* To weave tape or ribband.

तोतला **tót-la,** *adj.* Stutterer, stammerer, lisping, lisper, stuttering, stammering, speaking imperfectly as a child.

तोतलाना **totlána,** *v. n.* To lisp, to speak imperfectly as a child.

तोता **tó-ta,** *s. m.* A parrot ; the cock of a matchlock.

तोती **tó-tee,** *s. f.* A female parrot.

तोपड़ा **tóp-ra,** *s. m.* A fly ; a kind of pigeon.

तोपना **tóp-na,** *v. a.* To bury, to cover.

तोपाना **to-pá-na,** } *v. a.* To have buried,
तुपाना **too-pá-na,** } to cause to cover.

तोबड़ा **tób-ra,** *s. m.* The bag in which horses eat their corn.

तोमड़ी **tóm-ree,** *s. f.* A hollowed gourd (*Cucurbita lagenaria*).

तोय **tóyuh,** *s. m.* Water.

तोयकाम **toyuh-kám,** *s. m.* A sort of cane, growing in or near water (*Calamus fasciculatus*).

तोयकृच्छ **toyuh-kríchchh,** *s. m.* A sort of penance, drinking nothing but water for a fixed period.

तोयद **tó-yud,** *s. m.* A fragrant grass (*Cyperus rotundus*).

तोयघर **toyuh-dhúr,** *s. m.* A potherb (*Marsilia dentata*).

तोयपिप्पली tóyuh-píppul-ee, *s. f.* A plant (*Jussieua repens*).

तोयपुष्पी tóyuh-póoshpee, *s. f.* Trumpet flower.

तोयप्रसादन tóyuh-prusád-un, *s. m.* The clearing nut plant (*Strychnos potatorum*): the nut being rubbed upon the inside of a water jar, occasions the precipitation of the impurities of the water poured into it.

तोयवल्ली tóyuh-wúllee, *s. f.* A kind of gourd (*Momordica charantia*).

तोर tor, *s. f.* A kind of pulse; a net thrown over a woman's *palkee*.

तोरण tó-run, *s. m.* The ornamented arch of a door or gateway; decoration of a gate-post; a bundle of flowers enclosed in a cloth of gold tissue and hung at a gateway or door; strings of flowers suspended across gateways on public festivals.

तोरह tó-ruh, *s. m.* A number of trays, containing various dishes of food, presented to others by great men; a nobleman, a minister of state; pride. *Toruhposh, s. m.* A covering for dishes, &c. *Toruh-bundee, s. f.* The arrangement or sending out of trays of food as presents.

तोरी tór-hee, *s. f.* A trumpet.

तोरी tó-ree, *s. f.* A vegetable.

तोल tol, } *s. m.* Weight, weighing. *Toul*
तोल toul, } *tal*, Weighing and measuring.

तोला tóla, *s. m.* A *tola*, a weight of gold or silver; it is stated in books at 16 *mashus* of 5 *ruttees* or 6½ grains each, and weighs therefore 105 grains troy; in practice it is calculated at 12 *mashus* jeweller's weight, and weighs nearly double, or 210 grains.

तोष tosh, *s. m.* Pleasure, joy, happiness.

तोही tó-hee, *pron.* To or for thee, thee.

तौ tou, *adv.* Then, that time, in that case, moreover, that also, for, yes, well. *Tou bhee, adv.* Even then; still, yet, nevertheless. *Tou lon,* or, *Tou lug, adv.* Then, in that case, till, then, so long.

तौन toun, *adv.* So, in that manner, then.

तौसना tóuns-na, *v. a.* To be affected or overcome with heat.

तौन toun, *pron. correl.* That.

तौल toul, *s. m.* Weight, weighing. *Toul tal,* Weighing and measuring.

तौलना tóul-na, *v. a.* To weigh, to balance; to confront (*as two armies*). *Toulna nusuron men,* To estimate the worth of any one.

तौलवाई toul-wáee, } *s. f.* The price for
तौलाई tóul-aee, } weighing.

तौलाना tou-lá-na, *v. a.* To cause to be weighed.

तौलिया tóu-liya, *s. m.* } A vessel used by
तौली tóu-lee, *s. f.* } *Hindoos.*

तौही tóu-hee, *adv.* Then even, still, in that case only, at that very time.

तौहू tóu-hoo, *adv.* Still, then even, nevertheless.

त्युक्त tyukt, *adj.* Left, resigned, abandoned, deserted.

त्युजना tyújna, *v. a.* To quit, to abandon, to leave, or resign.

त्याग tyág, *s. m.* Abdication; leaving, abandoning, renouncing, parting from, separation, deserting.

त्यागना tyágna, *v. a.* To leave, to abandon, to desert, to forsake, to quit, to abdicate, resign.

त्यागिन tyágin, *s. m.* An abandoner, a deserter, but chiefly applied to the religious ascetic or him who abandons terrestrial objects, thoughts, passions, &c.

त्यागी tyágee, *part. act.* Leaving, relinquishing, abandoning. *s. m.* An abandoner, a deserter, but chiefly applied to the religious ascetic or him who abandons terrestrial objects, thoughts, passions, &c.

त्याज्य tyájyuh, *adj.* Fit to be left, forsaken, or avoided.

त्यों tyón, *adv.* So, in like manner, as; at the same time, then.

त्योंधा tyon-dha, *adj.* Dim-sighted, purblind.

त्रुंग trung, *m. f.* The city of *Hurischundr*, suspended, it is supposed in the air.

त्रुपा trúp-a, *s. f.* An unchaste woman (*a shame to her family*).

त्रुपारुंडा trúpa-rúnda, *s. f.* A whore, a harlot.

त्रय try, *adj.* Three.

त्रयी tryee, *s. f.* The three *Veds* collectively, that is, omitting the *Uthurvun,* which not being a text-book for the customary religious rites of the *Hindoos,* is considered very commonly rather as an appendix to the other three, than a fourth work of equal authority; a plant (*Conyza serratula*).

त्रयीधर्म tryee-dhurm, *s. m.* Duty enjoined by the *Veds,* modes of sacrifice, &c., prescribed by them.

त्रयोदशी tryodúsh-ee, *s. f.* The thirteenth day of the lunar fortnight.

त्रस्त trust, *adj.* Timid, fearful.

त्राण tran, *s. m.* Safety; preserving, protection; deliverance, salvation; a coat of mail. *Tran kurna,* To free, to protect. *Tran kurta, s. m.* A Saviour, a Deliverer.

त्राणी trá-nee, *s. m.* A Saviour, a Deliverer.

त्रायमाण trayumán, *adj.* A preserver, preserving.

त्रास trás, *s. m.* Fear, alarm, terror.

त्रासदायी tras-dáyee, *adj.* Terrifying, fear-exciting.

त्रासा trá-sa, } *adj.* Afraid.
त्रासित trá-sit, }

त्राह trah, ꞁ *interj.* Mercy! save! *Trahi*
त्राहि trahí, Ꞁ *Trahi kurna,* To complain, to repent of sin, to cry out for mercy.

त्राहिकार trahikár, *s. m.* Calling out for deliverance or mercy, cry for mercy.

त्रि tri, *adj.* Three.

त्रिकुट trí-kut, *s. m.* A plant (*Ruellia longifolia*).

त्रिकुटू tri-kút-oo, } *s. m.* The aggregate
तिरकुटा tír-koot-a, } of three spices, viz. black and long pepper, and dry ginger.

त्रिकुण्टक tri-kún-tuk, *s. m.* A sort of fish (*Silurus*); a plant (*Ruella longifolia*).

त्रिका trík-a, *s. f.* A triangular frame or bar across the mouth of a well, over which passes the rope of the bucket, or to which one end of it is tied to guard against its slipping; a frame at the bottom of a well, on which the masonry rests.

त्रिकालज्ञ trikal-úgyuh, *s. m.* A name of *Booddh,* founder of the *Bouddh* sect. *adj.* Omniscient; who knows or is acquainted with, the past, present, and future.

त्रिकालदर्शी trikal-dúrshee, *s. m.* A *Reeshi* or divine sage; a name of *Booddh. adj.* Omniscient.

त्रिकूट tri-kóot, *s. m.* The name of a mountain in the peninsula; any mountain with three peaks; sea salt prepared by evaporation.

त्रिकोण tri-kón, *s. m.* The vulva; a triangle.

त्रिगुण tri-gún, *s. m.* The aggregate of three human objects, or virtue, wealth, and love.

त्रिगुर्त्त tri-gúrtt, *s. m.* A country, in the northwest division of India, or *m. pl. Trigurtta,* its inhabitants: apparently part of *Lahore,* said by Mr. Wilford, to be the modern *Tahora,* but differently described in the various *Cosh.*

त्रिगुर्ता tri-gúrtta, *s. f.* A lascivious woman, a wanton.

त्रिगुण tri-góon, *adj.* Thrice, three times, triple; possessing the three *goons* or properties; the aggregate of the three qualities incident to human nature.

त्रिण trin, *s. m.* Grass, meadow grass.

त्रिणता trín-ta, *s. f.* The state or abstract property of grass.

त्रिणात्रिकेत trin-atri-két, *s. m.* A portion of the *Yujoor Ved;* a follower of that branch of the *Ved.*

त्रिदण्डी tri-dún-dee, *s. m.* A wandering devotee, one who carries three long bamboo staves

in his right hand; the religious man who has obtained a command over his words, thoughts and actions, or mind, body and speech.

त्रिदला tri-dúl-a, *s. f.* A creeping plant (*Cissus pedata*).

त्रिदूष tri-dúsh, *s. m.* A god, a deity, an immortal; from enjoying perpetual youth, or being subject, as well as mortals, to the three conditions, of birth, being, and destruction.

त्रिदूषाहार tri-dush-ahár, *s. m. Umrit* or Ambrosia.

त्रिदोष tri-dósh, *s. m.* Disorder of the three humours of the body, vitiation of the bile, blood, and phlegm.

त्रिपताक tri-put-ák, *s. m.* The forehead marked naturally with three horizontal lines.

त्रिपथ trí-puth, *s. m.* A place where three roads meet.

त्रिपुद tri-púd, *s. m.* A tripod.

त्रिपुदी tri-púd-ee, *s. f.* A creeper (*Cissus pedata*); the girth of an elephant.

त्रिपाद tri-pád, *s. m.* Fever (*personified*), the demon of fever is described in the *Poorans,* with three feet, and three heads, alluding probably to its three stages of cold, hot, and sweating.

त्रिपुण्ड tri-póond, *s. m.* Three curved horizontal marks made across the forehead with cow-dung ashes; they are worn especially by the followers of *Shiv,* or *Sukti,* and are indispensible in proceeding to worship the former.

त्रिपुर tri-póor, *s. f.* A district of Bengal, the modern *Tipperah.*

त्रिपौलिया tripóu-liya, *s. m.* A building with three doors or arches.

त्रिफला tri-phúl-a, *s. m.* A medicine composed of the three myrobalans.

त्रिवेणी tribén-ee, *s. f.* The conflux of three sacred rivers; especially that of the *Ganges, Jumna,* and supposed *Suruswutee,* under ground at *Allahabad,* which city, is also so named.

त्रिभङ्ग tri-bhún-ga, *adj.* Standing awry or bending (*properly with legs, loins, and neck bent*).

त्रिभङ्गी tri-bhúng-ee, *adj.* Having the position described under *tribhunga. s. f.* A species of poetical measure.

त्रिभुवन tri-bhóo-wun, *s. m.* The three worlds, viz. heaven, earth, and hell; the universe. *Tribhoowun-oujagur, adj.* Splendour of three worlds.

त्रिमधु tri-múd-hoo, *s. m.* A portion of the *Rig Ved;* a follower or student of the *Trimudhoo* section of the *Rig Ved.*

त्रिमार्गी tri-márggee, *s. f.* The meeting of three roads.

त्रिमूकुट tri-móo-koot, *s. m.* A mountain with three peaks.

त्रिमूर्ति tri-móortti, *s. m.* A *Jyn* saint ; the united form of *Bruhma, Vishnoo,* and *Shiv,* or the *Hindoo* triad ; one possessing three forms or modes of being. *s. f.* Trinity.

त्रियष्टि tri-yúsh-ti, *s. m.* A medicinal plant (*Mollugo pentaphylla*).

त्रिया tríya, *s. f.* A woman, maid, female, wife. *Tiriya-churitr, s. m.* Female wiles. *Tiriya-bed, s. m.* The science of women, knowledge of woman. *Tiriya-raj, s. m.* Amazon country, petticoat government.

त्रियामक tri-yámuk, *s. m.* Sin, as the impeder of the three objects of life.

त्रियामा tri-yáma, *s. f.* The *Yumoona* or *Jumna* river.

त्रिरात tri-rátr, *s. m.* Three nights collectively, or the duration of three nights.

त्रिलोक tri-lók, *s. m.* The three worlds, i. e. heaven, earth, and the regions under the earth ; the universe.

त्रिलोकी tri-ló-kee, *s. f.* The aggregate of the three worlds, or, heaven, earth, and hell collectively. *Trilokee-nuth, s. m.* Lord of the universe.

त्रिवर्ग tri-vúrg, *s. m.* Three human objects or pursuits, as, love, duty, and wealth ; three conditions of a king or state, prosperity, evenness and decay ; or loss, gain, equality ; the three qualities of nature, purity, blindness, and depravity.

त्रिवर्णक tri-vúrn-uk, *s. m.* A plant (*Ruellia longifolia*).

त्रिवेणी tri-vén-ee, *s. f.* A name of the Ganges ; the name is especially applied to the river at *Allahabad,* where it receives the *Jumna,* and is supposed to receive under ground the *Suruswutee.*

त्रिवृत्पर्णी trivrít-púrnee, *s. f.* A potherb (*Hilancha repens*).

त्रिशरण tri-shúr-un, *s. m.* A sanctified teacher of the *Jyn* sect ; the refuge or asylum of the three worlds.

त्रिशूल tri-shóol, *s. m.* A trident, a three pointed spike or spear, especially the crest of *Shiv.*

त्रिष्टुभ tri-shtóobh, *s. f.* A sort of metre, the stanza consisting of three lines of various lengths.

त्रिशृङ्ग tri-shring, *s. m.* A hill with three peaks ; a triangle.

त्रिशृङ्गी tri-shríng-ee, *s. m.* A kind of fish (*Cyprinus denticulatus*).

त्रिसन्ध्या tri-súndhiya, *adj.* The three periods of the day, or, dawn, noon, and eve.

त्रिसुपर्ण tri-soo-púrn, *s. m.* A portion of the *Rig* and *Yujoor Veds.*

त्रूटी tróo-tee, *s. f.* Loss, destruction.

त्रेता trét-a, *s. f.* The second *Yoog* or age of the *Hindoos,* said to consist of 1,296,000 years ; the silver age.

त्रिपुर try-poor, *s. m.* The modern city of *Tipperah* in Bengal.

त्रिविद्य try-vídyuh, *s. m.* A scholar in the three *Veds,* or one who possesses three sciences.

त्रोटकी tró-tuk-ee, *s. f.* A *Raginee,* or one of the female personifications of music.

त्रोटी tró-tee, *s. f.* The beak or bill of a bird ; a kind of pike (*Esox scolopax*).

त्वक twuk, *s. f.* The bark of the bamboo ; bark in general.

त्वक्कन्दुर twuk-kúndoor, *s. m.* A sore or wound.

त्वक्षीरा twuk-shéera, *s. f.* The manna of the bamboo.

त्वचा twúch-a, *s. f.* Skin ; bark, rind ; woody cassia.

त्वरा twúr-a, *s. f.* Haste, speed.

त्वरित twúr-it, *s. m.* Despatch, haste. *adv.* Quickly, swiftly. *adj.* Quick, swift, expeditious.

थ

थ thuh, The seventeenth consonant of the *Naguree* alphabet, and second of the dental class, being the aspirate of the preceding letter, and expressed by *th.*

थई thúee, *s. f.* A heap of clothes, &c.

थंब thumb,
थंभ thumbh, } *s. m.* A pillar, a post.

थंभना thúmbh-na, *v. n.* To cease, to be restrained, to stop ; to be supported.

थक thuk,
थक्का thúk-ka, } *s. m.* Clot, lump (*congealed*). *Thukkeh keh thukkeh, adj.* Congealed, thick, conglomerated.

थकथक thúk-thuk, *adj.* Very wet, drenched.

थकना thúk-na, *v. n.* To be wearied or fatigued, to tire, to fag.

थका thúk-a, *adj.* Tired, weary.

थकाना thuk-ána, *v. a.* To tire, harass, weary, fag, fatigue, jade.

थकित thúk-it, *adj.* Wearied, stopped, motionless, astonished.

थक्का thúk-ka, *s. m.* Clot, lump (*congealed*). *Thukkeh keh thukkeh, adj.* Congealed, thick, conglomerated.

थन thun, *s. m.* Udder. *Thundar,* An animal with a large udder, or having an udder.

थनी thún-ee, *s. f.* A blemish in horses.

थनेला thun-él-a, *s. m.* Inflamed breast (*of a woman*) ; name of an animal.

थनेश्वरी thun-ésh-wuree, *s. m.* A *Brahmun* of *Thuneshwur*, a famous *Hindoo* shrine in *Koorookshetr*, near *Kurnaul.*

थपक thúp-uk, *s. m.* A pat, a tap.

थपड़ा thúp-ra, *s. m.* A box, slap, claw, cuff.

थपड़ी thúp-ree, *s. f.* The clapping of hands. *Thupree bujana,* To clap the hands. *Thupree marna,* To hoot.

थपेड़ा thup-ér-a, *s. m.* A slap, a box, a clout, buffet; the scalp.

थप्पड़ thúp-pur, *s. m.* A box, a slap, claw, cuff.

थम thum, *s. m.* A pillar, a post.

थमड़ा thúm-ra, *adj.* Thick, corpulent.

थमना thúm-na, ⎫
थम्बना thúmb-na, ⎬ *v. n.* To cease, to be
थम्भना thúmbh-na, ⎭ restrained, to stop; to be supported.

थर thur, *s. m.* A lion or tiger's den.

थरथर thúr-thur, *adj.* Trembling.

थरथराना thur-thur-ána, *v. n.* To tremble, quiver, shiver, shake, quake, vibrate.

थरथराहट thur-thur-áhut, ⎫ *s. f.* Tremour,
थरथरी thúr-thur-ee, ⎬ shaking, trembling, quivering, shivering, vibration.

थरहरना thur-húr-na, ⎫
थरहराना thur-hur-ána, ⎬ *v. n.* To tremble,
थरौना thur-rána, ⎭ to quiver.

थल thul, *s. m.* Place, firm or dry ground; a lion's or tiger's den.

थलकना thúl-uk-na, *v. n.* To palpitate, to flutter.

थलचर thul-chúr, *adj.* Moving on land, terrestrial (*an animal*).

थलथल करना thúl-thul-kúrna, ⎫ *v. n.* To
थलथलाना thul-thul-ána, ⎬ undulate, to fluctuate as a thick or glutinous fluid, to shake as the flabby flesh of a fat man.

थलबेरा thul-béra, *s. m.* Place of abode, and means of attaining one's desires.

थलिया thúl-iya, *s. f.* A salver, a platter, a flat dish, generally of brass.

थुवई thu-wúee, *s. m.* A mason, a bricklayer, an architect.

था tha, *v. n. past tense,* Was.

थांग thang, *s. f.* A den of thieves.

थांगी tháng-ee, *s. m.* A receiver of stolen goods.

थांभ thambh, *s. m.* A post, a pillar, a support, prop, an obstacle.

थांभना thámbh-na, *v. a.* To support, to prop; to shield, protect, keep, retain, maintain,

to shelter; to prevent, withhold, restrain, calm; to stop, to pull up (*a horse*), to bear, assist, resist.

थांवला tháon-la, *s. m.* A mound or bason of earth about the root of a tree.   [tired.

थाकना thák-na, *v. n.* To fatigue, to be

थाती thá-tee, ⎫ *s. f.* A trust, what is
थाथी thá-thee, ⎬ given in charge, a charge.

थान than, *s. m.* A piece of cloth; a stall for cattle, a manger; a piece (*of coin*); as, *Ek than ushrufee,* One gold mohur. *Teenon than,* The private parts of a male.

थाना thá-na, *s. m.* A station, a guard; the inside of the lines of an army; a heap of bamboos.

थानी thá-nee, *s. m.* Householder, master of the house. *s. f.* A den of thieves.

थाप thap, *s. f.* A tap, a pat, a flap, paw; the sound of small drum.

थापना tháp-na, *v. a.* To patch (*as a wall with cowdung*); to tap. *s. f.* A religious ceremony performed at a certain season, at *Agra* and its vicinity.

थापा thá-pa, *s. m.* A mark of the paw.

थापी thá-pee, *s. f.* The noise of tapping; the instrument with which potters beat their earth, or with which terraces are beaten.

थाम tham, *s. m.* A post, a pillar, prop, support; an obstacle.

थांभना thámbh-na, *v. a.* To support, to prop; to shield, protect, keep, retain, maintain, to shelter; to prevent, withhold, restrain, calm; to stop, to pull up (*a horse*); to bear, assist, resist.

थार thar, ⎫
थाल thal, ⎬ *s. m.* A large flat dish.

थाला thá-la, *s. m.* The basin at the root of a tree for holding water; the excavation in which a tree is to be planted; a large flat dish.

थाली thá-lee, *s. f.* A salver, a platter, a flat dish; a mound or basin about the root of a tree for holding water.

थाह thah, *s. f.* Bottom, ford.

थाही thá-hee, *s. f.* Fordableness.

थिर thir, *adj.* Fixed, stable, settled, tranquil, calm, smooth.

थिरकना thir-úk-na, *v. n.* To set one's self off well in dancing, to dance with expressive action and gesture.

थिरता thír-ta, *s. f.* Rest, settlement, tranquillity, steadfastness.

थिराना thir-ána, *v. n.* To settle (*as liquor*).

थीर theer, *adj.* Tranquil, calm, smooth.

थुकथुकाना thook-thoo-kána, *v. n.* To spit on the mention of any disease, as a preservative against it, or, as a caution against an evil eye.

थूकबादैं thook-háee, *adj.* Base, contemptible (*fit to be spit upon*).

थूकाना thoo-ká-na, *v. a.* To cause to spit; to cause to reproach.

थूकदिला thóor-dil-a, *adj.* Miserly, narrowly.

थूतकारना thoot-kárna, *v. a.* To drive away scornfully.

थूथनी thóoth-nee, *s. f.* The mouth of a camel, horse, &c.

थूथाना thoo-thá-na, *v. a.* To frown, scowl, or pout.

थूपाना thoo-pána, *v. a.* To cause to be supported, propped or plastered.

थूलथूल thóol-thool, *adj.* Gently falling or dropping (*as water from a small height*).

थूक thook, *s. m.* Spittle, saliva. *Thook chutna*, To break one's promise. *Thook dena*, To leave, to give up. *Thook lugakur chhorna*, To treat with sovereign contempt. *Thook lugana*, To apply spittle (*a term of abuse and of most indecent meaning*).

थूकना thóok-na, *v. a.* To spit.

थूनी thóo-nee, *s. f.* A pillar, post, column.

थूथरा thóoth-ra, *s. m.* Mouth.

थूथना thóoth-na, *s. m.* ⎱ The mouth of a
थूथनी thóoth-nee, *s. f.* ⎰ camel, horse, &c.

थूनी thóo-nee, *s. f.* A pillar, post, column.

थूहर thóo-hur, *s. m.* A plant (*Euphorbia neriifolia*).

थेईथेई thé-ee-thé-ee, *s. m.* Merry-making. *The-ee-the-ee kurna*, To make merry.

थेगली thég-lee, *s. f.* A patch (*in a garment*).

थेयीथेयी théyee-théyee, *s. f.* Merry-making.

थेवा thé-wa, *s. m.* A stone set in a ring.

थैला thy-la, *s. m.* ⎫ A purse tied round
थैलिया thy-liya, *s. f.* ⎬ the waist; a bag;
थैली thy-lee, *s. f.* ⎭ the scrotum.

थोक thok, *s. m.* A mount, heap, ready money; share, portion. *Thokdar*, *s. m.* A wholesale dealer.

थोर thor, *s. m.* The spathe of a plantain tree before it shoots from the stem.

थोड़ा thó-ra, *adj.* A little, small, scarce, few, scanty, seldom, some, less. *Thora thora*, A little, by degrees. *Thora thora hona*, To be ashamed, to shrink with shame. *Thora-buhoot*, *adj.* More or less. *Thoreh seh thora*, *adj.* Very little.

थोतरा thót-ra, *adj.* Bruised and spoiled (*as the head of a mallet*); toothless.

थोथला thóth-la, *adj.* Blunt, not sharp, dull.

थोथा thó-tha, *s. m.* A medicine; an arrow without a point. *adj.* Hollow, empty; toothless. *Thothee bat*, *s. f.* Word without meaning, nonsense.

थोप thop, *s. m.* An ornament or mounting at the end of the pole of a *palkee*, &c.; head, topping.

थोपना thóp-na, *v. a.* To support, to prop; to plaster; to pile, to heap.

थोपियाना tho-pi-yána, *v. n.* To trickle.

थोपी thó-pee, *s. f.* Box, thump.

थोहर thó-hur, *s. m.* A plant (*Euphorbia neriifolia*).

द

द duh, The third letter of the dental class and eighteenth consonant in the *Naguree* alphabet, corresponding to the letter *d*, uttered with the point of the tongue pressed on the upper foreteeth.

दई dúee, *part.* Given; gift. *s. m.* Destiny, the Deity. *s. f.* The Godhead. *Duee lugna*, To be unfortunate. *Duee-mara*, *adj.* Struck by the Deity, accursed.

दंड dund, *s. m.* A stick, a staff; fine, penalty, punishment, castigation by amercement or putting to death; a measure of time, or 24 minutes.

दंडवत dúnd-wut, *s. f.* *Hindoo* salutation, bow, obeisance, prostration.

दंडी dún-dee, *s. m.* A mendicant who carries a staff in his hand; the penis.

दंदनाना dundun-ána, *v. n.* To enjoy one's self, to be contented and independent, to live at one's ease.

दंदारू dun-dá-roo, *s. m.* A blister, a pimple.

दंश dunsh, *s. m.* A gadfly; a tooth; the sting of a snake.

दंशन dúnsh-un, *s. m.* Biting, stinging.

दंशमूल dunsh-móol, *s. m.* A plant (*Hyperanthera morunga*).

दंशित dúnsh-it, *adj.* Bitten, stung.

दंशी dúnsh-ee, *s. f.* A small gadfly.

दंशेर dunsh-ér, *adj.* Mischievous, noxious.

दक्ष duksh, *s. m.* A son of *Bruhma*, said to have been born from the thumb of his right hand, for the purpose of peopling the world. *Duksh* is said to have had sixty daughters, of whom twenty-seven are represented as the nymphs who form the lunar asterisms, and wives of the moon: one of his daughters also was *Suti*, or *Doorga*, the wife of *Shiv*, and seventeen were married to *Kusyup*, and were the mothers of all created being. *Duksh* was on one occasion decapitated by

Shiv ; he is sometimes regarded as an *Uvutar* of *Bruhma* himself ; a *mooni* and legislator who flourished in the beginning of the *Treta yoog* ; a scholar ; a *pundit* ; a dexterous or clever man. *adj.* Clever, able, dexterous.

दृक्षता **dúksh-ta,** *s. f.* Dexterity, cleverness.

दृक्षाधर्ध्वंसकृत **dukshadhwúr-dwúns-krit,** *s. m.* A name of *Shiv.* *Duksh* having on one occasion made a sacrifice, to which he invited all the gods, except his son-in-law *Shiv,* and his wife *Suti,* they went unbid, and being received unpolitely, the latter threw herself into the fire, and was burnt ; a furious quarrel ensued between *Shiv* and *Duksh,* in which the god decapitated his father-in-law.

दृक्षिन **dúk-shin,** *adj.* Right (*not left*) ; south, southern.

दृक्षिणपूर्व्वा **dukshin-póorvva,** *s. f.* The south-east quarter.

दृक्षिना **dúkshin-a,** *s. f.* A present to *Brahmuns* upon solemn or sacrificial occasions, a fee, reward ; a form or figure of *Doorga,* in which the right side is said to be advanced ; donation to *Brahmuns,* personified as a goddess, said to be born from *Krishn's* right side.

दृक्षिनाग्नि **dúkshin-ágni,** *s. m.* One kind of sacred fire, that which is taken from the domestic or consecrated fire, and is placed to the south.

दृक्षिनाचल **dúkshin-áchul,** *s. m.* The *Muluya* mountain.

दृक्षिनामुख **dúkshin-ámookh,** *adj.* Turning the face southwards.

दृक्षिनायन **dúkshin-áyun,** *s. m.* Southing. *Dukshinayun sooruj,* The winter solstice, sun's southing, the period of the sun's being in the southern hemisphere, southern declination.

दृक्षिनीय **dúkshin-ćeyub,** *adj.* Meriting or deserving a reward.

दृक्षिनेन **dukshin-én,** *adv.* Southward, southerly.

दृक्षिय **dukshin-yuh,** *adj.* Meriting or deserving of a reward.

दृक्षी **dúkshee,** *adj.* Capable, able, well qualified.

दृक्षन **dúkhun,** *s. m.* South ; the southern part of India.

दृक्षनी **dúkhun-ee,** *adj.* Southern (*generally, things or persons from the south*). *Dukhunee poodeena,* Horse-mint.

दृक्षिन **dúkh-in,** *s. m.* South ; the southern part of India.

दृक्षिना **dúkhin-a,** *adj.* Southern. *s. f.* Southerly wind.

दृक्षिनायन **dukhin-áyun,** *s. m.* Southing. *Dukhinayun sooruj,* The winter solstice, sun's

southing, the period of the sun's being in the southern hemisphere, southern declination.

दृक्षिनी **dukhínee,** *adj.* Southern (*generally, things or persons from the south*). *Dukhinee poodeena,* Horse-mint.

दृगूर **dug-úr,** *s. m.* A kettle-drum.

दृगूरना **dug-úr-na,** *v. a.* To disbelieve a true testimony.

दृग्रा **dúg-ra,** *s. m.* Highway.

दृग्राना **dug-rá-na,** *v. a.* To propel, to roll.

दृगदुगा **dúg-dug-a,** *adj.* Shining.

दृगदुगाना **dug-dug-ána,** *v. n.* To glow, gleam, twinkle.

दृगदुगाहट **dug-dug-áhut,** *s. f.* Splendour, sparkling, twinkling (*as of a star*).

दृगुधना **dug-údh-na,** *v. a.* To burn ; to tease, vex ; to chide, threaten, upbraid, revile, pester.

दृगमगाना **dug-mug-ána,** *v. n.* To tremble.

दृगला **dúg-la,** *s. m.* A kind of quilted vest worn as armour.

दृग्ध **dugdh,** *adj.* Burnt, scorched, consumed by fire.

दृग्धकाक **dugdh-kák,** *s. m.* A raven, or perhaps the carrion crow.

दृनगुल **dún-gul,** *s. m.* A kind of chair.

दृनगा **dún-ga,** *s. m.* Wrangling, confusion, mutiny, sedition, rebellion.

दृनग्यत **dun-gyt,** *adj.* Mutinous, turbulent, mutineer, seditious.

दृच्छ **duchh,** *s. m.* See दृक्ष **duksh.**

दृच्छिना **dúchhina,** *s. f.* See दृक्षिना **dukshina.**

दृठना **dút-na,** *v. a.* To oppose, confute, fight.

दृरुकना **dur-úk-na,** *v. n.* To split, to be rent or torn, to crack.

दृरेरा **dur-ér-a,** *s. m.* Hard, impetuous rain.

दृर्हमूनडा **durh-móon-da,** *adj.* Beard-shaven, beardless.

दृर्हियल **dúrhi-yul,** *adj.* Having a long beard.

दृनड **dund,** *s. m.* A stick, a staff ; punishment, castigation by amercement or putting to death, fine, penalty ; a measure of time, or 24 minutes.

दृनडक **dúnd-uk,** *s. m.* A sort of metre, the stanza of which exceeds 27 syllables and may extend to 200.

दृनडक **dúnd-ka,** *s. f.* A country on the north-east coast of the peninsula, containing the celebrated forest *Dundkarunyuh,* in which *Ram* resided some time.

दृनडधुक्का **dund-dhúkka,** *s. f.* A sort of drum.

दंदताम्री dund-támree, *s. f.* A perforated copper vessel of given capacity, placed in a vessel of water : when filled with water it sinks, marking a certain portion of time.

दंदनीति dund-néeti, *s. f.* Ethics, the system of morals taught by *Chanyukyuh.*

दंदनीय dund-néeyuh, *adj.* Punishable, deserving punishment.

दंदपाल dund-pál, *s. m.* A small kind of fish (*Cyprinus barbiger?*)

दंदवत् dúnd-wut, *s. f. Hindoo* salutation, bow, obeisance, prostration.

दंदादंदी dúnda-dúndee, *s. f.* Single stick ; cudgelling, fighting with sticks or staves.

दंदायमान dunda-yumán, *adj.* Standing erect.

दंदित dúnd-it, *adj.* Punished, chastised, sentenced, fined.

दंदिन dún-din, *s. m.* A staff or mace-bearer.

दंदी dún-dee, *s. m.* A mendicant who carries a staff in his hand ; the penis.

दंदयुह dund-yúh, *adj.* Punishable, deserving punishment.

दतना dút-na, *v. a.* To oppose, confute, fight.

दतवन dút-wun, } *s. m.* A tooth-brush,
दतोन dut-óun, } generally of a twig.

दत्त dutt, *s. m.* The name of a king ; a title or surname of a man of the *Vys* or third tribe. *adj.* Given, presented, made over, assigned.

दत्तकपुत्र duttuk-póotr, *s. m.* A son given away by his natural parents to persons engaging to adopt him : one of the twelve heirs acknowledged by the old *Hindoo* law.

दत्तप्रदानिक dutt-prudánik, *s. m.* Resumption of a gift, taking back a thing given.

दत्तात्मन् dutt-átmun, *s. m.* A youth or orphan who gives himself to persons disposed to take the place of parents.

दत्तानुपकर्म्मन् duttánup-kúrmmun, *s. m.* Non-resumption of gifts.

दत्ति dútti, *s. f.* Gift, donation.

ददलाना dud-lána, *v. a.* To chide, to snub.

ददियाल dud-iyál, *s. m.* Descent (*by ancestors*), pedigree, ancestors, paternal grandfather's family.

ददोरा dud-ó-ra, *s. m.* A bump (*occasioned by the bite of an insect*).

दद्रु dúd-roo, *s. m.* Cutaneous and herpetic eruptions.

दद्रुरोगिन् dúdroo-rógin, *adj.* Herpetic, diseased by Herpes.

दद्रू dúd-roo, *s. m.* Herpetic eruptions.

दधि dúdhi, *s. m.* Sour, thick milk, milk, curdled or coagulated by heat, or by the addition of buttermilk : it is an article of food of general use and high estimation among the *Hindoos,* and is considered medicinally as the remedy, or preventative of most disorders. *Dudhi-kado,* Coagulated milk and clay, thrown by people at each other in sport, on the festival of *Krishn's* birth-day.

दधिपूष्पिका dúdhi-póosh-pika, *s. f.* A flower (*Clitorea ternata*).

दधिफल dudhi-phúl, *s. m.* The elephant or wood apple.

दधीच dudhéech, *s. m.* The name of a *mooni* or saint, famous for having devoted himself to death, that the gods might be armed with his bones in lieu of thunderbolts ; they being the only effective weapons against the demon *Taruk.*

दध्यानी dudh-yánee, *s. f.* A medicinal plant.

दंत dunt, *s. m.* A tooth ; an elephant's tusk or tooth.

दंतधावन dunt-dhá-wun, *s. m.* A tree yielding an astringent resin (*Mimosa catechu*) ; a plant (*Mimusops elengi*) ; a tooth-brush, or a fibrous stick used for cleaning the teeth.

दंतपत्रक dunt-pútruk, *s. m.* A kind of jasmine (*Jasminum pubescens*) : the petals, or leaves of the flower, resembling teeth in colour and shape : this comparision is frequent among the poets.

दंतपीर dunt-péer, *s. f.* The tooth-ache.

दंतपूष्प dunt-póoshp, *s. m.* A plant, the flower of which is compared to a tooth (*Strychnos potatorum*).

दंतमल dunt-múl, *s. m.* The tartar of the teeth.

दंतमांस dunt-máns, *s. m.* The gums.

दंतशठ dunt-shúth, *s. m.* Elephant or wood apple ; common lime (*Citrus acida*); a plant bearing an acid fruit (*Averrhoa carambola*).

दंतशठा dunt-shút-ha, *s. f.* Wood sorrel (*Oxalis monodelpha*).

दंतशान dunt-shán, *s. m.* A dentifrice, composed chiefly of the powdered fruit of the Chebulic myrobalan and green sulphate of iron.

दंतशूल dunt-shóol, *s. m.* The tooth-ache.

दंतार्वुद dunt-árv-vood, *s. m.* A disease of the teeth or gums ; gum boil, ulceration of the gums.

दंती dún-tee, *s. m.* An elephant. *adj.* Toothed, tusked.

दंतीबीज duntee-véej, *s. m.* A strong purgative nut, the fruit of the croton.

दंतुर dún-toor, } *adj.* Having large or
दंतेल dun-tél, } prominent tusks, tusk-
दंत्य dun-tyl, } ed (*an elephant, boar, &c.*)

दंत्य dún-tyuh, *adj.* Dental, of or belonging to the teeth (*as a class of letters in the Nuguree alphabet*).

दन्दनाना dundun-ána, *v. n.* To enjoy one's self, to be contented and independent, to live at one's ease.

दन्दारू dundároo, *s. m.* A blister, a pimple.

दन्ना dún-na, *s. m.* Membrum virile.

दपट dúp-ut, *s. f.* Course, gallop.

दपटना dúp-ut-na, *v. n.* To gallop, to rush; to rebuke, to reprimand.

दपटाना dup-tá-na, *v. a.* To gallop.

दपदपाना dup-dup-ána, } *v. a.* To
दपदप करना dup-dup kúrna, } shine.

दपदपाहट dupdup-áhut, *s. f.* Shining, splendour.

दबकना dúb-uk-na, *v. n.* To crouch, to sculk, to be awed, to lie in ambush, to lurk, to set (*a dog*), to twinkle. *Dubuk ana*, or, —*jana*, or, —*ruhna*, *v. n.* To sneak, to sculk. *Dubuk bythna, v. n.* To crouch.

दबकर dúb-kur, *s. f.* A trap.

दबकाना dub-ká-na, *v. a.* To snub, check, chide, threaten, awe, daunt; to conceal, hide.

दबकी dúb-kee, *s. f.* Ambush, crouching. *Dubkee marna*, To lie in ambush.

दबकीला dub-kée-la, } *adj.* Sculking, sculker.
दबकेल dub-kél, }

दबंग dub-úng, } *adj.* Ill-bred, brutish,
दबंगा dub-ún-ga, } barbarous, dolt, foolish, lout.

दबना dúb-na, *v. n.* To be snubbed, to crouch, to shrink, to be pressed down, be mowed down, give way, to be awed; to be concealed. *Dub chulna*, or, —*nikulna*, To be awed, be overpowered. *Dub jana*, To retire, to withdraw, to be mortified, to be suppressed. *Dub murna*, To be crushed to death. *Dubana, v. n.* To advance. *Dub sh paon*, With silent steps, softly, gently.

दबा dúb-a, *s. m.* Ambush. *Duba marna*, To lie in wait.

दबाना dub-ána, *v. a.* To press down; to snub, chide, keep under, to check, curb, restrain, repress, awe, depress, bow down, suppress. *Dubaeh dalna*, To keep concealed, to hide (*generally furtively*). *Duba marna*, To overcome, to get the better of; to crush to death. *Duba lena*, To encroach upon.

दबाव dub-áo, *s. m.* Strength, power, authority, pressure, crush, suppression, depression, resignation, submissiveness. *Dubao manna, v. a.* To stand in awe.

दबीला dub-ée-la, *s. m.* Name of a medicine; a paddle.

दबेपांव dúbeh-páon, *adv.* With silent steps, softly, gently.

दबैल dub-él, *s. m.* A subject, a person under dominion.

दबोचना dub-óch-na, *v. a.* To conceal, to hide (*generally furtively*).

दबोस dub-ós, *s. m.* A flint.

दबोसना dub-ós-na, *v. a.* To tope, to tipple.

दम dum, *s. m.* Taming, subduing; self-command, endurance of the most painful austerities; self-restraint, subduing the senses, suppressing the appetites, passions, &c.

दमक dúm-uk, *s. m.* A tamer, a subduer (*of the passions, appetites, &c.*). *s. f.* Ardour; glitter.

दमकना dúm-uk-na, *v. n.* To shine, to glow.

दमकल dúm-kul-a, *s. m.* A squirt, a fire-engine; a jack or crane (*for raising weights*).

दमरा dúm-ra, *s. m.* Gold, silver, riches.

दमरी dúm-ree, *s. f.* The eighth part of a pysa or pice. *Dumree keh teen teen hona*, To be ruined, demolished.

दमदमाना dum-dum-ána, *v. n.* To shake (*as the branch of a tree*).

दमन dúm-un, *s. m.* A hero; a kind of flower (*Artemisia*); taming, subduing.

दमना dúm-na, *v. n.* To glitter, to flash; to bend with elasticity, to spring.

दमाना dum-ána, *v. a.* To bend (*with elasticity*).

दमामा dum-áma, *s. m.* A large kettle-drum.

दम्पती dum-pútee, *m. du.* Husband and wife.

दम्भ dumbh, *s. m.* Arrogance, pride, boast; hypocrisy.

दम्भी dúm-bhee, *adj.* Hypocritical, proud. *s. m.* A hypocrite, an impostor.

दम्य dúm-yuh, *adj.* Subjected or tamed. *s. m.* A steer, a young bullock.

दया dya, *s. f.* A gift; affection, tenderness, sympathy, compassion, mercy, clemency; kindness, favor. [passion.

दयाकर dya-kúr, *adj.* Kind, shewing compassion.

दयाकृत dya-krít, *adj.* Compassionate.

दयामान dya-mán, *adj.* Charitable, merciful, kind.

दयायुक्त dya-yóokt, } *adj.* Kind, compas-
दयायुत dya-yóot, } sionate, benevolent, friendly.

दयाल dy-ál, } *adj.* Tender, compassion-
दयालु dy-áloo, } ate, merciful, gracious, liberal, generous, beneficent, kind.

दयालुत्व dyáloo-twúh, *s. m.* Tenderness, compassionateness.

दयावत dya-wút,
दयावन्त dya-wúnt, } *adj.* Merciful, tender, charitable, kind.
दयावान dya-wán,

दयाशील dya-shéel, *adj.* Kind, compassionate; affectionate.

द्यौ dy-óu, *pret.* Gave, given.

दयित dy-it, *adj.* Beloved, dear, desired.

दयिता dy-it-a, *s. f.* A wife.

दयिताधीन dyit-adhéen, *adj.* Hen-pecked, subject to a wife.

दर dur, *s. m.* Price.

दरकना dúr-uk-na, *v. n.* To split, rend, be torn, to crack.

दरका dúr-ka, *s. m.* Crack, crevice, cranny.

दरकाना dur-ká-na, *v. a.* To cause to crack or split.

दरदर dúr-dur, *s. m.* Cinnabar.

दरदरा dúr-dur-a, *adj.* Half-pounded, coarsely ground.

दरदा dúr-da, *s. f.* A country bordering on *Cashmeer*, the mountains about *Cashmeer* and above *Peshawur*. *s. m.* A tribe of barbarians.

दरबुहरा dur-búh-ra, *s. m.* An intoxicating spirit drawn from rice.

दरमा durma, *s. m.* A kind of mat.

दरस dúr-us, *s. m.* See दृश dursh.

दरही dur-hée, *s. f.* A fish, a sort of carp (*Cyprinus*).

दरा dúr-a, } *s. f.* A natural or artificial
दरी dúr-ee, } excavation in a mountain, a cave, a cavern, a grotto, &c.; a valley.

दरान्ती dur-án-tee, *s. f.* A sickle.

दरार dur-ár, *s. m.* A crack, a fissure, rift, rent, breach.

दरिद्र dúr-idr, *adj.* Poor, needy, indigent, distressed, wretched.

दरिद्रता duridr-ta, *s. f.* Poverty, indigence, wretchedness. [digent.

दरिद्री dur-íd-ree, *adj.* Poor, wretched, indigent.

दरीबा dur-ée-ba, *s. m.* A stall (*in a market*) where betel is sold.

दर्रू dúr-droo, *s. m.* Cutaneous eruption, Herpes.

दर्रूरोगी dúrdroo-rógee, *adj.* Herpetick, afflicted with Herpes.

दर्प durp, *s. m.* Pride, arrogance, boasting.

दर्पन dúr-pun, *s. m.* A mirror, looking-glass.

दर्ब durb, *s. m.* Wealth, property; substance, matter, a thing.

दर्भ durbh, *s. m. Koosa* or sacrificial grass (*Poa cynosuroides*); a kind of reed (*Saccharum spontaneum*); another species (*S. cylindricum*).

दर्राना dur-rá-na, *v. n.* To go straight and quickly, without fear or delay. *adj.* Straight forwards.

दर्व durv, *s. m.* Substance, thing, wealth.

दर्वी dúr-vee, *s. f.* A ladle or spoon.

दर्श dursh, *s. m.* Sight, seeing; the conjunction of sun and moon, or day of new moon when it rises invisible.

दर्शक dursh-úk, *adj.* Who or what shews, displays, explains, makes clear, &c. *s. m.* An exhibiter, one who points out or shews any thing.

दर्शन dúrsh-un, *s. m.* Sight, seeing, looking; aspect, appearance; interview; a *shashtr*, one of six religious or philosophical systems, the *Patunjul, Sankhyuh, Vyseshikuh, Nyayuh, Mimansa,* and *Vedant*; visiting any sacred shrine, worshipping in the presence of any image.

दर्शनधारी dúrshun-dháree, *adj.* Beautiful, handsome.

दर्शनप्रतिभ dúrshun-prutibhóo, *s. m.* A surety for appearance.

दर्शनी dúr-shun-ee, *adj.* Payable at sight (*a bill of exchange*). *s. f.* A bill of exchange payable at sight; offering, present. *adj.* Handsome, sightly. *Dursunee-juwan,* A beautiful youth.

दर्शनीय dúrshun-éeyuh, *adj.* Beautiful, handsome, agreeable; visible, to be seen.

दर्शनीयमानी durshunéeyu-mánee, *adj.* Vain, conceited, thinking one-self handsome.

दर्शित dúrsh-it, *adj.* Visible, apparent; shown, displayed; explained; seen.

दल dul, *s. m.* The leaf of a tree; a large army; a heap or quantity; wild rice. *Duldar,* *adj.* Fleshy, thick. *Dulwal,* Commander of an army.

दलक dúl-uk, *s. f.* Glitter.

दलकना dúl-uk-na, *v. n.* To glitter.

दलकपाठ duluk-pát, *s. m.* A folded petal or leaf.

दलकोश dul-kósh, *s. m.* A sort of jasmine (*Jasminum pubescens*).

दलदल dúl-dul, *s. f.* A quagmire, a slough, a bog.

दलदला dúl-dul-a, *adj.* Quaggy, boggy.

दलदलाना dul-dul-ána, *v. n.* To shake, to undulate.

दलदलाहट dul-dul-áhut, *s. f.* Tremour.

दलदली dúl-dul-ee, *adj.* Swampy.

दलउद्हृदय dul-ud-hrídy, *adj.* Broken-hearted, cut to the heart, &c.

दलन dúl-un, *s. m.* Breaking to pieces, dividing, tearing asunder, splitting.

दूलना dúl-na, r. a. To grind coarsely, to split pulse.

दूलनिर्मोक dul-nirm-mók, s. m. The *Bhoj putr* tree, the bark of which is used for wrapping woollens in, and for *hookah* snakes, &c.

दूलपुष्पी dul-póoshp-ee, s. f. A fragrant plant (*Pandanus odoratissimus*)

दूलबादूल dul-bá-dul, s. m. A mass of clouds; a large army; a large tent.

दूलमुसल करना dulmusul kúrna, v. a. To thrash, crumple, rumple, ruffle.

दूलवाना dul-wá-na, v. a. To cause to be coarsely ground (*corn*).

दूलवैया dul-wy-ya, s. m. One who grinds (*corn*).

दूलसूसा dul-sóo-sa, s. f. The fibre or vein of a leaf.

दूलहारन dul-há-run, ⎫ s. f. A woman
दूलहारी dul-há-ree, ⎭ whose business is to deal in grain.

दूलहारा dul-há-ra, s. m. One whose business is to sell grain.

दूलाढक dul-ádhuk, s. m. Sesamum growing wild or spontaneously; an aquatic plant (*Pistia stratioites*); a plant commonly called *Nagesur* (*Mesua ferrea*); a tree (*Mimosa sirisha*); a sort of jasmine (*Jasminum pubescens*).

दूलाना dul-á-na, v. a. To cause to be coarsely grounded.

दूलामूल dul-amúl, s. m. A tree (*Vangueria spinosa*).

दूछिद्र dul-ídr, s. m. ⎫ Wretchedness,
दूछिद्रता dul-ídr-ta, s. f. ⎭ poverty, indigence.

दूछिद्री dul-íd-ree, adj. Poor, wretched, indigent, needy, unfortunate.

दूलिया dúl-iya, s. m. Half-ground or coarsely pounded grain, split pulse.

दूलिहुन dúl-i-huu, s. f. Any sort of pulse which may be split, as *dal*.

दूली dúl-ee, s. f. A clod of clay or mould.

दूलेंती dul-én-tee, s. f. A handmill.

दूलेगुन्धि dul-égundhi, s. m. A plant (*Echites scholaris*).

दूवाग्नि duv-ágni, s. m. A wood on fire or the conflagration of a forest.

दूश dush, adj. Ten. *Duson-disa*, The ten regions, sides or quarters (*of the world*). *Duson dwar*, The ten passages for the actions of the faculties, viz., the eyes, ears, nostrils, mouth, penis, anus, and crown of the head. It seems, however, that properly there are only nine, the last not being acknowledged in any *Sunskrit* works of authority which have been consulted.

दूशकामजूव्युसन dushkám-júvyusun, s. m.

The aggregate of ten vices, proceeding from the quality of desire, viz. hunting, gambling, sleeping during the day, abusiveness, lechery, drunkenness, dancing, singing, playing and hypocrisy.

दूशगुण dúsh-goon, adj. Ten times, tenfold.

दूशग्राम dush-grám, s. m. A district or collection of ten villages.

दूशन dúsh-un, s. m. A tooth.

दूशपुर dúsh-poor, s. m. A fragrant grass (*Cyperus rotundus*); a district, part of *Malwa* in *Bundelkhund*.

दूशम dúsh-um, adj. Tenth.

दूशमाल dush-mál, s. m. A collection of ten garlands.

दूशमी dúsh-mee, s. f. The tenth day of the lunar fortnight; the tenth or last stage of human life, the last ten years of a century. *adj.* Very old or aged.

दूशमूल dush-mool, s. m. A tonic medicament prepared from the roots of ten plants.

दूशरथ dúsh-ruth, s. m. A proper name, a sovereign of *Ujodhya* or *Oude*, and father of *Ram*.

दूशलूक्षन dush-lúkshun, s. m. Ten marks or attributes.

दूशसूत dush-sút, adj. A thousand.

दूशसुहस्र dúsh-suhúsr, adj. A myriad.

दूशूहरा dushúh-ra, s. m. The tenth of *Jeth, shookl-puksh*, which is reckoned the birthday of *Gunga*: whoever bathes in the *Gunga* on that day is supposed to be purified from ten sorts of sins. The tenth of *Asin, shookl-puksh*, on which, after the worship and religious ceremonies performed during nine nights (*nururatree*), they throw the images of *Devee* into the river. On this day, it is said, *Ram* marched against *Ravun*, for which reason it is called *Vijy dusmee*: the day is celebrated with great pomp by *Hindoo* princes; the weapons and instruments of war are hallowed; and if war be intended, the campaign is then opened.

दूशा dúsh-a, s. f. A state, condition, period or time of life, as youth, manhood, old age, &c.; circumstances.

दूशांश dush-ánsh s. m. Tenth part.

दूशानिक dush-á-nik, s. m. A plant (*Croton polyandrum*).

दूशाफुल dush-a-phúl, s. m. Result of circumstances, or of condition of life.

दूशार्न dush-árn, s. m. A country, part of central *Hindoostan*, lying on the S. E. of the *Vind'hya* mountains.

दूशार्णा dush-árna, s. f. A river rising in the *Vind'hya* hills, the *Dosarene* of the ancients.

दूशार्ब dush-árb, s. m. A country in the

south of India, the kingdom of *Yudoo*. *m. pl.* The *Yaduv* or people of *Dusharh*.

दशावतार dúsh-avutár, *s. m.* A name of *Vishnoo*; the deity of whom there are said to have been ten descents from heaven, for the purpose of protecting or punishing mankind.

दशाविशेष dúsha-vishésh, *s. m.* Existing circumstances, peculiar condition.

दशी dúsh-ee, *s. f.* Thread; the unwove threads at the end of a piece of cloth.

दशीला dush-éela, *adj.* In good circumstances.

दशेन्द्रिय dushén-driya, *m. pl.* The ten organs of sense and action, viz., the skin, eye, tongue, nose, ear, organ of speech, hand, foot, anus, and pudendum.

दस dus, *adj.* Ten. *Duson disa, f. pl.* The ten regions, sides or quarters (*of the world*). *Duson dwar, m. pl.* The ten passages for the actions of the faculties; viz., the eyes, ears, nostrils, mouth, penis, anus, and crown of the head.

दसन dús-un, *s. m.* A tooth.

दसम dús-um,
दसवां dus-wan, } *adj.* Tenth.

दसमी dús-mee, *s. f.* The tenth day of the lunar fortnight.

दसहरा dusúhra, *s. m.* The tenth of *Jeth*, *shookl-puksh*, supposed to be the birth-day of *Gunga*: whoever bathes in the *Gunga* on that day is supposed to be purified from ten sorts of sins. The tenth of *Asin, shookl-puksh*, on which, after the worship and religious ceremonies performed during nine nights (*nuvuratree*), they throw the images of *Devee* into the river. On this day *Ram* is supposed to have marched against *Ravun*, for which reason it is called *Vijy dusmee*: the day is celebrated with great pomp by *Hindoo* princes; the weapons and instruments of war are hallowed; and if war be intended, the campaign is then opened.

दसी dús-ee, *s. f.* Thread; the unwove threads at the end of a piece of cloth.

दसीला dus-ée-la, *adj.* In good circumstances.

दसोखा dus-ó-kha, *s. m.* Moulting (*of birds*). *Dusokha jharna*, To moult.

दसोदिसा dúson-dís-a, *f. pl.* The ten regions, sides, or quarters (*of the world*).

दसोद्वार dúson-dwár, *m. pl.* The ten passages for the actions of the faculties; viz., the eyes, ears, nostrils, mouth, penis, anus, and crown of the head.

दसोंधा dus-óun-dha,
दसोंधी dus-óun-dhee, } *s. m.* A panegyrist.

दस्ता dús-ta, *s. m.* Zinc, tutenag, Lapis calaminaris.

दस्यु dús-yoo, *s. m.* An enemy; a thief; an oppressor, a violator, a committer of injustice, &c.

दस्युवृत्ति dúsyoo-vrítti, *s. f.* Theft, dishonest mode of subsistence.

दह duh, *s. m.* A deep whirlpool, very deep water, an abyss. *Kunwul-duh*, A place abounding in water-lilies.

दहक dúhuk, *s. f.* Ardour.

दहकना dúhuk-na, *v. n.* To burn, to be burnt, to be ruined, lost, destroyed; to regret.

दहकाना duh-ká-na, *v. a.* To burn, to kindle; to ruin, destroy, lose; to cause to regret; to heat, (*iron &c.*)

दहदह जलना duhur-duhur júlna, *v. n.* To burn with great fury.

दहत dúhut, *adj.* Scorching, burning.

दहन dúhun, *s. m.* Burning, combustion; fire, or the deity *Ugni*; the marking-nut plant; lead-wort (*Plumbago zeylanica, &c.*)

दहना dúh-na, *adj.* Right, the opposite of left.

दहनीय duhun-éeyuh, *adj.* To be or what may be burnt, combustible.

दहनोपल duhun-ópul, *s. m.* The sun-gem, a crystal lens.

दहुलना duhúlna, *v. n.* To shake, to tremble, to fear.

दहलाना duh-lána, *v. a.* To agitate.

दहसेर duh-séra, *s. m.* A weight of ten seers.

दहाई duháee, *s. f.* The figure ten; the tenth part; the decimal places of figures in arithmetic, the tens.

दहारना duhárna, *v. n.* To roar (*as a tiger*).

दहाना duhána, *v. a.* To burn.

दहित dúhit, *part. pass.* Burnt.

दहिना dúhina, *adj.* Right, the opposite of left.

दही duhée, *s. m.* Thick sour milk, coagulated milk. *Duheewala, s. m.* A seller of sour milk.

दहेंगर duhéngur, *s. m.* A vessel for carrying sour milk in (*particularly at festivals*).

दुएर duér,
दुहेल duhél, } *s. m.* A bird (*Coracias*).

दुहेंडी duhéndee, *s. f.* A vessel in which sour milk is kept.

दाइक dá-ik,
दाई dá-ee, } *s. m.* Giving, a donor, a giver.

दाई dá-ee, *s. f.* A milk-nurse; a midwife. *Daee ko sompna*, To put out to nurse. *Daee khilare*, A dry nurse. *Daee junaee, s. f.* A midwife. *Daee-pilaee, s. f.* A wet nurse.

दाऊ dá-oo, *s. m.* An appellation of a father or of an elder brother.

दाउदी dáoo-dee, *s. f.* A shrub that bears a flower like chamomile (*Chrysanthemum indicum*); a kind of firework like that shrub; a kind of armour. *adj.* Relating to David, of David.

दाएजा daeja, *s. m.* Dowry, dower.

दांएबांए dáen-baen, *adv.* On the right and left.

दांड dand, *s. m.* Fine, punishment, oppression, injustice, injury.

दांडमेंडा dánda-ménda, *s. m.* The frontier or boundary between the lands of two proprietors.

दांडी dán-dee, *s. f.* A balance.

दांत dant, *s. m.* A tooth. *Dant oonglee katna*, To bite the finger, is a term expressive of being surprised. *Dant kuchkuchana*, To grin, to shew the teeth. *Dant kutkutana*, *v. a.* To gnash the teeth. *Dant katee rotee khana*, To be the most intimate friend of any one. *Dant ka durd*, The tooth-ache. *Dant khutteh kurna*, To dishearten, to displease. *Dant tuleh oonglee dubana*, or, —*katna*, To stand in amaze, to be amazed, to wonder. *Dant nikalna*, To laugh, to grin; to express or confess inability and helplessness. *Dant pur churhana*, To detract from the virtues or praise of another. *Dant peesna*, To gnash the teeth, to grin. *Dant bujna*, or, —*bajna*, *v. n.* To chatter the teeth, squabble, wrangle, chattering of the teeth, squabbling, wrangling, sparring. *Dant rukhna*, or, —*hona kisee-pur*, To desire any thing exceedingly; to hate. *Dant lugna*, *s. m.* Trismus or locked-jaw. *Dant lana*, or, —*nikalna*, To teeth, grow (*as teeth*). *Danton sumeen pukurnee* (*lit. to bite the ground*), To be reduced to extremities, to suffer great pain. *Danton marna*, To gnash the teeth (*with anger*).

दांतन dán-tun, *s. m.* A tooth-brush made from the branch of a tree.

दांतपीसना dant-péesna, *v. n.* To gnash the teeth, to grin.

दांताकिलकिल dánta-kílkil, *s. f.* Quarrel.

दांती dán-tee, *s. f.* The tooth of a saw or other instrument, cog (*of a wheel*). *Dantee dena*, To insist upon. *Dantee purna*, *v. n.* To be notched or indented (*the edge of a tool*). *Dantee lugna*, To have a locked jaw.

दांव dáon, *s. m.* Ambuscade, ambush, snare; time, turn, opportunity, vicissitude; twisting of one another in wrestling. *Daon chulna*, To have the advantage. *Daon chulana*, To take advantage of. *Daon pukurna*, To wrestle. *Daon bythna*, To lie in ambush, to lurk.

दांवान dan-wán, *s. m.* Burning, stubble, &c.

दाक dak, *s. m.* A donor, one who makes presents, especially to *Brahmuns*; a sacrificer, one who pays all the expenses of the ceremony, and employs the officiating priests.

दाक्षायिणी dáksha-yínee, *f. pl.* The twenty-seven lunar mansions, considered mythologically as the daughters of *Duksh*, and wives of the moon. *s. f.* The nymph and asterism *Rohini*; a plant (*Croton polyandrum*).

दाक्षिकुंथा dákshi-kúntha, *s. f.* A place in the north of India, in the country of *Vuhleek* or *Bulkh*.

दाक्षिकुंथीय dákshi-kúntheeyuh, *adj.* Produced or born, &c. in *Dakshikuntha*.

दाक्ष्य dákshyuh, *s. m.* Cleverness, dexterity, ability.

दाख dakh, *s. f.* A raisin, grape.

दाग dag, *s. m.* Spot, stain, mark, scar, cicatrix, blemish, freckle, speck, a mark made by burning with a hot iron, brand, stigma, cautery. *Dag churhana*, or, —*lugana*, To vilify, to defame. *Dag dena*, To mark by burning with a hot iron, to cauterize, brand, scar; to blemish. *Dagdar*, *adj.* Scarred, cauterized, spotted, marked. *Dag lugna*, To be damaged, to get a bad name. *Dag lana*, To vilify. *Dag hona*, To be cauterized or scarred.

दागना dág-na, *v. a.* To cauterize, to mark by burning with a hot iron; to fire (*a gun*, &c.).

दारुक dár-uk, *s. m.* A tooth, a tusk.

दारिम dár-im, } *s. m.* The pomegranate
दारिम्ब dar-ímb, } tree, or its fruit, (*Punica granatum*).

दारिमपूष्पक dárim-póoshpuk, *s. m.* A medicinal plant (*Andersonia rohitaka*).

दारिमप्रिय dárim-príyuh, *s. m.* The parrot, as being fond of the pomegranate.

दाढ़ darh, *s. f.* A jaw-tooth, or grinder.

दाढ़ा dár-ha, *s. f.* A large tooth, a tusk.

दाढ़िका dár-bik-a, } *s. f.* The beard. *Dar-*
दाढ़ी dár-hee, } *hee bunana*, or, —*moondhna*, *v. a.* To shave.

दात dat, *s. m.* Bountifulness.

दातन dá-tun, *s. f.* A tooth-brush made of the branch of a tree.

दातव्य dat-úvyuh, *adj.* To be given, what may or ought to be given.

दाता dá-ta, *adj.* Liberal, generous. *subst.* Giver, benefactor, donor.

दात्रि dá-tri, *adj.* A donor, a giver, giving, bestowing.

दात्र datr, *s. m.* A sort of sickle, a large knife or da.

दाद dad, *s. m.* A ringworm, Herpes.

दादमूर्दन dad-múrdun, *s. m.* A plant used to cure the ringworm (*Cassia alata*).

दादरा dád-ra, *s. m.* A kind of song.

दादा dá-da, *s. m.* Paternal grandfather; elder brother.

दादी dá-dee, *s. f.* Paternal grandmother.

दादुर dá-door, *s. m.* A frog.

दादू dá-doo, *n. prop.* A *Hindoo* founder of a sect, born in the state of *Jypoor*. *Dadoo-pun-thee*, A follower of *Dadoo*.

दाधना dádh-na, *v. n.* To burn.

दान dan, *s. m.* Act of giving or bestowing; gift, donation; a present, a special gift; alms, charity; anything demanded by law or custom, as toll, &c.; the fluid that flows from the temples of an elephant in rut. *Danputtur, s. m.* A deed of conveyance or gift. *Dan-poon, s. m.* Charity, alms.

दानधर्म dán-dhurmm, *s. m.* Almsgiving, charity; the rules for making donations.

दानपति dan-púti, *s. m.* A liberal or munificent man.

दानपत्र dan-pútr, *s. m.* A deed of conveyance or gift.

दानयोग्य dan-yógyuh, *adj.* Fit for or meriting a donation.

दानव da-núv, *s. m.* A demon, a Titan or giant.

दानशील dan-shéel, *adj.* Liberal, munificent.

दाना dána, *s. m.* Grain in general, a grain, berry, seed, corn, speck, pimple.

दानी dá-nee, *adj.* Munificent, liberal, bountiful, charitable, giving.

दानेय dan-éeyuh, *adj.* Worthy of having any thing given, or worthy or fit to be given.

दाबना dáb-na, *v. a.* To press down, to suppress, to snub; to squeeze. *Dab rukha*, To conceal, to steal and conceal; to press (*particularly with the thighs*), to retain by pressure, to gripe (*as money*). *Dab lena*, To outgrow.

दाबानल dabánul, *s. m.* Fire in a forest.

दाम dam, *s. m.* Price, the twenty-fourth part of *pysa* or pice. *s. f.* A string, a cord, a thread or rope.

दामनी dámnee, *adj.* Relating to the artemisia flower. *s. f.* A string, a rope, especially for tying cattle.

दामलिप्त dam-lípt, *s. m.* A country, the modern district of *Tumlook*.

दामा dá-ma, *s. m.* A rope, a string, a cord.

दामासाह dam-a-sáh, *n. prop.* A merchant, who dying insolvent, his effects were divided among his creditors in proportion to their claims.

दामासाही dáma-sahee, *s. f.* Proportioning, equal assessment, dividend (*of a bankrupt's property*).

दामिनी dám-in-ee, *s. f.* Lightning.

दामी damee, *s. m.* An assessment. *Damee lugana*, To assess.

दामोदर dam-ó-dur, *s. m.* A name of *Krishn*: *Yusodha* his foster mother having in vain passed the folds of a rope round his body, whilst a child, to keep him in confinement.

दाम्भिक dám-bhik, *adj.* Hypocritical. *s. m.* A hypocrite; a kind of crane (*Ardea nivea*).

दायुह dáyuh, *s. m.* Inheritance; a nuptial present.

दायुक dá-yuk, *adj.* Liberal, giving, a donor.

दायुज dáyuja, *s. m.* A dowry, portion, nuptial present.

दायभाग dayubhág, *s. m.* Partition of heritage, apportioning inheritance, &c.

दायविभाग dáyuvibhág, *s. m.* Portioning or portion of inheritance, division of property amongst different heirs.

दाया dáya, *s.* Demand, claim, plaint.

दायाद dayád, *s. m.* A son; a kinsman, near or remote; an heir.

दायादव daya-dúv, *s. m.* An heir, a kinsman.

दायादी dayádee, *s. f.* A daughter, an heiress.

दायापवर्तन dáya-puvúrttun, *s. m.* Privation, forfeiture of property.

दायित dáyit, *adj.* Condemned, sentenced; awarded, adjudged.

दार dar, } *s. f.* A wife.
दारा dá-ra, }

दारचीनी dar-chée-nee, *s. f.* Cinnamon.

दारुन da-rún, *s. m.* The clearing nut plant (*Strychnos potatorum*).

दारुद dá-rud, *s. m.* A sort of poison brought from the country named *Durud*.

दाराधीन dar-ádheen, *adj.* Dependant upon a wife, subject to her.

दारिका dá-rik-a, *s. f.* A daughter.

दारिकादान darika-dán, *s. m.* Giving a daughter in marriage.

दारिद्र da-rídr, } *s. m.* Poverty, indi-
दारिद्र्य da-ridr-yúb, } gence, wretchedness.

दारिद्री da-ríd-ree, *adj.* Poor, indigent, needy, wretched, unfortunate.

दारी dá-ree, *s. f.* A female slave taken in war.

दारु dá-roo, *s. m.* Wood, timber; a sort of pine (*Pinus devudaroo*).

दारुज dá-rooj, *adj.* Made of wood, wooden, &c.

दारुण dá-roon, *adj.* Horrible, austere, terrific, frightful, fearful ; dreadful, shocking. *s. m.* Horror, horribleness ; lead wort (*Plumbago zeylanica*).

दारनिशा **dá-roo-nísh-a,** *s. f.* A plant (*Curcuma zanthorrhizon*).

दारमय **dároo-my,** *adj.* Made of wood, woody, wooden.

दारुस्त्री **da-roo-strée,** *s. f.* A doll.

दारहरिद्रा **dároo-hurídra,** *s. f.* A kind of Curcuma (*C. zanthorrhizon*).

दारू **da-róo,** *s. f.* Spirituous liquor ; gunpowder.

दारुरा **da-róo-ra,** *s. m.* }
दारुरी **da-róo-ree,** *s. f.* } Wine, spirituous liquor.

दार्ब्य **dárh-yub,** *s. m.* Hardness, fixedness, stability.

दार्व्विका **dárv-vik-a,** }
दार्व्वी **dárv-vee,** } *s. f.* A sort of collyrium from an infusion of the *Curcuma zanthorrhizon* ; a sort of potherb.

दाल **dal,** *s. f.* Pulse, vetches. *s. m.* A sort of grain (*Paspalum frumentaceum*). *Dal gulnee kisee kee, v. n.* To have an advantage, to avail.

दाला **dá-la,** *s. f.* Colocynth.

दालिद्र **da-lídr,** *s. m.* Poverty, indigence.

दालिद्री **da-lí-dree,** *adj.* Poor, indigent.

दालिम **dá-lim,** *s. m.* The pomegranate.

दाव **dáo,** *s. m.* A bill or kind of hatchet with a hooked point ; vicissitude, turn, opportunity, stake, wager, a stroke at any game ; a bet, &c. ; a forest, a forest on fire. *Dao bandhna,* or, *—budna,* To bet, to wager.

दावना **dáo-na,** *v. a.* To thrash, to tread.

दावा **dá-wa,** }
दाया **dá-ya,** } *s. m.* The husband of a nurse.

दावाग्नि **dav-ágni,** }
दावानल **dav-ánul,** } *s. m.* The conflagration of a forest, kindled by a tempest or some other cause.

दाश **dash,** *s. m.* A servant.

दाशपूर **dash-póor,** *s. m.* A fragrant grass (*Cyperus rotundus*).   [vince.

दाशेरक **dash-ér-uk,** *s. m. Malwa,* the province.

दास **das,** *s. m.* A servant, a slave ; a *Soodr* or man of the fourth tribe ; a *Soodr* affix or appellation.

दासुतव्यूह **da-sut-vúh,** *s. m.* Slavery, servitude.

दासदासी **das-dá-see,** *s. f.* The female slave of a slave ; male and female slaves.

दासपूर **das-póor,** *s. m.* A fragrant grass (*Cyperus rotundus*).

दासा **dá-sa,** *s. m.* A piece of wood sticking out from a wall to support the thatch or *chhuppur* ; a reaping-hook.

दासी **dasee,** *s. f.* A maid-servant.

दासीपूत्र **dásee-póotr,** *s. m.* The son of a slave girl.

दासयूह **das-yúh,** *s. m.* }
दासता **das-tá,** *s. f.* } Slavery, servitude.

दाह **dah,** *s. m.* Burning, combustion, conflagration, ardour, inflammation ; morbid heat ; actual or potential cautery. *Dah dena,* To light the funeral pile. *Dah rukhna,* To grudge.

दाहक **dá-huk,** *adj.* Burning, inflammatory ; cauterising, caustic. *s. m.* A plant (*Plumbago zeylanica*).

दाहज्वर **dah-jwúr,** *s. m.* Inflammatory fever.

दाहन **dá-hun,** *s. m.* Burning, reducing to ashes ; cauterising.

दाहना **dáh-na,** *v. a.* To burn. *adj.* Right (*not left*).

दाहसुर **dah-súr,** *s. m.* A place where dead bodies are burnt.

दाहहूरुन **dah-húrun,** *s. m.* The root of a fragrant grass (*Andropogon muricatum*) ; this root being woven into screens, and kept wet, for the purpose of excluding or tempering the hot winds.

दाहिन **dá-hin-a,** *adj.* Right (*opposed to left*).

दिक् **dik,** *s. m.* Quarter, region, side ; point (*of the compass*).

दिक्पति **dik-púti,** *s. m.* A regent of a quarter of the universe, as the Sun of the east ; Saturn of the west ; Mars of the south ; Mercury of the north ; Venus of the south-east ; *Rahoo* of the south-west ; *Chundr* of the north-west ; and Jupiter of the north-east.

दिक्पाल **dik-pál,** *s. m.* A regent of a quarter of the universe, as *Indr* of the east ; *Ugni* of the south-east ; *Yum* of the south ; *Nyrit* of the south-west ; *Vuroon* of the west ; *Muroot* of the north-west ; *Koover* of the north ; and *Eesan* or *Shiv* of the north-east : this word is applicable to the *Dikputis,* as that term is to these also.

दिक्शूल **dik-shóol,** *s. m.* An inauspicious planetary conjunction, as for the Sun and Venus to be in the west, &c.

दिखलाना **dikh-lá-na,** *v. n.* To shew, exhibit, denote, direct. *Dikhlaee dena,* To appear, be apparent, seem.

दिखलावा **dikh-láwa,** *s. m.* Shew, pageantry.

दिखाई **dikháee,** *s. f.* Shewing, show, display, appearance. *Dikhaee dena,* To appear.

दिखाऊ **dikháoo,** *adj.* Comely.

दिखाना **dikhá-na,** *v. a.* To cause to see, to shew, exhibit, display, expose.

दिखाव **dikháo,** *s. m.* Display, show.

दिग् **dig,** *s. m.* Quarter, region, tract, side,

- way; (in *compos.*) -wards, as *Oottur-dig,* North-wards; point (*of the compass*).

दिग्मन dig-únt, *s. m.* The horizon.

दिग्मार dig-ún-tur, *s. m.* Space, the atmosphere.

दिग्मबर dig-úm-bur, *adj.* Naked, unclad, unclothed; dressed in, or enveloped by the atmosphere, clouds, &c. *s. m.* A *Bouddh* mendicant, wearing coloured clothes, or going naked; any mendicant not wearing clothes; a name of *Shiv,* from his being naked; a *Jyn* of the great division, which represents the images of their saints, either naked or plainly attired.

दिग्वान् dig-wán,
दिग्वार dig-wár, } *s. m.* A watchman, a guard.

दिग्शूल dig-shóol, *s. m.* The quarter to which it is deemed unlucky to travel on particular days.

दिग्गज dig-gúj, *s. m.* An elephant of a quarter or point of the compass, one of eight supposed to be attached to the north, north-east, &c., supporting the globe.

दिग्गी díg-gee, *s. f.* A large tank, or reservoir, in form of an oblong square.

दिग्विजय díg-vi-jy, *s. m.* Subjugation of an extensive country, either in arms or controversy.

दिग्विजयी díg-vi-jyee, *s. m.* A conqueror or subjugator of an extensive tract of country, or the world.

दिग्विजयक्रम díg-vijy-krúm, *s. m.* Invasion, going forth to conquer the world.

दिग्विभाग díg-vi-bhág, *s. m.* A quarter or point of the compass.

दिग्व्यापी díg-vyápee, *adj.* Spreading through all space.

दिघी dighee, *s. f.* A large tank, or reservoir, in form of an oblong square.

दिठौना dit-hóu-na, *s. m.* A patch, an artificial mole on the face.

दिढ़ dirh,
दृढ़ drirh, } *adj.* Firm, strong.

दिढ़ता dírh-ta,
दृढ़ता drírh-ta, } *s. f.* Firmness, strength.

दिढ़ाना dir-hána, *v. a.* To prove, to strengthen.

दिति díti, *s. f.* One of the wives of *Kusyup,* and mother of the *Dytyus* or infernal race, opposed to the gods.

दित्युह dít-yuh, *s. m.* A Titan, a demon or giant.

दिधि didhi, *s. f.* Firmness, stability, fixed state of mind or being.

दिन din, *s. m.* Day. *Din katna,* To pass time with difficulty. *Din ko din, rat ko rat nuh janna,* To be totally absorbed in thought or busi-ness. *Din khoolna,* To begin to prosper after adversity. *Din gunwana,* To spend carelessly, or trifle away, time. *Din churhna,* The day being far advanced; the period of a woman's menstruation being protracted. *Din churhana,* To commence any business late in the day; to eat the bread of idleness, or earn one's wages without labour. *Din dhulna, v. n.* To grow late, to decline (*the sun*). *Din diya,* Day-light. *Din dhouleh, adv.* In daylight. *Din purna,* To be unfortunate. *Din phirna,* To begin to prosper (*after adversity*). *Din budin,* Day by day. *Din bhurneh,* Expresses time spent in pain and trouble. *Din moondna,* To grow late, to close (*the day*).

दिनकर din-kúr, *s. m.* The sun.

दिन्ज्योतिस् dín-jyótis, *s. m.* Sunshine, daylight.

दिनमान din-mán, *s. m.* The length of day.

दिनाई din-áee, *s. f.* A tetter, a ringworm.

दिनांत din-ánt, *s. m.* Evening, sun-set, close of day.

दिनारम्भ din-árumbh, *s. m.* Morning.

दिनावसान dín-avusán, *s. m.* Evening, close of day.

दिनी dín-ee, *adj.* Aged (*generally applied to animals*).

दिनौंध din-óun-dha, *s. m.* Disopia or day-blindness.

दिया díya, *s. m.* A lamp. *part. past.* Given. *s. m.* A gift.

दियासलाई díya-suláee, *s. f.* A match (*for catching fire*).

दिलवाना dil-wá-na, *v. a.* To cause to give or to pay.

दिलवाली dil-wá-lee, *s. m.* An inhabitant of *Delhi.*

दिलवैया dil-wy-ya, *s. m.* One who causes to give or pay.

दिलाना dil-ána, *v. a.* To cause to give, to occasion, consign, assign, to cause to yield, to cause to give up.

दिलासा dil-á-sa, *s. m.* Comfort, consolation, encouragement, support (*of mind*).

दिलीप dil-éep, *s. m.* The name of a king and ancestor of *Ram,* the ruler of *Delhi* or *Hustinapoor.*

दिल्ली dillee, *s. f.* The name of a city, once the metropolis of *Hindoostan,* called also *Shahjehanabad.*

दिवस dív-us,
दिवा dív-a, } *s. m.* A day.

दिवाकर diva-kúr, *s. m.* The sun.

दिवातन diva-tún, *adj.* Daily, diurnal, of or belonging to the day.

दिवानिश diva-nísh, *s. m.* Day and night.

दिवान्ध **divándh**, *adj.* Being blind by day. *s. m.* An owl.

दिवामध्य **diva-múdhyuh**, *s. m.* Mid-day, noon.

दिवारात्र **diva-rátr**, *s. m.* A day and night.

दिवारात्रि **díva-rátri**, *s. f.* Day or night; a day and night.

दिवाला **diwála**, *s. m.* Bankruptcy.

दिवाली **diwálee**, *s. f.* A *Hindoo* festival, celebrated on the day of the new moon of *Kartik*, when the *Hindoos*, after bathing in the Ganges, or other river, put on their best attire, perform a *sraddh*, and at night worship *Lukshmee*, and indulge in excessive gambling. The houses and streets are illuminated at night: and in *Hindoostan*, the night is universally spent in gaming.

दिवोदास **divo-dás**, *s. m.* A king of *Benares*, and founder of the Indian school of medicine.

दिव्य **dívyuh**, *adj.* Divine, celestial; beautiful, agreeable, charming; an ordeal; an oath.

दिव्यधर्मी **dívyu-dhúrm-mee**, *adj.* Virtuous, agreeable.

दिव्यपञ्चामृत **dívyu-púnch-amrit**, *s. m.* A mixture of five articles, *ghee*, curds, milk, butter and sugar.

दिव्यरत्न **dívyu-rútn**, *s. m.* The famous gem *Chintamuni*.

दिव्यरस **dívyu-rús**, *s. m.* Quicksilver.

दिव्यवस्त्र **dívyu-vústr**, *adj.* Clothed or invested in celestial raiment.

दिव्योपपादुक **divyóp-pádook**, *adj.* Divine, celestial, of heavenly birth or being.

दिश **dísh**, *s. f.* Region, space, quarter, part.

दिशा **dish-a**, *s. f.* Side, region, quarter, point (*of the compass*).

दिशाशूल **disha-shóol**, *s. m.* A sign in the heavens, consulted on commencing a journey; the quarter towards which it is deemed unlucky to travel on particular days.

दिसना **dísna**, *v. n.* To appear, be seen, to seem. *v. a.* To see.

दिसा **dís-a**, *s. f.* Side, region, quarter, point (*of the compass*). *Disa kurna*, To travel. *Disa jana*, or, —*phirna*, To go into the fields (*for a privy*).

दिसावर **dis-áwur**, *s. m.* A climate.

दिसावरी **dis-áwur-ee**, *s. f.* A sort of *pan* or betel leaf. *adj.* Foreign (*goods*).

दिहरा **díh-ra**, *s. m.* An idol temple.

दिहली **díh-lee**, *s. f.* A threshold.

दिहूरी **díhoo-ree**, *s. f.* Threshold, door. *Dihooredar*, *s. m.* A door-keeper.

दिल्ली **díllee**, *s. f.* Name of a city, the metropolis of *Hindoostan*, called also *Shahjuhanabad*.

दीक्षा **déeksha**, *s. f.* Sacrificing, offering oblations; receiving the initiatory *muntr* or incantation.

दीक्षित **déekshit**, *adj.* Initiated; performed (*as the Deeksha ceremony*).

दीक्षितृ **deekshí-tri**, *s. m.* A spiritual father, the communicator of the initiatory *muntr* or prayer.

दीखना **déekh-na**, *v. n.* To look, to appear.

दीठ **deeth**, } *s. f.* Sight, glance, look,
दीठि **déethi**, } vision.

दीधित **déedbit**, *s. f.* A ray of light, a sun or a moon beam; light in general.

दीन **deen**, *adj.* Poor, indigent, needy, distressed; humble. *Deen-dyal*, *adj.* Merciful to the poor: *Deen-nath*, Lord of the poor: *Deen-bundhoo*, The friend of the poor: are all epithets of the Deity.

दीनचेतन **deen-chétun**, *adj.* Distressed, dejected.

दीनता **déen-ta**, } *s. f.* Poverty, indi-
दीनताई **deen-táee**, } gence; humility.

दीनमुख **deen-móokh**, *adj.* Down-cast, of melancholy aspect.

दीना **dée-na**, *v. a.* To give, to grant, to yield, afford, allow, permit, emit, let, produce, lay (*eggs*). *s. m.* Giving.

दीनार **dee-nár**, *s. m.* A weight of gold; a coin, a *dinar*.

दीनो **dée-nou**, *3d pers. sing. per. tense* of दैना To give.

दीप **deep**, *s. m.* A lamp; an island; a continent, a region or clime of the earth.

दीपक **dée-puk**, *s. m.* A light, a candle, a lamp; an aromatic seed (*Ligusticum ajwaen*); a musical mode, sung at noon in the hot weather; a kind of firework. *adj.* Making luminous; kindling, inflaming.

दीपकिट्ट **deep-kítt**, *s. m.* Lamp-black, soot.

दीपकूपी **deep-kóo-pee**, } *s. f.* The wick of
दीपखोरी **deep-khó-ree**, } a lamp.

दीपध्वज **deep-dhwúj**, *s. m.* Lamp-black, the condensed smoke or soot of a lamp.

दीपन **dee-pún**, *adj.* Inflaming, light or heat-exciting; tonic, stimulant; stimulating, exciting.

दीपपुष्प **deep-póoshp**, *s. m.* The *Champac* (*Michelia chumpaca*).

दीपमाला **deep-mála**, } *s. f.* A row of
दीपमालिका **deep-málika**, } lamps, an illumination.

दीपवृक्ष **deep-bríksh**, *s. m.* The stand or stem of a lamp, a candlestick.

दीपशिखा deep-shíkha, *s. f.* The flame of a lamp.

दीवाली deep-álee, *s. f.* The day of new moon in the month *Aswin* or *Kartik* (*September-October*), a festival with nocturnal illuminations in honor of *Kartikeyuh*; the *Deewalee*, as it is usually termed; a row or range of lamps.

दीप्त deept, *adj.* Luminous, splendid, radiant.

दीप्ति déepti, *s. f.* Light, lustre, splendour.

दीमक dée-muk, *s. f.* The white ant.

दीर्घ deergh, *adj.* Long, applied either to space or time. *s. m.* The *Sal* tree; a long vowel.

दीर्घकण्टक déergh-kún-tuk, } *s. m.* A sort
दीर्घकन्धर déergh-kún-dhur, } of crane (*Ardea nivea*).

दीर्घकाल deergh-kál, *s. m.* A long time, a long period.

दीर्घकील deergh-kéel, *s. m.* A tree (*Alangium hexapetalum*).

दीर्घकेश deergh-kesh, *adj.* Long-haired.

दीर्घजङ्गुल deergh-júng-ul, *s. m.* A kind of fish.

दीर्घजङ्घ deergh-júng-ha, *adj.* Long-thighed. *s. m.* A crane, a camel.

दीर्घजिह्व deergh-jíbha, *s. m.* A snake.

दीर्घजीव deergh-jéev, *s. m.* Long life.

दीर्घजीवी deergh-jeevee, *adj.* Living or existing a long time.

दीर्घतनु deergh-tún-oo, *adj.* Tall, long.

दीर्घदर्शी deergh-dúr- shee, *adj.* Far-seeing, provident, wise. *s. m.* A wise or learned man, a seer, a prophet.

दीर्घदृष्टि deergh-drísh-ti, *s. m.* A wise or provident man. *adj.* Wise, provident, far-seeing.

दीर्घनिद्रा deergh-nídra, *s. f.* Death.

दीर्घनिश्वास deergh-nishwás, *s. m.* A long or deep-drawn sigh.

दीर्घपक्ष deergh-púksh, *s. m.* The fork-tailed shrike.

दीर्घपत्र deergh-pútr, *adj.* Long-leaved, longifolium. *s. m.* Garlic.

दीर्घपत्रक deergh-pútruk, *s. m.* Garlic; a thorny plant; a kind of *Bassia* growing in marshy places.

दीर्घपत्रा deergh-pútra, *s. f.* A sort of Eugenia.

दीर्घपर्ण deergh-púrn, *adj.* Long-leaved, longifolium.

दीर्घपल्लव déergh-púlluv, *adj.* Having long shoots or tendrils. *s. m.* The sun plant (*Crotolaria juncea*).

दीर्घपाद deergh-pád, *s. m.* A heron.

दीर्घफल deergh-phúl, *s. m.* A plant (*Cassia fistula*).

दीर्घमूल deergh-móol, *adj.* Having a long root. *s. m.* A kind of *Bilwa* tree; a sort of sensitive plant.

दीर्घमूला deergh-móola, *s. f.* A creeper (*Echites frutescens*); a plant (*Hedysarum gangeticum*).

दीर्घमूली deergh-móolee, *s. f.* A plant (*Hedysarum alhagi*).

दीर्घरात्र deergh-rátr, *s. m.* A long period; a long night.

दीर्घरोगी deergh-rógee, *adj.* Being long ill.

दीर्घबंश deergh-búns, *adj.* Being of an ancient family.

दीर्घवर्ण deergh-vúrn, *s. m.* A long vowel.

दीर्घवृन्त deergh-vrínt, *s. m.* A plant (*Bignonia Indica*).

दीर्घवृन्तिका deergh-vrín-tika, *s. f.* A plant (*Mimosa octandra*).

दीर्घशाख deergh-shákh, *s. m.* The *Sal* tree (*Shorea robusta*).

दीर्घसूत्र deergh-sóotr, *adj.* Dilatory, slow, tedious.

दीर्घसूत्रता deergh-sóotr-ta, *s. f.* Dilatoriness, tediousness.

दीर्घसूत्री deergh-sóotree, *adj.* Dilatory.

दीर्घस्वर deergh-swúr, *s. m.* A long vowel; a long note, a minim or semibreve.

दीर्घायु deergh-áyoo, *s. m.* Long life.

दीर्घायुष् deergh-áyoos, *adj.* Long-lived. *s. m.* The silk-cotton tree (*Bombax heptaphyllum*).

दीवट dée-vut, *s. f.* A lamp-stand.

दीवली déev-lee, *s. f.* A small lamp.

दीवा dée-wa, *s. m.* A lamp.

दीवाली dee-wá-lee, *s. f.* A leather strap, a belt.

दीवि déevi, *s. m.* The blue jay.

दीसना dées-na, *v. n.* To look, to seem, to appear, to be visible. *Deeseh, adj.* Like. *adv.* Likely.

दीक्षा déek-sha, *s. f.* Sacrificing, offering oblations; receiving the initiatory *muntr* or incantation.

दीक्षित déek-shit, *adj.* Initiated; performed (*as the Deeksha ceremony*).

दीक्षित्रि deek-shítri, *s. m.* A spiritual father, the communicator of the initiatory *muntr* or prayer.

दुन्दुभी dóon-doo-bhee, *s. m.* A large kettle-drum.

दुःख dookh, *s. m.* Pain, ail, ache, grief, sorrow, affliction, distress, unhappiness; difficulty, trouble; labour, fatigue; annoyance. *Dookh* ka mara, *adj.* Afflicted. *Dookh ka hurta,* *s. m.* Dispeller of grief or pain. *Dookh-daee,* or *Dookh-danee,* *adj.* Giving or occasioning pain, troublesome, vexatious. *Dookh pana,* To be afflicted. *Dookh bhurna,* To labour, to toil, to suffer distress or trouble. *Dookh-hurun,* Anodyne. *Dookh hurta,* Dispeller of grief or pain.

दुःखकर dookh-kúr, *adj.* Causing pain ; afflicting, occasioning sorrow or trouble.

दुःखछिन्न dookh-chhínn, *adj.* Afflicted, pained, distressed.

दुःखजीवी dookh-jéevee, *adj.* Living in pain or distress.

दुःखड़ा dóokh-ra, *s. m.* Misfortunes, calamities.

दुःखदग्ध dookh-dúgdh, *adj.* Afflicted, pained, distressed.

दुःखदाई dookh-dáee, } *adj.* Giving or
दुःखदानी dookh-dánee, } occasioning pain, troublesome, vexatious.

दुःखना dóokh-na, *v. n.* To ache, pain, smart.

दुःखबहुल dookh-búhool, *adj.* Painful, distressful, abounding with trouble, &c.

दुःखभागिन् dookh-bhágin, } *adj.* Suffering
दुःखभागी dookh-bhágee, } pain, having pain as their portion.

दुःखलभ्य dookh-lúbhyuh, *adj.* To be obtained or effected with difficulty.

दुःखसागर dookh-ságur, *s. m.* Deep distress ; the world.

दुःखहन dookh-hún, *adj.* Removing pain.

दुःखाना dookhána, *v. a.* To inflict pain, to torment, to hurt, to pain.

दुःखित dóo-khit, *adj.* Pained, suffering pain ; afflicted, in distress or pain, sick.

दुःखिया dóo-khi-ya, *adj.* In distress or pain, unfortunate, poor, indigent, afflicted.

दुःखियारा doo-khi-yára, *m.* } *adj.* Afflict-
दुःखियारी doo-khi-yáree, *f.* } ed, in distress or pain, sick, sorrowful, sad, wretched, grieved.

दुःखी dóo-khee, } *adj.* Suffering pain,
दुःखिन dóo-khin, } sorrowing ; afflicted, in distress or pain ; sick ; affected.

दुःशासन dooh-shás-un, *adj.* Ungovernable, ill-managed, intractable.

दुःशील dooh-shéel, *adj.* Ill-behaved, reprobate, abandoned.

दुःषम dooh-súm, *adj.* Improper, unseasonable.

दुःषमय dooh-súmuy, *s. m.* Time of affliction, distress or trouble.

दुःसह dooh-súhuh, *adj.* Intolerable, difficult to be borne.

दुःसाध्युः dooh-sádhyuh, *adj.* Difficult, arduous, not easily accomplished.

दुःस्पर्श dooh-spúrsh, *adj.* Difficult or unfit to be touched. *s. m.* A plant (*Hedysarum alhagi*).

दुःस्पर्शा dooh-spúrsh-a, *s. f.* A prickly sort of nightshade.

दोकरा dóok-ra, *s. m.* The fourth part of a *pysa* or pice.

दोकरी dóok-ree, *s. f.* A snaffle.

दुकान doo-kán, *s. f.* A shop.

दोगुन dóo-gun, *s. m.* A second degree or tone in music.

दोगुना dóo-gun-a, }
दोगूना dóo-goon-a, } *adj.* Two-fold, double.
दोगुन dóo-gun, }

दुग्ध doogdb, *s. m.* Milk.

दोग्धता dóogdh-ta, *s. f.* Milkiness, the nature of milk.

दुग्धताम्रेय doogdh-taléeyuh, *s. m.* Milk and mangoes, mango fool.

दुग्धफेन doogdh-phén, *s. m.* The froth or skim of milk, syllabub, cream.

दुग्धफेनी doogdh-phénee, *s. f.* A small medicinal shrub so called.

दुग्धिका dóog-dhi-ka, *s. f.* A sort of Asclepias (*A. rosea*): the *Hindee* derivative *Doodhee,* is also applied to *Euphorbia hirta* and *thymifolia.*

दुग्धिन dóogdhin, } *adj.* Milky, having
दुग्धी dóogdhee, } milk.

दुग्धिनिका doog-dhín-ika, *s. f.* A plant described as a red sort of *Apang* (*Achyranthes aspera*).

दूचित dóo-chit, } *adj.* Of two minds,
दूचिता dóo-chit-a, } wavering, distracted.

दूत doot, *interj.* Away! begone! avaunt! *s. f.* Splendour, light, beauty ; spite, malice. *Doot dubuk,* Reproof, reprimand.

दूतकार doot-kár, *s. m.* } A reproof.
दूतकारी doot-káree, *s. f.* } *Dootkarna,* *v. a.* To reprove.

दूताना doo-tá-na, *v. a.* To press down ; to snub, to chide, to keep under.

दूति dóo-ti, *s. f.* Splendour, light, beauty.

दूतदेना dóot-ta-dena, *v. a.* To drive away scornfully ; to deceive, balk, cheat.

दूद्धी dóoddhee, *s. f.* A medicinal herb (*Euphorbia hirta* and *thymifolia*).

दूधार doo-dhár, } *adj. f.* Milch, giving
दूधैल doo-dhyl, } milk.

दुन्द doond, } *s. m.* A sort of
दून्दम dóon-dum, } drum, a large
दून्दुभि dóon-doo-bhi, } kettle-drum.

दुण्डमार doondoo-már, *s. m.* A sort of red worm.

दुपट्टा doo-pútta, *s. m.* A kind of veil or a piece of linen in which there are two breadths. *Dooputta tankeh sona,* To draw the sheet over one's head (*either from security and carelessness or after death*). *Dooputta hilana,* or, —*phirana, v. a.* To hold out a flag of truce, to offer to surrender (*a fort.*)

दुपहरिया doo-púh-riya, *s. f.* A kind of flower (*Pentapetes phœnicea*). *adj.* Meridian.

दुबधा dóob-dha, *s. f.* Doubt, suspense, uncertainty, dilemma.

दुबला dóob-la, *adj.* Lean, thin, poor, barren, meagre; weak.

दुबलाई doob-láee, *s. f.* ⎱ Leanness,
दुबलापन dóobla-pún-a, *s. m.* ⎰ thinness,
दुबलापा dóob-la-pa, *s. m.* ⎰ meagreness.

दुभाषिया doo-bhá-shiya, *s. m.* An interpreter.

दुभुक dóo-bhook, ⎱ *s. m.* A famine, a scarcity.
दूभुक dóo-bhuk, ⎰

दुर door, *prep.* A depreciative particle, implying pain, trouble, (*bad, difficult, ill.*) Inferiority, (*bad, vile, contemptible*). Prohibition, (*away, hold, forbear.*) It corresponds in general to the English prefixes, *in, un,* &c., as infamous, unbearable, and the like. *Door-jun, s. m.* An enemy. *Door-din,* Day of adversity. *Door-nam, s. m.* Infamy. *Door-buchun, s. m.* Abuse. *Door-bul, adj.* Weak, nerveless, faint. *Door-bulta, s. f.* Weakness, faintness.

दुरना dóor-na, *v. n.* To be hidden, or concealed, to be absent, to disappear, to lurk.

दुरदृष्ट dóor-drisht, *s. m.* Bad luck, misfortune.

दुरन्त door-únt, *adj.* Ending ill, having a bad end.

दुरभिगृह door-bhigrúh, *s. m.* A tree (*Achyranthes aspera*).

दुरभिगृहा door-bhigruhá, *s. f.* Cowach.

दुराचार door-achár, ⎱ *adj.* Wicked, depraved, following evil practices; disregarding or deviating from established practices; irreligious, profligate.
दुराचारी door-acháree, ⎰

दुरात्मा door-átma, *adj.* Vile, wicked, bad. *s. m.* A rascal, a scoundrel, a villain.

दुरधर्ष door-adhúrsh, *s. m.* White mustard.

दुराना door-ána, *v. a.* To hide, to conceal.

दुरारोह door-ároh, *adj.* Of difficult ascent. *s. m.* The palm tree; the date tree.

दुरारोहा door-aróha, *s. f.* The silk-cotton tree.

दुरालुभ door-álubh, *adj.* Difficult of attainment.

दुरालूभा door-alúbha, *s. f.* A prickly plant, the *Juwasa* (*Hedysarum alhagi*).

दुरालाप door-álap, *s. m.* Abusive or scurrilous language, abuse.

दुरित dóor-it, *adj.* Sinful, wicked. *s. m.* Sin.

दुरिष्ठ door-íshth, *adj.* Very bad, very wicked. *s. m.* Great crime, extreme wickedness.

दुरी dóo-ree, *s. f.* The two on dice.

दुरोखा doo-róokha, *adj.* Double-faced; that which is the same on both sides, not having a wrong side.

दुरोत्तर door-óottur, *adj.* Unanswerable.

दुर्ग doorg, *adj.* Difficult of access or approach, inaccessible, impervious; impenetrable, impassable; difficult of attainment, unattainable. *s. m.* A fort, a strong-hold, a *Droog* or hill fort; a pass, a defile, a difficult or narrow passage over a stream, or a mountain, or through a wood, &c.

दुर्गकर्म doorg-kúrmm, *s. m.* Enterprize, difficult undertaking.

दुर्गत dóor-gut, *adj.* Poor, indigent, distressed; suffering pain or affliction.

दुर्गति door-gúti, *s. f.* Hell; poverty, indigence; meanness, abjectness.

दुर्गन्ध door-gúndh, *adj.* Ill-smelling, ill-scented, fetid. *s. m.* Any ill-smelling substance, stink, stench. *Doorgundh ana,* To stink.

दुर्गन्धी door-gún-dhee, *adj.* Ill-smelling.

दुर्गम door-gúm, *adj.* Inaccessible, difficult of access or approach; unattainable, difficult of attainment; deep, profound.

दुर्गमता door-gum-tá, *s. f.* Depth, profundity.

दुर्गा dóor-ga, *s. f.* The goddess *Doorga,* the wife of *Shiv,* and mother of *Kartikeyuh* and *Gunes;* also called *Ooma, Bhuwanee,* and *Parvutee:* as *Doorga* she is a goddess of terrific form and irascible temper, and particularly worshipped at the *Doorga pooja,* held in Bengal in the month of *Aswin* or about October; a word; a *Hindoo* book containing the narration of the goddess *Doorga.*

दुर्गाधिकारी doorg-ádhi-káree, ⎱ *s. m.* The governor of a fort, or fortress.
दुर्गाध्यक्ष doorg-ádhyuksh, ⎰

दुर्गानवमी doorga-núvumee, *s. f.* The ninth of the light half of *Kartik,* sacred to *Doorga* as *Jugguddhatree.*

दुर्गाश्रयण doorg-áshryun, *s. m.* Taking refuge in a fortress.

दुर्घट door-ghút, *adj.* Difficult of accomplishment, arduous.

दुर्जन dóor-jun, *adj.* Bad, wicked, vile; malicious, mischief-making. *s. m.* A bad man.

दुर्जनत्वह door-jun-twúh, *s. m.* ⎫ Wicked-
दुर्जनता door-jun-táee, *s. f.* ⎭ ness, villainy.

दुर्जय dóorj-jy, *adj.* Invincible, difficult to be subdued or overcome.

दुर्जर doorj-júr, *adj.* Difficult of digestion, indigestible.

दुर्जात doorj-ját, *adj.* Inauspiciously born or produced; improper. *s. m.* Misfortune, calamity; disparity, unconformity, impropriety.

दुर्जाति doorj-játi, *adj.* Vile, wicked; low, out cast.

दुर्नीत door-néet, *adj.* Ill-behaved, ill-governed; impolitic. *s. m.* Misconduct; impolicy.

दुर्नीति door-néeti, *s. f.* Impolicy; misconduct.

दुर्दम door-dúm, *adj.* Difficult to be subdued.

दुर्दर्श doord-dúrsh, *adj.* Difficult to be seen or met with.

दुर्दशा doord-dúsh-a, *s. f.* A state of calamity or misery, or adversity.

दुर्दिन door-dín, *s. m.* A dark or cloudy day; rain or cloudy and rainy weather.

दुर्दृष्ट door-drísht, *adj.* Ill-seen (*literally or figuratively*), ill-examined, imperfectly investigated; looked at with an evil eye.

दुर्दैव doord-dyv, *s. m.* Bad luck, misfortune.

दुर्नाम door-nám, *s. m.* Infamy, a bad name, obloquy, a discredit, slander.

दुर्नामा door-náma, *s. m.* Piles or hæmorrhoides.

दुर्नामी door-námee, *adj.* Infamous.

दुर्निवार door-niwár, *adj.* Difficult to be stopped, hindered, contradicted, &c.; invincible, unconquerable.

दुर्बल doorb-búl, *adj.* Feeble, thin, emaciated; weak, impotent, infirm, faint, powerless; poor.

दुर्बलता door-bul-tá, *s. f.* Feebleness, weakness, impotence.

दुर्बुद्धि door-bóoddhi, *adj.* Silly, ignorant.

दुर्भक्ष door-bhúksh, *adj.* To be eaten with difficulty.

दुर्भगा door-bhúg-a, *s. f.* A wife not loved or liked by her husband; a bad or ill tempered woman.

दुर्भाग्यह door-bhágyuh, *adj.* Unfortunate, unlucky.

दुर्भाव door-bháo, *s. m.* Bad disposition, ill-temper, bad behaviour, ill-manners.

दुर्भिक्ष door-bhíkah, *s. m.* Dearth, famine.

दुर्मति doorm-mút-i, *adj.* Silly, ignorant, simple, a blockhead. *s. f.* Folly, foolishness.

दुर्मना doorm-mún-a, *adj.* Sad, distressed, meditating or thinking sorrowfully.

दुर्मूख doorm-móokh, *adj.* Scurrilous, foul-mouthed; hideous, ugly.

दुर्मूष dóor-moos, *s. m.* A pounder, an instrument for pounding pavements with, a rammer.

दुर्मूल्यह doorm-móolyuh, *adj.* Dear, of an exorbitant price. *s. m.* Dearness, any thing of high price or value.

दुर्मेधा doorm-médha, *adj.* Of little or contemptible understanding, dull, stupid, ignorant, uninformed.

दुर्योधन dooryódhun, *s. m.* The elder of the *Kooroo* princes, and leader of the war against his cousins, the *Pandoos* and *Krishn.*

दुर्लभ doorl-lúbh, *adj.* Difficult of attainment or acquirement, hard to be got or met with; scarce, rare; excellent, eminent; dear, beloved. *s. m.* A plant, a sort of Hedysarum.

दुर्लभा doorl-lúbha, *s. f.* A sort of prickly nightshade.

दुर्लक्षण doorl-lúkshun, *s. m.* An evil mark, an unlucky sign, an evil omen.

दुर्वचन door-vúch-un, ⎫ *s. m.* Censure,
दुर्वाच्य door-váchyuh, ⎭ abuse; any unlucky or ill-omened speech.

दुर्वृत्त door-vrítt, *adj.* Vile, wicked, leading a low or infamous life, following disreputable habits or business, a cheat, a juggler, a rogue, a blackguard, &c.

दुर्वृत्ति door-vrítti, *s. f.* Leading a disreputable life, following a degrading business, &c.; juggling, fraud.

दुर्हृदय door-hrídy, *adj.* Evil-minded, bad-hearted.

दुलकी dóol-kee, *s. f.* Trot. *Doolkee jana,* or, —*chulna, v. n.* To trot.

दुलरा dóo-lur-a, *adj.* Two-fold, of two rows or strings. *s. m.* A necklace of two rows or strings.

दुलरी dóo-lur-ee, *s. f.* A necklace of two strings.

दुलत्ती doo-lúttee, *s. f.* A kick of the two hind legs of a quadruped. *Dooluttee marna,* To wince, to kick with the two hind legs.

दुलबन्द dool-búnd, *s. m.* A turband, or the fine cloth of one.

दुलमियान dool-miyán, *s. m.* A small purse.

दुलहन dóol-hun, ⎫
दुलहिन dóol-hin, ⎬ *s. f.* A bride.
दुलहिया dool-hyya, ⎭

दूल्हा dóol-ha, }
दूल्हा dóol-ha, } *s. m.* A bridegroom.

दुलाई doo-láee, *s. f.* A sheet or covering of two breadths used by females.

दुलाना doo-lá-na, *v. a.* To agitate, toss, shake.

दुलार dóo-lár, *s. m.* Love, affection.

दुशाला doo-shá-la, *s. m.* A pair of shawls.

दूषचर dóosh-chur-a, *adj.* Acting ill, behaving wickedly.

दूषरित doosh-chúr-it, *adj.* Misbehaving, doing or designing ill. *s. m.* Evil purpose or action, misconduct, error.

दूष्कर dóosh-kur, *adj.* Difficult to be done.

दूष्कर्म doosh-kúrmm, *s. m.* Wickedness, sin.

दूष्कर्मी doosh-kúrm-mee, *s. m.* A wicked person, a sinner, a criminal.

दूष्कूल doosh-kóol, *s. m.* A low family or race.

दूष्कुलीन doosh-koo-léen, *adj.* Of a low or degraded family.

दूष्कृत doosh-krít, *s. m.* Sin, crime, guilt.

दूष्कृती doosh-krít-ee, *adj.* Wicked, an evil doer.

दूःख dooshkh, *s. m.* Pain in general.

दुष्ट doosht, *adj.* Low, vile; wicked, depraved, bad, faulty; enemy.

दुष्टचारिणी doosht-chárinee, *f.* } *adj.*Wicked.
दुष्टचारी doosht-cháree, *m.* } ed.

दुष्टचेता doosht-chét-a, *adj.* Malevolent; stupid.

दुष्टता doosht-tá, *s. f.* Wickedness, badness, depravity.

दुष्टभाव doosht-bháo, *adj.* Innately bad.

दुष्टभावता doosht-bháota, *s.f.* Wickedness, innate depravity.

दुष्टमति doosbt-múti, *adj.* Wicked, depraved.

दुष्टा dóosh-ta, *s. f.* A harlot, a wanton.

दूष्णाम doosh-nám, *s. m.* Abuse.

दुस्पूर्श doo-spúrsh, *m.* } *adj.* Not to be
दुस्पूर्शा doo-spúrsh-a, *f.* } touched, unpleasant to the touch. *s. m.* A plant (*Hedysarum alhaji*).

दूष्प्रकृति doosh-prúkriti, *adj.* Of a bad nature or disposition.

दूष्प्राप doosh-práp, *adj.* Difficult of attainment, difficult to be got or reached.

दूष्प्राप्य doosh-práp-yuh, *adj.* Remote, unattainable, difficult of approach or attainment.

दुस्त्यज doos-tyúj, *adj.* Difficult to be relinquished or parted with.

दुस्सूर doos-súr, *s. m.* Double stakes at dice, &c., playing double or quits.

दूहन dóohun, *s. m.* Milking.

दूहना dóoh-na, *v. n.* To be milked.

दूहरा dóoh-ra, *adj.* Double.

दूहराना dooh-rá-na, *v. a.* To fold, to double, to repeat, to reduplicate.

दूहाई dooháee, *s. f.* Crying out for justice, exclamation; an oath, plaint. *Doohaee tihaee kurna,* To make reiterated complaints.

दूहाना doo-há-na, *v. a.* To cause to milk.

दूहार doo-hár, *s. m.* A milker.

दूहित dóo-hit-a, *s. f.* A daughter.

दूहितुपति dóohitoo-púti, *s. m.* A son-in-law, a daughter's husband.

दूहित्रि doo-hítri, *s. f.* A daughter.

दूहेला doo-héla, *adj.* Difficult, weighty.

दूह्यु dóohyuh, *adj.* To be milked, milkable.

दूआ dóoa, *s. m.* The two or deuce at cards, dice, &c.

दूगुना dóo-goo-na, *adj.* Double, two-fold.

दूज dooj, *s. f.* The second day of a lunar fortnight.

दूजबर dóoj-bur, *s. m.* A man who marries a second wife, a bigamist.

दूजा dóo-ja, *adj.* Second, other.

दूत doot, *s. m.* A messenger or envoy, a news-carrier; an ambassador; a go-between, an angel who passes between God and man.

दूतिका dóo-ti-ka, *s. f.* A female messenger, a confidant, &c.

दूतिया dóo-tiya, *adj.* Second.

दूती dóo-tee, *s. f.* A female messenger, a confidant, a procuress, a go-between, a bawd.

दूध doodh, *s. m.* Milk; the juice or milk of certain bushes. *Doodh-adharee,* *adj.* Living on milk. *Doodh-pilaee,* *s. f.* A wet nurse. *Doodh pilana,* To suckle. *Doodh burhna,* *v. n.* To be weaned (*a child*). *Doodh bhaee,* *s. m.* A foster-brother. *Doodh bhatee,* *s. f.* A ceremony performed the fourth day after marriage, wherein the bride and bridegroom eat milk, boiled rice, and sugar, together.

दूधल doodhúl, } *adj.* Giving much milk,
दूधार doodhár, } milch.

दूधिया dóo-dhi-ya, *adj.* Milky. *s. m.* Name of several plants with milky juice. *Doodhi-ya putthur,* A white stone of which plaster is made, and utensils are formed.

दूधी dóo-dhee, *adj.* Milky, containing milky juice. *s. f.* Starch; name of several plants with milky juice, as, various species of Asclepias, Echites, Euphorbia, &c. (*Asclepias rosea, &c.*)

2 G

दूना dóo-na, *adj.* Double, two-fold.

दूब doob, *s. m.* Name of a grass (*Agrostis linearis*).

दूबरूघसरू dóohroo-ghúsroo, *adj.* Unknown, insignificant, helpless, hiding through weakness.

दूबर dóo-bur, *adj.* Weak, lean ; difficult.

दूबिया dóo-bi-ya, *s. f.* A kind of green (*colour*), grass-green.

दूभक dóo-bhuk, *s. m.* A famine, a scarcity.

दूर door, *adj.* Distant, remote. *adv.* Far, far off ; widely, deeply. *Door bhagna*, To abstain from, to abhor, abominate, avoid, shun. *Door kurna*, To remove, to dispel, to reject, to avert, to keep at a distance. *Door hona*, To be removed, to be remote, or dispelled. *Door ho*, Begone, avaunt, be off !

दूरगामी door-gámee, *adj.* Going far.

दूरता dóor-ta, *s. f.* Remoteness, distance.

दूरदर्शन door-dúrshun, *s. m.* Foresight ; long-sightedness.

दूरदर्शी door-dúrshee, *adj.* Long-sighted, far-seeing (*literally or metaphorically*). *s. m.* A pundit, a learned man, a teacher ; a prophet, a seer ; a vulture.

दूरदृश door-drísh, *s. m.* A learned man ; a vulture.

दूरदृष्टि door-dríshti, *s. f.* Long-sightedness ; foresight.

दूरवासी door-vásee, *m.* ⎫ *adj.* Residing
दूरवासिनी door-vásinee, *f.* ⎭ in a foreign land, outlandish.

दूरस्थ doorústh, *adj.* Remote, far of.

दूरीकृत dooree-krít, *adj.* Removed, placed far off.

दूरीभूत dooree-bhóot, *adj.* Remote, far off.

दूर्वा dóorvva, *s. f.* Bent grass, the *Doob* (*Panicum dactylon*).

दूल्हा dóolha, *s. m.* A bridegroom.

दूषक dóo-shuk, *adj.* Ill, low, contemptible, infamous.

दूषण dóo-shun, *s. m.* Blame, fault, defect, offence.

दूषित dóo-shit, *adj.* Calumniated, falsely accused, especially of adultery ; contaminated, corrupted, spoiled ; violated ; blamed, censured.

दूषिता dóo-shit-a, *s. f.* A girl who has been violated or deflowered.

दूषी dóo-shee, ⎫ *s. f.* The secretion or
दूषीका dóo-shee-ka, ⎭ rheum of the eye.

दूष्युः dóosh-yuh, *adj.* Reprehensible, contemptible, vile, bad.

दूसर dóo-sur, *s. m.* The second.

दूसरा dóo-sra, *adj.* Second, other, an equal, a match. *Doosreh*, In the second (*place*), secondly.

दूहिया dóo-hiya, *s. m.* A kind of fire-place.

दृक्कर्ण drik-kúrn, *s. m.* A snake, whose eyes are his ears : in the opinion of the *Hindoos*, the snake has no visible external ear.

दृग drig, *s. m.* The eye.

दृग्गोल drig-gól, *s. m.* A small circle on the axis of the earth, within the greater circle of the armillary sphere, and accompanying each planetary circle.

दृङ्मण्डल dring-múndul, *s. m.* A small circle within the great circles of the armillary sphere, accompanying each planetary circle or orbit.

दृढ drirh, *adj.* Hard, firm ; able, powerful ; bulky, massive, solid ; strong ; confirmed.

दृढकाण्ड drirh-kánd, *s. m.* A bamboo.

दृढकारी drírh-káree, *adj.* Persevering, determined.

दृढता drírh-ta, *s. f.* Firmness, hardness ; steadiness ; solidity ; strength.

दृढनिश्चय drirh-níschy, *adj.* Certain, confirmed, corroborated, undoubted.

दृढफल drirh-phúl, *s. m.* The cocoanut.

दृढबन्धिनी drirh-bún-dhinee, *s. f.* A creeper (*Echites frutescens*).

दृढभक्ति drirh-bhúkti, *adj.* Faithful, devoted.

दृढमुष्टि drirh-móoshti, *adj.* Miserly, niggardly, close-fisted.

दृढलोमा drirh-lóma, *adj.* Having coarse hair on the skin. *s. m.* A wild hog ; coarse hair, bristles.

दृढसूत्रिका drirh-sóotri-ka, *s. f.* A plant, from the fibres of which bow strings are made.

दृढसौहृद drirh-soubríd, *adj.* Firm in friendship, constant.

दृढस्कन्ध drirh-skúndh, *s. m.* A plant, a sort of Mimusops.

दृढाङ्ग drirh-áng, *adj.* Firm-bodied, hard, strong. *s. m.* A diamond.

दृढाना drirhána, *v. a.* To strengthen ; to prove.

दृढाभक्ति drirha-bhúkti, *s. f.* A faithful mistress or wife.

दृढायुध drirha-yóodh, *s. m.* A hero, one firm in battle.

दृशा drísha, ⎫ *s. f.* The eye.
दृशी dríshee, ⎭

दृशोपम drish-ó-pum, *s. m.* The white lotus (*Nelumbium speciosum*).

दृश्युः drísh-yuh, *adj.* Visible, to be seen ; beautiful, pleasing. *s. m.* (*In arithmetic*), A given quantity or number.

दृश्ययुतवुः drish-yutwúh, *s. m.* Vision, sight.

दृष्ट drisht, *adj.* Seen, visible, apparent.

दृष्टकूट drisht-kóot, *s. m.* A riddle, an enigma.

दृष्टवत् drisht-wút, } *adj.* Seeing, behold-
दृष्टवान् drisht-wán, } ing, having seen.

दृष्टान्त drish-tánt, *s. m.* An example, illustration, a parable, simile, trope.

दृष्टि drishti, *s. f.* The eye ; sight, seeing, vision, view.

दृष्टिकृत drishti-krít, *s. m.* A flower (*Hibiscus mutabilis*).

दृष्टिनिपात dríshti-nipát, *s. m.* A look, a look at or on.

दृष्टिपात drish-ti-pát, *s. m.* A look, a glance.

देआरा de-ára, *s. m.* A white-ant hill.

देखना dékh-na, *v. a.* To see, to look at, view, observe, mark, inspect, behold, perceive, experience. *Dekhna bhalna,* To see, to look at. *Dekha dekhee, s. f.* Emulation, competition, the looking at each other, or being within sight (*of objects*).

देखवैया dekh-wyya, } *s. m.* A spectator,
दिखवैया dikh-wyya, } beholder, observer, viewer.

देखा dékh-a, *s. m.* Sight, seeing.

देखादेखी dékha-dékhee, *s. f.* Emulation, competition, the looking at each other, or being within sight (*of objects*).

देगम्बर deg-úm-bur, *adj.* Naked.

देजा déj-a, *s. m.* Dowry, portion.

देजू déj-oo, *s. m.* Part of a portion or dowry.

देन den, *verbal n.* To give, giving.

देनलेन dén-len, *s. m.* Pecuniary transactions upon interest, debts and credit ; barter, traffic.

देना dén-a, *v. a.* To give, to grant, to yield, afford, allow, permit, emit, let, resign, cause, occasion, produce, to lay (*eggs*). *s. m.* Giving. *Dena pana, s. m.* Profit and loss, settling of one's affairs.

देवदार deb-dár, *s. m.* The mast tree (*Uvaria longifolia*).

देवी déb-ee, *s. f.* A *Hindoo* goddess, the wife of any deity or divine being ; the goddess *Doorga* ; a queen.

देवरा déb-ra, *adj.* Left, opposite of right.

देमारना de-márna, *v. a.* To dash on the ground, to throw, to stamp.

देय déyuh, *adj.* To be given, fit or proper for a gift.

देरा dér-a, *s. m.* A dwelling, a tent.

देव deo, *s. m.* A deity, a god ; a husband's brother ; a term or surname applicable to a *Brahmun,* also to a man of the *Kayuth* class.

देवक dév-uk, *adj.* Divine, celestial, like a deity.

देवकर्दम dev-kúrddum, *s. m.* A fragrant paste of sandal, agallochum, camphor, and safflower.

देवकांदुर dev-kán-dur, *s. m.* Water-cresses.

देवकाष्ठ dev-kásth, *s. m.* A kind of pine (*Pinus devdaroo*).

देवकिरी dev-kír-ee, *s. f.* One of the female personifications of the modes of music.

देवकी dév-kee, *s. f.* Wife of *Vusoodev,* and mother of *Krishn.*

देवकीय dev-kéeyuh, *adj.* Divine, belonging or relating to a divinity.

देवकुंड dev-kóond, *s. m.* A natural spring.

देवकुसुम dev-kóosoom, *s. m.* Cloves.

देवगान्धारी dev-gandháree, *s. f.* One of the *Raginees,* or female personifications of the modes of music.

देवगायन dev-gáyun, *s. m.* A celestial quirister.

देवगिरी dev-gír-ee, *s. f.* One of the female personifications of music.

देवगृह dev-gríh, *s. m.* A celestial or planetary sphere, the dwelling of the gods ; a temple.

देवुत्ती dev-úttee, *s. f.* A sort of gull (*Larus ridibundus*).

देवथान dev-thán, *s. f.* The second day of the moon of *Kartik shookl-puksh,* on which *Vishnoo* is said to awake from his sleep of four months.

देवतरु dev-túr-oo, *s. m.* The holy fig tree ; a tree of paradise ; the tree of plenty ; any venerable and ancient tree ; usually the place of assembling in a village.

देवता dév-ta, *s. f.* A god, a deity or divine being ; divinity.

देवतार dev-tár, *s. m.* A kind of grass (*Andropogon serratus*).

देवतीर्थ dev-téerth, *s. m.* The part of the hand sacred to the gods, the tips of the fingers.

देवत्व dev-útwuh, *s. m.* Divinity, the abstract attribute of divine being.

देवदत्त dev-dútt, *adj.* Given by the gods, god-given, or given to the gods (*a name or epithet*).

देवदानी dev-dánee, *s. f.* A sort of creeper, commonly called *Huteeghosh.*

देवदारु dev-dá-roo, *s. m.* A species of pine (*Pinus devdaroo*): in Bengal it is usually applied to the *Uvaria longifolia,* and in the peninsula to another tree (*Erythroxylon siderosylloides*).

देवधान्य deo-dhányuh, *s. m.* A sort of grain cultivated in many parts of *Hindoostan* (*Andropogon Saccharatus*).

देवधूप dev-dhóop, *s. m.* A fragrant resin (*Bdellium*) used in incense.

देवनल dev-núl, *s. m.* A kind of reed (*Arundo bengalensis*).

देवनागरी dev-nágur-ee, *s. f.* The *Devnaguree* character used by the *Hindoos* in their sacred writings.

देवनासरवा dévna-múrwa, *s. m.* A shrub (*Ocymum*).

देवनिन्दक dev-nín-duk, *s. m.* A heretic, an unbeliever, a reviler of the gods.

देवनिन्दा dev-nín-da, *s. f.* Heresy, atheism.

देवनिर्मित dev-nírm-mit, *adj.* Natural, created.

देवपथ dev-púth, *s. m.* Heaven, the firmament, the celestial path or way.

देवपूजक dev-póojuk, *s. m.* A worshipper of idols, or the gods.

देवपूजा dev-póo-ja, *s. f.* Idolatry, the worship of the gods.

देवबल्लभ dev-búllubh, *s. m.* A tree used in dying (*Rottleria tinctoria*).

देवभवन dev-bhúvun, *s. m.* The holy fig tree ; paradise ; a temple.

देवमास dev-más, *s. m.* The eighth month of pregnancy.

देवर dév-ur, *s. m.* A husband's brother, particularly his younger brother.

देवरानी dévur-ánee, *s. f.* Husband's younger brother's wife.

देवरूपी dev-róopee, *adj.* Godlike, of divine form.

देवल dévul, *s. m.* A temple where idols are worshipped, a temple, a pagoda.

देवलता dev-lút-a, *s. f.* Double jasmine.

देवली dév-lee, *s. f.* A fish-scale ; the scale or scab of small-pox ; a small lamp.

देवलोक dev-lok, *s. m.* Heaven or paradise ; any one of the seven superior worlds, from earth to the highest or *Sutyuh lok*, in opposition to those below the earth ; the particular sphere or heaven of any divinity.

देववर dev-vúr, *s. m.* A divine boon or blessing.

देववाणी dev-vá-nee, *s. f.* The language of the gods, the *Sunskrit* language.

देववृक्ष dev-vríksh, *s. m.* A tree (*Echites scholaris*) ; a tree of heaven or paradise ; a plant yielding a fragrant resin (*Bdellium*).

देववृत dev-vrút, *s. m.* Any obligation or vow of a deity.

देवस्थान dev-sthán, *s. f.* A place of idols, a temple.

देवसभा dev-súb-ha, *s. f.* An assembly of the gods.

देवस्व devúswuh, *s. m.* The property applicable to religious purposes, endowments, &c.

देवा dév-a, *s. m.* A god, a deity ; a giver. *s. f.* A flower (*Hibiscus mutabilis*) ; a plant (*Marsilea quadrifolia*).

देवागत deva-gút, *s. f.* Sudden misfortune, accident.

देवाल dewál, *s. m.* A giver.

देवालय dev-áluy, *s. m.* A division of heaven, the residence of the gods ; a temple.

देवाला dewála, *s. m.* Bankruptcy.

देवालिया dewáliya, *adj.* Bankrupt.

देवाली dewálee, *s. f.* A *Hindoo* festival (*celebrated on the day of the new moon of Kartik*). The houses and streets are illuminated all night : and in *Hindoostan* the night is universally spent in gaming.

देवालेई déwa-lé-ee, *s. f.* Barter, traffic.

देवी dév-ee, *s. f.* A goddess, the wife of any deity or divine being ; the goddess *Doorga* ; a queen ; a plant (*Trigonella corniculata*).

देवीकूट devee-kútt, *s. m.* A town, the city of *Van*, probably *Davicottu* on the Coromandel coast.

देवोत्थान devot-thán, *s. f.* A place of idols, a temple.

देवोद्यान dev-od-yán, *s. m.* A sacred grove.

देश desh, *s. m.* A country, a region, whether inhabited or uninhabited, a territory.

देशकार desh-kár, *s. m.* A musical mode sung in the morning.

देशकारी desh-káree, *s. f.* A mode of music, a *Raginee*.

देशत्याग desh-tyág, *s. m.* Abandoning one's country, emigration.

देशधर्म desh-dhúrmm, *s. m.* Local law, the law or usage of the country.

देशनिकाला desh-nikála, *s. m.* Banishment, exile.

देशव्यवहार desh-vyuvhár, } *s. m.* Local
देशव्यवहार desh-beo-hár, } usage, custom of the country.

देशभाषा desh-bhá-sha, *s. f.* The language of the country, the vernacular dialect.

देशाख desh-ákh, *s. m.* A musical mode sung at noon in the spring.

देशाचार desh-achár, *s. m.* The custom and usage of the country.

देशाटन desh-átun, *s. m.* Wandering through the country.

देशाधिपति desh-ádhi-púti, *s. m.* The ruler of a country, a governor, a king.

देशान्तर desh-ántur, }
देशावर desh-áwur, } *s. m.* A foreign country.

देशावरी desh-áwur-ee, *s. m.* A kind of betel-leaf; a kind of dove.

देशी désh-ee, *adj.* Of or belonging to a country; indigenous. *s. f.* Appearance.

देश्य désh-yuh, *adj.* Local.

देह deh, *s. f.* The body. *Deh doorana,* To conceal or cover the privities. *Deh sumbhalna,* To keep up one's spirits, to be firm, to recover one's self.

देहक्षय deh-kshúy, *s. m.* Disease, sickness.

देहच्युत deh-chyóot, *adj.* Separated or detached from the body (*as excrement or the spirit, &c.*)

देहत्याग deh-tyág, *s. m.* Voluntary death; death in general.

देहयात्रा deh-yátra, *s. f.* Death, dying.

देहरा déhra, *s. m.* A temple where idols are worshipped by *Jyns,* a *Hindoo* temple.

देहली déh-lee, *s. f.* The threshold of a door, the lower part of the wooden frame of a door, or a raised terrace in front of it.

देहवत् deh-wút, }
देहवान् deh-wán, } *adj.* Corporeal, inhabiting a body.

देहात्मवादी dehátm-vádee, *s. m.* A *Charvak,* a materialist.

देहिन् déhin, }
देही déhee, } *adj.* Corporeal, embodied, having body; living, a living being.

देहो déhoo, *2d pers. sing. imper. of* Denoun, To give.

दैजा dy-ja, *s. m.* Dowry, portion.

दैत्य dyt-yuh, *s. m.* A demon, a Titan or giant of *Hindoo* mythology.

दैत्ययुग dyt-yujóog, *s. m.* An age of the demons, consisting of 12,000 divine years, or the sum of the four yoogs or ages of men.

दैन dyn, *adj.* Diurnal, daily, relating to a day. *s. m.* Poverty, wretchedness.

दैनिक dyn-ik, *adj.* Diurnal, of or relating to a day.

दैनिकी dyn-ik-ee, *s. f.* A day's hire or wages.

दैन्य dynyuh, *s. m.* Meanness, covetousness; poverty, humbleness.

दैया dy-ya, *s. f.* A mother; the stand that children run to in playing at hide and seek.

दैयो dy-yóu, Gave, given.

दैव dyv, *adj.* Of or relating to divinity or a deity, divine, celestial, &c. *s. m.* Destiny, fate, fortune.

दैवचिन्तक dyv-chín-tuk, *s. m.* A fatalist.

दैवचिन्ता dyv-chín-ta, *s. f.* Fatalism, reliance on fate.

दैवज्ञ dyvúg-yuh, *adj.* Prophetic, foretelling, acquainted with fate. *s. m.* An astrologer.

दैवज्ञा dyv-ugyá, *s. f.* A female fortune-teller.

दैवयोग dyv-yóog, *s. m.* An age of the gods or immortals.

दैवयोग dyv-yóg, *s. m.* The occurrence of any unforeseen event, the intervention of destiny.

दैवलेखक dyv-lékhuk, *s. m.* An astrologer, a fortune-teller.

दैववाणी dyv-vánee, *s. f.* A voice from heaven.

दैवागत dyva-gút, *s. f.* Sudden misfortune, accident.

दैवात् dyv-át, }
दैवी dy-vee, } *adv.* By chance, by accident, unavoidably, accidentally, fatally; at length.

दैव्य dyv-yuh, *s. m.* Fate, fortune.

दो do, *adj.* Two. *Do-kal, s. m.* Both worlds. *Do-gundee chittee,* A fomenter of quarrels; a go-between, one who flatters both parties in a dispute. (*Allusion to a game among children, who rub a tamarind seed on one side till a mark is made, then throw it like a die : the caster wins if the mark turns up. The seed thus prepared is called chittee: and if it be fraudulently marked on both sides, so as always to win, it is called do-gundee*). *Do-ghuriya, s. m.* The space of two hours. *Do-chulla, s. m.* A roof sloping two ways. *Do-chitaee, s. f.* Suspense, absence or abstraction of mind. *Do-chitta, adj.* Wavering, doubtful, of two minds, absent or abstracted (*in mind*). *Do-jiya, or Do-jeewa, adj.* Pregnant. *Do-jee teh hona,* To be pregnant. *Do-took, adj.* Two-pieced; clear, plain, clean. *Do-took hona,* To be adjusted, to be completed. *Do-dhara, adj.* Two edged (*sword*). *Do-purta, adj.* Double, of two folds. *Do-pulka,* (*having two eyelids*), *s. m.* A kind of pigeon; a kind of stone for a ring. *Do-puhur, s. f.* Mid-day, noon. *Do-puhriya, s. m.* A kind of flower (*Pentapetes phœnicea*). *adj.* Meridian. *Do-puhree, adj.* Of noon or mid-day. *Do-putta (two-breadthed), s. m.* A kind of veil or a piece of linen in which there are two breadths. *Do-putta tankeh sona,* To draw the sheet over one's head (*either from security and carelessness or after death*). *Do-putta hilana, or, —phirana, v. n.* To hold out a flag of truce, to offer to surrender (*a fort*). *Do-bhashiya, s. m.* An interpreter. *Do-rung, adj.* Piebald, of two colours; hypocrite. *Do-runga, adj.* Capricious, double-dealer. *Do-rungee, s. f.* The property of having two colours; duplicity, hypocrisy, double-dealing, deceit, capriciousness. *adj.* Of two colours, capricious, double-faced. *Do-lura, s. m.* A necklace of two strings. *Do-lohee, s. f.*

A scimitar made of two plates of steel joined together. *Do-soota*, *s. m.* A kind of cloth, the threads of which are double. *Do-sera*, *s. m.* A weight of two seers.

दोंकना dónk-na, *v. n.* To growl.

दोंकी dónk-ee, *s. f.* Bellows.

दोंर donr, *s. m.* A species of snake.

दोऊ dó-oo, *adj.* Both.

दोक dok, *s. m.* A two year old foal.

दोगारा do-gá-ra, *adj.* Twice, doubled; a musket carrying two balls.

दोजीवा do-jéewa, *adj.* Pregnant.

दोझा dó-jha, *adj.* Married to a second wife.

दोदना dód-na, *v. a.* To deny.

दोना dó-na, *s. m.* A flower (*a species of Artemisia*); leaves folded up in the shape of a cup for holding betel, flowers, sweetments, &c.

दोनाली do-ná-lee, *adj.* Double-barrelled (*a gun*).

दोनों dó-non, *adj.* Both. *Donon wukt milneh*, Expresses the evening twilight, when day and night meet.

दोपस्ता do-pústa, *adj.* Pregnant.

दोबर dó-bur, *adj.* Double.

दोबे dó-beh, *s. m.* A title of *Brahmuns*.

दोभयान do-bhy-án, *adj.* Two-fisted, ambidextrous, strong.

दोमुंहा do-móonha, *adj.* Having two mouths. *s. m.* A serpent which has two mouths (*Amphisbena*).

दोल dol, *s. m.* Swinging; a festival on the 14th of *Phalgoon*, the swinging of the juvenile *Krishn*; a litter, a swinging cot, a *dooly*; a swing. *Dol-mal kurna*, *v. a.* To wave, swing, undulate; hesitate.

दोलायमान dolayumán, *adj.* Swinging, being swung; doubting, perplexed, vacillating.

दोलिका dó-lik-a, *s. f.* A swing.

दोष dosh, *s. m.* Fault, blame, vice, defeat, blemish; sin, offence, transgression, crime; disorder of the humours of the body, or defect in the functions of bile, circulation, or wind. *Dosh hona*, To be sick after child-birth, from neglect of regimen.

दोषकल्पन dosh-kúlpun, *s. m.* Reprehending, condemning.

दोषग्राही dosh-grá-hee, *adj.* Malicious, malignant, censorious.

दोषन dósh-un, *s. m.* Objection, blame.

दोषना dósh-na, *v. a.* To accuse, to blame.

दोषवत dosh-wút, ⎫ *adj.* Faulty, defective;
दोषवान dosh-wán, ⎭ wicked.

दोषिक dó-shik, *adj.* Faulty, defective, bad.

दोषिन dó-shin, ⎫ *adj.* Faulty, defective;
दोषी dó-shee, ⎭ bad, wicked; criminal.

दोसाद do-sád, *s. m.* A low caste of *Hindoos*, residing in and about *Patna*, hog-keepers.

दोसी dó-see, *s. m.* Thick sour milk; a *Moosulman* milkman.

दोहरिका do-húr-ika, *s. f.* The *Prakrit* metre, called *Doha*; a stanza of four lines, containing thirteen and eleven syllabic instants alternately.

दोहत्तर do-húttur, *s. f.* A slap or pat with both hands. [son.

दोहता dóh-ta, *s. m.* Son-in-law, daughter's

दोहती dóh-tee, *s. f.* Daughter's daughter.

दोहद dó-hud, *s. m.* Wish, desire; the longing of a pregnant woman, especially as a sign of impregnation.

दोहदलक्षण dóhud-lúkshun, *s. m.* The foetus, the embryo, sometimes confounded with the womb.

दोहदवती dóhud-wút-ee, ⎫ *s. f.* A pregnant
दोहदान्विता dóhud-anvít-a, ⎭ nant woman longing for any thing.

दोहन dó-hun, *s. m.* A milk vessel, a milk pail; milking.

दोहना dóh-na, *v. a.* To milk.

दोहनी dóh-nee, *s. f.* A milk vessel, a milk pail.

दोहर dó-hur, *s. m.* A double sheet; a sheath.

दोहरा dóh-ra, *s. m.* A distich. *adj.* Double.

दोहराव doh-ráo, *s. m.* Repetition, doubling, reduplication.

दोहुलवती dóhul-wút-ee, *s. f.* A pregnant woman longing for any thing.

दोहा dóha, *s. m.* A couplet, distich.

दोहाई do-háee, *s. f.* A crying out for justice, exclamation; an oath, plaint (*crying twice alas!*) *Dohaee tihaee kurna*, To make reiterated complaints.

दोहान do-hán, *s. m.* A young bullock, a steer.

दोहिन dó-hin, *m.* ⎫ *adj.* A milker.
दोहिनी dó-hin-ee, *f.* ⎭

दौन doun, *s. m.* Fire.

दौंगरा dóung-ra, *s. m.* A heavy shower.

दौंजा dóunj-a, *s. m.* A scaffold.

दौर dour, *s. f.* Run, incursion, attack, assault, endeavour, struggle, effort, race, running, course, career, military expedition.

दौरधूप dour-dhóop, *s. f.* Labour and fatigue, toil, bustle. *Dourdhoop kurna*, To use great labour and exertion for the accomplishment of any object, to bustle, to toil.

दौड़ना dóur-na, *v. n.* To run, to gallop, course, drive, assault, rush, invade; toil.

दौड़ना धूपना dóurna dhóopna, *v. n.* To run violently, to use great exertion, to toil.

दौरा dóu-ra, *s. m.* A large basket (*without a lid*); a highwayman (*who robs on horseback*).

दौरक dou-rák, *s. m.* A racer, a runner.

दौरादौरी dóura-dóuree, *s. f.* Running, contest in running, race, hurry.

दौराना dou-rá-na, *v. a.* To cause to run or gallop, to run, drive, impel, actuate, expedite, speed, despatch.

दौराह dou-rá-ha, *s. m.* A messenger, runner, courier, guide.

दौरी dóu-ree, *s. f.* A drawn game at *Choupur*.

दौना dóu-na, *s. m.* A flower (*Artemisia Indica*); leaves folded up in the shape of a cup for holding betel, flowers, sweetmeats, &c.

दौरा dóu-ra, *s. m.* A large basket (*without cover*).

दौरात्म्य dour-átmyuh, *s. m.* Wickedness, depravity.

दौरी dóu-ree, *s. f.* A basket (*without a lid*); a rope with which a string of cattle are bound together.

दौर्गन्धि dour-gún-dhi, *s. f.* Fœtor, bad smell.

दौर्जन्य dour-jún-yuh, *s. m.* Wickedness, depravity, vileness.

दौर्वल्य dour-vúlyuh, *s. m.* Weakness, debility.

दौर्भाग्य dour-bhág-yuh, *s. m.* Ill luck, misfortune.

दौहित्र dou-hítr, *s. m.* A daughter's son.

दौहित्री dou-hít-ree, *s. f.* A daughter's daughter.

द्युतिला dyóo-til-a, *s. f.* A plant (*Hemionites cordifolia*).

द्यूत dyóot, *s. m.* Gaming, playing with dice, or any thing not possessing life.

द्यूतकार dyoot-kár, *s. m.* The keeper of a gaming house; a gambler.

द्यूतपूर्णिमा dyóot-póornim-a, *s. f.* The day of full moon in the month *Kurtik* (*October-November*), the night of which is spent in games of chance, in honor of the goddess of fortune, *Lukshmee*.

द्यूतसभा dyóot-súbha, *s. f.* A gaming house or assembly.

द्यूताधिकारी dyóot-adhikáree, *s. m.* The keeper of a gaming house.

द्योरानी dyó-ránee, *s. f.* Husband's younger brother's wife.

द्रविड़ drúv-ir, *s. m.* A man of an out-cast tribe, descended from a degraded *Kshuttree*.

द्रविड़ी drúv-ir-ee, *s. f.* One of the *Raginees* or female personifications of music.

द्रविणाशन drúvin-náshun, *s. m.* A plant (*Hyperanthera morunga*).

द्रव्य drúv-yuh, *s. m.* Wealth, property; substance, matter, thing; elementary substance, nine kinds of which are reckoned: viz. earth, water, fire, air, æther, time, space, soul, and intellect; a drug, a medicament, any thing used in medicine.

द्रव्यवत् druv-yuwút, } *adj.* Rich, wealthy.
द्रव्यवान् druv-yuwán, }

द्रव्यसंचय drúv-yu-súnchuy, *s. m.* Accumulation of property.

द्रव्यार्जन drúv-yárj-jun, *s. m.* Gain, acquisition, acquiring property.

द्राक्षा dráksha, *s. f.* A grape.

द्राघिमा drá-ghim-a, *s. m.* Length.

द्रावक drávuk, *adj.* Diuretic; solvent, discutient.

द्रावकर drav-kár, *s. m.* A kind of borax.

द्रावण drá-wun, *s. m.* The clearing nut; fusing.

द्राविका drá-vik-a, *s. f.* Saliva.

द्राविड़ drá-vir, *s. m.* A country, properly the coast of Coromandel, from Madras to Cape Comorin, or the country in which *Tumul* is spoken; a native of *Dravir* or *Dravid*; a Brahmun of *Dravir*, or rather of the south, five *Dravirs* being specified, or Dravir, Kurnat, Goojjerat, Muharashtr, and Telung.

द्राविड़ुक drá-vir-uk, *s. m.* Zedoary (*Curcuma zerumbet*); black salt.

द्राक्षा dráksha, *s. f.* A grape.

द्रुकिलिम droo-kíl-im, *s. m.* A tree, a sort of pine (*Pinus devdaroo*).

द्रुत droot, *adj.* Quick or swift; flown, escaped, run away.

द्रुतपद droot-púd, *s. m.* A quick pace or step. *adv.* Quickly.

द्रुम droom, *s. m.* A tree in general; a tree of *Swurg* or paradise.

द्रुमनख droom-núkh, *s. m.* A thorn, or claw of trees.

द्रुमव्याधि droom-vyádhi, } *s. m.* Lac, the
द्रुमामय droom-ámuy, } animal dye, or disease of trees.

द्रुमेश्वर droom-ésh-wur, *s. m.* The palm tree, or sovereign of trees.

द्रुसल्लुक droo-súlluk, *s. m.* A tree (*Chironjia sapida*).

द्रेकान drek-kán, *s. m.* The regent of one-third of a planetary sign, the *Decanus* of European astrology, whence the word is probably derived.

द्रोण dron, *s. m.* A measure of capacity, the same as an *Adhuk*; a measure of four *Adhuks*; in common use, a measure of thirty-two seers, or rather more than sixty-four lbs. avoirdupois; the sixteenth part of a *Kharee*, or forty-eight gallons; a proper name, the military preceptor of the *Pandoos*; a raven, or perhaps the carrion crow.

द्रोणकाक dron-kák, *s. m.* A raven.

द्रोणमुख dron-móokh, }
द्रोणीमुख dro-nee-móokh, } *s. m.* The capital of a district, the principal of four hundred villages.

द्रोह droh, *s. m.* Spite, malice, hatred, mischief, trespass, injury; offence, wrong; rebellion.

द्रोहचिन्तन droh-chín-tun, *s. m.* Injurious design, malice prepense; the wish, thought, or attempt to injure.

द्रोहाट dro-hát, *s. m.* A sort of metre, the *Doha* or stanza of *Hindee* poetry.

द्रोही dro-hee, }
द्रोहिया dró-hiya, } *adj.* Hurting, harming, endeavouring to hurt, mischievous, spiteful, malicious, malignant, inimical; rebellious.

द्रौणिकी dróu-nik-ee, *s. f.* A vessel holding a *dron* by measure.

द्वन्द्व dwund, *s. m.* A pair, a couple (*male and female especially*).

द्वन्द्वद्वह dwun-dwúh, *s. m.* A pair, a brace; a couple of animals, or male and female; union of the sexes or coupling.

द्वन्द्वचारी dwúndwuh-cháree, *s. m.* The ruddy goose, flying in couples.

द्वयाग्नि dwuyág-ni, *s. m.* A plant (*Plumbago zeylanica*).

द्वादश dwá dush, *adj.* The twelfth.

द्वादशी dwá-dush-ee, *s. f.* The twelfth day of the half month.

द्वापर dwá-pur, *s. m.* The third of the four *Yoogs* or great periods, comprising 864,000 years; doubt, uncertainty.

द्वार dwar, *s. f.* A door, a gate; a means, an expedient, a medium or way by which any thing takes place or is effected.

द्वार dwar, *s.* A door, a gate, or rather the door or gateway, a passage, an entrance; a way, a means, a medium or vehicle.

द्वारका dwár-ka, *s m. Dwarka*, the capital of *Krishn*, supposed to have been submerged by the sea, but represented by a small island off the north part of the *Malabar* coast.

द्वारपाल dwar-pál, *s. m.* A warder, a door-keeper.

द्वारबलिभुज dwar-wúli-bhóoj, *s. m.* The *Vuk*, a sort of crane (*Ardea nivea*).

द्वारा dwá-ra, *adv.* By means of.

द्वारिन् dwá-rin, }
द्वारी dwá-ree, } *s. m.* A porter, a warder, a door-keeper.

द्वि dwi, *dual only, adj.* Two.

द्विगुण dwí-goon, *adj.* Twice, two times; multiplied by two, doubled.

द्विगुणीकृत dwí-goonee-krít, }
द्विगुणीभूत dwí-goonee-bhóot, } *adj.* Doubled, increased, augmented.

द्विज dwij, *adj.* Twice-born. *s. m.* A man of either of the three first classes, a *Brahmun*, a *Kshuttree*, or a *Vys*, whose investiture with the characteristic string, at years of puberty, constitutes, religiously and metaphorically, their second birth.

द्विजकूटसित dwij-kóotsit, *s. m.* A tree (*Cordia myxa*).

द्विजदास dwij-dás, *s. m.* A *Soodr* or man of the fouth and servile tribe.

द्विजन्मा dwi-júnma, *adj.* Twice-born, regenerate. *s. m.* A Brahmun.

द्विजप्रिया dwij-príya, *s. f.* The moon-plant (*Asclepias acida*).

द्विजसेवक dwij-sévuk, *s. m.* A man of the fourth and servile tribe, a *Soodr*.

द्विजा dwij-a, *s. f.* A plant (*Siphonanthus Indicus*); gum olibanum.

द्विजायनी dwij-áyun-ee, *s. f.* The characteristic thread or cord which designates the three first classes of the *Hindoos*.

द्वितीय dwit-éeyuh, *adj.* Second.

द्वितीया dwit-éeya, *s. f.* A wife, according to the ritual, a woman wedded after the ceremony prescribed by the *Veds*, a second self as it were; the second day of the fortnight.

द्वितीयाभा dwit-eeyábha, *s. f.* A scitamineous plant (*Curcuma zanthorrhiza*). [ways.

द्विधा dwíd-ha, *adv.* Of two kinds, in two

द्विधातु dwi-dhá-too, *adj.* Having two natures.

द्विप dwip, *s. m.* A plant (*Mesua ferrea*).

द्विपथ dwi-púth, *s. m.* A place where two roads meet.

द्विपद dwi-púd, *adj.* Two-footed. *s. m.* A biped, including four genera, gods, demons, men, and birds.

द्विमुख dwi-móokh, *s. m.* A serpent. *s. f.* A leech.

द्विमुखाहि dwi-mookh-áhi, *s. m.* A sort of serpent (*Amphisbæna*).

द्विरुक्त dwir-óokt, *adj.* Repeated, said twice; said or told in two ways.

द्विरुक्ति dwir-óokti, *s. f.* Tautology, repetition.

द्विरूप dwi-róop, *adj.* Of two forms.

द्विविध dwi-vídh, *adj.* Of two kinds, in two ways.

द्विशुफ dwi-shúph, *s. m.* Any cloven-footed animal.

द्विसप्ताह dwi-suptáh, *s. m.* A fortnight.

द्विहृदया dwi-hrídya, *s. f.* A pregnant woman.

द्वीप dweep, *s. m.* An island, any land surrounded by water; the word is hence applied to the seven grand divisions of the terrestrial world, each of these being separated from the next by a peculiar and circumambient ocean: the seven *Dweeps*, reckoning from the central one, are *Jumboo, Koos, Pluksh, Salmulee, Krounch, Sak,* and *Pooshkur :* the central *Dweep,* or the known continent, is again portioned into ten divisions, likewise termed *Dweeps :* viz., *Kooroo, Chundr, Vursoon, Soumyuh, Nag, Koomarika, Gubhustiman, Tamrapoorn, Kuservo,* and *Indr.*

द्वीपी dwéepee, *adj.* Islander. *s. m.* A tiger.

द्वेष dwesh, *s. m.* Enmity, hate, hatred.

द्वेषी dwésh-ee, *adj.* Hostile, inimical, adverse, obnoxious. *s. m.* An enemy.

द्वेषयुह् dwésh-yuh, *adj.* Hateful, detestable.

द्वेषयुता dwésh-yuta, *s. f.* Aversion, dislike, detestableness.

द्वैत dwyt, *s. m.* Duplication, doubling or being doubled; duality, in philosophy, the assertion of two principles, as the distinctness of life and soul, spirit and matter, god and the universe.

द्वैतवादी dwyt-vádee, *s. m.* A philosopher who asserts two principles.

द्वैध dwydh, *adj.* Two-fold, of two sorts.

द्वैधीकरण dwydhee-kúrun, *s. m.* Making two, separating, disuniting.

द्व्यर्थ dwuyúrth, *adj.* Having two senses, meaning two things; having two objects. *s. m.* A two-fold meaning, double-entendre.

ध

ध dhuh, The nineteenth consonant in the *Naguree* alphabet; it is the aspirate of the preceding letter, and expressed by *dh,* as in mud-house, but a soft dental.

धंधका dhúndh-ka, *s. m.* A kind of drum.

धंधकी dhúndh-kee, *s. f.* A small drum.

धंधला dhúndh-la, *s. m.* Deception, trick.

धंधलाना dhundh-lá-na, *v. a.* To trick.

धंधा dhún-dha, *s. m.* Business, employment, work, avocation, occupation.

धंधार dhun-dhár, *adj.* Solitary.

धंधारी dhun-dhár-ee, *s. f.* Solitude.

धंधाला dhun-dhá-la, *s. f.* A procuress, a bawd.

धंसना dhúns-na, *v. n.* To be pierced, stuck into, to be penetrated, to be thrust into, to sink, to enter, run into.

धुकधुक dhúk-dhuk, *s. m.* } Palpitation,
धुकधुकी dhúk-dhuk-ee, *s. f.* } perturbation, apprehension.

धुकधुकाना dhuk-dhuk-ána, *v. n.* To palpitate.

धुकरुहजाना dhúk-ruh-jána, *v. n.* To be founded at a sudden disaster.

धुकेल dhuk-él, *s. m.* Shove, push, thrust. *Dhukel dena,* To push, to precipitate.

धुकेलना dhuk-él-na, *v. a.* To shove, to push, to jostle.

धुकेलू dhuk-él-oo, *s. m.* A pusher.

धुक्कमधुक्का dhúkkum-dhúkka, *s. m.* Shoving and jostling, justling.

धुक्का dhúk-ka, *s. m.* A shove, jolt, push, jog. *Dhukka dena,* To shove, push, jolt.

धुगरा dhúg-ra, } *s. m.* A paramour. *Dhug-*
धुग्गर dhuggúr, } *gur-baz, s. f.* An adulteress. *Kazee,* or, *Bukhshee ka dhuggur,* Independent of judge or general (*an expression of pride*).

धुगोलना dhug-ól-na, *v. n.* To roll, to wallow.

धुचुकना dhuchúkna, *v. n.* To give way, sink (*as a bog, slough, &c.*).

धुज dhuj, *s. m. f.* Shape, form; attitude, posture; figure, appearance, person. *Dhuj pulutna,* To change one's attitude in sword-playing, &c.

धुजभंग dhuj-bhúng, *s. m.* Impotency.

धुजा dhúj-a, *s. f.* A slip of cloth, a standard, a ship's pendant, a flag, a banner. *s. m.* Attitude, posture.

धुजीला dhuj-ée-la, *adj.* Well-looking, personable.

धुज्जी dhúj-jee, *s. f.* A slip of cloth or paper, a shred. *Dhujjian oorana,* To disgrace, to expose one to infamy. *Dhujjian kurna,* To tear to pieces.

धुर dhur, *s. m.* The body.

धुरुक dhúr-uk, *s. f.* Palpitation; fear.

धुरुकना dhúr-uk-na, *v. n.* To palpitate; to blaze.

धुरका dhúr-ka, *s. m.* Fear, doubt, suspense; palpitation; thunder.

धुरकाना dhur-ká-na, *v. a.* To affright, to frighten.

धड़धड़अडना dhúrdhur-júlna, *v. n.* To

burn with great fury. *Dhurdhur ruhna, v. n.* To flutter, to palpitate.

धुरधुराना dhurdhur-ána, *v. n.* To flutter, to palpitate.

धुरुक्का dhur-úkka, *s. m.* The sound of hammering, &c. ; frightening, alarming ; a crowd.

धुरुल्ला dhurúlla, *s. m.* The sound of hammering ; frightening, alarming, bullying, bravado ; a crowd.

धुरा dhúr-a, *s. m.* A party ; a weight. *Dhura bandhna,* To make up a standard to weigh by, with bricks or any thing else ; as, by having one weight (*of a pound suppose*) it is doubled, quadrupled, and so on, till the weight requisite is obtained.

धुराका dhur-áka, *s. m.* A crash, report of a gun, explosion.

धुरी dhúr-ee, *s. f.* A line, particularly the black lines made on the lips with *missee* ; a weight of five seers ; the quantity weighed at once.

धुरूआ dhúr-oo-a, ⎫ *s. m.* A bird, a kind
धुरूवा dhúr-wa, ⎰ of *myna* or jay.

धुत dhut, *s. f.* A word used to encourage elephants.

धुतीनगर dhut-éen-gur, *adj.* Ignoble, spurious.

धुतूरा dhut-óo-ra, *s. m.* A plant (*Datura fastuosa,* or *thorn-apple*).

धुतूरिया dhut-óo-riya, *adj.* A cheat, an impostor.

धुधुकना dhúdh-uk-na, *v. n.* To blaze.

धुधुच्छर dhudh-úch-chhur, *s. m.* In versification, certain words or letters, which are reckoned by poets to be unlucky. (*The letters,* ह *h,* ग *g,* न *n, in the beginning of a verse ;* र *r,* ज *j,* स *s, in the middle ; and* क *k,* ट *t,* ग्यु *gyu, in the end of a sentence are of this description*).

धुन dhun, *adj.* Fortunate. *interj.* Well done ! what happiness ! how fortunate. *s. m.* Fortune, prosperity, an expression of praise, thanks, riches, property of any description, thing, substance, wealth, opulence. *Dhun-putr, s. m.* An inventory of property. *Dhunman,* or, *Dhunwan, adj.* Affluent, rich, wealthy. *Dhun manna,* To thank. *Dhun-andh, adj.* Blinded with wealth or riches, purse-proud.

धुनंजय dhun-un-júy, *s. m.* Fire ; a tree (*Pentaptera arjuna*).

धुनक dhún-uk, *s. f.* Embroidery, lace.

धुनकटी dhun-kút-ee, *s. f.* The season for cutting rice.

धुनगर्बित dhun-gúrbbit, *adj.* Purse-proud.

धुनत्तर dhun-úttur, *adj.* Opulent, powerful.

धुनतृष्णा dhun-trishna, *s. f.* Covetousness.

धुनद् dhun-úd, *adj.* Beneficent, liberal, who gives away property, &c.

धुनदुंड dhun-dúnd, *s. m.* Fine, amercement.

धुनदर्प dhun-dúrp, *s. m.* Pride of wealth.

धुनदायी dhun-dáyee, *adj.* Liberal, munificent. *s. m.* A benefactor, a donor.

धुनंतुर dhun-ún-tur, ⎫ *n. prop.* The
धुनंतरी dhun-ún-tur-ee, ⎰ name of a physician in the court of *Indr. adj.* Powerful, strong, wealthy.

धुनपति dhun-púti, *s. m.* The god of riches, *Koover.*

धुनप्रिय dhun-príyuh, *adj.* Fond of wealth.

धुनप्रिया dhun-príya, *s. f.* A vegetable (*Ardisia solanacea*).

धुनमद् dhun-múd, *adj.* Proud, inflated with the pride of wealth.

धुनलोभ dhun-lóbh, *s. m.* Desire of wealth, greediness, avarice.

धुनवंत dhun-wúnt, ⎫
धुनवान dhun-wán, ⎬ *adj.* Wealthy, affluent, rich.
धुनाढ्य dhun-ádh-yuh, ⎭

धुनव्यय dhun-vyúy, *s. m.* Expenditure, extravagance.

धुनसंपत्ति dhun-súm-putti, *s. f.* Accumulation of wealth.

धुनसू dhun-sóo, *s. m.* The fork-tailed shrike.

धुनहरी dhun-húr-ee, *adj.* A thief, a pilferer. *s. f.* A sort of perfume commonly called *Chor.*

धुनहा dhun-há, *s. m.* A cultivator of rice. *adj.* (*Of a country*) in which rice is cultivated.

धुनहीन dhun-héen, *adj.* Poor, reduced to poverty.

धुनाधिकारी dhún-adhi-káree, *s. m.* An heir.

धुनाधिकारिणी dhún-adhi-kárinee, *s. f.* An heiress.

धुनार्जन dhun-árj-jun, *s. m.* Acquisition of property.

धुनार्थी dhun-árthee, *adj.* Seeking for wealth, covetous, miserly.

धुनाशा dhun-ásha, *s. f.* Thirst of wealth, longing after riches.

धुनाश्री dhun-ásh-ree, *s. f.* One of the musical modes.

धुनिक dhún-ik, *adj.* Pious. *s. m.* A creditor.

धुनिया dhún-iya, *s. m.* Coriander seed (*Coriandrum sativum*). *Dhuniyeh kee khopree men panee pilana, v. a.* To harass, to disturb, to tantalize.

धनिष्ठा dhun-ísh-tha, *s. f.* The twenty-fourth *Nukshutr* or lunar mansion; the dolphin; it comprises four stars and is figured by a drum or tabor.

धनी dhún-ee, *adj.* Rich, wealthy, fortunate; an epithet of the Deity. *s. m.* Owner, proprietor. *s. f.* A beam.

धनु dhún-oo, *s. m.* A bow; the sign *Sagittarius.*

धनुक dhún-ook, *s. f.* A bow. *Dhunook-dharee,* *s. m.* An archer. *Dhunook-dhur,* *s. m.* An archer, armed with a bow, an epithet of *Krishn. Dhunook-dhura,* *s. m.* A ceremony in honor of *Shiv. Dhunook-baeh,* *s. f.* Tetanus.

धनुकी dhún-oo-kee, *s. f.* The bow with which cotton is cleaned. *adj.* Arched.

धनुःपट dhun-oo-pút, *s. m.* A tree (*Buchanania latifolia*).

धनुःशाखा dhun-oo-shákha, *s. f.* A plant, from the leaves of which a tough thread is extracted, of which bow-strings were formerly made (*Sanseviera zeylanica*).

धनुर्धर dhun-oor-dhúr, *s. m.* An archer, a bowyer, one armed with a bow.

धनुर्धारी dhun-oor-dháree, *s. m.* An archer, a bowyer.

धनुर्माला dhun-oor-mála, *s. f.* A plant, from the leaves of which bow-strings were made.

धनुर्लता dhun-oor-lút-a, *s. f.* The moon-plant.

धनुष dhún-oosh, *s. m.* A bow.

धनेष dhun-ésh, *s. m.* The name of a bird with a very large bill (*Buceros*).

धनेश्वर dhun-ésh-wur, *s. m.* *Koover,* the Indian Plutus.

धन्नासेठ dhunna-séth, *adj.* Successful; true speaking.

धन्नोटा dhun-nó-ta, *s. m.* Cross beams that sustain the supports of thatch.

धन्य dhún-yuh, *adj.* Fortunate, well-fated, lucky; good, virtuous. *interj.* Well done! what happiness! how fortunate! an expression of praise, worthy of greatness or glory!

धन्याक dhun-yák, *s. m.* A plant bearing a small pungent seed used by the *Hindoos* as a condiment (*Coriandrum sativum*).

धन्वन्तरि dhun-wún-tur-i, *s. m.* The physician of the gods, said to have been produced at the churning of the ocean; a celebrated physician who appears to have been the founder of the *Hindoo* medical school.

धन्वयवास dhun-wuy-vás, *s. m.* A plant (*Hedysarum alhagi*).

धन्वा dhún-wa, *s. m.* A country scantily supplied with water, a desert, a waste; a firm spot, land, ground.

धनूी dhún-wee, *s. m.* An archer, a bowman; a name of *Urjoon;* a tree (*Pentaptera arjuna*); a wag, a wit, a sharp or shrewd man.

धप dhup, *s. m.* Voice, sound, noise, crack.

धपाड़ dhup-ár, *s. m.* Running, race.

धप्पा dúp-pa, *s. m.* A stain on cloth; a slap, box, thump, blow; deception.

धब्बा dhúb-ba, *s. m.* A stain on cloth.

धमक dhúm-uk, *s. f.* Noise of footsteps over-head, thumping, &c.; threat, threatening, awe. *s. m.* A blacksmith.

धमकना dhúm-uk-na, *v. n.* To throb, to shoot (as the pain of a head-ache); to palpitate, to thump; to flash, to glimmer.

धमका dhúm-ka, *s. m.* Great heat; threatening, chiding; thump, noise produced by the fall of any heavy body.

धमकाना dhum-ká-na, *v. a.* To threaten, menace, chide, snub, cow, daunt.

धमकाहट dhum-ká-hut, } *s. f.* Threaten-
धमकी dhúm-kee, } ing, threat, menace.

धमधमाना dhum-dhum-ána, *v. n.* To make a noise (with the feet by running about over-head).

धमधूसर dhum-dhóo-sur, *adj.* Corpulent.

धमाका dhum-áka, *s. m.* A kind of cannon carried on an elephant.

धमाचौकरी dhum-a-chóukree, *s. f.* Noise, tumult, bustle.

धमाधम dhum-a-dhúm, *s. m.* The sound of stamping, thumping.

धमार dhum-ár, *s. m.* A chime or time in music; running through fire on religious occasions (among *Mahomedan mendicants*).

धमाल dhum-ál, *s. m.* A chime or time in music; a kind of song which is sung during the *Holee,* or festival held at the approach of the vernal equinox; running through fire on religious occasions (among *Mahomedan fukeers*).

धमोका dhum-ó-ka, *s. m.* A kind of tambourin.

धमाल dhum-mál, *s. m.* Running through fire on religious occasions (among *Mahomedan mendicants*).

धरन dhúr-un, *s. f.* A beam; accent, tone; the navel (or rather the umbilical vein, perhaps the aorta or cœliack artery, as it is said to pulsate) which is supposed by the *Hindoo* physicians to be occasionally removed from its place, and thus to occasion various morbid symptoms. This is called *dhurun dignee,* or *naf tulna,* or, —*ookhurna,* and the cure is attempted by friction of the belly. *s. m.* Holding, possessing, having; a measure or weight; a breast, a female breast.

धरनी dhúr-nee, *s. f.* The earth. *Dhurnee-dhur,* *s. m.* A mountain; a name of *Sheshnag,* a fabulous serpent, said to uphold the earth ; a name of *Vishnoo*, in the form of a tortoise and of a boar.

धरणीकन्द dhur-nee-kúnd, *s. m.* An esculent root or bulb.

धरणीसूता dhurnee-soóta, *s. f.* A name of *Seeta*, the wife of *Ram*, earth-born, being turned up from the soil by a plough, as *Junuk* was ploughing a spot to prepare it for a sacrifice.

धरता dhúr-ta, *s. m.* A debtor.

धरती dhúrtee, *s. f.* The earth. *Dhurtee ka phool*, *s. m.* A mushroom.

धरधमकना dhur-dhum-úkna, *v. n.* To proceed with tumultuous rapidity ; to move with violence, to rush.

धरन dhúr-un, *s. f.* A beam.

धरना dhúr-na, *v. a.* To place, put down, lay, assume, put on, apply ; to give in charge ; to seize, catch, lay hold of, hold, keep. *Dhurna dena*, or, —*bythna*, A mode of extorting payment of a debt or compliance with any demand.

धरनी dhúrnee,
धरनेत dhur-nét, } *s. m.* A dun.

धरवाना dhur-wá-na, *v. a.* To cause to place, &c.

धरा dhúr-a, *s. f.* The earth.

धराना dhur-á-na, *v. n.* To owe.

धरित्री dhur-ít-ree, *s. f.* The earth.

धरीचा dhur-ée-cha, *s. m.* The second husband of a *Hindoo* widow among the lower classes : this connection, being contrary to the spirit of the *Hindoo* institutions, is formed without any particular ceremony, except marking the bride's head with minium.

धरोहर dhur-ó-hur, *s. f.* A trust, a charge, any thing given in charge, a deposite.

धर्त्ता dhúrt-ta, *s. m.* A debtor.

धर्म dhurmm, *s. m.* Virtue, moral and religious merit, according to the law and the *Veds*, justice ; usage, practice, the customary observances of caste, sect, &c. ; duty, especially that enjoined by the *Veds* ; fitness, propriety ; innocence ; any peculiar or prescribed practice or duty ; thus, giving alms, &c., is the *dhurm* of a householder ; administering justice, the *dhurm* of a king ; piety, that of a *Brahmun* ; courage, that of a *Kshuttree* ; law.

धर्मकार्य dhurm-káryuh, *s. m.* Any indispensable act of religion.

धर्मक्रिया dhurm-kríya, *s. f.* Righteous conduct, acting according to law ; any religious act.

धर्मक्षेत्र dhurm-kshétr, *s. m.* A plain in the north-west of India near *Delhi*, the scene of the great battle between the *Kooroos* and *Pundoos*.

धर्मगृहन dhurm-grúhun, *s. m.* Observance of moral or religious institutes, accepting or following the law.

धर्मचारिणी dhurm-chá-rin-ee, *s. f.* A virtuous woman, an honest wife.

धर्मचारी dhurm-chá-ree, *adj.* Virtuous, moral, dutiful.

धर्मचिन्तन dhurm-chín-tun, *s. m.* }
धर्मचिन्ता dhurm-chín-ta, *s. f.* } Virtuous reflection.

धर्मज्ञ dhurm-úgyu, *adj.* Knowing one's duty, conversant with virtue.

धर्मज्ञान dhurm-gyán, *s. m.* Knowledge of moral, legal, and religious duty.

धर्मण dhúrm-un, *s. m.* A sort of tree ; a kind of large snake, not poisonous.

धर्मत्व dhurm-út-wuh, *s. m.* Morality, piety ; inherent nature, peculiar property, &c.

धर्मद्रोही dhurm-dró-hee, *adj.* Wicked.

धर्मध्वजी dhurm-dhwúj-ee, *s. m.* A religious hypocrite or impostor, one who makes a livelihood by assumed devotion.

धर्मनिबन्ध dhurm-ni-búndh, *s. m.* Piety, virtue.

धर्मनिबन्धी dhurm-ni-bún-dhee, *adj.* Pious, holy, engaged in or conducive to virtue.

धर्मनिष्पत्ति dhurm-nish-pútti, *s. f.* Duty, moral or religious observance, discharge or fulfilment of duty.

धर्मपत्नी dhurm-pút-nee, *s. f.* A man's first wife and of the same class.

धर्मपुत्र dhurm-pútr, *s. m.* Glomerous fig tree (*Ficus glomerata*).

धर्मपुत्र dhurm-poótr, *s. m.* A name of the *Pandoo* prince *Yoodhisthir* ; one so considered, as a son for piety or duty.

धर्मप्रधान dhurm-prudhán, *adj.* Eminent in piety.

धर्मभागिनी dhurm-bhá-gin-ee, *s. f.* A virtuous and amiable wife.

धर्ममय dhurm-múy, *adj.* Moral, righteous, made up or replete with virtue, &c.

धर्ममूल dhurm-móol, *s. m.* The foundation of *Hindoo* law and religion (*the Veds*).

धर्मराज dhurm-ráj, *s. m.* A name of *Yum*, the regent of the dead ; of *Yoodhisthir* ; also of *Urjoon* ; a king in general.

धर्मरोधी dhurm-ró-dhee, *adj.* Illegal, immoral.

धर्मवत् dhurm-wút, *m.* }
धर्मवती dhurm-wút-ee, *f.* } *adj.* Virtuous, pious, upright, just.
धर्मवान् dhurm-wán, *m.* }

धर्मविवाह dhurm-viváh, *s. m.* Legal marriage of five sorts, as the *Brahma*, *Dyva*, *Arsha*, *Gandhurb*, and *Prajaputya*.

धर्मविवेचन dhurm-viv-échun, *s. m.* Judicial investigation.

धर्मशाला dhurm-shála, *s. m.* A court of justice, a tribunal.

धर्मशास्त्र dhurm-shástr, *s. m.* The body or code of *Hindoo* law; any work on the subject.

धर्मशील dhurm-shéel, *adj.* Virtuous, just, pious.

धर्मसंहिता dhurm-súng-hit-a, *s. f.* A code of laws, especially the work of some saint or divine person, as *Menu*, &c.

धर्मसभा dhurm-súb-ha, *s. f.* A tribunal, a court of justice.

धर्मात्मा dhurm-át-ma, *s. m.* A saint, a pious or virtuous person.

धर्माधर्मपरीक्षा dhurm-adhurm-puréeksha, *s. f.* Ordeal by drawing lots or slips of black and white paper.

धर्माधिकारी dhurm-adhi-káree, *s. m.* A judge.

धर्माध्यक्ष dhurm-adhyúksh, *s. m.* A magistrate, a judge, &c.

धर्मानुसार dhurm-anoosár, *s. m.* Conformity to law or virtue, course or practice of duty.

धर्मावतार dhurm-avutár, *s. m.* An incarnation of justice, used as a term of respect.

धर्मासन dhurm-ásun, *s. m.* The seat of the judge, the bench.

धर्मिष्ठ dhurm-íshth, *adj.* Very pious or virtuous.

धर्मी dhúr-mee, *adj.* Virtuous, pious, just.

धर्मोपदेश dhurm-óp-desh, *s. m.* Moral or religious instruction.

धर्मोपदेशक dhurm-op-déshuk, *s. m.* A *gooroo* or spiritual preceptor.

धव dhúv-uh, *s. m.* A husband; a tree (*Grislea tomentosa*).

धवल dhúv-ul, *adj.* White; handsome, beautiful. *s. m.* White (*the colour*); a tree (*Grislea tomentosa*); an inferior mode of music.

धवलपक्ष dhuv-ul-púksh, *s. m.* The fortnight of the moon's increase.

धवलमृत्तिका dhúvul-mríttika, *s. f.* Chalk.

धवलित dhúv-ul-it, *adj.* White, whitened.

धवलीकृत dhuv-ul-ee-krít, *adj.* White, made white.

धवलीभूत dhuv-ul-ee-bhóot, *adj.* Become white.

धवा dhúv-a, *s. m.* A caste of *palkee* bearers who are *Moosulmans*.

धसकना dhús-uk-na, *v. n.* To give way, to sink (*as a quagmire or slough*).

धसन dhús-un, *s. f.* A quagmire; the state of being thrust into.

धसना dhús-na, *v. n.* To be pierced, stuck into, to be penetrated, to be thrust into, to sink, to enter, run into.

धसम dhús-um, *s. m.* A swamp.

धसान dhus-án, } *s. m.* A slough, bog,
धसाव dhus-áo, } quagmire, a swamp.

धसाना dhus-ána, *v. a.* To cause to be thrust into, to sink.

धांगर dhán-gur, *s. m.* A caste whose business it is to dig the earth.

धांधना dhándh-na, *v. a.* To gormandize.

धांधुल dhan-dhúl, *s. f.* Wrangling, subterfuge, trick, cheating, juggle, chicanery. *Dhandhulpuna, s. m.* Chicanery, juggle, cheating, subterfuge.

धांधली dhándh-lee, *s. m.* A wrangler.

धांयधांय dháen-dháen, *s. f.* The report of cannon heard at a distance; a sound made by burning any thing.

धांविया dhan-wy-ya, *s. m.* A thrasher.

धांसना dháns-na, *v. n.* To cough (*a horse*).

धांसी dháns-ee, *s. f.* A cough (*of a horse*).

धार dháeh, *s. f.* A nurse.

धारमारना dháeh-márna, *v. n.* To cry, to groan. *Dhaeh mar rona,* To cry, to groan, to weep bitterly.

धक dhak, *s. f.* Pomp, glory; renown, fame; fear, terror; a tree (*Butea frondosa*); a post.

धाकर dhá-kur, *s. m.* A mongrel.

धाखा dhá-kha, *s. m.* A swing; a tree (*Butea frondosa*).

धागा dhá-ga, *s. m.* A thread. *Dhaga dalna, v. a.* To quilt.

धाटी dhá-tee, *s. f.* Advancing towards or confronting an enemy.

धार dhar, *s. f.* }
धारा dhá-ra, *s. m.* } A crowd, a multitude.

धात dhat, } *s. m.* Ore, metal, mineral;
धातु dhá-too, } *Sunskrit* root. *s. f.* Semen virile.

धातकी dhát-kee, *s. f.* A tree (*Grislea tomentosa*).

धातु dhá-too, *s. m.* A principle or humour of the body, as phlegm, wind and bile; any constituent part of the body, as blood, flesh, &c.; a primary or elementary substance, viz. earth, water, fire, air, and *Ukas* or atmosphere; the property of a primary element, odour, flavour, colour, touch, and sound; an organ of sense; a mineral, a fossil; a metal; a grammatical root.

धातुकाशीश dhátoo-kashéesh, *s. m.* Red sulphate of iron.

धातुप dha-tóop, *s. m.* The alimentary juice or chyle.

धातुभृत dhá-too-bhrít, *adj.* Promoting the animal secretions.

धातुमाचिक dhátoo-mákshik, *s. m.* A mineral substance, a sulphuret of iron.

धातुमारिणी dhátoo-márinee, *s. f.* Borax.

धातुराजक dhátoo-rájuk, *s. m.* Semen, the seminal fluid.

धातुवल्लभ dhátoo-vúllubh, *s. m.* Borax.

धातुवादी dhátoo-vádee, *s. m.* An assayer, a miner, a mineralogist.

धातुवैरी dhátoo-vyree, *s. m.* Sulphur.

धातुशेखर dhátoo-shékhur, *s. m.* Green sulphate of iron, or green vitriol.

धातुपुष्प dha-too-púl, *s. m.* Chalk.

धात्री dhá-tree, *s. f.* A mother, a foster-mother, a nurse; the earth; Emblick myrobalan.

धात्रीपुष्पिका dhátri-póosh-pika, *s. f.* A tree (*Grislea tomentosa*).

धात्रिका dhá-tri-ka, *s. f.* Emblick myrobalan.

धान dhan, *s. m.* The rice-plant, or rice before it is separated from the husk.

धाना dhá-na, *v. n.* To run, to make haste; to toil and labour, to drudge; to worship.

धानी dhá-nee, *s. f.* A kind of rice in the husk; a light green colour.

धानुक dhá-nook, *s. m.* A bowman, an archer; a watchman armed with a bow; a caste of hill people using bows and arrows.

धानुष्क dhá-nooshk, *s. m.* A bowyer, an archer.

धानुष्का dha-nóosh-ka, *s. f.* A tree (*Achyranthes aspera*).

धान्य dhán-yuh, *s. m.* Corn in general, but especially rice (*Oriza sativa*); coriander, a measure equal to four sesamum seeds.

धान्यराज dhan-yuráj, *s. m.* Barley.

धान्यवत dhan-yuwút, *adj.* Abounding in corn, having abundance of it.

धाप dhap, *s. f.* A foot measure; as far as a man can run without taking breath.

धाभाई dha-bháee, *s. m.* Foster-brother.

धाम dham, *s. m.* A dwelling, a house, a place.

धामनी dhám-nee, *s. f.* Any tubular vessel of the body.

धामवत dham-wút, *adj.* Splendid, luminous, eminent, exalted, illustrious.

धामा dhá-ma, *s. m.* A large cane basket.

धामिन dhá-min, *s. m.* A kind of serpent (*which is said to suck cows and to be harmless*); a kind of wood; a kind of bamboo.

धाएह dháeh, *s. f.* A nurse.

धाएहमारना dháeh-márna, *v. n.* To cry, to groan. *Dhaeh mar rona*, To cry, to groan, to weep bitterly.

धार dhar, *s. f.* A line, lineament; stream, current; edge (*of a sword, &c.*); sharpness. *Dhar pur marna*, or, *Dhar marna*, To contemn, to despise.

धार dhar, *s. m.* Debt; slight sprinkling rain; end, bound, a line or limit.

धारक dhá-ruk, *s. m.* A debtor.

धारन dhá-run, *s. m.* Holding, having, keeping, maintaining, bearing, upholding, sustaining, assuming.

धारना dhár-na, *s. f.* Continuance in rectitude, keeping in the right way; fortitude, firmness, steadiness, resolution; mental retention, memory. *v. a.* To hold, bear, have, keep, place, owe, sustain, support, uphold; to pour (*water*).

धारनी dhár-nee, *s. f.* Any tubular vessel of the body.

धारन dhá-run, *verbal n. s.* Holding, bearing, sustaining, upholding, assuming, keeping.

धारना dhár-na, *v. a.* To hold, bear, have, keep, place, owe, sustain, support, uphold; pour (*water*).

धारा dhá-ra, *s. f.* A stream, a current.

धारासार dha-ra-sár, *s. m.* A heavy fall of rain, a large drop or shower.

धारित dhá-rit, *adj.* Upheld, assumed, sustained.

धारी dhá-ree, *s. f.* A line, lineament; a small buttress; a plant used in dying (*Lythrum fruticosum : Grislea tomentosa*); (*used in comp.*) bearing, holding, having, wearing. *Dhareedar, adj.* Lined, striped, streaked.

धार्मिक dhár-mik, *adj.* Virtuous, pious, just.

धाव dhao, *s. m.* A plant (*Grislea tomentosa*).

धावक dhá-wuk, *adj.* Running, going, swift, expeditious; cleaning, what cleans or cleanses.

धावत dhá-wut, *adj.* Running, going quickly.

धावन dhá-wun, *s. m.* Going, motion; cleansing, purifying.

धावना dháo-na, *v. n.* To range, roam, rove; to run, run at, attack; to trudge; to worship.

धावनिका dháo-ni-ka, *s. f.* A prickly nightshade.

धावनी dháo-nee, *s. f.* A sort of creeping plant (*Hedysarum lagopodioides*).

धावमान dhao-mán, *adj.* Running, going, swift, expeditious.

धावा dhá-wa, *s. m.* Running; over-running an enemy's country, attack, assaulting; a stock, a store; crowding together; name of a tree. *Dhawa marna,* To go expeditiously from a distant place, to run on or about.

धावित dhá-wit, *adj.* Purified, cleaned, cleansed; gone, gone or run away; run to, advanced to or against.

धाह dhah, *s. f.* Cry, noise. *Dhah marna,* To cry, to groan.

धिक dhik, *adv.* An interjection of reproach or menace, or of contempt and aversion, fie, shame, &c.

धिक्कार dhik-kár, *s. m.* Disrespect, reproach, censure, contempt; curse, anathema.

धिक्कारना dhik-kár-na, *v. a.* To reproach, to curse.

धिक्कारी dhik-ká-ree, *adj.* Damned, cursed.

धिंगाना dhing-ána, *s. m.* Clamour, oppression.

धिमचा dhím-cha, *s. m.* A kind of tamarind.

धिया dhíya, *s. f.* A daughter.

धिरकार dhir-kár, *s. m.* Disrespect, reproach, censure, contempt; curse, anathema.

धिरकाल dhir-kál, *s. m.* A caste of people who work on bamboos.

धिराज dhir-áj, *s. m.* A potentate, a monarch, an emperor.

धिराना dhir-ána, *v. a.* To threaten, to bully.

धी dhee, *s. f.* Understanding, intellect.

धींग dheeng, ⎫
धींगड़ा dheeng-ra, ⎭ *s. m.* A paramour.

धींगाधांगी dhéenga-dhángee, *s. f.* Teasing.

धीदा dhée-da, *s. f.* A virgin, a maid.

धींद्रिय dhéen-driyuh, *s. m.* An intellectual organ, as the mind, the eye, ear, nose, tongue, and skin.

धीम dheem, *s. m.* Slowness; gentleness.

धीमत dhée-mut, *m.* ⎫ *adj.* Sensible,
धीमती dhée-mút-ee, *f.* ⎭ wise, learned.

धीमर dhée-mur, *s. m.* A fisherman; a caste of fisherman.

धीमा dhée-ma, *adj.* Slow, lazy; gentle, mild, temperate, abated, allayed. *Dheemeh dheemeh, adv.* Gently, softly.

धीमाई dhee-má-ee, *s. f.* Slowness, tardiness; gentleness, mildness.

धीमान dhee-mán, *adj.* Sensible, wise, learned.

धीर dheer, *adj.* Resolute, firm, steady, patient, sedate. *s. m.* Resolution, firmness, patience, deliberateness, sedateness.

धीरज dhee-ruj, *s. m.* ⎫ Patience, sedate-
धीरता dhéer-ta, *s. f.* ⎭ ness, gravity; firmness, deliberateness.

धीरत्व dheer-út-wuh, *s. m.* Firmness, fortitude.

धीरा dhée-ra, *adj.* Gentle, patient, deliberate, sedate, grave.

धीरिया dhée-riya, *s. f.* A daughter.

धीवर dhée-wur, *s. m.* A fisherman; a caste of fishermen.

धीवरी dhée-wur-ee, *s. f.* A fisherman's wife; a sort of harpoon for catching fish with.

धीवान dhée-wán, *adj.* Intelligent, renowned, famous.

धीशक्ति dhée-shúkti, *s. f.* An intellectual faculty or power of the understanding, as attention, comprehension, &c.

धूंगार dhoon-gár, *s. m.* Seasoning with which any thing is fried.

धूंगारना dhoon-gár-na, *v. a.* To season with spices.

धूंध dhoondh, *s. m.* Dim-sightedness; haziness, mistiness.

धूंधकार dhoondh-kár, *s. m.* Darkness, obscurity, mistiness.

धूंधराना dhoondh-rá-na, *v. n.* To be dull, misty.

धूंधला dhóondh-la, *adj.* Foggy, misty, dull.

धूंधलाई dhoondh-láee, *s. f.* Dimness, cloudiness, mistiness.

धूंधेला dhoon-dhél-a, *adj.* Knavish.

धूंवा dhóon-wa, *s. m.* Smoke.

धूकड़पूकड़ dhóokur-póokur, *s. f.* Palpitation, agitation.

धूकड़ी dhóo-kur-ee, *s. f.* A purse.

धूकधूकी dhóok-dhook-ee, *s. f.* An ornament worn on the breast; perturbation, anxiety, apprehension; consideration, reflection.

धूत्ता dhóot-ta, *s. m.* Trick, deception. *Dhootta dena,* To deceive.

धून dhoon, *s. f.* Inclination, propensity, application, diligence, perseverance, ardour, ambition, assiduity; pains in the bones; sound, musical sound.

धूनकना dhoo-núk-na, *v. a.* To card or comb (*cotton*).

धूनवी dhóon-wee, *s. f.* The bow with which cotton is carded.

धूनि dhóo-ni, *s. f.* Sound, musical sound.

धूनिया dhóo-ni-ya, *s. m.* A carder, a comber (*of cotton*).

धूनिहाव dhoo-ni-háo, *s. m.* Pains in the bones.

धूनेहा dhoo-néha, *s. m.* A carder of cotton, a comber.

धूनधूमार dhoon-dhoo-már, *s. m.* An insect (*Coccinella*).

धूनना dhóon-na, *v. a.* To comb, to card (*cotton*); to beat (*the head*). Sir dhoonna, To beat one's head with vexation, &c.

धूबला dhóobla, *s. m.* A petticoat, or any loose garment for covering the legs.

धूमला dhóom-la, *adj.* Blind, dim-sighted.

धूमलाई dhoom-lá-ee, *s. f.* Gloominess.

धूर dhoor, *s. m.* Beginning; limit, end. Dhoor srh dhoor tuk, From beginning to end.

धूरपद dhóor-pud, *s. m.* A kind of song.

धूरसांझ dhoor-sánjh, *s. f.* Dusk, twilight; evening.

धूरियाना dhoo-ri-yána, *v. a.* So throw dust; to winnow, to sift.

धूरी dhóo-ree, *s. f.* An axletree.

धूलवाना dhool-wá-na, *v. a.* To cause others to wash.

धूलाई dhoo-lá-ee, *s. f.* Washing; price of washing.

धूलाना dhoo-lá-na, *v. a.* To cause to wash.

धूलेंदी dhoo-lén-dee, ⎫ *s. f.* The first day
धूलंदी dhoo-lyn-dee, ⎰ of the month Chyt, on which it is the practice to scatter ashes.

धूवका dhóov-ka, *s. f.* The introductory stanza to a song, forming afterwards the burthen of each verse.

धूसतूर dhoos-tóor, *s. f.* Thorn-apple (*Datura fastuosa*).

धूस्सा dhóos-sa, *s. m.* Flannel, a kind of coarse stuff made of shawl-wool.

धूआँ dhóon-an, ⎫ *s. m.* Smoke.
धूवा dhóon-wa, ⎰

धूंधूर dhoon-dhúr, *s. f.* Fogginess, dulness.

धूंधरा dhoon-dhúr-a, *adj.* Foggy, dull, gloomy.

धूंधूंकार dhoon-dhoon-kar, ⎫ *s. m.* Heavy
धूंधूंकाल dhoon-dhoon-kál, ⎰ rain obscuring the whole heaven; gloomy weather, gloominess; desolateness; name of a game.

धूंवारा dhoon-wá-ra, *s. m.* A chimney.

धूंवाराना dhoon-wa-rána, *p. a.* To smoke.

धूनक dhóo-nuk, ⎫ *s. m.* Rosin, resin.
धूना dhóo-na, ⎰

धूनी dhóo-nee, *adj.* Persevering. *s. f.* Smoke; fumigation by way of exorcising one possessed; or, as a medical application; a fire lighted by a Hindoo mendicant, over which he sits, imbibing the smoke, by way of penance. It is often practised by them in the manner of dhurna, to

extort compliance with their demands: hence, Dhoonee dena, To dun, to importune; to smoke. Dhoonee lugane, To insist obstinately, or to persevere in a demand; fumigation by way of exorcising one possessed; or, as a medical application. Dhoonee lena, To inhale smoke, or undergo fumigation.

धूप dhoop, *s. m.* Incense, the aromatic vapour that proceeds from the combustion of any fragrant gum or resin, the use of which is authorized by the shasters; the perfume burnt by Hindoos at the time of worshipping. *s. f.* Sunshine, the heat of the sun. Dhoop-danee, *s. f.* A pot for keeping dhoop.

धूपकाला dhoop-kála, *s. m.* The hot weather.

धूपना dhóop-na, *v. a.* To smear with pitch, to pitch, to perfume.

धूपवृक्ष dhoop-bríksh, *s. m.* A species of pine (*Pinus longifolia*).

धूपांग dhoop-áng, *s. m.* Turpentine.

धूम dhoom, *s. m.* Smoke. *s. f.* Tumult, bustle, noise, fame, rumour, report.

धूमकेतु dhoom-kétoo, *s. m.* A comet or falling star.

धूमधाम dhoom-dhám, *s. f.* Pomp, parade, tumult, bustle, noise.

धूमप्रभा dhoom-prúbha, *s. f.* A supposed division of hell, the hell of smoke.

धूमरा dhóom-ra, ⎫ *adj.* Of a purple colour,
धूमला dhóom-la, ⎬ of the colour of smoke,
धूमा dhóo-ma, ⎰ compounded of black and red, purple.

धूर dhoor, *s. f.* Dust.

धूरधानी dhoor-dhá-nee, *s. m.* A tall stout fellow. *s. f.* A firelock (*without a chamber*).

धूरसंझा dhoor-sún-jha, *s. m.* Evening.

धूरादेना dhóora-déna, *v. a.* To deceive, to wheedle, to take in.

धूरियाबेला dhóoriya-béla, *s. m.* A species of jasmine.

धूरियामुल्लार dhóoriya-mullár, *s. m.* A musical mode (*particularly sung in the beginning of the rains*).

धूर्त dhoort, *adj.* Fraudulent, crafty, cunning, sly, dishonest, knavish, &c.; mischievous, injurious. *s. m.* A gamester, a rogue, a cheat.

धूर्तता dhoort-tá, *s. f.* Knavery, roguery, knavishness, cunning, slyness.

धूल dhool, ⎫ *s. f.* Dust.
धूलि dhóoli, ⎰

धूलुक dhóo-luk, *s. m.* Poison.

धूलिगूछछुक dhóoli-góoch-chhuk, *s. m.* The red vegetable powder thrown about at the spring festival called the Hoolee.

धूसना dhóos-na, v. a. To ram, to stuff; to butt (as horned cattle).

धूसर dhóo-sur, adj. Grey, of that colour. s. m. Grey (the colour); any thing of a grey tint.

धूसाधासी dhóosa-dhásee, s. f. Cramming and stuffing.

धूहा dhoo-há, s. m. A scarecrow.

धृत dhrit, adj. Possessed, held, contained.

धृतराष्ट्र dhrit-rásh-truh, s. m. A proper name, the father of Dooryodhun, and uncle of the Pandoo princes; a good king.

धृतात्मा dhrit-átma, adj. Firm, steady, calm, collected.

धृति dhríti, s. f. Steadiness, firmness; a metre, a stanza of four lines of eighteen syllables each.

धृतिमत dhriti-mút, m. } adj. Firm,
धृतिमती dhriti-mút-ee, f. } steady,
धृतिमान dhriti-mán, m. } calm.

धेंगामूष्टि dhénga-móoshti, s. f. Fisticuffs.

धेनू dhén-oo, s. f. A milch cow, one that has lately calved.

धेरा dhér-a, adj. Squint-eyed.

धेला dhél-a, s. m. Half a pice or pysa.

धैर्य dhyrj, s. m. Steadiness, firmness.

धैर्यकलित dhyrj-kúl-it, adj. Steady, calm, assuming firmness or composure.

धैवत dhy-wut, s. m. The sixth note of the gamut.

धोआ dhó-a, s. m. A present of fruit.

धोई dhó-ee, s. f. Pulse which has been soaked previous to boiling, a mash.

धोंधा dhón-dha, s. m. A small mound of earth; (met.) a pot-belly, a large belly.

धोंवाला dhon-wá-la, s. m. A chimney.

धोक dhok, s. f. Salutation, bowing down to idols.

धोकर dho-kúr, adj. Robust, athletic.

धोखा dhó-kha, s. m. Deceit, deception, delusion, blunder; disappointment; doubt, hesitation; a scarecrow; any thing imaginary, not real, a vapour resembling water at a distance, (French, mirage). Dhokha khana, To be deceived. Dhokha dena, To deceive.

धोड़ dhór, s. m. A sort of snake, a kind of water-snake.

धोता dhó-ta, adj. False, treacherous, perfidious.

धोती dhó-tee, s. f. A cloth worn round the waist, passing between the legs and fastened behind.

धोना dhó-na, v. a. To wash. s. m. Washing.

धोप dhop, s. f. A kind of sword.

धोब dhob, s. m. Washing.

धोबिन dhó-bin. s. f. A washer-woman, a washerman's wife.

धोबी dhó-bee, s. m. A washerman.

धोयेंदीदुकार dhoyéndee-dukár, s. f. A sour belch.

धोरुनि dhor-úni, s. f. Tradition.

धोरा dhó-ra, s. m. Name of a medicine.

धोवा dhó-wa, adj. Washed.

धोसा dhó-sa, s. m. A coarse kind of shawl.

धौ dhou, s. f. A kind of wood (Lythrum fruticosum; Grislea tomentosa).

धौन dhoun, s. m. A weight of 20 seers. pron. Whether. [asthma.

धौंक dhounk, s. f. Breathing, panting; the

धौंकना dhóunk-na, v. a. To blow with the bellows, &c.

धौंकनी dhóunk-nee, s. f. Bellows.

धौंज dhounj, s. f. Thought, consideration, contemplation, reflection.

धौंताल dhoun-tál, adj. Rich, wealthy; strong, stout; bold; vicious, mischievous.

धौंताली dhoun-tá-lee, s. f. Riches; strength; courage; viciousness, mischievousness.

धौंस dhouns, s. m. Assault, threatening.

धौंसधुरल्ला dhóuns-dhur-úlla, s. m. Blustering, bullying, tumult, the impetuous assault of a crowd or body of men.

धौंसा dhóuns-a, s. m. A large kettle-drum.

धौंसिया dhóuns-iya, s. m. The leader of a hue and cry or posse comitatus.

धौत dhout, adj. Washed, cleaned, purified.

धौतशिल dhóut-shil, s. m. Crystal.

धौर dhour, s. m. A large kind of dove.

धौरा dhóu-ra, }
धौला dhóu-la, } adj. White.

धौर्तिक dhóurt-tik, adj. Belonging to a cheat, knavish, fraudulent, dishonest, &c.

धौल dhoul, s. f. A thump, a rap, a slap.

धौल जड़ना dhoul júrna, } v. a. To thump.
धौल मारना dhoul márna, }
धौल लगाना dhoul lugána, } Dhoul lugna,
} v. n. To suffer loss.

धौलधुप्पा dhoul-dhúppa, s. m. Thumping and slapping.

धौला dhóu-la, adj. White. Dhoula-gir, s. m. Name of a mountain.

धौलाई dhou-láee, s. f. Whiteness.

धौलाना dhou-lá-na, } v. a. To thump,
धौलियाना dhou-li-yána, } to box, to slap, to cuff.

ध्यान dhyán, *s. m.* Meditation, contempla-tion, reflection, thought, consideration, imagination, advertency, but especially that profound and abstract consideration which brings its object fully and undisturbedly before the mind; mental representation of the personal attributes of the divinity to whom worship is addressed.

ध्यानयोग dhyan-jóg, *s. m.* The performance of religious abstraction.

ध्याना dhyán-a, *v. a.* To meditate on, to think on, to adore, to know.

ध्यानी dhyán-ee, *adj.* Considerate, contem-plative, given to meditation (*on divine matters*), religious.

ध्यानीय dhyan-éeyuh, *adj.* To be meditated upon.

ध्यानौन dhyan-óun, } *v. a.* To meditate
ध्यावनौन dhyao-nóun, } on, to think on, to adore, to know.

ध्रुव dhroov, *adj.* Fixed, stable, firm; true, right. *s. m.* The polar star or north pole itself.

ध्रुवतारा dhroov-tára, *s. m.* The polar star.

ध्रुवपद dhroov-púd, *s. m.* A kind of song.

ध्रुवा dhróo-va, *s. f.* A plant (*Hedysarum gangeticum*); a small tree, from the fibres of which bow-strings are made; the introductory stanza of a song, it is distinct from the verses of the song, after each of which it is again repeated as a burden or chorus; a virtuous woman.

ध्रू dhroo, *s. m.* The pole (*of the earth*), polar star.

ध्वंस dhwuns, *s. m.* Loss, destruction.

ध्वंसन dhwúns-un, *s. m.* Loss, destruction.

ध्वंसित dhwúns-it, *adj.* Lost, destroyed.

ध्वंसी dhwún-see, *s. f.* A mote in a sun-beam. *adj.* Destructive, destroying.

ध्वजा dhwúj-a, *s. m.* A flag or banner; a standard, a ship's pendant; a flag-staff.

ध्वजी dhwúj-ee, *s. m.* A standard-bearer.

ध्वनमोदी dhwun-mó-dee, *s. m.* The humble bee.

ध्वनि dhwún-i, *s. m.* Sound; the sound of a drum.

ध्वनित dhwún-it, *adj.* Sounded, making a noise as a drum, &c.

ध्वनिमाला dhwúni-ná-la, *s. f.* The *Vina* or lute; a pipe, a fife; a sort of trumpet.

ध्वांक्ष dhwanksh, *s. m.* Any aquatic bird, as a crane, a gull, &c. feeding upon fish.

न

न nuh, The twentieth consonant of the *Nagures* alphabet, having the sound of *n*. *adv.* No, not.

नंग nung, } *adj.* Naked; shameless.
नंगा núng-a, } *Nunga kurna*, To bare, to uncover. *Nunga jhooree, s. f.* Searching, exam-ining (*as people leaving a workshop, to prevent pil-fering*). *Nunga-madurzad*, Stark naked. *Nunga moonga*, or, *Nunga moonunga, adj.* Naked. *Nun-ga-sir*, Bareheaded. *Nunga tulwar*, A drawn sword. *Nungee shumsher*, A drawn sword; one who speaks his mind freely and without reserve. *Nungeh paon*, or, *Nungeh pyron*, Barefoot, bare-footed.

नंगटा núng-ta, *adj.* Naked.

नंगधड़ंग nung-dhur-úng, *adj.* Stark naked.

नंगियालेना núngiya-léna, *v. a.* To take and strip.

नंद nund, *s. f.* A sister-in-law, husband's sister. *s. m.* The foster-father of *Krishn*.

नंदन nún-dun, *s. m.* A son; the grove or garden of *Indr*, elysium.

नंदोला nun-dó-la, *s. m.* An earthen vessel.

नंदोसी nun-dó-see, } *s. m.* Husband's sis-
नंदोई nun-dó-ee, } ter's husband.

नंधना núndh-na, *v. n.* To begin.

नक nuk, (*In comp.*) Nose, as, *Nuk-ghis-nee, s. f.* Rubbing the nose on the ground in pros-tration, or by way of humiliation.

नकचूढ़ा nuk-chúrha, *adj.* Angry, fretful, ill-tempered, warm, passionate, fastidious.

नकछिकनी nuk-chhík-nee, *s. f.* A sternu-tatory plant.

नकटा nuk-ta, *adj.* Nose-clipt, noseless. *s. m.* A rogue; name of a bird.

नकरा núk-ra, *s. m.* An inflammation in the nose, the polypus.

नकतोरा nuk-tó-ra, *adj.* Droll, waggish, roguish. [ease.

नकवासा nuk-wása, *s. m.* Name of a dis-

नकसीर nuk-séer, *s. f.* The veins of the nose. *Nukseer phootna*, To bleed at the nose.

नकार nuk-ár, *s. m.* Refusal, denial.

नकारना nuk-ár-na, *v. a.* To refuse.

नकूट núk-oot, *s. m.* The nose.

नकूल núk-ool, *s. m.* The *Bengal* mungoose (*Viverra ichneumon*).

नकूलेष्टका núkool-ésht-ka, } *s. f.* A plant,
नकूलेष्टा nukool-ésh-ta, } the mun-goose if wounded in a conflict with a poisonous snake, is supposed to prevent the effects of the venom by the use of this plant.

नकूआ nuk-óo-a, *s. m.* The nose; a disease of the nose; the point of any thing.

नकेल nuk-él, *s. f.* The wooden or iron in-strument fixed to a camel's nose, and to which the string by which he is led is fastened; a cavesson.

नक्का núk-ka, *s. m.* The ace at cards, or on dice. *Nukka dooa,* A kind of game at dice.

नकी núk-kee, *s. f.* Speaking through the nose, nasal sound.

नकीमुंठ núkkee-móonth, *s. f.* Name of a game.

नकू nuk-kóo, *adj.* Infamous.

नक्रमाल nukt-mál, *s. m.* A tree (*Galedupa arborea*).

नकर nukr, *s. m.* An alligator; the nose.

नकरराज nukr-ráj, *s. m.* A shark.

नक्षत्र nuk-shútr, *s. m.* A star in general; an asterism in the moon's path or lunar mansion, of which twenty-eight, distinct in name, figure, and number of stars, are enumerated: the *Pouranic* and popular enumeration of those constellations is twenty-seven; *Ubhijit,* the twenty-seventh, being considered as formed of portions of the two contiguous asterisms, and not distinct from them. Besides the common division of the zodiac into twelve signs, the *Hindoos* divide it into twenty-seven *Nukshutrus,* each of which has its appropriate name, and two and a quarter of which are included in each sign.

नक्षत्रचक्र nukshútr-chúkr, *s. m.* A particular diagram for astrological purposes.

नक्षत्रमाला nukshútr-mála, *s. f.* A necklace containing twenty-seven pearls; the table of the asterisms in the moon's path.

नक्षत्री nuk-shút-ree, *adj.* Born under a lucky planet, fortunate.

नख nukh, *s. m.* A finger or toe nail. *Nukh sikh,* or, *Nukh-seh sikh-tuluk,* From top to toe, entirely, throughout, (*lit.*) from the (*toe*) nails to the hair on the crown of the head.

नख nukh, *s. m.* The string of a paper kite.

नखखादी nukh-khá-dee, *adj.* Who or what eats with nails or talons.

नखत núkh-ut, *s. m.* A star; a constellation.

नखुत्री nukhút-ree, *adj.* Fortunate, born under a lucky planet.

नखपद nukh-púd, *s. m.* A scratch, the mark of a finger nail.

नखरेखा nukh-rékha, *s. f.* } The marks left
नखलेखा nukh-lékha, } by the nails,
नखांक nukh-ánk, *s. m.* } a scratch.

नखियाना nukhi-yána, *v. a.* To claw, to scratch.

नखी núkhee, *s. f.* A perfume, a dried substance of a brown colour, and of the shape of a nail; apparently a dried shell-fish, used as a perfume; a vegetable perfume, different from the one above, though known by the same name *Nukhee. adj.* Nailed, clawed, having nails or talons.

नग nug, *s. m.* A mountain; the stone of a ring, or a stone on which a name, &c. is cut, a jewel, gem, precious stone.

नगचार nug-cháee, } *s. f.* Approach.
नगचाहुट nug-cháhut, }

नगचाना nug-chá-na, *v. n.* To approach.

नगज núg-uj, *adj.* Mountaineer.

नगना núg-na, *s. f.* Heart-pea (*Cardiospermum halicacabum*).

नगदौना nug-dóu-na, *s. m.* Wormwood.

नगन núg-un, *adj.* Naked.

नगपति nug-púti, *s. m. Himaleh,* the personified range of snowy mountains dividing India from Tartary, &c.

नगभिद् nug-bhíd, *s. m.* A plant (*Plectranthus scutellaroides*).

नगभू nug-bhóo, *adj.* Mountain, mountaineer.

नगर núg-ur, *s. m.* A town, a city. *Nugurnaree, s. f.* A courtezan.

नगरजन nugur-jún, *s. m.* Town's-folk, citizens.

नगरस्वरूपिनी nugur-swuróop-inee, *s. f.* A species of metre.

नगरी núg-ree, *s. f.* A town, a village. *adj.* Of or belonging to a town or village.

नगरोपांत nugur-opánt *s. m.* Suburb, skirts of the town.

नगाश्रय nug-áshruy, *adj.* Living in or frequenting mountains.

नग्न nugn, } *adj.* Naked. *s. m.* A nak-
नंग nung, } ed mendicant.
नूंगा nún-ga, }

नग्नउत्वुब nugn-útwub, *s. m.* Nudity, nakedness.

नग्नहू nugn-hóo, *s. m.* Ferment, a drug used to throw the mixture for spirituous liquors into fermentation.

नग्ना núgn-a, *s. f.* A naked woman.

नग्नात् nugn-át, *s. m.* A naked man, but especially a kind of religious mendicant, who wanders about without clothes; a *Bouddh,* a *Jyn.*

नग्निका núg-ni-ka, *s. f.* A girl before menstruation or about ten years old; a naked woman.

नग्नीकरण núgnee-kúrun, *s. m.* Stripping, undressing.

नग्नीकृत núgnee-krít, *adj.* Stripped, undressed, naked.

नचवाना nuch-wá-na, } *v. a.* To make to
नचाना nuch-á-na, } dance.

नचवैया nuch-wy-ya, *s. m.* A dancer.

नट nut, *s. m.* A dancer, a mimic, an actor, a tribe who are generally jugglers, rope-dancers, &c., a tumbler: in caste, the son of a degraded *Kshuttree* by a woman of the second class or caste; a sort of reed (*Arundo tibialis*, or, *A. karka*); a subordinate mode of music.

नठखट **nút-khut**, *adj.* Roguish, waggish, artful, trickish, shrewd. *s. m.* A cheat.

नठखटी **nut-khút-ee**, *s. f.* Trick, roguery, artifice, artfulness.

नठन **nút-un**, *s. m.* The art or act of dancing, pantomime, &c.

नठनारायण **nut-naráyun**, *s. m.* A *Rag* or mode of music, according to some, the sixth, or to others, a subdivision of *Deepuk* or of *Megh*.

नठपुत्रिका **nut-pútrika**, *s. f.* The egg-plant (*Solanum melongena*).

नठवर **nut-búr**, ⎫ *s. m.* A juggler, rope-
नठवा **nut-wá**, ⎭ dancer, mimic, actor, &c.; a chief dancer or actor.

नठमण्डन **nut-mún-dun**, *s. m.* Yellow orpiment.

नठा **nút-a**, *s. f.* A shrub (*Cæsalpinia bonduccella*).

नठिन **nút-in**, ⎫ *s. f.* A female rope-
नठिनी **nút-in-ee**, ⎭ dancer, tumbler, mimic, &c.

नठी **nút-ee**, *s. f.* A medicinal plant; a whore, a *nach* girl, a dancer, an actress; red arsenic.

नड **nur**, *s. m.* A sort of reed (*Arundo tibialis*, or, *A. karka*); a particular tribe whose employment is making a sort of glass bracelets.

नडकीय **nur-kée-yuh**, *adj.* Abounding in reeds (*a field*, &c.)

नडमीन **nur-méen**, *s. m.* A small fish, a kind of sprat haunting reedy places.

नडवान **nur-wán**, *adj.* Reedy, abounding in reeds.

नत **nút-uh**, *s. m.* The arc or distance of any planet from the zenith.

नतमुख **nút-mookh**, *adj.* Down-faced, looking down.

नतांश **nut-ánsh**, *s. m.* Zenith distance (*in Astronomy*).

नतांग **nut-áng**, *adj.* Bent, curved, bowed, stooping.

नतांगी **nut-ángee**, *s. f.* A woman.

नति **núti**, *s. f.* Bending, bowing, stooping; curvature, crookedness.

नतिनी **nút-in-ee**, *s. f.* Grand-daughter, daughter's daughter.

नतैत **nutyt**, *s. m.* A relative.

नथ **nuth**, *s. m. f.* A large ring worn in the nose (*on the left nostril*); a rope passed through the nose of a draught ox.

नथना **núth-na**, *s. m.* A nostril, a ring for the nose. *v. n.* To have the nose pierced (*a bullock*). *Nuth nah churhana*, To be angry or displeased.

नथनी **núth-nee**, *s. f.* A small ring worn in the nose; a ring inserted in the hilt of a sword.

नद **nud**, *s. m.* A river, applied only to one of which the personification is male, as the *Bruhmapootr, Sone, Indus*, &c.

नदी **núd-ee**, *s. f.* A river in general; the common personification of rivers being female.

नदीकान्त **nud-ee-kánt**, *s. m.* A tree (*Barringtonia acutangula*); a small tree (*Vitex negundo*).

नदीकान्ता **nud-ee-kánta**, *s. f.* The rose apple (*Eugenia jambu*); a shrub (*Leea hirta*).

नदीकूल **nud-ee-kóol**, *s. m.* The bank or shore of a river.

नदीकूलप्रिय **nud-ee-kool-príyuh**, *s. m.* A sort of reed (*Calamus rotang*).

नदीज **nud-éej**, *adj.* Aquatic, water-born; a tree (*Pentaptera arjuna*); the marshy date tree.

नदीतीर **nud-ee-téer**, *s. m.* The bank of a river.

नदीसर्ज **nud-ee-súrj**, *s. m.* A tree (*Pentaptera arjuna*).

नदेयी **nud-éyee**, *s. f.* A plant (*Premna herbacea*).

नदोल **nud-ó-la**, *s. m.* A large earthen pan.

नुनका **nún-ka**, *s. m.* A little child, a son: an expression of endearment.

नुनद **nún-ud**, ⎫
नंद **nund**, ⎪ *s. f.* A sister-in-law,
ननदिया **nún-diya**, ⎬ husband's sister.
ननदी **nún-dee**, ⎭

ननिहाल **nuni-hál**, *s. f.* Maternal grandfather's family.

नन्दन **nún-dun**, *s. m.* A son; the grove or garden of *Indr*, elysium. *adj.* Delighting, rejoicing, making pleased or happy.

नन्दिक **nún-dik**, ⎫ *s. m.* Toon, a tree,
नन्दिवृक्ष **nundi-vríksh**, ⎭ the wood of which resembles mahogany, and is used for furniture, &c. (*Cedrella Tuna*).

नन्दिनी **nún-din-ee**, *s. f.* Wife's sister.

नन्दोई **nun-dó-ee**, ⎫ *s. m.* Husband's sis-
नन्दोसी **nun-dó-see**, ⎭ ter's husband.

नन्दोला **nun-dó-la**, *s. m.* An earthen vessel.

नन्हा **nun-há**, *adj.* Small, diminutive, neat, nutty, tiny.

नपुंसक **nup-óon-suk**, *s. m.* A eunuch, a hermaphrodite; an impotent or imbecile man; the neuter gender. *adj.* Unmanly, coward.

नभ **nubh**, *s. m.* The sky, ether, atmosphere.

नभश्चर nubh-chúr, *adj.* What moves in the sky ; aerial. *s. m.* A bird ; a cloud ; air, wind.

नभःस्थित nubhusthít, *adj.* Abiding in heaven or in the sky. *s. m.* A division of the infernal regions, a hell.

नमः núm-uh, *s. m.* Salutation, reverence, bowing, obeisance, adoration.

नमकीन num-kéen, *s. f.* Pickled lemons.

नमत् núm-ut,) *adj.* Bending, stooping,
नमन núm-un,) bowed.

नमन núm-un, *adj.* Like, resembling.

नमसित num-us-ít, *adj.* Reverenced, respected, worshipped.

नमस्कार num-us-kár, *s. m.* Respectful or reverential address or salutation, adoration.

नमस्कारी num-us-káree, *s. f.* A sensitive plant.

नमस्य num-ús-yuh, *adj.* Venerable, respectable, entitled to salutation or civility.

नमस्यित num-us-yít, *adj.* Reverenced, respected, worshipped.

नमेरु num-éroo, *s. m.* The seed of the Eleocarpus.

नमेगुरु num-égooroo, *s. m.* A spiritual teacher.

नम्र numr, *adj.* Bending ; (met.) courteous.

नम्रता numr-tá, *s. f.* Condescension.

नम्रमुख numr-móokh, *m.*) *adj.* Looking
नम्रमुखी numr-móokhee, *f.*) down, having the head bent.

नयन ny-un, *s. m.* The eye.

नयना ny-na, *s. f.* The pupil of the eye.

नयनोत्सव nyn-ót-suv, *s. m.* A lamp ; any lovely or desired object.

नयनोपान्त nyn-opánt, *s. m.* The outer angle or canthus of the eye.

नयनौषध nyn-óu-shudh, *s. m.* Green sulphate of iron, or the salt in a state of partial decomposition by exposure to the atmosphere.

नया ny-a, *adj.* New. *Nyeh sir seh, adv.* Anew, afresh.

नर nur, *s. m.* Man, individually or generally, a man, a male, mankind. *adj.* Masculine, male.

नरक núr-uk, *s. m.* Hell, the infernal regions, including a number of places of torture of various descriptions.

नरककुण्ड nur-uk-kóond, *s. m.* A well or pit in Tartarus, eighty-six such are enumerated.

नरकट núr-kut,) *s. m.* A reed of which
नरकल núr-kul,) mats are made (*Arundo tibialis*).

नरकस núr-kus, *s. m.* The wind-pipe.

नरकस्था nur-kús-tha, *s. f.* The river of hell.

नरजा núr-ja, *s. m.* Small scales.

नरपति nur-púti, *s. m.* A king, a sovereign prince.

नरप्रिय nur-príyuh, *adj.* Favourable or friendly to mankind.

नरपूर nur-póor, *s. m.* One of the three *loks* or regions of the universe, the abode of man, the earth.

नरभू nur-bhóo, *s. f. Bharut Vursh,* India, or the central part of the known continent ; the birth-place of men.

नरमाना nur-má-na, *v. a.* To soften.

नरमेध nur-médh, *s. m.* A human sacrifice.

नररूप nur-róop, *adj.* Having the human form. *s. m.* The human form.

नररूपी nur-róo-pee, *adj.* Having the human form.

नरसिंग nur-sín-ga, *s. m.* A horn (*musical*), a wind instrument.

नरसिंगिया nur-sín-giya, *s. m.* One who plays on the horn.

नरसिंह núr-singh, *s. m.* The fourth *Uvutar* or incarnation of *Vishnoo,* which is said to have happened in the *Sut-joog,* upon the following occasion. *Hirnya Kusyup,* an impious prince, was enraged at his son *Pruhlad* for worshipping the Almighty, and tried every means of destroying him, by poison, by throwing him into fire, into the ocean, &c., yet *Pruhlad* lived. " If your God is present every where," says *Hirnya Kusyup,* " let him come from an alabastar pillar ;" on which, it is said, *Nursingh* appeared, with the lower part of a man and the upper of a lion, destroyed the father, and set the son on the throne, &c.

नरसों núr-son, *adv.* The fourth day past or to come, some days ago or hence.

नरहर nur-húr, *s. m.* Shank, leg.

नराधम nur-ádhum, *s. m.* A low or vile man, a wretch.

नरिया núr-iya, *s. f.* A tile.

नरी núr-ee, *s. f.* A kind of leather, skin ; a weaver's shuttle.

नरोख nur-óokh, *adj.* Male, masculine.

नरेट nur-ét, *s. m.*) The throat, the
नरेटा nur-ét-a, *s. m.*) wind-pipe. *Nure-*
नरेटी nur-ét-ee, *s. f.*) *tee dubana,* To throttle. [sovereign.

नरेन्द्र nur-éndr, *s. m.* A king, an anointed

नरेश nur-ésh,) *s. m.* A king.
नरेश्वर nur-ésh-wur,)

नर्तक núrt-tuk, *s. m.* An actor, a mimic ; a juggler, a dancer, a player of any description ; a reed (*Arundo karka*).

नर्तकी núrt-tuk-ee, *s. f.* An actress, female dancer or singing girl.

नर्तन núrt-tun, *s. m.* Dancing, gesticulating, acting.

नर्द्वटक nur-dwút-uk, *s. m.* A stanza of four parts, having seventeen syllables in each.

नर्मदा núrm-ud-a, *s. f.* The *Nermuda*, or *Nerbudda* river, which rising in the *Vindhya* mountains, runs westward to the gulph of Cambay.

नळ nul, *s. m.* A reed (*Arundo karka*); the name of a king, and hero of several poetical works famous among the *Hindoos*, especially the poem called *Nyshudh*; a tube, spout, joint of bamboo or other hollow wood; the bamboo which fowlers use to entangle game by applying bird-lime to the top of it. *Nul chulana*, Setting the bamboo in motion, denotes a magical practice adopted for the discovery of theft. Two pieces of split bamboo, of equal lengths, are applied to one another side by side, and held by two men, one at each end. It is said that any persons taken at random may be employed for this purpose. Then the magician pronounces certain incantations, the efficacy of which is pretended to be such that the bamboos spontaneously move towards the place where the thief or the stolen goods are, and drag the men along with them. *Nul dur nul*, One tube within another.

नळा núl-a, *s. m.* The ureters, urinary ducts. *Ahunee nula*, or *Bhooeen nula*, A sort of fireworks, roman candle, made of iron, buffalo-horn, or bamboo, placed on the ground. *Dum nula*, A variety of the above-mentioned, but with occasional globes of bright light bursting up. *Huth nula*, Of the like sort as above, but small, held in the hand.

नळिका núl-ik-a, *s. f.* A perfume.

नळिन núl-in, *s. m.* A lotus or water-lily (*Nelumbium speciosum*, or *Nymphæa nelumbo*); the Indian crane.

नळिनी núl-in-ee, *s. f.* An assemblage of lotus flowers; a place abounding in lotuses.

नळिया núl-iya, *s. m.* A caste whose employment is to catch birds with birdlime by means of the *nul*, or reed.

नळी núl-ee, *s. f.* A tube, pipe, spout; the windpipe, ureter, &c.; a gun-barrel; the bone of the leg, the tibia; a weaver's shuttle, or the little tube within the shuttle on which the woof is wound.

नळूआ nul-óo-a, *s. m.* A tube, a joint of bamboo to convey letters in; straw.

नल्व nulv, *s. m.* A furlong, a distance measured by four hundred cubits.

नव núv-uh, *adj.* New; nine.

नवउकलिका nuv-ukál-ika, *s. f.* A young woman, either one recently married, or one in whom menstruation has lately commenced.

नवग्रह nuv-ugrúha, *s. m. pl.* The nine planets, or sun, moon, five planets, and the ascending and descending nodes.

नवछात्र nuv-uchhátr, *s. m.* A student, a novice.

नवयौवना nuv-ujóvun-a, *s. f.* A girl just grown up to puberty.

नवता núv-ut-a, *s. f.* Novelty.

नवद्वार nuv-udwár, *adj.* Having nine doors; an epithet applied to the body, which has nine inlets or outlets, as the nostrils, ears, mouth, eyes, anus, &c.

नवनिधि nuv-uníd-hi, *s. f.* The treasure of *Koover*, the god of riches, consisting of nine fabulous gems.

नवनी nuv-ún-ee, *s. f.*
नवनीत nuv-un-éet, *s. m.* } Fresh butter.

नवफुळिका nuv-uphúl-ik-a, *s. f.* A bride, a newly married woman; a girl in whom menstruation has recently commenced.

नववधू nuv-ubúd-hoo, *s. f.* A bride, a newly married woman.

नवबाला nuv-ubála, *s. f.* A girl just grown up to puberty.

नवम núv-um, *adj.* Ninth.

नवमालिका nuv-umálik-a, *s. f.* Double jasmine (*Jasminum sambac*).

नवमी núv-um-ee, *s. f.* The ninth day of a lunar half month.

नवयौवना nuvu-yóu-vun-a, *s. f.* A young woman.

नवरत्न nuvu-rútn, *s. m.* Nine precious gems, or, a pearl, ruby, topaz, diamond, emerald, lapis lazuli, coral, sapphire, and one called *Gomed*; the nine men of letters at the court of *Vikrumadityuh*, or, *Dhunwunturee, Kshupunukuh, Umursingh, Sunkoo, Vetalubhutt, Ghutukurpur, Kalidas, Vuruhumihir,* and *Vururoochi.*

नवरात्र nuvu-rátr, *s. m.* The period of nine days, from the first of the light half of *Aswin* to the ninth; part of the time devoted to the worship of *Doorga*. [ling.

नवुल núv-ul, *adj.* Beautiful. *s. m.* A sap-

नववरिका nuvu-vúrika, *s. f.* A newly married woman.

नववस्त्र nuvu-vústr, *s. m.* New cloth.

नवशायक nuvu-sháyuk, *s. m.* A name given to any of the nine inferior classes, the cowherd, gardener, oilman, weaver, confectioner, water-carrier, potter, blacksmith, and barber.

नवश्राद्ध nuvu-shráddh, *s. m.* The first series of *Shraddhs* collectively, or funeral offerings on the first, third, fifth, seventh, ninth, and eleventh days after a person's demise.

नवसूतिका nuvu-sóotí-ka, *s. f.* A woman recently delivered.

नवा núwa, *adj.* New.

नवांश nuv-ánsh, *s. m.* A ninth, a ninth part.

नवाड़ा nuwára, *s. m.* A boat ; a particular kind of boat, a barge.

नवाना nuwána, *v. a.* To bend downwards, to bow ; to cause to submit to, to cause to stoop ; to double, to fold.

नवान्न nuv-ánn, *s. m.* New rice or grain ; a ceremony observed on first eating the rice, &c. of the last harvest.

नवाम्बर nuv-ám-bur, *s. m.* New and unbleached cloth.

नवारना nuwárna, *v. n.* To travel, to walk, to wander, to stray ; to go round, to surround ; to shut out, to exclude.

नवारी nuwáree, *s. f.* A flower, a sort of jasmine.

नवी núvee, *s. f.* The string with which a cow's feet are tied when milking, a tether.

नवीकृत núvee-krit, *adj.* Renewed, revived, done or made anew.

नवीन nuvéen, *adj.* New ; youthful.

नवीनता nuvéen-ta, *s. f.* Newness.

नवीभूत nuvee-bhóot, *adj.* Renewed, revived.

नव्युह núv-yuh, *adj.* New, recent, young, &c.

नशाक nush-ák, *s. m.* A bird, said to be a sort of crow.

नश्यन nush-yún, *adj.* Perishing, decaying, wasting, being destroyed.

नश्वर nush-wúr, *m.* ‌} *adj.* Mischievous,
नश्वरा nush-wur-á, *f.* } destructive.

नष्ट nusht, *adj.* Lost, destroyed, removed, annihilated.

नष्टचन्द्र nusht-chúndr, *s. m.* The moon on the fourth lunation of either half of *Bhadr.*

नष्टचेतन nusht-chét-un, *adj.* Fainted, insensible. [tion.

नष्टता nusht-tá, *s. f.* Destruction, annihila-

नष्टा nush-ta, *s. f.* An adulteress.

नसा nús-a, *s. f.* The nose.

नसाना nus-ána, *v. a.* To destroy, to annihilate, to spoil, to squander. *v. n.* To be destroyed or annihilated.

नसी nús-ee, *s. f.* A coulter, a ploughshare.

नसीठ nus-éeth *adj.* Ill-omened.

नस्त nust, *s. m.* A sternutatory, snuff, &c. ; the nose.

नस्ता nús-ta, *s. f.* A hole bored in the septum of the nose.

नस्युभ nús-yuh, *adj.* Nasal, relating or belonging to the nose. *s. m.* A sternutatory, snuff.

नह nuh, *s. m.* Nail (*of the finger, &c.*), talon. *Nuh lena,* To trip, to stumble.

नहुक núh-uk, *adj.* Meagre, lean.

नहट्टा nuhútta, *s. m.* A scratch with the nail or talon.

नहुनी nuhún-ee, *s. f.* An instrument for cutting nails ; a kind of chisel used in polishing and turning brass, &c.

नहुरनी nuhúr-nee, *s. f.* An instrument for paring the nails with.

नहुलवाना nuhul-wá-na, *v. a.* To cause to be bathed or washed.

नहलाना nuh-lá-na, *v. a.* To cause to bathe.

नहान nuhán, *s. m.* Bathing, ablution.

नहाना nuhán-a, *v. n.* To bathe, to wash.

नहानी nuhán-ee, *s. f.* Menses.

नहारमुंह nuhár-moonh, *adj.* Without eating.

नहारूआ nuhár-oo-a, *s. m.* A guinea worm (*Filaria medinensis*).

नहि núhi, *adv.* No, not.

नहियर núhiyur, *s. f.* Wife's family.

नहीं nuhéen, *adv.* No, not, nay.

नहींतो nuhéen-to, *adv.* Otherwise, else.

ना na, *adv.* No, not.

नाइन ná-in, *s. f.* Female of *Naee ;* a barber's wife.

नाई náee, }
नाऊ náoo, } *s. m.* A barber.

नांदिया nán-diya, *s. m.* The bull and vehicle of *Shiv.*

नाह nah, *adv.* No, nay.

नाक nak, *s. f.* The nose. *Nak kutana,* To dishonour. *Nak kutee honee,* To lose one's honour. *Nak churhana,* To be angry or displeased. *Nak rukhna,* To preserve one's honour. *Nak sukorna,* To turn up one's nose, to be displeased.

नाक nak, *s. m.* Heaven, paradise, ether, sky, atmosphere.

नाकड़ा nák-ra, *s. m.* An inflammation in the nose, the polypus.

नाका ná-ka, *s. m.* The extremity of a road ; the eye of a needle ; an alley, avenue, lane. *Nakeh bundee,* Shutting up a road.

नाका ná-ka, *s. m.* An alligator.

नाकुल ná-kool, *adj.* Relating or belonging to an ichneumon.

नाकुली ná-koo-lee, *s. f.* A plant ; the ichneumon plant, a vegetable supposed to furnish the mungoose with an antidote, when bitten in a conflict with a snake (*Serpent ophioxylon ?*)

नाक्षत्र na-kshútr, *s. m.* A month, one computed by the moon's passage through the twenty-seven mansions, or of thirty days of sixty *ghurees* each.

नाक्षत्रिक na-kshut-rik, *adj.* Relating or belonging to the lunar asterisms.

नाक्षत्रिकी na-kshút-rik-ee, *s. f.* The state or condition to which a person is subjected agreeably to the asterism presiding over his nativity.

नाग nag, *s. m.* A demigod so called, having a human face, with the tail of a serpent, and the expanded neck of the *Koluber Naga*; the race of these beings is said to have sprung from *Kudroo*, the wife of *Kusyup*, in order to people *Patal*, or the regions below the earth; a serpent in general, or especially the spectacle snake, or Cobra Capella (*Coluber Naga*); a small tree (*Mesua ferrea*); a sort of grass (*Cyperus pertenuis*); a tree used in dying (*Rottleria tinctoria*); one of the astronomical periods called *Kurun*: it is one of those termed invariable, and always corresponds to the last half of *Umavusya* or new moon.

नागकन्या nag-kún-ya, *s. f.* A race of females said to inhabit *Patal* or the regions under the earth, and to be of serpentine extraction, but very beautiful.

नागकेश्वर nag-késh-ur, *s. m.* A small tree (*Mesua ferrea*).

नागजिव्हा nag-jív-ha, *s. f.* A plant (*Asclepias pseudosarsa*).

नागजिव्हिका nag-jívhi-ka, *s. f.* Red arsenick.

नागजीवन nag-jéevun, *s. m.* Tin.

नागदन्त nag-dúnt, *s. m.* Elephant's tooth or ivory.

नागदन्ती nag-dún-tee, *s. f.* A sort of sunflower (*Heliotropium Indicum*).

नागदोन nag-dóun, *s. m.* A kind of wood, by touching which it is said that fetters spontaneously fall off.

नागदोना nag-dóu-na, *s. m.* A plant (*Artemisia vulgaris*).

नागन ná-gun, } *s. f.* A serpent (*fe-*
नागिनी ná-gin-ee, } *male*).

नागपंचमी nag-púnch-um-ee, *s. f.* A *Hindoo* holiday, the 5th of *Srawun*, *sookl-puksh*, on which day they worship a snake to procure blessings on their children.

नागपाश nag-pás, *s. m.* } A running noose
नागफांस nag-pháns, *s. f.* } of a rope, &c., a sort of noose or knot, used in battle to entangle an enemy.

नागपुष्प nag-póoshp, *s. m.* A tree used in dyeing (*Rottleria tinctoria*); a small tree (*Mesua ferrea*); a flower (*Michelia Champaca*).

नागफनी nag-phún-ee, *s. f.* A hedge plant (*Cactus Indica*).

नागवन्ध्य nag-bún-dhoo, *s. m.* The holy fig tree (*Ficus religiosa*).

नागवला nag-búl-a, *s. f.* A creeping plant (*Hedysarum lugopodioides*).

नागवेल nag-bél, *s. m.* Betel plant (*Piper betel*).

नागभाषा nag-bhá-sha, *s. f.* A *Prakrit* language, said to be used by the serpentine race who inhabit *Patal*.

नागभिद् nag-bhíd, *s. m.* A sort of snake (*Amphisbæna*).

नागमातृ nag-mátri, *s. f.* A name of *Munusa*, a goddess supposed to preside over snakes; red arsenic.

नागर ná-gur, *adj.* Clever, sharp, knowing (*as a buck, a blood, a wag, &c.*); town-born or bred. *s. m.* A sort of grass (*Cyperus pertenuis*); a form of writing, the *Dev-naguree* alphabet.

नागरंग nag-rúng, *s. m.* The orange; in India usually applied to the *Silhet* orange (*Citrus aurantium*).

नागरमूस्ता nágur-móosta, *s. f.* A grass (*Cyperus*).

नागरमोथा nágur-mótha, *s. m.* A sweet smelling grass (*Cyperus pertenuis, C. juncifolius, or, rush-leaved Cyperus*).

नागरी ná-gur-ee, *s. f.* A sort of Euphorbia; a clever or intriguing woman. *adj.* The most common *Hindee* character of writing, called *Dev-naguree*.

नागल ná-gul, *s. m.* A plough.

नागलोक nag-lók, *s. m.* The region under the earth, the abode of serpents and hydras, *Patal*: not being accessible to the sun, it is supposed to be illuminated by very resplendent jewels.

नागा ná-ga, *s. m.* A caste of *Hindoo* mendicants.

नागांग nag-áng, *s. m.* *Hustinapoor*, or ancient *Delhi*.

नागांचुला nag-án-chul-a, *s. f.* A stick or pole driven into a square piece of earth in the centre of a newly dug pond, a boring rod.

नागाभ nag-ábha, *s. m.* *Hustinapoor*, or ancient *Delhi*.

नागिन ná-gin, } *s. f.* A serpent (*fe-*
नागिनी ná-gin-ee, } *male*).

नागेश्वर nag-ésh-ur, *s. f.* A flower (*Mesua ferrea*), Indian rose chesnut.

नागेश्वरी nag-éshur-ee, *adj.* Of the colour of the *Nageshur*, yellow.

नागोद nag-ód, *s. m.* Armour for the front or the belly.

नागोदर nag-ó-dur, *s. m.* A breast-plate, a cuirass.

नागौर na-góur, } s. m. A country near
नागपास nag-pás, } Marwar.

नांघना nángh-na, v. a. To step across,
cross, jump over, pass, leap over.

नाच nach, s. m. Dance. Nach nuchana,
To make to dance ; to tease.

नाचना nách-na, v. n. To dance.

नाज naj, s. m. Contraction of Unaj, grain.

नाट nat, s. m. The Carnatic.

नाटक ná-tuk, s. m. An actor, acting, dancing, &c.; a play, a drama; the first of the ten
species of dramatic compositions of the first order.

नाटकीय na-tuk-éeyuh, adj. Dramatic.

नाटा ná-ta, adj. Dwarf, dwarfish, dapper,
short.

नाटापन na-ta-pún, s. m. Lowness (of stature).

नाटिका ná-tik-a, s. f. A short or light
comedy, the first of the dramas of the second order.

नाट्य nát-yuh, s. m. The science or art of
dancing or acting, or the union of song, dance,
and instrumental music.

नाट्यशाला nátyuh-shála, s. f. A theatre, a
building for dramatic exhibitions.

नाठ nath, s. m. Non-existence.

नाड़िका nár-ik-a, s. f. An Indian hour, or
twenty-four minutes.

नाड़िपत्र nári-putr, s. m. An esculent root
(Arum colocasia).

नाड़िमण्डल nári-mún-dul, s. m. The celestial equator.

नाड़ी ná-ree, s. f. Any tubular organ of the
body, as an artery, a vein, an intestine ; a fistulous sore, a fistula, a sinus ; an hour of twenty-
four minutes ; the pulse, either at the hand or feet,
&c.

नाड़ीच na-réech, s. m. An esculent root
(Arum colocasia).

नाड़ीनक्षत्र náree-nukshútr, s. m. The planet of a person's nativity.

नाड़ीव्रण naree-vrún, s. m. An ulcer.

नातर ná-tur, adv. (If) not (then) otherwise, else.

नाता ná-ta, s. m. Relationship, kin, alliance. Natehdar, s. m. f. Relation, relative.

नातिन ná-tin, s. f. Granddaughter, daughter's daughter.

नाती ná-tee, s. m. Grandson, daughter's
son.

नाथ nath, s. m. A master, a husband, a
lord ; an affix to the names of a class of Yogees,
as, Gorukhnath ; a rope passed through the nose
of a draft ox. s. f. A seton.

नाथना náth-na, v. a. To bore a bullock's
nose and put a string in it to guide him by.

नाथवत nath-wút, adj. Dependant, subservient, subject.

नाद nad, s. m. Sound in general ; a semicircle, used especially as an abbreviation or hie-
roglyphic in mystical works.

नादाहा na-da-há, s. m. A spout, a canal.

नादेयी na-deyée, s. f. A sort of reed growing usually near water (Calamus fasciculatus) ; a
plant (Premna herbacea) ; the China rose.

नाधना nádh-na, v. a. To yoke.

नानक ná-nuk, n. proper. Name of a religious mendicant, the founder of the sect of Sikhs.

नानकपंथी nának-pún-thee, } s. m. A Sikh,
नानकमता nának-mút-a, } or follower
नानकशाही nának-shá-hee, } of Nanuk.

नाना na-na, s. m. Maternal grandfather.
adj. Various, many. v. a. To bend, to bow.

नानाप्रकार nána-pruk-ár, } adj. Of various
नानाभांति nána-bhánti, } kinds, sorts,
modes, methods.

नानारूप nana-róop, adj. Multiform, various.

नानावर्ण nana-vúrn, adj. Variegated, many-
coloured.

नानाविध nana-vídh, adj. In various ways ;
of various sorts or kinds.

नानी ná-nee, s. f. Maternal grandmother.

नांद nand, s. f. A large earthen pan.

नांदिया nán-di-ya, s. m. The bull and vehicle of Shiv.

नांदीमुख nan-dee-móokh, s. m. A shraddh
or funeral obsequies performed on joyous occasions, as initiation, marriage, &c. in which nine
balls of meat are offered to the deceased father,
paternal grandfather, and great grandfather ; to the
maternal grandfather, great grandfather, and great
great grandfather ; and to the mother, paternal
grandmother, and paternal great grandmother.

नांधना nándh-na, v. a. To begin.

नाप nap, s. f. Measure.

नापजोख nap-jókh, s. f. Measuring and
weighing.

नापना náp-na, v. a. To measure, to weigh.

नापित ná-pit, s. m. A barber, a shaver, a
surgeon.

नापितशाला nápit-shála, s. f. A barber's
shop.

नाभक ná-bhuk, s. m. A myrobalan (Terminalia chebula).

नाभि ná-bhi, } s. f. The navel.
नाभी ná-bhee, }

नाभिगोलक nábhi-góluk, s. m. A prominent or ruptured navel.

नाभिछेदन nábhi-chhédun, s. m. Division of the umbilical cord.

नाभिनाड़ी nábhi-náree, } s. f. The umbili-
नाभिनाला nábhí-nála, } cal cord.

नाम nam, s. m. Name, appellation, character, fame, reputation, honour. *Nam nikalna*, To become celebrated ; to investigate the perpetrator of any crime. *Nam lekur mang-khana*, To beg alms in the name of another. *Nam lena*, To praise ; to repeat the name of God. *Nam hona*, To be conspicuous, famous, or renowned.

नामकरण nám-kurun, s. m. Naming a child first after birth ; acquiring or taking a name (*of honour*).

नामकरना nám-kúrna, v. a. To become famous.

नामडुबोना nam-doo-bóna, v. a. To lose one's honour or reputation.

नामदेना nam-déna, v. a. To give name to, to make conspicuous.

नामधरना nam-dhúr-na, v. a. To name, to fix a name on (*particularly a bad name*), to nickname, to miscal.

नामधरवाना nam-dhur-wána, v. a. To be defamed ; to give a name to a child.

नामना nám-na, v. a. To name, to praise, to panegyrise.

नामरखना nam rúkh-na, v. a. To name.

नामशेष nam-shésh, adj. Dead, deceased.

नाम होना nam hóna, v. n. To be conspicuous, famous, or renowned.

नामी होना namee hóna, v. n. To be celebrated.

नायक ná-yuk, s. m. A guide, a leader, a conductor ; a chief, a head, pre-eminent, principal ; a native officer of the lowest rank, corresponding to corporal in our corps ; a person well conversant in dancing, singing, &c.

नायन nú-yun, s. f. Female of *Naee*, a barber's wife.

नायिका ná-yik-a, s. f. Female of *Nayuk* ; a damsel, a lass ; the mistress of a house, particularly (*now*) of a brothel ; a bawd.

नार nar, s. f. A woman. s. m. Barrel of a gun ; the fibre of which rope is made ; the stalk of the lotus ; the neck.

नारक ná-ruk, m. } adj. Infernal, hellish.
नारकी nár-kee, f. } s. m. Hell or the infernal regions.

नारकी ná-ruk-ee, adj. Infernal, being in hell, condemned to, or deserving it.

नारंगी ná-rung-ee, s. f. An orange (*Citrus aurantium*).

नारद ná-rud, n. prop. The name of a *Hindoo* sage, the son of *Bruhma*, and one of the ten original *Moonis* or *Rishis* ; he is a friend of *Krishn*, a celebrated legislator, and inventor of the *Veena* or lute ; and who, by carrying tales, occasioned frequent quarrels among the gods ; (*met.*) a disputant, one fond of altercation.

नारविवार nar-bi-wár, s. m. The membrane in which the fœtus is enveloped, secundines.

नारा ná-ra, s. m. Red thread.

नारायण nará-yun, s. m. A name of *Vishnoo*, considered as the being who existed before all worlds and moved on the waters of creation.

नारायणक्षेत्र nará-yun-kshétr, s. m. Four cubits on either side of the stream of the Ganges.

नारायणतेल nara-yun-tyl, s. m. An oil of great reputed efficacy in many complaints, expressed from a variety of plants.

नारायणी nará-yun-ee, s. f. A name of *Lukshmee*, the goddess of prosperity, and wife of *Vishnoo* ; a plant (*Asparagus racemosa*). adj. Of or relating to *Narayun*.

नारिकेल na-ri-kél, } s. m. The cocoanut.
नारियल ná-ri-yul, }

नारिया ná-ri-ya, s. m. A person who feels the pulse.

नारी ná-ree, s. f. A woman in general, a female ; the pulse, an artery ; the umbilical cord ; a kind of greens.

नारीच na-réech, s. m. An esculent root (*Arum colocasia*).

नारीदूषण náree-dóoshun, s. m. A vice or breach of duty in a woman, of which six cases are reckoned, viz. drinking spirits, keeping bad company, quitting a husband, rambling abroad, and sleeping or dwelling in a strange house.

नारीप्रसंग náree-prusúng, s. m. Libertinism, lechery.

नारू na-róo, s. m. The guinea-worm.

नल nal, adv. Along with, accompanying. s. m. A tube ; barrel, bore, or chase of a gun ; the naval-string ; stalk of the lotus.

नाला ná-la, s. m. A rivulet, brook, canal, gutter, furrow, ravine.

नालकी nál-kee, s. f. A sort of sedan or litter, generally used by people of rank.

नालिका ná-li-ka, s. f. An esculent root (*Arum colocasia*).

नालिता ná-li-ta, s. f. A sort of potherb (*Hibiscus cannabinus*).

नाली ná-lee, s. f. A stalk or culm ; any tubular vessel of the body ; the pulse.

नालीव्रण nalee-vrún, s. m. A fistulous or sinous sore.

नाव nao, s. f. A boat, ship, vessel ; any thing long and hollow within.

नावना náo-na, *v. a.* To bend downwards, to bow ; to cause to submit to, to cause to stoop.

नाविक návik, } *adj.* Belonging to a ves-
नावकी náo-kee, } sel, a boat, &c. *s. m.* The helmsman of a vessel, the steersman, the pilot ; a sailor.

नाश nash, } *s. m.* Annihilation, loss, de-
नास nas, } struction, non-existence, death.

नाशक na-shúk, *s. m.* A destroyer.

नाशन násh-un, *s. m.* Destruction, perishing.

नाशपाती nash-pá-tee, *s. f.* A pear (*Pyrus communis*).

नाशयन nash-yún, *adj.* Destroying, annihilating.

नाशित násh-it, *adj.* Destroyed.

नाशिनी násh-in-ee, *f.* } *adj.* Destructive,
नाशी násh-ee, *m.* } destroying, a destroyer.

नास nas, *s. f.* Snuff. *Nasdan, s. m.* A snuff-box.

नास nas, *s. m.* Non-existence, annihilation, death.

नासक nás-uk, *s. m.* A destroyer.

नासना nás-na, *v. n.* To flee, to run away. *v. a.* To destroy.

नासपाल nas-pál, *s. m.* The rind of an unripe pomegranate (*used in dying*). *Naspalee rung,* The colour extracted from *Naspal*.

नासमझ na-súm-ujh, *adj.* Unintelligent, not understanding.

नासमझी na-súm-jhee, *s. f.* Ignorance.

नासा ná-sa, *s. f.* The nose. *s. m.* An inflammation in the nose, the polypus.

नासादचिशावर्ष nása-dukshin-ávurn, *s. m.* Wearing the nose-ring in the right nostril by women who have money and children.

नासाबंश nasa-vúush, *s. m.* The bridge of the nose.

नासावामवर्त्त nása-vama-vúrtt, *s. m.* Wearing the nose-ring in the left nostril, a mark of sorrow or distress.

नासाशोख nasa-shókh, *s. m.* Drying of the nostrils.

नासिका nás-ik-a, *s. f.* The nose.

नासिकामल násika-múl, *s. m.* The mucus of the nose, snot.

नासि nás-ti, *adv.* Non-existence, not so, it is not.

नास्तिक nás-tik, } *s. m.* An atheist, but
नास्तिकी nás-tik-ee, } applied by the orthodox *Hindoos* to any one who denies the divine

authority of the *Veds,* or doubts the legends of the *Poorans.*

नास्तिकता nas-tik-tá, *s. f.* Atheism, denial of the deity, of a future state, of the divinity of the *Veds* ; *Bouddhism,* heresy, &c.

नास्तिक nas-tík-yuh, *s. m.* Infidelity, atheism.

नास्तित्व nas-ti-twúh, *s. m.* Non-existence.

नास्य nás-yuh, *s. m.* The rein of an ox passed through the septum of the nostrils.

नाहर ná-hur, *s. m.* A tiger.

नाहि ná-hi, } *adv.* No, not.
नाहीं na-héen, }

निःकारन níh-ka-run, *adj.* Causeless, unfounded.

निःक्षिप níh-kshipt, *adj.* Thrown or sent away ; spent ; passed.

निःक्षेप níh-kshep, *s. m.* Throwing, sending, putting away ; spending ; passing (*as time*) ; wiping away (*as tears*).

निःफल níh-phul, *m.* } *adj.* Fruitless,
निःफला níh-phul-a, *f.* } barren.

निःसंशय níh-shun-suy, *adj.* Undoubted.

निःशङ्क níh-shunk, *m.* } *adj.* Fearless.
निःशङ्का níh-shun-ka, *f.* }

निःशब्द níh-shubd, *adj.* Silent, voiceless.

निःशेष níh-shesh, *adj.* Complete, entire.

निःश्रेयस् nih-shréyus, *s. m.* Final beatitude, the release of the soul from the body, and its reunion with the primary and universal spirit.

निःश्वास níh-shwas, *s. m.* Breathing out, expiration ; sighing.

निःसंग níh-sung, *adj.* Separated, unconnected.

निःसत्य níh-sutyuh, *adj.* False, untrue.

निःसत्यता níh-sutyutá, *s. f.* Insincerity, falsehood.

निःसरन níh-sur-un, *s. m.* Death, dying ; a means or expedient ; exit, a going forth, or out ; final beatitude.

निःसह níh-suhuh, *adj.* Intolerable, unbearable ; irresistible, unable to support or bear.

निःसहत्व níh-suhutwúh, *s. m.* Inability to bear or support ; impatience ; unendurance.

निःसार níh-sar, *adj.* Sapless, pithless ; worthless, vain, unsubstantial. *s. m.* A plant (*Trophis aspera*).

निःसुख níh-sookh, *adj.* Disagreeable, distressing ; unhappy.

निःस्नेहा níh-sneha, *s. f.* Linseed (*Linum utilitissimum*).

निःस्पृह níh-sprihuh, *adj.* Free from desire ; disregarding, indifferent to.

निःख níh-swub, *adj.* Poor, indigent.

निःखादु níh-swadoo, *adj.* Iusipid, taste-less.

निकंटक ník-un-tuk, *adj.* Happy, without enmity or opposition ; plain, easy.

निकंद ní-kund, *adj.* Rooted up, extirpated.

निकट ní-kut, *adj.* Near, proximate. *adv.* About, with.

निकती ník-tee, *s. f.* A balance, small scales.

निकपट ní-kup-ut, *adj.* Without deceit or fraud, sincere, candid.

निकम्मा ni-kúm-ma, *adj.* Useless, good for nothing.

निकर ni-kúr, *s. m.* A flock or multitude ; a heap, a bundle ; pith, sap, essence.

निकरना ni-kúr-na, *v. n.* To issue, to go forth or out, to be extracted, drawn, pulled or taken out, to come or get out, secede, depart, proceed, to be uttered, to appear, result, prove, to turn out, to escape, to rise, slip, spring.

निकलचलना níkul-chúlna, *v. n* To escape ; (met.) to surpass another, to be advanced or promoted ; to speak much or display one's talent (*spoken of a person who from the modesty of a stranger had formerly been silent*).

निकलजाना níkul-jána, *v. n.* To escape, to go away.

निकलना ní-kul-na, *v. n.* To issue, to go forth or out, to be extracted, drawn, pulled or taken out, to come or get out, secede, depart, proceed, to be performed or accomplished, to exceed, to be uttered, to be taken off, to be produced, to appear, result, to prove, to turn out, to begin, to be invented, to escape, to rise, to slip, to spring.

निकलपडना nik-ul-púr-na, *v. n.* To come out, to be drawn forth.

निकलभागना ník-ul-bhágna, *v. n.* To run away, to get off, to be off.

निकसना ní-kus-na, *v. n.* To issue, to go forth or out, to be extracted, drawn, pulled or taken out, to come or get out, secede, depart, proceed, to be uttered, to appear, result, prove, to turn out, to escape, to rise, slip, spring.

निकाई ni-ká-ee, *s. f.* The price paid for weeding a field ; the act of weeding.

निकाना ni-ká-na, *v. a.* To weed.

निकाम ni-kám, *adv.* Voluntarily, willingly, implying certainty.

निकाल ni-kál, *s. m.* Contrivance, outlet, issue, vent, discharge, expulsion, projection. *Nikal dalna,* To deduct, to strike out. *Nikal dena,* To cashier, to exclude, to expel, to eject, to discard, to drive or turn out. *Nikal lana,* To bring off. *Nikal lena,* To dig up, to take out, to extract.

निकालना ni-kál-na, *v. a.* To cause to issue, to take out, to turn out, to expel, to cause to exceed, to utter, to discover or find out, to invent, to take off, to exclude, to extract, protrude, deduce, extricate, to exhibit, to produce, put forth, hatch, to pull, to do, to perform, to accomplish, to pick.

निकास ni-kás, *s. m.* Skirts, suburbs, outer boundary of land attached to a town, &c., issue, outgoing, discharge, outlet, vent, source, origin, spring ; adjustment of accounts, accomplishment.

निकासना ni-kás-na, *v. a.* To cause to issue, to take out, to turn out, to expel, to utter, to discover or find out, to invent, to exclude, to extract, to deduce, to extricate, to produce.

निकासी ni-ká-see, *s. f.* Taxes collected on goods passing out of a town, duties, &c. *Nikasee kee chitthee, s. f.* A permit, a passport.

निकास्त ní-kás-ta, *s. m.* A prop, a pillar.

निकुंज ni-kóonj, *s. m.* An arbour, a bower, a place overgrown with creepers.

निकुंभ ni-kóombh, *s. m.* A plant (*Croton polyandrum*).

निकोचक ni-kó-chuk, *s. m.* A tree (*Allangium hexapetalum*).

निकोसना ni-kós-na, *v. a.* To grin.

निकृत ni-krít, *adj.* Dishonest, wicked, perverse ; low, base, vile.

निकृति ni-krí-ti, *s. f.* Wickedness, dishonesty.

निकृष्ट ni-krísht, *adj.* Outcast, despised, low, vile.

निक्षिप्त ni-kshípt, *adj.* Rejected, abandoned, foregone, given or thrown away.

निक्षेप ni-kshép, *s. m.* Abandoning, parting with, throwing away.

निखंग ni-khúng, *s. f.* A quiver.

निखट्टू ni-khút-too, *adj.* Idle, thriftless, merciless.

निखंड ni-khúnd, *adj.* Half, mid.

निखरना ni-khúr-na, *v. n.* To be peeled, skinned, cleaned, cleared, settled.

निखराना nikh-rá-na, *v. a.* To settle, to purify, to clear.

निखर्ब ni-khúrb, *adj. m.* Dwarfish, a dwarf. *s. m.* A billion.

निखर्बा ni-khúr-ba, *adj. f.* Dwarfish, a dwarf.

निखारना ni-khár-na, *v. a.* To strain ; to bleach, to clear.

निखिल ni-khíl, *adj.* All, entire, complete.

निखोट ni-khót, *s. m.* Plain dealer, any thing without blemish.

निखोरना ni-khór-na, } *v. a.* To peel, skin,
निखोरना ni-khór-na, } decorticate, clean.

निखोसना ni-khós-na, *v. n.* To grin.

निगड़ ni-gúr, *s. m.* An iron chain for the feet, a fetter, but especially the heel chains of an elephant ; fetters, the stocks.

निगत ni-gút, *adj.* Naked.

निगन्दना ni-gúnd-na, *v. a.* To quilt.

निगन्दा ni-gún-da, *s. m.* } Quilting.
निगन्दाई ni-gun-dáee, *s. f.* }

निगम ni-gúm, *s. m.* The holy writings or *Veds* of the *Hindoos* collectively ; certainty, assurance.

निगमन ni-gúm-un, *s. m.* Certain or logical conclusion, the winding up of a syllogism.

निगर ni-gúr, *s. m.* Eating, swallowing.

निगलना ní-gul-na, *v. a.* To swallow, gulp down.

निगाली ni-gá-lee, *s. f.* A small *hookka* snake, the wooden pipe of a *hookka* snake.

निगूढ ni-góorh, *adj.* Profound, obscure ; hidden, concealed.

निगूढार्थ ni-goorh-árth, *adj.* Having a hidden sense or purpose.

निगोड़ा ni-gó-ra, *s. m.* Wretch, wight.

निग्गर níg-gur, *adj.* Solid.

निग्रह ni-grúh, *s. m.* Aversion, disfavour, discouragement, dislike.

निघण्टु ni-ghún-too, *s. m.* A vocabulary, a collection of words or names.

निघाति ni-ghá-ti, *s. f.* An iron club or mace.

निघ्न nighn, *adj.* Docile, subservient, domestic, dependant.

निश्चय ní-chuy, *s. m.* Certainty.

निश्चिन्त ni-chínt, *adj.* Free from thought, anxiety, or care, unconcerned, careless, at leisure. *Nichint hona,* To be at leisure, to be disengaged, to have finished.

निश्चिन्ताई ni-chin-táee, *s. f.* Carelessness, fearlessness, thoughtlessness, unconcern, leisure.

निचोड़ ni-chór, *s. m.* The end or termination of any affair ; the burthen, or that on which any thing depends.

निचोड़ना ni-chór-na, *v. a.* To wring, squeeze, press, strain, express, to extort, exact.

निचोड़ू ni-chó-roo, *adj.* Rapacious.

निछावर ni-chhá-wur, *s. f.* A propitiatory offering, sacrifice, victim.

निज nij, *adj.* Own, particular, individual, personal. *Nij-ka, adj.* Own, peculiar. *Nij-tij seh,* Properly, as is requisite.

निझतिझ nijh-tijh, *s. f.* Correctness, propriety, good order.

निझाना ni-jhá-na, *v. a.* To spy, observe, behold.

निझोटना ni-jhót-na, *v. a.* To twitch.

निझोल ni-jhól, *adj.* Steady, easy-paced, walking or running smoothly without agitation (*epithet of an elephant*).

निठारा ni-tá-ra, *s. m.* Determination, final settlement, decree.

निठल्ला ni-thúl-la, *s. m.* Idleness. *adj.* Idle.

निठुर ni-thóor, *adj.* Harsh, obdurate, relentless, cruel ; sly, cunning, shrewd.

निठुरता ni-thoor-tá, } *s. f.* Cruelty, obstinacy.
निठुराई ni-thoor-áee, }

निडर ní-dur, *adj.* Fearless, dauntless. *adv.* Without fear, fearlessly.

निढाल ni-dhál, } *adj.* Still, motionless.
निढोल ni-dhól, }

नित nit, *adv.* or *adj.* Always, continually, eternally, ever, constant, invariable ; the base of an obtuse-angled triangle. *Nit-pruti,* or, *Nit-nit,* Constantly, perpetually.

नितऊठ nit-óoth, *adv.* Constantly.

नितम्ब ni-túmb, *s. m.* A woman's buttocks.

नितराम् nit-rám, *adv.* Always, continually, eternally.

नितूल ni-túl, *s. m.* One of the seven divisions of *Patal* or hell.

नितान्त ni-tánt, *adj.* Much, excessive. *adv.* Much, excessively.

निती nít-tee, *s. f.* Small scales, such as goldsmiths use.

नित्य nít-yuh, *adj.* Eternal, everlasting, continual, perpetual ; past, present, and future; regular, fixed, invariable. *adv.* Always, eternally, continually.

नित्यकर्म nítyu-kurm, *s. m.* Indispensable act or ceremony, as observance of the five great sacrifices, or any daily or necessary rite.

नित्यता nit-yutá, *s. f.* Perpetuity, eternity.

नित्यदा nit-yudá, *adv.* Always, constantly, and eternally.

नित्यदान nit-yudán, *s. m.* Daily alms.

नित्यप्रलय nityu-prúluy, *s. m.* The constant loss of living beings.

नित्ययुक्त nityu-yóokt, *adj.* Always busy or engaged in.

नित्ययौवन nityu-yóuvun, *adj.* Ever or always young.

नित्यानध्याय nítya-nudhyá-yuh, *s. m.* A period when the perusal of the *Veds* is invariably prohibited, as the day of full moon, new moon, the eighth and fourteenth days of the half month.

नित्यानित्य nít-ya-nít-ya, *adj.* Eternal and perishable, permanent and temporary.

निथर níth-ra, *adj.* Clear (*water whose impurity has subsided*).

निथारना ni-thár-na, *v. a.* To pour ; to purify water or other liquid by letting the feculent matter subside and pouring off the clear.

निद्र्मन ni-dúr-shun, s. m. An example or illustration ; injunction, precept ; authority, text.

निदाधकाल ni-dádh-kal, s. m. The hot season, two months previous to the rains, about May and June.

निदान ni-dán, adv. At last, at length, lastly, after all, altogether. s. f. (In medicine) Knowledge of the symptoms of diseases (Diagnosis).

निदिग्धिका ni-dig-dhí-ka, s. f. A sort of prickly nightshade (Solanum jacquini).

निदिष्ट ni-dísht, adj. Ordered, directed ; advised, enjoined ; explained, pointed.

निदेश ni-désh, s. m. Order, command, direction, instruction ; the word of command.

निदेशी ni-désh-ee, adj. Showing, directing, pointing out.

निद्रा ní-dra, s. f. Sleep, sleepiness, sloth.

निद्रायमान ní-dra-yumán, adj. Sleeping, asleep.

निद्रालु ni-drá-loo, adj. Sleeping, sleepy, drowsy, slothful. s. f. A sort of perfume.

निद्रित ní-drit, adj. Sleepy, drowsy.

निधड़क ní-dhur-uk, adv. or adj. Without fear, fearlessly, abruptly.

निधन ní-dhun, adj. Poor.

निधनता ni-dhun-tá, s. f. Poverty.

निधान ni-dhán, s. m. A Nidhi or divine treasure, belonging especially to Koover, the god of wealth ; a receptacle, a place or vessel in or on which any thing is collected or deposited ; place of cessation or rest ; a place, house, mansion, abode, the subject in which any quality inheres.

निधि ní-dhí, s. m. One of Koover's divine treasures, nine of which are enumerated, viz. The Pudm, Muhapudm, Sunkh, Mukur, Kuchchup, Mookoond, Nund, Neel and Khurb : their nature is not exactly defined, though some of them appear to be precious gems : according to the Tantrik system they are personified and worshipped as demigods ; a receptacle, a place of asylum or accumulation, as, a treasury, a granary, a nest, &c. ; a treasure, any sum or quantity of wealth or valuables.

निनद nín-ud,
निनाद nin-ád, } s. m. Sound in general.

निनाया niu-áya, s. m. A bug.

निनांवा ninán-wa, s. m. The thrush, aphthae.

निन्दक nín-duk, adj. Reproachful, abusive, scurrilous, censorious, querulous. s. m. A calumniator, scorner.

निन्दकाई nin-duk-áee, s. f. Querulousness, censoriousness.

निन्दन nín-dun, adj. Abusing, blaming. s. m. Reproach, censure, blame.

निन्दना nind-na, v. a. To vilify, defame, revile, reproach.

निन्दा nín-da, s. f. Censure, reproach, scorn, defamation, reproof, blame, abuse, reviling.

निन्दास nind-ás, s. f. Drowsiness.

निन्दासा nind-ása, adj. Sleepy, drowsy.

निन्दास्तुति nínda-stóoti, s. f. Irony, ironical praise.

निन्दित nin-dit, adj. Abused, reviled, reproved ; low, despicable, worthy of being reviled.

निन्द्य nínd-yuh, adj. Bad, vile, despicable, reprehensible.

निन्नान्वे nin-nán-weh, adj. Ninety-nine. Ninnanweh keh pher men purna, To be entirely absorbed in the acquisition of wealth ; to be involved in difficulties.

निप nip, s. m. The Kudumb tree (Nauclea cadamba).

निपट ní-put, adv. Very, exceedingly.

निपटना ni-pút-na, v. n. To terminate, to be finished.

निपटाना nip-tá-na, v. a. To settle, decide, conclude, terminate.

निपटारा nip-tá-ra, s. m. End, finishing.

निपटारू nip-tá-roo, s. m. Who finishes, terminates, &c.

निपतन ni-pút-un, s. m. Falling.

निपतित ni-pút-it, adj. Fallen, fallen down.

निपाठ ni-páth, s. m. Reading, study of the sacred books, or public perusal of popular poems.

निपात ni-pát, s. m. Death, dying ; falling, coming down, alighting ; irregularity (in grammar) ; a particle (in ditto).

निपान ni-pán, s. m. A trough or ditch near a well for watering cattle ; any reservoir of water.

निपुण ni-póon, adj. Clever, skilful, expert, conversant, eminent.

निपूता ni-póo-ta, adj. Childless, having no son.

निबटेरा nib-tér-a, s. m. Determination.

निबड़ना ni-búr-na, v. n. To be accomplished, to be spent, to be ended.

निबन्ध ni-búndh, s. m. Epistasis, suppression of urine or constipation ; binding, confinement.

निबल ní-bul, adj. Weak.

निबलाई ni-bul-áee, s. f. Weakness.

निबाड़न ni-bá-run, s. m. Ending, finishing, cessation, separation.

निबाड़ना ni-bár-na, v. a. To keep one's engagements, &c. ; to accomplish, to perform, manage ; to spend, to end ; to separate.

निवारन ni-bá-run, *s. m.* Prevention, hindering, forbidding, stopping.

निवारना ni-bár-na, *v. a.* To forbid.

निवाह ni-báh, *s. m.* Accomplishment, performance, sufficiency, supply, maintenance ; performing or keeping an engagement, keeping, guarding.

निवाहना ni-báh-na, *v. a.* To accomplish, achieve, perfect, perform ; to protect, to guard, to take care of ; to keep one's faith ; to behave ; to afford ; to conduct.

निबाहू ni-bá-hoo, *adj.* Lasting, permanent, sufficient for one's purpose.

निबेरना ni-bér-na, *v. a.* To end, to put an end to, complete, perform, finish, spend.

निबेरा ni-bér-a, *s. m.* End, finishing.

निवेदन ni-béd-un, *s. m.* An address, a petition, representation to a superior.

निभना níbh-na, *v. n.* To serve, succeed, pass, live, last, to be accomplished, perfected, or performed.

निभाना ni-bhá-na, *v. a.* To perform ; to guard ; to keep one's faith ; to behave ; to afford ; to conduct.

निमकी ním-kee, *s. f.* Pickled lemons.

निमकौरी nim-kóuree, *s. f.* The berry of the *Neem* tree (*Melia azad-dirachta*).

निमन ním-un, *adj.* Stout, strong, tight, good.

निमनाई nim-un-áee, *s. f.* Strength, stoutness.

निमनाना nim-ná-na, *v. a.* To strengthen, to ameliorate.

निमाना nim-á-na, *adj.* Simple, without guile ; singular, unlike to all others, sheepish.

निमिष ním-ikh, *s. m.* A moment (*of time*), a twinkling of the eye.

निमित्त nim-ítt, *s. m.* Cause, motive, instrumental cause ; for the sake of ; (*met.*) fortune.

निमिष ním-ish, *s. m.* The twinkling of an eye ; the twinkling of an eye considered as a measure of time.

निमीलन nim-ée-lun, *s. m.* Death, dying ; twinkling of the eye, shutting of the eyelids, winking.

निमेष nim-ésh, *s. m.* Twinkling of the eye ; a momentary space of time, the twinkling of the eye considered as a measure of time.

निम्न nimn, *adj.* Deep, profound (*literally or figuratively*) ; low (*ground*), stooping.

निम्नता nimn-tá, *s. f.* Depth, profundity.

निम्ब nimb, *s. m.* A tree (*Melia azad-dirachta*).

निम्बतरु nimb-túroo, *s. m.* The Coral tree

(*Erythrina fulgens*), it is considered as one of the trees of paradise.

निम्बू ním-boo, *s. m.* The common lime (*Citrus acida*).

नियत ní-yut, *adj.* Self-governed, subdued, restrained.

नियतात्मा niyut-átma, *adj.* Self-regulated, self-controuled or restrained.

नियताहार níyut-ahár, *adj.* Abstemious.

नियतेन्द्रिय níyut-éndriyuh, *adj.* Of restrained or subdued passions.

नियन्ता ni-yún-ta, *s. m.* A charioteer, a coachman ; a ruler, a governor, a master.

नियम ní-yum, *s. m.* Agreement, contract, engagement, assent, promise ; any religious observance voluntarily practised, as fasting, watching, pilgrimage, praying, &c. ; a religious observance or obligation in general ; rule, precept ; usage, practice.

नियमन ni-yum-ún, *s. m.* Binding, restraining, checking.

नियमित ni-yum-ít, *adj.* Regulated, prescribed.

नियर ní-yur, *adv.* Near.

नियराई ni-yur-áee, *s. f.* Nearness.

नियामक ni-yá-muk, *s. m.* A boatman, a sailor, a steersman ; a pilot, a helmsman ; a charioteer.

नियाय ni-yáyuh, *s. m.* Justice, equity, right, decision. *Niyayuh kurna*, To judge, to administer justice, to decide.

नियायक ni-ya-yúk, *s. m.* A judge.

नियायिक ni-ya-yík, *s. m.* A reasoner, arguer, logician, sophist.

नियायी ni-yá-yee, *s. m.* A distributor of justice ; a logician.

नियार ni-yár, *s. m.* Forage, fodder, food of cattle.

नियारा ni-yá-ra, *adj.* Apart, aloof, separate, distinct, different, extraordinary, uncommon. *s. m.* The scoria left after refining gold, silver, or other metals ; from which a minute portion of those metals is obtainable. *Niyareh, adv.* Apart.

नियारिया ni-yá-riya, *s. m.* One who extracts metals from their scoria. *adj.* Prudent, cautious, not easily imposed on.

नियुक्त ni-yóokt, *adj.* Engaged in, applying or attached to ; authorized, called, appointed.

नियुत ni-yóot, *adj.* A million ; ten hundred thousand.

नियुद्ध ni-yóoddh, *s. m.* Close fight, personal struggle.

नियोग ni-yóg, *s. m.* An order or command ; authority, appointment.

नियोगी ni-yó-gee, *adj.* Engaged in any pursuit, closely attached to it or engrossed by it ; appointed, authorized, entrusted with authority, &c. *s. m.* A minister, a deputy, an agent, &c.

नियोजन **ni-yó-jun,** *s. m.* Ordering, commanding, directing.

नियोजित **ni-yo-jít,** *adj.* Entrusted with, appointed to ; directed, ordered.

निर् **nir,** *adv.* Negation, privation. *prep.* Out, without (*on the outside*), without (*not having*).

निरक्ष **nir-úksh,** *adj.* Having no latitude. *s. m.* (*In astronomy*) The terrestrial equator. .

निरक्षदेश **nir-uksh-désh,** *s. m.* A first meridian, as *Lunka* or Ceylon, a place where the sun is always vertical, and the days and nights are equal ; the equatorial region.

निरकार **nir-un-kár,** ⎱ *adj.* Without form
निरकाल **nir-un-kál,** ⎰ (*the deity*), incorporeal.

निरकुश **nír-un-koosh,** *adj.* Unchecked, uncontrolled, self-willed.

निरखना **nir-úkh-na,** *v. a.* To look at, to view, to see.

निरंजन **nír-un-jun,** *adj.* Void of passion or emotion ; unstained, unblackened. *s. m.* The Supreme Being.

निरंजना **nir-un-jun-á,** *s. f.* The day of full moon.

निरतक **nír-tuk,** *s. m.* A dancer.

निरंतर **nír-un-tur,** *adj.* or *adv.* Without interstices ; without interval ; continuous ; uninterrupted, continual ; unbounded ; incessantly, constantly.

निरंतराभ्यास **níruntur-abhyás,** *s. m.* Private study, reading to one's self the sacred works ; diligent and uninterrupted pursuit, exercise, practice.

निरपराध **nír-up-radh,** ⎱ *adj.* Faultless,
निरपराधी **nír-up-rádhee,** ⎰ blameless.

निरपेक्ष **nír-up-eksh,** *adj.* Independent of, unconnected or unconcerned with ; careless, indifferent, negligent ; without purpose or hope.

निरर्थक **nír-ur-thuk,** *adj.* Vain, fruitless, unprofitable ; unmeaning, insignificant, obsolete.

निरस **ní-rus,** *adj.* Dry ; insipid, tasteless. *s. m.* Insipidity, want of flavour or passion ; dryness ; want of juice.

निरस्त **nir-úst,** *adj.* Expelled ; abandoned, deserted, left.

निरस्त्र **nír-ustr,** *adj.* Without or destitute of arms, weapons, &c.

निरहंकार **nír-hun-kar,** *adj.* Humble, free from pride.

निरा **nír-a,** *adj.* Mere, pure, only, unalloyed, single, simple.

निराकार **nír-a-kar,** *adj.* Devoid of form or figure, incorporeal ; the Divine Spirit, God.

निराकांक्षी **nír-a-kankshee,** *adj.* Content, without desire, not coveting any thing.

निरादर **nír-a-dur,** *adj.* Without respect ; of bad dispositions, disrespectful, unceremonious, unpolite, disrespected.

निराधार **nír-adhar,** *adj.* Without support or prop.

निरापद **nír-a-pud,** *adj.* Prosperous, fortunate.

निरामय **nír-amuy,** *s. m.* The wild goat ; a hog, a boar.

निरामालु **nír-a-maloo,** *s. m.* The wood apple.

निरामिषी **nír-a-mish-ee,** *adj.* Living without meat ; free from sensual desires.

निरायास **nír-a-yas,** *adj.* Not giving trouble, ready, easily attainable.

निरायुध **nír-a-yoodh,** *adj.* Unarmed, defenceless.

निरालस्य **nír-a-lusyuh,** *adj.* Not slothful, active.

निराला **nir-á-la,** *adj.* Apart, aloof, retired, lonely, private ; pure, mere, simple, unmixed, unalloyed ; rare, strange, odd, extraordinary. *Niraleh,* or, *Niraleh men,* Apart, in private.

निराश **nír-ash,** *adj.* Hopeless, despairing ; disappointed. [ing.

निराशिष **nír-ashis,** *adj.* Without a bless-
निराशी **nír-ashee,** *s. f.* Despair.

निराश्रय **nír-ash-ruy,** *adj.* Without refuge, destitute.

निराहार **nír-a-har,** *adj.* Fasting through necessity or choice.

निरिन्द्रिय **nír-in-driyuh,** *adj.* Imperfect, mutilated, maimed.

निरीक्षण **nir-ée-kshun,** *s. m.* Looking at, regarding, seeing ; expecting, hoping.

निरीक्षमान **nir-eeksh-mán,** *adj.* Looking at, regarding, hoping, expecting.

निरीक्षित **nir-eek-shit,** *adj.* Seen, beheld, looked at ; hoped, expected.

निरीछा **nir-ée-cha,** *s. f.* Looking at, regarding ; hope, expectation.

निरीश **nir-ée-sh,** *s. m.* The body of a plough.

निरुक्त **nír-ookt,** *adj.* Obscure, obsolete. *s. m.* One of the *Vedangs* or works considered as supplementary to and connected with the *Veds,* forming part of scriptural or sacred science ; glossarial explanation of obscure terms, especially those occurring in the *Veds.*

निरुक्ति **nír-ook-ti,** *s. f.* The *Vedang* or portion of scriptural science, which explains obscure and obsolete terms.

निरुत्तर nír-oot-tur, *adj.* Non-plussed, without an answer.

निरुपम nír-oo-pum, *adj.* Unequalled, having no resemblance or likeness.

निरूप ní-roop, *adj.* Without form (*the Deity*), incorporeal.

निरूपण ni-róo-pun, *s. m.* Ascertaining, determining.

निरूपित ni-róo-pit, *adj.* Ascertained ; appointed, deputed, directed to do any thing.

निरेखना ni-rékh-na, *v. a.* To behold, to spy, to look out.

निरोग ní-rog, } *adj.* In high health and
निरोगी ní-ro-gee, } spirits, healthy.

निर्गत nír-gut, *adj.* Gone out or forth ; expended, extinct, departed.

निर्गन्ध nír-gundh, *adj.* Inodorous, void of fragrance or smell.

निर्गन्धपुष्पी nír-gundh-póoshpee, *s. f.* The *Simul* or silk-cotton tree.

निर्गम nír-gum, *s. m.* Going forth or out, exit.

निर्गुण nír-goon, *adj.* Void of all properties ; bad, worthless, unskilful, having no good or estimable qualities ; unstrung, as a necklace. *s. m.* The Supreme Being, as being without passions or human qualities.

निर्गुणत्व nirgoon-twúh, *s. m.* The state of being free from all qualities, an attribute, especially of the Supreme Being.

निर्गुण्डी nir-goon-thée, *s. f.* A shrub (*Vitex negundo*) ; the root of the lotus.

निर्घण्ट nir-ghúnt, *s. m.* A vocabulary, an index.

निर्घिन nír-ghin, *adj.* Not odious, not detestable.

निर्चा nír-cha, *s. m.* A kind of greens (*Corchorus capsularis*).

निर्छल nír-chhul, *adj.* Simple, guileless.

निर्जन nír-jun, *adj.* Without a person or individual, desert, uninhabited, lonely, unpeopled, unfrequented.

निर्जर nír-jur, *adj.* Immortal, imperishable, undecaying. *s. m.* Ambrosia, the food of the gods.

निर्जल nír-jul, *adj.* Dry, desert, without water, void of water. *s. m.* A desert, a waste.

निर्जित nír-jit, *adj.* Conquered, subdued, overcome ; unconquered.

निर्जीव nír-jeev, *adj.* Lifeless, inanimate.

निर्झर nír-jhur, *s.* A cascade or torrent, the precipitous descent of water from mountains, &c.

निर्णय nír-nuy, *s. m.* Certainty, positive

conclusion ; investigation ; (*in law*) sentence, decision ; (*in logic*) complete ascertainment.

निर्णीत nir-néet, *adj.* Ascertained, determined ; sentenced, decreed.

निर्त nirt, *s. m.* Dance.

निर्तना nírt-na, *v. a.* To dance, to jump about playfully.

निर्तोना nir-tá-na, *v. a.* To make dance ; to make pure, to clean.

निर्दई nír-duee, } *adj.* Unkind, unmerci-
निर्दय nír-duy, } ful, unfeeling, cruel,
निर्दयी nír-duyee, } hard-hearted, devoid of pity or charity, merciless.

निर्दहन nír-duhun, *s. m.* Marking nut.

निर्दहनी nir-dúhun-ee, *s. f.* A sort of creeper, from the fibres of which bow-strings are made (*Sanseviera zeylanica*).

निर्दिष्ट nir-dísht, *adj.* Described, depicted, pointed out, shown ; ascertained, determined.

निर्देश nir-désh, *s. m.* Order, command ; description ; depicting, pointing out or exhibiting.

निर्दोष nír-dosh, } *adj.* Faultless, with-
निर्दोषी nír-do-shee, } out defect or blemish.

निर्द्वन्द nir-dwund, *adj.* Not double ; free from either of two alternatives, neither glad nor sorry, &c. ; not acknowledging two principles.

निर्धन nír-dhun, *adj.* Poor, indigent.

निर्धर्म nír-dhurm, *adj.* Impious, unrighteous, immoral, void of law or religion.

निर्धार nir-dhár, } *s. m.* Certainty, as-
निर्धारण nir-dhár-un, } certainment.

निर्धारित nir-dhá-rit, *adj.* Ascertained, determined.

निर्नमस्कार nír-num-us-kár, *adj.* Uncourteous.

निर्नाथ nír-nath, *adj.* Having no superior, master, protector, &c.

निर्नाथता nír-nath-ta, *s. f.* Being without a master ; widowhood.

निर्पक्ष nír-puksh, } *adj.* Helpless, friend-
निर्पक्ष nír-puchh, } less.

निर्फल nír-phul, *adj.* Fruitless.

निर्बंश nír-bunsh, *adj.* Childless, without offspring ; extinct (*as a race or family*).

निर्बन्धू nír-bun-dhoo, *adj.* Friendless, without relations.

निर्बल nír-bul, *adj.* Weak, feeble, powerless ; without strength.

निर्बलता nír-bul-tá, *s. f.* Weakness, feebleness, impotence, prostration of strength.

निर्बुष nír-bush, *adj.* Powerless, enfeebled.

निर्बिंसी nír-bis-ee, *s. f.* Zedoary (*a spicy*

plant somewhat like ginger in its leaves, but of a sweet scent, Amomum zedoaria : Curcuma zedoaria).

निर्बीज **nír-beej,** *adj.* Without seed, child-less ; extinct (*a race or family*).

निर्बुद्धि **nír-booddhí,** *adj.* Ignorant, unwise, void of understanding, senseless, irrational.

निर्बूझ **nír-boojh,** *adj.* Not to be under-stood, incomprehensible.

निवर **nír-byr,** *adj.* Free from hatred or enmity.

निर्भय **nír-bhuy,** *adj.* Fearless, undaunted.

निर्मद **nír-mud,** *adj.* Sober, quiet, unin-toxicated. *s. m.* An elephant after the frontal juice has ceased to exude, one out of rut.

निर्मनुष्य **nír-mun-oosh,** *adj.* Uninhabited, desolate.

निर्मम **nír-mum,** *adj.* Disinterested, claim-ing or wishing for nothing.

निर्ममत्व **nír-mum-twuh,** *s. m.* Disregard of worldly interests or possessions.

निर्मल **nir-mul,** *adj.* Clear, clean, free from dirt or impurities (*literally or figuratively*), pure, limpid, pellucid, transparent, spotless.

निर्मलता **nir-mul-tá,** *s. f.* Pureness, limpid-ness, pellucidness, clearness, transparency.

निर्मलत्व **nir-mul-twúh,** *s. m.* Purity, clean-ness (*physical or moral*).

निर्मली **nír-mul-ee,** *s. f.* A seed with which water is cleared (*Strychnos potatorum*).

निर्माण **nir-mán,** *s. m.* Manufacture, pro-duction, making ; pith, marrow, essence.

निर्माल्य **nir-mál-yuh,** *adj.* Clear, clean. *s. m.* The remains of an offering presented to a god; purity, clearness, cleanness.

निर्मित **nír-mit,** *adj.* Made; fabricated, artificial.

निर्मूल **nír-mool,** *adj.* Baseless, unfounded ; eradicated.

निर्मोही **nír-mo-hee,** *adj.* Not fascinated, without affection, free from attachment, unkind.

निर्यास **nir-yás,** *s. m.* Extract, decoction, infusion ; any natural exudation of a plant, as gum, milk, extract, &c.

निर्लज्ज **nír-lujj,** *adj.* Shameless, immodest, impudent.

निर्लिप्त **nír-lipt,** *adj.* Unsmeared, unanoint-ed ; undefiled, uncontaminated (*by passion, &c.*). *s. m.* A name of *Krishn.*

निर्लोभ **nír-lobh,** } *adj.* Without covet-
निर्लोभी **nír-lo-bhee,** } ousness, not covet-ous, void of avarice, contented.

निर्वण **nír-vun,** *adj.* Bare, open (*a country*).

निर्वाण **nir-ván,** *adj.* Liberated from exist-ence ; dead, deceased. *s. m.* Eternal happiness, emancipation from matter, and re-union with the deity : it is especially employed in this sense by the *Bouddhs* and *Jyns,* understanding by it per-fect and perpetual calm.

निर्वात **nír-vat,** *adj.* Calm, still, not windy, having ceased to blow. *s. m.* A calm.

निर्वाह **nír-váh,** *s. m.* Accomplishment, completion, an end ; carrying on, supporting, maintaining ; providing means ; sufficiency, ade-quacy.

निर्विकार **nír-vi-kar,** *adj.* Unchanged, un-altered, uniform.

निर्विघ्न **nír-vighn,** *adj.* Unobstructed. *s. m.* Absence of obstruction or impediment. *adv.* Freely, unobstructedly.

निर्विन्ध्या **nir-vín-dhya,** *s. f.* A river that rises in the *Vindhya* mountains.

निर्विवेक **nír-vivek,** *adj.* Foolish, undiscri-minating.

निर्विषी **nír-vish-ee,** *s. f.* A plant (*Curcuma zedoaria*).

निर्वीज **nír-veej,** *adj.* Seedless ; impotent.

निर्वीर्य **nír-veerj,** *adj.* Tame, feeble, spi-ritless ; impotent.

निर्वृत **nir-vrít,** *adj.* Ended, terminated ; happy, content ; emancipated ; free from occupa-tion or interest.

निर्वृत्ति **nir-vrítti,** *s. f.* Final emancipation from existence ; death ; happiness ; rest, repose, tranquillity, ceasing or abstaining from ; comple-tion, accomplishment, conclusion.

निर्वेद **nír-ved,** *adj.* Not having the *Veds,* infidel, unscriptural.

निर्वैर **nír-vyr,** *adj.* Friendly, without en-mity.

निवुरा **ní-vur-a,** *s. f.* A virgin, a girl un-married.

निवान **ni-wán,** *adj.* Low (*ground*).

निवाना **ni-wá-na,** *v. a.* To bend down-wards, to bow ; to cause to submit to, to cause to stoop ; to double, to fold.

निवार **ni-wár,** *s. m.* Hindering, opposition, impediment. *s. f.* Tape (*of a coarse kind*). *Niwar-baf,* A tape-weaver.

निवारण **ni-wá-run,** *s. m.* Hindering, op-posing, an impediment.

निवारना **ni-wár-na,** *v. a.* To prevent, to hinder, to prohibit.

निवारित **ni-wá-rit,** *adj.* Hindered, check-ed, opposed.

निवारी **ni-wá-ree,** *s. f.* A flower, a sort of jasmine.

निवाौना **ni-wáo-na,** *v. a.* To bend down-wards, to bow ; to cause to submit to, to cause to stoop ; to double, to fold.

निवास ni-wás, *s. m.* A house, a dwelling, a residence.

निवासी ni-wá-see, *m.* ⎫ *adj.* Dwelling,
निवासिनी ni-wa-sín-ee, *f.* ⎭ abiding in, inhabiting. *s. m. f.* An inhabitant.

निवृत्ति ni-vrít-ti, *s. f.* Final emancipation from existence; rest, repose, tranquillity.

निवेदन ni-véd-un, *s. m.* An address, a petition, representation to a superior.

निश nish, *s. f.* Night.

निःशङ्क ní-shunk, *adj.* Fearless, free from doubt or suspicion. *adv.* Boldly.

निशा nísh-a, *s. f.* Night.

निशाकर nish-a-kúr, ⎫
निशानाथ nish-a-náth, ⎭ *s. m.* The moon.

निशाचर nísh-a-chúr, *adj.* Nocturnal, night-walking, what goes or moves about by night. *s. m.* A Rakshus, a fiend, an imp or goblin, a demon; a robber, a thief; a nocturnal animal, an animal that watches and feeds by night.

निशाचरी nísh-a-chúr-ee, *s. f.* A woman who goes to an assignation, a harlot, a whore; a she-devil, a female fiend; a sort of perfume.

निशान्त ni-shánt, *adj.* Quiet, tranquil, patient. *s. m.* A house, a dwelling; the end of the night, or break of day.

निशान्तनारी nishánt-náree, *s. f.* A female, a house-wife.

निशान्ध nish-ándh, *adj.* Blind at night.

निशापुष्प nísh-a-pooshp, *s. m.* The white water-lily.

निशिपुष्पा níshi-póoshp-a, *s. f.* A flower (*Nyctanthes tristis*).

निशीथ nish-éet, *s. m.* Midnight; night.

निशेला nish-él-a, *adj.* Intoxicating, inebrient.

निशीत ni-shyt, *s. m.* A crane (*Ardea nivea*).

निश्चय nís-chuy, *s. m.* Certainty, ascertainment, positive conclusion; trust, belief, faith. *adj.* Actual, real, ascertained, certain, sure, indubitable. *adv.* Certainly, actually, indubitably.

निश्चर nish-chúr, *s. m.* A prowler.

निश्चरी nish-chur-áee, *s. f.* Prowling. *Nishchuraee kurna*, To prowl.

निश्चल nísh-chul, *adj.* Immovable, still, fixed.

निश्चला nísh-chúl-a, *s. f.* The earth.

निश्चलाङ्ग nish-chul-áng, *s. m.* A kind of crane (*Ardea nivea*); a mountain, a rock.

निश्चित nísh-chit, *adj.* Certain, ascertained, determined, concluded. *s. m.* Certainty, conclusion.

निश्चिन्त nísh-chint, *adj.* Thoughtless, inconsiderate, void of reflection; free from thought,
anxiety, or care, unconcerned, careless, at leisure. *Nishchint hona*, To be at leisure, to be disengaged, to have finished.

निश्चूर्ण nish-chóok-kun, *s. m.* A sort of tooth powder prepared of sulphate of iron, &c., it destroys the tartar, but blackens the teeth.

निश्चेष्ट nísh-chesht, *adj.* Powerless, helpless; incapable of effort.

निश्छिद्र nísh-chhidr, *adj.* Without flaw or defect; without vent, having no holes or rent.

निश्श्वास nísh-shwas, *s. m.* Breath expired, breathing out, expiration.

निषङ्ग ni-shúng, *s. m.* Union, meeting, association.

निषध ni-shúdh, *s. m.* The name of a mountain or mountainous range, forming one of the principal ranges of the universe, and described as lying immediately south of *Ilavrut*, and north of the *Himala* range; a country in the south-east division of India; the sovereign of *Nishudh*.

निषण्णक ni-shún-nuk, *s. m.* A sort of pot-herb (*Marsilea dentata*).

निषाद ni-shád, *s. m.* The first of the seven musical notes, or more properly the last and highest of the scale; a man of a degraded tribe, or an outcast, especially the son of a *Brahmun* by a *Soodr* woman. [den.

निषिद्ध ni-shíddh, *adj.* Prohibited, forbid-
निषिद्धता ni-shiddh-tá, *s. f.* ⎫ Prohibition,
निषेध ni-shédh, *s. m.* ⎭ forbiddance.

निषेक ni-shék, *s. m.* The ceremony performed upon impregnation taking place.

निषेध ni-shédh, *s. m.* Prohibition, negation.

निष्कण्टक nísh-kun-tuk, *adj.* Without thorns; free from trouble.

निष्कुन्थ nish-kúnth, *s. m.* A plant (*Capparis trifoliata*).

निष्कपट nísh-kup-ut, *adj.* Without fraud or deceit, open, artless, honest, sincere.

निष्कर्ष nísh-kursh, *s. m.* Certainty, ascertainment.

निष्काम nísh-kam, *adj.* Free from wish or desire. *adv.* Unwillingly.

निष्कारण nísh-karun, *adj.* Causeless, groundless.

निष्क्रमण nish-krúm-un, *s. m.* Going forth or out; taking a child for the first time out of the house, in the fourth month, considered as an essential ceremony, and accompanied by sacrifice, &c.

निष्ठा nish-thá, *s. f.* Confirmation; faith, belief.

निष्ठान nish-thán, *s. m.* Sauce, condiment.

निष्ठुर nish-thóor, *adj.* Harsh, contumelious (*as speech*); hard, solid.

निष्ठुरता nísh-thoor-tá, *s. f.* Harshness of speech, reviling, abuse.

निष्पत्ति nísh-putti, *s. f.* Completion, conclusion, termination, consummation.

निष्पन्न nish-púnn, *adj.* Done, finished, concluded, completed.

निष्पराक्रम nísh-pur-a-krum, *adj.* Weak, destitute of power.

निष्पादन nish-pá-dun, *s. m.* Doing, effecting, accomplishing; concluding; producing, causing, engendering.

निष्पादित nish-pa-dít, *adj.* Done, effected, made, produced.

निष्पाप nísh-pap, ⎫ *adj.* Sinless, innocent.
निष्पापी nísh-pa-pee, ⎭ cent.

निष्पुत्र nísh-pootr, *adj.* Sonless.

निष्पुरुष nísh-poo-roosh, *s. m.* A eunuch or impotent man; a coward.

निष्प्रयोजन nísh-pruyo-jun, *adj.* Causeless, groundless.

निष्पृह nísh-prih, *adj.* Content, not envying any person, nor coveting any thing; exempt from desires.

निष्फल nísh-phul, *adj.* Barren, unfruitful; seedless, impotent.

निष्फला nísh-phul-á, ⎫ *s. f.* A woman past
निष्फली nísh-phul-ée, ⎭ child-bearing, one in whom menstruation has ceased.

निश nis, *s. f.* Night.

निशंक ní-sunk, *adj.* Fearless, free from doubt or suspicion. *adv.* Boldly.

निशंकट ní-sun-kut, *adv.* Without trouble or difficulty; with ease.

निशंकोच ní-sun-koch, *adj.* Without contracting; without shame or reserve.

निशचर nis-chúr, *s. m.* A night-prowler.

निशचराई nis-chur-áee, *s. f.* Night-prowling. *Nischuraee kurna,* To prowl at night.

निशंधाई ní-sun-dhaee, *s. f.* Solidity.

निशंधि ní-sun-dhi, *adj.* Solid, tight, not leaky.

निसरना ní-sur-na, *v. n.* To issue, to go forth, to come out.

निसास ni-sás, *s. m.* Breath.

निशि ní-si, *s. f.* Night.

निसिंधु ni-sín-dhoo, *s. m.* A shrub (*Vitex negundo*).

निसेनी ni-sén-ee, ⎫ *s. f.* A wooden ladder,
निसेनी ni-sy-nee, ⎭ a ladder.

निष्कपट nís-kup-ut, *adj.* Without fraud or deceit, open, artless, honest, sincere.

निस्तार nis-tár, *s. m.* Release, acquittal, salvation, final liberation, beatitude.

निस्तारना nis-tár-na, *v. a.* To release, acquit; to beatify or exempt the soul from further transmigration.

निस्तारबीज nis-tar-véej, *s. m.* The cause of final liberation, faith in any deity, &c.

निस्तारा nis-tá-ra, *s. m.* Definitive settlement, decision, decree, adjustment; blessing.

निस्तेजस् nís-tej-us, *adj.* Dull, obscure; dull, spiritless; powerless, impotent.

निस्तोक nis-tók, *s. m.* Definitive settlement, decision, decree, adjustment.

निस्पंद ní-spund, *adj.* Still, steady, immoveable.

निस्पृह ní-sprih, *adj.* Content, unenvious.

निस्पृहा ní-spri-ha, *s. f.* A plant (*Gloriosa superba*).

निस्संदेह nís-sun-deh, *adj.* Free from doubt, undoubted. *adv.* Undoubtedly.

निस्वास nis-wás, *s. m.* Breath, aspiration.

निहंग ní-hung, *adj.* Naked; free from care. *Nihun lurla,* A careless child or person.

निहचय níh-chuy, *s. m.* Certainty, ascertainment.

निहत्था ní-huttha, *adj.* Unarmed.

निहाई ni-háee, *s. f.* An anvil.

निहाका ni-há-ka, *s. f.* An iguana or the Gangetic alligator.

निहानी ni-há-nee, *s. f.* The menses.

निहारना ni-hár-na, *v. a.* To look at, to regard, to watch, to look after, to spy, to see.

निहाल ni-hál, *adj.* Exalted, pleased, happy.

निहोरना ni-hóor-na, *v. n.* To condescend, to incline or bend downward, decline, to stoop, to bow, to lean.

निहोराना ni-hoo-rána, *v. a.* To cause to crook, to bend, to bow.

निहोरना ni-hóor-na, *v. n.* To bend downwards, to bow down, to incline, to stoop.

निहोरा ni-hó-ra, *s. m.* Favour, obligation, kindness; begging, requesting humbly, coaxing.

निक्षिप्त ni-kshípt, *adj.* Thrown or sent away.

निक्षेप ni-kshép, *s. m.* Throwing, sending, putting away.

नींद neend, *s. f.* Sleep. *Neend oochat hona,* To be unable to sleep, or to have sleep broken. *Neend bhur sona,* To sleep sound, to be at ease.

नींदना néend-na, *v. a.* To deny; to blame, to censure. *v. n.* To sleep.

नींदू neen-dóo, *s. m.* Sleeper.

नींबू néem-boo, *s. m.* Lemon, lime.

नीका née-ka, } *adj.* Good, beautiful, ele-
नीकौ née-kou, } gant; well.

नीच neech, *adj.* Low (*in stature*), short, dwarfish; low (*in condition*), vile, base, mean, vulgar. *Neech-oonch*, *s. f.* Inequality; the ups and downs of life.

नीचा née-cha, *adj.* Below, down, low. *Neecha ooncha*, Up and down, uneven ground, abrupt. *Neecheh sooron seh bolna*, To sing with a low voice, or hum a tune.

नीचाई nee-chá-ee, *s. f.* Lowness.

नीचे née-cheh, *adv.* Below, beneath, under, down. *Neecheh oopur*, Upside down. *Neecheh jana*, To descend, to submit, to subside, to succumb.

नीति née-ti, *s. f.* Polity, political science, treating especially of the administration of government, including the practice of morality in private life, both by the sovereign and his subjects.

नीतिकथा néeti-kútha, *s. f.* Any work on polity or good government.

नीतिज्ञ nee-tig-yúh, *s. m.* A statesman, a politician.

नीतिमत neeti-mút, *adj.* Moral, eminent for royal duties.

नीतिविद्या néeti-vídya, *s. f.* Political science.

नीतिशास्त्र néeti-shástr, *s. m.* The science of political ethics, or any work treating of it.

नीद need, *s. f.* Sleep.

नीप neep, *s. m.* The *Kudumb* tree (*Nauclea kadamba*); a species of Ixora (*I. bundhuca*); a sort of *Asoca* or *Nil Asoka*.

नीबू née-boo, *s. m.* Lemon, lime.

नीम neem, *s. m.* A tree (*Melia azaddirachta*), the margosa tree.

नीमन née-mun, *adj.* Strong; well-finished; solid.

नीमावत nee-má-wut, *s. f.* System of the followers of *Neemanund*, a *Hindoo* mendicant.

नीर neer, *s. m.* Water.

नीरज neer-új, *adj.* Aquatick. *s. m.* A sort of *Costus* (*C. speciosus*); a lotus in general; an otter.

नीरजस् née-ruj-us, *adj.* Having no pollen (*as a flower*). *s. f.* A woman not menstruating.

नीरथ née-ruth, *adj.* Fruitless, profitless, vain.

नीरस née-rus, *adj.* Dry, withered, insipid, devoid of taste, &c., morally or physically; tasteless, unpleasant.

नीरोग née-rog, *adj.* Healthy, free from sickness.

नीरोगता nee-rog-tá, *s. f.* Health.

नील neel, *adj.* Blue, dark blue or black.

नील neel, *s. m.* Indigo, blue (*Indigofera tinctoria*); the river *Nile*, the blue mountains, one of the principal ranges of mountains, dividing the world into nine portions, and lying immediately north of *Ilavrut* or the central division; one of the divine treasures of *Koover*; a gem (*the sapphire*); the blue or hill *Myna*, a bird so called; blue vitriol. *Neel ka math bigarna*, (*lit.*) A vat of indigo being spoiled, is used (*met.*) To express the persecutions of fortune; and on hearing something very wonderful and incredible. (*The phrase is said to originate from a notion entertained by dyers, that when their dye, through any accident, has been spoiled, it may be restored by telling some miraculous story*).

नीलक nee-lúk, *adj.* Blue (*stained or dyed blue*). *s. m.* One of the terms used in *Beej-gunit*, as we use the letters a, b, x, y, in algebra.

नीलकण्ठ néel-kunth, *s. m.* A bird (*Coracias bengalensis*); a name of *Muhadeo*: (he is called by this name because his throat was stained blue by swallowing the poison produced by overchurning the ocean, with the mountain *Mundur*, by the *Soors* and *Usoors*, to procure the *Umrit*); a gallinule; a sparrow; a wagtail; a peacock; *Morunga* (*Hyperanthera morunga*); a blue jay.

नीलकण्ठाक्ष neel-kunth-áksh, *s. m.* The *Elæocarpus* seed.

नीलकमल néel-kum-ul, *s. m.* The blue lotus.

नीलकुरण्टक neel-koo-róon-tuk, *s. m.* Blue Barleria (*B. cærulea*).

नीलक्रौञ्च neel-króunch, *s. m.* A sort of curlew or heron.

नीलगाव néel-gao, *s. f.* An animal (*known by the name of Leel-gaee and Rojh*), the whitefooted antelope of Pennant and *Antilope picta* of Pallas.

नीलज nee-lúj, *s. m.* Blue steel.

नीलझिण्टी neel-jhín-tee, *s. f.* Blue Barleria.

नीलपद्म néel-pudm, *s. m.* The blue lotus (*Nymphœa cærulea*).

नीलपाचन neel-pá-chun, *s. m.* Steeping or maceration of indigo.

नीलपाचनभाण्ड neel-pachun-bhánd, *s. m.* An indigo vat.

नीलपिच्छ neel-píchchh, *s. m.* A falcon.

नीलपुष्पिका neel-póoshp-ika, *s. f.* The indigo plant.

नीलपृष्ठ neel-príshth, *s. m.* A sort of fish, the *Rohi* (*Cyprinus denticulatus*).

नीलबरी neel-búr-ee, *s. f.* A lump of indigo.

नीलम néelum, } *s. m.* A gem of a blue
नीलमणि neel-múni, } colour, the sapphire.

नीलमृत्तिका néel-mrit-ti-ka, *s. f.* Iron pyrites; black mould.

नीलम्बर neel-úm-bur, *s. m.* Black or dark blue raiment.

नीललोह neel-lóh, *s. m.* Blue steel.

नीललोहित neel-ló-hit, *adj.* Purple, of a purple colour. *s. m.* A mixture of red and blue, purple.

नीलवर्ण neel-vúrn, *adj.* Blue, of a blue colour.

नीला née-la, *adj.* Blue, dark blue or black. *Neela-peela*, Black and blue. *Neela thotha*, Blue vitriol.

नीलाई neel-á-ee, *s. f.* Blueness.

नीलाङ्ग neel-áng, *s. m.* The Indian crane; the blue jay.

नीलाञ्जन neel-án-jun, *s. m.* Blue vitriol.

नीलाम neel-ám, *s. m.* Auction.

नीलाम्बर neel-ám-bur, *adj.* Dressed in dark blue cloth. *s. m.* Black or dark blue raiment.

नीलाश्मन् neel-ásh-mun, *s. m.* A blue stone, a sapphire.

नीलिका née-lik-a, *s. f.* A plant (*Nyctanthes tristis*), a species with blue flowers; the indigo plant.

नीलिनी née-lin-ee, *s. f.* Indigo (*Indigofera tinctoria.*)

नीलोपल neel-ó-pul, *s. m.* A blue stone (*Lapis lazuli*).

नीवा née-wa, *s. m.* Stillness.

नीसरना née-sur-na, *v. n.* To issue, to go forth, to come out.

नीहार nee-hár, *s. m.* Frost, hoar frost; heavy dew.

नूह nooh, *s. m.* Nail (*of the finger, &c.*), talon. *Nooh lena*, To trip, to stumble.

नूहटा noo-hútta, *s. m.* A scratch with the nail or talon.

नूतन nóo-tun, *adj.* New, recent, fresh, young, &c. [velty.

नूतनत्व noo-tun-twúh, *s. m.* Newness, no-

नूद nood, *s. m.* The mulberry tree (*Morus Indica*).

नूधा nóo-dha, *s. m.* A sort of tobacco.

नून noon, *s. m.* Salt.

नूनिया nóo-ni-ya, *s. f.* A sort of greens, purslain (*Portulaca oleracea*.)

नूपुर nóo-poor, *s. m.* A ring hollowed, about a finger and a half in breadth, used as an ornament for the ankles and toes. (*In it are bits of copper or iron, of the size of a vetch, which cause it to sound like a number of small bells, when the wearer walks*).

नृति nrí-ti, *s. f.* Dancing, the science or practice.

नृतू nrí-too, *s. m.* A dancer, a mimic, an actor.

नृत्य nrít-yuh, *s. m.* Dancing, acting, the actor's practice in general.

नृदेव nri-dév, *s. m.* A king.

नृधर्म nrí-dhurm, *s. m.* Manly property or duty.

नृप nrip, नृपति nri-púti, } *s. m.* A king, a sovereign.

नृपनीति nrip-néeti, *s. f.* Royal policy.

नृपद्रुम nrip-dróom, *s. m.* A tree (*Cassia fistula*).

नृपप्रिय nrip-príyuh, *s. m.* A thorny species of bamboo (*Bambusa spinosa*).

नृपांश nrip-ánsh, *s. m.* Revenue, the royal portion; of grain, a sixth, eighth, or twelfth; of fruits, &c., a sixth; and of merchandize, a fiftieth.

नृपाभीर nrip-a-bhéer, *s. m.* Music played at the royal meals.

नृपामय nrip-á-muy, *s. m.* Consumption.

नृपावर्त nrip-a-vúrt, *s. m.* A kind of gem.

नृपासन nrip-ásun, *s. m.* A throne.

नृपोचित nrip-ó-chit, *adj.* Kingly, princely, suited to a king.

नृवराह nri-vur-áh, *s. m.* The mythological boar, incarnation of *Vishnoo*.

नृसिंह nrí-singh, *s. m.* The fourth *Uvutar*, or supposed descent of *Vishnoo*, in the shape of a man, with the head and claws of a lion; a chief, a noble, a great or illustrious man.

ने neh, A particle affixed to the name of the agent with a transitive verb in a past tense.

नेओन ne-óon, *s. m.* Butter.

नेक nek, नेकू nék-oo, } *adj.* A little, little.

नेग neg, *s. f.* Presents at marriage and on other festive occasions made to relations and to particular servants, and considered by them as perquisites which they are entitled to.

नेगीजोगी négee-jógee, *adj.* Tenants and dependants, to whom it is customary to give the neg.

नेटा nét-a, *s. m.* Snot, snivel.

नेती nét-ee, *s. f.* A cord used to whirl round the churn-staff with.

नेत्र netr, *s. m.* The eye; the string of a churning rope.

नेत्रपिण्ड netr-pínd, *s. m.* The ball of the eye.

नेत्ररञ्जन netr-rún-jun, *s. m.* Collyrium.

नेत्ररोग netr-róg, *s. m.* Any disease of the eye.

नेत्रलोत netr-lót, *s. m.* A prisoner.

नेत्राम्बु netr-ámboo, *s. m.* A tear.

नेत्रोत्सव netr-ót-suv, *s. m.* Any pleasing or beautiful object.

नेत्रौषध netr-óushudh, *s. m.* Green sulphate of iron considered as a collyrium ; collyrium in general.

नेत्रौषधी netr-óushudh-ee, *s. f.* A drug.

नेदिष्ठ ned-íshth, *s. m.* A tree (*Alangium hexapetalum*).

नेपाल ne-pál, *n. prop.* The country of *Nepal.*

नेपालिका ne-pá-lik-a, *s. f.* Arsenic.

नेपुर né-poor, *s. f.* An ornament for the toes and feet, or worn on the ankles.

नेम nem, *s. m.* Vow, compact, agreement ; any religious observance voluntarily practised ; piety.

नेमधर्म ném-dhurm, *s. m.* Abstinence, good conduct.

नेमिचक्र nem-ee-chúkr, *n. prop.* A prince descended from *Pureekshit,* who is said to have removed the capital of India to *Kousambi,* after the inundation of *Hustinapoor.*

नेमी ném-ee, *adj.* Conscientious, abstemious, continent, chaste. *s. f.* A tree (*Dalbergia Oujeinensis*).

नेरूआ né-roo-a, *s. m.* Straw.

नेरे nér-eh, }
नेरौ ner-óu, } *adv.* Near, beside.

नेव néo, *s. f.* The foundation (*of a house, &c.*). Neo dalna, To lay the foundation.

नेवुंजी ne-wún-jee, *s. f.* Name of a flower.

नेवतना néot-na, *v. a.* To invite.

नेवता néo-ta, *s. m.* An invitation, or the presents sent along with an invitation to the person invited, or made by a guest.

नेवतना neo-tá-na, *v. a.* To invite.

नेवना néo-na, *v. n.* To stoop, to bow.

नेवर né-wur, }
नेवुल né-wul, } *s. f.* A sore in the feet of a horse.

नेवल né-wul, }
नेवला néo-la, } *s. m.* A weasel, a ferret, a mongoose (*Vivera mungo.*)

नेवाना ne-wá-na, *v. a.* To bend.

नेवार ne-wár, *s. f.* Tape.

नेवारना ne-wár-na, *v. a.* To shut out, to exclude.

नेह neh, *s. f.* Affection, kindness, love, friendship ; oil.

नेही ne-hee, *s. m.* A friend.

नेऋत ny-rit, *s. m.* The ruler of the south-west quarter.

नेऋती ny-rit-ee, *s. f.* The south-west quarter.

नैक nyk, *adj.* Many, various.

नैकट्य ny-kút-yuh, *s. m.* Proximity, vicinage.

नैकभेद nyk-bhéd, *adj.* Various, multiform, manifold.

नैकरूप nyk-róop, *adj.* Multiform.

नैगम ny-gúm, *s. m.* An *Oopnishud* or portion of the *Veds.*

नैज nyj, *adj.* Own.

नैजान ny-jána, *v. n.* To stoop.

नैन nyn, }
नैना ny-na, } *s. m.* The eye.

नैनसूख nyn-sóokh, *s. m.* Name of a flower.

नैना ny-na, *s. m.* A tether.

नैपाल ny-pal, *adj.* }
नैपालिक ny-pal-ík, } Produced in *Nepal* or brought from thence.

नैपाली ny-pál-ee, *s. f.* Double jasmine ; red arsenic ; *Sephalica* (*Nyctanthes tristis*).

नैपुण ny-póon, *s. m.* Dexterity, cleverness, skill.

नैपुण्य ny-póon-yuh, *s. m.* Dexterity, cleverness.

नैमिषारण्य nymish-árunyuh, *s. m.* A wood celebrated as the residence of the *Rishis,* to whom *Soutee* related the *Muhabhurut.*

नैयमिक ny-yum-ík, *adj.* According to rule, regular, enjoined.

नैया ny-ya, *s. m.* A boatman, a ferryman.

नैयायिक ny-ya-yík, *s. m.* A logician, a follower of the *Nyayuh* or logical philosophy.

नैराश्य nyr-ash-yuh, *s. m.* Despair.

नैऋत ny-rit, *s. m.* The ruler of the south-west quarter.

नैऋती ny-rit-ee, *s. f.* The south-west quarter.

नैरूक्त nyr-ookt, *adj.* Obsolete, uncommon, belonging to the glossary of the *Veds.*

नैर्गुण nyr-goon, *s. m.* Absence of qualities or properties.

नैर्मल्य nyr-mul-yuh, *s. m.* Cleanness, purity.

नैवेद्य ny-ved-yuh, *s. m.* An offering of eatable articles presented to a god, which may afterwards be distributed to his ministers or worshippers, especially when it has been presented to any form of *Vishnoo.*

नैहर ny-hur, *s. f.* A wife's mother's family.

नोकझोक nok-jhók, *s. f.* Pulling and hauling.

नोच noch, *s. m.* A pinch, a scratch.

नोचना nóch-na, *v. a.* To pinch, to gripe, to scratch, to claw.

नोन non, *s. m.* Salt.

नोना nó-na, *v. a.* To tie the feet of a cow when milking. *s. m.* A kind of custard apple (*Annona reticulata*).

नोनापानी nóna-pánee, *s. m.* Salt water, brine; sea water.

नोनिया nó-ni-ya, *s. m.* Purslain (*Portulaca oleracea*); a maker of or dealer in salt, a salt-petre manufacturer.

नोनी nó-nee, *s. f.* Efflorescence of salt on a wall.

नौ nou, *adj.* New, young, fresh, raw, newly.

नौकर nóu-kur, *s. m.* A servant.

नौकरी nóu-kur-ee, *s. f.* Service, attendance.

नौका nóu-ka, *s. f.* A boat.

नौखण्ड nou-khúnd, *s. m.* The nine climes or divisions of the earth; they are usually denominated the nine dweeps (*islands*), or Vurshus (*countries*), which constitute Jumboo dweep the centrical portion of the world, or the known world.

नौगरी nóu-gur-ee, *s. f.* An ornament for females worn on the wrist.

नौचन्दी nou-chúnd-ee, *adj.* Relating to the new moon.

नौची nóu-chee, *s. f.* A young girl kept by a bawd.

नौछावर nou-chhá-wur, *s. m.* A propitiatory offering, sacrifice, victim.

नौजोबना nou-jó-bun-a, *s. f.* Just grown up to puberty (*a girl*).

नौरहना nóurh-na, *v. n.* To bend; to incline downwards; to be obedient, to stoop.

नौहाना nour-hána, *v. a.* To bow, to bend.

नौतना nóut-na, *v. a.* To invite.

नौता nóu-ta, *s. m.* A portico; invitation. *adj.* Stooping.

नौध noudh, *s. m.* A young plant or fresh shoot or branch of a plant.

नौना nóu-na, *v. n.* To bend down, to bow, to incline downwards; to submit, to be obedient, to stoop.

नौमासा nou-má-sa, *s. m.* A feast given in the ninth month of pregnancy.

नौमी nóu-mee, *s. f.* The ninth day of a lunar fortnight.

नौरत्न nou-rútn, *s. m.* Nine precious gems, or a pearl, ruby, topaz, diamond, emerald, lapis lazuli, coral, sapphire, and one called *Gomed*; the nine men of letters at the court of *Vikrumadityuh*, or *Dhunwunturi, Kshupunuk, Umur Singh, Sunkoo, Vetalbhutt, Ghutkurpur, Kalidas, Vurahumihir*, and *Vururoochi*. *s. f.* An ornament worn on the arm and wrist and consisting of nine different gems.

नौलासी nou-lá-see, *adj.* Tender, soft.

नौशिख nóu-shikh, *s. m.* A novice, a student.

नौसादर nou-sá-dur, *s. m.* Sal ammoniac.

न्युकार nyuk-kár, *s. m.* Contempt, disrespect.

न्युग्रोध nyug-ródh, *s. m.* The Indian fig tree (*Ficus Indica*).

न्युग्रोधी nyug-ró-dhee, *s. f.* A plant (*Salvinia cucullata*).

न्यस्त nyúst, *adj.* Deposited, consigned, delivered.

न्याय nyáyuh, *s. m.* Propriety, fitness; the *Nyayuh* doctrine, logic, logical philosophy; policy, good government; justice, equity, reason, argument, disputation, sophistry. *Nyayuh shastr, s. m.* Logic. *Nyayuh kurna*, To administer justice, to decide.

न्यायक nyayúk, *s. m.* A judge.

न्यायता nyayutá, *s. f.* Fitness, propriety.

न्यायाचार nyayáchar, *s. m.* A virtuous man.

न्यायाधार nyayádhar, *s. m.* An example of virtue or propriety.

न्यायिक nyayík, *s. m.* A reasoner, arguer, logician, sophist.

न्यायिन् nyayín, *adj.* Right, fit; logical.

न्यायी nyayée, *s. m.* A distributor of justice; a logician.

न्याय्य nyayúh, *adj.* Right, proper, fit.

न्यार ny-ár, *s. m.* Forage, fodder, food of cattle.

न्यारा ny-ára, *adj.* Apart, aloof, separate, distinct, different, extraordinary, uncommon. *s. m.* The scoria left after refining gold, silver, or other metals, which a minute portion of those metals is obtainable. *Nyareh, adv.* Apart.

न्यारिया ny-áriya, *s. m.* One who extracts metals from their scoria. *adj.* Prudent, cautious, not easily imposed on.

न्याव nyáo, *s. m.* Justice, equity, right, decision. *Nyao kurna*, To judge, to administer justice, to decide.

न्यून nyoon, *adj.* Blameable, vile, wicked, despicable; less, deficient, defective.

न्यूनता nyoon-tá, *s. f.* Deficiency, inferiority.

न्यूनांग nyoon-áng, *adj.* Maimed, mutilated, imperfect.

न्यूनाधिक nyoon-ádhik, *adj.* Unequal, more or less.

न्यूनेन्द्रिय nyoon-éndri-yuh, *adj.* Imperfect, wanting some organ; as blind, deaf, &c.

न्योतना nyót-na, *v. a.* To invite.

न्योता nyó-ta, *s. m.* An invitation, or the presents sent along with an invitation to the person invited, or made by a guest.

न्योताना nyo-tá-na, *v. a.* To invite.

प

प puh, The twenty-first consonant of the *Naguree* alphabet, corresponding to the letter *p.*

पंपाना pun-pá-na, *v. a.* To cause to flourish, to promote the prosperity of another, to refresh.

पंवार pun-wár, *s. m.* A plant (*Cassia obtusifolia*); a tribe of *Rajpoots.*

पंवारा pun-wá-ra, *s. m.* A story, tale, fable.

पंवारिया pun-wá-riya, *s. m.* A bard, a storyteller.

पंवारी pun-wá-ree, *s. f.* A betel-garden.

पकड़ púk-ur, *s. f.* The act of seizing, seizure, capture, catch, hold; objection, difficulty.

पकड़ना púk-ur-na, *v. a.* To catch, lay hold of, seize, apprehend, take, capture, gripe, handle; to object.

पकड़ाना puk-rá-na, *v. a.* To cause to be caught, seized, or laid hold of; to deliver over, to give in charge, to hand.

पकना púk-na, *v. n.* To be dressed or cooked, to ripen; to suppurate (*as an inflammation, boil, &c.*); to turn grey (*hairs*). *Puka-pukaya,* Ready cooked.

पकला púk-la, *s. m.* A sore between the toes produced by moisture.

पकवाई puk-wá-ee, *s. f.* Price paid for cooking.

पकवान puk-wán, *s. m.* Sweetmeats, victuals fried in butter or oil.

पकवाना puk-wá-na, *v. a.* To cause to be dressed or cooked, to cause to ripen.

पका púk-a, *adj.* Ripe, mature, matured; boiled, dressed (*opposite to raw*), cooked, baked (*as bricks*), made of brick; cunning, knowing, instructed, firm, strong, proved, expert.

पकाई puk-á-ee, *s. f.* Ripeness.

पकाना puk-á-na, *v. a.* To ripen, to dress victuals, to cook, to bake.

पकाव puk-áo, *s. m.* Suppuration.

पकोरा puk-ó-ra, *s. m.* ⎫
पकोरी puk-ó-ree, *s. f.* ⎬ A kind of dish made of pease-meal.
पकोउरी puk-óu-ree, *s. f.* ⎭

पक्क pukk, ⎫ *adj.* Ripe, mature, matured; boiled, dressed (*opposite to raw*), cooked, baked (*as bricks*), made of
पक्का púk-ka, ⎭

2 M

---

brick; cunning, knowing, instructed, firm, strong, proved, expert. *Pukka kurna,* To establish a claim, agreement, or proposition, so that no doubt or subject of dispute can remain; to build with bricks.

पक्तिशूल pukti-shóol, *s. m.* Inflammation of the bowels, cholic.

पक्व puk-wúh, *adj.* Mature, dressed, cooked, matured by nature or by art; fully matured, on the eve of rottenness or decay; perfect, come to perfection; able, shrewd, experienced, mature (*as the understanding*); grey (*the hair*); digested.

पक्वकृत् puk-wuh-krít, *s. m.* The *Nimb* tree, the leaves of which are applied to phlegmonoid swellings to induce suppuration.

पक्वान्न puk-wán, *s. m.* Dressed food.

पक्वाशय puk-wá-shuy, *s. m.* The abdomen, the stomach.

पक्ष puksh, *s. m.* The half of a lunar month or fortnight, comprising fifteen days; a partisan; a friend; a side, a flank.

पक्षता puksh-tá, *s. f.* The taking up a side or argument.

पक्षधर puksh-dhúr, *s. m.* A partisan.

पक्षपात puksh-pát, *s. m.* Adopting a side or an argument whether right or wrong, partisanship; a partisan, an adherent, who or what sides with.

पक्षपातिता puksh-pati-tá, *s. f.* Adherence, friendship, fellowship.

पक्षपाती puksh-pátee, *s. m.* A partisan, a friend, an adherent.

पक्षाघात puksh-a-ghát, *s. m.* Palsy, hemiplegia.

पक्षिणी púk-shin-ee, *s. f.* ⎫
पक्षी púk-shee, *s. m.* ⎬ A bird.

पक्षिराज pukshi-ráj, *s. m.* King of the birds, usually applied to *Guroor.*

पक्षिशाला púkshi-shála, *s. f.* A nest, an aviary.

पक्ष pukh, *s. m.* A period of fifteen days, a fortnight; two; side, party, assistance, protection.

पखड़ी púkh-ree, *s. f.* A petal or flower-leaf.

पखरौटा pukh-róu-ta, *s. m.* A bit of gold or silver leaf covering a *beera* or mouthful of betel.

पखान pukhán, ⎫
पखाना pukhán-a, ⎬ *s. m.* A stone.

पखारना pukhár-na, *v. a.* To wash.

पखाल pukhál, *s. f.* A large leather bag for holding water, generally carried on bullocks, a water-bag.

पखावज pukhá-wuj, *s. f.* A kind of drum, a timbrel.

पखावजी pukhá wuj-ee, *s. m.* One who beats the *pukha-wuj,* a drummer.

पखेरू pukhér-oo, *s. m.* A bird.

पखेस pukhés, *s. m.* Mark, stamp.

पखौरा pukhóu-ra, *s. m.* The shoulder-blade.

पग pug, *s. m.* The foot. *Pug put tar bajna*, To beat time with the foot.

पगडंडी pug-dún-dee, *s. f.* A by-path, by-way, foot-path, track. *Pug-dundee lena*, To track, to trace.

पगड़ी púg-ree, *s. f.* A turband. *Pugree utukna*, To be obstinate, to persist or persevere. *Pugree chhuputna*, To practise deceit, to act treacherously.

पगडंडी pug-dún-dee, *s. f.* A by-path, by-way, foot-path, track. *Pug-dundee lena*, To track, to trace.

पगधारना pug-dhár-na, *v. n.* To travel, to go, to leave, to depart.

पगना púg-na, *v. n.* To be dipped in or covered with syrup ; (*met.*) to be in love.

पगला púg-la, *adj.* Foolish.

पगा púg-a, *s. m.* A rope fastened
पगहा pug-há, round the neck of a bullock, a tether.

पगार pug-ár, *s. m.* Mud kneaded or prepared for building walls or plastering.

पगिया púg-iya, *s. f.* A turband.

पगुराना pug-oo-rá-na, *v. n.* To ruminate, to chew the cud.

पंक punk, *s. m.* Mud, mire, clay.

पंककीर punk-kéer, *s. m.* A lapwing.

पंकगुरुक punk-gúr-uk, *s. m.* A small fish (*Macrognathus Pancalus*).

पंकग्राह punk-gráh, *s. m.* The *Mukur*, a marine monster.

पंकज punk-új, *s. m.* A lotus.

पंकधूम punk-dhóom, *s. m.* One of the divisions of hell.

पंकप्रभा punk-prubhá, *s. f.* A hell, the hell of mud or mire.

पंकवास punk-vás, *s. m.* A crab.

पंकशुक्ति punk-shóok-ti, *s. f.* A cockle.

पंकार pun-kár, *s. m.* An aquatic plant (*Vallisneria* ; also, *Trapa bispinosa*).

पंकुचर pun-kri-chúr, *s. m.* An osprey.

पंकेरू pun-ker-ooh, *s. m.* The Indian crane.

पंक्ती púnk-tee, *s. f.* A line, a row, or range ; a sort of metre, a stanza of four lines, each line consisting of ten syllables.

पंख punkh, *s. m.* A feather, a wing.

पंखड़ी púnkh-ree, *s. f.* A petal, a flower-leaf.

पंखा pún-kha, *s. m.* A fan.

पंखिया pún-khi-ya, *s. f.* A small fan. *s. m.* A kind of mendicant, who fans every body ; a wicked man.

पंखी pún-khee, *s. f.* A small fan ; a bird ; a kind of woollen cloth which comes from the hilly countries.

पंगत pún-gut, *s. f.* A row or line.

पंगला púng-la, *adj.* Bandy-legged, a crip-
पंगू pún-goo, ple.

पंगास pun-gás, *s. m.* A fish (*Silurus sagittatus*).

पंगू pún-goo, *adj.* Lame, crippled, halt, one who has lost his legs, &c., a cripple.

पंगुता pun-goo-tá, *s. f.* Deformity, mutilation.

पंगुल pún-gool, *s. m.* A horse of a glossy or silvery white colour.

पचखुना púch-khun-a, *adj.* Consisting of five parts or divisions (*a house, &c.*)

पचखा puch-khá, *s. f.* Six days from *Shrawun* to *Revtee*, on which several kinds of work are unlawful.

पचतोलिया puch-tó-liya, *s. m.* A kind of cloth.

पचन púch-un, *adj.* What cooks or matures, &c.

पचना púch-na, *v. n.* To be digested ; to rot ; to be consumed ; to take pains, to labour.

पचपच puch-puch, *s. m.* The noise made by walking in damp places.

पचपचाना puch-puch-ána, *v. n.* To be damp, to be wet ; to sweat.

पचपन púch-pun, *adj.* Fifty-five.

पचमहला puch-múh-la, *adj.* Of five stories (*a house*).

पचमेल puch-mél, *adj.* Mixed, confused.

पचउंपचा puch-úmp-cha, *s. f.* A species of Curcuma (*C. Zanthorhison*).

पचलुरा púch-lur-a, *adj.* Of five strings (*a necklace, &c.*)

पचलुरी púch-lur-ee, *s. f.* A necklace consisting of five rows or strings.

पचलोना púch-lo-na, *s. m.* A medicine composed of five kinds of salt.

पचादालना púcha-dálna, *v. a.* To digest, to rot, to ferment.

पचान्वे puch-án-veh, *adj.* Ninety-five.

पचाना puch-á-na, *v. a.* To digest, to cause to rot, to rot, to ferment.

पचाव puch-áo, *s. m.* Digestion.

पचास puch-ás, *adj.* Fifty.

पचासी puch-á-see, *adj.* Eighty-five.

पचीस puch-ées, *adj.* Twenty-five.

पचीसी puch-ées-ee, *s. f.* A game played

with cowries instead of dice, and so named from the highest throw, which is twenty-five.

पचूका puch-óo-ka, *s. m.* A squirt, a syringe.

पचोतरा puch-ó-tur-a, *s. m.* A duty of five per cent. on merchandize.

पचोनी puch-óu-nee, *s. f.* The stomach.

पचर púch-chur, *s. f.* A wedge. *Puchchur marna,* To tease, to harass, to distress.

पची puch-chée, *adj.* Adherent, sticking, joined; (*met. in music*) in unison. *Puchchee hona,* To be stuck together as with glue; to be in unison; to be strongly attached by love.

पचीकारी puchchée-káree, *s. f.* Mosaic; patching or darning of damaged cloth.

पच्छम puch-chhúm, | *s. m.* The west.
पच्छिम puch-chhím, |

पच्छी púch-chhee, *s. m.* An ally, an assistant, favourer, an advocate, a patron; a bird.

पच्छना puchhúr-na, *v. n.* To fall, to tumble down. *Puchhur jana, v. n.* To be overcome.

पछताना puchh-tá-na, *v. n.* To regret, repent, rue, grieve.

पछतावा puchh-tá-wa, *s. m.* Regret, penitence, contrition, concern, compunction, grief, sorrow, remorse.

पछहर puch-húttur, *adj.* Seventy-five.

पछना púchhna, *s. m.* The act of scarifying (*tattooing*); inoculation; a scarificator (*name of an instrument*). [*ing.*]

पछनी púchh-nee, *s. f.* Scarifying (*tattoo-*

पछवा púchh-wa, *s. f.* The westerly wind.

पछाड़ puchhár, *s. f.* A fall or throwing down; the act of winnowing. *Puchhar khana,* To fall down, to suffer pain.

पछाड़ना puchhár-na, *v. a.* To throw down, to abase, to conquer.

पछियाव puchhi-yáo, *s. f.* A westerly wind.

पछोड़ना puchhór-na, *v. a.* To winnow with a basket used for this purpose.

पजेब puj-eb, *s. f.* An ornament for the feet.

पजौरा puj-óu-ra, *adj.* Low, mean, shabby.

पच punch, *adj.* Five. *s. m.* A council, an assembly, a meeting, a company; arbitrators.

पचक punch-úk, *adj.* Five, or relating to five, made of five, bought with five, &c. *s. m.* Any collection or aggregate of five, a five.

पचकर्म punch-kúrm, *s. m.* Five actions of the body, vomiting, evacuation by bleeding or by stool, diseased excretion by fæces or purging, and blowing the nose.

पचकोण punch-kón, *s. m.* A pentagon.

पचकोल punch-kól, *s. m.* The aggregate of five spices, long-pepper, its root *Chai* or Piper Chavya, Plumbago, and dry ginger.

पचकोश punch-kó-sha, *s. m. pl.* The five sheathes supposed to invest the soul, or the *Unnumuyuh kosh,* that supported by food, the gross form; the *Pranu-muyuh kosh,* the organs of action; the *Muno-muyuh kosh,* the organs of perception, with the *munus* or mind; the *Vijnanuhmuyuh,* the same with the *Buddhi* or intellect; and the *Anundu-muyuh,* consisting of the elements of identity and divine wisdom.

पचकी pun-chúk-kee, *s. f.* A water-mill.

पचखन punch-khún-a, *adj.* Consisting of five floors, stories, or apartments (*a house, &c.*)

पचगव्य punch-gúvyuh, *s. m.* Five articles derived from the cow; milk, curds, clarified butter, cow's urine, and cow-dung.

पचगोन punch-góon, *adj.* Five times, fivefold.

पचतत्त्व punch-tútwub, *s. m.* The five elements collectively; (*in the Tuntrus*) the five essentials of certain rites; or wine, meat, fish, sexual intercourse, and mystic gesticulations.

पचतपा púnch-tup-a, *s. m.* An ascetic, who in the hot weather, sits amongst four fires, and has the sun for the fifth.

पचता púnch-ut-a, *s. f.* Death, dying. *i. e.* the separation of the five elements of whose aggregate the body consists.

पचतीर्थी pun-chu-téer-thee, *s. f.* Any five principal places of pilgrimage, especially *Visranti, Soukur, Nymish, Pruyag,* and *Pooshkur;* bathing on the day of the Equinox.

पचत्व pun-chu-twúh, *s. m.* Death.

पचधा pun-chu-dhá, *adv.* In five ways, five-fold.

पचनख punch-núkh, *s. m.* An elephant; a tortoise; a tiger; any animal having five toes or claws.

पचनद punch-núd, *s. m.* The *Punjab* or country of five rivers, viz. the *Yumoona, Sutudroo, Vepasa, Chundrubhaga,* and *Vitusthu.*

पचपचनख punch-punch-núkh, *s. m.* Five kinds of animals allowed to be killed and eaten, the hare, porcupine, alligator, rhinoceros, and tortoise.

पचपर्णी punch-púr-nee, *s. f.* A small shrub.

पचपल्लव punch-púlluv, *s. m.* The aggregate of five sprouts, viz. of the spondias, rose-apple, *Bel* or marmelos, citron, and wood-apple.

पचपात्र punch-pátr, *s. m.* Five plates collectively; a *Shraddh* in which offerings are made in five vessels.

पचपिरिया punch-píri-ya, *s. m.* Any person, *Hindoo* or other, who worships the five peers or saints of the *Muhomedans.*

पचप्राण punch-prán, *s. m. pl.* The five airs supposed to be in the body, and necessary to life.

पञ्चबन्ध punch-búndh, *s. m.* A fine equal to the fifth part of any thing lost or stolen.

पञ्चभद्र punch-bhúdr, *s. m.* A horse with five auspicious marks, or, spotted on the chest, back, face, and flanks ; a sauce or condiment of five vegetables.

पञ्चभूत punch-bhóot, *s. m.* The five elements : earth, air, fire, water, and *Akas.*

पञ्चभूताक्ष punch-bhoot-átma, *s. m.* Man as formed of the five elements.

पञ्चम púnch-um, *adj.* Fifth. *s. m.* One of the seven musical notes ; the seventh called *Punchum,* from being said to be performed by air drawn from five places ; the navel, the breast, the heart, the throat, and forehead ; one of the *Rags* or modes of music.

पञ्चमकार pun-chum-kár. *s. m.* The five essentials of the left hand, *Tuntr* ritual, viz. *Mudyuh,* wine, man's flesh, *Mutsyuh* fish, *Mythoon* copulation, *Moodra* gesticulation.

पञ्चमहायज्ञ punch-múha-yug, *s. m.* The five great sacraments of the *Hindoos,* or the worship of spirits, progenitors, gods, *Veds,* and mankind, by offerings of perfumes and flowers, obsequial rites, oblations with fire, the study of the *Veds,* and hospitality.

पञ्चमास्य punch-más-yuh, *s. m.* The *Koil* or Indian cuckoo.

पञ्चमी pún-chum-ee, *s. f.* The fifth day of a half month.

पञ्चमूल punch-móol, *s. m.* The assemblage of five roots, the *Bel,* Premna longifolia, Cassia, Gmelina arborea, and the trumpet-flower.

पञ्चमूली punch-móo-lee, *s. f.* A similar aggregate of five roots, considered as the smaller one, viz. Hedysarum gangeticum, H. lagopodioides, Solanum melongena, S. jacquini, and Tribulus lanuginosus.

पञ्चरत्न punch-rútn, *s. m.* A collection of five precious objects, o , gold, a diamond, a pearl, a ruby, an amethyst.

पञ्चलक्षण punch-lúk-shun, *s. m.* A *Pooran* or mythological poem : a *Pooran* should comprehend five topics, viz. the creation of worlds, their destruction and renovation, the genealogy of gods and heroes, the reigns of the *Munoos,* and the actions of their descendants.

पञ्चलोह punch-lóh, *s. m.* A metallic alloy containing five metals : copper, brass, tin, lead and iron.

पञ्चशाख punch-shá-kha, *s. m.* The hand.

पञ्चसुगन्धक punch-soo-gún-dhuk, *s. m.* The aggregate of five aromatic vegetable substances, viz., cloves, nutmeg, camphor, aloe wood, and *kukkola.*

पञ्चसूना punch-sóo-na, *s. m. pl.* The five things in a house by which animal life may be accidentally destroyed, viz., the fire place, the slab on which condiments are ground, the broom, the pestle and mortar, and the water-pot.

पञ्चाग्नि púnch-agni, *s. m.* A collection of five fires, amidst which a devotee performs penance during the summer season, or four fires lighted severally to the north, south, east and west, and the sun overhead ; five mystic fires supposed to be present in the body.

पञ्चाङ्ग punch-áng, *s. m.* Five modes of devotion, or silent prayer, burnt-offering, libations, bathing idols, and feeding *Brahmuns;* an almanac describing solar days, lunar days, and the periods of asterisms, *Yogs* and *Kuruns ;* reverence by extending the hands, bending the knees and head, and in speech and look.

पञ्चाध्याय punch-adhyáyuh, *s. m.* Five readings, sections, or chapters. *s. f.* The aggregate of five chapters of the *Shree Bhagwut,* detailing the sports of *Krishn* with the *Gopees.*

पञ्चामृत punch-ámrit, *s. m.* A mixture of milk, curds, sugar, *ghee,* and honey ; the aggregate of any five drugs of supposed efficacy.

पञ्चाम्ल punch-áml, *s. m.* The aggregate of five acid plants, viz., the jujube, pomegranate, sorrel, spondias, and citron.

पञ्चायत pun-chá-yut, *s. f.* A meeting of any particular society (*generally as a court of inquiry*) ; a jury, an inquest.

पञ्चायती pun-cha-yút-ee, *s. f.* Relationship.

पञ्चाल pun-chál, *s. m.* A country in the north of India.

पञ्चावन pun-chá-wun, *adj.* Fifty-five.

पञ्चेन्द्रिय punch-én-driyuh, *s. m.* The five organs of sense, viz., the eye, ear, nose, tongue, and skin ; or those of action, as hands, feet, windpipe, anus, and parts of generation.

पञ्चों pún-chon, *s. m.* Associates, friends.

पञ्चोरा pun-chó-ra, *s. m.* An earthen vessel with a narrow neck and a hole in the bottom : when filled with water and the mouth stopped, no water flows from the hole below till the hand or whatever stopped the mouth be removed. It is used as an experiment to illustrate the doctrine of the *horror vacui* by the followers of Aristotle.

पञ्छाल्ल pun-chhá-la, *s. m.* Tail of a paper kite.

पञ्छी pún-chhee, *s. m.* A bird in general.

पञ्जर pún-jur, *s. m.* A skeleton ; the ribs.

पञ्जरी púnj-ree, *s. f.* A rib.

पञ्जाब pun-jáb, *s. m.* Name of a country.

पञ्जाबी pun-já-bee, *adj.* Of or belonging to the *Punjab. s. m. f.* A native of *Punjab.*

पञ्जिका pún-ji-ka, *s. f.* The register or journal of *Yum,* the record of human actions.

पञ्जीरी pun-jée ree, *s. f.* A medicine composed of sugar, *ghee*, flour, &c. given to puerperal women ; caudle.

पट put, *adj.* Upside down, overturned. *s. m.* A shutter, the valve of a folding-door ; fine or coloured cloth, the sound of falling or beating.

पटकन pútkun, *s. f.* A knock, a fall. *Putkun khana*, To fall down. *Putkunee dena, v. a.* To dash on the ground, to throw against any thing with violence.

पटकना pút-uk-na, *v. a.* To dash against anything, to throw on the ground with violence, to knock. *v. n.* To crackle, to crack.

पटका pút-ka, पटूका put-óo-ka, } *s. m.* A cloth worn round the waist, a girdle. *Zuree putka*, The golden girdle (*an ensign conferred by the Peshwa on generals, who are invested with authority immediately by him*). *Putka bandhna*, To determine on, or prepare for any act. *Putka pukurna*, To hinder, to obstruct.

पटकाजाना pútka-jána, *v. n.* To fall from one's rank or estimation.

पटकाना put-ká-na, पटकारना put-kár-na, } *v. a.* To dash against anything, to throw on the ground with violence, to knock.

पटड़ा pút-ra, *s. m.* A plank ; a plank to sit on, a plank on which a washerman beats clothes ; unripe grain (*Cicer arietinum*). *Putra kur dena, v. n.* To deprive one of his power or strength, to convict an adversary and leave him without a reply.

पटन pút-un, *s. m.* Roofing.

पटना pút-na, *v. n.* To be paid, to be procured ; to be watered ; to fill ; to be covered, to be roofed, to be piled, &c. *s. m.* Name of a city, *Patna in Behar.*

पटनी pút-nee, पटौनी put-óu-nee, } *s. m.* A ferryman.

पटपट put-put, *s. f.* The sound of beating.

पटरा pút-ra, *s. m.* A plank, a plank to sit on, a plank on which a washerman beats clothes ; unripe grain (*Cicer arietinum*). *Putra kur dena, v. n.* To deprive one of his power or strength, to convict an adversary and leave him without reply.

पटरानी put-rá-nee, *s. f.* A queen who is installed or consecrated with the king, a princess.

पटरी pút-ree, *s. f.* A plank or board to write on ; a narrow slip or plank of wood, iron, &c.; the vanes of a venetian window ; a firm seat on horseback ; a title.

पटवाना put-wá-na, *v. a.* To provide money ; to water.

पटवार put-wár, पटवारी put-wá-ree, } *s. m.* One who keeps accounts of lands, a land steward.

पटसन put-sún, *s. m.* A plant (*Crotolaria juncea*).

पटसाल put-sál, *s. m.* A college, a school.

पटा pút-a, *s. m.* A foil, a wooden scimitar for cudgelling with ; a board on which *Hindoos* sit whilst eating their meals or performing religious ceremonies. *Puteh-baz*, A fencer, a cudgeller ; (*met.*) a coquette, a wanton, a strumpet. *Puta katna, v. a.* To discharge from service.

पटाक put-ák, *s. m.* A kind of bird ; a sound, a crash.

पटाका put-á-ka, *s. f.* A flag, a banner.

पटाखा put-á-kha, *s. m.* A cracker, a squib.

पटाना put-á-na, *v. a.* To irrigate, to water ; to prepare a *chouka* with cowdung dissolved in water ; to place the beams on the roof of a house ; to pay money.

पटापट put-a-pút, *s. m.* The sound of beating or of the falling of drops of rain.

पटापुर put-a-púr, *s. m.* Name of a fruit.

पटाव put-áo, *s. m.* Irrigating, flooding a field ; roofing a house with tiles, &c.

पटिया pút-iya, *s. f.* A slate or slab of stone.

पटीना put-ée-na, *s. m.* Name of a bird.

पटीमा put-ée-ma, *s. m.* The planks on which cloth is spread for printing.

पटीलना put-éel-na, *v. a.* To exact, to subdue ; to beat.

पटू pút-oo, *adj.* Clever, dexterous, skilful, diligent, smart, sharp.

पटुत्व pút-oo-twuh, *s. m.* Cleverness ; eloquence.

पटुआ pút-oo-a, *s. m.* A man who strings pearls, a braider, a maker of fringe and tape ; tow made from the Hibiscus cannabinus.

पटूका put-óo-ka, *s. m.* A cloth worn round the waist, a girdle. *Putooka bandhna*, To determine on, or to prepare for any act.

पटूस put-óot, *s. m.* पटूता put-óo-ta, *s. f.* } Vigour, virility, activity, skill.

पटेरा put-ér-a, *s. m.* Papyrus.

पटेल put-él, *s. m.* Cudgelling ; sovereignty ; a chief among the *Koonbee* tribe ; a title of *Mahrattas*, the head man of a village. *Putel dalna*, To interrupt, to throw obstacles in the way of a business ; to beat.

पटेला put-él-a, *s. m.* A kind of boat, flat-bottomed ; or log or beam used to roll or harrow ground.

पटेली put-él-ee, *s. f.* A small flat-bottomed boat.

पटैत put-úyt, *s. m.* A cudgeller.

पडेला put-úyla, *s. m.* A kind of boat, flat-bottomed; a log or beam used to roll or harrow ground.

पडोतन put-ó-tun, *s. m.* Roofing with planks or boards, transom.

पडोढिया put-ó-hiya, *s. m.* An owl.

पडौनी put-óu-nee, *s. m.* A ferryman.

पट्ट putt, *s. m.* Wove silk; a plant (*Corchorus olitorius*), from the fibres of the bark of which, called Jute, a coarse sackcloth and cordage are prepared; a royal grant or order written on copper, stone, &c.

पट्टन pút-tun, *s. m.* The name of a city.

पट्टदेवी putt-dévee, *s. f.* A principal queen.

पट्टरंग putt-rúng, *s. m.* A plant used in dyeing (*Cæsalpinia sappan*).

पट्टशाक putt-shák, *s. m.* A sort of potherb (*Corchorus capsularis*).

पट्टा pút-ta, *s. f.* An ornament of the forehead. *s. m.* A lock of hair; a dog-collar; name of harness; a deed, particularly a title deed to land or a deed of lease. *Putta toorana*, To flee, run away.

पट्टिल pút-til, *s. m.* A plant (*Cæsalpinia bonduccella*).

पट्टिलोध्र pútti-lódhr, *s. m.* A sort of tree, the bark of which is used as an astringent; the red species of the *Lodh* (*Symploces racemosa*).

पट्टी pút-tee, *s. f.* Plaster, a bandage, a fillet; a quarter of a place; the side pieces of the frame of a bedstead; a row or line; a kind of sweetmeat; division of the hair which is combed towards the two sides and divided by a line in the middle; a written order or patent. *Lusdar puttee*, Sticking plaster. *Puttee pukurkeh hiltek ruhna*, denotes excessive weakness and laziness. *Puttee torna*, To be bedrid. *Puttee seh puttee milana*, expresses the most intimate proximity.

पट्टू pút-too, *s. m.* A kind of woollen cloth, a cloth to cover with from rain, &c.

पट्ठा pút-tha, } *s. m.* A young full-grown
पठ puth, } animal, a youth, a wrestler; a sinew, a tendon; a plant with long leaves.

पठन pút-hun, *s. m.* Reading, reciting.

पठाना puthá-na, } *v. a.* To send.
पठौना put-hóu-na, }

पठित pút-hit, *adj.* Read, studied; recited, repeated.

पठिया pút-hiya, *s. f.* A young full-grown animal (*generally applied to kids, fowls, &c.*)

पठैया put-hy-ya, *part. pass.* Sent.

पठौना put-hóu-na, *v. a.* To send.

पड़ जाना púr jana, *v. n.* To lie down; to repose, to cease (*as the wind*), to abate.

पड़ना púr-na, *v. n.* To fall; to lie down, repose; to befall, happen, occur; to encamp; to drop; to be confined to bed by sickness. *Pur ruhna*, or, *Pureh ruhna*, To remain helpless, poor or destitute.

पड़पड़ाना pur-pur-ána, *v. n.* To prattle, to chatter; to throb with pain (*as the tongue from an acrid substance*).

पड़ाना pur-á-na, *v. a.* To lay down; to put to sleep, to cause to repose; to cull, to pluck, to gather.

पड़ापड़ pur-a-púr, *adv.* With reiterated strokes.

पड़ापाना púr-a-pána, *v. a.* To find or get easily.

पड़ाव pur-áo, *s. m.* Halting place; camp, encampment; an army; a crowd, an assembly.

पड़िया púr-iya, *s. f.* A female buffalo calf.

पड़ोस pur-ós, *s. m.* Neighbourhood.

पड़ोसिन pur-o-sín, *s. f.* A female neighbour.

पड़ोसी pur-ó-see, *s. m.* A male neighbour.

पढ़न púr-hún, *s. f.* The act of reading.

पढ़ना púrh-na, *v. a.* To read, repeat, say, decipher, speak.

पढ़नेवाला purh-ne-wála, *s. m.* Reader.

पढ़न्त pur-húnt, *s. f.* A reading, a spell.

पढ़यूल purh-yúl, *s. f.* Sweepings.

पढ़ा pur-há, *part. pass.* Read, learned, of much reading.

पढ़ागुना púrha-góon-a, *adj.* A learned, experienced man.

पढ़ाना pur-há-na, *v. a.* To cause or teach to read, to instruct, to teach, to teach to speak or sing (*as birds*).

पढ़िन pur-hín, *s. f.* A mullet.

पन pun, *s. m.* Measure of account, in *cowries* or shells, twenty *gundas* or eighty *cowries*; a stake at play, a bet, a wager; a vow, a promise, a resolution.

पन्ड pund, *s. m.* A catamite; a eunuch.

पन्डा pún-da, *s. f.* Wisdom, understanding; science, learning. *s. m.* A *Brahmun* who presides at the temple of an idol.

पन्डित pún-dit, *s. m.* A scholar, a teacher, a learned *Brahmun*, or one read in sacred science, and teaching it to his disciples. *adj.* Wise, learned. *Pundit-khanuh*, *s. m.* A prison, gaol.

पन्डिताई pun-dit-áee, *s. f.* The learning of a *Brahmun*, learning.

पन्डितानी pundit-ánee, *s. f.* The wife of a *Pundit*.

पन्डू pun-doo, *s. m.* A sovereign of ancient *Delhi*, and nominal father of *Yoodhishthir* and the other four *Panduv* princes.

पन्डूक pún-dook, *s. m.* A turtle-dove.

पन्डुबी pún-doo-bee, *s. f.* A water-fowl, the coot, the diver.

पन्डूरी pun-dóo-ree, *s. f.* A bird (*Falco*).

पत put, *s. f.* Good name, honour, character. *s. m.* Lord, master, husband.

पतङ्ग put-úng, *s. m.* A moth; a paper kite; the sun.

पतङ्गा put-úng-a, *s. m.* A spark. *Putunga hona,* To go rapidly about a business.

पतझड़ put-jhúr, *adj.* Without leaves. *s. f.* The fall of the leaf; autumn. *Put jhur hona,* To lose its leaves in autumn (*a tree*); (*met.*) to decay (*a person from old age*).

पतदिन put-dín, *adv.* Each day, always, constantly.

पतन pút-un, *s. m.* The act of falling; falling from dignity, virtue, &c.

पतनी pút-nee, *s. f.* A wife.

पतरिङ्गा put-rín-ga, *s. m.* A bird (*Merops viridis*).

पतरिया pút-ri-ya, } *s. f.* A prostitute.
पतुरिया put-óo-riya, } *Putooriya-baz,* A whoremonger.

पतला pút-la, *adj. m.* Fine, thin (*cloth or liquids*); lean, meagre, delicate, weak.

पतलाई put-láee, *s. f.* Thinness, fineness, meagreness, attenuation, weakness.

पतलो put-ló, *s. m.* The dead leaves fallen from a tree; the leaves cut off from the culm of a reed (*Saccharum spontaneum*) and used for thatching.

पतवार put-wár, } *s. f.* A rudder, helm.
पतवाल put-wál, }

पता pút-a, *s. m.* A sign, mark, symptom, hint, token, direction, address or place to which one is directed, label.

पताका put-á-ka, *s. f.* A standard, a flag or banner; a flagstaff; an emblem carried as an ensign or banner, a symbol, a sign; a mark.

पताकी put-á-kee, *s. m.* An ensign, a standard bearer.

पताल put-ál, *s. m.* The infernal regions or a place under the earth.

पति púti, *s. m.* A lord, master, owner; husband; a leaf.

पतिघ्नी put-ígh-nee, *s. f.* The murderess of her husband; a line on the hand, indicating that a woman will be faithless or treacherous to her husband.

पतित pút-it, *adj.* Fallen; fallen from virtue, abject, wicked, guilty, abandoned; degraded, outcast.

परितपावन pútit-páwun, *adj.* Purifying the guilty (*an epithet of the deity*).

पतित्व pu-ti-twúh, *s. m.* The conjugal state.

पतिप्राणा púti-prána, *s. f.* A faithful wife.

पतिम्बरा pút-im-bur-a, *s. f.* A bride choosing her husband; a pungent seed (*Nigella Indica*).

पतिया pú-ti-ya, *s. f.* A written opinion given by *Pundits*; a letter.

पतियाना pu-ti-yána, *v. a.* To confide in, to trust, to believe, to depend on.

पतियारा pu-ti-yára, *s. m.* Trust, confidence, belief, dependance.

पतिव्रत puti-vrút, *s. m.* Chastity.

पतिव्रता púti-vrút-a, *s. f.* A good and virtuous wife.

पतिसेवा púti-séva, *s. f.* Devotion to a husband.

पतोरी pu-tée-ree, *s. f.* A kind of mat.

पतील pu-téel, *adj.* Thin, fine.

पतीला pu-tée-la, *s. m.* A pan, a pot.

पतुकी pú-too-kee, *s. f.* A small pot, a pan.

पतुरिया pu-too-ríya, *s. f.* A prostitute.

पतोह put-óh, } *s. f.* Daughter-in-law,
पतोहू put-ó-hoo, } son's wife.

पतौवा put-óu-wa, *s. m.* A leaf.

पत्तन pút-tun, *s. m.* A town, a city; act of ordering goods from a manufacturer.

पत्तनी pút-tun-ee, *adj.* Commissioned, manufactured by order.

पत्तर pút-tur, *s. m.* A leaf; a letter, epistle; a deed; plate or clamp of metal.

पत्तल put-túl, *s. f.* A plate or trencher formed of leaves.

पत्ता pút-ta, *s. m.* A leaf; a trinket. *Putta hona,* To run away, to flee.

पत्ताल put-tál, *s. m.* The infernal regions or a place under the earth.

पत्ति pútti, *s. m.* A company, a platoon, consisting of one chariot, one elephant, three horse, and five foot.

पत्तिपंक्ति pútti-púnk-ti, *s. f.* A line of infantry.

पत्तिसंघति pútti-súng-huti, *s. f.* A body of troops.

पत्ती pút-tee, *s. f.* A leaf; hemp, of which an intoxicating potion is made.

पत्थर put-thúr, *s. m.* A stone, stone. *Putthur chhatee-pur rukhna,* To be patient by compulsion or from being without remedy. *Putthur puseejna,* To be softened or melted (*a stony heart*). *Putthur panee ho jana,* The melting of a stony heart; a difficult task to be facilitated. *Putthur-bazee, s. f.* Stone-throwing, playing with stones. *Putthur-sa phenk marna,* To reply rashly without understanding the meaning of one's question. *Put-*

thur-seh sir phorna, To teach or instruct a fool. *Putthur hona*, To be heavy; to be stable, to stand still; to be unmerciful.

पत्थरकला pútthur-kúl-a, *s. m.* A firelock.

पत्थरचटा pútthur-chút-a, *s. m.* A sort of greens; a skinflint; name of a serpent; a sort of fish. *adj.* One attached to his own house, who remains there even in distress.

पत्थरचूर putthur-chóor, *s. m.* A plant (*Plectranthus aromaticus*).

पत्थरफोड़ putthur-phór, *s. m.* A woodpecker (*Picus*).

पत्नी pút-nee, *s. f.* A wife.

पत्र putr, *s. m.* A leaf; the leaf of the Laurus cassia; the leaf of a book; gold-leaf, &c., any thin sheet or plate of metal.

पत्रगुप्त putr-góopt, *s. m.* A species of Euphorbia.

पत्ररङ्ग put-rúng, *s. m.* Red sanders (*Pterocarpus santalinus*).

पत्रनालिका putr-ná-ri-ka, *s. f.* The fibre or vein of a leaf.

पत्रपुष्प putr-póoshp, *s. m.* A plant, a red sort of Basil (*Ocymum pilosum*).

पत्रपुष्पक putr-póoshp-uk, *s. m.* A kind of birch, from the bark of which *Hookka* snakes, &c., are made.

पत्ररञ्जन putr-rún-jun, *s. m.* Embellishing a page, illuminating, gilding, &c.

पत्रशिरा putr-shír-a, *s. f.* The vein or fibre of a leaf.

पत्रा pút-ra, *s. m.* An almanack, an ephemeris, a calendar.

पत्राङ्क put-ránk, *s. m.* Page, paging.

पत्राङ्ग putr-áng, *s. m.* Red sanders (*Pterocarpus santalinus*); red or sappan wood (*Cæsalpinia sappan*); *Bhojputr*, a tree so called, a kind of birch.

पत्रिका pútri-ka, *s. f.* A leaf, a written leaf or page, a writing, a letter.

पत्रोपुष्कर putro-pús-kur, *s. m.* A tree (*Cassia esculenta*).

पत्रोर्ण putr-órn, *s. m.* A plant (*Bignonia Indica*).

पथ puth, *s. m.* A road, path, way.

पत्थरकला púthur-kúl-a, *s. m.* A firelock.

पत्थरचटा púthur-chút-a, *s. m.* A sort of greens; a skinflint; name of a serpent; a sort of fish. *adj.* One attached to his own house, who remains there even in distress.

पत्थरचूर puthur-chóor, *s. m.* A plant (*Plectranthus aromaticus*).

पत्थरफोड़ puthur-phór, *s. m.* A woodpecker (*Picus*).

पथराना puth-rá-na, *v. n.* To be petrified; to become hard (*a boil*), to indurate.

पथरी púth-ree, *s. f.* Grit, gravel; the flint of a musket; stone in the bladder, calculus; a gizzard.

पथरीला puth-rée-la, *adj. m.* Stony.

पथिक púth-ik, *s. m.* A traveller, a passenger, a way-farer; a guide, one who knows the way.

पथिद्रुम puthí-droom, *s. m.* A sort of *khyur* (*Mimosa alba*).

पथिन् púth-in, *s. m.* A division of hell.

पथ्य púth-yuh, *adj.* Proper, fit, suitable, agreeing with, but applied chiefly medically, with respect to diet, regimen, &c.

पथ्या puth-yá, *s. f.* Yellow myrobalan (*Terminalia chebula*).

पद pud, *s. m.* A foot; a footstep, the mark of a foot, step; a word; an inflected word; rank, dignity, character; station, degree, place; a foot or rather line of a stanza.

पदक púd-uk, *s. m.* An ornament of the neck.

पदक्रम pud-krúm, *s. m.* Step, pace.

पदच्युत pud-chyóot, *adj.* Fallen from station or dignity, disgraced.

पदना púd-na, ⎫ *adj.* Having the quality
पद्दो pud-dóo, ⎬ of letting wind; (*met.*)
पदोरा pud-ó-ra, ⎭ a coward.

पदबी púd-bee, *s. f.* A path, a road; rank, character; title, titular name, surname, patronymic.

पदभञ्जन pud-bhún-jun, *s. m.* Explanation of obscure or obsolete words; etymology.

पद्म púd-um, *s. m.* The lotus (*Nelumbium speciosum*, or *Prunus cerasus*), ten billions (according to the shastr), or one thousand billions (according to the Dustoor-ool-uml, or Royal ordinances of Ukbur).

पदवी púd-wee, *s. f.* A road, a path, a way; station, situation, rank, degree; place, site.

पदाङ्क pud-ánk, *s. m.* Foot-mark, vestige.

पदात pud-át, *s. m.* A footman, a pedestrian, a foot-soldier.

पदातिक pud-á-tik, *s. m.* A peon; a footman, or foot-soldier.

पदाना pud-á-na, *v. a.* To cause to let wind; (*met.*) to frighten or put to flight.

पदार्थ pud-árth, *s. m.* Thing, substantial or material form of being; a rarity, a good, a blessing, a delicacy or exquisite food; a category or predicament in logic, of which seven are maintained, viz., substance, quality, action, identity, variety, relation, and annihilation; another enumeration gives sixteen.

पदास pud-ás, *s. f.* Inclination to let wind, flatulency.

पदासन pud-á-sun, *s. m.* A footstool.

पदासां pud-á-sa, *adj. m.* Inclined to let wind, flatulent.

पदोरा pud-ó-ra, *adj.* Having the quality of letting wind ; (*met.*) a coward.

पदी púd-dee, *s. f.* A path, a way, an alley.

पदती pud-dhútee, *s. f.* A road, a line, a row or range ; a ritual, a manual, a work upon any act or ceremony, detailing the mode of its performance, and collecting the texts connected with it ; a family name, a surname or title ; manner, custom.

पद्म pudm, *s. m.* A lotus (*Nelumbium speciosum*), it is often confounded with the water-lily (*Nymphæa*) ; a large number, ten billions.

पद्मक púdm-uk, *s. m.* A kind of leprosy.

पद्मकाष्ठ pudm-káshth, *s. m.* A fragrant wood used in medicine, and described as cooling and tonic.

पद्मकी pud-múk-ee, *s. m.* The *Bhojputr* or birch tree, the bark is used for writing upon, and wrapping shawls, &c.

पद्मचारिणी pudm-chá-rin-ee, } *s. f.* A small
पद्मा púdm-a, } tree (*Hibiscus mutabilis*).

पद्मदर्शन pudm-dúr-shun, *s. m.* The resin of the Pinus longifolia.

पद्मपत्र pudm-pútr, *s. m.* A sort of Costus (*C. speciosus*).

पद्मपुष्प pudm-póoshp, *s. m.* A shrub (*Webera corymbosa*).

पद्ममुखी pudm-móo-khee, *s. f.* A sort of prickly nightshade.

पद्मराग pudm-rág, *s. m.* A ruby.

पद्मवर्णक pudm-vúrn-uk, *s. m.* A species of Costus (*C. speciosus*).

पद्मा púdm-a, *s. f.* The goddess of riches, *Lukshmee.*

पद्माकर pudm-á-kur, *s. m.* A large deep tank or pond ; one in which the lotus does or may grow.

पद्मात pudm-át, *s. m.* A sort of Cassia (*C. tora*).

पद्मावत pudm-á-wut, *n. prop.* A celebrated princess whose adventures are related in a romance entitled *Pudmawutee.*

पद्मावती pudm-a-wút-ee, *s. f.* The wife of the sage *Jurutkaroo* ; a river, the main stream of the Gunges, between the *Cossimbazar* river and the sea.

पद्मासन pudm-á-sun, *s. m.* A posture in religious meditation, sitting with the thighs crossed, one hand resting on the left thigh, the other held up with the thumb upon the heart, the eyes directed to the tip of the nose ; a seat or throne made in the shape of a lotus, one especially on which idols are placed.

पद्मिनी púd-min-ee, *s. f.* A woman of one of the four classes into which the sex is distinguished, the first and most excellent.

पद्मोत्तर pudm-ót-tur, *s. m.* Safflower.

पद्युह púd-yuh, *s. m.* Metre, verse.

पुधारना pu-dhár-na, *v. n.* To go, proceed, depart, arrive.

पन pun, } A termination affixed to nouns
पना púna, } to denote the abstract quality, and answering to the English terminations *ship, hood, ness,* &c., as *Luruk-pun,* Childhood ; *Buniya-pun,* The business of a Buniya.

पनकपड़ा pún-kup-ra, *s. m.* Soft cloth wetted and applied to a wound or sore.

पनगोटी pún-go-tee, *s. f.* Chicken-pox.

पनघट pun-ghút, *s. m.* A passage to a river, a stair or quay for drawing water.

पनच pún-uch, *s. f.* A bow-string.

पनचक्की pun-chúk-kee, *s. f.* A water-mill.

पनचोरा pun-chó-ra, *s. m.* An earthen vessel with a narrow neck and a hole in the bottom. When filled with water and the mouth stopped, no water flows from the hole below till the hand or whatever stopped the mouth be removed. (*It is used as an experiment to illustrate the doctrine of the horror vacui by the followers of Aristotle*). [*meat.*

पनतुवा pun-túwa, *s. m.* A kind of sweet-meat.

पनउपना pun-úp-na, *v. n.* To commence increasing in bulk (*a man, tree,* &c.) ; to prosper, to flourish, to thrive, to shoot, to grow, to be refreshed or restored.

पनपनाहट pun-pun-áhut, *s. f.* The whizzing of an arrow or shot.

पनपाना pun-pá-na, *v. a.* To cause to flourish, to promote the prosperity of another, to refresh.

पनबट्टा pun-bút-ta, *s. m.* A betel-box.

पनभत्ता pun-bhút-ta, *s. m.* A kind of drink made from rice.

पनवारा pun-wá-ra, *s. m.* A plate or dish made of leaves to eat on.

पनवारी pun-wá-ree, } *s. f.* A betel-gar-
पनवाड़ी pun-wá-ree, } den.

पनस pún-us, *s. m.* The bread-fruit tree (*Artocarpus integrifolia*).

पनसा pún-sa, *adj.* Insipid. *s. f.* A pustule, a malady, pustular and phlegmonoid inflammation of the skin or external organs.

पनसारहट्टा pun-sar-hútta, *s. m.* A quarter where are many druggists' shops.

पनसारी pun-sá-ree, *s. m.* A druggist.

पनसाल pun-sál, ⎫ *s. m.* A stand where
पनसाला pun-sá-la, ⎬ water is provided
पनसुल्ला pun-súl-la, ⎭ for passengers.

पनसोइ pun-só-ee, *s. f.* A small boat so called.

पनहाना pun-há-na, *v. a.* To cause the milk to come into the udders of animals.

पनहारा pun-há-ra, *s. m.* A man who carries water in pots on his head, or in a *banghy.*

पनहारिन pun-há-rin, ⎫ *s. f.* A woman who
पनहारी pun-há-ree, ⎬ carries water in
pots on her head. *s. m. f.* A faithless person, a promise-breaker.

पनहियारैं pun-hi-yáee, *adj.* Afflicted with the *fluor albus.*

पनही pun-hée, *s. f.* A slipper.

पना pún-a, A termination affixed to nouns to denote the abstract quality, and answering to the English terminations *ship, hood, ness,* &c., as *Buch-pun,* Infancy, childhood; *Khontu-pun,* Wickedness.

पनाना pun-á-na, *v. a.* To cause the milk to come into the udders of animals.

पनारी pun-á-ree, ⎫ *s. f.* A drain or pipe by
पनाली pun-á-lee, ⎬ which water runs off
from the roof of a house.

पनिया pún-i-ya, *s. m.* Water; a water-snake or any thing living in water.

पनियाना pun-i-yána, *v. n.* To irrigate, to water, to yield water.

पनियाला pun-i-yála, *s. m.* A fruit (*Flacourtia catafracta*).

पनीर pun-éer, *s. m.* Cheese.

पनीरक pun-ée-ruk, ⎫ *s. f.* A young flow-
पनेरी pun-ér-ree, ⎬ ering shrub.

पनीहा pun-ée-ha, *s. m.* Any thing living in water, aquatic; a water-snake.

पन्थ punth, ⎫ *s. m.* A road, path, way;
पन्था pun-thá, ⎬ a sect, a religious order.

पन्नग pun-núg, *s. m.* A snake.

पन्ना pún-na, *s. m.* A beverage; the upper part of a shoe; an emerald; a leaf.

पन्नी pún-nee, *s. f.* Tinfoil. *s. m.* A tribe of *Puthans.*

पपड़ा púp-ra, *s. m.* A crust.

पपड़ियाकथ púpriya-kuth, *s. f.* A kind of white-coloured *kuth* (extract of *Mimosa catechu*).

पपड़ी púp-ree, *s. f.* A scab, a scale, scurf; scales formed by the drying up of moist earth; thin cakes of bread.

पपड़ीला pup-rée-la, *adj.* Scurfy.

पपनी púp-nee, *s. f.* The eyelash.

पपीहा pup-ée-ha, *s. m.* A sparrow-hawk (*Falco nisus.*)

पपैया pup-úy-ya, *s. m.* A sort of child's whistle; a tree and its fruit (the *Papaw tree, Carica papaya*).

पपोटा pup-ó-ta, *s. f.* The eyelid.

पम्पा púm-pa, *s. f.* A river in the south of India.

पय puy, *s. m.* Milk, water. *adv.* On, upon, over, at, to, nevertheless, yet. *conj.* But. *s. f.* A fault.

पयस्खा puy-syá, *s. f.* A shrub (*Asclepias rosea*); a medicinal kind of moon-plant.

पयस्विनी puy-swín-ee, *s. f.* Milch-cow.

पयान puy-án, *s. m.* Departure.

पयाल puy-ál, *s. f.* Straw.

पयोधर puy-ó-dhur, *s. m.* A woman's breast; a sort of rush (*Scirpus kysoor*); a fragrant grass (*Cyperus rotundus, &c.*)

पयोधिक puy-ó-dhik, *s. m.* Cuttle-fish bone.

पयोनिधि puy-o-nídhi, *s. m.* The ocean.

पयोर puyór, *s. m.* The *khuyur* (*Mimosa catechu*).

पयोव्रत puyo-vrút, *s. m.* Living upon milk for a month, which with prayer and residence in a cow-house, is an expiation for receiving an unsuitable present; offering of milk to *Vishnoo,* and subsisting upon it for twelve days; also for one or for three days as a religious act.

पयोष्णी puy-ósh-nee, *s. f.* A river that rises in the *Vindhya* mountain.

पर pur, *adj.* Distant, removed, remote, far; other, different, strange, foreign. *adv.* and *conj.* Over, above, through, after, at, by, for, of; but, yet, however. *prep.* On, upon, at, notwithstanding.

परकना púr-uk-na, *v. a.* To inspect, to examine, to prove, to try.

परकाज púr-kaj, *s. m.* The business or interest of another.

परकाजी pur-ká-jee, *adj.* Attentive to the business or interest of others, serving others, beneficent.

परकान pur-kán, *s. m.* A trunnion.

परकाना pur-ká-na, *v. a.* To accustom, to habituate.

परकीय pur-kée-yuh, *adj.* Another, belonging to another.

परकीया pur-kée-ya, *s. f.* The mistress or wife of another.

परक्षेत्र pur-kshétr, *s. m.* Another's field; another's body; another man's wife.

परख púr-ukh, *s. f.* Inspection, examination, trial, proof, experiment.

पर्ख्ना púr-ukh-na, *v. a.* To inspect, to examine, to prove, to try.

पर्खाई pur-kháee, *s. f.* The act of examining ; the price paid for examination, inspection, trial or proof.

पर्खाना pur-khá-na, *v. a.* To cause to inspect, examine, try or prove.

पर्खैया pur-khy-ya, *s. m.* An inspector, examiner, prover, assayer.

पर्गाछ pur-gách, *s. m.* Epidendron.

पर्घटी pur-ghút-ee, *s. f.* A mould in which silver or gold in cast previous to working it ; apparency, clearness.

पर्चना púr-uch-na, *v. n.* To be made acquainted, to be introduced.

पर्चा púr-cha, *s. m.* Examination, trial, proof, experiment.

पर्चाना pur-chá-na, *v. a.* To introduce to a person, to engage in conversation.

पर्चूनिया pur-chóo-niya, *s. m.* A meal-merchant.

पर्चूनी pur-chóo-nee, *s. f.* The act of selling flour, meal, &c.

पर्छली pur-chút-ee, *s. f.* A small thatch thrown over mud walls.

पर्छना pur-úchh-na, *v. a.* To move a lamp or candle over the heads of a bride and bridegroom, to drive away evil spirits, propitiate good ones, &c. ; to kindle (*a fire*).

पर्छाईं pur-chhá-een, *s. f.* Image (*from shade or reflection*), shadow, shade. *Purchhaen upnee seh bhagna*, To be frightened at one's own shadow.

पर्छिद्र pur-chhídr, *s. m.* A fault or defect in another.

पर्जङ्क púr-junk, *s. m.* A bedstead.

पर्जतन् pur-jút-un, *s. m.* Travelling.

पर्जवट pur-ju-wút, *s. m.* Quit-rent, tax.

पर्जा púr-ja, प्रजा prúj-a, } *s. f.* A subject, tenant, renter, people.

पर्जित púr-jit, *adj.* Conquered, subdued.

पर्त púr-ut, *s. m.* A fold, plait, ply, layer, crust, incrustation, a stratum.

पर्तम pur-túm, *adj.* Greatest.

पर्तल púr-tul, *s. m.* The baggage of a horseman carried all on one bullock or *tuttoo*, a pack-horse, a pad-horse.

पर्तला púr-tul-a, *s. m.* Sword-belt, shoulder belt.

पर्ता púr-ta, *s. m.* A reel (*for winding thread*).

पर्ती púr-tee, *s. f.* Waste land.

पर्तीत pur-téet, प्रतीत pru-téet, } *s. f.* Faith, confidence, trust. *Purteet kurna*, To examine ; to believe ; to trust.

पर्दादा pur-dá-da, *s. m.* A great grandfather by the father's side.

पर्दार pur-dár, *s. f.* Another's wife.

पर्दारगमन purdár-gúm-un, *s. m.* Adultery, adulterous intercourse or intrigue.

पर्दुःख pur-dóokh, *s. m.* The pain or sorrow of another.

पर्देश pur-désh, *s. m.* A foreign country.

पर्देशी pur-désh-ee, *adj.* Foreign, exotic. *s. m.* A foreigner ; one residing abroad.

पर्दोषकीर्तन púrdosh-kéerttun, *s. m.* Scandal, calumny, censoriousness.

पर्द्वेषी pur-dwésh-ee, *adj.* Hostile, inimical, adverse.

पर्द्रव्य pur-drúv-yuh, *s. m.* Another's property. [another.

पर्द्रोही pur-dró-hee, *adj.* Tyrannising over

पर्धन pur-dhún, *s. m.* Another's wealth.

पर्धनास्वादनसुख púrdhun-aswádun-sóokh, *s. m.* Feeding luxuriously at another's expense.

पर्धर्म pur-dhúrm, *s. m.* Another's duty or business, the occupation of another caste.

पर्ण púr-un, *s. f.* A very quick time in music.

पर्नाना pur-ná-na, *s. m.* A great grandfather by the mother's side.

पर्नाला pur-ná-la, *s. m.* पर्नाली pur-ná-lee, *s. f.* } A gutter, a drain, a conduit. [but.

पर्न्तु púr-un-too, *conj.* Afterwards, also,

पर्न्त pur-úntr, *adj.* Subservient, obedient, dependant.

पर्पञ्च pur-púnch, *s. m.* Delusion, fraud, imposition, treachery, deceit, artifice.

पर्पञ्ची pur-pún-chee, *adj.* Insidious, fraudulent, artful.

पर्पद pur-púd, *s. m.* Eminence, high station ; final felicity.

पर्पराना pur-pur-ána, *v. n.* To smart.

पर्पराहट pur-pur-áhut, *s. f.* Acrimony, smart.

पर्परिगृह pur-puri-grúh, *s. m.* The family or dependants of another.

पर्पुष्ट púr-poosht, *s. m.* The *Kokila* or Indian cuckoo.

पर्पुष्टा pur-poosh-tá, *s. f.* A harlot, a whore ; a parasite plant.

पर्पूरन pur-póo-run, *adj.* Brimful.

पर्पैठ pur-pyth, *s. m.* A duplicate of a bill of exchange.

परब् púr-ub, *s. m.* A gem, a flat diamond; a festival, a holiday, an anniversary festival, a feast; a chapter, a section.

परबल púr-bul,) *adj.* Predominant, pre-
प्रबल pru-bul,) valent, violent, strong, powerful.

परबस púr-bus, *adj.* Depending on the will of another, under the authority of another, dependant, precarious.

परब्रह्म pur-brúmh, *s. m.* The Supreme Being.

परभाग pur-bhág, *s. m.* Excellence, superior merit, supremacy; good fortune, prosperity; the last part, residue, remainder.

परभूमि pur-bhóo-mi, *s. f.* A foreign or an enemy's country.

परभृत pur-bhrít, *adj.* Cherished or nourished by a stranger, fostered, adopted. *s. m.* The Indian cuckoo, which is supposed to leave its eggs in the nest of the crow to be hatched.

परम púr-um, *adj.* Best, most excellent; chief, principal, preceding, first, supreme.

परमगति púrum-gúti, *s. f.* Chief object or refuge, as a god, a protector; final felicity, eternal felicity, heavenly bliss.

परमत pur-mút, *s. m.* A different opinion or doctrine.

परमधाम pur-um-dhám, *s. m.* Paradise.

परमपद pur-um-púd, *s. m.* Eminence, high station; final felicity; heaven or beatitude.

परमराज pur-um-ráj, *s. m.* A supreme monarch.

परमल púr-mul, *adj.* Sweet-scented. *s. m.* Parched grain of *joar* or *bajra* (*Holcus sorgum* and *spicatus*).

परमहंस pur-um-húns, *s. m.* An ascetic, a religious man who has subdued all his senses by abstract meditation.

परमागति pur-um-águti, *s. f.* Translation to heaven, final beatitude.

परमाणु pur-um-ánoo, *s. m.* An atom, the invisible base of all aggregate bodies; thirty of them are supposed to form a mote in a sun-beam; the lowest measure of weight; a measure of time, the sun's passage past an atom of matter.

परमात्मा pur-um-át-ma, *s. m.* The Supreme Being, considered as the soul of the universe.

परमाद्वैत pur-um-ádwyt, *s. m.* Pure unitarianism.

परमानन्द pur-um-ánund, *s. m.* Great pleasure.

परमान्न pur-um-ánn, *s. m.* An oblation of rice to progenitors or gods, boiled with milk and sugar.

परमायुः pur-um-áyoo, *s. m.* The longest period of life, either in men or animals.

परमार्थ pur-um-árth, *s. m.* Spiritual knowledge; any excellent or important aim or object; the best sense; the first pursuit, the best end, virtue, merit.

परमार्थी pur-um-árthee, *adj.* Religious, seeking the best end, virtuous.

परमिलू pur-míl-oo, *s. f.* A kind of dance.

परमेव pur-méo, *s. m.* A gonorrhœa, a (*venereal*) clap, a gleet.

परमेश्वर pur-mésh-wur, *s. m.* The first and Supreme Lord, God, the Almighty.

परमपद pur-um-púd, *s. m.* Eternal felicity.

परम्पर pur-um-púr, *adj.* Traditionary or successive, proceeding from one to another, from father to son, &c. *s. m.* A great-great-grandson.

परम्परा pur-úm-pur-a, *s. f.* Race, progeny, lineage; order, method, continuous arrangement, regular series or succession; communication from one to another in succession, tradition.

परम्परीण pur-um-pur-éen, *adj.* Hereditary, what has come by inheritance or descent; traditional.

परू púr-roo, *s. m.* A potherb (*Eclipta prostrata*).

परला púr-la, *adj.* Of the other side.

परलोक pur-lók, *s. m.* Heaven, paradise.

परलोकगमम् purlok-gúm, *s. m.* Death, dying.

परवल púr-wul,) *s. m.* A plant (*Tricho-*
पटवल púl-wul,) *santhes dioica*).

परवश pur-wúsh, *adj.* Subservient, dependant, subject.

परवान pur-wán, *s. m.* The yard (*of a sail*). *Purwan churhna*, To grow up (*a phrase peculiar to women*).

परवाल pur-wál, *s. m.* A disease of the eyelids in which the eyelashes fall off, a stye or stythe.

परश pur-úsh, *s. m.* A kind of gem.

परशाद pur-shád,) *s. m.* Viand, victuals,
प्रसाद pru-sád,) food that has been offered to the deities; kindness, favour, blessing, gift; leavings of a great man or spiritual guide.

परशु púr-shoo, *s. m.* An axe, a hatchet.

परशुराम pur-shoo-rám, *s. m.* A hero and demi-god, the first of the three *Rams*, and the sixth *uvutar* or supposed descent of the god *Vishnoo*, who is said to have appeared in the world as the son of the sage *Jumudugni*, for the purpose of repressing the tyranny and punishing the violence of the *Kshuttrees* or military tribe, and contemporary with *Dushuruth Ram*. He is, from his father, called *Jumudugni*. *Renooka*, wife of *Jumudugni*, was interrupted in bringing water from the river by *Kartuveerj-Arjoon*, a prince of the *Kshuttrees*, who was sporting in the water with his thousand wives, for which *Purshooram's* father *Jumudugni* cursed him. The *Kshuttree* prince killed *Jumudugni*; and *Jumudugni* vowed not to leave a *Kshuttree* on the face of the earth; he is reported to have extirpated them twenty-one times; the women with child each time producing a new race; and, they say that there have been no *Kshuttrees* since; those so called being of spurious breed or *Vuruasunkurs*. *Purshooram* appears to typify the tribe of *Brahmuns*, and their contests with the *Kshuttrees*.

परश्वस् pur-shwús, *adv.* The day after to-morrow.

परस् púr-us, *s. m.* Touch.

परसना púr-us-na, *v. a.* To touch.

परसिया púr-si-ya, *s. m.* A reaping hook, a sickle.

परस्रूत pur-sóot, ⎫ *s. m.* The whites, *fluor*
प्रस्रूत pru-sóot, ⎭ *albus*.

परसों púr-son, *adv.* The day before yesterday; the day after to-morrow.

परसम्बन्ध púr-sum-bundh, *s. m.* Relation or connection with another.

परसम्बन्धी púr-sum-bun-dhee, *adj.* Related to another, belonging to another.

परस्पर púr-us-pur, *adj.* Mutual, interchanging. *adv.* Mutually, reciprocally.

परस्परानुमति púr-uspur-ánoo-muti, *s. f.* Mutual concurrence or assent.

परस्परोपकार púr-uspur-opkár, *s. m.* Mutual assistance; offensive and defensive alliance.

परस्परोपकारी púr-uspur-opkáree, *s. m.* An ally; an associate, a helper.

परस्मैपद purusmúy-púd, *s. m.* The transitive or active verb.

परहित pur-hít, *adj.* Friendly, benevolent; good or profitable for another.

परा púr-a, *prep.* (In comp.) Back, backward, reverse, over. *s. m.* A company, a body (of troops). [paste.

परांठा pur-án-tha, *s. m.* A kind of cake,

पराक pur-ák, *s. m.* A religious obligation of an expiatory kind, fasting for twelve days and nights, and keeping the mind attentive, and organs subdued; a sacrificial sword or scimitar.

पराक्रम pur-á-krum, *s. m.* Power, strength; valour, prowess.

पराक्रमी pur-a-krúm-ee, *adj.* Powerful, bold, strong, vigorous.

परांग pur-ág, *s. m.* The pollen or farina of a flower; fragrant powder used after bathing; the name of a mountain.

परांगमुख pur-áng-mookh, *adj.* Turning away, having the face averted.

पराचीन pur-a-chéen, ⎫ *adj.* Old, of former
प्राचीन pra-chéen, ⎭ times, ancient.

परःजय púr-a-juy, *s. m.* Overthrow, defeat, discomfiture.

पराजयमान pur-a-juy-mán, *adj.* Overcoming, surpassing, defeating.

पराजित pur-a-jit, *adj.* Conquered, defeated, overcome.

पराठा pur-á-tha, *s. m.* Bread made with butter or *ghee*, and of several layers, like pie-crust.

परात pur-át, ⎫ *s. f.* A large plate (of
पराती pur-á-tee, ⎭ brass).

परात्प्रिय purát-príyuh, *s. m.* A kind of reed (*Saccharum spontaneum*).

परादन pur-á-dun, *s. m.* A horse of the *Persian* breed.

पराधिकार púr-a-dhí-kar, *s. m.* Another person's office or post.

पराधिकारचर्चा pur-adhikár-churchcha, *s. f.* Officiousness, interference with another's concerns.

पराधीन pur-a-dhéen, *adj.* Dependant, subject, subservient, humble, under another.

पराधीनता pur-adhéen-ta, *s. f.* Subjection, dependance.

परान pur-án, ⎫ *s. m.* Breath; soul, life;
प्राण pran, ⎭ sweetheart, mistress.
Pran-puti, Soul's lord.

परानसा pur-án-sa, *s. f.* The practice of medicine, administering remedies.

परानां pur-á-na, *v. n.* To run, to flee.

परान्न pur-ánn, *adj.* Living at another's expense. *s. m.* Food supplied by another.

परान्नभोजी pur-ann-bhójee, *adj.* Living at another's cost.

पराभव pur-a-bhúv, *s. m.* Discomfiting, overcoming.

पराभूत pur-a-bhóot, *adj.* Defeated, discomfited, overcome.

परामर्ष pur-a-múrsh, *s. m.* Discrimination, discriminating, distinguishing, judgment; counsel, advice, consideration, reflection.

परामोधना pur-a-módh-na, *s. m.* Wheedling.

परायण pur-a-yún, *s. m.* Adherence to any pursuit, attachment to any object; dependance on. *adj.* Adhering or attached to; connected with, depending upon.

परायप pur-a-yútt, *adj.* Dependant, subject.

पराया pur-á ya, *adj.* Strange, foreign, belonging to another, extraneous, other, of another.

परारू pur-á-roo, *s. m.* A kind of gourd (*Momordica charantia*).

परार्थ pur-árth, *adj.* Having another object or sense, &c.; designed or purposed by another. *s. m.* For the sake or good of another.

परार्थवादी pur-arth-vádee, *adj.* Officious, intermeddling.

परार्द्ध pur-árddh-vuh, *s. m.* A great number, a lack of lacks of crores, or a number equal to half the term of *Brumh's* life, or as many mortal days as are equal to fifty of his years.

परााल pur-ál, *s. f.* Straw.

परावर्त pur-a-vúrtt, *s. m.* Reversal of a sentence.

परावर्तव्यवहार puravúrtt-byuvhár, *s. m.* Appeal (*in law*).

परावृत्त pur-a-vrítt, *adj.* Reversed (*as a judgment*).

परााशर pur-a-shúr, *n. prop.* The father of the poet *Vyas.*

परााशरी pur-a-shúr-ee, *s. m.* A beggar, a wandering mendicant.

परााश्रय pur-ásh-ruy, *adj.* Dependant or relying upon another. *s. m.* Dependance.

परााश्रया pur-ásh-ruya, *s. f.* A parasite plant.

परााश्रित pur-ásh-rit, *adj.* Subject, dependant.

परास pur-ás, *s. m.* A tree (*Butea frondosa*); oakum made of the bark of that tree.

परासू pur-á-soo, *adj.* Dead, expired.

परासूता pur-a-sóo-ta, *s. f.* Death, extinction; drowsiness, sleepiness.

परास्त pur-ást, *adj.* Defeated.

पराह pur-áh, *s. m.* The next day. *s. f.* Flight, a general emigration.

पराहन pur-á-hun, *s. m.* The afternoon, the latter part of the day.

परि púr-i, *prep.* (*In comp.*) About, around, round about, entirely.

परिकथा puri-kútha, *s. f.* A work of fiction, a tale, a story, the history or adventures of any fabulous person.

परिकल्पित puri-kúlpit, *adj.* Made, invented.

परिकीर्तन puri-kéerttun, *s. m.* Saying, telling; talking of, boasting.

परिक्रमा puri-krúm-a, *s. f.* Walking round or about, circumambulating, going about; act of going round to the right by way of adoration, circumambulation, going about.

परिक्रय puri-krúy, *s. m.* Redemption, purchasing or purchasing back; giving up part of a treasure to preserve the rest.

परिक्लिश puri-klísh, *s. m.* Vexation, trouble.

परिक्लिष्ट puri-klísht, *adj.* Vexed, annoyed.

परिक्षित purik-shít, *n. prop.* The name of a king, the son of *Ubhimunyoo*, and grandson of *Urjoon.*

परिखा puri-khá, *s. f.* A moat, a ditch surrounding a fort, &c.

परिख्यात puri-khyát, *adj.* Famous, celebrated.

परिख्याति puri-khyáti, *s. f.* Fame, reputation.

परिचय puri-chúy, *s. m.* Acquaintance, intimacy.

परिचर्या puri-chúrjya, *s. f.* Service, dependance; veneration, worship.

परिचारक puri-cháruk, *s. m.* A servant, an attendant.

परिचित puri-chít, *adj.* Known, acquainted with.

परिचेय puri-chéyu, *adj.* To be known as an acquaintance.

परिच्छेद puri-chhéd, *s. m.* Segment, division; the division of a book, a section or chapter.

परिजन puri-jún, *s. m.* Dependants, servants, family, followers.

परिनाम puri-nám, *s. m.* Maturity, fulness, ripeness; end, last stage or state.

परिनामदर्शी purinám-dursbee, *adj.* Who looks forward or to the end.

परितः puri-túh, *adv.* Around, every way, all round.

परिताप puri-táp, *s. m.* Pain, anguish; sorrow; a division of hell.

परितुष्ट puri-tóosht, *adj.* Pleased, delighted.

परितोष puri-tósh, *s. m.* Pleasure, satisfaction, delight.

परित्यक्त puri-tyúkt, *adj.* Void or deprived of, left, quitted, abandoned.

परित्याग puri-tyág, *s. m.* Abandonment, quitting, desertion.

परित्यागी puri-tyágee, *adj.* Abandoning, quitting.

परित्रान puri-trán, *s. m.* Preserving, protecting.

परिधान puri-dhán, *s. m.* A lower garment; vesture, clothes.

परिधि puri-dhí, *s. m.* The circumference of a circle; the disk of the sun or moon.

परिपक्व puri-pukwú, *adj.* Cooked, dressed; mature; shrewd, knowing; digested.

परिपक्वता puri-pukwú-ta, *s. f.* Maturity, perfection; shrewdness; digestion.

परिपन्थी puri-púnthee, *s. m.* An enemy, an antagonist; a robber, a highwayman, a bandit.

परिपाक puri-pák, *s. m.* Maturity, perfection; cleverness, shrewdness; digestion.

परिपाकिनी puri-pakín-ee, *s. f.* A drug (*Convolvulus turpethum*).

परिपाटी puri-pátee, *s. f.* Order, method, arrangement; arithmetic.

परिपालन puri-pálun, *s. m.* Protecting, cherishing.

परिपालित puri-pálit, *adj.* Protected, cherished.

परिपूष्कर puri-póosh-kur-a, *s. f.* A sort of cucumber (*Cucumis madraspatanus*).

परिपूजन puri-póo-jun, *s. m.* Worshipping, adoring.

परिपूजित puri-póo-jit, *adj.* Served, worshipped, adored.

परिपूर्ण puri-póorn, *adj.* Full, entire, complete; satisfied, content.

परिपूर्णता puri-póorn-ta, *s. f.* Completion, entireness, fulness; satiety or satisfaction.

परिपेल puri-pél, *s. m.* A fragrant grass (*Cyperus rotundus*).

परिप्लव puri-plúv, *s. m.* Bathing, immersing; inundation.

परिप्लुत puri-plóot, *adj.* Immersed, inundated; bathed.

परिभव puri-bhúv, } *s. m.* Disrespect, contempt, disgrace.
परिभाव puri-bháo, }

परिभाषा puri-bhásha, *s. f.* A technicality, a conventional term in any science; (*in grammar*) a maxim given by the ancient grammarians as a summary interpretation of the rules of *Panini*; (*in medicine*) prognosis; abuse, ridicule.

परिभोग puri-bhóg, *s. m.* Possession, enjoyment.

परिभ्रम puri-bhrúm, *s. m.* Wandering, going about; error.

परिभ्रष्ट puri-bhrúsht, *adj.* Fallen, degraded, deprived of.

परिमण्डल puri-mún-dul, *s. m.* A ball; a globe, a circle.

परिमण्डलता puri-múndul-ta, *s. f.* Rotundity, circularity.

परिमन्द puri-múnd, *adj.* Slow, dull.

परिमल puri-múl, *s. m.* An exquisite scent, especially arising from the trituration of fragrant substances; the trituration of perfumes.

परिमाण puri-mán, *s. m.* Measure; measuring.

परिमित puri-mít, *adj.* Meted, measured; regulated.

परिमितभोज purimít-bhóoj, *adj.* Temperate, abstemious.

परिमिताहार purimít-ahár, *adj.* Eating moderately.

परिमोहन puri-móhun, *s. m.* Fascinating, beguiling.

परिमोहिनी puri-móhin-ee, *f.* } *adj.* What
परिमोही puri-móhee, *m.* } is bewitching, fascinating.

परिम्लान puri-mlán, *adj.* Soiled, stained; waned, withered; diminished, impaired.

परिवर्त puri-vúrt, *s. m.* Going or turning back; turning round, revolving; exchange, barter; requital, return; the end of a period of four ages, or destruction of the world.

परिवा púri-wa, *s. f.* The first day of a lunar fortnight, the first of the moon's increase or wane.

परिवाद puri-vád, *s. m.* Abuse, reproach, reproof; charge, accusation.

परिवादक puri-vá-duk, *s. m.* An accuser, a plaintiff, a complainant or calumniator.

परिवादी puri-vá-dee, *s. m.* An accuser, a reprover; (*in law*) a plaintiff.

परिवार puri-wár, *s. m.* Family, attendants, dependants; dependant.

परिवारता puri-wárta, *s. f.* Subjection, dependance.

परिवास puri-vás, *s. m.* Abiding, abode.

परिवाह puri-váh, *s. m.* An inundation, an overflowing, natural or artificial.

परिविष्ट puri-vísht, *adj.* Surrounded, enclosed.

परिवृत्त puri-vrítt, *adj.* Gone round, revolved; exchanged.

परिवेदन puri-védun, *s. m.* Anguish, pain, misery; marriage, marrying.

परिवेषण puri-vésh-un, *s. m.* Surrounding, enclosing; serving up dinner, distributing food to guests, &c.

परिवेष्टन puri-vésh-tun, *s. m.* Surrounding, encompassing; circumference.

परिवेष्टित puri-vésh-tit, *adj.* Enclosed, surrounded, encompassed; covered, veiled.

परिव्याध puri-vyádh, *s. m.* A tree (*Pterospermum acerifolia*); a sort of reed growing in water (*Calamus fasciculatus*).

परिव्रज्या puri-vrújya, *s. f.* Ascetic devotion, religious austerity, abandonment of the world; leading the life of a mendicant.

परिव्राजक puri-vrá-juk, *s. m.* A religious mendicant.

परिशङ्कनीय puri-shun-kun-éeyuh, *adj.* To be doubted, to be feared or apprehended.

परिशाप puri-sháp, *s. m.* Cursing, reviling.

परिशुद्ध puri-shóoddh, *adj.* Cleaned, purified ; discharged, paid.

परिशेष puri-shésh, *s. m.* Remainder ; completion.

परिशोध puri-shódh, *s. m.* Cleansing, purifying, correcting ; discharging a debt or obligation.

परिशोष puri-shósh, *s. m.* Drying, evaporation.

परिश्रम puri-shrúm, *s. m.* Labour, trouble, pain, toil ; distress, fatigue.

परिश्रमी puri-shrúm-ee, *adj.* Active, laborious.

परिश्रान्त puri-shránt, *adj.* Overcome with distress or fatigue, exhausted, wearied.

परिश्रान्ति puri-shránti, *s. f.* Labour, trouble ; fatigue, exhaustion.

परिष्कार pur-ish-kár, *s. m.* Decoration, embellishment ; initiation, purification by essential rites.

परिष्कृत pur-ish-krít, *adj.* Adorned, decorated, embellished ; purified by initiatory rites.

परिष्कृतभूमि pur-ish-krit-bhóomi, *s. f.* An altar, or ground prepared for a sacrifice, or for the victim and the utensils employed.

परिसंख्या puri-sun-khyá, *s. f.* Total or complete enumeration or specification, implying exclusion of any other ; reckoning, enumerating.

परिसंख्यात puri-sun-khyát, *adj.* Counted, enumerated.

परिसमापन puri-sum-apún, *s. m.* Finishing entirely.

परिसमाप्त puri-sum-ápt, *adj.* Finished, done entirely.

परिसमाप्ति puri-sum-ápti, *s. f.* Entire completion.

परिसाधन puri-sa-dhún, *s. m.* Accomplishing, effecting ; determining, ascertaining.

परिसीमन् puri-séem-un, *s. m.* Boundary, extreme term or limit.

परिहरण puri-húr-un, *s. m.* Seizing, taking ; leaving, abandoning.

परिहरना puri-húr-na, *v. a.* To leave, forsake, abandon, desert ; to take away, to clear off.

परिहार puri-hár, *s. m.* Disrespect.

परिहास puri-hás, *s. m.* Mirth, sport, pastime.

परिहासवेदी puri-has-védee, *s. m.* A jester, a wag, a wit.

परिहीन puri-héen, *adj.* Waned, faded, wasted ; deserted by, deprived of.

परीक्षक pur-eek-shúk, *s. m.* An experimenter, an assayer, a prover ; an investigator, a judge.

परीक्षण pur-eek-shún, *s. m.* Trial, experiment, examination.

परीक्षा pur-eek-shá, *s. f.* Discrimination, investigation, examination, test, trial, experiment ; trial by ordeal of various kinds.

परीक्षित pur-eek-shít, *n. prop.* The grandson of *Urjoon*, to whom the *Bhagvut* was related.

परीक्षित pur-eek-shít, *adj.* Tried, examined, tested, proved.

परीधावी puree-dhá-wee, *s. m.* The fortyfirst year of the Indian cycle.

परीवर्त pur-ee-vúrtt, *s. m.* Exchange, barter.

परीवाद pur-ee-vád, *s. m.* Reproof, censure, abuse.

परीवार pur-ee-wár, *s. m.* Dependants, family, retinue.

परीवाह pur-ee-wáh, *s. m.* A natural inundation or overflow.

परीहास pur-ee-hás, *s. m.* Mirth, sport, amusement.

परु pur-óo, *s. m.* A knot or join tin a reed.

परुष pur-óosh, *s. m.* Harsh and contumelious speech, abuse ; yellow Barleria ; a sort of tree (*Xylocarpus granatum*).

परुषवचन pur-oosh-búchun, *s. m.* Harsh language, reproach, abuse.

परुषवाच् pur-oosh-vách, *s. f.* Harsh or contumelious speech.

परुषोक्ति pur-oosh-ókti, *s. f.* Abusive or harsh language.

परुषोक्तिक pur-oosh-óktik, *s. m.* An abuser, one uttering harsh and scurrilous language.

परोस pur-óos, *s. m.* The knot or joint of a cane or reed.

परे púr-eh, *adv.* Beyond, yonder, at a distance. *Pureh ruhna*, To remain at a distance.

परेखा pur-ékha, *s. m.* Regret, concern, contrition, repentance. *s. f.* Examination, trial.

परेत pur-ét, *adj.* Dead, defunct. *s. m.* A departed soul, a spirit of the dead, a kind of goblin, a ghost, a spirit, an evil spirit, a fiend.

परेतना pur-ét-na, *v. a.* To reel (*thread or yarn*).

परेता pur-ét-a, *s. m.* A reel (*for winding yarn*).

परेवा pur-éwa, *s. m.* A pigeon.

परेह pur-éh, *s. m.* Soup.

परोक्ष pur-óksh, *adj.* Invisible, imperceptible ; absent, past. *s. m.* An ascetic, a religious hermit ; invisibility, absence, secrecy ; (in *grammar*) past time or tense.

परोपकार púr-op-kar, *s. m.* Charity, benevolence, doing good to others, the helping of
others, beneficence.

परोपकारी pur-op-káree, *adj.* Benevolent,
charitable, good to others, acting for others, beneficent, hospitable.

परोपदेश pur-op-désh, *s. m.* Giving advice,
counselling, admonishing.

परोष्णी pur-úsh-nee, *s. f.* A cockroach.

परोस pur-ós, *s. m.* Vicinity.

परोसना pur-ós-na, *v. a.* To serve up dinner, to distribute food to guests, &c.

परोसा pur-ó-sa, *s. m.* A dish of food which
is sent to a friend.

परोसी pur-ó-see, *s. m.* A neighbour.

परोसिया pur-ó-syya, *s. m.* A distributer of
victuals to the guests, one who serves up dinner, a
waiter.

परोहन pur-ó-hun, *s. m.* Carriage, vehicle,
instruments of transportation.

परोक्ष pur-óksh, *adj.* Invisible, imperceptible; absent, past. *s. m.* An ascetic, a religious
hermit; invisibility, absence, secrecy; (*in grammar*) past time or tense.

पर्कंट pur-kút, *s. m.* A heron.

पर्कंटी purk-kút-ee, *s. f.* The waved-leaf fig
tree (*Ficus infectiosa*).

पर्चा púr-cha, *s. m.* Examination, trial,
proof, experiment.

पर्चाना pur-chá-na, *v. a.* To introduce to a
person, to engage in conversation.

पर्चूनिया pur-chóo-niya, *s. m.* A meal merchant.

पर्चूनी pur-chóo-nee, *s. f.* The act of selling
flour, meal, &c.

पर्छत्ती pur-chhúttee, *s. f.* A small thatch
thrown over mud walls.

पर्छा pur-chhá, *s. m.* Self-sown paddy
(*rice*); a spindle for winding thread on.

पर्छां pur-chhán, ⎫
पर्छांई pur-chháeen, ⎬ *s. f.* Image (*from
पर्छांवा pur-chhán-wa,* ⎭ *shade or reflection*), shadow,
shade. *Purchhaeen upnee seh bhagna*, To be
frightened at one's own shadow.

पर्ज purj, *s. f.* A musical mode or *raginee*;
handle of a shield. *Purjdar, adj.* Back-hilted (*a
scimitar*).

पर्जंक pur-júnk, *s. m.* A bedstead.

पर्जुनी púr-jun-ee, *s. f.* A sort of Curcuma
(*C. zanthorrhizon*).

पर्ण purn, *s. m.* A leaf; the *Pan* or betel
leaf; the *Pulas* tree (*Butea frondosa*).

पर्णनर purn-núr, *s. m.* A man of leaves, an
effigy stuffed with leaves, made to represent a per-

son deceased, whose body cannot be found, and
for whom obsequial rites are performed with this
representative.

पर्णमाचल purn-má-chal, *s. m.* The *Kum-
ranga*, an acid fruit (*Averrhoa carambola*).

पर्णलता purn-lút-a, *s. f.* The betel plant.

पर्णवल्ली purn-wúllee, *s. f.* A tree (*Butea
frondosa*).

पर्णशाला purn-shá-la, *s. f.* A hut of leaves
and grass, a hermitage.

पर्णासि purn-á-si, *s. m.* A sort of Basil
(*Ocymum sanctum*), with small leaves.

पर्णी púr-nee, *s. m.* A tree (*Butea frondosa*). *s. f.* An aquatic plant (*Pistia stratiotes*);
the leaf of the asafœtida (?).

पर्णोटज purn-ó-tuj, *s. m.* A hut of leaves,
the residence of holy anchorets, a hermitage.

पर्दादा pur-dá-da, *s. m.* A great grandfather by the father's side.

पर्दादी pur-dá-dee, *s. f.* A great grandmother by the father's side.

पर्दून purd-dún, *s. m.* Wind downwards,
letting wind.

पर्प purp, *s. m.* A wheel chair, or one on
which a cripple can move about.

पर्पट pur-pút, *s. m.* A medicinal plant
with bitter leaves (*apparently the Oldenlandia
biflora, though the Hindee name Papur is also
applied to the Gardenia latifolia*).

पर्पटद्रूम purput-dróom, *s. m.* Bdellium.

पर्पटी púr-put-ee, *s. f.* A thin crisp cake
made of any pulse.

पर्यंक purj-yúnk, *s. m.* A bedstead.

पर्यटन purj-yút-un, *s. m.* Wandering about,
roaming.

पर्यंत pur-jyúnt, *s. m.* Limit, term, boundary, extent.

पर्यवसान pur-jyu-wusán, *s. m.* End, conclusion.

पर्याय pur-jyáyuh, *s. m.* Order, arrangement, regular and methodical disposal or succession; manner, kind; opportunity, occasion; the
text of a vocabulary, or the order of the synonyms
for any term.

पर्ल púr-la, *adj.* Of the other side.

पर्व purv, *s. m.* A festival, a holiday, an
anniversary festival, feast.

पर्वकारी purv-káree, *s. m.* A *Brahmun* who
performs ceremonies for hire out of season.

पर्वगामी purv-gámee, *s. m.* A man who
associates with his wife on festival or holy days.

पर्वनिका purv-ník-a, *s. f.* Specks with
pain on the edge of the cornea of the eye.

पर्वत púr-vut, *s. m.* A mountain, a hill; a
kind of fish (*Silurus pabda*).

पर्व्वतकाक purvut-kák, *s. m.* A raven.

पर्व्वतवासी pur-vut-rásee, *adj.* Living, &c. in the mountains.

पर्व्वतात्रय pur-vut-áshruy, *adj.* Mountaineer, living, &c. in the mountains.

पर्व्वतिया pur-vut-íya, *s. m.* A kind of pumpkin.

पर्व्वतीय pur-vut-éeyuh, *adj.* Mountainous, mountaineer, &c.

पर्व्वसन्धि purv-sún-dhi, *s. m.* The full and change of the moon, the junction of the 15th and 1st of a lunar fortnight, or the precise moment of the full and change of the moon.

पर्व्वाल pur-wál, *s. m.* A disease in the eyelids in which the eyelashes fall off, a stye or stythe.

पर्व्वित pur-vít, *s. m.* A sort of fish (*Silurus pabda*).

पर्शु púr-shoo, *s. m.* An axe, a hatchet.

पर्शुराम pur-shoo-rám, *s. m.* The first of three *Rams*, being the sixth mythological *Uvutar* of *Vishnoo*, as the son of the *Mooni Jumudugni*.

पल pul, *s. m.* A moment, the 60th part of a *ghuree* or *dund* (2½ *puls* being equal to one *minute*). *Pul-ot*, For an instant. *Pul marteh, adv.* Immediately, instantly, in the twinkling of an eye. *Pul marna,* To make a motion of the eyelid.

पलउरी pul-uée, *s. f.* A young branch or spray of a tree.

पलक púl-uk, *s. m. f.* The eyelid; a moment.

पलंग púl-ung, *s. m.* A bed (*without curtains*), a bedstead. *Pulung-posh, s. m.* A coverlet, a counterpane.

पलंगरी pul-ung-rée, *s. f.* A small bedstead.

पलटन púl-tun, *s. f.* A battalion.

पलटना púl-ut-na, *v. n.* To return, to turn back, to retreat; to overturn, to rebound; to change.

पलट लेना púl-ut léna, ⎫ *v. a.* To take back,
पलटा लेना púlta léna, ⎭ to take in return, to take revenge.

पलटा púl-ta, *s. m.* Turn, stead, exchange, recompense, revenge, retaliation.

पलटा खाना púlta khána, *v. a.* To turn over head and heels; to overturn, to be tilted; to rebound.

पलटना pul-tá-na, *v. a.* To turn, cause to turn, return, convert, repel.

पलटाव pul-táo, *s. m.* Contradiction, reaction, rebound.

पलथा मारना pulthá márna, *v. n.* To sit down on the ground resting on the buttocks.

पलरा púl-ra, *s. m.* A scale, *i. e.* one side of a pair of scales.

पलथा मारना pulthá márna, *v. n.* To sit down on the ground resting on the buttocks.

पलथी pul-thée, *s. f.* A mode of sitting on the ground resting on the buttocks.

पलना púl-na, *v. n.* To be reared, nourished or fattened, to thrive.

पलवल pul-wúl, *s. m.* A vegetable (*Trichosanthes dioica*). *Pulwul-lutee,* The plant of *pulwul.*

पलवाना pul-wá-na, *v. a.* To cause to nourish, to bring up, &c.

पलवार pul-wár, *s. m.* A kind of boat.

पलवारी pul-wá-ree, *s. m.* Boatmen (*belonging to a pulwar.*)

पला púl-a, *s. m.* A spoon, ladle for taking out oil, &c.

पलाग्नि pul-ág-ni, *s. m.* Bile, the bilious humour.

पलांग pul-áng, *s. m.* The Gangetic porpoise.

पलांडु pul-án-doo, *s. m.* An onion.

पलाद pul-ád, *s. m. f.* A *Rakshus*, male or female.

पलाना pul-á-na, *v. a.* To flee, run away, escape.

पलानी pul-á-nee, *s. f.* ⎫
पलाव pul-áo, *s. m.* ⎭ Thatching.

पलाना pul-án-na, *v. a.* To saddle a horse or bullock.

पलायन pul-á-yun, *s. m.* Flight, retreat.

पलायनपरायण puláyun-puráyun, *adj.* Fugitive.

पलायमान pul-ayumán, *adj.* Running away.

पलाश pul-ásh, *s. m.* A tree bearing red blossoms (*Butea frondosa*); a sort of Curcuma (*C. reclinata*); ancient *Behar* or *Mugudha*.

पलाशक pul-á-shuk, *s. m.* Curcuma reclinata; the *Pulas* tree.

पलाश पपरा pulásh-púp-ra, *s. m.* The seeds of the Butea frondosa used in medicine.

पलाशाख pulash-ákhyuh, *s. m.* Asafœtida.

पलाशी pul-ásh-ee, *s. f.* Lac. *s. m.* A goblin; a sort of Mimusops (*M. kauki*).

पली púl-ee, *s. f.* A ladle used to take out oil with.

पलीत pul-éet, *s. m.* A ghost.

पलीता pul-ée-ta, *s. m.* A match (*of a gun*); a candle. *Puleeta chat jana,* To flash in the pan.

पलेथन pul-éthun, *s. m.* Dry flour laid under and over bread when it is rolled. *Pulethun pukana,* To contrive the ruin of any one. *Pulethun nikalna,* To beat severely.

पल्वेव pul-éo, *s. m.* Soup; pounded rice or flour put into soup to thicken it.

पल्वौठा pul-óu-tha, *adj.* First-born.

पल्लव pul-lúv, *s. m.* A sprout, a shoot, the extremity of a branch bearing new leaves, a twig.

पल्लवक pul-luv-úk, *s. m.* A kind of fish (*Cyprinus denticulatus*).

पल्ला púl-la, *s. m.* Space, distance; assistance; a border of cloths; a sheet (*generally applied to chints or shawl*); a bag; one shutter of a door, &c.; border, margin.

पल्ली púl-lee, *s. f.* A small village; a house lizard.

पल्लो pul-lóo, *s. m.* The hem or border of a garment. *Pulloodar*, A garment with a silver or gold border.

पल्हिन्दा pul hín-da, *s. m.* A shelf upon which water-pots are placed, a place where water is kept.

पवन púv-un, *s. f.* Air, wind, physical or personified as a deity. *s. m.* Regent of the winds, and of the north-west quarter. *Puvun ka poot*, The son of *Puvun*, i. e. The ape *Hunooman*.

पवनव्याधि puv-un-byádhi, *s. m.* Wind, as affected morbidly, or rheumatism, &c.

पवनाल puv-un-ál, *s. m.* A kind of grain (*Andropogon saccharatus*).

पवनाहुत puv-un-áhut, *adj.* Rheumatic.

पवाई puv-áee, *s. f.* A chain fastened to horses' legs to prevent their being stolen; chains with which the legs of a criminal are fastened, fetters; the leg of a boot or stocking.

पवित puv-ít, *adj.* Purified, cleansed.

पवित्र puv-ítr, *adj.* Pure, clean, purified physically or morally, holy, undefiled, nice. *s. m.* The brahminical cord.

पवित्रता puv-itr-tá, *s. f.* Purity, holiness.

पवित्रा puv-it-rá, *s. f.* Holy Basil (*Ocymum sanctum*); a river, a little to the north-west of *Hurdwar*, the *Pubur*; the twelfth of the light fortnight of *Shrawun*, a festival in honor of *Vishnoo*. *s. m.* The brahminical thread; a string of silken beads; a knotted piece of *Koosha* grass, used in religious ceremonies of the *Hindoos*.

पवित्री puv-ít-ree, *s. f.* A ring of *Koosha* grass (*Poa cynosuroides*), or of gold, silver, or copper, worn on the ring-finger and fore-finger by *Hindoos* during religious worship.

पशु púsh-oo, *s. m.* An animal in general, a beast.

पशुक púsh-oo-ka, *s. f.* Any small animal.

पशुक्रिया púsh-oo-kríya, *s. f.* Copulation, coition.

पशुगायत्री púsh-oo-gáyutree, *s. f.* A parody of the holy verse of the *Veds*, whispered into the ear of an animal about to be sacrificed.

पशुता push-oo-tá, *s. f.* The condition or nature of an animal, beastiality, brutality.

पशुत्व push-oo-twúh, *s. m.* Nature of an animal.

पशुधर्म púsh-oo-dhurm, *s. m.* Action or property of animals; promiscuous cohabitation; the marrying of widows.

पशुपुल्वुल púsh-oo-púlvul, *s. m.* A fragrant grass (*Cyperus rotundus*).

पशुपाल push-oo-pál, *s. m.* A herdsman.

पशुपालन push-oo-pálun, *s. m.* Tending or rearing cattle.

पशुरज्जु push-oo-rújjoo, *s. m.* A string or tie for fastening cattle.

पशुराज push-oo-ráj, *s. m.* A lion.

पशुरोमन् púsh-oo-rómun, *s. m.* The hair of an animal.

पशुहरीतकी púshoo-huréetkee, *s. f.* The hog-plum.

पश्चात push-chát, *adv.* After, afterwards, behind, westward.

पश्चाताप push-chat-táp, *s. m.* Repentance.

पश्चिम púsh-chim, *adj.* West, western; behind, after: *Hindoos* in their prayers, usually facing the east, and consequently having the west behind them.

पषान push-án, पखान pukhán, } *s. m.* A stone, a rock.

पसर pús-ur, *s. f.* Grazing cattle at night.

पसरना pús-ur-na, *v. n.* To be spread, stretched out, distended, expanded.

पसली pús-lee, *s. f.* A rib, the præcordia. *Puslee phuruknee*, A thrilling over the ribs, is applied to a perception of the condition of an absent person.

पसही pus-hée, *s. f.* A kind of wild rice growing in shallow ponds.

पसा pús-a, *s. m.* Two handfuls, as much as can be held in both hands open.

पसाई pus-áee, *s. f.* A kind of rice.

पसाना pus-á-na, *v. a.* To skim, to pour off superfluous water (*from boiled rice*).

पसारना pus-ár-na, *v. a.* To spread, distend, stretch out, reach, extend, expand, open, display.

पसारा pus-á-ra, *s. m.* Expansion, the act of spreading out. *Pusara kurna*, To procrastinate and find obstacles to an easy matter.

पसारी pus-á-ree, *s. m.* One who sells spices, a spicer.

पसीजना pus-éej-na, *v. n.* To perspire, to sweat, to melt; to compassionate.

पसीना pus-ée-na,
पसेव pus-éo, } s. m. Perspiration, sweat.
पसेवहा pus-év-ha,

पसूजना pus-óoj-na, v. a. To stitch.

पसताना pus-tá-na, v. n. To regret.

पह puh, s. f. Dawn. *Puh phutna*, v. n. To dawn, to grow luminous.

पहचान puh-chán, s. f. Acquaintance, knowledge, recognisance.

पहचानना puh-chán-na, v. a. To know, to recognise, to discriminate, to distinguish.

पहनावा puh-ná-wa, s. m. Clothing, dress.

पहिनना pu-hín-na, v. a. To put on, to wear, to dress. s. m. Dress, clothing.

पहर púhur, s. m. A division of time consisting of eight *ghurees*, a watch or three hours.

पहरना púhur-na, v. a. To put on clothes, to dress, to clothe one's self, to wear.

पहरा púh-ra, s. m. A watch, a sentinel; tour of watch; a corporal and six. *Puhra dena*, To watch. *Puhreh men dalna*, To give in charge to a watch or the guard. *Puhreh men purna*, To be given in charge to a watch or the guard.

पहराना puh-rá-na, v. a. To cause to dress, to clothe, invest, to dress.

पहरावनी puh-ráo-nee, s. f. A woman who dresses the guests at a wedding, a tirewoman; vestments bestowed on guests at a wedding, dress, clothing.

पहरिया púh-ri-ya,
पहरूआ púh-roo-a, } s. m. A watchman, a sentinel, guard.
पहरू puh-róo,

पहुल púhul, s. m. A flock of cotton; beginning; aggression; the side of a rectangular figure.

पहला púh-la, } adj. First. adv. Before,
पहिला pú-hi-la, } rather, soon.

पहले púh-leh, adv. At first, soon, rather. *Puhileh par*, On the other side.

पहाड़ puhár, s. m. A mountain. *Puhar-see-raten*, Long nights (especially of sorrow).

पहाड़ा puhár-a, s. m. The multiplication table (in arithmetic).

पहाड़िया puhár-iya, adj. Belonging to, or of a mountain. s. m. A mountaineer. [tain.

पहाड़ी puhár-ee, s. f. A hill, a small moun-

पहिनना puhín-na, v. a. To put on, to wear, to dress. s. m. Dress, clothing.

पहिया puhíya, s. m. A wheel.

पहिरावन puhi-rá-wun, s. f. Dress, clothing, &c.

पहिरावनी puhi-ráo-nee, s. f. A woman who dresses the guests at a wedding, a tirewoman; vestments bestowed on guests at a wedding, dress, clothing.

पहिरना puhír-na, v. a. To put on clothes, to dress, to clothe one's self, to wear.

पहिला púhila, adj. First. adv. Before, rather, soon.

पहिले púhileh, adv. At first, in the first place, first, sooner, before, chiefly, rather. *Puhileh par*, On the other side.

पहिलौटा puhiloú-ta, adj. First-born.

पहुंच puhóonch, s. f. Arrival, reach; sagacity, penetration; access, admittance; a receipt.

पहुंचना puhóonch-na, v. n. To arrive, reach, extend, amount, befall, belong.

पहुंचा puhóonch-a, s. m. The wrist.

पहुंचाना puhoon-chána, v. a. To cause to arrive, convey, transmit, bring, conduct, to cause, to occasion.

पहुंची puhóonch-ee, s. f. An ornament worn on the wrist, a kind of bracelet.

पहुरना puhóor-na, v. n. To lie down, to repose, to lie, to rest.

पहुनई puhoo-núee, s. f. Hospitality, entertainment.

पहुप púhoop, s. m. A flower.

पहेली puhélee, s. f. A riddle, an enigma.

पह्नव puh-núv, s. m. The name of one of the degraded *Kshuttree* races sentenced by *Sugur* to wear beards, perhaps a Parthian.

पह्निका puh-ník-a, s. f. A plant (*Pistia stratiwites*).

पक्ष puksh, s. m. The half of a lunar month or fortnight, comprising fifteen days; a partisan; a friend; a side, a flank.

पक्षता puksh-tá, s. f. The taking up a side or argument.

पक्षधर puksh-dhúr, s. m. A partisan.

पक्षपात puksh-pát, s. m. Adopting a side or an argument whether right or wrong, partisanship; a partisan, an adherent, who or what sides with.

पक्षपातिता puksh-pa-ti-tá, s. f. Adherence, friendship, fellowship.

पक्षपाती puksh-pá-tee, s. m. A partisan, a friend, an adherent.

पक्षाघात puksh-a-ghát, s. m. Palsy, hemiplegia.

पक्षिणी púksh-in-ee, } s. f. A bird.
पक्षी púksh-ee,

पक्षिराज pukshi-ráj, s. m. King of the birds, usually applied to *Guroor*.

पक्षिशाला púkshi-shála, s. f. A nest, an aviary.

पाई paée, s. f. A coin, the fourth part of an anna.

पांक pank, *s. m.* A bog, mire, mud, slough, quagmire.

पांक्त pánkt, *adj.* Linear, in or by line, or row.

पांगा pán-ga, *s. m.* Culinary salt obtained from sea sand (*as by the process in use on the sea coast of Bengal*).

पांच panch, *adj.* Five. *Panch-sat, s. f.* Perplexity.

पांचवां panch-wán, *adj.* Fifth.

पांजर pán-jur, *s. m.* The ribs, the side; a side or quarter.

पांडे pán-deh, } *s. m.* A title of *Brahmuns;*
पांडे pán-reh, } a school-master.

पांत pant, } *s. f.* A row; a line (*of*
पांती pántee, } *writing*); a note; a rank of soldiers.

पांतर pán-tur, *s. m.* A desert field.

पांयती pán-yutee, *s. f.* The foot of a bed.

पांव páon, *s. m.* Leg, foot. *Paon oothana,* or, — *chulana,* To go quickly. *Paon oorana,* To interfere unprofitably in any one's affairs. *Paon ooturna,* To be dislocated (*the foot*). *Paon ka ungootha, s. m.* The great toe. *Paon kampna,* or, — *thurthurana,* To fear to attempt any thing. *Paon kaim kurna,* To occupy a fixed habitation; to adopt a new resolution. *Paon kisee ka ookharna,* To move any person from his place, intention or resolution. *Paon kisee ka guleh men dalna,* To convict one by his own arguments. *Paon kee oonglee, s. f.* A toe. *Paon chul jana,* To totter, to become unstable. *Paon jumana,* To stand firmly. *Paon zumeen-pur nuh thuhurna* is used to express excessive joy. *Paon dalna,* To prepare for and commence an undertaking. *Paon digna,* To slip. *Paon tuleh mulna,* To give one pain, to annoy. *Paon torna,* To desist from visiting any person; to visit one very often; to be tired. *Dubeh paon ana,* To come gently and unperceived as a spy. *Paon dho dho peena (lit. to drink the water with which one's feet are washed*), denotes perfect confidence. *Paon nikalna,* To exceed one's proper limits; to withdraw from an undertaking; to be a ringleader in a criminal action. *Paon pukurna,* To beseech submissively; to prevent one from going. *Paon purna,* To entreat submissively. *Paon-pur paon rukhna,* To imitate or adopt the conduct of another, to walk in the steps of another; to sit at ease, to sit cross-legged. *Paon paon, adj.* Afoot. *Paon peetna,* To stamp with impatience. *Paon poojna,* To honour another; to avoid another. *Paon phook phook rukhna,* To do any thing carefully. *Paon phylakur sona (lit. to sleep with the legs extended*), is applied to signify perfect content and security. *Paon phylana,* To insist, to be obstinate. *Paon burhana,* To take the lead among one's equals; to desist from one's former courses. *Paon bhur jana,* Numbness of the feet, sleeping of

the feet. *Paon rugurna,* To go about foolishly and unprofitably; to be in the agonies of death. *Paon lugna,* To make obeisance. *Paon sabit rukhna,* To persevere firmly in a resolution. *Paon seh paon bandhna,* To watch one close. *Paon seh paon bhirana,* To be near. · *Paon sona,* To be numbed, to sleep (*the foot*).

पांवड़ा páonra, *s. m.* A cloth or carpet spread to walk on.

पांवपांव páon-páon, *adj.* Afoot, on foot.

पांवरोटी paon-rótee, *s. f.* A loaf of bread.

पांशव pan-shúv, *s. m.* Rock or fossil salt.

पांशु pán-shoo, *s m.* Manure.

पांशुका pán-shoo-ka, *s. f.* A fragrant plant (*Pandanus odoratissimus*).

पांशुकासीस pán-shoo-kasées, *s. m.* Sulphuret of iron.

पांशुज pan-shóoj, *s. m.* Salt extracted from soil, rock or fossil salt.

पांशुपुत्र pan-shoo-pútr, *s. m.* A potherb (*Chenopodium album*).

पांशूल pán-shool, *s. m.* A kind of tree (*Cæsalpinia bonducella*).

पांस pans, *s. m.* Manure, a dunghill. *Pans ho-jana,* To rot; to become mellow (*land*).

पांसना páns-na, *v. a.* To manure, to dung.

पांसा páns-a, *s. m.* A die.

पांसू páns-oo, *s. f.* The ribs.

पाईं pa-éen, *s. f.* Pins used by weavers to wind off the warp from.

पाईंती páeen-tee, *s. f.* The foot of a bed, the side towards the feet.

पाएह páeh, *s. m.* A peasant residing in one village and cultivating land belonging to another village.

पाक pak, *s. m.* An electuary medicine, confection.

पाकुर pákur, } *s. m.* The waved leaf
पाकरिया pakuríya, } Indian fig-tree (*Ficus venosa*).

पाकना pák-na, *v. a.* To boil in sirup.

पाकफुल pák-phul, *s. m.* The Caronda (*Carissa carondas*).

पाकरंजन pak-rún-jun, *s. m.* The leaf of the Laurus cassia.

पाकूल pakúl, *adj.* Producing maturity; suppurative, producing suppuration in a boil. *s. m.* A sort of Costus (*C. speciosus*).

पाकलि pá-kuli, *s. m.* A sort of plant (*Bauhinia candida*).

पाकली pá-kul-ee, *s. f.* A sort of cucumber (*Cucumis utilatissimus*).

पाकशाला pak-shála, } *s. m.* A kitchen.
पाकस्थान pak-sthán, }

पाकसंकृषी pak-súnr-see, *s. f.* A table-vice, a bench-vice.

पाक्य pák-yuh, *s. m. Bitlubun*, a medicinal salt, impregnated with iron; nitre, saltpetre.

पाक्ष्य pák-shyu, *adj.* Relating to a side or party.

पाखंड pa-khúnd, } *s. m.* Wickedness, de-
पाषंड pa-shúnd, } ceit, hypocrisy, heresy; a heretic, a heterodox *Hindoo*, adopting the exterior marks of the classes, but not respecting the ordinances of the *Veds*.

पाखंडी pa-khúndee, } *adj.* Hypocritical,
पाषंडी pa-shúndee, } deceitful, heretical.

पाखर pá-khur, *s. f.* Iron armour for the defence of a horse or of an elephant.

पाखा pá-kha, *s. m.* A shed, any small building leaning against the wall of a yard or area.

पाग pag, *s. f.* A turband; sirup.

पागल pá-gul, *s. m.* A fool, idiot, madman.

पागा pága, *s. m.* A troop of horse (*among Marhattas*), a stud.

पागुर pá-goor, *s. m.* Act of chewing the cud, rumination.

पागुराना pa-goo-rá-na, *v. a.* To chew the cud, to ruminate.

पाचक pá-chuk, *adj.* Digestive, tonic, what effects digestion. *s. m.* The bile which assists in digestion; a digestive, a stomachic, a solvent; a cook.

पाचन pá-chun, *adj.* Digestive; suppurative. *s. m.* A medicinal preparation, an infusion, a decoction, &c. of various drugs, chiefly carminatives or gentle stimuli given to bring the vitiated humours in fever, &c. to maturity, a sort of diet drink; a digestive.

पाचनक pa-chun-úk, *s. m.* Borax.

पाचनी pá-chun-ee, *s. f.* A sort of myrobalan (*Terminalia chebula*).

पाचुल pa-chúl, *adj.* Whatever causes digestion, &c.

पाछ pachh, *s. m.* The act of inoculating, inoculation.

पाछना páchh-na, *v. a.* To inoculate.

पाछें pách-hen, } *adv.* Behind, after, after-
पाछे pách-heh, } wards, in the absence.

पांचाल pán-chal, *adj.* Belonging to, dwelling in, ruling over, &c., the country of *Punchal. s. m.* The sovereign of *Punchal*; the company or association of five trades, the carpenter, weaver, barber, washerman, and shoemaker.

पाजीपना pájee-pún-a, *s. m.* Meanness.

पाट pat, *s. m.* Breadth (*of cloth or of a river*), expanse, extension; tow; silk; a mill-stone; a throne, seat; a board, shutter, plank, slab, plank on which washermen beat clothes.

पाटकृम pát-krim, *s. m.* A silk-worm.

पाटन pá-tun, *s. f.* A roof. *s. m.* Name of a city.

पाटना pát-na, *v. a.* To roof, to cover, to shut; to fill, fill up, overstock, heap, pile, accumulate; to water, irrigate; to pay.

पाटम्बर pat-úm-bur, *s. m.* Silk cloth, a silk garment.

पाटरानी pat-rá-nee, *s. f.* The queen or principal wife of a *Rajah*.

पाटल pa-túl, *adj.* Of a pink or pale red colour. *s. m.* Pale red, rose colour.

पाटला pá-tul-a, *s. f.* The trumpet-flower (*Bignonia suare-olens*).

पाटलिपुत्र pátuli-póotr, *s. m.* The name of a city, supposed to be the ancient *Palibothra*, and the modern *Patna*.

पाटलोपल pátul-ópul, *s. m.* A ruby.

पाटव pa-túv, *adj.* Clever, sharp, dexterous. *s. m.* Cleverness, talent; eloquence.

पाटविक pat-wík, *adj.* Cunning, crafty, fraudulent; clever, dexterous.

पाटिका pát-hik-a, *s. f.* A small shrub (*Abrus precatorius*).

पाटा pá-ta, *s. m.* A plank on which washermen beat clothes.

पाटिम pa-tín, } *s. m.* A sort of fish de-
पाटी pa-tée, } scribed as having many teeth.

पाटी pá-tee, *s. f.* The side pieces of a bedstead; a kind of mat; a kind of board on which children learn to write; divisions of the hair which is combed towards the two sides and parted by a line in the middle; a kind of sweetmeat.

पाटीर pa-téer, *s. m.* A pungent root, a sort of radish; sandal.

पाटूनी pa-tóo-nee, *s. m.* A ferryman.

पाठ path, *s. m.* Studying the *Veds* or sacred writings, considered as one of the five great sacraments of the *Hindoos*; reading, perusal or study in general; a lecture, lesson.

पाठक pa-thúk, *s. m.* A lecturer, a public reader of the *Pooruns* or other sacred works, or a *Pundit* who declares what is the law or custom according to the sacred writings; a spiritual preceptor; a reader, a student; he who gives lessons, a teacher, a professor; a title of *Brahmuns*.

पाठन pa-thún, *s. m.* Lecturing, teaching.

पाठभू path-bhóo, *s. f.* A place where the *Veds* are read or studied.

पाठमञ्जरी path-múnch-ree, *s. f.* A small bird (*Gracula religiosa*).

पाठशाला path-shála, *s. f.* A college, a school.

पाठशालिनी path-shá-lin-ee, *s. f.* A small bird (*Gracula religiosa*).

पाठा pat-há, *s. m.* A young animal full grown (*generally, a goat or elephant*), a youth or young wrestler.

पाठान pat-hán, *s. m.* Bdellium.

पठित pat-hít, *adj.* Instructed, taught, lectured.

पाठी pat-hée, *s. m.* He that gives lessons, a teacher, a professor; a *Brahmun*, especially one who has finished his sacred studies; a plant (*Plumbago zelanica*). *s. f.* A young goat; a kind of fish.

पाठीन pat-héen, *s. m.* A sort of fish (*Silurus boalis*); a public reader or lecturer on the *Poorans*, &c.

पाठ्य path-yúh, *adj.* To be read or studied.

पाड par, *s. f.* A scaffold.

पाड़ना pár-na, *v. a.* To let fall, to cause to fall, to knock or throw down; to finish, to kill; to collect lamp-black.

पाड़ा pá-ra, *s. m.* A quarter of a town, a ward.

पाड़ा pár-ha, *s. m.* A hog-deer (*Cervus porcinus*).

पाड़ी pár-hee, *s. f.* Crossing a river (*when travelling on it; a young buffalo, a buffalo calf*).

पाणि pá-ni, *s. m.* The hand.

पाणिग्रहीती páni-grihée-tee, *s. f.* A bride, one wedded according to the ritual.

पाणिग्रहण páni-grúhun, *s. m.* Marriage; laying hold of the hand; the junction of the hands of the bride and bridegroom, forming part of this ceremony.

पाणिग्रहणिक páni-gruhun-ík, *adj.* Matrimonial.

पाणिनि pánini, *s. m.* A *Mooni* and inspired grammarian.

पाणिनीय pani-néeyuh, *adj.* Connected with or derived from *Panini* the grammarian (as a scholar, a rule, &c.)

पाणिभज pani-bhóoj, *s. m.* The glomerous fig-tree (*Ficus glomerata*).

पाण्डुर pán-dur, *adj.* Pale or yellowish white. *s. m.* Pale or yellowish white (*the colour*); many-flowered jasmine.

पाण्डुरपुष्पिका pándur-póoshp-ik-a, *s. f.* A plant commonly called *Seetula* (*perhaps Phrynium dichotomum*).

पाण्डव pan-dúv, *s. m.* A descendant of *Pandoo*; especially applied to *Yoodhishthir* and his four brothers.

पाण्डिती pan-dit-ée, *s. f.* Scholarship, learning.

पाण्डु pán-doo, *adj.* Pale or yellowish white. *s. m.* Pale or yellowish white (*the colour*); the name of a sovereign of ancient *Delhi*, and nominal father of *Yoodhisthir* and the other four *Panduv* princes. *s. f.* A plant, commonly called *Mushani* (*Glycine debilis*).

पाण्डुकुम्बुल pándoo-kúmbul, *s. m.* A kind of stone (*Limestone or marble?*)

पाण्डुनाग pan-doo-nág, *s. m.* A plant (*Rottleria tinctoria*).

पाण्डुपुत्र pan-doo-póotr, *s. m.* Either of the *Panduv* princes.

पाण्डुभूम pan-doo-bhóom, *s. m.* A country with a light coloured soil.

पाण्डुमृत्तिका pán-doo-mríttika, *s. f.* The opal; a pale soil.

पाण्डुर pán-door, *adj.* Of a yellowish white colour. *s. m.* A pale or yellowish white; the white leprosy, vitiligo.

पाण्डुरद्रुम pan-door-dróom, *s. m.* A plant (*Echites antidysenterica*).

पाण्डुलोमा pan-doo-lóma, *s. f.* A plant (*Glycine debilis*).

पाण्डुवर्ण pan-doo-vúrn, *adj.* White. *s. m.* Whiteness.

पाण्डुशर्करा pándoo-shúrkkur-a, *s. f.* Light coloured gravel (*disease*).

पात pat, *s. m.* Falling; sin, wickedness; a leaf; an ornament worn in the upper part of the ear; a draught or check on a banker. *Paton-a-lugna*, applied to trees, indicates the fall of their leaves in autumn: metaphorically, the phrase signifies that one's power or ability is exhausted; and, this expression is often applied to patience exhausted by the scorn of a beloved person; or to a destitute condition from adverse fortune.

पातक pá-tuk, *s. m.* Sin, crime.

पातकवा pa-tuk-wá, *s. m.* A messenger.

पातकी pa-tuk-ée, *adj.* Wicked, sinful, a sinner.

पातञ्जल pa-tun-júl, *s. m.* The *Yog* system of philosophy.

पातुर pá-tur, *s. f.* A prostitute, a dancing girl. *adj.* Weak, lean.

पाता pá-ta, *s. m.* A leaf. *adj.* Preserved, protected.

पाताल pa-tál, *s. m.* The regions under the earth, and the abode of the *Nagas* or serpents; a sort of apparatus for calcining and subliming metals, formed of two earthen pots, the upper one inverted over the lower, and the two joined together by their necks with cement, and placed in a hole containing fire.

पाति páti, *s. m.* A master, a lord, a husband.

पातिक pá-tik, *s. m.* The Gangetic porpoise.

पातित pá-tit, *adj.* Lowered, depressed, humbled.

पातिली pá-til-ee, *s. f.* A small earthen vessel or pot, especially used by religious mendicants.

पाती pá-tee, *s. f.* A letter, a note, an epistle ; a leaf.

पातुक pa-tóok, *s. m.* An aquatic animal of a large size ; figuratively the water-elephant.

पात्र pa-trí, *adj.* Who or what protects or nourishes.

पात्रता pa-tri-tá, *s. m.* A plant (*Ocymum pilosum*).

पात्र pat-trúh, *s. m.* A preservative from sin, a preserver, a saviour.

पात्रता pat-trutá, *s. f.* The quality or power of a preservative from sin.

पात्र patr, *s. m.* A vessel in general, a plate, a cup, a jar, &c. ; a leaf ; a receptacle of any kind, what holds or supports. *adj.* Capable, worthy, able, eligible, fit.

पात्रता patr-tá, *s. f.* Capacity, fitness.

पाथना páth-na, *v. a.* To make up cow dung into cakes for fuel.

पाथर pá-thur, *s. m.* A stone.

पाथेय pa-théyuh, *s. m.* Provender, or provisions, &c. for a journey.

पाद pad, *s. m.* The foot ; a foot, a quarter ; the foot or line of a stanza ; the line of a hymn or stanza of the *Rig Ved* ; wind downwards.

पादकटक pad-kút-uk, *s. m.* An ornament for the feet or toes.

पादमण्डिर pad-gún-dir, *s. m.* Morbid enlargement of the legs and feet.

पादग्रहण pad-grúhun, *s. m.* Respectful obeisance, touching the feet of a *Brahmun* or superior.

पादघाबरा pad-gháb-ra, *adj.* Frightened out of one's wits.

पादचत्वर pad-chutwúr, *s. m.* The religious fig-tree (*Ficus religiosa*).

पादचापल्य pad-chapúl-yuh, *s. m.* Beating or shuffling with the feet.

पादचार pad-chár, *adv.* On foot.

पादचारी pad-chá-ree, *s. m.* A footman, a foot soldier.

पादज pa-dúj, *s. m.* A *Soodr*, or man of the fourth and servile class.

पादतल pad-túl, *s. m.* The sole or the lower part of the foot. *adv.* As low as or under the feet.

पाददारी pad-dáree, *s. f.* A chap in the feet, a chilblain.

पादन pád-na, *v. n.* To let wind.

पादुप pa-dúp, *s. m.* A footstool, a cushion, &c. for the feet.

पादुपरूढा pa-dup-róo-ha, *s. f.* A creeping or a parasite plant.

पादपा pad-pá, *s. f.* A shoe, a slipper.

पादप्रक्षालन pad-pruksh-álun, *s. m.* Washing the feet.

पादप्रणाम pad-prun-ám, *s. m.* Bowing to the feet, prostration.

पादप्रहार pad-pruhár, *s. m.* A kick.

पादमूल pad-mól, *s. m.* The heel.

पादरोहण pad-ró-hun, *s. m.* The Indian fig-tree.

पादवल्मीक pad-vulm-éek, *s. m.* Morbid enlargement of the legs and feet.

पादविक pad-vík, *s. m.* A traveller, a wayfarer.

पादशब्द pad-shúbd, *s. m.* The sound or noise of feet.

पादशाखा pad-shá-kha, *s. f.* A toe.

पादशोथ pad-shóth, *s. m.* Swelling of the feet, gout.

पादस्फोट pad-sphót, *s. m.* Kibe, chilblain, a sore or ulcer in the foot.

पादहत pad-hút, *adj.* Trodden on, kicked, touched with the feet.

पादहर्ष pad-húrsh, *s. m.* Tingling of the feet after pressure upon the crural nerves.

पादहारक pad-há-ruk, *s. m.* One who takes or steals any thing with his feet.

पादाङ्गुली pad-án-goo-lee, *s. f.* A toe.

पादाङ्गुष्ठ pad-an-góoshth, *s. m.* The great toe.

पादाङ्गुष्ठिका pád-an-góosh-thik-a, *s. f.* An ornament or ring worn on the great toe.

पादानोन pa-da-nón, *s. m.* Black salt, prepared by melting common salt with a small proportion of myrobalans : it contains sulphur.

पादार्द्ध pad-árddh, *s. m.* Half a line of a stanza.

पादासन pad-á-sun, *s. m.* A foot-stool.

पादाहत pad-á-hut, *adj.* Kicked, trodden, touched by the foot.

पादी pá-dee, *adj.* Footed, having feet. *s. m.* A footed aquatic animal, an amphibious animal.

पादुक pa-dóok, *adj.* Who or what goes on foot or with feet.

पादुका pá-doo-ka, *s. f.* A shoe, a slipper.

पाडू pá-doo, *s. f.* A shoe.

पादोदक pad-ó-duk, *s. m.* Water for the feet, especially that in which the feet of a *Brahmun* have been washed.

पादयूह pad-yúh, *s. m.* Water, &c. for cleaning the feet.

पादयूहपात्र pad-yuh-pátr, *s. m.* A metal vessel for washing the feet.

पाधा pá-dha, *s. m.* A school-master.

पान pan, *s. m.* Drinking in general; a hand; a leaf; betel leaf (*leaves of Piper betel*).

पानदान pan-dán, *s. m.* A box for holding betel or its apparatus.

पानपात्र pan-pátr, *s. m.* A glass, a drinking vessel.

पाना pána, *v. a.* To get, acquire, find, enjoy, suffer, overtake, reach, accept, obtain, attain. *s. m.* Finding, getting, &c.; a plant growing in stagnant water.

पानी pá-nee, *s. m.* Water; sperm; lustre, character, honour. *Panee kurna, v. a.* To abash; to facilitate. *Panee ka boolboola (a bubble of water)*, indicates instability. *Panee chulna, v. n.* To be afflicted with the fluor albus. *Panee jana, v. n.* To be afflicted with the fluor albus; to be disgraced; to shed tears. *Panee dena,* To offer a libation of water to satisfy the manes of a deceased person, after the corpse has been burnt. *Panee nuh mangna,* To be slain with the single stroke of a sword, &c., and die instantly. *Panee purna, v. n.* To rain. *Panee pee pee kosna,* To curse excessively (*i. e. till the throat, being dry, must be moistened by drinking*). *Panee bhurna,* To confess inferiority. *Panee murna, v. n.* To dry up, to be evaporated; to exhibit signs confirming a suspicion. *Panee men ag lugana,* To revive a contention which had subsided. *Panee seh putla kurna,* To abash, to put to shame.

पानीय pa-née-yuh, *adj.* Drinkable, to be drunk.

पानीयनकुल panee-yun-kóol, *s. m.* An otter.

पानीयपृष्ठज paneeyu-prish-thúj, *s. m.* An aquatic plant (*Pistia stratioites*).

पानीयमूलक paneeyu-móol-uk, *s. m.* A plant (*Serratula anthelmintica*).

पानीयामलक paneeya-múl-uk, *s. m.* A fruit (*Flacourtia cataphracta*).

पान्थ panth, *adj.* A traveller.

पान्हर pan-húr, *s. m.* A kind of reed.

पाप pap, *s. m.* Sin, fault, crime, wickedness, vice.

पापकर pap-kúr, *adj.* Wicked, abandoned.

पापकर्त्ता pap-kúrta, *adj.* Sinful, wicked, a sinner.

पापकृत् pap-krít, *adj.* Sinful, wicked, a sinner.

पापग्रह pap-grúh, *s. m.* Any ill-omened aspect of the stars, as the conjunction of the sun or *Boodh* with the moon in its last quarter; *Rahoo; Saturn; Mars.*

पापघ्न pap-úghn, *adj.* Removing sin.

पापचेली pap-chél-ee, *s. f.* A plant, commonly called *Uknidhi (Cissampelos hexandra).*

पापुर pá-pur, *s. m.* A thin crisp cake made of any grain of the pea kind. *Papur belna,* To undergo great labour or pain.

पापरा pap-rá, *s. m.* A plant (*Gardenia latifolia*).

पापराखार pap-ra-khár, *s. m.* Ashes of the plantain tree (*Musa paradisiaca*) used instead of salt for seasoning the cakes called *papur.*

पापदर्शी pap-dúrsh-ee, *adj.* Malevolent, looking at faults.

पापदृश्वन् pap-drísh-wun, *adj.* Conscious of guilt, knowing an act to be wicked.

पापनाशी pap-násh-ee, *adj.* Purifying, sin-destroying. [lant.

पापपति pap-púti, *s. m.* A paramour, a gal-

पापपूरुष páp-poo-roosh, *s. m.* A personification of all sin.

पापबुद्धि pap-bóoddhi, *adj.* Evil-minded, wicked.

पापमति pap-múti, *adj.* Of a corrupt mind, depraved.

पापमुक्त pap-móokt, *adj.* Freed from sin, liberated from all crime.

पापरोग pap-róg, *s. m.* A disease, considered as the punishment of sin in a former life; smallpox, leprosy.

पापसम्मित pap-súm-mit, *adj.* Equal in sin, of like.

पापा pa-pa, *s. m.* A weevil, an insect bred in rice.

पापात्मा pap-átma, *s. m.* A sinner, a reprobate, a wretch.

पापिन pa-pín, ⎫ *adj. f.* Sinful, bad,
पापिनी papín-ée, ⎭ a sinner, criminal, wicked (*woman*).

पापिष्ठ pa-píshth, *adj.* Very wicked.

पापी pá-pee, *adj.* Wicked, sinful, bad, a sinner, criminal.

पामन pá-mun, *adj.* Diseased with herpes.

पामर pá-mur, *adj.* Wicked, vile, low, base; stupid, as an idiot, a fool.

पामरी pám-ree, *s. f.* Silken clothes, silk dress; the wife of a man of inferior caste.

पामा pá-ma, *s. f.* Cutaneous eruption, herpes, scab.

पामारि pa-má-ri, *s. m.* Sulphur.

पायठ pa-yúth, *s. m.* A scaffold.

पायंती pá-yun-tee, *s. f.* The foot of a bed, the side towards the feet.

पायल pa-yúl, *adj.* Sure-footed, easy-paced (*an elephant*). *s. f.* An ornament for the foot or ankle; a bamboo ladder.

पायस pá-yus, *adj.* Made of or from milk or water. *s. m.* An oblation of milk, rice, and sugar.

पाया pá-ya, *s. m.* The leg or foot of a table, chair, &c.

पायिक pá-yik, *s. m.* A foot-soldier, a footman; a messenger, a harbinger.

पायिल pa-yíl, *adj.* Sure-footed, easy-paced (*an elephant*). *s. f.* An ornament for the foot or ankle.

पार par, *s. m.* The opposite bank or shore. *adv.* Over, across, on or to the other side, through, beyond. *adj.* Last, past, the end, the extremity. *Par kurna,* To ferry over, to cross; to finish, accomplish, carry through; to perforate, to transfix; to relieve; to carry off.

पारक pa-rúk, *adj.* What purifies, protects, cherishes, pleases, &c.; what enables any one to cross (*a river, or go through the world*).

पारखी par-khée, *s. m.* An examiner, a discriminator.

पारग pa-rúg, *adj.* Crossing, crossing over; going over or beyond the world.

पारगत par-gút, *adj.* Crossed, gone over the world, pure, holy. *s. m.* A *Jin* or *Jyn* deified teacher.

पारजायिक par-já-yik, *s. m.* An adulterer.

पारन pa-rún, *s. m.* A cloud; eating or drinking after a fast, breaking a fast.

पारद pa-rúd, *s. m.* Quicksilver.

पारदुंडक par-dún-duk, *s. m.* Name of a country, part of *Orissa.*

पारदारिक par-dár-ik, *s. m.* An adulterer.

पारदार्यु par-dárjyuh, *s. m.* Adultery.

पारदृश्वन par-drísh-wun, *adj.* Long-sighted, far-seeing, wise.

पारदेशिक par-désh-ik, *adj.* Foreign, abroad. *s. m.* A traveller; a foreigner.

पारदेश्यु par-désh-yuh, *m.* } *adj.* Belong-
पारदेशी par-désh-ee, *f.* } ing to another country. *s. m.* A traveller, one gone to a foreign country; a foreigner.

पारन pár-na, *s. m.* Breaking a fast. *v. a.* To finish, to accomplish.

पारमार्थिक par-már-thik, *adj.* Preferable, best, most desirable.

पारम्पर्य्यं par-um-púrj, *s. m.* Traditional in-

struction, tradition; continuous order or succession.

पारम्पर्य्योपदेश parum-purj-opdésh, *s. m.* Traditional instruction.

पारुल pá-rul, *s. m.* A plant (*Bignonia chelonoides,* or *Bignonia suave-olens*).

पारलौकिक par-lóu-kik, *adj.* Belonging or relating to the next world.

पारवती pár-vut-ee, *s. f. Doorga,* the wife of *Shiv.*

पारवार par-wár, *adv.* On both sides (*of a river*); quite through, through and through.

पारशव par-shúv, *s. m.* The son of a *Soodr* woman by a *Brahmun*; a son by another's wife, an adulterine; an iron weapon.

पारशीक par-shéek, *s. m.* Persia; a native of Persia; a Persian horse.

पारस pár-us, *s. m.* The philosopher's stone. *adj.* Persian.

पारसपत्थर párus-pútthur, *s. m.* The philosopher's stone.

पारसपीपल párus-péepul, *s. m.* A tree (*Hibiscus populnioides*).

पारसाल pár-sal, *s. m.* or *adv.* Last year.

पारसिक pár-sik, *s. m.* Persia.

पारसी par-sée, *s. m.* A Persian, the Persian language.

पारसीक par-séek, *s. m.* The kingdom of Persia; a Persian, an inhabitant of Persia; a Persian horse.

पारा pá-ra, *s. m.* Quicksilver, mercury. *s. f.* A river, said to flow from the *Pariyatr* mountains, or the centrical and western portion of the *Vindhya* chain.

पारापार par-a-pár, *s. m.* The two banks of a river.

पारायण par-a-yún, *s. m.* Totality, entireness, completeness; reading a *Pooran* or causing it to be read.

पारायणिक par-ayun-ík, *s. m.* A lecturer, a reader of the *Poorans.*

पारावत par-a-wút, *s. m.* A sort of ebony (*Diospyros glutinosa*).

पारावती par-a-wút-ee, *s. f.* A river in the peninsula; the fruit of the *Annona reticulata*; a form of song peculiar to the cowherds.

पारावार par-a-wár, *adv.* On both sides (*of a river*). *s. m.* Limit (*of sea*); sea, ocean.

पाराशर pa-ra-shúr, *n. prop.* A name of the poet *Vyas. s. m.* The rules of *Parashur* or *Vyas,* for the conduct of the mendicant orders.

पाराशरी pa-ra-shúr-ee, *s. m.* The religious mendicant or *Brahmun,* who having passed through the three stages of student, householder, and ascetic, leads a vagrant life, and subsists upon alms.

पारिकाङ्क्षी pari-káng-kshee, *s. m.* An ascetic, one who devotes his days to devout contemplation.

पारिजात pari-ját, *s. m.* A tree of paradise ; the coral tree (*Erythrina fulgens*).

पारिनाय्यु pari-náyuh, *s. m.* Property received at the time of marriage by a woman.

पारितथ्या pari-túthya, *s. f.* A trinket worn on the forehead, where the hair is parted.

पारितोषिक pari-tósh-ik, *adj.* Delighting, making happy. *s. m.* A reward, a gratuity.

पारिपन्थिक pari pún-thik, *s. m.* A robber, a thief, a highwayman.

पारिपात्र pari-pátr, ⎱ *s. m.* The name of a
पारियात्र pari-yátr, ⎰ mountain, apparently the centrical or western portion of the *Vindhya* chain, which skirts the province of *Malwa*.

पारिभद्र pari-bhúdr, *s. m.* The coral tree (*Erythrina fulgens*) ; the *Nimb* tree ; a sort of pine (*Pinus Devadaru*) ; the *Surul*, also a sort of pine (*P. longifolia*).

पारिभाव्य pari-bhávyuh, *s. m.* A drug, a sort of Costus (*C. speciosus*).

पारिषद pari-shúd, *s. m.* A spectator, a person present at an assembly or congregation.

पारी pá-ree, *s. f.* Time, tour, turn.

पारेन्द्र par-éendr, *s. m.* A lion ; a large snake (*Bou*).

पारूष्य pa-róosh-yub, *s. m.* Aloe wood or Agallochum.

पार्थक्य par-thúk-yuh, *s. m.* Severalty, individuality, difference.

पार्थिव par-thív, *adj.* Earthen, made or derived from earth ; ruling or possessing the earth. *s. m.* A king, a prince, an earthen vessel.

पार्वण par-vún, *s. m.* The general funeral ceremony to be offered to all the manes at the *Purv*, or junction of the sun and moon, at which double oblations are offered ; three cakes to the father, paternal grandfather, and great grandfather ; and three to the maternal grandfather, his father, and grandfather ; and the crumbs of each set to the remoter ancestors in each line.

पार्वत pár-vut, *s. m.* A tree called the large *Nimb* (*Melia sempervirens*).

पार्वती pár-vut-ee, *s. f.* A name of *Doorga*, in her capacity of daughter of *Himala*, the sovereign of the snowy mountains ; the olibanum tree (*Boswellia thurifera*) ; another tree (*Celtis orientalis*).

पार्वतीय par-vut-éeyuh, *adj.* Mountaineer.

पार्श्व pársh-wuh, *adj.* Near, proximate, by the side of. *s. m.* A side, the part of the body below the armpit ; side of any square figure.

पार्श्वगत parsh-wugút, *adj.* Close to, beside.

पार्श्वभाग parsh-wuh-bhág, *s. m.* The side, the flank.

पार्श्वशूल parsh-wushóol, *s. m.* Spasm of the chest, stitch.

पार्श्विक parsh-wík, *adj.* Lateral, belonging to the side, &c. *s. m.* A partisan, a sidesman, an associate or companion.

पाल pal, *s. m. f.* A sail ; a small tent ; layers of straw, leaves, &c., between which unripe mangoes are ripened.

पालक pá-luk, *adj.* Who or what protects, nourishes, &c. *s. m.* A cherisher, a protector, a guardian, a keeper ; a kind of greens (*a species of spinach*) ; a bedstead.

पालकजूषी páluk-jóohee, *s. f.* A medicinal plant (*Justicia nasuta* ; also, *Ixora undulata*).

पालकपुत्र pa-luk-póotr, *s. m.* An adopted son.

पालकरी pá-luk-ree, *s. f.* Blocks of wood placed under the feet of a bed to raise it. (*It is the custom to have two such blocks ready to raise the head of a bed, to give it a sloping position*).

पालकी pál-kee, *s. f.* A litter, a sedan. *Palkee nisheen*, Entitled to be carried in a *Palkee* (formerly this privilege was granted by a King or Viceroy). *Palkee suwar*, One who rides in a *Palkee*.

पालङ्क pa-lúnk, *s. m.* Olibanum tree (*Boswellia thurifera*) ; a sort of beet-root (*Beta bengalensis*) ; a hawk.

पालङ्की pa-lún-kee, *s. f.* Incense, the resin of the olibanum.

पालङ्क्या pa-lúnk-ya, *s. f.* Gum olibanum.

पालन pá-lun, *s. m.* Bringing up, preserving, guarding, protecting, cherishing, nourishing, rearing, breeding.

पालना pál-na, *v. a.* To guard, preserve, protect, bring up, rear, cherish, nourish, breed, educate, patronise. *s. m.* A cradle.

पाला pá-la, *s. m.* Frost, hoar-frost, snow ; trust, charge ; a heap of earth made by children to separate the two parties in a game called *kubuddee* ; leaves of a tree named *Jhurberee* (*a species of Zizyphus*). *Pala purna*, *v. n.* To snow. *Paleh purna*, *v. n.* To fall within the power of another.

पालागन pa-lá-gun, *s. m.* Obeisance by embracing the feet, reverence, respect, veneration.

पालाश pa-lásh, *adj.* Of a green colour ; belonging to the *Pulas* tree, made of its wood, &c. *s. m.* Green (*the colour*).

पालाशखण्ड pa-lash-khúnd, *s. m.* A country in India, the western part of *Behar*.

पालिक pa-lík, *s. m.* A cherisher, a protector, a guardian, a keeper.

पालित pa-lít, *adj.* Cherished, nourished.

पालिन्द pa-línd, *s. m.* A sort of jasmine (*Jasminum pubescens*).

पालिन्धी pa-lín-dhee, *s. f.* A plant, commonly called *Teoree* (*Convolvulus turpethum*), the black sort.

पाली pá-lee, *adj.* Who or what nourishes or protects. *s. m.* A cowherd. *s. f.* A battle between birds; a place where birds fight, a cockpit; a covering of a pot.

पाव pao, *s. m* A quarter, a fourth part.

पावक pá-vuk, *adj.* Who or what renders pure, a purifier, purificatory. *s. m.* Fire; a saint, a person purified by religious abstraction; a tree, the wood of which is used to procure fire by attrition (*Premna spinosa*); leadwort (*Plumbago zeylanica*); marking-nut plant (*Semicarpus anacardium*).

पावन pá-wun, *adj.* Purified, pure; purifying, expurgatory, purificatory. *s. m.* Water; penance, expiation, purification by acts of austerity and devotion; the Eleocarpus seed; a kind of grass (*Costus*).

पावनध्वनि páwun-dhwúni, *s. m.* A conch shell.

पावना páo-na, *v. a.* To get, acquire, find, enjoy, suffer, overtake, reach, accept, obtain, attain. *s. m.* Finding, getting, &c.; a plant growing in stagnant water.

पावमान pao-mán, *adj.* Purificatory, purifying.

पावला páo-la, *s. m.* A quarter of any coin (as of a rupee, &c.)

पावस pá-wus, *s. m.* The rainy season.

पावित pa-vít, *adj.* Purified.

पावी pá-wee, *adj.* Who or what purifies.

पाश pash, *s. m.* A fetter, a chain, a tye, the string for fastening tame animals, or the net or noose for catching birds, deer, &c.; a noose as a weapon of combat.

पाशक pá-shuk, *s. m.* A die, particularly the long sort used in playing *choupur.*

पाशबद्ध pash-búddh, *adj.* Noosed, snared, caught, or bound.

पाशबन्ध pash-búndh, *s. m.* A noose, a snare, a halter, a net, &c.

पाशा pá-sha, *s. m.* A die; a throw of dice.

पाशित pash-ít, *adj.* Tied, fettered, bound.

पाशी pá-shee, *s. m.* One armed with a net or noose.

पाशचात्य pash-chát-yuh, *adj.* Behind, being behind; subsequent; western.

पाशुक pa-shúk, *s. m.* An ornament for the feet.

पाशण्ड pa-shund, *s. m.* A heretic, an imposter, one who not conforming to the orthodox tenets of *Hindoo* faith, assumes the external characteristics of tribe or sect, a *Jyn*, a *Bouddh*, & c

पाषण्डी pa-shún-dee, *s. m.* A heretic.

पाषाण pa-shán, *s. m.* A stone in general.

पाषाणभेदी pashán-bhédee, *s. m.* A plant (*Plectranthus scutellaroides*).

पास pas, *s. m.* A rope, a noose. *adv.* At the side, near, beside, about, at.

पासा pá-sa, *s. m.* A die (plur. *paseh*, dice, the oblong dice with which *choupur* is played); a throw of dice.

पासी pá-see, *s. f.* A net; a rope with which the legs of a horse are bound. *s. m.* A fowler; one whose business it is to make or sell *taree*. (So named from the rope round his leg when he climbs the tar tree).

पाहत pa-hát, *s. m.* The mulberry tree (*Morus Indica*).

पाहन pa-hán, *s. m.* A stone.

पाहुन pá-hoon, *s. m.* A guest.

पाहुना pa-hoo-ná, *s. m.* A guest; a son-in-law.

पाहुनी pa-hoo-née, *s. f.* A female guest.

पाहू pa-hóo, *s. m.* A person.

पिओ pióo, *adj.* Beloved, dear. *s. m.* Husband, sweetheart, lover.

पिक pik, *s. m.* The Indian cuckoo (*Cuculus Indicus*).

पिकबन्धु pik-bún-dhoo, *s. m.* The mango tree.

पिकवयनी pik-by-un-ee, }
पिकवैनी pik-by-nee, } *adj.* Possessing a voice like the *Kokila:* an epithet of a female.

पिकाक्ष pik-áksh, *s. m.* A vegetable, and perfume, commonly called *Rochunee* (having red blossoms).

पिकाङ्ग pik-áng, *s. m.* A small bird, called also *Chatukeeya.*

पिकानन्द pik-á-nund, *s. m.* The spring season.

पिक्क pikk, *s. m.* A young elephant.

पिघलना pi-ghúl-na, *v. n.* To melt or to be melted, to be in fusion, to fuse, to flow (a metal).

पिघलाना pigh-lá-na, *v. a.* To melt, to fuse; to soften (an angry or a hard person), assuage, mollify.

पिघलाव pigh-láo, *s. m.* Fusion, flux.

पिङ्ग ping, *adj.* Of a tawny colour. *s. m.* Tawny (the colour).

पिङ्गकूपिशा ping-kúp-i-sha, *s. f.* A cockroach.

पिङ्गचूक्षु ping-chúk-shoo, *s. m.* A crab.

पिङ्गल pín-gul, *adj.* Of a tawny colour, brown, yellowish. *s. m.* Tawny (the colour), a dull brown, or yellow; a fabulous being in the form of a *Nag*, or serpent of the lower regions, to whom a treatise in prosody is ascribed, he is hence considered as a *Mooni*, or inspired and divine personage; the 51st year of the *Hindoo* cycle.

पिंगुलिका pin-gul-ík-a, *s. f.* A sort of crane.

पिंगाष ping-ásh, *s. m.* A sort of fish (*Pimelodius pangasius*).

पिंगूरा pin-góo-ra, *s. m.* A cradle.

पिचकना pich·úk-na, *v. n.* To be squeezed; to be shrivelled.

पिचकाना pich-ká-na, *v. a.* To squeeze, to press together, to shrivel, to wrinkle, to burst.

पिचकारी pich-ká-ree, *s. f.* A squirt, a syringe.

पिचंड pich-únd, *s. m.* The belly.

पिचंडिका pi-chún-dik-a, *s. f.* The instep.

पिचंडिल pi-chúnd-il, *adj.* Big-bellied, corpulent.

पिचपिचा pích-pich-a, *adj.* Flabby, watery, clammy.

पिचिंड pi-chínd, *s. m.* The belly or abdomen.

पिचिंडिल pi-chín-dil, *adj.* Big-bellied, corpulent, pot-bellied.

पिच्छु pí-choo, *s. m.* A sort of leprosy.

पिच्चुक pí-chook, *s. m.* A plant (*Vangueria spinosa*).

पिचूका pi-chóok-ka, *s. m.* A squirt.

पिचुमंद pi-choo-múnd, पिचुमर्द pi-choo-múrd, *s. m.* The *Nimb* tree (*Melia azad-dirachta*).

पिचूल pi-chóol, *s. m.* The tamarisk tree (*T. Indica*); a plant (*Barringtonia acutangula*); the diver or water-crow.

पिचट pich-chút, *s. m.* Inflammation of the eyes, ophthalmia.

पिच्छ pichchh, *s. m.* The tail of a peacock; a tail in general.

पिच्छलदला pích-chhul-dúl-a, *s. f.* The jujube (*Zizyphus jujuba*).

पिच्छवान् pichchh-wán, *adj.* Tailed, having a tail.

पिच्छितिका pich-chhí-tik-a, *s. f.* The *Sisoo* (*Dalbergia Sisu*).

पिच्छिला pich-chhíl-a, *s. f.* The silk cotton tree (*Bombax heptaphyllum*); a potherb (*Basella rubra and lucida*); a timber tree (*Dalbergia Sisu*); an esculent root (*Arum Indicum*).

पिच्छुलना pi-chhúl-na, *v. n.* To slip, to slide.

पिच्छलपाई pi-chhul-páee, *s. f.* The ghost of a woman.

पिछला píchh-la, *adj.* Hindermost, hind, hinder, latter, last, late, modern. *Pichhleh paon hutna*, To withdraw from one's agreement.

पिछवाड़ा pichh-wá-ra, *s. m.* पिछवाड़ी pichh-wá-ree, *s. f.* The rear, rearward, the back part. *adj.* Hinder, hindmost, hindermost, in the rear, abaft.

पिछाड़ी pi-chhá-ree, *s. f.* The rear; the ropes by which a horse's hind legs are tied. *adv.* In the rear, behind. *Pichharee marna*, To attack in the rear.

पिछानना pi-chhán-na, *v. a.* To know, to be acquainted with, to recognise.

पिछूत pi-chóot, *adv.* Behind, afterward. *s. m.* Back of a house.

पिछेत pi-chhét, *s. m.* The back of a house; a yard or enclosure behind a house.

पिछौरा pi-chhóu-ra, *s. m.* A cloth or sheet worn round the waist or thrown carelessly over the head.

पिछौरी pi-chhóu-ree, *s. f.* Diminutive of *Pichhoura*.

पिंजूत pin-jút, *s. m.* The concrete rheum of the eyes.

पिंजन pin-jún, *s. m.* A bow used for cleaning cotton.

पिंजर pin-júr, *adj.* Yellow or tawny, reddish yellow. *s. m.* A sort of colour, tawny brown, a reddish yellow, or a mixture of red and yellow; a horse, probably a bay or chesnut horse; yellow orpiment; a cage, the ribs or the cavity formed by them; the thorax.

पिंजरा pínj-ra, *s. m.* A cage. *Pinjra hona*, To be or grow lean.

पिंजुली pín-jul-ee, *s. f.* Two blades of *Koosa* grass used as a vessel, or to take up articles with at sacrifices.

पिंजिका pín-jik-a, *s. f.* A roll of cotton, from which the threads are spun.

पिंजियारा pin-ji-yára, *s. m.* One whose business it is to beat or separate cotton.

पिंजूल pin-jól, *s. m.* The wick of a lamp.

पिंजूष pin-jóosh, *s. m.* The wax of the ear.

पिंजेट pin-jét, *s. m.* The excretion, or concrete rheum of the eyes.

पिटुंकाकी pit-unk-ákee, *s. f.* Colocynth.

पिटुंकाष pit-unk-ásh, *s. m.* A species of pike (*Esox scolopax*).

पिटना pít-na, *v. n.* To be beaten.

पिटपिटिया pit·pít-iya, *adj.* Combing or carding (*wool, cotton, &c.*).

पिटारा pi-tá-ra, *s. m.* A large basket, a portmanteau.

पिटारी pi-tá-ree, *s. f.* A small basket, a portmanteau.

पिटुक pit-túk, *s. m.* The tartar or excretion of the teeth.

पिंडवाना pir-wá-ná, *v. a.* To cause to press, squeeze or pound.

पिंड pind, *s. m.* } An oblation to deceased ancestors, as a ball or lump of meat, or rice, mixed up with milk, curds, flowers, &c., and offered to the manes at the several *Shraddh* by the nearest surviving relations.
पिंडी pín-dee, *s. f.* }

पिंडगोस pind-gós, *s. m.* Gum myrrh.

पिंडतैलक pind-ty-luk, *s. m.* Incense, olibanum.

पिंडदान pind-dán, *s. m.* Presentation of the obsequial cake.

पिंडपुष्प pind-póoshp, *s. m.* The flower of the *Asoca* tree (*Jonesia Asoca*); the China rose; a lotus; a flower (*Tabernæmontana coronaria*).

पिंडपूष्पक pind-póoshp-uk, *s. m.* A potherb (*Chenopodium album*).

पिंडफला pind-phúl-a, *s. f.* A bitter gourd.

पिंडमुस्ता pind-móos-ta, *s. f.* A sort of grass (*Cyperus pertenuis*).

पिंडमूल pind-móol, *s. m.* The carrot (*Daucus carota*).

पिंडली pínd-lee, *s. f.* The calf of the leg.

पिंडवीज pind-véej, *s. m.* A flowering shrub (*Oleander odorum*).

पिंड pín-da, *s. m.* Body, person; a lump of clay; a bundle or ball of string, clew.

पिंडार pin-dár, *s. m.* A tree (*Trewia nudiflora*).

पिंडारा pin-dá-ra, *s. m.* A plunderer, a pillager (*among Murhattas*).

पिंडालु pind-á-loo, *s. m.* An esculent and medical root, described as sweet, cooling and diuretic.

पिंडिला pín-di-la, *s. f.* A sort of cucumber (*Cucumis Madraspatanus*).

पिंडी pín-dee, *s. f.* A long gourd (*Cucurbita lagenaria*); a sort of palm (*Phenix dactylifera*); a flowering shrub (*Tabernæmontana coronaria*, *flor. plen.*); the upper part of a *Shiv-ling*; a lump of any thing that may be contained in the fist; a small clue or ball of string; a small altar of sand a cubit square, on which oblations to the manes are offered.

पिंडीतक pin-dee-túk, *s. m.* A tree (*Vangueria spinosa*); a shrub (*Tabernæmontana coronaria*).

पिंडीतगर pin-dee-túg-ur, *s. m.* A plant, a species of Tabernæmontana.

पिंडोर pin-déer, *s. m.* Cuttle-fish bone.

पिंडूक pín-dook, *s. m.* A turtle-dove.

पिंडोल pin-dól, *s. f.* A kind of white earth used by the *Hindoos* to cover or wash the walls of their houses with.

पिंडोलि pin-dó-li, *s. f.* Orts, leavings of a meal, or fragments dropped from the mouth.

पिंड्याक pin-yák, *s. m.* Asafœtida.

पितपापड़ा pit-páp-ra, *s. m.* A medicinal plant (*Oldenlandia biflora*).

पितर pítur, *s. m. pl.* Fathers, fore-fathers, ancestors.

पितराई pitr-áee, *s. m.* A kinsman, a paternal relation from three generations. *s. f.* Verdigris.

पितरौ pit-róu, *s. m. dual*, Mother and father, parents.

पितलाना pit-lá-na, *v. n.* To be contaminated with verdigris (*as food, especially of an acid quality, kept in copper vessels*).

पिता pít-a, *s. m.* Father.

पितामह píta-múhuh, *s. m.* A paternal grandfather; a name of *Bruhm*, the great father of all.

पितामही píta-múhee, *s. f.* A paternal grandmother.

पितांबर pit-ám-bur, *s. m.* Silk cloth of a yellow colour; (*vulgarly*) a silk cloth.

पितिया pí-ti-ya, *s. m.* A paternal uncle, a father's brother.

पित्र pitr, *s. m.* A father.

पित्रिक pitrík, *adj.* Paternal, ancestral, parental, obsequial, relating or belonging to parents or progenitors.

पित्रिकर्म pitri-kúrm, *s. m.* }
पित्रिकार्य pitri-kárj, *s. m.* } Obsequial rites.
पित्रिक्रिया pitri-kríya, *s. f.* }

पित्रिगण pitri-gún, *s. m.* A class of progenitors, the sons of the *Rishis* or *Prujaputis*.

पित्रिग्रीष pitri-gríb, *s. m.* A burial ground, a cemetry.

पित्रिघातक pitri-ghá-tuk, *s. m.* A parricide.

पित्रितर्पण pitri-túrp-un, *s. m.* The part of the hand between the middle finger and thumb, sacred to the manes; gifts in honour of deceased relations, distributed at the *Shraddhs* or funeral ceremonies; the act of throwing water out of the right hand at seasons of ablution, by way of offering to the manes, or deceased ancestors in general.

पित्रितिथि pitri-títhi, *s. m.* Day of new moon, on which she rises invisible.

पित्रितीर्थ pitri-téerth, *s. m. Gaya*, the city so called, where the performance of funeral sacrifices is thought to be peculiarly efficacious and meritorious; the part between the fore-finger and thumb, sacred to the manes.

पित्रिदान pitri-dán, *s. m.* Gift in honour of deceased ancestors.

पिटपच pitri-púksh, *s. m.* The first or dark fortnight of the lunar *Asin* month.

पिट्रिपिट्र pitri-pitrí, *s. m.* A paternal grand-father.

पिट्रप्रसू pitri-prús-oo, *s. f.* A father's mother.

पिट्रप्राप्त pitri-prápt, *adj.* Received from a father; inherited patrimonially.

पिट्रबन्धु pitri-bún-dhoo, *s. m.* A remote or cognate kinsman by the father's side, as the son of the paternal grandfather's sister, of the paternal grandmother's sister, and of the father's maternal uncle.

पिट्रभक्ति pitri-bhúkti, *s. f.* Filial duty to a father.

पिट्रभोजन pitri-bhó-jun, *s. m.* Food offered to the manes.

पिट्रमन्दिर pitri-mún-dir, *s. m.* The paternal mansion; a cemetry.

पिट्रयज्ञ pitri-júg, *s. m.* Obsequial rites.

पिट्रलोक pitri-lók, *s. m.* The world or sphere of the manes: it is variously situated, but principally in the *Bhoovur* region or mid-heaven.

पिट्रवन pitri-vún, *s. m.* A cemetry, a place where dead bodies are burnt or buried.

पिट्रव्यूह pitrívyuh, *s. m.* A paternal uncle.

पिट्रश्राद्ध pitri-shráddh, *s. m.* The obsequial ceremony of a father.

पिट्रस्थान pitri-sthán, *s. m.* A guardian, a protector; the abode of the manes.

पिट्रस्वसा pitri-swús-a, *s. f.* An aunt, father's sister.

पिट्रहन् pitri-hún, *s. m.* A parricide.

पित्त pitt, *s. m.* Bile, the bilious humour.

पित्तघ्न pitt-úghn, *adj.* Antibilious.

पित्तघ्नी pitt-úgh-nee, *s. f.* A plant (*Menispermum glabrum*).

पित्तज्वर pitt-jwúr, *s. m.* Bilious fever.

पित्तल pittúl, *adj.* Bilious, relating to the bilious humour. *s. m.* Brass; the *Bhojputr* or Birch tree, of which the bark is used for writing upon, &c.

पित्तला pittul-á, *s. f.* A plant (*Jussieua repens*).

पित्तलाना pitt-lána, *v. n.* To be contaminated with verdigris (*as food, especially of an acid quality, kept in copper vessels*).

पित्ता pitta, *s. m.* Bile, the gall-bladder; (*ironically*) anger, emotion of mind. *Pitta nikalna,* To chastise. *Pitta murna,* To subside, cool (*anger*).

पित्तापड़ा pit-páp-ra, *s. m.* A medicinal plant (*Oldenlandia biflora*).

पिद्री píd-ree, *s. f.* A tom-tit.

पिद्दा píd-da, *s. m.* Name of a bird.

पिधान pi-dhán, *s. m.* A covering, a cover or concealment; a lid, a top or cover; a wrapper or cloak, &c.

पिन pin, *s. m.* A sound.

पिनकी pín-kee, *s. f.* Intoxication from eating opium; drowsiness, nodding.

पिनजियारा pin-ji-yára, *s. m.* One whose business it is to beat or separate cotton.

पिनपिनाना pin-pin-ána, *v. n.* To twang, to whiz.

पिनपिनाहट pin-pin-áhut, *s. f.* The whizzing of an arrow or shot.

पिनहाना pin-há-na, *v. a.* To clothe, to put on, to adorn, to dress.

पिनाक pin-ák, *s. m.* The bow of *Shiv*; a trident or three-pronged spear; the trident of *Shiv*.

पिनाकी pin-ák-ee, *s. f.* A musical instrument, a sort of viol.

पिन्ना pín-na, *s. m.* A cake of mustard seed remaining after the expression of the oil and given to cows, &c. for food.

पिन्नी pín-nee, *s. f.* A kind of sweetmeat.

पिपासन pip-á-sun, *adj.* Thirsty, thirsting.

पिपासा pip-á-sa, *s. f.* Thirst.

पिपासित pip-a-sít, } *adj.* Thirsty, athirst.
पिपासु pip-á-soo, }

पिपीतकी pip-ée-tuk-ee, *s. f.* The twelfth of the month *Vysakh*, when giving away water, is an act of merit.

पिपीलुक pip-ée-luk, *s. m.* A large black ant.

पिपीलिका pip-ée-lik-a, *s. f.* The common small red ant.

पिप्पटा pipp-tá, *s. f.* A kind of sweetmeat.

पिप्पल píp-pul, *s. m.* The holy fig-tree (*Ficus religiosa*).

पिप्पलूक pipp-lúk, *s. m.* A nipple.

पिप्पली pípp-lee, *s. f.* Long-pepper.

पिप्पलीमूल pipp-lee-móol, *s. m.* The root of long-pepper.

पिय píyuh, *adj.* Beloved. *s. m.* A husband, a lover, a sweetheart.

पियाना pi-yá-na, *v. a.* To give or cause to drink, to water.

पियार pi-yár, *s. m.* Love, affection, fondness. *Piyar kurna,* To fondle, caress.

पियारा pi-yá-ra, *adj. m.* Beloved.

पियारी pi-yá-ree, *adj. f.* Beloved, pleasant.

पियाल pi-yál, *s. m.* A fruit (*Chironjia sapida: Buchanania latifolia*).

पियास pi-yás, *s. f.* Thirst. *Piyas murna,* Applied to thirst without drinking. *Piyas boojha-*

na, To quench thirst. *Piyas marna*, To suffer thirst. *Piyas lugna*, To be thirsty.

पियासा pi-yá-sa, *adj. m.* Thirsty. *Piyaseh murna*, To be very thirsty.

पियासी pi-yá-see, *adj. f.* Thirsty.

पिराना pir-á-na, *v. n.* To have pain, to be painful, to pain, ache, ake.

पिरोना pir-ó-na, *v. a.* To thread (*as a needle*), to string (*as pearls*).

पिलई pil-úee, *s. f.* The spleen ; a disease from enlargement or inflammation of the spleen.

पिलचना pil-úch-na, *v. n.* To adhere.

पिलरी píl-ree, *s. f.* Forced meat.

पिलना píl-na, *v. a.* To attack, to assault. *v. n.* To be bruised, thrashed, treated, pressed, ground.   [cid.

पिलपिला píl-pil-a, *adj.* Soft, flabby, flaccid.

पिलपिलाना pil-pil-ána, *v. a.* To soften.

पिलपिलाहट pil-pil-áhut, *s. f.* Softness.

पिलाना pi-lá-na, *v. a.* To give or cause to drink.

पिलूआ píl-oo-a, *s. m.* A worm.

पिल्ला pílla, *s. m.* A puppy, whelp, cub.

पिल्लू pillóo, *s. m.* A worm.

पिवत् piv-út, } *adj.* Drinking.
पिवन् piv-ún, }

पिशंग pish-úng, *adj.* Of a tawny or brown colour. *s. m.* Tawny (*the colour*).

पिशंगता pish-ung-tá, *s. f.* Tawniness.

पिशंगी pish-úng-ee, *adj.* Brown, tawny.

पिशाच pish-ách, *s. m.* A sprite, a fiend, an evil spirit of a particular class, a demon, a spectre, a malevolent being, something between an infernal imp and a ghost, but always described as fierce and malignant.

पिशाचग्रस्त pish-ach-grúst, *adj.* Possessed of a demon, a demoniac.

पिशाचद्रू pish-ach-dróo, *s. m.* A tree (*Trophis aspera*), the favourite haunt of goblins.

पिशाचनी pish-ach-née, *s. f.* A female sprite or fiend.

पिशाब pish-áb, *s. m.* Urine.

पिशिता pish-it-á, *s. f.* Spikenard.

पिशुन písh-oon, *adj.* Cruel, wicked ; vile, low, contemptible ; stupid, a fool. *s. m.* A spy, an informer.

पिशुनवचन píshoon-vúchun, } *s. m.* Evil
पिशुनवाक्य pishoon-vákyuh, } speech, abuse, bad report, detraction, slander.

पिशुना pish-oon-á, *s. f.* A gramineous plant (*Trigonella corniculata*).

पिशुक pish-túk, *s. m.* A disease of the eyes, opacity of the cornea.

पिष्टुप pish-túp, *s. m.* A world, a division of the universe.

पिसना pís-na, *v. n.* To be reduced to meal, to be ground, bruised or broken to powder ; to be ruined or distressed ; (*met.*) to be desperately in love.

पिसाई pis-áee, *s. f.* Price paid for grinding.

पिसाच pis-ách, *s. m.* An evil spirit of a particular class, a demon, a spectre.

पिसाचनी pis-ach-née, *s. f.* A female sprite or spectre.

पिसान् pis-án, *s. m.* Meal, flour.

पिसाना pis-á-na, *v. a.* To reduce to meal, to grind.

पिसाब pis-áb, *s. m.* The act of making water.

पिस्सू pis-óo, *s. m.* A flea.

पी pee, *adj.* Beloved. *s. m.* A lover, a sweetheart, a husband.

पीक peek, *s. f.* The juice of the betel-leaf chewed and spit out. *Peekdan, s. m.* A vessel for holding betel spittle, a spitting-pot.

पीच peech, *s. f.* Rice-water, water in which rice has been boiled, rice-gruel.

पीचना péech-na, *v. a.* To tread under foot.

पीचू pee-chóo, *s. m.* The fruit of the Capparis.

पीछ peechh, *s. f.* Rice-water, water in which rice has been boiled, rice-gruel.

पीछवा péechh-wa, *s. m.* The hinder part (*of a saddle particularly*).

पीछा pée-chha, *s. m.* The hinder part, the rear ; pursuit, persecution, following ; absence. *Peechha kurna*, To pursue, to chase, to follow ; to recoil (*a gun, &c.*). *Peechha pherna*, To leave, to withdraw. *Peechha lena*, To pursue, to importune, to be obstinately persevering.

पीछे pée-chheh, *adv.* In the rear, after, behind, ago, afterwards, astern, in the absence. *Peechheh dalna*, To leave behind, to outstrip, to surpass. *Peechheh purna*, To dance attendance, to run after, to importune, to dun, to persecute, to torment, to be out-stripped. *Peechheh lugna*, To pursue, to follow.

पीजाना pee-jána, *v. a.* To drink or to be drunk ; to absorb ; to stifle one's passions ; to refrain from answering.

पींजना péenj-na, *v. a.* To clean cotton from the seeds.

पीटना péet-na, *v. a.* To beat, thrash, dash, strike, knock, pound. *Chhatee peetna*, To lament, regret, repent.

पीठ peeth, *s. m.* A stool, a seat, a chair. *s. f.* The back. *Peeth keh peechheh dal lena*, To protect, to defend. *Peeth keh peechheh purna*, To take refuge or shelter. *Peeth thokna*, To animate, encourage. *Peeth dena*, To run away, to flee, to turn tail; to turn, to shrink from, to veer; to turn away in displeasure. *Peeth pur hath pherna*, To pat on the back, to encourage. *Peeth pherna*, To turn one's back, to depart, to flee, to leave, to withdraw. *Peeth lugna*, To have a sore on the back (*a horse*); to mount or to back a horse. *Peeth lugana*, To throw down in wrestling.

पीठा pée-tha, *s. m.* A kiud of food made of rice and flour.

पीठियाठोंक péethiya-thónk, *adv.* Closely.

पोठौता pee-thóu-ta, *s. m.* Page (*of a book*).

पीड़ peer, *s. f.* Pain, labour (*in childbirth*).

पीड़क peer-úk, *adj.* What gives or causes pain.

पीड़ा pée-ra, *s. f.* Pain, anguish, suffering.

पीड़ाकर pee-ra-kúr, *adj.* Giving pain, afflicting, tormenting.

पीड़ित pee-rít, *adj.* Pained, suffering pain or distress; sick, afflicted.

पीढ़ा péer-ha, *s. m.* A stool or chair.

पीढ़ाबन्ध peerha-búndh, *s. m.* A preface or introduction to a book.

पीढ़ी peer-hée, *s. f.* A stool, a chair; a generation of progenitors.

पीण्ड peend, *s. m.* A roller.

पीत peet, *adj.* Of a yellow colour. *s. m.* Yellow (*the colour*). *s. f.* Love, affection, kindness, friendship. *Peet kee peet ruheh our meet ka meet hath lugeh*, Let friendship continue and the sweets or benefits of it will be obtained.

पीतकन्द péet-kund, *s. m.* The carrot.

पीतकाष्ठ péet-kashth, *s. m.* Yellow sanders.

पीतघोषा peet-ghó-sha, *s. f.* A sort of creeper with yellow flowers.

पीतचन्दन peet-chún-dun, *s. m.* A yellow fragrant wood, considered as a yellow species of *Sandal* wood.

पीतता peet-tá, *s. f.* Yellowness.

पीततुण्ड peet-tóond, *s. m.* The taylor-bird (*Sylvia sutoria*).

पीतदारु peet-dá-roo, *s. m.* A sort of pine (*Pinus Devadaru*); another kind of pine (*Pinus longifolia*).

पीततन peet-tún, *s. m.* The hog plum (*Spondias magnifera*); a tree (*Pentaptera tomentosa*); the waved-leaf fig-tree.

पीतपर्णी peet-púr-nee, *s. f.* A plant, commonly called *Bichhuti*; a name applied to the nettle, or a plant of the same class (*Tragia involucrata*).

पीतपादा peet-pá-da, *s. f.* A small bird, the *Myna* (*Turdus salica*).

पीतपुष्प peet-póoshp, *s. m.* A species of *Kurnikara*; a sort of Tabernæmontana.

पीतपुष्पी peet-póoshp-ee, *s. f.* Yellow barleria.

पीतफल peet-phúl, *s. m.* Trophis aspera.

पीतम pée-tum, *adj. superl.* Most beloved. *s. m.* A lover, a sweetheart, a husband.

पीतमणि peet-múni, *s. m.* A yellow gem, a topaz.

पीतमस्तक peet-mús-tuk, *s. m.* A small bird (*Loxia philippensis*).

पीतमण्ड peet-móond, *s. m.* A gallinule.

पीतम्बर pee-túm-bur, *s. m.* A silk cloth of yellow colour; (*vulg.*) a silk cloth.

पीतयूथी peet-yóo-thee, *s. f.* Yellow jasmine.

पीतरक्त peet-rúkt, *s. m.* A yellow coloured gem, perhaps the topaz.

पीतरस peet-rús, *s. m.* Turmeric (*Curcuma*).

पीतल pée-tul, *s. m.* Brass.

पीतल péet-la, *adj.* Brazen.

पीतलोह peet-lóh, *s. m.* Yellow brass, queen's metal, or a mixed metal.

पीतशाल peet-shál, *s. m.* A tree (*Pentaptera*).

पीतसार peet-sár, *s. m.* Sandal; a yellow gem, a topaz; a tree (*Alangium hexapetalum*).

पीतस्फटिक peet-sphút-ik, *s. m.* A precious gem, the topaz.

पीताम्बर peet-ám-bur, *s. m.* Silk cloth of a yellow colour; (*vulg.*) a silk cloth.

पीति péeti, *s. f.* Love, affection, kindness, friendship.

पीदड़ी péed-ree, *s. f.* A tom-tit.

पीन peen, *adj.* Heavy, fat, bulky, corpulent, large.

पीनक pée-nuk, *s. f.* Intoxication and drowsiness from opium.

पीनस pée-nus, *s. m.* Cold, catarrh; cold, affecting in the nose, inflammation of the schneiderian membrane. *s. f.* Chair or litter.

पीनसी pée-nus-ee, *adj.* Having a cold.

पीना pée-na, *v. a.* To drink; to smoke (*tobacco*). *s. m.* Drinking, &c.; the dregs or refuse (*of linseed, &c.*), the oil cake.

पीपल pée-pul, *s. m.* The holy fig-tree (*Ficus religiosa*). *s. f.* Long-pepper (*Piper longum*).

पीपला péep-la, *s. m.* The point of a sword.

पीपलामूल peep-la-móol, *s. m.* The root of the long-pepper tree.

पीपा pee-pa, *s. m.* A pipe, barrel, cask.

2 Q

पीब peeb, *s. f.* Pus, matter, corruption, purulent running.

पीबियाना pee-bi-yána, *v. n.* To suppurate.

पीबियाहट pee-bi-yáhut, *s. f.* Suppuration.

पीयु pée-yoo, *adj.* Beloved, dear. *s. m.* Husband, sweetheart, lover.

पीयूष pee-yóos, *s. m.* The food of the gods, ambrosia, nectar; the milk of a cow during the first seven days after calving.

पीर peer, *s. f.* Pain, ache, sickness; feeling, pity, compassion, mercy.

पीरा pée-ra, *adj.* Yellow.

पीराई pee-rá-ee, *s. m.* A tribe or caste who beat a kind of drum called *dhol.*

पीला pée-la, *adj.* Yellow.

पीलाई pee-lá-ee, *s. f.* Yellowness.

पीलाम pee-lám, *s. m.* Satin.

पीली pée-lee, *s. f.* A gold-mohur.

पीलीभीत pee-lee-bhéet *n. prop.* The name of a town in *Rohilkhund.*

पीलू pée-loo, *s. m.* A tree, applied in some places to the Careya arborea, and in others to the Salvadora persica; it is very commonly assigned also to all exotic and unknown trees; the blossom of the Saccharum sara; an insect.

पीलूपर्णी péeloo-púrnee, *s. f.* A plant (*Bryonia grandis*).

पीवुकर pee-vúk-kur, *s. m.* A tippler, a toper, a drinker.

पीवरी péev-ree, *s. f.* A plant (*Asparagus racemosus*).

पीवा pée-wa, *s. f.* Water.

पीसना pées-na, *v. a.* To grind, to triturate, to bruise, to powder; to gnash (*the teeth*). *s. m* The corn or grain for grinding.

पीहर pée-hur, *s. m.* Mother's house.

पीहू pée-hoo, *s. m.* A flea.

पुंज poonj, *s. m.* A heap, a quantity, a collection.

पुंलिंग póon-ling, *s. m.* The male organ; the masculine gender (*in grammar*).

पुंश्चिह्न poonshch-chính, *s. m.* The penis.

पुंसवन poons-wún, *s. m.* The first of the essential ceremonies of *Hindoo* initiation; a religious and domestic festival held on the mother's perceiving the first signs of a living conception.

पुंस्त्व poons-twúh, *s. m.* Semen virile; manhood, virility.

पुकार poo-kár, *s. f.* Bawl, calling out aloud, cry, call.

पुकारदेना pookár-déna, *v. a.* To proclaim publicly, to call.

पुकारना poo-kár-na, *v. a.* To call aloud, to bawl, to cry out, exclaim, shout.

पुखराज pookh-ráj, *s. m.* A topaz.

पुचकारा pooch-ká-ra, } *s. m.* A thin coat
पुचारा poo-chá-ra, } of clay for laying on a wall; the sponge of a gun. *Poochara dena*, To lay a thin coat of clay on the walls of a house; to white-wash a wall. *Poochara pherna*, To sponge a gun.

पुच्छ poochchh, *s. f.* A tail.

पुच्छवैया poochh-wy-ya, *s. m.* An inquirer.

पुजवाना pooj-wá-na, *v. a.* To cause to worship; to cause to fill or complete.

पुजाना poo-já-na, *v. a.* To cause to worship; to fill, to complete.

पुजापा poo-já-pa, *s. m.* The apparatus of worshipping.

पुंज poonj, *s. m.* A heap, quantity, collection.

पूत poot, *s. m.* A menstruum, solvent, flux.

पुट्ठा poot-thá, *s. m.* The buttock, the hip (*of an animal*).

पूरा póo-ra, *s. m.* A large parcel (*of physic, &c.*).

पुरिया póo-ri-ya, *s. f.* A parcel (*of physic, &c.*).

पूरी póo-ree, *s. f.* A skin with which a drum is made.

पुंडरीक poond-réek, *s. m.* The elephant of the south-east quarter; a sort of snake (*Amphisbena*); a sort of leprosy; a white lotus.

पुंडरीयक poond-rée-yuk, *s. m.* A flower (*Hibiscus mutabilis*); a drug commonly called *Poonderiya.*

पुण्य póon-yuh, *adj.* Virtuous, pure, righteous. *s. m.* Virtue, moral or religious merit; a good action.

पुण्यकर्मा póon-yuh-kúrma, *adj.* Pious, virtuous.

पुण्यगन्ध poon-yuh-gúndh, *s. m.* The *Chumpuk* flower (*Michelia champaca*).

पुण्यतीर्थ poon-yuh-téerth, *s. m.* A holy shrine or place of pilgrimage.

पुण्यतृण poon-yu-trín, *s. m.* White *Koosa* grass.

पुण्यदर्शन poon-yu-dúrshun, *s. m.* The blue jay.

पुण्यफल poon-yu-phúl, *s. m.* The reward or consequence of good actions.

पुण्यभू poon-yu-bhóo, *s. f.* The holy land of the *Hindoos*; the central part of *Asia*, bounded on the north by the *Himala*, on the south by the *Vindhya* mountains, and on the east and west by the sea.

पुण्यभूमि poon-yu-bhóomi, *s. f.* The holy land of the *Hindoos*; the mother of a male child.

पुषलोक poon-yu-lók, *s. m.* Heaven, para-dise. [righteous.

पुषवान poon-yu-wán, *adj.* Virtuous, pious,

पुषशील poon-yu-shéel, *adj.* Virtuous.

पुषस्थान poon-yu-sthán, *s. m.* A sacred place, holy ground.

पुष्या poon-yá, *s. f.* The commencement of collection for the new year. (*Used by land-hold-ers*).

पुष्याई poon-yá-ee, *s. f.* A virtuous action, performed (*according to those who hold the doctrine of the metempsychosis*) in one state of existence, the reward of which is received in a future trans-migration; merit of an ancestor rewarded in his descendants.

पुष्यात्मा póon-yu-átma, *adj.* Holy, pious.

पुष्योदय poon-yó-duy, *s. m.* Good fortune, as the result of virtuous acts in a former life.

पुत् poot, *s. m.* A hell to which the child-less are said to be condemned.

पुतला póot-la, *s. m.* An idol, image.

पुतली póot-lee, *s. f.* The pupil of the eye; an image, a puppet, an idol, a doll; the frog of a horse's hoof. *Pootlee ka tara kurna*, To honour or esteem as the apple of the eye.

पुताई poo-tá-ee, *s. f.* The act of plaster-ing; price paid.

पुत्र pootr, *s. m.* A son.

पुत्रकाम्या pootr-kám-ya, *s. f.* Wish or affec-tion for progeny.

पुत्रजीव pootr-jéev, *s. m.* A tree, from the fruit of which necklaces are made of supposed prolific efficacy (*Nigella Putranjiva*).

पुत्रपौत्रीण pootr-pou-tréen, *adj.* Descended from son to son.

पुत्रश्रेणी pootr-shrénee, *s. f.* A plant (*Sal-vinia cucullata*).

पुत्रिका póotri-ka, *s. f.* A daughter; a doll, a puppet.

पुत्रिकापुत्र pootri-ka-póotr, *s. m.* The son of a daughter, appointed to raise issue for her father; one of the twelve heirs acknowledged by the old *Hindoo* law; a grandson.

पुत्री póotree, *s. f.* A daughter; a plant (*Siphonanthus Indica*).

पुत्रेष्टि pootréshti, *s. f.* A sacrifice perform-ed for the purpose of obtaining children.

पुनःपुनः póonuh-póonuh, } *adv.* Repeated-
पुनःपुनर् póonuh-póonur, } ly, again and again.

पुनःपुना póonuh-póona, *s. f.* The *Poompoon* river in *Behar*.

पुनर् poo-núr, } *adv.* Again.
पुनरायुः póo-nur-áyuh, }

पुनरुक्त poon-ur-óokt, *adj.* Repeated, said over again. *s. m.* Tautology, repetition.

पुनरुक्ति poon-ur-óokti, *s. f.* Repetition, tautology.

पुनरुत्थान poon-ur-ootthán, *s. m.* Resur-rection.

पुनर्जन्मा poon-ur-júnma, *adj.* Re-born, born again.

पुनर्नवा poo-nur-núva, *s. f.* Hog-weed (*Boerhavia diffusa-alata*).

पुनर्भू poon-ur-bhóo, *s. f.* A virgin widow re-married.

पुनर्वसु poon-ur-vús-oo, *s. m.* The seventh of the lunar asterisms.

पुनवाना poon-wá-na, *v. a.* To cause to be abused or reproached by another.

पुनि póoni, *adv.* Again.

पुनीत poo-néet, *adj.* Pure, clean.

पुन्नक्षत्र poon-nukshútr, *s. m.* An asterism under which males are procreated.

पुन्ना póon-na, *v. a.* To abuse.

पुन्नाग poon-nág, *s. m.* A tree, from the flowers of which a yellowish dye is prepared (*Rot-tleria tinctoria*).

पुर poor, *s. f.* A city.

पुर poor, *s. m.* A town, a city; a place containing large buildings surrounded by a ditch, and extending not less than one *kos* in length, is called a city, a *Poor* or *Nugur*; if it extends not less than half a *kos*, it is called a *Khet*, or town; if less than that, a *Kurvut*, or small market town; and any cluster of houses less than that, is a *Gram*, or village.

पुरःसर pooruh-súr, *adj.* One who goes first or before. *s. m.* A leader, a preceder.

पुरनिया poo-run-íya, } *n. prop.* Name of
पुरेनिया poo-ry-niya, } a district and town, *Purneah* in *Bengal.*

पुरदेवता poor-dév-ta, *s. f.* The tutelary deity of a town.

पुरद्वार poor-dwár, *s. m.* A city gate.

पुरनिया poo-run-íya, *s. m.* An old man, an elder; a patron.

पुरन्दर poo-rún-dur, *s. m.* A sort of pep-per (*Piper chavya*).

पुरवासी poor-vá-see, *adj.* Inhabiting a city or town.

पुरुष्छद poo-rush-chhúd, *s. m.* A sort of grass (*Saccharum cylindricum*).

पुरुष्कार poo-rus-kár, *s. m.* Honouring, re-specting, worshipping.

पुरा póo-ra, *s. m.* A large village, a town, an assemblage of habitations.

पुराण poo-rán, *s. m.* A sacred and poetical

work, supposed to be compiled or composed by the poet *Vyas*, and comprising the whole body of *Hindoo* theology ; each *Pooran* should treat of five topics especially, the creation, the destruction and renovation of worlds, the genealogy of gods and heroes, the reigns of the *Munoos*, and the transactions of their descendants ; but great variety prevails in this respect, and few contain historical or genealogical matter. There are eighteen acknowledged *Poorans* : 1, *Bruhm* : 2, *Pudm*, or the lotus : 3, *Bruhmand*, or the egg of *Bruhm* : 4, *Ugni*, or fire : 5, *Vishnov* : 6, *Guroor*, his bird or vehicle : 7, *Bruhm-ryvurt*, or transformations of *Bruhm*, i. e. of *Krishn*, identified with the Supreme : 8, *Shiv* : 9, *Ling* : 10, *Narud*, son of *Bruhm* : 11, *Skund*, son of *Shiv* : 12, *Markundey*, so called from a *Mooni* of that name : 13, *Bhuvishyut*, or prophetic : 14, *Mutsyuh*, or the fish : 15, *Varah*, or boar : 16, *Koorm*, or tortoise : 17, *Vamun*, or dwarf, and 18, The *Bhagurut*, or life of *Krishn* ; which last is by some considered as a spurious and modern work : the *Bruhm-ryvurt* is also of very modern origin. The *Poorans* are reckoned to contain four hundred thousand stanzas. There are also eighteen *Oop-poorans*, or similar poems of inferior sanctity, and different appellations : the whole constitute the popular or poetical creed of the *Hindoos*, and some of them or particular parts of them, are very generally read and studied.

युराणा poo-rá-na,
युरातन poo-rá-tun, } *adj.* Old, ancient.
युरातम poo-rá-tum,

युराना poo-rá-na, *v. a.* To fill. *adj.* Old.

पुरी póo-ree, *s. f.* A city, a town.

पुरीमोह pooree-móh, *s. m.* The thorn-apple (*Datura*).

• पुरीष poo-réesh, *s. m.* Fæces, excrement, ordure.

पुरु póo-roo, *s. m.* The name of a king, the sixth monarch of the lunar line ; the farina of a flower. *s. f.* The name of a river, said to run a little to the north-west of the *Surwooti.*

पुरुखा poo-roo-khá, *s. m.* An old man, an elder, an ancestor.

पुरुखे poo-roo-khéh, *s. m.* Ancestors, ancestry.

पुरुष póo-roosh, *s. m.* A man, generally or individually, a male, mankind ; God, the Supreme Being.

पुरुषकार poo-roosh-kár, *s. m.* Manly act, virility ; effort, exertion ; any act of man, manhood.

पुरुषता poo-roosh-tá, *s. f.* Manhood, manliness ; valour.

पुरुषत्व poo-roosh-twúh, *s. m.* Manhood, virility, manly nature or property ; valour, prowess.

पुरुषद्वेषी póo-roosh-dwésh-ee, *adj.* Man-hating, misanthropic.

पुरुषद्वेषिणी póo-roosh-dwéshin-ee, *s. f.* An ill-tempered or factious woman.

पुरुषमात्र poo-roosh-mátr, *adj.* Of the height or measure of a man.

पुरुषवर्जित póoroosh-vúrjit, *adj.* Desolate, destitute of human beings.

पुरुषाः poo-roo-sháh, *s. m. pl.* Ancestors, the ancients, predecessors.

पुरुषाधम pooroosh-ádhum, *s. m.* A low man, an outcaste.

पुरुषाधिकार póoroosh-adhikár, *s. m.* Manly office or duty.

पुरुषायु póoroosh-áyoo, *s. m.* Life of man, human existence.

पुरुषार्थ poo-roosh-árth, *s. m.* A human object, as the gratification of desire, acquirement of wealth, discharge of duty, and final emancipation. *adv.* For or on account of man.

पुरुषाशी póoroosh-áshee, *s. m.* A *Rakshus*, a cannibal.

पुरुषोत्तम póoroosh-óttum, *s. m.* An excellent or superior man.

पुरूरवस् poo-roor-vús, *n. prop.* The son of *Booddh*, and second king of the lunar dynasty.

पुरेन poo-rén, *s. f.* The placenta ; the plant of the lotus.

पुरोधा poo-ro-dhá, } *s. m.* The family or
पुरोहित poo-ro-hít, } domestic priest, conducting all the ceremonials and sacrifices of a house or family.

पुरोहितानी poo-ro-hit-ánee, *s. f.* The wife of a *Poorohit*, or family priest.

पुर्खा póor-kha, *s. m.* An old man, an elder, an ancestor.

पुर्चक póor-chuk, *s. f.* Deceit, trick, coaxing.

पुर्वा póor-va, *s. f.* An easterly wind.

पुर्वाना poor-wá-na, *v. a.* To cause to fill.

पुर्वय्या poor-wy-ya, *s. f.* Easterly wind.

पूर्खा póor-kha, *s. m.* An old man, an elder, an ancestor.

पूर्खे póor-kheh, *s. m.* Ancestors, ancestry.

पूर्स póor-sa, *adj.* Of man's height. *s. m.* The extent of a man's reach in height when extending the arms and fingers, a fathom.

पूल pool, *s. m.* A bridge, an embankment. *Pool bandhna, v. a. (lit. To make a bridge)* To limit ; to abound.

पूलकित póol-kit, *adj.* Joyful.

पूलकी póol-kee, *s. m.* A sort of *Kudumb* (*Nauclea Cadamba*).

पुलपुला póol-poo-la, *adj.* Soft, flabby, flaccid.

पुलपुलाना pool-poo-lána, *v. n.* To fear, to dread ; to take a morsel into the mouth, and from the want of teeth, being unable to chew, to turn it about.

पुलपुलाहट pool-poo-láhut, *s. f.* Fear ; the act of turning about a morsel in the mouth.

पुलहाना pool-hána, *v. a.* To persuade.

पुलिन poo-lín, *s. m.* An island of alluvial formation, or one from which the water has recently withdrawn, or a small island or bank left in the middle of a river, upon the falling of the waters; any island.

पुलिन्द poo-lín-da, *s. m.* A bundle.

पुल्लिङ्ग póol-ling, *s. m.* The masculine gender (*in grammar*).

पुवाल poo-wál, *s. f.* Straw.

पुषित póosh-it, *adj.* Nourished, nurtured.

पुष्कर póosh-kur, *s. m.* The sky, heaven, atmosphere ; a lotus (*Nelumbium speciosum,* or *Nymphæa nelumbo*) ; a drug (*Costus speciosus*) ; a celebrated place of pilgrimage, now called *Pokur,* in the province of *Ajmere,* about four miles from the city of *Ajmere,* consisting of a small town on the bank of a lake, whence its name ; one of the seven great *dweeps* or divisions of the universe ; a pond or lake ; a mountain in *Pooshkur-dweep.*

पुष्करमूलक póoshkur-móoluk, *s. m.* The root of the Costus speciosus.

पुष्करिणी pooshkur-ín-ee, *s. f.* A square or large pond ; a piece of water, a lake.

पुष्कल poosh-kúl, *adj.* Excellent, eminent, chief, best ; much, many ; full, filled, complete. *s. m.* The mountain *Meroo* ; the holy place *Pooshkur.*

पुष्ट poosht, *adj.* Nourished, cherished ; fat ; restorative, provocative.

पुष्टई poosht-uée, *adj.* Restorative, provocative.

पुष्टता poosht-tá, *s. f.* Fatness ; invigoration, restorative power.

पुष्टाङ्ग poosht-áng, *adj.* Fat, fattened.

पुष्टि póosh-ti, *s. f.* Cherishing, nourishing.

पुष्टिकर poosh-ti-kúr, *s. m.* Any food or drug of a nutritive quality, or provocative.

पुष्टिद poosh-tíd, *adj.* Nourishing, cherishing.

पुष्टिदा poosh-tid-á, *s. f.* A plant (*Physalis flexuosa*).

पुष्प pooshp, *s. m.* A flower in general ; the menses ; the vehicle or car of *Koover* ; a disease of the eyes, specks on the eye, albugo.

पुष्पक pooshp-úk, *s. m.* Calx of brass ; the chariot of *Koover* ; a disease of the eyes, albugo, specks on the eye ; a bracelet of diamonds or jewels ; green vitriol.

पुष्पकरण्डक póoshp-kurun-dúk, *s. m. Uvuntee* or *Oujyn,* or the grove in its vicinity considered as sacred to *Muhadev.*

पुष्पकासीश pooshp-ka-séesh, *s. m.* The green sulphate of iron.

पुष्पकीट pooshp-kéet, *s. m.* Any insect affecting flowers.

पुष्पकेतु pooshp-két-oo, *s. m.* Calx of brass.

पुष्पचामर pooshp-chá-mur, *s. m.* A plant *Artemisia*) ; a fragrant plant (*Pandanus odoratissimus*), having a large bushy flower.

पुष्पदन्त pooshp-dúnt, *s. m.* The elephant of the north-west quarter.

पुष्पपथ pooshp-púth, *s. m.* The vulva.

पुष्पपुर pooshp-póor, *n. prop. Patalipootr,* or *Palibothra.*

पुष्पफल pooshp-phúl, *s. m.* Elephant or wood apple.

पुष्पमास pooshp-más, *s. m.* Spring.

पुष्परक्त pooshp-rúkt, *s. m.* A shrub (*Hibiscus phæniceus*).

पुष्परस pooshp-rús, *s. m.* The nectar or honey of flowers.

पुष्परेणु pooshp-rén-oo, *s. m.* The dust or farina of flowers.

पुष्परोचन pooshp-ró-chun, *s. m.* A plant (*Mesua ferrea*).

पुष्पवत pooshp-wút, *adj.* Having flowers, flowery.

पुष्पवाटी pooshp-vá-tee, *s. f.* A flower garden.

पुष्पशून्य pooshp-shóon-yuh, *adj.* Not bearing flowers, flowerless.

पुष्पसमय pooshp-súmuy, *s. m.* Spring.

पुष्पसार pooshp-sár, *s. m.* The nectar or honey of flowers.

पुष्पहीन pooshp-héen, *adj.* Flowerless, not flowering.

पुष्पहीना pooshp-héen-a, *s. f.* The glomerous fig-tree ; a woman whose menstruation has ceased, a barren woman.

पुष्पाञ्जन pooshp-án-jun, *s. m.* The calx of brass.

पुष्पाञ्जली pooshp-ánjul-ee, *s. f.* Presenting a nosegay of flowers, held in both hands opened, and hollowed.

पुष्पिका póoshp-ik-a, *s. f.* The tartar of the teeth ; the mucus of the glans penis or urethra.

पुष्पित pooshp-ít, *adj.* Flowered, in flower.

पुष्पिता pooshp-it-á, *s. f.* A woman during menstruation.

पुष्पिताग्रा pooshp-it-ágra, *s. f.* A form of metre ; the line consisting of four or six short syllables, a pyrrhic, or a dactyl, two trochees and a spondee.

पुष्पी póoshp-ee, *adj.* Flowering, bearing flowers.

पुष्य póosh-yuh, *s. m.* The eighth lunar asterism, comprising three stars, of which one is Cancer ; the month *Pous* (*December—January*).

पुष्यपुत्र pooshyuh-póotr, *s. m.* An adopted son. *Poospoot kurna,* To adopt.

पुस्तक poos-túk, *s. m.* A book, a manuscript.

पूहुप póo-hup, *s. m.* A flower.

पूआ póo-a, *s. m.* A pancake.

पून poon, *s. m.* A sound of letting wind.

पूंगी póon-gee, *s. f.* Flute, pipe ; a kind of pipe played on by jugglers.

पूंछ poonchh, *s. f.* A tail.

पूंछना poonchh-na, *v. a.* To wipe.

पूंछार poon-chhár, *adj.* Tailed.

पूंजी póon-jee, *s. f.* A capital in trade, stock, principal sum, fund.

पूग poog, *s. m.* The betel-nut tree (*Areca faufel,* or *catechu*) ; a heap, a quantity, a multitude ; the fruit of the faufel, the betel-nut.

पूगफल poog-phúl, *s. m.* The areca nut.

पूगरोट poog-rót, *s. m.* The marshy date tree (*Phœnix,* or *Elate paludosa*).

पूछ poochh, *s. f.* Inquiry, investigation. *Poochh-pachh, s. f.* Inquiry, interrogation.

पूछना póochh-na, *v. a.* To ask, inquire, question, interrogate.

पूछी póo-chhee, *s. f.* The tail of a fish.

पूजक poo-júk, *adj.* Worshipping, a worshipper.

पूजत poo-jút, *adj.* Worshipping, reverencing.

पूजन poo-jún, *s. m.* Worship, worshipping.

पूजना póoj-na, *v. a.* To adore, reverence, worship, venerate.

पूजनीय pooj-née-yuh, ⎫ *adj.* To be wor-
पूजमान pooj-mán, ⎭ shipped or reverenced, *deserving respect, venerable.*

पूजा póo-ja, *s. f.* Worship, culture, respect, homage of superiors, or adoration of the gods.

पूजारी poo-já-ree, *s. m.* A worshipper.

पूजित poo-jít, *adj.* Worshipped, adored, reverenced.

पूज्य póoj-yuh, *adj.* Worshipful, venerable, fit for or deserving adoration, &c. *s. m.* A father-in-law.

पूज्यमान poojyu-mán, *adj.* Being reverenced or respected.

पूट poot, *s. m.* A bone lying over the tail of a cow. [abuse.

पूटकी poot-kée, *s. f.* The anus ; a term of

पूठ pooth, *s. m.* The buttock, the hip.

पूठा poo-thá, *s. m.* The paper or paste board cover of a book.

पूरा póo-ra, *s. m.* A kind of cake made of pease-meal.

पूनी póo-nee, *s. f.* Rolls of cotton prepared for spinning.

पूत poot, *s. m.* A son.

पूतना póot-na, *s. f.* Yellow myrobalan (*Terminalia chebula*) ; the name of a female demon killed by *Krishn* ; a disease, atrophy and wasting in a child, ascribed to the malignant operations of the female fiend *Pootna.*

पूतफल poot-phúl, *s. m.* The jack fruit.

पूतरी poot-rée, *s. f.* ⎫ A puppet, an image.
पूतला poot-lá, *s. m.* ⎭

पूतली poot-lée, *s. f.* A small puppet or image ; the apple of the eye.

पूतात्मा poot-átma, *s. m.* A saint, an ascetic, a pure or purified person ; a man of a cleanly person, or purified by ablution.

पूति póoti, *s. f.* Purity, purification.

पूतिक poo-tík, *s. m.* Grey bonduc (*Cœsalpinia bonducella*).

पूतिकर्णक póoti-kúrn-uk, *s. m.* Fetid ulceration of the ear.

पूतिकमुख póotika-mookh, *s. m.* A bivalve shell.

पूतिकाष्ठ pooti-káshth, *s. m.* A sort of pine (*Pinus Devadaru*).

पूतिफला pooti-phúl-a, *s. f.* A plant (*Psoralea corilifolia*).

पूतिफली pooti-phúl-ee, *s. f.* A medicinal plant (*Serratula anthelmintica*).

पूतिवृक्ष pooti-vríksh, *s. m.* A plant (*Bignonia Indica*).

पूतिशारिजा póoti-shá-rij-a, *s. f.* The pole or civet cat.

पूतियंध poot-yúnd, *s. m.* The musk-deer ; an insect with a fetid smell, the winged bug.

पूदीना poo-dée-na, *s. m.* Garden mint (*Mentha sativa*).

पूनसलाई poon-sul-áee, *s. f.* A thin roller on which cotton is prepared for spinning.

पूनी poo-née, *s. f.* Rolls of cotton prepared for spinning.

पूनों póo-non, ⎫ *s. f.* The day of full moon.
पून्यो poon-yó, ⎭

पूप poop, *s. m.* A cake.

पूपला póop-la, *s. f.* A sort of sweet cake, fried with *ghee* or oil.

पूपाली poo-pá-lee, *s. f.* A sort of cake or biscuit, made of meal or barley, half baked or fried.

पूय póo-yuh, } *s. m.* Pus, matter, dis-
पूयन poo-yún, } charge from an ulcer, wound or sore.

पूयालस poo-yá-lus, *s. m.* Suppuration at the joints, white swelling.

पूरक poo-rúk, *adj.* Filling, completing, or that which fills or completes.

पूरन poo-rún, *adj.* Filling, completing; full, filled, complete, perfect, accomplished, entire, total, exact, ripe. *s. m.* Act of filling, completing or making up; multiplication (*in arithmetic*); a fragrant grass (*Cyperus rotundus*).

पूरनी poor-née, *s. f.* The cross threads in weaving a piece of cloth.

पूरब póo-rub, *s. m.* The east. *adj.* Eastern; former, prior, preceding.

पूरा póo-ra, *adj.* Full, complete, entire, exact, perfect, sufficient, just, total, ripe, powerful. *Poora kurna, v. a.* To fill, to fulfil, to accomplish, to complete; to re-imburse.

पूराई poo-ra-ée, *s. f.* Fulness, completion.

पूरित poo-rít, *adj.* Filled, full, complete.

पूरिया póo-ri-ya, *s. f.* A musical mode or *raginee.*

पूरी poo-rée, *s. f.* A kind of fresh cake fried in butter or *ghee.* [kind.

पूरुष póo-roosh, *s. m.* Man, male, man-
पूर्ण poorn, *adj.* Full, filled, complete, perfect, accomplished; all, entire, total; strong, powerful, able; exact; ripe.

पूर्णकाम poorn-kám, *adj.* Satisfied, satiated.

पूर्णकुम्भ poorn-kóombh, *s. m.* A water-vessel, one filled with holy water, used at the consecration of a king; a full cup or jar.

पूर्णपात्र poorn-pátr, *s. m.* A full cup or vessel; a vessel filled with clothes or ornaments, which are scrambled for by the guests and relations at a festival; a vessel full of rice, presented as a sacrifice to the superintending and officiating priests: it is properly a measure of 256 handfuls of rice; it may also be composed of as much as will satisfy one great eater.

पूर्णमा poorn-má, } *s. f.* The day of
पूर्णमासी poorn-másee, } full moon.

पूर्णमास poorn-más, *s. m.* A monthly sacrifice, performed on the day of full moon.

पूर्णा poor-na, *v. a.* To weave (*as a spider*). *v. n.* To be filled. *Chouk oorna,* To make chequers or squares.

पूर्णाहुति poorn-áhooti, *s. f.* The oblation presented at the conclusion of a religious sacrifice, the final oblation; the burnt-offering which completes any ceremony.

पूर्ति póortti, *s. f.* Fulness, completion.

पूर्ती póort-tee, *adj.* Filling, completing.

पूर्ब poorb, *adj.* Anterior, prior, former, preceding; east, eastern.

पूर्बार्द्ध poorb-árddh, *adj.* The former or prior half.

पूर्बी póor-bee, *s. f.* A *raginee* sung before evening. *adj.* Eastern, from the east; a kind of rice from the east or Bengal.

पूर्व poorv, *adj.* First, former, prior, preceding, initial; east, eastern; before, in front of.

पूर्वक poorv úk, *adj.* Prior, before, preceding.

पूर्वकाल poorv-kál, *s. m.* Former time.

पूर्वकालीन poorv-ka-léen, *adj.* Ancient, belonging to former times.

पूर्वकृत poorv-krít, *adj.* Done formerly, or in a prior existence.

पूर्वगंगा poorv-gún-ga, *s. f.* The *Nermuda* river, formerly called the Ganges.

पूर्वज poor-vúj, *adj.* Born or produced before either in time or place; eastern, born in the east; elder. *s. m.* An elder brother.

पूर्वजा poorv-já, *s. m. pl.* The deified progenitors of mankind; ancestors, progenitors in general.

पूर्वदिक् poorv-dík, } *s. f.* The eastern
पूर्वदिश poorv-dísh, } region.

पूर्वदेश poorv-désh, *s. m.* The eastern country, or eastern part of India.

पूर्वदेह poorv déh, *s. m.* A former body, a prior existence.

पूर्वपक्ष poorv-púksh, *s. m.* A proposition, an assertion; the first part of an argument, to which assent or refutation is necessary; the first half of a lunar month.

पूर्वपर्वत poorv-púr-vut, *s. m.* The eastern mountain, behind which the sun is supposed to rise.

पूर्वफाल्गुनी poorv-phúl goonee, *s. f.* The eleventh lunar asterism; the first *Phulgoonee*, the twelfth *Nukshutr*, being termed *Oottura*, or subsequent: this asterism figured by a conch contains two stars, one of which is Leonis.

पूर्वभाद्रपदा póorv-bhadr-púd-a, *s. f.* The first of the two lunar asterisms, and twenty-sixth of the whole, containing two stars.

पूर्वरात्र poorv-rátr, *s. m.* The first part of the night.

पूर्वलक्षण poorv-lúkshun, *s. m.* Indication of something about to occur, as sickness, &c.

पूर्वशैल poorv-shyl, *s. m.* The eastern mountain, behind which the sun is supposed to rise.

पूर्वसन्ध्या poorv-sún-dhya, *s. f.* Dawn, daybreak.

पूर्व póor-va, *s. m.* A small village.

पूर्वफाल्गुनी póorva-phál-goonee, *s. f.* The eleventh lunar asterism.

पूर्वभाद्रपद póorva-bhadr-pud, *s. m.* The twenty-sixth lunar asterism.

पूर्वाभिमुख póorv-ábhi-mookh, *adj.* Facing the east.

पूर्वाभ्यास póorv-abhyás, *s. m.* Former practice, or experience.

पूर्वार्द्ध poorv-árddh, *s. m.* The first or east half of any thing.

पूर्वाषाढ़ा póorv-ashárha, *s. f.* The first of two constellations, each called *Asharha,* and the 20th of the lunar asterisms, containing two stars, of which one is Sagitarii.

पूर्वाह्न poorv-ánh, *s. m.* The first part of the day, the forenoon.

पूर्वी póor-vee, *adj.* Eastern, from the east; a kind of rice from the east or Bengal. *s. f.* A *raginee* sung before evening.

पूर्वोत्तर poorv-óttur, *s. m.* The north-east.

पूला póo-la, *s. m.* A bundle or truss of grass or straw. *Pooleh tuleh gooxran kurna (lit. To live under a bundle of straw),* implies a very destitute condition.

पूली póo·lee, *s. m.* A small bundle of any grass or straw, &c.

पूष poosh, *s. m.* The eighth mansion of the moon, comprising three stars in Cancer; the mulberry (*Morus Indica*).

पूस poos, *s. m.* The ninth solar month, the full moon of which is near *Pooshyuh,* three stars in Cancer.

पृक्का prik-ká, *s. f.* A gramineous plant (*Trigonella corniculata*).

पृच्छक prich-chhúk, *s. m.* An inquirer, an investigator, an inquisitive person.

पृच्छन prich-chhún, *s. m.* Asking, inquiring.

पृच्छा prich-chhá, *s. f.* Asking, questioning, a question or inquiry.

पृतना prit-ná, *s. f.* An army; a small army or division consisting of 243 elephants, as many chariots, 729 horse, and 1215 foot.

पृथक् pri-thúk, *adj.* Separate, apart. *adv.* Separately, severally.

पृथक्करण prithúk-kúrun, *s. m.* Separating, distinguishing.

पृथक्कृत prithúk-krít, *adj.* Separated, sundered, made distinct.

पृथक्त्व prithuk-twúh, *s. m.* Individuality, separateness, severalty.

पृथक्त्वचा prithúk-twúch-a, *s. f.* A plant, commonly called *Moorva (Sanseviera zeylanica).*

पृथक्पूर्णी prithúk-púrnee, *s. f.* A plant (*Hemionites cordifolia*).

पृथगात्मा prithúg-átma, *s. m.* Individualised spirit, or that of an individual, as detached from universal spirit or the soul of all.

पृथग्गुण prithug-góon, *adj.* Having distinct properties.

पृथग्विध prithug-vídh, *adj.* Various, multiform, diversified.

पृथ्वी príth-vee,
पृथिवी pri-thí-vee, } *s. f.* The earth.

पृथिवीतल pri·thi-vée-tul, *s. m.* The surface of the ground.

पृथिवीनाथ prithivée-nath,
पृथिवीपति prithivée-puti,
पृथिवीपाल prithivée-pal } *s. m.* A king, a sovereign, a ruler.

पृथु pri-thóo, *n. prop.* The fifth monarch of the solar dynasty in the second age; an ancient *Raja,* son of *Ven, Raja* of *Bettoor:* he was married to a form of the goddess *Lukshmee,* taught men to cultivate the earth, &c. *s. f.* A pungent seed (*Nigella Indica*); a medicinal substance, commonly called *Hingooputree.*

पृथूदर pri-thóo-dur, *adj.* Large-bellied, stout, corpulent. *s. m.* A ram.

पृथ्वी prith-vée, *s. f.* The earth; a pungent seed (*Nigella Indica*); a medicinal substance and condiment, perhaps the leaf of the asafœtida plant, *Hingooputree.*

पृथ्वीभर prith-vee-bhúr, *s. m.* A species of the *Atyasti* metre.

पृश्निका prísh-nik-a, *s. f.* An aquatic plant (*Pistia stratioites*).

पृश्निपर्णी príshni-púrnee, *s. f.* A plant (*Hemionites cordifolia: Hedysarum lagopodioides*).

पृष्ट prisht, *adj.* Asked, inquired.

पृष्ठ prishth, *s. m.* The back; the rear, the last, the back or hinder part of any thing.

पृष्ठदृष्टि prishth-dríshti, *s. m.* A bear, from looking behind him.

पेई pe-ée, *s. f.* A small basket, a portmanteau.

पें pen, *s. m.* An imitative sound.

पेंग peng, *s. f.* The exertion made by people in a swing, when two persons keep the swing in motion without assistance from by-standers. *s. m.* A bird (*Gracula chattareah*).

पेंजनी pénj-nee, *s. f.* Little bells fastened round the feet of pigeons and of children.

पेठ penth, *s. f.* A market.

पेंड pend, *s. f.* Pace, step ; a rising ground, an eminence.

पेंताना pen-tá-na, *s. m.* The foot of a bed, the side towards the feet.

पेंदा pén-da, *s. m.* The bottom (*of a vessel, box, pot, &c.*)

पेखना pékh-na, *s. m.* A play, farce, sham, comedy. *v. a.* To see.

पेखनिया pekh-ní-ya, *s. m.* A player, an actor.

पेचक péch-uk, ⎱ *s. m.* An owl.
पेचा péch-a, ⎰

पेचु péch-oo, *s. m.* An esculent root (*Arum colocasia*).

पेट pet, *s. m.* The belly ; the womb, pregnancy ; the bore (*of a gun, &c.*) ; cavity, capacity. *Pet ana,* To be purged. *Pet katna,* To pinch one's belly, to starve one's self ; to be griped. *Pet ka dook dena,* To starve. *Pet ka purda, s. m.* The omentum. *Pet ka panee nuh hilna,* is applied to the steady motion of a horse which does not agitate the rider. *Pet kee ag, s. f.* Maternal affection. *Pet kee ag boojhana,* To eat something. *Pet kee baten, s. f.* Bosom secrets. *Pet keh paon bahur nikalna,* To practise baseness or vitiousness. *Pet gurgurana,* To have borborygmi. *Pet girna,* To miscarry (*a female*), abortion, miscarriage. *Pet girana,* To cause an abortion. *Pet chulna,* or *chhootna,* To be purged, to have a diarrhœa or flux. *Pet julna,* To be very hungry. *Pet jaree hona,* To be fluxed, to be purged. *Pet dalna,* To procure abortion. *Pet dikhana,* To complain of poverty and hunger. *Pet pukna,* To burst with laughter. *Pet panee hona,* To be violently purged, to have watery stools. *Pet palna,* To be able to live decently ; to be selfish. *Pet peeth ek hona,* To be greatly emaciated. *Pet peeth butana,* To implore (?). *Pet ponchhun,* The last child of a woman. *Pet posoo, adj.* Glutton. *Pet phoolna,* To burst with laughter. *Pet burhana,* To eat voraciously ; to encroach on the share or rights of another. *Pet bandhna,* To eat less than one's appetite demands. *Pet-bhur, adv.* Bellyful. *Pet bhurna,* To fill one's belly ; to be satisfied. *Pet marna,* To commit suicide, to stab one's self. *Pet men pythna,* To worm one's self into the secrets of another, to become intimate. *Pet men lena,* To endure, have patience. *Pet rukhana,* To get with child. *Pet ruhna,* To be pregnant. *Pet lug jana,* To be starving with hunger. *Pet lug ruhna,* To be very hungry. *Petwalee, adj. f.* Pregnant. *Pet seh, adj.* Pregnant. *Pet seh hona,* To be pregnant. *Pet hurburana,* To have a griping or inclination to stool.

पेटक pét-uk, *s. m.* A basket for holding clothes, books, &c.

पेटा pét-a, ⎱ *s. f.* A basket, a large bas-
पेटी pét-ee, ⎰ ket.

2 R

पेटारा pet-á-ra, *s. m.* A large basket, a portmanteau.

पेटार्थी pet-ár-thee, ⎱ *adj.* Gluttonous, epi-
पेटार्थू pet-ár-thoo, ⎰ curean.

पेटिया péti-ya, *s. m.* A pension, daily food, board.

पेटी pét-ee, *s. f.* A belly-band, a girth ; a portmanteau ; a box, a tumbril, a case ; the thorax, chest. *Petee lurna,* or *-marna, v. a.* To copulate.

पेटू pét-oo, *adj.* Gluttonous, epicurean.

पेटौखा pet-óu-kha, *s. m.* A looseness, purging, flux.

पेठा pét-ha, *s. m.* A kind of gourd.

पेड़ per, *s. f.* A tree, a plant. *Per lugana,* To plant trees.

पेड़ना pér-na, *v. a.* To press (*oil by means of a mill*), to squeeze, to rack.

पेड़ा pér-a, *s. m.* A kind of sweetmeat made with curds ; a globular mass of leaven prepared for baking.

पेड़ी pér-ee, *s. f.* A kind of sweetmeat made with curds ; a kind of betel-leaf ; the indigo plant after being once cut ; the trunk of a tree.

पेड़ू pér-oo, *s. m.* The belly below the navel, the pubes.

पेंदा pén-da, *s. m.* The bottom (*of a vessel, box, pot, &c.*)

पेनी pén-ee, *adj. f.* Sharp.

पेम pem, *s. m.* Love, friendship.

पेमी pém-ee, *adj.* Affectionate, lover.

पेय péyuh, *s. m.* Water, milk. *adj.* Drinkable, drink.

पेयी peyée, *s. f.* A small basket, a portmanteau.

पेयूष peyóosh, ⎱ *s. m.* The milk of a cow
पेयूष peyós, ⎰ which has calved within seven days, biestings.

पेरू péroo, *s. m.* A turkey.

पेरोज per-ój, *s. m.* The turquoise.

पेल pel,
पेलउर pel-úr, ⎱ *s. m.* A testicle.
पेलड़ा pel-rá, ⎰

पेलना pél-na, *v. a.* To shove, to push ; to stuff, to cram ; to express, to squeeze out.

पेलपाल pel-pál, *part.* Shoving, pushing, &c.

पेला pél-a, *s. m.* A testicle ; fault, oppression ; a prop, a support.

पेलू pél-oo, *adj.* A wrestler.

पेबरी peó-ree, *s. f.* A kind of yellow colour (*said to be obtained from the urine of a cow, fed on* the flowers of Butea frondosa, or according to others, on the leaves of the mango tree).

पेवसी peó-see, *s. f.* The milk of a cow which has calved within seven days.

पेशाब pesh-áb, *s. m.* Urine. *Peshab-bund,* *s. m.* Strangury.

पेशी pésh-ee, *s. f.* Spikenard (*Valeriana jatamansi*).

पेषण pesh-ún, *s. m.* Reducing to dust or powder; a hand-mill, a stone and muller, any apparatus for grinding or pounding; a plant (*a sort of Euphorbia with three lobes, commonly called Tekanta-sij*).

पेषणी pesh-un-ée, *s. f.* A stone, slab, on which condiments, &c. are ground with a muller.

पे puy, *s. m.* Milk, water. *adv.* On, upon, over, at, to, nevertheless, yet. *conj.* But.

पेंचना pynch-na, *v. a.* To winnow.

पेंचा pynch-a, *s. m.* Return, retribution, a loan, repayment of a loan.

पेंजनी pynj-nee, *s. f.* Little bells fastened round the feet of pigeons and of children.

पेंड pynd, *s. f.* Pace, step; a rising ground, an eminence.

पेंडा pynd-a, *s. m.* A road, highway, path. *Pynda marna,* To stop a road; to rob in the road.

पेंताना pyn-tá-na, *s. m.* The foot of a bed, the side towards the feet.

पेंतालीस pyn-tá-lees, *adj.* Forty-five.

पेंतीस pyn-tées, *adj.* Thirty-five.

पेंसठ pyn-suth, *adj.* Sixty-five.

पेकड़ा py-kur-a, *s. m.* ⎫ Iron chains on a
पेकड़ी py-kur-ee, *s. f.* ⎭ culprit's legs, fetters; ornamental rings worn on the ankles.

पेकी py-kee, *s. m.* One who carries about a *hookka* for hire at a fair or in a camp.

पेगू py-góo, *s. m.* A sort of green-coloured stone (*brought from Pegu*).

पेज pyj, *s. m.* A vow, a promise. *Pyj kurna,* *v. a.* To make a vow.

पेठ pyth, *s. m.* A duplicate (*of a bill of exchange*); entrance, ingress, admission, access.

पेठना pyth-na, *v. n.* To penetrate, enter, rush or run into, pervade.

पेठालना py-thál-na, *v. a.* To force in, to make to penetrate, to thrust, to run in, to introduce, to insinuate.

पेढ़ी py-ree, *s. f.* A ladder, a staircase; a flight of steps. [an eminence.

पेंड pynd, *s. f.* Pace, step; a rising ground,

पेंडा pyn-da, *s. m.* A road, highway, path. *Pynda marna,* To stop a road; to rob in the road.

पतरा py-tur-a, *s. m.* Flourishing about before cudgelling, &c.

पेतला py-túl-a, *adj.* Shallow.

पैतृक py-trík, *adj.* Paternal, ancestral, belonging or relating to the father or to progenitors, hereditary, inherited from a father.

पैतृकभूमि pytrik-bhóomi, *s. f.* Father-land, the country of one's ancestors; a paternal estate.

पैत्तिक pyt-tík, *adj.* Biliary, bilious.

पैत्रिक py-trík, *adj.* Paternal, ancestral.

पैदल py-dúl, *adv.* On foot. *s. m.* Infantry.

पैन pyn, *s. m.* A reservoir of water; a rill.

पैना py-na, *s. m.* A goad. *adj. m.* Sharp.

पैनाना py-ná-na, *v. a.* To sharpen.

पैनाला py-ná-la, *s. m.* A gutter, a spout.

पैया py-ya, *s. m.* A wheel.

पयान py-yán, *s. m.* Departure.

पयाल py-yál, *s. f.* Straw.

पैर pyr, *s. m.* The foot.

पैरना pyr-na, *v. n.* To swim.

पैराई py-rá-ee, *s. f.* Place of swimming or distance over which it is necessary to swim; art of swimming; wages for teaching to swim.

पैराक py-rák, *s. m.* A swimmer.

पैराकी py-rá-kee, *s. f.* Act or art of swimming.

पैराना py-rá-na, *v. a.* To cause to swim.

पैराव py-ráv, *adj.* Beyond man's depth, where it is necessary to swim.

पैरी py-ree, *s. f.* An ornament worn on the legs.

पैल pyl, *n. prop.* A sage, the promulgator of the *Rik Ved.*

पैला py-la, *s. m.* A vessel for measuring grain.

पैवन्दीबेर py-wúndee-ber, *s. m.* An engrafted ber (*Zizyphus jujuba*).

पैशाच py-shách, *adj.* Infernal, demoniacal, relating or belonging to a *Pisach* or goblin. *s. m.* A mode of marriage, the ravishment of a girl by her lover.

पैशुन्य py-shóon-yuh, *s. m.* Depravity, wickedness.

पैसा py-sa, *s. m.* A copper coin, a *pice;* money, cash. *Pysa oorana,* To spend extravagantly; to take the money of another by theft or deceit. *Pysa khana,* To spend extravagantly, to waste; to subsist by wages or the produce of labour; to take bribes; to embezzle. *Pysa doobona,* To sink money, to lay out money without return. *Pysa doobna,* To be sunk (*money*). *Pysa phar phar kurna,* To turn the penny. *Pyseh lugana,* To lay out or expend money. *Pyseh-wala, adj.* Moneyed; worth one *pysa. Pyseh son durbar bundna,* To bribe, to give bribes.

पयसार py-sár, *s. m.* Access, ability, admission.

पोआ pó-a, *s. m.* A very young serpent; a nursling of any animal; a plant.

पोआना po-á-na, *v. a.* To warm by the sun or the steam of water, to bask.

पोईस po-ées, *interj.* Ho! holla! (*calling to people in the road to get out of the way*), have a care!

पोंकना pónk-na, *v. n.* To be fluxed.

पोंका pón-ka, *s. m.* The ship-worm (*Teredo navalis*).

पोंगा pón-ga, *s. m.* A blockhead; a sort of drum; a thin joint of bamboo. *adj.* Empty.

पोंछन pón-chhun, *s. m.* Wiping; a rag, &c. with which any thing is wiped; any thing thrown away after wiping.

पोंछना pónchh-na, *v. a.* To wipe.

पोंटा pón-ta, *s. m.* Snot.

पोंठी pón-thee, *s. f.* A kind of small fish (*Cyprinus chrysoparius*).

पोखर pó-khur, *s. m.* A pond, a lake.

पोट pot, *s. f.* A bundle, a ball, a package; a spout.

पोटगुल pot-gúl, *s. m.* A reed (*Arundo tibialis*); a sort of grass (*Saccharum spontaneum*).

पोटला pót-la, *s. m.* A large bundle.

पोटलिका pót-lik-a, *s. f.* A bundle or packet.

पोटली pót-lee, *s. f.* A bundle, a parcel.

पोटा pó-ta, *s. m.* An unfledged bird; the eyelid; the crop or craw (*of birds*); the stomach; the mucus of the nose, snot. *s. f.* A woman having a beard.

पोरहा pór-ha, *adj.* Strong, firm.

पोरहाई por-há-ee, *s. f.* Strength, firmness.

पोत pot, *s. m.* ⎤ The young of any ani-
पोती pó-tee, *s. f.* ⎦ mal.

पोत pot, *s. f.* A vessel, a ship, a boat. *s. m.* Nature, disposition, quality; glass beads, beads.

पोतकी pót-kee, *s. f.* A potherb (*Basella lucida*).

पोतुज po-túj, *s. m.* An animal that produces young at once without the intervention of any medium; elephants and some other animals being supposed in *Hindoo* physiology to carry the young without the aid of an ovarium or uterus.

पोतरा pót-ra, *s. m.* Baby-cloths, clouts.

पोतरी pót-ree, *s. f.* The afterbirth.

पोतना pót-na, *v. a.* To besmear, to plaster.

पोतरा pót-ra, *s. m.* Baby-cloths, clouts.

पोता pó-ta, *s. m.* Grandson, son's son.

पोतिया pó-ti-ya, *s. m.* A cloth worn at the time of bathing; a plaything.

पोती pó-tee, *s. f.* Grand-daughter, son's daughter.

पोथ poth, *s. m.* A small glass bead.

पोथकी póth-kee, *s. f.* Red pimples on the eyelids.

पोथा po-thá, *s. m.* A large book.

पोथी po-thée, *s. f.* A book.

पोदना pód-na, *s. m.* A bird (*Sylvia olivacea*).

पोदनी pód-nee, *s. f.* Female of *Podna*.

पोना pó-na, *v. a.* To string (*pearls*), to thread (*a needle*).

पोपनी póp-nee, *s. f.* A wind instrument (*of music*) made by children, of the seeds of mango and the leaves of the Borassus; any wind instrument.

पोपला póp-la, *adj.* One whose teeth are fallen out, toothless.

पोय póyuh, *s. f.* ⎤ A kind of vegetable
पोया póy-a, *s. m.* ⎦ (*Basella alba and rubra*).

पोर por, *s. f.* The space or interval between two joints or articulations (*of the body, or of a bamboo, sugar-cane, &c.*) *Por-por, adv.* Every joint.

पोरी pó-ree, *s. f.* A joint of bamboo, sugar-cane, &c.

पोरूआ po-róo-a, *s. m.* A joint or phalanx of the fingers; a joint of the tamarind.

पोलुक pó-luk, *s. m.* Straw bands at the ends of a staff, used with a *churkhee*, to frighten and restrain a furious elephant.

पोला pó-la, *adj.* Soft, hollow.

पोली pó-lee, *s. f.* A term of abuse, simpleton.

पोष posh, *s. m.* Nourishing, cherishing.

पोषक pó-shuk, *s. m.* A nourisher, cherisher.

पोषण po-shún, *s. m.* Nourishing, cherishing, breeding, rearing.

पोषना pósh-na, *v. a.* To breed, to rear, to foster, to nourish, to tame.

पोष्य pósh-yuh, *adj.* To be cherished or taken care of.

पोष्यपुत्र póshyuh-póotr, *s. m.* An adopted son.

पोष्यवर्ग póshyuh-vúrg, *s. m.* A class of persons or objects to be cherished, as parents, children, guests, and the sacred fire.

पोसना pós-na, *v. a.* To breed, rear, foster, nourish, tame.

पोह poh, *s. f.* Dawn of day.

पोहना póh-na, *v. a.* To make bread.

पौ pou, *s. f.* The one or ace on dice; a stand where water is provided for passengers. *Pou phutna*, To dawn (*morning*).

पौंडा póun-da, *s. m.* A kind of sugar-cane.

पौंसवन poun-súv-un, *s. m.* One of the *Sunskars* or essential ceremonies of the *Hindoo* religion; a religious observance, held when signs of a living conception take place.

पौढ़ना póurh-na, *v. n.* To repose, to lie down, to rest.

पौढ़ा pour-há, *adj.* Strong, firm; wide, broad.

पौढ़ाई pour-há-ee, *s. f.* Strength, firmness; breadth.

पौंड्रक pound-rúk, *s. m.* The pale straw-coloured species of sugar-cane; a man of a mixed caste, from the *Vysyuh* and female of the distiller caste, whose business it is to boil sugar.

पौंड्रवर्द्धन poundr-várddhun, *s. m.* A country, one of the divisions of central India (*Behar*).

पौत्तलिक póuttul-ik, *s. m.* A worshipper of idols.

पौत्र poutr, *s. m.* A son's son, a grandson.

पौत्रिक pou-trík, *adj.* Belonging to a son or a grandson.

पौत्री póutree, *s. f.* A grand-daughter, either in the male or female line, though more usually implying a son's daughter.

पौधा póu-dha, *s. m.* A young tree, plant, sapling.

पौन poun, *s. f.* Air, wind. *adj.* A quarter less (*than one or any given number*); three quarters.

पौनरुक्त poun-ur-óokt, *s. m.* Tautology.

पौनर्भव poun-ur-bhúvuh, *s. m.* One of the sons or heirs admitted by the old *Hindoo* law; the son of a twice-married woman.

पौनुब póu-nub, *s. m.* A spoon with holes
पौना póu-na,   in it like a colander for skimming with, &c.

पौने póu-neh, *adj.* One quarter less (*either of one, or of the aggregate number which may follow*).

पौर pour, *s. m.* A fragrant grass. *s. f.* A gate, a door.

पौरसख्य pour-us-khúh, *s. m.* Connexion or equality by inhabiting the same city for ten years, fellow-citizenship.

पौरणिक pou-ran-ík, *adj.* Of or belonging to the *Poorans. s. m.* A *Brahmun* well read in the *Poorans.*

पौरिया póu-ri-ya, *s. m.* A door-keeper, a porter.

पौरी póu-ree, *s. f.* A gate, a door.

पौरुष póu-roosh, *adj. subs. m.* The measure of a man, equal to the height to which he reaches with both arms elevated, and the fingers extended. *adj.* The property of manhood, virility, manliness; action, or action incidental to the state of humanity; semen virile.

पौरुषता pou-roosh-tá, *s. f.* Manhood, manly strength or spirit.

पौरोहित्य pou-ro-hit-yúh, *s. m.* The character or functions of family priest.

पौर्णमासी pourn-má-see, *s. f.* The day of
पौर्णिमा pour-ním-a,   full moon.

पौर्वदेहिक pourv-déhik, *adj.* Belonging to a former body or existence.

पौर्विक pour-vík, *adj.* Prior, primary, former.

पौली póu-lee, *s. f.* A gate, a door.

पौवा póu-wa, *s. m.* A quarter; a weight or measure of a quarter of a *seer.*

पौष poush, *s. m.* The ninth *Hindoo* solar month, the full moon of which is near *Pooshyuh*, three stars in Cancer, December-January.

पौष्करिणी poush-kur-ín-ee, *s. f.* A large pond or reservoir.

पौष्टिक poush-tík, *adj.* Preservative, protective, nutritive, &c.; nutritious, fattening.

पौष्प poushp, *adj.* Flowery, floral, relating or belonging to flowers, &c.

पौष्पक poushp-úk, *s. m.* The oxide of brass, considered as a collyrium.

पौष्पी póushp-ee, *s. f.* A name of *Palibothra.*

पौह pouh, *s. m.* A stand where water is kept ready for travellers.

प्याना py-ána,   *v. a.* To give or cause to
प्याओना py-áona,   drink, to water.

प्यार py-ár, *s. m. f.* Love, affection, fondness.

प्यारा py-ára, *adj. m.* Beloved. *Pyara janna*, To esteem.

प्यारी py-áree, *adj. f.* Beloved, pleasant.

प्याल py-al, *s. f.* A fruit (*Chironjia sapida*); straw.

प्यास py-ás, *s. f.* Thirst. *Pyas boojhana*, To quench thirst. *Pyas murna*, applied to thirst, which vanishes without drinking. *Pyas murna*, To suffer thirst. *Pyas lugna*, To be thirsty.

प्यासा py-ása, *adj. m.* Thirsty. *Pyaseh murna*, To be very thirsty.

प्यासी py-ásee, *adj. f.* Thirsty.

प्र pruh, *prep. in compos.* Forth, for, forward; off, abroad, away: (*English* pre-, for-, fore-).

प्रकट pruk-út, *adj.* Displayed, unfolded, manifest, apparent.

प्रकटित pruk-ut-ít, *adj.* Manifested, displayed; evident, apparent; opened, expanded.

प्रकटीकृत pruk-ut-ee-krít, *adj.* Made manifest, open or visible.

प्रकम्प pru-kúmp, *s. m.* Shaking, trembling.

प्रकम्पन pru-kúmp-un, *adj.* Trembling violently. *s. m.* A hell.

प्रकम्पमान prukump-mán, *adj.* Shaking, trembling violently.

प्रकर prúk-ur, *s. m.* Aloe wood (*Agallochum*).

प्रकरण pruk-ur-ún, *s. m.* An introduction, a prologue or prelude; a chapter, a section, a book, a place of pausing or stopping.

प्रकर्ष prukúrsh, *s. m.* (*In grammar*) The effect of the prefix प्र (*pruh*) upon roots.

प्रकाण्ड prukánd, *s. m.* The stem of a tree, the part between the root and the branches; excellence, happiness.

प्रकार prukár, *s. m.* Sort, kind, species; way, mode, method, manner.

प्रकाश prukásh, *adj.* Open, manifest, blown, expanded; famous, celebrated; public. *adv.* Openly, publicly. *s. m.* Sunshine, lustre, light; expansion, diffusion, manifestation; the word being equally applicable to physical or moral subjects, as the blowing of a flower, diffusion of celebrity, the publicity of an event, or the manifestation of a truth; publicity.

प्रकाशक prukash-úk, *adj.* What irradiates, what makes open or apparent, &c. *s. m.* An illuminator, an expounder, an illustrator.

प्रकाशता prukash-tá, *s. f.* Manifestation, visibility; luminousness.

प्रकाशन prukash-ún, *s. m.* Illuminating, giving light; making clear or manifest.

प्रकाशमान prukash-mán, *adj.* Splendid, brilliant, radiant.

प्रकाशित prukash-ít, *adj.* Evident, apparent, manifest, visible; published, promulgated.

प्रकाशी prukásh-ee, *s. m.* A discoverer.

प्रकीर्ण prukéern, *adj.* Spread abroad, published, promulgated; expanded, open. *s. m.* A *Chowree*, a cow-tail used as a fan; a chapter, a section.

प्रकीर्ति prukéerti, *s. f.* Fame, celebrity; declaration.

प्रकीर्तित prukéert-tit, *adj.* Declared, explained, said, revealed; celebrated, renowned.

प्रकुपित prukóop-it, *adj.* Enraged, incensed.

प्रकृत prukrít, *adj.* Made, completed, accomplished.

प्रकृति prúkriti, *s. f.* Nature; in philosophy, the passive or material cause of the world, as opposed to the active or spiritual; and in mythology, a goddess, the personified will of the Supreme in the creation, identified with *Maya* or illusion, and in an especial manner the prototype of the female sex: in some systems *Prukriti* is considered the same with the Supreme Being; the natural state or condition of any thing; a form of metre, consisting of a stanza of four lines, each line containing twenty-one syllables. (*In anatomy*), Temperament, the predominance of one of the humours at the time of generation.

प्रकृतितुरल prúkriti-túrul, *adj.* Volatile, fickle.

प्रकृतिस्थ prukrit-ísth, *adj.* Natural, genuine, unmixed; inherent, innate.

प्रकृष्ट prukrisht, *adj.* Chief, principal, preeminent.

प्रकृष्टत्व prukrisht-twúh, *adj.* Eminence, superiority.

प्रकोप prukóp, *s. m.* Irritation, provocation, enraging.

प्रकोपन prukóp-un, *s. m.* Irritating, provoking.

प्रकोपित prukop-ít, *adj.* Irritated, provoked.

प्रक्रम prukrúm, *s. m.* Proceeding, going; leisure, opportunity.

प्रक्रिया prúkriya, *s. f.* Bearing royal insignia.

प्रक्षालन prukshá-lun, *s. m.* Cleaning, washing.

प्रक्षालित pruksha-lít, *adj.* Washed, cleansed.

प्रक्षिप्त prukshípt, *adj.* Thrown, cast, hurled.

प्रक्षीण prukshéen, *adj.* Decayed, wasting.

प्रखर prukhúr, *adj.* Very hot or acrid.

प्रख्यात prukhyát, *adj.* Celebrated, famous, notorious.

प्रख्याति prukhyáti, *s. f.* Publicity, notoriety; praise, eulogium, fame.

प्रगट prug-út, *adj.* Obvious, notorious, public, issued out, apparent, manifest, visible.

प्रगटता prugut-tá, *s. f.* Visibility, publicity, manifestation.

प्रगटना prugut-ná, *v. n.* To issue forth, to become manifest, to appear.

प्रगमन prugúm-un, *s. m.* Progress, advance.

प्रगल्भ prugúlbh, *adj.* Bold, confident; prompt, ready; resolute, energetic; strong, able.

प्रगल्भता prugulbh-tá, *s. f.* Energy, resolution; confidence, boldness; power, eminence.

प्रगाढ prugárh, *adj.* Much, excessive; hard, difficult; hard, firm. *s. m.* Pain, privation, penance.

प्रगोपण prugop-ún, *s. m.* Protection, preservation, salvation.

प्रग्रह prugrúhun, *s. m.* Taking, seizing, assuming.

प्रघट prughút, *adj.* Obvious, notorious, public, issued out, apparent, manifest, visible.

प्रघटी prughút-ee, *s. f.* A mould in which silver or gold is cast previous to working it; apparency, clearness.

प्रघन prughún, *s. m.* A sort of bean (*Phaseolus mungo*).

प्रचण्ड pruchúnd, *adj.* Excessively hot or burning; intolerable, insupportable; wrathful, passionate; violent, strong. *s. m.* A sort of Nerium with white flowers.

प्रचण्डमूर्ति pruchúnd-móortti, *s. m.* A tree (*Tapia cratæva*).

प्रचरित pruchúr-it, *adj.* Pursued, practised (*as an art or business*).

प्रचलत pruchul-út, *adj.* Prevailing, circulating, being customary or current; being recognised (*as authority or law, &c.*)

प्रचलन pruchúl-un, *s. m.* Circulating, being customary or current.

प्रचलित pruchúl-it, *adj.* Current, customary, circulating, prevailing; recognised, received (*as authority or law, &c.*)

प्रचार pruchár, *s. m.* Custom, usage; conduct; currency; appearance, manifestation.

प्रचित pruchít, *s. m.* A species of metre.

प्रचुर pruchóor, *adj.* Much, many.

प्रचेल pruchél, *s. m.* A yellow fragrant wood.

प्रचोदन pruchódun, *s. m.* Saying, enjoining, prescribing; a rule or law; sending, directing.

प्रचोदित pruchodít, *adj.* Prescribed, directed; sent.

प्रचोदिनी pruchódin-ee, *s. f.* A prickly night-shade (*Solanum jacquini*).

प्रच्छना pruch-chhun-á, *s. f.* Asking, addressing, inviting.

प्रच्छद pruch-chhúd, *s. m.* A wrapper, a cover.

प्रच्छन्न pruch-chhún, *adj.* Covered, clothed; unavowed, disguised; private, concealed, secret. *s. m.* A private door within a house; a lattice, a loop-hole; any private door.

प्रच्युत pruchyót, *adj.* Fallen from, deviated from.

प्रजा prúj-a, *s. f.* Progeny, offspring; people, subjects; a subject, tenant, renter.

प्रजाधर्म pruja-dhúrm, *s. m.* The duty of children or of subjects.

प्रजापति pruja-púti, *s. m.* A name of

Bruhm; the epithet common to ten divine personages, who were first created by *Bruhm*; some authorities make them only seven in number; others reduce them to three; and others make them twenty-one; king, sovereign, lord of subjects, prince; father; son-in-law, daughter's husband; potter.

प्रजाहित pruja-hít, *adj.* Favourable or good for children or subjects, &c., kind to them, useful to them, &c.

प्रजीवन pru-jée-vun, *s. m.* Livelihood, subsistence.

प्रज्ञ prúgyuh, *adj.* Wise, learned.

प्रज्ञा prug-yá, *s. f.* A clever or sensible woman; understanding, wisdom, knowledge.

प्रज्ञात prug-yát, *adj.* Known, understood; famous, notorious.

प्रज्ञान prug-yán, *adj.* Wise, learned. *s. m.* Knowledge, wisdom.

प्रज्ञावान् prug-ya-wán, *adj.* Wise, intelligent.

प्रज्वलित prujwúlit, *adj.* Blazing, radiant.

प्रण prun, *s. m.* Promise, agreement, vow, resolution.

प्रणति prúnuti, *s. f.* Salutation, reverence, obeisance, courtesy.

प्रणय prunúy, *s. m.* Affection, friendly or fond regard; acquaintance; asking, begging; affectionate solicitation; final emancipation or beatitude; trust, confidence; reverence, obeisance.

प्रणयी prunuyée, *adj.* Affectionate, kind; intimate, familiar. *s. m.* A husband or lover.

प्रणव prunúv, } *s. m.* The mystical
प्रणवक prun-wúk, } name of the deity,
or syllable Om.

प्रणाद prun-ád, *s. m.* A disease of the ear, a noise or buzzing in the ear from thickening of the membranes, &c.

प्रणाम prun-ám, *s. m.* Respectful or reverential salutation, addressed especially to a Brahmun or deity.

प्रणाल prun-ál, *s. m.* } An issue from a
प्रणाली prun-ál-ee, *s. f.* } pond, a drain,
a gutter, a water-course, a conduit.

प्रणाश prunásh, *s. m.* Loss, destruction.

प्रणाशी prunáshee, *adj.* Destroying.

प्रणिधान prunidhán, *s. m.* Great effort, stress, energy; profound religious meditation; access, entrance.

प्रणिपतन prúni-pútun, *s. m.* Saluting, bowing or doing homage to.

प्रणिपात pruni-pát, *s. m.* Salutation, reverence, obeisance.

प्रणी prún-ee, *adj.* Resolute.

प्रतल prutúl, *s. m.* One of the seven principal divisions of the lower regions.

प्रतान prut-án, *s. m.* A disease, fainting, epilepsy.

प्रताप prutáp, *s. m.* Majesty, dignity, glory, the possession of rank and power, the high spirit arising from the possession of these; spirit, energy; splendour, brilliancy.

प्रतापन prutáp-un, *s. m.* A hell.

प्रतापवान् prutap-wán, *adj.* Majestic, glorious, potent.

प्रतापस prutap-ús, *s. m.* A species of gigantic Asclepias with white flowers.

प्रतापी prutáp-ee, *adj.* Shining, splendid; dignified, powerful; glorious, potent.

प्रतारक prutáruk, *s. m.* A cheat.

प्रतारण prutár-un, *s. m.* } Fraud, cheating,
प्रतारणा prutar-ná, *s. f.* } deceit, overreaching, trick.

प्रतारित prutar-ít, *adj.* Cheated, deceived, tricked.

प्रति prúti, *prep.* Again, against, back again, for, in exchange, instead, each.

प्रतिकर्म pruti-kúrma, *s. m.* Retaliation, requital; remedy, redress.

प्रतिकार pruti-kár, *s. m.* Revenge, retaliation; remedying, counteracting.

प्रतिकूल pruti-kóol, *adj.* Contrary, adverse, cross-grained, reverse, inverted; contradictory, cross, perverse.

प्रतिकूलता pruti-kool-tá, *s. f.* Opposition, hostility.

प्रतिक्रिया pruti-kríya, *s. f.* Return, requital, retaliation; remedying, counteracting.

प्रतिक्षण pruti-kshún, *adv.* Momentarily, every moment.

प्रतिगर्जन pruti-gúr-jun, *adj.* Echoing, reverberating.

प्रतिग्रह pruti-grúh, *s. m.* Proper donation to *Brahmuns*, whatever is a fit present to a *Brahmun* at suitable periods; the acceptance of such a gift.

प्रतिघात pruti-ghát, *s. m.* A return blow, repulse, rebound; warding off a blow; preventing, prohibiting.

प्रतिघातन pruti-ghát-un, *s. m.* Killing, slaughter.

प्रतिघाती pruti-ghát-ee, *adj.* Repelling; repulsing; hostile, opposed to.

प्रतिचिन्तन pruti-chíntun, *s. m.* Thinking repeatedly, considering, meditating upon.

प्रतिछाया pruti-chháya, *s. f.* An image, a statue, a bas-relief, a picture.

प्रतिजिह्वा pruti-jívha, *s. f.* The uvula, or soft palate.

प्रतिजीवन pruti-jéevun, *s. m.* Resuscitation.

प्रतिज्ञा pruti-gyá, *s. f.* Promise, agreement, engagement, assent; admission, acknowledgment. (*In logic*) The proposition, the assertion to be proved.

प्रतिज्ञात prutig-yát, *adj.* Promised, agreed; admitted, acknowledged; propounded, asserted.

प्रतिज्ञापत्रक prutigyá-pútruk, *s. m.* A bond, a written contract.

प्रतिताल pruti-tál, *s. m.* A kind of air or melody.

प्रतिदान pruti-dán, *s. m.* The return or redelivery of a deposit; barter, exchange; giving back or in return for.

प्रतिदिन pruti-dín, *adv.* Day by day, every day.

प्रतिदिशा pruti-dísh-a, *adv.* Every where, all around.

प्रतिध्वनि pruti-dhwúni, *s. f.* } Echo, an
प्रतिध्वान pruti-dhwán, *s. m.* } echo, reiterated or re-
प्रतिनाद pruti-nád, *s. m.* } peated sound, resonance.

प्रतिनिधि prúti-nídhi, *s. m.* A resemblance of a real form, an image, a statue, a picture, &c.; a surety; a substitute.

प्रतिनिश pruti-nísh, *adv.* By night, every night.

प्रतिपत pruti-pút, } *s. f.* The first day of
प्रतिपद् pruti-púd, } a lunar fortnight, the first of the moon's increase or wane; rank, consequence.

प्रतिपत्ति pruti-pútti, *s. f.* Fame, reputation; knowledge, determination, ascertainment.

प्रतिपद् pruti-púd, *adj.* or *adv.* Step by step, at each step; continually, every moment.

प्रतिपन्न pruti-punn, *adj.* Known, understood, ascertained, determined.

प्रतिपादन pruti-pádun, *s. m.* Gift, donation; ascertaining, determining, rendering clear or intelligible.

प्रतिपालक pruti-pá-luk, *adj.* Who or what protects or defends. *s. m.* A king; a protector, a cherisher, a patron.

प्रतिपालन pruti-pál-un, *s. m.* Protecting, defending, cherishing, patronising, protection, fostering, rearing, breeding.

प्रतिपालना pruti-pálna, *v. a.* To preserve, to keep, to cherish.

प्रतिपुरुष pruti-póo-roosh, *adv.* Every man, man by man.

प्रतिपूजक pruti-póojuk, *s. m.* A reverer, one who does homage.

प्रतिपूजन pruti-póojun, *s. m.* Exchange of civilities, mutual obeisance or reverence; offering homage or respect.

प्रतिप्रसव **pruti-prúsuv**, *s. m.* Precept for an act which under other circumstances is forbidden.

प्रतिफल **pruti-phúl**, *s. m.* Return, requital, retaliation.

प्रतिबन्ध **pruti-búndh**, *s. m.* Obstacle, impediment.

प्रतिबन्धक **prúti-búndhuk**, *adj.* Impeding, obstructing, an obstructer or opposer. *s. m.* An impediment.

प्रतिबिम्ब **pruti-bímb**, *s. m.* An image or picture; the reflection of an image or figure from a mirror.

प्रतिभय **pruti-bhúy**, *adj.* Formidable, fearful, frightful. *s. m.* Fear.

प्रतिभा **pruti-bhá**, *s. f.* Understanding, intellect, especially as opening or expanding; sharpness, brilliancy of conception; light, splendour.

प्रतिभाव **pruti-bháo**, *s. m.* Corresponding character or disposition.

प्रतिभिन्न **pruti-bhínn**, *adj.* Separated, divided.

प्रतिभू **pruti-bhóo**, *s. m.* A surety.

प्रतिभेदन **pruti-bhéd-un**, *s. m.* Piercing, cutting, penetrating; separating, dividing.

प्रतिमा **prútima**, *s. f.* A resemblance, a figure, an image, a likeness, a picture; an idol, a statue.

प्रतिमान **prutim-án**, *s. m.* Resemblance, an image, a picture.

प्रतिमास **pruti-más**, *adv.* Every month, monthly.

प्रतिमूषिका **pruti-móoshik-a**, *s. f.* A kind of rat.

प्रतियोग **pruti-yóg**, *s. m.* Opposition, contradiction, controversy; co-operation, association.

प्रतियोगिता **prúti-yogitá**, *s. f.* Mutual co-operation; opposition.

प्रतियोगी **pruti-yógee**, *s. m.* An opponent; a partner, an associate.

प्रतिरक्षण **pruti-rúkshun**, *s. m.* Preserving.

प्रतिरात्र **pruti-rátr**, *s. m.* Every night.

प्रतिरूप **pruti-róop**, *s. m.* A picture, an image, the counterpart of any real form.

प्रतिरोध **pruti-ródh**, *s. m.* Opposition, impediment.

प्रतिरोधक **pruti-ródhuk**, } *s. m.* A thief, a
प्रतिरोधी **pruti-ródhee**, } robber.

प्रतिलुम्भ **pruti-lúmbh**, *s. m.* Censure, reviling, abuse.

प्रतिलोम **pruti-lóm**, *adj.* Left, not right; reverse, inverted; low, vile, base, depraved.

प्रतिवचन **pruti-vúch-un**, *s. m.* A reply, an answer, a rejoinder; an echo.

प्रतिवाक्य **pruti-vákyuh**, *s. m.* A reply, an answer.

प्रतिवाच् **pruti-vách**, *s. f.* An answer, a reply.

प्रतिवाणि **pruti-váni**, *s. f.* An answer; a rejoinder.

प्रतिवादी **pruti-vádee**, *s. m.* A defendant, a respondent.

प्रतिवासी **pruti-vásee**, *adj.* A neighbour, neighbouring.

प्रतिविम्ब **pruti-vímb**, *s. m.* A resemblance or counterpart of real forms, as a picture, an image, a shadow, &c.

प्रतिविषा **pruti-vísh-a**, *s. f.* A plant (*Betula*).

प्रतिशङ्का **pruti-shúnka**, *s. f.* Constant fear or doubt.

प्रतिश्या **pruti-shyá**, *s. f.* Catarrh.

प्रतिषिद्ध **pruti-shíddh**, *adj.* Forbidden, prohibited.

प्रतिषेध **pruti-shédh**, *s. m.* Prohibition, forbidding, exception, contradiction.

प्रतिष्ठ **prutíshth**, *adj.* Famous.

प्रतिष्ठा **prutish-thá**, *s. f.* Fame, celebrity; a form of metre, consisting of a stanza of four lines, of four syllables each; consecration of a monument erected in honour of a deity, or of the image of a deity; endowment of a temple, portioning or marrying a daughter, &c.

प्रतिष्ठान **prutish-thán**, *s. m.* Site, situation; the capital of the early kings of the lunar dynasty, opposite to *Allahabad*; the capital of *Sáliváhan*, in the *Dukhin*.

प्रतिष्ठित **prutish-thít**, *adj.* Famous, celebrated; consecrated; endowed, portioned; placed, situated; established, fixed.

प्रतिसर **pruti-súr**, *s. m.* Cicatrizing or healing, as a sore; a form of magic or incantation; a string worn round the hand at nuptials.

प्रतिसर्ग **pruti-súrg**, *s. m.* The portion of a *Pooran*, which treats of the destruction and renovation of the world; secondary creation, or the creation of the world by the agency of *Bruhma*, and other divine beings as the agents of one Supreme Being.

प्रतिस्पर्द्धा **prúti-spúrddha**, *s. f.* Emulation, rivalry, the wish or effort to excel or overcome.

प्रतिस्पर्द्धी **pruti-spúrddhee**, *adj.* Envious, emulous, a rival; refractory, rebellious.

प्रतिस्याय **prúti-syáyuh**, *s. m.* Catarrh.

प्रतिहत **pruti-hút**, *adj.* Disappointed; opposed, obstructed; fallen, overthrown.

प्रतिहति **pruti-húti**, *s. f.* Disappointment.

प्रतिहास **pruti-hás**, *s. m.* A shrub (*Nerium odorum*).

प्रतिहिंसा pruti-hínsa, *s. f.* Retaliation, revenge.

प्रतीक prut-éek, *adj.* Contrary, adverse; inverted, reversed, against the natural order or state. *s. m.* A limb, a member; a part, a portion.

प्रतीकार prut-ee-kár, *s. m.* Revenge, retaliation; obviating, correcting; remedying, administering medicines.

प्रतीक्षक prut-éekshuk, *adj.* Expecting; looking at.

प्रतीक्षण prut-eekshún, *s. m.* Looking to or at, considering, referring to; respecting; expecting, waiting for.

प्रतीक्षा prut-éeksha, *s. f.* Reference, regard to, consideration, looking to or at; hope, expectation.

प्रतीक्षी prut-éekshee, *adj.* Expecting, looking or waiting for.

प्रतीची prut-éechee, *s. f.* The west quarter.

प्रतीचीन prut-éecheen, } *adj.* West, western.
प्रतीच्य prut-éechyuh, }

प्रतीत prut-éet, *adj.* Famous, celebrated, renowned; known. *s. f.* Faith, confidence, trust. *Pruteet kurna,* To examine; to believe; to trust.

प्रतीति prut-éeti, *s. f.* Knowledge, understanding; fame, notoriety.

प्रतीयमान prut-eeyumán, *adj.* Being believed or trusted.

प्रतीर prutéer, *s. m.* A shore or bank.

प्रतीवाप prut-eeváp, *s. m.* Calcining or fluxing metals; throwing one substance into another to alter its form or state; adding any thing to a medicine during or after decoction; a public danger or calamity, as a plague, &c.

प्रतूनी prut-óo-nee, *s. f.* Pain shooting from the rectum along the bowels.

प्रत्यक्पर्णी prut-yuk-púrnee, } *s. f.* A
प्रत्यक्पुष्पी prut-yuk-póoshp-ee, } plant (*Achyranthes aspera*).

प्रत्यक्श्रेणी prut-yuk-shrénee, *s. f.* A plant, commonly called *Duntee*; a plant (*Salvinia cucullata*).

प्रत्यक्ष prut-yúksh, *adj.* Perceptible, perceivable, present, cognizable by any of the organs of sense.

प्रत्यक्षदर्शन prut-yúksh-dúrshun, *s. m.* A witness, an eye-witness.

प्रत्यक्षप्रमाण prut-yúksh-prumán, *s. m.* Ocular or visible proof.

प्रत्यक्षी prut-yúkshee, *adj.* Seeing, perceiving, consciousness of what is perceptible.

प्रत्यवेक्षित prutyúkshee-krít, *adj.* Manifested, displayed, made present or visible.

प्रत्यङ्ग prut-yúng, *s. m.* An organ of perception. *adv.* On the body, or the limbs severally.

प्रत्यनन्तर prut-yúnun-tur, *adv.* Next in succession.

प्रत्यन्त prut-yúnt, *adj.* Bordering, skirting, contiguous. *s. m.* The country of the *Mlechchhus* or savages.

प्रत्यय prut-yúy, *s. m.* Trust, faith, belief, confidence; knowledge, apprehension; an affix to roots and words forming derivatives and inflections.

प्रत्ययित prut-yuyít, *adj.* Trusted, confidential.

प्रत्ययी prut-yuyée, *adj.* Trusting, believing, having faith in.

प्रत्यवाय prut-yuváyuh, *s. m.* Disappearance, either of what exists, or non-production of what does not exist.

प्रत्यश्मन् prut-yúshm-un, *s. m.* Red chalk.

प्रत्यहम् prut-yuhúm, *adv.* Day by day, every day.

प्रत्यादिष्ट prut-ya-dísht, *adj.* Removed, set aside; informed, apprised; warned, cautioned; declared (*as from heaven*).

प्रत्यादेश prut-ya-désh, *s. m.* Information, apprising, informing; warning, caution; heavenly annunciation or declaration.

प्रत्याशा prut-yá-sha, *s. f.* Hope, expectation, desire.

प्रत्याशी prut-yá-shee, *adj.* Hoping, expecting.

प्रत्याहार prut-ya-hár, *s. m.* (*In grammar*) Combination of two or more letters of the alphabet to form a class of letters.

प्रत्युक्ति prut-yóokti, *s. f.* Answer, reply.

प्रत्युत्तर prut-yóottur, *s. m.* A rejoinder, a reply to an answer, an answer.

प्रत्युत्थान prut-yootthán, *s. m.* Rising from a seat, as a mark of respect.

प्रत्युत्पन्न prut-yoot-púnn, *adj.* Reproduced, regenerated; (*in arithmetic*) multiplied. *s. m.* Multiplication; the product of a sum in multiplication.

प्रत्युद्गमन prut-yood-gúmun, *s. m.* Rising from a seat as a mark of respect, &c.; going forth or out, going to meet any one, &c.

प्रत्युपकार prut-yoop-kár, *s. m.* Requital of aid or assistance, mutual assistance.

प्रत्युपकारी prut-yoop-káree, *adj.* Requiting a favour or kindness.

प्रत्यूष prut-yóosh, *s. m.* The morning, dawn, day-break.

प्रत्येक prut-yék, *adv.* Singly, one by one, one at a time.

प्रथम prúthum, *adj.* First, prior, before, initial; chief, principal.

प्रथमसाहस prúthum-sáhus, *s. m.* The first or lowest degree of fine or punishment.

प्रथा pruthá, *s. f.* Fame, celebrity.

प्रथित prut-hít, *adj.* Famous, celebrated; made known, declared.

प्रथिति pruthí-ti, *s. f.* Celebrity, notoriety.

प्रथुक pru-thóok, *s. m.* The young of any animal.

प्रदक्षिण pru-dúkshin, *adj.* Reverential salutation, by circumambulating a person or object, keeping the right side towards them.

प्रदर prud-úr, *s. m.* A disease of woman (*Menorrhagia*).

प्रदर्शक pru-dúrsh-uk, *s. m.* A teacher, an expounder; a prophet.

प्रदर्शन pru-dúrsh-un, *s. m.* Shewing; explaining generally, not exclusively; explaining or specifying; prophecying.

प्रदर्शित pru-dúrsh-it, *adj.* Mentioned, specified; shewn; prophecied.

प्रदान prudán, *s. m.* A gift, donation.

प्रदिक् prudík, } *s. f.* Intermediate point
प्रदिश prudísh, } of the compass, or half quarter, as north-east, south-west, &c.

प्रदीप prudéep, *s. m.* A lamp.

प्रदीपन prudéep-un, *s. m.* A sort of mineral poison, of a red colour, and caustic operation.

प्रदेश prudésh, *s. m.* A place in general, a country, a district, &c.; a foreign country, abroad.

प्रदेह prudéh, *s. m.* Unguent, unction.

प्रदोष prudósh, *s. m.* Evening, the first part of the night; fault, offence, defect, transgression.

प्रधान prudhán, *s. m.* Nature, the natural state of any thing, or the cause of the material world; the Supreme God; chief, principal; the first companion of a king, his minister, his eunuch, or confidant, &c.; a president, courtier, noble, leader, chief, minister or counsellor of state.

प्रधानता prudhán-ta, *s. f.* Excellence, superiority, supremacy.

प्रधानधातु prudhán-dhátoo, *s. m.* Semen virile.

प्रधानमन्त्री prudhán-múntree, *s. m.* Prime minister.

प्रधानोत्तम prudhán-óttum, *adj.* Eminent, illustrious.

प्रध्वंस prudhwúns, *s. m.* Destruction, loss.

प्रध्वंसी prudhwúnsee, *adj.* Destroying, annihilating.

प्रणाम prunám, *s. m.* Salutation, bow, obeisance.

प्रणाल prun-ál, *s. m.* } A water-course, a
प्रणाली prun-álee, *s. f.* } canal; a gutter, a drain, a conduit.

प्रपञ्च prupúnch, *s. m.* Opposition; delusion, deceit, trick or fraud, imposition, treachery, artifice; prolixity, copiousness, in style or composition; error, illusion.

प्रपञ्चित prupunch-ít, *adj.* Erring, mistaken; tricked, deceived, beguiled; declared fully, explained, treated at length.

प्रपञ्ची prupúnch-ee, *adj.* Insidious, fraudulent, artful.

प्रपलायन prupuláyun, *s. m.* Flight, running away. [ed.

प्रपलायित prupulayít, *adj.* Routed, defeat-

प्रपलायी prupulayée, *s. m.* A fugitive, one who deserts his cause.

प्रपितामह prupíta-múhuh, *s. m.* A paternal great grandfather.

प्रपितामही prupíta-múhee, *s. f.* A paternal great grandmother.

प्रपुन्नाड prupoonár, *s. m.* A sort of Cassia (*C. tora*).

प्रपुन्ना prupóon-na, *s. f.* A sort of grass (*Hedysarum alhaji*).

प्रपूरिका prupóo-rik-a, *s. f.* A prickly nightshade (*Solanum Jacquini*).

प्रपौण्डरीक prupound-réek, *s. m.* A small herbaceous plant, used in medicine, and as a perfume, commonly called *Poonderya*; in medicine it forms the basis of applications to ulcers and bad eyes.

प्रपौत्र prupóutr, *s. m.* A great grandson.

प्रपौत्री prupóutree, *s. f.* A great granddaughter.

प्रफुल्ल pruphóoll, *adj.* Blown, as a flower; smiling; glad, pleased; shining.

प्रफुल्लनयन pruphóoll-nyun, *adj.* Having full or sparkling eyes.

प्रफुल्लवदन pruphooll-vúdun, *adj.* Having a cheerful or smiling countenance, looking gay or happy.

प्रफुल्लित pruphoollít, *adj.* Blooming, in blossom; gay, lively, cheerful.

प्रबन्ध prubúndh, *s. m.* Continuous application or action, continuance, uninterruptedness; a connected discussion, or narrative; a kind of song; style, composition (*of a discourse*).

प्रबन्धकल्पना prubúndh-kúlp-na, *s. f.* A feigned story, a work of imagination, whether founded in fact or not.

प्रबल prubúl, *adj.* Strong, powerful, predominant, prevalent, violent.

प्रबाल prubál, *s. m.* Coral.

प्रवास prubás, *s. m.* Travelling, journey, journeying, sojourning in a foreign country, abroad.

प्रवासी prubásee, *s. m.* A traveller.

प्रवाह prubáh, *s. m.* Stream, flood, flow, current, tide; breadth of a river.

प्रवीण prubéen, *adj.* Skilful, intelligent, accomplished, knowing, clever.

प्रवीनता prubeentá, *s. f.* Skill, accomplishment, cleverness, knowledge.

प्रबुद्ध prubóoddh, *adj.* Wise, learned.

प्रवेश prubésh, *s. m.* Entrance, admittance, access.

प्रवेशी prubéshee, *adj.* Penetrating.

प्रबोध prubódh, *s. m.* Vigilance, wakefulness, active or vigilant state of being; intellect, understanding; knowledge, wisdom; sense, consciousness; demonstration, consolation, persuasion; awaking, either from ignorance or sleep.

प्रबोधन prubodhún, *s. m.* Awakening, arousing, exciting, reviving; instructing; persuasion, persuading, production of conviction.

प्रबोधिता prubodhit-á, *s. f.* A species of the *Utijugutee* metre.

प्रभुव prubhúvuh, *adj.* Born, produced; superior, powerful; the operative cause, or immediate origin of being, as the father or mother, &c.

प्रभा prubhá, *s. f.* Light, radiance, splendour.

प्रभाकर prubha-kúr, *s. m.* The sun; the moon.

प्रभाकीट prubha-kéet, *s. f.* The fire-fly.

प्रभान्जन prubhan-jún, *s. m.* A tree (*Hyperanthera morunga*).

प्रभात prubhát, *s. m.* Morning, dawn, daybreak.

प्रभाती prubhát-ee, *adj.* Sung in a tune (*or raginee*) peculiar to the morning.

प्रभान prubhán, *s. m.* Light, radiance, shining.

प्रभाव prubháo, *s. m.* Majesty, dignity, magnanimity, high spirit; power, strength, influence; spirit.

प्रभास prubhás, *s. m.* A place of pilgrimage, in the west of India.

प्रभू prubhóo, *s. m.* Strong, able; always, eternal; a superior, an owner, a proprietor, a master or mistress, &c. *s. m.* A master, a lord, principal.

प्रभुता prubhoo-tá, *s. f.* Greatness, power, government, supremacy, lordship or sovereignty, superiority, influence.

प्रभुभक्त prubhoo-bhúkt, *adj.* Faithful, devoted.

प्रभृति prúbhriti, *s. f.* Manner, kind; etcetera, others, rest, remainder (*in composition*).

प्रभेद prubhéd, *s. m.* Kind, sort, difference.

प्रमुग्न prumúgn, *adj.* Immersed, drowned.

प्रमथा prumuthá, *s. f.* Yellow myrobalan (*Terminalia chebula*).

प्रमथालय prúmuth-áluy, *s. m.* Hell, or abode of pain.

प्रमद prumúd, *adj.* Mad, intoxicated, figuratively with passion or literally with liquor; impassioned. *s. m.* Joy, pleasure, delight, rapture.

प्रमदा prumud-á, *s. f.* A woman, a handsome woman.

प्रमा prum-á, *s. f.* True knowledge, or knowledge exempt from all error; consciousness, perception.

प्रमाण prum-án, *s. m.* Cause, motive; limit; proof, testimony, authority, verification, attestation; instance, example; measure, quantity; detail; a scripture, a work of sacred authority. *adj.* Authentic, actual, substantial, real, approved of, admissible, agreeable, acceptable. *Pruman churhna*, To rise to a high rank.

प्रमाणपूरुष prumán-póoroosh, *s. m.* An umpire, an arbitrator, a judge.

प्रमाणाभाव prumán-ábhao, *s. m.* Want or absence of proof or authority.

प्रमाणिक pruman-ík, *adj.* Proper, creditable; reverend. *s. m.* Chairman of an assembly.

प्रमाणिका pruman-ik-á, *s. f.* A species of the *Unooshtoobh* metre.

प्रमाणीकरण prumánee-kúrun, *s. m.* Establishing or admitting as authority or proof.

प्रमातामह prumáta-múhuh, *s. m.* A maternal great grandfather.

प्रमातामही prumáta-muhée, *s. f.* A maternal great grandmother.

प्रमाद prumád, *s. m.* Inadvertence, carelessness, error, inaccuracy.

प्रमादी prumá-dee, *adj.* Heedless, careless, indifferent, incautious, inconsiderate, unreflecting.

प्रमित prum-ít, *adj.* Known, understood, established, proved; measured.

प्रमिताक्षरा prúmit-akshur-á, *s. f.* A species of the *Jugutee* metre.

प्रमुख prumóokh, *adj.* Chief, principal; best, most excellent; first. *s. m.* A chief, a sage, any respectable man; a tree used for dyeing (*Rottleria tinctoria*).

प्रमुख्बल prum-ookh-twúh, *s. m.* Superiority, predominance.

प्रमुद prumóod, ⎫ adj. Pleased, glad,
प्रमुदित prumóod-it, ⎰ content, happy.

प्रमेह pruméb, s. m. Urinary affection, as change in the colour, quantity, or consistence of the urine; twenty-one varieties are enumerated, including diabetes, gonorrhœa, &c.

प्रमोचन prumóchun, s. m. Liberating, setting free.

प्रमोचनी prumochun-ée, s. f. A sort of cucumber.

प्रमोद prumód, s. m. Pleasure, happiness, delight.

प्रमोदित prumodít, adj. Happy, delighted.

प्रमोदी prumódee, adj. Happy, delighted; delighting, making happy.

प्रमोह prumóh, s. m. Fascination; fainting, insensibility.

प्रयत्न pruyútn, s. m. Continued and persevering effort, exertion; act, action; (in logic) active effort of three kinds, engaging in any act, prosecuting it, and completing it; caution, care.

प्रयत्नवान् pruyutn-wán, adj. Active, zealous, enterprising, assiduous, persevering.

प्रयाग pruyág, s. m. Sacrifice, oblation; a celebrated place of pilgrimage, the confluence of the Ganges and Jumna, with the supposed subterranean addition of the Suruswutee, the modern Allahabad. The term in composition is applied to many places of reputed sanctity, situated at the confluence of two rivers, as Dev-pruyag, Roodr-pruyag, Kurn-pruyag, and Nund-pruyag, in the Himala mountains, which with Pruyag or Allahabad, constitute the five principal places so termed, and where worship is deemed peculiarly efficacious. Allahabad is one of the places where Bruhma is supposed to have consummated ten Uswumedhs or sacrifices of the horse, in commemoration of his recovery of the four Veds from Sunkhasoor.

प्रयाण pruy-án, s. m. Going forth or to a distance; departure; death; march of an assailing force, attack, invasion.

प्रयाणकाल pruyan-kál, s. m. Time of departure; death.

प्रयास pruyás, s. m. Trouble, labour, fatigue; desire for or pursuit of any object.

प्रयुक्त pruyóokt, adj. Endowed with, possessing as an attribute, &c.; associated or connected with; compact, closely united.

प्रयोग pruyóg, s. m. Occasion, cause, motive, object, consequence, result; device, contrivance; example, comparison; act, action.

प्रयोगी pruyógee, adj. Having some object in view, calculated for some particular purpose.

प्रयोजक pruyojúk, adj. Who or what causes or induces any act; who or what deputes or appoints. s. m. A founder or institutor of any ceremony; a law-giver, a legislator.

प्रयोजन pruyójun, s. m. Cause, occasion; motive, origin; purpose, object, intention, design; use, exigence.

प्रयोजनी pruyójunee, adj. Necessary, requisite.

प्रयोजनवान् pruyojun-wán, adj. Designing, purposing.

प्रयोज्य pruyójyuh, s. m. Capital, principal; a servant, a slave.

प्रलय prúluy, s. m. The end of a Kulp, or destruction of the world; death, dying, loss, destruction, dissolution, annihilation; fainting, syncope, loss of sense or consciousness. s. f. A general destruction, such as at the flood or resurrection; (met.) vexation, fatigue, oppression, languor, disgust.

प्रलाप prulápp, s. m. Unmeaning or incoherent speech; discourse, conversation.

प्रलेपक prulepúk, adj. Who or what anoints, smears, &c.

प्रलोठन prulothún, s. m. Rolling on the ground, heaving, tossing (as of the ocean).

प्रलोठित prulothít, adj. Rolling, heaving, tossing.

प्रलोभ prulóbh, s. m. Desire, cupidity.

प्रलोभन prulobhún, s. m. Allurement, inducement; attraction, attracting, seducing.

प्रवर prúvur, s. m. Offspring, descendants; family, race, kindred.

प्रवरललित prúvur-lúlit, s. m. A species of the Ushtee metre.

प्रवर्त pruvúrt, s. m. Engaged in, undertaking; excitement, stimulus.

प्रवर्तक pruvurttúk, adj. Inciting, stimulating, inducing, who or what sets in action. s. m. The original instigator of any act, the author, the principal.

प्रवसन pruvúsun, s. m. Going abroad, sojourning in a foreign country.

प्रवह pruvúh, s. m. One of the seven Vayoos or winds.

प्रवारण pruvarún, s. m. Prohibition, objection, opposition.

प्रवास pruvás, s. m. A temporary or foreign residence, a habitation away from home.

प्रवासत् pruvasút, adj. Dwelling or being abroad or absent.

प्रवासन pruvasún, s. m. Dwelling abroad, sojourning, lodging; exile.

प्रवासी pruvásee, adj. A traveller, a sojourner, one living away from home.

प्रवाह pruváh, s. m. Stream, current, flow, continuous passage.

प्रवाहिका pruváhika, s. f. Diarrhœa.

प्रविख्याति pruvikhyáti, *s. f.* Celebrity, reputation.

प्रविभक्त pruvibhúkt, *adj.* Partitioned, divided, separated, shared.

प्रविभाग pruvibhág, *s. m.* Division, a part.

प्रविर pruvír, *s. m.* A yellow fragrant wood.

प्रविष्ट pruvísht, *adj.* Entered, gone in or into; entered upon (*as an affair*), engaged in.

प्रवीण pruvéen, *adj.* Skilful, clever, conversant.

प्रवीणता pruveentá, *s. f.* Proficiency, skill.

प्रवीर pruvéer, *adj.* Best, most excellent. *s. m.* A hero, a warrior; a chief, a person of rank or distinction.

प्रवृत्त pruvrítt, *adj.* Fixed, settled, determined, done; engaged in, undertaking, occupied.

प्रवृत्ति pruvrítti, *s. f.* Activity, occupation, active life, as opposed to contemplative devotion; prosecution, perseverance; addiction to, predilection for; tidings, intelligence; continuous flow, stream, current; *Oujein* or any holy place; (*in arithmetic*) the multiplier.

प्रवेक्षण pruvekshún, *s. m.* Foreseeing.

प्रवेक्षित pruvekshít, *adj.* Foreseen, anticipated.

प्रवेक्ष्यत् pruvekshyút, *adj.* Foreseeing, anticipating.

प्रवेट pruvét, *s. m.* Barley.

प्रवेणि pruvéni, *s. f.* The hair twisted, and undecorated, as worn by women in the absence of their husbands.

प्रवेणी pruvénee, *s. f.* Unornamented hair.

प्रवेल pruvél, *s. m.* The yellow variety of kidney bean.

प्रवेश pruvésh, *s. m.* Entrance.

प्रवेशक pruvesh-úk, *adj.* Who or what enters. *s. m.* An entry.

प्रवेशन pruvesh-ún, *s. m.* The entrance to a house; entering, entrance.

प्रशंसन prushun-shún, } *s. m.* Praising, eulogising.
प्रशंसन prushun-sún, }

प्रशंसा prushun-sá, *s. f.* Praise, eulogium.

प्रशंसनीय prusun-sunéeyuh, *adj.* To be praised, praiseworthy.

प्रशंसा prushun-sá, *s. f.* Praise, applause, flattery, commendation.

प्रशंसित prushun-sít, *adj.* Praised, eulogised.

प्रशमन prush-mún, *s. m.* Killing, slaughter; pacifying, tranquillising.

प्रशस्त prushúst, *adj.* Happy, well, right; good, excellent, best.

प्रशस्ति prushústi, *s. f.* Excellence, eminence; eulogy.

प्रशान्त prushánt, *adj.* Calmed, calm, tranquillised.

प्रशान्तात्मा prushánt-átma, *adj.* Peaceful, calm, composed.

प्रशान्ति prushánti, *s. f.* Calm, quiet, tranquillity, moral or physical.

प्रशासन prushásun, *s. m.* Governing, ruling.

प्रश्न prushn, *s. m.* A question, a demand, an inquiry.

प्रश्नदूती prushn-dóotee, *s. f.* A riddle, an enigma, an intricate or enigmatical question.

प्रश्नी prúshnee, *s. f.* An aquatic plant (*Pistia stratioites*).

प्रष्टा prúshtu, *adj.* Asking, demanding, an asker or questioner.

प्रष्ठ prushth, *adj.* A leader, a conductor, one who goes first or before; prior, preceding; chief, principal, best.

प्रष्ठी prush-thée, *s. f.* The wife of a leader or chief.

प्रसक्त prusúkt, *adj.* Eternal, constant, continual; obtained, gained, attained; attached to, devoted to (*person or thing*), engaged in. *adv.* Continually, incessantly, eternally.

प्रसक्ति prusúkti, *s. f.* Adherence or attachment to.

प्रसङ्ग prusúng, *s. m.* Introduction, insertion; association, connexion.

प्रसन्न prusúnn, *adj.* Pleased, rejoiced, delighted; complacent, gracious, favourable, kind. *Prusunn kurna*, To please. *Prusunn hona*, To be pleased with, to like.

प्रसन्नता prusunn-tá, *s. f.* Favour, kindness, being pleased with.

प्रसन्नमुख prusunn-móokh, *m.* } *adj.* Agreeable
प्रसन्नमुखी prusunn-móokhee, *f.* } looking, smiling, looking pleased.

प्रसव prusúv, *s. m.* Bringing forth, bearing (*as young*); birth, production.

प्रसवक prusúvuk, *s. m.* A tree, commonly called *Peeya* (*Buchanania latifolia*).

प्रसवत् prusuvút, *adj.* Bearing.

प्रसवन्ती prusuvúntee, *s. f.* A woman in labour.

प्रसववन्धन prusúv-búndhun, *s. m.* The footstalk of a leaf or flower.

प्रसवी prusúv-ee, *adj.* Having or bearing young.

प्रसाद prusád, *s. m.* Favour, kindness, blessing, gift, propitiousness, approbation; food that has been offered to an idol, or of which a spiritual teacher has partaken.

प्रसादी prusádee, *adj.* Offered to idols.

प्रसाधक prusadhúk, *adj.* Who or what accomplishes or perfects.

प्रसाधन prusá-dhun, *s. m.* Accomplishing, effecting.

प्रसाधनी prusádhunee, *s. f.* A drug, commonly called *Siddhi.*

प्रसाधित prusadhít, *adj.* Accomplished, completed, done.

प्रसार prusár, } *s. m.* Spreading, ex-
प्रसारण prusarún, } tending, expanding.

प्रसारित prusarít, *adj.* Stretched, expanded, extended.

प्रसारी prusáree, *adj.* Spreading, expanding.

प्रसिद्ध prusíddh, *adj.* Famous, celebrated ; notorious ; adorned, ornamented.

प्रसिद्धि prusíddhi, *s. f.* Fame, celebrity ; notoriety.

प्रसू prusóo, *s. f.* A mother.

प्रसूत prusóot, *s. m.* The whites, fluor albus. *adj.* Born.

प्रसूता prusóota, *s. f.* A woman who has borne a child, or one who is recently delivered.

प्रसूति prusóoti, *s. f.* Bringing forth (*as young*) ; birth, production ; offspring, children, a son or daughter.

प्रसून prusóon, *adj.* Born, produced. *s. m.* A flower, a bud, a blossom ; fruit.

प्रसूती prusóutee, *s. f.* puerperal women.

प्रस्कन्दन prus-kúndun, *s. m.* } Purging, di-
प्रस्कन्दिका pruskúndika, *s. f.* } arrhœa.

प्रस्तर prústur, *s. m.* A stone or rock ; a jewel, a precious stone.

प्रस्ताव prustáo, *s. m.* Opportunity, occasion, season ; occasional or introductory eulogium.

प्रस्तावना prustáo-na, *s. f.* Commencement, introduction.

प्रस्ताविक prustavík, *adj.* Suited to the occasion, appropriate, seasonable.

प्रस्तुत prústoot, *adj.* Said, declared ; praised, panegyrised ; accomplished, done.

प्रस्थ prusth, *adj.* Expanding, spread. *s. m.* A measure of quantity, forty-eight double handfuls ; table-land on the top of a mountain.

प्रस्थपुष्प prusth-póoshp, *s. m.* A sort of *Toolsee*, or Basil with small leaves.

प्रस्थान prusthán, *s. m.* Going forth, proceeding, departing ; march of an assailant ; march.

प्रस्थापन prusthápun, *s. m.* Sending away ; appointment on an embassy.

प्रस्थापित prusthapít, *adj.* Sent, despatched.

प्रस्फुट prus-phóot, *adj.* Blown, expanded.

प्रस्मृति prusmríti, *s. f.* Forgetfulness, forgetting.

प्रस्राव prusráv, *s. m.* Urine.

प्रहर prúhur, *s. m.* A watch, an eighth part of the day, or a division of time consisting of eight *ghurees,* or about three hours.

प्रहरकलिका pruhúrun-kúlika, *s. f.* A species of the *Surkuree* metre.

प्रहरी prúhuree, } *s. m.* A watchman, a
परहिया púhriya, } bellman, a sentinal.

प्रहर्षिणी pruhurshinée, *s. f.* A species of the *Utijugutee* metre.

प्रहर्षित pruhurshít, *adj.* Delighted, very happy.

प्रहसत् pruhúsut, *adj.* Laughing, laughing heartily.

प्रहसन pruhúsun, *s. m.* Loud, violent or hearty laughter ; mirth, merriment ; sarcasm, satire ; reproof, ridicule, irony.

प्रहसन्ती pru-husún-tee, *s. f.* Arabian jasmine.

प्रहार pruhár, *s. m.* Striking, wounding, killing ; a blow, a stroke.

प्रहारी pruháree, *s. m.* A striker, smiter, destroyer, debaser, humbler.

प्रहास prubás, *s. m.* Loud laughter.

प्रहासी pruhásee, *adj.* Laughing aloud ; diverting, causing laughter.

प्रहेलिका pruhélika, *s. f.* An enigma, a riddle, a puzzling or enigmatical question.

प्रहृष्ट pruhrísht, *adj.* Pleased, delighted.

प्रह्लाद pruhlád, *s. m.* Pleasure, joy, happiness ; the name of *Hirnyakshu's* pious son and regent of one division of *Patal.*

प्रह्लादित pruhladít, *adj.* Rejoiced, delighted.

प्राक् prak, *adv.* Before, prior, preceding, in place or time ; east, eastern ; at dawn, early in the morning.

प्राकार pra-kár, *s. m.* An inclosure, a fence, a rampart, particularly a surrounding wall, &c., elevated on a mound of earth.

प्राकृत prá-krit, *adj.* Low, common, vulgar, thence especially applicable to a provincial and peculiar dialect of the Sunskrit language ; natural ; belonging to or derived from the philosophical *Prukriti,* illusory, material, &c. *s. m.* Any dialect not *Sunskrit,* it is especially spoken by the female characters and the inferior personages of plays.

प्राकृतज्वर prakrit-jwúr, *s. m.* Common or usual fever, occurring from affections of the wind, bile, and phlegm, severally, in as many seasons, or the rains, autumn, and spring.

प्राकृतप्रलय **prákrit-prúluy**, *s. m.* The total dissolution of the world.

प्राकृतमित्र **prákrit-mítr**, *s. m.* A natural friend or ally.

प्राक्काल **prak-kál**, *s. m.* Former age or time.

प्राक्कालीन **prak-ka-léen**, *adj.* Anterior, ancient, of a former time.

प्राक्तन **prak-tún**, *adj.* Old, ancient ; prior, anterior, preceding, former.

प्राक्तनकर्म **praktun-kúrm**, *s. m.* Fate, destiny ; any act formerly done.

प्राक्फल्गुनी **prak-phúl-goonee**, *s. f.* The eleventh of the lunar asterisms.

प्रागभाव **prag-bháo**, *s. m.* Antecedent privation, the non-existence of any thing which may yet be. In law, the non-possession of property that may be possessed.

प्रागल्भ्य **pra-gúlbh-yuh**, *s. m.* Confidence, boldness, determination ; arrogance, effrontery.

प्रागामी **prag-gámee**, *adj.* Going before, a precursor.

प्राग्ज्योतिष **prag-jyótish**, *s. m.* A country, *Kamroop*, part of *Assam*, being the scene of *Bruhma's* penance.

प्रागभाव **prag-bháo**, *s. m.* Prior existence ; superiority, excellence.

प्राग्युह् **prág-yuh**, *adj.* Chief, principal.

प्राचार **pra-chár**, *adj.* Contrary to rectitude, deviating from the ordinary institutions and observances.

प्राचार्य **pra-chárj**, *s. m.* A scholar, a pupil.

प्राची **pra-chée**, *adj. f.* East, eastern. *s. f.* The east.

प्राचीन **pra-chéen**, *adj.* East, eastern ; former, prior, ancient, old, of former times, ancient. *s. f.* A bound hedge, a fence, a wall.

प्राचीनता **pracheen-tá**, *s. f.* Antiquity.

प्राचीनपनस **prachéen-pun-us**, *s. m.* A tree (*Ægle marmelos*).

प्राचीना **pra-chéen-a**, *s. f.* A plant (*Cissampelos hexandra*).

प्राचीनामलक **prachéen-ámluk**, *s. m.* A fruit (*Flacourtia cataphracta*).

प्राचीर **pra-chéer**, *s. m.* A bound hedge, a fence, a wall, an inclosure, a rampart.

प्राच्य **prách-yuh**, *adj.* Eastern, easterly. *s. m.* The eastern country, the country south and east of the *Suruswuttee*, which flows from the north-east to the south-west.

प्राजापत्य **prája-pútyub**, *s. m.* A form of marriage, the gift of a girl respectfully, by her father to her lover ; a name of *Allahabad* or *Pruyag* ; a sort of penance, eating once a day for three days in the morning, once in the night for three days, subsisting three days on food given as alms, and fasting three days more ; a particular sacrifice performed before appointing a daughter to raise issue in default of male heirs ; the asterism *Rohinee*.

प्राजापत्या **prája-putyá**, *s. f.* Giving away the whole of one's property before entering upon the life of an ascetic or mendicant.

प्राज्ञ **prág-yuh**, *adj.* Patient in investigation ; wise, clever, sensible. *s. m.* A *pundit*, a learned or wise man ; a skilful or clever man.

प्राज्ञबल **prag-yutwúh**, *s. m.* Learning, wisdom.

प्राज्ञमान **prag-yumán**, *s. m.* Respect for learned men.

प्राज्ञमानी **prag-yumánee**, *adj.* Respecting learned men.

प्राज्ञा **prag-yá**, *s. f.* Knowledge, understanding.

प्राज्ञा **prag-yá**, ⎫ *s. f.* A clever or intelligent woman.
प्राज्ञी **prag-yée**, ⎭

प्राज्ञी **prag-yée**, *s. f.* The wife of a *Brahmun*.

प्राञ्जलि **pran-júli**, *s. f.* Putting the hands together to the forehead, a mark of respect.

प्राड्विवाक **prad-vi-vák**, *s. m.* A judge, a magistrate.

प्राण **pran**, *s. m.* Air inhaled, inspiration, breath ; air, wind ; life, vitality, soul ; poetical talent or inspiration ; a title of *Bruhm*, the Supreme Spirit ; an aspiration in the articulation of letters ; sweetheart, mistress. *Pran-puti*, Soul's lord.

प्राणक **pran-úk**, *s. m.* An animal or sentient being ; a plant (*Celtis orientalis*).

प्राणत्याग **pran-tyág**, *s. m.* Abandoning life, dying, suicide.

प्राणधारण **pran-dhá-run**, *s. m.* Sustenance, supporting life.

प्राणनाथ **pran-náth**, *s. m.* A husband.

प्राणान्त **pran-únt**, *s. m.* A sort of collyrium.

प्राणन्ती **pran-úntee**, *s. f.* Sneezing ; hickup.

प्राणप्रतिष्ठा **pran-prutish-thá**, *s. m.* The ceremony of imparting life to an idol.

प्राणप्रदा **pran-prúd-a**, *s. f.* A medicinal plant, commonly called *Riddhi*.

प्राणबाध **pran-bádh**, *s. m.* Extreme peril or distress, fear of life.

प्राणमय **pran-múy**, *adj.* Living, breathing, endowed with breath or life.

प्राणमयकोष **pranmuy-kósh**, *s. m.* One of the cases or investitures of the soul, the vital or organic case.

प्राणयात्रा pran-yátra, *s. f.* Support of life, subsistence.

प्राणव्यय pran-vyúy, *s. f.* Death, expenditure of life.

प्राणसंयम pran-sún-yum, *s. m.* A peculiar religious exercise ; suspending the breath.

प्राणसमा pran-súm-a, *s. f.* A wife, considered as equal to, or as life.

प्राणहर pran-húr, *adj.* Destructive, taking away life.

प्राणहारी pran-háree, *adj.* Mortal, deadly.

प्राणाधिनाथ pran-adhi-náth, *s. m.* A husband, as lord over life.

प्राणान्त pran-ánt, *s. m.* Death.

प्राणान्तिक pran-ánt-ik, *adj.* Fatal, destructive of life ; capital (*as punishment*). *s. m.* Murder, assassination.

प्राणापहारी prana-puháree, *adj.* Deadly, fatal.

प्राणायाम pran-ayám, *s. m.* Breathing in a peculiar way through the nostrils, during the mental recitation of the names or attributes of some deity. It is differently performed : the *Vydyus* or followers of the *Ved* close the right nostril first with the thumb, and inhale breath through the left, then they close both nostrils, and finally open the right for exhalation : the followers of the *Tuntrus* close the left nostril first, and exhale also through it.

प्राणी prá-nee, *adj.* Living, breathing, having life. *s. m.* An animal, a sentient or living being, an animated being.

प्राणीपीड़ा pránee-péera, *s. f.* Cruelty to animals.

प्राणीमाता pránee-máta, *s. f.* A mother.

प्राणीहिंसा pránee-hínsa, *s. f.* Doing harm to any living creature.

प्राणीहित pranee-hít, *adj.* Favourable or good for living beings.

प्राणेश pran-ésh, *s. m.* A husband, as sovereign of life.

प्राणेशा pran-esh-á, *s. f.* A wife.

प्रातः prátuh, ⎫ *s. m.* Early
प्रातःकाल pratuh-kál, ⎬ morning, day-
प्रातःसमय prátuh-súmuy, ⎭ break, dawn of day.

प्रातर pra-túr, *adv.* Morning, dawn.

प्रातर्भोजन pratur-bhó-jun, *s. m.* Breakfast, the morning meal.

प्रातिपदिक práti-púd-ik, *s. m.* A crude noun, a noun before any of its inflections are formed with appropriate affixes.

प्रात्ययिक prat-yuyík, *adj.* Trusty, confidential, having faith in. *s. m.* A surety.

प्राथमिक pra-thum-ík, *adj.* First, of the first, initial, initiative.

प्राथम्य pra-thúm-yuh, *s. m.* Firstness, priority.

प्रादक्षिण pra-dukshin-yúh, *s. m.* Circumambulation.

प्रादुर्भाव pra-door-bháo, *s. m.* Appearance, manifestation.

प्रादेश pra-désh, *s. m.* Place, country.

प्राधान्य pra-dhán-yuh, *s. m.* Supremacy, superiority.

प्रान्त prant, *s. m.* Edge, margin, border, end.

प्रापक pra-púk, *adj.* Procuring, causing to obtain ; obtaining, who or what obtains.

प्रापण pra-pún, *s. m.* Obtaining.

प्रापित pra-pít, *adj.* Procured.

प्राप्त prapt, *adj.* Obtained, gained, received, procured ; fixed, placed ; proper, right.

प्राप्तकाल prapt-kál, *adj.* Fated, destined, one whose fated time has come ; opportune, in season.

प्राप्तबुद्धि prapt-bóoddhi, *adj.* Enlightened, instructed, intelligent ; recovering, becoming conscious (*after fainting*).

प्राप्तार्थ prapt-árth, *adj.* Successful, having gained an object.

प्राप्तावसर prapt-avusúr, *adj.* Opportune, seasonable, taking or finding occasion.

प्राप्ति prápti, *s. f.* Gain, profit, income, produce, advantage, benefit, acquiring, getting, obtaining ; improvement, success.

प्राप्य práp-yub, *adj.* Attainable, obtainable.

प्राबल्य pra-búl-yuh, *s. m.* Power, vigour ; predominance.

प्राभव pra-bhúvub, *s. m.* Superiority, pre-eminence.

प्रामाणिक pra-man-ík, *adj.* Exercising or proceeding from some evidence or authority, &c. ; being of authority. *s. m.* A president, the chief or head of a trade, &c. A learned man, one who supports his arguments by reference to books, &c.

प्रामाण्य pra-mán-yuh, *s. m.* Authority, proof.

प्रामाद्य pra-mád-yuh, *s. m.* A tree (*Justicia adhenatoda*). *s. m.* Madness, frenzy, fury, intoxication.

प्राय práyuh, *adj.* Like, resembling (*used in composition*). *s. m.* Fasting to death, as a religious or penitentiary act, and especially after abandoning all worldly goods, and desires ; quantity, abundance.

प्रायण pra-yún, *s. m.* Death, voluntary death.

प्रायश्चित्त prayush-chítt, *s. m.* Expiation, penance.

प्रायश्चित्तविधि prayushchitt-vídhi, *s. f.* Rules for penance or expiation.

प्रारब्ध pra-rúbdh, *adj.* Begun, beginning. *s. f.* Fortune, fate, lot, destiny, predestination, venture, chance.

प्रारम्भ pra-rúmbh, *s. m.* Beginning.

प्रार्थक prar-thúk, *adj.* Asking, an asker, a solicitor.

प्रार्थना prárth-na, *s. f.* Asking, begging, petition, prayer.

प्रार्थनीय prarth-néeyuh, *adj.* To be asked or begged. *s. m.* The third or *Dwapur* age of the world.

प्रार्थित prar-thít, *adj.* Asked, begged, solicited.

प्रालब्ध pra-lúbdh, *s. f.* Fortune, fate, lot, destiny, predestination, venture, chance.

प्रावट pra-vút, *s. m.* Barley.

प्रावीण्य pra-véen-yuh, *s. m.* Cleverness, skilfulness.

प्रावृत pra-vrít, *s. m.* A veil, a wrapper, a cloak or mantle.

प्रावृत्ति pra-vrítti, *s. f.* An inclosure, a fence, a bound hedge.

प्रावृष् prá-vrish, *s. f.* The rainy season, two months, about July and August.

प्रावृषायणी právrish-áyunee, *s. f.* Cowach (*Curpopogon pruriens*).

प्रावृषेण्य právrish-ényuh, *s. m.* The *Kudumb* tree (*Nauclea Cadamba*).

प्रास pras, *s. m.* A bearded dart.

प्रासक prá-suk, *s. m.* A die, dice.

प्रासङ्गिक pra-sung-ík, *adj.* Innate, inherent; inseparably connected with.

प्रासाद pra-sád, *s. m.* A temple, a palace, a building consecrated to a deity, or inhabited by a prince.

प्रिय príyuh, *adj.* Beloved, dear, desired. *s. m.* A husband, a lover; a sort of drug, commonly called *Riddhi*.

प्रियक príyuk, *s. m.* A tree (*Nauclea Cadumba*); a tree (*Pentaptera tomentosa*).

प्रियकार priyukár, *adj.* Kind, favourable, affectionate, doing good to, or treating kindly.

प्रियकृत priyukrít, *adj.* Kind, friendly, a friend, a benefactor.

प्रियङ्गु priyúngoo, *s. m.* A medicinal plant, and perfume, described in some places as a fragrant seed; panick seed (*Punicum italicum*).

प्रियतम priyutúm, *adj.* Dearest, most beloved. *s. m.* A favourite friend, beloved, lover, sweetheart, husband.

प्रियतर priyutúr, *adj.* Dearer, more dear.

प्रियता priyutá, *s. f.* Love, affection.

प्रियदर्शन príyudúrshun, *adj.* Handsome, lovely, good looking. *s. m.* A tree (*Mimusops kauki*).

प्रियभाषण priyubháshun, *s. m.* Speaking kindly.

प्रियमान priyumán, *adj.* Beloved, affectionate.

प्रियभावुक príyum-bhávook, *adj.* Become dear to or beloved by.

प्रियभावुकता príyum-bhavook-tá, *s. f.* Amiability, becoming beloved, the state or condition.

प्रियवर्णी priyuvúrnee, *s. f.* A creeping plant (*Echites frutescens*).

प्रियवादी priyuvádee, *adj.* Sweet or pleasant spoken, flattering, a flatterer.

प्रियसख priyusúkh, *s. m.* A tree (*Mimosa catechu*).

प्रियसखी priyusúkhee, *s. f.* A female friend or companion, a confidante.

प्रियसन्देश príyusundésh, *s. m.* A tree bearing a fragrant flower (*Michelia Champaca*).

प्रिया príya, *adj. f.* Beloved, dear; mistress, sweetheart. *Heh priyeh*, My dear!

प्रियाख्य priyákhyub, *adj.* Announcing good tidings.

प्रियाल priyál, *s. m.* A tree, commonly called *Piyal* (*Buchanania latifolia*).

प्रीत preet, *adj.* Gracious, kind, affectionate; beloved, dear to. *s. m.* Pleasure, delight.

प्रीतम pree-túm, *adj. superl.* Dearest, most beloved. *s. m.* A favourite, friend, beloved, lover, sweetheart, husband.

प्रीति préeti, *s. f.* Love, affection, regard; the second of the twenty-seven astronomical *yogs*.

प्रीतिदान preeti-dán, *s. m.* A kind or friendly present.

प्रीतिदाय préeti-dáyuh, *s. m.* A gift or token of affection.

प्रीतिपूर्वक préeti-póorvuk, *adv.* Through favour or kindness.

प्रीतिमान preeti-mán, *adj.* Kind, affectionate.

प्रेक्षण prekshún, *s. m.* Any public show or spectacle, a sight.

प्रेक्षा préksha, *s. f.* Seeing, viewing, observing.

प्रेक्षित prekshít, *adj.* Seen, beheld, looked at.

प्रेत pret, *adj.* Dead, deceased. *s. m.* A departed soul, a spirit of the dead, a ghost, a goblin, a sprite, an evil spirit, fiend.

प्रेतनी prét-nee, *s. f.* A female ghost, demon or evil spirit.

प्रेतकर्म pret-kúrm, *s. m.* Funeral or obsequial rites.

प्रेतगृह pret-gríh, *s. m.* A cemetry, a burial ground.

प्रेतनदी pret-núdee, *s. f.* The river of hell.

प्रेतपक्ष pret-púksh, *s. m.* The dark half of the month.

प्रेतलोक pret-lók, *s. m.* The region of disembodied spirits, in which they remain for one year, or until the obsequial rites are completed.

प्रेम prem, *s. m.* Love, affection, friendship, kindness, tender regard. *Premrung-rata, adj.* Coloured with the die of love, strongly attached, or in love, loving.

प्रेमपर prem-púr, *adj.* Affectionate, loving, constant.

प्रेमी prém-ee, *adj.* Affectionate, lover.

प्रेरण pre-rún, *s. m.* Sending, directing.

प्रेरित prerít, *adj.* Sent, directed, despatched.

प्रेष्ठ preshth, *adj.* Most or very dear.

प्रेष्ठा presh-thá, *s. f.* A wife.

प्रोक्त prokt, *adj.* Said, declared.

प्रोत्साह prot-sáh, *s. m.* Effort, exertion; stimulus, incitement.

प्रोत्साहक prot-sahúk, *s. m.* The instigator or adviser of any act, or, in law, of any crime.

प्रोत्साहन prot-sahún, *s. m.* Instigating, exciting, stimulating.

प्रोत्साहित prot-sahít, *adj.* Incited, instigated, stimulated, encouraged.

प्रोष्ठ proshth, *s. m.* A sort of carp (*Cyprinus Pausius*).

प्रोष्ठपदा proshth-púd-a, *s. f.* One of the constellations, the twenty-sixth or twenty-seventh, containing stars in the wing of *Pegasus.*

प्रोहित pró-hit, *s. m.* A family priest conducting all the ceremonials and sacrifices of a house or family.

प्रोक्षण prók-shun, *s. m.* Killing animals in sacrifice, immolation of victims; killing, slaughter; sprinkling with water, &c.; a text to be repeated when animals are offered.

प्रोक्षित pro-kshít, *adj.* Sprinkled; killed, slaughtered; offered in sacrifice.

प्रौढ prourh, *adj.* Full grown; confident, bold, arrogant; able, clever.

प्रौढता prourh-tá, *s. f.* Strength, firmness; breadth.

प्रौढा prourhá, *s. f.* A woman from thirty years of age to fifty-five. *adj.* Strong, firm.

प्रौढि próurhi, *s. f.* Enterprise, zeal, confi-dent or audacious exertion; investigation, controversy, discussion.

प्रोष्ठपद próushth-pud, *s. m.* The month *Bhadr* (*August-September*).

प्रोष्ठपदी proushth-púd-ee, *s. f.* Full moon in *Bhadr.*

प्लुक्ष pluksh, *s. m.* Waved-leaf fig-tree (*Ficus infectoria*); another tree (*Hibiscus populneoides*); the holy fig-tree (*Ficus religiosa*); one of the seven *Dweeps* or continents, into which the world is divided.

प्लव pluv, *s. m.* A diver or bird so called (*Pelicanus fusicollis*); waved-leaf fig-tree (*Ficus infectoria*); a sort of grass (*Cyperus rotundus*); fragrant grass in general, or another sort.

प्लवन plúv-un, *s. m.* A deluge, an inundation.

प्लक्ष plaksh, *s. m.* The fruit of the Hibiscus populneoides.

प्लाव plav, *s. m.* Submersion.

प्लिहन plihún, *s. m.* }
प्लिहा plihá, *s. f.* } The spleen.

प्लीहघ्न plee-húghn, *s. m.* A medicinal plant (*Andersonia rohitaka*).

प्लीहन plee-hún, *s. m.* } The spleen; the
प्लीहा plee-há, *s. f.* } organ or the disease of it, as in English: in the latter sense, however, it is equally applied to the enlargement of the mesenteric glands, &c.

प्लीहशत्रु pleeh-shútroo, *s. m.* A medicinal plant, commonly called *Rohera* or *Rohinee* (*Andersonia rohitaka*).

प्लीहारि plee-hári, *s. m.* The holy fig-tree (*Ficus religiosa*), deemed an enemy to the spleen.

प्लुत ploot, *s. m.* The third sound given to vowels, the protracted or continuous sound, being three times the length of the short vowel, and occupying three moments in its utterance.

फ

फ phuh, The twenty-second consonant of the *Naguree* alphabet, the aspirate of the preceding letter, and expressed by *ph.*

फंका phún-ka, *s. m.* A handful (*or rather mouthful*) of any thing eaten by being chucked in the mouth. *Phunka marna,* To eat by chucking into the mouth, to chuck food into the mouth.

फंगा phún-ga, *s. m.* A grasshopper.

फंदना phúnd-na, *v. n.* To be imprisoned.

फंदलाना phund-lána, *v. a.* To ensnare, to entrap.

फंदा phún-da, *s. m.* A noose, a net, a snare; perplexity, difficulty.

फंसना phúns-na, *v. n.* To be entangled, to

stick, to be involved (*in calamity, &c.*), to be en-snared, noosed or entrapped, to be caught.

फंसवाना phuns-wá-na, *v. a.* To cause to noose, strangle, &c.

फंसाव phun-sáo, *s. m.* Entanglement.

फंसियारा phun-si-yára, *s. m.* A footpad who strangles passengers or travellers.

फकड़ी phúk-ree, *s. f.* The act of treating with rudeness.

फकिया phúk-iya, *s. f.* A slice, a piece of fruit.

फकोड़िया phuk-ó-riya, *s. m.* A fop, an ab-surd prattler, an indecent talker.

फकोड़ियत phuk-o-riyát, *s. f.* Absurdity.

फककर phuk-kúr, *s. m.* Wrangling, mutual abuse, brawl, raillery. *Phukkur-bas*, An abuser, an indecent chatterer.

फकिका phúk-ki-ka, *s. f.* A sophism; a trick; illusion; fraud.

फगूआ phúg-oo-a, *s. m.* The season of the *holee*; presents made during the *holee* holidays.

फंका phún-ka, *s. m.* ⎫ A handful (*or ra-*
फंकी phún-kee, *s. f.* ⎬ *ther mouthful*) of any thing eaten by being chucked into the mouth. *Phunka marna*, To eat by chucking into the mouth, to chuck food into the mouth.

फंगा phún-ga, *s. m.* A grasshopper.

फंजिका phún-ji-ka, *s. f.* A plant (*Sipho-nanthus Indica*); a species of Hedysarum (*H. alhagi*).

फंजिपूतिका phúnji-póotrika, *s. f.* A plant (*Salvinia cucullata*).

फटक phút-uk, *s. m.* Crystal.

फटकना phút-uk-na, *v. a.* To winnow; to dust, to shake or knock off any light thing which slightly adheres (*as crumbs from a table-cloth or dust from a table*). *v. n.* To be separated. *s. m.* The tape in a pellet-bow which strikes the ball.

फटकरी phút-kur-ee, *s. m.* Alum.

फटकी phút-kee, *s. f.* A fowler's net; a large cage; a rope tied to a tree to frighten birds with its sound.

फटना phút-na, *v. n.* To be torn, split, rent, broken, cracked, to burst, split.

फटपड़ना phut-púr-na, *v. n.* To be pro-duced plentifully; to become fat suddenly; to be confounded with too much business.

फटफटाना phut-phut-ána, *v. a.* To shake or flap or clap the wings as birds just going to fly; to give a sound as the shoes of a person walking.

फटा phút-a, *s. m.* A crack. *Phuteh men paon dena*, To interfere in any thing.

फटिक phút-ik, *s. m.* Crystal.

फड़ phur, *s. f.* A gaming-house where dice are played; a place where goods are exposed for sale; the shafts or pole of a carriage. *Phur-bas*, *s. m.* A player at dice, a gamester; a prater, a talkative fellow. *Phur-bazee*, *s. f.* Gambling, play-ing at dice.

फड़क phúr-uk, *verbal n. f.* Fluttering, flutter, vibrating, throbbing, palpitating.

फड़कना phúr-uk-na, *v. n.* To flutter, to vibrate with convulsive involuntary motion, as the eyelids or other muscles; to throb, to palpitate; to writhe (*the shoulders, &c.*)

फड़काना phur-ká-na, *v. a.* To cause to flutter, to cause convulsive motion in the muscles, &c.; (*met.*) to shew.

फड़की phúr-kee, *s. f.* A coarse skreen.

फड़फड़ाना phur-phur-ána, *v. n.* To flutter, to wave, to twinkle, to move with convulsive mo-tion.

फड़फड़िया phur-phúr-iya, *s. m.* A flutterer. *adj.* Quick, swift.

फड़ाना phur-ána, *v. a.* To cause to be torn, split or cleaved.

फड़िंगा phúr-in-ga, *s. f.* A cricket.

फड़िया phúr-iya, *s. m.* A pedlar, a retailer; the keeper of a gaming-house or dice-table.

फन phun, *s. m.* The expanded hood or neck of the *Cobra de capello*, &c. *Phun oothana*, *v. a.* To spread the hood (*a snake*).

फनकर phun-kúr, *s. m.* A snake, especially the *Cobra de capello*, or *Coluber naja*.

फनधर phun-dhúr, *s. m.* A snake.

फनमणि phun-múni, *s. m.* A jewel sup-posed to be in the head of a snake.

फनवान phun-wán, *s. m.* A snake.

फनिकेशुर phúni-késhur, *s. m.* Mesua fer-rea.

फनिखेल phuni-khél, *s. m.* A quail.

फनिझुक phunij-jhúk, *s. m.* A plant, call-ed also *Muroua*.

फनिझुका phunij-jhúk-a, *s. f.* A plant, commonly called *Ramdooti*, apparently a sort of Basil with small leaves.

फनी phún-ee, *s. m.* A snake.

फनींद्र phun-éendr, ⎫ *s. m.* The
फनीशुर phun-éeshwur, ⎬ great ser-pent *Ununt*.

फदफदाना phud-phud-ána, *v. n.* To fer-ment (*as sour milk, curds, &c.*); to be inflamed with lust.

फन phun, *s. m.* The expanded hood or neck of the *Cobra de capello*, &c.

फनगा phún-ga, *s. m.* A grasshopper.

फनफनाना phun-phun-ána, *v. n.* To hiss (*as a snake*); to spring up suddenly (*as a fast-growing plant*); to move about briskly (*as a play-ful child*).

फुन्दना phúnd-na, *v. n.* To be imprisoned.

फुन्दलाना phund-lána, *v. a.* To ensnare, to entrap.

फुन्दा phún-da, *s. m.* A noose, a net, a snare ; perplexity, difficulty.

फुन्दाना phun-dá-na, *v. a.* To cause to jump or leap over.

फुफसा phúph-sa, *adj.* Swelled ; insipid.

फाफूंदी phuphóon-dee, *s. f.* Mouldiness.

फुफोला phuphó-la, ⎫ *s. m.* A blister.
फुपोला phupóla, ⎬ *Phupholeh phoot-*
neh, v. n. To be blistered ; it is used to express the mind being blistered, to be afflicted. *Phu-pholeh dil keh phorneh,* To satisfy a revenge that has long been rankling in one's breast.

फुब phub, *s. f.* Embellishment, ornament, dress.

फुबकना phúb-uk-na, *v. n.* To shoot forth (*as a plant*).

फुबता phúb-ta, *adj.* Pertinent, fit.

फुबती phúb-tee, *s. f.* Ornament, conjec-turing what a person is by his dress. *Phubtee kuhna, v. a.* To say what is conjectured by one's dress.

फुबन phúb-un, *s. f.* Embellishment, or-nament.

फुबना phúb-na, *v. n.* To become, befit, fit.

फुबीला phub-éela, *adj.* Becoming, fit.

फुर phur, *s. m.* A shield ; a fruit.

फुरक phúr-uk, *s. m.* A shield.

फुरकना phúr-uk-na, *v. n.* To flutter, to vibrate with convulsive involuntary motion, as the eyelids and other muscles ; to throb, to palpitate ; to writhe (*the shoulders, &c.*)

फुरचा phúr-cha, *s. m.* Clearing away or dispersion (*of clouds or of a multitude of people*) ; fair weather ; decision, definitive sentence (*of a judge*).

फुरचाना phur-chá-na, *v. a.* To decide, to give a final sentence.

फुरछा phur-chhá, *adj.* Pure, honest, fair, candid, fair (*not cloudy*). *Phurchha kurna, v. a.* To clean, to settle, to sweep.

फुरछाना phur-chhá-na, *v. a.* To clean, to wipe, to settle, to clear away (*the clouds, &c.*)

फुरफुन्द phur-phúnd, *s. m.* Deceit, trick, wickedness.

फुरफुन्दिया phur-phún-diya, *adj.* Deceitful, treacherous, wicked.

फुरसा phúr-sa, *s. m.* An axe, hatchet.

फुरूरा phurúh-ra, *s. m.* ⎫ A vane, a pen-
फुरूरी phurúh-ree, *s. f.* ⎬ nant. *adj.*
Half dried.

फुरिया phúr-iya, *s. f.* A kind of bordered vestment worn by *Hindoos* ; a contractor for reap-ing.

फुरी phúr-ee, *s. f.* A shield, target ; one of several fishes.

फुरुवुक phur-oo-vúk, *s. m.* A betel-box.

फुरोहा phuróoha, *s. m.* An instrument for raking together.

फुरेठा phur-rá-ta, *s. m.* A piece of bam-boo ; a sound made by the flying of a flag or the breathing of a horse.

फुरराना phur-rá-na, *v. n.* To fly (*as a flag*).

फुरराrस phur-rás, *s. m.* A tree (*its leaves resemble those of the Cypress or of the Tamarisk, and make a whistling noise in the wind : whence the name*).

फुल phul, *s. m.* The fruit of any plant, fruit in general ; fruit (*metaphorically*), result, effect, produce, consequence ; children, progeny ; gain, profit, acquisition, advantage ; recompense, reward ; the blade of a sword or knife, the head of an arrow, spear, &c. ; a sort of fragrant berry and drug, commonly called *Kukoli* ; a nutmeg ; a ploughshare ; the quotient of a sum (*in arith-metic*). *Phuldar, adj.* Fruitful. *Phul pana,* To reap the reward of (*good or bad actions*). *Phul-phularee,* Fruits of various kinds.

फुलुक phul-úk, *s. m.* A shield ; a bone, the *os frontis*, or bone of the forehead ; a plant (*Mesua ferrea*).

फुलकामना phul-kámna, *s. f.* Desire of any consequence.

फुलकी phúl-kee, *adj.* Having or being armed with a shield, &c. *s. m.* A sort of fish, commonly called *Phulees.*

फुलकेशुर phul-késhur, *s. m.* The cocoa-nut tree.

फुलकोशुक phul-kóshuk, *s. m.* The scrotum or testicles.

फुलकृष्ण phul-kríshn, *s. m.* A small fruit of a black colour (*Carissa carandas*).

फुलगृहि phul-grúhi, *adj.* Fruitful, bearing fruit in due season.

फुलखून्दन phul-khún-dun, *s. m.* Disap-pointing.

फुलचूमस phul-chúm-us, *s. m.* The bark of the Indian fig, ground and eaten with curds, by way of penance.

फुलजनक phul-jún-uk, *adj.* Fruitful, pro-ducing fruit. [&c.

फुलूत phul-út, *adj.* Yielding fruit, profit,

फुलतार phul-tár, *s. m.* The fruit bearing *tar,* the female palm.

फुलत्रुय phul-trúy, *s. m.* The three sorts of fruit collectively, the *Puroosh,* and the *Gmeli-na arborea ;* the three myrobalans.

फलत्रिक phul-trík, *s. m.* The three myrobalans collectively.

फलद phul-úd, *adj.* Yielding or bearing fruit, results, &c. *s. m.* A tree.

फलदाता phul-dáta, *adj.* Giving fruit, rewarding or giving the fruit of good or bad actions.

फलन phul-ún, *s. m.* Fructifying, bearing fruit, producing consequences.

फलना phúl-na, *v. n.* To produce or bear fruit; to result, to be produced; to be fortunate.

फलनिवृत्ति phul-nivrítti, *s. f.* Cessation of consequences.

फलनिर्वृत्ति phul-nirvrítti, *s. f.* Final consequence or result.

फलनिष्पत्ति phul-nish-pútti, *s. f.* Bearing fruit; yielding profit or desired results.

फलपाक phul-pák, *s. m.* The ripening of fruit; the fulness of consequences; the *Coronda.*

फलपाकान्ता phul-pak-ánta, *s. f.* An annual plant, dying after bearing fruit.

फलपूर phul-póor, *s. m.* Common citron (*Citrus medica*).

फलप्राप्ति phul-prápti, *s. f.* Obtaining the desired result or fruit.

फलबूझौवल phul-boo-jhóu-wul, *s. m.* A game (called also *munkela*): "think of a number, double it, add ten to it, take five from it, &c. how much remains?" "twenty-one," "the number was eight."

फलभोग phul-bhóg, *s. m.* Receipt or enjoyment of consequences; possession of rent or profit, usufruct.

फलभोगी phul-bhó-gee, *adj.* Who receives the profits, consequences, &c.

फलवान् phul-wán, } *adj.* Bearing fruit;
फलवत् phul-wút, } yielding results, or consequences.

फलश्रेष्ठ phul-shréshth, *s. m.* The mango.

फलसम्पत् phul-súm-put, } *s. f.* Prosperity,
फलसम्पद् phul-sum-púd, } success.

फलसिद्धि phul-síd-dhi, *s. f.* Realizing an object, reaping the fruit of any act.

फलहानि phul-háni, *s. f.* Loss of fruit or profit.

फलाकाङ्क्षी phul-akánkshee, *s. f.* Hope or expectation of favourable consequences.

फलाङ्ग phul-áng, *s. f.* A stride.

फलाना phul-ána, *v. a.* To make fruitful, to fructify, to cause to produce.

फलापेक्षा phul-apéksha, *s. f.* Regard to or expectation of consequences.

फलाशी phul-áshee, *adj.* Living on fruits.

फलास phul-ás, *s. m.* A step, a stride.

फलित phul-ít, *adj.* Fruitful, bearing fruit; successful, yielding a result.

फलिया phúl-iya, } *s. f.* A cod, a pod (*or*
फली phúl-ee, } *the seed*) of any leguminous plant, but particularly of peas; a loop. *Phulee-kush, s. m.* A hook for drawing the strings through the holes by which the walls of a tent are laced to the top.

फलियाना phul-iyána, *v. n.* To bear fruit.

फली phúl-ee, *s. f.* A cod, a pod, (*or the seed*) of any leguminous plant, but particularly of peas; a loop. *Phulee-khus, s. m.* A hook for drawing the strings through the holes by which the walls of a tent are laced to the top. *s. f.* A shield; a medicinal plant, commonly called *Priyungoo.*

फली phúl-ee, *adj.* Bearing fruit, fruitful, productive of consequences. *s. m.* A sort of fish, commonly called *Phuluee* (*Mystus kapirat*).

फलूआ phul-óo-a, *s. m.* A knotted fringe.

फलेरूहा phuleroohá, *s. f.* The trumpet-flower (*Bignonia suave-olens*).

फलोत्तमा phul-óttum-a, *s. f.* The fruit arising from sacred study.

फलोदय phul-ó-duy, *s. m.* Gain, profit; joy, happiness; consequence, result.

फलोद्देश phul-oddésh, *s. m.* Regard to results.

फल्गु phúl-goo, *s. f.* The opposite-leaved fig-tree (*Ficus oppositifolia*); the name of a river which is said to run underneath *Gya*; a red powder, usually of the root of wild ginger, coloured with sappan wood, and thrown over one another by the *Hindoos* at the *Holee* festival.

फल्गुन phúl-goon, *s. m.* The month *Phalgoon.*

फल्गुनी phúl goo-nee, *s. f.* The constellation *Phulgoonee.*

फल्यु phúl-yuh, *s. m.* A bud, a flower.

फलुकी phúl-luk-ee, *s. m.* A fish caught in ponds, commonly called *Phuluee* (*Mystus kapirat*).

फसकर phus-kúr, *s. m.* Sitting on the ground with legs extended.

फसकना phus-úk-na, *v. n.* To split, burst, break.

फसकाना phus-ká-na, *v. a.* To burst, split, break; loosen, slacken.

फसना phús-na, *v. n.* To stick (*as in mud or in a narrow passage*), to be caught, to be noosed or ensnared, to be imprisoned, to be impeded, to be entangled, to be involved (*in calamity, &c.*)

फसफसा phus-phús-a, *adj.* Flabby, loose, not rigid.

फसाङ्क phus-a-kóo, *adj.* Bad tobacco.

फुसाना phus-á-na, v. a. To cause to stick (as in mud, &c.), to mire, entangle, embroil, catch, to cause to be imprisoned, to squash.

फुहुरना phuhúr-na, v. n. To fly (as a flag).

फुहराना phuhrána, v. n. To fly, wave, stream (as a flag in the air), to flutter.

फांक phank, s. f. A slice, a piece of fruit.

फांकड़ phan-kúr, s. m. A fop.

फांकना phánk-na, v. a. To chuck into the mouth from the palm of the hand (grain, meal, &c.); to squander.

फांकी phán-kee, s. f. A slice or piece of fruit; an objection (in logic).

फांड phand, ⎫ s. m. A noose, snare,
फांदा phán-da, ⎬ net; (met.) perplexity, difficulty.

फांदना phánd-na, v. a. To jump over, to leap over.

फांदी phán-dee, s. f. A bundle of 50 or 100 sugar-canes.

फांपना phámp-na, v. n. To swell.

फांफूड़ pham-phúr, s. m. A hole, an orifice.

फांस phans, s. m. A splinter (of bamboo, &c.); a noose; an impediment.

फांसना pháns-na, v. a. To noose, to ensnare, to entrap, to throttle, to strangle, to choak. v. n. To be impeded, to stick (as in mud); to be perplexed.

फांसा pháns-a, s. m. A noose; an impediment.

फांसी pháns-ee, s. f. A noose, a loop, halter, strangulation. Phansee dena, To strangle. v. a. To strangle, to hang. Phansee purna, v. n. To be hanged. Phansee lugana, v. a. To kill one's self by strangling.

फाग phag, s. m. Red powder (sprinkled in the time of the Holee); the act of throwing coloured powders in the Holee, the gambols of the Holee.

फागुन phá-goon, s. m. The name of the 11th month, the full moon of which is near Poorvaphul-goonee, February-March.

फाटक phá-tuk, s. m. A gate, a large shutter; an obstruction, impediment, a check; the bar of a court of justice, where the plaintiff and defendant take their station.

फाटना phát-na, v. n. To be torn, to be broken, split, rent, torn asunder, &c.

फरखाऊ phar-khaóo, adj. Ravenous; ravenous beast, &c.

फरखाना phar-khána, v. a. To worry.

फारना phár-na, v. a. To tear, rend, split, break, cleave (wood, &c.), to tear open, burst, rip.

फाड़ phá-ra, adj. Cut, slit, torn, rent.

फानि phá-ni, s. f. Flour or meal mixed with curds.

फाल phal, s. m. The share of a plough. s. f. A lump of betel-nut (Areca); a step.

फालसा phál-sa, s. m. A fruit (Grewia asiatica).

फालगून phál-goon, s. m. A tree (Pentaptera Arjuna); the eleventh Hindoo month, February-March.

फालगूनी phál-goo-nee, s. f. Day of full moon in the month Phalgoon, on which the Holee or great vernal festival of the Hindoos is celebrated; a name common to the eleventh and twelfth lunar asterisms, distinguished by the epithets first and last.

फाव pháo, s. m. A small quantity given above the quantity purchased, to boot.

फावड़ा pháo-ra, s. m. Mattock, spade, hoe.

फावड़ी pháo-ree, s. f. A crutch on which a Jogee leans; a piece of wood or staff with a support at each end, which is held in both hands and laid horizontally, in performing the exercise of dund; an instrument like a small rake or hoe for removing a horse's dung.

फाहा phá-ha, s. m. A flock of cotton wet with utr or scented water.

फिंकना phínk-na, v. n. To be thrown.

फिकाना phik-ána, v. a. To cause or teach to throw.

फिकारना phik-árna, v. a. To bare or uncover the head, to unplait the hair of the head.

फिकैत phikyt, s. m. A thrower (of a spear, &c.)

फिंगुक phin-gúk, s. m. The fork-tailed shrike.

फिट phit, s. m. Curse, malediction. adv. Fy! Phit phit, Curse on it! fy upon it!

फिटकरी phít-kur-ee, s. f. Alum.

फिटकार phit-kár, s. f. Curse, malediction, removing something to a distance.

फिटकारना phit-kár-na, v. a. To curse.

फिटकिरी phít-kir-ee, s. f. Alum.

फिटाना phit-á-na, v. a. To beat up and mix, to froth.

फिर phir, adv. Again, then.

फिरकी phír-kee, s. f. A whirligig, any thing turning as on an axis.

फिरजाना phir-jána, v. n. To return, to revolt; to be distorted; to warp.

फिरउत phir-ut, s. m. Rejected things; money paid by a lewd woman to her paramour.

फिरतारूबना phírta-rúbna, v. n. To wander, to perambulate, to walk about.

फिरना phír-na, v. n. To turn, return, walk

about, go round, circulate, roll, whirl, to wheel, wander, travel, ramble, change, revolt.

फिरती phir-tee, *part. f.* or *s. f.* Returning, return, homeward-bound. *Phirtee ka bhara,* The hire of a return boat, carriage, &c.

फिराना phir-ána, *v. a.* To cause to turn, whirl, wheel, make to go about, return, change, roll, shift, wander.

फिराव phir-áo, *s. m.* Return, restitution, rotation, turning.

फिरनी phír-nee, *s. f.* A whirligig, any thing turning as on an axis.

फिलसना phil-ús-na, *v. n.* To slip.

फिली phíl-lee, *s. f.* The leg.

फिश phish, *interj.* Pish! pshaw! tush!

फिसफिसाना phis-phis-ána, *v. n.* To be terrified.

फिसलना phis-úl-na, *v. n.* To slip, to slide, to err. *adj.* Slippery.

फिसलुहा phis-luhá, *adj.* Slippery.

फिसलाना phis-lá-na, *v. a.* To cause to slip, slide or err.

फिसलाहट phis-lá-hut, *s. f.* Slipperiness.

फींचना phéenchna, } *v. a.* To wash
फींचडालना phéench-dálna, } cloth, to rinse, squeeze.

फीक pheek, *s. f.* The point of a scourge.

फीका phée-ka, *adj.* Weak, vapid, tasteless, insipid; pale, sallow, light (*in colour*).

फुंकार phoon-kár, *s. f.* Hiss (*of a snake*).

फुंकारना phoon-kár-na, *v. n.* To hiss (*as a snake*).

फुंकारी phoon-ká-ree, *s. f.* Hissing (*of a snake*). *Phoonkaree marna,* To hiss (*a snake*).

फुंगी phóon-gee, *s. f.* A sprout, a bud, the point of an ear of corn.

फुंहार phoon-hár, *s. f.* The small drops of rain. [d'eau.]

फुंहारा phoon-há-ra, *s. m.* A fountain, a jet

फुकना phóok-na, *s. m.* A bladder.

फुकनी phóok-nee, *s. f.* A blowpipe; a firelock or pistol.

फुट phoot, *adj.* Odd, unpaired.

फुटकर phoot-kúr, *adj.* Odd, unpaired; separate, dispersed (*as a horseman*).

फुटकी phóot-kee, *s. f.* A blot, spot, stain. *adj.* Odd, unpaired.

फुड़िया phóo-ri-ya, *s. f.* A sore, a pimple, a boil.

फुत phoot, *interj.* Expression of disregard or contempt (*Phoo, hoot.*)

फुतकार phoot-kúr, *adj.* Arrogant, contemptuous, disdainful.

फुदकना phoo-dúk-na, *v. n.* To jump, leap, hop (*applied to small birds*), to dance about in token of delight.

फुदकी phóod-kee, *s. f.* A bird (*Certhia tula*).

फुनगी phóon-gee, *s. f.* A sprout, a bud, the point of an ear of corn, &c.

फुनुंग phoo-núng, *s. f.* Top, summit.

फुनसी phóon-see, *s. f.* A pimple.

फुनिया phóo-niya,
फुन्नी phóon-nee, } *s. f.* Penis puerilis.
फुन्नो phóon-no,

फुँदना phóond-na, *s. m.* A tassel.

फुप्फा phoop-phá, *s. m.* The husband of a paternal aunt.

फुप्फी phóop-phee, *s. f.* A paternal aunt.

फुफकार phooph-kár, *s. f.* The hissing of a snake.

फुफकारना phooph-kar-na, *v. n.* To hiss (*a snake*).

फुफियासास phóophiya-sás, *s. f.* The sister of a father-in-law.

फुफेरा phoophéra, *m.* } *adj.* Descended
फुफेरी phoophéree, *f.* } from, or related through a paternal aunt. *Phoophera bhaee,* The son of a paternal aunt; cousin. *Phoopheree buhin,* Daughter of a paternal aunt.

फुर phoor, *adj.* True, right.

फुर्र phoorr, *s. m.* The noise of a bird, as a partridge or quail, suddenly taking wing; or of a small quantity of gunpowder exploding.

फुरफुराना phoor-phoo-rána, *v. n.* To tremble; to wave (*as hair in the wind*).

फुरफुरी phóor-phoo-ree, *s. f.* Trembling, quivering, tremour, palpitation.

फुरहारी phoor-há-ree, *s. f.* Horripilation.

फुर्त phoort,
फुर्ती phoort-ée, } *s. f.* Activity, quickness, alertness, agility.

फुर्तीला phoor-tée-la, *adj.* Quick, nimble, active, smart, alert, expert.

फुलका phóol-ka, *adj.* Inflated, puffed up; light. *s. m.* A blister; a kind of cake or small loaf; an area or arena for wrestlers.

फुलकारना phool-kárna, *v. n.* To inflate, to swell out (*as a snake's hood*), to expand.

फुलकारी phool-kúree, *s. m.* Flowered cloth.

फुलकी phóol-kee, *s. f.* A cake or raised bread.

फुलझुरी phool-jhúr-ee, *s. f.* A kind of firework like a fountain.

फुलवारी phool-wáree, *s. f.* A flower-garden.

फुलहथा phool-hútha, *s. m.* Cudgelling.

फुलाना phoo-lá-na, v. a. To cause to swell, to inflate, distend ; to fatten ; (met.) to make proud or to puff up with flattery.

फुलासरा phoo-lás-ra, s. m. Flattery.

फुलेल phoo-lél, s. m. Oil impregnated with the essence of flowers by steeping them in it, essence (as a perfume).

फुलौरी phoo-lóu-ree, s. f. Bread or cake made of fruit and pulse, and fried in ghee or oil.

फुल phool, adj. Blown, opened, expanded as a flower.

फुलदामन् phool-dámun, s. m. A species of the Utidhriti metre.

फुलनयन phool-nyun, adj. Full or large-eyed ; smiling, looking happy.

फुललोचन phoo-lóchun, adj. Full-eyed ; looking pleased or happy. s. m. A large full eye ; a species of the antelope.

फुलवत् phool-wút, } adj. Blossoming,
फुलवान् phool-wán, } blowing.

फुली phóol-lee, s. f. A disorder in the eye, the albugo.

फुसफुसाना phoos-phoo-sána, v. n. To whisper.

फुसफुसावट phoos-phoo-sá-wut, s. f. Whispering, buzzing in the ear.

फुसलाऊ phoos-láoo, } s. m. A coax-
फुसलौनिया phoos-lóu-niya, } er, a wheed-ler, a seducer.

फुसलाना phoos-lána, v. a. To coax, wheedle, cajole, flatter, instigate, entice, seduce.

फुसाहिन्द phoo-sa-hínda, adj. Disgusting, stinking.

फुक्का phóos-ka, adj. Weak, without strength, slack (as a knot).

फुआ phóoa, s. f. Father's sister, paternal aunt ; a lizard.

फूंक phoonk, s. f. Act of blowing, a puff, a blast, blowing up (fire, &c.) Phoonk dena, To set on fire. Phoonk-phoonk-kur paon dhurna, To act or walk carefully and cautiously.

फूंकना phóonk-na, v. a. To blow with the breath ; to blow up (a fire, &c.), to inflame, set on fire, kindle, to blow (a horn, trumpet, &c.)

फूंकारना phoon-kár-na, v. n. To hiss (as a snake), to snort.

फूंही phóon-hee, }
फींहार phon-hár, } s. f. Small rain.
फूहार phoo-hár, }

फूकना phóok-na, v. To blow.

फूकर phóo-kur, s. m. A fine sensible young fellow.

फूट phoot, s. f. A kind of melon (Cucumis momordica) ; a ripe cucumber bursting elasti-

cally (as the Cucumis utilatissimus : and Momordica mixta) ; odd, unpaired ; difference of opinion, dissension, discord ; separation ; a flow, breach, break. Phoot purna, To arise (dissension). Phoot-phoot, or phoot-kur rona, To weep excessively. Phoot bikhera, adj. Scattered, dispersed. Phoot ruhna, To be broken ; to be dispersed ; to be unpaired. Phoot hona, To be divided in opinion.

फूटन phoo-tún, s. f. Wrangling, disagreement, misunderstanding.

फूटना phóot-na, v. n. To be broken, to be broken into or broken down ; to be dispersed, to be separated, to separate, to be unpaired ; to burst, split ; to be made public, to transpire ; to arise (as a smell), or to burst forth ; to get promotion or advancement.

फूटला phóot-la, adj. Bad (coin).

फूटा phóo-ta, adj. Broken.

फूटी phóo-tee, s. f. Disagreement, disparity.

फूफा phoo-phá, s. m. Father's sister's husband.

फूफी phóo-phee, s. f. Father's sister, paternal aunt.

फूफू phóo-phoo, s. m. f. Father's sister's husband, or father's sister.

फूल phool, s. m. A flower, a blossom ; boss, stud, bunch of ribands, &c. a cockade ; the menses, of which children are the fruit ; a swelling ; bones of a dead person after the fleshy parts are burned ; lights or fire (seen at night) ; pl. a ceremony performed in honor of a deceased person on the third day after his death. Phool oothna, v. n. To be performed (a ceremony in honor of the dead), to complete the forty days of mourning. Phool jana, v. n. To swell, to be delighted, to be pleased ; to become fat. Phool jhurna, v. n. To speak eloquently ; to fall from a lamp (drops of burning oil). Phool purna, v. n. To break out (a fire). Phool bythna, v. n. To be glad.

फूलकोबी phóol-kobee, s. f. A cauliflower.

फूलना phóol-na, v. n. To blossom, to blow, to flower ; to be pleased, to be in health and spirits, i. e. to bloom, to flourish ; to swell, to be inflated, to be puffed up (with pride, &c.)

फूला phóo-la, adj. Swelled ; blossomed. Phoola nuh sumana, Not to be able to contain one's self from delight, to be overjoyed, to exult.

फूलाव phoo-láo, s. m. A swelling.

फूली phóo-lee, s. f. A disorder in the eye, the albugo.

फूस phoos, s. m. Old dry grass or straw. Phoos men chingaree dalna, To excite contention or strife.

फूसका phóos-ra, }
फूसरा phóos-ra, } s. m. A rag.

फूसी phóo-see, s. f. Chaff.

फूहुर phóo-hur, *adj.* Undisciplined, un-educated; stupid; obscene, foolish, rude (*applied to women*). *s. f.* A bad house-wife, a slut or slattern.

फूहुरपन phoohur-pún, *s. m.* Stupidity; obscenity; foolishness.

फूहरा phooh-rá, *adj.* Talking obscenely.

फूहा phoo-há, *s. m.* A fictitious teat of pap, formed of cotton or other substance, by which milk is given to a young goat or the like, when unable to suck the mother.

फूहार phoo-hár, } *s. f.* Small rain.
फूही phoo-hée, }

फेंक phenk, *s. f.* Throw, cast. *Phenk dena, v. a.* To throw away.

फेंकना phénk-na, *v. a.* To throw, to fling, to dart, to let fly (*a hawk, &c. at game*), to set off (*a horse*) at full speed, to gallop.

फेंकाव phen-káo, *adj.* Requiring to be thrown.

फेंट phent, } *s. f.* Waist-band, a belt.
फेंट phynt, } *Phent bandhna,* To get ready, to resolve.

फेंटना phént-na, *v. a.* To mix, to beat (*as eggs, &c.*), to triturate.

फेंटा phén-ta, } *s. f.* Waist-band; a small
फेंटा phyn-ta, } turband.

फेंटी phén-tee, *s. f.* A skein (*of thread, &c.*)

फेट phet, *s. f.* The waist when bound with a belt.

फेटना phét-na, *v. a.* To mix by trituration.

फेटा phét-a, *s. m.* A small turband; a waist-band without a fringe.

फेन phen, *s. m.* Froth, foam; cuttle-fish bone, supposed to be the indurated foam of the sea.

फेनक phen-úk, *s. m.* Cuttle-fish bone.

फेनका phen-uk-á, *s. f.* The soap berry.

फेनता phen-tá, *s. f.* Frothiness, vapour.

फेनल phen-úl, *adj.* Frothy, foamy.

फेनवस् phen-wút, *adj.* Frothy, foaming, bubbling.

फेना phén-a, *s. m.* Foam, froth.

फेनाना phen-ána, } *v. n.* To foam, to
फेनाना phyn-ána, } froth.

फेनायमान phen-ayumán, *adj.* Foaming, frothing.

फेनिल phen-íl, *adj.* Frothy, foamy. *s. m.* The soap plant (*Sapindus detergens*); the fruit of the jujube; the fruit of the *Vangueria spinosa.*

फेनी phén-ee, *s. f.* A kind of sweetmeat.

फेनूस phen-oos, *s. m.* Biesting, the milk of a cow, &c. for some days after calving.

फेफुरी phéphur-ee, *s. f.* Inability to move.

फेर pher, *s. m.* Turning, turn, return, change, meander, maze, curvature, twisting, coil, fold, circumference; equivocation, ambiguity; difficulty, distance. *adv.* Again, back. *Pher khana,* To wind (*as a river*), to meander; to go round about; to meet with perplexities. *Pher dena,* To return, to restore, refund. *Pher purna,* To differ. *Pher-phar, adj.* Alternate. *Pher-phar kurna,* To alternate. *Pher-men dalna,* To throw obstacles in the way of another.

फेरना phér-na, *v. a.* To turn, turn back, invert, reverse, avert, turn away, to make to walk backwards and forwards, to bring or carry back, to shift, repeat; plaster, stroke. *Sir-pur hath pherna,* To deceive by coaxing. *Hath pherna,* To caress, to fondle.

फेरव pher-úv, *adj.* Fraudulent, crafty, a rogue or cheat; malicious, noxious, injurious.

फेरा phér-a, *s. m.* Turning, circuit, peram-bulation; a roll; a wooden frame with which lime, sand, &c. is measured.

फेराफेरी phéra-phéree, *s. f.* Walking backwards and forwards, going and coming; returning, alternating, alternation.

फेरी phér-ee, *s. f.* Act of going round to the right by way of adoration, circumambulation, going about.

फेरीवाला phéree-wála, *s. m.* A pedlar.

फेरू phér-oo, *s. m.* A jackal.

फेंटा phyn-ta, *s. f.* Waist-band; a small turband.

फेनाना phy-ná-na, *v. n.* To foam, to froth.

फैलना phyl-ná, *v. n.* To be spread, to spread; to be expanded, dilated, diffused, scatter-ed or dispersed; to become public.

फैलाना phy-lá-na, *v. a.* To spread, scatter, expand, diffuse, widen, stretch out, extend, distend, dilate, publish, proclaim, to branch out. *Hath phylana,* To beg.

फैलाव phy-láo, *s. m.* Spread, expansion, extension, diffusion, publication, display, extent; plenty, profusion.

फैलावा phy-lá-wa, *s. m.* Prolixity.

फोंक phonk, *s. f.* The notch of an arrow. *adj.* Hollow, not solid (*particularly jewels*).

फोंफी phon-phée, *s. f.* A pipe, a tube; any thing perforated or hollow.

फोंहार phon-hár, *s. f.* Small rain.

फोक phok, *s. m.* Dregs, sediment, grains. *adj.* Hollow.

फोकट pho-kút, *s. m.* An indigent person.

फोकड़ pho-kúr, *s. m.* Dross, refuse, trash, grains.

फोड़ना phór-na, *v. a.* To break, split, burst, disclose, divulge or betray (*a secret*).

फोड़ा phó-ra, *s. m.* A boil, sore, abscess, imposthume.

फोला phó-la, *s. m.* A blister.

ब

ब buh, The twenty-third consonant of the *Naguree* alphabet, corresponding to the letter *b*, and often confounded with the analogous semivowel ब or *v*, with which some grammarians consider it to be at all times optionally interchangeable.

बंक bunk, *s. m.* A bending, a curvature, the reach or bend of a river.

बंकाई bunk-áee, *s. f.* A bending, curvature, the reach or bend of a river.

बंग bung, *s. f.* Calx of tin given internally as aphrodisiack; a name of *Bengal*.

बंगरी búng-ree, *s. f.* An ornament worn on the wrist (*properly made of glass*), a bangle.

बंगला búng-la, *s. m.* A kind of thatched house, a summer-house; a sort of betel-leaf or pan so called.

बंगा búng-a, *s. m.* A joint or bamboo root.

बंगाला bung-ála, *n. prop.* Name of *Bengal*.

बंगी búng-ee, *s. f.* A humming top.

बंचना búnch-na, *v. n.* To be read or perused.

बंझोटी bunjh-ótee, *s. f.* A medicine taken to produce barrenness.

बंटवाना bunt-wá-na, *v. a.* To distribute, to cause to be shared.

बंटवैया bunt-wyya, } *s. m.* A divider, a
बंटैत buntyt, } distributer.

बंटाना bun-tá-na, *v. a.* To share, divide, participate.

बंडी bún-dee, *s. f.* A short robe, a short full *Jamuh.*

बंडेरी bun-dér-ee, *s. f.* A ridge pole, the ridge of a house.

बंडोहा bun-dó-ha, } *s. m.* A whirlwind, a
बवंडर buv-ún-dur, } devil.

बंवर bún-wur, } *s. m.* A creeper, a
बंवंड bún-wund, } vine.

बंस buns, *s. m.* Race, lineage, family, offspring, descendant; a bamboo.

बंसलोचन buns-lóchun, *s. m.* The manna or sugar of the bamboo: it has been found by analysis to contain saliceous earth.

बंसावली buns-áwulee, *s. f.* A genealogy.

बंसी bún-see, *s. f.* A flute; a fishing hook; (*in comp.*) Of the race or lineage.

बंसीबट bunsee-bút, *s. m.* The fig-tree under which *Krishn* was accustomed to play the lute.

बक buk, *s. m.* A crane (*Ardea torra* and *putsa*). *Buk dhyan lugana,* To act with dissimulation. *s. f.* Prattle, chat, foolish talk, garrulity. *Buk jhuk, s. f.* Prattle, chat, &c. *Buk jhuk kurna,* To prattle, to chatter, to gabble. *Buk lugnee,* Talkativeness, garrulity.

बकची búk-chee, *s. f.* A plant the seed of which is used to cure the itch (*Conyza* or *Serratula anthelmintica*).

बकझक buk-jhúk, *s. f.* Prattle, chat, foolish talk, garrulity.

बकना búk-na, *v. n.* To prate, chatter, chat, jabber, babble, cackle.

बकबक buk-buk, *s. f.* Prattle, foolish talk, babble, clack, gabble. *Buk buk kurna,* To prattle, chatter, gabble.

बकबकाना buk-buk-ána, *v. n.* To prattle, chatter, clack.

बकरा búk-ra, *s. m.* A he-goat.

बकरी búk-ree, *s. m. f.* A goat (*generally*), a female goat.

बकला búk-la, *s. m.* Bark, skin, rind, shell (*of a fruit*), husk.

बकवाद buk-wád, *s. f.* Prattle, foolish talk.

बकवादी buk-wá-dee, *s. m.* One who talks foolishly, an idle talker, prater, cackler.

बकवास buk-wás, *s. f.* Talkativeness.

बकवाहा buk-wá-ha, *m.* } *part. act.* A
बकवाही buk-wá-hee, *f.* } chatterer, an idle talker.

बकसा búk-sa, *adj.* Astringent.

बकसूआ buk-sóo-a, *s. m.* The tongue of a buckle.

बकसैला buk-sy-la, *adj.* Astringent.

बकायन buk-á-yun, *s. f.* A tree (*Melia sempervirens*).

बकारा buk-á-ra, *s. m.* A forerunner, a harbinger; a traveller.

बकिया búk-iya, *s. f.* A clasp-knife, a penknife.

बकुल búk-ool, *s. m.* A tree (*Mimusops elengi*).

बकेलू buk-él-oo, *s. m.* The root of a grass of which rope is made.

बकोटना buk-ót-na, *v. a.* To lacerate with the nails, to claw, to scratch.

बककम búk-kum, *s. m.* Sappan or red wood (*Cæsalpinia sappan*).

बकुल buk-kúl, *s. m.* Bark, skin, rind, shell (*of a fruit*), husk.

बकी búk-kee, *part. act.* Talkative; a prater, chatterer, jabberer.

बक्ता buk-tá, *s. m.* A speaker in general. *adj.* Eloquent, loquacious, talkative.

बख़ bukh, *s. m.* The world.

बखरी búkh-ree, *s. f.* A cottage, a house.

बखान bukhán, *s. m.* Explanation, praise, description, definition.

बखानना bukhánna, } *v. a.* To
बखान करना bukhán kúrna, } praise, commend; explain, define, relate.

बखार bukhár, *s. m.* } A storehouse, a
बखारी bukháree, *s. f.* } granary.

बखिया búkhiya, *s. m.* A kind of stitch, strong quilting. [quilt.

बखियाना bukhiyána, *v. a.* To stitch, to

बखी búkhee, *s. f.* The side under the armpit.

बखेड़ा bukhéra, *s. m.* Wrangling, a tumult, broil, contention, dispute, quarrel.

बखेड़िया bukhér-iya, *adj.* Quarrelsome, captious; a wrangler, a brawler.

बखेरना bukhérna, *v. a.* To scatter.

बग bug, *s. m.* A crane (*Ardea torra* and *putea*).

बगचाल bug-chál, *s. f.* Walking slowly (*like a crane*).

बगछुंदा छगना bug-chhúnda lúgna, *v. n.* To be stupified or petrified with fear at the sight of a tiger.

बगछूट bug-chhóot, *s. f.* Galloping. *Bug-chhoot dourna*, To gallop.

बगऊ bug-úr, *s. m.* A kind of rice.

बगरा bug-rá, *s. m.* Trouble; cheat, deceit. *Bugra kurna*, To avoid the payment of one's debts or the performance of one's promise.

बगरिया bug-ríya, *adj.* A deceitful person.

बगउदना búg-ud-na, *v. n.* To return; to be spoiled.

बगदाना bug-dá-na, *v. a.* To cause to return, to put to the rout.

बगपाती bug-pá-tee, *s. f.* The side under the armpit.

बगपाँती bug-pán-tee, *s. f.* A row or line of cranes.

बगरेंडी bug-rénd-ee, *s. f.* A plant (*Jatropha curcus*).

बगला búg-la, } *s. m.* A crane or heron
बगऊला búg-oo-la, } (*Ardea torra* and *putea*). *Bugla bhugut*, A hypocrite.

बगहंस bug-húns, *s. m.* A bird, a grey goose.

बगारना bug-ár-na, *v. a.* To throw away; to spread over.

बगिया búg-iya, } *s. f.* A little garden.
बगीचा bug-ée-cha, }

2 u 2

बगूला bug-óo-la, *s. m.* A whirlwind.

बघनूहा bugh-núha, *s. m.* A medicinal herb with a fragrant root.

बघना bugh-ná, *s. m.* The teeth and nails of a tiger which are hung round the neck of a child.

बघार bughár, *s. m.* The spices which are mixed with food to give it relish; seasoning, condiment.

बघारना bughárna, *v. a.* To season.

बघी búghee, *s. f.* A horsefly.

बघेल bughél, *s. m.* A tribe of *Rajpoots*.

बघेला bughéla, *s. m.* A *Rajpoot* of the *Bughel* tribe; a tiger's whelp, a young tiger.

बंकाई bun-káee, *s. f.* A bending, curvature, reach or bend of a river.

बंग bung, *s. f.* Calx of tin given internally as an aphrodisiack; a name of *Bengal*.

बंगरी búng-ree, *s. f.* An ornament worn on the wrist (*properly made of glass*), a bangle.

बंगला búng-la, *s. m.* A kind of thatched house, a summer-house; a sort of betel-leaf or *pan* so called.

बंगा búng-a, *s. m.* A joint of bamboo root.

बंगाला bun-gá-la, *n. prop.* A name of *Bengal*.

बंगालिन bung-a-lín, *s. f.* A woman of *Bengal*.

बंगाली bun-gá-lee, *s. m.* An inhabitant of *Bengal*.

बंगी búngee, *s. f.* A humming top.

बच buch, *s. f.* Orris root.

बचकाना buch-kána, *adj.* Small (*generally applied to shoes and clothes*). *s. m.* A dancing boy.

बचकानी buch-ká-nee, *s. f.* A girl adopted by an old prostitute.

बचती búch-tee, *s. f.* Residue, remainder, surplus.

बचन búch-un, *s. m.* Speech, talk, discourse, word, expression; promise, agreement. *Buchun chhorna*, To break one's promise. *Buchun dalna*, To question, to ask, to inquire. *Buchun torna*, To break one's word. *Buchun dena*, To promise, to agree. *Buchun nibhana*, or, *—palna*, To abide by a promise. *Buchun bundh kurna*, To bind by promise. *Buchun bundh hona*, To give one's word, to promise, to be agreed upon. *Buchun manna*, To obey. *Buchun marna*, To conclude an agreement. *Buchun lena*, To receive a promise. *Buchun harna*, To promise, to agree, to give or pledge or plight one's word, to affirm.

बचनदत्त búchun-dútt, *adj.* Betrothed, espoused.

बचना búch-na, *v. n.* To be saved, be spared, to escape, avoid, remain unexpended, recover.

बचपन buch-pun, *s. m.* Childhood, infancy.

बचाना buch-ána, *v. a.* To save, preserve, protect, secure, reserve, extricate, spare, defend, guard, leave, avoid, conceal.

बचाव buch-áo, *s. m.* Protection, defence, safety, security, preservation, salvation, escape.

बच्चा búch-cha, *s. m.* A child, the young of any animal.

बच्छनाग buchchh-nág, *s. m.* A vegetable poison.

बछ buchh, *s. m.*
बछड़ा búchh-ra, *s. m.* } A calf.
बछरू buchh-róo, *s. m.*

बछिया buchhíya, *s. f.* A (*female*) calf.

बछेरा buchhéra, *s. m.* A colt.

बछेरी buchhéree, *s. f.* A foal, filly.

बजना búj-na, *v. n.* To be sounded, to sound, to be famous. *s. m.* A rupee (*used among brokers*).

बजन्त्री buj-ún-tree, *s. m.* One who plays on musical instruments. *Bujuntree-muhal, s. m.* The quarter inhabited by musicians ; a brothel ; taxes on musicians and female dancers.

बजबजाना buj-buj-ána, *v. n.* To effervesce with noise in putrefying.

बजरबट्टू bújur-búttoo, *s. m.* A kind of fruit.

बजरा búj-ra, *s. m.* A boat for travelling in, a pleasure boat of a larger kind.

बजवाना buj-wá-na, *v. a.* To cause to sound, to cause to play on an instrument of music.

बजाक buj-ák, *s. m.* A kind of serpent.

बजाना buj-á-na, *v. a.* To sound, to play upon an instrument, to perform or execute (*music*), to beat (*a drum, &c.*)

बजालाना buj-á-lána, *v. n.* To perform, accomplish, execute, effect, obey.

बजिद होना bujíd-hóna, *v. n.* To be in earnest, to be importunate, to insist.

बज्र bujr, *s. m.* A thunderbolt ; a diamond. *adj.* Hard. *Bujr pureh oospur,* May lightning fall on him ! (*an expression used in cursing any one*).

बज्रंग bujr-úng, *s. m.* A title of *Hunooman.*

बज्रंगी bujr-úngee, *s. f.* A kind of *tiluk* or mark made on a *Hindoo's* forehead with red-lead.

बूझना bújh-na, *v. n.* To be insnared, to be caught (*as game*); to stick.

बझाना bujhána, *v. a.* To entangle, insnare (*as game*), to entrap.

बट but, *s. m.* The Indian fig-tree (*Ficus Indica*) ; a single cowrie.

बटई butuée, *s. f.* The art of making gold thread.

बटखरा bút-khur-a, *s. m.* A weight.

बटना bút-na, *v. a.* To twist, to form by convolution (*as ropes*) ; to divide, share ; gain, make profit. *v. n.* To be divided, to be twisted. *s. m.* An instrument with which ropes are twisted.

बटपार but-pár, *s. m.* Highwayman, footpad, villain, cut-throat, assassin.

बटपारी but-pár-ee, *s. f.* Highway-robbery.

बटया bút-ya, *s. f.* A silken cord adorned with three fringes, which women use to tie their hair behind ; a narrow passage ; a small measure of weight.

बटरी bút-ree, *s. f.* A small cup.

बटलोही but-ló-hee, *s. f.* A brass vessel in which *Hindoos* dress their food.

बटवाना but-wá-na, *v. a.* To cause to twist, &c.

बटवार but-wár, *s. m.* A tax-gatherer who collects a tax levied in kind.

बटवारा but-wá-ra, *s. m.* A share.

बटाई but-áee, *s. f.* Hire paid for twisting ropes, &c.

बटाऊ but-aóo, *s. m.* A traveller, a robber.

बटिया bút-iya, *s. f.* A narrow passage ; a small measure of weight.

बटुआ but-óoa, *s. m.* A purse, a small bag (*generally used for holding betel-nut, &c.*); a brass vessel in which *Hindoos* dress their food.

बटेर but-ér, *s. f.* A kind of quail (*Perdrix olivacea*).

बटोर but-ór, *s. m.* A gathering, a crowd, a resort.

बटोरना but-ór-na, *v. a.* To gather up, collect, purse, accumulate. [farer.

बटोही but-ó-hee, *s. m.* A traveller, a way-

बट्टा bútta, *s. m.* Deficiency ; exchange or discount ; defect, blemish, injury, offence ; a ball (*of wood or stone*) ; a box in which gems are kept, a casket. *Butta-dhar,* and *Bhutta-dhal, adj.* Level, even. *Butteh-baz,* A juggler. *Butteh-bazee,* The performance of a juggler, juggling, sleight of hand.

बड़ bur, *s. m.* The Bengal fig-tree (*Ficus Bengalensis, or Indica*) ; (*in comp.*) a contraction of बड़ा bura, Great : as, *Bur-bola,* A noisy talkative person : *Bur-bhukooa,* A blockhead : *Bur-peta, adj.* Big-bellied ; a great eater ; greedy, avaricious.

बड़ना búr-na, *v. n.* To enter.

बड़बड़ bur-bur, *s. f.* Muttering, the lightheaded talk of a person in a delirium.

बड़बड़ाना bur-bur-ána, *v. a.* To mutter, grumble, chatter nonsense, talk light-headedly, rave.

बड़बड़िया bur-búr-iya, *part. act.* A chatterer, a mutterer, a grumbler.

बड़वा búr-wa, *s. f.* A mare; the nymph *Uswinee*, or the personified asterism which is designated by a horse's head.

बड़वाग्नि bur-wágni, *s. m.* Submarine fire.

बड़वानल bur-wa-núl, *s. m.* Submarine fire; in mythology, a being consisting of flame, but with the head of a mare, who sprang from the thighs of *Oorwa*, and was received by the ocean.

बड़वामुख bur-wa-móokh, *s. m.* Submarine fire; the infernal regions.

बड़हल búr-hul, *s. m.* A sweet and acid fruit of a yellowish red colour and nearly round.

बड़हेला bur-hél-a, *s. m.* A wild hog.

बड़ा búr-a, *adj.* Large, great, big, greater, senior, elder, eldest, principal, &c. *Bura kurna*, To enlarge, exalt, promote; extinguish, put out (*a lamp, &c. as to use the direct phrase is deemed unlucky*). *Bura rusta pukurna*, To die. *Bureh petwala hona*, To be patient.

बड़ाई bur-áee, *s. f.* Greatness, largeness, excellence, bulk, bulkiness, bigness; magnifying, boasting. *Buraee kurna*, or, —*marna*, To extol, magnify, boast, vaunt. *Buraee dena*, To honour.

बड़ाना bur-ána, *v. a.* To talk in one's sleep or in a delirium.

बड़ापन bur-a-pún, *s. m.* Greatness, grandeur, dignity.

बड़ापा bur-a-pá, *s. m.* Grandeur, dignity, elevation.

बड़ी búr-ee, *s. f.* A dish made of pulse.

बड़ूंखा bur-óon-kha, *s. m.* A kind of sugar-cane with long joints.

बड़ेमीयां búreh-méeyan, *s. m.* An old man; Sir! (*applied to an elderly man*).

बड़ई bur-húee, *s. m.* A carpenter.

बढ़ता burh-tá, *s. m.* ⎫ Increase, augmen-
बढ़ती burh-tée, *s. f.* ⎬ tation, enhance-
ment, overplus, more, promotion, aggrandizement, elevation.

बढ़न bur-hún, *s. f.* A carpenter's wife.

बढ़ना búrh-na, *v. n.* To increase, enlarge, go on, proceed, advance, exaggerate, grow, rise, swell, to be promoted, to amount, lengthen.

बढ़नी búrh-nee, *s. f.* A broom; advance made for cultivation or manufacture or a contract.

बढ़हुल bur-húl, *s. m.* A small round and acid fruit.

बढ़ाना bur-há-na, *v. a.* To increase, augment, enlarge, lengthen, make advance, forward, exalt, elevate, raise, promote, aggrandize, rear up, extend, stretch out, amplify, dilate; to extinguish; to shut up (*a shop*); to remove the table-cloth.

बढ़ालाना burhá-lána, *v. a.* To bring forward, to lead on (*an army*).

बढ़ाव burháo, *s. m.* Prolongation, advancement, increase, enlargement.

बढ़ावा bur-há-wa, *s. m.* Population; excitement, flattery.

बढ़िया búr-hiya, *adj.* High-priced.

बढ़ेला bur-héla, *s. m.* A wild hog.

बढ़ोतर bur-hó-tur, *s. m.* ⎫ Interest, pro-
बढ़ोतरी bur-ho-tur-ée, *s. f.* ⎬ fit, advantage.

बढ़ंत bur-húnt, *s. f.* Increase.

बणिकपथ bún-ik-puth, *s. m.* Traffick, commerce.

बणिकपुत्र bun-ik-póotr, *s. m.* The son of a merchant, or a young merchant or trader.

बणिकपुत्री bun-ik-póotree, *s. f.* A young woman of the *Buniya* tribe.

बणिग्भाव bún-ig-bhao, *s. m.* Traffic, trade, commerce.

बणिज् bún-ij, *s. m.* A merchant, a trader; the sixth of the astronomical periods called *Kurun*, corresponding to the half of a lunar day; trade, traffic.

बणिज्य bun-íjyuh, *s. m.* Trade, traffic.

बणिया bún-iya, *s. m.* A shop-keeper, a merchant (*usually a corn-chandler*).

बत but, *s. m.* The worm which is destructive to shipping (*Teredo*).

बत but, *contraction of* बात bat, A word, affair; or of बात bat, Wind, generally used in composition; as, *But-bahuree*, *adj.* External, foreign. *But burhao*, *s. m.* Prolixity, talkativeness, chicanery, wrangling. *But-buna*, An orator, a sophist. *But sonha kurna*, To ventilate. *But-kuhao*, *s. m.* Talk, conversation.

बतक bút-uk, *s. f.* A duck.

बतकहा but-kúha, *adj.* Loquacious, conversible.

बतकहाव but-kuháo, *s. m.* ⎫ Loquacity,
बतकही but-kuhée, *s. f.* ⎬ conversibleness, discourse, dialogue.

बतक्कड़ but-úk-kur, *adj.* Loquacious, talkative.

बतराना but-rá-na, *v. n.* To talk, converse, speak.

बतलाना but-lá-na, *v. a.* To shew, explain, point out, denote, teach, inform, express, signify, adduce, account for.

बता bút-a, *s. m.* A bamboo lath, a thin slip of bamboo; an oblong stone on which powders are levigated.

बताना but-á-na, *v. a.* To point out, to shew, indicate, signify, explain, teach, tell; to appear. *s. m.* An upper turband ; a small bracelet of metal.

बतास but-ás, *s. f.* Wind, air. *Butas-phenee, s. f.* A kind of sweetmeat, sugar-cakes.

बतासा but-á-sa, ⎫ *s. m.* A kind of sweet-
बताशा but-á-sha, ⎭ meat, sugar-cakes (*of a spongy texture, or filled with air, as the word implies*) ; a bubble.

बतियाना but-i-yána, *v. a.* To speak, talk, say, converse, discourse.

बती bút-ee, *s. f.* A word.

बतूनी bu-tóo-nee, *adj.* A tattler, an idle talker.

बतोली but-ó-lee, *s. f.* Buffoonery.

बतौरी but-óu-ree, *s. f.* A flatulent or œde-matous swelling.

बत्ती bút-tee, *s. f.* A candle ; a wick, a match, a stick (*of sealing-wax, &c.*) ; a tent or bougie.

बत्तीस buttées, *adj.* Thirty-two.

बत्तीसा buttéesa, *s. m.* A medicine com-posed of thirty-two ingredients, usually given to mares after foaling.

बत्तीसी buttéesee, *s. f.* A set of teeth ; any aggregate consisting of thirty-two parts. *Butteesee dikhana, v. a.* To shew teeth ; to laugh, to scoff or make faces at any one.

बत्सुल bútsul, *adj.* Affectionate, kind.

बत्सा bútsa, *s. m.* A kind of rice.

बथुआ buthóoa, *s. m.* A kind of greens or potherbs (*Chenopodium album*).

बद bud, *s. f.* A bubo.

बदन búd-un, *s. m.* The mouth, face, countenance.

बदना búd-na, *v. a.* To wager, to bet ; to settle, to predestinate, to take (*as witness*), to obey, acknowledge, agree, not to refuse.

बदरीछदा búdree-chhúd-a, *s. f.* A kind of perfume, apparently a dried shell-fish ; a tree, apparently a species of the *Zizyphus.*

बदरीपुत्रक búdree-pútruk, *s. m.* A sort of perfume, a leaf.

बदरीफला búdree-phúl-a, *s. f.* A plant, commonly called blue *Sephalika* or *Nyctanthes.*

बदरीशैल budree-shyl, *s. m.* A part of the *Himalaya* range, and a celebrated place of pil-grimage, the *Budrinath* of modern travellers, or a town and temple on the west bank of the *Uluknunda* river, in the province of *Shrinugur.*

बदुल búd-ul, *s. m.* A cloud ; exchange, substitution. *adv.* In change, for.

बदुलना búd-ul-na, *v. a.* To change, ex-change, alter.

बदला búd-la, *s. m.* Exchange, lieu, stead,

a substitute, recompense, revenge, requital. *Budla lena, v. a.* To alter ; retaliate, take revenge. *Budleh,* In exchange, in return for.

बदलाई bud-láee, *s. f.* Price of exchange.

बदलाना bud-lá-na, *v. a.* To cause to alter, to change.

बदली búd-lee, *s. f.* Exchange, relief (*of watches*) ; cloudiness ; a small bit of cloud.

बदसुला bud-súl-a, *s. m.* A hogsty.

बदा búd-a, *adj.* Predestinated.

बदाबदी bud-a-búd-ee, *adv.* With emula-tion, or rivalship, contentiously.

बदि búdi, ⎫ *s. f.* The dark half of the
बदी búd-ee, ⎭ lunar month from full moon to new moon, the wane of the moon.

बदूल bud-dúl, *s. m.* A cloud.

बद्ध buddh, *adj.* Bound, tied ; checked, suppressed ; fixed, firm ; withheld.

बद्धकोप buddh-kóp, *adj.* One who governs or suppresses wrath.

बद्धमूल buddh-móol, *adj.* Fast or firmly rooted.

बद्धशिख buddh-shíkh, *adj.* Young, a pupil, a child, one whose hair has not been shaven.

बद्धशिखा buddh-shíkha, *s. f.* A sort of pun-gent root, called by some a kind of garlic.

बद्धाञ्जुलि buddh-ánjooli, *adj.* Saluting re-spectfully, putting the hands joined to the forehead.

बद्धी búd-dhee, *s. f.* An ornament worn round the neck, hanging down to the waist and crossing behind and before ; a belt, a sash, brace (*of a carriage, &c.*)

बध budh, *s. m.* Killing, slaughter, slaying, murder.

बधक budhúk, *s. m.* A slaughterer, a killer.

बधकांक्षी budhu-kánkshee, *adj.* Wishing death.

बधकाम्या budh-kámya, *s. f.* Intent or de-sire to kill. [ment.

बधदुंड búdh-dund, *s. m.* Capital punish-

बधना búdh-na, *v. a.* To smite, to kill. *s. m.* A kind of pot with a spout to it, a vessel for drinking water from.

बधस्थली búdh-sthul-ee, *s. f.* ⎫ A place of
बधस्थान búdh-sthan, *s. m.* ⎭ slaughter or execution.

बधाई budháee, *s. f.* ⎫ A song in congra-
बधावा budháwa, *s. m.* ⎭ tulation ; pre-sents, &c. carried to the house of a woman on the sixth or fortieth day after childbirth.

बधिक budh-ík, *s. m.* A huntsman, sports-man, fowler, killer, slayer, executioner.

बधिया búdh-iya, *s. f.* A bullock, any cas-trated animal.

बधिर búdh-ir, *adj.* Deaf.

बधू búdh-oo, *s. f.* A woman, a wife, daughter-in-law, lady.

बधोपाय búdh-o-páyuh, *s. m.* Instrument or means of putting to death.

बध्य búdh-yuh, *adj.* Deserving death; condemned to death.

बध्यता budh-yutá, *s. f.* Fitness to be killed.

बध्यभूमि búdhyuh-bhóomi, *s. f.* ⎱ A place of
बध्यस्थान búdhyuh-sthán, *s. m.* ⎰ public execution.

बन bun, *s. f.* A forest, a wood. *Bun-kunda,* or *Bun-gontha, s. m.* Cowdung found in the forests. *Bun-jatra, s. f.* The pilgrimage through the 84 forests of *Bruj. Bun jharna,* or, —*marna,* or, —*mujharna,* To beat the forests.

बनखंड bún-khund, *s. m.* A forest.

बनचर bún-chur, *s. m.* A monkey.

बनज bún-uj, *s. m.* Trade, traffic, merchandise, commerce.

बनजर bún-jur, *s. f.* Waste land.

बनजारा bun-já-ra, *s. m.* A grain-merchant, a carrier of grain.

बनजारी bun-já-ree, *s. f.* A kind of tent used by *Bunjaras. adj. f.* Half-boiled (*grain*).

बनत bún-ut, *s. f.* Lace, a ribband studded with spangles.

बनतराई bun-tur-áee, *s. f.* A plant (*Luffa*).

बनपूरना bun-púr-na, *v. n.* To succeed, answer, suit, come to pass.

बनबास bun-bás, *s. m.* Living in the forest.

बनबासी bun-bá-see, *adj.* Inhabiting the forest.

बनबिलाव bun-bil-áo, *s. m.* A wild cat.

बनभांटा bún-bhan-ta, *s. m.* Wild (*byngun*) egg-plant (*Solanum melongena*).

बनमानूष bun-má-noos, *s. m.* A man of the woods, a wild man, an ourang-ootang.

बनमाल bun-mál, *s. f.* A garland of various flowers reaching to the feet: usually of the flowers of the *toolsee* (*Ocymum sanctum*), *koond* (*Jasminum multiflorum*), *munda* (*Asclepias gigantea*), *parijat* (*Erythrina fulgens*), and lotus.

बनरा bún-ra, *s. m.* A bridegroom.

बनरी bún-ree, *s. f.* A bride.

बनवाई bun-wáee, *s. f.* Price paid for making any thing.

बनवास bun-wás, *s. m.* Living in a wood, separated from one's family; (*met.*) disinherited (*a son*).

बनवैया bun-wy-ya, *s. m.* A maker.

बनसी bún-see, *s. f.* A fishing hook; (*in comp.*) Of the race or lineage; a flute. *Bunsee-but,* The fig-tree under which *Krishn* was accustomed to play the flute.

बना bún-a, *s. m.* A bridegroom; *part.* Made, prepared, having made, &c.

बनात bun-át, *s. f.* Woollen cloth, broad cloth.

बनाती bun-át-ee, *adj.* Woollen.

बनाना bunána, *v. a.* To make, prepare, form, fashion, shape, do, fabricate, build, compose, perform, make to agree, adjust, adorn, reconcile, pluck (*a fowl*), to dress (*victuals*), to mend, repair, invent, rectify, mock, feign.

बनायाजाना bunáya-jána, *v. n.* To be making, to be in hand.

बनाव bun-áo, *s. m.* Preparation, decoration, dressing, decking one's self; concord, understanding, reconciliation. *Bunao kurna,* To adorn, bedeck, decorate.

बनावट bun-a-wút, *s. f.* Make, invention, affectation, contrivance, fabrication, formation, fiction, sham.

बनावना bun-áo-na, *v. a.* To make, to prepare.

बनावरी bun-áo-ree, *s. f.* Preparation.

बनासपती bunás-púttee, *s. f.* Forest leaves.

बनिज bún-ij, *s. m.* Trade, traffic, merchandise, commerce.

बनिता bún-it-a, *s. f.* A wife, a woman.

बनिया bún-iya, *s. m.* A shop-keeper, a merchant (*usually a corn-chandler*).

बनियायन buniyayún, *s. f.* Wife of a *Buniya.*

बनी bún-ee, *s. f.* A bride.

बनेला bun-él-a, *adj.* Wild.

बनैटी bun-úy-tee, ⎱ *s. f.* A torch lighted
बनेटी bun-ét-ee, ⎰ at both ends and whirled round so as to form a double circle of fire.

बनैनी bun-úy-nee, *s. f.* Wife of a *Buniya* (*shop-keeper, &c.*)

बनैयाकंडा bunyya-kúnda, *s. m.* Cow dung dried for fuel (*not made up*).

बनैला bun-úy-la, *adj.* Wild.

बन्दनवार bundun-wár, *s. f.* A wreath or garland of leaves and flowers suspended across gateways on marriages or public festivals.

बन्दर bún-dur, *s. m.* A monkey.

बन्दरखुट्ट bundur-khútt, *s. m.* A sore that does not heal; a running sore, an issue.

बन्दरिया bundur-íya, ⎱ *s. f.* A female mon-
बन्दरी búnd-ree, ⎰ key.

बन्दा bún-da, } s. m. Mistletoe, a kind of
बंडा bún-da, } Epidendron (*Epidendrum tesselatum*).

बन्दी bún-dee, s. f. An ornament worn on the forehead; a dress shorter than the *Jama*. s. m. A tribe called *Bhat*, who are generally bards or panegyrists; a bard.

बन्दीगृह bundee-gríh, s. m. A place of confinement, a prison.

बन्दीजन bundee-jún, s. m. A sort of ornament; a bard.

बन्दूहा bun-doo-há, s. m. A whirlwind.

बन्दोर bun-dór, s. f. A female slave.

बन्दोल bun-dól, s. m. The child of a slave.

बन्ध bundh, s. m. A pledge, a deposit. s. m. f. A binding, a bandage, a tie or fetter; bondage, imprisonment; binding, tying. *Bundh men purna, ya, ana,* To become a captive.

बन्धक bun-dhúk, s. m. Binding, confinement; a pledge, a pawn, a deposit.

बन्धकी bún-dhuk-ee, s. f. An unchaste woman, a harlot, a wanton; a barren woman.

बन्धतन्त्र bundh-túntr, s. m. A complete army, or one with its four divisions, of chariots, elephants, horse, and foot.

बन्धन bún-dhun, s. m. Binding, tying, confining, fastening; bandage, bond; bondage, imprisonment; obstacle, hinderance.

बन्धनग्रन्थि búndhun-grúnthi, s. m. The knot of a ligature.

बन्धनरज्जु búndhun-rújjoo, s. f. Any rope or string used for tying.

बन्धना búndh-na, v. n. To be tied, fastened, bound, continuous or uninterrupted, kept, enclosed, laid, formed or composed. *Bundhee moothee,* An undisclosed intention.

बन्धनालय búndhun-áluy, s. m. A prison.

बन्धाई bun-dháee, s. f. Bond, binding, fastening.

बन्धान bun-dhán, s. m. Pension, a fixed allowance made to any one.

बन्धाना bun-dhá-na, v. a. To bind, fasten, shut, &c.

बन्धानी bun-dhá-nee, s. m. One whose business it is to carry stone, timber, &c. slung over his shoulder; a pensioner; a gunner, artilleryman.

बन्धू bún-dhoo, s. m. A kinsman, a relation, but especially a distant or cognate kinsman, and subsequent in right of inheritance to the gentile or *Sugotr*; the *Bundhoo*, is of three kinds: the kinsman of the person himself, of his father, or his mother, as his father's brother's son, and his mother's sister's or brother's son; and the same reckoning upwards, as his father's father's sister's son, &c.; a friend; a brother; a flower (*Pentapetes phœnicea*).

बन्धुजन bundhoo-jún, s. m. A relation, a friend.

बन्धुजीव bundhoo-jéev, s. m. A flower (*Pentapetes phœnicea*).

बन्धुता bundhoo-tá, s. f. A multitude of relations or friends; relationship, friendship.

बन्धुत्व bundhoo-twúh, s. m. Relationship, friendship.

बन्धुदत्त bundhoo-dútt, adj. Given by a kinsman. s. m. One kind of female property, that given to a girl at her marriage by her own relations.

बन्धुर bun-dhóor, s. m. A flower (*Pentapetes phœnicea*); a drug commonly called *Birung*; a crane; a drug commonly called *Reeshubh*.

बन्धुरा bun-dhoo-rá, s. f. A whore, a prostitute.

बन्धुवा bún-dhoo-wa, s. m. A prisoner, one bound, a captive. [relationless.

बन्धुहीन bun-dhoo-héen, adj. Friendless,

बन्धूक bun-dhóok, s. m. A shrub bearing a red flower (*Pentapetes phœnicea*, but also applied to the *Ixora Bundhooc*); a tree (*Pentaptera tomentosa*).

बन्धूकपुष्प bun-dhóok-pooshp, s. m. A tree (*Pentaptera tomentosa*).

बन्धेज bun-dhéj, s. m. Parsimony; stability, steadiness, persistence.

बन्ध्यूब bundhyúb, adj. Barren, unfruitful, not bearing fruit in due season; detained, confined, under arrest.

बन्ध्या bun-dhyá, s. f. A childless woman; a barren cow; a perfume, commonly called *Bala*.

बनना bún-na, v. n. To be made, to be prepared, to be mended or adjusted; to chime, to agree, to fall in with, to do, to answer, to serve, to be, to become, to avail, to counterfeit, to succeed. s. m. A bridegroom. *Buna choona,* Dressed, decked out, arranged. *Bunna thunna,* To be fully adorned or prepared, to be decked out. *Buna bunaya,* Finished, ready made, complete, entire, perfect. *Buna ruhna,* To remain waiting.

बनाफिर bunna-phír, s. m. A tribe of *Rajpoots*.

बनहा bun-há, s. m. A conjurer.

बनहाई bun-háee, s. f. A female conjurer, an enchantress.

बपंश bup-únsh, s. m. Patrimony, heritage.

बपा होना búp-a hóna, v. n. To be raised, established, or pitched.

बपुरा bup-oo-rá, } adj. Helpless.
बपुरी bup-oo-rée, }

बपौती bup-óu-tee, s. f. Paternal estate; patrimony, heritage. [bath.

बफ़ारा bu-phá-ra, s. m. Vapour, vapour

बबर búb-ur, *s. m.* One who crops the manes of horses.

बबराखेरी búbra-khéree, *s. f.* Quarrelling, dissention.

बबरी bub-rée, *s. f.* Cropped hair, tresses; the act of cropping (*especially the manes of horses*).

बबरूता bub-róo-ta, *s. m.* A clown, a lout, bumpkin, clumsy young man.

बबुवा búb-oo-wa, *s. m.* A child, a boy (*a term of fondness*).

बबूर bub-óor, ⎫ *s. f.* A tree of the Mimosa
बबूल bub-óol, ⎭ kind (*there are several species, but the commonest is Arabica*), the Acacia tree.

बबेसिया bub-ésiya, *adj.* Talking nonsense. *s. m.* A catamite.

बबेसी bub-ésee, *s. f.* The piles.

बबू bub-úy, *s. m.* The seed of a sweet-scented herb (*Ocymum pilosum*); a sort of bird.

बब्बी búbbee, *s. f.* A kiss.

बभ्रू búbh-roo, *adj.* Large, great; tawny, &c., bald-headed through disease. *s. m.* A large ichneumon; the name of a sage; a tawny or brown colour.

बम bum, *s. f.* A spring (*of water*); a fathom; a measuring rod.

बम bum, An interjection addressed to *Shiv* (*much used by pilgrims to the temple of Byjnuth or Vydyunath*).

बमकना búm-uk-na, *v. n.* To swell.

बमन búm-un, *s. m.* Vomit, emetic. *Bumun kurna*, To vomit.

बमील bum-éel, *s. m.* A sort of grass.

बया bya, *s. m.* The little bird that learns to fetch and carry, &c., and which the *Hindoos* teach to snatch the ornamental patch or wafer from the forehead of their mistresses (*Loxia Indica*); an assizer.

बयार by-ár, *s. f.* Wind, air.

बयाला by-ála, *adj.* Flatulent.

बयालीस by-a-lées, *adj.* Forty-two.

बयासी by-a-sée, *adj.* Eighty-two.

बर bur, *adj.* Best, excellent. *s. m.* A boon, a blessing, a choice, a good; a bridegroom, a son-in-law; the Indian fig-tree. *s. f.* Asparagus racemosus. *conj.* But, moreover, even. *Bur-daee*, Giver of a choice or blessing.

बरून bur-ún, *conj.* Moreover, but, even, rather.

बराव bur-áo, *s. m.* Abstinence.

बरूई bur-úee, *s. m.* A seller of betel-leaf, a cultivator of betel.

बरूखना búr-ukh-na, *v. n.* To rain.

बरगत búr-gut, *s. m.* The Indian fig-tree (*Ficus Indica*).

बरगा búr-ga, *s. m.* A rafter.

बरगेल bur-gél, *s. m.* An ortolan (*Alauda*).

बरजतिया búr-jut-iya, *s. m.* An innocent kind of snake.

बरजना búr-uj-na, *v. a.* To forbid, to prohibit.

बरूनी búr-un-ee, *s. f.* An eye-lash.

बरत búr-ut, *s. m.* A meritorious act, a fast, a vow, a religious rite or penance; use. *s. f.* A thong, leathern girth, rope. *part.* Flaming, blazing.

बरतन búr-tun, *s. m.* A dish, plate, basin, &c., vessel, utensil.

बरतना bur-út-na, *v. a.* To consider, to reflect.

बरता búr-ta, *part. pass.* That which has been used.

बरतना bur-tá-na, *v. a.* To distribute. *s. m.* Old clothes.

बरद búr-ud, *s. m.* A bull, a bullock.

बरदान bur-dán, *s. m.* A wedding gift (*to a bride*); the answer to a prayer addressed to God or to a saint.

बरदार búr-dar, *adj.* Wide, broad (*cloth*).

बरदी búr-dee, *s. f.* A drove of cattle loaded.

बरदैत bur-dyt, *s. m.* A panegyrist, a bard.

बरध búr-udh, *s. m.* A bull, a bullock.

बरधना búr-udh-na, *v. n.* ⎫
बरधाना bur-dhá-na, *v. a.* ⎭ To bull a cow.

बरन búr-un, *s. m.* Colour, sort, class; tribe (*among the Hindoos*), as Brahmun, Kshuttriyuh, Vyshyuh, and Shoodr; a letter of an alphabet; praise, description. *conj.* Moreover, but even, rather. *Burun kurna*, To hire a priest for the performance of a sacrifice or any religious ceremony.

बरनन búr-nun, *s. m.* Description, recital, explanation, praise. *Burnun kurna*, To explain, describe, extol, praise.

बरना búr-na, *n. prop.* A rivulet running past the north of *Benares*. *s. m.* A fruit tree (*Crateva tapia*). *v. a.* To marry. *v. n.* To burn.

बरनी búr-nee, *s. f.* An eye-lash.

बरपा करना búr-pa kúrna, *v. a.* To raise, pitch, establish, produce, set on foot, cause, occasion, introduce.

बरपा रहना búr-pa rúhna, *v. n.* To continue firm or standing.

बरपा होना búr-pa hóna, *v. n.* To be raised, set on foot, pitched, established, produced, occasioned.

बरबरी búr-bur-ee, *s. f.* A peculiar kind of goat (*from Barbary*).

बरबस búr-bus, *s. m.* Strength, vigour; prowess, bravery.

बरभसिया bur-bhús-iya, *adj.* Affected, an old person who affects the manners of youth.

बरमला búr-mul-a, *adj.* Public, conspicuous.

बरमा búr-ma, *s. m.* A kind of gimlet or borer worked with a string.

बरयार bur-yár, *adj.* Strong, violent.

बरयारा bur-yár-a, *adj.* Strong, violent. *s. m.* A medicinal herb so called.

बररना bur-rá-na, *v. a.* To talk in one's sleep or in a delirium.

बरवट búr-wut, *s. m.* A tumour in the belly.

बरवट búr-wut, *s. f.* A kind of snake.

बरवह búr-wúh, *s. m.* A bird that feeds on fish.

बरवा búr-wa, *s. f.* A *raginee* or musical mode by which deer and serpents are said to be tamed.

बरस búr-us, *s. m.* Rain; a year; an intoxicating drug made of opium. *Burus-ganth, s. f.* The ceremony of tying a knot on the anniversary birth-day of a child; birth-day.

बरसवान bur-us-wán, *adj.* Annual, anniversary.

बरसौरी bur-sóu-ree, *s. f.* An annual tax or rent.

बरहा bur-há, *s. m.* A field where cows feed.

बरहेला bur-héla, }
बरहेला bur-héla, } *s. m.* A wild hog.

बरा búr-a, *s. m.* Cakes made of ground pulse fried in oil, or ghee. *adj.* Large, great.

बरात bur-át, *s. f.* The marriage procession.

बराती bur-at-ée, *s. m.* The company and attendants at a marriage.

बराना bur-ána, *v. n.* To abstain, to withdraw.

बरारा bur-ára, *s. f.* A thong, a rope (*particularly of a swing*).

बराव bur-áo, *s. m.* Abstinence.

बराह bur-úh, *s. m.* A boar; the third *Uvutar* or mythological incarnation of *Vishnoo* in the form of a boar.

बरियाई bur-iyáee, *s. f.* Boast, exultation.

बरियार bur-iyár, *adj.* Strong, violent.

बरियारा bur-iyára, *adj.* Strong, violent. *s. m.* A medicinal herb so called.

बरी búr-ee, *s. f.* Quicklime; a dish made of pulse; wedding garment. *adj.* Strong, powerful.

बरीस bur-ées, *s. m.* A year.

बरुण búr-oon, *s. m.* The god of water; a tree (*Cratæva tapia*, or, *Capparis trifoliata*).

बरेज bur-éj, *s. m.* A betel-garden.

बरेठन bur-éthun, *s. f.* A washerwoman.

बरेठा bur-étha, *s. m.* A washerman.

बरेरा bur-ér-a, *s. f.* A wasp.

बरे bur-úy, *s. m.* A seller of betel-leaf, a cultivator of betel.

बरेन bur-úyn, *s. f.* A (*female*) seller of betel-leaf, or rather cultivator of betel.

बरोठा bur-ó-tha, }
बरोठा bur-óu-tha, } *s. m.* A washerman; a vestibule.

बर्ग burg, *s. m.* An assembly of people of one class, a multitude of similar things; a class of letters pronounced on the same part of the mouth (*as the gutturals, palatals, &c.*); the square of a number.

बर्गी búrg-ee, *s. m.* The *Marhattas* are so called.

बर्छा bur-chhá, *s. m.* }
बर्छी bur-chhée, *s. f.* } A (*long slender*) spear, a javelin, dart. *Bur-chha*, or, *Bur-chhee-burdar*, A spearman.

बर्छत bur-chhyt, *s. m.* A spearman.

बर्न burn, *s. m.* Colour, sort, class; a tribe (*among the Hindoos*), as, Brahmun, Kshuttriyuh, Vyshyuh, Shoodr; a letter of an alphabet; praise, description.

बर्नन burn-ún, *s. m.* Description, recital, explanation, praise. *Burnun kurna*, To explain, describe, extol, praise.

बर्नना búr-nu-na, *v. a.* To explain, describe, praise.

बर्नमाला burn-mála, *s. f.* An alphabet.

बर्नसंकर búrn-sun-kur, *s. m.* A person of a tribe originating in the intercourse of a man of one tribe with a woman of another.

बर्त burt, *s. m.* Use, practice.

बर्तन búr-tun, *s. m.* A dish, plate, bason, &c.; vessel, utensil.

बर्तना búrt-na, *v. a.* To use.

बर्तमान burtumán, *adj.* Present, existent; the present tense.

बर्मा búr-ma, *s. m.* A kind of gimlet or borer worked with a string.

बर्माना bur-má-na, *v. a.* To bore.

बर्मा burm-há, *n. prop.* The people of *Ava* are so called.

बराहुत bu-rá-hut, *s. f.* Chattering, prate, rant.

बर्ष bursh, *s. m.* Rain; a year.

बर्षवां burs-wán, *adj.* Annual, anniversary.

बर्षा búr-sha, ⎫ s. f. The rains, the third
बर्खा búr-kha, ⎬ season (*of the six*), from
the 15th of *Asharh* to the 15th of *Bhadoo*; rain.

बर्षाओ bur-sháoo, ⎫ *part. act.* Raining.
बर्खाओ bur-kháoo, ⎬

बर्सात bur-sát, s. f. The rainy season, the
rains.

बर्साती bur-sát-ee, s. f. A disorder in horses,
the farcy.

बर्षाना bur-shána, v. a. To cause to rain, to
shower down ; to rain.

बर्षाशन bur-shá-shun, s. m. Yearly pay or
subsistence.

बर्षौरी bur-shóu-ree, s. f. An annual tax or
rent.

बरसना búrus-na, v. n. To rain.

बर्सात bur-sát, s. f. The rainy season, the
rains.

बर्साती bur-sát-ee, s. f. A disorder in horses,
the farcy.

बर्साना bur-sá-na, v. a. To cause to rain, to
shower down.

बर्सी búr-see, s. f. An annual ceremony in
commemoration of deceased relations.

बर्ही bur-hée, s. f. A peacock.

बल bul, s. m. A coil, twist, crook, convo-
lution ; side, direction. *Bul khana,* To be twisted.
Buldar, adj. Crooked, twisted, coiled, convoluted.
Bul dena, v. a. To twist.

बल bul, s. m. Power, strength ; semen
virile ; a name of the elder brother of *Krishn,*
Bulram; name of the king of *Patal* or the infer-
nal·regions ; a sacrifice, an offering. *Bul beh,*
interj. Bravo ! *Bul jana,* or, *Bul bul jana,* To be
sacrificed. *Bul dena,* or, *Bul kurna,* To sacrifice.

बलुकना búl-uk-na, v. a. To open ; to speak
indistinctly from excessive joy or intoxication.

बलगना bul-gún-a, s. m. A sob.

बलताड़ bul-tár, s. m. The male palm or
toddy tree (*Borassus flabelliformis*).

बलतोड़ bul-tór, s. m. A pimple, a sore, a
small boil (*supposed to be caused by the breaking or
pulling out of a hair, as the word imports*).

बलद búl-ud, s. m. A bullock that carries
a burden.

बलदाओ bul-dáoo, ⎫ s. m. A cowherd,
बलदिया búl-diya, ⎬ a bullock-driver, a
बलदी búl-dee, ⎭ drover, a grain-merchant.

बलदेव bul-déo, s. m. A name of *Bulram.*

बलदेवा bul-déva, s. f. A medicinal plant,
commonly called *Trayuman.*

बलना búl-na, v. n. To burn.

2 x 2

बलनिग्रह bul-nígruh, s. m. Weakening, reducing strength or power.

बलबकरा bul-búk-ra, s. m. A person who
dies in a battle, &c. without doing any thing.

बलबलाना bul-bul-ána, v. n. To ferment (*as
sour milk, curds, &c.*) ; to be inflamed with lust ;
to make a noise (*a camel*) from lust.

बलभद्र bul-bhúdr, s. m. A strong or robust
man.

बलभाना bul-bhána, v. a. To allure.

बलम búl-um, ⎫ s. m. A lover, a husband.
बलमा búl-ma, ⎬

बलरांड bul-ránd, s. f. A widow who lost
her husband while very young.

बलराम bul-rám, n. prop. The elder brother of *Krishn.*

बलवत्ता bul-wútta, s. f. Strength, power.

बलवन्त bul-wúnt, ⎫ adj. Strong, powerful,
बलवान bul-wán, ⎬ able-bodied, stout,
बलवाला bul-wála, ⎭ lusty.

बलवर्द्धन bul-vúrddhun, adj. Strengthen-
ing, ennobling.

बलवा búl-wa, s. m. A tumult, riot, sedition, mutiny, alarm.

बलहून bul-hún, s. m. Phlegm, the phlegmatic humour.

बलही bul-hée, s. f. A faggot.

बलहीन bul-héen, adj. Weak, infirm.

बलहीनता bul-heen-tá, s. f. Exhaustion,
weakness, prostration of strength, infirmity from
fatigue or age, &c.

बला búl-a, s. m. An aquatic and medicinal
plant (*Sida rhombifolia, rhomboidea,* and *cordifolia*).

बलाईलेना buláee-léna, ⎫ v. a. To draw the
बलाएंलेना buláen-lena, ⎬ hands over the
head of another in token of taking all his misfortunes upon one's self (*generally practised by women*).

बलाका bul-á-ka, s. f. A sort of crane.

बलांचिता bul-ánchi-ta, s. f. A sort of *Veen*
or lute, called also *Ram's* lute.

बलाट bul-át, s. m. A sort of bean.

बलात्कार bul-at-kár, s. m. Violence, oppression, exaction ; (*in law*) the detention of the
person of a debtor by his creditor, and the violent
measures taken by the latter (*flogging, &c.*) to recover his debt.

बलात्मिका bul-át-mik-a, s. f. A sort of sun-
flower (*Heliotropium Indicum*).

बलान्वित bul-án-wit, adj. Strong, powerful.

बलावल bul-a-búl, adj. Strong and weak.

बलाय bul-áyuh, *s. m.* A plant (*Capparis trifoliata*).

बलालक bul-á-luk, *s. m.* The Caronda (*Carissa carandas*).

बलाश bul-ásh, *s. m.* The phlegmatic humour.

बलि búli, *s. m.* An oblation, a religious offering in general ; presentation of food to all created beings, one of the five great sacraments of the *Hindoo* religion : it consists in throwing a small parcel of the offering, *ghee* or rice, or the like, into the open air at the back of the house ; an animal, or one which is fit for an oblation ; a king and *Dytyuh*, also *Muha Buli*, the virtuous sovereign of *Muhabulipoor*, tricked out of the dominion he had obtained over earth and heaven, by *Vishnoo*, in the *Vamun* or dwarf *Uvutar*, and left, in consideration of his merits, the sovereignty of *Patal*, or the infernal regions.

बलिदान bulidán, *s. m.* An act of sacrificing, or offering victims in sacrifice to God.

बलिन bul-ín, *adj.* Shrivelled, wrinkled, flabby, flaccid.

बलिहार bulihár, *s. m.* } Sacrifice. *Buli-*
बलिहारी buliháree, *s. f.* } *haree jana,* To be sacrificed.

बली búl-ee, *adj.* Strong, powerful, robust, stout. *s. f.* A wrinkle, skin shrivelled by old age ; the fold of skin in stout persons, especially females, upon the upper part of the belly, or between the ensiform cartilage and the navel.

बलूआ bul-oo-a, *adj.* Sandy.

बलूरना bul-óor-na, *v. a.* To scratch, to tear with the nails.

बलूला bul-óo-la, *s. m.* A bubble.

बलेंडा bul-én-da, *s. m.* A whirlwind ; a ridge-pole (*of a cottage*).

बलेंडी bul-én-dee, *s. f.* A ridge-pole (*of a cottage*).

बलैया लेना bulyya léna, *v. a.* To draw one's hands over the head of another in token of taking his misfortunes on one's self (*generally practised by women*).

बल्य búl-yuh, *adj.* Strong, vigorous. *s. m.* Semen virile.

बल्लभ bullúbh, *adj.* Dear, beloved. *s. m.* A favourite, a friend ; a superintendant, a master.

बल्लम búllum, *s. m.* A spear. *Bullum-burdar,* A spearman.

बल्ला búlla, *s. m.* A pole or boat-hook.

बल्ली búllee, *s. f.* A prop, a pole, a long pole to steer or move a boat with. *Bullee marna,* To push or move (*a boat*).

बवंडर buwún-dur, *s. m.* A whirlwind, a devil.

बवाई buwáee, *s. f.* A kibe, blister or chap on the foot, chilblain.

बवासीर bu-wa-séer, *s. pl.* The piles or hemorrhoids.

बवाहा buwahá, *adj.* Pocky, affected with Lues venerea.

बवेसिया buwésiya, *adj.* Talking nonsense, a babbler. *s. m.* A catamite.

बस bus, *s. m.* Power, will, command, advantage, authority. *Bus ana,* To be obtained, to come into one's power. *Bus kurna,* To overpower, to bring to submission.

बसगित bus-gít, *s. f.* Residence.

बसन bús-un, *s. m.* Cloth ; a dress, a habit, a suit of clothes, apparel, attire.

बसना bús-na, *v. n.* To dwell, inhabit, settle, reside, abide, to be peopled.

बसनी bús-nee, *s. f.* A purse.

बसन्त bús-unt, *s. f.* The spring ; one of the musical modes of the *Hindoos* ; the first of the six seasons, comprising *Chyt* and *Bysakh* ; the small-pox ; a phrase peculiar to the *Bengalees. Busunt phoolna, v. n.* To put forth the blossoms of mustard plants. *Ankhon men busunt phoolna,* To dazzle. *Busunt kee khubur,* Knowledge of, or care about, futurity.

बसन्ती bus-ún-tee, *adj.* Of yellow colour.

बसराना busúr-ána, *v. n.* To come to an end ; to succeed, to get away from. *Busur kurna, v. a.* To bring to an end, to finish, accomplish, execute, spend, pass. *Busur jana, v. n.* To be finished, to pass away. *Busur le-jana, v. a.* To bring to an end, finish, accomplish, execute, acquit one's self of, outstrip. *Busur hona, v. n.* To be finished, ended, spent, or passed.

बसाना bus-á-na, *v. a.* To people, to colonize, to cause to dwell, to bring into cultivation, to settle a country.

बसूधा bús-oo-dha, *s. f.* The world, the earth.

बसूला bus-oo-la, *s. m.* A kind of axe used by carpenters, an adze.

बसूली bus-óo-lee, *s. f.* An instrument for cutting bricks.

बसेंधा bus-én-dha, *adj.* Stinking.

बसेरा bus-éra, *s. m.* A time before evening when birds return to their nest ; a night's lodging ; a bird's roost, a bird remaining on its roost. *Busera kurna,* To roost.

बसोबास bus-o-bás, *s. m.* Home, dwelling-place, residence, country.

बस्त bust, *s. f.* Thing, matter, substance, chattels, goods, baggage.

बस्त्र bustr, *s. m.* Cloth, clothes, raiment, apparel.

बक्रा bus-trá, *s. m.* A plant (*Callicarpa Americana*).

बस्ती bús-tee, *s. f.* An abode, a village, a peopled or inhabited place, a population.

बस्ना bús-na, *s. m.* Cloth, a wrapper, pack-cloth.

बहुकना buhúk-na, *v. n.* To be balked, to be disappointed, to be deceived, to stray, to be intoxicated.

बहकाना buh-ka-na, *v. a.* To balk, disappoint, mislead, deceive, beguile.

बहुंगी buhún-gee, *s. f.* A bamboo stick with ropes hanging from each end for slinging baggage to, which is carried on the shoulder.

बहजाना búh-jána, } *v. n.* To flow, pass ;
बहिजाना búhi-jána, } to go or swim with the stream ; to be ruined, to be destroyed.

बहता buhta, *part. act.* Running (*water*), afloat. *Buhteh panee men hath dhona*, To pay attention to one's friends, or to attend to one's own duty or affairs while the opportunity is favourable ; to make hay while the sun shines.

बहत्तर buhút-tur, *adj.* Seventy-two.

बहधा búh-dha, *s. f.* Pain, distress ; obstruction, hindrance, prevention.

बहन búhun, } *s. f.* A sister.
बहिन búhin, }

बहना búh-na, *v. n.* To flow, to glide ; to float ; to blow, to pass away, drive.

बहनेऊ buh-néoo, } *s. m.* A sister's husband, a brother-in-law.
बहनोई buh-nóee, }

बहनेली búhun-élee, *s. f.* An adopted sister.

बहबहा buh-buhá, *adj.* Flowing, gliding along ; brave, bold ; public, notorious.

बहर buhr, *s. f.* A fleet.

बहरा búh-ra, *adj.* Deaf.

बहरिया búh-riya, *adj.* A stranger.

बहरी búh-ree, *s. f.* A falcon, a female hawk (*Falco calidus*). *Buhree-bucha, s. m.* The male of the *Buhree*.

बहल búhul, *s. f.* A two-wheeled car (*for riding in, not for baggage*), a coach, a carriage.

बहलना búhul-na, *v. n.* To be diverted, to be amused.

बहलाना buh-lá-na, *v. a.* To divert, amuse, recreate.

बहलिया buhúl-iya, *s. m.* A kind of servant armed with bow, arrow, &c., a huntsman.

बहली búh-lee, *s. f.* A two-wheeled car (*for riding in, not for baggage*), a coach, a carriage.

बहसना búhus-na, *v. a.* To argue, dispute, debate, talk.

बहादेना búha-déna, *v. a.* To set afloat, demolish, destroy, ruin, impoverish, deprive of felicity or fortune.

बहाना buhána, *v. a.* To make flow, set afloat or adrift, float, launch, swim away.

बहा फिरना búha phírna, } *v. n.*
बहा बहा फिरना búha búha phírna, } To wander, to be in a distressed condition, to be intoxicated.

बहाव buháo, *s. m.* A flood, a flooding, flow, flux, afflux, effusion, fluidity.

बहिजाना búhi-jána, *v. n.* To flow, pass ; to go or swim with the stream ; to be ruined, to be destroyed.

बहिन búhin, *s. f.* A sister.

बहिर आना búhir ána, *v. n.* To issue, to come out.

बहिरा búhira, *adj.* Deaf.

बहिराना buhirána, *v. a.* To divert, to amuse, to recreate.

बहिर्देश búhir-desh, *s. m.* Remote or foreign country.

बहिर्मुख búhir-mookh, *s. m.* The neglect or violation of any moral or religious duty. *adj.* Impious.

बहिला búhil-a, *adj. f.* Barren (*generally applied to cattle*).

बही buhée, *s. f.* A book not stitched at the sides but at the ends ; a register, book of accounts, ledger.

बहीर buhéer, } *s. f.* The baggage, &c. of
बहीर buheer, } an army.

बहीरोबोना buhéero-bóona, *Idem.*

बहु búhoo, *adj.* Much, many ; large, great.

बहुक búhook, *s. m.* A plant (*Asclepias gigantea*).

बहुकंटक búhoo-kúntuk, *s. m.* A prickly plant (*Hedysarum alhagi*) ; the marshy date tree.

बहुकाल búhoo-kál, *s. m.* A long time.

बहुगंध búhoo-gúndh, *s. m.* Olibanum.

बहुगंधा búhoo-gúndha, *s. f.* Arabian jasmine.

बहुगुण búhoo-goon, *m.* } *adj.* Many
बहुगुणा búhoo-góona, *f.* } times ; having many good qualities.

बहुत búhoot, *adj.* Much, many, more, most. *Buhoot yar hona*, To become more intimate than formerly.

बहुतात buhoot-át, *s. f.* Excess, abundance.

बहुतायत búhoo-táyut, *s. f.* Abundance, plenty, multitude.

बहुतेरा búhoo-téra, *adj.* Many, much, very much, abundant, most.

बहुत्रुह buhoo-trúh, *adv.* In many ways or places, &c.

बहुत्वह buhoo-twúh, *s. m.* Plurality, multitude, muchness, abundance.

बहुत्वक्क buhoo-twúkk, *s. m.* The *Bhoj*, or Birch tree.

बहुदर्शी búhoo-dúrshee, *adj.* Experienced.

बहुदुग्धिका búhoo-dóogdhi-ka, *s. f.* A plant, yielding a caustic milky juice (*Euphorbia of various sorts*).

बहुदृष्ट buhoo-drísht, *adj.* Experienced.

बहुदोष buhoo-dósh, *adj.* Full of faults or defects, very wicked, very bad.

बहुधन buhoo-dhún, *adj.* Wealthy, rich.

बहुधा buhoo-dhá, *adv.* In many ways, sorts, &c., usually, generally, mostly, often.

बहुधागत búhoo-dha-gút, *adj.* Dispersed, scattered.

बहुपटु búhoo-pútoo, *adj.* Very clever.

बहुपत्र buhoo-pútr, *s. m.* Talc.

बहुपत्री búhoo-pútree, *s. f.* A drug (*Trigonella fœnum-grecum*).

बहुपर्णी búhoo-púrnee, *s. f.* A medicinal plant (*Trigonella fœnum-grecum*).

बहुपुत्र buhoo-póotr, *adj.* Having many children. *s. m.* A tree (*Echites scholaris*).

बहुपुत्री búhoo-póotree, *s. f.* A plant (*Asparagus racemosus*).

बहुप्रवाह búhoo-pruváh, *adj.* Flowing in many streams.

बहुवचन búhoo-búch-un, *s. m.* The plural number (*in grammar*).

बहुफल búhoo-phul, *adj. m.* Fertile, fruitful. *s. m.* The *Kudumb* tree (*Nauclea Cadamba*).

बहुफली búhoo-phúl-ee, *adj. f.* Fertile, fruitful. *s. f.* The opposite-leaved fig-tree.

बहुभाग्य búhoo-bhágyuh, *adj. m.* }
बहुभाग्या búhoo-bhágya, *adj. f.* } Fortunate.

बहुमान búhoo-mán, *s. m.* Respect, reverence.

बहुमूर्ति búhoo-móortti, *adj.* Multiform.

बहुमूल búhoo-móol, *adj.* Many-rooted, having many roots.

बहुमूल्य búhoo-móolyuh, *adj.* Costly, precious.

बहुर búhoor, *adv.* Again.

बहुरंगी búhoo-rúngee, *adj.* Various, or variable (*in colour*); changeable.

बहुरना búhoor-na, *v. n.* To return, to come back.

बहुराना búhoo-rána, *v. a.* To bring back, to cause to return.

बहुरि búhoori, *adv.* Again.

बहुरिया búhoo-riya, *s. f.* A daughter-in-law.

बहुरूप búhoo-róop, *adj.* Multiform. *s. m.* Mimickry.

बहुरूपा búhoo-róopa, *s. m.* A chameleon.

बहुरूपिया búhoo-róopiya, } *s. m.* An actor,
बहुरूपी búhoo-róopee, } a mimick.

बहुरूप्य búhoo-róopyuh, *s. m.* Mimickry.

बहुरेखा búhoo-rékha, *s. m. pl.* Wrinkles, furrows, marks of care or pain.

बहुरों búhooron, *adv.* Again.

बहुल búhool, *adj.* Much, many.

बहुलत्वह búhool-twúh, *s. m.* Abundance.

बहुवचन búhoo-rúch-un, *s. m.* The plural number (*in grammar*). [*myra*].

बहुवार búhoo-var, *s. m.* A fruit (*Cordia*

बहुविध búhoo-vidh, *adj.* Various, multiform, of many sorts or kinds.

बहुबीज búhoo-véej, *adj.* Having many or much seed. *s. m.* The custard-apple (*Annona squamosa*).

बहुबीर्य्य búhoo-véerjyuh, *s. m.* Belleric myrobalan (*Terminalia belerica*).

बहुव्रीहि búhoo-vréehi, *s. m.* One of the forms of grammatical composition, the compounding two or more words to furnish an epithet or attributive ; as, बहुमाल buhoo-mal, Having many necklaces.

बहुशत्रु búhoo-shútroo, *adj.* Having many enemies.

बहुशाख búhoo-shákh, *adj.* Having many branches or ramifications.

बहुसूता búhoo-sóota, *s. f.* A plant (*Asparagus*).

बहुसू búhoo-sóo, *s. f.* The mother of many children.

बहू buhóo, *s. f.* A daughter-in-law, a son's wife, a wife.

बहूबार buhoo-ár, *s. m.* A fruit (*Cordia myra*, and *Cordia latifolia*).

बहेरा buhéra, *s. m.* A fruit, the Belleric myrobalan (*Terminalia belerica*).

बहेतू buhétoo, *s. m.* A vagabond, vagrant, wanderer.

बहेलिया buhélia, *s. m.* A fowler ; a tribe of *Hindoos*.

बह्मनेता búhm-néta, *s. m.* A young *Brahmun*.

बांक bank, *s. m.* A crook, curvature, bending ; a reach or turning of a river ; fault, offence, wickedness. *s. f.* A semicircular ornament worn on the arms ; a kind of dagger ; an exercise with the dagger ; a settee.

बांकपट्टा **bank-pútta,** *s. m.* A kind of fencing with (*wooden*) dagger and cutlass.

बांकपन **bank-pun,** *s. m.* Foppishness, debauchery, disorderly conduct.

बांका **bánka,** *s. m.* A fop, beau, coxcomb, buck, bravo, bully ; a knife or hook to cut bamboo with. *s. f.* Name of a river. *adj.* Crooked, foppish, coxcombish, arrant.

बांकाचूर **banka-chóor,** *s. m.* A fop, beau, coxcomb, bully, bravo.

बांगा **bán-ga,** *s. m.* Raw cotton.

बांचना **bánch-na,** *v. a.* To read.

बांछा **bán-chha,** *s. f.* Wish, desire.

बांछित **ban-chhít,** *adj.* Desired, wished, longed-for.

बांजर **bán-jur,** *adj.* Lying waste or fallow (*land*).

बांझ **banjh,** *adj.* Barren.

बांट **bant,** *s. m.* Share, distribution ; a weight (*i. e. the standard by which things are weighed*) ; food given to a cow while she is milked. *Bant chont,* Share, distribution.

बांटना **bántna,** *v. a.* To share, distribute, divide, participate, dispose.

बांडा **bán-da,** *adj.* Tail-less. *s. m.* A serpent which has lost its tail.

बांडी **bán-dee,** *s. f.* A cudgel, a kind of dress.

बांदा **bán-da,** *s. m.* The name of a place in *Boondelkhund* ; a parasite plant which grows on trees (*Epidendrum, particularly tesselatum*).

बांदी **bán-dee,** *s. f.* A female slave, a bond-maid.

बांध **bandh,** *s. m.* An embankment ; confinement, imprisonment.

बांधना **bándh-na,** *v. a.* To bind, tie, fasten, shut, stop water, embank ; to invent, contrive, devise, stop, pack, aim, build, compose, form, put, settle.

बांधनू **bandh-nóo,** *s. m.* A mode of dying, in which the cloth is tied in different places, to prevent the parts tied from receiving the die ; slander, plot, plan ; a kind of silk cloth, a kind of parrot.

बां बां करना **ban-ban kúrna,** *v. a.* To prate idly, to talk foolishly.

बांस **bans,** *s. m.* A bamboo ; a measure of about ten feet, used to measure tanks, ditches, and excavations in general. (*A cube of one buns is called a chouka.*) *Bans pur churhna,* *v. n.* To be branded with infamy.

बांसफोड़ **bans-phór,** *s. m.* Name of a caste who work on bamboos.

बांसरी **báns-ree,** *s. f.* A flute, fife, pipe.

बांसली **báns-lee,** *s. f.* A flute, fife, pipe ; a purse.

बांसा **ban-sa,** *s. m.* The bridge of the nose.

बांसी **bán-see,** *s. f.* Flute, fife, pipe. *adj.* Made of bamboo.

बांसुरी **bán-soo-ree,** *s. f.* Flute, fife, pipe.

बांह **banh,** *s. f.* The arm ; guarantee, protector or security (*as when a man trusts himself in the power of an enemy, a third person, who engages to return him to his house or fort in security, is his banh*). *Banh pukurna,* To protect. *Banh tootna,* To be destitute of friends or protectors. *Banh dena,* To assist. *Banh guhna,* To protect. *Banh churhana,* To get ready, to prepare.

बांहियां **ban-hiyán,** *s. m.* A patron.

बा **ba,** *adv.* Or, either.

बाई **ba-ée,** *s. f.* Mistress, lady (*among Marhattas*) ; a dancing girl. *Baee-jee,* *s. f.* The mother bawd.

बाईस **ba-ées,** *adj.* Twenty-two.

बाईसी **baée-see,** *s. f.* The royal army (*so called, because composed of the troops of twenty-two soobuhs*) ; a command of 22,000 men. *Baee-see tootna,* To attack with one's whole force.

बाईहा **baee-há,** *s. m.* Rheumatism.

बक **bak,** *s. m.* Language, dialect, speech.

बकला **bák-la,** *s. m.* A bean.

बकस **bá-kus,** *s. m.* A bush of which charcoal is made for the manufacture of gunpowder (*Justicia adhatoda,* or, *gandarussa*).

बकयुह **bák-yuh,** *s. m.* A sentence, speech, a word.

बाखर **bá-khur,** } *s. m.* An area or courtyard ; several houses contained within one enclosure, a drug used as a ferment.
बाखल **bá-khul,** }

बाग **bag,** *s. f.* A rein, a bridle. *Bag morna,* To turn the reins : and this phrase is applied to the drying up of the small-pox ; thus, when the pustules begin to blacken and dry up, they say, *Seetla neh bag moree,* or, *Mata neh bag moree.* *Bag lena,* To take the rein ; to curb or pull up (*a horse, &c.*) *Bag hath seh chhootna,* The reins to have slipped from the hand, denotes the loss of choice, power or controul.

बागडोर **bag-dór,** *s. f.* A long rein with which horses are led.

बागा **bá-ga,** *s. m.* A vestment ; honorary dress.

बागी **bá-gee,** *s. m.* A horseman.

बाघ **bagh,** *s. m.* A tiger.

बाघन **ba-ghún,** } *s. f.* A tigress.
बाघनी **bagh-née,** }

बाघम्बर **bagh-úm-bur,** *s. m.* A tiger's skin.

बाघ bá-gha, *s. m.* A tiger.

बाघी bá-ghee, *s. f.* A bubo.

बाचक bá-chuk, *part. act.* Speaker; (*in grammar*) an explanatory particle.

बाचा bá-cha, *s. f.* Speech, language, word; affirmation, agreement, promise.

बाच्य bách-yuh, *s. m.* A sentence (*in grammar*). *adj.* Speakable, fit to speak.

बाछ bachh, *s. f.* Selection; the corner of the lip. *adj.* Useless.

बाछना bách-na, *v. a.* To choose, to select.

बाछा bá-chha, *s. m.* A calf, or the young of any animal.

बाजगाज baj-gáj, *s. m.* The sound or clangour of various musical instruments.

बाजन bá-jun, }

बाजन बाजा bájun-bája, } *s. m. pl.* Musical instruments.

बाजना báj-na, *v. n.* To sound (*as a musical instrument*); to be published, to resound.

बाजरा báj-ra, *s. m.* A kind of grain, Indian corn (*Holcus spicatus*).

बाजा bá-ja, *s. m.* A musical instrument.

बाजागाजा bája-gája, *s. m.* The sound or clangour of various musical instruments.

बाजी bá-jee, *s. m.* A horse.

बाजू bá-joo, *s. m.* An ornament worn on the arm, a bracelet.

बाट bat, *s. f.* Road, highway, path. *s. m.* A weight or measure of weight.

बाटिका bá-tik-a, *s. m.* A villa.

बाटी bá-tee, *s. f.* A habitation, dwelling-house, home, a garden-house.

बाटे घाटे báteh-gháteh, *adv.* Somewhere or other.

बाड़ bar, *s. f.* Edge (*of a sword, knife, &c.*), verge, edge, margin, a fence, a hedge, a line (*of soldiers*); a place below *Patna*. *Bar oorana,* To fire a volley. *Bar chirwana,* or, —*chirna,* To sharpen. *Bar jharna,* To fire a volley. *Bar dilwana,* or, —*dena,* To sharpen, to grind; to excite, to instigate, to animate. *Bar pukrana,* To encourage, to teach. *Bar bandhna,* To enclose a field with thorns. *Bar rukhna,* To sharpen.

बाड़व bá-ruv, *s. m.* Submarine fire; a *Brahmun*.

बाड़वानल bar-wa-núl, *s. m.* Submarine fire.

बाड़ा bá-ra, *s. m.* An enclosure; alms, charity.

बाड़िया bá-ri-ya, *s. m.* A whetter (*of swords, knives, &c.*)

बाड़ी bá-ree, *s. f.* An enclosed piece of ground, a garden, orchard, kitchen-garden; a house with the garden, orchard, &c., attached to it; cotton.

बाढ़ barh, *s. f.* Increase, promotion; a flood.

बाढ़ना bárh-na, *v. n.* To increase, enlarge, go on, proceed, advance, exaggerate, grow, rise, swell, to be promoted, to amount, lengthen.

बान ban, *s. f.* Temper, quality, manners. *s. m.* An arrow, a rocket used in battle; name of an *Usoor*, son of *raja Buli*; the boar or swell of the tide in the Indian rivers; a kind of rope made of *moonj*, used to form the bottoms of beds, as well as for other purposes.

बानिज्य ba-níj-yuh, *s. m.* Trade, traffic, merchandise.

बानी bá-nee, *s. f.* Speech, voice, language; name of the goddess *Suruswutee*.

बान्डा bán-da, *adj.* Tail-less. *s. m.* A serpent which has lost its tail.

बात bat, *s. f.* Speech, language, word, saying, report, discourse; account, subject, question, cause, business, affair, matter, circumstance, particular, article. *Bat kurna,* To converse, to talk, speak, say, address. *Bat katna,* To interrupt. *Bat ka butukkur kurna,* To multiply words, to talk much on little. *Bat kee bat,* Unmeaning orders, commands not expected to be obeyed, words of course. *Bat kee bat men, adv.* Instantly. *Bat kuhao, s. m.* Conversation, chitchat. *Bat koorsee nisheen hona,* To be acceptable or approved of, a word or speech. *Bat gurhna,* To speak to the purpose, to (*speak so that one's words*) have effect or make impression. *Bat chulana,* To converse, to start a subject. *Bat cheet, s. f.* Conversation, chitchat, confabulation, discourse, talk. *Bat talna,* To put off, to excuse one's self. *Bat dalna,* To throw away one's words, to ask in vain. *Bat dhurana,* To persist in making excuses, to put off, to evade. *Bat pana,* To accomplish one's wishes, to effect one's purpose. *Bat phenkna,* To jeer, to mock, to speak at (*but not to*). *Bat pherna,* To equivocate. *Bat burhana,* To prolong a contest. *Bat bunana,* To make up a story, to make excuses. *Baten soonana,* To abuse, to speak harshly. *Baten soonua,* To receive abuse or harsh reproof. *Bat bandhna,* To sophisticate, to prevaricate. *Bat bigarna,* To mar a plot, to spoil. *Bat marna,* To turn off, to evade, to divert a discourse, &c. *Bat men kooch kurna,* To perform a business in a short time, to lose no time in doing any thing. *Bat rukhna,* To assist, to agree, to comply. *Bat ruhna,* To make good one's words. *Bat lugana,* To calumniate, to insinuate something maliciously.

बात bat, *s. m.* Pain in the joints, rheumatism.

बाती bá-tee, *s. f.* A candle; the wick of a lamp; a tent or bougie put into a wound to keep it open.

बातूनिबा ba-tóo-nia, *s. m.* A talkative, conversible, entertaining person.

बातूनी ba-tóo-nee, *adj.* Conversible, talkative, chatty, entertaining.

बाद bad, *s. m.* Accusation, dispute, assertion, affirmation ; rheumatism. *Bad kurna,* To argue.

बादर bá-dur, } *s. m.* A cloud.
बादल bá-dul, }

बादला bád-la, *s. m.* Gold or silver thread or wire, brocade.

बादानुबाद bad-anoo-bád, *s. m.* Altercation.

बादली bád-lee, *s. f.* Silver cloth.

बादी bá-dee, *s. m.* A speaker, an accuser, a plaintiff, an enemy, a mischief-maker, disputant, an arguer. *Badee-chor,* An inveterate thief.

बादुर bá-door, *s. m.* A flying-fox, a bat.

बाध badh, *s. m.* Opposing, hindering.

बाधक ba-dhúk, *adj.* What hinders, opposes, pains, &c.

बाधन bádhun, *s. m.* Pain ; impeding, opposing.

बाधा bá-dha, *s. f.* Pain, distress ; obstruction, hinderance, prevention.

बाधित bá-dhít, *adj.* Obstructed, impeded ; pained, tormented.

बान ban, *s. f.* Temper, quality, manners. *s. m.* An arrow, a rocket used in battle ; the name of an *Usoor,* son of *raja Buli* ; the high tide in the Indian rivers commonly called the Bore ; a kind of rope made of *moonj,* used to form the bottoms of beds as well as for other purposes.

बानगी bán-gee, *s. f.* A pattern, a muster.

बानप्रस्थ ban-prústh, *s. m.* One who retires from the world with his wife and family, and is supposed to pass his life in devotion in the forests ; an anchoret or hermit.

बानर bá-nur, *s. m.* A monkey.

बानवे bán-weh, *adj.* Ninety-two.

बाना bá-na, *s. m.* Habit, profession ; fashion in dress, peculiar to individuals or to bodies taken individually (*so, regimentals may be called bana*) ; uniformity ; a kind of weapon ; a veil ; the woof in weaving. *Bana bandhna,* To be ready, to be determined.

बाना bá-na, *v. a.* To open.

बानी bá-nee, *s. f.* The price paid for a work ; ashes ; the thread with which cloth is woven ; speech, voice, language ; name of the goddess *Suruswutee.*

बानीबोनी bánee-bónee, *s. f.* The price of weaving.

बानूआ ba-nóo-a, *s. m.* Name of a waterbird.

बानूसा ba-nóo-sa, *s. m.* } A kind of cloth.
बानूसी ba-noo-see, *s. f.* }

2 Y

बान्दा bán-da, *s. m.* Name of a place in *Bundelkhund.*

बान्धव bán-dhuv, *s. m.* A relation, a kinsman ; a friend.

बाप bap, *s. m.* Father. *Bap kurna,* To consider as a father. *Bap mera* (*my father !*) and, *Bap reh* (*O father !*), are exclamations expressive of surprise, grief, &c.

बापरा bap-rá, } *adj.* Helpless, poor.
बापरौ bap-róu, }

बाफ baph, *s. f.* Steam, vapour.

बाबनी bab-née, *s. f.* A snake's hole.

बाबर bá-bur, *s. m.* A kind of sweetmeat.

बाबा bá-ba, *s. m.* Father, dad ; sire ! sir ! child ! *Baba jan,* Dear child !

बाबू bá-boo, *s. m.* A child ; a prince ; Master (*a title given by Hindoos, equivalent to Mr. or 'Squire*).

बाम bam, *s. f.* An eel (*Ophidium simack*).

बामअंग bám-ung, *s. m.* The left side.

बामन bá-mun, *s. m.* A dwarf.

बाम्भनी bambh-née, } *s. f.* A snake's hole.
बाम्भी bam-bhée, }

बाम्हन báh-mun, *s. m.* A *Brahmun.*

बाम्हनी báh-mun-ee, *s. f.* The wife of a *Brahmun* ; name of a medicinal herb, the moonplant ; a stye on the eye-lids ; a lizard.

बाम्हनहत्ती báhmun-húttee, *s. f.* Name of a plant (*Ovieda verticellata*).

बायन bá-yun, *s. m.* Sweetmeat, cakes, &c. distributed at marriages and other ceremonies.

बायब bá-yub, *adj.* Apart, separate, distinct ; strange. *Yih bat bayub hy,* This is another thing.

बायां bá-yan, *adj.* Left (*hand, &c.*) *s. m.* The bass part in music, the base sound (*especially of tubla, dholuk, and pukhawuj*), which are played on with the left hand. *Bayan paon poojna,* To acknowledge the cunning of an artful person.

बार bar, *s. f.* Time, occasion, delay ; a girl not exceeding sixteen ; verge, edge. *s. m.* A day of the week ; door ; water ; child ; hair ; prohibition, obstacle. *Bar lugana, v. a.* To delay, to hesitate.

बारदेना bar-déna, *v. a.* To load, give charge ; to impose, give trouble, encumber ; to give admission, to give leave.

बारन ba-rún, *s. m.* Forbidding, prohibiting, preventing ; an elephant.

बारना bar-ná, *v. n.* To leave off, separate. *v. a.* To forbid, prohibit.

बारना bár-na, *v. a.* To kindle, light.

बारम्बार bar-um-bár, *adv.* Often, frequently, repeatedly.

बारह bá-ruh, *adj.* Twelve. *Baruh bat hona,* To be vagabond, ruined, or harassed. *Baruh-duree, s. f.* A summer-house.

बाराखुरी bára-khúree, *s. f.* The combination of the consonants with the symbols of the vowels.

बारादुरी bára-dúr-ee, *s. f.* A summer-house.

बारासिंगा bára-sínga, *s. m.* A stag (*Cervus elaphus*).

बाराह ba-ráh, *s. m.* A hog.

बारिद bá-rid, *s. m.* A cloud.

बारी bá-ree, *s. m.* A window; the name of a caste of *Hindoos* whose business it is to sell torches and leaves which are used as platters; an ornament worn in the ear and nose; a garden, an orchard, a house; a girl not exceeding sixteen; time, tour, turn. *Baree-kee tup,* An intermittent fever. *Bareedar,* An attendant who waits in turn with others.

बारुनी bá-roo-nee, *s. f.* Spirituous liquors.

बारू ba-róo, *s. f.* Land. *s. m.* A child.

बारू ba-róo, } *s. f.* Gun-powder.
बारूत baróot, }

बाल bal, *adj.* Ignorant, unwise, uninstructed; young, infantine, a child.

बाल bal, *s. m.* } An infant, a child; it
बाला bá-la, *s. f.* } usually means the young child, under five years old, but is equally applicable till sixteen years of age.

बाल bal, *s. m.* Hair. *Bal gopal,* Family. *Bal churitr,* Tricks of children. *Bal bandhee kowree marna,* To shoot at without missing, to act with great care, not to mistake. *Bal bal,* Hair by hair, every hair. *Bal beeka,* A bent or disordered hair, is used to express " the smallest harm or inconvenience;" *so, Bal beeka nuh howeh,* Let not a hair be disordered (*let not the least harm be done*).

बाल bal, *s. f.* An ear or spike of corn; a crack in a cup or glass. *s. m.* The thread on which sugar is crystallized. *Baldar,* A cracked vessel (*of china, glass, &c.*)

बालुक bá-luk, *s. m.* A boy, an infant.

बालुकत्व báluk-twúh, } *s. m.* Childhood,
बालुकपन báluk-pún, } childishness.

बालका bal-ká, *s. m.* A young follower of a *Jogee* or *Sunnyasee.*

बालुकीय báluk-éeyuh, *adj.* Childish, infantine.

बालछुर bal-chhúr, *s. f.* Name of a medicine or perfume.

बालतोर bal-tór, *s. m.* A pimple.

बालना bál-na, *v. a.* To kindle, to light.

बालबचे bál-búchcheh, *s. pl.* Children.

बालभोग bal-bhóg, *s. m.* An offering to *Krishn* presented early in the morning.

बालुम ba-lúm, *s. m.* A lover or beloved person; a husband; a kind of cloth. *Balam kheera, s. m.* A sort of cucumber in season in the rains (*a variety of Cucumis sativa*).

बालरांड bál-rand, *s. f.* A widow, who, when very young, lost her husband.

बालराज bal-ráj, }
बालवायुज bal-váyuj, } *s. m.* Lapis lazuli.
बालसूर्य bal-sóorj, }

बाला bá-la, *s. f.* A female child, a girl not exceeding sixteen; a medicinal and fragrant plant. *s. m.* An ear-ring; a male child, a boy. *Bala-chand,* The new moon.

बालातप bala-túp, *s. m.* The rays of the rising sun.

बालापन bala-pún, *s. m.* Childhood, infancy.

बालाभोला bála-bhóla, *adj.* Innocent, artless as a child. *s. m.* An artless child.

बालि báli, } *s. m.* A monkey, the son of
बाली bálee, } *Indr,* killed by *Ram.*

बालिनी bá-lin-ee, *s. f.* The constellation *Uswinee.*

बालिश bá-lish, *s. m.* A pillow.

बाली bá-lee, *s. f.* A female child; an ear-ring worn in the ear passing through the centre of it.

बालीश ba-léesh, *s. m.* Pain in making water, from gravel, &c.

बालू bá-loo, *s. m.* A drug commonly called *Elubalook.*

बालूक bá-look, *s. m.* A drug and perfume.

बालूका bá-loo-ka, *s. f.* Sand, gravel.

बालूकागुर bálooka-gúr, *s. m.* A sort of fish (*Cheilodipterus culius and butis*).

बालूकामय bálooka-múy, *adj.* Sandy, gravelly.

बालू bá-loo, *s. f.* Sand.

बालूक ba-lóok, *s. m.* A sort of poison.

बालूचुरी báloo-chúr-ee, *adj.* (*Silk cloth*) made in *Baloochur* near *Moorshedabad.*

बालेयुह baléyuh, *s. m.* } A plant (*Sipho-*
बालेयुशाक baléyuh-shák, } *nanthus Indica*).

बालोपवीत baló-puv-éet, *s. m.* The sacrificial thread, or a substitute for it as worn by children; a cloth covering the privities.

बालयुह bál-yuh, *s. m.* Childhood.

बाव bao, *s. f.* Wind, air; the venereal disease. *Bao ka rookh butana,* To cheat, to impose on, to deceive. *Bao khana,* To live in pleasure and enjoyment ; to court one's inspirations, *i. e. to* protract a miserable existence. *Bao bundes, s. f.* Sophistry, exaggerated praise of a worthless being. *Bao bandhna,* To prevail over an adversary by flattery or invective without argument. *Bao bhuree khal,* Of light estimation. *Bao surna,* Wind being discharged backwards.

बावग **bá-wug,** *s. m.* Seed-time.

बावगोला **báo-góla,** *s. m.* The colick, flatulency.

बावझक **bao-jhúk,**⎫ *adj.* A prattler, trifling talker, babbler.
बावभक **bao-bhúk,**⎭

बावड़ी **báo-ree,** *s. f.* A large well.

बावन **bá-wun,** *adj.* Dwarfish, diminutive. *s. m.* The fifth supposed incarnation of *Vishnoo* in the form of a dwarf.

बावन **bá-wun,** *adj.* Fifty-two.

बावना **báo-na,** *adj.* Dwarfish.

बावबतास **báo-but-ás,** *s. f.* Possession by a demon or devil, misfortune, calamity.

बावरा **báo-ra,** *adj.* Mad, insane, crazy.

बावरी **báo-ree,** *s. f.* A large well.

बावला **báo-la,** *adj.* Mad, insane, crazy.

बावली **báo-lee,** *s. f.* A large well into which people descend by steps to get water; the drag (*thing or animal with which hawks, dogs, &c. are taught to hunt*); a trick. *Baolee dena,* To initiate, to train.

बावलेना **bao-léna,** *s. m.* Name of a defect in horses.

बावसूल **bao-sóol,** *s. m.* The colick.

बाशीन **ba-shéen,** *s. f.* The female of a kind of hawk or falcon.

बास **bas,** *s. m.* Abode, residence. *s. f.* Smell, scent, odour.

बासक **bá-suk,**⎫ *s. m.* The chief of serpents, which is
बासुकी **bá-soo-kee,**⎭ fabled to support the universe, and which was used as a string to whirl the mountain *Mundur* in churning the ocean for the *umrit,* &c.

बासन **bá-sun,** *s. m.* A basin, plate, dish, goblet, pot, &c.

बासना **bás-na,** *s. f.* Desire, inclination, choice. *v. a.* To scent, to perfume.

बासर **bá-sur,** *s. m.* A day.

बासा **bá-sa,** *s. m.* Lodging, abode, dwelling, temporary residence.

बासी **bá-see,** *adj.* Stale ; perfumed. *adj. m.* (*used substantively*) Inhabitant ; as, *Bun-basee,* Inhabitant of the woods. *Basee kurna,* To make stale, to vomit.

बाह **bah,** *s. m. f.* The arm.

बाहन **bá-hun,** *s. m.* A vehicle, carriage,

any animal or other conveyance on which a person rides.

बाहना **báh-na,** *v. a.* To shoot, to discharge a weapon ; to comb (*the hair*).

बाहुर **bá-hur,**⎫ *adv.* Without, out, outside, abroad, away. *adj.* Foreign.
बाहिर **bá-hir,**⎭

बाहिरह **bá-hir-uh,** *s. m.* The left side (*in sword exercise, &c.*)

बाहिरी **bá-hir-ee,** *adj.* Outward, outer, outside, extraneous, foreign ; stranger, foreigner.

बाहु **bá-hoo,** *s. f.* An arm.

बाहुज **bá-hooj,** *s. m.* Sesamum growing wild or spontaneously.

बाहुदा **bá-hoo-da,** *s. f.* The name of a river, said to arise in the snowy chain of the *Himaluy,* and probably the modern *Behut,* the classical *Hydaspes.*

बाहुभूषा **báhoo-bhóosha,** *s. f.* An armlet, an ornament worn round the upper arm.

बाहुमूल **bahoo-móol,** *s. m.* The arm-pit.

बाहुयुद्ध **bahoo-jóoddh,** *s. m.* Close fight, personal struggle, boxing, wrestling.

बाहुल्य **ba-hóol-yuh,** *s. m.* Plenty, abundance, quantity.

बिआरी **bi-ár-ee,** *s. f.* Supper.

बिंजन **bin-jún,** *s. m.* Sauce, condiments, particularly vegetables dressed with clarified butter, &c. and added to flesh or fish ; (*in grammar*) a consonant.

बिंदाल **bin-dál,** *s. f.* A medicinal herb.

बिंब **bimb,** *s. m.* The name of a tree bearing a red fruit (*Momordica monadelpha,* or, *Byronia grandis*).

बिक **bik,** *s. m.* A wolf.

बिकट **bik-út,** *adj.* Difficult ; terrible.

बिकना **bík-na,** *v. n.* To be sold, to sell. *Bik jana,* (*met.*) To be dependant on, to be obliged.

बिकराल **bik-rár,**⎫ *adj.* Terrific, ugly.
बिकराल **bik-rál,**⎭

बिकुल **bik-úl,** *adj.* Restless, uneasy, troubled.

बिकसना **bik-ús-na,** *v. n.* To blow or expand (*as a flower*) ; to be delighted, to smile.

बिकसित **bik-us-ít,** *adj.* Expanded, blown (*as a flower*) ; delighted.

बिकाऊ **bik-áoo,** *adj.* Saleable, for sale.

बिकाना **bik-ána,** *v. a.* To sell.

बिकार **bik-ár,** *s. m.* The change of any thing from its original state, deterioration ; disease.

बिकाल **bik-ál,** *s. m.* Afternoon.

बिकाव **bik-áo,** *s. m.* Sale, vent.

विकास bik-ás, *s. m.* Shining, blooming, expansion, display ; pleased, happy, delighted.

विकी bík-kee, *s. m.* A partner (*at play, &c.*)

विकी bík-ree, *s. f.* Sale.

विखरना bik-húrna, *v. n.* To be scattered, dispersed or dishevelled ; to become angry.

विगंध big-úndh, *s. f.* Stink, fetor.

विगड़ना big-úr-na, *v. n.* To be spoiled, damaged or marred, to fail of success, miscarry, to quarrel, disagree, be at variance, be enraged.

विगड़ी bíg-ree, *s. f.* Spoil, damage, misunderstanding between friends, war, battle.

विगति bí-gut-i, *s. f.* Badness.

विगहा bíg-ha, *s. m.* A quantity of land containing twenty *kutthas* or 120 square feet.

विगाड़ big-ár, *s. m.* Violation, difference, quarrelling, discord, misunderstanding, damage, injury. *Bigar kurna, v. a.* To quarrel, to forfeit friendship. *Bigar pur ana, v. n.* To be ready to quarrel.

विगाड़ना big-árna, *v. a.* To spoil, mar, damage, injure, ruin, bungle ; to cause misunderstanding between friends.

विघन bíg-hun, *s. m.* Hinderance, stop, prevention, interruption.

विच bich, *adv.* In, among, between.

विचकना bich-úk-na, *v. n.* To be disappointed, to be balked ; to sprain ; to run away, to retreat ; to withdraw a consent which has been given.

विचकन्ना bich-kúnna, *s. m.* An ornament worn in the anterior lobe of the ear.

विचकाना bich-kána, *v. a.* To balk, disappoint, to break one's promise.

विचकलना bich-úl-na, *v. n.* To turn, to bend, slip, break one's promise, infringe.

विचवई bich-wúee, | *s. m.* A mediator,
विचवानी bich-wánee, } interposer, arbitrator, agent, ambassador.

विचार bich-ár, *s. m.* Consideration, reflection, contrivance, judgment, opinion, thought, apprehension, will.

विचारक bich-ar-úk, *part. act.* Investigator, judge, inspector.

विचारत bich-ar-út, *part.* Reflecting, thinking.

विचारना bich-ar-na, *v. a.* To consider, reflect, think, investigate, comprehend, apprehend, conceive, judge.

विचाली bich-á-lee, *s. f.* Straw.

विचित्र bich-ítr, *adj.* Variegated, various ; wonderful.

विचौलिया bich-óu-liya, *s. m.* A mediator, interposer, arbitrator, agent, ambassador.

विछू bích-chhoo, *s. m.* A scorpion, the sign Scorpio of the Zodiac.

विछुरना bich-húr-na, | *v. n.* To separate,
विछुरना bich-hóor-na, } to be separated.

विछराव bichh-ráo, *s. m.* Separation.

विछना bíchh-na, *v. n.* To be spread, to spread.

विछराहट bichh-rá-hut, *s. f.* Separation.

विछलना bich-húr-na, | *v. n.* To be separated, to separate,
विछलना bich-húl-na, } to slip, slide, to slip out of place, to sprain, to turn away the face.

विछवाना bichh-wá-na, *v. a.* To cause to spread.

विछाता bich-há-ta, *s. m.* A stinging nettle (*Urtica interrupta*).

विछा देना bichhá déna, *v. a.* To spread ; (*metonim.*) To knock down, to drub.

विछाना bichhá-na, *v. a.* To spread, to extend.

विछूरना bich-hóor-na, *v. n.* To separate, to be separated.

विछूवा bich-hóoa, *s. m.* A sort of dagger ; an ornament worn on the toes.

विछोरना bich-hórna, *v. a.* To separate.

विछोह bich-hóh, | *s. m.* Separation, absence.
विछोहा bich-hóha, }

विछोना bich-hóuna, | *s. m.* Bedding, bedclothes, bed, carpetting.
विछोना bich-hóna, }

विजना bíj-na, *s. m.* A fan.

विजली bíj-lee, *s. f.* Lightning ; a thunderbolt.

विजायठ bij-ayúth, *s. m.* A bracelet worn on the arm, an armlet.

विजाला bij-ála, *adj.* Seedy, turned to seed.

विजिया bij-iya, *s. f.* Hemp (*Cannabis sativa*).

विजे bijuy, *s. m.* Triumph. *Bijuy-dusmee* (*the victorious tenth*), The tenth of *Aswin sookl puchh*, the anniversary of *Ram's* victory over *Rawun.*

विजेयी bijuy-ée, *adj.* Conqueror, vanquisher.

विजोग bijóg, *s. m.* Separation, absence, (*especially of lovers*). *adj.* Separate, parted.

विजोगी bijógee, *s. m. f.* An unfortunate, or miserable person.

विझकना bij-húk-na, *v. n.* To be alarmed.

विझकाना bijh-ká-na, *v. a.* To frighten, to scare, to alarm.

विठप bit-úp, *s. m.* A tree.

विठवा bit-wá, *s. m.* A son.

विठाना bit-ána, *v. a.* To scatter, sprinkle.

विटिया bit-iyá, *s. f.* A daughter.

विटोना bit-óna, *v. a.* To scatter, sprinkle. *s. m.* A son.

विटोरा bit-óu-ra, *s. m.* A heap of the cakes of dried cow-dung.

विठाना bit-hána, विठलाना bith-lána, } *v. a.* To cause to sit down, to seat, set, settle.

वित bit, *s. m.* Wealth, substance, thing ; ability, power, means.

वितना bít-na, *v. n.* To pass.

वितरन bit-urún, *s. m.* Giving charity, donation, alms.

वितरना bit-úr-na, *v. a.* To bestow.

विताना bit-ána, *v. a.* To pass.

वितीत bit-éet, *adj.* Passed, gone.

वित्त bitt, *s. m.* Wealth, substance, thing ; ability, power, means.

वित्ता bítta, *s. m.* A span.

वित्तिया bíttiya, *s. m.* A dwarf (*i. e. a span high*).

वित्थरना bit-húr-na, वित्थुरना bit-hóor-na, } *v. n.* To be scattered, to be sprinkled, to be spread.

वित्थराना bith-rá-na, *v. a.* To scatter, to sprinkle.

वित्था bit-há, *s. f.* Pain, affliction, distress.

वित्थारना bit-hár-na, *v. a.* To cause to scatter, to cause to sprinkle.

वित्थारी bit-há-ree, *s. f.* Cleansing the warp.

वित्थुरना bit-hóor-na, *v. n.* To be scattered, to be sprinkled, to be spread.

विद bid, *s. f.* A little pit into which children in play endeavour to throw balls or marbles.

विदरी bid-ree, *s. f.* A kind of tutenag inlaid with silver; used to make *hookka* bottoms, cups, &c., and, so called from *Beeder*, the name of a city and province.

विदा bíd-a, *s. f.* Dismission, taking leave, farewell, adieu. *Bida kurna*, To bid farewell, to dismiss.

विदारन bid-á-run, *s. m.* Tearing, rending, breaking, cleaving, splitting, severing, dividing.

विदारना bid-ár-na, *v. a.* To tear, rend.

विदाहना bid-áh-na, *v. a.* To turn the plough over a field after the seed is come up, to plough immediately after sowing for the purpose of covering the seed ; to harrow.

विदेस bid-és, *s. m.* A foreign country, another country.

विदेसी bid-ésee, *adj.* Foreigner.

विदोरना bid-ór-na, *v. a.* To screw ; to mock at, to laugh at, to ridicule.

विद्या bid-yá, *s. f.* Science, knowledge, intellect.

विद्याधर bid-ya-dhúr, *s. m.* A sort of demigod or attendant in the celestial courts.

विद्यार्थी bid-yár-thee, *s. m.* A student.

विद्याबान bid-ya-wán, *adj.* Scientific, learned.

विद्वान bid-wán, *adj.* Learned in the *Beds.*

विध bidh, *s. f.* A sacred precept, rule, order, law, statute, direction, decree, injunction ; manner, mode, kind, sort. *s. m.* Name of *Bruhma*, providence.

विधना bídh-na, *v. n.* To be pierced or perforated.

विधवा bídh-wa, *s. f.* A widow.

विधुवा bid-húwa, *s. m.* The Deity.

विधाता bid-há-ta, *s. m.* He who has predestinated, i. e. the deity *Bruhma*; Providence.

विधान bid-hán, *s. m.* Common practice, precept, direction.

विधावट bid-há-wut, *s. f.* Perforation.

विध्वंस bid-húns, *s. m.* Non-existence, annihilation, slaughter.

विन bin, विना bín-a, } *adv.* Without, except, unless, not. *Bin-janeh*, Without knowing, unwittingly. *Bin-daneh panee*, Without eating and drinking. *Bin mareh touba kurna*, To fear without a cause.

विनबाई bin-wáee, *s. f.* Price paid for weaving.

विनसना bin-ús-na, *v. n.* To spoil, deteriorate, perish.

विना bín-a, *adv.* Without, except, unless, not.

विनाई bin-áee, विनावट bin-á-wut, } *s. f.* Weaving.

विनास bin-ás, *s. m.* Annihilation, disappearance, destruction.

विनौना bin-óu-na, *v. a.* To adore, venerate, revere, laud.

विनौला bin-óu-la, *s. m.* The seed of the cotton tree. (*It is said to be very fattening food for cattle*). *Binoula chabna*, To say unpleasant things.

विनौली bin-óu-lee, *s. f.* Hail (*of a small kind*).

विन्ती bín-tee, *s. f.* An apology, submission, solicitation.

बिन्द bind, / s. f. A spot, a dot, a mark;
बिन्दी bín-dee, / the dot over a letter representing the nasal termination.

बिन्धना bíndh-na, v. a. To sting, bite. v. n. To be bored or pierced.

बिन्ना bín-na, v. a. To knit; to weave. v. n. To be picked.

बिपत bíp-ut, / s. f. Adversity, calamity,
बिपत्ति bip-útti, / misfortune, distress.
बिपता bíp-ta, /

बिपरना bip-úr-na, v. a. To attack, to assault.

बिपरीत bip-ur-éet, part. Contrary, opposite. s. f. Mischief, ruin.

बिप्र bipr, s. m. A Brahmun.

बिफरना bip-húr-na, v. n. To be perverse, refractory, disobedient, cross, obstinate, pert.

बिफे bíp-huy, s. m. Thursday.

बिमल bím-ul, adj. Clean.

बिमान bim-án, s. m. A car or chariot of the gods (sometimes serving us a seat or throne, and at others carrying them through the skies self-directed and self-moving).

बिमुख bím-ookh, adj. Having the face averted, turned from, averse.

बिया bíya, s. m. Seed.

बियारी biyáree, s. f. / Supper.
बियालू biyáloo, s. m. /

बियाह biyáh, s. m. Marriage. Biyah kurna, To marry. Biyah ruchana, To celebrate a marriage. Biyah-lana, To take in marriage, to bring home a wife, to marry.

बियाहता biyah-ta, f. / adj. Married.
बियाहा biyahá, m. /

बियाहन biya-hún, s. m. Marrying, marriage, to marry. Biyahun-jog, adj. Fit for marriage, marriageable.

बियाहना biyáh-na, v. a. To give or take in marriage, to marry.

बियोग biyóg, s. m. Separation, absence (especially of lovers).

बियोगी biyógee, s. m. A lover suffering the pain of absence.

बिरकत bír-kut, s. m. A kind of fukeer who has relinquished the world. adj. Wearied, disgusted.

बिरचन bír-chun, s. m. Flour made from the fruit of the ber (Rhamnus jujuba).

बिरता bír-ta, s. m. Substance, ability, power.

बिरती bír-tee, s. m. Name of a plant (a species of Panicum).

बिरुद bír-ud, s. m. Fame, reputation, panegyrick.

बिरनी bír-nee, s. f. A wasp; a small grain.

बिरमना bir-úm-na, v. n. To stop, to remain, to delay.

बिरमाना bir-má-na, v. a. To stop; to tame, to reduce to obedience, to allure.

बिरला bír-la, adj. Scarce, uncommon, rare, wonderful; delicate, fine.

बिरवा bír-wa, s. m. A plant, a tree.

बिरवाही bir-wá-hee, s. f. An orchard. Birwahee kurna, To make an orchard; to enclose with a hedge.

बिरसना bir-ús-na, v. n. To stay, to remain.

बिरह bír-uh, s. m. Separation, parting, absence, especially the separation of lovers.

बिरहन bír-hun, adj. f. (A woman) suffering the pangs of absence in love, (a female lover) separated from the object of her affection.

बिरहा bír-ha, s. m. Separation, parting, absence, especially the separation of lovers; a kind of song peculiar to washermen.

बिरहिया bír-hiya, adj. Amorous, sensual, suffering the pangs of absent love.

बिरही bír-hee, adj. m. Suffering the pangs of absence in love, separated from one's love.

बिराजना bir-áj-na, v. n. To be conspicuous or splendid; to enjoy one's self; to live in health, ease, content, and independence.

बिरात bir-át, s. m. The embodied spirit. n. prop. Name of a sovereign.

बिराना bir-ána, adj. Strange, foreign; belonging to another, of another. v. a. To mock.

बिराम bir-ám, adj. Uneasy, unquiet, agitated.

बिराोना bir-áo-na, v. a. To vex.

बिरिया biriyán, s. f. Time.

बिरेजा bir-éeja, s. m. Galbanum.

बिरुद्ध bir-óoddh, adj. Opposite, opposed to, contrary to, against.

बिरूप bir-óop, adj. Disfigured, deformed, ugly. Biroop hona, To be disgraced.

बिरोग bir-óg, s. m. Separation, absence.

बिरोगन bir-ógun, adj. f. Separated, distressed from separation.

बिरोध bir-ódh, s. m. Enmity, quarrel, contention, dispute, contrariety, opposition.

बिरोधी bir-ódhee, adj. Quarrelsome.

बिल bil, / s. m. A hole, burrow.
बिला bíl-a, /

बिलकना bil-úk-na, v. n. To sob, to cry violently (as a child); to long for, to desire eagerly.

विलूखना bil-úkh-na, v. a. To see, to look at, to perceive, to behold. v. n. To be displeased.

विलग bil-úg, adj. Separate. s. m. Separation, disunion, difference. Bilug manna, v. n. To be displeased, to be angry or offended.

विलगना bil-úg-na, v. n. To separate, to be separated ; to curdle, to turn (as milk).

विलगाना bil-gána, v. a. To separate, to disjoin.

विलगाव bil-gáo, s. m. Separation.

विलंगना bil-úng-na, v. a. To climb, to ascend.

विलचना bil-úch-na, v. a. To extract, to select (as passages from books), to pick.

विलटना bil-út-na, v. n. To become bad.

विलनी bíl-nee, s. f. A stye or stithe, the disorder in the eyelids.

विलबिलाना bil-bil-ána, v. n. To be restless, to be tormented with pain, to complain from pain or grief, to lament, to blubber.

विलंभ bil-úmbh, s. m. Delay, procrastination, tardiness.

विलंभना bil-úmbh-na, v. n. To stay, tarry, delay.

विलरा bíl-ra, s. m. A he-cat ; a kind of cloth.

विलुलाना bil-ul-ána, v. n. To lament.

विलल्ला bil-úlla, adj. Foolish, simple, silly.

विलसना bil-ús-na, v. n. To be pleased, to be satisfied, to be delighted.

विलस्त bil-ust, s. f. A span.

विलुहबूंद bíluh-búnd, s. m. Settlement, regulation.

विलहुरा bil-húr-a, s. m. A kind of basket (long and narrow) generally used for holding pan.

विलहुरी bil-úh-ree, s. f. A ladle for taking out oil ; a small basket for holding betel-leaf

विलाई bil-áee, s. f. A she-cat ; a grater for scraping pumpions, &c.

विलाईकंद bilàee-kúnd, s. m. Name of a medicine.

विलांड bil-ánd, s. f. A span.

विलाना bil-ána, v. n. To vanish, to retire, to be lost. v. a. To cause to vanish, to dissipate, to dispose of, to distribute.

विलाप bil-áp, s. m. Lamentation, a complaint.

विलापना bil-áp-na, v. n. To lament, to bewail.

विलार bil-ár, } s. m. A male cat.
विलाव bil-áo, }

विलावल bil-áwul, s. f. Name of a raginee.

विलास bil-ás, s. m. Pleasure, delight.

विलासी bil-ásee, adj. Voluptuous, addicted to pleasure.

विलोकना bil-ók-na, v. a. To see, look at, behold.

विलोना bil-óna, } v. a. To churn.
विलोउना bil-óuna, }

विल्ला bílla, } s. m. A male cat.
विलार billár, }

विल्लाना billána, v. n. To weep or complain from grief or pain.

विल्ली bíllee, s. f. A she-cat ; the bolt of a door, a bar.

विल्लीलोतन bíllee-lótun, s. m. Valerian.

विषनी bísh-nee, s. m. A rake, a debauchee, a lecher. adj. Delicate, nice, showy in dress.

विषेष bish-ésh, s. m. Particular circumstance. adj. Peculiar, special, particular, abundant. adv. Particularly, specially.

विषेषता bish-esh-tá, s. f. Abundance.

विश्रांत bish-ránt, adj. Rested, reposed.

विश्रांति bish-ránti, s. f. Rest, repose, cessation from toil or occupation.

विश्राम bish-rám, s. m. Rest, ease, repose, pause, a stop, a pause in writing. Bishram lena, To rest, to repose, to pass the night (particularly used by wandering fukeers).

विष bish, } s. m. Poison, venom ; (met.)
विख bikh, } it is sometimes applied to bitter things. Bikhdhur, A snake.

विषखपरा bísh-khúpra, s. m. The name of a medicinal plant (Trianthema pentandra).

विषखोपरा bish-khópra, s. m. The name of an animal of the lizard kind, about a yard long, and said to be venemous (Lacerta iguana).

विषम bísh-um, adj. Unequalled (in a bad sense), difficult, bad, afflictive. Bishum-jwur, s. m. An inflammatory fever, a high fever.

विषय bísh-uy, } s. m. An object of sense,
विखय bíkh-uy, } any thing perceivable by the senses ; as, colour, sound, odour, flavour, and contact ; an affair, matter, &c.

विषयी bish-uy-ée, } adj. Sensual, worldly.
विखयी bikh-uy-ée, }

विषहा bish-há, } adj. Venemous (as rep-
विखहा bikh-há, } tiles).

विषेला bish-éla, } adj. Venemous.
विषियर bish-iyúr, }

विष्टी bísh-tee, s. f. Rain.

विष्था bish-thá, s. f. Ordure.

विष्णु bísh-un, n. prop. (in Hindoo mythology), The Deity in the character of Preserver.

बिष्णपद bishn-púd, *s. m.* A particular song in the name of *Vishnoo*.

बिष्मज्वर bishm-jwúr, *s. m.* An inflammatory fever, a high fever.

बिसखपरा bis-khúpra, *s. m.* The name of a medicinal plant (*Trianthema pentandra*).

बिसखोपरा bis-khópra, *s. m.* The name of an animal of the lizard kind, about a yard long, and said to be venemous (*Lacerta iguana*).

बिसन bís-un, *s. m.* Evil, fault; desire, lust.

बिसनपट bisun-pút, } *s. m.* A habit of indulging desire.
बिसनपन bisun-pún, }

बिसनी bís-nee, *s. m.* A rake, a debauchee, a lecher. *adj.* Delicate, nice, showy in dress.

बिसबिसाना bis-bis-ána, *v. n.* To yield a sound as in the fermentation of putrefying vegetables or of vinous liquors.

बिसमार bis-már, *s. m.* The name of a bush.

बिसराना bis-rá-na, *v. n.* To forget, to cause to forget, to mislead.

बिसरना bis-úr-na, *v. n.* To forget, to be forgotten.

बिसाखा bis-ákha, *s. f.* The name of the 16th mansion of the moon.

बिसात bis-át, *s. f.* Means, capital stock, estate.

बिसाती bis-á-tee, *s. m.* One who sells every kind of things, a pedler, a haberdasher.

बिसांध bis-ándh, } *s. f.* Fetor, fetidness, stink.
बिसायंध bis-áyundh, }

बिसान bis-án, *s. f.* An offensive smell (*as of fish, onions, &c.*)

बिसाना bis-ána, *v. a.* To purchase.

बिसारना bis-ár-na, *v. a.* To forget.

बिसाल bis-ál, *adj.* Great, large.

बिसाह bis-áh, *s. f.* Purchase.

बिसाहना bis-áh-na, *v. a.* To buy, to purchase.

बिसूरना bis-óor-na, *v. n.* To cry slowly, to sob.

बिसेला bis-éla, *adj.* Venemous.

बिस्तार bis-tár, *s. m.* Spreading out, abundance, copiousness, prolixity, diffusion.

बिस्तारना bis-tár-na, *v. a.* To spread out, to extend, to diffuse.

बिसूइया bis-tóo-iya, } *s. f.* A lizard.
बिसूई bis-tóo-ee, }

बिहुन bíhun, *s. m.* A seed.

बिहनौर bih-nóur, *s. f.* A seed-plot, nursery (*for plants*).

बिहफे bíh-phuy, *s. m.* Thursday.

बिहबल bíh-bul, *adj.* Agitated, alarmed, overcome with fear or agitation, beside one's self, unable to restrain one's self.

बिहरना bihúr-na, *v. n.* To rejoice, to take pleasure. *v. a.* To enjoy, to take pleasure in, to rejoice, to delight.

बिहरी bíh-ree, *s. f.* A subscription to raise a certain sum, assessment, quota, rate, share.

बिहाई bihá-ee, *s. f.* A spirit supposed to tease infants by whispering alternately sad and pleasing things in their ears which is the cause of their laughing and crying when asleep or awake.

बिहाग bihág, *s. m.* Name of a *raginee*.

बिहान bihán, *s. m.* Morrow, morning.

बिहाना bihána, *v. n.* To spend or pass (*the time*).

बिहाने biháneh, *adv.* Early, soon.

बिहार bihar, *s. m.* Diversion, amusement, sport. *Bihar-usthul*, Place of amusement. *n. prop.* Name of a province.

बिहारी bihár-ee, *adj.* Sportive. *n. prop.* A name of *Krishn*, also name of a *Hindoo* poet.

बी bee, A vocative particle used in speaking to women; Lady. *conj.* Also, even.

बींदा béen-da, *s. m.* A roll of paper.

बींधना béendh-na, *v. a.* To bore.

बीउर bee-úr, *s. f.* Seed-bed, seed-plot.

बीउर bée-ur, *s. m.* A hole (*of a snake, rat, &c.*)

बीक beek, *s. m.* A wolf.

बीघा bée-gha, *s. m.* A quantity of land containing twenty *kutthas* or 120 feet square.

बीच beech, *adv.* In, into, among, between, during. *s. m.* Middle, midst, centre; difference; quarrel, hostility. *Beech kee oonglee, s. f.* The middle finger. *Beech purna, v. n.* To differ, to raise a quarrel between. *Beech bichao*, Mediation, interposition, arbitration. *Beech bichao kurna*, To mediate, interpose. *Beechon beech, s. m.* The very middle, the very midst.

बीछा bée-chha, *s. m.* A scorpion; the sign Scorpio.

बीज beej, *s. m.* Seed, sperma genitale (*viri aut mulieris*).

बीजक bée-juk, *s. m.* A ticket tied to goods or on bags to mark their contents, price, &c., a list, an invoice.

बीजना béej-na, *s. m.* A fan.

बीजाबर खंड béejabur-khund, *s. m.* A forest.

बीजार bee-jár, *adj.* Seedy.

बीजी bée-jee, *s. f.* A weasel, a mongoose (*Vivera Ichneumon*).

बीझना béejh-na, *v. a.* To tear up the earth with the horns; to push, to shove, to shoulder.

बीट beet, *s. f.* Dung of any animal; a factitious salt containing sulphur.

बीटना béet-na, *v. n.* To spill, to scatter.

बीठा bee-tha, *s. m.* An annular cushion put on the head to carry a pot of water on.

बीड़ा bee-ra, *s. m.* A betel-leaf made up with a preparation of the areca nut, spices and chunam ; a thong tied to the hilt of a sword by which it is retained in the scabbard, a sword knot. *Beera oothana, v. a.* To undertake a business. *Beera dalna,* To propose a premium for the performance of a task. (*These expressions originate in a custom that prevailed of throwing a beera of betel into the midst of an assembly, in token of proposal to any person to undertake some difficult affair then requisite to be performed ; and the person who took up the betel bound himself to perform the business in question*).

बीन been, *s. f.* A kind of stringed instrument, a sort of lute.

बीण्डा béen-da, *s. m.* A roll of paper.

बीतना béet-na, *v. n.* To pass, to come to pass, happen, befall.

बीन been, *s. f.* A kind of stringed instrument, a sort of lute.

बीनड़ी béen-dee, *s. f.* The hair twisted or plaited behind ; a tail.

बींधना béendh-na, *v. a.* To bore.

बीबी bée-bee, *s. f.* A lady, a wife.

बीमा bée-ma, *s. m.* Insurance.

बीर beer, *s. m.* A hero ; a brother ; a jewel worn in the ear. *s. f.* A tusk ; a sister. *adj.* Brave.

बीरता beer-tá, *s. f.* Prowess, valour.

बीरन bée-run, *s. m.* Brother.

बीरबहूटी béer-búhoo-tee, *s. f.* A small insect with a back red and soft like velvet, scarlet-fly, or lady-fly.

बीरा bée-ra, *s. m.* A betel-leaf made up with a preparation of the areca nut, spices and chunam.

बीरी bée-ree, *s. f.* A betel-leaf made up with spices, &c.; the colour which adheres to the lips from chewing betel ; a composition which being rubbed on the teeth stains their interstices of a red colour.

बीर्य beerj, *s. m.* Seed ; sperma genitale (*viri aut mulieris*) ; power, strength.

बीस bees, *adj.* Twenty.

बीसा bée-sa, *s. m.* A dog which has twenty nails.

बीसी bée-see, *s. f.* A measure of grain. *adj.* Twenty, a score.

बुंदा bóon-da, *s. m.* A point, a dot.

बुंदिया bóon-diya, *s. f.* A kind of sweet-meat like drops.

बुंदेला boon-dél-a, *s. m.* A *Rajpoot* of *Bundelkhund.*

बुकठ boo-kút, } *s. m.* A claw.
बुकटा book-tá, }

बुकनी bóok-nee, *s. f.* Powder.

बुकलाना book-lá-na, *v. n.* To talk incoherently to one's self, to act or talk foolishly.

बुक्का bóok-ka, *s. m.* Handful.

बुकी bóok-kee, *s. f.* A cloth brought over the shoulders under the armpits and tied behind ; a handful. *Book-kee marna,* To pass a cloth under the armpits and tie it behind.

बुजना bóoj-na, *s. m.* A cloth used by menstruous women, a pessary. [water.

बुजहरा boo-júh-ra, *s. m.* A vessel for warm

बुझना bóojh-na, *v. n.* To be extinguished, to be put out, to be quenched (*thirst*), to be damped or dejected (*the spirits, &c.*)

बुझाना booj-hána, *v. a.* To extinguish, to make to comprehend, to demonstrate, to push as with argument, to persuade, assure, instruct, signify, to cause to believe.

बुड़ाना boo-rána, *v. a.* To cause to sink.

बुड्ढा bood-dhá, *adj.* Old.

बूढ़भस boorh-bhús, *adj.* Affecting in old age the manners of youth.

बूढ़वा boorh-wá, *adj.* Aged.

बूढ़ापा boor-há-pa, *s. m.* Old age.

बूढ़िया boor-híya, *s. f.* An old woman.

बूंदा bóon-da, *s. m.* A kind of ornament worn on the ears.

बूत boot, *s. m.* A hazard table ; a blow with the fist.

बूताना boo-tá-na, *v. a.* To extinguish.

बूत्ता bóot-ta, *s. m.* Overreaching, fraud, trick, take in. *Bootta dena,* To overreach.

बुद्ध booddh, *s. m.* A wise or learned man, a sage ; the planet Mercury ; Wednesday ; the ninth *Uvutar* or *Hindoo* incarnation and the apparent founder of the religion of the *Booddhus.*

बुद्धि bóod-dhi, *s. f.* Sense, knowledge, wisdom, understanding, intellect, discretion.

बुद्धिभृत booddhi-bhrít, *adj.* Wise, intelligent.

बुद्धिमत booddhi-mút, *m. adj.* Wise, learned ; famed, known.

बुद्धिमान booddhi-mán, *m.* }
बुद्धिवान booddhi-wán, *m.* } *adj.* Idem.
बुद्धिमती booddhi-múti, *f.* }

बुद्धिहीन booddhi-héen, *adj.* Ignorant, silly, a fool.

2 z

बुद्धिहीनता booddhi-heentá, *s. f.* Folly, ignorance.

बुद्धीन्द्रिय booddh-éendriyuh, *s. m.* An organ of intellect, as the mind, eye, ear, nose, tongue and skin.

बुदबुद bóod-bood, *s. m.* A bubble.

बुदबुदाना bood-bood-ána, *v. n.* To mutter, to grumble.

बुध boodh, *s. m.* The son of the moon, and regent of the planet Mercury, with whom he is identified ; a wise or learned man, a sage.

बुधजन boodh-jún, *s. m.* A wise man.

बुधवार boodh-wár, *s. m.* Wednesday.

बुधित boo-dhít, *adj.* Known, understood.

बुनना bóon-na, *v. a.* To weave, to intertwine.

बुभुक्षा boo-bhóoksha, *s. f.* Hunger.

बुभुक्षित boo-bhookshít, *adj.* Hungry.

बुर boor, *s. f.* Pudenda fœminæ.

बुरबोला boor-bóla, *adj.* Scurrilous.

बुरभसिया boor-bhús-iya, *adj.* Affected, an old person who affects the manners of youth.

बुर्ला bóor-la, *s. m.* A wasp.

बुरा bóo-ra, *adj.* Bad, worse. *Boora manna, v. a.* To take amiss or ill or as an affront, to be displeased or affronted. *Boora lugna, v. n.* To be unpleasant.

बुराई booráee, *s. f.* Mischief, badness, evil, wickedness. *Booraee pur oothna,* or, *Booraee pur kumur bandhna,* To resolve on mischief.

बुर्ज boorj, *s. m.* A cable.

बुर्जरी boor-jur-ee, *s. f.* A term of abuse (*applied to a woman*).

बुर्द boord, *s. f.* A term used at chess when the king only, on one side, remains on the board ; (*hence also*) an opportunity of making some acquisition.

बुर्हा boor-há, *adj* Wicked, bad.

बुल bool, *s. f.* Pudenda fœminæ.

बुलबुला bóol-boo-la, *s. m.* A bubble.

बुलवाना bool-wána, *v. a.* To cause to call or to send for.

बुलाक boo-lák, *s. m.* An ornament worn on the nose.

बुलाना boo-lá-na, *v. a.* To call, invite, bid.

बुला भेजना boolá-bhéjna, *v. a.* To send for.

बुलालाना boolá-lána, *v. a.* To summon.

बुलाहट boolá-hut, *s. f.* Calling, call, a summons, bidding.

बुल्ला bóol-la, *s. m.* A bubble.

बूहनी bóoh-nee, *s. f.* Handsel, first sale.

बूहरी bóoh-ree, *s. f.* Fried or parched barley.

बुहारन boo-há-run, *s. f.* Sweepings.

बुहारना boo-hár-na, *v. a.* To sweep.

बुहारी boo-há-ree, *s. f.* A broom.

बुहारू boo-há-roo, *s. m.* A sweeper.

बूआ bóoa, *s. f.* A sister ; an aunt by the father's side.

बूई bóoee, *s. f.* A word used to frighten children, a goblin.

बूंद boond, *s. f.* A drop. *Boond kee boond,* Rectified, twice distilled (*spirit, &c.*)

बूंदा bóon-da, *s. m.* A large drop. *Boonda bandee,* Small and interrupted dropping of rain.

बूंदी bóon-dee, *s. f.* Drops of rain ; name of a place ; a kind of sweetmeat.

बूकना bóok-na, *v. a.* To reduce to powder, to powder, pulverize, grind.

बूका bóo-ka, *s. m.* Powder ; small pearls.

बूचना bóochna, *v. n.* To sit in a confined posture, to crouch.

बूचा bóo-cha, *m.* }
बूची bóo-chee, *f.* } *adj.* Ear-cropt, without ears.

बूझ boojh, *s. f.* Understanding, comprehension, thought.

बूझना bóojh-na, *v. a.* To understand, comprehend, think.

बूझाई booj-háee, *s. f.* Teaching, instruction.

बूट boot, *s. m.* A kind of pulse, chick-pea (*Cicer arietinum*).

बूटा bóo-ta, *s. m.* A flower (*particularly worked on cloth or painted on paper, &c.*), a bush, a shrub. *Boota-kudd,* Is applied to describe the small stature and exquisite proportion of a beloved person. *Booteh-dar,* Flowered (*cloth*).

बूटी bóo-tee, *s. f.* Drugs ; flowers or sprigs (*on muslin*).

बूड़ना bóor-na, *v. n.* To dive ; to be immerged, to drown, to dip.

बूड़ मरना boor-múrna, *v. n.* To be drowned, to drown.

बूड़िया bóo-riya, *s. m.* A diver.

बूड़ी bóo-ree, *s. f.* A point of a spear ; a spike in the end of a staff.

बूता bóo-ta, *s. m.* Strength, power, ability.

बूबू boo-boo, *s. f.* A sister ; (*on the west of India*) a lady, a favourite concubine or one of superior rank.

बूर boor, *adj.* Barren (*land*). *s. f.* Chaff, husk. *Boor ka luddoo,* A sort of sweetmeat made with the husk of grain. (*The confectioners avow the imposition and cry out to passengers, " you will*

repent if you eat it, or regret not tasting it."
Hence great men are sometimes called *Boor ka luddoo, when they make a practice of encouraging their
dependants to hope, but do nothing for them at last
as, dancing attendance on them and neglecting
them are each likely to produce regret. The term
also means, any person or thing, which is fair without and foul within, or that promises well but turns
out ill)* ; a well-looking, but stupid fellow.

बूरा **bóo-ra**, *s. m.* A coarse kind of sugar ;
saw-dust ; powder.

वृंद **brind**, *s. m.* A heap, a multitude, a
quantity, an aggregation.

वृंदा **brín-da**, *s. f.* A plant worshipped by
the *Hindoos* commonly called *Toolsee* (*Ocymum
sanctum, or sacred basil: this shrub is said to be a
female metamorphosed ; the circumstance however
is variously told*).

वृंदावन **brin-da-bún**, *s. m.* Name of a place
in the vicinity of *Muthoora*, and the scene of
Krishn's sports with the *Gopees* ; a wilderness of
Toolsee trees.

वृक **brik**, *s. m.* A wolf.

वृक्ष **briksh**, } *s. m.* A tree in general.
वृच्छ **brichh**, }

वृथा **brít-ha**, *adj.* Abortive, vain, in vain.

वृद्ध **briddh**, *adj.* Old.

वृहस्पति **bríhus-púti**, *s. m.* The regent of
the planet Jupiter identified astronomically with
the planet : in mythology he is the preceptor of
the gods ; Thursday.

वृहस्पतिवार **bríhus-puti-bár**, *s. m.* Thursday.

बे **beh**, A vocative particle used contemptuously, you fellow ! you rascal ! sirrah ! O !

बेंग **beng**, *s. m.* A frog, paddock, toad.

बेंट **bent**, *s. m.* A handle.

बेंडा **bén-da**, *adj.* Crooked, athwart, awry.

बेंधना **béndh-na**, *v. a.* To plait, braid.

बेग **beg**, *s. m.* Celerity, haste, rapidity ;
(*adverbially*) with haste, quickly, soon ; dung.

बेगार **beg-ár**, *s. m.* A person forced to work
with or without pay.

बेगारी **beg-áree**, *s. f.* The act of pressing or
forcing to work. *Begaree lena*, To take forcibly
or press, with or without pay.

बेगी **bég-ee**, *adv.* Quickly.

बेंग **beng**, *s. m.* A frog, paddock, toad.

बेचना **béch-na**, *v. a.* To sell.

बेजू **béj-oo**, *s. m.* The name of an animal
that feeds on carcases (*Ursus Indicus: Indian
badger*).

बेझा **bej-há**, *s. m.* A butt or mark for archers.

बेटा **bét-a**, *s. m.* A son, a child. *Beta kur
lena*, To adopt a son.

बेटी **bét-ee**, *s. f.* A daughter.

बेठन **bét-hun**, *s. m.* The envelope, in which
cloth purchased is folded up, to which the purchaser is entitled ; packcloth, wrapper.

बेर **ber**, *s. m.* An enclosure. *Ber bundee
kurna*, To enclose a field.

बेड़ा **bér-a**, *s. m.* A raft, a float ; the raft
which is floated by the *Mahomedans* in honour of
Khwaja Khizr. (*Besides the anniversary bera offered to propitiate him, hundreds of smaller ones
with lamps may be seen on Thursdays of the month
Bhadon particularly, which are offered by the Mahomedans to this saint). Bera par kurna, or
lugana, To relieve from distress, to remove difficulties, to help one through a business (lit. to ferry
over a raft). Bera par hona, To obtain deliverance from misfortune or distress, to succeed.*

बेड़िया **bér-iya**, *s. m.* The name of a caste
of *Hindoos* ; dimin. of *bera*.

बेड़ी **bér-ee**, *s. f.* Irons fastened to the legs
(*of criminals, elephants, &c.*), fetters ; a basket
used to irrigate fields with.

बेड़ना **bérh-na**, *v. a.* To enclose with a
fence, to surround ; to pound (*cattle, &c.*) ; to
drive away cattle.

बेढ़ा **ber-há**, *adj.* Crooked. *s. m.* Paling,
railing.

बेन **ben**, } *s. f.* A flute, pipe, fife.
बेनू **bén-oo**, }

बेत **bet**, *s. f.* A cane, a ratan (*Calamus
rotang*).

बेताल **bet-ál**, *s. m.* A dead body supposed
to be occupied and animated by an evil spirit ;
name of a demon.

बेद **bed**, *s. m.* A *Ved*, or the *Veds* in the
aggregate. The original *Ved* is believed by the
Hindoos to have been revealed by *Bruhma*, and
to have been preserved by tradition until it was
arranged in its present order by a sage, who thence
obtained the surname of *Vyas* or *Vedvyas*, that is,
compiler of the *Veds*. He distributed the Indian
sacred books into four parts, which are severally
entitled, *Rig, Yujoosh, Sam*, and *Uthurv* ; and
each of them bears the common name of *Ved*.

बेदन **béd-un**, } *s. f.* Pain, sickness,
बेदना **béd-un-a**, } ache.

बेदवा **bed-wá**, *s. m.* A reader of the *Veds*.

बेदांत **bed-ánt**, *s. m.* The name of a particular *Hindoo* philosophical system.

बेदांती **bed-ánt-ee**, *s. m.* One who is conversant in the *Vedant* system.

बेदिका **béd-ik-a**, *s. f.* An altar, platform.

बेदी **béd-ee**, *s. f.* An altar.

बेध **bedh**, *s. m.* Bore, crack, hole.

बेधड़क bedhúr-uk, ⎫ adj. Without fear or
बेधड़का bedhúr-ka, ⎭ doubt, fearless.

बेधना bédh-na, v. a. To pierce, to perforate, to bore.

बेधिया béd-hiya, ⎫ s. m. A borer, one who
बेधी bed-hée, ⎭ perforates gems, &c.

बेन ben, s. f. A flute, pipe, fife.

बेना bén-a, s. m. Name of a grass, *Khus* (Andropogon muricatum); a fan.

बेनी bén-ee, s. f. The hair twisted behind.

बेब beb, s. f. A sort of grass.

बेमात bem-át, s. f. A step-mother. *Bemat-bhaee,* A brother born of a different mother by the same father, a half-brother by the father's side.

बेर ber, s. m. The name of a fruit, that of the jujube (*Zizyphus jujuba*); also the name of the tree; time, turn, bout, vicissitude, delay, while.

बेरबेर bér-ber, adv. Often, frequently, over and over, repeatedly, again and again.

बेरी bér-ee, s. f. The tree of *Zizyphus jujuba.*

बेल bel, s. m. The name of a fruit (*Crateva, or Eagle marmelos*). s. f. A creeper, climber; tendril (*of a vine*); descendants, offspring.

बेलन bél-un, s. m. A rolling pin.

बेलना bél-na, s. m. A rolling pin. v. a. To spread out, to laminate.

बेलनी bél-un-ee, s. m. A branch.

बेलबूटा bel-bóo-ta, s. m. A shrub, bush or creeper; flowers (*on cloth*).

बेला bél-a, s. f. A while, a time; name of a shrub (*Jasminum zambac*); a cup; an instrument of music resembling a fiddle.

बेलि bél-i, ⎫ s. f. A creeper, climber; ten-
बेली bél-ee, ⎭ dril (*of a vine*).

बेलू bél-oo, Rolling.

बेलौ bel-óu, adj. Dispirited, heartless.

बेपारी beo-pá-ree, s. m. A merchant.

बेोरा béo-ra, s. m. Difference, distinction; account, explanation, history, detail of circumstances, an account of particulars or detailed account (*in book-keeping.*)

बेरेवार beo-rewár, adj. Explicitly, distinctly.

बेोहर beo-húr, s. m. A loan.

बेोहरा beo-húr-a, s. m. A creditor, a lender.

बेोहार beo-hár, s. m. Profession, calling, trade, negociation, transaction, practice, custom.

बेवान bewán, s. m. The vehicle of self-moving car of a Hindoo deity; a Hindoo bier.

बेसन bés-un, s. m. The flour or meal of pulse (*particularly of Chuna, Cicer arietinum*).

बेसनी bés-un-ee, adj. Made of or mixed with *besun.*

बेसनबूटी bésun-óutee, s. f. A cake made of pease-meal.

बेसुर bés-ur, s. m. The small ring worn in the nose.

बेसुरा bes-úr-a, s. m. A kind of falcon (*Falco nisus*).

बेसूरा bésoor-a, adj. Out of tune.

बेस्या bés-ya, ⎫ s. f. A courtezan, harlot,
बेस्वा bés-wa, ⎭ prostitute.

बेह beh, s. m. A hole, a perforation.

बेहड़ behúr, adj. Uneven, abrupt, rugged.

बेहिन्ना behinna, s. m. A comber, a carder (*of cotton*).

बैंगन byn-gun, s. m. The egg-plant (*Solanum melongena*).

बैंगनी byn-gun-ee, ⎫ adj. Purple (*the co-
बैंजनी byn-jun-ee, ⎭ lour of the Solanum melongena*).

बैंटा byn-ta, s. m. The handle of an axe or hatchet.

बैंदा byn-da, s. m. A mark placed on the forehead as a preparative to devotion among the Hindoos.

बैंदी byn-dee, s. f. An ornamental circlet made with a coloured earth or unguent on the forehead and between the eye-brows; an ornament worn by women on the forehead.

बैकाल by-kál, s. m. Afternoon.

बैकुंठ by-kóonth, s. m. A name of *Vishnoo*; the heaven or paradise of *Vishnoo.*

बैगन by-gun, s. m. The egg-plant (*Solanum melongena*).

बैगुंती by-gún-tee, s. f. A sort of wood.

बैजंती by-jún-tee, s. f. A flag or standard; the standard of *Vishnoo.*

बैजंती माला byjúntee mála, s. f. A necklace especially worn by *Vishnoo* in his several forms, and composed of the following jewels, produced from the five elements of nature; namely, the sapphire, from the earth; the pearl from water; the ruby, from fire; the topaz, from air; and the diamond, from space or ether.

बैठक by-thúk, s. f. ⎫ A seat, a place where
बैठका byth-ká, s. m. ⎭ people meet to sit and converse, a bench. s. f. Act or state of sitting, sitting; a kind of exercise.

बैठना bythna, v. n. To sit, to be unemployed or idle; to ride (*on a horse*); to visit a person in grief for the purpose of condolence; to sit in *dhurna*, or as a dun.

बैठवा byth-wan, adj. Flat.

बैठा byt-ha, s. m. A paddle.

बेठाना byt-hána, ⎤ v. a. To cause to sit
बेठारना byt-hárna, ⎬ down, seat, set, set-
बेठालना byt-hálna, ⎦ tle, place, station,
apply, plant, calm, becalm.

बेन byn, s. f. A flute, pipe, fife. s. m. f.
A word, speech.

बेतरनी by-túr-nee, s. f. A river, according
to the Hindoos, which is to be crossed by the dead
on their way into the world of spirits, like the Styx
of the ancients ; a river in Orissa.

बेतरा by-tur-a, s. f. Dry ginger.

बेद byd, s. m. A physician.

बेदक by-duk, s. m. The practice or science
of physic.

बेदिक by-dik, s. m. A Brahmun well versed
in the Veds.

बेन byn, s. f. A flute, pipe, fife. s. m. f.
A word, speech.

बेना by-na, s. m. An ornament worn on
the forehead.

बेना byna, s. m. Sweetmeats, cakes, &c.,
distributed at marriages and other ceremonies.

बेन्दा bynda, s. m. A mark placed on the
forehead as a preparative to devotion among the
Hindoos.

बेन्दी byndee, s. f. An ornamental circlet
made with a coloured earth or unguent on the
forehead and between the eyebrows ; an ornament
worn by women on the forehead.

बेपार by-pár, s. m. Traffick, trade, business, labour.

बेपारी by-pá-ree, s. m. A merchant.

बेमात्र by-mátr, s. m. A brother born of a
different mother by the same father.

बेया by-a, s. m. The name of the little
bird that learns to fetch and carry, & c., and which
the Hindoos teach to snatch the ornamental patch
or wafer from the forehead of their mistresses
(Loxia Indica) ; an assizer.

बेयाकरन bya-kúrun, s. m. Grammar.

बेयाकरनी bya-kúrun-ee, s. m. A grammarian.

बेयान by-án, s. m. Birth, act of parturition. Char byan gaeh, A cow that has calved
four times. Ek byan jamuk, Having produced
two calves at a birth.

बेयाना by-ána, v. n. To be delivered of
young (applied to animals only), to calve, foal,
farrow, litter, pup, yean.

बेयाला by-ála, adj. Flatulent.

बेर byr, s. m. Enmity, hostility, animosity, revenge. Byr lena, v. a. To revenge.

बेरख by-rukh, s. m. Banner, ensign, colours.

बेरन by-rún, s. f. A female enemy.

बेरागन by-rá-gun, s. f. A female byragee.

बेरागा by-rá-ga, s. m. A small crooked
stick, which a byragee places under his armpit to
lean upon as he sits.

बेरागी by-rá-gee, s. m. The religious asce-
tick, or he who abandons terrestrial objects,
thoughts, passions, &c., a kind of wandering fukeer
who practises certain austerities.

बेराग्य by-rágyuh, s. m. Penance, devotion,
the act of leaving the pleasures of the world.

बेरी by-ree, s. m. An enemy, a foe.

बेल byl, s. m. A bull, an ox; (met.) a
blockhead.

बेला by-la, s. m. A species of bird.

बेष्नौ bysh-nou, adj. Of or relating to Vishnoo. s. m. A follower of Vishnoo.

बेष bys, s. m. The third of the four Hindoo
tribes or vurns ; name of a tribe of Rajpoots : (a
prince of that tribe reigned at Dounria-Khera ; his
dominions, which extended over a great part of
Oude, on the north bank of the Ganges, are still
called Bys-wara) ; age.

बेसुंदर by-sún-dur, s. m. Fire, or its deity.

बेसनी bys-nee, s. f. A female of the Bys
caste.

बेसवाडा bys-wára, s. m. The residence of
Bys, the nativity of Bys.

बेसाख by-sákh, s. m. The first solar month
of the Hindoos, the full moon of which is near
Vishakha (four stars in Libra and Scorpio) ; April-
May.

बेसाखा by-sákha, s. m. A crutch ; a club
armed with iron ; a club consecrated in the month
of Bysakh.

बेसाखी by-sá-khee, adj. Growing in the
month of Bysakh, or relating to that month. s. f.
A large kind of Myrobalan or citron fruit; the
day of full moon in the month Bysakh ; the day
on which the sun enters the sign Aries.

बेसान्दू by-sán-doo, adj. Sedentary, idle.

बोआई bo-áee, s. f. Sowing, the act of
sowing, seed time.

बोआना bo-ána, v. a. To cause to sow. v. n.
To stink, to emit a smell, to smell.

बोआरा bo-ára, s. m. Seed time.

बोइया bóiya, s. m. A small basket.

बोंट bont, s. m. A stalk.

बोक bok, ⎤ s. m. A he-goat, a ram.
बोकरा bók-ra, ⎦

बोकरी bók-ree, s. f. A she-goat.

बोच boch, s. m. An alligator.

बोचा bó-cha, s. m. A kind of sedan, a chair
palkee.

बोझ bojh, s. m. A load, burthen. Bojh

pukurna, To affect consequence or to give one's self airs (*generally spoken in raillery*). *Bojh sir pur hona*, Is applied to a task, the performance of which is become indispensable.

बोझना **bójh-na**, *v. a.* To load ; to scald or parch rice.

बोझल **boj-húl**, } *adj.* Loaded, heavy.
बोझेल **boj-hél**, }

बोटी **bó-tee**, *s. f.* A morsel or lump of meat.

बोरना **bór-na**, *v. a.* To cause to dive, to immerse, drown, sink.

बोंदी **bón-dee**, *s. f.* The germ of a plant after the flower is shed.

बोटू **bó-too**, *s. m.* A he-goat.

बोदली **bód-lee**, *adj. f.* A simple woman, a trollop ; a woman who lives with a *benuwa fukeer* and dresses like a man.

बोदा **bó-da**, *adj.* Weak, faint-hearted, low-spirited.

बोद्धा **bod-dhá**, *adj.* Intelligent, ingenious, sensible.

बोध **bodh**, *s. m.* Wisdom, intellect, understanding, knowledge.

बोधक **bod-húk**, *s. m.* A teacher.

बोधन **bod-hún**, *s. m.* } Knowledge ;
बोधनी **bod-hun-ée**, *s. f.* } teaching, informing ; awakening, arousing.

बोधना **bódh-na**, *v. a.* To wheedle.

बोना **bó-na**, *v. a.* To sow.

बोनी **bó-nee**, *s. f.* The season of sowing.

बोबा **bó-ba**, *s. m.* Goods and chattels, property ; a bundle.

बोर **bor**, *adj.* Deep. *s. m.* Studs of gold or silver.

बोरा **bó-ra**, *s. m.* A canvas bag (*particularly for holding two maunds of rice*), a sack ; a kind of bean like French beans (*Dolichos catsang*).

बोरो **bó-ro**, *s. m.* Rainbow ; the name of a kind of rice which is cut in March.

बोल **bol**, *s. m.* Myrrh ; word, speech, talk, conversation ; words of a song.

बोलचाल **bol-chál**, *s. f.* Conversation, confabulation, diction.

बोलता **ból-ta**, *part. act.* (Used substantively), The faculty of speech ; soul, life.

बोलना **ból-na**, *v. n.* To speak, talk ; to sound, emit sound, to articulate ; to tell, to say. *Bol oothna*, To speak out, to exclaim. *Bol chalna*, To converse, speak together. *Boleh so bolna*, To speak repeatedly.

बोलबाला **bol-bála**, *s. m.* A kind of benediction. *Bol bala hona*, To prosper.

बोली **bó-lee**, *s. f.* Speech, dialect, language ;

conversation, talk, saying. *Boles kurna*, To jeer, to jest.

बोंड **bound**, *s. m.* A creeper, a vine.

बोंडना **bóund-na**, *v. n.* To intwine (*creepers or vines*).

बोंडियाना **boun-di-yána**, *v. n.* To twine ; to run irregularly or in a crooked path with turnings and windings.

बोछार **bou-chhár**, *s. m.* Driving rain, wind and rain, drift.

बौद्ध **bouddh**, *s. m.* A *Buddhist*.

बौना **bóu-na**, *adj.* Dwarfish. *s. m.* A dwarf ; the fifth supposed *Uvutar* or incarnation of the deity.

बौनी **bóu-nee**, *s. f.* A female dwarf.

बौरहा **bour-há**, } *adj.* Mad, insane.
बौरा **bóu-ra**, }

बौराना **bou-rá-na**, *v. n.* To be mad, to madden.

बौरापन **bou-ra-pún**, *s. m.* Madness.

बौराहा **bou-rá-ha**, *adj.* Mad, insane.

बौला **bóu-la**, *adj.* Toothless.

बौहा **bou-há**, *adj.* Pocky.

बौहाई **bou-háee**, *s. f.* A woman afflicted with venereal disease.

व्याकरण **bya-kúrun**, *s. m.* Grammar.

व्याकरणी **bya-kúrunee**, *s. m.* A grammarian.

व्याकुल **bya-kóol**, *adj.* Perplexed, confounded, restless, agitated (*in mind*), uneasy.

व्याध **byadh**, *s. m.* A hunter, a fowler.

व्याधि **byá-dhi**, *s. m.* Sickness, disease in general, ail, ailment, pain, anguish.

व्यान **byán**, *s. m.* Birth, act of parturition.

व्याना **byána**, *v. n.* To be delivered of young (*applied to animals only*), to calve, foal, farrow, litter, pup, yean.

व्यापना **byáp-na**, *v. a.* To pervade, occupy, effect, operate, work, act, affect.

व्यालु **byá-loo**, *s. m.* Supper.

व्यास **by-ás**, *s. m.* A celebrated saint and author, the supposed original compiler of the *Veds* and *Poorans* ; also the founder of the *Vedant* philosophy.

ब्याह **by-áh**, *s. m.* Marriage. *Byah kurna*, To marry. *Byah ruchana*, To celebrate a marriage. *Byah lana*, To take in marriage, to bring home a wife, to marry.

ब्याहन **bya-hún**, *s. m.* Marrying, marriage, to marry. *Byahun-jog, adj.* Fit for marriage, marriageable.

ब्याहना **byáh-na**, *v. a.* To give or take in marriage, to marry. *Byahee juna*, To be married (*a woman*).

ब्याहता byah-tá, *f.* }
ब्याहा byahá, *m.* } *adj.* Married.

ब्योंगा byón-ga, *s. m.* The instrument with which leather is scraped and cleaned. *Byonga phira nuheen,* His hide has not been curried yet (*said of a spoiled child, &c.*)

ब्योंत byónt, *s. m.* Shape, fashion, the act of cutting out clothes.

ब्योंतना byónt-na, *v. a.* To cut or shape clothes.

ब्योपार byo-pár, *s. m.* Traffick, trade, business, labour.

ब्योपारी byo-páree, *s. m.* A merchant.

ब्योरा byó-ra, *s. m.* Difference, distinction; account, explanation, history, detail of circumstances.

ब्योहार byo-hár, *s. m.* Profession, calling, trade, negociation, transaction, practice, custom.

ब्रज bruj, *s. m.* Name of a district, containing the several villages of *Muthoora, Gokul, Brindavun,* &c., being about 168 miles in circumference.

ब्रत brut, *s. m.* A meritorious act, a fast, a vow, a religious rite or performance; use. *s. f.* A thong, leathern girth, rope; flaming, blazing. *Brutee, s. m.* One who fasts.

ब्रथा brut-há, *adj.* Abortive, vain, in vain.

ब्रषभ bruk-húbh, *s. m.* A bull.

ब्रह्म bruhm, *s. m.* God; the all-pervading, the divine cause and essence of the world from which all things are supposed to proceed and to which they return; spirit, the very soul. *Bruhmustruh,* A fabled weapon, which, consecrated by a formula addressed to *Bruhma,* deals infallible destruction to those against whom it is discharged. *Bruhm-duytyuh,* An apparition, Satan, ghost. *Bruhm-bhoj,* Feeding of Brahmuns. *Bruhm-rakhus,* A kind of demon. *Bruhm-ratri, s. f.* A night of *Bruhma,* comprising a thousand ages of the gods, or 216,000,000 of those of mortals. *Bruhm-sesh,* The leavings of Brahmuns. *Bruhm-hutya,* The murder of a *Brahmun;* sacrilege. *Bruhm-hutyara, s. m.* A murderer of a *Brahmun. Bruhm-hutyaree, s. f.* A murderess of a *Brahmun.*

ब्रह्मउचर्ज bruhm-uchúrj, *s. m.* The profession or way of life of a religious student, or *Bruhmucharee.*

ब्रह्मचारिणी bruhm-chárinee, *s. f.* A woman leading a life of continence.

ब्रह्मचारी bruhm-ucháree, *s. m.* A religious student, a *Brahmun* from the time of his investiture with the sacerdotal thread, till he becomes a householder, a person who continues with his spiritual teacher studying the *Ved,* a *pundit* learned in the *Ved,* an ascetic; by the *Tuntrus* it is assigned to persons whose chief virtue is the observance of continence; and it is assumed by many religious vagabonds.

ब्रह्मजन्म bruhm-júnm, *s. m.* Second or spiritual birth, investiture.

ब्रह्मन bruh-mun, *n. prop.* A *Brahmun.*

ब्रह्मबान bruhm-bán, *s. m.* A fabled weapon, which, consecrated by a formula addressed to *Bruhma,* deals infallible destruction to those against whom it is discharged.

ब्रह्मउग्युह bruhm-úgyuh, *s. m.* A sage, one who has spiritual wisdom.

ब्रह्मज्ञान bruhm-gyán, *s. m.* Spiritual wisdom, divine knowledge.

ब्रह्मतत्त्वुह bruhm-tútwuh, *s. m.* The true knowledge of Supreme Spirit.

ब्रह्मउत्व bruhm-útv, *s. m.* Godhead.

ब्रह्मदूंद bruhm-dúnd, *s. m.* A curse, an anathema.

ब्रह्मदूर्भा bruhm-dúrbha, *s. f.* A plant (*Ligusticum ajwaen*).

ब्रह्मदारू bruhm-dároo, *s. m.* The mulberry (*Morus Indica*).

ब्रह्मनिर्वाण brúhm-nirwán, *s. m.* Absorption into or identification with the Supreme.

ब्रह्मपूत्र bruhm-póotr, *s. m.* A kind of poison; the *Burampooter* river; a place of pilgrimage, probably the source of the stream.

ब्रह्मपूत्री bruhm-póotree, *s. f.* The *Suruswuttee* river.

ब्रह्मलोक bruhm-lók, *s. m.* A division of the universe, the supposed eternal residence of the spirits of the pious.

ब्रह्मवादी bruhm-vádee, *s. m.* A follower of the *Vedant* system of philosophy, one who maintains all things are Spirit; a defender or expounder of the *Veds.*

ब्रह्मशासन bruhm-shásun, *s. m.* An edict or grant, &c. addressed to *Brahmuns.*

ब्रह्मस्वरूप bruhm-swuróop, *adj.* Of the nature of spirit, of the same essence as the Godhead.

ब्रह्मा brúh-ma, *s. m.* The Deity in the character of Creator, or matter personified.

ब्रह्मांड bruh-mánd, *s. m.* The globe, the world; (*in creation there are said to have been innumerable Bruhmands or worlds;*) the top of the head.

ब्रह्मावत्त bruh-ma-wútt, *s. m.* The country to the north-west of *Delhi,* lying between the rivers *Suruswutee* and *Drishudwuttee.*

ब्रह्मासन bruh-másun, *s. m.* A posture suited to devout and religious meditation.

ब्राह्मण bráh-mun, *s. m.* A man of the first *Hindoo* tribe, a Brahmun.

ब्राह्मणी bráh-mun-ee, *s. f.* The wife of a *Brahmun,* a female of the *Brahmun* caste.

ब्रह्मण्युः brah-mún-yuh, *s. m.* The state, quality, or business of a *Brahmun*, brahmunhood.

ब्राह्यः brá-hiyuh, *s. m.* The worship or veneration of *Brahmuns* ; astonishment.

भ

भ bhuh, The twenty-fourth consonant of the *Naguree* alphabet, and aspirate of the last letter, or *bh*.

भंटवास bhunt-wás, *s. m.* Name of a grain, the fruit of the *Koee* or water-lily.

भंबेरी bhum-béree,
भंभेरी bhum-bhér-ee, } *s. f.* A butterfly.

भंभोरना bhum-bhór-na, *v. a.* To bite and mumble (*as a dog*), to worry.

भंवर bhún-wur, *s. m.* A whirlpool, eddy, vortex.

भंवर bhun-wúr,
भंवरा bhun-wra, } *s. m.* A large black bee ; a climbing plant, a creeper.

भंवरकूली bhún-wur-kúlee, *s. f.* A collar or halter (*for a dog, goat, &c.*)

भंसना bhúns-na, *v. n.* To float.

भई bhúee, *past tense or part. of the verb, subs.* Was, became, become.

भकसी bhúk-see, *s. f.* A dungeon, a dark room.

भकूआ bhúk-oo-a, *adj.* Foolish.

भकूआना bhuk-oo-ána, *v. n.* To be stupified.

भकोसना bhuk-ós-na, *v. a.* To devour, stuff, eat.

भक्त bhukt, *adj.* Attached or attentive to, devoted to, engrossed by ; pious, desirous. *s. m.* An adorer, a devotee, a votary, a zealot ; a *Hindoo* performer for entertainment, a dancer, a player. *Bhukt-raj, s. m.* King or lord of the devout, an epithet of the deity.

भक्तता bhukt-tá, *s. f.* Devotedness, implied faith in and attachment to.

भक्ताई bhuk-táee, *s. f.* Faith, devotedness, religion.

भक्ति bhúk-ti, *s. f.* Religion, faith, devotedness, attachment, desire ; service, worship ; belief.

भक्तिमत bhúkti-mút, *m.*
भक्तिमान bhukti-mán, *m.*
भक्तिमती bhukti-mút-ee, *f.* } *adj.* Faithful, devoted to.

भक्तिवंत bhukti-wúnt, *adj.* Devoted, religious, pious.

भगत bhúg-ut, *s. m.* An adorer, a devotee, a votary, a zealot ; a *Hindoo* performer for entertainment, a dancer, a player. *adj.* Pious ; desir-

ous. *Bhugut khelna, v. n.* To act (*a play*), to imitate, to mimick. *Bhugut hona, v. n.* To be initiated as a devotee, to be affiliated to a religious order.

भगतन bhug-tún, *s. f.* Wife of a *Bhugut* ; (*ironically*) a lewd woman, a prostitute, a whore.

भगताई bhug-táee, *s. f.* Piety, devotion, religiousness.

भगतिया bhúg-tiya, *s. m.* A dancing boy.

भगंदर bhug-úndur, *s. m.* A fistula (*in ano*).

भगल bhúg-ul, *s. m.* Affectation, hypocrisy, trick, deception. *Bhugul nikalna, v. a.* To affect, to play a trick, to pretend poverty.

भगलिया bhug-líya, *s. m.* Trick, cheat, imposture ; impostor, cheat.

भगली गहना bhúg-lee gúhna, *s. m.* False jewels, trinkets.

भगवत bhug-wút,
भगवान bhug-wán, } *adj.* Respectable, worshipful, adorable, divine, glorious, illustrious. *s. m.* God, the Deity, the Supreme Being.

भगवंत bhug-wúnt, *adj.* Divine. *s. m.* God, the Deity.

भगवां bhug-wán, *s. m.* Cloth dyed with *geroo* (*a kind of red chalk or ochre*).

भगवान bhug-wán, *adj.* Divine, glorious. *s. m.* God, the Deity, the Supreme Being.

भगाना bhug-ána, *v. a.* To cause to flee or escape, to cause to run away, to drive away.

भगिनी bhúg-in-ee, *s. f.* A sister.

भगीरथ bhug-éeruth, *s. m.* A king whose austerities, it is said, brought *Gunga*, the river, from heaven.

भगेल bhug-él, *s. f.* Overthrow, defeat. *s. m.* A runaway, a deserter.

भगोंहा bhug-on-ha, *s. m.* The reddish colour extracted from *geroo*.

भगोरा bhug-óra,
भगू bhúg-goo, } *s. m.* A runaway, a deserter, a fugitive.

भग्न bhugn, *adj.* Torn, broken ; overcome, defeated.

भग्नास bhugn-ás, *adj.* Disappointed.

भगूनी bhúg-nee, *s. f.* A sister.

भंग bhung, *s. f.* Hemp (*Cannabis sativa*). *s. m.* Breaking, splitting ; defeat, discomfiture. *adj.* Broken, torn, overcome, defeated.

भंगरा bhúng-ra, *s. m.* Name of an herb (*Eclipta or verbesina prostrata*).

भंगुन bhung-ún, *s. f.* The wife of a *hulalkhor* or sweeper ; a female drinker of *bhung*.

भंगना bhúng-na, *s. f.* A kind of fish.

भंगराज bhung-ráj,
भंगा bhun-gá, } *s. m.* Name of a bird.

भझगन bhun-gán, *s. m.* A sort of fish (*Cyprinus Banggana*).

भझी bhún-gee, *s. f.* Fracture, division, separation; fraud, deception, trick, disguise. *s. m.* A caste of sweepers or *hulalkhors*; a drinker of bhung.

भझेरन bhun-gér-un, *s. f.* A female seller of bhung.

भझेरा bhun-gér-a, *s. m.* One who sells bhung.

भचक bhúch-uk, *adj.* Alarmed, aghast, starting. *Bhuchuk rukna*, To be amazed or astonished at a sudden or unexpected event.

भचकना bhuch-úk-na, *v. n.* To be astonished or amazed.

भझत bhuj-út, *adj.* Serving, waiting upon; enjoying carnally.

भझन bhúj-un, *s. m.* Service, adoration, worship; a hymn; possessing or enjoying carnally. *Bhujun kurna*, To say prayers, to worship.

भझना bhúj-na, *v. n.* ⎫ To flee, to run
भझिआना bhuji-jána, ⎭ away.

भझना bhúj-na, *v. a.* To worship, to count one's beads, to adore.

भझनीक bhuj-néek, *s. m.* A singer, an adorer.

भझझक bhun-júk, *adj.* Who or what breaks, severs, divides, destroys, &c.

भझझत bhun-jút, *adj.* Breaking, destroying.

भझझन bhun-jún, *adj.* Breaking, destroying; afflicting.

भझझाना bhun-já-na, *v. a.* To change money.

भट bhut, *s. m.* A warrior, a soldier, a combatant; a barbarian, or outcast of a particular tribe. *s. f.* An oven, a furnace, a kiln; curse, misfortune. *Bhat purna, v. n.* To be cursed, to be unfortunate, to be lost (*lit. to fall into the fire*).

भटई bhut-íee, *s. f.* Praise, panegyrick, the encomiums of a *Bhat* or bard.

भटकटई bhut-kut-áee, ⎫ *s. f.* The name of
भटकटैया bhut-kutúya, ⎭ a prickly plant (*Solanum jacquini*).

भटकना bhát-uk-na, *v. n.* To go astray, to stray, wander, miss the right path, lose (*the way*).

भटका bhút-ka, *adj.* Astray.

भटकाना bhut-ká-na, *v. a.* To mislead, bewilder, deceive, scare, cause to wander.

भटपरना bhut-púrna, *v. n.* To be cursed, to be unfortunate, to be lost (*lit. to fall into the fire*).

भटियारपन bhutiyár-pán, *s. m.* The business of a *bhutiyara*.

भटियारा bhutiyára, *s. m.* A sutler, an innkeeper, one who prepares victuals for travellers in a *sara*.

भटियारिन bhutiyarín, ⎫ *s. f.* A female *bhu-*
भटियारी bhutiyarée, ⎭ *tiyara* or sutler.

भठऊ bhút-oo, *interj.* O sister!

भट्ट bhutt, *s. m.* A philosopher, a learned man, especially one conversant with the philosophical systems; a title of *Marhatta Brahmuns*.

भट्टाचार्य bhútta-chárj, *s. m.* The most learned of the learned.

भट्टी bhút-tee, *s. f.* A furnace, a kiln.

भट्टा bhut-thá, *s. m.* A furnace, a kiln, oven, brick-kiln.

भट्ठी bhut-thée, *s. f.* A furnace, a kiln.

भठियाना bhuthi-yána, *v. n.* To go down the river; to ebb (*the tide*).

भठियाल bhuthi-yál, *adj.* With the current, *i. e.* down the river and not with the flood tide. *s. m.* A kind of *mursecya* or elegiac verses sung in praise of *Husun* and *Hoosyn*.

भड़ bhur, *s. m.* A large boat, a lighter.

भड़क bhúr-uk, *s. f.* Splendour, blaze, flash, glare, show; perturbation, agitation, alarm, starting, shyness (*in animals*).

भड़कना bhúr-uk-na, *v. n.* To start, to shrink, to be scared, to be alarmed; to be blown up into a flame.

भड़काना bhur-kána, *v. a.* To frighten, to scare, to blow up into a flame, to kindle (*a fire*).

भड़कीला bhur-kéela, *adj.* Splendid, glittering, flashy, gaudy.

भड़कैल bhur-kél, *adj.* Shy, skittish, coy, wild, untamed.

भड़ऊंग bhur-úng, *adj.* Simple, undesigning, silly, artless, having the quality of telling secrets without reserve.

भड़भड़िया bhur-bhúr-iya, *adj.* Simple, candid, without guile.

भड़भूंजन bhur-bhóon-jun, *s. f.* A woman who parches grain.

भड़भूंजा bhur-bhóon-ja, *s. m.* A man who parches grain.

भड़ुरिया bhur-ur-íya, *s. m.* A conjurer.

भड़ूआ bhúr-ooa, *s. m.* A pimp, one who lives on what a prostitute earns.

भड़ूआई bhur-ooáee, *s. f.* Pandarism, pimping; the wages of prostitution.

भड़ूत bhur-úyt, ⎫ *s. m.* A tenant, a les-
भड़ूती bhur-úytee, ⎭ see.

भनक bhun-úk, *s. f.* A low sound, a distant sound, hum.

भनित bhun-ít, *adj.* Sounded, spoken, uttered.

भंटा bhún-ta, *s. m.* The egg-plant (*Solanum melongena*).

भभ्ड bhund, *s. m.* A mimic, a jester, a buffoon, an actor; confusion, spoiling. *Bhund hona,* To be destroyed, to be spoiled.

भभ्डक bhun-dúk, *s. m.* A wagtail.

भभ्डसार bhund-sár, } *s. f.* The provision
भभ्डसाल bhund-sál, } which is previously reserved for years.

भभ्डसाली bhund-sálee, *s. m.* One who reserves provision for years.

भभूड bhún-da, *s. m.* A vessel, a large earthen pot. *Bhunda phootna,* To be disclosed (*a secret*).

भभ्डार bhun-dár, *s. m.* A place where household goods are kept, a storehouse.

भभ्डारा bhundára, *s. m.* A feast of *Jogees, Sunnyasees,* &c.

भभ्डारी bhun-dáree, *s. m.* A house-steward, one who has charge of the store-house, a treasurer, purveyor.

भभ्डरिया bhun-dér-iya, } *s. m.* An actor.
भभ्डेला bhun-dél-a, }

भभ्डेलुन bhun-del-ún, *s. f.* An actress.

भभ्डौवा bhun-dóu-wa, *s. m.* Satire, ribaldry.

भद् bhud, *s. f.* A slap, a crash.

भद्भद् bhud-bhud, *s. m.* Sound made by the fall of a fruit or by the walking of a person, &c.

भद्भदाना bhud-bhud-ána, *v. a.* To make a sound by striking two bodies together; to strike repeatedly.

भद्भदाहट bhud-bhud-áhut, *s. f.* Sound made by the fall of fruits.

भदाक bhud-ák, *s. m.* A crash, the noise made by any thing falling; as, *Bhudak seh gir pura,* It fell with a crash.

भदाका bhud-áka, *s. m.* A sound.

भदेसल bhud-és-ul, *adj.* Ill-shaped, ugly, awkward, clumsy.

भद्दा bhúd-da, *adj.* Stupid, senseless, dull.

भद्र bhudr, *adj.* Happy, prosperous, lucky, propitious. *s. m.* Prosperity, fortune, happiness; a fragrant grass (*Cyperus*); a wagtail. *Bhudr hona, v. n.* To be clean or purified by shaving one's head and beard after mourning or in a holy place.

भद्रक bhud-rúk, *adj.* Beautiful, pleasing, agreeable; respectable, worthy, estimable; lucky, fortunate. *s. m.* A sort of grass (*Cyperus pertenuis*); a sort of pine (*Pinus devadaru*). *s. f.* Advantage, produce; nature, genius, reason; beauty, goodness, pleasantness.

भद्रकाली brudr-kálee, *s. f.* A fragrant grass (*Cyperus pertenuis,* or, *rotundus*).

भद्रगन्धिका bhudr-gúndhi-ka, *s. f.* A creeping plant (*Asclepias pseudosarsa, the narrow-leaved variety*).

भद्रचूड bhudr-chóor, *s. m.* A sort of Euphorbia (*E. tirucalli*).

भद्रदारु bhudr-dároo, *s. m.* A sort of pine (*Pinus devadaru*).

भद्रनामा bhudr-náma, *s. m.* The woodpecker.

भद्रपदा bhudr-púd-a, *s. f.* A name given to the 26th and 27th lunar asterisms.

भद्रपर्णा bhudr-púrna, *s. f.* A shrub (*Pæderia fœtida*).

भद्रपर्णी bhudr-púrnee, *s. f.* A tree (*Gmelina arborea*); a shrub (*Pederia fœtida*).

भद्रमुस्तक bhudr-móostuk, *s. m.* A fragrant grass (*Cyperus pertenuis*).

भद्रयव bhudr-yuv, } *s. m.* The seed of the
भद्रजौ bhudr-jou, } *Echites* or *Wrightea antidysenterica.*

भद्रवल्ली bhudr-wúllee, *s. f.* Arabian jasmine (*Jasminum zambac*); the large *Bengal* creeper (*Gaertnera racemosa*).

भद्रा bhud-rá, *s. f.* An unlucky moment; the 2d, 7th, and 12th days of the lunar month.

भद्राकरण bhudrá kúrun, *s. m.* Shaving.

भद्रारक bhudr-áruk, *s. m.* One of the eighteen minor *Dweeps* or divisions of the world.

भद्राश्व bhudr-áshv, *s. m.* One of the four *Muha Dweeps,* into which the known world is divided, according to some systems; or according to another system, one of the nine *Khunds,* or smaller divisions of the continent; in either case it is the east division.

भद्रासन bhudr-ásun, *s. m.* A throne; a peculiar posture, in which abstract meditation is performed by the devotee; the legs bent, and crossed underneath, and turned so as to bring the ancles in contact with the perineum, whilst the soles of the feet are held close to the sides.

भद्री bhúd-ree, *s. m.* An astrologer, a palmister.

भद्रोदनी bhudr-ódnee, *s. f.* A plant (*Sida cordifolia*).

भबुकना bhub-úk-na, *v. n.* To be enraged, to rush on with rage; to catch fire; to run with great rapidity (*a horse*).

भबका bhúb-ka, *s. m.* An alembic, a still; a kind of drinking vessel with a large mouth.

भबकाना bhub-kána, *v. a.* To kindle, light; to provoke, exasperate, enrage; to spur a horse.

भबकी bhúb-kee, *s. f.* Threat.

भबभर bhub-bhúr, *s. m.* Solicitude, alarm. *Bhubbhur purna, v. n.* To be alarmed, to be frightened.

भबभल bhub-bhúl, *adj.* Fat.

भबक bhub-húk, *s. f.* Sudden bursting

forth of flame ; forcible expulsion of water from a fountain or pipe ; smell arising suddenly.

भबकना bhub-húkna, *v. n.* To simmer, to bubble ; to emit steam, fume, boil.

भभर bhub-húr, *s. m.* Solicitude, alarm. *Bhubhur purna, v. n.* To be alarmed, to be frightened.

भभरना bhub-húrna, *v. n.* To be solicitous, to be alarmed, to be frightened.

भभराना bhubh-rána, *v. n.* To swell (*particularly the face*).

भभूका bhub-hóo-ka, *s. m.* Blaze, flame, explosion. *adj.* Red (*as a coal, sometimes applied to the splendour of a beloved person's countenance*) ; splendid, beautiful.

भभूत bhub-hóot, *s. f.* Ashes of cowdung which *fukeers* rub over their bodies.

भमना bhúm-na, *v. n.* To revolve.

भमभेरी bhum-bhér-ee, *s. f.* A butterfly.

भमी bhúm-ee, *s. f.* Revolution, whirling, going round, wandering.

भय bhuy, *s. m.* Fear, alarm, fright, dread, terror ; the flower of the *Trapa bispinosa. Bhuy khana,* To be afraid, to be frightened.

भयकारक bhuy-káruk, *adj.* Terrifying, frightening.

भयङ्कर bhuy-únkur, *adj.* Fearful, formidable, frightful, horrible, terrific.

भयचक bhuy-chúk, *adj.* Alarmed, aghast, starting. *Bhuychuk ruhna,* To be amazed or astonished at a sudden or unexpected event.

भयदर्शी bhuy-dúrshee, *adj.* Fearful, frightful.

भयमान bhuy-mán, *adj.* Frightened, alarmed, terrified, afraid.

भयस्थान bhuy-sthán, *s. m.* Seat or part exposed to peril or hurt.

भयहू bhuy-hóo, *s. f.* Sister-in-law, younger brother's wife.

भया bhúya, } *past tense or part. of*
भई bhuée, *fem.* } *the verb subs.* Was, became, become.

भयातुर bhuy-átoor, *adj.* Afraid, distressed or distracted with fear, terrified.

भयानक bhuy-ánuk, *adj.* Frightful, formidable, terrific, terrible, fearful, dreadful, alarming, dismal.

भयापा bhuy-ápa, } *s. m.* Brotherhood,
भयापत bhuy-apút, } friendship.

भयार्त्त bhuy-ártt, *adj.* Frightened, afraid.

भयावना bhuy-áona, *adj.* Terrible, frightful.

भयो bhuyó, *part.* Was, became, become.

भर bhur, *adj.* Full, as much as, as far as,

up to, whole, all, bulk, size, every, each. As, *Oomr bhur,* All lifetime. *Kos bhur,* A kos ; whereas, *Bhur kos,* would mean a full *kos. Bans bhur,* The height or length of a bamboo. *Bhur mukdoor,* or *Mukdoor bhur,* To the best of one's power, with all one's might. *Ser bhur,* A seer.

भरका bhúr-ka, *s. m.* Slaked lime.

भरकाना bhur-kána, *v. a.* To slake (*lime*).

भर जाना bhur jána, *v. n.* To be filled ; to be lined (*a bitch*) ; to be broken-winded (*a horse from severe exercise*).

भरण bhur-ún, *s. m.* Cherishing, maintaining, nourishing, supporting.

भरणी bhur-née, *s. f.* The name of the second lunar asterism, containing three stars (*Musca*) and figured by the pudendum muliebre.

भरत bhúr-ut, *n. prop.* The younger brother of *Ram. Bhurut khund, s. m.* One of the nine divisions of the world, between *Lunka* and *Soomeroo* ; India.

भरत bhur-út, *s. m.* A mixed metal composed of copper and lead.

भरतवर्ष bhurut-vúrsh, *s. m.* India. (*Bhurut, the son of Dooshyuntuh, is supposed to have been the first emperor or monarch of all India*).

भरदेना bhur-déna, *v. a.* To pay ; to fill ; to reimburse ; to darn.

भरद्वाज bhur-dwáj, *s. m.* A skylark.

भरुन bhúr-un, *adv.* Up to, to, till ; filling, satisfying.

भरना bhúr-na, *v. a.* To fill, load, charge, satisfy, perform, daub, pay, liquidate or discharge (*a debt, fine, &c.*), to undergo, suffer. *v. n.* To be filled, to abound, heal (*a wound*).

भरनी bhúr-nee, *s. f.* Weft, woof.

भरपाना bhur-pána, *v. a.* To be paid, to receive the full amount ; (*met.*) it is used when a person is disappointed, *Mynneh bhur paya,* I am paid.

भरपूरन bhur-póorun, *adj.* Brimful, overflowing, quite full, replete.

भरभराना bhur-bhur-ána, *v. n.* To swell and be glossy (*particularly the face, as in fever*).

भरभरी bhur-bhúr-ee, *s. f.* A swelling, a sore.

भरभांड bhur-bhánd, *s. m.* The name of a prickly poppy (*Argemone Mexicana.*)

भरम bhúr-um, *s. m.* Error, mistake, suspicion, apprehension, perplexity, doubt ; credit, character, reputation. *Bhurum gunwana, v. a.* To lose character.

भरमाना bhur-mána, *v. a.* To deceive ; to excite by throwing out temptation ; to perplex, to alarm.

भरमी bhúr-mee, *adj.* Suspicious.

भरमीला bhur-mée-la, *adj.* Ambiguous, doubtful, confounded, scrupulous.

भरवाना bhur-wána, *v. a.* To cause to fill, to cause to load, to cause to charge.

भरा bhúr-a, *adj.* Full, replete.

भराना bhur-ána, *v. a.* To fill, to cause to fill.

भरावट bhur-áwut, *s. f.* Filling, stuffing.

भरी bhúr-ee, *s. f.* The weight of one *sicca* weight or one *tola.*

भरैत bhur-úyt, } *s. m.* A tenant, a les-
भरैती bhur-úy-tee, } see.

भरोसा bhur-ósa, *s. m.* Hope, dependance, reliance, faith, assurance, confidence. *Bhurosa kurna,* To hope, to rely (*on*).

भर्त bhurt, *s. m.* A mixed metal composed of copper and lead; the name of a bird (*a species of lark*), a skylark.

भर्ता bhúr-ta, } *s. m.* Vegetables boiled or
भोर्ता bhóor-ta, } fried and broken in the hand.

भरतिया bhúr-tiya, *s. m.* A brasier, a worker in the metal called *bhurt.*

भर्ती bhúr-tee, *s. f.* Completion; filling; loading, lading, cargo, burden (*of a ship, &c.*); (*vulgarly used for*) promotion. *Bhurtee kurna,* To recruit, load.

भर्ता bhúrt-ta, *adj.* A cherisher, nourisher, protector, holder, supporter. *s. m.* A husband; a lord, master.

भर्तना bhúrts-na, *s. m.* Threat, menace. *s. f.* Reproach, abuse, cursing, reviling.

भर्रा bhúr-ra, *s. m.* A panic. *Fouj men bhurra pura,* The army was seized with a panic.

भल bhul, *adj.* Good, well. *Bhul ghoriya,* Having a good horse; a cavalier. *s. m.* Side, direction. *Sir keh bhul,* Head-foremost, headlong.

भलका bhúl-ka, *s. m.* A gold patch fixed on the nose ring; a kind of bamboo; dawn of day.

भलता bhul-tá, *s. f.* A shrub (*Pæderia fœtida*).

भलमनसात bhul-múnsát, *s. f.* Humanity, benignity, civility.

भलमनसी bhul-mún-see, *s. f.* Good-nature, benevolence.

भला bhúl-a, *adj.* Good, excellent, benevolent, kind, healthy, well, virtuous, righteous, sound; strange, wonderful, admirable, comical, droll. *Bhula admee, s. m.* A person of respectability, a gentleman; (*iron.*) a silly fellow. *Bhula manna,* To take well.

भलाई bhul-áee, *s. f.* Goodness, good health, welfare.

भलचंगा bhúla-chúnga, *adj.* In good order, in health, perfect, hale, well.

भलूक bhul-lúk, *s. m.* A bear.

भलपूछी bhull-póoch-chhee, *s. f.* A plant (*Hedysarum lagopodioides*).

भलिका bhúl-lík-a, *s. f.* Marking nut.

भलुक bhúl-look, }
भलूक bhul-lóok, } *s. m.* A bear.

भव bhúvuh, *s. m.* Being, existing, existence, the world; a name of *Shiv. Bhuvuh-sagur,* The ocean of the world or of existence.

भवन bhuv-un, *s. m.* A house, a dwelling; the place of abiding or being, scite, field, spot, &c.

भवनाशिनी bhuvun-áshinee, *s. f.* The *Surjoo* river, which runs from the *Himaluh* chain and falls into the *Goggrah,* with which it is then confounded.

भवानी bhuv-ánee, *s. f.* The goddess *Parvutee* or *Doorga,* in her pacific and amiable form.

भवितव्य bhuv-itúv-yuh, *adj.* To be or become, what is to be.

भवितव्यता bhuv-itúv-yutá, *s. f.* Fate, destiny.

भविष्य bhuv-íshyuh, *adj.* Future, what will be.

भविष्यत् bhuv-ish-yút, *adj.* What is to be, what will be, future.

भविष्यत्वक्ता bhuvishyút-vúkta, *s. m.* A prophet, one who foretells things to come.

भवैया bhuvúy-a, *s. m.* A dancer.

भषिरा bhúsh-ir-a, *s. f.* A sort of beet (*Beta Bengalensis*).

भस bhus, *s. m.* Ashes.

भसकना bhús-uk-na, *v. n.* To fall.

भसूड bhus-úd, *s. f.* Pudendum muliebre; mons veneris.

भसना bhús-na, *v. n.* To float.

भसभसा bhús-bhus-a, *adj.* Flabby, loose (*as meat*).

भसुम bhús-um, }
भसम bhusm, } *s. f.* Ashes.

भसाना bhus-ána, *v. a.* To launch, to set afloat.

भसम bhusm, *s. f.* Ashes.

भसमूक bhusm-úk, *s. m.* A disease of the eyes, thickening of the membranes, and indistinctness of vision; morbid appetite, constant craving for food, with general decay.

भसमगर्भा bhusm-gurbhá, *s. f.* The *Sisoo* tree, or a variety of it (*Dalbergia Sisu*).

भसमंत bhus-múnt, *s. m.* Ashes.

भसमीकरण bhúsmee-kúrun, *s. m.* Calcining.

भस्मीकृत **bhusmee-krít**, *adj.* Reduced to ashes; calcined (*as a metal*).

भयराना **bhuh-rána**, *v. n.* To shiver, tremble, totter, stagger.

भुक्षुक **bhuk-shúk**, *adj.* Gluttonous, voracious, gourmand; a feeder, an eater, who or what eats.

भुक्षुन **bhuk-shún**, *s. m.* Eating.

भुक्षुनीय **bhuk-shun-éeyuh**, *adj.* Eatable, to be eaten.

भुक्षित **bhuk-shít**, *adj.* Eaten.

भुक्ष्य **bhuksh-yúh**, *adj.* Eatable.

भांग **bhang**, *s. f.* Hemp (*Cannabis sativa*), of which an intoxicating liquor is made.

भांज **bhanj**, *s. f.* Twist, twisting.

भांजना **bhánj-na**, *v. a.* To put into circular motion, to twist, to turn on a lathe, to wave, to brandish; to break, destroy.

भांजा **bhán-ja**, *s. m.* A sister's son, a nephew.

भांजी **bhán-jee**, *s. f.* A sister's daughter, a niece; interruption; hinderance; tale-bearing. *Bhanjee khana, v. a.* To give malicious intelligence. *Bhanjee-khor, s. m.* An interrupter, a tale-bearer. *Bhanjee dena,* or,—*marna, v. a.* To interrupt, to put a stop to, to break in upon.

भांट **bhant**, *s. m.* A medicinal plant (*Clerodendron infortunatum : Volkameria infortunata*).

भांटा **bhán-ta**, *s. m.* The egg-plant (*Solanum melongena*).

भांड **bhand**, *s. m.* An earthen pot; a mimic, an actor.

भांडना **bhánd-na**, *v. a.* To abuse.

भांडा **bhán-da**, *s. m.* A large earthen pot; estate, equipage. *Bhanda phootna, v. n.* To lose one's character.

भांडीर **bhan-déer**, *s. m.* The Indian fig-tree.

भांडैती **bhan-dytee**, *s. f.* Mimickry, buffoonery.

भांत **bhant**, } *s. f.* Manner, mode, method, kind, sort. *Bhant*
भांति **bhánti**, } bhant, adj. Various.

भांवर **bhán-wur**, } *s. f.* Revolution, circulation. *Bhan-*
भांवरी **bhánwur-ee**, } culation. *Bhanwur purna,* or *Bhanwee phirna, v. n.* To circle, to circumambulate; to be sacrificed.

भाई **bháee**, *s. m.* Brother; comrade.

भाईचारा **bhaee-chára**, *s. m.* Brotherhood, fraternity, quality or property of brother.

भाईन **bha-éen**, *adj.* Terrible, awful.

भाईबंद **bhaee-búnd**, *s. m.* Brotherhood, relations, kindred, friends, comrades.

भाकसी **bhák-see**, *s. f.* A kiln.

भक्त **bhakt**, *s. m.* A follower, a dependant, one to whom food is regularly given.

भक्तिक **bhak-tík**, *s. m.* One who is fed by another, a dependant, a retainer.

भाखना **bhákh-na**, *v. a.* To speak, say, tell, call.

भाखा **bhá-kha**, *s. f.* Speech, language, dialect.

भाग **bhag**, *s. m.* A portion, a share, a part; fate, fortune, destiny, lot, luck; a degree, the 360th part of the circumference of a great circle; a fraction. *Bhag jagna, v. n.* To be very fortunate or prosperous. *Bhag bhurosa,* Consolation.

भाग जाना **bhag jána**, *v. n.* To run away, to flee, to abscond.

भागुर **bha-gúr**, *s. f.* Flight, a general emigration, escape, immediate danger.

भागना **bhág-na**, *v. n.* To flee, to run away.

भागमान **bhag-mán**, *adj.* Fortunate.

भागमानी **bhag-mánee**, *s. f.* Good fortune, prosperity.

भागलपूरी **bhágul-póoree**, *s. m.* A kind of cloth from *Bhagulpoor*, made of silk and cotton.

भागवत **bhag-wút**, *s. m.* A celebrated poem.

भागवान **bhag-wán**, *adj.* Fortunate, rich.

भागाभाग **bhag-a-bhág**, *s. m.* Flight, running away.

भागिनेय **bhagin-éyuh**, *s. m.* A sister's son.

भागी **bhá-gee**, *m.* } *adj.* Who or what
भागिनी **bhágin-ee**, *f.* } shares; a co-heir or heiress.

भागी **bhá-gee**, *s. m.* A partner, sharer, participator. *adj.* Fortunate.

भागीरथ **bhagée-ruth**, *s. m.* A pious monarch at whose intercession the river Ganges, it is said, first descended from heaven.

भागीरथी **bhagée-thee**, *s. f.* The Ganges.

भाग्य **bhág-yuh**, *s. m.* Destiny, fortune, good or ill luck.

भाग्यवंत **bhag-yuh-wúnt**, } *adj.* Fortunate,
भाग्यवान **bhag-yuh-wán**, } rich.

भाग्यहीन **bhagyuhéen**, *adj.* Unfortunate, wretched, poor.

भाजन **bhá-jun**, *s. m.* Any vessel, as a pot or cup, a plate, &c.; (*in arithmetic*) division.

भाजना **bháj-na**, *v. n.* To flee, to run away. *v. a.* To fry.

भाजुर **bhá-jur**, *s. f.* Flight.

भाज्य **bháj-yuh**, *adj.* Divisible, to be portioned or divided. *s. m.* A portion, a share, an inheritance; (*in arithmetic*) the dividend.

भाट **bhat**, *s. m.* Name of a tribe; a bard.

भाटन bhat-ún, *s. f.* The wife of a *Bhat*.

भाठा bhát-ha, *s. m.* A current or stream, the ebb-tide.

भाठियाल bhathi-yál, *adj.* Down, below, down the river, with the stream.

भाठी bhát-hee, *s. f.* Down the river, with the current.

भाड़ bhar, *s. m.* A furnace, kiln (*particularly for parching grain*).

भाड़ा bhára, *s. m.* Hire, fare.

भांड bhand, *s. m.* An earthen pot; a mimic, an actor.

भांडना bhánd-na, *v. a.* To abuse.

भांडा bhán-da, *s. m.* A large earthen pot; estate, equipage. *Bhanda phootna, v. n.* To lose one's character.

भांडार bhan-dár, *s. m.* A place where household goods are kept, a storehouse.

भांडारी bhan-dáree, *s. m.* A house-steward, one who has charge of the store-house, a treasurer, purveyor.

भात bhat, *s. m.* Boiled rice.

भाता bháta, *s. m.* An extra allowance to troops on service.

भादों bhá-don, ⎱ *s. m.* Name of the fifth
भाद्र bhadr, ⎰ solar month, August-September, when the moon is full near the wing of Pegasus.

भाद्रपद bhadr-púd, *s. m.* The month *Bhadr*.

भाद्रपदा bhadr-pud-á, *s. f.* A name common to the twenty-sixth and twenty-seventh lunar asterisms, distinguished by the epithets prior, and subsequent, or *poorv* and *oottur*.

भानमती bhán-mut-ee, *s. f.* A female juggler, an actress.

भाना bhána, *v. n.* To be approved of, to please, to suit, to fit.

भानु bhá-noo, *s. m.* The sun. *s. f.* A handsome woman.

भानुमती bhánoo-mút-ee, *adj.* Beautiful, handsome.

भानुवार bhanoo-wár, *s. m.* Sunday.

भान्ना bhánna, *v. a.* To put into circular motion, to twist, to turn on a lathe, to wave, brandish; to break, destroy.

भाफ bhaph, *s. f.* Steam, vapour, exhalation.

भाफना bháph-na, *v. a.* To conceive, guess, comprehend.

भावी bha-bée, *adj.* Future, about to be, predestined.

भाभी bha-bhée, *s. f.* A brother's wife.

भामिन bha-mín, *adj.* Angry, passionate.

भामिनी bha-min-ée, *s. f.* A passionate woman.

भार bhar, *s. m.* A load, a weight, a burthen; a weight of gold equal to two thousand *pulus*; weight, gravity, fagot.

भारत bhá-rut, *s. m. Bharutvursh* or India proper, so called from *Bhurut*, the son of *Dooshyuntuh*, whose patrimony it was; the great sacred epic poem of the *Hindoos*, which contains the account of *Joodhishthir's* war.

भारद्वाज bhar-dwáj, *s. m.* A skylark.

भारवाह bhár-wah, *s. m.* A porter, a bearer of burthens.

भारवृक्ष bhar-bríksh, *s. m.* A fragrant substance commonly called *Kakshee*, considered variously as a vegetable or mineral product.

भारा bhá-ra, *s. m.* A load, burthen.

भारी bhá-ree, *adj.* Heavy, weighty; of importance, valuable; big, great, fat, large; grave, steady, patient; strong, loud, thick; burdensome, troublesome. *s. m.* A porter, carrier of burthens. *Bharee-bhurkum, adj.* Grave, sedate. *Bharee putthur choomkur chhorna,* To withdraw from a difficult or impracticable undertaking.

भार्या bharj-já, *s. f.* A wife, espoused according to the ritual of the *Veds*; a married woman; a musical mode, the wife of a Deity presiding over a musical mode.

भार्यातिक bharjja-tík, *s. m.* A henpecked husband, one overruled by his wife.

भार्यात्व bharjja-twúh, *s. m.* The condition or state of a wife.

भल bhal, *s. f.* The point of an arrow; the forehead; fortune. *s. m.* A bear.

भाला bhá-la, *s. m.* A spear (*about seven cubits long*).

भलांक bhal-ánk, *s. m.* A sort of fish, commonly called the *Rohi* (*Cyprinus Rohita*); a sort of potherb.

भालूक bhá-look, ⎱ *s. m.* A bear.
भालू bhá-loo, ⎰

भाल्यत bhá-lyt, *s. m.* A spearman.

भाव bhao, *s. m.* State or condition of being; natural state of being, innate property, disposition, nature; meaning, purpose, intention; sentiment, passion, choice, liking, will, notion, idea; blandishment; gesticulation, acting, pantomime, expressing a meaning by signs; a sudden idea or emotion of the mind; living, being; existence, thing. *Bhao butana, v. a.* To gesticulate.

भाव bhao, *s. m.* Price, value, rate; friendship.

भवई bhawuée, *adj.* About to be, future, predestined.

भावक bha-wúk, *s. m.* The external expression of amatory sentiments; friend, lover.

भावज bhá-wuj, *s. f.* A brother's wife.

भावता bháo-ta, *adj.* Amiable, dear, beloved, love.

भावना bháo-na, *s. m.* Mental perception, recollection, the present consciousness of past ideas or perceptions; imagination; religious and abstract meditation; looking about (*literally or figuratively*), observing, investigating; consideration, anxiety, apprehension, contemplation, doubt, thought, concern.

भावुह bhá-wuh, *s. f.* A younger brother's wife.

भाविक bha-wík, *adj.* Natural, innate; sentimental, relating to feeling, &c.

भावित bha-wít, *adj.* Animated, inspired; thoughtful, anxious, apprehensive, alarmed.

भावी bha-wée, *adj.* Future, what will be or what is about to be, proximately future.

भावें bhá-wen, *postpos. mas.* In the sentiment, perception, mind, notion or idea.

भाव्य bháv-yuh, *adj.* What must, will, or ought to be.

भाषा bhá-sha, bhá-kha, *s. f.* Speech, dialect, language; common or vernacular speech; one of the *Raginees*.

भाषित bha-shít, *adj.* Spoken, uttered, said.

भासना bhás-na, *v. n.* To be known, to appear.

भासूर bha-sóor, *s. m.* A species of Costus (*C. speciosus*); a husband's elder brother.

भास्कर bhas-kúr, *adj.* Resplendent, shining. *s. m.* The sun; the name of a celebrated *Hindoo* astronomer, author of the *Siddhant Shiromuni* and other works.

भास्वर bha-swúr, *adj.* Shining, radiant. *s. m.* The sun; a day; a sort of Costus (*C. speciosus*).

भिखरी bhíkh-ree, *s. f.* An unfilled grain, a shrivelled grain.

भिखारी bhik-háree, *s. m.* A beggar.

भिगाना bhig-ána, ⎱ *v. a.* To wet, moisten,
भिगोना bhig-óna, ⎰ steep.

भिजवाना bhij-wána, *v. a.* To cause to send.

भिजाना bhij-ána, *v. a.* To cause to be wet, to wet, moisten, steep; to cause to send.

भिटनी bhít-nee, *s. f.* A nipple.

भिड़ना bhír-na, *v. n.* To close (*as two armies*), to join battle, to come together, to be joined, to shoulder, to join, to be placed together touching each other, to be continuous.

भिड़ाना bhir-ána, *v. a.* To join, to place close to, to close; to cause to fight.

भिड़ा bhir-há, *s. m.* A wolf.

भिंडी bhín-dee, *s. f.* The name of a vegetable (*Hibiscus esculentus*).

भित्ति bhitti, *s. f.* A wall of earth or masonry.

भिनकना bhín-ukna, *v. n.* To buzz (*as a fly*); to be covered with flies, to swarm.

भिनभिनाना bhinbhin-ána, *v. n.* To buzz (*as a fly*), to hum (*as a bee, &c.*)

भिनभिनाहट bhin-bhin-áhut, *s. f.* Buzzing (*of a fly*), buzz, hum (*of a bee*).

भिन्न bhinn, *adj.* Separate, apart, distinct, other, different; (*in arithmetic*) a fraction. *Bhinn bhinn,* Various, one by one, severally.

भिन्नूक bhin-núk, *s. m.* A heterodox sectary, a *Bouddh*, a seceder.

भिन्नगूनन bhinn-góonun, *s. m.* Multiplication of fractions.

भिन्नघन bhinn-ghún, *s. m.* Cube of a fraction.

भिन्नभागहर bhinn-bhag-húr, *s. m.* Division of fractions.

भिन्नवत् bhinn-vút, *adj.* Divided, scattered.

भिन्नवर्ग bhinn-vúrg, *s. m.* Square of a fraction.

भिन्नव्यवकलित bhinn-uvyúv-kúlit, *s. m.* Subtraction of fractions.

भिन्नसंकलित bhinn-súnkul-it, *s. m.* Addition of fractions.

भिन्नाना bhinná-na, *v. n.* To have a singing in the ears, to be giddy; to sound (*as shot, brass pots, &c.*)

भिन्सार bhin-sár, *s. m.* Dawn of day.

भिलावा bhil-áwan, ⎱ *s. m.* A nut used for
भिलावन bhil-áwun, ⎰ marking clothes, &c. (*Semicarpus anacardium*).

भिलौंजी bhil-óunjee, *s. f.* The seed of the *bhilawan.*

भिक्षा bhík-sha, *s. f.* Begging, asking; the thing obtained by begging, alms.

भिक्षापात्र bhiksha-pátr, *s. m.* A beggar's bowl, a vessel for collecting alms.

भिक्षुक bhik-shóok, *s. m.* A beggar.

भी bhee, *conj.* Also, too, even, and.

भीख bheekh, *s. f.* Begging, charity, alms. *Bheekh mangna,* To ask alms, to beg.

भीगना bhéeg-na, ⎱ *v. n.* To be wet. *Rat*
भींगना bhéeng-na, ⎰ *bheegna,* is applied to the night passing in mirth and musical entertainment.

भींचना bhéechna, *v. a.* To squeeze, compress, crush.

भीजा bhée-ja, *adj.* Wet, moist.

भीठा bhée-ta, *s. m.* An old house, a former residence (*provided some vestige remain*).

भीड़ bheer, *s. f.* Multitude, crowd, mob, throng; a press of work, trouble, difficulty.

भीत bheet, *adj.* Afraid, frightened, fearful, timid. *s. m.* Fear, alarm, apprehension. *s. f.* A wall, or breadth of a wall. *Ochheh kee preet jon baloo kee bheet,* The friendship of the mean is like a wall of sand (*i. e. unstable*).

भीतर bhée-tur, *adj.* Within.

भीतरिया bheetur-íya, *adj.* (*used substantively*), The people who live in a house, not strangers, domestic; men who preside at a temple (*i. e. bhundaree, a steward; poojaree, a priest; rusoiya, a cook*); those among the guests at a wedding feast who eat in company with the relations of the bride (*those who partake of the feast without being called buhuriya*).

भीतरी bhéet-ree, *adj.* Inward, inside, internal, inner, inferior.

भीति bhéeti, *s. f.* Fear, apprehension.

भीना bhée-na, *adj.* Wet. *s. m.* Sister's husband, brother-in-law.

भीम bheem, *n. prop.* One of the five *Pandoo* princes. *adj.* Horrible, fearful, dreadful, terrible, terrific. *s. m.* Horror, terror.

भीमसेनी bheem-sén-ee, *s. f.* A kind of camphire.

भीरु bhée-roo, *s. f.* A timid woman; a plant (*Asparagus racemosus*); a sort of prickly nightshade.

भील bheel, *s. m.* A barbarian of a particular tribe, a savage race dwelling especially along the course of the *Nurmuda* (*Nerbudda*), and subsisting chiefly by plunder.

भीषण bhée-shun, *adj.* Horrible, terrific, formidable. *s. m.* Horror, terror, the property that excites fear; the olibanum tree (*Boswellia thurifera*).

भीष्म bheeshm, *adj.* Horrible, terrific, fearful. *s. m.* Horror, horribleness.

भुक्त bhookt, *adj.* Eaten, eating (*either that which is eaten, or the person who has eaten*).

भुगतना bhoo-gútna, *v. a.* To enjoy, suffer, receive the reward of virtue or the punishment of crime, to be requited.

भुगतमान bhoo-gutmán, *adj.* Fit to enjoy, deserving punishment.

भुगताना bhoog-tána, *v. a.* To cause to enjoy, to distribute, requite.

भुग्गा bhóog-ga, *adj.* Simple, foolish.

भुच्च bhooch, *adj.* Barbarous, ignorant.

भुचंग bhoo-chúng, *s. m.* Name of a bird (*Lanius cærulescens*).

भुचंपा bhoo-chúmpa, *s. m.* Name of a tree (*Kæmpferia rotunda*).

भुज bhooj, *s. m. f.* The arm (*above the elbow*); the perpendicular or shortest side of a right-angled triangle. *Bhooj bundh, s. m.* An ornament worn on the arm, an armlet. *Bhooj bhurna,* To embrace. *Bhooj mool,* The upper part of the arm near the shoulder.

भुजंग bhoo-júng, } *s. m.* A serpent.
भुजंगम bhoo-júng-um, }

भुजंगा bhoo-júnga, *s. m.* A kind of shrike (*Lanius cærulescens*). *Bhoojungeh sorena,* To be in great distress and poverty; to spread false reports.

भुजना bhóoj-na, *s. m.* Parched or scorched grain.

भुजा bhóo-ja, *s. f.* The arm (*above the elbow*).

भुजिया bhóo-jiya, *s. f.* Greens.

भुट्टा bhóot-ta, *s. m.* Indian corn (*Zea mays*).

भुंडली bhóond-lee, *s. f.* A kind of worm covered with hair, the palmer-worm.

भुतना bhóot-na, *s. m.* A small devil, an imp, a demon, a ghost.

भुतनी bhóot-nee, *s. f.* A female devil.

भुतुहा bhoo-tuhá, *adj.* Devilish, peevish, fierce.

भुतियाना bhoo-tiyána, *v. n.* To be like a devil.

भुनना bhóon-na, *v. n.* To be parched, grilled, fried, broiled; to be changed (*money*).

भुभुक्षित bhoo-bhookshít, *adj.* Hungry.

भुरभुरा bhóor-bhoo-ra, *adj.* Dry and in the state of powder.

भुरभुराना bhoor-bhoo-rána, *v. a.* To throw or sprinkle salt or sugar upon meat.

भुराना bhoo-rána, *v. a.* To wheedle.

भुलसना bhoo-lúsna, *v. n.* To be singed or scorched.

भुलाना bhoo-lána, *v. a.* To cause to forget, to cause to be forgotten; to inveigle, mislead, bewilder, deceive, fascinate, coax, amuse.

भुलावा bhoo-láwa, *s. m.* Deception, fraud, cheat, deceit, feint. *Bhoolawa dana,* To deceive, to play a trick.

भुवः bhóovuh, *s. m.* Heaven, ether, sky or atmosphere.

भुवंग bhoo-wúng, *s. m.* A snake.

भुवन bhóo-wun, *s. m.* A world; water; heaven; man, mankind.

भुस bhoos, *s. m.* Bran, husk, chaff. *Bhoos pur burat,* An assignment on chaff: i. e. that from which nothing can be obtained.

भुसेरा bhoo-séra, } *s. m.* A place where
भुसेला bhoo-séla, } corn or chaff is kept.

भुसौंदा bhoo-sóunda, *s. m.* A hole or place to put chaff in.

भ bhoo, *s. f.* The earth ; place, scite, the place of being or abiding.

भूरँचम्पा bhooéen-chúmpa, *s. m.* A kind of fire-works like a flower-pot (*resembling those commonly called Unar*).

भूरँडोल bhooéen-dól, *s. m.* An earth-quake.

भूँ bhoon, *s. f.* Ground, land, earth.

भूँरँ bhoon-éen, *s. f.* The earth, ground ; a kind of caterpillar covered with hair and destructive to *ber* trees.

भूँचम्पा bhoon-chúmpa, *s. m.* The name of a plant (*Kæmpferia rotunda*).

भूँसना bhóonsna, *v. n.* To bark.

भूआ bhóoa, *s. f.* Father's sister ; a worm, a caterpillar.

भूकदम्ब bhoo-kudúmb, *s. m.* A plant (*Ligusticum ajwaen*).

भूकम्प bhoo-kúmp, *s. m.* An earthquake.

भूख bhookh, *s. f.* Hunger, appetite. *Bhookhon murna*, To die with hunger, to famish, to starve.

भूखन bhoo-khún, *s. m.* Ornament, embellishment, decoration, an ornament, a jewel, dress.

भूखा bhóo-kha, *adj.* Hungry.

भूगोल bhóo-gol, *s. m.* The terrestrial globe, the earth. [line.

भूचक्र bhoo-chúkr, *s. m.* The equinoctial

भूजन्तु bhoo-júntoo, *s. m.* An earth-worm.

भूजम्बू bhoo-júmboo, *s. f.* Wheat ; the fruit of the *Vikunta* (*Flacourtia sapida*).

भूजेल bhoo-jél, *s. m.* A species of bird.

भूर bhoor, *s. f.* Sandy ground, soil in which much sand is mixed.

भूरुल bhoo-rúl, *s. m.* Talc, mica.

भूँदपैरा bhoond-pyra, *adj.* Unlucky, ill-omened.

भूत bhoot, *adj.* Been, become ; being, existing ; gone, past. *s. m.* A demon, a goblin, a fiend, a ghost, an apparition, a malignant spirit haunting cemetries, lurking in trees, animating carcases, and deluding or devouring human beings ; the past preterite tense ; an element (*the Hindoos reckon five elements, earth, fire, water, air, and akas or ether*).

भूतगण bhoot-gún, *s. m.* A class of sprites or goblins.

भूतगन्धा bhoot-gúndha, *s. f. Moora*, a sort of perfume.

भूतजटा bhoot-jút-a, *s. f.* Indian spikenard (*Valeriana jatumansi*).

भूतनाशन bhoot-náshun, *s. m.* Marking-nut plant (*Semicarpus anacardium*) ; the Eleocarpus seed.

भूतनी bhóot-nee, *s. f.* A female demon or goblin.

भूतूल bhoo-túl, *s. m.* The earth, the face of the earth.

भूतवास bhoot-vás, *s. m.* Beleric myrobalan (*Terminalia belerica*).

भूतविक्रिया bhoot-víkriya, *s. f.* Epilepsy, possession by evil spirits.

भूतवेशी bhoot-véshee, *s. f.* A species of Nebari (*Nyctanthes tristis*).

भूतवृक्ष bhoot-vríksh, *s. m.* A tree (*Trophis aspera*) ; a species of Bignonia (*B. Indica*).

भूतसञ्चार bhoot-sunchár, *s. m.* Possession by evil spirits.

भूतात्मा bhoot-átma, *s. m.* The body ; the elementary or vital principle, or the proximate cause of life and action.

भूतारि bhoot-ári, *s. m.* Asafœtida.

भूताविष्ट bhoot-avísht, *adj.* Occupied or possessed by a devil.

भूतावेश bhoot-avésh, *s. m.* Possession by a devil or evil spirit.

भूदार bhoo-dár, *s. m.* A hog.

भूदेव bhoo-dév, *s. m.* A *Brahmun*.

भूधर bhoo-dhúr, *s. m.* A mountain.

भूनाग bhoo-nág, *s. m.* An earth-worm.

भूनिम्ब bhoo-nímb, *s. m.* A species of Gentian, commonly called Cherayta (*Gentiana cherayta*).

भूनना bhoonna, *v. a.* To parch, grill, broil, toast, fry, inflame.

भूप bhoop, *s. m.* A sovereign, a prince, a king.

भूपति bhoo-púti, } *s. m.* A king, a sovereign ; a landlord, a Raja.
भूपाल bhoo-pál, }

भूपाली bhoo-pálee, *s. f.* Name of a *raginee*.

भूभुल bhóo-bhul, *s. m.* Hot ashes, embers.

भूमि bhóomi, *s. f.* Land, earth, the earth ; place, scite in general ; the base of any figure in geometry.

भूमिकम्प bhoomi-kúmp, *s. m.* An earth-quake.

भूमिचम्पक bhoomi-chúmpuk, *s. m.* A plant (*Kæmpferia rotunda*).

भूमिजम्ब bhoomi-júmboo, *s. f.* A tree (*Premna herbacea*).

भूर bhoor, *s. f.* Charity given to poor people, alms ; a spring, a fountain. *Bhoor bantna, v. a.* To give alms to a numerous assembly of the poor.

भूरा bhóo-ra, *adj.* Fair, auburn or brownish (*as hair*).

भूरि bhóori, *adj.* Much, many.

भूरिधामन bhoori-dhámun, *adj.* Splendid, bright; illustrious.

भूरिलाभ bhoori-lábh, *adj.* Very profitable or beneficial. *s. m.* Great gain.

भूरुंडी bhoo-róondee, *s. f.* A sort of sunflower (*Heliotropium Indicum*).

भूर्जपत्र bhoorj-pútr, *s. m.* The *Bhojputr*, a tree growing in the snowy mountains, a kind of birch; the bark is used for writing on, and very generally for *hookka* snakes.

भूल bhool, *s. f.* Forgetfulness, error, mistake, miss, blunder.

भूलता bhóolta, *s. f.* A worm, an earthworm.

भूलना bhóolna, *v. n.* To forget, err, go astray, be misled or deceived, mistake, blunder, miss, omit, stray, to be forgotten.

भूलाबिसरा bhoola-bísra,
भूलाभूतका bhoola-bhútka, } *adj.* Missing the road, (*generally a person*) calling another in consequence of some accident, &c., not intentionally to pay a visit.

भूलोक bhoo-lók,
भूर्लोक bhoor-lók, } *s. m.* The earth, the habitation of mortals.

भूषण bhoo-shún, *s. m.* Ornament, embellishment, a dress, jewel, decoration.

भूषित bhoo-shít, *adj.* Adorned, decorated, dressed.

भूसा bhóo-sa, *s. m.* Husk, chaff.

भूसी bhóo-see, *s. f.* Chaff, bran.

भूस्वर्ग bhoo-swúrg, *s. m.* The mountain *Soomeroo* (*a heaven on earth*).

भूस्वामी bhoo-swámee, *s. m.* A landlord, a landholder.

भृकुटी bhrí-kootee, *s. f.* the eyebrow; a frown, a contraction of the eyebrows.

भृगु bhrígoo, *n. prop.* The name of a celebrated *Mooni*.

भृंग bhring, *s. m.* A large black bee, the humble bee.

भृंगक bhring-úk, *s. m.* A bird, a sort of shrike (*Lanius Malabaricus*).

भृंगराज bhring-ráj, *s. m.* A spreading shrub (*Eclipta or Verbesina prostrata, or perhaps more properly, Verbesina scandens*); a sort of bird, apparently the variety of shrike termed *Malabar* (*Lanius Malabaricus*).

भृंगी bhríngee, *s. f.* A kind of wasp (*Vespa solitaria*); a large black bee, a humble bee.

भृंगीफल bhringee-phúl, *s. m.* The hogplum. [er.

भृत bhrit, *s. m.* A servant, a hired labour-

भृति bhríti, *s. f.* Wages, hire; nourishment, maintenance.

भृत्युह bhrít-yuh, *s. m.* A dependant, a servant, a slave.

भृत्या bhrit-yá, *s. f.* Hire, wages.

भृष्ट bhrisht, *adj.* Fried.

भेंगा bhén-ga, *adj.* Squint-eyed.

भेंट bhent, *s. f.* Interview, visit; a present.

भेंटना bhéntna, *v. a.* To meet with, to visit.

भेक bhek, *s. m.* A toad, a frog.

भेकी bhék-ee, *s. f.* The female of the frog, or a small frog; a kind of creeper (*Hydrocotyle Asiatica*).

भेख bhekh, *s. m.* Disguise, assumed appearance, semblance. *Bhekh-dharee, adj.* Putting on the dress, assuming the appearance.

भेजना bhéj-na, *v. a.* To send, transmit; utter, ejaculate.

भेजा bhéja, *s. m.* The brain.

भेट bhet, *s. f.* Meeting, interview; a present to a superior.

भेटन bhét-un, *verbal s.* To meet, meeting, &c.

भेटना bhét-na, *v. a.* To meet, join; to make a present (*to a superior*).

भेटी bhétee, *s. f.*
भेटू bhétoo, *s. m.* } A stalk, a stem.

भेर bher, *s. m.* A ram, a sheep.

भेरना bhér-na, *v. a.* To shut, close.

भेरा bhér-a, *s. m.* A ram.

भेरिया bhér-iya, *s. m.* A wolf. *Bheriya dhusan, s. m.* A multitude crowded together like sheep in a pen, the act of following the example of another.

भेरी bhér-ee, *s. f.* An ewe.

भेद bhed, *s. m.* A secret, secrecy, mystery; separation, distinction, kind, sort, species, difference; disunion, disagreement. *Bhed lena,* To spy, to pry into, to work one's self into confidence, to sound.

भेदक bhed-úk, *adj.* A breaker, who or what breaks or divides. *s. m.* A mischief-maker.

भेदकर bhed-kúr, *adj.* Separating, disuniting; causing disunion.

भेदुकिया bheduk-iya,
भेदिया bhéd-iya, } *s. m.* A scout, a spy.
भेदी bhédee, }

भेदी bhédee, *s. m.* The ratan.

भेदी bhédee, } *adj.* Intelligent. *s. m.*
भेदिया bhédiya, } A scout, a secret-keeper.

भेदू bhedóo, *s. m.* A secret-keeper, a confidant.

भेना bhéna, *s. f.* Sister.

भेर bher, *s. f.* A kind of pipe, a musical instrument, a kettle-drum.

भेरी bhéree, *s. m.* A piper.

भेला bhéla, *s. m. Semicarpus anacardium.*

भेली bhélee, *s. f.* A lump of coarse sugar (*or goor*).

भेव bheo, *s. m.* A state or condition of being, innate property, nature, disposition.

भेष bhesh, *s. m.* Disguise, assumed likeness, counterfeit dress, semblance, guise, garb.

भेषज besh-új, *s. m.* A remedy, a drug, a medicament; a kind of fennel (*Nigella Indica*).

भैंस bhyns, *s. f.* A female buffalo.

भैंसा bhynsa, *s. m.* A male buffalo.

भैंसादाद bhynsa-dád, } *s. m.* A kind of
भैंसियादाद bhynsiya-dád, } ring-worm.

भैंकुर bhy-únkur, *adj.* Terrific, terrible, horrible.

भैंआतुर bhyá-toor, *adj.* Distressed or distracted with fear, terrified.

भैंआनक bhy-ánuk, *adj.* Frightful, terrible, formidable, fearful, dreadful, alarming, dismal.

भैंचक bhy-chúk, *adj.* Alarmed, aghast, starting.

भैंमान bhy-mán, *adj.* Frightened, alarmed, terrified, afraid.

भैंया bhy-a, *s. m.* Brother.

भैंयापा bhy-ápa, *s. m.* Brotherhood, friendship.

भैंरव bhy-rúv, *adj.* Formidable, horrible, terrific. *s. m.* A name of *Shiv*, but more especially an inferior manifestation or form of the deity, eight of which are called by the common name *Bhyruvuh*, and are severally termed *Usitanguh, Rooroo, Chunduh, Krodh, Oonmutt, Kooputi, Beeshun,* and *Sunghar,* all alluding to terrific properties of mind or body; the name of a river; a musical mode, that which is calculated to excite emotions of terror.

भैंरवी bhy-ruv-ee, *s. f.* The name of a *raginee.*

भैंरारी bhy-rá-ree, *s. f.* The name of a *raginee.*

भैंरौं bhy-ron, *s. m.* The name of a musical mode sung at dawn in autumn: (*It is represented by Muhadev with the Ganges flowing from his head, and the rag issuing from that deity's mouth*); a name of *Shiv.*

भैंहू bhy-hóo, *s. f.* Sister-in-law, younger brother's wife.

भों bhon, *s. f.* The eyebrow.

भोंकरा bhónk-ra, *adj.* Very fat.

भोंकना bhónk-na, *v. a.* To thrust, to drive (*as a nail*).

भोंकस bhon-kús, *s. m.* A wizard who preys upon children (*or men or women*) till he brings them to the grave.

भोंघरा bhon-ghúr-a, *s. m.* A vault, a cavern, a cellar.

भोंडा bhón-da, *adj.* Ill-shaped, uncouth, mis-shapen, useless, bad, ugly, unlucky.

भोंथा bhon-thá, } *adj.* Blunt, obtuse.
भोंथरा bhonth-rá, }

भोंदू bhon-dóo, *adj.* Silly, quiet, mild, artless, simple.

भोंपू bhon-póo, *s. m.* A horn, wind instrument.

भोई bhóee, *s. m.* A chair porter, a *palkee* bearer, a bearer; a white cat.

भोकस bhó-kus, *s. m.* A wizard, sorcerer, magician.

भोकना bhókh-na, *v. a.* To bark.

भोग bhog, *s. m.* Pleasure, enjoyment, satisfaction; suffering; possession; eating, victuals; (*in arithmetic*) the numerator of a fraction. *Bhog kurna,* To enjoy, to suffer.

भोग bhog, *s. m.* Abuse, rudeness.

भोगना bhóg-na, *v. n.* To enjoy, to suffer.

भोगा bhó-ga, *s. m.* Fraud, trick, deceit, illusion, deception, imposition, treachery, roguery, cheat.

भोगी bhó-gee, *adj.* Jovial, jolly.

भोग्य bhógyuh, *adj.* To be enjoyed.

भोज bhoj, *s. m.* A country, *Patna* and *Bhagulpore;* the name of a sovereign of *Oojein,* who is supposed to have flourished about the end of the tenth century: he was a celebrated patron of learned men, and the nine gems or poets, and philosophers, often ascribed to his era; eating, feast.

भोजकूट bhoj-kút, *s. m.* The country of *Bhoj,* the present *Bhojpore,* or the vicinity of *Patna* and *Bhagulpore.*

भोजन bhó-jun, *s. m.* Eating, food, victuals. *Bhojun kurna,* To eat, to feed.

भोजनीय bhojun-éeyuh, } *adj.* To be eaten,
भोज्य bhój-yuh, } edible. *s. m.* Food.

भोजपत्र bhoj-pútr, *s. m.* The bark of a tree, said to be a kind of birch, used in making *hookka* snakes.

भोजपूर bhoj-póor, *n. prop.* A country near *Chhupra.*

भोट bhot, } *s. m.* A country, pro-
भोटांग bhot-áng, } bably *Bootan.*

भोटिया bhó-tiya, *s. m.* An inhabitant of *Bootan.*

भोरुल bhó-rul, *s. m.* Talc, mica.

भोता bhó-ta, *adj.* Blunt, dull.

भोपा bhó-pa, *s. m.* A kind of *fukeer*, a magician.

भोमीरा bho-mée-ra, *s. f.* Coral.

भोर bhor, *s. f.* Dawn of day. *Bhor hona*, To be finished, to be terminated.

भोला bhó-la, *adj.* Simple, artless, undesigning, innocent, harmless, meek.

भोली bhó-lee, *adj. f.* Innocent, artless. *Bholee baten*, Innocent prattle.

भोसरा bhós-ra, *s. m.*
भोसरी bhós-ree, *s. f.* } Vulva magna.
भोसा bhó-sa, *s. m.*

भौं bhoun, *s. f.* The eyebrow. *Bhoun terhee kurna, v. a.* To scowl, frown, browbeat, look angrily raising the eyebrows. *Bhouen tannee*, To knit the eyebrows.

भौंकना bhóunkna, *v. n.* To bark; (*met.*) to talk foolishly.

भौंचाल bhoun-chál, *s. m.* An earthquake.

भौंर bhounr, *s. m.* A whirlpool.

भौंरा bhóunra, *s. m.* A large black bee enamoured of the lotus.

भौंरियाना bhoun-riyána, *v. a.* To whirl, to turn.

भौंरी bhóun-ree, *s. f.* Feathered hair; name of a defect in horses.

भौंवरकली bhoun-ur-kúl-ee, *s. f.* A kind of halter (*for horses or dogs*).

भौंसना bhóuns-na, *v. n.* To bark.

भौ bhou, *s. m.* Fear.

भौचक bhou-chúk, *adj.* Aghast.

भौजाई bhou-jáee, }
भौजी bhóu-jee, } *s. f.* A brother's wife.

भौतिक bhou-tík, *adj.* Relating or appertaining to evil spirits.

भौना bhóu-na, *v. n.* To revolve.

भौनास bhou-nás, *s. m.* A post driven into the ground for chaining an elephant to.

भौमी bhou-mée, *adj. f.* Earthly, terrestrial, produced in or relating to the earth.

भ्रंश bhrunsh, *s. m.* Falling, declining from a height, or from propriety; falling from or off.

भ्रम bhrum, *s. m.* Error, ignorance, mistake, misapprehension; apprehension, perplexity, doubt.

भ्रमण bhrúm-un, *s. m.* Whirling, going round; wandering, literally or figuratively; going about, perambulation.

भ्रमत bhrum-út, *adj.* Going round, whirling, revolving; roving; erring.

भ्रमर bhrúm-ur, *s. m.* A large black bee; vertigo, epilepsy.

भ्रमि bhrúmi, *s. f.* Error, blunder, mistake.

भ्रमी bhrúm-ee, *adj.* Whirling, going round or about.

भ्रष्ट bhrusht, *adj.* Fallen, lost; vicious, depraved, fallen from virtue, debased, polluted, abominable, dissolute. *Bhrusht kurna, v. a.* To pollute, to seduce. *Bhrusht hona, v. n.* To be polluted; to calcine.

भ्रष्टराज्य bhrusht-rájyuh, *adj.* Deposed, deprived of a kingdom.

भ्रात्रि bhrátri, *s. m.* A brother, a uterine brother.

भ्रातृक bhra-trík, } *adj.* Fraternal, bro-
भ्रातृय bhra-tréeyuh, } therly, of or belonging to a brother.

भ्रान्त bhrant, *adj.* Whirled, revolved; blundering, mistaken.

भ्रान्ति bhránti, *s. f.* Error, mistake, ignorance; going round, whirling, revolving; going about, wandering.

भ्रान्तिमान् bhranti-mán, *adj.* Erring, mistaking; wandering.

भ्रमूक bhram-úk, *s. m.* A cheat, a rogue.

भ्रमर bhrám-ur, *s. m.* Epilepsy.

भ्रमरी bhrámur-ee, *adj.* Epileptic.

भ्रू bhroo, *s. f.* An eye-brow.

भ्रूण bhroon, *s. m.* The embryo or fœtus, a child.

भ्रूणहत्या bhroon-hutyá, *s. f.* Murder of the fœtus, procuring or causing abortion.

भ्रूभंग bhroo-bhúng, *s. m.* A frown.

म

म muh, The twenty-fifth consonant of the *Naguree* alphabet, corresponding to the letter म.

मंजन munjun, *s. m.* Tooth-powder, dentifrice; cleaning the person by wiping, bathing or rubbing it with oil or fragrant unguents.

मंजना munjna, *v. n.* To be polished, to be cleaned, to be scoured.

मंजीरा munjéera, *s. m.* A musical instrument, a kind of cymbal.

मंझोला munjhóla, *adj.* Middle, middlemost, middling.

मंझोली munjhólee, *s. f.* A smallish sort of car or carriage on two wheels.

मंड़ूआ munr-ooá, *s. m.* } Name of a grain
मंडूई munr-ooée, *s. f.* } (Cynosurus corocanus).

मकड़ा múk-ra, *s. m.* A kind of grain; a spider.

मकड़ाना muk-rána, v. a. To move by winding about or crookedly ; (met.) to be averse or act contrary.

मकड़ी múk-ree, s. f. A spider. *Mukree ka jala*, s. m. A spider's web ; hence (*met.*) any thing very fine and slender.

मकर múk-ur, s. m. A marine monster, confounded usually with the crocodile and shark, but properly a fabulous animal : as a fish it might be conjectured to be the horned shark, or the unicorn fish ; but it is often drawn, as in the pictured signs of the Zodiac, with the head and fore legs of an antelope, and the body and tail of a fish : it is the emblem of the god of love ; one of the signs of the zodiac, corresponding with Capricorn, and like the Greek representation of that sign, being an animal in the foreparts, and ending in the tail of a fish.

मकरन्द múk-rúnd, s. m. The nectar or honey of a flower ; the *Kokila* or Indian cuckoo ; a fragrant kind of mango ; a kind of Jasmine (*Jasminum pubescens*).

मकरन्दवती mukrund-wút-ee, s. f. The trumpet-flower (*Bignonia suave-olens*).

मकरोना muk-róna, v. a. To wet (*slightly*).

मकुट múk-oot, s. m. A crest, a head-dress, a crown, a tiara.

मको muk-ó, s. m. A species of Solanum (*S. nigrum ?*).

मकोड़ा muk-óra, s. m. A large ant.

मकोह muk-óeh, s. m. Sarsaparilla.

मकखन muk-khún, s. m. Butter.

मकखी muk-khée, s. f. A fly ; the sight of a gun. *Mukkhee oorana*, To flatter or perform servile offices for any one ; to have ulcers on the body (*so as to be constantly employed in driving away the flies from them*) ; to be a good marksman (*so as to hit a fly with a ball or arrow*). *Mukkhee-choos*, A miser, a niggard, a skinflint. *Mukkhee jhulna*, To have venereal ulcers. *Mukkhee marna*, To idle, to be unemployed, to trifle, to fool.

मख mukh, s. f. Sacrifice, oblation.

मखन muk-hún, s. m. Butter.

मखना mukhná, s. m. A kind of elephant which has no tusks ; a cock without spurs.

मखनिया mukhun-íya, s. m. Butterman.

मखी muk-hée, s. f. A fly.

मग mug, s. m. A road. *Mug dekhna*, To expect, to wait for.

मगध mug-údh, s. m. A country, South *Behar* ; an inhabitant of that country ; a bard, whose peculiar province is to sing the praises of a chief's ancestry in his presence, a family bard or minstrel.

मगन múg-un, } adj. Plunged, dived, immersed ; sunk, drowned-
मग्न mugn, } ed ; delighted, pleased, glad, happy, cheerful, joyful.

मगनता mug-un-tá, s. f. Transport, rapture, cheerfulness, vivacity, delight.

मगर múg-ur, } s. m. An alligator.
मगरमच्छ mugur-múchchh, } gator.

मगरा múg-ra, adj. Proud, haughty, presumptuous, fastidious, arrogant, insolent, cross, obstinate, stubborn, impatient, refractory.

मगराई mug-ráee, s. f. Obstinacy, stubbornness, refractoriness, insolence.

मगरापन mugra-pún, s. m. Haughtiness, obstinacy, refractoriness.

मगराही mugra-hée, s. f. Arrogance.

मगरेला mug-réla, s. m. A small blackish, triangular, pyramidical shaped seed of a very pungent smell (*Nigella Indica*).

मगसिर mug-sír, s. m. The eighth solar month.

मगुही muguhée, adj. Belonging to *Mugudh* (a thing).

मगहया mug-hya, s. m. Inhabitant of *Mugudh* ; a caste of Brahmuns.

मगाना mug-ána, v. a. To send for.

मगुरी múg-ooree, s. f. A fish, a species of Silurus (*S. pelorius*).

मग्न mugn, adj. Plunged, dived, immersed ; sunk, drowned.

मघ mugh, s. m. One of the *dweeps* or divisions of the universe ; a country, that of the modern *Mugs*, or Arracan ; a drug.

मघन mug-hún, adj. Odoriferous.

मघया mughuyá, s. m. Inhabitant of *Mugudh* ; a caste of Brahmuns.

मघा mug-há, s. f. The tenth lunar asterism, containing five stars figured by a house, a Leonis, Regulus.

मघी mug-hée, adj. Belonging to *Mugudh* (a thing). s. f. A sort of grain.

मुंका mún-ka, s. m. A rosary, a bead (*of gold ?*) ; the vertibræ of the neck. *Munka dhulukna* (lit. the bending of the neck), To be at the point of death.

मुंगत mung-út, } s. m. A beggar, a borrower.
मुंगता mung-tá, } rower.

मुंगनी mung-née, s. f. Betrothing, asking in marriage ; a loan. *Mungnee dena*, To lend.

मुंगरा múngra, s. m. The ridge of a house.

मुंगुल mún-gul, adj. Auspicious, propitious, conferring happiness, prosperity, &c. ; beautiful, pleasing, agreeable. s. m. Welfare, happiness; the planet Mars or its deified personification; Tuesday. *Mungul-achar, s. m.* Festivity, rejoicing, congratulation, a song of congratulation, a marriage song or Epithalamium.

मङ्गलकोटी **múngul-kótee**, *s. f.* A sort of carpet made at *Mungulkot.*

मङ्गलवार **mungul-wár**, *s. m.* Tuesday

मङ्गलसमाचार **múngul-sumachár**, *s. m.* Glad tidings, the Gospel.

मङ्गलामुखी **mungul-amóokhee**, *s. m. f.* A musician or singer.

मङ्गली **mungul-ée**, *adj.* Triumphant, rejoicing. *Mungulee log*, People employed on rejoicings.

मङ्गवाना **mung-wána**, *v. a.* To cause to ask for, to send for.

मङ्गसिर **múng-sir**, *s. m.* Name of a month, the first of the *Hindoo* year, according to some systems, or the eighth.

मङ्गाना **mungána**, ⎫ *v. a.* To send
मङ्गभेजना **munga-bhéjna**, ⎬ for, to ask for, to call for.

मङ्गूला **mun-góola**, *s. m.* A small tassel.

मङ्गेतर **mun-gétur**, *s. m. f.* One to whom a man or woman is betrothed.

मचक **múch-uk**, *s. f.* Pain in the joints.

मचकना **múch-uk-na**, *v. n.* To have pain in the joints; to creak (*as a bedstead, &c.*)

मचकाना **much-kána**, *v. a.* To wink.

मचना **múch-na**, *v. n.* To be made, to be committed, to be perpetrated, to be produced.

मचमच **much-much**, An imitative sound.

मचमचाना **much-much-ána**, *v. n.* To creak (*as a bedstead or other thing heavily laden*).

मचउलना **much-úlna**, *v. n.* To be perverse, refractory, disobedient, cross, obstinate.

मचउलपन **much-ul-pún**, *s. m.* ⎫ Pertness,
मचलाई **much-laée**, *s. f.* ⎬ perverseness, obstinacy.

मचला **múch-la**, *adj.* Perverse, refractory, disobedient, cross, obstinate, restiff, pert.

मचलाना **much-lána**, *v. n.* To be sick at the stomach, to feel nausea; to pretend ignorance.

मचलापन **muchla-pún**, *s. m.* ⎫ Stubborn-
मचलाहट **muchla-hút**, *s. f.* ⎬ ness.

मचलाहा **much-láha**, *adj.* Squeamish, stubborn.

मचान **much-án**, *s. m.* A platform, scaffold, stage, raised seat.

मचाना **much-ána**, *v. a.* To make, cause, stir up, excite, commit, perpetrate, produce.

मचमच **much-amúch**, *adj.* Filled up, stuffed full.

मचिया **múch-iya**, *s. m.* A stool, a chair.

मचियाव **muchiyáo**, *s. m.* Honey.

मचोड़ना **much-órna**, *v. a.* To twist, to break by twisting.

मच्छ **muchchh**, *s. m.* A fish in general; the name of the first *Uvutar* or incarnation, when *Vishnoo* is said to have appeared in the shape of the small fish *suphuree*, to *Sutyuvruta* or *Huyugreev*, to warn him of the general deluge, and desire him to place the four *Veds* in the boat which he (*Vishnoo*) would preserve. The fish was first taken up by *Huyugreev* in his hands when bathing, being then of the size of the *suphuree (or ponthee)*, but it grew too large for being contained in a tank, river, &c. and was carried to the sea, where, afterwards it supported the ark with its horn. *Sutyuvruta* lived about 3000 years before Christ.

मच्छर **much-chhúr**, *s. m.* A musquito, a gnat. *Muchchhur kee jhool ka chor*, One who would steal the minutest thing, a petty pilferer.

मच्छी **much-chhée**, *s. f.* A kiss.

मच्छ **muchhh**, *s. m.* A fish in general.

मच्छंदर **muchh-úndur**, *n. prop.* Name of a *Jogee. s. m.* A rat. *adj.* Stupid.

मच्छली **muchh-lée**, *s. f.* A fish.

मच्छवा **muchh-wá**, *s. m.* A fisherman.

मज **muj**, *adj.* Ripe, mellow.

मजीठ **muj-éeth**, *s. f.* A drug used for dying red (*Rubia manjith*).

मजीत **mujeet**, *adj.* Cheap, that which is sold at an under price; bought at second hand.

मजीरा **muj-éera**, *s. m.* Small cymbals.

मजूर **muj-óor**, *s. m.* A labourer, carrier, porter.

मज्जा **muj-já**, *s. f.* Marrow, pith, sap.

मझला **mújh-la**, *adj.* Middling.

मझार **muj-hár**, *s. m.* The middle, centre; in the middle, in.

मझारी **muj-háree**, *adv.* In the midst.

मझेली **muj-hélee**, *s. f.* A small cart.

मझोला **muj-hóla**, *adj.* Middling.

मझोली **muj-hólee**, *s. f.* A smallish sort of car or carriage on two wheels.

मञ्च **munch**, *s. m.* A bed, a bedstead; a platform, a scaffold; an elevated shed raised on bamboos in a cornfield, &c. where a watchman is stationed to protect the corn from cattle, birds, wild beasts, &c.; a sort of throne or chair of state, or the platform on which it is raised, the dais.

मञ्जन **mún-jun**, *s. m.* Tooth-powder, dentifrice; cleaning the person by wiping, bathing or rubbing it with oil or fragrant unguents.

मञ्जना **múnj-na**, *v. n.* To be polished, to be cleaned, to be scoured.

मञ्जर mun-júr, *s. f.* The blossom (*of a tree*).

मञ्ज mún-ja, *s. m.* A bedstead ; a sort of throne or chair of state.

मञ्जार mun-jár, *s. m.* A cat.

मञ्जीरा mun-jéera, *s. m.* A musical instrument, a kind of cymbal : (*it consists of two small brass cups tied together with a string, and played upon by striking one against another*).

मटक mút-uk, } *s. f.* Coquetry, ogling.
मटकन mut-kún, }

मटकना mút-kun-a, *s. m.* A small vessel for taking water out of a larger.

मटकना mut-úkna, *v. n.* To wink, ogle, coquet.

मटका mút-ka, *s. m.* A large earthen jar or pot.

मटकाना mut-kána, *v. a.* To wink, ogle, twinkle.

मटकी mut-kée, *s. f.* A child's coral, or plaything which infants suck ; a small earthen pot or jar ; a wink, a twinkle, closing the eyes.

मटकोठा mut-kótha, *s. m.* A house of earth.

मटर mút-ur, *s. m.* A pea (*Pisum sativum*).

मटरा mút-ra, *s. m.* A kind of pea ; a kind of silk cloth.

मटरी mut-rée, *s. f.* A kind of pea.

मटरोला mut-réela, *adj.* Mixed with peas.

मटियाना mut-iyána, *v. n.* To wink at, connive, suffer, tolerate.

मटियारा mut-iyára, *s. m.* Arable land, rich soil.

मटियाव mut-iyáo, *s. m.* Sufferance, toleration.

मट्टी múttee, } *s. f.* Earth. *Muttee kurna,*
मिट्टी mittee, } To ruin or destroy. *Muttee khana,* To eat flesh. *Muttee dalna,* To conceal the crime or fault of another. *Muttee dena,* To bury. *Muttee pukurna,* To bite the ground ; to be overcome or overturned ; to be perverse or obstinate, to resist. *Mittee pur lurna,* To dispute about land. *Muttee men milana,* To be ruined or disgraced. *Muttee hona,* To become weak or faint, to be ruined.

मट्ठा mut-thá, *s. m.* Buttermilk.

मठ muth, *s. m.* A school, a college, the residence of young *Brahmuns,* prosecuting sacred studies ; a building inhabited by ascetics of the same order ; a pagan temple.

मठरी múth-ree, *s. f.* A sort of sweetmeat.

मठा mut-há, *adj.* Slow.

मठोर mut-hór, *s. m.* A jar.

मठोली mut-hólee, *s. f.* Onanism.

मरियाना mur-iyána, *v. a.* To paste.

मरोर mur-ór, *s. f.* Twist, flexion, turn, writhe, convolution, contortion. *Muror bas,* An affected person.

मरोरना mur-órna, *v. a.* To twist, writhe, contort, distort, gripe, yearn.

मरोरा mur-óra, *s. m.* A twisting of the bowels, pain in the bowels, flux, gripes.

मरोरी muróree, *s. f.* Twisting, twist, flexion, writhe, convolution.

मरहुन mur-hún, *s. f.* Lining, heading (*of a drum, &c.*)

मरहना múrh-na, *v. a.* To cover (*as a book with leather or a drum with parchment*), to gild, to case.

मरहा mur-há, *adj.* Lined, headed, covered or topped (*as a drum with parchment*).

मरही mur-hée, *s. f.* A cottage, a temple.

मरहय्या mur-hyya, *s. f.* A cottage, a hut.

मणि múni, *s. m.* A gem, a jewel, a precious stone.

मणिमय muni-múy, *adj.* Composed of gems.

मणिमाला múni-mála, *s. f.* A necklace, a zone, a fillet, &c., of precious stones.

मण्ड mund, *s. m.* Scum, skimmings, froth, foam, barm, &c. ; pith, essence.

मण्डन mún-dun, *s. m.* Ornament, decoration, jewels, trinkets, &c.

मण्डप mun-dúp, *s. m.* A temporary building, an open shed or hall adorned with flowers and erected on festival occasions, as at marriages, &c. ; an open temple or building consecrated to a deity.

मण्डल mun-dúl, *s. m.* A circle, orb, sphere, disk of the sun or moon, halo, circumference ; a round tent ; an officer employed in villages, an exciseman, a province, a region, a district, extending twenty, or according to some authorities, forty *Yojuns* every way ; the country or empire over which the twelve princes termed *Chukruvurtees* are supposed to have ruled, perhaps the peninsula of India.

मण्डलाकार múndul-akár, *adj.* Round, circular.

मण्डलाना mund-lána, *v. n.* To make a circuit, to hover (*as birds, &c.*), to be enveloped.

मण्डलिया mundul-íya, *s. m.* A tumbler pigeon.

मण्डली mundul-ée, *s. f.* An assembly, a corporation.

मण्डवा mund-wá, *s. m.* An alcove, an arbour, a bower, a shed.

मण्डा mún-da, *s. m.* A kind of sweetmeat.

मण्डित mun-dít, *adj.* Ornamented, adorned, overlaid (*with gold, &c.*), covered (*with dust*).

मंडियाना mundi-yána, v. a. To starch.

मंडी mún-dee, s. f. A market, a particular market for any one thing.

मंडूआ mun-dóoa, s. m. An alcove, an arbour, a bower; a shed.

मंडूक mun-dóok, s. m. A frog; a flower (*Bignonia Indica*).

मंडूकी mun-dóokee, s. f. A female or small frog; a plant (*Siphonanthus Indica*, or, *Hydrocotyle Asiatica*).

मंढना múndh-na, v. a. To cover (*as a book with leather, or a drum with parchment*), to gild, to case.

मंढप mun-dhúp, s. m. A small round temple or cell.

मंढवाना mundh-wána, v. a. To cause to cover (*a book, drum, &c. with parchment*).

मंढा mun-dhá, s. m. A temporary building, an open shed or hall, adorned with flowers and erected on festive occasions, as at marriages, &c.

मंढाया mun-dháya, adj. Starched.

मंढियाना mun-dhiyána, v. a. To starch.

मंढी mun-dhée, s. f. A *jogee's* hut or place of abode.

मत mut, s. m. Purpose, intention, wish, mind (*as to have a mind to any thing*); knowledge; doctrine, tenet, belief, opinion. s. f. Manner, method, way, mode, system; wisdom, understanding, intellect. *Mutheen*, Void of understanding. *neg. part.* No, do not.

मतंग mut-úng, s. m. An elephant.

मतना mút-na, s. m. A kind of sugar-cane.

मतराना mut-rána, v. a. To persuade.

मतलानाजीका mut-lána-jéeka, v. n. To be sick at the stomach, to feel nausea.

मतवत mutwút, adj. Drunken, like one intoxicated.

मतवाला mut-wála, adj. Intoxicated, drunken, drunk.

मतहीन mut-héen, } adj. Stupid, igno-
मतिहीन muti-héen, } rant.

मता mút-a, s. m. Counsel, advice.

मति múti, s. f. Understanding, intellect; wish, desire, inclination.

मतिभ्रम muti-bhrúm, s. m. } Error, mis-
मतिभ्रान्ति muti-bhránti, s. f. } take, misapprehension.

मतिमान muti-mán, adj. Sensible, clever, intelligent.

मत्त mutt, adj. Intoxicated (*drunk with liquor*), intoxicated (*with pride, passion, &c.*)

मत्राना mutrána, v. a. To persuade.

मत्सुर mut-súr, adj. Envious; niggardly, covetous.

मत्सुरा mut-sur-á, s. f. Envy, impatience of another's success or prosperity; passion, anger; a gnat, a musquito.

मत्सुरिनी mut-sur-ínee, f. } adj. Wicked,
मत्सुरी mut-sur-ée, m. } depraved, bad; envious.

मत्स्य mút-syuh, s. m. A fish in general; a particular fish, probably the *suphuree*, or the fish in which *Vishnoo* is said to have been incarnate in his fish *Uvutar*; a country, enumerated amongst the midland divisions of India (*Dinajpoor and Rungpoor*); one of the *Poorans*.

मत्स्यराज mutsyuh-ráj, s. m. The *Rohi*, a sort of fish (*Cyprinus Rohita*); the country called *Mutsyuh*.

मथन mut-hún, s. m. Churning.

मथना múth-na, v. a. To churn; to knead, to work. s. m. A churn-staff.

मथनिया muth-níya, s. f. A churn.

मथनी muth-née, s. f. A churn-staff.

मथा mut-há, s. m. The forehead.

मथित mut-hít, s. m. Butter-milk, without any watery admixture.

मथिन mut-hín, s. m. A churning stick.

मथुरा mút-hoo-ra, s. f. A town in the province of *Agra*, celebrated as the birth-place, and early residence of *Krishn*, and still an object of pilgrimage amongst *Hindoos*.

मथुरिया muthoo-ríya, s. m. A caste of *Brahmuns* of *Muthoora* (*Muttra*).

मथुरनी muthoor-née, s. f. The female of *Muthooriya*.

मथौट muthóut, s. m. Contribution, subscription, capitation.

मथौरा muthóura, s. m. A parasol, parapluie, umbrella.

मद mud, s. m. Spirituous or vinous liquor; inebriety, intoxication; pride, arrogance.

मदन múd-un, s. m. Love, lust; *Kamdev*, the *Hindoo* Cupid; a medicinal plant, *Datura*; the plant called *mynphul* (*Gardenia dumetorum: Vangueri a spinosa*). *Mudun-ban*, s. m. Name of a flower.

मदनवश mud-un-vúsh, adj. Subdued by love, in love.

मदमाता mud-máta, m. } adj. Drunk, in-
मदमाती mud-mátee, f. } toxicated.

मदार mud-ár, s. f. A plant (*Asclepias gigantea*).

मदारिया mud-aríya, s. m. The followers of *Mudar*, a Mahomedan mendicant.

मदारी mud-áree, s. m. A juggler.

मदिक mud-ík, *adj.* Proud.

मदिरा múd-ir-a, *s. f.* Wine, spirits, spirituous or vinous liquor.

मदुरसी mud-góorsee, *s. f.* A sort of fish.

मद्य múd-yuh, *s. m.* Wine, vinous or spirituous liquor.

मद्यपीत mudyu-péet, *adj.* Drunk, a drunkard.

मद्यमाता mudh-máta, *adj.* Intoxicated, drunk.

मधु múd-hoo, *s. m.* Spirituous liquor; the nectar or honey of flowers; honey; the season of spring; the month Chyt (March-April).

मधुकर múdhoo-kúr, *s. m.* A bee; a plant (Achyranthes aspera); a fruit, the round sweet lime.

मधुकोष mudhoo-kósh, *s. m.* The honey-comb or hive.

मधुतृण mudhoo-trín, *s. m.* Sugar-cane.

मधुप múdhoop, *s. m.* A bee.

मधुपर्क mudhoo-púrk, *s. m.* A dish of curds, ghee and honey, to be offered to a respectable guest on his arrival.

मधुमय mudhoo-múy, *adj.* Sweet, luscious.

मधुमाखी mudhoo-mákhee, *s. f.* A honey-bee.

मधुमास mudhoo-mát, *s. m.* A Raginee or musical mode.

मधुमाता múdhoo-máta, *adj.* Intoxicated, drunk.

मधुमास mudhoo-más, *s. m.* The month Chyt (March-April).

मधुर múdhoor, *adj.* Sweet; pleasing, agreeable, liked.

मधुरस mudhoo-rús, *s. m.* Sweetness (in flavour); sweetness (in speech).

मधुरी mudhoo-rée, *adj.* Sweet.

मधूकरी mudhóok-ree, *s. f.* A kind of bread baked on live coals (used among the fukeers); victuals given in alms to pilgrims.

मधूलुक mudhóo-luk, *s. m.* A sort of Bassia, growing in watery or mountainous situations; sweetness.

मध्य múdh-yuh, *adj.* Middle, intermediate. *adv.* Amongst, amidst, amid. *s. m.* The middle, centre.

मध्यदेश mudhyuh-désh, *s. m.* The middle region; part of India, bounded by Koorookshetr on the north, Allahabad on the south, the Himaluy mountains on the east, and the Vindhya mountains on the west; comprising therefore the modern provinces of Allahabad, Agra, Delhi, Oude, &c.; the northern limit is elsewhere defined to be the disappearance of the Suruswutes.

3 C

मध्यभाग mudhyuh-bhág, *s. m.* The centre.

मध्यम mudh-yúm, *adj.* Middle, centrical, intervening, intermediate, middling, temperate. *s. m.* One of the seven musical notes, the fifth note of the Hindoo gamut.

मध्यमलोक mudhyúm-lók, } *s. m.* The earth,
मध्यलोक mudhyu-lók, } the world of mortals.

मध्यमा mudhyum-á, *s. f.* The middle finger.

मध्यवर्ती mudhyuh-vúrttee, *adj.* Central, middle; being amongst or amidst. *s. m.* A mediator.

मध्यस्थ mudh-yústh, *adj.* Centrical, middle. *s. m.* A middle man, an umpire, and arbitrator, a mediator.

मध्यस्थता mudhyusth-tá, *s. f.* Middle state or character.

मध्याह्न mudh-yánh, *s. m.* Midday, noon.

मन mun, *s. m.* Mind, heart, soul, spirit, inclination. Mun-chor, Heart-stealer. Mun-durawurdee, *adj.* Fanciful, invented (speech or story). Mun-poorun, Confidence, satisfaction of mind. Mun-bhana, *v. n.* To be agreeable to the mind. *adj.* Grateful to the mind. *s* A sweetheart, mistress. Mun-bhana moondiya hilana, To shake the head at what one approves of, to pretend to refuse that which one secretly desires. Mun-man, s. Heart's desire, choice. Mun-manta, or Mun-mana, *adj.* Agreeable, pleasing, satisfactory, to one's heart's wish or content. *s.* A mistress, sweetheart. Mun-maneh, As the mind may desire. Mun-marruhna, To suffer grief with patience. Mun-lugun, Heart-attachment, heart-engaging. Mun-lana, To fix the mind upon, to be attentive, to apply to. Mun-heen-men, In the very soul.

मन mun, *s. m.* A weight (40 ser or) seventy-eight pounds.

मनका munka, *s. m.* A rosary, a bead; the vertebræ of the neck. Munka dhulukna, To be at the point of death.

मनकामना mun-kámna, *s. f.* Desire, wish.

मनगरा mungúra, *adj.* Powerful.

मनघटा mun-ghút-a, *s. m.* The raised masonry round the mouth of a well.

मनचला mun-chúl-a, *adj.* Assiduous, intent, eager, active, bold.

मनजन munjún, *s. m.* Tooth-powder, dentifrice; cleaning the person by wiping, bathing, or rubbing it with oil or fragrant unguents.

मनत mun-út, *s. f.* Acknowledgment.

मनन mún-un, *s. m.* Minding, understanding.

मनभावन mun-bháwun, } *adj.* Acceptable,
मनभावना mun-bháona, } agreeable, pleasant, amusing, charming.

मनमथ mun-múth, *s. m.* Cupid.

मनमारना mun-márna, *v. a.* To resist one's own inclination, to be grieved or troubled in mind.

मनमोहन mun-móhun (*heart ravishing*). *s. m.* A sweetheart, mistress; a name of *Krishn.*

मनमौज mun-móuj, *s. m.* Self-conceit.

मनमौजी mun-móujee, *adj.* Self-conceited.

मनस् mun-ús, *s. m.* The mind, or considered as the seat of perception and passion, the heart; the intellect, the understanding.

मनसरवा mun-súrwa, *s. m.* A man, male.

मनसा mún-sa, } *s.f.* The goddess
मनसादेवी munsa-dévee, } of the serpent race, and the particular protectress against their venom.

मनसा mún-sa, *s. f.* Wish, desire, intention, design, purport, purpose.

मनसिज mun-síj, } *adj.* Mental, intellectu-
मनस्क mun-úsk, } al.

मनसेरू mun-séroo, *s. m.* A man.

मनस्कार mun-uskár, *s. m.* The attention of the mind to its own sensations, consciousness of pleasure or pain.

मनस्ताप munus-táp, *s. m.* Mental distress.

मनहरन mun-húrun, *s. m.* Heart-stealing.

मनहारी mun-háree, *adj. m.* Heart-stealer.

मनहूं munuhóo, *adv.* Suppose, as if, like.

मनाना mun-ána, *v. a.* To persuade, cause to agree (*to any thing*), conciliate, propitiate, sooth, coax, assuage, appease, put in mind; to do, act, perform, make. *Munana-dunana,* To appease, conciliate.

मनार्थ mun-árth, *s. m.* Intention, desire, purpose.

मनि múni, } *s. f. m.* A gem, a jewel.
मन mun, }

मनिहार muni-hár, *s. m.* A person who makes or sells (*choorees*) the glass bracelets, which the women wear on their wrists.

मनिहारी muni-háree, *s. f.* The trade in jewels, &c.

मनीथनी múnee-thúnee, *s. m.* A blemish in horses.

मनु mún-oo, *s. m. Menu,* the legislator and saint, the son of *Bruhma,* or a personification of *Bruhma* himself, the creator of the world, and progenitor of mankind; the name is however a generic term, and in every *Kulp* or interval from creation to creation, there are fourteen successive *Menus* presiding over the universe for the period of a *Munwuntura,* respectively : in the present creation there have been the six following *Menus:* *Menu* called also *Swuyumbhooruh,* the supposed revealer of the code of law possessed by the Hin-

doos, *Swurochisha, Oottum, Tamus, Ruyvut,* and *Chakshoosh ;* the seventh or the present *Menu* is *Vuyvuswut,* or *Ruyvut* the second. A man in general.

मनुज mun-óoj, *s. m.* A man in general.

मनुजा mun-oojá, *s.f.* A woman.

मनुषी mun-ooshée, *s. f.* A woman, the wife or female of the man.

मनुष्य mun-óoshyuh, *s. m.* Man, a man, mankind.

मनुष्यत्व munooshyu-twúh, *s. m.* The state or condition of man, manhood, humanity.

मनुहार mun-oohár, } *adj. f.* Charming,
मनुहारी munooháree, } fascinating, delighting, captivating the mind.

मनुसा mun-óoa, *s. f.* A kind of cotton. *s. m.* Puss (*a cat*); mind, soul, life.

मनो mún-o, *adv.* Like, as if.

मनोगत mun-ógut, *adj.* Seated in the mind.

मनोगुप्त mun-ógoopt, *adj.* Thought or meditated on secretly.

मनोज्ञ mun-ógyuh, *adj.* Beautiful, handsome, lovely, pleasing, agreeable.

मनोनीत mun-onéet, *adj.* Chosen, preferred.

मनोरथ mun-óruth, *s. m.* Wish, desire, design, intention. [pleasing.

मनोरम mun-órum, *adj.* Beautiful, lovely,

मनोल्लास mun-olóulyuh, *s. m.* Fancy, caprice, whim.

मनोहर mun-ohúr, *adj.* Heart-ravishing, beautiful, lovely, pleasing.

मनोहारिणी mun-oharín-ee, *f.* } *adj.* Beau-
मनोहारी mun-oháree, *m.* } tiful, pleasing, agreeable, lovely.

मनौती mun-óutee, *s. f.* Bail, security, a person referred to to pay the debt, &c. of another, surety, assurance, acknowledgment.

मन्त्र muntr, *s. m.* A division of the *Veds ;* a mystical verse or incantation ; a formula sacred to any individual deity ; a charm, philter, spell, incantation ; secret consultation, private advice. *Muntr-juntr,* Incantation, exorcism.

मन्त्रगुप्ति muntr-góopti, *s. f.* Secret counsel.

मन्त्रना muntr-ná, *s. f.* Advising, counselling in private, advice.

मन्त्री mun-trée, *s. m.* A counsellor or adviser, a king's counsellor or minister ; enchanter.

मन्थ munth, *s. m.* A churning stick ; a dish made of barley-meal with *ghee* and water, a sort of gruel or porridge ; a disease of the eyes, cataract or opacity ; rheum, excretion of the eyes.

मन्थन mun-thún, *s. m.* Agitating, stirring, churning.

मन्थनी mun-thun-ée, *s. f.* A churn.

मन्द mund, *adj.* Abated, slow, tedious, dull, foolish; bad, ill; low (*as a tone*). *s. m.* The planet Saturn; Saturday. *Mund-guti,* Slow (*in*) pace. *adv.* Slowly, softly. *Mund-mund, adv.* Gently, softly.

मन्दता mund-tá, *s. f.* Dulness, littleness, slowness, feebleness, badness.

मन्दबुद्धि mund-bóoddhi, *adj.* Stupid, foolish.

मन्दभाग्य mund-bhágyuh, *adj.* Wretched, unhappy, unfortunate.

मन्दमति mund-múti, *adj.* Dull, stupid, slow of apprehension.

मन्दयमान mund-yumán, *adj.* Slow, tardy.

मन्दर mún-dur, *adj.* Large, bulky. *s. m.* The mountain *Mundur,* with which the ocean is said to have been churned by the *Soors* and *Usoors,* after the deluge, for the purpose of recovering the sacred things lost in it during that period; the *Mundur* tree or one of the trees of paradise; *Swurg* or the paradise of the *Hindoos.*

मन्दरा mun-dur-á, *adj.* Squat, dapper.

मन्दहास्य mund-hásyuh, *s. m.* A smile, a gentle laugh.

मन्दा mundá, *adj.* Gentle, mild, affable, cheap, abated, allayed, slow, tardy; little.

मन्दात्मा mund-átma, *adj.* Slow of apprehension, dull.

मन्दादर mund-ádur, *adj.* Disregarding, neglecting, disrespecting.

मन्दायमान mund-ayumán, *adj.* Delaying, going tardily.

मन्दार mun-dár, *s. m.* One of the five trees of *Swurg;* the coral tree (*Erythrina fulgens*); swallow wort (*Asclepias gigantea*).

मन्दिकूकुर múndi-kóokoor, *s. f.* A sort of fish.

मन्दिर mún-dir, *s. m.* A house, dwelling, temple.

मन्नत mun-nút, *s. f.* Acknowledgment.

मन्ना mun-ná, *v. n.* To be soothed, propitiated.

मन्मथ mun-múth, *s. m.* A name of *Kam,* the god of love; love, amorous passion or desire.

मन्मथी mun-múth-ee, *adj.* Amorous, impassioned, in love.

मन्वन्तर mun-wún-tur, *s. m.* The reign of a *Menu,* a period equal to seventy-one ages of the gods, or 306,720,000 years of mortals, or with its *Sundhi* or interval of universal deluge, 308,448,000 years; fourteen *Munwunturas* constitute a *Kulp,* the grand period of creation and destruction, or

4,320,000,000 years; each *Munwuntura* is governed by its distinct *Menu,* and is provided with its own *Indr,* and minor deities; according to *Hindoo* cosmogony there have been innumerable *Munwunturas* since the first creation of the world.

मन्वान mun-wán, *adj.* Thinking, conceiving; minding, regarding.

मपुतखपुत múput-khúput, *s. f.* Measure.

मपना múpna, *v. n.* To be measured.

मपवाना mup-wána, *v. a.* To cause to measure.

मपान mup-án, *s. m.* Measure.

मपाना mup-ána, *v. a.* To cause to be measured.

मम mum, *pron.* My, mine.

ममता mum-tá, *s. f.* Pride, arrogance, self-sufficiency; the interest or affection entertained for other objects from considering them as belonging to, or connected with, one's self, affection.

ममतायुक्त mumta-jóokt, *adj.* Selfish. *s. m.* A miser, a niggard.

ममियासुर múmiya-súsoor, *s. m.* Husband or wife's maternal uncle.

ममियासास múmiya-sás, *s. f.* Husband or wife's maternal aunt.

ममेरा mum-éra, *adj.* Relating to the maternal uncle; as, *Mumera bhaee,* Mother's brother's son, cousin. *Mumeree buhin,* Mother's brother's daughter.

ममोडा mum-óra, *s. m.* Twist; ache, pain (*particularly in the bowels*).

मय muy, (*in comp.*) Composed of, chiefly consisting or made of.

मयना múy-na, *s. f.* A bird, a kind of jay (*Coracias Indica*).

मया múy-a, *s. f.* Kindness, pity, sympathy, compassion, mercy, feeling, affection.

मयी muyée, *s. f.* A harrow; a ladder.

मयूख muyóokh, *s. m.* The pin or gnomon of a sun-dial.

मयूर muyóor, *s. m.* A peacock; a flower, the coxcomb (*Celosia cristata*); a plant (*Achyranthes aspera*).

मयूरचूडा muyoór-chóora, *s. f.* Coxcomb (*Celosia cristata*).

मयूरारि muyoorári, *s. m.* A chameleon, a lizard.

मयूरी muyoorée, *s. f.* A peahen.

मरक múr-uk, *s. m.* Epidemic or pestilential disease.

मरकचा mur-kúch-a, *s. m.* The ridge of a house.

मरकट mur-kút, *s. m.* A monkey, an ape.

मरकत mur-kút, *s. m.* An emerald.

मरकर múr-kur, (lit. *having died*,) *adv.* With difficulty.

मरकुहा mur-kuhá, ⎫
मरखूना mur-khún-a, ⎬ *adj.* Addicted to beating, striking, or butting (*a man or animal*).
मरखाहा mur-kháha, ⎭

मरखूपना mur-khúpna, *v. n.* To die.

मरगुल mur-gúl, *adj.* Fried (*fish*).

मरघट mur-ghút, *s. m.* The place where *Hindoos* burn their dead.

मर जाना múr-jana, *v. n.* To die.

मर जीया mur-jéeya, *s. m.* A diver.

मरन múr-un, *s. f.* Death, dying.

मरदनियां murdun-iyán, *s. m. pl.* Attendants whose business it is to rub oil, perfumed paste, &c. over the body.

मरना múr-na, *v. n.* To die, expire, cease ; (*met.*) to desire vehemently, to set one's heart upon any thing, to dote. *s. m.* Dying.

मरपच mur-púch, *adj.* Rotten, fermented, macerated.

मरपचना murpuch-ná, *v. n.* To suffer pain or sorrow ; to labour excessively.

मरभूखा mur-bhóokha, *adj.* Starved to death, greedy, voracious, ravenous.

मरम múr-um, *s. m.* Secret meaning or purpose, a secret, any thing hidden or recondite.

मरमर múr-mur, *s. m.* Sound made by treading upon dry leaves, &c.

मरमराना mur-murána, *v. a.* To creak as a new shoe (*an imitative sound*).

मररूहना mur-rúhna, *v. n.* To be dead ; to be deeply in love.

मरवाना mur-wána, *v. a.* To cause to be beaten, to cause to be killed.

मरषा múr-sha, *s. m.* A pot-herb (*Amaranthus oleraceus*).

मरहट्टा mur-hútta, *s. m.* A *Marhatta*.

मराल mur-ál, *s. m.* A sort of goose with red legs and bill, or perhaps the Flamingo ; a duck.

मरिच múr-ich, *s. f.* Pepper.

मरियल múr-iyul, *adj.* Lean, emaciated, much reduced by sickness.

मरी múr-ee, *s. f.* The plague.

मरीच mur-éech, *s. f.* Pepper (*Piper nigrum*).

मरीचि mur-éechi, *s. f.* A ray of light, a sun-beam. *s. m.* A saint, the son of *Bruhma*, and one of the *Prajuputis*, and *Bruhmadikas*, or first created beings and sovereigns of the world ; a niggard, a miser.

मरीचिका mureechiká, *s. f.* The mirage,

vapour which in hot and sandy countries especially appears at a distance like a sheet of water.

मरू múr-oo, *s. m.* A region or soil destitute of water, sands, a desert ; the province of *Marwar*.

मरूवा múr-oon, *s. m.* A strong-scented plant (*Artemisia vulgaris*) ; *Ocymum pilosum*.

मरूभू mur-oo-bhóo, *s. m.* The province of *Marwar*.

मरूस्थल mur-oo-sthúl, *s. m.* A desert, a dry and desert tract. *adj.* Barren, dry, without water, desert.

मरोर mur-ór, *s. f.* Twist, flexion, turn, writhe, convolution, contortion. *Muror-bas*, An affected person.

मरोरना mur-órna, *v. a.* To twist, writhe, contort, distort, gripe, yearn.

मरोरफूली murór-phúlee, *s. f.* A plant (*Helicteres isora*), the fruit of which is used in medicine.

मरोरा mur-óra, *s. m.* A twisting of the bowels, pain in the bowels, flux, gripes.

मरोरी mur-óree, *s. f.* Twisting, writhing.

मरोलि mur-óli, *s. m.* The *Mukur*, a marine monster, apparently the *Monodon* or *Unicorn*, and usually confounded with the crocodile or shark.

मरोह mur-óh, *s. f.* Affection, kindness, humanity, pity.

मरोही mur-óhee, *adj.* Affectionate.

मर्कट múr-kut, *s. m.* A monkey or ape.

मर्कटी murkut-ée, *s. f.* A small or female monkey.

मर्कटेंदु murkut-éndoo, *s. m.* A sort of ebony (*Diospyros melanoxylon*).

मर्त्तव्य murttúv-yuh, *adj.* Mortal, what must or should die.

मर्त्य múrttyuh, *s. m.* A man, a mortal.

मर्त्यलोक murttyuh-lók, *s. m.* The earth, the world, the habitation of mortals.

मर्दन murd-dún, *s. m.* Rubbing, anointing, bruising, trampling, treading down, grinding, pounding.

मर्दित murd-dít, *adj.* Rubbed, anointed, &c.

मर्म murmm, *s. m.* Secret meaning or purpose, a secret, any thing hidden or recondite.

मर्मर múrmmur, *s. m.* The rustling sound of cloth on dry leaves.

मर्मरी murmmur-ée, *s. f.* A sort of pine (*Pinus Devadaru*).

मर्मज्ञ murmmúgyuh, *s. m.* A learned or intelligent man or *Brahmun*.

मर्मवेदी murmm-védee, *s. m.* An acute and intelligent man.

मर्य्याद murj-ják, } *s. f.* Station, rank,
मर्य्यादा murj-jáda, } dignity, respect, continuance in the right way, propriety of conduct, steadiness, rectitude.

मर्य्यादिक murjja-dík, *adj.* Respectable.

मज्ज mul, *s. m.* Excretion of the body, as serum, semen, blood, marrow, urine, fæces, earwax, nails, phlegm, tears, rheum, and sweat; dirt, filth; dreg, sediment; rust.

मज्जकना múl-uk-na, *v. n.* To walk like a chairman, &c. (*trotting and raising the shoulders*).

मज्जङ múl-ung, *s. m.* A kind of *dervis*; a kind of bird.

मज्जङी mul-úng-ee, *s. m.* A salt-maker.

मज्जत múl-ut, *s. m.* A worn rupee or other coin.

मज्जदज múl-dul, *s. m.* Rubbing, grinding.

मज्जन múl-un, *s. m.* Rubbing, grinding, &c.

मज्जना múl-na, *v. a.* To rub, tread on, trample on, anoint.

मज्जबा múlba, *s. m.* Rubbish.

मज्जमज múl-mul, *s. f.* Muslin.

मज्जमास mul-más, *s. m.* An intercalary month.

मज्जमेट mul-mét, *adj.* Ruined; decided (*in dispute*). *Mulmet kurna*, To destroy, raze. *Mulmet hona*, To be ruined, to perish.

मज्जय mul-úy, *s. m.* A mountain or mountainous range, from which the best *Sandal* wood is brought, answering to the western *Ghats* in the peninsula of India; the country that lies along the *Muluy* range, or the west coast of the peninsula, *Muluyalim*, or *Malabar*; one of the minor *dweeps* or divisions of the world.

मज्जयज mul-uy-új, *s. m. Sandal* wood.

मज्जया muluyá, *s. f.* A plant, commonly called *Teoree* (*Convolvulus turpethum*).

मज्जयागीरी muluya-géeree, *s. m.* The colour of *Sandal* wood.

मज्जयाचज muluya-chúl, *s. m.* The mountain *Muluy*.

मज्जवाई mul-wáee, *s. f.* Price of scouring, rubbing, &c.

मज्जाई muláee, *s. f.* Cream.

मज्जागिर mul-ágir, *s. m.* A mountain or mountainous range, from which the best *Sandal* wood is brought, answering to the western *Ghats* in the peninsula of India.

मज्जागीरी mul-a-géeree, *s. m.* The colour of *Sandal* wood.

मज्जामा mul-ána, *v. a.* To cause to rub, grind, or scour.

मज्जार mul-ár, *s. f.* A *Raginee* or musical mode sung during the rains.

मज्जिच múl-ichh, *adj.* An unclean race, those make no distinction between clean and unclean food, a barbarian or one speaking any language but *Sunskrit* and not subject to the usual *Hindoo* institutions.

मज्जिन múl-in, *m.* } *adj.* Dirty, filthy,
मज्जिना mul-in-á, *f.* } foul, vile, bad; foul (*figuratively*), soiled with crime or vice, sinful, depraved.

मज्जिनता mul-in-tá, *s. f.* Filth, impurity; vileness.

मज्जिनमुख mul-in-móokh, *adj.* Cruel, fierce, savage; vile, wicked.

मज्जिनी mul-ín-ee, *s. f.* A woman during menstruation.

मज्जिया múl-iya, *s. m.* A small vessel of wood, or of the shell of a cocoa-nut, for holding the oil used in unction.

मज्जिष्ठ mul-íshth, *m.* } *adj.* Very foul or
मज्जिष्ठा mul-ish-thá, *f.* } unclean; very wicked. *s. f.* A woman during menstruation.

मज्जीन mul-éen, *adj.* Filthy, foul, dirty; sad, vexed, indisposed, disturbed, troubled.

मज्जूक mul-óok, *s. m.* A kind of worm.

मज्जेच्छ mul-échh, *adj.* An unclean race, those who make no distinction between clean and unclean food, a barbarian or one speaking any language but *Sunskrit* and not subject to the usual *Hindoo* institutions.

मज्जेपुंज mul-epúnj, *adj.* Aged above ten years (*a horse*).

मज्जैया mul-úyya, *s. m.* Name of a mountain.

मज्ज mull, *adj.* Strong, stout, athletic, robust. *s. m.* A wrestler, a boxer, by birth.

मज्जभू mull-bhóo, *s. f.* A palæstrum or arena, a place for athletic contests; it is also applied to the site of any conflict, as a field of battle, &c.

मज्जयाचा mull-játra, *s. f.* A match of wrestling or boxing.

मज्जयुद्ध mull-jóoddh, *s. m.* Wrestling, boxing.

मज्जार mullár, } *s. f.* One of the *Ragi-*
मज्जारी mullarée, } *nees* or divisions of the musical mode *Megh* sung during the rains.

मज्जिका mullik-á, *s. f.* Arabian Jasmine (*Jasminum zambac*).

मज्जिगन्धि múlli-gúndhi, *s. m.* Aloe wood.

मज्जू múlloo, *s. m.* A bear.

मज्जास muwás, *s. m.* Protection, refuge, asylum, retreat.

मज्ज mush, *s. m.* A musquito.

मज्जक músh-uk, *s. m.* A gnat, a mosquito;

a kind of cutaneous eruption, the formation of small pustules or warts ; a leather water-bag.

मशहरी mush-húr-ee, *s. f.* Musquito curtains, bed curtains of gauze, or of any thin substance, used to keep off musquitoes.

मशरंगी mush-rúng-ee, *s. f.* A kind of pulse fried.

मशी músh-ee, *s. f.* Ink ; the stalk of the *Nyctanthes tristis.*

मश्ट musht, *s. f.* Silence. *Musht marna,* To remain silent.

मशक mús-uk, *s. m.* A gnat.

मशकना mús-uk-na, *v. n.* To be torn, split, rent, burst.

मशकाना mus-kána, *v. a.* To tear, rend, split, burst.

मशन mus-ún, *s. m.* A medicinal fruit (*Serratula anthelmintica*).

मशबिद mus-bírd, *s. m.* A wart, a fleshy excrescence or swelling.

मशमशाना mus-mus-ána. *v. n.* To suppress one's sentiments from fear.

मशलना mús-ul-na, *v. a.* To bruise, crush, break with the hand.

मशहरी mus-úh-ree, *s. f.* Curtains (*of a bed*), mosquito curtains.

मशा mús-a, *s. m.* A wart, a fleshy excrescence.

मशान mus-án, *s. m.* A place where a dead body is burnt or buried, a cemetry.

मशार mus-ár, *s. m.* An emerald.

मशि mús-i, *s. m.* } Ink.
मशी mús-ee, *s. f.* }

मशिधान musi-dhán, *s. m.* } An inkstand.
मशिधानी musi-dhánee, *s. f.* }

मशी mús-ee, *s. f.* Ink.

मशीन mus-éen, *s. m.* A vetch, pulse.

मशीना mus-éena, *s. f.* Linseed (*Linum utilatissimum*).

मशीह mus-éeh, *n. prop.* Messiah, Christ, the Anointed, the Saviour of the world.

मशीहाई museehái, } adj. Of the Messiah.
मशीही museehée, } *s. m.* A follower of Christ, a Christian.

मशूड़ा mus-óora, *s. m.* The gums (*of the teeth*).

मशूर mus-óor, *s. f.* A sort of pulse or lentil (*Ervum hirsutum,* and *Cicer lens*).

मशूरिया mus-óoriya, } *s. f.* A kind of
मशूरी mus-óoree, } small-pox.

मशें mús-en, *s. f. pl.* Down, small hairs on the lips before the beard grows.

मशोसना mus-ósna, *v. a.* To twist ; to squeeze, wring ; to regret, to grieve.

मशोसा mus-ósa, *adj.* Twisted ; grieved, afflicted. *s. m.* Affliction, remorse, regret.

मस्तक mús-tuk, *s. m. f.* The head, the skull ; the forehead ; the head or top of any thing.

मसूल mus-tóol, *s. m.* Mast of a ship.

मस्सा mús-sa, *s. m.* A wart, a fleshy excrescence.

महंगा muhúnga, *adj. m.* Dear, high-priced, expensive.

महंगी muhung-ée, *s. f.* Dearth, scarcity, famine. *adj. f.* Dear.

मह़क múhuk, *s. f.* Odour, perfume, fragrance.

महकना muhúkna, *v. n.* To exhale agreeable smells, to emit odour, to perfume.

महकाना muhukána, *v. a.* To exhale (*agreeable scent*), to perfume.

महकीला muhuk-éela, *adj.* Odoriferous, fragrant, spicy, aromatic.

महक्क muhúkk, *s. m.* Diffusive fragrance.

महत múhut, *adj.* Great, glorious ; large, bulky ; excellent, illustrious. *s. f.* Greatness, grandeur, dignity.

महतो muhtó, *s. m.* A person employed by the land-holder to collect the rent from a village, a land-bailiff.

महतारी muh-táree, *s. f.* A mother.

महत्व muhuttwúh, *s. m.* Greatness, either in bulk or rank.

महदाश्रय múhud-ásruy, *adj.* Dependant upon or attached to the great.

महना múh-na, *v. a.* To churn.

महन्त múbunt, *s. m.* A monk, an abbot, prior, a religious superior, a chief of the *fukeers.*

महन्ताई muhuntáee, *s. f.* The business of a *Muhunt.*

महर múbur, *s. m.* A chief. *s. f.* A woman, wife, female.

महरा múhra, *s. m.* A *palkee*-bearer.

महराई muhráee, *s. f.* The business of a *palkee*-bearer ; a kind of song among the cowherds.

महरि múhri, *s. f.* A woman.

महर्लोक muhur-lók, *s. m.* A division of the universe ; a region said to be one *crore* of *yojuns* above the polar star, and to be the abode of those saints who survive a destruction of the world.

महल्लक muhullúk, *s. m.* A eunuch employed in a *Haram.*

महा múha, *adj.* Great, illustrious ; very, extremely.

मह‍ाकन्द muha-kund, s. m. Garlic; a very large esculent root, a sort of yam.

महाकाय muha-káyuh, adj. Large, bulky, stout.

महाकाल muha-kál, s. m. A name or rather a form of *Shiv*, in his character of the destroying deity, being then represented of a black colour, and of aspect more or less terrific. *Shiv* or *Muha-kal* may be considered as a personification of time that destroys all things.

महाकाली muha-kálee, s. f. The wife of the preceding deity, and a terrific form of *Doorga*.

महाकुल muha-kool, adj. Eminent by birth, of good family or extraction.

महाकुलीन muha-kooléen, adj. Of good family.

महाकूप muha-kóop, s. m. A large or deep well.

महाकूल muha-kóol, adj. Of a good family.

महाकोड muha-kórh, s. m. A species of leprosy (*great leprosy*), perhaps the elephantiasis.

महाजन muhájun, s. m. A banker, money-dealer, merchant; a good or trust-worthy person.

महाजनी muha-junée, s. f. The business of a *Muhajun*; interest.

महाज्ञान muha-ján, adj. Very wise.

महाजाल muha-jál, s. m. A seine.

महादोल muha-dól, s. m. A large and splendid sort of sedan or *palkee*.

महात्म muhá-tum, s. m. Greatness, gran-deur, rank, dignity; the benefit supposed to be de-rived from any good work.

महातमप्रभा muhatúm-prubhá, s. f. The lowermost division of *Nuruk* or hell.

महातल muha-túl, s. m. The fifth in de-scent of the seven *patals* or regions under the earth, said to be inhabited by various races of evil beings, as the *Nags*, *Usoors*, *Dyts*, &c.

महातिक्त muha-tíkt, adj. Very bitter. s. m. The large *Nimb* tree (*Melia sempervirens*).

महातीक्ष्ण muha-téeshn, adj. Very sharp (*as flavour*), or literally (*as a weapon*), or figura-tively (*as perception, &c.*)

महातेजा múha-téja, adj. Very bright; very energetic or vigorous.

महात्मा muhátma, adj. Liberal, lofty-mind-ed, magnanimous.

महादन्त muha-dúnt, s. m. An elephant with large tusks; an elephant's tusk.

महादेव muha-dév, s. m. *Shiv*, one of the principal *Hindoo* gods.

महाधातु múha-dhátoo, s. m. Gold.

महानन्द muha-núnd, s. m. Eternal eman-cipation or beatitude.

महानरक múha-núruk, s. m. One of the hells or divisions of Tartarus.

महानिद्रा múha-nídra, s. f. Death, dying.

महानिम्ब muha-nímb, s. m. A large kind of *Nimb* tree (*Melia sempervirens*).

महानिशा múha-nísha, s. f. Midnight.

महानील muha-néel, s. m. The emerald.

महानुभाव muhánoo-bháo, adj. Magnani-mous, liberal. s. m. A gentleman.

महापक्षी múha-púkshee, s. f. An owl.

महापथ muha-púth, s. m. The principal path or entrance to a town or house, &c., a main road, a highway; the end of life, the way of all flesh.

महापातक múha-pátuk, s. m. A crime of the highest degree, as, killing a *Brahmun*, stealing gold from a priest, drinking spirits, adultery with the wife of a spiritual teacher, and associating with persons who have committed these offences; great crime in general.

महापातकी múha-patukée, s. m. An offender in the highest degree.

महापाप múha-páp, s. m. Atrocity, great sin; heinous crime or sin in general.

महापापी múha-pápee, adj. Atrocious, great sinner.

महापासक múha-pásuk, s. m. A religious mendicant.

महापूरुष múha-póoroosh, s. m. A great man, a holy man.

महापुष्पा múha-póoshpa, s. f. A flower (*Clitoria ternatea*).

महाप्रभु múha-prúbhoo, s. m. A holy man, a saint; a king.

महाप्रलय múha-prúluy, s. m. A destruc-tion of the world said to occur after every period of 4,320,000,000 years; a total destruction of the universe happening after a period commensurate with the life of *Bruhma*, or 100 years, each day of which is equal to the period first stated, and each night of which is of similar duration; at the expi-ration of this term, the seven *Loks*, with the saints, gods, and *Bruhma* himself, are said to be annihi-lated.

महाप्रसाद múha-prusád, s. m. The meat which is offered to the deity (*especially to Juggun-nath*) and afterwards distributed.

महाबली muha-búl-ee, adj. Very powerful.

महाब्राह्मण múha-bráhmun, s. m. A priest who officiates at funeral ceremonies; and is first fed after the mourning for a dead person.

महाभाग muha-bhág, adj. Virtuous in a high degree, pure, holy; eminent, exalted.

महाभागता múha-bhagtá, s. f. Possession of the eight cardinal virtues, clemency, &c.; exalted station or merit.

मयाभारत múha-bhárut, *s. m.* A grand epic poem by *Vyas-dev*, containing an account of the dissensions and wars of the *Kooroos* and *Pandoos*, two great collateral branches of the house of *Bharut*, so called from *Bhurut* its founder; the great war of the descendants of *Bhurut*.

मयाभीत muha-bhéet, *adj.* Very timid, pusillanimous, cowardly.

मयाभीता múha-bheetá, *s. f.* A sort of sensitive plant (*Mimosa pudica*).

मयामांष muha-máns, *s. m.* Human flesh. (*One who takes money on giving his daughter in marriage is said to sell muhamans, human flesh*).

मयामाया múha-máya, *s. f.* Doorga; worldly illusion or unreality.

मयामाष muha-másh, *s. m.* A kind of bean (*Dolichos catjang*).

मयामूल्य muha-móolyuh, *adj.* Costly, precious. *s. m.* A ruby.

मयामेद muha-méd, *s. m.* The coral tree (*Erythrina Indica*); a drug, classed amongst the principal drugs, and described as a tonic, and stimulant.

मयायज्ञ muha-júgyuh, *s. m.* An essential sacrifice, a sacrament of the *Hindoo* religion: five acts are enumerated of this description, severally considered as due to the *Veds*, to the gods, to man, to the manes, and to all created beings; they are respectively, study of scripture, offering of sacrifice to the gods, hospitable treatment of guests, libation of water, &c. to deceased progenitors, and the casting of food on the ground or in water as an offering to the gods, to spirits, &c.

मयायन्त्र muha-júntr, *s. m.* Any great mechanical work, as a lock or dyke.

मयायशा múha-júsha, *adj.* Illustrious, celebrated.

मयायुग muha-jóog, *s. m.* A great *Joog*; the aggregate of the four ages, or a period of four million, three hundred and twenty thousand years.

मयाराज muha-ráj, *s. m.* A sovereign, an emperor; great king, excellency.

मयाराजा múha-rája, *s. m.* A *Hindoo* emperor.

मयाराजाधिराज muharája-dhiráj, *s. m.* A paramount sovereign, an emperor.

मयारात्र muha-rátr, *s. m.* Midnight.

मयारानी múha-ránee, *s. f.* An empress.

मयालय muha-lúy, *s. m.* God, the Supreme Being; a place of refuge, a sanctuary, an asylum.

मयालोह muha-lóh, *s. m.* The loadstone.

मयावठ muhawúth, *s. m.* Rain which falls in the month of *Magh*.

मयावत muhawút, *s. m.* An elephant driver or keeper.

मयावन muha-vún, *s. m.* A large forest.

मयावर muháwur, *s. m.* Lac, the red animal die so called extracted from lac insects.

मयाविष muha-vísh, *s. m.* A small venemous snake, supposed to be two-headed.

मयाविषुव múha-víshoov, *s. m.* The *Sunkranti* or moment of the sun's entering *Aries*; the vernal equinox, but varying several days from the European computation.

मयावीचि múha-véechi, *s. f.* One of the divisions of Tartarus.

मयाशंख muha-shúnkh, *s. m.* A thousand millions.

मयाशय muha-shúy, *adj.* Magnanimous, liberal, munificent.

मयासत्व muha-sútwuh, *adj.* Good, virtuous, just.

मयासांतपन múha-santúpun, *s. m.* A sort of penance; subsisting for six successive days respectively, on cow's urine, cow-dung, milk, curds, *ghee*, and water in which *Koosa* grass has been boiled, and fasting on the seventh day; instead of one day some authorities assign a period of three days to each, considering the first as the common *Santupun* penance; others omit the two last periods, making it last fifteen days.

मयासाहस múha-sáhus, *s. m.* Excessive violence, brutal assault.

मयासुख muha-sóokh, *s. m.* Copulation.

मयासूक्ष्म múha-sóokshm, *adj.* Subtile, fine, minute.

मयाहास muha-hás, *s. m.* A horse-laugh.

मयि múhi, *s. f.* The earth.

मयिमा múhima, *s. f.* Greatness in general, literal or figurative.

मयिष múhish, *s. m.* A buffalo.

मयिषाक्ष muhish-áksh, *s. m.* A plant, supposed to be the *Bdellium* tree.

मयिषी muhishée, *s. f.* A female buffalo.

मयी muhée, *s. f.* The earth; a river, the *Muhee* which rises in the province of *Malwa*, and after pursuing a westerly course of about 280 miles, falls into the upper part of the gulph of Cambay.

मयीतल muhée-tul, *s. m.* The surface of the earth.

मयीना muhéena, *s. m.* A month; monthly pay. *Muheena churhna*, To be in arrears. *Muheena-dar*, A monthly servant.

मयीप muhéep,
मयीपति mubee-púti, } *s. m.* A sovereign, a king.
मयीपाल muhee-pál,

मयीमय muhee-múy, *adj.* Earthen, made of earth or clay.

मयीरूह muhée-rooh, *s. m.* A tree.

मुहीलता muhee-lút-a, *s. f.* An earth-worm.

मुहुआ múhooa, } *s. m.* Name of a tree
मुहुआ muhóoa, } (*Bassia latifolia*) bearing flowers which are sweet, and from which a spirituous liquor is distilled. The nuts afford an oil used instead of butter.

मुहूरत muhóorut, } *s. m.* A division of
मुहूर्त muhóortt, } time, equal to 12 *kshuns* or 48 minutes.

मुहेंद्र muhéndr, *s. m. Indr*, the ruler of *Swurg*; a range of mountains, one of the seven principal chains in *Bharut Vursh* or India, and apparently the northern part of the *Ghats* of the peninsula.

मुहेर muhér, *s. m.* } A dish, consisting
मुहेरी muherée, *s. f.* } of rice or other grain, boiled in some milk.

मुहेला muhéla, *s. f.* A food given to horses, consisting of boiled kidney beans (*Phaseolus max*), a mash.

मुहेश muhésh, *s. m.* } *Shiv.*
मुहेश्वर muhésh-wur, }

मुहोक्ष muhóksh, *s. m.* A large bull or ox.

मुहोका muhóka, *s. m.* A bird (*Cuculus castaneus*).

मुहोत्सव muhót-suv, *s. m.* A great festival.

मुहोत्साह muhót-sah, *adj.* Persevering, diligent, making strenuous and unremitting exertion. *s. m.* Diligence, effort, exertion.

मुहोदय muhóduy, *s. m. Kunouj*, the ancient city and district; final beatitude, emancipation from vitality and absorption into the divine essence, prosperity, elevation, eminence.

मुहोदार muhodár, *adj.* Mighty, powerful.

मुहोद्यम muhód-yum, *adj.* Diligent, persevering, making strenuous and unremitting effort. *s. m.* Great effort, energy, exertion.

मुहोसा muhósa, *s. m* A freckle.

मुहोषुध muhóu-shudh, *s. m.* Garlic; a plant (*Betula*); long-pepper.

मुहोषधि muhóu-shúdhi, *s. f.* A sort of grass, commonly called *Doob*; a kind of sensitive plant (*Mimosa pudica*).

मुहोषधी muhóu-shudhée, *s. f.* Dry ginger; a potherb (*Hingta repens*).

मुह्यु muhyóu, *s. m.* Buttermilk.

मुक्षिका mukshiká, *s. f.* A bee.

मा ma, *s. f.* Mother; a name of *Luchhmee*.

माई máee, *s. f.* Mother.

माएं maéen, *s. f.* Aunt.

मां man, *postpos.* In. *s. f.* Mother.

मांग mang, *s. f.* A line on the top of the head where the hair is parted; a betrothed dam-sel; prow; division. *Mang nikalna*, To divide the hair in a straight line on the top of the head.

मांगचिकनी mang-chíknee, *s. f.* Name of a bird.

मांगदेना mang-déna, *v. a.* To borrow for another, to ask for and give.

मांगना máng-na, *v. a.* To ask for, require, demand, beg, pray, crave, solicit, want, desire, seek, betroth, will. *Mang tang kurna*, To ask for.

मांगनी mángnee, *s. f.* Asking or betrothing in marriage.

मांगलेना mang-léna, *v. a.* To borrow.

मांगी mang-ée, *s. f.* A loan, what is borrowed. *part.* Betrothed (*a woman*).

मांज manj, *s. m.* Pus, matter, serum.

मांजना mánj-na, *v. a.* To scour, scrub, clean.

मांझ manjh, *s. m.* The middle, in the middle, in; a *Raginee* or musical mode; a kind of verse. *Manjhdhar, s. f.* The mid-stream.

मांझत man-jhút, *s. f.* State, dignity.

मांझा mán-jha, *s. m.* A paste mixed with pounded glass, and applied to the string of a kite, to cut that of another with; a feast given by a bridegroom previous to the wedding; the trunk of a tree.

मांझी mán-jhee, *s. m.* Master of a vessel, a boatman, sailor, steersman, helmsman.

मांड mand, *s. m.* Rice-water, rice-gruel, starch, paste.

मांडना mánd-na, *v. a.* To rub, tread or trample down; to knead; to make, stir, excite, commit, perpetrate, produce; to starch.

मांडा mán-da, *s. m.* Film, speck (*on the eye*); a kind of bread.

मांडी mán-dee, *s. f.* Starch (*made of rice-flour*).

मांढा mán-dha, *s. m.* A temporary building, an open shed or hall, adorned with flowers and erected on festive occasions, as at marriages, &c.

मांद mand, *s. f.* Faded, a dull colour; a dunghill; the den of a wild beast.

मांस mans, *s. m.* Flesh, meat.

मांसी mans-ée, *s. f.* Indian spikenard (*Valeriana Jatamansi*).

मांसभक्ष mans-bhúksh, *adj.* Eating flesh, carnivorous.

माकंद ma-kúnd, *s. m.* The mango.

माकंदी ma-kún-dee, *s. f.* Emblic myrobalan.

माखन má-khun, *s. m.* Butter.

मागध má-gudh, *adj.* Belonging to, or produced in the province of *Mugudh* or south *Behar*.

s. m. A bard, a minstrel, whose duty it is to recite the praises of sovereigns, their genealogy, and the deeds of their ancestors, in their presence, and to attend on the march of an army, and animate the soldiers by martial songs. The minstrel forms a particular caste, said to spring from a *Vys* father and *Kshutree* mother; in mythology they are said to have been created at once by the will of *Shiv*. Under the name of *Bhats*, they are still numerous in the west of India, where they are a privileged tribe.

मागधा magudhá, *s. m. pl.* The inhabitants or people of *Mugudh*.

मागधी magud-hée, *s. f.* A kind of jasmine (*Jasminum auriculatum*); long-pepper (*Piper longum*); a sort of Cardamoms grown in *Guzerat*; a dialect of *Sunskrit*, one of the principal forms of *Prakrit*, and nearly the same as that used in the sacred books of the *Bouddhs* and *Jyns*.

मागना mág-na, *v. a.* To ask for.

माघ magh, *s. m.* One of the months of the *Hindoo* year (*January-February*).

माघी mag-hée, *s. f.* A potherb (*Hingsta repens*).

मांगलिक man-gul-ík, *adj.* Propitious, tending to good fortune.

मांगल्य man-gúl-yuh, *s. m.* Welfare, propitiousness.

माचा má-cha, *s. m.* A large bedstead or platform; a frame or stage on which they sit to drive away birds, &c. from corn-fields. *Machator, adj.* A lazy person who never stirs from his bed; a kind of soldier among the *Rajpoots*, very indolent and much addicted to opium, but active and brave when roused.

माची má-chee, *s. f.* A harrow; a small bedstead. [China.

माचीन ma-chéen, *s. m.* Name of a country,

माछर má-chhur, *s. m.* A mosquito.

माछी má-chhee, *s. f.* A fly.

माजाई ma-jaée, *f.* ⎱ *adj.* Born of the
माजाया ma-jayá, *m.* ⎰ same mother.

माजूफल majoo-phúl, *s. m.* A gall-nut.

मझधार majh-dhár, *s. f.* Mid-stream.

मांजिष्ठ man-jishth, *m.* ⎱ *adj.* Of a red
मांजिष्ठी man-jishthée, *f.* ⎰ colour.

माटी má-tee, *s. f.* Earth.

माठा má-tha, *s. m.* Buttermilk. *adj.* Perverse, lazy, obstinate.

माठू ma-thóo, *s. m.* A buffoon (*a term of reproach*).

मारनी marnee, *s. f.* Paste.

मारिया má-riya, *adj.* Lean, thin.

मानव ma-núv, *s. m.* A child; a man (*in a contemptuous sense*), a manikin.

मानवक man-vúk, *s. m.* A child, a boy not exceeding sixteen years of age, a manikin.

माणिक्य man-íkyuh, *s. m.* A ruby.

मात mat, *s. f.* Accent, a vowel; mother.

मातंग ma-túng, *s. m.* An elephant.

मातना mát-na, *v. n.* To be intoxicated.

माता má-ta, *s. f.* Mother; the small-pox. *adj.* Drunk, intoxicated.

मातापितृ máta-pítri, *m. du.* Mother and father.

मातामह máta-múhub, *s. m.* A maternal grandfather.

मातामही máta-múhee, *s. f.* A maternal grandmother.

मातुल ma-tóol, *s. m.* A maternal uncle.

मातुलपुत्रक mátool-póotruk, *s. m.* The son of a maternal uncle.

मातुला ma-toolá, ⎱ *s. f.* The wife of
मातुलानी matoolánee, ⎬ a maternal uncle,
मातुली matoo-lée, ⎰ &c.

मातृ matri, *s. f.* A mother.

मातृघातुक matri-ghátoek, *s. m.* A matricide.

मात्र matr, *adv.* Only, solely (*exclusive and identical, the very thing*).

मात्रक matrúk, *adj.* Mere, only, solely.

मात्रा mátra, *s. f.* A vowel (*point or symbol*); a dose, an ingredient.

मत्सर mat-súr, *adj.* Envious, or impatient of another's prosperity.

मत्सर्य mat-súrj, *s. m.* Envy, malice.

माथा má-tha, *s. m.* The forehead; prow; the ridge of a thatch. *Mutha thunukna* (*lit. ringing or throbbing of the forehead*), implies a presentiment of the conclusion, from certain marks observed in the commencement of an affair: and it is generally understood to indicate an unfortunate termination. *Mutha rugurna* (*lit. to rub the forehead, viz. on the ground*), To implore humbly (*of the Deity, a saint, or a king*). *Matheh pur churhna, v. a.* To tyrannise, to oppress.

माथीलेना máthee-léna, *v. a.* To make even (*particularly a thatch*).

माथुर má-thoor, *s. m.* An inhabitant of *Muthoora* (*Muttra*); a caste of *Kayusths*, also of *Brahmuns*.

मादक ma-dúk, *adj.* Intoxicating.

मादकता maduk-tá, *s. f.* Intoxication.

माधवी ma-dhuv-ée, *s. f.* A large creeper (*Gærtnera racemosa*).

माधूर्य ma-dhóorj-yuh, *s. m.* Sweetness of flavour or disposition.

माध्वी madh-wée, *s. f.* Spirituous liquor; a sort of fish.

माधूक madh-wéek, *s. m.* Spirituous liquor, distilled from the blossoms of the *Bassia latifolia* ; wine, spirit distilled from grapes.

मान man, *s. m.* Character, dignity, honor, respect ; arrogance, haughtiness, pride ; blandishment ; measure in general, whether of weight, length or capacity. *adj.* Like. *Man-gooman, s. m.* Dignity, state, honour. *Man-goun,* Respect.

मान man. *adv.* Suppose, grant.

मानक ma-núk, *s. m.* A plant, of which the root is sometimes eaten (*Arum indicum*).

मानता man-tá, *s. f.* Vow, promise.

माननीय manun-éeyuh, *adj.* To be respected or revered.

मानव ma-núv, *s. m.* A man, man ; a boy.

मानवत man-wút, *m.* } *adj.* Proud,
मानवती man-wut-ée, *f.* } haughty, high-spirited.

मानवर्जित man-vurjjít, *m.* } *adj.* Humble, lowly
मानवर्जिता man-vurjjittá, *f.* }

मानवी ma-nuv-ée, *s. f.* A woman.

मानस ma-nús, *adj.* Mental. *s. m.* The mind, the seat or faculty of reason and feeling ; the lake *Manus* or *Mansurowur* in the *Himaluy* mountains.

मानसत्व manus-twúh, *s. m.* Thoughtfulness.

मानसम्वान man-sunwán, *s. m.* Welcome.

मानहू man-hóo, *adv.* Suppose, grant, as if, like, resembling.

मानिक má-nik, *s. m.* A kind of gem, ruby. *Leed ka manik,* A horse.

मानिकजोर manik-jór, *s. m.* A bird (*Ardea leucocephala*).

मानिता má-nita, *s. f.* Pride, dignity.

मानिनी má-nin-ee, *adj. f.* Proud, arrogant, haughty.

मानी ma-née, *adj.* Proud, haughty.

मानूष ma-nóosh, *s. m.* A man.

मानूषी ma-noosh-ée, *s. f.* A woman.

मानूष्य ma-nóosh-yuh, *s. m.* Manhood, manliness, humanity, the state or quality of a man or mortal.

मानो má-no, *adv.* Suppose, grant, as if, as. *s. m.* A cat.

मान्ना mán-na, *v. a.* To respect, regard, mind, attend to, observe, obey, heed, believe, accept, acknowledge, receive, experience, agree, allow, accede, assent, confess, consent, grant, admit, take, assume, trust, yield, submit, suppose, own, permit, to be set on. *Boora manna,* To take amiss, to take as an affront. *Bhula manna,* To take in good part.

मान्य mán-yuh, *adj.* Respectable, venerable.

3 D 2

माप map, *s. m.* Measure.

मापन map-ún, *s. m.* Measure, measuring.

मापना máp-na, *v. a.* To measure. *Mapa shorba our ginee duliyan,* is applied to express scarcity of provision, also penurious economy.

माबाप ma-báp, *s. m.* Parents.

मामक má-muk, *adj.* Selfish. *s. m.* A miser, a niggard.

मामा ma-ma, *s. m.* A maternal uncle.

मामी ma-mée, *s. f.* An aunt, maternal uncle's wife.

मामीपीना mámee-péena, *v. a.* To shew partiality.

माम् ma-móo, *s. m.* An uncle, mother's brother ; a snake. (*Phrase used at night when it is deemed unlucky to call a serpent by its proper name*).

माया máya, *s. f.* Kindness, pity, sympathy, compassion, mercy, feeling, affection ; fraud, trick, deceit, illusion ; philosophical illusion, idealism, unreality of all worldly existence. *Mayapatr, adj.* Rich, opulent, wealthy.

मायापट् máya-pút-oo, *adj.* Delusive, expert in deceiving.

मायामय maya-múy, *adj.* Illusive, deceptive.

मायावी maya-vée, *s. m.* A juggler, a conjurer.

मायिक ma-yík, *adj.* Illusory, deceptive.

मार mar, *s. f.* Beating ; battle ; a blow ; (*in comp.*) killing, killer. *Mar kootaee, s. f.* Beating and bruising. *Mar khanee,* To get a drubbing. *Mar girana,* To knock down. *Mar dalna,* To kill, smite. *Mar dena,* To smite, to beat. *Mar-dhar, s. f.* Thumping and beating severely. *Mar purna,* To be beaten. *Mar peet, s. f.* Beating and bruising, drubbing. *Mar murna,* To commit suicide ; to fall in battle after killing some of the enemy. *Mar lana,* To rob, to take by robbery. *Mar lena,* To smite, overcome, conquer. *Mar sukna,* To be able to beat. *Mar hutana,* To overcome, to beat and drive back. *Mar harna,* To beat severely.

मार mar, } *s. m.* Plague, pestilence,
मारक mar-úk, } epidemic.

मारकत már-kut, *adj.* Emerald, of the colour of an emerald.

मारग már-ug, *s. m.* A road, path, way ; the anus.

मारन mar-ún, *s. m.* Killing, slaughter. *Marunhara, s. m.* Smiter, slayer.

मारना már-na, *v. a.* To smite, strike, hit, kill, slay, beat, bang, drive, shoot, punish, mortify, cast, mar, blight, blast, spoil, ruin, conquer, crack, destroy, break, fine, take, set, smother, stamp, sting, stop, calm, throw, toss, quench, run. *s. m.* Striking, &c.

मारवा mar-wá, ¦ *s. m.* A musical mode.
मारू ma-róo,

मारा má-ra, *adj.* Beaten, smitten, slain; foundered or overturned (*a boat, &c.*) *s. m.* A victim. *Mara purna,* To be killed or slain. *Mara mara phirna,* To wander. *Mara maree,* Mutual beating, scuffle, fray, bickering, broil.

मारा जाना mára-jána, *v. n.* To be slain; to be overcome; to be overturned or sunk (*a boat, &c.*); to be cut off (*a caravan, detachment, &c.*)

मारात्मक mar-átmuk, *adj.* Murderous.

मारित mar-ít, *adj.* Killed, slain.

मारी ma-rée, *s. f.* Plague, epidemic.

मारू ma-róo, *s. m.* A warlike musical instrument, a kettledrum. *adj.* (*in comp.*) Smiting, striking; striker, killer.

मारे máreh, *subst. mas. inflect.* (By) reason, (on) account, (for) the sake, for.

मार्ग marg, *s. m.* A road, path, way; search, seeking, inquiry; the anus.

मार्गशिर marg-shír, *s. m.* The month *Ugruhayun* (*November-December*).

मार्जन márj-un, *s. m.* Cleaning, cleansing, wiping; cleaning the person, by wiping, bathing, or rubbing it with oil or fragrant unguents; sprinkling with water for purification before the performance of religious ceremonies.

मार्जार marj-ár, *s. m.* ¦ The common cat;
मार्जारी marj-arée, *s. f.* ¦ the wild or pole cat.

माल mal, *s. m.* Wrestler, boxer, prize-fighter. *s. f.* A necklace, a garland.

मालकंगनी mal-kúng-nee, *s. f.* Celastrus (*Staff tree*).

मालुका má-luk-a, *s. f.* A garland.

मालकोष mal-kós, *s. m.* A musical mode.

मालती mal-tée, *s. f.* Great-flowered jasmine (*Jasminum grandiflorum*); a bud, a blossom; a flower (*Bignonia suave-olens*); a shrub (*Echites caryophyllata*); a creeper (*Gærtnera racemosa*).

मालपूआ mal-póoa, *s. m.* A kind of sweetmeat, a pancake.

मालव ma-lúv, *s. m.* The province of *Malwa,* or *m. pl.* The people of that province.

मालश्री mal-srée, *s. f.* A *Raginee* or musical mode.

माला má-la, *s. f.* A garland, a necklace, a string or wreath of flowers; a chaplet of flowers; a string of beads, a *Hindoo* rosary; a book.

मालाकार mala-kár, *s. m.* A flower-seller, a florist, a gardener.

मालाफल mala-phúl, *s. m.* The seed of the Eleocarpus, of which common rosaries are made.

मालिन ma-lín, ¦ *s. f.* The wife of a
मालिनी ma-lin-ée, ¦ flower-gatherer, or a female vender of garlands, &c.

माली má-lee, *s. m.* A florist, a gatherer and vender of flowers, a gardener.

माल्य mál-yuh, *s. m.* A garland, a wreath; a chaplet, a garland for the forehead.

माल्यवत् malyuh-wút, ¦ *s. m.* A mountain-
माल्यवान् malyuh-wán, ¦ ous range, described as one of the smaller mountains of India proper; lying eastward of mount *Meroo.*

मावस má-wus, *s. f.* The conjunction of the sun and moon, the change of the moon.

मावा má-wa, *s. f.* Substance; starch; the yolk of an egg; leaven; milk inspissated by boiling.

माष mash, *s. m.* A sort of vetch or kidney-bean (*Phaseolus max,* or, —*radiatus*).

माषपर्णी mash-púrnee, *s. f.* A sort of leguminous shrub (*Glycine debilis*).

माषा má-sha, *s. m.* A jeweller's or goldsmith's weight, variously reckoned at five, eight or ten *ruttees* or seeds of the *Abrus precatorius:* the weight in common use is about seventeen grains troy.

मास mas, *s. m.* The month, a month, the twelfth part of the *Hindoo* year, it is usually a lunar one, consisting of thirty *Tithis,* but it may be a *Soura* or solar month, being equal to the sun's passage through a sign of the zodiac; there is also a *Sawun* month, consisting of thirty risings and settings of the sun; a *Nukshutr* month, or month regulated by the lunar asterisms; and a fifth description of month called *Varhusputyuh,* depending on the motions of the planet Jupiter; the lunar month also being of two kinds, as reckoned from the new or from the full moon, completes six different modes of monthly computation.

मास mas, *s. m.* Flesh, meat.

मासकबार mas-kub-ár, *s. m.* The last day of a month.

मासुन ma-sún, *s. m.* A medicinal seed (*Serratula anthelmintica*).

मासा má-sa, *s. m.* A small weight consisting of eight *ruttees.*

मासांत mas-ánt, *s. m.* Day of new-moon.

मासिक mas-ík, *adj.* Monthly, relating or belonging to a month; payable in a month (*a debt, &c.*); hired by the month (*a servant*); lasting for a month; happening or occurring at the end of a month, what will occur a month hence, &c. *s. m.* A particular *Shraddh,* or obsequial sacrifice performed every day of new moon.

मासी ma-sée, *s. f.* Mother's sister, maternal aunt. [old.

मासीन ma-séen, *adj.* Of a month, a month

माहाकुल maha-kóol, *adj.* Of a respectable family.

माहाजनिक máha-jún-ik, *adj.* Fit for or suitable to great persons.

माहात्मिक mahat-mík, *adj.* Glorious, majestic ; magnanimous ; of great sanctity or honour.

माहात्म्य mahátmyuh, *s. m.* Majesty, greatness, might ; the peculiar efficacy or virtue of any divinity or sacred shrine, &c. ; a work, giving an account of the merits of any holy place or object.

माहाराजिक maha-rájik, *adj.* Imperial, royal, fit for a king, &c.

माहिं máhin, *adv.* In.

माहुर má-hoor, *s. m.* Poison.

माहू ma-hóo, *s. m.* A kind of Scolopendra or Julus which is said to get into the brain through the ears, and by its bite to occasion excessive pain and even death.

मिंह minh, *s. m.* Rain.

मिंगनी mingnee, *s. f.* Goat's or sheep's dung.

मिचकारना mich-kárna, *v. a.* To rinse.

मिचना mích-na, *v. n.* To shut, to close.

मिचराना mich-rána, *v. a.* To eat without an appetite. *Michur-michur kurna,* Eating without an appetite.

मिचौलना michoul-ná, *v. a.* To shut or cover the eye.

मिटना mit-ná, *v. n.* To be effaced, to expire.

मिटाना mit-ána, *v. a.* To efface, erase, obliterate, blot out, abrogate, abolish.

मिटिया mítiya, *s. f.* An earthen pot.

मिट्टी mittee, } *s. f.* Earth. *Mittee pukurna,*
मट्टी muttee, } To bite the ground ; to be overcome or overturned ; to be perverse or obstinate, to resist. *Mittee dena,* To bury. *Muttee pur lurna,* To dispute about land. *Muttee dalna,* To conceal the crime or fault of another. *Muttee kurna,* To ruin or destroy. *Muttee men milna,* To be ruined or disgraced. *Muttee khana,* To eat flesh. *Muttee hona,* To become weak or faint, to be ruined. [slow.

मिट्ठा mit-thá, *s. m.* A kiss. *adj.* Sweet ;

मिट्ठी mit-thée, *s. f.* A kiss.

मिठरी mith-rée, *s. f.* A sort of sweetmeat.

मिठाई mit-haée, *s. f.* A sweetmeat ; sweetness.

मिठास mit-hás, *s. f.* Sweetness.

मित mit, *adj.* Measured.

मितवाच mit-vách, *adj.* Prudent in speaking, of measured speech.

मिताशन mit-áshun, *adj.* Abstemious, moderate in diet, eating little and sparingly.

मिति miti, *s. f.* Measuring, measure ; proof, evidence.

मिती mít-ee, *s. f.* Date ; interest.

मित्र mitr, *s. m.* A friend.

मित्रता mitr-tá, } *s. f.* Friendship, friend-
मित्राई mitráee, } liness.

मित्रद्रोह mitr-dróoh, *s. m.* A false or treacherous friend.

मित्रभेद mitr-bhéd, *s. m.* Breach of friendship.

मित्रलाभ mitr-lábh, *s. m.* Acquirement of a friend or friendship, forming friendship, &c.

मिथस् mit-hús, *adv.* Mutually, reciprocally.

मिथुन mít-hoon, *s. m.* A couple, a pair, a brace, male and female ; copulation ; union, junction. *s. m.* The sign of the zodiac *Gemini.*

मिथुनीभाव mithoonée-bháo, *s. m.* Amorous inclination.

मिथ्या míth-ya, *adv.* Falsely, untruly. *adj.* False, counterfeit.

मिथ्याचार mithyá-chár, *adj.* Acting falsely.

मिथ्यादृष्टि mithya-dríshti, *s. f.* Denial of future existence, atheism, heresy.

मिथ्याप्रतिज्ञ míthya-prutígyuh, *adj.* Treacherous, guilty of a breach of promise.

मिथ्यामति míthya-múti, *s. f.* Error, ignorance, mistake.

मिथ्यावादी míthya-vádee, *adj.* Lying, a liar.

मिन्ती mín-tee, *s. f.* An apology, submission, solicitation.

मियां miyan, *s. m.* Sir ! an address expressive of kindness, master. *Miyan admee,* A respectable person.

मिर्गी mír-gee, *s. f.* The epilepsy.

मिर्गीहा mir-gee-há, *s. m.* One afflicted with the epilepsy, one epileptic.

मिर्च mirch, *s. f.* Pepper. *Gol-mirch,* Black-pepper. *Lal-mirch,* Capsicum or red pepper.

मिर्चा mír-cha, } *s. m.* Chili pepper
मिर्चाई mir-cháee, } (*Capsicum frutescens*).

मिर्था mír-tha, *adj.* False, lying, untrue.

मिर्दंग mir-dúng, *s. f.* A kind of drum, a tabour. (*A kind of long drum, much longer than the dhol and broader at the middle than at either end*).

मिर्दंगिया mir-dúng-iya, } *s. m.* A beater
मिर्दंगी mir-dúng-ee, } of the *mirdung,* a tabourer.

मिर्धा mír-dha, *s. m.* An officer employed by government in villages, an overseer, exciseman.

मिलन míl-un, *s. m.* Mixing with, being in contact with, associating with, &c.; agreement; encountering, meeting; to meet, to mix, &c.

मिलनसार mil-un-sár, *adj.* Civil, affable, sociable, friendly, familiar, intimate, convivial. *Milunsaree, s. f.* Sociableness, friendliness, affability, civility, concord, agreement.

मिलना mil-na, *v. n.* To be mixed or confounded, to blend, meet, join, to be met with, to attain, occur, to be got, to associate, agree, accord, fit, tally, suit, to be united, to become connected (*with*), to coalesce, correspond. *Milna joolna, or Milna jhoolna,* To meet cordially, to have unrestricted intercourse. *Milna hilna, v. n.* To act together, to coalesce, to be together, to join. *Mileh jooleh ruhna,* To live together in harmony.

मिलवाना mil-wá-na, *v. a.* To cause to mix, &c.

मिलाना mil-ána, *v. a.* To mix, to blend; to cause to meet, to join, attach, connect, adjust, accord, fit, unite, apply, introduce, cement, close, compare, reconcile, assimilate, agree, find, get, meet, visit.

मिलाप mil-áp, *s. m.* Agreement, reconciliation, accommodation, mixing, coalescence, combination, union, concord, understanding, adjustment, pacification, visit, meeting.

मिलापी mil-ápee, *adj.* Civil, affable, sociable, friendly, familiar, intimate, convivial.

मिलाव mil-áo, *s. m.* Mixture, mixing, accord, unison, assimilation.

मिलित míl-it, *adj.* Mixed, united, combined or connected with; found, met with, encountered.

मिश्री mísh-ee, *s. f.* A sort of fennel (*Anethum panmorium*); Indian spikenard; common anise.

मिश्र mishr, *adj.* Mixed, mingled, blended. *s. m.* Mixing, mixture; a title of *Brahmuns,* who were brought to India from *Saku-dweep* by *Krishn* in order to cure the leprosy of his son *Sambuh;* also a title of some *Brahmuns* from *Mithila,* &c.; a *Hindoo* physician; a respectable person.

मिश्रण mish-run, *s. m.* Mixing, uniting; (*in Arithmetic*) Addition.

मिश्रित mísh-rit, *adj.* Respected, respectable; mixed, mingled; added.

मिष mish, ⎫ *s. m.* Fraud, trick, deception;
मिस mis, ⎭ pretence, sham, stratagem; envy.

मिषी mísh-ee, *s. f.* Spikenard (*Valeriana Jatamansi*); a sort of fennel (*Anethum panmorium, &c.*)

मिष्ट misht, *adj.* Sweet, sugary.

मिष्टान्न mish-tánn, *s. m.* Sauce, gravy, seasoning, a mixture of sugar and acids, &c. eaten with bread or rice.

मिसना mís-na, *v. n.* To be ground, to be pulverized.

मिसी mís-ee, *s. f.* A sort of fennel (*Anethum panmorium*); another kind (*A. sowa*); spikenard (*Valeriana Jatamansi*); a sort of lovage (*Ligusticum ajwaen*); common anise (*Pimpinella anisum*).

मिसी mís-ee, ⎫ *s. f.* A powder (*made of*
मिस्सी mís-see, ⎭ *vitriol, &c.*) with which the teeth are tinged of a black colour. *adj. f.* Made of vetches. *Misee-dan,* A box of gold, silver or other metal for holding *misee.*

मिहदी míh-dee, ⎫ *s. f.* A plant from the
मेंहदी ménh-dee, ⎭ leaves of which a red die is prepared, with which the natives stain their hands and feet (*Lawsonia inermis*).

मिहना míh-na, *s. m.* Sarcasm. *Mihna phenkna,* To sneer.

मिहरा míh-ra, *s. m.* A man who appears in the habit of a woman.

मिहराऊ mih-rároo, ⎫
मिहरिया míhriya, ⎬ *s. f.* A woman.
मिहरी míhree, ⎭

मिहाना mihána, *v. n.* To grow damp.

मिहानी mihánee, *s. f.* A churn.

मींगी méeng-ee, *s. f.* Marrow.

मींजना méenj-na, *v. a.* To rub, scour.

मीच meech, *s. f.* Death.

मीचना méech-na, ⎫ *v. a.* To close the
मीछना méechh-na, ⎭ eyes, shut, wink.

मीजना méej-na, *v. a.* To rub with the hands.

मीजू mee-jóo, *s. m.* Lentil.

मीठा mee-thá, *adj.* Sweet; slow. *s. m.* A very active vegetable poison; name of a fruit; a kiss.

मीठिया méethi-ya, *s. m.* ⎫
मीठी mée-thee, *s. f.* ⎬ A kiss.

मीना mée-na, *s. f.* A caste of *Hindoos* professedly thieves.

मीत meet, *s. m.* A friend, a lover; a cup.

मीतन mee-tún, *s. f.* A female namesake or friend.

मीता mée-ta, *s. m.* A namesake; a pitcher; a porringer, a cup.

मीन meen, *s. m.* A fish; the sign of the zodiac *Pisces*; the name of the first incarnation of *Vishnoo*.

मीनरंगा meen-rúnga, *s. m.* A kingfisher.

मीना mée-na, *s. f.* A caste of *Hindoos* professedly thieves.

मीनघाती méena-ghátee, *s. m.* A crane; a fisherman.

मीनाण्ड meen-ánd, *s. m.* Fish-spawn, roe, milt.

मीमांसक meem-ansúk, *s. m.* A follower of the *Meemansa* philosophy.

मीमांसा meemánsa, *s. f.* One of the philosophical systems of the *Hindoos*, or rather a twofold system, the two parts of which form two of the six *Dursuns* or schools of philosophy; the first part, the *Poorv Meemansa*, or *Meemansa* simply, originates with the *Mooni Juymini*, and illustrates the *Kurm-kand* of the *Veds*, or the practical part (*the ritual*) of religion and devotion, including also moral and legal obligations. The second part, or *Oottur Meemansa*, ascribed to *Vyas*, is the same as the *Vedant*, founded on the *Jnan-kand* or theological portion of the *Veds*, and treating of the spiritual worship of the Supreme Being or soul of the universe.

मीमियाना meemiyána, *v. n.* To bleat (*a kid*).

मीलन mée-lun, *s. m.* Twinkling, blinking, winking.

मीवा méewa, *s. f.* The worm of the intestines, Ascarides, &c.

मीशी mée-shee, *s. f.* A kind of leather, chamois.

मीसना mées-na, *v. a.* To grind, pulverize, tweak, twitch, rumple, crumple.

मुंह moonh, *s. m.* Mouth, face, countenance, presence, aspect, orifice; respect, complaisance; (*met.*) power, fitness, qualification, pretence, ability.

मुंहनाल moonhnál, *s. m. f.* The mouthpiece of a *hookka*.

मुकरना moo-kúr-na, *v. a.* To deny.

मुकरी móok-ree, *s. f.* A kind of short poem of frequent use in the *Bruj* dialect, the peculiarities of which are these. It consists of four lines, each composed of four trochees. In the three first, the speaker, a female, appears to talk of her lover; but on the question being put by a friend, applies the whole to some other object. Hence the name from *mookurna*, To deny.

मुकुट móo-koot, *s. m.* A crown, crest, diadem, tiara.

मुकुन्द moo-kóond, *s. m.* Gum olibanum; a precious gem; quicksilver.

मुकुर móo-koor, *s. m.* A mirror.

मुकुल móo-kool, *s. m.* An opening bud.

मुकुलित moo-kool-ít, *adj.* Half-closed (*as a bud*); half-shut (*as the eye*), blinking, winking.

मुक्का móok-ka, *s. m.* } A thump, a blow
मुक्की mook-kée, *s. f.* } with the fist, buffet.

मुक्त mookt, *adj.* Released, liberated, loosed, let go; liberated from corporal existence, finally happy. *s. m.* The spirit released from mundane existence, and re-integrated with its divine original.

मुक्त mookt, *s. m.* A pearl. *s. f.* Release, pardon, absolution from sin, salvation, deliverance of the soul from the body and exemption from further transmigration. *adj.* Released, absolved, freed from corporal existence, finally happy.

मुक्ता mookt-á, } *s. m.* A pearl.
मुक्ताफल mookta-phúl, }

मुक्त móokta, *adj.* Much, many.

मुक्तावली mookt-áwulee, *s. f.* A pearl necklace.

मुक्ति móokti, *s. f.* Final beatitude, the delivery of the soul from the body and exemption from further transmigration; the (*imaginary*) reabsorption of the emancipated spirit into its great primary source, identification (*according to Hindoo ideas*) with God; liberation, setting or becoming free or loose.

मुख mookh, *s. m.* The mouth, the face. *adj.* First, initial; chief, pre-eminent, principal.

मुखपूरण mookh-póorun, *s. m.* A mouthful.

मुखाग्नि mookh-ágni, *s. m.* Fire put into the mouth of the corpse at the time of lighting the funeral pile; a sacrificial or consecrated fire.

मुखिया mookh-iyá, } *adj.* Chief, primary,
मुख्य mookh-yúh, } principal.

मुख्यता mookh-yutá, *s. f.* Pre-eminence, being best or chief.

मुद्गर moog-dúr, *s. m.* A mallet; a club used to exercise with in the manner of dumb-bells.

मुग्ध moogdh, *adj.* Lovely, beautiful; stupid, ignorant, an idiot, a fool; simple, silly.

मुग्धता moogdh-tá, *s. f.* Loveliness; ignorance, stupidity; simplicity.

मुग्धा moog-dhá, *s. f.* A young and lovely female.

मुच्छा moochcha, *s. m.* A large lump of flesh or meat.

मुजरा móoj-ra, *s. m.* Allowance, premium, deduction; obeisance, respects, visit, audience. *Moojra kurna*, To make obeisance, pay respects, wait on, visit. *Moojreh-gah*, Place of visiting, audience, salutation, &c.

मुझ moojh, *pron.* Me.

मुंज moonj, *s. m.* A sort of grass, from the fibres of which a string is prepared, of which the triple thread worn by the *Brahmun* as a girdle should be formed (*Saccharum munja*); the *Brahminical* girdle, or in common use, the sacred string or cord.

मुटाई mootáee, *s. f.* } Fatness, plump-
मुतापा moo-tápa, *s. m.* } ness, bigness,
bulkiness.

मुट्ठी moot-thée, *s. f.* Fist, grasp (*of the hand*), clutch, hand, handful.

मुठ mooth, *s. f.* The fist, blows with the fist, clutch, grasp. *Mooth-murd*, *s. m.* A robber, a ruffian.

मुठिया moothi-yá, *s. m.* A handful.

मुठोली moo-thó-lee, *s. f.* Onanism.

मुड़ना mćor-na, *v. n.* To be turned back, to be bent, twisted, turned, to turn, bend, twine.

मुड़ियाना moorhiyána, *v. n.* To be twisted, to be writhed.

मुण्ड moond, *adj.* Shaved, bald, having no hair on the head; low, mean. *s. m.* The head, the forehead, a bald pate; the trunk of a lopped tree; a head-man. *Moond-mal*, A necklace of human heads.

मुण्डकारी मारना moond-káree márna, To lie round with the knees to the belly.

मुण्डक moond-úk, *s. m.* A barber.

मुण्डन moond-ún, *s. m.* Shaving; the first shaving of a child (*a religious ceremony among the Hindoos*); shearing, cutting.

मुण्डना moond-ná, *v. n.* To be shaved.

मुण्डला moond-lá, *adj.* Shaved.

मुण्डवाना moond-wána, *v. a.* To cause to be shaved.

मुण्डा móon-da, *s. m.* The head, the head of a paper kite. *s. f.* Bengal madder (*Rubia manjeth*). *adj.* Shaven, bald; uncovered; a kind of uncovered *palkee*.

मुण्डाना moon-dána, *v. a.* To shave.

मुण्डासा moond-ása, *s. m.* A kind of small turban.

मुण्डित moond-ít, *adj.* Bald, shorn, shaven.

मुण्डितशिरा móondit-shír-a, *adj.* Bald-pated, shaven-headed.

मुण्डिया móon-diya, *s. m.* The head.

मुण्डी móon-dee, *s. m.* A barber. *s. f.* A medicinal plant (*Sphæranthus indicus*).

मुण्डीरी moon-déeree, *s. f.* A plant, described as a creeper, bearing a red and yellow flower, and commonly called by the same name, *Moondeeree*.

मुण्डू moon-dóo, *s. m.* A *sunyasee*, a *gosaeen*.

मुण्डेर moon-dér, } *s. f.* The coping of
मुण्डेरी moon-dér-ee, } a wall.

मूतना móot-na, *adj.* One who pisses much, a piss-a-bed.

मूतास moot-ás, *s. f.* Desire or inclination to piss.

मूतासा moot-ása, *adj.* Desirous of pissing.

मूतिहर mooti-húr, *s. m.* Straw, &c. mixed with horse's urine.

मूतिहरी mootih-ree, *s. f.* A hole in which the dirt of a stable (*particularly urine*) is collected.

मुद mood, *s. f.* Pleasure, delight, joy.

मुदा móo-da, *s. f.* Happiness, joy.

मुदित mood-ít, *adj.* Pleased, delighted. *s. m.* Pleasure, happiness.

मुद्ग moodg, *s. m.* A sort of kidney-bean (*Phaseolus mungo*).

मुद्गर mood-gúr, *s. m.* A mallet, a mace, a weapon formed like a carpenter's hammer; a staff, armed with iron, and larger at the lower extremity, used for breaking clods of earth, &c.; a carpenter's hammer; a sort of flower, said to be a kind of jasmine, perhaps *Jasminum sambac*, the wild variety.

मुद्रा móod-ra, *s. f.* A seal, a signet; a seal ring; the mark of a seal or similar impression, a stamp, print, coin, medal, &c.; a ring worn by *Jogees* in their ears.

मुद्रांकित mood-ránkit, *adj.* Stamped, sealed.

मुद्रित mood-rít, *adj.* Sealed; marked, stamped, struck.

मुनक्का moo-núk-ka, *s. m.* A species of raisin.

मुनमुन moon-moon, *s. m.* Puss puss, a mode of calling a cat.

मुनि móo-ni, } *s. m.* A holy man, a sage,
मुनी móo-nee, } a pious and learned person, endowed with more or less of a divine nature, or having attained it by rigid abstraction and mortification; the title is applied to the *Rishis*, the *Bruhmudiks*, and to a great number of persons distinguished for their writings, considered as inspired, as *Panini*, *Vyas*, &c.; an ascetic, a devotee.

मुनिया móo-niya, *s. f.* The female of the little birds called amadavats (*or lal*, *Fringila amandava*).

मुनिस्थान moonis-thán, *s. m.* A hermitage, the abode or retirement of holy sages.

मुनीश moon-éesh, *s. m.* A saint, or chief of the saints or sages.

मुन्दना móond-na, *v. n.* To be shut, closed, contracted. *v. a.* To close.

मुन्द्रा móon-dra, *s. m.* A ring, a collar.

मुन्द्री moon-drée, *s. f.* A ring, a finger-ring.

मुमाखी moo-mákhee, *s. f.* A honey-bee.

मुमानी moo-mánee, *s. f.* An aunt, mother's brother's wife.

मुमूर्षु moo-móor-shoo, *s. m.* A man at the point of death, a dying man.

मुरई moo-ruée, *s. f.* A radish.

मुरकाना moor-kána, *v. n.* To twist, to writhe.

मुरकी móor-kee, *s. f.* An ornament worn in the ear ; the tragus of the ear.

मुरगीवाला móorgee-wála, *s. m.* A poulterer.

मुरचंग moor-chúng, *s. f.* A jew's-harp.

मुरझाना moor-jhána, *v. n.* To wither, fade, pine, droop, to be dejected or dispirited.

मुरुंद moo-rúnd, *s. m.* A country on the north-west of *Hindoostan*, called also *Lumpuk*, and now *Lamgan. m. pl.* The inhabitants of *Lamgan.*

मुरुंद करना moorúnda kúrna, *v. a.* To tie.

मुरमुरा móor-moora, *s. m.* A kind of food, rice pressed flat and eaten raw. (*So named in imitation of the sound which it gives in chewing*).

मुरला móor-la, *adj.* Toothless. *s. m.* A peacock.

मुरली móor-lee, *s. f.* A flute, a pipe, a fife. *Moorlee-dhur, s. m.* A name of *Krishn.*

मुरहा moor-há, *s. m.* Convolution. *adj.* Twisted.

मुरही moor-hée, *s. f.* A twist, contortion, writhe, convolution.

मुराई moo-raée, *s. m.* One whose business it is to grow and sell vegetables.

मुरेला moo-réla, *s. m.* A peachick.

मुर्रा móor-ra, *s. m.* A squib.

मुलतानी mool-tánee, *s. f.* A musical mode. *adj.* Of *Mooltan. Mooltanee muttee, s. f.* Armenian bole (*lit. earth of Mooltan*).

मुलहठी mool-húttee, *s. f.* A medicinal root, liquorice.

मुलाई moo-laée, *s. f.* Appraisement, valuation.

मुलाना moo-lána, *v. a.* To appraise.

मुष्कें बांधना mooshken bandhna, } *v. a.*
मुष्कें चढाना mooshken churhána, } To pinion, to tie the hands behind the back.

मूशल móo-shul, *s. m.* A club, a mace ; a pestle for cleaning rice.

मुषित moo-shít, *adj.* Stolen, robbed.

मूष्क mooshk, *s. m.* The scrotum ; the testicle.

मुष्ट moosht, *s. m.* Theft, robbery.

मुष्टमार moosht-már, *s. m.* A pilferer, robber. *Mooshtmar kur bythna,* To sit with the knees held up, by the arms clasped round them, towards the face.

मुष्टामुष्टि móoshta-móoshti, *s. m.* Thumping and pulling, fisticuffs, boxing.

मुष्टी móosh-tee, *s. f.* The fist, the closed hand ; filching, stealing.

मुष्टीपात mooshtee-pát, *s. m.* Pummelling, boxing.

मुष्टीबंध mooshtee-bund, *s. m.* Clenching the fist.

मुष्टीमुष्टि móoshtee-móoshti, *adv.* Fist to fist (*fighting*), fisticuffs.

मुसकान moos-kán, *s. f.* A smile, a grin.

मुसकाना moos-kána, *v. n.* To smile, grin, smirk.

मुसकुराई moos-koo-raée, } *s. f.* Smiling,
मुसकुराहट moos-koo-rahút, } grinning, laughing, smile, smirk.

मुसकुराना moos-koo-rána, *v. n.* To smile, grin, smirk, simper.

मुसल móo-sul, *s. m.* A pestle, a wooden pestle used for cleaning rice ; a club.

मुसलमान moo-sul-mán, *s. m.* A Mahomedan.

मुसलमानी moo-sul-mánee, *s. f.* The Mahomedan religion ; circumcision ; a female *Moosulman* ; of or relating to a *Moosulman.*

मुसाना moo-sána, *v. a.* To cause to steal.

मुस्तक móos-tuk, *s. m.* A fragrant grass (*Cyperus rotundus*) ; a sort of poison.

मूहरा móoh-ra, *s. m.* Van, vanguard.

मूहरी móoh-ree, *s. f.* The cuff of the sleeve of a jacket, or the extremity of the leg of a pair of trousers, the bore (*of a gun, &c.*)

मुहाना moo-hána, *s. m.* The mouth (*of a river, &c.*), inlet, outlet.

मुहासा moo-hása, *s. m.* A pimple (*on the face in youth*).

मुहूर्त moo-hóortt, *s. m.* A division of time, the thirtieth part of a day and night, or an hour of forty-eight minutes.

मूआ móoa, *adj.* Dead, lifeless, dull. *Mooa-badul, s. m.* Sponge. *Mooa-sho,* A washer of dead bodies.

मूंकी móon-kee, *s. f.* A blow with the fist.

मूंग moong, *s. f.* A kind of pulse (*Phaseolus mungo*). *Moong-phulee, s. f.* The ground-nut or pig-nut of the West Indies (*Arachis hypogæa*).

मूंगची moong-chée, } *s. f.* A dish made
मूंगरी moong-rée, } with *moong.*

मूंगा móon-ga, *s. m.* Coral.

मूंगिया móon-giya, *s. m.* A colour (*red coral-coloured*).

मूंछ moonch, } *s. f.* Whiskers.
मूंछ moonchh, }

मूंज moonj, *s. f.* A grass of which ropes are made (*Saccharum munja*).

मूंड moond, *s. m.* The head. *Moond pana,* To coax, to wheedle. *Moond bhera,* Butting (*as rams*).

मूंड़चूरा moond-chóora, *s. m.* A kind of pillar.

मूंड़ना móond-na, *v. a.* To shave; to instruct, convert, or make a disciple of; to wheedle out of any thing. *Oolteh oostooreh seh moondna,* To cheat one.

मूंड़ला móond-la, *adj.* Shaved.

मूंड़ी móon-dee, *s. f.* The head.

मूंढा moon-dhá, *s. m.* The shoulder, a lump; a stool, a footstool.

मूंदना móond-na, *v. a.* To shut, cover, close, imprison, involve.

मूंदरी móond-ree, *s. f.* A ring for the finger.

मूंह moonh, *s. m.* Mouth, face, countenance, presence, aspect, orifice; respect, complaisance; power, fitness, qualification, pretence, ability. *Moonh undhera,* Twilight; evening; dusk, obscure. *Moonh-ukhree, adj.* Verbal. *Moonh upna-sa lekeh phir jana,* To return disappointed from any enterprise, to fail of success. *Upna-sa moonh lena,* is used to denote failure of success. *Moonh ana,* Salivation. *Moonh-a-moonh, adj.* Brimful. *Moonh ootur jana,* To have the face shrunk or withered by weakness and emaciation. *Moonh kurna,* To confront, to compare; to give abuse; to burst or open (*as an abscess*); to make the first attempt at seizing game (*a young hound or other animal used in hunting*); to turn one's face, or direct one's steps towards any particular object or place. *Moonh ka nuwala,* Any thing easily attained. *Moonh ka phoohur,* Abusive. *Moonh kala, s. m.* Disgrace. *Moonh kala kurna,* To incur disgrace; to punish, to disgrace. *Moonh kee loee ooturne,* To lose the sense of shame. *Moonh keh konweh oor janeh,* To look blank or any occasion. *Moonh kholna,* To abuse. *Moonh-chung,* A jew's-harp. *Moonh churhna,* To become intimate with, to attach one's self to; to face, to confront. *Moonh chulana,* To bite (*or to be inclined to bite, as a horse*). *Moonh chirana,* To make mouths. *Moonh chor,* Shame-faced, bashful, timid, sheepish. *Moonh choree,* Bashfulness. *Moonh chhipana,* To hide one's face (*from bashfulness*). *Moonh terha kurna,* To make wry faces. *Moonh thuthana,* To slap one's face, to box the ears. *Moonh dalna,* To beg, to request. *Moonh tukna,* To be astonished or afflicted. *Moonh torna,* To harass. *Moonh to dekho,* Look at his face! (*applied to a person who pretends or aspires to something beyond his power or capacity*). *Moonh topa, s. m.* Bribe. *Moonh thuthana,* To make mouths or faces, to fashion the face. *Moonh dikhaee, s. f.* A present given by the friends of the family and the women of the neighbourhood on their first visit to a bride. *Moonh dikhana,* To shew one's face, to appear with confidence and satisfaction. *Moonh dekhkur bat kurna,* To flatter, to speak what one supposes will be agreeable to one's hearers. *Moonh dekhna,* To look up to (*for aid, &c.*); to have a regard for one; to be astonished or helpless. *Moonh dekh ruhna,* To stare at with surprise. *Moonh dekheh kee preet,* Apparent friendship or affection, shew of friendship before a person whom you pay no regard to in absence. *Moonh pur gurm hona,* To behave disrespectfully in the presence of a superior. *Moonh pur lena,* To tell, relate. *Moonh pur kuwaee oornee* (*lit. To have a squib or rocket discharged against one's face*), To change colour. *Moonh pusarna,* To gape (*with surprise, &c.*) *Moonh pana,* To get into one's good graces; to presume on the favor of another. *Moonh phirna,* To turn away from, to be displeased with, to be disgusted. *Moonh pherna,* To abstain from. *Moonh phylana,* To presume, to desire much, to gape. *Moonh bund kurna,* To hold one's tongue. *Moonh bunana,* To make mouths or faces, to fashion the face. *Moonh bana,* To open the mouth, to gape. *Moonh barna,* To refrain. *Moonh bigurna,* To be displeased; to have the taste blunted or depraved. *Moonh bigarna,* To frown, to make faces. *Moonh-bola, adj.* Nominal, in name or appellation. *Moonh-bola bhaee,* or *Moonh-bolee buhin,* An intimate friend (*lit. one called a brother or sister*). *Moonh-bharee, s. f.* A bribe, a sop. *Moonh manga, (as)* demanded, requested or asked for by word of mouth. *Moonh marna,* To stop one's mouth, to silence; to feed; to desire. *Moonh men panee ana,* To desire with eagerness. *Moonh morna,* To turn away, to abstain or desist from any thing. *Moonh rukhna,* To keep on good terms with. *Moonh lugna,* To have the mouth burned by any pungent substance; to become intimate, to be familiarized, to become a favourite. *Moonh lugana,* To familiarize, to be intimate with inferiors, to favor, to countenance. *Moonh lutkana,* To be down in the mouth, to make a long face. *Moonh lekeh ruk-jana,* To be silent from shame. *Moonh sookurna,* To change colour. *Moonh seh phool jhurneh,* To abuse, to reproach.

मूंहाँ moon-hán, *s. m.* Soreness in the mouth, the aphthæ or thrush, salivation. *Moonhan-moonh,* Tête-à-tête, face to face, brimful, topful. *Moonhan-moonhee, s. f.* Altercation, squabble, wrangle.

मूक mook, *adj.* Dumb.

मूका móo-ka, *s. m.* The fist; a thump, blow; a spy-hole.

मूकी móo-kee, *s. f.* A thump, a blow of the fist.

मूखा mookhá, *s. m.* The ridge of a thatch, the topping or coping of a wall.

मूखी mookhée, *s. m.* A kind of pigeon. *s. f.* A thump.

मूगरी móogree, *s. f.* A mallet for beating cloths with.

मूछकाना mooch-kána, *v. a.* To sprain.

मूछना moochná, *s. m.* Pincers, tweezers. *v. a.* To pinch, shut, close.

मूछ moochh, *s. f.* Whiskers. *Moochh mu-*

rora rotee tora, One who is proud of eating the bread of idleness.

मूछाकरे moochh-ákreh, *s. m.* Stiff and bushy whiskers.

मछैल moo-chhyl, *adj.* Having large whiskers.

मूठ mooth, *s. f.* Handle, hilt, fist, hand, handful; name of a game. *Mooth-kee-mooth,* Handful after handful, repeated handfuls.

मठरा móoth-ra, *s. m.* A kind of printing consisting of spots on cloth, leather, &c.

मूठा moo-thá, *s. m.* A handle.

मूठिया móo-thi-ya, *s. m.* A handful.

मठी móo-thee, *s. f.* The fist.

मूढ moor, *s. m.* The head.

मूढ moorh, *adj.* Foolish, stupid, ignorant, brutal. *s. m.* An idiot, a fool, a simpleton. *Moorh-mun,* Stupid in mind.

मूढता moorh-tá, *s. f.* Folly, silliness, ignorance.

मूढात्मा moorh-átma, *adj.* Foolish, a fool.

मूत moot, *s. m.* Urine, piss.

मूतना móot-na, *v. n.* To piss.

मूत्र mootr, *s. m.* Urine, piss.

मूत्रकृच्छ्र mootr-krichchhr, *s. m.* Strangury; urinary affection in general, as gravel, &c.

मूत्रदोष mootr-dós, *s. m.* Gonorrhœa, considered as an urinary complaint.

मूत्रमार्ग mootr-márg, *s. m.* The urethra.

मूत्रशूक mootr-shóok, *s. m.* Milky urine, depositing a thick white sediment.

मूत्राघात mootr-aghát, *s. m.* Suppression of urine.

मूत्रातीत mootr-atéet, *s. m.* Difficulty or slow passage of urine.

मूना móo-na, *v. n.* To die.

मूनू móo-noo, *adj.* Little.

मूरख móo-rukh, *adj.* Foolish, ignorant, stupid, idiot, fool. *Moorukh-ganth,* The insisting of an ignorant fellow upon what he says, stubbornness.

मूरखता moorukhtá, *f.*
मूरखताई moorukhtáee, *f.* } *s.* Barbarism, folly, ignorance, stupidity.
मूरखपना moorukhpúna, *m.*

मूरत móo-rut, *s. f.* A statue, image, an idol, a picture, a resemblance, form, figure, body; a person (*term used by Byragees*).

मूर्ख moorkh, *adj.* Foolish, ignorant, stupid, idiotic.

मूर्खता moorkh-tá, } *s. f.* Barbarism, folly, ignorance, stupidity.
मूर्खताई moorkh-táee,

मूर्च्छन moorch-chhún, *adj.* Fainting, swooning. *s. m.* Fainting, syncope, swooning.

मूर्च्छा móorch-chha, *s. f.* Fainting, loss of consciousness or sense.

मूर्च्छित moorch-chhít, *adj.* Fainting, fainted, insensible.

मूर्च्छा móorchha, *s. f.* A swoon, stupefaction. *Moorchha ana,* To swoon.

मूर्च्छित moorchhít, *adj.* Fainted, in a swoon, insensible, entranced.

मूर्ति móortti, *s. f.* The body; figure, form, body in general, or any definite shape or image.

मूर्तिमान् moortti-mán, *adj.* Material, substantial, having shape or substance; incarnate.

मूर्धा moor-dhá, *s. m.* The head.

मूल mool, *s. m.* Origin, root, race, generation, principal or capital sum of money; text (*of a book, opposed to comment*); name of the nineteenth lunar mansion. *adj.* Really.

मूलिया móo-liya, *adj.* Born while the moon is in mool (*Scorpionis, which is considered unlucky*).

मूली móo-lee, *s. f.* A radish.

मूल्य móol-yuh, *s. m.* Price.

मूष moosh, *s. m.* A rat, a mouse.

मूषक moo-shúk, *s. m.* A rat, a mouse; a thief.

मूषन moo-shún, *s. m.* Stealing, pilfering.

मूषिक mooshík, *s. m.* A rat, a mouse; a thief, a plunderer.

मूषित moo-shít, *adj.* Stolen.

मूसना móos-na, *v. a.* To pilfer, steal, filch, defraud, snatch or seize by force.

मूसरा móos-ra, *s. m.* A rat.

मूसरी moos-rée, *s. f.* A mouse.

मूसल moo-súl, *s. m.* A wooden pestle.

मूसला móos-la, *s. m.* A taproot; the fusiform receptacle of a many-seeded fruit (*as of the Artocarpus, Annona, &c.*) *Moosladhar burusna,* To rain very heavily.

मूसा móo-sa, *s. m.* A mouse, a rat.

मूसाई moosaée, *s. f.* Judaism (*following of Moses*).

मृग mrig, *s. m.* A deer, an antelope; the fifth lunar constellation *Mrigsirus. Mrig-chira, s. m.* Name of a small bird. *Mrig chhala,* The skin of any antelope worn and used as a bed by devotees. *Mrig-nabhi, s. m.* Musk, a bag of musk. *Mrig-nynee,* Deer-eyed. *Mrig-mud,* Musk. *Mrig-lochunee,* Having an eye like the deer. *Mrig-sala,* A deer park.

मृगतृष mrig-trísh, *s. f.* Vapour floating over sands or deserts, and appearing at a distance like water; sultry vapour, mirage.

मृगनेत्री mrig-nétree, *s. f.* A woman with beautiful eyes, or eyes like a deer.

मृगभोजनी mrig-bhójunee, *s. f.* Bitter apple or colocynth.

मृगया mrig-yá, *s. f.* Chase, hunting.

मृगराज mrig-ráj, *s. m.* A lion.

मृगशिरा mrig-shíra, *s. m.* The fifth lunar mansion, containing three stars.

मृगादनी mrig-ádunee, *s. f.* Colocynth (*Cucumis coloquintida*).

मृगी mríg-ee, *s. f.* A doe, a female deer; the epilepsy.

मृगेन्द्र mrig-éndr, *s. m.* A lion.

मृत mrit, *adj.* Dead, expired, extinct, defunct. *s. m.* Death.

मृतक mrit-úk, *s. m.* A dead body, a corpse.

मृतकल्प mrit-kúlp, *adj.* Insensible, fainted.

मृतस्नान mrit-snán, *s. m.* Funeral ablution, bathing after mourning.

मृतकीरा mrit-kíra, *s. f.* An earth worm.

मृत्ताल mrittál, *s. m.* A sort of fragrant earth, also called *Surat* earth.

मृत्तिका mríttika, *s. f.* Earth, clay, soil.

मृत्यु mrít-yoo, *s. m.* Death, dying.

मृत्युञ्जय mrityoon-júy, *s. m.* A name of *Shiv,* as the conqueror of death.

मृदङ्ग mrid-úng, *s. m.* A tabour, a small drum; a double drum.

मृदङ्गिया mri-dúng-iya, *s. m.* A beater of
मृदङ्गी mri-dung-ée, } the *mridung,* a tabourer.

मृदु mrí-doo, *adj.* Soft; blunt, not sharp; gentle, mild.

मृदुता mridoo-tá, *s. f.* Softness.

मृषा mrishá, *adv.* Falsely; uselessly, in vain.

में men, *adv.* In, among, between, at. *Men seh,* From within, out of.

मेंगनी méng-nee, *s. f.* The dung of goats, sheep, camels, &c.

मेंड mend, *s. f.* A bank (*raised to separate fields*), a border, bank (*of a pond, river, &c.*), dam, dike. *Mend purna,* The rising of waves in the sea.

मेंडक men-dúk, *s. m.* } A frog; the rump
मेंडकी mend-kée, *s. f.* } of a horse. *Mend-kee ko zoukam hona* (*lit. a frog having caught cold*), expresses pride or consequential airs assumed by worthless persons.

मेंडा ménda, *s. f.* the brim of a well.

मेंडियाना men-diyána, *v. n.* To skirt, to enclose with a bank.

मेंढा men-dhá, *s. m.* A ram; the swell of the tide called the boar.

मेंह menh, *s. m.* Rain. *Menh chhootna,* To rain hard. *Menh burusna,* To rain.

मेंहदी ménh-dee, *s. f.* A plant, from the leaves of which a red die is prepared, with which the natives stain their hands and feet (*Lawsonia inermis*).

मेख mekh, *s. m.* A ram; the sign Aries; a tent-pin, a pin, a peg, a nail.

मेखला mékh-la, *s. f.* A woman's girdle or zone; the sacrificial string of a *Brahmun* when made of deer skin; a triple zone or string worn round the loins by the three first classes; the gird of the *Brahmun* should be of the fibres of the *moonj* or of *koosa* grass, that of the *Kshuttree* of a *moorwa,* or bowstring, and that of the *Vys* of a thread of the *sun.*

मेखली mékh-lee, *s. f.* A sackcloth.

मेघ megh, *s. m.* A cloud; a fragrant grass (*Cyperus rotundus*); a musical mode appropriated to the wet season and last watch of the night before the first dawn of the day, and said to have proceeded from the head of *Bruhma,* or else from the sky. *Megh-puti, s. m.* Lord of the clouds. *Megh-burun, adj.* Of the colour of the clouds. *Megh-raj, s. m.* The thunderer.

मेघकाल megh-kál, } *s. m.* The rains, the
मेघागम megha-gúm, } rainy season.

मेघगर्जन megh-gúrjjun, *s. m.* Thunder.

मेघज्योतिष megh-jyótis, *s. m.* A flash or lightning or the fire of it.

मेघतिमिर megh-tímir, *s. m.* Cloudiness, cloudy or rainy weather.

मेघदीप megh-déep, *s. m.* Lightning.

मेघद्वार megh-dwár, *s. m.* Sky, heaven, ether.

मेघनाद megh-nád, *s. m.* The noise or grumbling of clouds; the *Pulas* tree (*Butea frondosa*); a sort of *Amaranth* (*Amaranthns polygamus*).

मेघमाला megh-mála, *s. f.* A gathering or succession of clouds.

मेघराग megh-rág, *s. m.* One of the six modes of music.

मेचक méch-uk, *s. m.* Sulphuret of antimony.

मेटना mét-na, *v. a.* To effect, erase, blot out, wipe out, annihilate, annul, cancel, expiate, atone for; to thwart.

मेटोला mét-oola, *s. f.* A tree (*Spondias mangifera*).

मेढ़शृंगी mérh-shring-ee, *s. f.* A milky plant, the fruit of which is crooked, and therefore compared to a ram's horn (*Asclepias geminata*).

मेढ़ा medhá, *s. m.* A ram.

मेथी **méthee**, *s. f.* The plant fenugreek (*Trigonella fenugræcum*).

मेद **med**, *s. m.* Adeps, fat, the supposed proper seat is the abdomen; morbid or unnatural corpulency.

मेदस्वी **medus-wée**, *adj.* Robust, stout, strong; fat, corpulent.

मेदा **med-á**, *s. f.* A drug, described as a sort of root resembling ginger, brought from the *Moorung* district: it is one of the eight principal medicaments, and is said to be of cooling and emollient properties, and of particular use in fever and consumption.

मेदिनी **med-in-ée**, *s. f.* The earth.

मेदोधरा **med-ódhra**, *s. f.* A membrane in the abdomen, containing the fat, the omentum.

मेदोवृद्धि **médo-bríddhi**, *s. f.* Corpulence; enlargement of the scrotum.

मेध **medh**, *s. m.* Sacrifice, offering, oblation.

मेधा **medhá**, *s. f.* Apprehension, conception, understanding.

मेधावी **medháwee**, *adj.* Intelligent, comprehending, of ready comprehension or conception.

मेधि **médhi**, *s. m.* A post fixed in the centre of a threshing-floor or barn, to which the cattle are attached, as they turn round it to tread out the corn.

मेधिर **medhír**, *adj.* Intelligent, possessing a ready and just apprehension.

मेन्धी **mén-dhee**, *s. f.* A plant, from the leaves of which a reddish dye is prepared, with which the palms of the hands, tips of the fingers, soles of the feet, and finger-nails are stained (*Lawsonia inermis*).

मेमना **mém-na**, *s. m.* A kid.

मेरा **mér-a**, *pron.* 1*st pers. poss. masc.* My, mine.

मेरू **mér-oo**, *s. m.* The sacred mountain *Meroo*, in the centre of the seven continents, compared to the cup or seed-vessel of the lotus, the leaves of which are formed by the different *Dweeps*: its height is said by the *Hindoos* to be 84,000 *Yojuns*, sixteen thousand of which are below the surface of the earth: the shape is variously described, as square, conical, columnar, spherical, or spiral; and the four faces of it are of various colours, or white towards the east, yellow to the south, black to the west, and red towards the north: the river Ganges falls from heaven on its summit, and flows thence to the surrounding world in four streams; the southern branch is the Ganges of India, the northern running into Tartary, is the *Bhudrsoma*, the eastern is the *Sita*, and the western the *Chukshoo* or *Oxus*: on the summit of *Meroo Bruhma* resides, attended and worshipped by the *Rishis, Gundhurvs,* &c.; the regents of the points of the compass occupy the corresponding faces of the mountain, the whole of which consists of gold and gems: considered in any but a fabulous light, mount *Meroo* appears to mean the high land of Tartary, immediately to the north of the *Himaluy* mountains.

मेरूक **mér-ook**, *s. m.* Fragrant resin, incense.

मेरू **meróo**, *s. m.* An axis.

मेरो **meró**, *pron.* My, mine.

मेल **mel**, *s. m.* Connexion, relationship, agreement, combination, intimacy, concord, reconciliation, union, association, mixture, mixing, meeting, assemblage; a meeting or assemblage of people, a set, a fair, a court of justice, a counterpart.

मेलना **mel-ná**, *v. a.* To thrust in, stuff in, cram, penetrate, force in.

मेला **mél-a**, *s. m.* A fair, a large concourse of people collected at stated periods for religious or commercial purposes, as at *Hurdwar*, a mixed assemblage of *fukeers* or *sauds*. *Mela thela, s. m.* A crowd, a concourse of people. *Mela milna*, To meet full in the face.

मेली **mél-ee**, *s. m.* A partaker. *adj.* Friendly, sociable.

मेव **mev**,
मेवड़ा **mév-ra**,
मेवाती **mewátee**, } *s. m.* A tribe inhabiting the mountainous province of *Mewat*, much addicted to robbing.

मेष **mesh**, *s. m.* A ram; the sign Aries; a kind of drug.

मेषी **mésh-ee**, *s. f.* An ewe.

मेह **meh**, *s. m.* Urinary disease, especially inflammatory affection of the urethra, including gonorrhœa, &c.; urine, piss.

मेहतर **méh-tur**, *s. m.* A sweeper.

मेहतरानी **mehtur-ánee**, *s. f.* Female of *mehtur*; also a female inn-keeper.

मेहना **méh-na**, *s. m.* A taunt. *Mehna marna, v. a.* To taunt.

मेहुन्हा **mehun-há**, *s. m.* A taunter.

मैं **myn**, *pron.* I.

मैका **my-ká**, *s. m.* Kindred, relations, mother's family.

मैत्र **mytr**, *adj.* Of or belonging to a friend, friendly, amicable.

मैत्री **my-tree**, *s. f.* Friendship; the seventeenth lunar asterism.

मैथिल **my-thíl**, *adj.* Belonging to, born in, &c. *Mithila*.

मैथुन **my-thóon**, *s. m.* Venery, coition, copulation; union, association; marriage.

मैनफल myn-phúl, *s. m.* A fruit used in medicine (*Vangueria spinosa*).

मैनसिल myn-síl, *s. m.* Red arsenic (*Realgar*).

मैना my-na, *s. f.* A bird, a kind of jay (*Coracias Indica*).

मैभा my-bhá, *s. f.* A step-mother.

मैया my-yá, *s. f.* Mother.

मैल myl, *s. f.* Dirt, filth, rust, scum. *Myl katna*, To refine, to purify. *Myl chhantna*, To fine, strain, purify, clarify. *Myl bythna*, To gather a crust.

मैला my-lá, *adj.* Dirty, nasty, foul, defiled. *Nyla kurna*, To dirty, tarnish, foul. *Myla-koochyla*, *adj.* Dirty. *Myla hojana*, To tarnish, to become turbid, to be dirty.

मैहिका my-hik-á, *s. m.* A male buffalo.

मैहिकी my-hik-ée, *s. f.* A female buffalo.

मो mo, *pron.* (in *Bruj*), Me. *Mo-koun*, To me, me.

मोंढा mon-dhá, *s. m.* The shoulder; a lump; a stool, a footstool.

मोंरी mónh-ree, *s. f.* A kennel, a drain.

मोखा mó-kha, *s. m.* A small hole in a wall for admitting light and air, an air-hole, an aperture.

मोगरा móg-ra, *s. m.* A mallet, a pounder, a rammer; a flower, great double *Arabian* or *Tuscan jasmine* (*Jasminum sambac* : *Magorium*).

मोगरी móg-ree, *s. f.* A mallet for beating cloths, &c. with.

मोघ mogh, *adj.* Vain, useless, fruitless. *s. f.* Trumpet-flower (*Bignonia suave olens*).

मोघग्यान mogh-gyán, *adj.* Cultivating vain knowledge or any but religious wisdom.

मोघास mogh-ás, *adj.* Indulging vain hopes.

मोच moch, *s. m.* Strain, sprain, twist; a tree (*Hyperanthera morunga*).

मोचक mó-chuk, *s. m.* The silk-cotton tree (*Bombax heptaphyllum*); the plantain (*Musa sapientum*); a liberator.

मोचन mo-chún, *s. m.* Liberating, setting free; release, acquittal; theft, robbery. *s. f.* A saddler's or shoemaker's wife.

मोचना moch-ná, *v. a.* To let go, to set free, to shed, put off, extinguish.

मोचरस moch-rús, *s. m.* The gum of the silk-cotton tree.

मोचा mó-cha, *s. m.* A large lump of flesh; a plantain tree (*Musa sapientum*).

मोचाट mo-chát, *s. m.* A kind of pungent seed (*Nigella Indica*).

मोचिनी mo-chin-ée, *s. f.* A prickly nightshade.

मोची mó-chee, *s. m.* A saddler, a shoemaker, a cobbler.

मोच्छ mochh, *s. m.* Release, liberation, deliverance, absolution, salvation, beatitude, final and eternal happiness, the liberation of the soul from the body, and its exemption from further transmigration.

मोट mot, *s. f.* A package, bundle, bale, a load; amount, total; a leather bucket for raising water; vetches, lentils.

मोटकी mot-kée, *s. f.* One of the *Raginees* or female personifications of the musical modes; a mattock, pickaxe; a fat woman.

मोटरा mót-ra, *s. m.* A bundle.

मोटरी mot-rée, *s. f.* A small bundle, parcel, knapsack.

मोटला motla, ⎫ *adj.* Fat, plump, corpu-
मोटा mó-ta, ⎭ lent, thick, coarse, great, large, big, bulky, gross.

मोटाई mo-táee, *s. f.* ⎫ Fatness, corpu-
मोटापन mota-pún, *s. m.* ⎬ lency, thick-
मोटापा motá-pa, *s. m.* ⎭ ness, coarseness, bigness, bulk, bulkiness, grossness.

मोटिया mó-tiya, *s. m.* A porter.

मोठ moth, *s. f.* A bundle, package, bale, a load; amount, total; a leather bucket for raising water; vetches, lentils.

मोड़ mor, *s. m.* A turn, twist, convolution, writhe, sprain; fistula. [screw.

मोड़ना mór-na, *v. a.* To twist, turn, bend,

मोढ़ा mór-ha, *s. m.* A stool; the shoulder.

मोतरा mót-ra, *s. m.* Spavin.

मोतिया mó-tiya, *s. m.* A flower (*Jasminum sambac*).

मोतियाबिंद motiya-bínd, *s. m.* A kind of blindness (*Guta serena*).

मोती mó-tee, *s. m.* A pearl. *Motee keesee ab ooturnee*, To be disgraced. *Motee koot-kur bhurneh*, To be very bright (*applied to an eye*). *Motee pironeh*, To string pearls; (*met.*) to speak eloquently; to weep (*the tears being compared to pearls*).

मोतीचूर motee-chóor, *s. m.* A kind of sweetmeat; a certain description of eye among pigeons.

मोथरा móth-ra, *s. m.* A disease in horses, splint, spavin.

मोथा mo-thá, *s. m.* A kind of grass the root of which is used in medicine (*Cyperus rotundus*).

मोद mod, *s. m.* Joy, delight, happiness, pleasure.

मोदक mo-dúk, *adj.* Delighting, rejoicing, causing happiness or delight. *s. m.* A sort of sweetmeat.

मोदित mo-dít, *adj.* Pleased, delighted. *s. m.* Pleasure, delight.

मोदी mó-dee, *s. m.* A merchant, a shop-keeper, a grain-merchant, a steward, a providore. *Modee-khana*, A pantry, a grain-merchant's shop.

मोधू mó-dhoo, *adj.* Guileless, artless, simple, foolish.

मोनी mó-nee, *s. f.* Point, end.

मोम mom, *s. m.* Wax. *Mom kee nak*, A person of a fickle disposition. *Mom-jama, s. m.* Wax-cloth, cere-cloth. *Mom-dil, adj.* Tender-hearted. *Mom-buttee, s. f.* A wax-candle. *Mom-roughun*, Wax and oil mixed together.

मोमिया mó-miya, *s. m.* A mummy.

मोमियाई mo-miyáee, *adj.* Of or like a mummy. *s. f.* A medicine.

मोमी mó-mee, *adj.* Waxen; of the colour of wax; (*applied to chints*) prepared after stamping by covering the flowers with wax to prevent their being spoiled by other colours afterwards applied.

मोर mor, *s. m.* A peacock; twist, turn. *Mor-punkhee, s. f.* A kind of pleasure boat, a barge. *Mor-mookoot, s. m.* A crown or crest like that of the peacock.

मोरचंग mor-chúng, *s. f.* A jew's-harp.

मोरछल mor-chhúl, *s. m.* A fan for driving away flies (*especially of peacock's feathers*), a brush.

मोरनी mornée, *s. f.* A peahen.

मोरा mó-ra, *pron.* Mine, my.

मोरी mó-ree, *s. f.* A pipe or subterraneous passage (*for water*).

मोल mol, *s. m.* Purchase; price. *Mol thuhrana*, To appraise, estimate, value. *Mol-tol*, Fixing a price; traffic, purchasing. *Mol burhana, v. a.* To enhance. *Mol-lena, v. a.* To buy, to purchase.

मोषक mo-shúk, *s. m.* A thief.

मोषन mo-shún, *s. m.* Stealing.

मोषा mo-shá, *s. f.* Stealing, theft.

मोषना mós-na, *v. a.* To pilfer, steal, filch, defraud, snatch or seize by force.

मोह moh, *s. f.* Fainting, loss of consciousness or sense; ignorance, folly, foolishness; it is applied especially to that spiritual ignorance which leads men to believe in the reality of worldly objects, and to addict themselves to mundane or sensual enjoyment; error, mistake; bewilderment, distraction; pity, compassion, sympathy, kindness, affection, allurement, fascination, love. *Moh men ana*, To faint, as at the sudden appearance of a friend or mistress. *Moh lena*, To attach, allure, fascinate, charm, captivate.

मोहन mó-hun, *adj.* Fascinating, stupefying, depriving of sense or understanding. *s. m.* Copulation; temptation, seduction, the overpower-ing of reason and reflection by worldly or sensual allurements. *Mohun-bhog, s. m.* A kind of sweetmeat. *Mohun-mala, s. f.* An ornament, a string or necklace composed of gold beads and corals.

मोहना moh-ná, *v. a.* To fascinate, enchant, charm, allure, delude. *adj.* Fascinating, captivating, charming, winning.

मोहनी moh-née, *s. f.* An enchantress; fascination, a charm, a philter. *adj. f.* Fascinating, depriving of the powers of reflection, stupefying.

मोहाना mo-hána, *s. m.* The mouth (*of a river, &c.*), inlet, outlet.

मोहि móhi, *pron.* To me, me.

मोहित mo-hít, *adj.* Faint, senseless, charmed, fascinated; beguiled, deceived.

मोहिनी móhin-ee, *f.* }
मोही mo-hée, *m.* } *adj.* Illusive, fallacious, beguiling. *s. f.* An enchantress, a whore.

मोहिनी mó-hin-ee, *s. f.* A kind of jasmine, called also *Tripoora-malee*.

मोक्ष moksh, *s. m.* Final and eternal happiness, the liberation of the soul from the body, and its exemption from further transmigration; death; liberation, freedom.

मोक्षक moksh-úk, *s. m.* A deliverer, a liberator.

मोक्षित moksh-ít, *adj.* Let go, liberated, at large.

मौ mou, *s. m.* Honey.

मौख्य móukh-yuh, *s. m.* Pre-eminence.

मौग्ध mougdh, *s. m.* Simplicity, silliness; ignorance.

मौंजी móun-jee, *s. f.* The girdle of a *Brahmun* made of three strings of *moonj* grass.

मौंजीबन्धन móunjee-búndhun, *s. m.* Investiture with the distinguishing cord.

मौर mour, *s. m.* A kind of high crowned hat, worn by the bridegroom at the time of marriage.

मौर्ह्य mourhyu, *s. m.* Ignorance, folly, especially spiritual folly.

मौन moun, *s. m.* }
मौनता moun-tá, *s. f.* } Silence, taciturnity.

मौना mouná, *s. m.* A large jar; a basket.

मौनी mou-née, *adj.* Silent, taciturn. *s. f.* A small round basket, a work-basket. *s. m.* A class of mendicants who observe perpetual silence, an ascetic, a hermit, a religious sage, one who has overcome his passions and retired from the world.

मौमाखी mou-mákhee, *s. f.* A honey-bee.

मौर mour, *s. m.* The blossom of a tree, especially of the mango.

मौराना mou-rána, *v. n.* To blossom (*as the mango tree*).

मौर्ख्य móurkh-yuh, *s. m.* Stupidity, folly, fatuity.

मौलना móul-na, *v. n.* To bloom, bud, blossom (*the mango tree*); to intoxicate (*as bhung, &c.*)

मौलसरी moul-súr-ee, *s. f.* A tree (*Mimusops elengi*).

मौलिक moul-ík, *adj.* Of inferior rank or caste among *Kuyuths.*

मौली mou-lée, *s. f.* A lock of hair on the crown of the head; hair ornamented and braided round the head; a diadem, a tiara; the head; the earth.

मौसा móu-sa, *s. m.* An uncle, mother's sister's husband.

मौसी móu-see, *s. f.* An aunt, mother's sister.

मौसेरा mou-séra, *adj. m.* Belonging or related to the mother's sister's husband; as *Mousera bhaee*, A cousin, son of a mother's sister. *Mousree buhin*, Daughter of a mother's sister.

म्लान mlan, *adj.* Foul, dirty; languid, weary; faded, withered.

म्लानि mlá-ni, *s. f.* Weariness, languor; foulness, filth; fading, decay.

म्लेच्छ mlechchh, *s. m.* The generic term for a barbarian or foreigner, that is, for one speaking any language but *Sunskrit*, and not subject to the usual *Hindoo* institutions; a sinner, a criminal.

म्लेच्छजाति mlechchh-játi, *s. m.* A barbarian, or a man of an outcast race. The tribes enumerated under this head by *Munoo*, but who are by him said to be properly, degraded *Khuttrees*, appear to be chiefly the inhabitants of the countries bordering immediately upon India, both to the north and south.

म्लेच्छदेश mlechchh-dés, *s. m.* The countries bordering on India, or those inhabited by people of a different faith and language; defined to be any where the black antelope is not found.

म्लेच्छभोजन mlechchh-bhójun, *s. m.* Wheat.

म्लेच्छवाक् mlechchh-vák, *adj.* Speaking a barbarous dialect.

म्लेच्छित mlech-chhít, *adj.* Spoken incorrectly or barbarously. *s. m.* Foreign or barbarous language; ungrammatical speech.

य

य yuh, The twenty-sixth consonant of the *Nuguree* alphabet, or semivowel *y*: in some provinces it is pronounced *j*.

यजमान juj-mán, *s. m.* An employer of priests at a sacrifice, the person who institutes its performance, and pays the expense of it; a customer, a person to whose custom, *Brahmuns*, barbers, and some others, have a legal claim. (*The hereditary Brahmun, or barber, &c. of a village must be paid his fee, whether you choose to employ him or another person*).

यजुर्वेद yujoor-véd, *s. m.* One of the four *Veds.*

यजुस् yúj-oos, *s. m.* The *Yujoor* or *Yujoos*, one of the four *Veds*: it is divided into two principal portions, the white and black: both portions of this *Ved* are very full on the subject of religious rites, and the prayers peculiar to it are chiefly in measured and poetical prose.

यज्ञ júg-yuh, *s. m.* A sacrifice, a ceremony in which oblations are presented.

यज्ञकर्म júgyuh-kúrmm, *s. m.* Any sacrificial act or ceremony.

यज्ञपशु júgyuh-púsoo, *s. m.* A horse; any animal offered in sacrifice. [sel.

यज्ञपात्र júgyuh-pátr, *s. m.* A sacrificial vessel.

यज्ञपुरुष júgyuh-póoroosh, *s. m.* A name of *Vishnoo.*

यज्ञभूमि júgyuh-bhóomi, *s. f.* Place prepared for a sacrifice, or where it is offered.

यज्ञसिद्धि júgyuh-siddhi, *s. f.* Performance of sacrifice; obtaining the objects of a sacrifice.

यज्ञसूत्र júgyuh-sóotr, *s. m.* The characteristic thread, worn by the three principal classes of *Hindoos.*

यज्ञस्थान jugyuh-sthán, *s. m.* A place of sacrifice.

यज्ञिय jugiyúh, *adj.* Proper for or suitable to a sacrifice.

यज्ञियदेश jugiyuh-dés, *s. f.* The country of the *Hindoos*: those districts in which the ritual and institutes of the *Hindoo* system are enforced; properly the country in which the black deer or antelope is native.

यज्ञशाला júgyuh-shála, *s. f.* A temple, a shrine, a place of sacrifice.

यज्ञोपवीत jugyó-puv-éet, *s. m.* The sacrificial cord, originally worn by the three principal castes of *Hindoos.*

यज्ञोपवीती jugyó-puvéetee, *s. m.* A *Brahmun*, &c. invested with the sacred thread.

यतन jút-un, *s. m.* Striving, making effort or exertion; carefulness, remedy, care, effort, endeavour.

यतनीय jútun-éeyuh, *adj.* To be exerted or persevered, to be made as an effort.

यतव्रत yut-vrút, *adj.* Firm to an engagement or vow.

यति yúti, jútí, *s. m.* A sage, whose passions are completely under subjection; a religious mendicant, especially one of the *Jyn* sect.

यती jút-ee, *s. m.* A sage with subdued passions.

यतेन्द्रिय jut-éndriyuh, *adj.* Chaste, pure, of subdued passions.

यत्न jutn, *s. m.* Effort, exertion, perseverance, energy.

यत्नवत jutn-wút, ⎫ *adj.* Persevering, diligent, making effort or exertion.
यत्नवान jutn-wán, ⎬
यत्नी jutnee, ⎭

यत्र yutr, *adv.* Where, in what place.

यथा yuthá, *adv.* As, according to.

यथाकर्तव्य yuthá-kurtúvyuh, *adj.* What is right or proper to be done.

यथाकल्प yutha-kúlp, *adv.* As designed.

यथाकाम yutha-kám, *adv.* At pleasure, as you please.

यथाकामी yútha-kámee, *adj.* Wilful, independant, uncontrolled, following one's own inclinations.

यथाक्रम yutha-krúm, *adv.* In order, orderly, successively, methodically.

यथातथा yútha-tuthá, *adv.* In any way, any how.

यथाभिमत yuthá-bhimút, *adv.* According to one's wish or purpose.

यथामुखीन yútha-mookhéen, *adj.* Like, resembling, shewing similarly or reflecting.

यथार्थ yuthárth, *adj.* Right, proper; according to the sense. *adv.* Properly, suitably.

यथार्थता yutharth-tá, *s. f.* Rectitude, propriety, fitness.

यथावकाश yuthao-kásh, *adv.* According to opportunity.

यथावत yutha-vút, *adv.* Truly, exactly, as it was, according to law or usage.

यथावसर yutha-vusúr, *adv.* According to opportunity.

यथाविधि yútha-vídhi, *adv.* According to rule.

यथाशक्ति yútha-shúkti, *adv.* Extent of capability, as much as possible.

यथाशास्त्र yútha-shástr, *adv.* According to the *Shastrus*, agreeably to scripture.

यथासुख yútha-sóokh, *adv.* Happily.

यथास्थित yutha-sthít, *adv.* Circumstantially, relating a thing as it happened.

यदा yúd-a, *adv.* When, at what time.

यदि yúdi, *adv.* If.

यदु yúdoo, *n. prop.* The name of a king, the ancestor of *Krishn*, and the eldest son of *Yuyati*, the fifth monarch of the lunar dynasty; a country on the west of the *Jumna* river about *Muthoora* and *Vrindavun*, over which *Yudoo* ruled, and named after him.

यदुनाथ yudoo-náth, *s. m.* A name of *Krishn*, as lord of *Yudoo*.

यदुवंश yudoo-búns, *s. m.* The tribe of *Yudoo*.

यदुवंशी yudoo-búnsee, *s. m.* A descendant of *Yudoo*.

यद्यपि yudyúpi, *adv.* Although.

यन्त्र yuntr, juntr, *s. m.* A machine in general, any implement or apparatus; a musical instrument; a dial; an observatory; a diagram of a mystical nature or astrological character; an amulet. *Juntr-muntr, s. m.* Juggling, conjuring, enchanting by figures and incantations.

यन्त्रणा juntr-ná, *s. m.* Pain, anguish, affliction.

यन्त्री jun-trée, *s. m.* An instrument for drawing wire; a conjurer, a juggler, a wizard.

यम jum, *adj.* Twin, fellow, one of a pair or brace. *s. m.* The deity of *Nuruk* or hell, and judge of departed souls; he is often identified with death and time. *Jum-diya, s. m.* A candle or illumination sacred to *Jum*, lighted on the 13th of *Kartik, Krishn-puksh*, i. e. three days before the *dewalee*.

यमक júm-uk, *adj.* Twin, fellow, one of a pair or twins.

यमदूत jum-dóot, *s. m.* An infernal spirit, the messenger or minister of *Jum*, employed, it is said, to bring the souls of the dead to *Jum*'s judgment-seat, and thence conduct them to their final destination.

यमन yúm-un, *s. m.* A musical mode; a *Yuvun*, which formerly meant an Ionian or Greek, but is now applied to both the *Mahomedan* and European invaders of India, and it is often used as a general term for any foreign or barbarous race.

यमल júm-ul, *s. m.* A pair, a brace, a couple.

यमुना yúm-oona, *s. f.* The *Jumna* river, which rises on the south side of the *Himaluy* range, at a short distance to the north-west of the source of the Ganges, and which after a course of about 378 miles falls into that river immediately below *Allahabad*.

यलाफिल्ला yúla-phyla, *adj.* Unconfined, extended, spread, at ease.

यव jou, *s. m.* Barley (*Hordeum hexastichon*); the measure of a barley corn, considered as equal to six mustard seeds; the mark between the joints of the finger. *Jou jou hisab lena*, To take a strict account.

यवक्षार yuvukshár, juvukhár, *s. m.* Saltpetre, nitre, nitrate of potash.

यवन yúv-un, *s. m.* A country, probably Bactria, or it may be extended from that colony to Ionia (*to which word it bears some resemblance*), or still further to Greece ; by late *Hindoo* writers, it is most commonly applied to Arabia ; a *Yuvun*, apparently originally a Greek, but since applied to both the *Mahomedan* and European invaders of India, and often used as a general term for any foreign or barbarous race.

यवनाचार्य्यं yúvun-achárjj, *s. m.* An astronomical writer, frequently quoted by ancient *Hindoo* astronomers : perhaps Ptolemy, or the Greek astronomers collectively.

यवनाल yuvun-ál, *s. m.* A sort of grass, very generally cultivated, and the grain extensively eaten (*Andropogon* or *Holcus bicolor*.)

यवनी yuv-un-ée, *n. prop.* A female *Yuvun*.

यवफल jou-phúl, *s. m.* A medicinal plant (*Wrightea antidysenterica*).

यवमध्य jou-múdhyuh, *s. m.* A form of penance, diminishing the food daily during the dark fortnight, fasting on the new moon, and gradually augmenting the food till the full moon.

यवानी juvánee, *s. f.* A plant (*Ligusticum ajwaen*).

यवास juwás, *s. m.* A flower (*Hedysarum alhagi*).

यश jus, *s. m.* Celebrity, reputation, glory, fame, renown, name, character, luck ; splendour, lustre ; praise, eulogium. *Jus-upjus, s. m.* Good or bad (*name, fame or character*). *Jus-put, adj.* Reputable, renowned.

यशस्कर jusus-kúr, *adj.* Rendering famous, conferring celebrity.

यशस्काम jusus-kám, *adj.* Ambitious, desirous of fame or glory.

यशस्वन् jusus-wán, } *adj.* Famous, cele-
यशस्वी jusus-wée, } brated, renowned, famed.

यष्टि yúsh-ti, *s. m.* } A staff, a stick ; a
यष्टी yush-tee, *s. f.* } staff armed with iron, &c. used as a weapon, a club, a mace.

यष्टिक yush-tík, *s. m.* A bird, the lapwing.

यष्टिमधु jústi-múdhoo, *s. m.* Liquorice, or the root of the *Abrus precatorius*, which is used for it.

यह yuh, *pron.* This, he, she, it, these, the, to this degree.

यहाँ yuhán, *adv.* Here, hither ; at the above, near, with. *Yuhan-ka-yuheen,* In the very same place, exactly here. *Yuhan-tuk,* To this pitch, to this degree, thus far, hitherto.

यहीं yuhéen, *adv.* This very, in this very place, here.

यहूदी yuhóodee, *s. m.* A Jew, a Hebrew.

यक्ष yuksh, *s. m.* A demigod.

यक्षिणी yukshin-ée, *s. f.* A female fiend.

यक्ष्मा yuksh-má, *s. m.* Pulmonary consumption.

या ya, *pron.* This.

याँ yan, *adv.* Contraction of *Yuhan,* Here, hither.

याग yág, *s. m.* A sacrifice, any ceremony in which offerings and oblations are presented.

याचक ya-chúk, ja-chúk, *adj.* Beggar, mendicant, asking, one who asks or solicits.

याचना yach-ná, jach-ná, *s. f.* Asking, begging.

याचित ja-chit, *adj.* Asked, begged, solicited.

याजक ja-júk, *s. m.* An officiating priest, a *Brahmun* who conducts any part of a sacrifice.

याजन ja-jún, *s. m.* Conducting a sacrifice, or causing its performance.

याज्ञिक jag-yík, *s. m.* A sacrificer, an institutor of a sacrifice.

याज्ञिय jagyiyúh, *adj.* Fit for sacrifice.

याज्य jáj-yuh, *s. m.* Property or presents derived from officiating at sacrifices.

यातना yát-na, *s. f.* Pain, agony, sharp or acute pain ; the pains of hell.

यातायात yata-yát, *s. m.* Coming and going ; transmigration.

यात्रा játra, *s. f.* Going, moving, proceeding, marching, travelling ; departure, march, journey ; a festival but especially the procession of idols, &c. ; going on pilgrimage.

यात्राकरण játra-kúrun, *s. m.* Setting forth on a journey, a march, &c.

यात्रिक ja-trík, *s. m.* A pilgrim, a traveller.

यात्री ja-trée, } *s. m.* A pilgrim.
यात्रु ja-tróo, }

याथार्थिक ya-thar-thík, *adj.* Just, true, right.

यादव ja-dúv, *s. m. Krishn,* as descended from the family of *Yudoo.*

यान yan, *s. m.* Any vehicle or form of conveyance, as a carriage, a litter, a horse, an elephant, &c.

यापन já-pun, *s. m.* Spending or passing away time.

याबू ya-bóo, *s. m.* A poney, a galloway.

यामनी yám-nee, *adj.* Of or relating to *Yuvuns.*

यामिनी yám-in-ee, *s. f.* Night. *Yaminee-bhasha, s. f.* The language or dialect of *Yuvuns.*

यावक ja-wúk, *s. m.* The red colour procured from the lac insect.

यावज्जीव ya-vujjéev, } *adv.* For life, as
यावज्जीवन jáwuj-jéevun, } long as life.

यावत् ja-wút, *adv.* As much as; as many as; as long as; as far as; unto, until.

यावन yá-vun, *m.*
यावनी ya-vun-ée, *f.* } *adj.* Belonging or relating to a *Yuvun*, Ionian, Mahomedan, &c.

याही ya-hée, *pron. dem. object. case*, This, to this.

यिह yih, *pron.* This, he, she, it, these, the, to this degree.

यिही yihée, *pron.* This very, the same, itself.

युक्त yookt, *adj.* Joined, combined, united, identified; right, fit, proper; possessing, endowed with, as virtues, qualities, &c.

युक्तरसा yookt-rúsa, *s. f.* A plant (*Mimosa octandra*).

युक्ति yóokti, *s. f.* Union, connection, joining; propriety, fitness; contrivance, dexterity, art, skill, policy, project.

युग yoog, *s. m.* An age of the world, or great period, as the *Sut* or *Kreet, Treta, Dwapur*, and *Kuli*; a term used in the game of *Chousur* (*the opposite of a blot, two or more men standing on the same square*); a pair, a couple, a brace. *Joog-joog, adv.* Constantly, eternally. *Joog phorna, v. a.* To cause a difference between friends, to fall out. *Joog-an-joog*, Ages of ages, from age to age, for ages.

युगपत् joog-pút, *adv.* At one time, at once; together, conjointly.

युगल joo-gúl, *s. m.* A pair, a brace, a couple.

युगान्त joog-ánt, *s. m.* A destruction of the universe; the end of an age.

युगान्तबन्धु joog-ánt-búndhoo, *s. m.* A real friend, a friend in need.

युग्म joogm, *s. m.* A pair, a couple, a brace.

युत joot, *adj.* Joined, combined, connected; endowed with, possessed of.

युद्ध jooddh, *s. m.* War, battle, contest, conflict.

युधिष्ठिर joodhis-thír, *s. m.* The elder of the five *Panduv* princes, and leader in the great war between them and the *Kooroos*, in the beginning of the fourth age; the nominal son of *Pandoo*, whom he succeeded in the sovereignty of India.

युध्मान joodhmán, *adj.* Fighting, warring.

युवती joo-vut-ée, *s. f.* A young woman, one from sixteen to thirty.

युवराज joovuráj, *s. m.* A young prince, especially the heir apparent, associated to the throne.

युवराज्य joovuráj-yuh, *s. m.* The dignity of heir apparent and associate in the throne.

युव jóo-va, *s. m.* A young man or one of the virile age, or from sixteen to seventy.

यूं yoon,
यों yon, } *adv.* Thus, in this manner. *Yoon nuh yoon*, One way or other, somehow or other. *Yoon-heen*, In this very manner, thus, accidentally, by chance, causelessly, easily, cursorily.

यूका jóo-ka, *s. f.* A louse.

यूथ jooth, *s. m.* A multitude of birds or beasts, a herd, a flock.

यूथी joo-thée, *s. f.* A sort of jasmine (*Jasminum auriculatum*.)

यूप joop, *s. m.* A sacrificial post, a pillar usually made of bamboos, or the wood of the *Khudir*, to which the victim at a sacrifice is bound; a trophy, a column erected in honour of a victory.

यूष joos, *s. m.* Pease soup, pease porridge, the water in which pulse of various kinds has been boiled.

ये yeh, *pron. plur.* These, they.

योग jog, *s. m.* Junction, joining, union; combination, association, meeting, conflux; fitting; a fortunate moment, opportunity, occasion; penance, devotion, religious meditation, spiritual worship of God, or union with the Supreme Being by means of abstract contemplation; certain divisions of a great circle, measured upon the ecliptic; propriety, fitness. *adj.* Possible, capable, fit. *Jog-maya, s. f.* A deceptive power which *Jogees* are supposed to possess.

योगनाविक jogna-vík, *s. m.* A sort of fish (*Silurus ascita*).

योगपट्ट jog-pútt, *s. m.* A cloth drawn round the lower extremities of the ascetic as he squats to perform religious abstraction.

योगवाही jog-váhee, *s. m.* A menstruum or medium for mixing medicines. *s. f.* Alkali; quicksilver.

योगसेवा jog-sév-a, *s. f.* Practising religious abstraction.

योगासन jog-ásun, *s. m.* A religious posture, the position in which the devotee sits to perform the religious exercise called *Jog*.

योगिनिद्रा jógi-nidra, *s. f.* Light sleep, wakefulness.   [sprite.

योगिनी jogin-ée, *s. f.* A female fiend or

योगी jó-gee, *s. m.* A devotee, an ascetic in general; a magician, a conjurer.

योगेश्वर jog-éshwur, *s. m.* A principal sage or ascetic; a magician; a deity, the object of devout contemplation.

योग्य jóg-yuh, *adj.* Clever, accomplished, skilful; powerful, able; fit, proper, suitable.

योग्यता jogyuh-tá, *s. f.* Fitness, suitableness, propriety, capability, ability.

योजन yó-jun, jó-jun, *s. m.* God, the Supreme Being, the soul of the world; a measure of distance equal to four *kros* or *kos*, will be exactly nine miles; other computations make the *Jojun* but about five miles, or even no more than four miles and a half; joining, union, junction.

योद्धा jod-dhá, *s. m.* A warrior, a soldier, a combatant.

योधन jodhún, *s. m.* Fighting, warring, battle.

योधापन jodha-pún, *s. m.* Heroism, bravery, prowess.

योधी jo-dhée, *s. m.* A warrior.

योनि jó-ni, *s. f.* The vulva.

योनिनासा jóni-nása, *s. f.* The upper part of the vulva, or the union of the labiæ.

योनिलिंग jóni-líng, *s. m.* The clitoris.

योन्यर्सा jonyúr-sa, *s. m.* An affection of the vulva, Menorrhagia, or prolapsus uteri.

योषित jo-shít, *s. f.* A woman in general.

यों youn, *adv.* Thus, in this manner.

यौतक you-túk, *s. m.* A nuptial gift, presents made to a bride at her marriage by her father or friends; some consider it also implying a gift to the bridegroom.

यौन joun, *m.* ⎱ *adj.* Relating to the
यौनी jou-née, *f.* ⎰ womb or place of origin, uterine; connected by female alliance, marriage, &c.

यौवन jou-vún, *s. m.* Youth, manhood.

यौवनदर्प jouvun-dúrp, *s. m.* Pride of youth, rashness, conceit.

यौवनदशा jóuvun-dúsa, *s. f.* The period of youth, adolescence.

यौवनवती jouvun-vútee, *f.* ⎱ *adj.* Youth-
यौवनवान् jouvun-wán, *m.* ⎰ ful.

र

र ruh, The twenty-seventh consonant of the *Nagures* alphabet, corresponding to the letter *r*.

रई ruée, *s. f.* A churning staff, bran.

रंक runk, *s. m.* A poor man.

रंहट rún-hut, *s. m.* A wheel for drawing water with.

रंश runs, *s. f.* A ray, a sun-beam.

रक्त rukt, *adj.* Red, of a red colour. *s. m.* Blood. *Rukt-chundun, s. m.* Red sandal-wood, red sanders, or sapan wood.

रक्तकोढ rukt-kórh, *s. m.* A kind of leprosy in which the part affected is red.

रक्तगुल्म rukt-góolm, *s. m.* A disease, a hard lump in the abdomen of the female after conception, perhaps scirrhus of the ovarium; a clot of blood.

रक्तचूर्ण rukt-chóorn, *s. m.* Red lead.

रक्तता rukt-tá, *s. f.* Redness.

रक्तधातु rukt-dhátoo, *s. m.* Red chalk or red orpiment; copper.

रक्तपा rukt-pá, *s. f.* A leech.

रक्तपात rukt-pát, *s. m.* Spilling of blood.

रक्तपित्त rukt-pítt, *s. m.* Plethora, spontaneous hæmorrhages from the mouth, nose, rectum and cuticle, accompanied with fever and headache, vomiting, purging, &c.

रक्तपित्ती rukt-píttee, *s. f.* A painful and itchy eruption supposed to arise from excess of blood and bile; a plant used for the cure of this disease.

रक्तमय rukt-múy, *adj.* Bloody, full or consisting of blood.

रक्तलोचन rukt-lóchun, *adj.* Red-eyed.

रक्तवर्ण rukt-vúrn, *adj.* Red, of a red colour.

रक्तहीन rukt-héen, *adj.* Bloodless, coldblooded.

रक्ताम्बर rukt-ámbur, *adj.* Dressed in red.

रक्ताम्बरा rúkt-ambur-á, *s. m.* Any vagrant devotee wearing red garments.

रक्तालू rukt-áloo, *s. m.* A sort of yam, (*Dioscorea purpurea*).

रखक rukhúk, *s. m.* A keeper.

रखछोरना rukh-chhórna, *v. a.* To place; to keep; to have; to give in charge.

रखदेना rukh-déna, *v. a.* To put down, to place; to keep, to put by.

रखन rukhún, *s. m.* Keeping, charge, protection.

रखना rúkh-na, *v. a.* To keep, put, place, have, hold, possess, preserve, reserve, save, lay, set, station, apply, ascribe, impute, esteem, consider, have, own, stop.

रखलेना rukh-léna, *v. a.* To take in charge, to take into keeping or service, to engage.

रखवाई rukh-wáee, *s. f.* The price paid for keeping, &c.

रखवाना rukh-wána, *v. a.* To cause to keep, place, &c. *Rukhwa lena*, To take in charge.

रखवारा rukh-wára, ⎤ *s. m.* A keeper, guard,
रखवाल rukh-wál, ⎬ shepherd, cowherd,
रखवाला rukhwála, ⎦ goatherd.

रखवाली rukh-wálee, *s. f.* Keeping, guarding, custody, grazing cattle.

रखाना rukh-ána, *v. a.* To give in charge, to cause to keep, put, place. *Rukh lena*, To take in charge.

रखिया rúkh-iya, *s. f.* Protection, keeping.

रखी rúkh-ee, *s. f.* A tribute paid to a *Sikh* chief for protection. *s. m.* A protector, guardian. *adj.* used *sub.* Grass which has been preserved for cattle, cut down and dried, hay.

रखैया rukhyya, *s. m.* Keeper, protector.

रगड़ rug-úr, *s. f.* Attrition, friction, rubbing, abrasion.

रगड़ना rug-úr-na, *v. a.* To rub, scour, grate, fret, abrade, excoriate.

रगड़ा rug-rá, *s. m.* Quarrelling; rubbing, polishing; a collyrium.

रगड़ाझगड़ा rúgra-jhúg-ra, *s. m.* Quarrel, debate, discussion.

रगना rúg-na, *v. a.* To be attached to, to be in love with.

रगेद rug-éd, *s. f.* Pursuit, chase.

रगेदना rug-éd-na, *v. a.* To pursue, chase, hunt.

रघु rúgh-oo, *s. m.* A sovereign of *Oude,* the great grandfather of *Ramchundr;* the family or descendants of *Rughoo.*

रघुबंश rughoo-búns, *s. m.* The race or family of *Rughoo;* hence also the name of a poem by *Kalidas,* which treats of the ancestors of *Ram,* from *Duleep* to that prince, and his descendants to *Ugnivurn.*

रङ्क runk, *adj.* Niggardly, avaricious, a miser. *s. m.* A poor man.

रंग rung, *s. m.* Paint, colour, tint, dye, hue; dancing, acting, singing, amusement, merriment, pleasure; suit (*at cards*). *Rung oor jana,* To change colour, to be afraid. *Rung ooturna,* To become pale; to be grieved. *Rung kurna,* To enjoy, to lead a life of pleasure. *Rung churhna,* To be elated with liquor. *Rung dekhna,* To look at or examine the state, condition, result, conclusion or consequence of any thing. *Rung-bhung,* Spoiling of sport. *Rung-muhull,* An apartment for festive or voluptuous enjoyment. *Rung marna,* To win (*in gaming: an expression taken from the game of choupur*). *Rung-ruliyan, s. f. pl.* Merriment, pleasure, mirth, pleasant society of a lover. *Rung ratna,* To be affected or imbued (*with love*), to become attached to any one. *Rung-roop, s. m.* Colour, form, appearance. *Rung lugana,* To colour; to excite a quarrel.

रंगत rúng-ut, *s. f.* Colour.

रंगना rúng-na, *v. a.* To colour, to die.

रंगभूति rung-bhóoti, *s. m.* The day of full moon in the month *Aswin* (*September-October*), on the night of which *Lukshmee* descended, promising wealth to all who were awake: the night is spent in playing ancient chess, in *naches,* &c.

रंगभूमि rung-bhóomi, *s. f.* A field of battle; a stage, a theatre, a place where dancing is exhibited.

रंगरस rung-rús, *s. m.* Delight, melody, pleasure.

रंगवाई rung-wáee, *s. f.* The price paid for colouring (*particularly for dyeing*).

रंगवैया rung-wyya, *s. m.* A dier.

रंगशाला rung-shála, *s. f.* A hall for public exhibitions, as *naches,* plays, &c., a ball-room, a theatre.

रंगाई rung-áee, *s. f.* The price paid for dying; a certain space of time during which a cloth is dyed.

रंगाना rung-ána, *v. a.* To colour.

रंगावट rung-áwut, *s. f.* Colour, colouring.

रंगी rúng-ee, *adj.* Impassioned, having propensity or passion. *s. m.* A dier. *s. f.* Chintz, the colour of which will not stand washing; a kind of cloth peculiar to *Khyrabad.*

रंगीला rung-éela, *s. m.* A rake. *adj.* Gaudy, fine, showy, airy, buxom.

रचक ruch-úk, *s. m.* A maker, a composer.

रचना rúch-na, *v. n.* To be made, to be created, to be prepared; to be set to work, to be employed, to be about (*a business*); to stain, to colour; to love, to like; to keep time in music; to penetrate; to predestinate. *v. a.* To make, form, invent, prepare, compose, perform. *s. f.* Forming, composing, creating, making, invention; created thing, work, workmanship.

रचाना ruch-ána, *v. a.* To set to work, to set a going; to make, to do; to make merry; to stain the hands, feet, &c. with *menhdee,* &c.; to celebrate.

रचित rúch-it, *adj.* Made, manufactured; . written, composed.

रच्छक ruchhúk, *s. m.* A protector, keeper, guard, watchman, redeemer.

रच्छा ruchhá, *s. f.* Protection, guarding, keeping, preservation, defence, patronage, safety.

रज ruj, *s. m.* Dust; the pollen of flowers; the menstrual excretion; the secondary property of humanity, the quality of passion, which produces sensual desire, worldly coveting, pride and falsehood, and is the cause of pain.

रजक rúj-uk, *s. m.* A washerman.

रजकी ruj-uk-ée, *s. f.* A washerman's wife or a washerwoman.

रजजाना ruj-jána, *v. n.* To be satisfied.

रजत rúj-ut, *s. m.* Silver.

रजनी ruj-née, *s. f.* Night.

रजनीकर rujnee-kúr, *s. m.* The moon.

रजनीगन्ध rujnee-gúndh, *s. m.* The tuberose (*Polianthes tuberosa*).

रजनीचर rujnee-chúr, *s. m.* A *rakshus,* a ghost, goblin; a thief; a watchman.

रजनी मुख rujnee-móokh, *s. m.* Evening, beginning of the night.

रजनीचासा rújnee-hása, *s. f.* A flower (*Nyctanthes arbor tristis*), which blossoms at night and diffuses a powerful scent after sun-set.

रुजवारा ruj-wára, *s. m.* A kingdom, a country under the control of a *raja*.

रजस ruj-ús, *s. m.* The second condition of humanity, the quality or property of passion; that which produces sensual desire, worldly coveting, pride and falsehood, and is the cause of pain; dust; the dust or pollen of a flower; the menstrual evacuation.

रजस्वला ruj-swúla, *s. f.* A woman during menstruation.

रजित ruj-ít, *adj.* Affected, moved, attracted, or excited by.

रजोगुण rújo-goon, *s. m.* One of the three characters or dispositions assigned by the *Hindoos* to the human mind, they are, first *Sutwuh*, Goodness, benevolence; *Rujuh*, Passion or love of sensual enjoyment or of pleasure; *Tumuh*, Darkness, ignorance, delusion, promptitude to the vindictive passions. These are all exhibited in the *Hindoo* Triad: in *Bruhma*, *rujuh* prevails; in *Vishnoo*, *sutwuh*; and in *Shiv*, *tumuh*.

रजोबन्ध rujo-búndh, *s. m.* Suppression of menstruation.

रज्जु rújjoo, *s. m.* A rope, a cord, a tie, a string.

रञ्जक run-júk, *adj.* What excites or affects; what colours, &c. *s. m.* A colourist, a painter, a dyer; a stimulus, an inciter of affection, &c.; biliary humour on which vision depends. *s. f.* Priming powder. *Runjuk oorna*, To flash in the pan (*priming*). *Runjuk oorana, v. a.* To burn priming, to flash in the pan. *Runjuk-dan, s. m.* Priming pan or fire-pan. *Runjuk pilana, v. a.* To prime.

रञ्जन run-jún, *s. m.* Colouring, dyeing, painting, &c.; affecting the heart, exciting passion, &c.; red *sandal* or sapan wood.

रञ्जित run-jít, *adj.* Moved or affected.

रट rut, *s. f.* Repetition, iteration.

रटना rút-na, *v. a.* To repeat, iterate, order or demand repeatedly.

रण run, *s. m.* War, battle.

रणकामी run-kámee, *adj.* Desirous of war, wishing to fight.

रणगढ़ा run-gurhá, *s. m.* Lines of entrenchment.

रणवन run-vún, *s. m.* A wilderness.

रणस्तम्भ run-stúmbh, *s. m.* A trophy, a pillar.

रणाङ्गन run-ángun, *s. m.* A field of battle.

रणोत्साह run-otsáh, *s. m.* Prowess.

रण्ड rund, *s. m.* A tree (*Palma christi*: *Ricinus vulgaris*).

रण्डक run-dúk, *s. m.* A barren tree.

रण्डसाला rund-sála, *s. m.* Widow's dress, widow's weeds.

रण्डा rún-da, *s. f.* A plant (*Salvinia cucullata*); a widow.

रण्डापरो rúnda-púro, } *s. m.* Widowhood.
रण्डापा rundá-pa, }

रण्डिया run-diyá, *s. f.* A widow; a woman.

रण्डी rún-dee, *s. f.* A woman (*in a bad sense*) *Rundee-baz*, A whoremonger. *Rundeebazee, s. f.* Whoring, fornication.

रण्डूआ run-dóoa, *s. m.* A widower.

रत rut, *adj.* Occupied or engaged by, actively intent on. *s. m.* Coition, copulation.

रतकेल rut-kél, *s. m.* Venery, coition.

रतजगा rut-júga, *s. m.* Watching all night on religious occasions (*a female ceremony*), vigil.

रतन rút-un, *s. m.* A jewel, gem, a precious stone; the pupil of the eye. *Rutun-jurit*, Set with jewels. *Rutun-singhasun, s. m.* A throne adorned with precious stones.

रतनार rut-nár, *s. m.* Red colour.

रतनिधि rut-nídhi, *s. m.* A wagtail.

रतनियां rut-níyan, *s. m.* A kind of rice.

रतवाही rut-wáhee, *s. f.* An attack in the night; a concubine who comes at night.

रताना rut-ána, *v. n.* To rut, to be lewd.

रतायनी rut-áyunee, *s. f.* A whore, a harlot.

रतार्थिनी rut-árthinee, *s. f.* A libidinous woman, a wanton harlot.

रतार्थी rut-árthee, *adj. m.* Libidinous, lascivious.

रतालू rut-áloo, *s. m.* A yam (*Dioscorea*).

रति rúti, *s. f.* Passion, desire; coition, copulation.

रतिक्रिया rúti-kríya, *s. f.* Copulation.

रतिसत्वरा rúti-sutwúra, *s. f.* A plant (*Trigonella corniculata*), perhaps considered as an aphrodisiac.

रती rútee, *n. prop.* The Venus of the *Hindoos*. *s. f.* A weight equal to eight barley-corns; fortune. *Rutee chumuknee*, To begin to prosper, to flourish.

रतीवत rutee-wút, } *adj.* Fortunate, prosperous, flourishing.
रतीवन्त rutee-wúnt, }

रतोन्ध rut-óun-dha, *s. m.* Blindness at night, nyctalopia.

रतोन्धिया rut-oun-dhiyá, *adj.* Blind at night.

रत्ती rúttee, *s. f.* A weight equal to eight

barley corns; fortune. *Ruttee chumuknee*, To begin to prosper, to flourish.

रत्न **rutn**, *s. m.* A jewel, a gem, a precious stone; any thing the best of its kind, or figuratively, the jewel of the species.

रत्नकुंदल **rutn-kúndul**, *s. m.* Coral.

रत्नजोत **rutn-jót**, *s. f.* A plant; a medicine, said to be good for the eyes.

रत्नमंजरी **rutn-mún-juree**, *s. f.* Name of a flower.

रत्नमय **rutn-múy**, *adj.* Gemmed, full or made of gems.

रत्नमाला **rutn-mála**, *s. f.* A necklace of precious stones; a book in astronomy; a flower.

रत्नवत **rutn-wút**, *adj.* Having gems.

रत्नवृक्ष **rutn-vríksh**, *s. m.* Coral.

रत्नसिंघासन **rutn-singhásun**, *s. m.* A throne adorned with precious stones.

रत्नाकर **rutn-ákur**, *s. m.* The ocean; a jewel mine.

रत्नावली **rutn-ávulee**, *s. f.* A necklace of gems.

रथ **ruth**, *s. m.* A car, a war chariot; a carriage in general, any vehicle or mode of conveyance; a four-wheeled carriage (*not used for baggage*), a coach, chariot.

रथकार **ruth-kár**, *s. m.* A maker of cars, a coach-maker.

रथयात्रा **ruth-játra**, *s. f.* A festival at which the chariots go in procession: in *Bengal* and *Orissa* it is applied to the procession of the car of *Krishn*, as *Juggunnath*, on the second of the light fortnight of *Asharh*.

रथवान **ruth-wán**, *s. m.* A coachman, charioteer.

रथवानी **ruth-wánee**, *s. f.* Coachmanship.

रथांग **ruth-áng**, *s. m.* A wheel; the ruddy goose (*Anas casarca*).

रथी **rúthee**, *s. m.* The owner of or rider in a car.

रद **rud**, }
रदन **rúd-un**, } *s. m.* A tooth.

रदछद **rud-chhúd**, *s. m.* A lip.

रदा **rúd-da**, *s. m.* A layer of a wall, the work of a day.

रदी **rúd-dee**, *s. m.* Rejected things, especially waste paper.

रन **run**, *s. m.* Battle, war, combat. *Runbhoomi*, *s. f.* Field of battle.

रनबन **run-bún**, *s. m.* A wilderness.

रनवास **run-wás**, *s. m.* The seraglio of a *raja*, the female apartments.

रंदा **rundá**, *s. m.* A hole; a loop-hole, an embrasure, an air hole.

रंधना **rúndh-na**, *v. n.* To be boiled (*victuals*).

रंध्र **rundhr**, *s. m.* A hole, a fissure, a cavity, a chasm; a fault, a defect.

रपट **rúp-ut**, *s. f.* Fatigue, hard labour; slipperiness; chase.

रपटना **rúp-ut-na**, *v. n.* To slip, slide.

रपरपाना **rup-rup-ána**, *v. n.* To gallop hard.

रबूर **rub-úr**, *s. f.* Fatigue, fruitless labour, trudging.

रबूरना **rub-úr-na**, *v. n.* To fatigue one's self, to run about fruitlessly.

रबरा **rúb-ra**, *adj.* Fatigued.

रबराना **rub-rána**, *v. a.* To fatigue, to cause to run about uselessly.

रबड़ी **rub-rée**, *s. f.* Thick milk.

रबि **rúbi**, *s. m.* The sun. *Rubi-bar*, *s. m.* Sunday.

रमचेरा **rum-chéra**, *s. m.* A common appellation of a slave.

रमन **rum-ún**, *s. m.* Sporting, playing; dalliance, amorous sport; coition, copulation.

रमनी **rumun-ée**, *s. f.* An agreeable woman, a wife.

रमनीक **rum-néek**, *adj.* Pleasant.

रमनीय **rum-un-éeyuh**, *adj.* Beautiful, pleasing.

रमनीयता **rúmuneeyutá**, *s. f.* Agreeableness, pleasantness.

रमन्युह **rum-ún-yuh**, *s. m.* Sport, pleasure, wanton sport or dalliance.

रमत **rum-út**, *adj.* Playing, sporting.

रमदूफूट **rúmdoo-phúttoo**, *s. m. pl.* Populace, the vulgar (or *tag, rag, and bobtail*).

रमना **rúmna**, *v. n.* To turn; to roam, go, range, wander. *s. m.* A pack or chase (*for game*). *v. a.* To enjoy, to have connexion with.

रमाना **rum-ána**, *v. a.* To entice, to beguile; to take possession of.

रंभा **rum-bhá**, *s. f.* A plantain; a harlot, a whore; delight.

रम्यक **rum-yúk**, *s. m.* One of the minor *dweeps* or divisions of the world, lying to the north of *Iluvrit*.

रुलना **rúl-na**, *v. n.* To be mixed.

रुलाना **rul-ána**, *v. a.* To mix.

रव **ruv**, *s. m.* Sound in general, cry, noise, &c.

रवन्ना **ruvúnna**, *s. m.* A servant who attends at the gate of the women's apartments to purchase articles that are required.

रूआ **rúv-a**, *s. m.* Gold or silver filings; a grain or particle of sand, dust, gunpowder, &c.

रवांश ruv-áns, *s. m.* A kind of bean (*Dolichos sinensis*).

रवि rúvi, *s. m.* The sun.

रविकांत ruvi-kánt, *s. m.* The sun-stone, a sort of crystal.

रविमंडल rúvi-múndul, *s. m.* The disk of the sun.

रविमार्ग rúvi-márg, *s. m.* The sun's path.

रसना rús-na, *s. f.* The tongue; a woman's girdle or zone.

रश्मि rús-mi, *s. m.* A ray of light.

रस rus, *s. m.* Juice, humour, essence; flavour, taste, as sweet, salt, pungent, bitter, sour, and astringent; taste, sentiment, or emotion, as an object of poetry or composition; eight sentiments are usually enumerated, *Sringar* or love, *Hasyuh* or mirth, *Kuroona* or tenderness, *Roudr* or anger, *Veer* or heroism, *Bhyanuk* or terror, *Veebhuts* or disgust, *Udbhoot* or surprise, *Sant*, tranquillity or content, or *Vatsulyuh*, paternal tenderness, is sometimes considered as the ninth; affection of the mind, passion; exudation, a fluid, a liquid; semen virile; relish, enjoyment; quicksilver, mercury.

रसकर्पूर rus-kurp-póor, *s. m.* A white sublimate or a muriate of mercury, made in close vessels with sulphur, mercury, and common salt; the crystals formed in the first operation are sublimed a second time, which seems to be the only essential difference between this and the preparations called *Rusupooshpuh.*

रसज्ञ rusúgyuh, *adj.* Discriminating or acquainted with tastes, sentiments, &c. *s. m.* A poet, a writer, who understands the different *Rusus* or sentiments to be described, an alchymist, one who has obtained a command over the magical properties of mercury; a physician, a medical preparer and administerer of mercurial and chemical compounds.

रसज्ञता rúsug-yutá, *s. f.* Poetical skill or taste; knowledge of flavours; alchymy.

रसज्ञा rusugyá, } *s. f.* The tongue.
रसना rusuná, }

रसधातु rus-dhá-too, *s. m.* Quicksilver.

रसनिवृत्ति rús-nivrítti, *s. f.* Loss of taste, flavour, &c.

रसपुष्प rus-póoshp, *s. m.* A preparation of mercury, a kind of muriate formed by subliming in close vessels, a mixture of sulphur, mercury, and common salt.

रसभस्मन् rus-bhúsm-un, *s. m.* Calx or oxide of mercury.

रसमसा rus-mús-a, *adj.* or *part.* Wet with perfumed essences or perspiration.

रसमसाना rus-mus-ána, *v. n.* To wet with perfumed essences or perspiration.

रसरा rús-ra, *s. m.* A rope.

रसराज rus-ráj, *s. m.* Quicksilver.

रसरी rus-rée, *s. f.* String, cord.

रसवत rus-wút, *s. f.* A kind of collyrium, extracted from the root of the *Amomum anthorrhiza.*

रसवाद rus-wad, *adj.* Exciting quarrels.

रसवान rus-wán, *adj.* Well-flavoured; tasteful, applied to a composition, &c.

रससिंदूर rus-síndoor, *s. m.* A sort of factitious cinnabar, made with zinc, mercury, blue vitriol, and nitre fused together: the compound is used as an escharotic.

रसाञ्जन rus-án-jun, *s. m.* A sort of collyrium, prepared either with the calx of brass, or with the *Amomum anthorrhiza.*

रसातल rus-a-túl, *s. m. Patal;* the seven infernal regions under the earth, and the residence of *Nagus, Usoors, Dyts,* and other monstrous and demoniacal beings: this is not to be confounded with *Nuruk* or Tartarus, the proper hell or abode of guilty mortals after death; the lowest of the seven divisions of *Patal.*

रसाना rus-ána, *v. a.* To solder.

रसायन rus-áyun, *s. m.* Alchymy, chemistry; the employment of mercury in medicine; a medicine composed of mercury and other metals; slowness, mildness. *Rusayunee, s. m.* A chymist.

रसाल rus-ál, *s. m.* The sugar-cane; the mango tree (*Mangifera Indica*).

रसालसा rus-al-sá, *s. f.* A tubular vessel of the body, a nerve, a tendon, &c.

रसावुल rus-a-wúl, *s. m.* A kind of dish (*rice and the juice of sugar-cane boiled together*).

रसिक rús-ik, *adj.* Flavoured, having taste or flavour; tasteful, as a composition, &c.; sentimental. *s. m.* A libertine. *adj.* Witty.

रसिकाई rus-ik-áee, *s. f.* Cunningness, shrewdness, amorousness.

रसिया rús-iya, *s. m.* A rake, one who enjoys life, a voluptuary.

रसियाना rus-iyána, *v. n.* To be moist, to be juicy; to commence ripening, to ooze.

रसी rús-ee, *adj.* Humorous; impassioned.

रसीला rus-ée-la, *adj.* Juicy, luscious; voluptuous, rakish.

रसून rús-oon, *s. m.* Garlick.

रसे rús-eh, *adv.* Softly.

रसेंद्र rus-éndr, *s. m.* Quicksilver; the philosopher's stone, the touch of which turns iron to gold.

रसोइया rus-óiya, *s. m.* A cook.

रसोई rus-óee, *s. f.* Victuals; cookroom, kitchen.

रसोत rus-óut, *s. f.* A kind of collyrium, extracted from the root of the *Amomum anthorrhiza.*

रस rús-yuh, *adj.* Juicy. *s. m.* Blood.

रस्सा rús-sa, *s. m.* Rope, cable.

रस्सी rús-see, *s. f.* String, cord, rope.

रहकल ruh-kúl, ⎱ *s. m.* A small can

रहकला ruh-kul-á, ⎰ non, a swivel, field-piece; a cart.

रहचोला ruh-chóla, *s. m.* Flattery, agreeable conversation.

रहजाना ruh-jána, *v. n.* To wait, stay, delay, desist, give up.

रहुट rúhut, *s. m.* A wheel for drawing water with.

रहटा ruh-tá, *s. m.* A spinning-wheel.

रहरू rúh-roo, *s. m.* A cart.

रहत rúhut, *s. m.* Staying, remaining.

रहते ruh-téh, *adv.* (*In the*) remaining; in the presence, during, notwithstanding.

रहन ruhún, *s. f.* Manner, method.

रहना ruh-ná, *v. n.* To stay, stop, remain, be, exist, last, stand, continue, lie, live, inhabit, dwell, reside, escape. *Ruhnewala,* Inhabitant.

रहमार ruh-már, *s. m.* A robber, highwayman.

रहला rúh-la, *s. m.* A kind of pulse, *chuna (Cicer arietinum).*

रहवा ruh-wá, *s. m.* A slave (*not purchased*).

रहवाई ruh-wáee, *s. f.* House-rent.

रहवैया ruh-wyya, *s. m.* An inhabitant, dweller.

रहस rúhus, *adv.* Solitary, private, in private, secretly, privily. *s. m.* Waggery, merriment; trampling, treading under foot; solitariness, privacy; copulation.

रहसना ruhus-ná, *v. n.* To be pleased, to rejoice.

रहस्य ruhús-yuh, *adj.* Private, secret. *s. m.* A secret, a mystery, any thing hidden, recondite or mysterious.

रहाइस ruháis, *s. f.* ⎱ Stay, halt, delay,

रहाव ruháo, *s. m.* ⎰ abode, residence, continuance.

रहित rúhit, *adj.* Free from, devoid of, destitute, void of.

रक्षक ruk-shúk, *s. m.* A guardian, a protector.

रक्षण ruk-shún, *s. m.* Preserving, protecting, defending.

रक्षन् ruk-shún, *adj.* Preserving, guarding, protecting.

रक्षस ruk-shús, *s. m.* An evil spirit.

3 G

रक्षा rúk-sha, *s. f.* Protection, guarding, keeping, preservation, defence, patronage, safety.

रक्षित ruk-shít, *adj.* Preserved, protected, defended; kept, detained.

रक्षण rukshn, *s. m.* Preserving, guarding, defence, protection.

रक्ष्यमान rukshyumán, *adj.* Preserved.

राई raée, *s. f.* A kind of mustard seed with small grains (*Sinapis ramosa*). *Raee-kaee,* Broken to small pieces or atoms.

राईया raeeyá, *s. m.* Chaff of wheat, bran; a species of mustard with large seeds.

राह ráeh, *s. m.* A *Hindoo* title, prince, chief. *Raeh-rayan, s. m.* A *Hindoo* title, (*lit.*) the chief of princes; the *Dewan* of the *Khalisa,* or chief treasurer.

रायता ráeta, *s. m.* Pumpkins, &c. pickled in sour milk.

रायबांस raebáns, *s. m.* A kind of spear.

रायबेल raebél, *s. f.* A flower so called.

रंग rang, *s. f.* ⎱ Pewter, tin.

रंगा ráng-a, *s. m.* ⎰

रंगभूरा rang-bhúr-a, *s. m.* A toyman.

रंझन ran-jhún, ⎱ *s. m.* Sweetheart;

रंझना ranjh-ná, ⎰ Leander, the lover of

रंझा ran-jhá, ⎰ Hero (*who is called* in *Hindee Heer*).

रंड rand, *s. f.* A widow; a woman. *Rand ka sand,* Son of a widow, a spoilt child.

रांडा rán-da, *adj.* Barren. (*The mango fish without roes are so called; and the word is particularly applied to unproductive trees, such as the male palm, &c.*)

रंडापा ran-dá-pa, *s. m.* Widowhood.

रंडनी rand-née, *s. f.* Parsley.

रंडपरोस rand-pur-ós, *s. m.* Neighbourhood.

रांधना rándh-na, *v. a.* To cook, to dress food.

रांपी rán-pee, *s. f.* An iron instrument for scraping leather, scraper for leather.

रांभना rámbh-na, *v. n.* To low, bellow, cry out.

राकस rákus, *s. m.* A demon, an evil spirit.

राका rá-ka, *s. f.* Full moon, or the day of full moon.

राख rakh, *s. f.* Ashes.

राखना rákh-na, *v. a.* To keep, to put.

राखी rá-khee, *s. f.* An amulet, or string which *Hindoos* tie round their arms on a certain festival, held in the full moon of *Srawun,* or, *Sawun,* in honour of *Krishn.*

राग rag, *s. m.* A mode in music (*there being six in number*), music, song, tune : the modes are, *Bhyruv, Maluv, Sarung, Hindol, Vusunt, Deepuk,* and *Megh* ; anger, passion ; love. *Rag chhana, v. n.* To be in concert. *Rag-mala, s. f.* A treatise on music (*being nothing more than a collection of pictures, exhibiting the traditional history of the primary and subordinate modes, and the subjects appropriated to each*). *Rag rung, s. m.* Music. *Rag-sagur, s. m.* A song composed of many *Rags* or musical modes.

रागचूब rag-chóon, *s. m.* A tree yielding an astringent resin or extract, the wood of which is used in dying (*Mimosa catechu*).

रागना rág-na, *v. a.* To begin to sing.

रागिनी rag-in-ée, *s. f.* A mode in music (*there being thirty of the Raginees in number*).

रागी rá-gee, *adj.* Passionate, impassionate. *s. m.* A singer ; a libertine, a lover.

राघव ra-ghúv, *s. m.* A sort of fish.

राचना rách-na, *v. n.* To be affected or imbued (*with love*), to be strongly attached.

राछ rachh, *s. m.* Apparatus.

राज raj, *s. m.* Government, sovereignty, royalty, reign, kingdom. (*In comp.*) Prince, king.

राज raj, *s. m.* A mason, a bricklayer.

राजकन्या raj-kúnya, *s. f.* A princess.

राजकर raj-kúr, *s. m.* Tax or toll imposed by the king.

राजकमेद raj-kuséroo, *s. m.* A fragrant grass (*Cyperus*).

राजकार्य raj-kárj, *s. m.* Royal duties, state affairs.

राजकीय rajuk-éeyuh, *adj.* Royal, kingly.

राजकुमार raj-koomár, *s. m.* A king's son, a prince.

राजकुल raj-kóol, *s. m.* A royal race ; a prince, a king.

राजगादी raj-gádee, *s. f.* King's cushion or throne.

राजगुरू raj-góoroo, *s. m.* The king's spiritual preceptor.

राजपीव raj-gréev, *s. m.* A sort of flat freshwater fish.

राजतिलक raj-tíl-uk, *s. m.* The royal mark on the forehead, coronation.

राजतेजस् raj-téjus, *s. m.* Majesty, kingly dignity.

राजल rajutwúh, *s. m.* Sovereignty, royalty.

राजदण्ड raj-dúnd, *s. m.* Punishment ordered by the king ; a baton, a sceptre.

राजदर्शन raj-dúrsh-un, *s. m.* A levee, an audience.

राजद्वार raj-dwár, *s. m.* The gate of the palace.

राजद्रोह raj-dróh, *s. m.* Oppression, tyranny ; rebellion.

राजद्रोही raj-dróhee, *s. m.* A rebel, a traitor.

राजधन raj-dhún, *s. m.* Royal revenue or right to property.

राजधर raj-dhúr, *s. m.* The prime minister of a *raja.*

राजधर्म raj-dhúrm, *s. m.* Royal duty ; the duty of the military tribe.

राजधानी raj-dhánee, *s. f.* A royal city, a capital, a metropolis.

राजधुरा raj-dhóora, *s. f.* Royal state or function, government.

राजना ráj-na, *v. n.* To shine, to be adorned.

राजनीति raj-néeti, *s. f.* Regal polity, civil and military government ; the art of government, the duties of a prince both in peace and war.

राजनील raj-néel, *s. m.* The emerald.

राजपट्ट raj-pútt, *s. m.* A gem, said to be an inferior kind of diamond brought from *Virat Des,* a country in the north-west of India ; a tiara or royal fillet. *s. f.* King's cushion, throne.

राजपुत raj-pút, *s. m.* A *Hindoo* title, prince.

राजपत्नी raj-pút-nee, *s. f.* A queen.

राजपुत्र raj-póotr, *s. m.* A *Kshuttree* or man of the military tribe.

राजपूत raj-póot, *s. m.* A descendant of a *raja* ; the name of a tribe.

राजपूती raj-póo-tee, *s. f.* Courage, prowess in war.

राजबंसी raj-bún-see, *s. m.* Descendant of a *raja* ; a *Rajpoot* tribe.

राजभवन raj-bhúvun, } *s. m.* A royal re-
राजभूवन raj-bhóo-bun, } sidence, a palace.

राजभोग raj-bhóg, *s. m.* Victuals placed before idols at noon.

राजमन्दिर raj-mún-dir, *s. m.* A palace, a royal residence.

राजमार्ग raj-márg, *s. m.* A royal road, one passable for horses and elephants, and forty cubits broad.

राजयुद्धा raj-joodhwá, *s. m.* An enemy, a rebel, one making war against a prince.

राजयोग्य raj-jóg-yuh, *adj.* Proper or suitable for a sovereign, princely, royal.

राजराज raj-raj, *s. m.* An emperor, a universal monarch, or king of kings.

राजरोग raj-róg, *s. m.* A mortal disease ; a consumption.

राजलक्षण raj-lúkshun, s. m. Royal insignia; any natural mark indicating royalty.

राजलेख raj-lékh, s. m. A royal letter or order.

राजवंशी raj-vún-see, s. m. The descendant of a *raja*; a tribe of *Rajpoots*.

राजवंश्य raj-vúns-yuh, adj. Of royal parentage or descent.

राजवत् raj-wút, adj. Royal, kingly.

राजवारा raj-wára, s. m. The country of *rajas*.

राजवीजी raj-vée-jee, adj. Springing from a royal race.

राजशासन raj-shás-un, s. m. A royal edict.

राजस raj-ús, adj. Relating to, or derived, &c. from the quality of passion.

राजसत्ता raj-sútta, s. f. Majesty, royal dignity.

राजसभा raj-subhá, s. f. A royal assembly or court.

राजसर्प raj-súrp, s. m. A large kind of snake (*Boa*), the king of snakes.

राजसूय raj-sóoyuh, s. m. A sacrifice performed only by a universal monarch, attended by his tributary princes.

राजसेवक raj-sévuk, s. m. A courtier, a royal attendant.

राजस्व rajus-wúh, s. m. Royal revenue, impost, duty, tax.

राजहंस raj-húns, s. m. A white goose with red legs and bill, or more properly perhaps the flamingo.

राजहासुक raj-hás-uk, s. m. A sort of large fish (*Cyprinus niloticus*).

राजा rá-ja, s. m. A king, a prince.

राजाज्ञा raj-ágya, s. f. A royal edict or command.

राजाधिराज raj-adhi-ráj, s. m. A paramount sovereign.

राजावर्त raja-vúrt, s. m. A gem, described as an inferior sort of diamond, brought from the country *Virat*.

राजावली raj-áwulee, s. f. A line of kings, a royal dynasty or genealogy.

राजी rá-jee, s. f. A row, a line.

राजीव ra-jéev, s. m. A large fish (*Cyprinus niloticus*).

राजेन्द्र raj-éndr, s. m. An emperor.

राजेश्वर raj-éshwur, s. m. A sovereign, prince, a lord, a governor.

राज्य ráj-yuh, s. m. A government, a country, a principality, a kingdom; administration or exercise of sovereignty or government.

राज्यच्युत rájyuh-chyóot, s. m. A prince who has lost his government.

राज्यच्युति ráj-yuh-chyóoti, s. f. Deposal, loss of sovereignty.

राज्यभंग rájyuh-bhúng, s. m. Subversion of a sovereignty.

राज्यभ्रंश rájyuh-bhrúns, s. m. Deposal or loss of a kingdom.

राज्यभ्रष्ट rájyuh-bhrúsht, s. m. A deposed sovereign.

राज्यरक्षा rájyuh-rúksha, s. f. Protection or defence of a kingdom.

राज्याधिकार rájyuh-adhikár, s. m. Government of a kingdom; right or title to a sovereignty.

राढ rarh, s. m. A country or district, part of Bengal west of the *Hooghly* river.

राना rá-na, s. m. A *Hindoo* title of a prince or *raja*.

रानी ra-née, s. f. A *Hindoo* queen or princess.

रात rat, s. f. Night. *Adhee rat*, Midnight. *Rat thorse our sang buhoot*, Is applied to express a hurry of business with little time to perform it in; also great expense with a small income. *Ruton-rat*, In the middle of the night.

रातना rat-ná, v. a. To dye (*with colour*), to stain. v. n. To be strongly attached or in love (*lit.* stained with the die of love).

राता rá-ta, adj. Red; died, coloured.

रातौंधा rat-óundha, s. m. Nyctalopia, night blindness.

रात्रि rátri, } s. f. Night.
रात्री rat-rée, }

रात्रिचर rátri-chúr, adj. Going or moving at night. s. m. A goblin, a fiend, a ghost or evil spirit; a thief, a robber; a guard, a patrole.

राद rad, s. f. Pus, matter.

राधानगरी rádha-núgree, s. m. A kind of silk cloth made at *Radha-nugur*.

राना rá-na, s. m. A *Hindoo* title of a prince or *raja*.

रानी ra-née, s. f. A *Hindoo* queen or princess.

राब rab, s. f. Sirup.

राबड़ी rab-rée, s. f. A kind of food like pap.

राम ram, n. prop. A name common to three incarnations of *Vishnoo*, or *Pursooram*, the son of the *Mooni Jumudugni*, born at the commencement of the second or *Treta Joog*, for the purpose of punishing the tyrannical kings of the *Kshuttree* race; *Ramchundr*, the son of *Dusruth*, king of *Oude*, born at the close of the second age, (or 1600 years B. C.) to destroy the demons who infested the earth, and especially *Ravun*, the *Dyt* sovereign of *Ceylon*; and *Bulram*, the elder and half brother of *Krishn*, the son of *Rohini*, born at the end of the *Dwapur* or third age. *Ram kuha-nee*, *s. f.* The *Ramayun*; a long story. *Ram doo-haee*, *s. f.* An asseveration, by *Ram*, by God. *Ram-bhuti*, *s. f.* Calling out for redress, complaint. *Ram! Ram!* A *Hindoo* form of salutation.

रामकरी ram-kúr-ee,⎫ *s. f.* One of the
रामकली ram-kúl-ee, ⎬ *Raginees* or fe-
रामकेली ram-kél-ee,⎭ male personifications of the musical modes.

रामगिरि ram-gíri, *s. m.* The name of a mountain, variously applied, but especially assigned to a mountain called *Compteh* or *Chitrkoot* in *Bundelkhund*, and to another near *Nagpore*, called now *Ramtek*.

रामजनी ram-jún-ee, *s. f.* A *Hindoo* dancing-girl, a prostitute.

रामतुरई ram-toorúee, *s. f.* A vegetable, Ochra (*Hibiscus esculentus*).

रामतुलसी ram-tóolsee, *s. f.* A plant (*Ocymum gratissimum*).

राममून ram-móon, *s. m.* A kind of goat.

रामसर ram-súr, *s. m.* A sort of wood; a kind of reed.

रामानन्दी rama-núndee, *s. m.* A class of *Hindoo* mendicants, followers of *Ramanund*.

रामायण ram-áyun, *s. m.* The first epic poem of the *Hindoos*, recording the adventures of *Ram*, the son of *Dusruth*, sovereign of *Oude*, written by the poet *Valmeeki*; a name of several poems on the life and adventures of *Ram*.

रामावत ramá-wut, *s. m.* System of *Hindoo* mendicants.

राय ráeh, *s. m.* A *Hindoo* title, prince, chief. *Raeh-rayan*, *s. m.* A *Hindoo* title, (*lit.*) The chief of princes; the *Deewan* of the *Khalisa*, or chief treasurer.

रायता raetá, *s. m.* Pumpkins, &c. pickled in sour milk.

रायबांस rae-báns, *s. m.* A kind of spear.

रायबेल rae-bél, *s. f.* A flower so called.

रायमनिया ráe-mún-iya,⎫ *s. m.* A kind of
रायमनी ráe-mún-ee, ⎬ rice (*in the
husk.*)

रार rar,⎫ *s. f.* Wrangling, quarrel, fray.
रार rar,⎭

रारी ra-rée,⎫ *adj.* Quarrelsome, contenti-
रारी ra-rée,⎭ ous.

राल ral, *s. m.* Resin, the resinous or fragrant exudation of the *Shorea robusta*, rosin, pitch; saliva.

राव ráo, *s. m.* A prince.

रावचाव rao-chao, *s. m.* Gaiety, amuse-

ment, dalliance, merriment, mirth; affection, endearment.

रावटी ráo-tee, *s. f.* A kind of tent.

रावण rá-wun, *s. m.* The sovereign of *Lunka* or *Ceylon*, said to have been killed by *Ramchundr*.

रावत ra-wút, *s. m.* A hero; a sweeper (*of a particular caste*).

रावरा rao-rá,⎫ (*In Bruj.*) *pron.* Yours.
रावरो rao-ró,⎭

राशि ráshi, *s. m.* A heap, a quantity; a sign of the zodiac; a part and its divisor, or numerator and denominator.

राशिचक्र ráshi-chúkr, *s. m.* The zodiac.

राशिभाग ráshi-bhág, *s. m.* A fraction.

राशिभोग ráshi-bhóg, *s. m.* Passage of a planet through a sign of the zodiac.

राशिकरण ráshi-kúrun, *s. m.* Heaping, piling, gathering.

राशिकृत ráshi-krit, *adj.* Heaped, piled, gathered.

राष्ट्र rashtr, *s. m.* An inhabited country or realm, a region.

राष्ट्रिका rash-trik-á, *s. f.* A prickly sort of night-shade (*Solanum jacquini*).

रास ras, *s. f.* Reins of a bridle; usury; adoption. *Ras-una*, To be agreeable. *Ras lena*, *v. a.* To adopt a son.

रास ras, *s. m.* A festival among the cowherds, including songs and dance, especially the circular dance as performed by *Krishn* and the *Gopees* or cowherdesses; a heap; a sign of the zodiac.

रासचक्र ras-chúkr, *s. m.* The zodiac.

रासधारी ras-dhá-ree, *s. m.* A dancing-boy, who imitates the *Ras* of *Krishn*.

रासयात्रा ras-játra, *s. f.* A festival in honour of *Krishn* on the full moon of *Kartik*.

रासी rás-ee, *adj.* Of middling breed (*a horse*); indifferent, so so.

रासना ras-ná, *s. f.* A plant (*Mimosa octandra*); another plant (*the serpent Ophioxylon?*); a sort of perfume.

रांहना ráh-na, *v. a.* To roughen a millstone (*by digging little pits in its surface with a small pickaxe*).

राहु rá-hoo, *s. m.* Typhon or the dragon that is supposed to devour the sun or moon during an eclipse; the ascending node.

राहुग्रास ráhoo-grás, *s. m.* Immersion of a planet in an eclipse.

राहुग्राह ráhoo-gráh, *s. m.* An eclipse of the sun or moon.

राक्षस rak-shús, *adj.* Infernal, demoniacal. *s. m.* An evil spirit, a demon, a vampire, a fiend,

but who appears to be of various descriptions and
is either a powerful Titan or enemy of the gods in
a superhuman or incarnate form, as *Ravun* and
others.

राक्षस्ब्याह rákshus-byáh, *s. m.* A form of
marriage, the violent seizure and rape of a girl
after the repulse or destruction of her relatives.

राक्षसी rakshus-ée, *s. f.* A female fiend, the
female of *Rakshus.* *adj.* Demoniacal, devilish.

रिक्त rikt, *adj.* Empty, void. *s. m.* A vacuity, a vacuum.

रिक्तता rikt-tá, *s. f.* Vacuity, void, space.

रिक्तहस्त rikt-húst, *adj.* Empty-handed.

रिचा rich-á, *s. f.* A magical invocation, a
mystical prayer of the *Veds.*

रिझवैया rijh-wyya, *adj.* Having the quality
of being pleased.

रिझाना rijhá-na, *v. a.* To please; (*met.*)
to plague, tease, perplex.

रिताना rit-ána, *v. a.* To cause to empty.

रितु rít-oo, *s. f.* Season, weather. The
Hindoos divide the year into six seasons, viz. *Vusunt, Greeshm, Vursha, Surud, Him,* and *Sisir.*

रिद्धिríd-dhi, *s. f.* Increase, wealth, prosperity.

रिपु ríp-oo, *s. m.* An enemy.

रिपुता rípoo-tá, *s. f.* Hostility, enmity.

रिषि ríshi, *s. m.* A saint.

रिष्टक risht-úk, *s. m.* The soap-berry plant
(*Sapindus of several species*).

रिष्टपुष्ट risht-póosht, *adj.* Fat.

रिस ris, *s. f.* Anger, passion, vexation.

रिसना rís-na, *v. n.* To drop slowly.

रिसहा ris-há, *adj.* Passionate.

रिसाना ris-ána, } *v. n.* To be displeas-
रिसियाना ris-iyána, } ed, vexed, angry,
provoked.

री ree, *f.* A vocative particle used by way
of disrespect or admiration generally, (*in addressing females*), holla! bravo! O!

रींगना réeng-na, *v. n.* To creep, to plod.

रीछ reenchh, }
रीछ reechh, } *s. m.* A bear.

रींधना réendh-na, *v. a.* To dress (*victuals*),
to cook.

रीझ reejh, *f.* Choice, approbation, love,
desire, wish; pleasing, satisfying. *Reejh-puchaoo,
s. m.* A person who conceals his inclination. *Reejh
puchana, v. a.* To conceal one's gratification.

रीझना reejh-ná, *v. n.* To be pleased, to be
gratified, to be delighted.

रीठा ree-thá, *s. m.* A fruit, soap-wort,
soap-nut (*Sapindus saponaria*).

रीठिया ree-thi-yá, *s. f.* A small *Reetha*
(*fish*).

रीर reerh, *s. f.* The backbone.

रीढ़ी reer-hée, *s. f.* A young mango.

रीता rée-ta, *adj.* Empty.

रीति réeti, *s. f.* Usage, custom, practice,
rite, habit, regulation, rule, local or traditionary
observance.

रीर reer, *s. m.* Noise.

रीरियाना reeriyána, *v. n.* To cry (*as a
child*); to murmur. *v. a.* To importune, to beg
earnestly.

रीस rees, *s. f.* Anger, passion, vexation.

रुंदना roondna, *v. n.* To be trod or trampled on.

रुंधाना roondh-jána, *v. n.* To be confined,
restrained or afflicted (*in mind*).

रुक rook, *s. m.* Stoppage.

रुकन rook-ún, *s. f.* Stopping.

रुकना róok-na, *v. n.* To stop, to be hindered, to be enclosed, to be prohibited.

रुकवैया rook-wyya, *s. m.* A preventer.

रुकाना roo-kána, *v. a.* To cause to enclose,
surround, stop, hinder.

रुकाव roo-káo, *s. m.* }
रुकावट roo-ká-wut, *f.* } Prevention, hinderance, deten-
tion, backwardness.

रुखाई roo-kháee, *s. f.* Plainness, dryness;
unkind looks, indifference.

रुग्न roogn, *adj.* Bent, crooked, curbed;
diseased, sick, infirm.

रुच rooch, *s.* Desire, wish, avidity, desire of or pleasure from eating; light, lustre.

रुचना róoch-na, *v. n.* To excite desire; to
be agreeable.

रुचि róochi, *s. f.* Hunger, appetite, taste,
sentiment.

रुण्ड roond, *s. m.* A headless body.

रुदन róodun, *s. m.* Weeping, wailing.

रुद्ध rooddh, *adj.* Obstructed, stopped,
shut up; opposed, stopped, impeded.

रुद्राक्ष rood-ráksh, *s. m.* A tree (*Eleocarpus
ganitrus*).

रुधिर róo-dhir, *s. m.* Blood.

रुपना róop-na, *v. n.* To be at bay, to stop.

रुपहरा roo-púh-ra, *adj.* Of silver.

रुपया roo-pyya, *s. m.* A coin so called, a
rupee.

रुलना róolna, *v. n.* To roll, be rolled or
pulverized.

रुलाना roo-lána, *v. a.* To cause to cry,
to vex, displease, afflict.

रूसना róos-na, *v. n.* To be angry, to be

displeased, to have a misunderstanding with a friend.

रूष्ट roosht, *adj.* Angry, displeased.

रूक्ष rooksh, *adj.* Harsh, unkind; rough, hard; rugged, uneven.

रूई roo-ée, *s. f.* Cotton. *Rooee-dar, adj.* Quilted with cotton, stuffed with cotton.

रूईहा rooee-há, *s. m.* A seller of cotton.

रूंगटा róong-ta, *s. m.* The short hairs of the body. *Roongteh khureh hona, v. n.* The standing of the hairs on end (*from cold, fear, &c.*)

रूंघट roon-ghút, *s. f.* Dirt, filth.

रूंधना róondh-na, *v. a.* To surround, to enclose (*as with a hedge*); to watch. *v. n.* To be restrained; to be confounded, to be astonished.

रूक rook, } *s. f.* To boot.
रूकन róokun, }

रूख rookh, *s. m.* A tree. *adj.* Plain, unseasoned. *Rookh-churha, s. m.* A monkey.

रूखुर roo-khúr, *s. m.* A sort of devotee.

रूखरा rookh-rá, *s. m.* A small tree.

रूखा róo-kha, *adj.* Dry, plain, rough, harsh, unkind, unfriendly, pure, simple, unseasoned. *Rookha sookha, adj.* Plain, blunt, harsh (*words, &c.*)

रूखाई rookhá-ee, *s. f.* Roughness, plainness, dryness, unfriendliness. [sel.

रूखानी rookhá-nee, *s. f.* A carpenter's chisel.

रूखी róo-khee, *s. f.* A squirrel.

रूच्छ roochh, *adj.* Stern. *s. m.* A violator.

रूज rooj, *s. m.* An insect very troublesome to birds.

रूझा roo-jhá, *adj.* An animal (*or bird more particularly*) much teased by the insect *rooj.*

रूठना róoth-na, *v. n.* To have a misunderstanding with a friend, to be cool, to quarrel, to be angry or displeased.

रूठनी rooth-née, *adj.* Quarrelsome. *s. f.* A species of sensitive plant (*Mimosa natans*).

रूठारूठी roothá-roothée, *s. f.* Mutual coolness, misunderstanding.

रूढ़ roorh, *adj.* Hard, stiff, rough, grim, cross.

रूप roop, *s. m.* Countenance, form, shape, figure, appearance, face, picture, beauty, manner, mode, method; silver. *Roop-nidhan,* Receptacle or abode of beauty. *Roop-rus,* Killed or calcined silver. *Rup-sagur,* Ocean of beauty.

रूपजस्त roop-júst, *s. m.* Pewter.

रूपवती roop-wút-ee, *adj. f.* Well-shaped, elegant, beautiful, handsome (*a woman*).

रूपवान roop-wán, *adj.* Well-shaped, beautiful, handsome.

रूपहला roopúh-la, *adj.* Silvered, made of silver, silver.

रूपा róo-pa, *s. m.* Silver.

रूपी roo-pée, (*used in compos.*) In form or figure, having the shape or figure of.

रूमती room-tée, *s. f.* Subterfuge, trick, wrangling.

रूमी róo-mee, *s. m.* A Grecian. *Roomee-mustkee, s. f.* Gum mastick.

रूसना róos-na, *v. n.* To be angry, to be displeased, to have a misunderstanding with a friend.

रूसी róo-see, *s. f.* Scurf.

रे reh, *m.* A vocative particle used by way of disrespect or admiration generally; holla! bravo! O!

रेंक renk, *s. f.* Braying (*as of an ass*).

रेंकना rénk-na, *v. n.* To bray (*as an ass*).

रेंगना réng-na, *v. n.* To creep, to plod.

रेंगनी réng-nee, *s. f.* A medicinal plant.

रेंट rént, *s. m.* A wheel for drawing water with; snivel, snot.

रेंटा rént-a, *s. m.* Snot, snivel.

रेंड rend, *s. m.* } Palma christi (*Ricinus*
रेंडी rénd-ee, *s. f.* } *vulgaris*). *Rendee ka tel, s. m.* Castor-oil.

रेंडी rén-dee, *s. f.* A small melon.

रेख rekh, } *s. f.* Writing, line, mark,
रेखा rekhá, } fate, destiny.

रेघारी reghár-ee, *s. f.* A furrow.

रेणु rénoo, *s. f.* Dust.

रेतूह retúh, } *s. m.* Semen virile.
रेतून ret-ún, }

रेत ret, *s. f.* Sand; filings.

रेतना rét-na, *v. a.* To file, polish, thrum.

रेतूल ret-úl, *adj.* Sandy. *s. f.* Sand, sandy ground.

रेतला ret-lá, *adj.* Sandy.

रेता ret-á, *s. m.* Sand.

रेताई ret-aée, *s. f.* Price paid for filing or polishing.

रेतियाना retiyána, *v. a.* To file, to polish.

रेती rétee, *s. f.* Sandy ground on the shore of a river; a file.

रेतीला retéela, *adj.* Sandy.

रेतूआ retóoa, *s. m.* A fileman, a filer, a polisher.

रेफ reph, *s. m.* The letter *r*, with the inherent short vowel.

रेलना rél-na, *v. a.* To shove, push, rush.

रेलपेल rel-pel, *s. f.* Abundance, plenty; crowd, bustle.

रेला rél-a, *s. m.* A flood; a line or string of animals; rushing, rush, push, shove, assault.

रेवड़ी rév-ree, *s. f.* A kind of sweetmeat. *Revree keh pher men purna, v. n.* To be involved in difficulties.

रेवती rév-tee, *s. f.* The last of the lunar asterisms, containing thirty-two stars, figured by a tabor.

रेवा réwa, *s. f.* The *Nerbudda* or *Nurmuda* river, which rises in the mountain *Umrkoot* or *Umurkuntuk*, in the province of *Gondwana*, and runs nearly due west about 750 miles, when it falls into the sea below *Baroach.*

रेह reh, *s. f.* (*mittee*) Fossil alkali, used for washing and making soap.

रेहरू réh-roo, *s. m.* A sled, a sledge.

रेहला reh-lá, *s. m.* A vetch.

रेही rehée, *s. f.* Fossil alkali.

रेहूपेहू réhoo-péhoo, *s. f.* Abundance.

रैंकना rynkna, *v. n.* To bray (*as an ass*).

रैदास rydás, *s. m.* The leader of a *Hindoo* sect.

रैन ryn, *s. f.* Night.

रोआई roáee, *s. f.* Lamentation.

रोआं róan, *s. m.* Hair of the body, down, wool.

रोआना ro-ána, *v. a.* To make cry, to vex, displease.

रोआस ro-ás, *s. f.* Inclination to cry.

रोआसा ro-ás-a, *adj.* Inclined to cry, vexed, displeased, afflicted.

रोएं ro-én, *s. f.* The hair on the arms, &c., bristle, pile, nap, down. *Roen budulna,* To become sleek and fat (*a horse*), to change his coat.

रोंगटी róng-tee, } *s. f.* Wrangling, subter-
रोंटगी ront-gée, } fuge, trick, cheat.

रोंट ront, *s. f.* Trick, subterfuge.

रोंटना rónt-na, *v. a.* To deny.

रोंटिया ront-iyá, *adj.* Treacherous.

रोंपना rómp-na, *v. a.* To plant, to transplant.

रोक rok, *s. f.* Prevention, prohibition, stop, restraint, let, hinderance. *Rok-tok,* Let and hinderance, opposition, resistance.

रोक rok, *s. m.* }
रोकर rok-ur, *s. f.* } Ready money, cash.

रोकरिया rokur-íya, *s. m.* A cash-keeper, treasurer.

रोकन rok-ún, *s. f.* An obstacle.

रोकना rók-na, *v. a.* To enclose, surround, stop, block, fend, prevent, restrain, hinder, coerce, detain, interrupt, prohibit.

रोकू ro-kóo, *s. m.* A preventer.

रोग rog, *s. m.* Sickness, disease in general, or a disease.

रोगग्रस्त rog-grúst, *adj.* Sick, diseased.

रोगभू rog-bhóo, *s. f.* The body.

रोगराज rog-ráj, *s. m.* Consumption.

रोगलक्षण rog-lúkshun, *s. m.* The symptoms or sign of a disease, or of its progress.

रोगशान्तक rog-shant-úk, *s. m.* A physician or alleviator of sickness.

रोगशान्ति rog-shánti, *s. f.* Cure or alleviation of disease.

रोगहर rog-húr, *adj.* Curative, medicinal.

रोगहारी rog-háree, *adj.* Curative, medicinal. *s. m.* A physician.

रोगिनी rogín-ee, *f.* } *adj.* Diseased, ill, sick,
रोगी rogée, *m.* } affected with sickness or disease.

रोगिया ro-giyá, *adj.* Sick, diseased, ill.

रोचक ro-chúk, *s. m.* A stomachic, a carminative, any medicine, fruit or fossil, supposed to strengthen the tone of the stomach and restore lost appetite.

रोचना rochun-á, *s. m.* A yellow pigment, supposed to be the concrete bile of the cow, or according to some authorities, to be found in the head of the animal, used as a medicine, a dye, and perfume.

रोज roj, } *s. m.* Lamentation.
रोजरा roj-rá, }

रोझ rojh, *s. m.* The painted or white-footed antelope (*Antelope picta*).

रोट rot, } *s. m.* Thick bread; (*met.*)
रोटा ró-ta, } Sweetmeats offered to *Hunooman*.

रोटी ró-tee, *s. f.* Bread.

रोड़ा ró-ra, *s. m.* A stone, a fragment of stone or brick, a brickbat.

रोदन ró-dun, *s. m.* Weeping, crying; a tear, tears.

रोध rodh, *s. m.* A bank, a shore.

रोधन ro-dhún, *adj.* Impeding, that which impedes or obstructs, an obstacle, a hinderer or hindrance. *s. m.* Impeding, obstructing.

रोना róna, *v. n.* To cry, to weep; to be displeased, to be melancholy. *adj.* Addicted to crying. *s. m.* Lamentation, grief. *Ro dena,* To cry, to weep; to be displeased, to be filled with indignation. *Ronee soorut, adj.* Of a sad countenance. *s. f.* A melancholy or rueful countenance.

रोपक ro-púk, *adj.* Who or what plants, raises, &c.

रोपन ro-pún, *s. m.* Planting; raising.

रोपना róp-na, *v. a.* To sow, to plant; to defend, block, fend.

रोपित ro-pít, *adj.* Planted; raised.

रोम rom, *s. m.* Down, small hair of the body.

रोमकूप rom-kóop, *s. m.* A pore of the skin.

रोमवत् rom-wút, } *adj.* Hairy, woolly.
रोमम् ro-mús,

रोमविकार rom-bikár, } *s. m.* Horripila-
रोमांच rom-ánch, tion, erection or rigidity of the hair of the body, conceived to be occasioned by, and to express, exquisite delight.

रोमांचित rom-án-chit, *adj.* Having the hair of the body erect, considered as a proof of exquisite pleasure ; enraptured, delighted.

रोमावली róma-vúl-ee, *s. f.* A line of hair across the middle of the belly or navel.

रोर ror, *s. f.* Noise, clamour, outcry ; fame.

रोरोकर roró-kur, *adv.* With difficulty, labour and pain.

रोलना ról-na, *v. a.* To roll, plane, polish, smooth ; to select, pick.

रोलाना ro-lá-na, *v. a.* To cause to cry, weep.

रोली ró-lee, *s. f.* A mixture of rice, turmerick and alum, with acid, used to paint the forehead.

रोस ros, *s. m.* Anger, wrath, rage. *Ros kurna,* To be angry, to be displeased.

रोशन ro-shún, *m.* } *adj.* Angry, passion-
रोशना ro-shun-á, *f.* ate.

रोसवाहन ros-váhun, *adj.* Angry, feeling and displaying wrath.

रोसना rós-na, *v. n.* To be angry, to be displeased, to have a misunderstanding with a friend.

रोहग ró-hug, *s. m.* The name of a mountain, Adam's peak in *Ceylon.*

रोहट ró-hut, *s. f.* Weeping, crying, tears.

रोहिनी ró-hin-ee, *s. f.* The fourth lunar asterism, figured by a wheeled carriage, and containing five stars.

रोहित ro-hít, } *s. m.* The *Rohi* fish (*Cy-*
रोहू ro-hóo, *prinus Rohita*).

रोहिष ro-hís, *s. m.* A sort of grass ; the *Rohi,* a kind of fish ; a deer said to resemble an ass.

रौंदन roun-dún, *s. m.* Trampling, treading under foot.

रौंदना róund-na, } *v. a.* To trample on,
रौंधना róundh-na, to tread down, to ride over.

रौद्र roudr, *adj.* Formidable, fearful, terrific ; violent, wrathful, irascible. *s. m.* Wrath, rage ; heat, warmth.

रौद्रता roudr-tá, *s. f.* Fierceness, formidableness.

रौना rouná, *s. m.* Bringing home a wife to consummate a marriage.

रौमुक roum-úk, } A kind of salt,
रौमलवण róum-lúvun, according to some authorities, brought from a mountain in *Ajmere,* but in fact procured from a salt lake near the town of *Sambhur,* about twenty miles west of *Jynugur.*

रौर rour, *s. f.* Noise, clamour outcry ; fame.

रौरव rour-úv, *adj.* Formidable, horrible, terrific. *s. m.* One of the divisions of hell.

रौल róu-la, *s. m.* Noise, tumult, sedition, alarm.

रौहीन rou-hín, *s. m. Sandal* wood.

रौहिनेय róuhin-éyuh, *s. m.* An emerald.

रौहिष rou-hísh, *s. m.* A sort of deer ; the *Rohi* fish ; a kind of grass.

ख

ख luh, The twenty-eighth consonant of the *Naguree* alphabet, the letter *L.*

लकच lúk-uch, } *s. m.* A species of the
लकूच lúk-ooch, bread-fruit tree (*Artocarpus Lacucha*).

लकुर lúk-ur, *s. m.* Wood, a cudgel, beam, bar. *Lukur-baz,* A cudgel-player. *Lukur-bazee. s. f.* Cudgel-playing, fencing.

लकुरहारा lukur-hára, *s. m.* A wood-cutter, wood-seller, woodmonger.

लकरा lúkra, *s. m.* A hyena ; a large piece of wood.

लकड़ी lúk-ree, *s. f.* Wood, timber, a staff, stick. (*met.*) *adj.* Stiff.

लकीर luk-éer, *s. f.* A line, lineament, streak.

लकूट lúk-oot, *s. m.* A staff, a stick, a club.

लखना lúkh-na, *v. a.* To see, look at, perceive, behold ; to understand. *v. n.* To disappear.

लखपती lukh-pút-ee, *adj.* Rich.

लखलखाना lukh-lukhána, *v. n.* To gasp, or pant with heat or thirst (*as birds*).

लखलूट lukh-lóot, *adj.* Extravagant.

लखा luk-há, *s. pl.* Hundreds of thousands.

लखाव luk-haóo, *adj.* Significant.

लखाव luk-háo, *s. m.* Act of seeing or perceiving.

लखिया lúk-hiya, *s. m.* A spectator.

लखेरा luk-héra, *s. m.* A varnisher.

लखौटा luk-hoúta, *adj.* Besmeared with lac. *Lukhouta kurna,* To smear with lac, to glaze.

लुग lug, *adv.* To, as far as, near, till, until, up to, close to, whilst, during.

लुगचलना lug-chúlna, *v. n.* To follow closely, to court friendship.

लुगड़ lug-úr, *s. m.* A kind of hawk.

लुगन lúg-un, ⎫ *s. f.* A moment, the rising
लुग्न lugn, ⎭ of a sign of the zodiac; affection, attachment, friendship, love; espousal, appointing the day of marriage. *s. m.* A large flat hollow copper utensil in the form of a bason.

लुगना lúg-na, *v. n.* To be applied, to apply, to begin, to be fixed, to be attached, to be close (*to*), adjoin, to touch, to be employed, to be imputed, to attain (*to*), to reach, to suit, to join, to close, to be, to belong, to become, to happen, to befall, to seem, to taste, to be connected (*with*), to regard. *Lug ruhna,* To continue without interruption, to continue fixed. *Luga ruhna,* To be occupied or busy (*in*).

लुगभग lúg-bhug, *adj.* Close, near, about, almost, by, thereabout.

लुगवाना lug-wána, *v. a.* To apply, to fix, to cause to apply, cause to put or plant, &c.

लुगातार lug-atár, *adj.* Successive, incessant.

लुगान lug-án, *s. m.* Stopping or making fast (*a boat, &c.*)

लुगाना lug-ána, *v. a.* To apply, to close, to attach, join, fix, affix, ascribe, impose, lay, add, place, put, plant, set, inflict, shut, spread, fasten, connect, plaster, put to work, employ, engage, use, impute, report any thing in the way of scandal or malice. *Lugana boojhana,* To excite quarrels. *Luga marna,* To calumniate. *Luga lena,* To attach to one's self, to conciliate, to win.

लुगाव lug-áo, *s. m.* Application, connexion, contact, adherence, symmetry, series, relation, intercourse.

लुगावट lug-áwut, *s. f.* Connexion, application.

लुगित lúg-it, *adj.* Connected with, attached to.

लुगूड़ lúg-oor, *s. m.* A staff, a stick; an iron club, or one bound with iron.

लुगूर lúgoor, *s. m.* A club, a stick.

लुगूरहस्त lugoor-húst, *s. m.* A man armed with a stick.

लुगूहन lugoon-hán, *adj.* Pleasing, beautiful, delightful, alluring.

लुगूआ lug-óoa, *s. m.* A paramour.

लुग्गा lúg-ga, *s. m.* Affection, attachment; a pole with which a boat is impelled. *Lugga nuh khana,* To be incompatible, inconsistent (*with*), not comparable (*with*).

लुग्गी lúg-gee, *s. f.* A pole, a staff, gibstaff.

लुग्न lugn, *adj.* Attached to, intent on; joined to, connected with. *s. m.* The rising of a

3 H

sign, its appearance above the horizon; the oblique ascension, or the divisions of the equator, which rise in succession with each sign in an oblique sphere; also defined as the arc of the equator, which passes the meridian in the same time with each sign of the ecliptic; in popular acceptation it is the moment of the sun's entrance into a zodiacal sign.

लुग्ना lugn-á, *s. m.* A bard, a panegyrist.

लुघु lúg-hoo, *adj.* Light, not heavy; small, little; insignificant, mean, low; short (*as a vowel*). *Lughoo-deeth,* Short-sighted. *Lughoo-belah, adv.* Shortly.

लुघुगर्ग lughoo-gúrg, *s. m.* A kind of fish, probably a variety of the *Pimelodus.*

लुघुचेत lúghoo-chéta, *adj.* Low-minded, frivolous.

लुघुता lughoo-tá, *s. f.* Lightness; meanness, insignificance.

लुघुदुन्दुभी lúghoo-doondoobhée, *s. m.* A small kettledrum.

लुघुमांस lughoo-máns, *s. m.* The Francoline partridge.

लुघुमित्र lughoo-mítr, *s. m.* A friend or ally of little power or value.

लुघुमूल lughoo-móol, *s. m.* In algebra, the least root with reference to the additive quantities.

लुघूकरण lughóo-kúrun, *s. m.* Reducing in weight or consequence; thinking little of, contemning.

लुघ्वाचार lughva-hár, *adj.* Temperate, abstemious.

लुङ्क lunk, *s. f.* The reins, the loins.

लुङ्का lún-ka, *s. f.* The capital of *Ravun* in *Ceylon;* the name is extended also to the island, which according to the notions of the *Hindoos,* is much more considerable in size, and lies further from the continent than in reality; it is described as being equal to 1-12th of the equatorial circumference of the earth, and is one of the places lying under the first meridian, whence the longitude is computed; it is thus placed in the Eastern ocean, south of *Ceylon,* and according to Wilford is the peninsular of *Malacca:* according to some *Hindoo* accounts also, it is distinct from *Ceylon,* from which island *Lunka* is said to be just visible.

लुङ्कायिका lunká-yika, *s. f.* A plant (*Trigonella corniculata*).

लुङ्कस्थायी lúnka-sthayee, *s. m.* A plant (*Euphorbia Tirucalli*),

लुङ्कोपिका lunk-ópika, *s. f.* A gramineous plant (*Trigonella corniculata*).

लुङ्ग lung, *s. m.* Limping, lameness.

लुङ्ग lung, ⎫ *adj.* Lame, cripple.
लुङ्गड़ा lúngra, ⎭

लुङ्गड़ाना lung-rána, *v. n.* To limp.

लंगर lún-gur, *s. m.* An anchor. *Lungur oothana*, To weigh anchor. *Lungur dalna*, To cast anchor. *Lungur pur hona*, To be at anchor.

लंगरी lúng-ree, *s. f.* A large shallow pan, made of metal, and generally used to knead bread in, or at meals for serving rice.

लंगूचा lun-góo-cha, *s. m.* A sausage.

लंगूर lun-góor, *s. m.* A baboon.

लंगोट lun-gót, *s. m.* ⎫ A cloth worn be-
लंगोटा lungó-ta, *s. m.* ⎬ tween the legs
लंगोटी lungó-tee, *s. f.* ⎭ to conceal the
privities. *Lungot-bund, s. m.* A bandage to which the *lungot* is fastened ; one devoted to celibacy. *Lungotiya-yar, s. m.* An old friend (*from childhood*), a very intimate friend, a crony.

लंघन lun-ghún, *s. m.* Fasting, abstinence ; leaping, springing, going by leaps or jumps ; jumping over or beyond ; exceeding, transgressing, disregarding propriety, going beyond proper bounds.

लंघना lúngh-na, *v. n.* To be jumped over, to be passed over, to pass. *v. a.* To jump or leap over.

लंघुनी lunghun-ée, *s. f.* Fast, fasting.

लचक lúch-uk, *s. f.* Spring, elasticity, bending.

लचकता luch-úk-ta, *adj.* Elastic.

लचकना luch-úk-na, *v. n.* To spring, to bend.

लचका lúch-ka, *s. m.* Jolt ; a barge, a kind of boat. *part.* Bent.

लचकाना luch-ká-na, *v. a.* To jolt, to strain.

लचना lúch-na, *v. n.* To bend, to bow.

लचलचाना luch-luch-ána, *v. n.* To be clammy, or glutinous ; to be elastic.

लचर lúch-ur, *s. m.* A foolish fellow, a simpleton.

लचाना luch-ána, *v. a.* To bend, to bow, to crook.

लछन luch-chhún, *s. m.* Sign, mark ; symptom, feature.

लछा luch-chhá, *s. m.* A bundle (*of thread*), a ball or skein of thread, &c.

लजकारिका luj-kárika, *s. f.* The sensitive plant (*Mimosa pudica*).

लजलजा luj-lúj-a, *adj.* Clammy, glutinous, viscous.

लजलजाना luj-luj-ána, *v. a.* To soften.

लजलाज luj-láj, *n. prop.* Name of the inventor of chess.

लजवाना luj-wána, *v. a.* To shame, to cause to blush.

लजाना luj-ána, *v. n.* To be ashamed, or abashed, to blush.

लजालू luj-áloo, *s. m.* ⎫ A kind of sensitive
लजवंती luj-wún-tee, *s.* ⎬ plant (*Mimosa natans*, or, *pudica*). *adj.* Bashful.

लजियाना luj-iyána, *v. n.* To be abashed, to be ashamed.

लजीला luj-éela, *adj.* Bashful, modest.

लज्जत luj-jút, *adj.* Being ashamed, blushing, shrinking.

लज्जमान lujj-mán, *adj.* Being ashamed.

लज्जा lúj-ja, *s. f.* Shame, modesty, bashfulness.

लज्जाकर lujja-kúr, ⎫ *adj.* Shameful,
लज्जाकारी lujja-káree, ⎬ causing or occasioning shame.

लज्जान्वित lujjan-vít, *adj.* Ashamed, bashful.

लज्जामान lujja-mán, ⎫ *adj.* Ashamed, mo-
लज्जित luj-jít, ⎬ dest, abashed.

लज्जारहित lújja-rúhit, *adj.* Shameless, immodest.

लज्जालू luj-já-loo, *s. m.* A sensitive plant (*Mimosa pudica*).

लज्जावती lújja-vút-ee, *f.* ⎫
लज्जावान lujja-wán, *m.* ⎬ *adj.* Modest, bashful.
लज्जाशील lujja-shéel, *m.* ⎭

लज्जाहीन lujja-héen, *adj.* Shameless, impudent.

लज्जित luj-jít, *adj.* Ashamed, modest.

लज्जा luj-jyá, *s. f.* Modesty, bashfulness.

लट lut, *s. f.* Tangled hair, a clotted lock (*of hair*) ; a tadpole. *Lut jana*, To become entangled.

लठ lut, *s. m.* A blockhead, a fool, one speaking ignorantly or foolishly ; fault, defect.

लटक lút-uk, *s. f.* Hanging, dangling ; an affected motion in blandishment and coquetry.

लटकचाल lútuk-chál, *s. f.* Affected gait, coquetry.

लटकन lút-kun, *s. m.* Any thing hanging ; drops worn in the ears ; a pendant ; ringlet ; a fruit with which clothes are dyed yellow ; name of a green handsome bird, which often remains hanging by the feet ; a stand for water-pots ; the drops of a crystal lustre.

लटकना lut-úk-na, *v. n.* To hang, to dangle.

लटका lút-ka, *s. m.* Incantation, conjuring rod, a philter, a quack medicine or nostrum.

लटकाना lut-ká-na, *v. a.* To hang, dangle, append, suspend.

लटकाव lut-káo, *s. m.* Suspension, hanging.

लटपट lut-pút, *adj.* Staggering, tripping ; folded, tangled.

लटपटा lút-put-a, *adj.* Playful, wanton, frisky, humorous ; irregularly folded (*a turband*).

लटपटाना lút-put-ána, *v. n.* To stagger, to trip.

लटपटी lut-pút-ee, *s. f.* Stumbling, staggering, swaggering.

लटा lút-a, *adj.* Reduced (*by sickness, &c.*), lean, emaciated.

लटाई lut-áee, *s. f.* A kind of roller on which the string of a kite is wound.

लटापटा lút-a-pút-a, *s. m.* Baggage, furniture, effects.

लटूरी lut-óo-ree, *s. f.* A small curl or lock of hair. *Lutooriyan, s. f. pl.* Tangled short hair.

लठोरा lut-óra, *s. m.* Name of a bird (*Lanius*).

लटू lút-too, *s. m.* A child's top. *Luttoo hona, v. n.* To fall in love, to be enamoured.

लटठर lut-thúr, *adj.* Slack, remiss.

लट्ठा lút-tha, *s. m.* A beam.

लठ luth, *s. m.* A stick, club, cudgel. *Luthbazee, s. f.* Cudgelling.

लठपठ luth-púth, *adj.* Wet, soaked, drenched.

लठालठी luthá-luthée, *s. f.* Mutual beating with cudgels.

लठियाना luthi-yána, *v. a.* To belabour, cudgel, cane.

लड़ lur, *s. f.* A string (*of pearls, &c.*), a thread, a row ; a strand of a rope or cord ; a party. *Lur men ruhna,* To be in one's party.

लड़कपन lur-uk-pún, *s. m.* Childhood, boyhood.

लड़कबुद्धि lúruk-bóoddhi, *s. f.* Childishness, the wisdom of a child.

लड़का lúr-ka, *s. m.* A boy, child, infant, babe. *Larka bala, s. m.* Child. *Lurka-lurkee,* Boys and girls, children.

लड़काई lur-káee, *s. f.* Childhood, boyhood, the being of a child or children.

लड़कापन lurka-pún, *s. m.* Childhood, boyhood.

लड़की lúr-kee, *s. f.* A girl.

लड़खुराना lur-khur-ána, *v. n.* To stagger, trip; to stutter, stammer.

लड़ना lúr-na, *v. n.* To fight, quarrel, contend, battle, war. *s. m.* Fighting.

लड़न्त lur-únt, *s. f.* Fighting, contending.

लड़बड़ाना lur-bur-ána, *v. n.* To stutter, stammer ; to stagger, reel.

लड़बावला lur-báo-la, *adj.* Mad, foolish.

लड़ाई lur-áee, *s. f.* Battle, quarrel, war, fight, fighting. *Luraee kurna,* To war, fight, give battle.

लड़ांका lur-án-ka, *adj.* Quarrelsome, warlike.

लड़ाक lur-ák, } *adj.* Quarrelsome, good-
लड़ाका lur-áka, } fighter.

लड़ाना lur-ána, *v. a.* To make fight, to fight, to bait ; to play.

लड़ियाना lur-iyána, *v. a.* To thread, to string.

लड़ी lúr-ee, *s. f.* A string (*of pearls, &c.*)

लड़ूक lud-dóok, *s. m.* A class of sweetmeats, or a sweetmeat; a sort of ball made with flour fried with oil or *ghee*, and mixed with sugar and spices, and distinguished into different kinds according to some slight varieties in its less essential ingredients.

लड़ू lúd-doo, *s. m.* A kind of sweetmeat, made chiefly of sugar, with the addition of cocoanut kernel rasped, and cream, and formed into the shape of large boluses or balls. *Mun keh luddoo khana,* To build castles in the air. *Thug keh luddoo kha bythna,* To be distracted, foolish, or intoxicated. (*Spoken of one who talks or acts absurdly in opposition to his usual good sense :*) an allusion taken from sharpers who join a party of travellers, and having got into their confidence, entertain them with sweetmeats impregnated with *Datura,* or other intoxicating drug, that they may rob them with impunity while under its stupifying influence.

लड़बा lúr-ba, *s. m.* } A cart.
लड़िया lur-híya, *s. f.* }

लड़ियाना lur-hiyána, *v. a.* To double hem a garment.

लड़ही lur-hée, *s. f.* A small cart.

लंड lund, *s. m.* Penis.

लंडूरा lun-dóo-ra, *adj.* Tail-less, docked ; (*a person*) without friends, forlorn.

लत lut, *s. f.* Bad habits, whim, whimsey. (*In compos.*) contraction of *lat,* kick. *Lut-khora, adj.* Kicked, beaten; contemptible, mean. (*subst.*) A slave ; a threshold. *Lut-koondun,* Ignominious treatment. *Lut-kob, adj.* Beating, cudgelling. *Lut-khana,* To suffer a kick or beating. *Lut-suda, adj.* Of bad habits, vicious. *Lut-murdun kurna,* To trample or tread on. *Lut-murdun men purna,* To be trampled under foot or disgraced.

लत lut, *s. f.* The hanging branch of a creeper.

लतर lút-ur, *s. f.* An old shoe.

लतरी lut-ree, *s. f.* An old shoe ; a kind of vetch.

लता lút-a, *s. f.* A creeper, a vine, a creeping or winding plant in general ; a vegetable and medicinal substance, the musk-creeper said to grow in the *Dukhin*

लुताकाम luta-kám, *n. prop.* Name of a most famous woman.

लुताब lutár, *s. f.* Calumny, labour.

लुतारना lut-ár-na, *v. a.* To work, to cause to toil, exhaust by labour, fatigue, jade, bring down, affront, insult.

लुताद्रुम luta-dróom, *s. m.* A timber tree (*Shorea robusta*).

लुतिका lúti-ka, *s. f.* A twining plant.

लुतिया lútiya, *adj.* Of bad habits.

लुतियाना lut-iyána, *v. a.* To kick.

लुत्ता lútta, *s. m.* A rag, tatter, scrap of cloth.

लुत्ती lúttee, *s. f.* The string of a child's top; a cloth tied to the end of a pole to direct the flight of pigeons; a kick when swimming. *Luttee kurna*, To run away.

लुथुरना luthúr-na, *v. n.* To be draggled.

लुथेरना luthérna, *v. a.* To draggle or besmear with dirt.

लुदना lúd-na, *v. n.* To be loaded, to be laden.

लुदफुन्दा lud-phúnda, *s. m.* Packing and loading.

लुदाना lud-ána, *v. a.* To load. *Ludwána, v. a.* To cause to load or lade.

लुदाव lud-áo, *s. m.* A load; an arched roof or terrace.

लुप lup, *s. f.* A handful, the space in the palm of the hand closed so as to hold water.

लुपक lúp-uk, *s. f.* A flash (*of lightning, &c.*); the spring (*of a tiger, &c.*), bounce, snatch.

लुपकना lup-úk-na, *v. n.* To flash (*as lightning*), to spring, bounce or rush forth or upon, to attack.

लुपका lúp-ka, *s. m.* A snatch; nimbleness; a bad custom or habit.

लुपकी lúp-kee, *s. f.* A stitch.

लुपची lúp-chee, *s. f.* A scate.

लुपझुप lup-jhúp, *adj.* Nimble.

लुपट lúp-ut, *s. f.* Odour; warmth, glow.

लुपटना lup-út-na, } *v. n.* To cling, stick,
लुपटाना lup-tá-na, } adhere together.

लुपट lúp-ta, *s. m.* A kind of molasses; relation, connexion; a sort of grass (*Panicum verticillatum*).

लुपटी lúp-tee, *s. f.* Pap, any glutinous liquid food.

लुपलुप lúp-lup, *adj.* Nimble, quick. *Luplup khana*, To eat quickly.

लुपसी lúp-see, *s. f.* A glutinous kind of food, pottage, pap, spoonmeat.

लुपाटिया lup-átiya, *s. m.* A tattler, a liar.

लुपाटी lup-á-tee, *s. f.* Lying, tattling.

लुपानक lup-á-nuk, *adj.* Slender, thin.

लुपेट lup-ét, *s. m. f.* A fold, a ply, envelope, twist, bandage, fillet. *Lupet-jhupet*, or, — *supet, s. f.* Evasion, subterfuge.

लुपेटन lup-etún, *s. f.* A roller on which cloth is wound in the loom, a button, &c.

लुपेटना lup-étna, *v. a.* To wrap up, to fold, enclose, pack, roll, furl.

लुपेटवाँ lup-etwán, *adj.* Twisted, ornamented with gold or silver thread wound round it.

लुप्पा lúp-pa, *s. m.* Brocade, gold or silver cloth.

लुबरखुन्दा lúbur-khúnda, *m.* } A mischiev-
लुबरखुन्दी lúbur-khúndee, *f.* } ous child.

लुबरचुताई lúbur-chutáee, *s. f.* Giving the breast to a child when it contains no milk.

लुबरसुबर lúbur-súbur, *s. m.* Tittle-tattle, nonsense.

लुबरा lúbra, *s. m.* A liar, a tattler. *adj.* Left-handed.

लुबरो lubró, *adj. f.* False and talkative (*a woman*).

लुबनी lúb-nee, *s. f.* The pot in which *taree* is collected from the tree.

बुबरघुत्ता búbur-ghútta, *adj.* Fastidious, fretful, touchy.

लुबलुबा lúb-luba, *s. m.* The pancreas. *adj.* Clammy, glutinous.

लुबलोस lublós, *adj.* Naked, shapeless. *s. f.* Flattery.

लुबार lub-ár, *s. m.* A liar, a talker.

लुबी lúb-ee, *s. f.* The juice of the sugarcane when boiling into sugar.

लुबेदा lub-éda, *s. m.* A club.

लुबेरा lub-éra, *s. m.* A fruit (*Cordia myxa*).

लुब्ध lubdh, *adj.* Gained, acquired, obtained, received, got.

लुब्धचेता lubdh-chéta, *adj.* Recovered, restored to one's senses, come to a right mind.

लुभ्युः lúbhyuh, *adj.* Attainable, procurable.

लुमकाना lum-kána, *v. n.* To stretch out the hands to take any thing.

लुमकाना lum-kána, }
लुमहा lúm-ha, } *s. m.* A hare, a rabbit.
लुम्भा lum-bhá, }

लुमछुर lum-chhúr, *s. f.* A long musket.

लुमछुरा lum-chhúr-a, *adj.* Tall.

लुम्पट lúm-put, *adj.* False, lying, dissolute, lecher, libertine. *s. m.* A lecher, a libertine, a whoremonger, a gallant. *Kuchh-lumput, adj.* Incontinent, dissolute, lewd.

लम्पटता lúmput-ta, *s. f.* Libertinism, dissoluteness.

लम्बर lúm-bur, *s. f.* A fox.

लम्बा lúm-ba, *adj.* Long, tall. *Lumba kurna*, To lengthen, to extend ; to beat, to drub.

लम्बाई lum-báee, *s. f.* } Length. *Lum-*

लम्बान lum-bán, *s. m.* } *baee-chouraee, s. f.* Size, length and breadth ; (*met.*) pomp, glory, pride.

लम्बाना lum-bá-na, *v. a.* To lengthen.

लम्बिका lúm-bik-a, *s. f.* The uvula or soft palate.

लम्बित lum-bít, *adj.* Suspended, depending, falling or hanging down.

लम्बियां करना lúmbiyan kúrna, *v. a.* To prance.

लम्बी lúm-bee, *adj. f.* Long, tall ; a kind of bounding pace in a horse. *Lumbee kurna*, To make a horse capriole, or throw out his forelegs. *Lumbee sans bhurnee, v. n.* To regret, to lament.

लम्बू lum-bóo, *adj.* Long, tall.

लम्भा lum-bhá, *s. f.* A sort of chain enclosure or fence.

लय luy, *s. f.* Equal time in music and dancing, tone, melody, modulation, symphony, singing in tune ; ardent affection or desire, immersion or absorption.

लयारी ly-áree, *s. m.* A wolf.

लर्छा lúr-chha, *s. m.* A skein.

ललक lúl-uk, *s. f.* A sudden gush of water, &c. ; (*met.*) whim, fancy, caprice.

ललकना lúl-uk-na, *v. n.* To attack.

ललकाना lul-ká-na, *v. a.* To excite quarrel, to set on to fight.

ललकारना lul-kár-na, *v. a.* To call, bawl after, halloo after, challenge, set up the war whoop. *v. n.* To bawl out insultingly.

ललगन्दा lúl-gun-da, *s. m.* A monkey.

ललगन्दी lúl-gun-dee, *s. f.* The female monkey.

ललचाना lul-chá-na, *v. n.* To be tantalized, to long. *v. a.* To excite desire, to tantalize, to covet.

ललदम्बू lul-dúmboo, *s. m.* A flower (*Nerium odorum*).

ललन lúl-un, *s. m.* Pleasure, sport, pastime.

ललना lul-un-á, *s. f.* A wanton woman.

लला lúl-a, *s. m.* A boy.

ललाट lul-át, *s. m.* The forehead ; fate, destiny, fortune.

ललाटरेखा lulát-rékha, *s. f.* A line on the forehead, supposed to indicate long life ; a coloured sectarial mark on the forehead.

ललाटिका lul-átika, *s. f.* An ornament worn on the forehead, a jewel or star suspended there, or a kind of tiara bound over it ; a mark made with *Sandal* on the forehead.

ललित lúl-it, *s. f.* A *Raginee* or musical mode. *adj.* Beautiful, lovely.

ललिता lul-it-á, *s. f.* A woman in general ; a wanton.

ललियाना lul-iyána, *v. a.* To coax, wheedle, beg earnestly ; to redden.

लली lúl-ee, *s. f.* A girl. *adj.* Impotent.

ललोपत्तो lúllo-pútto, *s. m.* Wheedling, coaxing, flattering, adulation.

लव lúv-uh, *s. m.* A minute division of time, the sixtieth part of the twinkling of an eye ; a larger division of time, or 36 twinklings of the eye, or about ⅓ a second ; (*in arithmetic*) the numerator of a fraction.

लवक luv-úk, *adj.* Who or what cuts, reaps, &c.

लवंग lúv-ung, *s. m.* The clove tree (*Myristica caryophyllata*) ; cloves, the fruit.

लवन lúv-un, *adj.* Salt, saline. *s. m.* Sea salt, rock or fossil salt ; factitious salt or salt obtained by boiling clay found near the sea-shore, or any earth impregnated with saline particles ; the saline or salt taste, saltness.

लवनखानि lúvun-kháni, *s. m.* A salt mine in general, or the district of *Sambhur* in *Ajmere*, celebrated for its fossil salt.

लवनसमुद्र lúvun-súmoodr, *s. m.* The sea of salt water.   [*hoot.*

लवना luvun-á, *s. f.* A small river in *Tir-*

लवनाकर luvun-akúr, *s. m.* A salt mine.

लवनाम्बु lúvun-ámboo, *s. m.* The sea, or salt water.

लवनोत्तम lúvun-óttum, *s. m.* Nitre ; rock or river salt.

लवन lúv-un, *s. m.* Reaping.

लवा lúv-a, *s. m.* A kind of quail (*Perdix chinensis*).

लवाक luv-ák, } *s. m.* A sickle, a reap-

लवानक luv-ánuk, } ing-hook.

लुष्टम पुष्टम lúshtum-púshtum, *adj.* Topsy-turvy, with difficulty, with much ado.

लुशून lúsh-oon, *s. m.* Garlic (*Allium sativum*) ; a freckle.

लुस lus, *s. m.* Tenacity, viscosity, glutinousness, clamminess. *Lusdar, adj.* Viscous, glutinous, clammy. *Lusduree, s. f.* Tenacity, viscosity, glutinousness.

लुसकना lus-úk-na, *v. n.* To become viscous, to become moist (*or stiff, as a field*).

लुसना lús-na, *v. n.* To become, to befit ; to shine.

रुसरुसा lus-lús-a, *adj.* Viscous, clammy, glutinous, adhesive, ropy.

रुसरुसाना lus-lus-ána, *v. n.* To be clammy or glutinous, to agglutinate.

रुसित lus-ít, *adj.* Seen, evident.

रुसियाना lus-iyána, *v. n.* To be viscous, to be clammy.

रुसोरा lus-óra, *s. m.* A glutinous fruit (*Cordia myxa*).

रुसी lus-sée, *s. f.* Milk and water.

रुहुंगा luhún-ga, *s. m.* A petticoat (*or a mere skirt, which is tied round the loins and extends to the feet or ground*).

रुहुक lúhuk, *s. f.* Glitter, flash.

रुहुकना lúhuk-na, *v. n.* To be kindled or lighted, to rise up into a flame ; to glitter, flash, glance, shine ; to wave (*as herbage before the wind*) ; to warble, quaver.

रुहुकाना luh-kána, *v. a.* To warble, to quaver ; to cause to shine or glitter ; to blow up a fire.

रुहकारना luh-kárna, *v. a.* To fondle, to pat and encourage a horse, &c.

रुहकावट luh-ká-wut, *s. f.* Glittering, flashing.

रुहकीला luh-kée-la, *adj.* Glittering.

रुहकौवर luh-kóu-vur, *s. m.* Rice-milk eaten by bride and bridegroom.

रुहना lúh-na, *v. a.* To find, get, experience. *v. n.* To avail, answer, boot, signify, accrue. *s. m.* Outstanding debt ; fate, destiny.

रुहबर lúh-bur, *s. m.* A kind of parroquet.

रुहबेरा luh-bér-a, *s. m.* Name of a plant.

रुहुर lúhur, *s. f.* A wave, a large wave or surf, undulation ; whim, fancy, vision ; the effect of the poison of a snake ; a waving pattern in embroidery ; emotion.

रुहुरना luhúr-na, *v. n.* To wave, to undulate.

रुहुरबुहुर lúhur-búhur, *s. f.* Prosperity.

रुहरा lúh-ra, *s. m.* Quaver, shake, trill (*in music*).

रुहराना luh-rá-na, *v. n.* To tantalize ; to undulate, fluctuate, wave ; to play loosely, to put off.

रुहरालुगाना lúhra-lugána, *v. a.* To evade ; to avoid performing an agreement.

रुहरिया lúh-riya, *adj.* Waved, a mode of dyeing or painting.

रुहरी lúh-ree, *adj.* Inconstant, capricious, whimsical.

रुहुर्रा luhúrra, *s. m.* Name of a grain, Bajra (*Holcus spicatus*). [ing.

रुहलुहा luh-luhá, *adj.* Blooming, flourish-

रुहलुहाना luh-luhána, *v. n.* To bloom, to be verdant, to flourish.

रुहलोट luh-lót, *adj.* Borrowing and never paying.

रुहसन lúh-sun, *s. m.* Garlic (*Allium sativum*) ; a freckle.

रुहसनिया luh-sun-íya, *s. m.* Name of a precious stone.

रुहसोरा luh-só-ra, *s. m.* Name of a glutinous fruit (*Cordia myxa : Cordia latifolia*).

रुहू lúhoo, *s. m.* Blood. *Luhoo-loohan*, Covered with blood, bloody.

रुहूआ luhoo-á, *s. m.* Name of a plant.

रुक luksh, *s. m.* A lak, one hundred thousand.

रुकुन lúk-shun, *s. m.* A mark, a spot ; an indication, a predicate, any thing by which an object is designated or distinguished ; a symptom or any indication of actual disease.

रुकित luk-shít, *adj.* Seen ; marked.

रुकमुन luksh-mún, *n. prop.* The son of *Dusuruth*, the half-brother and faithful companion of *Ramchundr*.

रुकी lúksh-mee, *s. f.* One of the principal female deities of the *Hindoos*, the wife of *Vishnoo*, and goddess of wealth and prosperity ; fortune, success, prosperity ; beauty, splendour.

रुकीवान lukshmee-wán, *adj.* Prosperous, fortunate, wealthy, thriving ; beautiful.

रुकयुभ lúksh-yub, *adj.* To be seen or noted. *s. m.* A mark, a butt ; a mark, a sign ; a lak, a hundred thousand.

लाई láee, *s. f.* Parched rice mixed with sugar.

लांक lank, *s. f.* Quantity, measure ; the loins ; bird-lime ; chaff. [o ver.

लांघना lángh-na, *v. a.* To overleap, to pass

लाप lamp, *s. f.* Bound, leap, spring.

लाख lakh, *s. m.* Gum lac, a kind of wax formed by the *Coccus lacca*. *adj.* A hundred thousand. *Lakh lugana*, To shut up or conceal.

लाखना lákh-na, *v. a.* To apply lac.

लाखी la-khée, *s. f.* A red colour procured from lac.

लाग lag, *s. f.* Striking, hitting, fixing, a stroke ; enmity, rancour, spite, grudge ; affection, love ; cost, expenditure ; a secret ; approach. *Lag lugna*, To fall in love.

लागत lá-gut, *s. f.* Expense, cost.

लागी lá-gee, *s. f.* A mark, butt ; affection, love.

लागू la-góo, *adj.* Desirous, adhering to.

लाघव la-ghúv, *s. m.* Health ; lightness, delicacy, minuteness ; meanness, insignificance ; frivolity.

लांगूल lan-gúl, *s. m.* A plough; the penis.

लांगूलिक lan-gúl-ik, *s. m.* One of the thirty-four species of the fixed, or mineral and vegetable poisons.

लांगूल lan-góol, *s. m.* A hairy tail (*as a horse's, &c.*); the penis.

लाज laj, *s. f.* Bashfulness, modesty, shame.

लाजवंत laj-wúnt, *adj.* Modest, bashful, chaste, decent.

लाझा lá-jha, *s. m.* Viscosity, tenacity, glutinousness.

लात lat, *adj.* Old or worn, dirty, spoiled, shabby (*as clothes, ornaments, &c.*). *s. f.* An obelisk, a pillar.

लाठा lá-ta, *s. m.* A kind of food eaten by the poor (*Muhooa, pounded with grain*).

लाठ lath, *s. f.* A pillar, an obelisk, a club or staff; the vertical part of an oil-mill.

लाठी lá-thee, *s. f.* A staff, club, stick, crutch. *Lathee pathee*, Beating with sticks, a club or stick.

लाड़ lar, *s. m.* Lovingness, coaxing, caress, play, sport, playfulness of a child. *Lar lurana*, To fondle (*a child*).

लाड़ला lár-la, *adj.* Darling, dear.

लात lat, *s. f.* A kick. *Lat marna*, To kick.

लाद lad, *s. f.* Load; bowel. *Lad-phand*, *s. f.* Loading and packing.

लादना lád-na, *v. a.* To load, lade, freight.

लादिया lá-diya, *s. m.* A loader.

लादी lá-dee, *s. f.* A small load (*particularly a washerman's*).

लाडू lá-doo, *adj.* Fit to carry a load. *Ladoo kurna*, To mount a horse or colt for the first time.

लाना lá-na, *v. n.* To bring, adduce, induce, introduce, persuade, apply; to breed, produce, make.

लाफना láph-na, *v. n.* To jump.

लाभ labh, *s. m.* Gain, profit, produce; gain in general, acquirement, acquisition. *Labh kurna*, To attain.

लाभालाभ labh-alábh, *s. m.* Profit and loss.

लार lar, *s. m.* Saliva, spittle.

लाल lal, *adj.* Darling, dear. *s. m.* An infant boy, a son; spittle, saliva; name of a bird (*the male of Fringilla amandava*). *Lal-boojhukkur*, An intelligent person, one who comprehends quickly, or who readily divines what has happened or is to happen from certain symptoms: but the term is generally used ironically for a wise-acre, an ignorant foolish person who pretends to more sense than his neighbours.

लालच lá-luch, *s. m.* Longing, covetousness, greediness, selfishness, avarice, occasion, view, want. *Laluch kurna*, To covet, to long for.

लालची lál-chee, *adj.* Covetous, interested, selfish.

लालरी lal-rée, *s. f.* A kind of ruby; a false stone resembling a ruby.

लालन lá-lun, *adj.* Wheedling, coaxing. *s. f.* A mistress, sweetheart.

लालसा lál-sa, *s. f.* Ardent desire; regret, sorrow, missing, wishing for any person or object absent; soliciting, asking; the longing of pregnant women.

लाला lá-la, *s. f.* Saliva, spittle. *s. m.* Sir, master, a school-master.

लालाटिक lal-átik, *adj.* Relating to fate or destiny.

लालामेह lala-méh, *s. m.* Passing mucous urine.

लालित lá-lit, *adj.* Loved, desired; cherished, treated tenderly; coaxed, wheedled, seduced.

लालित्य la-lít-yuh, *s. m.* Beauty, loveliness; gaiety; gracefulness.

लालिन la-líin, } *s. m.* A seducer.
लाली lá-lee, }

लालिनी la-lin-ée, *s. f.* A wanton.

लालेपूरना láleh-púrna, *v. n.* To be extremely desirous and unable fully to express one's wishes.

लाव láo, *adj.* Cutting down. *s. m.* A rope (*particularly that drawn by bullocks at a well*); the cable of a boat.

लावनिकी lávun-íkee, *adj. f.* Lovely, beautiful.

लावण्य lavún-yuh, *s. m.* Saltness, the taste or property of salt; beauty, loveliness.

लावलाव lao-lao, *s. m.* Covetousness, avarice.

लावसाव lao-sao, *s. m.* Profit, advantage.

लावा lá-wa, *s. m.* Parched grain. *s. f.* A sort of quail (*Perdix chinensis*).

लावालूटरा láwa-lóotra, *s. m.* A tale-bearer.

लावू la-vóo, *s. f.* A pumpkin gourd (*Cucurbita lagenaria*).

लासा lá-sa, *s. m.* Any thing clammy or glutinous; the milk of plants; size.

लाह lah, *s. m.* A kind of cloth resembling gauze; advantage, welfare; lac.

लाहा lá-ha, *s. m.* Advantage.

लाही lá-hee, *s. f.* Name of a plant; a fine sort of cloth.

लाक्षा lak-shá, *s. f.* Lac, a red dye, or an insect which is analogous to the cochineal insect, and like it forms when dried and prepared, a dye of a red colour; the nest is formed of a resinous substance which is used as sealing-wax, and is usually termed shel lac.

लाबामय láksha-túroo,] s. m. The *Pulas*
लाबावृब láksha-bríksh,] tree (*Butea frondosa*).

लाबाप्रसादन láksha-prusádun, s. m. The red *Lodh*, a tree from the bark of which an astringent infusion is prepared, which is used to fix colour in dyeing.

लिकुच lík-ooch, s. m. A sort of bread-fruit tree (*Artocarpus lacucha*).

लिक्षा lík-ks, s. f. A nit, a young louse.

लिखतं likh-túng, s. m. A writing, paper, deed.

लिखत likh-út, adj. Writing. s. f. Writing, inscription.

लिखन likhún, s. f. Scripture, writing ; a writing, a written document.

लिखना líkh-na, v. a. To write.

लिखनी likh-nee, s. f. A pen. *Likhnee-das*, s. m. A writer, an amanuensis, copyist.

लिखंत likhúnt, s. m. Predestination, fate.

लिखलेना likh-léna, v. a. To copy, to write.

लिखा líkha, s. m. Fate, predestination, destiny, writing. adj. Written.

लिखाई likháee, s. f. The wages of writing ; the labour of writing ; the art or business of writing.

लिखाना likhá-na, v. a. To cause or teach to write, to get written.

लिखाव likháo, s. m.] Act of writing.
लिखावट likhá-wut, s. f.]

लिखित líkhit, adj. Written. s. m. Scripture, writing ; a writing, a manuscript, a written book or paper.

लिंग ling, s. m. A sign, a token ; the penis ; the phallus, or *Shiv* under that emblem ; gender.

लिंगन ling-ún, s. m. Embracing.

लिंगनाश ling-nás, s. m. Loss of the penis.

लिंगार्चन ling-árch-chun, s. m. Worship of the *Ling* or phallus.

लिंगिवेष liugi-vésh, s. m. The dress or the insignia of a religious student, the skin, staff, bowl, &c. ; the dress or appearance of a follower of *Shiv*.

लिंगी líng-ee, s. m. A worshipper of *Shiv* in the phallic type.

लिझरी líjh-ree, s. f. Afterbirth, placenta.

लिटाना lit-ána, v. a. To cause to lie or repose, to lay.

लिट्टी lít-tee, s. f. Balls or thick cakes of bread baked on coals.

लिथुरना lithúr-na, v. n. To be draggled.

लिथारना lithár-na, v. a. To draggle.

लिपटना lip-út-na, v. n. To cling, adhere together, stick.

लिपटाना lip-tá-na, v. n. To cling, stick, adhere together.

लिपटाव liptáo, s. m. Adhesion.

लिपरी lip-ree, s. f. An old ragged turband.

लिपना líp-na, v. n. To be plastered, smeared or washed over.

लिपवाना lip-wána, v. a. To cause to plaster, smear or wash over.

लिपाई lip-áee, s. f. Smearing, plastering.

लिपि lípi,] s. f. Writing in general,
लिपी líp-ee,] handwriting ; a writing, a written paper or book, &c.

लिपिकर lipi-kúr,] s. m. A scribe, a wri-
लिपिकार lipi-kár,] ter.

लिप्त lipt, adj. Smeared, anointed, plastered, spread ; embraced, united, connected with, &c. ; defiled or contaminated by.

लिबलिबा líb-lib-a, s. m. The pancreas.

लिब्बा líb-ba, s. m. A slap.

लिम lim, s. f. Unjust censure, calumny ; indication, trace. [monger.

लिम्पट lím-put, s. m. A lecher, a whore-

लिये líyeh, adv. For, on account of.

लिलाट lil-at,] s. m. The forehead ; fate,
लिलार lil-ár,] destiny, fortune.

लिलाना lil-ána, v. n. To long for.

लिवाना liwána, v. a. To cause to take.

लिवालाना liwá-lána, v. a. To bring.

लिवैया liwy-ya, s. m. Taker.

लिसौड़ा lis-óura, s. m. Name of a glutinous fruit (*Cordia myxa*).

लिहारा lihár-a, adj. Vile, base, mean, contemptible.

लीक leek, s. f. Marks of a carriage wheel, rut, path, track, trace, stain, ignominy, disgrace.

लीख leekh, s. f. A nit, the egg of a louse.

लीचजाना leech-jána, v. n. To submit, to succumb, to subside.

लीचर lée-chur, adj. Stingy.

लीची lée-chee, s. f. A china fruit (*Scytalia litchi*).

लीझी lee-jhée, s. f. Dregs (*of a dye, or of any thing that has been chewed*), sediment.

लीतरा léet-ra, s. m. An old shoe.

लीद leed, s. f. The dung of horses and elephants.

लीन leen, adj. Embraced, clung or adhered to ; melted, dissolved ; absorbed, immersed.

लीपरी léep-ree, s. f. A rag ; a small turband.

लोपना léep-na, v. a. To plaster, to be-smear.

लीबर lée-bur, s. m. Rheum (of the eyes).

लीम leem, s. m. Concord, peace.

लीमू lée-moo, s. m. A lime, a lemon, also the tree (Citrus medica).

लीर leer, s. f. A strip or slip of cloth.

लील leel, s. f. Indigo. adj. Blue.

लीलकंठ leel-kúnth, s. m. A bird (Coracias Bengalensis).

लीलना léel-na, v. a. To swallow, to gulp.

लीला lée-la, s. f. Play, sport, pastime in general; amorous or wanton sport.

लीलावती léela-wútee, s. f. A wanton or sportful woman; a work on arithmetic.

लूक look, s. m. A falling star; varnish.

लूकना lóok-na, v. n. To lie hid, to be con-cealed.

लूकुंद्रा lookúndra, s. m. A rake, a profli-gate.

लूक ló-ka, adj. Hid, concealed.

लूकांजन look-án-jun, s. m. An ointment, by applying which to a man's eyes he is said to become invisible.

लूकाना look-ána, v. a. To hide, to conceal.

लूगाई loo-gáee, s. f. Woman.

लूच looch, adj. Pure, mere, stark naked. Looch-buhadur, s. m. A vagabond.

लूचपन looch-pún, s. m. Libertinism, ra-kishness.

लूचरा lóoch-ra, s. m. A spider.

लूचा lóoch-cha, s. m. A vagabond, a liber-tine, a rake, a profligate. adj. Low, mean.

लूचामी looch-chá-mee, s. f. Libertinism.

लूजलूजा looj-lóoj-a, adj. Clammy, gluti-nous, viscous.

लूंजा lóon-ja, adj. Lame of a hand or hands, having lost the use of hands and feet.

लूटना lóot-na, v. n. To be plundered, to be squandered.

लूटवैया loot-wy-ya, s. m. A squanderer, a prodigal, spendthrift, plunderer.

लूतूस loo-tús, ⎱ s. m. Plundering, ruin,
लूतुस lóot-tus, ⎰ devastation.

लूटाना loo-tá-na, v. a. To squander, spend or expend, to cause to plunder or be plundered; to cause to wallow or roll about. Loota-loota-kur marna, To beat severely.

लूटिया lóo-tiya, s. f. A small pot.

लूटेरा loo-téra, ⎱ s. m. A squanderer, pro-
लूटेरू loo-téroo, ⎰ digal, spendthrift, plunderer.

लूरका lóor-ka, s. m. A Hindoo ornament worn in the ears.

लूरूखना loo-rúkh-na, v. n. To roll, to fall (or roll) off, to slip, to slide.

लूरखोरी loor-khóoree, s. f. Rolling; flat-tery, coaxing, wheedling, fawning.

लूरबुकना loor-búkna, ⎱ v. n. To roll, to be
लूरना lóorh-na, ⎰ spilt. Loorh jana, To die.

लूरहाना loor-hána, v. a. To cause to roll, to spill.

लूरहिया lóor-hiya, s. f. A stone pestle with which materials are triturated on a stone.

लूरहियाना loor-hiyána, v. a. To double hem a garment.

लूनतूक loon-túk, s. m. A sort of potherb (Chironia centauroides, &c.)

लूंदा lóon-da, adj. Tail-less, tail-cropt, docked.

लूतरा lóot-ra, s. m. A sycophant, a tell-tale, a babbler, a tattler, backbiter.

लूपरी lóop-ree, s. f. Pap.

लूपलूप loop-loop, s. m. Lapping (as of a dog drinking).

लूप्त loopt, adj. Gone, lost, disappeared.

लूप्तता loopt-tá, s. f. Disappearance, non-existence.

लूबदी lóob-dee, s. f. Poultice, cataplasm.

लूब्ध loobdh, adj. Covetous, greedy, desir-ous, cupidinous. s. m. A lecher, a libertine.

लूबधूक loob-dhúk, s. m. A hunter; a liber-tine, a rake, whore-monger; a covetous or greedy man.

लूभाना loo-bhána, v. a. To excite desire, tantalize, allure, entice.

लूहुंदा loo-hún-da, s. m. An iron pot.

लूहरा lóoh-ra, s. m. A younger, junior, cadet.

लूहांगी loo-háng-ee, s. f. A staff armed with iron.

लूहान loo-hán, adj. Bloody.

लूहार loo-hár, s. m. A blacksmith.

लूहारिन loo-har-ín, s. f. The female of Loohar.

लू loo, s. f. A hot wind.

लूआट loo-át, adj. Half-burnt (wood), a brand.

लूई ló-ee, s. f. A round lump of dough prepared for making into bread or cakes.

लूक look, s. f. A hot wind.

लूकट ló-kut, adj. Half-burnt (wood), a brand.

लूकटी lóok-tee, s. f. A wooden poker, or stake burnt at one end; a fox.

लूकना look-na, *v. n.* To be scorched by the sun or hot wind, to have a coup de soleil. *v. a.* To see.

लूकवाई look-wáee, *s. f.* Conflagration.

लूका lóo-ka, *s. m.* Pieces of burning matter thrown out from a conflagration. *Looka lugana,* To inflame or excite quarrels, &c.

लूख lookh, *s. f.* A flame. *Lookh chulana,* To charm, fascinate.

लूट loot, *s. f.* Plunder. *Loot-baz,* A plunderer, a murderer.

लूटखूट loot-khóot, *s. f.* Plundering and ravaging.

लूटना lóot-na, *v. a.* To plunder, pillage, spoil ; to squander. [ing.

लूटपाट loot-pát, *s. f.* Plunder and sack-

लूटालूट loot-a-lóot, *s. f.* Plundering.

लूंग्रा lóon-gra, *adj.* Salt, brackish.

लूनी lóon-nee, *s. f.* The salt that effloresces from walls, &c. ; butter.

लूता lóo-ta, *s. f.* A spider ; local inflammation produced by the urine of a spider.

लून loon, *s. m.* Salt.

लूनिया lóo-niya, *adj.* Salt, brackish. *s. m.* Purslain (*Portulaca oleracea*) ; a pioneer ; a saltmaker ; name of a tribe or caste of *Buniya.*

लूनी lóo-nee, *s. f.* The salt that effloresces from walls, &c. ; butter.

लूम loom, *s. m.* A tail ; a hairy tail, as a horse's, a monkey's, &c.

लूला lóo-la, *adj.* Lame of the hands.

लूलूआ loo-loo-á, *s. m.* A paw.

लूह looh, *s. f.* A hot wind.

ले leh, *part.* Having taken. *imper.* Take. *adv.* Till, to ; from. *interj.* Come ! well !

लेई lé-ee, *s. f.* Paste.

लेंडी lén-dee, *s. f.* Goat's dung ; a cur, a country dog. *adj.* Impotent.

लेंढा lén-dha, *s. m.* Smut, mildew ; a flock of goats or sheep, a pack of dogs.

लेख lekh, *s. m.* A letter, an epistle.

लेखक lékhuk, *s. m.* A writer, a scribe, a clerk, a copyist, an amanuensis, accountant.

लेखकी lekhuk-ée, *s. f.* The business of a writer.

लेखन lékhun, *s. m.* Writing, scripture ; the bark of the *Bhoj* tree, which is used for writing on in *Nepal* and Upper *Hindoostan.*

लेखनी lékh-nee, *s. f.* A pen, a reed.

लेखा lékha, *s. m.* Account, reckoning.

लेख्य lékhyuh, *s. m.* A letter, an epistle.

लेख्यपत्र lékhyuh-pútr, *s. m.* A written paper, a writing, a letter.

लेख्यस्थान lékhyuh-sthán, *s. m.* An office, a country-house, &c.

लेजाना leh-jána, *v. a.* To take away, carry, convey, run away with, export, submit, refer, win.

लेट let, *s. m.* Mortar, plaster, chunam.

लेटना lét-na, *v. n.* To repose, lie down, lie, rest.

लेत let, *s. m.* Plaster, paste, batter.

लेन len, *verbal n.* To take, taking.

लेनदेन len-den, *s. m.* Traffic, trade, barter, buying and selling.

लेना lén-a, *v. a.* To take, accept, assume, get, hold, pick, win, receive, buy. *Leh ana, v. n.* To bring, fetch.

लेप lep, *s. m.* Plaster, ointment ; plastering, smearing ; mortar, plaster, chunam.

लेपक lep-úk, } *s. m.* A bricklayer, a plas-
लेपी lép-ee, } terer.

लेपड़ना leh-púrna, *v. a.* To lie with ; to involve another in one's disgrace.

लेपना lép-na, *v. a.* To plaster, besmear.

लेपालक leh-páluk, *s. m.* An adopted child, adopted, a fosterchild.

लेपालना leh-pálna, *v. a.* To adopt, rear, bring up, father. [ing.

लेपालेप lep-alép, *s. m.* Complete plaster-

लेप्य lép-yuh, *s. m.* Plastering, spreading or smearing ointment, mortar, &c.

लेमरना leh-múrna, *v. a.* To calumniate.

लेरखना leh-rúkhna, *v. a.* To provide, keep ready, procure, reserve.

लेरुहना leh-rúhna, *v. n.* To cheat, to pilfer.

लेरू léroo, } *s. m.* A calf.
लेरुआ leroo-á, }

लेला léla, *s. m.* A lamb.

लेलूट lelóot, *adj.* Borrowing and never paying.

लेलेना leléna, *v. a.* To take, receive, accept of, take by force, extort, bereave.

लेव lev, *s. m.* Plaster falling from a wall.

लेवा léwa, *s. m.* Taker ; plaster, that which is spread on the outside of a new pot ; udder.

लेवादेई léwa-dé-ee, *s. f.* Traffic, trade, taking and giving.

लेवार lewár, *s. m.* Mud (*to plaster a wall with*).

लेवास lewás, *s. m.* Plaster.

लेवैया lewy-ya, *s. m.* Taker.

लेश lesh, *s. m.* Mark, sign, effect. *adj.* Small, little. *s. m.* Smallness, littleness ; a little.

लेसना lés-na, *v. a.* To plaster, spread, daub ; to kindle ; to foment (*a quarrel*).

लेसालेस lesalés, *s. m.* Plastering.

लेहुन léhun, *s. m.* Licking, tasting with the tongue.

लेहना léhna, *s. m.* Pasture, provender.

लेहिन léhin, *s. m.* Borax.

लेह्य léh-yuh, *adj.* To be licked. *s. m.* The food or beverage of the gods, nectar, ambrosia.

लेस lys, *adj.* Ready, brought. *s. m.* A kind of vinegar; a practising arrow; a spring.

लो lo, *imper.* Take, hold. *interj.* Lo! look, see, there now.

लोई lóee, *s. f.* Blanket, flannel; splendour of the countenance, honor.

लों lon, *adv.* Till, to, up to.

लोंग long, } *s. f.* A clove *(Caryophyllus*
लोंग loung, } *aromaticus). Loung-chura,*
s. m. A kind of dish prepared from pease-meal.

लोंदा lón-da, *s. m.* A lump of clay, clod.

लोक lok, *s. m.* Man, mankind; people; a world, a division of the universe: in general three *Loks* are enumerated, or heaven, hell, and earth: another classification enumerates seven, exclusive of the infernal regions; or *Bhoor-lok*, the earth, *Bhoovur-lok*, the space between the earth and the sun, the region of the *Moonis, Siddhis, &c. Swurg-lok*, the heaven of *Indr*, between the sun and the polar star, *Muhur-lok*, the usual abode of *Bhrigoo* and other saints: during the conflagration of these lower worlds, the saints ascend to the next, or *Jun-lok*, which is described as the abode of *Bruhma's* sons; above this is the sixth world or the *Tupo-lok*, where the deities called *Vyragees* reside; the seventh world *Sutyu-lok*, or *Bruhm-lok*, is the abode of *Bruhma*, and translation to this world exempts beings from further birth: the three first worlds are destroyed at the end of each *Kulp* or day of *Bruhma*; the three last at the end of his life, or of 100 of his years; the fourth *Lok* is equally permanent, but is uninhabitable from heat at the time the three first are burning. Another enumeration calls these seven worlds, earth, sky, heaven, middle region, place of births, mansion of the blest, and abode of truth, placing the sons of *Bruhma* in the sixth division, and stating the fifth or *Jun-lok* to be that, where animals destroyed in the general conflagration are born again; sight, seeing.

लोक lók-na, *v. a.* To catch.

लोकक्रत् lok-krít, *s. m.* The Creator, *Bruhma*.

लोकजित् lok-jít, *s. m.* A conqueror of the world.

लोकत्रय lok-try, *s. m.* The three worlds, heaven, earth, and hell.

लोकनाथ lok-náth, *s. m.* A sovereign of the universe.

लोकनीय lok-néeyuh, *adj.* Visible, to be seen.

लोकपाल lok-pál, *s. m.* A king, a sovereign; a divinity who is supposed to protect the regions, or the sun, moon, fire, wind, *Indr, Yum, Vuroon* and *Koover.*

लोकप्रसिद्ध lok-prusíddh, *adj.* Notorious, well known.

लोकरञ्जन lok-rún-jun, *s. m.* Popularity gaining public confidence.

लोकरा lók-ra, *s. m.* Tatters, torn clothes.

लोकान्तर lok-án-tur, *s. m.* Another world.

लोकालोक lok-alók, *s. m.* A mountainous belt surrounding the outermost of the seven seas and bounding the world.

लोखुर lo-khúr, *s. m.* Tools, old iron pots, pans, hardware.

लोग log, *s. m.* People, folk.

लोगाई lo-gáee, *s. f.* Woman.

लोचुक lo-chúk, } *s. m.* A ball or lump
लोचुना lo-chun-á, } of flesh or meat; stibium or lamp-black, &c. so used.

लोचन ló-chun, *s. m.* The eye.

लोचनकुर्कट lóchun-kúrkut, } *s. m.* A
लोचनमस्तक lóchun-mústuk, } flower *(Celosia cristata).*

लोचनामय lóchun-ámuy, *s. m.* Diseased affection of the eye, Ophthalmia.

लोटुन ló-tun, *s. m.* Tumbling, rolling; a kind of pigeon, tumbler; a bush.

लोटना lót-na, *v. n.* To wallow, roll about, flounce, sprawl.

लोटनापोटना lót-na-pótna, *v. n.* To wallow, to roll or turn over.

लोटपुटिया lot-póotiya, *s. m.* Water-cresses.

लोटपोट lot-pot, *adj.* Wallowing, tumbling and tossing, rolling about, restless. *Lot-pot hona*, To be in love.

लोटा ló-ta, *s. m.* An earthen pot *(for cooking)*, a pipkin, a small metal pot, generally of brass or tinned iron.

लोटासूजी lóta-sújee, *s. f.* A kind of earth containing fossil alkali.

लोरहा lor-há, *s. m.* A stone pestle with which materials are triturated on a stone.

लोना ló-na, *adj.* Salt, brackish; barren or salt *(land). s. m.* Purslain *(Portulaca oleracea)*; the salt that effloresces from walls, &c.

लोथ looth, *s. f.* A corpse, dead body.

लोथरा loth-rá, *s. m.* } A lump of flesh.
लोथरी loth-rée, *s. f.* }

लोथा ló-tha, *s. f.* A bag, a sack, stupe.

लोथी lo-thée, *s. f.* A staff, club *(knotted)*.

शोटी ló-dee, *s. m.* A caste among the Puthans.

शोध lodh, }
शोधर lodhr, } *s. m.* A tree, the bark of which is used in dyeing (*Symplocos racemosa*); a medicine.

शोधा ló-dha, *s. m.* Name of a tribe, a husbandman.

शोधिया ló-dhiya, *s. m.* Name of a tribe.

शोन lon, *s. m.* Salt. *Lon mirch lugana*, To speak hyperbolically or in lofty diffuse language.

शोना ló-na, *adj.* Salt, brackish; barren or salt (*land*). *s. m.* Purslain (*Portulaca oleracea*); the salt that effloresces from walls, &c.

शोनापन lona-pún, *s. m.* Saltness.

शोनार lo-nár, *s. m.* Salt lands; a place where salt is produced, a salt-pit.

शोप lop, *s. m.* Rejection, cutting off in general, especially used as a grammatical term for dropping letters, syllables, &c.; disappearance, destruction; erasure; (*in compos. with a verb*) vanished, disappeared.

शोपरी lóp-ree, *s. f.* A lump of any thing moist; a poultice composed of flour, turmeric, and oil or clarified butter.

शोबान lo-bán, *s. m.* A kind of gum, incense, benzoin (*resin*).

शोबिया ló-biya, *s. m.* A kind of bean (*Dolichos sinensis*).

शोभ lobh, *s. m.* Avarice, covetousness, cupidity, intense or greedy desire.

शोभना lóbh-na, *v. n.* To be enamoured.

शोभमोहित lobh-móhit, *adj.* Beguiled or overcome by cupidity.

शोभविरुह lobh-virúh, *adj.* Free from cupidity.

शोभी ló-bhee, *adj.* Desirous, cupidinous, covetous, greedy, avaricious.

शोम lom, *s. m.* A tail, a hairy tail; the hair of the body; the base of a triangle, &c.; a piquet, out-post, or sentry.

शोमकर्ण lóm-kurn, *s. m.* A hare.

शोमकूप lom-kóop, *s. m.* A pore of the skin.

शोमरी lóm-ree, *s. f.* A fox.

शोमविष lóm-vish, *s. m.* An animal whose hair is supposed to be poisonous, as a tiger, &c.

शोमुष lóm-ush, *adj.* Hairy, covered with or made of hair; woollen.

शोमुसपर्णिनी lómus-púrninee, *s. f.* A plant (*Glycine debilis*).

शोमुसमार्जर lómus-márjar, *s. m.* The polecat.

शोमसा lom-shá, *s. f.* A plant (*Leea hirta*);

Indian spikenard (*Valeriana Jatamansi*); cowach (*Carpopogon pruriens*); green vitriol; Orris root.

शोमसार lom-sár, *s. m.* The emerald.

शोमहर्षण lom-húrshun, *s. m.* Horripilation, erection of the hair of the body.

शोयन ló-yun, *s. m.* The eye.

शोर lor, *s. m.* An ear-ring, drop, pendant; a tear.

शोल lol, *adj.* Shaking, tremulous. *s. m.* Tears, the fluid in which the eyes appear sometimes to be overwhelmed, undulation, glimmer.

शोलुक ló-luk, *s. m.* An ear-ring, drop, pendant.

शोला ló-la, *s. m.* A suppository, a kind of solid clyster.

शोलिका ló-lika, *s. f.* A sort of dock or sorrel (*Rumex vesicarius*).

शोलुप ló-loop, *adj.* Very desirous or covetous, wishing, longing for, greedy, insatiable.

शोष्ट losht, *s. m.* A clod, a lump of earth; rust of iron or iron filings.

शोष्टमय losht-múy, *adj.* Made of a clod or of earth.

शोष्टू lósh-too, *s. m.* A lump of earth.

शोह loh, *s. m.* Iron, either crude or wrought; steel; Aloe wood or Agallochum.

शोहकंटक loh-kún-tuk, *s. m.* A thorny shrub.

शोहकांत loh-kánt, *s. m.* The loadstone.

शोहकार loh-kár, *s. m.* A blacksmith, or ironsmith.

शोहकिट्ट loh-kítt, *s. m.* Rust of iron, or iron filings.

शोहचूर्ण loh-chóorn, }
शोहचून loh-chóon, } *s. m.* Iron filings.
शोहचूर loh-chóor, }

शोहज lo-húj, *s. m.* Bell-metal; rust of iron, or iron filings.

शोहजित loh-jít, *s. m.* The diamond (*as conquering in hardness the iron*).

शोहुंडा lo-húnda, *s. m.* An iron pot.

शोहद्रावी loh-drávee, *s. m.* Borax (*as fusing metals*).

शोहमय loh-múy, *adj.* Made of iron.

शोहमारुक loh-már-uk, *s. m.* A plant (*Achyranthes triandra*).

शोहसार loh-sár, *s. f.* An iron mine.

शोहा ló-ha, Iron. *Loh-lath, s. m.* An iron mace or club. *Loha bujana*, To fight with swords.

शोहान lo-hán, *adj.* Bloody.

शोहानी lo-hánee, *s. f.* Name of a caste among *Puthans*.

शोहाभिसार lohá-bhisár, *s. m.* Lustration

of arms, ceremonies performed on the 9th of the light half of the month *Aswin*; formerly a ceremony observed by princes before opening a campaign, but now usually confined to the domestic decoration and worship of the soldier's weapons.

लोहार lo-hár, *s. m.* A blacksmith.

लोहारिन lo-harín, *s. f.* The female of *Lohar.*

लोहित ló-hit, *adj.* Red, of a red colour. *s. m.* Red, the colour; blood.

लोहितक lohi-túk, *s. m.* A ruby; calx of brass.

लोहितानन lóhit-ánum, *adj.* Red-faced. *s. m.* An ichneumon.

लोहिया ló-hiya, *adj.* Of iron.

लोही ló-hee, *s. f.* A lump, a mouthful; a kind of silk-cloth; dawn just before sunrise.

लोहू ló-hoo, *s. m.* Blood. *Lohoo dalna*, To spit blood. *Lohoo phutna*, To have leprosy. *Lohoo bythna*, To pass blood by stool. *Lohooloohan, adj.* Covered with blood, bloody.

लों loun,
लों lon, } *adv.* Till, to, up to.

लोंग loung, *s. f.* A clove (*Caryophyllus aromaticus.*)

लोंगचूरा loung-chúra, *s. m.* A dish prepared from pease-meal.

लोंदा loún-da, *s. m.* A boy, a slave boy, lad, brat. *Lounda-bazee, s. f.* Sodomy.

लोंदिया loundíya, } *s. f.* A girl, a slave girl,
लोंदी loun-dée, } a servant girl, bondmaid.

लौ lou, *s. f.* The flame of a candle, any pointed flame. *Lou lagana*, To be constant in prayer, devotion, &c. *Lou lagnee*, The frequent and long continued repetition of any saying (*particularly of a lover calling on his mistress, or of a dying man on God*), to have a constant desire or craving (*for any thing*).

लौकना lóuk-na, *v. a.* To see.

लौका lóu-ka, *s. m.* A kind of pompion (*Cucurbita lagenaria*); lightning, flash, glitter, coruscation.

लौकायतिक lóuka-yútik, *s. m.* An atheist, a materialist, a *Bouddh.*

लौकिक lóu-kik, *adj.* Mundane, worldly, human, what prevails amongst or is familiar to mankind; ceremonial, ceremonious.

लौकिकता loukik-tá, *s. f.* Worldliness; worldly currency, or custom.

लौकी lóu-kee, *s. f.* A kind of pompion.

लौट lout, *s. m.* Turning over, inverting; returning.

लौटना lóut-na, *v. n.* To turn over; to turn back, return.

लौटाना lou-tá-na, *v. a.* To turn over, to invert; to turn back, to return, give back, reject.

लौंग्रा lóun-gra, *s. m.* Name of a medicine.

लौना lóu-na, *s. m.* Balancing, making scales equal. *v. a.* To reap.

लौनी lóu-nee, *s. f.* Wages in kind to reapers in harvest time.

लौंद lóund, *s. m.* An intercalary month.

लौह louh, *adj.* Iron, made of iron. *s. m.* Iron.

लौहार louhár, *s. m.* A trance.

ल्यारी lyáree, *s. m.* A wolf.

व

व vuh, The twenty-ninth consonant of the *Naguree* alphabet, or more properly the semivowel *v*; it is often confounded with the labial consonant or ब buh, with which it is also optionally interchangeable.

वंस vuns, *s. m.* Race, lineage, family.

वंसक vuns-úk, *s. m.* A small fish (*Cynoglosus lingua*).

वंसचरित vuns-chúritr, *s. m.* A genealogical table or list, the history of a race or dynasty, &c.

वंसपरम्परा vuns-púrum-pura, *s. f.* Family, lineage, descent.

वंसभोज्युः vuns-bhójyuh, *s. m.* Hereditary estate.

वंसरोचना vuns-róchuna, } *s. f.* An earthy concre-
वंसलोचन vuns-lóch-un, } tion of a milk-white colour, formed in the hollow of the bamboo.

वंसवृद्धि vuns-vríddhi, *s. f.* Prosperity of a family.

वंससमाचार vuns-sumachár, *s. m.* Family usage.

वंसावली vuns-ávulee, *s. f.* A pedigree, a genealogy.

वंसिक vúns-ik, *adj.* Belonging or relating to a family, a bamboo, &c.

वंसी vún-see, *s. f.* A pipe, fife, flute.

वंसीधर vunsee-dhúr, *s. m.* A piper; a name of *Krishn.*

वक vuk, *s. m.* A crane (*Ardea nivea*); a tree (*Sesbana grandiflora*).

वकपुष्प vúk-pooshp, *s. m.* A tree (*Æschynomene grandiflora*).

वकूल vúk-ool, *s. m.* A plant (*Mimusops elengi*).

वक्तव्य vuk-túv-yuh, *adj.* Fit or proper to be said or spoken.

वक्ता vúk-ta, *s. m.* A speaker.

वक्र vukr, *adj.* Crooked, curved, bowed or bent; indirect, evasive.

वक्रगामी vukr-gámee, *adj.* Who or what goes tortuously; fraudulent, dishonest.

वक्रता vukr-tá, *s. f.* Crookedness, wickedness; craft, cunning; evasive or indirect speech.

वक्रपुष्प vukr-póoshp, *s. m.* The *Sesbana grandiflora.*

वक्री vuk-rée, *adj.* Crooked; dishonest, fraudulent.

वक्रीभाव vukree-bháo, *s. m.* Curvature, curve; fraudulent or dishonest disposition.

वक्रोक्ति vukr-ókti, *s. f.* Equivoque, evasion, pun, the covert expression of something else than the words used naturally imply, either from the manner in which they are uttered, or some other sense of which they are susceptible; hint, insinuation; sarcasm.

वङ्क vunk, *s. m.* The bend or elbow of a river, the winding course of a stream; crookedness.

वङ्ग vung, *s. m.* Bengal, or the eastern parts of the modern province.

वचन vúch-un, *s. m.* Speech, speaking; a sentence, a text, a dictum, an aphorism, a rule.

वचनकर vuchun-kúr, *adj.* Obedient. *s. m.* The author or enunciator of a precept.

वचनक्रम vuchun-krúm, *s. m.* Discourse, order of words.

वचनग्राही vúchun-gráhee, *adj.* Compliant, conformable, submissive, humble.

वचनमात्र vuchun-mátr, *s. m.* Mere words, assertion unsupported by facts.

वचा vúch-a, *s. f.* Orris root (*Acorus calamus*).

वज्र vujr, *adj.* Hard, impenetrable, adamantine. *s. m.* A thunderbolt in general, or the thunderbolt of *Indr*; the diamond, (*the gem being considered analogous in hardness to the thunderbolt, or in fact to be the same substance.*)

वज्रपात vujr-pát, *s. m.* A thunderbolt, a stroke of lightning.

वज्रपुष्प vujr-póoshp, *s. m.* The blossom of the sesamum.

वज्रवध vujr-búdh, *s. m.* Death by lightning; cross multiplication.

वज्रमय vujr-múy, *adj.* Hard, adamantine; hard-hearted.

वज्रवल्ली vujr-vúllee, *s. f.* A species of sunflower (*Heliotropium*).

वज्राघात vujr-aghát, *s. m.* A thunderbolt or stroke; a sudden calamity.

वज्राभ्यास vujr-abhyás, *s. m.* Cross multiplication.

वञ्चक vun-chúk, *adj.* Fraudulent, crafty. *s. m.* A jackal; a rogue, cheat.

वञ्चन vunch-ún, *s. m.* Cheating, fraud.

वञ्चित vúnch-it, *adj.* Tricked, deceived, cheated.

वञ्चुक vúnch-ook, *adj.* Crafty, fraudulent, dishonest.

वट vut, *s. m.* The large Indian fig-tree (*Ficus Indica*).

वटु vútoo, *s. m.* The *Bruhmcharee* or religious student, after his investiture with the sacred thread; a lad, a youth in general; a flower (*Bignonia Indica*).

वटुक vút-ook, *s. m.* A lad, a young man in general.

वटा vúd-a, *s. f.* Pulse ground and fried with oil or butter.

वडिशी vúr-ish-ee, *s. f.* A fish-hook.

वण्टुक vunt-úk, *s. m.* A part, a portion, a share.

वण्टन vunt-ún, *s. m.* Portioning, partitioning, dividing.

वण्ड vund, *s. m.* A man who is circumcised or has no prepuce.

वत् vut, *adv.* As, like, similar; this is more generally considered as an affix to words; as, *Pushoo-vut*, like a beast.

वत्स vuts, *s. m.* A calf; a year.

वत्सक vuts-úk, *s. m.* A child, a calf; a medicinal plant (*Wrightea antidysenterica*).

वत्सतर vuts-túr, *s. m.* A steer.

वत्सनाभ vuts-nábh, *s. m.* An active poison, also called *Meetha zuhur*, the root of the aconite ferox brought from *Nepal*.

वत्सर vúts-ur, *s. m.* A year.

वत्सरीय vútsur-éeyuh, *adj.* Annual, yearly.

वत्सुल vuts-úl, *adj.* Affectionate, kind. *s. m.* Affection, fondness.

वत्सलता vutsul-tá, *s. f.* Tenderness, affection.

वदन vúd-un, *s. m.* The mouth, the face.

वदाल vud-ál, *s. m.* A sheat-fish (*Silurus Boalis*).

वधू vúdhoo, *s. f.* A son's wife; a wife in general.

वन vun, *s. m.* A forest, a wood, a grove.

वनकचु vun-kúchoo, *s. m.* A species of Arum (*A. calocasia*).

वनचारी vun-cháree, *adj.* Forester, savage.

वनराज vun-ráj, *s. m.* A lion.

वनवास vun-vás, *s. m.* Living in the woods, as a hermit, &c.

वनवासी vun-vásee, *s. m.* An anchoret, a hermit; a forester.

वनविड़ाल vun-virál, *s. m.* A sort of wild cat (*Felis caracal*).

वनस्थायी vun-stháyee, *adj.* Being or abiding in a wood. *s. m.* A hermit, an anchoret.

वनस्थित vun-sthít, *adj.* Situate or being in a forest.

वनस्पति vúnus-púti, *s. m.* A tree that bears fruit but no apparent blossoms, as several species of the fig, the jack, &c.; a tree in general; an ascetic.

वनान्त vun-ánt, *s. m.* The skirts of a wood.

वनाश्रय vun-ásruy, *s. m.* Dwelling in a forest.

वनिता vún-it-a, *s. f.* A woman in general; a beloved woman, a wife, a mistress.

वन्दन vund-ún, *s. m.* Obeisance to a *Brahmun* or superior by touching the feet, &c.

वन्दना vund-ná, *s. f.* Praise, praising, especially the gods or great men.

वन्दनी vund-née, *s. f.* Reverence, worship, adoring.

वन्दनीय vund-néeyuh, *adj.* Praise-worthy, to be eulogized or praised.

वन्दा vúnd-a, *s. f.* A parasite plant (*Epidendrum tessellatum, &c.*); any parasite plant.

वन्दी vún-dee, *s. f.* A captive, a prisoner, a man or beast confined. *s. m.* A panegyrist, a bard, a herald, a servant whose duty it is to proclaim the titles of a great man as he passes along, or a poet, who sings the praises of a prince in his presence, or accompanies an army to chaunt martial songs; a praiser, a flatterer.

वन्द्य vúnd-yuh, *adj.* To be praised, commendable, laudable.

वन्य vúnyuh, *adj.* Forest, savage, wild, produced in a wood, &c.

वन्या vun-yá, *s. f.* A multitude of groves; a quantity of water, a flood, a deluge; a plant (*Physalis flexuosa*).

वपन vúp-un, *s. m.* Sowing seed; shaving; semen virile.

वप्ता vup-tá, *s. m.* A sower, a planter, &c.; a father, a progenitor.

वमन vúm-un, *s. m.* Vomiting, causing vomiting, an emetic. [miting.

वमी vúm-ee, *adj.* Vomiting, sick. *s. f.* Vo-

वयस् vy-us, *s. m.* Age, time of life.

वयस्क vy-ús-kuh, *adj.* Relating to age, aged.

वयस्य vy-ús-yuh, *adj.* Relating to age, aged. *s. m.* A contemporary, an associate or companion.

वर vur, *s. m.* A boon, a blessing, especially in the gift of a *Brahmun* or deity; a bridegroom. *adj.* Best, excellent.

वर्ना vúr-na, *s. f.* A rivulet, running past the north of *Benares*, into the Ganges, now called the *Burna*.

वरखालु vúrund-áloo, *s. m.* The castor oil tree (*Ricinus communis*).

वरद vur-úd, *adj.* Granting a prayer, conferring a boon, propitious, favourable.

वरदान vur-dán, *s. m.* Granting a boon.

वरप्रदान vur-prudán, *s. m.* Conferring a boon.

वररूहना vur-rúhna, *v. n.* To be victorious, to have the advantage, to gain.

वरुल vúr-ul, *s. m.* A wasp.

वर्ला vúr-la, *adv.* On this side of a river, &c.

वराटक vúr-a-túk, *s. m.* The small shell called a *Cowrie*, and used as a coin.

वरानसी vur-án-see, *s. f. Benares.*

वराह vur-áh, *s. m.* A hog; a name of *Vishnoo*, in the third *Uvutar* or descent, in which he is said to have assumed the shape of a boar; one of the eighteen smaller *Dweeps* or divisions of the universe.

वरिष्ठ vur-íshth, *adj.* Best, dearest, most preferable or beloved.

वरीयान् vur-ee-yán, *s. m.* The eighteenth of the astronomical periods called *Yogs*.

वरुण vúr-oon, *s. m.* The deity of the waters and regent of the west.

वरेह vúr-eh, *adv.* On this side, near. *Vareh girna*, To fall short.

वर्ग vurg, *s. m.* A class, a tribe, a multitude of similar things, whether animate or inanimate; as, *Kuh-vurg*, the class of gutteral letters; *Tri-vurg*, a class of three objects, as love, duty, and wealth; the *Soodr-vurg*, the *Soodr* tribe; a chapter, a book, a section; a square number (*in arithmetic*).

वर्गघन vurg-ghún, *s. m.* The square of a cube.

वर्गमूल vurg-móol, *s. m.* A square root.

वर्जन vurj-jún, *s. m.* Quitting, abandonment, shunning, avoiding.

वर्जनीय vurj-jun-éeyuh, *adj.* Improper, censurable, wicked, proper to be avoided.

वर्जित vurj-jít, *adj.* Abandoned, avoided; excluded, excepted.

वर्ण vurn, *s. m.* A tribe, a class, a caste, an order; colour, hue, tint; a letter of the alphabet; (*in arithmetic*) a co-efficient.

वर्णक्रम vurn-krúm, *s. m.* Order of caste or tribe; alphabetical arrangement, the alphabet.

वर्णगत vurn-gút, *adj.* Algebraic.

वर्णधर्म vurn-dhúrm, *s. m.* The particular occupation or duty of each caste or tribe.

वर्णन vúrn-un, *s. m.* Describing, expatiating, explaining, pointing out qualities or excellencies, &c.

वर्णना vurn-un-á, *s. f.* Praise, panegyric.

वर्णमाला vurn-mála, *s. f.* The alphabet.

वर्णरेखा vurn-rékha, *s. f.* A white aluminous fossil often confounded with chalk, of which it is considered a species.

वर्णश्रेष्ठ vurn-sréshth, *adj.* Of a good tribe, caste, kind, &c. *s. m.* A Brahmun.

वर्णसंकर vurn-súnkur, *s. m.* Mixture or confusion of castes; a man or tribe of mixed origin, or from a father and mother of different castes.

वर्णहीन vurn-héen, *adj.* Outcaste.

वर्णाश्रम vurn-ásrum, *s. m.* The class and state of a person.

वर्णित vurn-ít, *adj.* Described, explained.

वर्तन vurttún, *s. m.* Livelihood, subsistence.

वर्तमान vurtt-mán, *adj.* Being, existing, living, being present; dwelling or abiding in; (*in grammar*) the present tense.

वर्ति vúrtti,
वर्ती vúrttee,
} *s. f.* The wick of a lamp.

वर्तिका vurtti-ká, *s. f.* A quail; the wick of a lamp.

वर्तुल vúrttool, *adj.* Round, circular, globular, spherical.

वर्धन vurd-dhún, *adj.* Growing, thriving. *s. m.* Increasing, growing, thriving; augmenting, causing to increase.

वर्धमान vurddh-mán, *adj.* Prosperous, thriving; increasing, growing.

वर्धित vurd-dhít, *adj.* Grown, expanded, increased; thriven.

वर्ला vúr-la, *adv.* On this side of a river, &c.

वर्वटी vurv-vútee, *s. f.* A sort of bean (*Dolichos catjang*).

वर्ष vursh, *s. m.* A year; a division of the known continent, of which nine are reckoned, viz. *Kooroo, Hirunmuy, Romanuk, Ilavrut, Huri, Ketoomala, Bhadrasruh, Kinnur,* and *Bhurut; Jumboo Dweep,* or India.

वर्षण vursh-ún, *s. m.* Raining, rain.

वर्षत् vursh-út, *adj.* Raining, showering, sprinkling.

वर्षपर्वत vursh-púrv-vut, *s. m.* A mountainous range, supposed to separate the various *Vurshus* or divisions of the globe from each other: six ranges are enumerated from south to north, viz. *Himuvan, Hemukoot, Nishuddh, Neel, Swet,* and *Sringee,* or *Sringuvan; Meroo* constitutes the seventh.

वर्षशत vursh-shút, *s. m.* A century.

वर्षसहस्र vursh-suhúsr, *s. m.* A thousand years.

वर्षा vúrsha, *m. pl.*
वर्षाकाल vursha-kál, *s. m.*
} The rains or rainy season, containing two months, according to the *Hindoo* classification of the seasons, which some systems consider to be *Sravun* and *Bhadr,* and others *Bhadr* and *Aswin;* the duration of the monsoon is however longer, being reckoned from *Asarh* to *Kartik,* or from the middle of June to the beginning of October.

वर्षायुत vursh-áyoot, *s. m.* Ten thousand years.

वर्षावसान vursháv-sán, *s. m.* Autumn, the autumnal season.

वर्ष्यक vurshyk, *adj.* Yearly, annual.

वर्ही vur-hée, *s. m.* A peacock.

वला vúl-a, *adv.* Near, hither.

वलाका vul-áka, *s. f.* A small kind of crane.

वल्कल vúl-kul, *s. m.* The bark of a tree.

वल्मीक vulm-éek, *s. m.* The poet *Valmeeki.*

वल्लभ vullúbh, *adj.* Beloved, desired, dear. *s. m.* A lover, a husband, a friend; a superintendant, an overseer.

वश vush, *adj.* Humbled, subdued, tamed, overpowered; enthralled, subdued by charms and incantations, fascinated, charmed, enchanted. *s. m.* Authority, supremacy, mastership; subjection submission, the state of being completely tamed and overpowered.

वशिता vush-it-á, *s. f.* Fascinating, bewitching; subjection, holding in order or subjection.

वशिष्ठ vush-íshth, *s. m.* A *Rishi* or divine sage of the first order; he is also a *Bruhmadhika,* a *Prujaputi,* and one of the seven stars of Ursa Major.

वशी vúsh-ee, *s. m.* A sage with subdued passions.

वशीकरण vúshee-kúrun, *s. m.* Subduing or overcoming by drugs, charms, &c., enchanting, charming; subduing in general.

वशीकृत vúshee-krit, *adj.* Bewitched, fascinated, subjected to another's will.

वशीभूत vushee-bhóot, *adj.* Subjugated, subject to another's will.

वशीर vushéer, *s. m.* A pungent fruit resembling pepper (*Pothos officinalis*).

वश्युब vúshyub, *adj.* Docile, tame, humble, governable.

वश्यता vush-yutá, *s. f.* Humility, subjugation, disposition to, or fitness for subjection.

वश्यात्मा vúshyu-átma, *adj.* Of a subdued mind.

वसती vús-ut-ee, *s. f.* A house, a dwelling; abiding, abode, residence.

वसन vús-un, *s. m.* Cloth or clothes.

वसन्त vús-unt, *s. m.* The season of spring, or its deified personification; dysentery, diarrhœa; small-pox.

वसनकुसुम vúsunt-kóosoom, *s. m.* A tree (*Cordia myxa and latifolia*).

वसनोत्सव vúsunt-ótsuv, *s.* The celebration of the return of spring, formerly held on the full moon of *Chytr*, but now on the full moon of *Phalgoon*, being identified with the *Dol jatra* or *Holi*.

वसीठ vus-éeth, *s. m.* An agent, an ambassador.

वसु vúsoo, *s. m.* Wealth, thing, substance.

वसूक vús-ook, *s. m.* A fossil salt, brought from a district in *Ajmere*, *Sambhur* salt.

वसुदा vusoo-dá, *s. f.* The earth.

वसुदेव vusoo-dév, *s. m.* The father of *Krishn.*

वसुमान vusoo-mán, *adj.* Wealthy, rich.

वसूक vus-óok, *s. m. Sambhur* salt; the *Sesbana grandiflora.*

वस्तु vústoo, *s. m.* Thing, matter, substance.

वस्तुतस् vustoo-tús, *adv.* In fine, in fact, essentially, substantially.

वस्तुमात्र vustoo-mátr, *s. m.* Outline of any subject, skeleton of a discourse.

वस्तुहानि vústoo-háni, *s. f.* Loss of substance or property.

वस्त्र vustr, *s. m.* Cloth, clothes, raiment.

वस्त्रभेदी vustr-bhédee, *s. m.* A tailor.

वस्त्रांचल vustr-ánchul, *s. m.* The end or hem of a garment.

वसन vusn, *s. m.* Cloth, clothes.

वह vuh, *pron.* That, he, she, it, the; (*occasionally like veh*), they, those.

वहुरे vuhúee, *s. f.* Side, quarter, way.

वहला vúh-la, *s. m.* Attack, onset.

वहां vúhan, *adv.* There, thither, yonder. *Vuhan ka vuhan*, In that very place.

वहिर्देश vuhir-dés, *s. m.* A foreign country.

वहिर्भूत vuhir-bhóot, *adj.* Expelled, excluded.

वही vúhee, *pron.* He himself, that very.

वह्नि vúhni, *s. m.* Fire, or its deity *Ugni.*

वा va, *adv.* Or, whether. *conj.* and. *pron.* Him, her, it, that.

वां van, *adv.* There, that place.

वांसी váns-ee, *s. f.* The manna of the bamboo.

वाक् vak, *s. m.* Word, language, speech.

वाकचपुल vak-chúpul, *adj.* Frivolous, inconsistent (*in speech*).

वाकचापल्य vak-chapúl-yuh, *s. m.* Gossiping, chattering, idle or improper talk.

वाकछल vak-chhúl, *s. m.* Prevarication, equivocation.

वाकपटु vak-pútoo, *adj.* Eloquent, able in speech.

वाकपटुता vak-pútoo-ta, *s. f.* Eloquence.

वाक्य vákyuh, *s. m.* A sentence; a rule or aphorism; speech; a word.

वाक्यखण्डन vákyuh-khuudun, *s. m.* Refuting or criticising an assertion.

वाग्दत्त vag-dútt, *adj.* Promised.

वाग्दत्ता vag-dútta, *s. f.* A virgin betrothed.

वाग्दोष vag-dósh, *s. m.* Speaking ill, defamation, abuse.

वाच vach, *s. f.* Speech; speaking; a phrase, a proverb or adage.

वाचक vách-uk, *s. m.* A word; a speaker.

वाचनिक vach-ník, *adj.* Verbal.

वाचा vá-cha, *s. f.* Speech.

वाचाट vachát, } *adj.* Talkative, chatter-
वाचाल vachál, } ing, gabbling, talking much and idly or blamably.

वाचिक va-chík, *adj.* Verbal. *s. m.* News, tidings, intelligence.

वाचिकपत्र váchik-pútr, *s. m.* A letter, a despatch; a newspaper, a gazette.

वाचिष्रे va-chhíreh, *s. m. pl.* Praising, applauding; bravo! well done! aha!

वाजिपृष्ठ vaji-príshth, *s. m.* Globe amaranth.

वाजपेय vaj-péyuh, *s. m.* A particular sacrifice.

वाजी vájee, *s. m.* A plant (*Justicia adhenatoda*).

वाजीकर vajee-kúr, *adj.* Aphrodisiac.

वाजीकरण vájee-kúrun, *s. m.* Stimulous or excitement of amorous desires by aphrodisiacs, &c.

वाञ्छन van-chhún, *s. m.* Wishing, desiring.

वाञ्छा van-chhá, *s. f.* Wish, desire.

वाञ्छित van-chhít, *adj.* Wished, desired, longed for.

वाञ्छिनी van-chhin-ee, *s. f.* A libidinous woman, a wanton.

वाञ्छी van-chhée, *adj.* Wishing, desirous.

वाट vat, *s. f.* A road.

वाटिका vá-tika, *s. f.* The site of a house or building.

बाढ़ी vá-tee, *s. f.* A house, a building; a garden, an orchard, a plantation.

बार var, A termination (*in composition*), denoting place or enclosure.

बाड़ी vá-ree, *s. f.* An orchard, a court-yard for trees and plants.

बान van, *s. m.* An arrow.

बानिज्यु vaníjyuh, *s. m.* Traffic, trade.

बानी vá-nee, *s. f.* Speech, sound.

बात vat, *s. m.* Air, wind; rheumatism, gout, inflammation of the joints; air, wind, as one of the humours of the body.

बातक va-túk, *s. m.* A plant (*Marsilea quadrifolia*).

बातकी va-tuk-ée, *adj.* Rheumatic, gouty.

बातज्वर vat-jwúr, *s. m.* Fever arising from vitiated wind.

बातपित्त vat-pítt, *s. m.* Rheumatism attended with fever.

बातफूल vat-phóoll, *adj.* Inflated, puffed up with wind.

बातरक्त vat-rúkt, *s. m.* Acute gout or rheumatism.

बातरोग vat-róg, *s. m.* Rheumatism, gout.

बातरोगी vat-rógee, *adj.* Rheumatic, afflicted with gout or rheumatism, especially of the acute kind.

बातवृद्धि vat-vríddhi, *s. f.* Swelled testicle.

बातव्याधि vat-vyádhi, *s. f.* Any morbid affection attributed to disorder of the wind.

बातबेरी vat-vyree, *s. m.* The castor oil tree.

बातशूल vat-shóol, *s. m.* Cholic with flatulence.

बातारि vat-ári, *s. f.* The castor oil tree; a plant (*Asparagus racemosus*).

बातीय vatée-yuh, *adj.* Windy, relating or belonging to wind, &c.

बातूल va-tóol, *adj.* Gouty, rheumatic. *s. m.* A whirlwind, a gale, a hurricane.

बात्सल्य vat-súl-yuh, *s. f.* Tenderness, affection, fondness.

बाद vad, *s. m.* Discourse, dispute, assertion, discussion; a plaint, an accusation.

बादयुद्ध vad-jóoddh, *s. m.* Controversy, dispute.

बादसाधन vad-sádhun, *s. m.* Argument, maintaining a controversy.

बादानुबाद vad-anoo-vád, *s. m.* Attack and rejoinder, plaint and reply.

बादी vá-dee, *adj.* Speaking, discoursing; asserting, declaring. *s. m.* A sage, an expounder of the law and *Shastrus*; a plaintiff, an accuser.

बाद्य vád-yuh, *s. m.* Any musical instrument.

बाद्युभांड vádyuh-bhánd, *s. m.* A multitude of musical instruments, a band.

बान van, *s. m.* A heavy sea, the rolling of water from wind, &c.; hence the high tide in the Indian rivers, commonly called the Bore (*particle in compos.*) Possessing, endowed with, &c., as *Dhun-van*, Possessing wealth, rich.

बानप्रस्थ van-prústh, *s. m.* The *Brahmun* of the third order, who has passed through the conditions of student and householder, and has left his house and family for lonely meditation in woods and wilds; the hermit, the anchoret; a tree (*Bassia latifolia*); the *Pulas* tree (*Butea frondosa*).

बानर ván-ur, *s. m.* } An ape, a monkey.
बानरी van-ur-ée, *s. f.* }

बापूल va-púl, *s. m.* A kind of holy basil, distinguished as the black species of *Toolsee* (*Ocymum sanctum*).

बापी vá-pee, *s. f.* A large oblong pond, a pool, a lake.

बाम vam, *adj.* Left, not right; vile, base, wicked.

बामता vam-tá, *s. f.* Perverseness, contrariety; wickedness.

बामन vá-mun, *adj.* Short, dwarfish, a dwarf; low, vile, base. *s. m.* Vishnoo in his character of the dwarf, in which he is said to have appeared on his fifth descent from heaven, to prevent *Buli* from obtaining dominion of the three worlds.

बामनी vamun-ée, *s. f.* A female dwarf.

बामा vá-ma, *s. f.* A woman.

बामाचार vam-achár, *s. m.* The doctrine of the *Tuntrus*, according to one system; the left hand ritual, the use of flesh, spirits, &c. forming part of the *Vamachar* ceremonies.

बामाचारी vam-acháree, *s. m.* A follower of the left hand portion of the *Tuntrus*.

बायन vá-yun, *s. m.* Sweetmeats or cakes, forming a light refreshment, which is not supposed to be any breach of a religious fast, sweetmeats or cakes, part of an offering to a deity, or prepared on particular occasions, as marriages, &c., and sent as presents to friends and acquaintances.

बायब va-yúv, *adj.* Windy, relating or belonging to wind.

बायबी vayúv-ee, *s. f.* The water or region of the wind; the north-west.

बायु vá-yoo, *s. m.* Air, wind, or its personified deification; the air of the body; morbid affection of the windy humour.

बायुकोन vayoo-kón, *s. m.* The north-west.

बायुग्रस्थ vayoo-gúnd, *s. m.* Flatulence, indigestion.

वायुगुल्म vayoo-góolm, *s. m.* A whirlpool, an eddy; a whirlwind, a hurricane.

वायुग्रस्त vayoo-grúst, *adj.* Affected by wind, flatulent, epileptic.

वायुनिवृत्ति váyoo-nivritti, *s. f.* Calm, lull; cure of windy disorders.

वायुभक्षण váyoo-bhúkshun, *s. m.* Fasting, living on air.

वायुसम vayoo-súm, *adj.* Like wind, unsubstantial; swift.

वार var, *s. m.* A blow, wound, gash, assault.

वार var, *s. m.* A day of the week; a multitude, a quantity, a heap; the near bank of a river, on this side. *s. f.* Leisure; delay, waiting, patience; time.

वारक vá-ruk, *adj.* Opposing, obstructing, an obstacle or agent of resistance.

वारण var-ún, *s. m.* Resistance, opposition, prohibition, obstacle or impediment; defence, protecting, guarding; warding off a blow, guarding, warding.

वारन vár-un, *s. m.* Offerings, oblations; sacrifices.

वारना vár-na, *v. a.* To surround, encircle, go round; to offer (*in sacrifice, &c.*) Vares pharee hona, To go round any body (*as a sign of being an offering or sacrifice for his welfare*), to devote one's self for any one (*a practice chiefly of women*).

वारा vá-ra, *s. m.* Cheapness, thrift; benefit, gain; a victim. *adj.* Cheap.

वाराणसी var-án-see, *s. f.* The holy city, *Benares.*

वारपार vara-pár, } *adv.* On this side and
वार्पार vár-par, } that, on both sides; through and through, across. *s. m.* Bounds.

वारि vári, *s. m.* Water.

वारिकंटक vári-kún-tuk, *s. m.* An aquatic plant (*Pistia stratiotes*;) another plant (*Trapa bispinosa*).

वारिकर्पूर vári-kurpóor, *s. m.* The *Ilis* or *Hilsa fish* (*Cluponodon Ilisha*).

वारिचर vari-chúr, *adj.* Aquatic, living or moving in water. *s. m.* A fish.

वारिज var-íj, *adj.* Aquatic, born or produced in or by water. *s. m.* A conch-shell; any bivalve shell.

वारित vár-it, *adj.* Hindered, prevented, impeded.

वारिद var-íd, *adj.* What yields water. *s. m.* A cloud.

वारिधि varídhi, } *s. m.* The sea, the
वारिनिधि vári-nídhi, } ocean.

वारिपूर्णी vári-púrnee, } *s. f.* An aquatic
वारिमूली vari-móolee, } plant (*Pistea stratioites*).

वारिप्रवाह vári-pruváh, *s. m.* A cascade, a water-fall; a current or flows of water.

वारिरथ vari-rúth, *s. m.* A raft, a float.

वारिवदन vári-vúdun, *s. m.* A fruit (*Flacourtia cataphracta*).

वारुणी vá-roo-nee, *s. f.* Any spirituous liquor, or more properly a particular kind prepared from hogweed, ground with the juice of the date or palm, and then distilled; the west, the region of *Vuroon*; the 25th lunar asterism, of which *Vuroon* is the ruling deity.

वार्ता vártta, *s. f.* Tidings, news, intelligence; rumour, report; a word.

वार्तिक vart-tík, *adj.* Relating to news; commentary, explanatory. *s. m.* A gloss, a commentary, especially a supplementary explanation.

वार्द्धक vard-dhúk, *s. m.* Old age; the infirmity, &c. of old age.

वार्षिक vars-ík, *adj.* Yearly, annual; growing, &c. in the rainy season, or fit for or suited to it, &c.

वार्हत var-hút, *s. m.* The fruit of the *Solanum jacquini.*

वाल val, *s. m.* Revenge.

वाल val, } *s. m.* Denotes (*in compos.*)
वाला wála, } agent, doer, keeper, man, inhabitant, master, lord, possessor, owner: as *Rukhwal*, or, —wala, A keeper; *Nao-wala*, A boatman; *Dillee-wal*, or, —wala, An inhabitant of *Delhi. Ghur-wala*, Master or keeper of a house. *Likhne-wala*, Writer. *Hone-wala*, Becoming, about to be.

वाली wálee, *s. f.* Feminine of *wala*.

वाल्मीक val-méek, *s. m.* The author of the *Ramayun.*

वावदूक vav-dóok, *adj.* Talking much, gabbling, prattling.

वावदूकता vav-dook-tá, *s. f.* Garrulity, loquaciousness.

वाशा vá-sha, *s. m.* A plant (*Justicia ganderussa*).

वासित vas-ít, *adj.* Perfumed, scented.

वाशिष्ठी vashish-thée, *s. f.* The *Goomtee* river, which rising in the *Kemaon* hills, pursues a winding and south easterly course, and passing *Lucknow* and *Jonpoor* falls into the Ganges below *Benares.*

वास vas, *s. m.* A house, a habitation; site, situation, abode, or place of staying or abiding; perfuming.

वासन vás-un, *s. m.* Cloth, clothes; abiding, abode.

वासन्त va-súnt, *adj.* Vernal, relating to the season of spring, suitable to it, produced in it, &c.

वासर vá-sur, *s. m.* A day.

वासित vas-ít, *adj.* Perfumed, scented; peopled, populous, flourishing (*a country*).

वासी vás-ee, *adj.* Abiding, staying.

वासु vá-soo, *s. m.* A name of *Vishnoo*; the soul, or the Supreme Being considered as the soul of the universe.

वास्तव vás-tuv, *adj.* Determined, demonstrated, fixed, substantiated; real, substantial.

वास्तव्य vastúv-yuh, *adj.* To be abided or dwelt in, to be fixed as a habitation.

वास्तूक vas-tóok, *s. m.* A potherb (*Chenopodium album, and other edible species*).

वास्य vás-yuh, *s. m.* Vapour; tears.

वाहक vá-huk, *s. m.* A horseman; a porter, a carrier.

वाहन vá-hun, *s. m.* A vehicle, a conveyance of any kind, as a horse, an elephant, a carriage.

वाहि váhi, *pron. object. case, sing.* Him, her, it, that, to him, to her, to it, to that.

वाहिनी váhin-ee, *s. f.* An army; a body of forces consisting of 81 elephants, 81 cars, 243 horse, 405 foot, a cohort, a battalion.

वाहिनीपति váhinee-púti, *s. m.* A general, a commanding officer.

वाह्य váh-yuh, *adj.* Outer, external.

वि vi, *prep.* Denoting disunion, separation, division, distinction; away, apart, distinct.

विकट vík-ut, *adj.* Large, great; formidable, frightful, hideous, horrible.

विकण्टक vikúnt-uk, *s. m.* A herbaceous plant (*Hedysarum alhagi*).

विकम्पित vi-kúmp-it, *adj.* Trembling, tremulous, agitated; palpitating, heaving.

विकर्णिक vikúrn-ik, *s. m. Suruswut*, a district in the north-west of *Hindoostan*, generally considered as part of the *Punjab*, though sometimes confounded with *Cashmeer*.

विकर्म्मक्रिया víkurmm-kríya, *s. f.* Illegal or immoral act.

विकल vikúl, *adj.* Confused, confounded, agitated; the 1-60th of a *Kula*, the second of a degree.

विकल्प vikúlp, *s. m.* Error, ignorance, mistake; doubt, indecision; (*in rhetoric*) antithesis of opposites; (*in grammar*) admission of more than one form or rule.

विकसित vik-us-ít, *adj.* Blown, as a flower, budded, opened.

विकार vikár, *s. m.* Change of form or nature, alteration or deviation from the natural state; sickness, disease, change from the state of health.

विकाल vikál, *s. m.* Twilight.

विकाश vikásh, *s. m.* Display, manifestation, open or splendid appearance.

विकाशता vikash-tá, *s. f.* Appearance, display.

विकाशन vikásh-un, *s. m.* Manifestation.

विकृत vikrít, *adj.* A verse, estranged. *s. m.* Disgust, aversion.

विकृताकार vikrit-akár, *adj.* Changed in aspect, form or appearance.

विकृती vikrít-ee, *s. f.* Change of any kind, as of purpose, mind, form, nature, &c. either permanent or temporary; sickness, disease, change from the natural or healthy state.

विक्रम vikrúm, *s. m.* Heroism, prowess, heroic valour; great power or strength; overpowering, overcoming.

विक्रमादित्य vikrum-adítyuh, *n. prop.* The name of a celebrated prince, the sovereign of *Ougein*, and reputed founder of an æra still in use amongst the *Hindoos*, commencing 56 years before the Christian æra.

विक्रमी víkrum-ee, *s. m.* A lion; a hero.

विक्रय vikrúy, *s. m.* Sale, selling, vending.

विक्रयी vikruyée, *s. f.* A seller, a vender.

विक्रान्त vikránt, *adj.* Valiant, mighty; overcoming, victorious. *s. m.* A hero, a warrior.

विक्रीत vikréet, *adj.* Sold.

विख्यात vikhyát, *adj.* Known, notorious, famous.

विख्याति vikhyáti, *s. f.* Fame, celebrity, notoriety.

विख्यापन vikhyapún, *s. m.* Explaining, expounding.

विगुण vígoon, *adj.* Bad, worthless.

विगूढ vigóorh, *adj.* Concealed, hidden.

विग्रह vigrúh, *s. m.* The body; extension, diffusion; war, battle; opposition, encounter.

विघात vighát, *s. m.* Impediment, obstacle.

विघ्न vighn, *s. m.* Obstacle, impediment.

विघ्नकारी vighn-káree, *adj.* Impeding, obstructing.

विघ्ननाशक vighn-náshuk, *adj.* Who or what removes difficulties, &c.

विघ्ननाशन vighn-náshun, *s. m.* Removing obstacles.

विघ्नसिद्धि vighn-síddhi, *s. f.* Removal of obstacles.

विघ्नित vighnít, *adj.* Stopped, prevented, obstructed, impeded.

विचुल vichúl, *adj.* Unsteady, unfixed, moving, going.

विचुलन víchul-un, *s. m.* Fickleness, unsteadiness.

विचक्षण vichúkshun, *adj.* Clever, able, wise, sensible.

विचार vichár, *s. m.* The exercise of judgment or reason on a present object, investigation, consideration, deliberation.

विचारक vichar-úk, }
विचारकर्ता vichar-kúrtta, } *s. m.* An investigator, a judge.

विचारित vichar-ít, *adj.* Judged, discussed, determined, decided.

विचाल vichál, *adj.* Intervening, intermediate.

विचित्र vichítr, *adj.* Variegated, spotted; painted, coloured.

विच्छेद vichhéd, *s. m.* Separation, disjunction; prohibition, prevention.

विजन víjun, *adj.* Private, lonely, solitary.

विजयी víjuy, *s. m.* Victory, triumph, conquest.

विजयमान vijuy-mán, *adj.* Victorious, triumphant.

विजया víjuya, *s. f.* Hemp (*Cannabis sativa*), or the tops of the plant used as a narcotic.

विजयी vijuyée, *adj.* Victorious, triumphant, conquering.

विजाति vijáti, *s. f.* A different species or tribe.

विजित víjit, *adj.* Conquered, defeated.

विजितेन्द्रिय vijit-éndríyuh, *adj.* Of subdued organs or passions.

विज्ञ vígyuh, *adj.* Skilful, able, clever, conversant; wise, learned.

विज्ञता vigyutá, *s. f.* Wisdom, learning.

विज्ञात vigyát, *adj.* Celebrated, famous, known, notorious; known, understood.

विज्ञान vigyán, *s. m.* Knowledge, science, learning worldly knowledge or wisdom.

विज्ञापन vigyapún, *s. m.* Teaching, instruction, communication of knowledge not religious; representing, informing.

विज्वर víjwur, *adj.* Exempt from decay; free from fever.

विटप vitúp, *s. m.* A new shoot; a branch.

विटसारिका vít-sárika, *s. f.* A bird, a sort of thrush; a variety of the bird, usually though inaccurately, called *Myna* in Bengal.

विडम्बना vidumb-ná, *adj.* Afflicting, distressing.

विडम्बित vidumb-ít, *adj.* Low, poor, abject, distressed.

विक्राल virál, *s. m.* A cat.

विदूरुज vidóo-ruj, *s. m.* The lapis lazuli.

वितुण्डा vítunda, *s. f.* Controversy, argument, the subversion of another's opinion or interpretation and establishment of one's own; criticism.

वितद्रु vitúdroo, *s. f.* The name of a river, said to be situated in the *Punjab*.

वितरण víturun, *s. m.* Gift, donation; abandoning, quitting; passing, crossing.

वितर्क vitúrk, *s. m.* Reasoning, discussion.

वितल vitúl, *s. m.* One of the seven divisions of *Patal*, the second in descent below the earth.

वितस्ति vitústi, *s. f.* A long span measured by the extended thumb and little finger; considered equal to twelve fingers.

वितान vitán, *s. m.* An awning, a canopy.

वितृष्ण vítrishn, *adj.* Content, satisfied, free from desire.

वितृष्णता vitrishn-tá, *s. f.* Satiety, satisfaction; content.

वित्त vitt, *s. m.* Wealth, property, thing, substance.

वित्तवान vitt-wán, *adj.* Rich, wealthy.

वित्तहीन vitt-héen, *adj.* Poor, indigent.

विदुग्ध vidúgdh, *adj.* Clever, shrewd, knowing; burnt. *s. m.* A libertine, a lecher, an intriguer; a learned or clever man, a scholar, a *Pundit*.

विदुग्धता vidugdh-tá, *s. f.* Sharpness, shrewdness, cleverness.

विदुर víd-ur, *s. m.* The Indian prickly pear (*Cactus Indicus*).

विदा víd-a, *s. f.* Dismission, taking leave, farewell, adieu.

विदारण vidár-un, *s. m.* Tearing, breaking, splitting, severing, dividing.

विदारना vidár-na, *v. a.* To tear, to rend.

विदित víd-it, *adj.* Known, understood.

विदिश vidísh, }
विदिक् vidík, } *s. f.* An intermediate point of the compass.

विदूरुज vidóoruj, *s. m.* The lapis lazuli.

विदेश vidésh, *s. m.* A foreign country, abroad; any place away from home.

विदेशगमन videsh-gúmun, *s. m.* Travelling, going abroad.

विदेशज videsh-új, *adj.* Foreign, exotic.

विदेशी vidésh-ee, *adj.* Foreign, foreigner, exotic.

विदेह vídeh, *adj.* Incorporeal, without body.

विद्युमान् vidyumán, *adj.* Being, being present or in existence.

विद्या vidyá, *s. f.* Knowledge, learning, science, whether sacred or profane, though more especially the former.

विद्यादान vidya-dán, *s. m.* Giving knowledge or science.

विद्याप्राप्ति vidya-prápti, *s. f.* Acquirement of knowledge; acquisition made by or through learning.

विद्याभ्यास vidya-bhyás, *s. m.* Study, diligent application.

विद्यार्थी vidyárthee, *s. m.* A pupil, a student.

विद्यालय vidya-lúy, *s. m.* A school, a college.

विद्यालाभ vidya-lábh, *s. m.* Acquisition of learning; acquirement by or through learning.

विद्यावान vidya-ván, *adj.* Learned, possessed of learning or science.

विद्याहीन vidya-héen, *adj.* Ignorant, uninstructed.

विद्युत vid-yóot, *s. f.* Lightning.

विद्रुम vid-róom, *s. m.* Coral.

विद्वान vidwán, *adj.* Intelligent, wise; learned.

विद्वेष vidwésh, *s. m.* Enmity, hatred.

विद्वेषी vidwéshee, *adj.* Inimical, hostile, hating. *s. m.* An enemy.

विध vidh, *s. m.* Form, formula, rule; manner, kind, sort.

विधवा vídh-wa, *s. f.* A widow.

विधवावेदन vídhwa-védun, *s. m.* Marrying a widow.

विधान vidhán, *s. m.* Act, action, general or particular, though more especially the performance of such acts or rites as are prescribed in the sacred books of the *Hindoos*; rule, precept, ordinance, injunction; form, mode, manner.

विधि vídhi, *s. m.* A sacred precept, an act or rite prescribed by the *Veds* for effecting certain consequences; rule, form, formula.

विधूर vidhoor, *s. m.* Separation; agitation of mind from terror or distress, &c.

विधेय vidhéyuh, *adj.* Compliant, tractable, governable; to be done, what is or ought to be practised.

विध्वंस vidhwúns, *s. m.* Aversion, disrespect, enmity, dislike; destruction.

विध्वंसी vidhwúns-ee, *adj.* Hostile, adverse; destroying.

विन vin, *pron.* 3d *pers. pl.* (*same as* oon), Them, those.

विनत vín-ut, *adj.* Bent, bowed, stooping; crooked, curved; humble, modest.

विनति vín-ti, *s. f.* Bowing, bending; humility, modesty.

विनय vín-uy, *s. m.* Affability, modesty, humility, mildness; reverence, obeisance; decorum, decency, propriety of conduct or behaviour.

विनष्ट vinúsht, *adj.* Lost, destroyed.

विनष्टि vinúshti, *s. f.* Disappearance, destruction.

विना vína, *adv.* Without, except.

विनाथ vináth, *adj.* Deserted, unprotected, unowned.

विनाश vinásh, *s. m.* Disappearance, destruction, loss, annihilation.

विनाशक vinashúk, *adj.* Destroying, a destroyer.

विनाशित vinash-ít, *adj.* Destroyed.

विनाशी vináshee, *adj.* Destroyer, destructive; perishing, being destroyed; undergoing change or transformation.

विनिपात vinipát, *s. m.* Falling, falling down, (*literally or figuratively, or from a height, or from dignity, virtue, &c.*); calamity, unavoidable evil.

विनिपातशंसी vinipát-shúnsee, *adj.* Portentous, announcing misfortune or destruction.

विनिमय vini-múy, *s. m.* Barter, exchange.

विनीत vinéet, *adj.* Modest, humble; compliant.

विनीतात्मा vinéet-átma, *adj.* Well-behaved; humbled, lowly.

विनोद vin-ód, *s. m.* Eagerness, vehemence; play, sport, pastime; pleasure, gratification.

विन्दु vín-doo, *s. m.* A drop of water or any liquid; a spot, a dot, a mark; the dot over a letter representing the nasal termination.

विन्ध्य vindh-yuh, *s. m.* The *Vindhya* or *Bindh* mountain, or the mountainous range which runs across India from the province of *Behar*, nearly to *Guzerat*, and properly divides *Hindoostan* from the *Dekhin*.

विन्ध्याचल vindhya-chúl, *s. m.* The *Vindhya* range of mountains.

विन्ध्याटवी vindhya-túvee, *s. f.* The great *Vindhya* forest, which appears to have spread at one time from near *Muthoora* to the *Nermuda*.

विन्ध्यावासिनी vindhya-vásinee, *s. f.* A name of *Doorga*; a village and temple sacred to *Doorga*, under the forms of *Yog maya* and *Bhog maya*, and a place of great resort amongst the *Hindoos*, situated about three miles from *Mirzapoor* on the Ganges.

विन्याक vinyák, *s. m.* A tree (*Echites scholaris*).

विन्यास vinyás, *s. m.* Assemblage, collection, collecting or depositing any thing; site, place, receptacle, that in or on which any thing is placed or deposited.

विन्हें vín-hen, *pron.* 3d *pers. sing. (same as oonheen),* Them, those, to them, &c.

विपत्काल víput-kál, *s. m.* Time of calamity or misfortune, adversity.

विपत्ति viputti, *s. f.* Adversity, calamity, misfortune.

विपत्तियुक्त viputti-jóokt, *adj.* Unfortunate.

विपत्तिरहित viputti-rúhit, *adj.* Prosperous, happy.

विपत्सागर víput-ságur, *s. m.* Heavy calamity.

विपथ víputh, *s. m.* A bad road.

विपद् vípud,
विपत् víput,
विपदा víp-da, } *s. f.* Calamity, adversity, misfortune.

विपदुद्धार vípud-ooddhár, *s. m.* Extrication from misfortune.

विपद्ग्रस्त vipud-grúst, *adj.* Overtaken by or involved in calamity.

विपद्युक्त vipud-yóokt, *adj.* Unhappy, unfortunate.

विपद्रहित vípud-rúhit, *adj.* Prosperous.

विपरीत vip-réet, *adj.* Reverse, inverse, opposite, contrary.

विपरीतता vipuréet-tá, *s. f.* Contrariety, reverse or opposite state or condition.

विपक्ष vípuksh, *adj.* Opposed or adverse to, contrary, inimical. *s. m.* An enemy, an adversary; a disputant, an opponent.

विपक्षता vipúkshutá, *s. f.* Hostility, enmity, opposition; controversy, contradiction in argument.

विपक्षपात vipúkshupát, *adj.* Indifferent, impartial.

विपल vípul, *s. m.* A moment, an instant, either a *Pul* or second; a simple breathing.

विपाक vipák, *s. m.* Cooking, dressing.

विपाशा vi-pásha, *s. f.* The *Vipasa,* or *Beyah* river in the *Punjab.*

विपिन vípin, *s. m.* A wood, a forest.

विपुल vípool, *adj.* Large, great; broad; deep, profound.

विपुलता vipool-tá, *s. f.* Magnitude, extent.

विप्र vipr, *s. m.* A *Brahmun.*

विफल víphul, *adj.* vain, idle, unmeaning, fruitless, useless.

विफलता viphultá, *s. f.* Unprofitableness, fruitlessness.

विभक्त víbhukt, *adj.* Divided, portioned, partitioned; separated, parted; distinct.

विभूति vibhúti, *s. f.* Part, portion; a division, a partition; inflexion of nouns, declension.

विभव víbhou, *s. m.* Substance, thing, property, wealth; supreme or superhuman power.

विभाग vibhág, *s. m.* Part, portion, share; partition of an inheritance; (*in arithmetic*) the numerator of a fraction.

विभीषण vibhée-shun, *adj.* Fearful, formidable, terrific, horrible.

विभु víbhoo, *adj.* Omnipresent, all-pervading; always, eternal.

विभुता vibhoo-tá, *s. f.* Power, supremacy.

विभूति vibhóoti, *s. m.* Superhuman power; power, dignity, dominion.

विभूतिमान vibhóoti-mán, *adj.* Superhuman.

विभूषण vibhóoshun, *s. m.* Ornament, decoration.

विभूषित vibhóo-shit, *adj.* Adorned, decorated.

विभ्रम víbhrum, *s. m.* Error, mistake, blunder; hurry, flurry; doubt, apprehension.

विभ्रान्ति vibhránti, *s. f.* Error, confusion.

विमल vímul, *adj.* Clean, pure, (*either literally, as clothes, &c., or figuratively, as the heart or mind*).

विमलमणि vímul-múni, *s. m.* Crystal.

विमलात्मा vímul-átma, *adj.* Pure, undefiled.

विमात्रि vímatri,
विमाता vímata, } *s. f.* A step-mother, a father's wife.

विमान vimán, *s. m.* A car or chariot of the gods, sometimes serving as a seat or throne, and at others carrying them through the skies self-directed and self-moving; any car or vehicle.

विमार्ग vimárg, *s. m.* A bad road; a wrong road, literally or figuratively, evil conduct.

विमुक्त vímookt, *adj.* Loosed, liberated.

विमुक्ति vímookti, *s. f.* Liberation, especially final emancipation from future existence.

विमुख vímookh, *adj.* Averted, having the face cast down or turned away; opposed.

विमुखता vimookhtá, *s. f.* Turning away; opposition.

विमुखी vímookhee, *adj.* Averted, turned away; hostile, averse to or from.

विमूढात्मा vimóorh-átma, *adj.* Beguiled, foolish.

विमोक्ष vímoksh, *s. m.* Liberation, freedom, being or letting loose.

विमोचन vimóchun, *s. m.* Liberating.

विमोचित vimóchit, *adj.* Liberated, set free.

विमोहन vímohun, *s. m.* Seducing, tempting, confounding the mind and exciting the passions (*the act*).

विमोहनी vimóhunee, adj. Fascinating, seducing, bewitching, tempting, (the instrument or agent).

विमोहित vímohit, adj. Fascinated, beguiled.

विम्ब vimb, s. m. The disk of the sun or moon; an image, a picture, a shadow, a reflected or represented form; the gourd of the *Momordica monadelpha.*

विमलान vimlán, adj. Fresh, pure, free from soil or decay; refreshed.

वियोग viyóg, s. m. Absence, separation, especially of lovers; disunion, disjunction.

वियोगी viyógee, adj. Separated, absent, remote, apart. s. m. The ruddy goose.

विरक्त vírukt, adj. Averse, indifferent, free from inclination or affection; stoical, void of attachment to worldly objects.

विरक्तभाव vírukt-bháo, adj. Disinclined to, disliking.

विरक्ति virúkti, s f. Aversion, disinclination; absence of a ection.

विरचित virúchit, adj. Made, prepared, effected; written, composed.

विरजा vírja, s. f. A plant; a sort of grass, commonly called *Doob.*

विरुन vir-ún, s. m. A fragrant grass (*Andropogon schœnanthum*).

विरत vírut, adj. Stopped, ceased, rested.

विरति virúti, s. f. Stop, cessation, term, rest.

विरुल vír-ul, m. ⎱ adj. Fine, delicate, thin
विरला vír-la, f. ⎰ (but with interstices);
loose, relaxed; apart, wide, separated by an interval; remote, rare, occurring at distant or repeated intervals of time.

विरस vírus, adj. Insipid.

विरह viruh, s. m. Separation, parting, absence, especially the separation of lovers.

विरहित viruhít, adj. Void of, exempt or free from.

विरहिनी viruhínee, f. ⎱ adj. Separate, sun-
विरही viruhée, m. ⎰ dered, absent or apart from. s. f. A woman absent from her husband or lover.

विराग virág, s. m. The absence of desire or passion, indifference, philosophy, the disregard of all sensual enjoyment.

विरागी virágee, adj. Void of passion or desire.

विराजत virajút, adj. Shining, splendid, handsome.

विराजमान virajmán, adj. Splendid, brilliant, handsome.

विराट virát, s. m. A country, one of the midland divisions of India, probably *Berar.*

विराटज viratúj, s. m. An inferior sort of diamond, said to be found in the country of *Virat.*

विराल virál, s. m. A cat.

विरुद्ध viróoddh, adj. Opposed, hindered; reverse, contrary, opposite; inconsistent (in argument), incongruous, a nonsequitur; hostile, averse.

विरुद्धता virooddh-tá, s. f. Opposition, contrariety; incongruity; enmity.

विरूप viróop, adj. Deformed, monstrous; unnatural.

विरूपक viróopuk, adj. Frightful, hideous; deformed, mis-shapen.

विरेक virék, s. m. A purgative.

विरोध viródh, s. m. Enmity, animosity; opposition, contradiction; war.

विरोधी viródhee, adj. Inimical, adverse, hostile; opposing; obstructive; contradictory, inconsistent; quarrelsome, contentious. s. m. An enemy, an opponent.

विल vil, s. m. A hole, a chasm, a vacuity; a cave, a cavern.

विलज्ज vilújj, adj. Shameless, impudent, unabashed.

विलम्ब vilúmb, s. m. Slowness, tardiness, delay.

विलम्बना vilumbná, s. m. Delaying, retarding.

विलय víluy, s. m. Destruction of the world; destruction in general; liquefaction.

विलयन viluy-ún, s. m. Destroying; corroding, eating away; liquefying; attenuating (as the fluids of the body); an attenuant; an escharotic.

विलसन vilúsun, s. m. Sporting, dallying.

विलाप vilâp, s. m. Lamentation, the language of grief and distress.

विलास vilás, s. m. Sport, pastime, play, especially amorous pastime, dalliance, wantonness.

विलासिनी vilasín-ee, s. f. A woman; a whore, a harlot.

विलासिनी vilasín-ee, f. ⎱ adj. Wanton,
विलासी vilasćé, m. ⎰ sportive, dallying.

विलासी vilásee, s. m. A sensualist, an enjoyer.

विलोकन vilókun, s. m. Sight, seeing, looking.

विलोकना vilok-ná, v. a. To see, to look, to view.

विलोकनीय vilókun-éeyuh, adj. Agreeable, beautiful, fit to be seen or looked at.

विलोकित vilokít, adj. Seen, beheld.

विलोचन viló-chun, *s. m.* The eye.

विलोचनपात vilóchun-pát, *s. m.* A glance, a look.

विलोटक vilótuk, *s. m.* A sort of fish (*Cupea cultrata*).

विलोर्ण vilórna, *v. a.* To shake, to churn.

विलोभन vilóbhun, *s. m.* Allurement, attraction, temptation, seduction; beguiling, perplexing.

विलोम vilóm, *adj.* Reverse, opposite, contrary, backward.

विलोमक्रिया vilom-kríya, *s. f.* Rule of inversion.

विलोमत्र्यराशिक vilóm-tryrásik, *s. m.* Rule of three inverse.

विलोमविधि vilóm-vídhi, *s. f.* Rule of inversion.

विलोवना vilóvna, *v. a.* To churn.

विल्ल vill, *s. m.* A pit, a hole.

विल्व vilv, *s. m.* A fruit tree, commonly named *Bel* (*Ægle marmelos*); the fruit of the *Bel*.

विवर vívur, *s. m.* A hole, a chasm, a vacuity; fault, defect.

विवरण vivúrun, *s. m.* Explanation, exposition, gloss, comment; detailing, describing.

विवर्जन vivúrj-jun, *s. m.* Abandoning, leaving, shunning.

विवर्जित vivurj-jít, *adj.* Left, abandoned, avoided, shunned.

विवर्ण vívurn, *s. m.* A man of a low caste, one of degrading occupation, an outcaste.

विवश vívus, *adj.* Independant; uncontrouled, unrestrained, unsubdued; sedate at the period of death, or having the soul free from worldly cares and fears.

विवस्त्र vívustr, *adj.* Unclothed, naked.

विवक्षा vivúksha, *s. f.* Wish, desire.

विवक्षित vivukshít, *adj.* Wished, desired.

विवक्षिता vivukshitá, *s. f.* Purpose, wish.

विवाद vivád, *s. m.* Contest, contention.

विवादी vivádee, *adj.* Disputing, contending, a litigant.

विवासन vivásun, *s. m.* Exile, banishment.

विवाह viváh, *s. m.* Marriage.

विवाहित vivahít, *m.* }
विवाहिता vivahit-á, *f.* } *adj.* Married.

विविध vívidh, *adj.* Various, multiform, of many sorts.

विवेक vivék, *s. m.* Discrimination, judgment.

विवेकता vivektá, *s. f.* Judgment, discrimination, the faculty or property of judgment.

विवेकी vivékee, *adj.* Judicious, discriminative. *s. m.* A sage, a philosopher, a judge.

विवेचन vivéchun, *s. m.* Discrimination, judgment, distinguishing truth from falsehood.

विशङ्क víshunk, *adj.* Fearless, undaunted.

विशस्त्र víshustr, *adj.* Disarmed, unarmed.

विशाकार vishakár, *s. m.* A plant (*Euphorbia of various kinds*).

विशाखा vishákha, *s. f.* The sixteenth lunar asterism.

विशाल vishál, *adj.* Great, large; great, eminent, illustrious.

विशालता vishaltá, *s. f.* Magnitude, bulk; eminence, distinction.

विशिष्ट víshisht, *adj.* Endowed with, possessed of, having, inherent or attached to.

विशेष vishesh, *s. m.* Sort, kind, manner; excellence, superiority.

विशेषण visheshún, *adj.* Discriminative, attributive.

विशेष्य visheshyúh, *adj.* Principal, primary, chief. *s. m.* A name, a substantive.

विशोक víshok, *adj.* Without grief, happy.

विश्रान्त vishránt, *adj.* Rested, reposed; calm, composed.

विश्रान्ति vishrántí, *s. f.* Rest, repose, cessation from toil or occupation.

विश्राम vishrám, *s. m.* Rest, repose; pause, stop, cessation; tranquillity, composure.

विश्व víshwuh, *adj.* All, entire, whole, universal. *s. m.* The world, the universe; a deity of a particular class in which ten are enumerated who are worshipped particularly at the funeral obsequies in honor of deceased progenitors in general, and receive an oblation of clarified butter at the daily and domestic *Shraddh.*

विश्वकर्मा víshwuh-kúrmma, *s. m.* The son of *Bruhma*, and artist of the gods.

विश्वका vishwuh-ká, *s. f.* A sort of gull (*Larus ridibundus*).

विश्वकृत् víshwuh-krít, *s. m.* The creator, the maker of all things.

विश्वजन víshwuh-jún, *s. m.* All men, mankind.

विश्वजित् víshwuh-jít, *adj.* All-subduing.

विश्वदेवा víshwuh-déva, *s. f.* A plant (*Hedysarum lagopodioides*).

विश्वधारी víshwuh-dháree, } *adj.* All-sustaining.
विश्वम्भर vishwumbhúr, }

विश्वराज् víshwuh-ráj, *s. m.* A universal sovereign.

विश्वरूप vishwuróop, *adj.* Taking all forms, existing in all forms, universal, omnipresent. *s. m. Vishnoo.*

विश्वरोचन vishwuróchun, *s. m.* An esculent root (*Arum colocasia*).

विश्वव्यापक víshwuh-vyápuk, *adj.* All-pervading, everywhere diffused.

विश्वव्यापी víshwuh-vyápee, *adj.* All-diffused or prevading.

विश्वव्याप्ति víshwuh-vyápti, *s. f.* Universal diffusion or permeation.

विश्वसारक víshwuh-sáruk, *s. m.* The prickly pear (*Cactus Indicus*).

विश्वसृष्टा víshwusríshta, *s. m.* The creator of all, God.

विश्वा vishwá, *s. f.* A tree, the bark of which is said to be used in dyeing red, commonly called *Utees* (*Betula*).

विश्वात्म vishwátm, *s. m.* The soul of the world, the universal spirit, God.

विश्वामित्र víshwa-mítr, *s. m.* A *Mooni*, the son of *Gadhi*, originally of the military order, but who became by long and painful austerities a *Bruhmurshi*, in which character he appears in the *Ramayun*, as the early preceptor and counsellor of *Ram.*

विश्वास vishwás, *s. m.* Trust, faith, confidence.

विश्वासकृत vishwás-krít, *adj.* Inspiring confidence or faith.

विश्वासघात vishwás-ghát, *s. m.* Violation of trust, treachery.

विश्वासघातक vishwás-ghátuk, *s. m.* A traitor, one who betrays confidence.

विश्वासपात्र vishwás-pátr, *s. m.* A confidential agent, one worthy to be trusted.

विश्वासभङ्ग vishwás-bhúng, *s. m.* Breach of faith, violation of confidence.

विश्वासी vishwásee, *adj.* Trusting, confiding in ; honest, trusty.

विश्वेश्वर vishwéshwur, *s. m. Shiv*, under a form or appellation in which especially he is worshipped at *Benares*, where a celebrated temple is appropriated to him in the character of lord or god of the universe.

विष vish, *s. m.* Poison, venom.

विषघाती vish-ghátee, *adj.* Antidotic, an antidote. *s. m.* A tree (*Mimosa sirisa*).

विषधि víshuni, *s. m.* A sort of snake.

विषधर vísh-dhúr, *adj.* Venemous, poisonous. *s. m.* A snake.

विषनाशन vish-náshun, *s. m.* A tree (*Mimosa sirisa*); an antidote; removing or curing poison.

विषनाशी vish-náshee, *adj.* Antidote.

विषभक्षण vish-bhukshun, *s. m.* Taking poison.

विषभुजङ्ग vish-bhoojúng, *s. m.* A poisonous snake.

विषम víshum, víkhum, *adj.* Difficult (*of access*), rough, uneven ; difficult, &c. (*of comprehending*), as a book ; painful, difficult, troublesome (*in general*) ; odd (*in numbers*) ; fearful ; frightful, awful.

विषमज्वर vishum-jwúr, *s. m.* A violent fever ; irregularly remittent fever.

विषमन्त्र vish-múntr, *s. m.* A snake-catcher, one who by pretended charms, &c. attracts snakes and cures the bite ; a charm for curing snake bites.

विषमसाहस víshum-sáhus, *s. m.* Temerity, daring.

विषय víshuy, *s. m.* Any object of sense, any thing perceivable by the senses, as colour, form, flavour, odour and sound ; an object in general, as of affection or desire, &c. ; worldly object or pursuit, affair, business, transaction, &c.

विषयी vishuy-ée, *s. m.* An epicurean, a sensualist, one heedful of objects of sense or attentive to worldly objects ; a materialist, one who denies the existence of any thing which is not an object of sense ; a man of business or of the world.

विषविद्या vísh-vidya, *s. f.* The administration of antidotes, the cure of poisons by drugs or charms.

विषवैद्य vísh-vydyuh, *s. m.* A dealer in antidotes, one professing by charms, &c. to cure the bite of a snake.

विषसूचक vish-sóochuk, *s. m.* The Greek partridge (*Perdix rufa*).

विषहर vish-húr, *adj.* An antidote, removing venom.

विषहृदय vish-hírduy, *adj.* Malicious, malignant, cherishing hatred or hostility.

विषाण vishán, *s. m.* The horn of an animal ; the tusks of an elephant ; the tusk or fang of the boar.

विषाणी vishanée, *s. m.* Any animal with horns.

विषाद vishád, *s. m.* Lassitude, dejection, lowness of spirits, want of energy.

विषादी vishadée, *adj.* Dejected, disconsolate, sorrowful.

विषापह vish-ápuh, *adj.* Antidotic, an antidote.

विषापहा vísh-apuhá, *s. f.* A kind of birth wort (*Aristolochia Indica*).

विषालु vish-áloo, *adj.* Venemous, poisonous.

विषुव víshoov,
विषुवत् vishoov-út, } *s. m.* The equinox.

विषुवच्छाया víshoov-chháya, *s. f.* The shadow of the gnomon at noon when the sun is in the equinoctial points.

विषववदिन víshoov-dín, *s. m.* The day of the equinox.

विष्टम्भ vish-túmbh, *s. m.* A disease, obstruction of urine or fæces, ischury, constipation; paralysis, loss of motion.

विष्टर vish-tár, *s. m.* A seat, stool, chair, couch; the seat of the *Brahmun*, either real or in effigy, as presiding at a sacrifice.

विष्टि víshti, *s. f.* The seventh of the variable *Kuruns*, or astronomical periods so termed, each answering to half a lunar day.

विष्ठा víshtha, *s. f.* Fæces, ordure.

विष्णु víshnoo, *s. m.* One of the three principal *Hindoo* deities, and the preserver of the world.

विष्णुक्रान्ता víshnoo-kránta, *s. f.* A flower (*Clitorea ternatea*).

विष्णुपद víshnoo-púd, *s. m.* The sky, heaven, atmosphere.

विष्णुपदी víshnoo-púdee, *s. f.* One of the twelve *Sunkrantis* or periods at which the sun enters a sign of the zodiac, especially the first sign after the equinox.

विष्णुवल्लभा víshnoo-vullubhá, *s. f.* A plant (*Echites caryophyllata*); a small fragrant shrub (*Ocymum sanctum*).

विष vis, *pron.* 3d pers. sing. inflect. (same as *oos*), Him, her, it, that, &c.

विसर्ग visúrg, *s. m.* The soft aspirate, marked by two perpendicular dots (:), and as the substitute of the letters स or र, the termination of various inflexions both of nouns and verbs.

विसर्जन visúrjun, *s. m.* Gift, donation; quitting, relinquishing, dismissing, sending away.

विषे víseh, *pron.* 3d pers. sing. (same as *ooseh*) Him, her, it, to him, to her, &c.

विस्तर vís-tur, *s. m.* A bed.

विस्तार vis-tár, *s. m.* Spreading, extension, diffusion; vastness, expanse; breadth, amplitude.

विस्तीर्ण vis-téern, *adj.* Spread, expanded.

विस्तृत vistrít, *adj.* Spread, diffused, extended.   [cle.

विस्तृति vistriti, *s. f.* The diameter of a cir-

विस्पष्ट vispúsht, *adj.* Apparent, manifest, open; plain, intelligent.

विस्फोट visphót, *s. m.* } A boil, a pustule;
विस्फोटा visphotá, *s. f.* } small-pox.

विस्मय vísmuy, *s. m.* Wonder, surprise, astonishment.

विस्मयी vismúyee, } *adj.* Astonished, sur-
विस्मित vísmit, } prised.

विस्मृत vísmrit, *adj.* Forgotten.

विस्मृति vismriti, *s. f.* Forgetting, forgetfulness.

विस्वर víswur, *adj.* Discordant, unharmonious.

विस्वाद viswád, *adj.* Insipid, flavourless.

विहुङ्ग vihúng, }
विहुङ्गम vihung-úm, } *s. m.* A bird.

विहुरण víhurun, *s. m.* Taking off or away; going about for pleasure or exercise.

विहार vihár, *s. m.* Play, sport, pastime.

विहारी viharée, *adj.* Playful, sportive; taking pleasure or relaxation.

विहीन vihéen, *adj.* Abandoned, left, deserted, deprived of.

विक्षिप्त víkshipt, *adj.* Thrown, cast; agitated, bewildered, perplexed; foolish.

विक्षेप vikshép, *s. m.* Casting, throwing; confusion, perplexity; celestial latitude.

बीज veej, *s. m.* Seed (*of plants, &c.*); cause, origin in general; semen virile; algebra, analysis.

बीजकोश veej-kósh, *s. m.* Any seed-vessel.

बीजकोशी veej-kóshee, *s. f.* A pod, a legume.

बीजगणित veej-gúnit, *s. m.* Algebra.

बीजन veejún, *s. m.* A fan.

बीटिका véetika, *s. f.* The betel plant (*Piper betel*); the preparation of the Areca nut with spices and chunam, and enveloped in the leaf of the Piper betel, betel, *puun*.

बीणा véena, *s. f.* The Indian lute, a fretted instrument of the guitar kind, usually having seven wires or strings, and a large gourd at each end of the finger board: the extent of the instrument is two octaves: it is supposed to be the invention of *Narud*, the son of *Bruhma*, and has many varieties, enumerated according to the number of strings, &c.

बीर veer, *adj.* Heroic; powerful, mighty. *s. m.* A hero, a warrior, a champion.

बीरता veer-tá, *s. f.* Heroism.

बीरभद्र veer-bhúdr, *s. m.* A distinguished warrior.

बीर्य्य véerjyuh, *s. m.* Strength, vigour, power; semen virile; heroism, valour; seed (*of plants, &c.*)

बीर्य्यवान् veerj-wán, *adj.* Strong, stout, robust.

बीर्य्यविरहित véerj-virúhit, *adj.* Devoid of power or vigour, &c.

बीर्य्यविशिष्ट véerj-vishísht, *adj.* Possessed of courage, vigour, &c.

बीर्य्यहानि véerj-háni, *s. f.* Loss of vigour or courage; impotence.

बीर्य्यहीन veerj-héen, *adj.* Seedless; cowardly.

बुषीं woonhéen, *adv.* That very (*time, place, &c.*), immediately, exactly there, on the spot, in that very manner.

बुतना wóot-na, } *adj.* That much.
बितना wít-na, }

बुह wooh, *pron.* That, he, she, it, the; (*occasionally like veh*), they, those.

बुहां woohán, *adv.* There, thither, yonder.

बुहीं woohéen, *adv.* That very (*time, place, &c.*), immediately, exactly there.

बृक vrik, *s. m.* A wolf.

बृजि vríji, *s. f.* A country, probably that to the west of *Delhi* and *Agra*, or the modern *Bruj.*

बृत्त vritt, *adj.* Practice, profession, means of gaining a subsistence; a circle.

बृत्तखण्ड vritt-khúnd, *s. m.* Sector or segment of a circle.

बृत्तांत vrittánt, Tidings, rumour, intelligence; a tale, a story.

बृत्ति vrítti, *s. f.* Livelihood, profession, means of acquiring subsistence; circumference of a circle.

बृथा vrítha, *adv.* Useless, fruitless; in vain.

बृद्ध vriddh, *adj.* Old, aged, ancient. *s. m.* An old man, or one past seventy.

बृद्धता vriddhtá, *s. f.* Old age.

बृद्धसेवा vríddh-séva, *s. f.* Reverence for old age.

बृद्धा vriddhá, *s. f.* An old woman, either one past child-bearing or one with grey hair.

बृद्धावस्था vriddh-avusthá, *s. f.* The condition or period of old age.

बृद्धि vríddhi, *s. f.* Increase, augmentation in general, as in bulk, consequence, wealth, &c.; rise, ascending, mounting; prosperity, success; the eleventh of the astronomical *Yogs*, or *Yog* star of the 11th lunar mansion; the increase of the digits of the sun or moon; enlargement of the scrotum, either from swelled testicle or hydrocele or other morbid affections; interest, usury, especially returning the principal (*as in the case of seed corn lent*), with a proportionate increment.

बृद्धिमान vríddhi-mán, *adj.* Augmented, increased; rich; prosperous.

बृद्धिश्राद्ध vríddhi-shráddh, *s. m.* A sacrifice to progenitors on any prosperous occasion, as the birth of a son, &c.

बृन्द vrind, *s. m.* A heap, a multitude, a quantity.

बृन्दा vrín-da, *s. f.* Holy basil (*Ocymum sanctum*).

बृश्चिक vríshchik, *s. m.* A scorpion; the sign Scorpio.

बृष vrish, vrikh, *s. m.* A bull; the sign of the zodiac Taurus.

बृष्टि vríshti, *s. f.* Rain.

बृष्टिकाल vríshti-kál, *s. m.* The rainy season.

बृहज्जन vrihujjún, *s. m.* A great or illustrious man.

बृहत् vrihút, *adj.* Great, large.

बृहद्गूह vrihud-góoh, *s. m.* A country, described as lying behind the *Vindhya* mountains, near the province of *Malwa*, and perhaps comprising *Bundelkhund*, or the adjoining district.

बृहस्पति vrihuspúti, *s. m.* The regent of the plant Jupiter, identified astronomically with the planet.

बृहस्पतिचक्र vríhusputi-chúkr, *s. m.* The cycle of 60 years.

बृहस्पतिवार vríhusputi-wár, *s. m.* Thursday.

बृक्ष vriksh, *s. m.* A tree in general.

बृक्षचर vriksh-chúr, *s. m.* A monkey.

बृक्षछाया vriksh-chháya, *s. f.* The shade of a single tree; the shade of many trees, or a grove.

बृक्षधूप vriksh-dhóop, *s. m.* Turpentine.

बृक्षनाथ vriksh-náth, *s. m.* The Indian fig-tree, as lord of trees.

बृक्षमय vriksh-múy, *adj.* Abounding with trees.

बृक्षरोपण vriksh-rópun, *s. m.* Planting trees.

वेकुट vekút, *s. m.* A sort of fish (*perhaps the common Bhekti*).

वेग veg, *s. m.* Speed, dispatch, velocity. *adv.* Quickly, speedily.

वेगवान vegwán, *adv.* Quickly, speedily.

वेगिता vegitá, *s. f.* Speed, quickness.

वेगी végee, *adj.* Swift, fleet, rapid.

वेणी vénee, *s. f.* Unornamented and braided hair; assemblage of water, as the conflux of rivers, &c., as at *Allahabad*, where the *Gunga*, *Yumoona*, and as is supposed, the *Suruswuti*, all coming from the north, unite: this and other similar places, thence receive the name of *Triveni.*

वेणु vénoo, *s. m.* A flute, a pipe.

वेणुवाद venoo-vád, *s. m.* A player on a flute.

वेतन vétun, *s. m.* Hire, wages.

वेतना wétna, *adj.* So much, that much.

वेतस vetús, *s. m.* The ratan (*Calamus rotang*).

वेताल vetál, *s. m.* A sprite, a goblin, especially one supposed to haunt cemeteries and animating dead bodies.

वेत्ता vettá, *adj.* Knowing, understanding, acquainted with. *s. m.* A sage, one who knows the nature of the soul and God.

वेब vetr, *s. m.* A reed, a cane, the ratan.

वेबवती vetr-wútee, *s. f.* The *Betwa* river, which rises in the province of *Malwa,* and following a north-easterly course for about 340 miles, falls into the *Jumna* near *Calpee.*

वेद ved, *s. m.* A *Ved,* the generic term for the sacred writings or scripture of the *Hindoos,* supposed to have been revealed by *Bruhma,* and after being preserved by tradition for a considerable period, to have been arranged in the present form by *Vyas:* the principal *Veds* are three in number, the *Rich, Yugoos,* and *Sam,* to which a fourth, the *Uthurv,* is usually added, and the *Itihas* and *Poorans,* or ancient history and mythology, are sometimes considered as a fifth.

वेदूगुह vedúgyuh, *s. m.* A *Brahmun* skilled in the *Veds.*

वेदून ved-ún, *s. m.*
वेदना ved-ná, *s. f.* } Pain, smart, agony.

वेदपूयुह ved-póonyuh, *s. m.* The sanctity of the *Veds.*

वेदमाता ved-máta, *s. f.* The mystical prayer or *Gayutree,* personified as the mother or source of the *Veds.*

वेदव्यास ved-vyás, *s. m.* The *Mooni Vyas,* the compiler and arranger of the *Veds.*

वेदांग vedáng, *s. m.* A sacred science, considered as subordinate to, and in some sense, a part of the *Veds :* six sciences come under this denomination, viz. *Siksha,* or the science of pronunciation and articulation ; *Kulp,* the detail of religious ceremonies ; *Vyakurun* or grammar; *Chhund,* prosody ; *Jyotish,* or astronomy ; and *Nirookti,* or the explanation of the difficult or obscure words and phrases that occur in the *Veds.*

वेदांत vedánt, *s. m.* The theological part of the *Veds :* considered collectively it is contained in the numerous passages or chapters of the *Veds* termed *Oopunishuds,* which inculcate an abstract and speculative monotheistical worship, and these have been further explained and illustrated by later writers : the founder of the school is *Vyas,* and subsequently *Sunkur-acharyuh* is its most eminent teacher.

वेदांती vedantée, *s. m.* A follower of the *Vedant* philosophy.

वेदाभ्यास védabhyás, *s. m.* The repetition of the mystical syllable *Om* ; study of the *Veds.*

वेदिका védika, *s. f.* A quadrangular open shed in the middle of a court-yard, erected for various purposes ; ground prepared for sacrificial ceremonies, a rude kind of altar.

वेदी véd-ee, *s. f.* Ground for placing the vessels used at an oblation, or for binding the victim, or lighting the sacrificial fire ; it is more or less raised and of various shapes ; an altar, &c. *s. m.* A *Pundit,* a learned *Brahmun,* a teacher.

वेदोक्त ved-ókt, *adj.* Scriptural, taught or declared in the *Veds.*

वेध vedh, *s. m.* Perforation, piercing ; depth (*in measurement*).

वेधूक vedhúk, *adj.* Sharp, piercing, a piercer or perforator.

वेधन védhna, *v. a.* To pierce, perforate.

वेधनी vedh-née, *s. f.* An instrument for piercing an elephant's ear ; a small gimblet or perforating instrument used to pierce gems, shells, &c.; an auger, a gimblet, &c., or any similar instrument.

वेधित vedhít, *adj.* Pierced, perforated.

वेधी vedhée, *adj.* Piercing, perforating.

वेला véla, *s. f.* Time.

वेश vesh, *s. m.* Dress, decoration.

वेशदान vesh-dán, *s. m.* The sun-flower.

वेशधारी vesh-dháree, *s. m.* A hypocrite, a false devotee.

वेशुर vésh-ur, *s. m.* A mule.

वेश्या vesh-yá, *s. f.* A harlot, a prostitute, a whore ; a plant (*Cissampelos hexandra*).

वेष vesh, *s. m.* Ornament, dress, decoration.

वेष्टन vesh-tún, *s. m.* Surrounding, encompassing.

वेष्टित vesh-tít, *adj.* Surrounded, encompassed, enclosed ; bound round, enveloped, wrapped up.

वेसुर vés-ur, *s. m.* A mule.

वेंछना vynchh-na, *v. a.* To skin.

वैकाल vykál, *s. m.* Evening, afternoon.

वैकुंठ vy-kóonth, *s. m.* A name of *Vishnoo ;* the paradise or world of *Vykoonth* or *Vishnoo ;* its site is variously described, either as in the northern ocean, or on the eastern peak of mount *Meroo.*

वैकांत vykant, *s. m.* A kind of gem, said to resemble a diamond, and to be of similar properties ; it is also considered to be a burnt diamond, and to be the common loadstone or magnet.

वैणिक vyn-ik, *s. m.* A lutist, a player on the *Veena* or Indian lute.

वैतरणी vyturúnee, *s. f.* The river of hell.

वैदिक vyd-ík, *adj.* Scriptural, derived from or conformable to the *Veds.*

वैदूर्य vy-dóorj, *s. m.* A gem of a dark colour, the lapis lazuli.

वैदेशिक vy-déshik, *adj.* Foreign, stranger.

वैद्य vydyuh, *s. m.* A physician.

वैभव vy-bhúvuh, *s. m.* Grandeur, wealth.

वैयाकरण vya-kúrun, *adj.* Grammatical, relating to grammar. *s. m.* A grammarian.

बेर vyr, *s. m.* Enmity, hostility.

बेराग vyrág, *s. m.* Absence of worldly passion or desire.

बेरागी vyrágee, *s. m.* An ascetic, a devotee, one who has subdued his worldly desires : at present the term in common use is applied to a particular class of religious mendicants.

बेराग्य vyrágyuh, *s. m.* Subjection of the appetite and passions, absence of worldly desires.

बेरिता vyritá, *s. f.* Enmity.

बेरिनी vyrin-ée, *f.*　} *adj.* Hostile, inimical.
बेरी vyree, *m.*　　　}

बेरी vy-ree, *s. m.* An enemy.

बेशाख vyshákh, *s. m.* The month in which the moon is full near the southern scale (*April-May*), the first month in the *Hindoo* calendar.

बेशाखी vyshákhee, *s. f.* The day of full moon in the month *Vysakh.*

बेश्य vyshyuh, *s. m.* A man of the third or agricultural and mercantile tribe.

बेश्यक्रिया vyshyuh-kríya, *s. f.* Trade, agriculture.

बेश्यनी vysbyuh-née, *s. f.* A woman of the *Vyshyuh* caste.

बेषम्य vyshúm-yuh, *s. m.* Inequality, unevenness ; solitariness, singleness.

बेष्णव vyshnúv, *adj.* Relating or belonging to *Vishnoo. s. m.* A follower of *Vishnoo.*

बेष्णवी vyshnuvée, *s. f.* A flower (*Clitoria ternatea*) ; sacred basil (*Ocymum sanctum*).

बेसा vysa, *adv.* or *adj.* In that manner, so, that like, such. *Wysa ka wysa,* Such as before.

बेसाही vysahée, *adv.* In the same manner.

बेसें vysen, *adv.* Freely, without cost, gratis.

बों won, *adv.* In that manner, so. *Won ka wonhee,* Exactly the same as before or originally.

बोद wod, *adj.* Wet, moist, damp.

बोदाल wodál, *s. m.* A sheat fish (*Silurus Boalis*).

बोल wol, *s. m.* Gum, myrrh.

बुक्त vyukt, *adj.* Wise, learned ; evident, manifest, apparent ; individual, specific.

बुक्ति vyukti, *s. f.* Individuality ; appearance, manifestation ; case, inflexion, or the proper form of any inflected word.

बुग्र vyugr, *adj.* Bewildered, perplexed, distracted.

बुग्रता vyugr-ta, *s. f.* Perplexity, anxiety.

बुङ्गूल vyúngool, *s. m.* The 60th part of a digit or *Ungool.*

बुजन vyújun, *s. m.* A fan.

बुञ्जक vyúnjuk, *s. m.* A sign, a mark, a symbol.

बुञ्जन vyúnjun, *s. m.* Sauce, condiment ; a consonant.

बुतिक्रम vyúti-krúm, *s. m.* Inverted or retrograde order, inversion, reverse ; contrariety, opposition in general.

बुतिरिक्त vyúti-ríkt, *adj.* Different, distinct.

बुतिरेक vyutirék, *s. m.* Difference, separateness.

बुतीत vyutéet, *adj.* Past, gone.

बुतीपात vyútee-pát, *s. m.* Great and portentous calamity, or a portent ; the seventeenth of the astrological *Yogs.*

बुथा vyútha, *s. f.* Pain.

बुथाकर vyútha-kúr, *adj.* Painful, excruciating.

बुथारहित vyútha-rúhit, *adj.* Free from pain.

बुभिचार vyúbhi-chár, *s. m.* Following improper courses, doing what is prohibited or wicked.

बुभिचारिनी vyúbhi-chárinee, *s. f.* A wanton woman, an unchaste wife.

बुभिचारी vyubhi-cháree, *adj.* Following or doing what is improper ; going astray.

बुय vyúy, *s. m.* Expenditure, expending ; destruction, disappearance.

बुर्थ vyurth, *adj.* Useless, vain, unprofitable ; unmeaning.

बुर्थता vyurth-tá, *s. f.* Unprofitableness, uselessness ; absence of meaning, nonsense.

बुवकलन vyúv-kúlun, *s. m.* Subtraction.

बुवच्छेद vyuv-chhéd, *s. m.* Dividing, separating.

बुवधान vyuv-dhán, *s. m.* Intervening, intervention, space.

बुवधायक vyuv-dháyuk, *adj.* Intervening, intermediate, separating.

बुवसाय vynv-sáyuh, *s. m.* Effort, exertion, perseverance, industry ; following any business or profession ; plan, device, trick.

बुवसायी vyuv-sáyee, *adj.* Active, energetic ; engaged in business.

बुवस्था vyuvústha, *s. f.* Separating, placing remote or apart ; a decree, a written declaration of the law, applied in practice to the written extracts from the codes of law, stated as the opinions of the *Hindoo* law officers attached to the courts of justice ; an engagement, an agreement, a contract.

बुवहार vyuvhár, *s. m.* Usage, custom ; profession, business ; the practice of the courts, or civil and criminal law, judicial procedure, administrative justice, as the examination of evidence, &c.; contests at law, law suit, litigation.

व्यवहारिक vyuv-hárik, *adj.* Customary, usual; engaged in customary duty or avocation; connected with or relating to legal process; litigant, being party to a suit.

व्यवहारी vyuv-háree, *adj.* Litigant, litigating, engaged in a law suit; relating to legal process; customary, usual; following one's ordinary affairs or avocation.

व्यवहार्य vyuv-háryuh, *adj.* To be observed or practised, as a duty or avocation, customary, usual; actionable, subject to legal process.

व्यस्त vyust, *adj.* Confounded, confused, bewildered; pervaded, penetrated, spread.

व्यस्तता vyust-ta, *s. f.* Agitation, bewilderment; inherence.

व्याकरण vyá-kúrun, *s. m.* Grammar; explaining, expounding.

व्याकरणी vyá-kúrunee, *s. m.* A grammarian.

व्याकुल vyakóol, *adj.* Confounded, bewildered, perplexed, overcome with fear, &c.

व्याकुलता vyakool-tá, *s. f.* Perplexity, agitation, alarm.

व्याकुलमान vyakóol-múna, *adj.* Agitated, flurried, bewildered.

व्याकुलित vyakoolít, *adj.* Agitated, flurried, perplexed.

व्याख्या vyakhyá, *s. f.* Exposition, explanation, gloss, comment.

व्याख्यान vyakhyán, *s. m.* Explaining, expounding.

व्याघात vyaghát, *s. m.* Obstacle, impediment; the thirteenth of the astronomical *Yogs.*

व्याघाती vya-ghátee, *adj.* Who or what opposes, resists, beats, &c.

व्याघ्र vyaghr, *s. m.* A tiger.

व्याघ्रनखी vyághr-núkhee, *s. f.* A tiger's claw, a sort of perfume; a scratch or impression of the finger nails.

व्याज vyaj, *s. m.* Deceit, fraud, craft, cunning; disguise, either of purpose or person; wickedness.

व्याध vyadh, *s. m.* A hunter, one who lives by killing deer, &c.; a low or wicked man.

व्याधि vyádhi, *s. m.* Sickness, disease in general.

व्याधित vya-dhít, *adj.* Sick, ill, diseased.

व्याधिरहित vyádhi-rúhit, *adj.* Free from disease, convalescent.

व्यान vyan, *s. m.* One of the five vital airs, that which is diffused throughout the body.

व्यापक vyáp-uk, *adj.* Diffusive, comprehensive, spreading or extending widely.

व्यापकता vyapuk-tá, *s. f.* Diffusion, pervadence.

व्यापना vyáp-na, *v. n.* To spread through or throughout, to pervade, penetrate.

व्यापार vyapár, *s. m.* Occupation, business, trade, profession; exercise, practice.

व्यापारी vyapáree, *adj.* Busy, occupied; exercising, practising.

व्यापी vyápee, *adj.* Diffusive, comprehensive.

व्याप्त vyapt, *adj.* Pervaded, occupied or penetrated by; celebrated, famous; filled, full.

व्याप्ति vyápti, *s. f.* Pervading, inherence; universal permeation, omnipresence.

व्याप्तिमान vyapti-mán, *adj.* Diffusive, pervading.

व्याप्यता vyapyutá, *s. f.* Capacity of being penetrated or essentially affected by.

व्याम vyam, *s. m.* A fathom, or the space between the tips of the fingers of either hand when the arms are extended.

व्यायाम vyayám, *s. m.* Fatigue, labour; gymnastics.

व्यवहारी vyav-háree, *adj.* Usual, customary; juridical, judicial, legal. *s. m.* A counsellor, a minister.

व्यास vyas, *s. m.* A celebrated sage and author, the supposed original compiler of the *Veds* and *Poorans,* also the founder of the *Vedant* philosophy; diffusion, extension; the diameter of a circle.

व्युत्क्रम vyoot-krúm, *s. m.* Inverted order, irregular arrangement.

व्युत्पत्ति vyoot-pútti, *s. f.* Science, learning; formation of words, derivation, etymology.

व्युत्पन्न vyoot-púnn, *adj.* Learned, conversant or proficient in literature; derived, formed as a derivative word; generated, begotten.

व्यूह vyooh, *s. m.* Military array, the arrangement of troops in various positions.

व्रण vrun, *s. m.* A tumour, a boil; an ulcer, a wound.

व्रत vrut, *s. m.* Any meritorious act of devotion, the voluntary or vowed observance, or imposition of any penance, austerity, or privation, as fasting, continence, exposure to heat and cold, &c.

व्रती vrutée, *adj.* Engaged in or observing a religious vow or obligation. *s. m.* An ascetic, a devotee, one engaged in the observance of a vow or penance.

व्रात्य vrát-yuh, *s. m.* A *Brahmun,* or man of the three first classes, in whose youth the customary observances have been omitted, and who has not received his investiture with the sacrificial thread.

ब्रात्या vratyá, *s. f.* A female of a fallen *Brahmun*, &c.

बीड़ा vréera, *s. f.* Shame, bashfulness, modesty.

बीड़ित vree-rít, *adj.* Ashamed, modest.

बीहि vréehi, *s. m.* Rice of various kinds.

श

श shuh, The thirtieth consonant of the *Naguree* alphabet; and corresponds to *sh* pronounced softly, as in *shun*.

शक shúkuh, *s. m.* A sovereign, any prince who gives his name to an era, especially applied to *Salivahun*; a particular caste, the followers or descendants of *Sakuh*, or *Salivahun*.

शकट shúk-ut, *s. m.* A cart.

शकटिका shúkut-ík-a, *s. f.* A small cart, a toy-cart.

शकरभूता shúkur-bhút-a, *s. m.* A kind of sweetmeat made of rice, butter and sugar.

शकुन shúk-oon, *s. m.* Any lucky or auspicious object or omen.

शकुनि shú-kooni, *s. m.* A bird; one of the astronomical periods called *Kuruns*.

शकुल shúk-ool, *s. m.* A fish.

शकुलगुन्ध shukool-gúnd, *s. m.* A kind of fish, the gilt-head.

शकुलार्भक shúkool-árbhuk, *s. m.* A sort of gilt-head (*Sparus emarginatus*).

शक्त shukt, *adj.* Able, capable, strong, powerful.

शक्तता shukt-tá, *s. f.* Ability, power.

शक्ति shúkti, *s. f.* Power, ability, strength, prowess; the energy or active power of a deity.

शक्तिमान shukti-mán, *adj.* Powerful, mighty.

शक्तिहीन shukti-héen, *adj.* Powerless, impotent.

शक्य shúk-yuh, *adj.* Possible, practicable, to be effected or done.

शक्यता shukyutá, *s. f.* Possibility.

शक्रगोप shukr-góp, *s. m.* An insect of a red colour (*Coccinella* or *lady-bird of various species*).

शक्रधनूष shukr-dhúnoos, *s. m.* The bow of *Indr*, the rainbow.

शक्रभूभ्व shukr-bhóobhva, *s. f.* Colocynth (*Cucumis coloquintida*).

शक्राशन shukr-áshun, *s. m.* A medicinal plant (*Wrightea antidysenterica*).

शङ्करा shunkur-á, *s. m.* Name of a musical mode.

शङ्कर shún-kur, *s. m.* The name of a celebrated teacher of the *Vedant* philosophy.

शङ्कराभरण shunkur-ábhurun, *s. m.* Name of a musical mode.

शङ्का shún-ka, *s. f.* Fear, terror, apprehension; doubt, uncertainty.

शङ्कामय shunka-múy, *adj.* Fearful, afraid.

शङ्काहीन shunka-héen, *adj.* Free from doubt or apprehension.

शङ्कित shunk-ít, *adj.* Alarmed, frightened; doubtful, uncertain.

शङ्कु shún-koo, *s. m.* The trunk of a lopped tree; a javelin; a pin, a stake, a pale; the gnomon of a dial, usually twelve fingers long; the scate fish (*Raia Sankur*).

शङ्कोच shun-kóch, *s. m.* A scate fish.

शङ्ख shunkh, *s. m.* The conch shell used by the *Hindoos*; a large number, ten or a hundred billions.

शङ्खिनी shun-khínee, *s. f.* A description of woman, one of the four classes into which females are divided in erotic writings: the *Shunkhínee* is described as tall, with long hair, neither stout nor thin, of irascible disposition and strong passions.

शठ shuth, *adj.* Wicked, depraved, perverse, dishonest. [vity.

शठता shuth-tá, *s. f.* Wickedness, depra-

शण shun, *s. m.* Hemp (*Cannabis sativa*); Bengal Sun, a plant from which a kind of hemp is prepared (*Crotolaria juncea and other kinds*).

शणसूत्र shun-sóotr, *s. m.* The fibre or flax of the *Sun* plant, or string made from it; cordage, twine.

शणेर shun-éer, *s. m.* A rock or small island in the midst of the river *Sons*; an insular spot inclosed by the branches of the *Surjoo*, where it falls into the Ganges above *Chhupra*, at *Bhrigoorasrum* or *Bhugrasun*: called also the bank of the *Durduree*.

शण्ड shund, *s. m.* A bull at liberty.

शत shut, *s. m.* A hundred.

शतगुण shut-góon, *adj.* A hundred times, a hundred fold.

शतुद्रू shut-údroo, *s. f.* *Setlej* river, which rises in the *Himaluy* mountains, in the vicinity it is supposed of the *Ravun krud* or lake, and running to the S. W. unites in the *Punjab* with the *Beya* or *Vipasa*, when it forms the Hyphasis of the Greeks, and falls into the Indus below *Mooltan*.

शतपदी shut-púd-ee, } *s. f.* A centipede,
शतपाद shut-pád, } jaulus.

शतभिषा shut-bhísha, *s. f.* The twenty-fifth lunar mansion, containing 100 stars.

शतमूली shut-móolee, *s. f.* A plant (*Asparagus racemosus*).

शतलक्ष shut-lúksh, *s. m.* A hundred Lakhs, ten millions.

शतवर्ष shut-vúrsh, *s. m.* A century.

शतवेधी shut-védhee, *s. m.* A sort of dock or sorrel (*Oxalis monadelpha*, or, *Rumex vesicarius*).

शतसहस्र shut-suhúsr, *s. m.* A hundred thousand.

शत्रु shútroo, *s. m.* An enemy, a foe, an adversary.

शत्रुता shutroo-tá, *s. f.* Hostility, enmity.

शनि shúni, *s. m.* The planet Saturn or its regent.

शनिप्रिय shúni-príyuh, *s. m.* The emerald or sapphire.

शनिवार shúni-wár, *s. m.* Saturday.

शनुयशनुय shúnuy-shúnuy, *adv.* Slowly, tardily.

शनैश्चर shunyschúr, *s. m.* The planet Saturn or its mythological personification.

शपथ shúputh, *s. m.* An oath, asseveration by oath or ordeal; an imprecation, a curse.

शपन shúp-un, *s. m.* An oath, confirmation of the truth by oath or ordeal; abuse, imprecation, cursing, malediction.

शप्त shupt, *adj.* Cursed, anathematized. *s. m.* A sort of grass (*Saccharum cylindricum*).

शप्पा shúppa, *s. m.* A butt, or mark for archers.

शफरी shúph-ree, *s. f.* A small fish (*Cyprinus Sophore*).

शब्द shubd, *s. m.* Sound, word, voice; (*in grammar*) A declinable word, as noun, pronoun, &c.

शब्दकार shubd-kár, *adj.* Sounding, sonorous.

शब्दचोर shubd-chór, *s. m.* A plagiary.

शब्दयोनि shubd-yóni, *s. f.* A root, a radical word.

शब्दशास्त्र shubd-shástr, *s. m.* Philology, grammar, &c.

शम shum, *s. m.* Quiet of mind, stoicism, indifference; abstract meditation on *Bruhma*, or God; quiet, tranquillity, rest, calm; final happiness, emancipation from human existence.

शमन shúmun, *s. m.* Killing animals for sacrifice, immolation; mental tranquillity, calmness, indifference.

शमित shumit, *adj.* Pacified, appeased; quiet, tranquil, sedate, calm.

शमी shúm-ee, *adj.* Tranquil, pacific, tranquillized. *s. f.* A legume or pod; a tree (*Acacia Suma*); a shrub (*Serratula anthelmintica*).

शमीपुत्री shúmee-pútree, *s. f.* A sort of sensitive plant (*Mimosa pudica*).

शमीर shum-éer, *s. m.* A small variety of the *Mimosa Suma*.

शम्बूक shum-bóok, *s. m.* A bivalve shell; a conch shell; a snail.

शयन shúyun, *s. m.* Sleep; a bed, a couch; copulation.

श्यालु shyáloo, *adj.* Sleepy, slothful, sluggish.

शुज्या shujyá, *s. f.* A bed, a couch, a sopha.

शर shur, *s. m.* A sort of reed or grass (*Saccharum Sara*); an arrow.

शरट shúrut, *s. m.* A lizard, a chameleon; safflower, the plant.

शरण shúrun, *s. m.* A house; a preserver, a protector, what or who protects or preserves; preservation, protection, defence.

शरणागत shúrun-águt, *adj.* Refugee, appellant, one who comes for protection or refuge.

शरणार्थी shúrun-árthee, *adj.* Unfortunate, wretched, involved in calamity or ruin, and dependant on others for protection or aid.

शरण्य shurun-yúh, *adj.* To be protected or aided, poor, miserable, helpless. *s. m.* A protection, a protector, that which or who affords refuge and defence; a house, protection, defence.

शरत्काल shúrut-kál, *s. m.* The autumnal season.

शरत्कालीन shúrut-kaléen, *adj.* Autumnal.

शरद् shurud, *s. f.* The season of autumn or the sultry season; the two months succeeding the rains; according to the *Vydikus*, comprising the months *Bhadr* and *Aswin*, and according to the *Pouranikus*, *Aswin* and *Kartik*, fluctuating thus from August to November.

शरभ shúrubh, *s. m.* A fabulous animal, supposed to have eight legs, and to inhabit particularly the snowy mountains.

शरमल्ल shurmúll, *s. m.* A small bird, considered as a variety of the *Salic* or *Myna* (*Turdus gosalica*).

शरयु shúr-joo, *s. f.* The *Serjoo* river.

शरल shúrul, *adj.* Upright, honest.

शरलता shurul-tá, *s. f.* Uprightness, sincerity.

शराट shuráta, *s. m.* Sound, noise, voice.

शराटि shur-áti, ⎤ *s. f.* A sort of bird
शराटी shurálee, ⎦ (*Turdus ginginianus*).

शराबोर shurabór, *adj.* Soused, dripping wet.

शराव shuráo, *s. m.* A lid, a cover; a shallow cup or dish; a platter.

शरासन shurásun, *s. m.* A bow.

शरीर shuréer, *s. m.* The body.

शरीरबन्धक shuréer-bundhúk, *s. m.* A hostage.

शरीरसंस्कार shuréer-sunskár, *s. m.* Purification of the body by various ceremonies at conception, birth, initiation, death, &c.

शरीरी shuréeree, *adj.* Embodied, corporeal, having body.

शर्करा shurkrá, *s. m.* Clayed or candied sugar ; gravel (*the disease*).

शर्म्मा shurm-má, *adj.* Happy, glad. *s. m.* A name or appellation common to *Brahmuns.*

शर्व्वरी shúrv-vur-ee, *s. f.* Night ; a woman.

शल्बीन shulbéen, *s. f.* Vice in a horse.

शलभ shulúbh, *s. m.* A grasshopper ; a locust.

शलाका shuláka, *s. f.* A thin slip of bamboo, serving when tipped with sulphur for a match ; a ruler ; a fibrous stick used as a brush or pencil.

शलीता shuléeta, *s. m.* A canvass sack, &c. in which baggage is fastened previously to being loaded on cattle.

शलूका shulóoka, *s. m.* A child's bib.

शल्यशास्त्र shúlyuh-shástr, *s. m.* That part of surgery which treats of the extraction of extraneous substances lodged in the body.

शल्योद्धार shúlyuh-oddhár, *s. m.* Extraction of foreign substances from the body.

शल्लक shullúk, *s. m.* A plant (*Bignonia Indica*).

शल्लकी shulluk-ée, *s. f.* The gum Olibanum tree (*Boswellia thurifera*).

शल्लकीद्रव shullukée-drúv, *s. m.* Incense, Olibanum.

शव shuv, *s. m.* A dead body, a corpse.

शवर shúvur, *s. m.* A barbarian, one inhabiting the mountainous districts of India, and wearing the feathers of the peacock, &c. as decorations.

शवसाधन shuv-sádhun, *s. m.* A mystical and magical ceremony performed with a dead body.

शशक shúshuk, *s. m.* A hare or rabbit.

शशस्थली shúshusthúlee, *s. f.* The *Doab*, the country between the *Ganges* and *Jumna* rivers.

शशिलेखा shúshi-lékha, *s. f.* A digit of the moon.

शशी shúsh-ee, *s. m.* The moon.

शस्त्र shustr, *s. m.* A weapon in general ; (*or especially such as is used in the hand*) a sword, a scymitar. *Shustr-dharee, adj.* Armed.

शस्त्रकार shustr-kár, *s. m.* An armourer.

शस्त्राभ्यास shústr-abhyás, *s. m.* Military exercise or practice.

शस्य shúsyuh, *s. m.* Corn, grain in general.

शस्यभक्षक shúshyuh-bhukshúk, *adj.* Graminivorous.

शाक shak, *s. m.* A potherb in general, or any leaf, flower, fruit, stalk, root, &c. used as a vegetable ; one of the seven *Dweeps* or divisions of the world ; the sixth, surrounded by the sea of milk or white sea ; an era, a period usually commencing with some celebrated prince, as *Yoodhishthir, Vikrumadityuh, Salivahun,* &c. thence denominated *Sakesurus,* &c. ; the term in ordinary use is applied especially to the era of *Salivahun,* commencing 76 or 78 years after the Christian era.

शाकभरी shákum-bhúree, *s. f.* A city, supposed to be the modern *Sambhur.*

शाकभरीय shákum-bhuréeyuh, *s. m.* A fossile salt brought from a lake in the vicinity of *Sambhur,* a town in *Ajmere.*

शाक्त shakt, *s. m.* A worshipper of the female principle.

शाखा shákha, *s. f.* A branch, the branch of a tree.

शाखी shákhee, *s. m.* A tree.

शाटक shatúk, *s. m.* } A petticoat.
शाटी shatée, *s. f.* }

शाठ्य sháth-yuh, *s. m.* Wickedness, villainy.

शान shan, *s. m.* A touchstone ; a whet or grindstone.

शान्त shant, *adj.* Calm, tranquil, pacified ; allayed, alleviated ; stilled, hushed (*as wind, &c.*) ; meek, humble.

शान्तता shant-tá, *s. f.* Quietness, calmness, meekness.

शान्तात्मा shant-átma, *adj.* Calm, composed, of resigned or composed spirit.

शान्ति shánti, *s. f.* Quiet, tranquillity stoicism ; rest, repose ; remission, alleviation.

शाप shap, *s. m.* Oath, affirmation by oath or ordeal ; curse, imprecation.

शापग्रस्त shap-grúst, *adj.* Having incurred or suffering under a curse.

शापित shapít, *adj.* Sworn.

शापोद्धार shap-oddhár, *s. m.* Deliverance from a curse or its effects.

शाम sham, *n. prop.* A name of *Krishn.*

शामा shamá, *s. m.* A little bird ; a grain (*Panicum colonum,* or *frumentaceum*).

शामी लगाना shámee lugána, *v. a.* To shoe with iron.

शाम्बुक shám-book, *s. m.* A bivalve shell.

शारीरिक shareer-ik, *adj.* Relating to the body, corporeal.

शल shal, *s. m.* A kind of fish (*Ophiocephalus urahl*); a tree (*Shorea robusta*). *s. f.* A Shawl.

शलपर्णी shal-púrnee, *s. f.* A shrub (*Hedysarum gangeticum*).

शाला shála, *s. m.* A house; a hall.

शालि sháli, *s. m.* Rice in general, but especially in two classes: one like white rice growing in deep water, and the other a red sort, requiring only a moist soil.

शालिवाहन sháli-váhun, *s. m.* A sovereign of India, whose capital was *Pruteeshthan*, in the *Dekhin*, and institutor of the era now called *Suka*, beginning 76 or 78 years after Christ.

शाली shálee, *adj.* Made of *shawl*.

शालमली shalumlée, *s. f.* The silk-cotton tree (*Bombax heptaphyllum*).

शासन shásun, *s. m.* An order, an edict, a command; a writing, a deed, a written contract or agreement; governing, ruling, government.

शासनपत्र shásun-pútr, *s. m.* A plate of copper, a stone or sheet of paper, &c. on which an edict or grant is inscribed.

शासनीय shasun-éeyuh, *adj.* To be governed or directed.

शास्ति shásti, *s. f.* A command, an order; governing, ruling; correction, punishment.

शास्त्र shastr, *s. m.* An order or command; scripture, science, institutes of religion, law or letters, especially considered as of divine origin or authority; used singly it implies works of literature or science in general, and it is therefore customarily connected with some other word to limit its application, as the *Vedant Shastrus*, or treatises of philosophical theology, the *Dhurm Shustrus*, books of law, &c.; it is also applied to less important branches of knowledge, as the *Kavyuh Shastrus*, or poetical works, *Shilpi Shastrus*, works on the mechanical arts, and *Kam Shastrus*, or erotic compositions; in the singular number it is also used comprehensively to signify the body of all that has been written on the subject, as *Dhurm Shastr*, the institutes or code of law, *Kavyuh Shastr*, poetry, *Ulunkar Shastr*, rhetoric, &c.; a book in general.

शास्त्रज्ञ shastr-úg, *adj.* Acquainted with the *Shastrus*, skilled in the knowledge of law and religion especially.

शास्त्रविरुद्ध shastr-viróoddh, *adj.* Contrary to law or religion, illegal, forbidden.

शास्त्रानुसार shastr-anoosár, *s. m.* Conformity to sacred ordinances.

शास्त्री shás-tree, *s. m.* A *pundit*, a teacher of holy science, or one skilled in it.

शास्त्रीय shastrée-yuh, *adj.* Scriptural, authorized by or conformable to sacred institutes.

शास्त्रोक्त shastr-ókt, *adj.* Said or declared in a work of sacred authority.

शास्य shás-yuh, *adj.* Punishable, deserving punishment.

शिंशपा shins-pá, *s. f.* A tree (*Dalbergia Sisu*).

शिखर shíkhur, *s. m.* The peak or summit of a mountain; point, end, top in general.

शिखरी shikh-rée, *adj.* Crested, peaked, pointed.

शिखा shíkha, *s. f.* Point, top in general; a crest; a lock of hair on the crown of the head; flame.

शिखावल shikha-vúl, *adj.* Crested, pointed.

शिखी shíkhee, *adj.* Crested; having a lock of hair on the top of the head. *s. m.* A peacock.

शितुद्रु shitúdroo, *s. f.* The *Setlej* river.

शितिरत्न shiti-rútn, *s. m.* A sapphire.

शितिसारक shiti-sáruk, *s. m.* A sort of ebony (*Diospyros glutinosa*).

शिथिल shíthil, *adj.* Loose, lax, flaccid, flabby; languid, inert, feeble.

शिथिलता shithil-tá, *s. f.* Relaxation, looseness.   [relaxed.

शिथिलबल shithil-búl, *adj.* Weakened,

शिर shir, *s. m.* The head.

शिरःकपाली shíruh-kupálee, *s. m.* A devotee carrying a human skull as his emblem.

शिरःपीडा shíruh-péera, *s. f.* Pain of the head, head-ache.

शिरा shíra, *s. f.* Any vessel of the body, really or supposed to be, of a tubular form, as a nerve, a tendon, a gut, &c.

शिराल shirál, *adj.* Veiny, tendinous, skinny, showing the tendons or veins.

शिरीष shiréesh, *s. m.* A kind of tree (*Acacia Sirisa*).

शिरोमणी shiró-múnee, *s. f.* } A gem worn
शिरोरत्न shiro-rútn, *s. m.* } in a crest, or on the top of the head.

शिरोरोग shiro-róg, *s. m.* Disease of the head.

शिला shíl-a, *s. f.* A stone, a rock; a flat stone on which condiments, &c. are ground with a muller.

शिलाजतु shíla-jútoo, *s. m.* Bitumen; red chalk.

शिलाजित् shíla-jít, *s. m.* Bitumen.

शिलाधातु shíla-dhátoo, *s. m.* Chalk; red chalk; a white fossil substance; an aluminous earth of a white colour, and thence considered to be a kind of chalk.

शिलापुष्प shila-póoshp, *s. m.* Storax or Benzoin.

शिलामय shila-múy, *adj.* Made of stone.

शिलारस shila-rús, *s. m.* Incense, Benjamin or Olibanum.

शिलावल्का shíla-vúlka, *s. f.* A medicinal substance said to be of cooling and lithonthriptic properties, commonly termed *Silabak*; a sort of lichen or moss.

शिल्प shilp, *s. m.* Any art, any manual or mechanical art.

शिल्पकर्म shilp-kúrmm, *s. m.* Manual labour, handicraft.

शिल्पकार shilp-kár, *s. m.* An artisan, a mechanic.

शिल्पविद्या shilp-vidyá, *s. f.* Art, mechanical or manual skill.

शिल्पिनी shilpínee, *s. f.* A drug or herb, a kind of grass said to be known by the name of *Luhanusipi*, and described as sweet and cooling, and bearing seeds of tonic and restorative properties.

शिल्पिशाला shílpi-shála, *s. f.* A workshop, a manufactory.

शिल्पिशास्त्र shílpi-shástr, *s. m.* A treatise or set of treatises on works of art.

शिल्पी shilpée, *adj.* An artist, an artificer or artisan; belonging or relating to a mechanical profession or art.

शिव shiv, *s. m.* The deity *Shiv*, the most formidable of the *Hindoo* triad, the destroyer of creation : the adoration of which he is the object, is of a more gloomy nature in general than that of the rest, and he is the particular god of the *Tantriks* or followers of the books called *Tuntrus*.

शिवधातु shiv-dhátoo, *s. m.* The milk-stone, opal or chalcedony. [*Benares.*]

शिवपुरी shiv-póoree, *s. f.* The city of

शिवरात्रि shiv-rátri, *s. f.* A celebrated festival in honor of *Shiv* on the fourteenth of the moon's wane or dark fortnight in *Magh.*

शिवालय shiv-áluy, } *s. m.* Any temple de-
शिवाला shiv-ála, } dicated to *Shiv.*

शिशिर shíshir, *adj.* Cold, frigid, chilly, freezing. *s. m.* Frost.

शिशिरकाल shishir-kál, *s. m.* The cold season, comprising two months from about the middle of January to that of March.

शिशु shíshoo, *s. m.* The young of man or any animal, a child, a calf, a pup, &c.; a pupil, a scholar.

शिशुक shíshook, *s. m.* A porpoise; another fish resembling a porpoise.

शिशुता shishoo-tá, *s. f.* Boyhood, pupilage; childhood.

शिशुपाल shishoo-pál, *s. m.* The sovereign of a country in the central part of India or *Chhedi*, opposed to *Krishn* and slain by him.

शिष्ट shisht, *adj.* Obedient, docile; ordered, commanded, disciplined, trained.

शिष्टता shisht-tá, *s. f.* Good behaviour, urbanity, civility; docility.

शिष्टसभा shisht-súbha, *s. f.* A council of state, an assembly of chief officers.

शिष्टसमाचार shisht-sumachár, *s. m.* History or tradition of eminent persons.

शिष्टाचार shisht-achár, *adj.* Well-behaved. *s. m.* Good manners, proper behaviour.

शिष्य shísh-yuh, *s. m.* A pupil, a scholar.

शिक्षक shiksh-úk, *adj.* A learner, a teacher.

शिक्षा shikshá, *s. f.* Learning, study, the acquisition of knowledge.

शिक्षाशक्ति shíksha-shúkti, *s. f.* Dexterity, skill.

शिक्षित shikshít, *adj.* Skilful, clever, conversant; disciplined, exercised; docile; studied, learned.

शीकर shéekur, *s. m.* Thin rain, or rain driven by wind.

शीघ्र sheeghr, *adj.* Quick, speedy. *s. m.* (*In astronomy*) Parallax. *adv.* Soon, quickly, swiftly, speedily.

शीघ्रगामी sheeghr-gámee, *adj.* Going quick or expeditiously.

शीघ्रता sheeghr-tá, *s. f.* Quickness, speed.

शीत sheet, *adj.* Cold, chilly, frigid. *s. m.* Cold, coldness; cold weather or the six months of the rainy, dewy and cold seasons.

शीतकाल sheet-kál, *s. m.* Cold weather, winter.

शीतता sheet-tá, *s. f.* Cold, coldness.

शीतल sheet-úl, *adj.* Cold, chilly, frigid. *s. m.* Cold, coldness.

शीतलता sheetul-tá, *s. f.* Coldness, coolness.

शीतहर sheet-húr, *adj.* Removing cold.

शीतांशु sheet-ánsoo, *s. m.* Camphor.

शीतार्त sheet-ártt, *adj.* Cold, chilled, shivering, suffering or shrinking from cold.

शीताश्मन् sheet-áshm-un, *s. m.* The moon gem, crystal.

शीर्ण sheern, *adj.* Thin, small, slender; wasted, withered, decayed.

शीर्णता sheern-tá, *s. f.* Emaciation, withering.

शीर्ष sheersh, *s. m.* The head.

शीर्षछेद sheersh-chhéd, *s. m.* Decapitating.

शील sheel, *adj.* Well-behaved, well-disposed. *s. m.* Good conduct or disposition.

शीलवान sheel-wán, *adj.* Of a good or amiable disposition.

शीशम shéeshum, *s. f.* A kind of wood (*Dalbergia Sisu*).

शुक shook, *s. m.* A parrot.

शुक्ति shóokti, *s. f.* A pearl oyster; a small shell; a cockle.

शुक्तिमान shookti-mán, *s. m.* One of the seven principal mountains or mountainous ranges of India.

शुक्र shookr, *s. m.* The planet Venus; semen virile.

शुक्रवार shookr-wár, *s. m.* Friday.

शुक्ल shookl, *adj.* White, of a white colour. *s. m.* White (*the colour*); one of the astronomical *Yogs.*

शुक्लकन्थूक shookl-kunthúk, *s. m.* A kind of gallinule or water-hen.

शुक्लता shookl-tá, *s. f.* Whiteness.

शुक्लपक्ष shookl-púksh, *s. m.* The light half of a month, the fifteen days of the moon's increase, or from new to full moon.

शुचि shóochi, *adj.* White; clean, cleansed, purified; pure, pious, exempt from passion or vice.

शुचिता shoochi-tá, *s. f.* Purity, cleanness.

शुचिमुनि shóochi-múni, *s. m.* Crystal.

शुंठी shóonthee, *s. f.* Dry ginger.

शुंड shoond, *s. m.* An elephant's proboscis or trunk.

शुद्ध shooddh, *adj.* Pure, purified, clean, cleansed; faultless, correct.

शुद्धता shooddh-tá, *s. f.* Purity, cleanness, freedom from soil or defect.

शुद्धमति shooddh-múti, *adj.* Of pure and sincere purpose, honest, free from guile; intelligent.

शुद्धि shóod-dhi, *s. f.* Purity, purification; innocence established by ordeal or trial, acquittal.

शून्य shóon-yuh, *adj.* Empty, void. *s. m.* A cypher.

शुभ shoobh, *adj.* Happy, well, right, fortunate, auspicious; handsome, beautiful. *s. m.* Good, good fortune, auspiciousness, happiness; one of the astrological *Yogs.*

शुभकर shoobh-kúr, *adj.* Propitious, producing good, &c.

शुभकर्म shoobh-kúrmm, *s. m.* Pious or virtuous act; reputable occupation or employment.

शुभग shoo-bhúg, *adj.* Fortunate, propitious.

शुभंकर shoo-bhúnkur, *adj.* Propitious, auspicious, conferring happiness or fortune.

शुभदन्ती shoobh-dúntee, *s. f.* The female elephant of the North West quarter.

शुभफल shoobh-phúl, *s. m.* Happy result or consequence.

शुभलग्न shoobh-lúgn, *s. m.* An auspicious moment.

शुभशील shoobh-shéel, *adj.* Of a good disposition.

शुभांग shoobh-áng, *adj.* Handsome, elegant. *s. f.* A handsome woman.

शुभाचार shoobh-achár, *adj.* Virtuous.

शुभाशुभ shoobh-áshoobh, *adj.* Prosperous and unfortunate, good and evil. *s. m.* Good and ill-fortune.

शुभ्र shoobhr, *adj.* White; shining. *s. m.* White (*the colour*).

शुभ्रकृत shoobhr-krít, *s. m.* The thirty-sixth year of the Indian cycle.

शुंभपूर shumbh-póor, *s. m.* A city and district, perhaps the modern *Sumbhulpoor*, in the district of *Gondwana.*

शुशकार्ण shoosh-kárna, *v. n.* To encourage or stimulate a dog to the chase, by the sound *shoosh.*

शुशकारी shoosh-káree, *s. f.* Impelling a dog to the chase.

शुष्क shooshk, *adj.* Dry, dried.

शुष्कता shooshktá, *s. f.* Dryness.

शूद shóoh-da, *s. m.* A rake, prodigal, debauchee, blackguard, scoundrel, vagabond. *Shoohda shikusta*, Ruined and wretched.

शूदपन shoobda-pún, *s. m.* Raking, rakishness, debauchery, dissoluteness.

शूकीट shook-kéet, *s. m.* A caterpillar.

शूकर shóokur, *s. m.* A hog.

शूकापूत shooka-póott, *s. m.* A gem, perhaps amber.   [subtile.

शूक्ष्म shookshm, *adj.* Minute, small, fine,

शूद्र shoodr, *s. m.* A man of the fourth or servile tribe.

शूद्री shóodree, *s. f.* The wife of a *Shoodr.*

शून्य shóon-yuh, *adj.* Empty, void. *s. m.* Heaven, sky, ether; a cypher; a vacuum.

शून्यता shóonyutá, *s. f.* Vacuity, emptiness; unreality, the false or illusory nature of all existence.

शून्यवादी shóonyuvádee, *s. m.* A *Bouddh*; an atheist.

शूर shoor, *s. m.* A hero; a boar.

शूरण shoo-rún, *s. m.* An esculent root (*Arum campanulatum*); a plant (*Bignonia Indica*).

शूरता shoor-tá, *s. f.* Heroism, prowess.

शूर्प shoorpp, *s. m.* A winnowing basket.

शूल shool, *s. m.* Sharp pain in general, or especially in the belly, as cholic, &c., or in the joints from rheumatism or gout; a weapon, a pike, a dart; an astrological *Yog*, that of the 9th lunar mansion.

शूलसूत्र shool-shútroo, *s. m.* The castor oil plant (*Ricinus communis*).

शूलहत् shool-hút, *s. m.* Asafœtida.

शूली shoolée, *adj.* Suffering sharp pain, having the cholic, &c.

शृगाल shrigál, *s. m.* A shakal or jackal.

शृंखल shrinkhúl, *s. m.* A belt or chain worn round a man's body; a chain, a fetter in general.

शृंग shring, *s. m.* A horn; the top of a mountain.

शृंगार shrin-gár, *s. m.* Love; copulation, coition; red lead.

शृंगारी shrin-gáree, *adj.* Feeling or relating to the passion of love; stained with red lead. *s. m.* Dress, decoration.

शृंगि shríngi, *s. f.* A sort of sheat fish (*Silurus Singio*).

शृंगी shring-ée, *adj.* Horned; crested, peaked.

शेखर shékhur, *s. m.* A garland of flowers worn on the crown of the head; a crest.

शेफालिका shephálika, *s. f.* A flower (*Nyctanthes arbor-tritis*).

शेष shesh, *s. m.* Remainder, leavings, rest, balance.

शेषकाल shesh-kál, *s. m.* The last term, the time of death.

शेषरात्रि shes-rátri, *s. f.* The last watch of the night.

शेषावस्था shesh-avústha, *s. f.* The last state or condition of life.

शैत्य shytyuh, *s. m.* Cold, coldness.

शैथिल्य shy-thíl-yuh, *s. m.* Looseness, laxity; flaccidity.

शैल shyl, *adj.* Mountainous, mountaineer, &c.; stony, rocky. *s. m.* A mountain; Bitumen; storax; a sort of collyrium.

शैव shyv, *s. m.* A worshipper of *Shiv.*

शैवाल shyvál, *s. m.* An aquatic plant (*Vallisneria octrandra*).

शोक shok, *s. m.* Sorrow, grief.

शोकभंग shok-bhúng, *s. m.* Dissipating or removing sorrow.

शोकार्त्त shok-ártt, *adj.* Pained, afflicted by sorrow.

शोचित shochít, *adj.* Sorrowful, afflicted.

शोण shon, *s. m.* The *Sone* river, which rises in the table-land of *Umerkuntuk*, and running first northerly and then easterly for 500 miles, falls into the Ganges above *Patna*; a flower (*Bignonia Indica*); a red sort of sugar-cane.

शोणरत्न shon-rútn, *s. m.* A ruby.

शोणित sho-nít, *adj.* Red, crimson, purple. *s. m.* Blood; saffron.

शोणितोपल shónit-ópul, *s. m.* A ruby.

शोथ shoth, *s. m.* Swelling, intumescence.

शोथघ्न shothúghn, *adj.* Discutient, removing swellings.

शोथघ्नी shothúghnee, *s. f.* Hogweed (*Boerhavia diffusa*).

शोधक shodhúk, *adj.* Who or what cleanses, purifies, &c. (*In arithmetic*) The subtrahend.

शोधन sho-dhún, *s. m.* Cleaning, cleansing, purifying; correcting, freeing from faults or errors; correcting, as a writing; subtraction (*in arithmetic*); payment, acquittance; green vitriol.

शोभन shobhún, *adj.* Beautiful, handsome; propitious, auspicious. *s. m.* The fifth *Yog.*

शोभमान shobh-mán, *adj.* Fair, splendid, shining.

शोभा sho-bhá, *s. f.* Light, lustre, radiance, splendour; beauty.

शोभांजन shobh-ánjun, *s. m.* A tree, the *Sujina* or *Suhujna* (*Hyperanthera morunga*); the legumes, blossoms and leaves are esculent, and the root of the young tree is used as a substitute for horse-radish: in medicine the root is used as a rubefacient externally, as a stimulant internally, and the expressed oil of the seeds is employed to relieve arthritic pains, &c.

शोभित sho-bhít, *adj.* Beautified, decorated.

शोला shó-la, *s. m. Æschynomene paludosa*: the wood of which, being very light and spongy, is used by fishermen for floating their nets; a variety of toys, such as artificial birds and flowers, are made of it: garlands of those flowers are used in marriage ceremonies: when charred it answers the purpose of tinder.

शोख shokh, *s. m.* Pulmonary consumption; drying; intumescence, swelling.

शोखन sho-khún, *s. m.* Suction, sucking; drying up.

शौच shouch, *s. m.* Purification by ablution, &c. from personal defilement; purification at given periods from defilement caused by the death of a relation, &c.; purity, cleanness, freedom from defilement.

शौंडिक shound-ík, *s. m.* A distiller and vender of spirituous liquors.

शौंडिकी shoundik-ée, *s. f.* A female keeper of a tavern or dram shop.

श्रौर्य्य shóuryuh, *s. m.* Valour, heroism, prowess.

श्मशान shmushán, *s. m.* A cemetry, a place where dead bodies are burnt or buried.

श्मशानवासी shmushán-wásee, *adj.* A ghost, a gole, a sprite, male or female, abiding in cemeteries, &c.

श्याम shyam, *adj.* Black or dark blue. *s. m.* A sacred fig-tree at *Pruyag* or *Allahabad.*

श्यामता shyam-tá, *s. f.* Blackness.

श्यामभास shyam-bhás, *adj.* Black as jet, of a glossy black hue.

श्यामल shyamúl, *adj.* Of a black or dark blue colour.

श्यामा shyáma, *s. f.* A small singing bird with black plumage, called *Shama.*

श्यामक shyamák, *s. m.* A kind of grain generally eaten by the *Hindoos* (*Panicum frumentaceum*, also *P. colonum*), called also *Sanwan.*

श्यालक shyáluk, *s. m.* A wife's brother.

श्यालकी shyaluk-ée, *s. f.* A wife's sister.

श्येन shyen, *s. m.* A hawk, a falcon.

श्येनी shyenée, *s. f.* The female hawk.

श्रद्धान shrudd-dhán, *adj.* Trusting, believing; venerating, respecting.

श्रद्धा shruddhá, *s. f.* Respect, reverence; wish, desire; faith, belief; purity.

श्रद्धाकृत shruddha-krít, *adj.* Done with faith.

श्रद्धान्वित shruddhan-wít, *adj.* Believing, faithful.

श्रद्धामय shruddha-múy, *adj.* Believing, full of faith.

श्रद्धायुक्त shruddha-jóokt, *adj.* Having faith, believing.

श्रद्धारहित shruddha-rúhit, *adj.* Distrusting, unbelieving.

श्रद्धालु shruddh-áloo, *adj.* Faithful, believing; wishing, desirous. *s. f.* A pregnant woman longing for any thing.

श्रद्धावान shruddha-wán, *adj.* Believing, trusting, having faith.

श्रम shrum, *s. m.* Weariness, fatigue; labour, exertion, toil.

श्रमण shrum-ún, *s. m.* A religious character, an ascetic, a *Yuti,* one devoted to meditation for the purpose of obtaining final emancipation from existence, probably the Sarmanes of the Greek writers.

श्रमार्त्त shrum-ártt, *adj.* Exhausted, overcome with fatigue.

श्रमी shrum-ée, *adj.* Wearying, tiring, undergoing or incurring weariness or fatigue; laborious, diligent.

श्रवण shrúvun, *s. f.* The ear; hearing.

श्रवणा shruvuná, *s. f.* The twenty-third of the lunar asterisms, represented by three footsteps, and containing three stars.

श्रवणेन्द्रिय shrúvun-éndriyuh, *s. m.* The organ of hearing, the ear.

श्रविष्ठा shruvishthá, *s. f.* The twenty-fourth lunar asterism.

श्राद्ध shraddh, *adj.* Faithful, believing. *s. m.* A funeral ceremony observed at various fixed periods and for different purposes, consisting of offerings with water and fire to the gods and manes, and gifts and food to the relations present and assisting *Brahmuns :* it is especially performed for a parent recently deceased, or for three paternal ancestors, or for all ancestors collectively, and is supposed necessary to secure the ascent and residence of the souls of the deceased in a world appropriated to the manes.

श्रान्त shrant, *adj.* Wearied, fatigued; calmed, tranquil.

श्रान्ति shránti, *s. f.* Weariness, exhaustion.

श्रावक shrávuk, *s. m.* The lay votary of a *Booddh* or *Jyn.*

श्रावण shrávun, *s. m.* The month *Sravun* (*July-August*).

श्रावणी shravunée, *s. f.* Day of full moon in the month *Sravun.*

श्री shree, *s. f.* Fortune, prosperity, success, thriving; wealth; beauty, splendour, lustre; light; the three objects of life collectively, or love, duty, and wealth.

श्रीचक्र shree-chúkr, *s. m.* A magical diagram; the circle of the globe or earth.

श्रीफल shree-phúl, *s. m.* A fruit tree (*Ægle marmelos*).

श्रीमत् shree-mút, *m.* } *adj.* Wealthy, opu-
श्रीमति shree-mútee, *f.* } lent; pleasing beautiful; prosperous, fortunate, thriving; famous, illustrious.

श्रीमुख shree-móokh, *s. m.* The seventh year of the Indian cycle.

श्रीयुक्त shree-jóokt, } *adj.* Famous, illustri-
श्रीयुत shree-jóot, } ous; fortunate, wealthy.

श्रीरस shree-rús, *s. m.* Turpentine.

श्रीराग shree-rág, *s. m.* The third of the personified musical modes.

श्रीहस्तिनी shree-hústinee, *s. f.* The sunflower (*Heliotropium Indicum*).

श्रुत shroot, *adj.* Heard; understood. *s. m.* Sacred science, holy writ, &c.

श्रुति shróoti, *s. f.* The *Veds.*

श्रेणी shrénee, *s. f.* A line, a row, a range.

श्रेयः shreyúh, *s. m.* Final happiness ; good fortune, auspiciousness, prosperity.

श्रेष्ठ shreshth, *adj.* Best, excellent, most excellent, pre-eminent ; oldest, senior.

श्रेष्ठता shreshth-tá, *s. f.* Superiority, excellence. [stream.

श्रोत shrot, *s. m.* The ear ; the current of a

श्रोतव्य shrotúv-yuh, *adj.* To be heard or listened to.

श्रोता shróta, *s. m.* A hearer.

श्लाघा shlá-gha, *s. f.* Praise, panegyric, flattery, eulogium.

श्लाघ्य shlághyuh, *adj.* Venerable, respectable, praiseworthy, entitled to praise or veneration.

श्लेष्मा shlesh-ma, *s. m.* The phlegmatic humor, one of the three principal humors or fluids of the body.

श्लोक shlok, *s. m.* A verse, a stanza.

श्वशुर shwúsoor, *s. m.* A father-in-law, a wife's or husband's father.

श्वश्रू shwushróo, *s. f.* A mother-in-law.

श्वन् shwan, *s. m.* A dog.

श्वानी shwánee, *s. f.* A bitch.

श्वास shwas, *s. m.* Breath, breathing.

श्वित्र shwitr, *s. m.* Whiteness of the skin, vitiligo.

श्वित्री shwitrée, *adj.* Affected with vitiligo or whiteness of the skin.

श्वेत shwet, *adj.* White. *s. m.* White (*the colour*) ; the planet *Venus* or its regent *Sookr* ; the sixth range of mountains, dividing the known continent, the white mountains separating the *Vershus* of *Hirunmuy* and *Romunuk* ; one of the minor *Dweeps* or divisions of the world ; in fable the White Island, identified geographically by Wilford with Britain.

श्वेतद्वीप shwet-dwéep, *s. m.* The white island, or a minor division of the universe so called : also termed *Chundr Dweep*, and supposed by Wilford to be Britain.

श्वेतधातु shwet-dhátoo, *s. m.* Chalk ; the milk-stone, opal or chalcedony.

श्वेतसूर्प shwet-súrp, A tree (*Tapia crateva*) ; a white snake. [phant.

श्वेतहस्ती shwet-hústee, *s. m.* A white ele-

श्वेतार्क shwyt-árk, *s. m.* Gigantic swallow-wort (*Asclepias gigantea*), with white flowers.

ष

ष shuh, The thirty-first consonant of the *Naguree* alphabet, corresponding to *sh*, pronounced in some schools *kh*.

षट् khut, *adj.* Six.

षट्कर्म्मा khut-kurmmá, *s. m.* The six acts proper for a *Brahmun (collectively)*, or teaching the *Veds*, holy study, offering sacrifices, conducting them for others, giving, accepting gifts ; six acts allowable to a *Brahmun* for subsistence, or gleaning, accepting gifts, asking alms, agriculture, trade, and tending cattle, or according to some lending money at interest ; the six acts taught in the *Tuntrus*, or killing, infatuating, enthralling, expelling, exciting animosity, and the stopping or privation of any faculty.

षट्कोण khut-kón, *s. m.* A hexagon, a six-angled figure.

षडङ्ग khurúng, *s. m.* Six parts of the body collectively, as the two arms, two legs, and the head and waist ; the six supplementary parts of the *Veds*, or grammar, prosody, astronomy, pronunciation, the meaning of unusual terms, and the ritual of the *Hindoo* religion.

षड्गुण khur-góon, *adj.* Six-fold, six times. *s. m.* An assemblage of six qualities or properties.

षड्विध khur-vídh, *adj.* In six ways, of six kinds.

षण्ड shund, *s. m.* A bull at liberty.

षण्ढ khundh, *s. m.* A eunuch.

स

स suh, The thirty-second consonant of the *Naguree* alphabet, corresponding to *s*.

सं sun, *adv.* (*In compos.*) With, together with, &c.

संकची súnkchee, *s. f.* A scate.

संकट súnkut, *s. m.* Vexation, misfortune, pang, agony, pain, anguish. *Sunkut-chouth*, A *Hindoo* holiday, in the month of *Magh*, sacred to *Gunesh*.

संका sunká, *s. f.* Fear, terror, doubt, suspicion.

संकार sunkár, *s. f.* A sign, nod, wink, beckoning. *Sunkarna*, *v. a.* To beckon, nod, wink or make a signal, to hint.

संकोच sunkóch, *s. m.* Shame, bashfulness, reserve, diffidence ; a scate.

संकोचन sunkóchun, *s. m.* The act of shrinking.

संकोची sunkóchee, *adj.* Bashful, reserved, diffident.

संक्रान्ती sunkrántee, *s. f.* The sun's entering into a new sign.

संकल्प sunkulp, *s. m.* A solemn vow or declaration of purpose. *Sunkulpna*, *v. a.* To give alms (*by making a religious vow*), to vow.

संख sunkh, *s. m.* A conch which the *Hindoos* blow, a shell ; a kind of ornament. *adj.* Simple, artless. *Dupol sunkh, adj.* Promising much and performing nothing.

संखाडली sunkhahóolee, *s. f.* A medicinal plant (*Andropogon aciculatum ?*)

संखिनी sunkhínee, *s. f.* A description of women. (*The Sunkhinee are described as tall, with long hair, neither stout nor thin, of irascible disposition and strong passions*).

संख्या sunkhyá, *s. f.* A number. *s. m.* Arsenic.

संग sung, *adv.* Along with.

संगत súngut, *s. f.* Coition ; collection, congregation, company, society ; a place where the *Sikhs* celebrate their religious ceremonies. *adj.* Apposite, proper. *Sungutee, s. m. f.* Companion, comrade.

संगम súngum, *s. m.* Coition ; meeting, conflux, union.

संगर súngur, *s. m.* Lines, entrenchment.

संगसी súngsee, *s. f.* Pincers, forceps.

संगी sungée, *s. m.* A companion, a comrade, an accomplice.

संगीत sungéet, *s. m.* The exhibition of a song, dancing and music as a public entertainment ; the art and science of music and dancing. *Sungeet durpun,* A book on music. *Sungeet-nach,* A kind of dance.

संग्रह sungrúh, *s. m.* A compilation.

संग्रहनी sungruhúnee, *s. m.* A disorder, an irregular state of the bowels, costiveness alternately with a diarrhœa.

संग्राम sungrám, *s. m.* Battle, war.

संघात sunghát, *s. m.* Companionship, society, assemblage. *Sunghatee, s. m.* A companion, a friend, an associate.

संघिया sunghíya, *s. m.* A companion.

संचय sunchúy, *s. m.* Purse, capital, stock, saving, heaping up, hoard.

संचार sunchár, *s. m.* Entrance, penetration ; beginning, commencement ; the entering of the planets into a new sign.

संचारिका sunchárika, *s. f.* A bawd, a procuress.

संचित sunchit, *adj.* Hoarded, collected.

संछेप sunchhép, *adj.* Abridged, short. *Sunchhepun, s. m.* Abridgment, abbreviation, conciseness, brevity.

संज्ञा sungyá, *s. f.* A noun ; a metaphor, an idiomatical phrase.

संन्यासी sunnyásee, *s. m.* A *Brahmun* of the fourth order, a religious mendicant.

संपत sumpút, *s. f.* Affluence, wealth, riches, prosperity.

3 N

संपन्न sumpúnn, *adj.* Perfect, complete, endowed with.

संपूर्ण sumpóorn, *adj.* Perfect, full, complete, all, the whole.

संवत sumbút, *s. m.* A year ; an era. *Sumbut bandhna,* To establish an era.

संबंध sumbúndh, *s. m.* Connexion, affinity, relation ; rhyme, metre. *Sumbundhee, s. m.* Relation ; son or daughter's father-in-law.

संबोधन sumbódhun, *s. m.* Comfort, soothing, encouragement, the act of consoling ; vocative case.

संभव sumbhúv, *adj.* Possible, fit, right, proper, suitable.

संभलना sumbhúlna, *v. n.* To be supported, to stand, stop, to be firm, to recover one's self from a fall, &c.

संभालना sumbhálna, *v. a.* To support, prop, sustain, hold up, assist, help ; to shield, protect, stop, retain, restrain, check, repress.

संभावना sumbháona, *s. f.* Probability.

संभोग sumbhóg, *s. m.* Enjoyment ; coition.

संभ्रम sumbhrúm, *s. m.* Esteem, respect, honour, awe.

संमान sunmán, *s. m.* Respect, esteem, reverence, regard. *Sunmanee, adj.* Polite, civil ; respectful.

संमुख sunmóokh, *adv.* Opposite, confronting, in face, over against.

संयम sunjúm, *s. m.* Restraint, forbearance, soberness, abstinence from particular food on certain days. *Sunjumee, adj.* Who or what checks, restrains, curbs, &c., sober, temperate, abstemious. *s. m.* A saint, a sage, one who subdues or controuls his passions.

संयुक्त sunjóokt, *adj.* Joined with, connected, attached ; mixed, blended ; endowed with, possessed of.

संयोग sunjóg, *s. m.* Intimate union or association ; adherence, junction, conjunction ; accident, event, occurrence, chance, hap, luck.

संयोगी sunjógee, *s. m.* An ascetic who does not observe a vow of continence, but has a family.

संलग्न sunlúgn, *adj.* Joined, united, adherent.

संवत sumvút, *s. m.* A year ; an era.

संवत्सर sumvútsur, *s. m.* A year.

संवरना sunwúrna, *v. n.* To be dressed, prepared or arranged, to be decorated, to suit, prosper.

संवाद sumvád, } *s. m.* Communication of
संबाद sumbád, } intelligence ; information, news.

संवारना sunwárna, *v. a.* To prepare, dress,

deck, decorate, adjust, adorn, arrange, accomplish.

संशय súnshuy, *s. m.* Doubt, uncertainty ; dread, apprehension.

संशयात्मा sunshuy-átma, *s. m.* A sceptic.

संशयान sunshuyán, *adj.* Dubious, uncertain.

संशयापन्न sunshuy-apunn, *adj.* Affected with doubt, hesitating, dubious ; doubtful, uncertain.

संशयालु sunshúy-aloo, *adj.* Dubious, doubting, sceptical.

संशनाना sunsunána, *v. n.* To jingle, to ring ; to faint ; to simmer. *Sunsunahut, s. f.* An imitative sound, ringing, jingling ; simmering ; fainting.

संसय sunsúy, *s. m.* Doubt, apprehension fear, anxiety.

संसर्ग sunsúrg, *s. m.* Union, proximity, approximation, contact ; acquaintance, familiarity, intercourse ; sensual attachment.

संसर्गी sunsúrgee, *adj.* Familiar, friendly, keeping company, acquainted, an acquaintance.

संसार sunsár, *s. m.* The world, the habitation of mortals.

संसारी sun-sáree, *adj.* Worldly, mundane.

संस्कार suns-kár, *s. m.* Completing, accomplishing, finishing, perfecting ; an essential and purificatory rite or ceremony amongst the Hindoos ; purification, consecration.

संस्कृत sun-skrít, *adj.* Wrought, made, artificially produced ; excellent, best ; decorated, ornamented. *s. m.* Language formed by perfect grammatical rules, the classical and sacred language of the Hindoos.

संस्थान sun-sthán, *s. m.* A place where four roads meet ; form, figure, shape ; fabrication, construction ; a vicinity, a neighbourhood, a common place of abode.

संस्पर्श sun-spúrsh, *s. m.* Touching, contact, laying hold of.

संहत sung-hút, *adj.* Compact, close ; collected, assembled.

संहतता sung-huttá, *s. f.* Compactness ; approximation, contact.

संहति súng-huti, *s. f.* Assemblage, collection, heap ; union, junction ; compactness.

संहार sung-hár, *s. m.* Destruction, loss ; the destruction of the world ; making away, killing, murdering. *adj.* Killed.

संहारना sung-hárna, *v. a.* To kill, to make away with.

संहिता sung-hitá, *s. f.* An arrangement of the text of the *Veds* into short sentences ; a compendium, a collection more or less compressed of laws, legends, &c.

सकुठ súkut, *adj.* Bad, vile. *s. m.* A small tree (*Trophis aspera*) ; a cart ; the name of a *Hindoo* holiday.

सकुंटक sukúntuk, *adj.* Thorny, prickly ; troublesome, perilous, *s. m.* An aquatic plant (*Vallisneria*).

सकत súkut, *s. f.* Power, strength, ability ; the energy or active power of a deity ; the female organ as the counterpart of the phallick personification of *Shiv*, and worshipped either literally or figuratively by a sect of *Hindoos*, thence termed *Saktus*.

सकना súkna, *v. n.* To be able.

सकरा súkra, *adj.* Small (*not having room enough*), narrow, strait.

सकराई suk-ráee, *s. f.* Smallness, want of room, narrowness.

सकराना sukrána, *v. a.* To straiten, to deprive of necessary room ; to cause to accept (*bill, &c.*)

सक्रांत sukránt, *s. f.* The entering of the sun into a new sign.

सकर्म्मुक sukúrmmuk, *s. m.* (*In grammar*) The transitive verb.

सकल súkul, *adj.* All, whole, entire.

सकाना sukána, *v. n.* To be sorrowful, to be wearied.

सकार sukár, *s. m.* Dawn of day, morning.

सकारन sukárun, *adj.* Having a cause, originating from a cause.

सकारना sukárna, *v. a.* To accept (*a bill of exchange, &c.*)

सकारी sukáree, *s. f.* Dawn of day, morning.

सकाल sukál, *adv.* Betimes, early in the morning.

सकुच sukooch, *s. f.* Shrinking, awe, fear, shame.

सकुचना súkoochna, *v. n.* To fear, to be afraid of, to be in awe of, to be abashed, to apprehend, to be apprehensive.

सकुचाना súkooch-ána, *v. n.* To be abashed, to be afraid. *v. a.* To abash.

सकुल्यह sukólyuh, *s. m.* A kinsman, one of the same family name and common origin.

सकेत sukét, *adj.* Narrow, strait. *s. f.* Want, distress.

सकेतना sukét-na, *v. a.* To tighten, to straiten.

सकेलना sukélna, *v. n.* To shrink, to shrivel, to gather up (*the limbs, as a tortoise*).

सकेला sukéla, *s. m.* A kind of iron.

सकोच sukóch, *s. m.* Regard, respect, esteem.

सुकोरना sukorna, *v. n.* To shrink, to draw up (*the limbs*), to gather up, shrivel, tighten, contract. *v. a.* To contract, draw up.

सुकोप sukóp, *adj.* Angry, displeased.

सुकोरा sukóra, *s. m.* A small earthen vessel.

सुकोरी sukóree, *s. f.* A saucer.

सुक्तूक suktóok, *s. m.* A species of poison.

सुक्तूफूला súktoo-phúla, *s. f.* A tree (*Mimosa Suma*).

सखा sukhá, *s. m.* A friend; an associate, a companion.

सखित्वह sukhi-twúh, *s. m.* Friendship.

सखी sukhée, *s. f.* A woman's female friend or companion, a confidante, &c.

सखीजन sukhee-jún, *s. f.* A female friend or confidante.

सख्युह súkhyuh, *s. m.* Friendship.

सुगन्ध súgundh, *adj.* Fragrant, ordoriferous.

सुगपूहता sug-púhta, *s. m.* Greens dressed with pulse.

सुगर súgur, *adj.* Poisonous. *s. m.* A sovereign of *Ujodhya*.

सुगर्व्व sugúrvv, *adj.* Proud; elated.

सुगा súga, *adj.* Related (*of the same parents*), full, own; a relative, a kin. *s. m.* Kin. *Suga bhaee,* Own brother.

सुगाई sugaée, } *s. f.* Relationship by
सुगावत sugawút, } the same parents, consanguinity, relationship, kin; betrothing for marriage; second marriage of a woman of low tribe. *Sugaee kurna,* To contract a marriage, to affiance, to betroth.

सुगुण súgoon, *adj.* Having or endowed with properties, qualities, &c.

सुगन súgoon, *s. m.* Augury, omen.

सुगोती sugótee, *s. f.* Animal food, meat, flesh.

सुगोत्र sugótr, *adj.* Being of one family, of kin, related. *s. m.* A distant kinsman.

सुघन sughún, *adj.* Thick (*as a head of hair, clouds, wood, &c.*).

सुकुट súnkut, *adj.* Narrow, contracted. *s. m.* Difficulty, trouble, vexation, misfortune, pang, agony, pain, anguish.

सुकर súnkur, *s. m.* Mixing, blending, confounding; a mixed caste or race, one proceeding from the promiscuous intercourse of the four tribes in the first instance, and again from their commerce with the descendants of such a connexion, or the indiscriminate cohabitation of those descendants amongst one another: most *Hindoos* of the present age are of one of the many branches of this race, the highest of which is impure and

inferior to the *Soodr*: under this term (*Sunkur*) two kinds of men are included according to the *Ramayun,* the one denominated *yonisunkur*, mixed or degraded by birth, and the other, *achursunkur,* degraded by conduct.

सुकर्षण sun-kúrshun, *s. m.* Attracting, drawing.

सुकल sun-kúl, *s. m.* Collection, quantity; addition (*in arithmetic*).

सुकलन sun-kulún, *s. m.* Contact, junction; addition (*in arithmetic*).

सुकलित sun-kulít, *adj.* Heaped, piled, arranged; added. *s. m.* Addition (*in arithmetic*).

सुकल्प súnkulp, *s. m.* Volition, will, resolve, mental determination; a solemn vow or declaration of purpose.

सुकल्पना sunkulp-ná, *v. a.* To give alms (*by making a religious vow*), to vow.

सुकीर्ण sun-kéern, *adj.* Crowded, confused.

सुकीर्त्तन sun-kéerttun, *s. m.* Celebrating, praising; honour, glorification.

सुकूचित súnk-oochit, *adj.* Unblown, unopened; abashed.

सुकूल súnkool, *adj.* Crowded, confused, filled with so as to be impervious.

सुकेत sun-két, *s. m.* Engagement, agreement; sign, gesture, gesticulation.

सुकेतस्थान sunket-sthán, *s. m.* A place of assignation.

सुकोच sun-kóch, *s. m.* Shutting, closing, contracting, contraction; shame, bashfulness, reserve, diffidence; a sort of fish, a scate (*Raia Sancura*).

सुकोचन sun-kóchun, *s. m.* Astringing; causing to shrink or close; the act of shrinking.

सुकोची sun-kóchee, *adj.* Bashful, reserved, diffident.

सुक्रम sun-krúm, *s. m.* Going, moving, travelling; the passage of a planetary body through the zodiac.

सुक्रान्त sun-kránt, *adj.* Entered (*into a new sign*).

सुक्रान्ति sun-kránti, *s. f.* The actual passage of the sun or other planetary bodies from one sign of the zodiac into another.

सुक्षेप sunkshép, *s. m.* Abridgment, abbreviation, conciseness, compression.

सुख्युता sunkhyutá, *s. f.* Number, numeration, counting.

सुख्या sún-khya, *s. f.* Number in general, or a number, a numeral. *s. m.* Arsenic.

सुग sung, *s. m.* Meeting, encountering; joining, uniting.

सुगत sún-gut, *s. m.* Friendship, acquaintance; union, meeting.

सड्गति sún-guti, *s. f.* Meeting, union ; association, intercourse ; coition ; collection, congregation, company, society ; a place where the *Sikhs* celebrate their religious ceremonies.

सड्गम sún-gum, *s. m.* Meeting, union, junction, the encounter of persons, the association of friends or lovers, the confluence of rivers ; coition ; (*in astronomy*) Planetary conjunction.

सड्गर sun-gúr, *s. m.* War, battle ; misfortune, calamity ; promise, assent, agreement ; lines, entrenchment.

सड्गसी sung-sée, *s. f.* Pincers, forceps.

सड्गी sungée, *adj.* Uniting with, going to or with, attached ; libidinous, lustful, desirous. *s. m.* A companion, a comrade, an accomplice.

सड्गीत sun-géet, *s. m.* The exhibition of song, dancing, and music, as a public entertainment ; the art or science of music and dancing.

सड्गोपन sun-gó-pun, *s. m.* Hiding, concealment.

सड्ग्रह sungrúh, *s. m.* A compilation and abridgment ; quantity, collection.

सड्ग्रहण sun-gruhún, *s. m.* Collecting, compiling.

सड्ग्रहणी sun-gruhunée, *s. f.* Diarrhœa, dysentery.

सड्ग्राम sun-grám, *s. m.* War, battle.

सड्घ sungh, *s. m.* Flock, multitude, number, a collection of living beings either of the same or different species ; a heap, a quantity in general.

सच such, *adj.* True. *s. m.* Truth. *adv.* Indeed ; in earnest, actually, truly.

सचमुच such-múoch, *adj.* or *adv.* True, truly.

सचराचर suchur-áchur, *adj.* All whether animate or inanimate.

सचाई suchée, *s. f.* Truth, veracity, honesty, probity, authenticity.

सचि súchi, *s. m.* Friendship, intimacy, connexion.

सचेत suchét, *adj.* With circumspection, with caution, with reflection or consideration, mindful, conscious, attentive, cautious.

सचेतन suchet-ún, *adj.* Rational ; conscious, sensible.

सचेष्ट suchésht, *adj.* Active, making effort.

सचोटी suchóutee, *s. f.* Fidelity, rectitude, honesty, truth.

सच्चा súchcha, *adj.* True, genuine, real, honest, just, sincere, faithful, sure.

सच्चाई such-cháee, *s. f.* Truth, veracity, honesty, probity, authenticity.

सचिदानन्द súchchi-dánund, *s. m. Bruhm* or the Supreme Spirit.

सज suj, *s. m.* Shape, ornament, appearance, preparation. *Sujdar,* Well-shaped, handsome.

सजधज suj-dhuj, *s. f.* Preparation and appearance.

सजन sújun, *s. m. f.* A respectable person, a sweetheart, a mistress.

सजना súj-na, *v. n.* To be prepared ; to fit, to become, to beseem. *v. a.* To dress, to ornament, to accoutre, to adjust, to rectify. *s. m.* A respectable person, a sweetheart, a mistress.

सजल sújul, *adj.* With water, watery, wet, filled with or containing water.

सजला súj-la, *s. m.* Third brother of four or more.

सजवाना sujwána, *v. a.* To cause to prepare.

सजाई sujáee, *s. f.* The price paid for making belts or scabbards ; preparation.

सजाति sújati, *adj.* Of the same sort or species, of the same tribe, &c.

सजाना sujána, *v. a.* To cause to prepare.

सजाव sujáo, *s. m.* Preparation, ornament.

सजावट sujawút, *s. f.* Preparation ; contrivance.

सजीला suj-éela, *adj.* Well-shaped, handsome, graceful.

सजीव sujéev, *adj.* Alive, living.

सज्जन sujjún, *adj.* Of good family, wellborn ; respectable, reputable ; good, virtuous. *s. m. f.* A respectable person, a sweetheart, a mistress.

सज्जा sújja, *adj.* Armed, accoutered ; ornamented, decorated. *s. f.* Dress, decoration ; armour, mail.

सज्जी súijee, *s. f.* A kind of mineral alkali, natron, impure carbonate of Soda.

सञ्चय sún-chuy, *s. m.* Heap, quantity, number, multitude ; purse, capital, stock, store, saving, heaping up, hoard.

सञ्चयी sun-chuy-ée, *adj.* Who collects, gathers, heaps or hoards up.

सञ्चार sun-chár, *s. m.* Difficult progress ; a gem supposed to be in the head of a serpent.

सञ्चारिका sun-chárika, *s. f.* A female messenger or go-between ; a bawd.

सञ्चित sún-chit, *adj.* Accumulated, collected, gathered.

सञ्चिता sun-chit-á, *s. f.* A plant (*Salvinia cucullata*).

सज्ञान sugyán, *adj.* With knowledge ; knowing, intelligent, wise. *Sugyanes, adj.* Wise, intelligent.

सटक sút-uk, *s. f.* An elastic rod, thick at one end and thin at the other.

सटकना **sútuk-na**, *v. n.* To run away, to disappear, to flee, to sheer off.

सटकाइ **sut-káee**, *s. f.* Taperingness, vanishing of a tapering body at the extreme point, disappearance.

सटकाना **sutkána**, *v. a.* To balk, to disappoint, to cause to disappear.

सटना **sútna**, *v. n.* To join, to adhere, to stick, to unite.

सटपटाना **sutputána**, *v. n.* To be confounded, to be surprised.

सटल **sutúl**, *s. f.* Foolish prattle, falsehood. *Sutules*, *s. f.* Chattering nonsense, falsehood.

सटाना **sut-ána**, *v. a.* To unite, stick, make adhere.

सटासट **sut-asút**, *s. f.* Sticking or striking together, adhering, uniting.

सटिया **sútiya**, *s. f.* A stick.

सटी **sút-ee**, *s. f.* Zedoary (*Curcuma zerumbet*, but applied also to the *Curcuma amada*).

सटीसटी **sútee-sútee**, *adj.* Joined, glued, stuck together, crowded.

सटीक **sutéek**, *adj.* Accompanied or explained by a commentary.

सट्टाबट्टा **suttá-buttá**, *s. m.* An amour, combination, collusion.

सठ **suth**, *adj.* Cunning; ignorant.

सठियाना **suthiyána**, *v. n.* To be turned of sixty years; to be decrepid, or in one's dotage, to be superannuated.

सठोड़ा **suthóra**, *s. m.* A sweetmeat, consisting of meal, sugar, ginger, spices, &c. (*particularly given medicinally to child-bed women, and distributed, as caudle is, to gossips*).

सड़क **súr-uk**, *s. f.* A road.

सड़न **súr-un**, *s. f.* Rottenness, rot, putrefaction.

सड़ना **súr-na**, *v. n.* To rot; to ferment.

सड़ा **súr-a**, *adj.* Rotten, musty, stinking.

सड़ाना **sur-ána**, *v. a.* To cause to rot; to make ferment, to steep.

सड़ाहट **sur-ahút**, *s. f.* Rottenness, mustiness.

सड़ाहिन्द **sur-áhind**, *s. f.* A disagreeable smell, fumette, smell of putrid meat.

सनसूत्र **sun-sóotr**, *s. m.* Packthread.

सण्ड **sund**, *s. m.* A eunuch.

सण्डसी **súnd-see**, *s. f.* Tongs, pincers.

सण्डा **sún-da**, *adj.* Strong, fat, stout. *s. m.* Hardened excrement, Scybala.

सण्डास **sundás**, *s. m.* A necessary, a water closet (*opening into the streets*), a sink.

सण्डासा **sun-dása**, *s. m.* Large pincers.

सण्डासी **sun-dásee**, *s. m.* A class of *Hindoo* mendicants.

सत् **sut**, *adj.* True; right, actual; good, virtuous. *s. m.* The True God, the always present and all-pervading spirit; power, strength, essence, the principal of goodness; juice, sap; virtue; truth. *adv.* Actually.

सतमासा **sut-mása**, *s. m.* A feast given in the seventh month of pregnancy.

सतमी **sútmee**, *s. f.* The seventh lunar day.

सतरह **sút-ruh**, *adj.* Seventeen.

सतराना **sut-rána**, *v. n.* To be angry.

सतलड़ा **sut-lúr-a**, *adj.* Seven-fold, of seven strings or rows (*a chain of pearls, &c.*)

सतलड़ी **sut-lur-ée**, *s. f.* A necklace of seven strings.

सतवन्ता **sutwúnta**, *adj.* Virtuous, chaste, honest, adhering to truth.

सतसठ **sút-suth**, *adj.* Sixty-seven.

सतसैया **sut-syya**, *s. f.* The name of a book written by *Biharee-lall* (*an inhabitant of Gwalior*), containing 700 distiches or dohas in *Brij-bhakha*.

सतहत्तर **sut-húttur**, *adj.* Seventy-seven.

सताना **sut-ána**, *v. a.* To tease, vex, fret, trouble, afflict, ail, harm, interrupt, annoy, grieve, harass. *Satáoo*, *s. m. f.* Vexer, teaser, tormentor.

सती **sút-ee**, *adj. f.* Chaste, virtuous, constant. *s. f.* A virtuous wife; in ordinary use applied especially to the wife who burns herself with her husband's corpse.

सतीत्व **sutéetwuh**, *s. m.* Virtuousness or purity in a wife.

सतीर्थ **súteerth**, *s. m.* A fellow-student, the pupil of the same spiritual preceptor.

सतीला **sut-éela**, *adj.* Powerful, strong.

सतीबाड़ **sútee-wár**, *s. f.* A tomb, grave, burning ground, the place where a *sutee* is burned.

सतूआ **sutóoa**, *s. m.* Parched grain, reduced to meal and made into a paste. *adj.* (*Applied to a kind of ginger*) Pulverable, free from threads or fibres. *Sutooa sunkrant*, The entering of the sun into *Aries*, on which day the meal of parched grain is distributed to the *Brahmuns*.

सत्कर्म **sút-kurmm**, *s. m.* A good act, piety, virtue; hospitality; funeral obsequies.

सत्कार **sut-kár**, *s. m.* Reverence, respect; hospitable treatment or reception; doing good, a pious action.

सत्क्रिया **sut-kríya**, *s. f.* Funeral or obsequial ceremonies; doing good, charity, virtue, &c.; salutation, welcome, courtesy; hospitality.

सत्तम **suttúm**, *adj.* Best, excellent; very venerable or respectable; most virtuous.

सत्तर **súttur**, *adj.* Seventy. *Suttura-buhuttura*, *adj.* Old, decrepid, doting.

सुत्ता sútta, *s. f.* Being, existence; goodness, excellence. *s. m.* Power, strength.

सुतारेस suttáees, *adj.* Twenty-seven.

सुतानबे suttánweh, *adj.* Ninety-seven.

सुतावन suttawún, *adj.* Fifty-seven.

सुतासी suttasée, *adj.* Eighty-seven.

सुतार suttóor, *s. m.* An enemy.

सुतू suttóo, *s. m.* Parched grain, reduced to meal and made into a paste.

सुत्तु súttwuh, *s. m.* One of the three *Goons* or properties of man and nature, the quality of excellence or goodness; substance, thing; vigour, power; essence; a substantive noun.

सुत्तुगून súttwugóon, *s. m.* The property of goodness.

सुतुता suttwutá, *s. f.* Purity, goodness.

सुतपथ sut-púth, *s. m.* A good road; correct or virtuous conduct, doctrine, &c.

सुतपात्र sut-pátr, *s. m.* A worthy or virtuous person.

सुतपुत्र sut-póotr, *s. m.* A virtuous son.

सुतपुरुष sut-póoroosh, *s. m.* A worthy or spirited man.

सुतफल sút-phul, *s. m.* The pomegranate.

सुत्य sút-yuh, *adj.* True; sincere, honest, speaking the truth. *s. m.* Truth; an oath; the first *Yoog* or age, the golden age, comprising one million seven hundred and twenty-eight thousand years; the uppermost of the seven *Loks* or worlds, the abode of *Bruhm*, and heaven of truth.

सत्यता sutyutá, *s. f.* Truth, trueness.

सत्यम् sutyúm, *adv.* Indeed, verily, a particle of interrogation, and asseveration.

सत्ययुग sutyujóog, *s. m.* The first of the four *Yoogs* or ages, the period of general virtue and purity, or the golden age, comprising a term of 1,728,000 years.

सत्यलोक sutyulók, *s. m.* The uppermost of the seven *Loks* or worlds, the abode of *Bruhm*, and heaven of truth.

सत्यवचन sútyu-vúchun, *s. m.* Speaking truth.

त्यवादी sútyuh-vádee, *adj.* Who speaks truth.

सत्यसाक्षी sútyuh-sákshee, *s. m.* An unexceptionable witness.

सत्यात्मा sutyátma, *s. m.* A virtuous and upright man.

सत्यानाश sutyanás, *s. m.* (*a term of imprecation signifying*) Depravation, destruction. *Sutyanas kurna*, To make the ruin, destruction, or mischief (*of any one or any thing*). *Sutyanas jana*, or, — *hona*, To be the depravation, destruction, ruin, &c. (*of any one or any thing*), to be destroyed or ruined.

सत्यानाशी sutyanásee, *adj.* Depraved, bad, destroyed, damaged; a thorny plant.

सत्यानृत sutya-nrít, *s. m.* Commerce, trade, traffic (*being a mixed practice of truth and lies*).

सुत्व sútvuh, *s. m.* The quality of excellence or goodness.

सुत्वर sutwúr, *adj.* Quick, expeditious. *adv.* Quickly, swiftly.

सुत्वरता sutwurtá, *s. f.* Quickness, speed.

सुत्संग sut-súng, *s. m.* Association with the good.

सुत्वांस sut-wánsa, *adj.* Child born in the seventh month.

सुथराव suth-ráo, *s. m.* A heap of slain.

सुथवारा suth-wára, *s. m.* A sweetmeat given to a childbed woman.

सुथिया súthiya, *s. m.* A surgeon; a mark in form of a cross, the four arms of which are bent at right angles, prefixed in vermilion by *Hindoos* to their account books at the commencement of a new year; the same figure is formed on the ground with flour, at marriages and other ceremonies.

सुदन súdun, *s. m.* A place, house, mansion. [*ate.*

सुदय súduy, *adj.* Benevolent, compassionate.

सुद्या sudya, *s. f.* The female of the little bird called Amadavat; a kind of mendicant.

सुदस्य sudúsyuh, *s. m.* Any person present at an assembly, a spectator, an assessor, a member, &c.

सुदा súda, *adv.* Always, at all times.

सुदागति súda-gúti, *s. m.* Final happiness, emancipation from life; the Supreme Spirit.

सुदाचार sud-achár, *s. m.* Virtuous conduct.

सुदात्म sud-átma, *adj.* Good, virtuous.

सुदानन्द sud-anúnd, *adj.* Always happy.

सुदानर्त sud-anúrtt, *s. m.* A wagtail.

सुदापुष्पी súda-póoshpee, *s. f.* A shrub, gigantic swallow-wort, the white variety.

सुदाफल suda-phúl, *s. m.* The cocoanut tree; the glomerous fig-tree; the jack (*Artocarpus integrifolia?*); the Bel (*Ægle marmelos*).

सुदाव्रत suda-vrút, *s. m.* Alms, or food distributed daily to the poor, travellers, &c.

सुदाशिव súda-shív, *s. m.* Shiv.

सुदासुहागुन súda-soohágun, *s. f.* A bird (*Trogon dilectus*); a flower (*Hibiscus phœniceus, the white variety*); a kind of mendicant dressed like a woman.

सुदिया sudya, *s. f.* The female of the little bird called Amadavat.

सुदुत्तर sud-óottur, *s. m.* A proper or good reply.

सदृश sudrísh, *adj.* Like, similar.

सदृशता sudrish-tá, *s. f.* Likeness, sameness.

सदेश sudésh, *adj.* Near, proximate ; of the same country or place.

सदेह sudéh, *adj.* With body. *adv.* Bodily.

सद्गति sud-gúti, *s. f.* Felicity or fortune ; good conduct.

सद्गुण sud-góon, *adj.* Good, pure, virtuous ; excellent, eminent.

सद्भाव sud-bháo, *s. m.* A pure or holy disposition or nature ; a good temper ; amiability, kindly feeling ; the property of goodness.

सधन súdh-na, *v. n.* To be fully instructed or disciplined.

सधर्मी súdhurmmee, *adj.* Observing the same customs or laws.

सधवा sudh-wá, *s. f.* A wife, whose husband is living.

सधाना sudhána, *v. a.* To train animals ; to perform.

सन sun, *s. m.* Name of a plant (*Crotalaria juncea*), a kind of flax ; a tree (*Pentaptera tomentosa*).

सनसनाना sunsunána, *v. n.* To jingle, to ring ; to faint.

सनसूत्र sun-sóotr, *s. m.* Packthread, or a net made of it.

सनपात sun-pát, *s. m.* A disease in which the body is seized with universal chilliness, deliquium : it is explained by the *Hindoo* physicians to be that in which the three humours, bile, phlegm and atrabilis are corrupted.

सना súna, *s. m.* Senna.

सनातन sunátun, *adj.* Eternal, continual, perpetual ; firm, fixed, permanent.

सनाथा sunátha, *s. f.* A woman whose husband is living.

सनिया súniya, *s. m.* A kind of *Tusur* cloth.

सनीचर sun-éechur, *s. m.* Saturn, Saturday.

सनीचरा sunée-churá, *adj.* Unlucky (*fellow*). *s. m.* Name of a mountain near *Gwalior*.

सन्त sunt, *s. m.* A kind of devotee, a saint. *adj.* Pious, virtuous.

सन्तति suntúti, *s. f.* Race, lineage ; a son, a daughter, offspring, progeny.

सन्तप्त suntúpt, *adj.* Distressed, afflicted, wretched.

सन्त súnta, *adj.* Depraved ; miserly.

सन्तान suntán, *s. m.* Family, race, lineage ; offspring, progeny, a son or daughter, children.

सन्ताप suntáp, *s. m.* Heat, burning heat ; affliction, sorrow, pain, distress, misery, repentance.

सन्तापी suntapée, *adj.* Sad, sorrowful.

सन्ती súntee, *s. m.* A succedaneum.

सन्तुष्ट sun-tóosht, *adj.* Satisfied, gratified, delighted, content, pleased.

सन्तेह súnteh, *adv.* Instead, stead.

सन्तोष suntósh, suntókh, *s. m.* Content, patience, satiety, satisfaction, joy, pleasure, delight happiness, gratification. Suntokh kurna, To be patient, to be content.

सन्तोषी suntokhée, *adj.* Patient, contented ; consoled, comforted, gratified.

सन्दिग्ध sundígdh, *adj.* Doubted, questioned, doubtful.

सन्देश sun-désh, *s. m.* News, tidings, information ; a message.

सन्देशी sun-deshée, *s. m.* A messenger.

सन्देह sun-déh, *s. m.* Doubt, uncertainty, suspicion, apprehension, hesitation, anxiety.

सन्देही sun-dehée, *adj.* Doubtful, scrupulous, distrustful, suspicious.

सन्धान sun-dhán, *s. m.* Spying, prying into secrets. Sundhan pana, *v. a.* To trace, to discover.

सन्धाना sundhána, *s. m.* } Pickles, &c., acid
सन्धानी sundhánee, *s. f.* } preparation of the *Bel* and other fruits.

सन्धि súndhi, *s. m.* Union, junction, connexion, combination ; peace, making peace, pacification ; a hole, a chasm.

सन्ध्या sundhyá, *s. f.* Twilight, either morning or evening ; a period of time, forenoon, afternoon, or mid-day.

सन्ध्याकाल súndhya-kál, *s. m.* Twilight.

सन्ध्यासमय súndhya-súmuy, *s. m.* Evening twilight.

सन्नति súnnuti, *s. f.* Reverence, obeisance, reverential salutation.

सन्न sunna, *v. n.* To be impregnated ; to be stained, soiled, smeared or defiled ; to be kneaded, mixed up (*as flour, dough, earth, &c.*)

सन्नाटा sunnáta, *s. m.* The roaring of the waves, rumbling noise made by wind and rain at a distance, sound, bluster.

सन्निकर्ष sunni-kúrsh, *s. m.* } Proximity,
सन्निधान sunni-dhán, *s. m.* } approxima-
सन्निधि sunnídhi, *s. f.* } tion, nearness.

सन्निपात sunni-pát, *s. m.* Morbid state of the three humours.

सन्निहित sunnihít, *adj.* Near, proximate, at hand, present.

सन्मान sun-mán, *s. m.* Respect for the good ; respect, esteem, reverence, regard.

सन्मानी sun-mánee, *adj.* Polite, civil ; respectful.

सम्मुख sún-mookh, adj. Opposite, confronting, in face, over against.

सन्यास sunnyás, s. m. Abandonment of all worldly affections and possessions.

सन्यासी sunnyasée, s. m. The *Brahmun* of the fourth order, the religious mendicant; an ascetic, a devotee.   [tion.

सपथ supúth, s. f. An oath, an assevera-

सपदि súpdi, adv. Instantly, in a moment, quickly, swiftly.

सपना súp-na, s. m. A dream.

सप्न supn, } s. m. A dream. *Supn-*
सपना súpna, } *dosh, s. m.* Nocturnal pollution. *Supna-bicharee, s. m.* An interpreter of dreams.

सपल्लव supúlluv, adj. With sprouts, shoots, or twigs (*a pot, &c. in times of rejoicing*).

सपक्ष súpuksh, s. m. A partisan, a follower, an adherent, one of the same side or party.

सपूत supóotr, } s. m. A tractable and duti-
सपूत supóot, } ful son.

सपोला supóla, } s. m. A young snake
सपोलिया supóliya, } just hatched.

सप्तमी suptumée, s. f. The seventh day of the fortnight.

सप्ताह suptáh, s. m. A week.

सफरी súphree, s. f. A small glistening fish, commonly termed *Poonthee*, a sort of carp (*Cyprinus Sophore*).

सफल súphul, adj. Productive, fruitful, bearing fruit, yielding a profit, &c.

सब sub, adj. All, every, the whole, total. (*In the inflection of the plural this word generally becomes Subhon*). *Sub koochh,* Every thing, all. *Sub koee,* Every body, every one. *Sub khowwa,* Omnivorous, one who eats all kinds of food without exception. *Sub misree kee hyn duliyan (all are pieces of sugar*), is applied to denote equality or similitude of state, form, &c.

सबल súbul, adj. Powerful, forcible.

सबलाई subulaée, s. f. Power, force, strength.

सबेर subér, adj. Early, soon, in good time.

सबेरा subéra, s. m. Morning, dawn.

सबेरे súbereh, adv. In the morning, early, soon.

सबोतर subótur, adj. Everywhere.

सब्द subd, s. m. Sound in general; a sound, a word; (*in gram.*) a declinable word, as a noun, pronoun, &c.; a song (*among Nanuk-punthees*).

सभय súbhuy, adj. Fearing, fearful.

सभा subhá, s. f. An assembly, meeting, company.

सभापति súbha-púti, s. m. The president of an assembly.

सभासद subha-súd, s. m. One of a company, an assistant at an assembly or meeting; (*in law*) an assessor.

सभ्य súbhyuh, adj. Trusted, confidential, faithful. s. m. An assistant at an assembly; an assessor.

सभ्यता subhyutá, s. f. Politeness, refinement in manners.

सम sum, adj. All, whole, entire; like, similar. s. m. A tone in music.

समझ súmujh, s. f. Understanding, comprehension, knowledge, opinion, conception, thought, mind.

समझना sumujh-ná, v. a. To understand, comprehend, suppose, think, conceive, consider, deem, fancy, perceive, apprehend, know, come to an understanding (*with*).

समझवार sumujh-wár, adj. Prudent, wise, considerate.

समझाना sumjhá-na, v. a. To make comprehend, to explain, to account for, to convince, describe, inform, satisfy, undeceive, warn, admonish, instruct, apologize.

समझावा sum-jháwa, } s. f. Act of ex-
समझौती sum-jhóutee, } plaining, convincing or giving confidence.

समंजस sumúnjus, adj. Proper, right, fit. s. m. Propriety, fitness.

समता sumtá, s. f. Sameness, similarity, equality, similitude, parallelism, resemblance, comparison, parity.

समदर्शी súm-durshee, s. m. Impartial, equally viewing both sides.

समदुःख súm-dookh, adj. Sympathizing, feeling for another's woe.

समधन súm-dhun, s. f. Child's mother-in-law.

समधमिलावा sumudh-miláwa, s. m. The mutual embracing of two *Sumdhees.*

समधियाना sumdhi-yána, s. m. The family of a child's father-in-law.

समधी sum-dhée, s. m. Child's father-in-law.

समभाव sum-bháo, adj. Of like nature or property. s. m. Equability; sameness.

समभूमि sum-bhóomi, s. f. Even ground.

समय súmuy, s. m. Time; leisure, opportunity; season, fit or proper time for any thing.

समर súmur, s. m. War, battle, conflict.

समर्थ sumúrth, adj. Strong, powerful; able, adequate to, capable. s. m. Strength, power.

समर्थक sumurthúk, s. m. Aloe wood (*Amyris agallocha*).

समर्थता sumurth-tá, *s. f.* Strength, power, prowess; ability, capability, adequacy.

समर्थी sumurthée, *adj.* Strong, powerful.

समर्पण sum-úrpun, *s. m.* Delivering, consigning, committing, entrusting to another.

समर्पित sum-urpít, *adj.* Delivered, made over, consigned.

समर्याद súmurjád, *adj.* Correct in conduct.

समल súmul, *adj.* Dirty, muddy, filthy.

समस्त súm-ust, *adj.* All, whole, entire, complete.

समा súm-a, } *s. m.* Time, season; plenty,
समन suman, } abundance; state, condition; concord, harmony, unison. *Sumabundhna v. n.* To be in concert.

समाई sumáee, *s. f.* Endurance; patience; capability.

समाख्या sum-ákhya, *s. f.* Fame, reputation.

समाख्यात sum-akhyát, *adj.* Famed, celebrated; notorious, public.

समागत sumagút, *adj.* Arrived, approached; met, encountered; united, joined.

समागति súma-gúti, *s. f.* Arrival, approach; union, joining; encountering, meeting; similar condition or progress.

समागम sumagúm, *s. m.* Union, junction; arrival, approach; association, acquaintance, intercourse; encounter, meeting.

समाचार sum-achár, *adj.* Equal or like in virtuous conduct. *s. m.* Information, tradition, news, tidings, intelligence, advice, account of circumstances or health, &c.

समाज sum-áj, *s. m.* A multitude, a number (*of any thing except beasts*); an assembly, a meeting; apparatus; society.

समाजी sumajée, *s. f.* Musicians that attend dancers.

समाधान sum-adhán, *s. m.* Religious meditation; promising, declaring; consolation, comfort, solace, pacification, adjustment, the act of satisfying.

समाधि sumádhi, *s. f.* Tomb of a *Jogee,* particularly where *Hindoos,* from religious motives, submit to be buried alive; deep and devout meditation; an exercise of austerity among *Jogees,* whereby they are supposed to acquire the power of suspending during their pleasure the connexion between their soul and body.

समान sum-án, *adj.* Like, akin, alike, similar, equal, adequate; one, uniform, same. *s. f.* Equality, level, rank.

समानकालीन sumán-kaléen, *adj.* Occurring or produced at the same period.

समानजन्मा sumán-júnma, *adj.* Of equal age.

समानता suman-tá, *s. f.* Sameness, resemblance, equality, likeness; community of kind or quality.

समान sum-ána, *v. n.* To be contained in, to go into.

समापन sum-ápun, *s. m.* Conclusion, completion, finish.

समापन्न sum-apúnn, *adj.* Finished, done, completed, concluded.

समापित sum-apít, } *adj.* Finished, done,
समाप्त sumápt, } concluded, completed, accomplished, perfected.

समाप्ति sumápti, *s. f.* End, conclusion, completion, perfection, finish.

समाली sum-álee, *s. f.* A collection of flowers, a nosegay, &c.

समालू sum-áloo, *s. m.* A plant (*Vitex trifolia* and *negundo*).

समाव sumáo, *s. m.* Room, space.

समावेश sum-avésh, *s. m.* Entrance.

समास sum-ás, *s. m.* Contraction, abridgment, conciseness; composition of words, formation of compound terms (*in grammar*).

समिति súmiti, *s. f.* Sameness, likeness, equality.

समिध súmidh, *s. f.* Fuel, wood, grass, &c. employed to kindle or light a fire.

समीकरण súmee-kúrun, *s. m.* (*In arithmetic*) Equation.

समीप suméep, *adj.* Near, contiguous, proximate, at hand. *postpos. mas.* Near.

समीपता sumeeptá, *s. f.* Proximity, contiguity.

समीपी suméepee, *s. f.* Proximity, nearness.

समुचित súmoochit, *adj.* Fit, right, proper.

समुच्चय sumoochchúy, *s. m.* Assemblage, collection, either in thought or fact; conjunction of words or sentences.

समुत्पत्ति sum-ootpútti, *s. f.* Origin, production, birth.

समुत्पन्न sum-ootpúnn, *adj.* Born, produced.

समुत्सव sum-ootsúv, *s. m.* Festivity.

समुदय sum-óoduy, *s. m.* Ascent, rise; rising (*as of the sun, &c.*)

समुदाय súmoodáyuh, *s. m.* Multitude, quantity, number, heap. *adj.* Aggregate.

समुद्र súmoodr, *s. m.* A sea, an ocean.

समुद्रकफ sumoodr-kúph, *s. m.* Cuttle-fish bone.

समुद्रतट sumoodr-tút, *s. m.* The sea coast.

समुद्रतीर sumoodr-téer, *s. m.* The sea shore.

समुद्रफेन sumoodr-phén, *s. m.* The dorsal scale or Cuttle-fish bone (*Sepia officinalis*).

समुद्रलवण sumoodr-lúvun, *s. m.* Sea salt.

समुद्रवह्नि sumoodr-vúhni, *s. m.* Submarine fire.

समुद्रसोख sumoodr-sókh, *s. m.* A medicine (*Convolvulus argentius*).

समुद्रान्त sumoodr-ánt, *s. m.* The sea shore. *adv.* As far as the sea.

समुद्रान्ता sumoodr-ánta, *s. f.* A shrub (*Hedysarum alhagi*); the cotton plant; a gramineous plant (*Trigonella corniculata*).

समुद्राव sumoodr-ároo, *s. m.* A shark; a large fabulous fish, perhaps intending the whale, hyperbolically described.

समुद्रिक sumóo-drik, *s. f.* Palmistry, fortune-telling, the art of physiognomy.

समुद्रिकी sumoodríkee, *s. m.* A fortune-teller, a physiognomist, a palmister.

समुद्रिय sumoodríyuh, *adj.* Marine, oceanic, maritime.

समूचा sumóocha, *adj.* Entire, whole.

समूह sumóoh, *s. m.* Assemblage, aggregate in general, heap, number, multitude, quantity, &c.

समें súmen,
समय súmuy,
समया súmuya,
} *s. m.* Time, season; leisure, opportunity.

समेट sumét, *s. f.* An astringent, a medicine used by women for constringing purposes; contraction.

समेटना sumetná, *v. a.* To collect together, to amass; to constringe, contract, compress, brace, to cause to shrivel or shrink.

समेत sumét, *adv.* With, along with, together with.

समो sumó, *s. m.* Season, time.

समोना sumóna, *v. a.* To cool warm water by mixing it with cool water.

सम्पत्ति súm-putti, *s. f.* Prosperity, success, increase of wealth, power, or happiness; a sort of medicinal root.

सम्पद् sumpúd, *s. f.* Success, prosperity, increase of any favourable kind, or of wealth, fame, power, &c.; advancement in good qualities, perfection, excellence; a necklace of pearls, &c.

सम्पन्न sum-púnn, *adj.* Accomplished, completed, effected, obtained; prosperous, fortunate, thriving, happy.

सम्पर्क sumpúrk, *s. m.* Mixture, mingling, contact, union, junction; copulation.

सम्पादक sum-padúk, *adj.* Who or what fulfils, accomplishes, &c.

सम्पादन sumpádun, *s. m.* Gaining, acquiring; accomplishing, effecting.

सम्पादित sumpadít, *adj.* Attained, obtained, gained, gotten; effected, accomplished.

सम्पुट súmpoot, *s. m.* A casket, a covered box.

सम्पूर्ण sumpóorn, *adj.* Whole, entire; complete, finished.

सम्पूर्णता sumpoorn-tá, *s. f.* Fulness, completion.

सम्प्रति súm-pruti, *adv.* Now, at present, at this time.

सम्प्रदान sum-prudán, *s. m.* Gift, donation; (*in grammar*) the dative case.

सम्प्रदाय súmprudáyuh, *s. m.* Traditional doctrine, what has been transmitted from one teacher to another, and is established as of sacred authority.

सम्प्रसाधन sum-prusádhun, *s. m.* Effecting, accomplishing, performing well or completely.

सम्प्रस्थान súm-prusthán, *s. m.* Setting out on a journey.

सम्प्राप्त sum-prápt, *adj.* Attained, obtained, gotten.

सम्प्राप्ति sum-prápti, *s. f.* Obtaining, getting, acquisition.

सम्प्रीत sum-préet, *adj.* Well pleased, delighted.

सम्प्रीति sum-préeti, *s. f.* Attachment, affection; delight.

सम्बन्ध sum-búndh, *s. m.* Connexion, affinity, relation; connexion by birth or marriage, relationship; rhyme, metre; (*in grammar*) the possessive case.

सम्बन्धी sum-búndhee, *adj.* Related to, a relation, a connexion; connected with, belonging or relating to. *s. m.* A relation; son or daughter's father-in-law.

सम्बुद्धि sum-bóoddhí, *s. f.* The vocative case.

सम्बोधन sumbódhun, *s. m.* Calling, addressing, calling to; the vocative case; comfort, soothing, encouragement, the act of consoling.

सम्भलना súm-bhulna, *v. n.* To be supported, to stand, stop, be firm, recover one's self from a fall, &c.

सम्भव sum-bhúv, *s. m.* Capacity, appropriateness, adaptation; possibility; consistency, compatibility.

सम्भालना sum-bhálna, *v. a.* To support, prop, sustain, hold up, assist, help; to shield, protect, stop, retain, restrain, check, repress.

सम्भावना sum-bháona, *s. f.* Considering, reflecting; fitness, suitableness; adequacy, competency; possibility; probability; (*in grammar*) the sense of the potential mood.

सम्भावित sum-bhavít, *adj.* Possible.

सम्भाषण sumbháshun, *s. m.* Conversation, discourse.

सम्भू súmbhoo, *s. m.* A parent, a progenitor.

सम्भोग sum-bhóg, *s. m.* Enjoyment, pleasure, delight; coition, copulation.

सम्भोगी sum-bhógee, *adj.* Sensual, sensualist.

सम्भोजन súm-bhojun, *s. m.* A meal partaken together, a convivial party.

सम्भ्रम súmbhrum, *s. m.* Esteem, respect, reverence, honour, awe.

सम्मत súmmut, *adj.* Assented or agreed to, concurred in, approved of; conformable to. *s. m.* Opinion, sentiment.

सम्मति súmmuti, *s. f.* Wish, desire; agreement, ascent, similarity of opinion or purpose; approbation.

सम्मान summán, *s. m.* Respect, homage.

सम्मान्य summányub, *adj.* Respectable, honourable.

सम्मित summít, *adj.* Like, similar, same; of equal measure or extent; meted, measured.

सम्मुख súmmookh, *adj.* Encountering, facing, in front of.

सम्मुखीन summookhéen, *adj.* Before, in front or in face of.

सम्मुग्ध summóogdh, *adj.* Fascinated, bewildered; stupified, astounded.

सम्मोद summód, *s. m.* Pleasure, delight.

सम्मोह summóh, *s. m.* Ignorance; folly; beguilement, fascination; stupefaction.

सम्मोहित summohít, *adj.* Beguiled, fascinated; enraptured, overcome with delight.

सम्यक् súm-yuk, *adv.* All, wholly; properly, fitly, in the right manner.

सयन súyun, *s. m.* Sleep, repose.

सयान suyán, *s. m.* Cunning, shrewdness.

सयाना suyána, *adj.* Cunning, artful, shrewd, sly, knowing, sagacious, clever, prudent; mature (*in understanding*), grown up.

सर sur, *s. m.* An arrow; a lake, a pool.

सरकड़ा sur-kúra, सरकण्डा sur-kúnda, *s. m.* A reed (*Saccharum procerum*).

सरकना súr-ukna, *v. n.* To be moved, to remove, move, stir, to get out of the way, budge.

सरकाना surkána, *v. a.* To remove, put on one side, to move out of the way.

सर्गुण súr-goon, *adj.* All qualities, possessing all qualities (*an epithet of the Deity*).

सरट surut, *s. m.* A lizard, a chameleon.

सरदा súr-da, *s. m.* A kind of musk-melon.

3 o 2

सरन súr-un, सरना sur-ná, *s. f.* An asylum, shelter, protection.

सरना súr-na, *v. n.* To be performed, to be carried on, to issue, to be ended.

सरनागत surnágut, *s. m.* A refugee, one who has come for protection or refuge.

सरनागतवत्सल surunágut-vútsul, *adj.* Merciful to those come for sanctuary, an epithet of the Deity.

सरप súr-up, *s. m.* A serpent.

सरपट súr-put, *s. f.* Galloping. *Surput phenkna*, To set off in a gallop.

सरपत sur-pút, *s. m.* A kind of reed, or reed-grass (*Saccharum procerum*).

सरबस surbús, *s. m.* Every thing, whole property.

सरुल súr-ul, *adj.* Plain, artless, honest, sincere, simple, candid, upright; perpendicular, straight. *s. m.* A sort of pine (*Pinus longifolia*); a bird (*Pavo bicalcarata*).

सरुला surul-á, *adj.* Upright, tall, straight. *s. f.* A variety of the plant called *Teori*.

सरवर survur, *s. m.* A lake, pond, tank. *Surwur, adj.* Equal.

सरुस súr-us, *adj.* Best, excellent, prime; more, abundant, plenty.

सरसराना sur-surána, *v. n.* To creep along as a snake, to make the noise a snake does when creeping.

सरसा súr-sa, *adj.* Best, excellent, prime; more, abundant, plenty.

सरसाई sur-sáee, *s. f.* Increase, abundance, excellence.

सरसों súr-son, *s. f.* A species of mustard (*Sinapis dichotoma*).

सरस्वत sur-swút, *adj.* Elegant.

सरस्वती surswutée, *s. f.* The wife of *Bruhma*, the goddess of speech and eloquence, the patroness of music and the arts, and the inventress of the *Sunskrit* language and *Devnaguree* letters; a river, the *Sursooty*, which rises in the mountains bounding the north-east part of the province of *Delhi*, whence it runs in a south-westerly direction, and is lost in the sands of the great desert in the country of the *Bhutti*: according to the *Hindoos* the river only disappears in this place, and continuing its course under ground, joins the *Ganges* and *Jumna* at *Allahabad*.

सरा súra, *s. m.* An earthen cover of a pot.

सराई sur-áee, *s. f.* A small cover.

सराप sur-áp, *s. m.* Curse, imprecation. *Surap dena*, To curse.

सरापना sur-ápna, *v. a.* To curse.

सराव sur-áo, *s. m.* A lid, or a shallow cup or saucer used as such.

सरावक surâwuk, *s. m.* A *Hindoo* tribe; the followers of the *Jyn* religion; the laity.

सरावन sur-áwun, *s. m.* A harrow.

सराह suráh, *s. f.* Praise, commendation.

सराहन surahún, *s. m.* Praising.

सराहना surahná, *v. a.* To praise, commend, approve, applaud, celebrate.

सरिगम surigúm, *s. m.* The gamut; sol-faing, sol-mization.

सरी sur-ée, *s. f.* The shaft of an arrow; a reed of which arrows are made.

सरीखा sur-éckha, *adj.* Like, resembling; so.

सरूप suróop, *adj.* Like, resembling. *s. m.* Own or natural shape or form, appearance, identity, shape, form, a spectacle; with form, with appearance.

सरूपता surooptá, *s. f.* Likeness, resemblance.

सरूपी suróopee, *adj.* In its own shape, as it really appears.

सरेखा surékha, *s. f.* The ninth mansion of the moon, consisting of five stars, probably in Cancer. *adj.* Cunning, sly.

सरेस surésh, *s. m.* Glue, starch.

सरोज surój, *s. m.* A lotus.

सरोता suróta, *s. m.* A kind of scissars for cutting betel-nut.

सरोग súrog, *adj.* Sick, diseased.

सरोवर sur-óvur, *s. m.* A lake or large pond, any piece of water deep enough for the lotus to grow.

सरोही surohée, *s. f.* A kind of scimitar.

सरौंज súrounj, *s. f.* A kind of seed.

सर्जि súrjji, *s. f.* Natron, alkali.

सर्प surp, *s. m.* A snake, a serpent.

सर्पगन्धा surp-gúndha, *s. f.* A plant, perhaps the same as the serpent ophioxylon.

सर्पछत्र surp-chhútr, *s. m.* A mushroom.

सर्पफणुज surp-phúnuj, *s. m.* The snakestone, a gem or pearl said to resemble in form the berry of the *Abrus precatorius*, and to be found in the head of the snake.

सर्पमणि surp-múni, *s. m.* The snake-stone or carbuncle, or a jewel said to be found in the head of a snake, possessing also alexipharmic properties.

सर्पहन surp-hún, *s. m.* An ichneumon, a mungoose.

सर्वगुहन surbgúhun, *s. m.* A total eclipse.

सर्व surv, *adj.* All, whole, entire, complete, universal.

सर्वकारी surv-káree, *adj.* The maker of all things.

सर्वकाल surv-kál, *s. m.* All seasons or times.

सर्वकालीन surv-kaléen, *adj.* Of all times or seasons.

सर्वग survúg, *adj.* Going every where, all-pervading.

सर्वगत surv-gút, *adj.* Omnipresent, universally diffused.

सर्वगन्ध surv-gúndh, *s. m.* A class of four aromatics, or *Kukkol*, cloves, agallochum, and gum benjamin.

सर्वजगत् surv-júgut, *s. f.* The universe, the whole world.

सर्वजित् surv-jít, *adj.* All-subduing, irresistible; all-surpassing, excellent, incomparable. *s. m.* The twenty-first year of the cycle.

सर्वज्ञ survúgyuh, *adj.* Omniscient, all-wise.

सर्वज्ञता survúgyutá, *s. f.* Omniscience.

सर्वतेजस surv-tejús, *s. m.* All-splendour or power.

सर्वतेजोमय surv-tejomúy, *adj.* Made, comprising or consisting of all-splendour or power.

सर्वतोभद्र survutobhúdr, *adj.* Every where auspicious. *s. m.* A temple or palace of a square form, with an entrance opposed to each point of the compass.

सर्वत्र survútr, *adv.* Every where, in all places; always, at all times.

सर्वथा surv-thá, *adv.* In all ways, by all means; assuredly, certainly.

सर्वदमन surv-dúmun, *adj.* All-subduing, irresistible.

सर्वदर्शी surv-dúrshee, *adj.* All-seeing.

सर्वदा survudá, *adv.* Always, at all times.

सर्वदुःखक्षय súrv-dookh-kshúy, *s. m.* Final emancipation from transmigration.

सर्वधन surv-dhún, *s. m.* Whole wealth or property; (in arithmetic) total of a sum in progression.

सर्वधारी surv-dháree, *s. f.* The twenty-second year of the cycle.

सर्वनाम surv-nám, *s. m.* A pronoun.

सर्वनाश surv-násh, *s. m.* Total destruction, destruction of all.

सर्वपूर्णता súrv-poorntá, *s. f.* Entire completion or fulness, complete preparation or provision.

सर्वप्रिय surv-príyuh, *adj.* Generally or universally beloved; generally friendly, loving all.

सर्वभुक्ष surv-bhúksh, *adj.* Omnivorous, eating all or any thing, all-devouring.

सर्वभाव surv-bháo, *s. m.* Whole disposition, all one's thoughts and purpose.

सर्वभूत surv-bhóot, *s. m.* All the elements; all created things.

सर्वमय surv-múy, *adj.* General, universal, comprehensive, comprehending.

सर्वरात्र surv-rátr, *s. m.* The whole night.

सर्वलोक surv-lók, *s. m.* The universe.

सर्वविद् surv-víd, } *adj.* Omniscient, all-

सर्ववेदी surv-védee, } wise.

सर्वसमता surv-sumtá, *s. f.* Sameness or identity with all things; equanimity, equal regard for all.

सर्वसह surv-súhuh, *adj.* All-enduring, bearing all things with patience and firmness. *s. m.* Bdellium.

सर्वस्व survúswuh, *s. m.* Whole property or possessions; substance, whole essence of any thing.

सर्वस्वदण्ड survúswuh-dúnd, *adj.* Fined in all one's property. *s. m.* Confiscation of property.

सर्वस्वहरण survúswuh-húrun, *s. m.* Confiscation of a whole property.

सर्वस्वामी surv-swámee, *s. m.* A universal monarch; the owner or master of all.

सर्वहार surv-hár, *s. m.* Total confiscation.

सर्वाङ्ग surv-áng, *s. m.* The whole body.

सर्वात्मा surv-átma, *s. m.* The supreme or universal spirit; all beings collectively.

सर्वाधिकार surv-adhikár, *s. m.* General control or superintendance.

सर्वाधिकारी surv-adhikáree, *s. m.* A general or head superintendant.

सर्वार्थम् surv-arthúm, *adv.* For or on account of all.

सर्वाश्रय surv-ásruy, *adj.* Giving shelter or protection to all.

सर्वेश surv-ésh, *s. m.* Supreme or universal monarch; the Supreme Being.

सर्वौषधिगण surv-óushudhi-gún, *s. m.* A class of certain principal drugs, consisting of *Moora, Valeriana Jatamansi, Orris root, Benzoin, Zedoary, Koork,* or *Costus speciosus,* red saunders, and *Cyperus.*

सर्वौषधिरस surv-óushudhi-rús, *s. m.* The juice or infusion of a number of plants as used at a royal inauguration.

सर्षप surshúp, *s. m.* A sort of mustard (*Sinapis dichotoma*); a kind of poison.

सलज्ज sulújj, *adj.* Bashful, modest, ashamed.

सलना súlna, *v. n.* To pierce, prick, perforate, enter. *s. m.* A rivulet.

सलसलाना sul-sulána, *v. n.* To creep (*as a snake*), to make the noise a snake does when creeping.

सलाई suláee, *s. f.* A needle, or piece of wire for tinging the eyelids with a collyrium: also used for depriving people of sight, which is effected by drawing it while hot close over the eyes of the sufferer; a lead pencil.

सलाका suláka, *s. f.* A rule, a ruler; a probe.

सलिता súlita, *s. f.* A river.

सलिल súlil, *s. m.* Water; liquid.

सलूना sulóono, *s. f.* The full moon in *Sawun,* at which time the ornament called *rakhee* is tied round the wrist.

सलूप sulóop, *s. m.* A little.

सलून sulón, *adj.* Salted (*food*). *s. m.* Name of a district.

सलूना sulóna, *adj.* Salted, salt, seasoned; tasteful; beautiful, expressive (*a countenance*).

सलूनी sulónee, *adj.* Seasoned, tasteful; beautiful (*when applied to a mistress*).

सलुकी sullukée, *s. f.* The gum Olibanum tree (*Boswellia thurifera*).

सल्लम súllum, *s. m.* A kind of coarse cloth.

सल्लू sulló, *s. m.* A thong, narrow slips of leather with which shoes are stitched.

सल्ली sulló, *adj.* Foolish (*a woman*).

सवर्ण suvúrn, *adj.* Like, resembling; of the same tribe or class; of the same kind, homogeneous.

सवा súva, *adj.* With a quarter, a quarter more.

सवाई suwáee, *s. m.* A title of the *Rajah* of *Jypore*; a quarter more.

सवाङ्ग suwáng, *s. m.* Mimickry, acting, imitation, disguise, sham. *Suwang lana,* To imitate, &c.

सवाङ्गी suwángee, *s. m.* An actor, a mimick.

सवाचना suwáchna, *v. a.* To try, to prove.

सवाद suwád, *s. m.* Relish, flavour, taste, sweetness; pleasure.

सवाया suwáya, } *adj.* A quarter added.

सवैया suwyya, }

सविलास suvilás, *adj.* Wanton, sportive.

सविस्मय suvísmuy, *adj.* Astonished, surprised.

सव्य súvyuh, *adj.* Left, left hand; south, southern; reverse, contrary, backward.

सशङ्क sushúnk, *adj.* Fearful, doubtful.

सशोक sushók, *adj.* Sorrowful, sad. *adv.* Sorrowfully.

सशुंशय susúnshuy, *adj.* Doubtful, uncertain.

सस्ता sústa, *adj.* Cheap.

सस्ताई sus-táee, *s. f.* Cheapness.

सुस्तान sus-tána, v. n. To rest.

सस sús-a, s. m. A hare.

ससुर súsoor, s. m. Father-in-law.

सस्य sús-yuh, s. m. Fruit ; corn, grain.

सहुकार suhukár, s. m. A fragrant sort of mango ; assistance.

सहुकारिता suhukárita, s. f. Co-operation, assistance.

सहुकारी suhukáree, adj. An assistant or associate. s. m. A helper.

सहगमन súhugúmun, s. m. Going with, accompanying ; a woman's burning herself on the funeral pile with her deceased husband.

सहचर suhuchúr, s. m. A companion, a follower.

सहचरी suhuchúree, s. f. A wife ; a woman's female friend or confidante.

सहचारी suhucháree, adj. A companion, an attendant.

सहज súhuj, adj. Easy, not difficult, facile. adv. Easily. Suhuj-soobhaohee, With natural ease.

सहजना súhujna, s. m. A tree, the root of which supplies the place of horseradish (Guilandina morunga : Hyperanthera morunga).

सहत्व suhutwúh, s. m. Sufferance, endurance ; association, union.

सहन súhun, adj. Patient, enduring, suffering, bearing. s. m. Bearing, enduring.

सहनहार suhunhár, adj. Sufferable, bearable, tolerable. [port.

सहना súhna, v. n. To bear, endure, sup-

सहमरण suhumúrun, s. m. Concremation, a widow's burning herself with the corpse of her husband.

सहराना suhrána, v. n. To thrill, have the hairs stand on end. v. a. To stroke, rub gently, tickle, titillate ; to tire, harass, tease.

सहरावन suhráwun, s. f. Titillation.

सहरी suhrée, s. f. A fish, the small carp (Cyprinus chrysopareius).

सहलाना suhlána, v. a. To stroke, rub gently, tickle.

सहलाहट suhláhut, s. f. Gentle rubbing, stroking, titillation.

सहवैया suh-wyya, s. m. A sufferer.

सहस súbus, s. m. The month Ugruhayun (November-December); the winter season ; strength, power.

सहसा súhsa, adv. Quickly, precipitately, inconsiderately, without consideration or pause.

सहसान suhsán, adj. Patient, enduring.

सहस्य suhúsyuh, s. m. The month Poush (December-January).

सहस्र suhúsr, s. m. A thousand.

सहस्रदंत suhusr-dúnt, s. m. A sort of sheat fish (Silurus pelorius).

सहस्रयुग suhusr-jóog, s. m. A period of a thousand ages.

सहस्राक्ष suhusr-áksh, adj. Thousand-eyed : used figuratively, vigilant, all-perceiving, all-inspecting, all-powerful.

सहस्री suhusrée, s. m. Commander or prefect of a thousand.

सहाई suhaée, s. m. Aider, assistant, helper.

सहाऊ suhaóo, adj. Tolerable.

सहाव suháo, s. m. Bearing, endurance.

सहाना suhána, s. m. A musical mode.

सहाय suháeh, s. m. A companion, a follower, an adherent ; a patron, a helper.

सहायक suhayúk, s. m. A succourer, aider, ally.

सहायता suhaetá, s. f. Aid, help, assistance, friendship.

सहायवान suhaewán, adj. Befriended, assisted, accompanied.

सहारा suhára, s. m. Assistance, aid, help, association. Suhara kurna, To abet.

सहार्थ suhárth, adj. Synonimous, having the same meaning.

सहित suhít, adj. Accompanied by, in company with, associated with. adv. With, together with.

सहिराना suhirána, v. n. To thrill, have the hairs stand on end. v. a. To stroke, rub gently, tickle, titillate ; tire, harass, tease.

सहिष्णु suhíshnoo, adj. Patient, enduring, resigned.

सहिष्णुता suhishnootá, s. f. Patience, resignation.

सही suhée, An emphatical particle, (it is) true or correct or good ; very well !

सहेजना suhéjna, v. a. To try ; to adjust ; to provide.

सहेली suhélee, s. f. A woman's female companion, a handmaid, damsel, concubine.

सहोदर suhódur, s. m. A brother of whole blood, one by the same father and mother. Suhodur bhaee, Full brother.

सहोल suhól, s. m. A plummet.

सहोटी suhóutee, s. f. A kind of doorframe.

सह्य súhyuh, adj. To be borne or suffered.

सा sa, adj. Like, resembling (most commonly by way of adjunct, like the English ish), as Kala-sa, Blackish ; an adjunct the meaning of which is at times scarcely perceptible, though often it seems to give intensity to the preceding word, as *Buhoot-sa*, Much, many, very much.

साऊ **saóo,** *adj.* Tractable. *s. m.* A relation.

साऊंगी **saóongee,** *s. f.* A support on which the pole of a cart is propped.

सांई **sáeen,** *s. m.* Lord, master; (*met.*) a mendicant; the deity; an imitative sound, as of wind.

सांक **sank,** *s. f.* Fear; the asthma; a lump of a sweetmeat (*particularly of Julebee*).

सांकर **sán-kur,** ⎫ *s. f.* A chain; a kind of
सांकरी **sánk-ree,** ⎰ female ornament; a strait, a narrow lane; (*met.*) difficulty. *adj.* Tight, narrow, close, strait, strict.

सांकल **sánk-ul,** *s. f.* A chain.

सांखू **san-khóo,** *s. m.* A bridge; a kind of wood (*Shorea robusta*).

सांग **sang,** *s. f.* A spear or javelin, all of iron. *s. m.* Disguise, mimickry, sham acting, imitation; a scene. *Sang kurna,* *v. a.* To act foolishly. *Sang lana,* To imitate, to mimick.

सांगी **sangée,** *s. f.* A support on which the pole of a cart is propped.

सांगीत **sangéet,** *s. m.* The exhibition of song, dancing and music as a public entertainment; the art or science of music and dancing.

सांगूस **san-góos,** *s. f.* A scate.

सांघर **sán-ghur,** *s. m.* A wife's son by a former husband. ⎡act, real.

सांच **sanch,** *adj.* True, proper, correct, ex-

सांचा **sán-cha,** *s. m.* A mould.

सांझ **sanjh,** *s. f.* Evening.

सांझा **san-jhá,** *s. m.* ⎫ Images of cow-dung
सांझी **san-jhée,** *s. f.* ⎰ made by children in the month of *Asin, Krishn-puksh,* to represent idols.

सांठ **sant,** ⎫ *s. f.* Joining, sticking; con-
सांठ **santh,** ⎰ federacy, collusion; a stick for threshing corn with, a flail.

सांटा **sán-ta,** *s. m.* A stick or whip with which elephants are beaten at the time of fight; a spur.

सांठना **sánth-na,** *v. a.* To join thread, to join, splice, to stick together.

सांड **sand,** ⎫ *s. m.* A bull; a stallion;
सांढ **sanr,** ⎰ (*met.*) an independant, extravagant fellow.

सांडनी **sand-née, sanr-née,** *s. f.* A female camel, a dromedary. *Sandnee-suwar,* One who rides on a camel.

सांडा **sán-da,** *s. m.* Name of an animal resembling a lizard (*the oil of which is said to have restorative powers*).

सांत **sant,** *adj.* Calm, tranquil, pacified, appeased. *Sant kurna,* To appease, pacify. *Sant hona,* To be appeased or pacified.

सांती **sán-tee,** *prep.* Instead. *s. f.* Stead.

सांप **samp,** *s. m.* A snake, a serpent.

सांपन **samp-ún,** *s. f.* A female snake.

सांभर **sám-bhur,** *s. m.* The name of a town, near *Ajmere,* in the vicinity of which is a lake, from which salt is extracted; the salt itself.

सांवला **sáon-la,** *adj.* Of a dark or sallow (*complexion*).

सांवा **sán-wa,** *s. m.* A very small grain (*Panicum frumentaceum*).

सांस **sans,** *s. f.* Breath, sigh. *Sans ooltee lene,* To gasp or draw in breath (*as a person in agony*). *Sans bhurna,* To sigh, to regret. *Sans rookna,* To be smothered or throttled. *Sans rokna,* *v. a.* To suffocate, to stifle.

सांसना **sáns-na,** *v. a.* To snub, distress, threaten.

सांसा **sánsa,** *s. m.* Imagination, reflection, fancy, fear, apprehension.

सांसारिक **san-sárik,** *adj.* Worldly, of or belonging to the world.

साका **sá-ka,** *s. m.* An era. *Saka kurna,* To establish an era; (*met.*) to distinguish one's self by heroic actions. *Sakeh-bundh,* *s. m.* A king who has established an era.

साकार **sákar,** *adj.* Having form or shape.

साख **sakh,** *s. f.* Trust, credit, reputation; season.

साखा **sákha,** *s. f.* A branch.

साखी **sakhée,** *s. m.* An evidence, a witness, an eye-witness.

साक्षात **sakhyát,** *adj.* Evident, conspicuous. *adv.* Before, in the presence of.

साग **sag,** ⎫ *s. m.* Greens, edible ve-
सागपात **sag-pát,** ⎰ getables, culinary herbs, potherb. *Sagpat hona,* To become soft.

सागर **sá-gur,** *s. m.* The ocean; to bathe the bones of *Sugur's* 60,000 sons the *Ganges* is said to have been led by *Bhugeeruth,* his great-great grandson, to the ocean, at the place now called *Gunga-Sagur.*

सागून **sa-góon,** *s. f.* Teak wood or tree (*Tectona grandis*).

सांकुल **sán-kul,** *s. f.* A chain.

सांख्य **sánkh-yuh,** *adj.* Numeral, relating to number. *s. m.* A system of philosophy, ascribed originally to the *Mooni Kupil.*

सांग **sang,** *adj.* Having all the members. *s. m.* Disguise, mimickry, sham, acting, imitation; a scene. *Sang kurna,* *v. a.* To act foolishly. *Sang lana,* To imitate, to mimick.

साच sach, *adj.* True.

साज saj, *s. m.* Preparation, harness, accoutrements.

साजन sáj-un, *s. m.* A sweetheart, a lover.

साजना sáj-na, *v. a.* To prepare, dress, decorate, bedeck, regulate. *v. n.* To become, fit, suit.

साझा sá-jha, *s. m.* Partnership, association.

साझी sá-jhee, *s. m.* A partner, associate.

साटवाट sátbat, *s. f.* Combining, leaguing, confederating.

साठ sath, *adj.* Sixty.

साठी sa-thée, *s. m.* A kind of rice produced in the rains (*so called, because it ripens in 60 days from the time of sowing*).

साड़ी sá-ree, *s. f.* A dress consisting of one piece of cloth worn by *Hindoo* women round the body and passing over the head.

साढ़े sarhée, *s. m.* The spring harvest or grain cut in the spring.

साढ़ू sar-hóo, *s. m.* A wife's sister's husband.

साढ़े sarhéh, *adj.* (*used with nouns of number denotes*) With a half (*of one, or of the aggregate number in addition to the number specified*).

सात sat, *adj.* Seven. *Sat panch kurna,* To be in doubt, to be unable to decide what to do. *Sat sumoondur,* The name of a game.

सातवाँ satwan, *adj.* Seventh.

सातिसार sati-sár, *adj.* Dysenteric, afflicted with dysentery.

सात्विक sat-wik, *adj.* Spontaneous, sincere ; relating to or proceeding from the *Sutwuh* quality, honest, true, good, gentle, amiable, &c.

साथ sath, *adv.* With, together, along with. *s. m.* Society, company. *Sath iskeh,* Along with this ; besides, moreover. *Sath ooskeh,* Along with that, although, notwithstanding. *Sath dena,* To join, associate with. *Sath-wala,* A comrade, a companion. *Sathon-sath,* Together with, along with.

साथिन sa-thin, *s. f.* A female companion.

साथी sa-thée, *s. m.* A companion, comrade, ally, accomplice, associate. *Suthee-sath,* Together, in one company.

सादर sá-dur, *adj.* Respectful. *adv.* Respectfully.

सादरा sád-ra, *s. m.* A kind of song.

सादृश्य sa-drísh-yuh, *s. m.* Resemblance, similarity.

साध sadh, *adj.* Virtuous, righteous, good, holy. *s. m.* A religious person, a mendicant. *s. f.* Desire.

साधक sa-dhúk, *adj.* Completing, perfecting, finishing, who or what effects or completes ; holy, devotee. *s. m.* A practiser.

साधन sá-dhun, *s. m.* Accomplishing, effecting ; practice.

साधना sádh-na, *v. a.* To familiarize gradually to any habit, to teach, learn, habituate, accustom, to use, practise, regulate, pacify, correct, rectify, settle, fix or determine, accomplish. *s. f.* The act of familiarizing by habitude, practice ; accomplishment.

साधारन sa-dhárun, *adj.* In common ; common.

साधारनधर्म sadhárun-dhúrmm, *s. m.* Common or universal duty, conduct to be observed by all castes or orders, as humanity, &c.

साधु sá-dhoo, *adj.* Pious, virtuous, good, pure, honest. *s. m.* A merchant ; a kind of mendicant.

साधुता sa-dhootá, *s. f.* Goodness, honesty, correctness, piety.

साधुपुष्प sadhoo-pooshp, *s. m.* A flower (*Hibiscus mutabilis*).

साधुवृक्ष sadhoo-vríksh, *s. m.* The *Kudumb* tree (*Nauclea Cadamba*).

साधुशील sádhoo-séel, *adj.* Virtuous, righteous, wisely or virtuously inclined.

साध्य sádh-yuh, *adj.* Accomplishable, attainable ; practicable, easy. *s. m.* The twenty-second astronomical *yog.*

सान san, *s. f.* A whetstone, a grindstone.

सानबूझना san-boojhána, *v. a.* To make one understand by hints.

सानी sánee, *s. f.* Chaff or straw mixed with grain (*particularly, that from which oil has been expressed*), as food for cattle.

सानु sánoo, *s. m.* Table-land, level ground on the top or edge of a mountain.

सान्त्वन sán-twun, *s. m.* Conciliation, reconcilement.

सानना sán-na, *v. a.* To knead, to mix up (*flour, dough, earth, &c.*), to impregnate, stain, soil, smear, defile ; to whet.

सन्निध्य sannídh-yuh, *s. m.* Proximity, vicinity.

साप sap, *s. m.* Imprecation, curse.

सापुन sá-pun, *s. m.* A disorder in which the hair gradually falls off.

सापना sapna, *v. a.* To curse.

सापराध saprádh, *adj.* Faulty, offending.

सापिन sapín, *s. f.* A female snake.

साफल्य sa-phúlyuh, *adj.* Productiveness, fruitfulness.

सावधान sabdhán, *adj.* Attentive, cautious.

साबर sá-bur, *s. m.* An elk ; a leather of elk's or any kind of deer's hide for bedding ; a small anvil.

सावरमंत्र **sábur-múntr,** *s. m.* A spell composed in colloquial language.

साबूत **sa-bóot,** *adj.* Whole, entire.

साम **sam,** *s. m.* The third of the four *Veds,* the prayers of which composed in metre, are always sung or chanted.

सामग्री **samugrée,** *s. f.* Furniture, tools, apparatus, articles, materials, scenery.

सामर **sá-mur,** *s. m.* A kind of salt.

सामर्थ्य **samúrth,** *s. f.* Ability, power.

सामर्थी **sa-múrthee,** *adj.* Powerful, mighty, able, capable.

सामर्थ्य **sa-múrthyuh,** *s. m.* Ability, power.

सामा **sá-ma,** *s. f.* Apparatus, provisions, furniture, articles.

सामाजिक **sama-jík,** *s. m.* An assistant or spectator at an assembly, &c.

सामान्य **sam-ányuh,** *adj.* Common, general, generic, universal.

सामान्यलक्षण **samányuh-lúkshun,** *s. m.* A generic or specific character.

सामान्या **samanyá,** *s. f.* A female who is common to all men, a harlot.

सामी **sámee,** *s. f.* A ferrule. *adv.* In front, fronting, before, confronting, opposite.

सामीप्य **saméepyuh,** *s. m.* Proximity, nearness.

सामुद्रिक **samóodrik,** *s. f.* Palmistry, chiromancy, fortune-telling, the art of physiognomy.

सामना **sám-na,** }
सामहना **samh-na,** } *s. m.* Encountering, confronting, facing, front, opposition. *Samna kurna,* To confront, oppose, encounter.

सामने **sámneh,** }
सामहने **samh-neh,** } *adv.* In front, fronting, before, confronting, opposite.

साम्बर **sámbur,** *s. m.* An elk.

सायंकाल **sáyung-kál,** *s. m.* Eventide, evening.

साया **sáya,** *s. m.* Shade.

सार **sar,** *adj.* Best, excellent. *s. m.* The pith or sap of trees, &c.; strength, vigour; the essence of any thing, the essential or vital part of it, quintessence; value, worth; manure; iron; the piece used in playing *choupur.*

सारंग **sá-rung,** *s. m.* A musical mode; a peacock; a snake, a serpent; a cloud; the cry of a peacock; a deer; a woman; water; the name of a country; a lamp; the *Nymphea lotus.*

सारंगिया **sarún-giya,** *s. m.* A fiddler.

सारंगी **sá-rungee,** *s. f.* A musical instrument like a fiddle.

सारता **sar-tá,** *s. f.* Strength, substance; essence.

सारथी **sar-thée,** *s. m.* A charioteer.

सारना **sár-na,** *v. a.* To perform, accomplish, effect, complete, make, mend, manure.

सारलोह **sár-loh,** *s. m.* Steel.

सारवत् **sar-vút,** *adj.* Substantial, having pith, substance, strength, &c.

सारवर्जित **sar-vúrjjit,** *adj.* Pithless, sapless.

सारस **sár-us,** *s. m.* }
सारसी **sarusée,** *s. f.* } The Indian crane, male and female, (*Ardea Sibirica*).

सारस्वत **saruswút,** *s. m. pl.* The people of the *Suruswut* country, or the north-west part of the province of *Delhi.*

सार **sára,** *adj.* All, the whole. *s. m.* Wife's brother, brother-in-law.

सारार्थ **sar-árth,** *s. m.* Abridgment.

सारिका **saríka,** *s. f.* A bird (*Turdus salica*); also a myna (*Gracula religiosa*).

सारी **sarée,** *s. f.* Cream; a dress consisting of one piece of cloth worn by *Hindoo* women round the body and passing over the head.

सारू **saróo,** *s. f.* A bird, a starling.

सर्पी **sarppée,** *s. f.* The ninth lunar asterism.

सार्वभौम **sarv-bhóum,** *s. m.* An emperor, a universal monarch.

सार्वलौकिक **sarv-lóukik,** *adj.* Universally known, prevailing throughout the universe.

सार्ववर्णिक **sarv-vúrnik,** *adj.* Of every kind or sort; belonging or relating to every tribe, &c.

साल **sal,** *s. m.* A common timber tree (*Shorea robusta*); a thorn; perforation, bore, mortise, a hole made by driving a pin into the ground, &c. *s. f.* A house, place; a school. *s. m.* A jackal.

सालग्राम **salgrám,** *s. m.* A stone, a species of Ammonite common in the *Gundhuk* river, and worshipped by the *Vyshnuvs,* as a type of *Vishnoo.*

सालुन **sál-un,** }
सालना **sál-na,** } *s. m.* Meat or fish, &c. eaten with bread or rice.

सालना **sál-na,** *v. a.* To penetrate, perforate, bore, prick, pierce, drill. *v. n.* To ache, to be in pain, to smart.

सालपूर्णी **sal-púrnee,** *s. f.* A shrub (*Hedysarum gangeticum*).

सालपुष्प **sal-póoshp,** *s. m.* A shrub (*Hibiscus mutabilis*).

सालरस **sal-rús,** *s. m.* The resinous juice of the *Sal* tree.

सालबाहन **sal-váhun,** *s. m.* The sovereign *Salivahun.*

सालसा sál-sa, *s. m.* Sarsaparilla.

साला sála, *s. m.* A wife's brother, brother-in-law ; (*in compos. mostly*), house, place.

साली sálee, *s. f.* Sister-in-law, wife's sister, especially younger sister.

सालू sáloo, *s. m.* A kind of red cloth (*dyed with Morinda*).

सालोतरी sal-ótree, *s. m.* A horse-doctor.

सावक sávuk, *s. m.* A child, the young of animals.

सावकास savukás, *s. m.* Leisure, opportunity.

सावज sávuj, *adj.* Savage, wild. *s. m.* Sport, game, (*i. e. wild animals for the chase.*)

सावधान savudhán, *adj.* Careful, cautious, attentive.

सावधानी savudhánee, *s. f.* Caution, attention.

सावन sávun, *s. m.* The name of the fourth Hindoo month, July-August. *Savun hureh nuh Bhadon sookheh (Flourishing in summer and not fading in autumn)*, is applied to express continuance in the same state or situation.

सावन्त sa-wúnt, *adj.* Brave, heroic. *s. m.* A hero.

सावन्ती sa-wúntee, *s. f.* Valour, heroism, bravery.

सास sas, *s. f.* A mother-in-law.

सासन sá-sun, *s. m.* Order, edict, command ; a patent, a grant.

सासना sás-na, *v. a.* To chastise, admonish.

साह sah, *s. m.* A merchant, a shop-keeper ; an innocent person.

साहस sáhus, *s. m.* Violence ; courage, spirit, valour, resolution.

साहसी sáhusee, *adj.* Violent ; resolute, brave, bold, undaunted, determined, daring.

साहाय्य saháyuh, *s. m.* Friendship, fellow-ship ; help, succour ; alliance.

साहित्य sahítyuh, *s. m.* Society, association, connexion, combination.

साहिल sahíl, *s. m.* A plumb-line ; a porcupine.

साही sahée, *s. f.* A porcupine.

साहूकार sahookár, *s. m.* A great merchant.

साहूकारी sahoo-káree, *s. f.* Traffic, trade, commerce.

साहूल sahóol, *s. m.* A plummet.

साक्षात् sakshát, *adv.* Before, in presence, in sight ; as, like ; evidently, manifestly.

साक्षी sákshee, *adj.* Witnessing, seeing, an eye-witness ; attesting, testifying, evidence. *s. m.* A witness (*in law*), an evidence, an eye-witness.

साक्ष्य sákshyuh, *s. m.* Testimony, evidence.

सिंगरा singrá, *s. m.* A powder-horn.

सिंगरी singreé, *s. f.* A small powder-horn for priming with.

सिंगिया singíya, *s. m.* A sort of poison.

सिंगोटी singóutee, *s. f.* A polishing tool made of horn ; an ornament of metal on the horns of a bullock.

सिंघारा singhára, *s. m.* *Trapa natans ;* a handkerchief folded diagonally.

सिंघ singh, *s. m.* A lion ; Leo, the sign of the zodiac ; a title used by *Hindoos. Singhpour,* The grand entrance gate (*to a palace, &c.*)

सिंघकेशर singh-késhur, *s. m.* A lion's mane ; a plant (*Mimusops elengi*).

सिंघद्वार singh-dwár, *s. m.* A gate, an entrance, especially the chief gate of a mansion or palace.

सिंघनाद singh-nád, *s. m.* War-cry, war-hoop, shouting or roaring upon making an onset.

सिंघनादक singh-náduk, *s. m.* The roar or yelp of a lion ; war-cry.

सिंघनादका singh-náduka, *s. f. Hedysarum alhagi.*

सिंघनी singh-née, *s. f.* A lioness.

सिंघपूर्णी singh-púrnee, *s. f.* A plant (*Justicia adhenatoda*).

सिंघपूच्छी singh-póochchhee, *s. f.* A plant (*Hedysarum lagopodioides*).

सिंघल sing-húl, *s. m.* Tin ; brass ; Cassia bark ; *Ceylon.*

सिंघासन sing-hásun, *s. m.* A throne.

सिकता síkta, *s. f.* Gravel or stone (*the disease*).

सिकना síkna, *v. n.* To be toasted or parched.

सिकरी sikrée, *s. f.* A staple (*of a lock*).

सिख sikh, *s. m.* A disciple, a scholar, a pupil, an apprentice ; a people living in the *Punjab.*

सिखनावद sikh-náwud, *s. m.* Tuition.

सिखर síkhur, *s. m.* Three or more strings tied together forming a support to hang any thing on ; the cords of a *buhungee,* in which the baskets rest ; top, summit, peak, pinnacle.

सिखरन sikhúrun, *s. m.* A kind of dish made of coagulated milk and sugar.

सिखाई sikháee, *s. m.* Teaching, instruction.

सिखाना sikhána, *v. a.* To teach ; (*met.*) to admonish, chastise.

सिगरौ sígrou, *adj.* All, every, the whole.

सिंगा sínga, *s. m.* A trumpet.

सिंगार singár, *s. m.* Dress, ornament, embellishment, decoration. *Singar-rus, s. m.* One of the nine *Rus* or sentiments, that of love.

सिंगारना singárna, *v. a.* To dress, decorate, embellish.

सिंगारहार singar-hár, *s. m.* The weeping Nyctanthes (*Nyctanthes arbor-tristis*).

सिंगारिया singáriya, *s. m.* One whose business is to dress an idol.

सिंगौटी singóutee, *s. f.* A polishing tool made of horn; an ornament of metal on the horns of a bullock.

सिंघाड़ा singhára, *s. m. Trapa natans;* a handkerchief folded diagonally.

सिच्छुक sichchhúk, *s. m.* A preacher, teacher.

सिच्छा sichchhá, *s. f.* Tuition, sermon, doctrine, teaching.

सिझाना sijháua, *v. a.* To tan, boil, seeth, melt.

सिटकारी sitkáree, *adj.* Fusiform, tapering.

सिटी sittée, *s. f.* Whistling.

सिट्ठी sitthée, *s. f.* Dross, lees.

सिठाई sitháee, *s. f.* Insipidity, tastelessness.

सिर sir, *s. f.* Madness.

सिरन sírun, *adj. f.* Mad (*women*).

सिरबिलिला sir-bilílla, *adj.* Mad.

सिरा sir-á, *m.* }
सिरी sir-ée, *f.* } *adj.* Mad.

सित sit, *adj.* White. *s. m.* White (*the colour*); the planet Venus.

सितंग sit-úng, *s. m.* Palsy, numbness, being chilled with cold.

सितंगी sit-úngee, *adj.* Palsied, paralytic, numbed.

सितचिंघ sit-chính, *s. m.* A sort of fish (*Lacerta scincus*).

सितरी sítree, *s. f.* Sweat.

सिताक sit-áuk, *s. m.* A kind of fish (*Lacerta scincus*).

सितोपल sit-ópul, *s. m.* Chalk, or a mineral substance of similar appearance, considered as a variety. *s. m.* Crystal.

सिथुल síthul, *adj.* Cold, cool; stupified, benumbed (*with fear, &c.*)

सिद्ध siddh, *adj.* Accomplished, effected, completed; celebrated, famous; valid (*in law*); demonstrated, proved (*in logic*); finished. *s. m.* A divine personage of undefined attributes or character; a sort of demigod or spirit, inhabiting the middle air, or region between the earth and sun; an inspired or prophetic writer, as *Vyas* and others, or one to whom the past, present and future, are supposed to be known; a sage, a seer; the twenty-first of the astronomical *yogs*; an

adept, a magician, one who by the performance of certain mystical and magical rites has acquired superhuman powers; an ascetic who by mystical and austere practices has effected, one or all of five purposes, viz. the affluence, the form, or the society of the gods, residence in the divine *Loks*, or identification with a deity.

सिद्धधातु siddh-dhátoo, *s. m.* Quicksilver.

सिद्धरस siddh-rús, *adj.* Mineral, metallic. *s. m.* Quicksilver.

सिद्धसाधन siddh-sádhun, *s. m.* The performance of magical rites, &c. or the materials employed in magical or alchemical processes.

सिद्धान्त sid-dhánt, *s. m.* Demonstrated conclusion, established truth, result, consequence; a system of science.

सिद्धान्ती sid-dhántée, *s. m.* A follower of the *Mimansa* philosophy; a demonstrator, one who establishes his conclusions.

सिद्धि síddhi, *s. f.* Fulfilment, accomplishment; a *yog*, either the sixteenth of the astronomical periods termed *yogs*, or the nineteenth of the twenty-eight astrological *yogs*; prosperity, success; accuracy, correctness; validity (*in law*); the result or fruit of the adoration of the gods or of ascetic severities; the supposed acquirement of supernatural powers by the completion of magical, mystical, or alchemical rites and processes.

सिधारना sidhárna, *v. n.* To go, set off, depart.

सिधावट sidháwut, *s. f.* Candour; simplicity.

सिनक sín-uk, *s. m.* Blowing the nose, snot.

सिनकना sín-ukna, *v. a.* To blow the nose.

सिन्दूर sindóor, *s. m.* Red-lead, minium.

सिन्धु síndhoo, *s. m.* The ocean, the sea; the Indus; the country along the Indus or *Sindh*

सिन्धुपुष्प sindhoo-póoshp, *s. m.* A conch.

सिन्धुलवण síndhoo-lúvun, *s. m.* Rock salt.

सिप्रा síp-ra, *s. f.* A river near *Oojein*.

सिमट sím-ut, *s. f.* Act of collecting, condensing or constringing; tone, elasticity. *Simut jana,* To shrivel, to shrink.

सिमटना sím-utna, *v. n.* To be concentrated, to shrink, to be contracted or drawn together, to shrivel.

सियान siyán, *s. m.* Cunning, shrewdness. *Siyanpun, s. m.* Cunning, art.

सियाना siyána, *adj.* Cunning, artful, sly, shrewd, knowing, sagacious, clever, prudent; mature (*in understanding*), grown up.

सियार siyár, }
सियाल siyál, } *s. m.* A jackal.

सिर sir, *s. m.* The head, the top. *Sir oothatehee pamal hona,* To be crushed in the commencement of one's undertaking. *Sir oothana*, To rebel, to rise up against one. *Sir kuta*, Beheaded, decapitated. *Sir kurna*, To begin. *Sir karhna*, To become conspicuous. *Sir keh zor*, With all *(one's)* might. *Sir ko kudum kurna*, To go quickly but with respect. *Sir khoojana*, To court punishment. *Sir churhkeh murna*, To lay the guilt of one's blood at the door of another. *Sir churha*, *adj.* Proud, haughty. *Sir churhana*, To exalt; to assume, to be arrogant; to shew respect. *Sir doolana*, or *Sir dhoonna*, To shake the head from affliction. *Sir doob*, *adj.* Perfectly wet. *Sir torna*, To subdue. *Sir dhurna*, To be obedient. *Sir nuwana*, To be humble, to be obedient. *Sir pupolna bheja khana*, To shew kindness externally and harbour enmity in one's breast. *Sir pur khak dalna*, To lament. *Sir pur churhana*, To spoil *(a child, &c.)*; to raise an inferior above one's self; to shew respect. *Sir purustee kurna*, To protect, to aid. *Sir peetna*, To lament. *Sir phirana*, To labour in vain. *Sir pherna*, To revolt from obedience. *Sir marna*, To take great pains, to search diligently. *Sir moondana*, To quit one's connexions and adopt a life of mendicity. *Sir seh kufun bandhna*, To engage in a desperate undertaking, giving up all regard to one's own safety. *Sir seh sirwah*, The conducting of an affair depends on the leader or head.

शिरकी **sir-kee**, *s. f.* A kind of reed of which mats are made, reed-grass *(the upper joint of Saccharum procerum)*; a sort of mat to keep off rain.

शिरखप **sir-khúp**, *adj.* Resolute *(soldier)*, adventurous.

शिरखपी **sir-khupée**, *s. f.* Resolution, perseverance, enterprise. [*form.*

शिरजना **sír-ujna**, *v. a.* To create, produce,

शिरफुटौवर **sír-phutouvúr**, *s. m.* Wrangling; affectation of civility with internal hatred.

शिरसींग **sir-séeng**, *adj.* Rebellious, mutinous.

शिरहाना **sir-hána**, *s. m.* The head part or side of any thing *(as of a tomb or bedstead)*, the place where the head rests or reclines.

शिरा **síra**, *s. m.* Head, extremity, end.

शिराजाल **sir-ajál**, *s. m.* Enlargement of the vessels of the eye.

शिरात **sír-át**, *adj.* Cold, becoming cold.

शिराना **sir-ána**, *v. n.* To cool. *v. a.* To make cold, to cool; to set afloat, to float, to set off, to despatch.

शिरिस **síris**, *s. m.* A tree *(Mimosa serisa)*.

शिरोत्पात **sir-otpát**, *s. m.* Redness and inflammation of the eyes.

शिरी **sirrée**, *adj.* Mad, insane.

शिल **sil**, } *s. f.* A stone, a rock; a flat
शिला **síla**, } stone on which condiments, &c. are ground with a muller.

शिलपट **sil-pút**, *adj.* Smooth, even, level.

शिलबट्टा **sil-bútta**, *s. m.* Two stones with which spices, paint, &c. are ground.

शिलवाना **sil-wána**, *v. a.* To cause to sew or stitch.

शिलाई **siláee**, *s. f.* The price of sewing; seam, sewing.

शिलाजित **sila-jít**, *s. m.* Storax.

शिलाना **silána**, *v. a.* To cause to sew or stitch.

शिलारूस **sila-rús**, *s. m.* Storax.

शिली **sílee**, *s. f.* A whetstone; a small kiln; the trunk of a tree; plank; a teal.

शिव **siv**, *s. m.* An Indian deity, *Muhadev.*

शिवरात्री **sivrátree**, *s. f.* A festival held on the 14th of the dark fortnight in the month of *Phalgoon (February-March)*, in honor of the birth of the *Ling* or phallus.

शिवाना **siwána**, *s. m.* Verge, limit, boundary, landmark.

शिवार **siwár**, *s. m.* Green vegetation at the bottom of pools or other water *(Vallisneria spiralis or octandra)*.

शिवाला **siwála**, *s. m.* A temple of *Muhadev.*

शिसुकना **sisukná**, *v. n.* To sob.

शिसकी **sís-kee**, *s. f.* Sobbing. *Siskiyan bhurna*, To sob.

शिहुरना **sihurná**, *v. n.* So shiver, to shake with cold.

शिहरा **síhra**, *s. m.* A chaplet, a garland, wreath *(worn on the head by a bridegroom and bride at the marriage ceremony)*.

शिहराऊ **sih-raóo**, *adj.* Tiresome, tedious.

शिहराना **sih-rána**, *v. n.* To thrill, to have the hairs stand on end. *v. a.* To stroke, rub gently, tickle, titillate; to tire, harass, tease.

शिहूरना **sihúrna**, *v. n.* To shiver, shake with cold; to scrape.

शींक **seenk**, *s. f.* The culm of the grass *(Andropogon muricatum)* of which brooms are made.

शींकुर **séenk-ur**, *s. m.* The flower of the *Seenk.*

शींका **séenk-a**, *s. m.* A groove.

शींकिया **séenkiya**, *adj.* Striped.

शींग **seeng**, *s. m.* A horn.

शींगरा **séeng-ra**, *s. m.* A powder-horn.

शींगा **séenga**, *s. m.* A horn *(musical)*.

शींगिया **séengiya**, *s. m.* A kind of poison.

शींगी **séengee**, *s. f.* A kind of fish *(Silurus pungentissimus)*; a cup for cupping; a small horn *(musical)*. *Seengee lugana*, To cup.

शींचना **séenchna**, *v. a.* To irrigate, to water.

सींचाई seenchaée, *s. f.* The price paid for irrigation or watering.

सींची seenchee, *s. f.* The season for watering fields, &c.

सींह seenh, *s. m.* A hedge-hog.

सीकरी seekree, *s. f.* A wire-chain.

सीख seekh, *s. f.* Admonition, lesson, learning, study.

सीखना seekhna, *v. a.* To learn, to acquire.

सींचना seech-na, *v. a.* To water, to irrigate.

सीज seej, *s. m.* A species of Euphorbia, the milky hedge-plant (*Euphorbia nerifolia* or *antiquorum*).

सीजना seej-na, *v. n.* To exude, filtrate, sweat; to seeth, boil, dissolve or become soft by boiling; to be received (*as money*), liquidated (*as a debt*).

सीटी seetee, *s.f.* Whistling. *Seetee bujana,* To whistle. *Seetee bundhna,* or, —*goom hona,* or, —*bhoolna,* To be distracted or confounded, to become senseless. *Seetee-bas,* A whistler.

सीठ seeth, *s. f.* } Dregs of betel, or any
सीठी see-thée, } thing that has been chewed.

सीठना seeth-ná, *s. m.* } Abusive songs
सीठनी seeth-née, *s. f.* } sung by women at weddings.

सीठा sée-tha, *adj.* Tasteless, insipid, weak, vapid, pale, pithless, sickly, faded.

सीढी séerhee, *s.f.* A ladder, stair, step; degree.

सीत seet, *s. f.* Cold or chilness; dew, wet, wetness.

सीतकाल seet-kál, *s. m.* Winter.

सीतज्वर seet-jwúr, *s. m.* Ague.

सीतरस seet-rús, *s. m.* The flux, dysentery.

सीतल see-túl, *adj.* Cool, cold; stupified, benumbed (*with fear, &c.*)

सीतलचीनी séetul-chéenee, *s. f.* Allspice (*Myrtus pimenta*).

सीतलपाटी séetul-pátee, *s. f.* A kind of fine, cool mat.

सीतला séetla, *s. f.* Small-pox.

सीता seetá, *s. f.* The daughter of *Junuk* and wife of *Ramchundr.*

सीताङ्ग seet-áng, *s. m.* Palsy.

सीताफल seeta-phúl, *s. m.* The custard-apple (*Annona squamosa*).

सीधा sée-dha, *adj.* Straight, right, direct; opposite; simple; fair, candid, upright. *s. m.* Provisions, victuals (*undressed*), forage. *Seedha kurna,* To straighten.

सीधाई seedhaée, *s. f.* Straightness, directness; simplicity; candour, uprightness.

सीधी seedhee, *s. f.* Straightness.

सीना sée-na, *v. a.* To sew, to stitch.

सीप seep, *s. f.* A shell; a kind of mango.

सीपी séepee, *s. f.* A shell.

सीमा sée-ma, *s. f.* A boundary, a limit, restriction, a landmark, or mound, &c. serving to fix the limits of estates, &c.

सीमावृक्ष seema-vríksh, *s. m.* A tree serving as a boundary mark.

सीमासन्धि séema-súndhi, *s. m.* The meeting of two boundaries.

सीरा séera, *adj.* Cool. *s. m.* A kind of sweetmeat made of meal and sugar.

सील seel, *s. m.* Nature, quality, disposition; good conduct or disposition, steady and uniform observance of law and morals. *s. f.* Cold, dampness. *Ankhon men seel hona,* To be polite, generous, &c.

सीलवान seelwán, *adj.* Of good or amiable disposition, benevolent, well-conducted.

सीला sée-la, *adj.* Damp, wet, cool.

सीवन sée-wun, *s. m.* Sewing, stitching, a seam.

सीवनी see-wunée, *s. f.* The frenum of the prepuce.

सीवली seev-lée, *s. m.* Name of a caste whose business it is to draw juice from the date or tar trees.

सीस sees, *s. m.* The head. *Sees-phool, s. m.* An ornament for the head (*worn by females*).

सीसा sée-sa, *s. m.* Lead.

सीसों see-són, *s. m.* A kind of wood, or name of a tree (*Dalbergia sisoo*).

सीह seeh, *s. m.* A hedge-hog.

सु soo, *adv.* A particle and prefix analogous to good, well, &c. and implying reverence, worship, honour. (*In Bruj*) *adv.* From, by, with, of, as *Ja-soo,* From or of whom: it is also sometimes used for *so,* He, she, it, they, &c.

सुंघाना soonghána, *v. a.* To cause to smell.

सुकचाना sook-chána, *v. n.* To be abashed, to be afraid. *v. a.* To abash.

सुकटा sook-tá, *adj.* Lean, thin, dry, emaciated.

सुकटी sook-tée, *adj. f.* Lean, thin, dry, emaciated. *s. f.* Dried fish.

सुकुडना soo-kúrna, *v. n.* To be shrunk or contracted, to shrink; to draw in, collect, gather up, constrain, shrivel, dwindle.

सुकर sóo-kur, *adj.* Easy, practicable, attainable. *s. m.* The planet Venus; Friday; Sperma genitale.

सुकवार sook-wár, *adj.* Delicate, feeble.

सुकाल soo-kál, *s. m.* Goodness of seasons; plenty, abundance.

सुकुचना soo-koochna, *v. n.* To fear, to be afraid of, to be in awe of, to be abashed, to apprehend, to be apprehensive.

सुकुमार soo-koomár, *adj.* Soft, delicate, smooth, tender; youthful, young.

सुकृत sóokrit, *adj.* Virtuous, pious; done well, well performed, properly, ably, &c. *s. m.* Virtue, a good action, moral merit; kindness, bounty.

सुकृती sóo-krítee, *adj.* Virtuous, pious, good; benign, benevolent.

सुक्रिया sóokriya, *s. f.* A good action, a good work; a moral or religious observance.

सुख sookh, *s. m.* Ease, tranquillity, pleasure, delight, easy circumstances, content, happiness. *Sookh pana,* To get ease, leisure, rest, &c.

सुखचैन sóokh-chyn, *s. m.* Ease, rest, leisure, tranquillity.

सुखतला sookh-túla, *s. m.* A piece of leather placed on the sole within the shoe.

सुखद sookhúd, *adj.* Salubrious, pleasant; conferring or affording pleasure, &c.

सुखदर्शन sóokh-dursún, *s. m.* A shrub, the juice of which is given for the ear-ache (*Crinum Asiaticum* and *zeylanicum*).

सुखदाई sookh-daée, } *adj.* Ease-afford-
सुखदायक sookh-dayúk, } ing, comforter, giver of ease or content.

सुखदान sookh-dán, *s. m.* Giving of ease or of comfort or of content.

सुखदास sookh-dás, *s. m.* A kind of rice.

सुखधाम sookh-dhám, *s. m.* Abode of happiness, &c.

सुखपूर्वक sookh-póorvuk, *adv.* Easily, without difficulty.

सुखभाग sookh-bhág, *s. m.* Happiness, good fortune.

सुखभागी sookh-bhágee, *adj.* Happy, delighted.

सुखमय sookh-múy, *adj.* Full or consisting of happiness, delightful.

सुखसाध्य sookh-sádhyuh, *adj.* Easy of accomplishment or attainment.

सुखाना soo-khána, } *v. a.* To dry; to
सुखलाना sookh-lána, } emaciate, to cause to pine away; to evaporate.

सुखार्थ sookh-árth, *adv.* For the sake of ease, happiness, &c.

सुखार्थी sookh-arthée, *adj.* Seeking or wishing for happiness.

सुखाला sookhála, *adj.* Easy, not difficult, facile.

सुखास्वाद sookh-aswád, *adj.* Well-flavoured; delightful, agreeable. *s. m.* Enjoyment, flavour.

सुखित soo-khít, } *adj.* At ease, happy,
सुखिया soo-khíya, } tranquil, contented,
सुखी soo-khée, } comfortable, pleasant, possessing happiness or pleasure.

सुखिस्वभाव sóokhi-swubháo, *s. m.* A happy or contented disposition.

सुखेच्छा sookh-échchha, *s. f.* Hope or desire of happiness.

सुखोदय sookh-óduy, *s. m.* Realization or occurrence of pleasure.

सुख्यात sookh-yát, *adj.* Celebrated, famous.

सुख्याति sookh-yatí, *s. f.* Fame, celebrity.

सुगन्ध soo-gúndh, *adj.* Fragrant, sweet-smelling. *s. m.* Good smell, fragrance, odour, perfume. *Soogundh-rash,* Name of a flower.

सुगन्धिता soo-gúndh-itá, *s. f.* Fragrance, pleasant scent, such as is produced by the trituration of perfumes.

सुगम soo-gúm, *adj.* Accessible, good (*as a road*); easy, practicable; plain, intelligible.

सुगुप्त soo-góopt, *adj.* Secret, well hidden or kept secret. *adv.* Secretly, privily.

सुगुप्ति soo-góopti, *s. f.* Closeness, secrecy.

सुगरी soo-gruée, *s. f.* A musical mode sung in the afternoon.

सुघर soo-ghúr, *adj.* Elegant, accomplished, beautiful, virtuous.

सुघराई soogh-raée, *s. f.* Elegancy, accomplishment. [ed, clean.

सुच sooch, *adj.* Pure, undefiled, unpollut-

सुचकना soochúkna, *v. n.* To be astonished or startled.

सुचित sóo-chit, *adj.* Thoughtless, easy, at leisure, disengaged; attentive, careful; occupied.

सुचिन्ता sóo-chinta, *s. f.* Due reflection or consideration.

सुचेत soo-chét, *adj.* Attentive, mindful, careful, aware, cautious.

सुजन sóo-jun, *adj.* Virtuous, good, respectable; kind, benevolent.

सुजनता soo-juntá, *s. f.* Goodness, benevolence, kindness.

सुजसी soo-jusée, *adj.* Renowned.

सुजाति soo-játi, *adj.* Of a good tribe or species.

सुजान soo-ján, *adj.* Intelligent, wise, knowing.

सुजाना soo-jána, *v. a.* To cause to swell.

सुझाना soo-jhána, *v. a.* To shew, to make understand.

सुज्ञान soogyán, *s. m.* Wisdom, intelligence, sagacity.

सुड्कून sóot-koon, *s. f.* A rod.

सुड़कना soo-tóok-na, *v. a.* To swallow by gulps and with a noise.

सुड़की sóor-kee, } *s. f.* Act of suddenly
सुड़की soo-rúkkee, } slackening the string of a paper kite.

सुरूप soo-rúp, *s. f.* Sipping, or sucking up (*as broth*), or the noise made thereby.

सुरूपना soo-rúpna, *v. n.* To sip.

सुरूकना soo-róokna, *v. a.* To swallow by gulps.

सुडौल soo-dóul, } *adj.* Well-formed, well-
सुडब soo-dhúb, } shaped, elegant, grace-
सुडाल soo-dhál, } ful.

सुडौलदेही soodóul-dehée, *s. f.* Gracefulness of bodily shape, handsomeness.

सुत soot, *s. m.* A son.

सुता sóo-ta, *s. f.* A daughter.

सुतार soo-tár, *s. m.* A carpenter; time, opportunity.

सुतारी soo-táree, *s. f.* An awl, a bodkin.

सुतार्थी soot-árthee, *adj.* Desirous of having a son.

सुथन soo-thún, *s. m.* Trousers.

सुथरा sóothra, *adj.* Neat, beautiful, elegant, adorned, excellent, well.

सुथराई sooth-raée, *s. f.* Neatness, beauty, elegance, goodness.

सुथरासाही sóothra-sáhee, *s. m.* A follower of *Soothrasah,* a religious mendicant.

सुदंती soo-dúntee, *s. f.* The female elephant of the north-west quarter.

सुदर्शन soo-dúrshun, *adj.* Handsome, good-looking. *s. m.* The discus of *Krishn;* the rose-apple (*Eugenia jambu*).

सुदी sóo-dee, *s. f.* The light half of the lunar month.

सुदुराचार soo-doorachár, *adj.* Very wicked, abandoned, a profligate.

सुदुर्लभ soo-dóorlubh, *adj.* Difficult to be attained, unattainable.

सुदुष्कर soo-dóoskur, *adj.* Very difficult.

सुदृढ soo-drírh, *adj.* Solid, firm. *adv.* Very hard or firm.

सुध soodh, *s. f.* Memory, remembrance, sensation, consciousness, notice, care, intelligence. *adj.* Accurate, correct; pure, clean, unpolluted. *Be-soodh, adj.* Beside one's self.

सुधबुध soodh-boodh, *s. f.* Correct knowledge, perception, sense, care.

सुधलेना soodh-léna, *v. a.* To take care of, accommodate, look after, inquire into.

सुधरना sóo-dhurna, *v. n.* To be correct, to be or seem right or good, to be mended, to avail, to succeed or answer.

सुधा sóo-dha, *s. m.* Nectar, the beverage of immortality and sustenance of the gods; the nectar or honey of flowers.

सुधं sóo-dhan, *adv.* Together, with.

सुधांशु soodh-ánsoo, } *s. m.* The moon, as
सुधाकर soodhákur, } being the supposed mine or repository of the beverage of the gods.

सुधाना soodhána, *v. a.* To put in mind, to cause to remember.

सुधारना soo-dhárna, *v. a.* To adorn, adjust, arrange, rectify, mend.

सुधी soo-dhée, *s. m.* A *pundit,* a learned man or teacher; an intelligent person.

सुन soon, *adj.* Insensible, without sensation, palsied.

सुनकातर soon-kátur, *s. m.* A kind of snake.

सुनबहरी soon-búhree, *s. f.* A disease (*Elephantiasis*).

सुनसर soon-súr, *s. m.* An ornament.

सुनसान soon-sán, *adj.* Void, dreary, desolate and silent, still, lonely, dismal.

सुनहरा soonuhrá, } *adj.* Golden.
सुनहरी soonuhrée, }

सुनाना soonána, *v. a.* To cause to hear, to inform, to advise, tell, bid, warn.

सुनापत soonapút, *s. f.* Stillness, dreariness.

सुनाभ soo-nábh, *s. m.* A mountain; part of the ranges of southern India.

सुनार soo-nár, *s. m.* A goldsmith.

सुनारिन soonarín, } *s. f.* A goldsmith's
सुनारनी soo-narnée } wife.

सुनारी soo-náree, *adj.* Clever. *s. f.* The business of a goldsmith; a good handsome woman.

सुनावनी soo-náonee, *s. f.* Tidings of any one having died abroad.

सुनिद्रा soo-nídra, *s. f.* Sound sleep.

सुनीत soo-néet, *adj.* Well-behaved; politic. *s. m.* Good conduct; policy.

सुनीति soo-néeti, *s. f.* Propriety of behaviour, good manners.

सुनीलक soo-néeluk, *s. m.* The blue shrike; the emerald or sapphire.

सुन्दर sóon-dur, *adj.* Beautiful, handsome, comely, seemly; good, virtuous.

सुन्दरता soondur-tá, } *s. f.* Beauty,
सुन्दरताई soondurtaée, } handsomeness.

सुन्दरी soondur-ée, *adj. f.* Beautiful, handsome; a handsome woman. *s. f.* Beauty, comeliness; a small timber tree (*Heritiera minor*).

सुन्धावट soondhávut, *s. m.* Smell, perfume, odour, scent, an earthy smell.

सुन्ना soon-ná, *v. a.* To hear, hearken, listen or attend to. *s. m.* Hearing; a cypher.

सुपत्र soo-pútr, *s. m.* The leaf of the *Laurus cassia.*

सुपथ soo-púth, *s. m.* A good road; good conduct.

सुपक्ष soo-púksh, *s. m.* The party which has justice on its side; the fortunate half of the month, i. e. from the new to the full moon.

सुपक्षी soo-púkshee, *s. m.* An advocate of the just cause.

सुपात्र soo-pátr, *adj.* Worthy, fit, creditable. *s. m.* An able or clever man; a vessel of earthenware, &c.

सुपारा soo-pára, *s. m.* Glans penis.

सुपारी soo-páree, *s. f.* Betel-nut (*Areca catechu*); glans penis.

सुपूत soó-pootr, } *s. m.* An excellent, a
सुपूत soo-púot, } tractable or dutiful son.

सुप्त soopt, *adj.* Sleeping, asleep; senseless, numbed. *s. m.* Sleep, deep or sound sleep.

सुप्रकाश soo-prukásh, *adj.* Manifest, apparent; public.

सुप्रतिष्ठा soo-prutishthá, *s. f.* Consecration, erection (*as of a temple or idol*).

सुप्रसन्न soo-prusúnn, *adj.* Well-pleased, favouring, favourable.

सुफल soo-phúl, *adj.* Bearing good fruit (*literally or figuratively*), fruitful, profitable, useful.

सुफेन soo-phén, *s. m.* Cuttle-fish bone.

सुबन्ध soo-búndh, *adj.* Well-secured, having a good binding.

सुबास soobás, *s. f.* Sweet smell, fragrance, odour, perfume.

सुबुद्धि soo-bóoddhi, *adj.* Wise, clever, intelligent.

सुभ soobh, *adj.* Good, pleasant, agreeable, happy, fortunate, auspicious.

सुभगा soo-bhugá, *s. f.* A woman beloved by her husband, a favourite wife; a respectable and auspicious mother.

सुभद्र soo-bhúdr, *adj.* Propitious, auspicious, fortunate.

सुभाव soo-bháo, *s. m.* Good disposition, nature, natural state, property, disposition. *adj.* Well-disposed, of good quality.

सुभासुभ soobhasóobh, *compound adj.* Good and bad, lucky and unlucky.

सुभीता soo-bhéeta, *s. m.* Opportunity, convenience, accommodation, time, leisure.

सुमङ्गल soo-múngul, *adj.* Very fortunate or auspicious.

सुमत soo-mút, *adj.* Friendly, well or kindly disposed.

सुमति soo-múti, *s. f.* Friendship, kindness; benevolence; good conscience.

सुमुन soo-mún, *adj.* Handsome, beautiful. *s. m.* Wheat.

सुमनोहर soo-munóhur, *adj.* Very agreeable, pleasing, beautiful.

सुमरन sóom-run, *s. m. f.* Remembrance (*continual theme*), mentioning. *s. f.* A small rosary, or string of beads.

सुमरना sóo-murna, *v. a.* To remember, to keep in memory; to mention, Soomir, *s. m.* Remembrance.

सुमेर soo-méroo, *s. m.* The sacred mountain *Meroo*, allegorically represented as composed of gold and gems, and the residence of the gods; (*in astronomy*) the north-pole.

सुमेल soo-mél, *adj.* Suitable, affable, of pleasing manners.

सुम्बा sóomba, *s. m.* A sponge-staff, a ramrod.

सुर soor, *s. m.* A god, a deity; tone, voice, accent, note; a vowel. Soor milana, To sing in tune.

सुरंग sóo-rung, *s. f.* A mine; a hole cut in a wall to break into a house, &c.; a gallery, subterraneous passage, an adit. *s. m.* Red colour. *adj.* Red-coloured, light bay or chesnut (*horse*).

सुरंगधातु sóorung-dhátoo, *s. m.* Red chalk.

सुरत sóo-rut, *s. f.* Recollection, consideration, reflection, memory, attention, caution, accuracy; copulation, coition.

सुरता soor-tá, *adj.* Mindful, considerate, attentive, prudent, intelligent, accurate.

सुरतीला soor-téela, *adj.* Considerate, prudent.

सुरधूप soor-dhóop, *s. m.* Resin, turpentine.

सुरभि soorúbhi, *adj.* Fragrant, sweet-smelling. *s. m.* Nutmeg.

सुरस soo-rús, *adj.* Sweet; well-flavoured, sapid, juicy.

सुरसुराना soor-soorána, *v. n.* To creep along as a snake, to make the noise a snake does when creeping.

सुरसराहट soor-sooráhut, *s. f.* Creeping (*sensation*), titillation.

सुरसुरी sóor-sooree, *s. f.* Titillation; an insect bred in grain.

सुरा sóora, *s. f.* Spirituous liquor.

सुरुकना sóo-rook-na, *v. a.* To swallow by gulps.

सुरूप soo-róop, *adj.* Handsome, well-formed, beautiful.

सुरत soo-ryt, } *s. f.* A paramour, a
सुरेतिन soorytin, } mistress, a concubine.

सुखलगा sóo-lugna, *v. n.* To light, to be

kindled, to be inflamed; to burn without smoke or flame.

सुलगाना sool-gána, v. n. To light, to inflame, to kindle.

सुलझना soo-lújhna, v. n. To be unravelled or disentangled.

सुलझाना sool-jhána, v. a. To unravel, to disentangle.

सुलभ sóo-lubh, adj. Easy, feasible, attainable, of easy acquisition or attainment, not difficult to be obtained or effected.

सुलवाना soolwána, v. a. To cause to put to sleep.

सुलक्षण soo-lúkshun, s. m. Good distinguishing mark or character. adj. Clearly or strongly distinguished by (marks, features, or) character.

सुलाना soo-lána, v. a. To cause or put to sleep, to repose; to kill, to murder. Soola dena, To kill, to murder.

सुलेमानी soolymánee, s. m. An onyx.

सुवक्ता soo-vuktá, adj. Eloquent.

सुवचन soo-vúchun, s. m. Eloquence, speaking well or elegantly.

सुवर्ण soo-vúrn, adj. Of a good tribe or caste; brilliant, bright; of a good colour. s. m. Gold; a sort of Sandal-wood; a kind of red chalk or ochre.

सुवर्णगणित soovúrn-gunít, s. m. (In arithmetic) Allegation medial.

सुवाना soo-wána, v. a. To cause to sleep.

सुवास soo-vás, s. m. A pleasant or reputable dwelling; an agreeable perfume.

सुविक्रम soo-víkrum, s. m. Prowess, valour.

सुविचार soo-vichár, s. m. Deliberate or due consideration.

सुविध soo-vídh, adj. Of a good kind, in a good or easy way. adv. Easily.

सुवेशी soo-véshee, adj. Well-dressed, ornamented, decorated.

सुवैया soo-wyya, s. m. A sleeper.

सुशील soo-shéel, adj. Well-disposed, of good temper or disposition.

सुशीलता soosheel-tá, s. f. Natural amiability, excellence of temper or disposition.

सुषुप्त soo-shóopt, adj. Fast asleep.

सुषुप्ति soo-shóopti, s. f. Deep sleep, profound repose, entire insensibility.

सुसकारना soos-kárna, v. n. To sibilate, to hiss (as a snake).

सुसताना soos-tána, v. n. To rest.

सुसमय soo-súmuy, s. m. A season of plenty, a good season.

सुसर sóo-sur, सुसरा sóos-ra, s. m. Father-in-law.

सुसरार soos-rár, सुसराल soos-rál, s. f. Father-in-law's house or family.

सुस्थ soosth, adj. Well, healthy.

सुस्थता soosth-tá, s. f. Health.

सुस्थिर soo-sthír, adj. Firm, steady, stable; resolute, cool.

सुहुरना soo-húrna, v. n. To trail, to drag.

सुहाग soo-hág, s. m. Auspiciousness, good fortune; the affection of a husband.

सुहागन soo-hagún, s. f. A woman beloved by her husband, a favourite wife, a married woman whose husband is alive.

सुहागपिटारा soohág-pitára, s. m. A casket of jewels presented by the bridegroom to his bride.

सुहागलहर soohág-lúhur, s. f. A cool refreshing breeze.

सुहागा soo-hága, s. m. Borax.

सुहाता soo-háta, adj. Agreeable, pleasant, charming.

सुहाना soo-hána, adj. Agreeable, pleasant, charming. v. n. To be agreeable, to please, to be liked or approved of.

सुहारना soohárna, v. a. To trail, to drag.

सुहाल soo-hál, s. m. सुहाली soo-halée, s. f. Bread (or cakes) fried in butter.

सुहावन soohávun, adj. Agreeable, pleasant, charming.

सुहावना soohávuna, adj. Agreeable, pleasant, charming. v. n. To be agreeable, to please, to be liked or approved of.

सुहृदय soo-hríduy, adj. Good-hearted.

सूअर sóo-ur, s. m. A hog. Soour ka gosht, Pork.

सूअरी soo-urée, s. f. A sow.

सूआ sóo-a, s. m. A parrot, paroquet; a needle with which gunny bags are sewed, a packing needle, an awn of corn.

सूई soo-ée, s. f. A needle. Sooee ka senbul, A bubble. Sooee keh nakeh seh khoodaee ko nikalna, Applied to express the performance of things apparently impossible. Sooiya, adj. Pointed.

सूंगरा sóong-ra, s. m. A buffalo calf.

सूंगा soongá, s. m. Clitoris.

सूंघ soongh, s. f. Smell.

सूंघन soon-ghún, s. f. Any thing to smell to snuff, smelling.

सूंघना sóonghna, v. a. To smell.

सूंघनी soongh-née, s. f. Snuff.

सूंठ soont, s. f. Silence. Soont bhurna, or,

—*marna*, To be silent. *Soont mareh jana*, To depart in silence.

खूंड soond, *s. f.* Proboscis of an elephant.

खूंडा soondá, *s. m.* A weevil, or small insect in corn.

खूंड़ी soon-rée, *s. m.* A distiller and vender of spirituous liquors.

खूंतना sóont-na,
खूंथना sóonth-na, } *v. a.* To strip leaves off vegetables; to draw (*a sword*).

खूंस soons, *s. m.* A porpoise.

खूकटा sóok-ta, *adj.* Lean, weak.

खूकना sóok-na, *v. n.* To dry, to become dry.

खूकर soo-kúr, *s. m.* A hog; a sort of deer (*the hog-deer*).

खूकवा sook-wá, *s. m.* A kind of vetch.

खूका soo-ká, *adj.* Dry.

खूका soo-ká, *s. m.*
खूकी soo-kée, *s. f.* } A quarter of a rupee piece.

खूकास sookás, *s. m.* Leisure.

खूकछूरी sookh-chhúree, *s. f.* A consumption, atrophy.

खूखना sóokh-na, *v. n.* To dry, dry up, evaporate, fall away, pine away, emaciate, shrivel, dwindle, wither.

खूखा sóo-kha, *adj.* Dry. *s. m.* Dry tobacco eaten with betel-leaf; a consumption, atrophy. *Sookha dhan*, Rice burnt up by the sun's rays.

खूगंध soogundh, *s. f.* Perfume, fragrance. *adj.* Fragrant. *Soogundh-suna*, Impregnated or mixed with perfume.

खूगा sóo-ga, *s. m.* A paroquet.

खूचक soo-chúk, *s. m.* A teacher, an instructor; a needle.

खूचित soochít, *adj.* Thoughtless, at leisure, disengaged, at ease; careful, attentive; occupied.

खूची soo-chée, *s. f.* A needle.

खूचीपुत्र sóochee-putr, *s. m.* An index (*to a work*).

खूछम sóochhum, *adj.* Subtile, fine, slender, minute, small; shrill.

खूछमता sóochhumtá, *s. f.* Subtileness, minuteness; shrillness.

खूज sooj,
खूजन sóo-jun, } *s. f.* Swelling.

खूजना sóoj-na, *v. n.* To swell, to rise.

खूजा soojá, *s. m.* A borer, a gimlet, an auger, an awl.

खूजी sóo-jee, *s. f.* Meal, flour (*ground coarse*).

खूजी soo-jée, *s. m.* A tailor. *s. f.* A needle.

खूझ soojh, *s. f.* Sight.

खूझना sóojh-na, *v. n.* To be visible, to be seen, to appear, to seem, to be able to be seen.

खूडोल soo-dóul, *adj.* Well-shaped, graceful.

खूत soot, *s. m.* Thread, yarn; a silver thread; a stamen (*in botany*), a tendril; a charioteer, a carpenter. *Soot-boontee*, A kind of needlework.

खूतक soo-túk, *s. m.* Impurity from childbirth or miscarriage.

खूतना sóot-na, *v. n.* To sleep.

खूतल soo-túl, *s. m.* A division of the lower regions, the sixth in descent.

खूतला soot-lá, *s. m.* Reins of a carriage; the little skin that rises backwards near the nails, at the end of the fingers.

खूतली sóot-lee, *s. f.* String, twine.

खूतिका sootí-ka, *s. f.* A woman recently delivered.

खूती sóotee, *adj.* Made of cotton-thread, threaden.

खूतीमास sootee-más, *s. m.* The last month of pregnancy.

खूत्र sootr, *s. m.* A thread in general; a rule, a precept, in morals or science.

खूथून soo-thún, *s. f.* Drawers.

खूथनी sooth-née, *s. f.* Drawers; an edible root (*Dioscorea fasciculata*).

खूद्र soodr, *s. m.* A person of the fourth or servile tribe among the *Hindoos*.

खूद्रानी soodránee, *s. f.* A female of the *Soodr* caste.

खूधा soo-dhá, *adj.* Proper, true; straight; simple, artless.   [ness.

खूधाई soo-dháee, *s. f.* Simplicity, artless-

खून soon, *adj.* Empty, vacant.

खूना soo-ná, *adj.* Empty, desert, void.

खूनू sóonoo, *s. m.* A son.

खूप soop, *s. m.* A kind of basket for winnowing corn with.

खूपाबेना sóopa-béna, *s. m.* A kind of bird, a swallow (*Hirundo apus batassia*).

खूपारा soo-pára, *s. m.* Glans penis.

खूपियारी sóopi-yáree, *s. f.* Betel-nut.

खूबर soobúr, *adj.* Impure, alloyed (*silver*).

खूबरन soobúrun, *s. m.* Pure gold. *adj.* Golden.

खूबस soobús, *s. m.* A pleasant dwelling.

खूबास soobás, *s. m.* A pleasant dwelling; a pleasant smell, fragrance.

खूभाव soo-bháo, *s. m.* Good disposition, good nature. *adj.* Well-disposed.

सूम soom, *s. m.* A miser.

सूर soor, *s. m.* A hero; the sun; tenesmus.

सूरज sóo-ruj, *s. m.* The sun.

सूरजगहन sóoruj-gúhun, *s. m.* Eclipse of the sun.

सूरजमूखी sóoruj-móokhee, *s. f.* Sun-flower (*Helianthus annuus*); a kind of fan or parasol.

सूरता soor-tá, *s. f.* Valour, heroism. *Soorta-dharee*, Heroic.

सूरदास soor-dás, *n. prop.* A *Hindee* poet and singer who was blind; hence a blind man, among the *Hindoos*, is called *Soordas*.

सूरबीर soor-béer, *s. m.* A hero.

सूरमूलार soor-mulár, *s. m.* A musical mode.

सूरमा soor-má, *adj.* Bold; brave.

सूरमापन soorma-pún, *s. m.* Bravery, heroism.

सूरा soorá, *s. m.* A hero.

सूर्ज soorj, *s. m.* The sun.

सूर्जग्रहन soorj-grúhun, *s. m.* Eclipse of the sun.

सूर्जमण्डल soorj-múndul, *s. m.* The orb or disc of the sun.

सूर्जमूखी soorj-móokhee, *s. f.* Sun-flower (*Helianthus annuus*).

सूर्जसंक्रांति soorj-sunkránti, *s. f.* The sun's entrance into a new sign.

सूर्जास्त soorj-ást, *s. m.* Sunset.

सूर्जोदय soorj-óduy, *s. m.* Sunrise.

सूल sool, *s. m. f.* Colick; a trident, pike, dart; the point of a spear; a thorn; compassion, tenderness. *s. m.* Situation, condition.

सूली sóo-lee, *s. f.* An empaling stake. *Soolee dena*, or, —*churhana*, To empale.

सूवा sóo-va, *s. m.* A parrot, paroquet; a needle with which gunny bags are sewed, a packing needle, an awn of corn.

सूस soos, ⎫ *s. m.* A porpoise (*Del-*
सूसमार soos-már, ⎭ *phinus*).

सूसंदेस soo-sundés, *s. m.* Good tidings.

सूसी soo-sée, *s. f.* A kind of cloth.

सूहा soo-há, *adj.* Red, crimson. *s. m.* A musical mode.

सूहाकूसूम्भा sóoha-koosoombhá, *adj.* Red as the dye of safflower.

सूक्ष्म sooksm, *adj.* Little, small; minute, atomic; fine, delicate; ingenious, subtle.

सूक्ष्मता sooksm-tá, *s. f.* Fineness, subtilty.

सूक्ष्मदर्शी sooksm-dúrshee, *adj.* Acute, quick, sharp-sighted, intelligent.

सूक्ष्मबुद्धि sooksm-bóoddhi, *adj.* Sharp, shrewd, intelligent, acute. *s. f.* Mental acumen.

सृजना sríj-na, *v. a.* To create, produce, form.

सृष्ट srisht, *adj.* Created, made.

सृष्टि sríshti, *s. f.* Creation, creating; the creation, the world; nature, natural property or disposition.

से seh, *adv.* From, of, out of, by, with, at, since, to, through, than.

सेंक senk, *s. m.* Toasting, fomentation. *Senk sank kurna*, To toast or warm.

सेंकना sénk-na, *v. a.* To toast, parch, warm before, or with, any thing hot, to foment, to incubate (*eggs*).

सेंकरा senk-ra, *adj.* Hundred.

सेंगरी seng-rée, *s. f.* A pod, siliqua (*particularly the siliqua of the radish*).

सेंठा sen-thá, *s. m.* ⎫ A kind of reed (*of*
सेंठी sen-thée, *s. f.* ⎭ *which morhas are* *made*), reed-grass (*Saccharum Sara*).

सेंत sent, *adv.* Gratis, free of cost.

सेंतना sént-na, *v. a.* To adjust, to put to rights.

सेंतमेत sent-met, *adv.* Gratis, free of cost.

सेंद send, *s. f.* A vegetable (*Cucumis Madraspatanus*).

सेंदूर sen-dóor, *s. m.* Red-lead, minium.

सेंध sendh, *s. m.* A hole made in a wall by thieves.

सेंधना séndh-na, *v. a.* To mine.

सेंधा sén-dha, *s. m.* Rock-salt.

सेंधिया sén-dhiya, *s. m.* Poison; a housebreaker; a *Marhatta* tribe (*probably so named as originating on the banks of the river Sindh*).

सेंधी sen-dhée, *s. f.* The juice of the wild date tree (*Phœnix sylvestris*).

सेंहुआ sénhooa, *s. m.* A tetter.

सेचन séch-un, *s. m.* Sprinkling, aspersion.

सेज sej, *s. f.* A bed, a couch.

सेजबन्द sej-búnd, *s. m.* A cord for fastening bedding to the bedstead.

सेठ seth, *s. m.* A wholesale merchant, banker. [brush.

सेठन sethún, *s. f.* A whisk, a kind of

सेत set, *adj.* White.

सेतदीप set-déep, *s. m.* The white island or a minor division of the universe so called, and supposed by Wilford to be Britain.

सेतु sétoo, *s. m.* A bridge.

सेतुबन्ध setoo-búndh, *s. m.* The ridge of rocks extending from the south extremity of the *Coromandel* coast towards the island of *Ceylon*,

सेदना séd-na, *v. a.* To stupe, to foment.

सेन sen, *s. m.* A hawk.

सेना séna, *s. f.* An army.

सेनानी sen-ánee, } *s. m.* A general, the
सेनापति séna-púti, } commander of an army.

सेम sem, *s. m.* The flat bean.

सेमल sém-ul, *s. m.* The silken or a coarse kind of cotton, or the tree producing it (*Bombax heptaphyllum*).

सेर ser, *s. m.* Name of a weight.

सेराना ser-ána, *v. a.* To set afloat; to despatch; to cool.

सेरुआ serooá, *s. m.* The head and foot parts of a bed-frame.

सेल sel, *s. m.* A spear.

सेला séla, *s. m.* A kind of sheet constituting a part of dress, especially worn and given in presents in the *Dukkhin*; a royal tiger.

सेलिया séliya, *s. m.* Tabby, puss.

सेली selée, *s. f.* A necklace (*of threads*) worn by mendicants, a sash, a belt.

सेव sev, *s. m.* A kind of sweetmeat; an apple. *s. f.* Service, worship, attendance on.

सेवक sev-úk, *s. m.* A servant, a worshipper, a votary.

सेवकाई sevuk-áee, *s. f.* Service.

सेवरा sev-rá, *s. m.* A mendicant of the *Jyn* faith; *Trophis aspera.*

सेवती sev-tée, *s. f.* A white rose (*Rosa glandulifera*).

सेवन sev-ún, *s. m.* Sewing, darning, stitching; service. *verbal n.* Serving, to serve.

सेवना sév-na, *v. a.* To attend on, serve; to brood, rear, sit, incubate, hatch.

सेवरा sév-ra, *s. m.* Half-baked earthenware.

सेवा sév-a, *s. f.* Service, servitude; worship, homage; addiction to, attendance on.

सेवारी sewáree, *s. f.* Sugar that has been purified with *siwar*, the green vegetation at the bottom of rivers or other water.

सेवई sevúeen, *s. f.* Vermicelli.

सेष sesh, *s. m.* Remainder, end; the king of the serpent race, as a large thousand-headed snake, at once the couch and canopy of *Vishnoo* and the upholder of the world, which rests on one of its heads.

सेषनाग ses-nág, *s. m.* The king of the serpent race.

सेसुर ses-úr, *s. m.* The gripe of a bow; name of a play at cards.

सेही sehée, *s. f.* A porcupine.

सेहुंड sehóond, *s. m.* A species of Euphorbia, or indeed a general name for plants of that kind; the milk-hedge plant (*Euphorbia antiquorum, &c.*)

सै suy, *adj.* Hundred. *s. f.* Success.

सैंकरा synk-rá, *adj.* Hundred.

सैंगुर syn-gúr, *s. m.* The beau of *Sumee* or *Mimosa Suma.*

सैंतना synt-na, *v. a.* To adjust, to put to rights.

सैंतालीस syntálees, *adj.* Forty-seven.

सैंताव syntáo, *s. m.* Arrangement.

सैंतीस syntées, *adj.* Thirty-seven.

सैंकड़ा sykra, *adv.* A hundred per cent.

सैतना sytna, *v. a.* To take care of, keep carefully, husband.

सैन syn, *s. m.* Sleeping, repose. *s. f.* An army, forces; a wink, sign, token, hint, a signal. *Syn kurna,* To beckon.

सैनासैनी syná-synée, *s. f.* Mutual tokens, signs, hints, or signals.

सैंध्व syn-dhúv, *adj.* Produced or born in *Sindh. s. m.* A horse; rock-salt.

सैन्यूह synyúh, *s. f.* An army.

सैल syl, *s. m.* A mountain.

सैहरन sy-húrun, *s. f.* Sufferance.

सैहरुचे sy-huruće, *s. m.* Sufferer.

सो so, *pron.* That, he, she, it; so.

सोअर so-úr, *s. m.* The chamber of a puerperal woman.

सोआ só-a, *s. m.* Fennel (*Anethum sowa*).

सोई so-ée, *pron.* That very, he himself.

सों sou, *postpos.* From, with, through, than.

सोंटा sont-a, *s. m.* A club, mace, pestle. *Sonteh-burdar,* A mace-bearer; a person in the retinue of the great, armed with a short curved club, generally covered with silver.

सोंठ sonth, *s. f.* Dry ginger; (met.) a miser. *Sonth kee nas nuh lena,* To be very covetous. *Sonth kee see nas leh ruha,* To endure, to wait patiently, to suffer.

सोंठूराछ sonthoo-ráeh, *adj.* Hard, miserly.

सोंदी sondée, *s. f.* The wash in which washermen steep their cloth.

सोंधना sóndh-na, *v. a.* To rub cloth in mud preparatory to washing; to mix, to smear.

सोंधा son-dhá, *s. m.* A composition of fragrant substances used for washing the hair; smelling like that of a new earthen vessel when wetted or from parching of pulse.

सोंधारट son-dhahút, s. f. Fragrance ; a smell like that of new earth.

सोंधे sondhéh, adj. Fragrant, smelling like new earth.

सोंपना sómpna, v. a. To deliver over, commit to charge, give, consign, resign, entrust, deposite.

सोंह sonh, s. f. An oath.

सोंहखिलाना sonh-khilána, v. a. To adjure, to swear.

सोंहडालना sonh-dálna, v. a. To conjure.

सोंहदेना sonh-dena, v. a. To adjure.

सोंहीं sonhéen, adv. Face to face, opposite, before, in front.

सोक sok, s. m. The holes in a bedstead through which the strings for bracing it pass ; affliction, grief, lamentation, sorrow.

सोखना sókh-na, v. a. To soak up, dry up, absorb.

सोग sog, s. m. Affliction, grief, sorrow, lamentation, anguish.

सोगी sogée, adj. Afflicted, grievous.

सोच soch, s. m. Consideration, reflection, thought, meditation.

सोचना sóch-na, v. a. To consider, think, meditate, advert, reflect, imagine, conceive.

सोज soj, s. f. Swelling.

सोझ sojh, s. f. Straightness.

सोझा so-jhá, adj. Straight.

सोत sot, s. f. ⎫ A spring, a fountain, a
सोता sóta, s. m. ⎬ jet d'eau, a stream, a
rivulet, an arm (of the sea),

सोता sóta, part. pres. Asleep. s. m. Asleep, sleeping.

सोथ soth, s. f. Swelling, intumescence.

सोदरा sodur-á, adj. Born of the same mother ; an own brother.

सोध sodh, s. f. Discharge (of debt) ; correction, search inquiry, collection.

सोधना sódh-na, v. a. To pay, to discharge (a debt), to liquidate ; to collate ; to refine metals.

सोन son, s. m. Name of a river ; name of a flower (Bignonia indica).

सोनुहरा sonúh-ra, ⎫ adj. Golden.
सोनुहला sonuh-lá, ⎬

सोनुहलापानी sonúhla-pánee, s. m. Gilding.

सोना sóna, v. n. To sleep ; (met.) to die. s. m. Gold. Soneh-ka nuwala, An expensive banquet, a delicious morsel.

सोनिया son-íya, s. m. One who separates gold from ashes, &c. in the mint.

सोपान sopán, s. f. A ladder, a scale.

सोभना sóbh-na, v. n. To become, befit.

सोभा só-bha, s. f. Beauty, splendour, show, ornament, dress, decoration.

सोभायमान sobhayumán, adj. Beautiful, splendid conspicuous, adorning.

सोभाव sobháo, s. m. Nature, natural state, property or disposition, genius.

सोम som, s. m. The moon ; a mountain or mountainous range, the mointains of the moon.

सोमतीर्थ som-téerth, s. m. A place of pilgrimage in the west of India.

सोमपत्र som-pútr s. m. A sort of grass (Saccharum cylindricum).

सोमराज som-ráj, s. m. Black cumin seed (Serratula anthelmintica).

सोमराजी som-rájee, s. m. A medicinal plant (Serratula anthelmintica).

सोमवत som-wút, adj. Lunar. adv. Like the moon.

सोमवार som-wár, s. m. Monday.

सोरठ so-rúth, s. f. Name of a musical mode.

सोरठा sor-thá, s. m. A metre in Brujbhakha.

सोलह sóluh, adj. Sixteen. Soluhwan, adj. Sixteenth.

सोह soh, s. f. Ornament, dress, decoration.

सोहन só-hun, s. f. A file ; a whetstone. s. m. f. A kind of sweetmeat. s. m. A lover, a friend. adj. Pleasing.

सोहना sóh-na, v. n. To become, to beseem. v. a. To weed.

सोहागा so-hága, s. m. Borax.

सोही só-hee, adv. Before, face to face, opposite, in front.

सौ sou, adj. A hundred. Sou sir ka hona lit. possessing a hundred heads ; so that, if one or several be cut off, others still remain), Implies excessive perseverance, energy or obstinacy.

सौंपना sóump-na, v. a. To deliver over, commit to charge, give, consign, resign, intrust, deposite.

सौंफ sounph, s. f. Anise seed (Pimpinella anisum).

सौंरा sóunra, s. m. Soot, or any thing of a black colour.

सौकर sóu-kur, m. ⎫ adj. Hoggish, swin-
सौकरी sou-kur-ée, f. ⎬ ish.

सौगन्ध sou-gúndh, adj. Fragrant. s. f. Perfume, fragrance.

सौगन्धसना sougúndh-súna, adj. Impregnated or mixed with perfume.

सौगन्ध sou-gúndhyuh, s. m. Odour, fragrance.

शौच souch, *s. m.* Purification by ablution, &c. ; ablution.

शौजन्य sou-júnyuh, *s. m.* Kindness, compassion ; friendship ; goodness.

शौत sout,
शौतन sout-ún, } *s. f.* Rival (*wife*), contemporary wife. (*One wife is sout to another*).

शौतियादाह sóutiya-dáh, *s. f.* Malice of a rival wife.

शौतेला sou-téla, *adj.* Belonging or relating to *Sout*, of one father by different mothers ; as, *Soutela bhaee*, Step-brother ; *Soutelee buhin*, Step-sister.

शौन्दर्य soun-dúrj, *s. m.* Beauty, loveliness.

शौभाग्य sou-bhágyuh, *s. m.* Auspiciousness, good fortune ; the fourth of the astronomical *yogs*.

शौभाग्यवान् sou-bhagyuwán, *adj.* Auspicious, fortunate.

शौमिक soum-ík, *adj.* Lunar.

शौर sour, *adj.* Solar. *s. m.* Name of a fish.

शौरभ sou-rúbh, *s. m.* Fragrance ; saffron.

शौरमास sour-más, *s. m.* A solar month.

स्कन्ध skundh, *s. m.* The shoulder ; a book, a section, a chapter ; the trunk of a tree.

स्खलन skhúlun, *s. m.* Stumbling, slipping, tripping ; stumbling or falling from virtue.

स्तन stun, *s. m.* The female bosom or breast.

स्तनमुख stun-móokh, *s. m.* A nipple.

स्तब्ध stubdh, *adj.* Stopped, blocked, or shut up.

स्तम्भ stumbh, *s. m.* A post, a pillar, a column ; hindrance, obstruction.

स्तम्भन stum-bhún, *s. m.* Stopping, hindering, obstruction ; a styptic, an astringent.

स्तव stuv, *s. m.* Praise, eulogium, panegyric.

स्तावक sta-vúk, *s. m.* A praiser, a panegyrist.

स्तुति stooti, *s. f.* Praise, eulogy.

स्तोत्र stotr, *s. m.* Praise, eulogium.

स्त्री stree, *s. f.* A woman or female in general.

स्त्रीजित stree-jít, *s. m.* A henpecked husband.

स्त्रीधर्म stree-dhúrm, *s. m.* Duty of woman ; the menstrual excretion.

स्त्रीराज्य stree-rájyuh, *s. m.* The kingdom of women, a country placed by some in the direction of *Bhot*.

स्त्रीलिङ्ग stree-líng, *s. m.* Feminine gender.

स्त्रीवश stree-rús, *s. m.* Subjection to women.

स्त्रैण stryn, *adj.* Female, feminine. *s. m.* The nature of woman.

स्थल sthul, *s. m. f.* Place, site, soil, dry or firm ground ; part (*of a book*).

स्थलज sthul-új, *adj.* Terrene, terrestrial, what is produced on land.

स्थलसीमा sthul-séema, *s. m.* A boundary, a land-mark.

स्थान sthan, *s. m.* Place, spot, site, situation ; a house, a dwelling, an abode, a residence ; a section, a chapter, a book ; office, appointment ; degree, station.

स्थानी sthanée, *adj.* Having place or fixation, placed, abiding, permanent, &c.

स्थापन sthá-pun, *s. m.* Placing, fixing, founding, erecting, causing to stand.

स्थापित sthapít, *part. pass.* Established, placed, fixed, founded, erected.

स्थायी sthayée, *adj.* Steady, firm, unchangeable, invariable.

स्थायीभाव sthayee-bháo, *s. m.* Fixed or permanent condition.

स्थायुक sthayóok, *adj.* Stationary ; steady, firm.

स्थाली sthalée, *s. f.* An earthen pot or boiler.

स्थावर sthá-wur, *adj.* Fixed, stationary, stable, immovable.

स्थित sthit, *adj.* Steady, firm, immovable ; determined, resolved, decreed, established.

स्थिति sthíti, *s. f.* Stay, staying, being fixed or stationary.

स्थिर sthir, *adj.* Firm, fixed, stable, steady, immovable ; hard, solid ; permanent, durable, lasting ; firm, steady (*morally*) ; cool, collected ; constant, faithful ; mild, tranquil ; settled, steadfast.

स्थिरचेता stir-chetá, *adj.* Firm, resolute, steady, constant.

स्थिरता sthirtá, *s. f.* Stability, firmness ; moral firmness, fortitude.

स्थिरमति sthir-múti, *adj.* Steady, firm, deliberate.

स्थिरात्मा sthir-átma, *adj.* Firm, resolute, unmoved ; stable, steady.

स्थूना sthooná, *s. f.* The post or pillar of a house.

स्थूल sthool, *adj.* Fat, corpulent, bulky ; large, great ; coarse.

स्थूलता sthooltá, *s. f.* Coarseness, bulkiness.

स्थूलबुद्धि sthool-bóoddhi, *adj.* Stupid, dull.

स्थैर्य sthyrj, *s. m.* Firmness, stability ; firmness of mind, resolution, fortitude.

स्थौल्य sthóulyuh, *s. m.* Bulk, size, coarseness, largeness.

स्नान snan, *s. m.* Bathing, ablution, purification by bathing.

स्नानीय snanéeyuh, *adj.* Ablutionary.

स्नेह sneh, *s. m.* Affection, kindness, friendship, love ; oil.

स्नेहवान sneh-wán, *adj.* Affectionate.

स्नेही snehée, *adj.* Kind, affectionate, friendly. *s. m. f.* Friend, lover, mistress.

स्पर्धा spurd-dhá, *s. f.* Envy, emulation, rivalry.

स्पर्धी spurd-dhée, *adj.* Envious, emulous.

स्पर्श spursh, *s. m.* Touch, contact.

स्पष्ट spusht, *adj.* Evident ; manifest, apparent ; clear, easy, intelligible.

स्पृहा sprihá, *s. f.* Wish, desire. *Sprihee, adj.* Desirous.

स्फटिक sphútik, *s. m.* Crystal.

स्फटिकमय sphutik-múy, *adj.* Made of crystal.

स्फटी sphutée, *s. f.* Alum.

स्फाटिक sphátik, *adj.* Crystalline, made, &c. of crystal. *s. m.* Crystal.

स्फुट sphoot, *adj.* Blown, opened, expanded (*as a flower*) ; apparent, manifest, evident ; known, understood.

स्फूर्ति sphóortti, *s. f.* Throbbing, palpitating, shaking.

स्फोटक sphótuk, *s. m.* A boil, a tumour.

स्मरण smúrun, *s. m.* Recollecting, remembering, memory, recollection.

स्मरणीय smúrun-éeyuh, *adj.* Fit or proper to be remembered.

स्मरन smúrun, *adj.* Remembering, recollecting, considering.

स्मृति smríti, *s. f.* Recollection, remembrance, memory ; law, the body of law ; a law book, a code of laws.

स्यानपन syan-pún, *s. m.* Cunning, art.

स्याना syaná, *adj.* Cunning, artful, shrewd, sly, knowing, sagacious, clever, prudent ; mature (*in understanding*), grown up.

स्यार syar, *s. m.* A jackal.

स्लेष slesh, *s. m.* A pun, a double meaning.

स्वकार्य्य swukárj, *s. m.* Own business or duty.

स्वकुटुम्ब swukootúmb, *s. m.* Own family.

स्वकुल swukól, *s. m.* Own family or race.

स्वकृत swukrít, *adj.* Done or made by one's self, self-performed.

स्वच्छ swuchchh, *adj.* Pure, clean, clear, free from stain or soil ; transparent, pellucid.

स्वच्छता swuchchh-tá, *s. f.* Purity, transparency, &c.

स्वच्छन्द swuchchhúnd, *adj.* Unrestrained, uncontrolled, independant, self-willed ; spontaneous ; acting to one's own opinion or inclination.

स्वजन swújun, *s. m.* A distant kinsman.

स्वज्ञाति swugyáti, *s. f.* Kindred, kin. *s. m.* A kinsman.

स्वतन्त्र swutúntr, *adj.* Unrestrained, uncontrolled, self-willed ; independant, free, absolute.

स्वतन्त्रता swutuntr-tá, *s. f.* Independance, absoluteness, wilfulness.

स्वदेश swudésh, *s. m.* Native country, home.

स्वधर्म swudhúrm, *s. m.* Peculiar duty or occupation.

स्वनगर swunúgur, *s. m.* Own or native town.

स्वनाश swunásh, *s. m.* Self-destruction.

स्वप्न swupn, *s. m.* Sleep. Dreaming, a dream.

स्वप्नदोष swupn-dósh, *s. m.* Nocturnal pollution.

स्वप्नविचार swupn-bichár, *s. m.* Interpretation of dreams.

स्वप्नविचारी swupn-bicháree, *s. m.* An interpreter of dreams.

स्वभाव swubháo, *s. m.* Nature, natural state, property or disposition.

स्वभूमि swubhóomi, *s. f.* Own land or estate ; native country.

स्वयंवर swuyum-vúr, *s. m.* The public choice of a husband by a princess, from a number of suitors assembled for the purpose.

स्वयंवरा swúyum-vúra, *s. f.* A girl choosing her husband.

स्वयम्भू swuyum-bhóo, *s. m.* Bruhma ; the self-existent.

स्वर swur, *s. m.* An accent ; a vowel ; a note in music ; tone, voice.

स्वरूप swuróop, *s. m.* Natural state or condition, nature. *adj.* Similar, like.

स्वर्ग swurg, *s. m.* Heaven, the residence of deified mortals ; the sky.

स्वर्गगमन swurg-gúmun, *s. m.* Going to heaven.

स्वर्गति swur-gúti, *s. f.* Going to heaven, future felicity ; death.

स्वर्गलोक swurg-lók, *s. m.* Paradise.

स्वर्गारोहण swurg-aróhun, *s. m.* Ascending to heaven.

स्वर्गीय swurgéeyuh, *adj.* Heavenly, divine, celestial.

स्वर्ग्य swúrgyuh, *adj.* Heavenly, paradisiacal.

स्वर्ण swurn, *s. m.* Gold.

स्वर्णक swurn-úk, *adj.* Golden, of gold.

स्वर्णचीरी swurn-kshéeree, *s. f.* A medicinal kind of moon-plant, said to be brought from the *Himalay* mountains.

स्वर्णगैरिक swùrn-gyrik, *s. m.* A kind of ochre, golden ochre.

स्वर्णचूड़ा swurn-chóora, *s. m.* The blue-jay.

स्वर्णपुष्पी swurn-póoshpee, *s. f.* The *Cassia fistula ;* a medicinal sort of moon-plant.

स्वर्लोक swur-lók, *s. m.* Heaven.

स्वल्प swulp, *adj.* Very small ; very few.

स्ववृत्ति swuvrítti, *s. f.* Own, or peculiar duty or occupation.

स्वस्ति swústi, *adv.* A particle of benediction ; an auspicious particle ; a term of sanction or approbation, (*so be it, amen.*)

स्वस्तिमान् swusti-mán, *adj.* Happy, auspicious.

स्वस्तिवाचन swusti-váchun, *s. m.* A religious rite, preparatory to any important observance, in which the *Brahmuns* strew boiled rice on the ground, and invoke the blessings of the gods on the ceremony about to commence.

स्वांग swang, *s. m.* Mimickry, acting, imitation, disguise, sham. *Swang lana,* To imitate, &c.

स्वांगी swangée, *s. m.* An actor, a mimick.

स्वागत swá-gut, *s. m.* Welcome, salutation.

स्वाति swáti, *s. f.* The star Arcturus, or fifteenth lunar asterism, consisting of but one star.

स्वाद swad, *s. m.* Taste, flavour, relish ; sweetness ; pleasure. *Swadee, s. m.* A taster.

स्वादक swad-úk, } *adj.* Delicious, relishing,
स्वादल swad-úl, } of high flavour.

स्वादु swádoo, *adj.* Sweet ; agreeable, desired ; grateful to the palate, dainty, delicate.

स्वाधिकार swa-dhikár, *s. m.* Own or peculiar office or station.

स्वाधिपत्य swádhi-pútyuh, *s. m.* Supreme sway, royalty, sovereignty.

स्वाधीन swa-dhéen, *adj.* Independant, uncontrolled, being one's own master ; absolute, despotic.

स्वाधीनता swadheen-tá, } *s. f.* Independ-
स्वाधीनी swa-dheenée, } ance, liberty, freedom.

स्वान swan, *s. m.* A dog.

स्वाभाविक swa-bhawík, *adj.* Natural, peculiar, inherent.

स्वामित्व swami-twúh, *s. m.* Ownership, mastership ; sovereignty, &c.

स्वामी swámee, *adj.* Owner, proprietor, lord, master or mistress. *s. m.* A master, a lord ; a sovereign, a prince, a monarch ; a husband, a lover ; a spiritual preceptor ; the Divine Being ; a class of mendicants.

स्वामीद्रोह swamee-dróh, *s. m.* Injuring one's master, treachery, perfidy.

स्वाराज्य swa-rájyuh, *s. m.* Final felicity ; heaven.

स्वार्थ swarth, *adj.* Having one's own object. *s. m.* Mundane affairs, desire, object, end, aim, &c.; same meaning ; own object or desire ; self-interest, selfishness.

स्वार्थिक swar-thík, *adj.* Expressing its own or literal meaning ; having one's own object ; answering its purpose or object, successful, useful, profitable.

स्वार्थी swarthée, *adj.* Selfish.

स्वास swas, } *s. m.* Breath, respiration,
स्वासा swasá, } breathing ; life.

स्वीकार swéekar, *s. m.* Promise ; assent, agreement.

स्वेच्छा swech-chhá, *s. f.* Wilfulness, following one's own purpose or inclination.

स्वेत swet, *adj.* White.

स्वेद swed, *s. m.* Warmth, heat ; prespiration, sweat.

स्वेदज swedúj, *adj.* Engendered by heat and damp, as insects and worms.

स्वैरुन swyrún, *s. m.* An adulterer.

स्वैरिणी swyrinée, *s. f.* An unchaste wife, an adulteress ; a wanton woman.

स्वैरी swyrée, *adj.* uncontrolled, self-willed.

ह

ह huh, The thirty-third consonant of the *Naguree* alphabet.

हंकाना hun-kána, *v. a.* To drive out or away.

हंकार hun-kár, *s. m.* Cry, outcry, bawling, calling ; driving.

हंकारना hun-kárna, *v. a.* To bawl to, to call, to halloo after, to brave ; to drive, to drive away, to excel.

हंकारी hun-káree, *adj.* Proud, self-conceited.

हंफैल hum-phyl, *adj.* Short-winded.

हंस huns, *s. m.* A goose, a gander, a swan, a duck ; *Bruhm,* the supreme soul.

हंसक huns-úk, *s. m.* The flamingo.

हंसगमनी huns-gúmunee, *adj.* Walking gracefully as the swan (*a woman*).

हंसगामिनी huns-gáminee, *s. f.* A graceful woman.

हंसना húns-na, *v. n.* To laugh, deride.

हंसमुख húns-mookh, *adj.* Cheerful, merry, laughing, facetious, jocular, jolly, jovial, blithe, blithsome.

हंस hunsa, *s. m.* Laughing, laughter.

हंसाई hunsáee, *s. f.* Ridicule.

हंसाना hunsána, *v. a.* To cause to laugh, to tickle.

हंसिया húnsiya, *s. m.* A sickle.

हंसी húnsee, *s. f.* Sport, fun, mirth, laughter, laugh, ridicule.

हंसुआ húnsooa, *s. m.* A sickle.

हंसोड़ hunsór, *adj.* Facetious, jocular, merry, cheerful. *s. m.* A wag.

हंसोड़पन hunsor-pún, *s. m.* Facetiousness, jocularity.

हुकबुकाना hukbuk-ána, *v. n.* To be confused or irresolute (when any thing is to be done), to be aghast.

हुकला húkla, *adj.* Stuttering, stammering.

हुकलाना huk-lána, *v. n.* To stammar, stutter, falter.

हुकलाहा hukláha, *s. m.* A stammerer.

हुकारना hukárna, *v. a.* To drive oxen or other cattle in a circle, as when treading out grain.

हुक्काबुक्का húkka-búkka, *adj.* Confused (when any thing is to be done), aghast.

हुगना húg-na, *v. n.* To go to stool, to evacuate fæces, to dung.

हुगनेटी hugnétee, *s. f.* A field or place to which people repair to ease themselves; podex.

हुगभरना hug-bhúrna, *v. n.* To be polluted with excrement, to go to stool.

हुगाना hugána, *v. a.* To cause to go to stool.

हुगास hugás, *s. f.* Inclination to go to stool, tenesmus. *Hugas-buttukh,* A restless fidgetting person.

हुचकोला huch-kóla, } *s. m.* A jolt, a shock.
हुचका húch-ka,

हुचुरमुचुर húchur-múchur, *s. m.* Dispute, cavil, excuse.

हुट hut, *s. f.* Obstinacy, perverseness, crossness, unpersuadableness, disobedience; teasing; allegation.

हुटकना hutúk-na, *v. n.* To be repulsed, driven back, to retreat, move, stop, boggle.

हुटकाना hutkána, *v. a.* To stop.

हुटकाहुटकी hútka-hútkee, *s. f.* Driving back, struggling.

हुटताल hut-tál, *s.f.* Shutting up all the shops in a market (on account of oppression, &c.)

हुटना hútna, *v. n.* To go or fall back, to be driven back, to retire, recede, move, budge, shrink, flinch, to be defeated.

3 R

हुटवा hut-wá, *s. m.* A person employed in a market to measure rice, grain, &c.

हुटवाई hut-waée, *s. f.* The office of a hut-wa.

हुटाकुटा húta-kúta, *adj.* Stout and active, robust, vigorous.

हुटाना hut-ána, *v. a* To repel, drive backwards, to back, to worst, to foil.

हुटिया hutíyá, *s. f.* A market.

हुट hutt, *s. m.* A market, a movable market, a fair.

हुट्टाकुट्टा hútta-kútta, *adj.* Stout and active, robust, vigorous.

हुट्टी huttée, *s. f.* A petty market or fair.

हुठ huth, *s. m.* Violence; oppression; rapine. *s. f.* Obstinacy, perverseness, crossness, unpersuadableness, disobedience; teasing; allegation. *Huth kurna,* or *Huth kee tekpur hona,* To resist or disobey obstinately, to be perverse or peevish.

हुठधर्मी huth-dhúrmee, *adj.* Perverse, obstinate.

हुठना húth-na, *v. n.* To be peevish, perverse or pettish.

हुठी hut-hée, *adj.* Peevish, obstinate, perverse.

हुठीला hut-héela, *adj.* Teasing (child), pettish, perverse, obstinate, peevish.

हुर hur, *s. f.* A nut (Myrobalan); an ornament resembling that fruit. *s. m.* Bilboes, the stocks.

हुरकुट hur-kút, *s. m. Acanthus ilicifolius.*

हुरगीला hur-géela, *s. m.* A bird, the gigantic crane (Ardea argala).

हुरजोरा hur-jóra, *s. m.* A medicinal plant (Cissus quadrangularis).

हुरफूटन hur-phóotun, *s. m.* Pains in the bones.

हुरबुराना hur-burána, *v. n.* To be confused, to hurry.

हुरबुरिया hur-búriya, *adj.* Easily agitated; irritable, hasty.

हुरबुरी hur-búree, *s. f.* Hurry, alarm, uproar, riot, disorder, hastiness, hubbub.

हुरहुराना hur-hurána, *v. n.* To shudder, to shiver; to crash, to rattle.

हुरहुराहट hur-huráhut, *s. f.* Crack, crash, sound.

हुरहुरी hur-húree, *s. f.* The twang of a bow.

हुरा hur-á, *s. m.* A sky-rocket.

हुराहुरी húra-húree, *s. f.* The twang of a bow.

हुड्डा húdda, *s. m.* A wasp; bone; spavin.

Huddeh mothreh nikalna, (*lit.*) To break out in spavins and œdematous swellings: (*met.*) To adopt an evil conduct.

हुड्डी **húddee**, *s. f.* A bone; the hard part in the centre of a carrot or other similar root.

हुड्डीला **huddéela**, *adj.* Bony.

हुंडा **húnda**, *s. m.* A caldron, an earthen pot or boiler. *Hunda phorna, v. a.* (*lit.* To break the pot), To disclose a secret, to let the cat out of the bag.

हुंडाना **hundána**, *v. a.* To banish, expel, drive out of a city, disgrace (*by public punishment*); to move round.

हुंडिका **hundiká**, } *s. f.* An earthen pot or
हुंडी **hundée**, } boiler.

हुत **hut**, *s. m.* Multiplication. *interj.* Begone! fy!

हुतना **hút-na**, *v. a.* To kill.

हुत्या **hut-yá**, *s. f.* Murder, slaughter, killing, slaying.

हुत्यारा **hut-yára**, *s. m.* A murderer, assassin, wretch, villain. *adj.* Inhuman, bloody.

हुत्यारी **hut-yarée**, *s. f.* A murderess, a female murderer.

हुथ **huth**, *s. m.* Hand.

हुथकटी **huth-kútee**, *s. f.* Name of a cut with the sword, which is intended to take off or disable the adversary's hand.

हुथकड़ी **huth-kúree**, *s. f.* A handcuff, fetter, manacle.

हुथखुंडा **huth-khúnda**, *s. m.* Habit, custom, knack.

हुथचुपूआ **huth-chupooá**, *s. m.* Snack, share.

हुथछूट **huth-chhóot**, *s. m.* A beater.

हुथझोला **huth-jhóla**, *s. m.* A hand-barrow.

हुथनाल **huth-nál**, *s. f.* A small cannon carried on elephants, &c.

हुथनी **huthnée**, *s. f.* A female elephant.

हुथफूल **huth-phóol**, *s. m.* A kind of firework.

हुथफेर **huth-phér**, *s. m.* Sleight of hand (*in a money-changer*), changing a good for a bad rupee for the purpose of imposition; borrowing. *Huth pher lena*, To borrow.

हुथबूली **huth-búlee**, *s. f.* Strength of hand, force; dishonesty.

हुथरस **huth-rús**, *s. m.* Amorous dalliance, toying; self-pollution, onanism.

हुथूरी **huthúree**, *s. f.* A handle, a winch (*of a spinning-wheel*).

हुथलेवा **huth-léwa**, *s. m.* A ceremony in marriage among *Hindoos*. (*The hands of the bride and bridegroom are joined palm to palm with some flour put between them*).

हुथा **huthá**, *s. m.* A handle; a shovel, a baker's peel; a sleeve.

हुथिया **huthiyá**, *s. m.* The 13th mansion of the moon, Corvus; the breaking up of the rains. *Huthiya kee rah*, The milky-way.

हुथियाना **huthiyána**, *v. a.* To seize.

हुथियार **huthiyár**, *s. m. f.* A tool, arms, weapon, implements, apparatus.

हुथियारबंद **huthiyar-búnd**, *adj.* Armed.

हुथियारबांधना **huthiyar-bándhna**, *v. a.* To arm.

हुथी **huthée**, *s. f.* A brush for rubbing down horses with, or rather a hair-glove; a rubber.

हुथेला **huthéla**, *s. m.* A thief, a robber.

हुथेली **huthélee**, *s. f.* The palm of the hand.

हुथौटी **huthóutee**, *s. f.* Dexterity, art, skill.

हुथौरा **huthourá**, *s. m.* A sledge-hammer.

हुथौरी **huthourée**, *s. f.* A small hammer.

हुथ्याई **huth-yaée**, *s. f.* Murder, slaughter, violence.

हुदियाना **hudiyána**, *v. n.* To hesitate; to be alarmed or apprehensive, to shrink.

हुदियाहुट **hudiyahút**, *s. f.* Scrupulousness, sheepishness, shyness.

हुदियाहा **hudiyahá**, *adj.* Sheepish, shamefaced, timid, bashful, scrupulous.

हुनन **hún-un**, *s. m.* Killing, destroying; injuring, hurting, striking; (*in arithmetic*) multiplication.

हुनना **hún-na**, *v. a.* To kill, to give a blow, to smite.

हुनुमान **hunoomán**, *s. m.* The monkey chief *Hunooman*, the friend, ally, and spy of *Ramchundr*, in his invasion of *Lunka*.

हुंता **huntá**, *s. m.* A murderer, a slayer.

हुप **hup**, *s. m.* Act of suddenly snatching with the mouth and swallowing.

हुपझुप **hup-jhúp**, *adj.* Quick. *Hup-jhup khana*, To eat quickly and voraciously.

हुफहुफाना **huph-huphána**, *v. n.* To pant, to be out of breath.

हुबरा **hub-rá**, *adj.* Ill-shaped, clumsy.

हुमेव **hum-éo**, *s. m.* Vanity, egotism, arrogance, pride.

हुय **huy**, *s. m.* A horse; the yak.

हुयगंधा **huy-gundhá**, *s. f.* A plant (*Physalis flexuosa*).

हुयग्रीव **huy-gréev**, *s. m.* A prince of the *Dyts*, who during *Bruhma's* sleep at the end of a *Kulp* stole the *Veds*: in the recovery of them, he was slain by *Vishnoo*, after his descent as the *Mutsya* or fish *Uvutar*.

हुयाझमा **huy-áshna**, *s. f.* The gum Olibanum tree.

हर hur, *s. m.* (*In arithmetic*), A divisor; also division; a rogue, a wag; a plough; a name of *Mahadeo*. *Hurbhoom ka raj,* A country or place in which injustice prevails. *Hurbhog, s. m.* Anarchy, confusion, uproar.

हरक hur-úk, *s. m.* (*In arithmetic*), A divisor; also division.

हरख hurúkh, *s. m.* Blowing, blooming; delight, joy, happiness, pleasure.

हरखना hurúkhna, *v. n.* To blow (*as a flower*); to be delighted.

हरखित hurkhít, *adj.* Pleased, delighted, rejoiced.

हरगुनी hur-góonee, *adj.* Skilful, clever.

हरन húr-un, *s. m.* Theft, plunder, seizing, carrying off or away, taking away by force; subtraction; the hand; semen verile; (*in arithmetic*) dividing, division. *Hurun-dookh,* Taking away or dissipating grief or trouble.

हरता hurtá, *s. m.* A thief, a stealer, a taker away.

हरताल hurtál, *s. f.* Orpiment.

हरन húr-un, *s. m.* A deer or antelope, hart.

हरना hur-ná, *s. m.* A stag, a buck, a male antelope; a pommel (*of a saddle*). *v. a.* To seize on, to take by force; to steal, spoil, plunder, take away.

हरनी hur-née, *s. f.* A doe, a hind.

हरनौटा hur-nóuta, *s. m.* A fawn.

हरफारेवरी húrpha-revrée, *s. f.* Name of a sour fruit (*Averrhoa acida : Cicca disticha : Phyllanthus cheramela*).

हरमुष्ट hurmóoshta, *adj.* Stout, robust, active.

हरमुष्टी hurmóoshtee, *s. f.* Robustness; thick-headedness.

हरसिंगार hur-singár, *s. m.* The weeping Nyctanthes (*Nyctanthes arbor-tristis*).

हरा húra, *adj.* Green, fresh; verdant.

हराई huraée, *s. f.* Greenness, freshness, verdure.

हराना hurána, *v. a.* To win, overcome, beat (*at cards*), to foil, worst, weary, tire.

हरावल huráwul, *s. m.* The advanced guard of an army, the vanguard.

हरिचन्दन huri-chúndun, *s. m.* A yellow and fragrant sort of Sandal-wood.

हरिन hur-ín, *s. m.* A deer or antelope, hart.

हरिनी hurinée, *s. f.* A doe, a hind; a woman, one of the four kinds, the same as the *Chitrini*.

हरित húrit, *adj.* Green, of a green colour.

हरिताल huritál, *s. m.* Yellow orpiment.

हरिताश्मन् hurít-áshmun, *s. m.* Blue vitriol; a turquoise; an emerald.

हरिदेव huri-dév, *s. m.* The asterism *Sravuna.*

हरिद्रा huri-drá, *s. f.* Turmeric.

हरिद्वार huridwár, *s. m.* The town of *Hurdwar,* where the Ganges descends into the level land of *Hindoostan.*

हरिन्मुनि húrin-múni, *s. m.* An emerald.

हरिभुक्त huri-bhúkt, *s. m.* A worshipper of *Vishnoo.*

हरिभजन húri-bhújun, *s. m.* Adoration of *Vishnoo.*

हरियल huriyúl, *s. m.* A green pigeon (*Columba hurriala*).

हरियाला huriyála, *adj.* Verdant, green, grassy.

हरियाली huriyalée, *s. f.* Greenness, freshness, verdure; grass.

हरीतकी hureetkée, *s. f.* Yellow or chebulic myrobalan (*Terminalia chebula*); seven varieties of this are distinguished.

हरीरा hureerá, } *adj.* Verdant, green; a
हरीला hureelá, } coward, a run-away.

हरीवा hureewá, *s. m.* A kind of paroquet.

हरेरा hurerá, *adj.* Verdant. *s. m.* A vegetable, verdure.

हरौटी huroutée, *s. f.* A cane, staff.

हर्रा hur-rá, *s. m.* An astringent nut, myrobalan (*Terminalia chebula* or *citrina*).

हर्त्ता hurttá, *s. m.* A thief, a stealer, a taker away.

हर्ष hursh, *s. m.* Joy, mirth, pleasure, delight, happiness.

हर्षना hursh-ná, *v. n.* To blow (*as a flower*); to be delighted.

हर्षित hursh-ít, *adj.* Pleased, rejoiced, happy, delighted, gladdened, made glad or happy.

हर्षोदय hursh-óduy, *s. m.* Appearance or occurrence of happiness.

हल hul, *s. m.* A plough; the afterbirth. *Hul-jota,* A tiller, a ploughman.

हलका húlka, *adj.* Light (*in weight or character*), debased, mean, silly, easy, soft, cheap. *Hulka kurna,* To lighten, exonerate, ease, assuage, debase, abase, depreciate, affront. *Hulka janna,* To disdain, disesteem.

हलकाई hulkaée, *s. f.* Lightness, levity.

हलकाना hulkána, *v. a.* To abet.

हलकापन hulka-pún, *s. m.* Lightness, levity, vanity, despicableness.

हलकोण hulkórna, *v. a.* To gather, to collect; to billow, to wave.

हलचल húl-chul, *s. f.* Fright, perturbation, hubbub, tumult, anarchy.

हलदिया huldiyá, *s. m.* A kind of poison; the jaundice; a class of merchants. *adj.* Yellow.

हलदी húldee, *s. f.* Turmeric (*Curcuma longa*).

हलपना hulúp-na, *v. n.* To toss or tumble about, to shudder in a fever.

हलफुल hul-phúl, *s. f.* Affability; hurry, perturbation.

हलरावना hul-ráona, *v. a.* To amuse, play with, dandle.

हलवाहा hulwáha, *s. m.* A ploughman.

हलवाही hulwahée, *s. f.* Tillage, ploughing.

हलहल hulhúl, *s. m.* A mortal poison.

हलहला hul-húla, *s. m.* Poison.

हलहलाट hulbulát, *s. m.* Trembling thro' fever or fear.

हलहलाना hulhulána, *v. n.* To shake (*from the effect of an ague, &c.*); to tremble. *v. a.* To shake, to cause to tremble.

हलहलिया hulhuliyá, *s. m.* Poison.

हलहली hulhulée, *s. f.* Sickness, disease; an ague.

हलाई hulaée, *s. f.* Ploughing.

हलाहल hulahúl, *s. m.* Poison.

हलिया huliyá, *s. m.* A herd (*of oxen*), drove, flock (*of cows*).

हलियाना huliyána, *v. n.* To nauseate.

हलोरा hulorá, *s. m.* A wave, billow, surge.

हलोर्ना hulórna, *v. a.* To collect, to gather.

हल्ला húlla, *s. m.* Uproar, tumult; assault.

हवन húvun, *s. m.* Sacrifice, offering, oblation.

हव्यु húv-yuh, *s. m.* An offering to the gods.

हसत् hus-út, *adj.* Laughing, smiling.

हसन hús-un, *s. m.* Laughter, laughing.

हसाई husáee, *s. f.* Ridiculing.

हसाना husána, *v. a.* To make (*one*) laugh, to cause to laugh.

हस्त hust, *s. m.* The hand; the thirteenth lunar asterism, designated by a hand, and containing five stars; a cubit measured by the hand and arm, or from the elbow to the tip of the middle finger.

हस्ति hustí, *s. m.* An elephant.

हस्तिदन्त husti-dúnt, *s. m.* Ivory.

हस्तिनी hustinée, *s. f.* A female elephant; a description of women, the worst of the four classes.

हस्तिनापुर hústina-póor, *s. m.* Ancient *Delhi*, the capital of *Yoodhishthir* and his brethren, the remains of which still exist, about 57 miles north-east of the modern city, on the banks of the old channel of the Ganges.

हस्तिमद husti-múd, *s. m.* The juice that exudes from an elephant's temples when in rut.

हस्ती hustée, *s. m.* An elephant.

हस्ली huslée, *s. m.* The collar-bone, clavicle; a collar (*of gold or silver, &c.*) worn round the neck as an ornament.

हा ha, *adv.* An interjection of weariness; of sorrow, pain; an exclamation of pleasure; a term of reproach.

हां han, *adv.* Yes, ay, indeed, by the by, forsooth; here, hither, &c. *Han kuhna*, To agree.

हांक hank, *s. f.* Cry, call, bawling, calling to (*loud*); driving. *Hank marna*, To bawl after, to call to.

हांकना hánk-na, *v. a.* To drive; to bawl to.

हांकपुकार hank-pookár, *s. f.* Uproar, outcry.

हांकाहांक hanka-hánk, *s. m.* Driving.

हांकी hán-kee, *s. f.* A vessel in which they make *sewya* or vermicelli; a sieve.

हांगर hán-gur, *s. m.* A shark.

हांडना hánd-na, *v. n.* To wander, to ramble.

हांडी han-dée, } *s. f.* A pot, a caldron.
हांड़ी han-rée, }

हांपना hámp-na, } *v. n.* To pant, to be
हांफना hámph-na, } out of breath.

हांस hans, *s. m.* A duck, a goose, a swan.

हांसी han-sée, *s. f.* Laughter, laughing, joke, derision.

हांहीं han-héen, *adv.* Yes.

हाट hat, } *s. f.* A market, a movable
हाठ hath, } market or fair, a shop.

हाटू hatóo, *s. m.* A market-man.

हार har, *s. m.* A bone.

हाड़जोड़ा har-jóra, *s. m.* A plant (*Cissus quadrangularis*).

हात hat, *s. m.* The hand.

हाथ hath, *s. m.* The hand; a cubit; possession, power.

हाथ आना hath ána, *v. n.* To come into one's possession or power, to be gained or obtained.

हाथ उठाना hath oothána, *v. a.* To leave off, refrain from, desist, abandon, relinquish, resign, cease; to salute by raising the hand to the head; to beat; to give alms.

हाथ बाट लेना hath ót léna, *v. a.* To receive with both hands open and stretched out together.

हाथ कमरपर रखना hath kúmur pur rúkhna, v. n. To be very feeble.

हाथ करना hath kúrna, v. a. To subdue, to have possession.

हाथ कानों पर रखना hath kánon pur rúkhna, v. n. To be astonished; to deny vehemently.

हाथ खैंचना hath khynchna, v. a. To refrain, desist, abstain.

हाथ चाटना hath chátna, v. a. To relish any food exceedingly, to lick one's lips.

हाथ चालाकी hath chalákee, s. f. Expertness.

हाथ जोड़ना hath jórna, v. a. To supplicate, intreat earnestly. [bestow.

हाथ झाड़ना hath jhárna, v. a. To give,

हाथ झूठा होना hath jhóota hóna, v. n. To have the hands defiled; to lose the power of the hands.

हाथ डालना hath dálna, v. a. To thrust or put the hand (in or on), to meddle, to interfere (in); to encroach.

हाथ देना hath déna, v. a. To concern one's self in or about; to make a bargain by taking hold of the hands of the other party under a cloth. (A practice chiefly used in settling the price of horses and jewels.)

हाथ धोना hath dhóna, v. a. To be disappointed, to be hopeless, to relinquish.

हाथ पकड़े लेजाना hath púkreh lejána, v. n. To hand a person.

हाथ पड़ना hath púrna, v. n. To come into one's possession.

हाथ पत्थर तले दबना hath putthúr túleh dúbna, v. n. To be helpless, to be unable to act.

हाथ पसारना hath pusárna, v. a. To ask, to beg.

हाथ पांव फूल जाने hath paon phool jáneb, v. n. To be distressed or confounded.

हाथ पांव फैलाना hath paon phylána, v. a. To extend one's business or schemes.

हाथ पांव मारना hath paon márna, v. a. To strive, endeavour, strain, toil, struggle. v. n. To be agitated; to sprawl.

हाथ फूल hath phóol, s. m. A plant (Pothos).

हाथ फेंकना hath phénkna, v. a. To fence.

हाथ फेरना hath phérna, v. a. To stroke, to caress, to coax.

हाथ बंद होना hath bund hóna, v. n. To be much engaged in business, to have no leisure; to be poor or indigent.

हाथ बढ़ाना hath burhána, v. a. To endeavour to get any thing; to gain possession of the property of others.

हाथ बांधना hath bándhna, v. a. To join the hands in a supplicating posture.

हाथ बैठना hath bythna, v. n. To acquire perfection in any art by practice.

हाथ भरना hath bhúrna, v. n. To have the hands wearied or fatigued.

हाथ मलना hath múlna, v. n. To regret, repent, lament.

हाथ मारना hath márna, v. a. To promise; to acquire, to plunder; to wound with a sword.

हाथ मिलाना hath milána, v. n. To claim equality; to prepare to wrestle.

हाथ में रखना hath men rúkhna, v. a. To possess, to hold in subjection.

हाथ रोकना hath rókna, v. a. To prevent.

हाथ लगना hath lúgna, v. n. To come to the hand, to be got, obtained, acquired.

हाथ लगाना hath lugána, v. a. To put or thrust the hand (in), to meddle (in), to handle; to reprove, punish, torment; to be employed in any business.

हाथ समेटना hath sumétna, v. a. To refrain from giving, &c.

हाथा hathá, s. m. The hand; possession, power.

हाथाजोड़ी hathá-jóree, s. f. A plant (Lycopodium imbricatum).

हाथाफची hathá-phuchée, s. f. A sort of game.

हाथांची करना hathá-banhée kúrna, v. n. To scuffle or struggle together.

हाथी háthee, s. m. An elephant; the 13th mansion of the moon.

हाथीदांत hathee-dánt, s. m. Elephant's tooth, ivory.

हाथीवान hathee-wán, s. m. An elephant-driver.

हाथी हाथ करना hathee hath kúrna, v. a. To act in concord, to pull together.

हाथों हाथ hathon háth, adv. Out of hand, overhand, quickly, expeditiously. Hathon hath le-jana, To carry away quickly, to snatch away at once or suddenly.

हान han, } s. f. Loss, privation, deficiency, harm, injury,
हानि háni, } slaughter. Hanee, adj. Occasioning loss.

हापुर hapur, s. f. A seed-bed (or rather nursery) for sugar-cane.

हाय háeh, } interj. Alas! ah!
हायहाय háeh-háeh, } s. f. A sigh.
Haeh marna, To sigh.

हायन hayún, s. m. A year; a sort of rice.

हार har, s. m. A string or garland or necklace of pearls, &c., a wreath, a chaplet (of flowers, worn as a necklace); a flock (of cattle); pasturage. s. f. Loss, forfeiture, discomfiture. part. act. Being overcome.

हार har, s. m. (In arithmetic), A divisor, also the denominator of a fraction.

हारक har-úk, s. m. A thief; a cheat, a rogue; a gambler; a tree (Trophis aspera); a plunderer, a ravisher, one who carries off any thing; (in arithmetic), a divisor.

हारजीत har-jéet, s. m. Gambling, hazard. Harjeet kurna, To gamble.

हारना hár-na, v. n. To be overcome, to be unsuccessful, to lose (in play), to be tired out. v. a. To lose.

हारमाना har-mánna, v. a. To give up a dispute, to give up in despair, to acknowledge all lost.

हारसिंगार har-singár, s. m. The weeping Nyctanthes (Nyctanthes arbor-tristis).

हारा hára, (In compos.) denotes the performer of any act, dealer in any article, as lukur-hara, A woodman; marneh-hara, A striker.

हारा hára, s. m. A necklace of pearls, &c.

हारियल hariyul, s. m. A green pigeon (Columba hurriala). adj. Of a green colour.

हारू haroo, s. m. A loser.

हार्द hardd, s. m. Affection, kindness.

हार्ज harj, s. m. Beleric myrobalan.

हल hal, adj. Quick. s. m. A plough.

हलना hálna, v. n. To shake.

हाला hála, s. f. Wine, vinous or spirituous liquor.

हालाडोला hála-dóla, s. m. Shaking, agitation; an earthquake.

हलाहल hala-húl, s. m. A sort of poison.

हालाहलधर halahúl-dhúr, s. m. A small black and venemous snake.

हालाहली hála-hulée, s. f. Wine, spirituous liquor.

हालिम hálim, s. m. Cress, cresses (Lepidum sativum).

हाव hao, s. m. Any feminine act of amorous pastime, or tending to excite amorous sensations, coquetry, blandishment, dalliance, airs.

हावभाव hao-bháo, s. m. Dalliance, blandishment, charm, attraction, welcome.

हास has, s. m. Laughing, laughter.

हासकर has-kúr, adj. Causing laughter, merry, ridiculous.

हासिका hasiká, s. f. Laughter, mirth.

हासी hasée, adj. Laughing, smiling.

हास्तिन hastín, adj. Elephantine, large, as big as an elephant.

हास्तिनपुर hástin-póor, s. m. Ancient Delhi.

हास्य hásyuh, adj. Laughable, ridiculous. s. m. Laughter, laughing, mirth.

हाहा haha, s. m. Flattery, importunity, earnest request, supplication. Haha khana, To flatter, wheedle, intreat, beseech. adv. An interjection of surprise, or grief, or pain, alas!

हाहाकार haha-kár, s. m. The noise or uproar of battle; lamentation, sound of grief or pity; consternation.

हिंडोल hin-dól, s. m. A musical mode, sung in the morning of spring.

हिंडोला hin-dóla, s. m. A swing, a cradle; a song describing the swing, and sung during that exercise.

हिंसक hin-súk, adj. Mischievous, malignant, ferocious, savage. s. m. A beast of prey; an enemy.

हिंसन hin-sún, s. m. Injuring, hurting.

हिंसा hin-sá, s. f. Injury, mischief, &c.; slaughter, killing, slaying.

हिंसालु hins-áloo, adj. Mischievous, hurtful.

हिंस्र hinsr, adj. Mischievous, hurtful, injurious; murderous; formidable, terrible; fierce, savage.

हिंस्रुक hin-srúk, s. m. A beast of prey.

हिक्का híkka, s. f. Hiccough.

हिंगु hín-goo, s. m. Asafœtida.

हिंगुल hín-gool, s. m. Vermilion.

हिचकना híchuk-na, v. n. To draw back from, to decline, to shrink, to waver, to boggle.

हिचकाना hich-kána, v. a. To jolt.

हिचकिचाना hich-kichána, v. n. To doubt, hesitate, be in suspense, falter.

हिचकिची hich-kíchee, s. f. Hesitation. Hichkichee bandhna, To gnash the teeth.

हिचकी hich-kée, s. f. The hiccough.

हिजड़ा híj-ra, s. m. An hermaphrodite, a eunuch.

हिंडन hin-dún, s. m. Wandering, roaming; copulation.

हिंडोर hin-déer, s. m. Cuttle-fish bone, considered to be the indurated foam of the sea; a tonic, a stomachic.

हित hit, adj. Suitable, proper, fit, worthy, right; friendly, affectionate, kind; useful. s. m. A good, a benefit; love, friendship, affection, benevolence.

हितकर hit-kúr, adj. Friendly, kind, favourable. s. m. A benefactor.

हितकार hit-kár, } s. m. A friend, bene-
हितकारी hit-karée, } factor.

हितकारी hit-káree, s. f. Friendship, love.

चितवान hit-wán, *adj.* Friendly, favourable, doing good to.

चितू hitóo, *s. m. f.* A friend.

चितैषी hityshée, *adj.* Seeking another's welfare.

चितोपदेश hitopdésh, *s. m.* Friendly or proper advice.

चिनचिनाना hinhinána, *v. n.* To neigh.

चिनौता hin-outá, *s. f.* Supplication, humility.

चिमाल hin-tál, *s. m.* The marshy date tree (*Phœnix* or *Elate paludosa*).

चिन्दी hindée, *adj.* Indian, relating to India.

चिन्दू hin-dóo, *s. m.* An Indian, a gentoo; (*met.*) a mole or lock (*of a mistress*).

चिन्दूवान hindoo-wán, *s. m.* A water-melon.

चिन्डोल hin-dól, *s. m.* A swing; one of the musical modes.

चिम him, *s. m.* Frost, snow; cold.

चिमकर him-kúr, *adj.* Frigorific, cold.

चिमवत him-wút, *adj.* Cold, freezing, chilly, frosty.

चिमालय him-áluy, *s. m.* The *Hymala* range of mountains, which bounds India on the north, and separates it from Tartary; the Imaus and Emodus of the ancients, giving rise to the Ganges and Indus, and many other considerable rivers, and containing the highest elevations in the world.

चिमावती híma-wutée, *s. f.* A sort of moon-plant.

चिया híya, *s. m.* Heart, breast, mind, soul, life.

चियाव hiyáo, *s. m.* Courage, bravery.

चियो hiyó, *adv.* The sound made when calling cattle.

चियौ hiyóu, चिरद hírud, चिरदा hírda, } *s. m.* Heart, breast, mind, soul, life.

चिरदावल hirdáwul, *s. m.* A defect in horses. (*It is a feather or curling lock of hair on the breast, which is reckoned unlucky for the rider*).

चिरन hír-un, *s. m.* A deer or antelope, hart.

चिरनौटा hir-noutá, *s. m.* A fawn.

चिराना hirána, *v. a.* To lose, to mislay.

चिरकी hir-kée, *s. f.* Shift, contrivance.

चिलुकना hil-úkna, *v. n.* To writhe or suffer contortions (*from affliction or pain; chiefly applied to children*).

चिलुक रुहना híluk rúhna, *v. n.* To cling to.

चिलकोर hilkór, *s. f.* Agitation, fluctuation; a wave, a billow.

चिलकोरा hil-kóra, *s. m.* A wave, a billow, a surge.

चिलकोरना hilkórna, *v. a.* To agitate, shake, disturb, perplex. *v. n.* To fluctuate, to waver.

चिलुग्ना hil-úgna, *v. n.* To be hung on, to be entangled, to adhere, stick to; to be constant.

चिलगाना hil-gána, *v. a.* To hang, suspend.

चिलना híl-na, *v. n.* To shake, be moved, be agitated, to move; to be familiarized, be tamed.

चिलमिल जाना hilmil jána, *v. n.* To be mixed; to be intimate; to be jumbled together.

चिलमोची hil-móchee, *s. f.* A potherb (*Hingtsha repens*).

चिलसा hil-sá, *s. f.* A fish (*Clupea alosa*).

चिला híl-a, *adj.* Domesticated, tame. *s. m.* Slime, mud.

चिलाना hil-ána, *v. a.* To move, shake, agitate; to familiarize, tame; to cause to swim.

चिलामिला híla-míla, *adj.* Amicable, attached.

चिलोरा hilóra, *s. m.* A wave, billow, surge.

चिलोरी मार्ना hilorée márna, *v. a.* To heave, to rise (*as the sea*).

चिलोर्ना hil-órna, *v. n.* To billow, to wave.

चिवाव hiwáo, *s. m.* Courage.

चिसका hís-ka, *s. m.* Imitation, copying; contention, rivalry, emulation. *Hiska kurna*, To copy, imitate, ape, vie (*with*).

चिसकाचिसकी híska-hískee, *s. f.* Mutual emulation.

ही hee, *emphatic affix* or *adverb*, Very exactly, even, indeed, truly, only.

हींग heeng, *s. m.* Asafœtida. *Heeng hugna*, To void by stool involuntarily; (*met.*) to pine.

हींसना héensna, *v. n.* To neigh, to make a noise (*as a horse when kicking*).

हीक heek, *s. m.* Sickness at the stomach, qualm; disgust.

हीजड़ा héejra, *s. m.* A species of eunuch.

हीन heen, *adj.* Deficient, defective, little, abated; left, abandoned, quitted; wasted, worn, decayed; void of, free from.

हीनजाति heen-játi, *adj.* Outcaste, vile, degraded.

हीनवर्ण heen-vúrn, *adj.* Of a low caste, outcaste, vile.

हीर heer, *s. m.* Essence; pith, energy, vigour. *adj.* Essential, pure. *n. prop.* Hero, the celebrated mistress of Leander, called by the Indians, *Ranjha*.

हीरक heerúk, हीरा heerá, } *s. m.* The diamond.

हीरामन heeramún, *s. m.* A kind of paroquet (*Psitacus*).

हीरावल heera-wúl, *s. m.* A kind of chequered blanket worn by mendicants.

हील heel, } *s. m.* Mud, slime, ooze.
हीला heelá, }

हीही hee-hee, *adv.* An interjection of surprise, (ah, ha!)! an interjection of laughter, (hee, hee!).

हुंकार húon-kár, *s. m.* Uttering a menacing sound, roaring, bellowing.

हुरका húorka, *s. m.* Pining (*particularly applied to children separated from parents*).

हुरदुंगा hoor-dúnga, *adj.* Turbulent.

हुरदुंगी hoor-dúngee, *s. f.* Turbulence.

हुरहुरी hoor-hóoree, *s. f.* The twang of a bow.

हुरुक húorook, *s. m.* A kind of drum in form like an hour-glass (*generally played on by bearers*).

हुंडवी hoond-wée, } *s. f.* A bill of exchange. *Hoondee-wal*, An exchange merchant.
हुंडी hoon-dée, }

हुंडाभारा húonda-bhára, *s. m.* Contract for transportation of goods, including the payment of duties.

हुंडार hoon-dár, *s. m.* A wolf.

हुंडावन hoon-dávun, } *s. m.* Exchange, or price paid for a bill of exchange.
हुंडियाव hoon-diyáu, }

हुंडी húon-dee, *s. f.* A bill of exchange.

हुंडीवाल hoondee-wál, *s. m.* An exchange merchant.

हुत hoot, *adj.* Offered with fire, burnt as an oblation. *s. m.* Oblation.

हुरगूंदा hoor-góonda, *s. m.* A sort of vegetable. [*viscosa*].

हुरहुर hoor-hoor, *s. m.* A plant (*Cleome*

हुरुकनी hoorook-née, *s. f.* A dancing-girl, a whore, a courtezan, a harlot.

हुर्रा hoorrá, *s. m.* Dispersion (*of an army, an assembly, &c.*), general jail-delivery.

हूर्सा húorsa, *s. m.* A stone on which sandalwood is ground.

हुलकारना hool-kárna, *v. a.* To set on (*as a dog on a bull*), to instigate, to halloo on.

हुलसना hoo-lúsna, *v. n.* To be rejoiced, pleased, delighted.

हुलसाना hool-sána, *v. a.* To cheer, rejoice, delight, exhilarate, gladden.

हुलास hoolás, *s. f.* Snuff. *s. m.* Alacrity, joy, gladness.

हुल्लड़ hoollúr, *s. m.* Alarm, tumult, uproar, commotion, bustle, disturbance, riot.

हूं hoon, (I) am. *adv.* Too, also, yes, well, very, exactly.

हूं hoon kúrna, *v. a.* To make the sound *hoon*, in anger, from fear, or as an incantation, &c.

हुंहां hoon-hán, *s. m.* Uproar.

हूक hook, *s. f.* Pain, stitch, ache, shooting pain, twitch. *Hook-hook-kur rona*, To weep with sobbing, or with repeated burstings forth.

हूचना húoch-na, *v. a.* To miss, to err, to mistake.

हूर hoor, } *s. f.* Striving, wrangling.
हूराहूरी hóora-hóoree, }

हून hoon, *s. m.* A (*Madras*) coin, called also a pagoda.

हूल hool, *s. f.* A thrust, stab, an attack. *Hool dena*, *v. a.* To goad, thrust, push, drive, impel, urge.

हूलना hóolna, *v. a.* To goad, thrust, push, drive (*an elephant*).

हूहा hoo-há, *s. m.* Report, rumour, popular fame; a storm; pageantry, ostentation.

हृद hrid, } *s. m.* The heart; the mind, the faculty or seat of thought and feeling; knowledge.
हृदय hríduy, }

हृष्ट hrisht, *adj.* Pleased, glad, delighted; laughing, smiling.

हृष्टपुष्ट hrisht-póosht, *adj.* Well-conditioned, well fed and happy.

हे heh, A vocative particle, O!; a particle of calling out to, or challenging.

हेंगा hénga, *s. m.* A harrow.

हेठ heth, *adv.* Below, down, under.

हेठा hethá, *adj.* Indolent, pusillanimous, cowardly, low.

हेठापन hetha-pún, *s. m.* Cowardice.

हेत het, } *s. m.* Cause, origin, motive, meaning, object, intention, theme, reason, account.
हेतू hetóo, }

हेम hem, *s. m.* Gold.

हेमकूट hem-kóot, *s. m.* One of the ranges of mountains dividing the known continent into nine *Vurshus* : this range is the second south of *Ilavrit*, or the central division, and is immediately to the north of the *Himaluy*, forming with it the boundaries of the *Kinnur Vurshum*.

हेमक्षीरी hem-kshéeree, *s. f.* A medicinal sort of moon-plant.

हेमतूरो hem-túroo, *s. m.* The thorn-apple.

हेमतार hem-tár, *s. m.* Blue vitriol.

हेमंत hem-únt, *s. m.* The cold season, winter, the two months *Ugruhayun* and *Poush*, or about November-December.

हेरना hérna, *v. a.* To look after, to observe, see ; to search for, to hunt, chase, pursue, catch, stop.

रेलना hélna, _v. n._ To swim.

रेला helá, _s. f._ Wanton dalliance, lascivious endearment; disrespect, contempt.

रेला मारना héla-márna, _v. a._ To shove, launch, dash through water.

रेंगा hyn-ga, _s. m._ A harrow.

रेक hyk, _s. m._ A horse.

रो ho, A vocative particle, _Ho!_

रो आना ho-ána, _v. n._ To have gone to and returned.

रोंकना hónk-na, _v. n._ To pant, to puff and blow.

रोंठ honth, _s. m._ The lip.

रोंठी honthée, _s. f._ The bit of a bridle.

रोके hókeh, _adv._ Through, by.

रो चुकना ho-chóokna, _v. n._ To be finished.

रो जाना ho-jána, _v. n._ To have happened, to become.

रोठ hoth, _s. m._ The lip.

रोड़ hor, _s. f._ A wager, an agreement, a bargain, a bet. _Hor budna_, To wager, bet, &c. _Hor bandhna_, To bargain, &c. _Hor lagana, v. a._ To wager; to make an agreement. _v. n._ To be positive, obstinate, or perverse. _Hor karna_, To lose a wager, &c.

रोरुल hó-rul, _s. m._ Talc, mica.

रोत hot, _s. f._ Ability, means.

रोतव ho-túv, _s. m._ Predestination, destiny.

रोतव्यता hotúv-yutá, _s. f._ Fate, destiny.

रोता hóta, _s. m._ Wealth.

रोता जाता hóta-játa, _s. m._ Coming and going.

रोते hotéh, _adv._ In the being, during, in the presence.

रोते रोते hóteh-hóteh, _adv._ Gradually.

रोना hóna, _v. n._ To be, to exist, to become, to belong, have, serve, answer, accrue, come, do, stand; to die. _s. m._ The being or becoming.

रोन्हार hon-hár, _adj._ What is to happen; possible, feasible, hopeful.

रोम hom, _s. m._ Burnt-offering, the casting of clarified butter, &c. into the sacred fire, as an offering to the gods, accompanied with prayers or invocations, according to the object of the sacrifice.

रोमना hóm-na, _v. a._ To perform the sacrifice of the _hom._

रोमी homée, _s. m._ The offerer of an oblation.

रोला hóla, _s. m._ The chickpea having been parched in the pod.

रोली hólee, _s. f._ The great festival held at the approach of the vernal equinox; the song which is sung during the festival.

रो लेना ho-léna, _v. n._ To be completed.

रोंस houns, _s. f._ Desire, wish, want, ambition, lust. _Houns kurna_, To desire.

रोका hóuka, _s. m._ Cupidity, covetousness, greediness.

रोले hóuleh, _adv._ Gently, slowly.

रोवा houwá, _s. m._ A bugbear, a hobgoblin.

रुद hrud, _s. m._ A deep lake, a large or deep piece of water.

रुस्वुह hrúswuh, _adj._ Short, low in stature; short, as a vowel.

क्ष

क्ष kshuh, The thirty-fourth consonant of the _Naguree_ alphabet, and pronounced as _ksh._

चयरोग kshuyee-róg, _s. m._ Consumption.

क्षन kshun, _s. m._ A measure of time equal to four minutes; a moment or instant. _adv._ For a moment.

क्षनमात kshun-mátr, _adv._ Momentary, but for a moment.

क्षनांतर kshun-ántur, _adv._ A minute afterwards, the next moment.

क्षनिक kshun-ík, } _adj._ Momentary, tran-
क्षनी kshun-ée, } sient.

क्षत्री kshútree, _s. m._ A man of the second or military and regal class.

क्षम kshum, _adj._ Able, adequate; fit, appropriate, suitable, proper. _s. m._ Propriety, fitness.

क्षमना kshúmna, _v. a._ To pardon, to forgive.

क्षमा kshumá, _s. f._ Patience, forbearance; pardon forgiveness.

क्षमायुक्त kshuma-jóokt, } _adj._ Patient, en-
क्षमावान kshuma-wán, } during, forbearing.

क्षय kshuy, _s. m._ Loss, waste, destruction, removal, &c.; a destruction of the universe; consumption; sickness in general; decay, wasting away; (in _algebra_) negative quantity, minus.

क्षयकाल kshuy-kál, _s. m._ The end of all things, the period of destruction.

क्षयकास kshuy-kás, _s. m._ A consumptive or phthisical cough.

क्षयनाशिनी kshuy-náshinee, _s. f._ A plant (_Celtis Orientalis_).

क्षयवायु kshuy-váyoo, _s. m._ The wind that is to blow at the end of the world.

चयरोग kshuy-róg, _s. m._ Consumption.

क्षयरोगिणी kshuy-roginée, *f.* ⎱ Consump-
क्षयरोगी kshuy-rógee, *m.* ⎰ tive, hectic.

क्षयसम्पद् kshuy-sumpúd, *s. f.* Total loss,
ruin, destruction.

क्षयी kshuyée, *adj.* Wasting, decaying;
consumptive.

क्षविका kshuviká, *s. f.* A kind of rice.

क्षान्त kshánt, *adj.* Patient, enduring.

क्षान्ति kshánti, *s. f.* Patience, forbearance,
endurance.

क्षार kshar, *s. m.* Salt; ashes; borax,
borate of soda; alkali, either soda or potash;
caustic alkali; one species of cautery; a factitious
or medicinal salt, commonly called black salt.

क्षारकर्म kshar-kúrm, *s. m.* Applying caustic alkali (*lapis infernalis*) to proud flesh, &c.

क्षारमृत्तिका kshar-mrittiká, *s. f.* Saline
soil, especially an impure sulphate of soda.

क्षाररस kshar-rús, *s. m.* A salt or alkaline
flavour.

क्षारवृक्ष kshar-vríksh, *s. m.* Any tree
yielding abundant potash, as the plantain, &c.

क्षिति kshíti, *s. f.* The earth; loss, destruction, wane; the period of the destruction of
the universe.

क्षितिपाल kshiti-pál, *s. m.* A king, a prince.

क्षीण ksheen, *adj.* Thin, emaciated, feeble;
thin, slender; wasted, diminished, worn away;
destroyed, lost; poor, miserable.

क्षीणता ksheen-tá, *s. f.* Slenderness, delicacy; thinness, emaciation; diminution, decay.

क्षीणवान ksheen-wán, *adj.* Wasted, decayed.

क्षीणशक्ति ksheen-shúkti, *adj.* Weak, feeble,
impotent.

क्षीर ksheer, *s. m.* Water; milk.

क्षीर ककोलिका ksheer-kakólika, *s. f.* A
drug, and one of the eight principal medicaments
of the *Hindoos*: it is a root from the *Himaluy.*

क्षीरस्फुटिक ksheer-sphútik, *s. m.* A precious stone, described as a milky crystal (*opal or
cat's eye?*).

क्षीरी ksheerée, *adj.* Milky, yielding milk;
having milk. *s. m.* A sort of *Mimusops.*

क्षीरोद ksheer-ód, *s. m.* The sea of milk,
one of the seven seas surrounding as many worlds.

क्षुद्र kshoodr, *adj.* Small, little; mean,
low; mean, niggardly, avaricious; poor, indigent.

क्षुद्रता kshoodr-tá, *s. f.* Smallness, minuteness; inferiority, insignificance, meanness.

क्षुद्रबुद्धि kshoodr-bóoddhi, *adj.* Simple,
silly, ignorant.

क्षुद्ररोग kshoodr-róg, *s. m.* A minor disease, one of little importance.

क्षुधा kshoodhá, *s. f.* Hunger.

क्षुधार्त्त kshoodhártt, ⎱ *adj.* Hungry, hun-
क्षुधित kshoodhít, ⎰ gered.

क्षुर kshoor, *s. m.* A razor; a horse's
hoof.

क्षुरी kshóoree, *s. f.* A knife.

क्षेत्र kshetr, *s. m.* A field; a wife; a pure
or sacred spot, a place of pilgrimage, as *Benares*,
&c.; plane figure, geometry; a diagram.

क्षेत्रज्ञ kshetrúg, *adj.* Clever, dexterous,
skilful; a husbandman, &c. *s. m.* The soul, the
emanation of the divinity residing in the body.

क्षेत्रसीमा kshetr-séema, *s. f.* The boundaries of a meadow or field, or holy place.

क्षेद kshed, *s. m.* Sorrowing, moaning.

क्षेप kshep, *s. m.* Throwing, casting; (in
arithmetic) additive quantity, addendum.

क्षेपण kshepún, *s. m.* Throwing, casting.

क्षेम kshem, *adj.* Happy, well, prosperous,
right, &c. *s. m.* Happiness, well being; final
emancipation or eternal happiness; the proper
term of civil address to a *Vys.*

क्षेमकर kshem-kúr, *adj.* Propitious, conferring happiness or good fortune.

क्षेमवान kshem-wán, *adj.* Happy, prosperous.

क्षौणि kshóuni, *s. f.* The earth.

क्षौद्र kshoudr, *s. m.* Honey; a flower
(*Michelia champaca*).

क्षौर kshour, *s. m.* Shaving the head;
shaving in general.

क्षौरिक kshour-ík, *s. m.* A barber.

क्षौरी kshourée, *s. f.* A razor.

क्ष्मा kshma, *s. f.* The earth.

क्ष्मातल kshma-túl, *s. m.* The surface of the
earth.

क्ष्मापति kshma-púti, ⎱ *s. m.* A king, a
क्ष्मभृत् kshma-bhrít, ⎰ prince.

Printed in the United States
144310LV00004BA/115/A

9 781436 724913